*Contemporary Authors*®

# NEW REVISION SERIES

# Contemporary

# Authors®

## A Bio-Bibliographical Guide to Current Writers in Fiction, General Nonfiction, Poetry, Journalism, Drama, Motion Pictures, Television, and Other Fields

## NEW REVISION SERIES
### volume 122

GALE®

THOMSON
™
GALE

Detroit • New York • San Diego • San Francisco • Cleveland • New Haven, Conn. • Waterville, Maine • London • Munich

# Contemporary Authors, New Revision Series, Vol. 122

**Project Editor**
Scot Peacock

**Editorial**
Katy Balcer, Shavon Burden, Sara Constantakis, Anna Marie Dahn, Alana Joli Foster, Natalie Fulkerson, Arlene M. Johnson, Michelle Kazensky, Julie Keppen, Joshua Kondek, Thomas McMahon, Jenai A. Mynatt, Judith L. Pyko, Mary Ruby, Lemma Shomali, Susan Strickland, Maikue Vang, Tracey Watson, Denay L. Wilding, Thomas Wiloch, Emiene Shija Wright

**Research**
Michelle Campbell, Tracie A. Richardson, Robert Whaley

**Permissions**
Kim Davis, Shalice Shah-Caldwell

**Imaging and Multimedia**
Dean Dauphinais, Robert Duncan, Leitha Etheridge-Sims, Mary K. Grimes, Lezlie Light, Dan Newell, David G. Oblender, Christine O'Bryan, Kelly A. Quin, Luke Rademacher

**Composition and Electronic Capture**
Carolyn A. Roney

**Manufacturing**
Stacy L. Melson

**LIBRARY OF CONGRESS CATALOG CARD NUMBER 81-640179**

ISBN 0-7876-6714-5
ISSN 0275-7176

Printed in the United States of America
10 9 8 7 6 5 4 3 2 1

# Contents

---

**Indexing note:** All *Contemporary Authors* entries are indexed in the *Contemporary Authors* cumulative index, which is published separately and distributed twice a year.

**As always, the most recent Contemporary Authors cumulative index continues to be the user's guide to the location of an individual author's listing.**

---

# Preface

*Contemporary Authors* (*CA*) provides information on approximately 115,000 writers in a wide range of media, including:

- Current writers of fiction, nonfiction, poetry, and drama whose works have been issued by commercial publishers, risk publishers, or university presses (authors whose books have been published only by known vanity or author-subsidized firms are ordinarily not included)

- Prominent print and broadcast journalists, editors, photojournalists, syndicated cartoonists, graphic novelists, screenwriters, television scriptwriters, and other media people

- Notable international authors

- Literary greats of the early twentieth century whose works are popular in today's high school and college curriculums and continue to elicit critical attention

A *CA* listing entails no charge or obligation. Authors are included on the basis of the above criteria and their interest to *CA* users. Sources of potential listees include trade periodicals, publishers' catalogs, librarians, and other users.

## How to Get the Most out of *CA*: Use the Index

The key to locating an author's most recent entry is the *CA* cumulative index, which is published separately and distributed twice a year. It provides access to *all* entries in *CA* and *Contemporary Authors New Revision Series* (*CANR*). Always consult the latest index to find an author's most recent entry.

For the convenience of users, the *CA* cumulative index also includes references to all entries in these Gale literary series: *Authors and Artists for Young Adults, Authors in the News, Bestsellers, Black Literature Criticism, Black Literature Criticism Supplement, Black Writers, Children's Literature Review, Concise Dictionary of American Literary Biography, Concise Dictionary of British Literary Biography, Contemporary Authors Autobiography Series, Contemporary Authors Bibliographical Series, Contemporary Dramatists, Contemporary Literary Criticism, Contemporary Novelists, Contemporary Poets, Contemporary Popular Writers, Contemporary Southern Writers, Contemporary Women Poets, Dictionary of Literary Biography, Dictionary of Literary Biography Documentary Series, Dictionary of Literary Biography Yearbook, DISCovering Authors, DISCovering Authors: British, DISCovering Authors: Canadian, DISCovering Authors: Modules* (including modules for Dramatists, Most-Studied Authors, Multicultural Authors, Novelists, Poets, and Popular/Genre Authors), *DISCovering Authors 3.0, Drama Criticism, Drama for Students, Feminist Writers, Hispanic Literature Criticism, Hispanic Writers, Junior DISCovering Authors, Major Authors and Illustrators for Children and Young Adults, Major 20th-Century Writers, Native North American Literature, Novels for Students, Poetry Criticism, Poetry for Students, Short Stories for Students, Short Story Criticism, Something about the Author, Something about the Author Autobiography Series, St. James Guide to Children's Writers, St. James Guide to Crime & Mystery Writers, St. James Guide to Fantasy Writers, St. James Guide to Horror, Ghost & Gothic Writers, St. James Guide to Science Fiction Writers, St. James Guide to Young Adult Writers, Twentieth-Century Literary Criticism, 20th Century Romance and Historical Writers, World Literature Criticism,* and *Yesterday's Authors of Books for Children.*

## A Sample Index Entry:

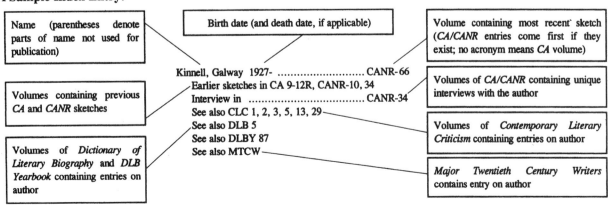

# How Are Entries Compiled?

The editors make every effort to secure new information directly from the authors; listees' responses to our questionnaires and query letters provide most of the information featured in *CA*. For deceased writers, or those who fail to reply to requests for data, we consult other reliable biographical sources, such as those indexed in Gale's *Biography and Genealogy Master Index,* and bibliographical sources, including *National Union Catalog, LC MARC,* and *British National Bibliography.* Further details come from published interviews, feature stories, and book reviews, as well as information supplied by the authors' publishers and agents.

*An asterisk (\*) at the end of a sketch indicates that the listing has been compiled from secondary sources believed to be reliable but has not been personally verified for this edition by the author sketched.*

# What Kinds of Information Does An Entry Provide?

Sketches in *CA* contain the following biographical and bibliographical information:

- **Entry heading:** the most complete form of author's name, plus any pseudonyms or name variations used for writing

- **Personal information:** author's date and place of birth, family data, ethnicity, educational background, political and religious affiliations, and hobbies and leisure interests

- **Addresses:** author's home, office, or agent's addresses, plus e-mail and fax numbers, as available

- **Career summary:** name of employer, position, and dates held for each career post; resume of other vocational achievements; military service

- **Membership information:** professional, civic, and other association memberships and any official posts held

- **Awards and honors:** military and civic citations, major prizes and nominations, fellowships, grants, and honorary degrees

- **Writings:** a comprehensive, chronological list of titles, publishers, dates of original publication and revised editions, and production information for plays, television scripts, and screenplays

- **Adaptations:** a list of films, plays, and other media which have been adapted from the author's work

- **Work in progress:** current or planned projects, with dates of completion and/or publication, and expected publisher, when known

- **Sidelights:** a biographical portrait of the author's development; information about the critical reception of the author's works; revealing comments, often by the author, on personal interests, aspirations, motivations, and thoughts on writing

- **Interview:** a one-on-one discussion with authors conducted especially for *CA*, offering insight into authors' thoughts about their craft

- **Autobiographical essay:** an original essay written by noted authors for *CA*, a forum in which writers may present themselves, on their own terms, to their audience

- **Photographs:** portraits and personal photographs of notable authors

- **Biographical and critical sources:** a list of books and periodicals in which additional information on an author's life and/or writings appears

- **Obituary Notices** in *CA* provide date and place of birth as well as death information about authors whose full-length sketches appeared in the series before their deaths. The entries also summarize the authors' careers and writings and list other sources of biographical and death information.

## Related Titles in the *CA* Series

*Contemporary Authors Autobiography Series* complements *CA* original and revised volumes with specially commissioned autobiographical essays by important current authors, illustrated with personal photographs they provide. Common topics include their motivations for writing, the people and experiences that shaped their careers, the rewards they derive from their work, and their impressions of the current literary scene.

*Contemporary Authors Bibliographical Series* surveys writings by and about important American authors since World War II. Each volume concentrates on a specific genre and features approximately ten writers; entries list works written by and about the author and contain a bibliographical essay discussing the merits and deficiencies of major critical and scholarly studies in detail.

## Available in Electronic Formats

**GaleNet.** *CA* is available on a subscription basis through GaleNet, an online information resource that features an easy-to-use end-user interface, powerful search capabilities, and ease of access through the World-Wide Web. For more information, call 1-800-877-GALE.

**Licensing.** *CA* is available for licensing. The complete database is provided in a fielded format and is deliverable on such media as disk, CD-ROM, or tape. For more information, contact Gale's Business Development Group at 1-800-877-GALE, or visit us on our website at www.galegroup.com/bizdev.

## Suggestions Are Welcome

The editors welcome comments and suggestions from users on any aspect of the *CA* series. If readers would like to recommend authors for inclusion in future volumes of the series, they are cordially invited to write the Editors at *Contemporary Authors*, Gale Group, 27500 Drake Rd., Farmington Hills, MI 48331-3535; or call at 1-248-699-4253; or fax at 1-248-699-8054.

# Contemporary Authors Product Advisory Board

The editors of *Contemporary Authors* are dedicated to maintaining a high standard of excellence by publishing comprehensive, accurate, and highly readable entries on a wide array of writers. In addition to the quality of the content, the editors take pride in the graphic design of the series, which is intended to be orderly yet inviting, allowing readers to utilize the pages of *CA* easily and with efficiency. Despite the longevity of the *CA* print series, and the success of its format, we are mindful that the vitality of a literary reference product is dependent on its ability to serve its users over time. As literature, and attitudes about literature, constantly evolve, so do the reference needs of students, teachers, scholars, journalists, researchers, and book club members. To be certain that we continue to keep pace with the expectations of our customers, the editors of *CA* listen carefully to their comments regarding the value, utility, and quality of the series. Librarians, who have firsthand knowledge of the needs of library users, are a valuable resource for us. The *Contemporary Authors* Product Advisory Board, made up of school, public, and academic librarians, is a forum to promote focused feedback about *CA* on a regular basis. The seven-member advisory board includes the following individuals, whom the editors wish to thank for sharing their expertise:

- **Anne M. Christensen,** Librarian II, Phoenix Public Library, Phoenix, Arizona.

- **Barbara C. Chumard,** Reference/Adult Services Librarian, Middletown Thrall Library, Middletown, New York.

- **Eva M. Davis,** Youth Department Manager, Ann Arbor District Library, Ann Arbor, Michigan.

- **Adam Janowski, Jr.,** Library Media Specialist, Naples High School Library Media Center, Naples, Florida.

- **Robert Reginald,** Head of Technical Services and Collection Development, California State University, San Bernadino, California.

- **Katharine E. Rubin,** Head of Information and Reference Division, New Orleans Public Library, New Orleans, Louisiana.

- **Barbara A. Wencl,** Media Specialist, Como Park High School, St. Paul, Minnesota.

# International Advisory Board

Well-represented among the 115,000 author entries published in *Contemporary Authors* are sketches on notable writers from many non-English-speaking countries. The primary criteria for inclusion of such authors has traditionally been the publication of at least one title in English, either as an original work or as a translation. However, the editors of *Contemporary Authors* came to observe that many important international writers were being overlooked due to a strict adherence to our inclusion criteria. In addition, writers who were publishing in languages other than English were not being covered in the traditional sources we used for identifying new listees. Intent on increasing our coverage of international authors, including those who write only in their native language and have not been translated into English, the editors enlisted the aid of a board of advisors, each of whom is an expert on the literature of a particular country or region. Among the countries we focused attention on are Mexico, Puerto Rico, Spain, Italy, France, Germany, Luxembourg, Belgium, the Netherlands, Norway, Sweden, Denmark, Finland, Taiwan, Singapore, Malaysia, Thailand, South Africa, Israel, and Japan, as well as England, Scotland, Wales, Ireland, Australia, and New Zealand. The sixteen-member advisory board includes the following individuals, whom the editors wish to thank for sharing their expertise:

- **Lowell A. Bangerter,** Professor of German, University of Wyoming, Laramie, Wyoming.

- **Nancy E. Berg,** Associate Professor of Hebrew and Comparative Literature, Washington University, St. Louis, Missouri.

- **Frances Devlin-Glass,** Associate Professor, School of Literary and Communication Studies, Deakin University, Burwood, Victoria, Australia.

- **David William Foster,** Regent's Professor of Spanish, Interdisciplinary Humanities, and Women's Studies, Arizona State University, Tempe, Arizona.

- **Hosea Hirata,** Director of the Japanese Program, Associate Professor of Japanese, Tufts University, Medford, Massachusetts.

- **Jack Kolbert,** Professor Emeritus of French Literature, Susquehanna University, Selinsgrove, Pennsylvania.

- **Mark Libin,** Professor, University of Manitoba, Winnipeg, Manitoba, Canada.

- **C. S. Lim,** Professor, University of Malaya, Kuala Lumpur, Malaysia.

- **Eloy E. Merino,** Assistant Professor of Spanish, Northern Illinois University, DeKalb, Illinois.

- **Linda M. Rodríguez Guglielmoni,** Associate Professor, University of Puerto Rico—Mayagüez, Puerto Rico.

- **Sven Hakon Rossel,** Professor and Chair of Scandinavian Studies, University of Vienna, Vienna, Austria.

- **Steven R. Serafin,** Director, Writing Center, Hunter College of the City University of New York, New York City.

- **David Smyth,** Lecturer in Thai, School of Oriental and African Studies, University of London, England.

- **Ismail S. Talib,** Senior Lecturer, Department of English Language and Literature, National University of Singapore, Singapore.

- **Dionisio Viscarri,** Assistant Professor, Ohio State University, Columbus, Ohio.

- **Mark Williams,** Associate Professor, English Department, University of Canterbury, Christchurch, New Zealand.

# *CA* Numbering System and Volume Update Chart

Occasionally questions arise about the *CA* numbering system and which volumes, if any, can be discarded. Despite numbers like "29-32R," "97-100" and "213," the entire *CA* print series consists of only 263 physical volumes with the publication of *CA* Volume 214. The following charts note changes in the numbering system and cover design, and indicate which volumes are essential for the most complete, up-to-date coverage.

| | |
|---|---|
| *CA* **First Revision** | • 1-4R through 41-44R (11 books)<br>*Cover:* Brown with black and gold trim.<br>There will be no further First Revision volumes because revised entries are now being handled exclusively through the more efficient *New Revision Series* mentioned below. |
| *CA* **Original Volumes** | • 45-48 through 97-100 (14 books)<br>*Cover:* Brown with black and gold trim.<br>101 through 214 (114 books)<br>*Cover:* Blue and black with orange bands.<br>The same as previous *CA* original volumes but with a new, simplified numbering system and new cover design. |
| *CA* **Permanent Series** | • *CAP*-1 and *CAP*-2 (2 books)<br>*Cover:* Brown with red and gold trim.<br>There will be no further Permanent Series volumes because revised entries are now being handled exclusively through the more efficient *New Revision Series* mentioned below. |
| *CA* **New Revision Series** | • CANR-1 through CANR-122 (122 books)<br>*Cover:* Blue and black with green bands.<br>Includes only sketches requiring significant changes; **sketches are taken from any previously published CA, CAP, or CANR volume.** |

| If You Have: | You May Discard: |
|---|---|
| *CA* First Revision Volumes 1-4R through 41-44R and *CA Permanent Series* Volumes 1 and 2 | *CA* Original Volumes 1, 2, 3, 4 and Volumes 5-6 through 41-44 |
| *CA* Original Volumes 45-48 through 97-100 and 101 through 214 | **NONE:** These volumes will not be superseded by corresponding revised volumes. Individual entries from these and all other volumes appearing in the left column of this chart may be revised and included in the various volumes of the *New Revision Series*. |
| *CA New Revision Series* Volumes *CANR*-1 through *CANR*-122 | **NONE:** The *New Revision Series* does not replace any single volume of *CA*. Instead, volumes of *CANR* include entries from many previous *CA* series volumes. All *New Revision Series* volumes must be retained for full coverage. |

# A Sampling of Authors and Media People Featured in This Volume

## Gary S. Becker

Becker is one of the most respected economists of the famous Chicago school. Mentored by Milton Friedman, Becker helped move the study of economics into territory previously unexplored with his many books about subjects such as racial discrimination, crime, and the family unit. This body of work garnered Becker the Nobel Prize in Economics in 1992. His titles include *Accounting for Tastes,* a 1996 collection of the economist's essays, and the 2000 volume authored with Kevin M. Murphy, *Social Economics: Market Behavior in a Social Environment.*

## Breyten Breytenbach

At the height of his literary acclaim, Breytenbach, South Africa's leading Afrikaner poet, was imprisoned by the government of his fellow Afrikaners for clandestine activities against its apartheid system of racial laws. Although he was released in 1982, Breytenbach remained an outspoken critic of the oppression of blacks and other minorities. His books include *The True Confessions of an Albino Terrorist* and 2000's *Lady One: Of Love and Other Poems.*

## Gayl Jones

Jones's novels *Corregidora* and *Eva's Man,* in addition to many of the stories in her collection *White Rat,* offer stark, often brutal accounts of black women whose psyches reflect the ravages of accumulated sexual and racial exploitation. In *Corregidora* Jones reveals the tormented life of a woman whose female forebears—at the hands of one man—endured a cycle of slavery, prostitution, and incest over three generations. In 1999 Jones published the novel *Mosquito.*

## Donald Justice

Justice is an award-winning poet known for his mastery of the form. His first published book, *The Summer Anniversaries,* which established Justice's reputation for attention to the craft of poetry writing, was the 1959 Lamont Poetry Selection, while the 1973 publication *Departures* received a National Book Award nomination and *Selected Poems* won the Pulitzer Prize in 1979. In 1998 Justice issued *Orpheus Hesitated beside the Black River: Poems, 1952-1997.*

## Doris Lessing

Lessing, whose long career as a novelist, short story writer, and essayist began in the mid-twentieth century, is considered among the most important writers of the modern postwar era. Since her birth in 1919 in Britain's sphere of influence in Persia (now Iran), Lessing has traveled widely, in geographical, social, political, psychological, and literary terms. These travels, as expressed in her writing, offer readers insights into life at distant outposts of the British Empire and at its core. Lessing published *The Sweetest Dream* in 2002.

## Dav Pilkey

A highly regarded and popular author and illustrator of children's books, Pilkey combines lowbrow humor and broad parodies with a subtle moral often thrown into the mix. Among his popular books are those from the "Dragon," "Captain Underpants," and "Big Dog and Little Dog" series. His individual creations have also garnered high praise, including *The Paperboy,* which was named a Caldecott Medal Honor Book.

## Kristine Kathryn Rusch

A prolific and popular writer, Rusch has had a great deal of influence on the genres of science fiction and fantasy writing toward the end of the twentieth century. The cofounder of Pulphouse Publishing, which issued the quarterly *Pulphouse: The Hardback Magazine,* Rusch also served as the editor of the *Magazine of Fantasy & Science Fiction.* In 2001, she received the Hugo Award for Best Novelette, for *Millennium Babies.*

## Ed Sikov

Sikov is a film scholar who specializes in Hollywood comedies from the 1930s through the 1970s. His first book, *Screwball: Hollywood's Madcap Romantic Comedies,* argues against the notion that the madcap romantic comedies of the 1930s and 1940s were produced to alleviate the sufferings of a nation weighed down by the Great Depression. Instead, according to Sikov, the films were a direct response to the restrictions the government imposed on showing sexuality on-screen. He is also the author of *Mr. Strangelove: A Biography of Peter Sellers,* published in 2002.

# Acknowledgments

Grateful acknowledgment is made to those publishers, photographers, and artists whose work appear with these authors' essays. Following is a list of the copyright holders who have granted us permission to reproduce material in this volume of *CA*. Every effort has been made to trace copyright, but if omissions have been made, please let us know.

## Photographs/Art

**Joan Abelove:** Abelove, photograph by Tony Dougherty. Reproduced by permission.

**Sebastian Barry:** Barry, photograph. © Jerry Bauer. Reproduced by permission.

**Gary S. Becker:** Becker, photograph. © Ralf-Finn Hestoft/Corbis Saba. Reproduced by permission.

**George Birimisa:** Birimisa, photograph by James McColley Eilers. Reproduced by permission.

**Peter J. Bowler:** Bowler, photograph. Reproduced by permission.

**Breyten Breytenbach:** Breytenbach attending the Writers Parliament in Lisbon, photograph. © Adanson James/Corbis Sygma. Reproduced by permission.

**Kenelm Burridge:** Burridge, photograph. Courtesy of K. O. L. Burridge. Reproduced by permission.

**John Canemaker:** Canemaker, photograph by Joe Henson. Reproduced by permission of John Canemaker.

**Lewis H. Carlson:** Carlson, photograph. Reproduced by permission.

**Paula S. Fass:** Fass, photograph. Reproduced by permission.

**Robert Fraser:** Fraser, portrait. Reproduced by permission.

**Thomas L. Friedman:** Friedman, photograph. © 1989, Jerry Bauer. Reproduced by permission.

**William H. Frist:** Frist, Tennessee senator, photograph. AP/Wide World Photos. Reproduced by permission.

**Peter J. Gomes:** Gomes, photograph. © Jerry Bauer. Reproduced by permission.

**Robert Graysmith:** Graysmith, photograph by Margot Graysmith. Reproduced by permission.

**Philip Grierson:** Grierson, photograph. Reproduced by permission.

**Barbara Hambly:** Hambly, photograph by Jay Kay Klein. © Jay Kay Klein. Reproduced by permission.

**Kathryn Harrison:** Harrison, photograph. © Jerry Bauer. Reproduced by permission.

**Guida M. Jackson:** Jackson, photograph. Reproduced by permission.

**Julie Johnston:** Johnston, photograph. Courtesy of Melissa Johnston. Reproduced by permission.

# A

## ABELOVE, Joan 1945-

*PERSONAL:* Born 1945; daughter of a businessman; married Steve Hoffman, 1987; children: Andrew. *Education:* Barnard College, B.A., 1966; City University of New York, Ph.D. (anthropology), 1978.

*ADDRESSES: Agent*—c/o Ginger Knowlton, Curtis Brown, Ltd., Ten Astor Place, New York, NY 10003. *E-mail*—JoanAndy@aol.com

*CAREER:* Taught emotionally disturbed boys in a state hospital; part-time teacher of anthropology at colleges in the New York, NY, area 1978-84; technical writer, 1984—.

*MEMBER:* Author's Guild, SCBWI.

*AWARDS, HONORS: Go and Come Back* chosen as one of one of *Globe and Mail* columnist Susan Perren's ten best juvenile books of 1998; Notable Children's Books and Best Books for Young Adults selections, both American Library Association, Best Books commendations, *Publishers Weekly* and *School Library Journal,* Editor's Choice designation, *Booklist,* Blue Ribbon Book designation, *Bulletin of the Center for Children's Books,* Fanfare selection, *Horn Book,* Book of Distinction, *Riverbank Review,* Pick of the Lists, American Booksellers Association, Editors' Choice, *Kliatt,* Booklinks' Lasting Connections, Pick of the Lists selection, American Booksellers Association, and *Los Angeles Times* Book Prize finalist, all

*Joan Abelove*

1999, all for *Go and Come Back;* Best Books for Young Adults selection, American Library Association, Best Book of the Year commendation, *Publishers Weekly,* and Books for the Teenage designation, New York Public Library, all 2000, all for *Saying It Out Loud.*

*WRITINGS:*

*Go and Come Back,* DK Ink (New York, NY), 1998.
*Saying It Out Loud,* DK Ink (New York, NY), 1999.

Contributor of story, "Sproing!," to *Lost and Found,* edited by M. Jerry Weiss, Forge (New York, NY), 2000; also contributor to *In My Grandmother's House,* edited by Bonnie Christensen, HarperCollins (New York, NY), 2003.

*WORK IN PROGRESS:* A novel.

*SIDELIGHTS:* Joan Abelove spent two years in the Amazon jungle of Peru in the 1970s doing her doctoral research in cultural anthropology. She drew on this experience in writing her young adult novel *Go and Come Back.* The narrator is a teenaged girl, Alicia, a member of the fictional Isabo tribe in the fictional village of Poincushmana. The Isabos have no word that equals goodbye. Their word used in parting is *catanhue,* which translated means "go and come back." Joanna and Margarita, two American graduate students, come to the village to study and take notes on the culture of the Isabos. The Isabos consider the two women stingy, because they refuse to share their possessions. Isabo cultural dictates that food and supplies be divided equally by all, and the villagers consider stealing from those who will not share a lesser sin than not sharing. The white women are criticized for not washing their hair when bathing. The villagers refer to them as "old white ladies," even though they are in their twenties. "The situation provides countless opportunities for misunderstandings by the observer and the observed, most of them a source of humor for the reader and tension for the participants," wrote a *Horn Book* reviewer. "By juxtaposing these two radically different cultures, Abelove provides humorous yet respectful insight into both."

Alicia is promised to her sister's husband, and she is trying to avoid the marriage. She adopts a sickly abandoned baby, but is unable to save its life. Alicia becomes closer to Joanna and Margarita, whose attitudes are changed as they begin to understand and accept their differences. A reviewer wrote in *Kirkus Reviews* that through the narrator's eyes, "readers will watch the outsiders' adjustments to the rhythms and customs they are studying, as they shed much of their physical

and cultural baggage." Alicia also gains new perspectives, especially when the women take her for a plane ride and she sees her village from high above. Pam Gosner wrote in *School Library Journal* that the anecdotal information "never overwhelms the narrative," and called *Go and Come Back* a "compelling novel." "There is not enough plot to the novel, but by its end the reader has nonetheless become attached to the characters and their relationships," wrote Jen Nessel in the *New York Times Book Review.* "We are left with a lot to think about in our own culture—why we think the things we think and do the things we do." "Full of life and packed with characters that by turns irritate and enlighten, *Go and Come Back* is a startling, vibrant read," concluded a *Booklist* reviewer. "Abelove seamlessly constructs a culture that may feel more real to readers than their own," wrote a *Publishers Weekly* reviewer. Since writing *Go and Come Back,* Abelove has been asked to visit schools and libraries, where she gives a presentation that includes slides of her trip to the Amazon, showing pictures of the actual people whom she has woven into her story.

Abelove's next book, *Saying It Out Loud,* was inspired by the author's memories of her mother's death from a brain tumor, when Abelove was sixteen. Humorous and serious by turns, the novel finds sixteen-year-old Mindy attempting to navigate her changing, conflicted relationship with her mother, all the while anticipating her mother's impending death. Her father, a rigid, bigoted, and unemotional man, provides her with neither guidance nor comfort during the final months of her mother's life. "Her isolation is palpable," commented a reviewer for *Horn Book.* Feeling shut out of her father's attempts to say good-bye to his wife, Mindy goes to the hospital on her own to make her peace with a mother who is unable to communicate with the outside world. This visit so unnerves her that she never returns.

At the outset of the novel, Mindy's father dominates her life. His influence is not pleasant, but when he withdraws into his own grief, the girl feels a void. She fills this emptiness by seeking solace in friendships—with her best friend Gail, Gail's happy-go-lucky little brother Andrew, a caring neighbor, and a schoolmate named Bobby who shows a growing interest in her. Mindy's own recollections of experiences with her mother allow her to express her sadness, guilt, and sometimes even anger. While many of the book's events are unusually sad, such as those that relate to the worsening condition of Mindy's mother as her tumor progresses, others reflect the typical experiences of teens growing up in the 1960s.

*Saying It Out Loud* received praise from critics for its realistic depiction of adolescent emotion. A *Publishers Weekly* writer rated it "a stirring, psychologically truthful novel." Deborah Stevenson, a contributor to *Bulletin of the Center for Children's Books,* noted the novel's "particularly authentic . . . depiction of strain laying bare a family's secrets." Describing Abelove's second novel as "a quiet book," *Voice of Youth Advocates* reviewer Judy Sasges added that "Mindy copes with death and spiritual questions, and challenges authority with strength and maturity." "[Mindy's] isolation is palpable," wrote *Horn Book* critic Nancy Vasilakis. And a writer for *Booklist,* Susan Dove Lempke, stated that Abelove writes this "melancholy but ultimately hopeful story with delicacy of word and feeling and creates three powerful, memorable characters in the members of the family." Taken with *Go and Come Back, Saying It Out Loud* proves the author's ability to write "books that are not only very complex but also vibrant and infused with tenderness."

To create the character of Mindy, Abelove drew on many specific memories of her own adolescence. "The books Mindy talks about are some of my favorite books as a kid," she said in an interview with *Authors and Artists for Young Adults.* She also "had first hand experience being raised by a father who adamantly did not want his daughter to marry anyone who wasn't Jewish."

In addition to writing her novels, Abelove has worked as a technical writer since the 1980s. "I work every day, 9 to 5, writing technically," she explained. "Writing fiction is entirely dissimilar," she added. "The skills barely overlap." While technical writing requires reviewing and distilling factual information, fiction is a creative act, the first step of which is finding the right voice. "Once I find the voice of the storyteller, the story tells itself," Abelove once explained. Commenting on making the transition between technical writing and creating fiction, Abelove implied that the two disciplines nourish each other. She commented to Jennifer M. Brown in *Publishers Weekly,* "When you write, there's always something back there. . . . There's always this little idea scooper going on."

## BIOGRAPHICAL AND CRITICAL SOURCES:

*BOOKS*

Abelove, Joan, *Go and Come Back,* DK Ink (New York, NY), 1998.
*Authors and Artists for Young Adults,* Volume 36, Gale (Detroit, MI), 2000.

*PERIODICALS*

*Booklist,* March 1, 1998, Ilene Cooper, review of *Go and Come Back,* p. 1129; November 15, 1998, review of *Go and Come Back,* p. 585; January 1, 1999, review of *Go and Come Back,* p. 782; September 1, 1999, review of *Saying It Out Loud,* p. 126.
*Book Report,* January-February, 1999, Sherry Hoy, review of *Go and Come Back,* p. 58.
*Bulletin of the Center for Children's Books,* October, 1999, Deborah Stevenson, review of *Saying It Out Loud,* pp. 44-45; June 1, 2000, review of *Go and Come Back,* p. 1875.
*English Journal,* November, 1999, Chris Crowe, review of *Go and Come Back,* p. 150.
*Horn Book,* May-June, 1998, Nancy Vasilakis, review of *Go and Come Back,* pp. 337-338; September-October, 1999, Nancy Vasilakis, review of *Saying It Out Loud,* p. 605.
*Kirkus Reviews,* January 15, 1998, p. 108.
*Kliatt,* September, 1999. p. 4.
*Magpies,* July, 1999, p. 36.
*New York Times Book Review,* Jen Nessel, June 21, 1998, review of *Go and Come Back.*
*Publishers Weekly,* February 2, 1998, p. 91; June 29, 1998, Jennifer M. Brown, "Joan Abelove," p. 26; August 9, 1999, review of *Saying It Out Loud,* p. 353; November 1, 1999, review of *Saying It Out Loud,* p. 57; June 5, 2000, review of *Go and Come Back,* p. 96; July 9, 2001, p. 70.
*School Library Journal,* March, 1998, Pam Gosner, review of *Go and Come Back,* p. 208; September, 1999, Barbara Auerbach, review of *Saying It Out Loud,* p. 218.
*Voice of Youth Advocates,* October, 1999, Judy Sasges, review of *Saying It out Loud,* p. 254.

*ONLINE*

*Downhomebooks.Com,* http://www.downhomebooks. com/ (August, 2003), interview with Abelove.

## ADA, Alma Flor 1938-

*PERSONAL:* Born January 3, 1938, in Camagüey, Cuba; daughter of Modesto A. (a professor) and Alma (a teacher and certified public accountant; maiden name, Lafuente) Ada; married Armando Zubizarreta, 1961 (divorced, 1971); married Jörgen Voss, 1984 (divorced, 1995); children: (first marriage) Rosalma, Alfonso, Miguel, Gabriel. *Education:* Universidad Complutense de Madrid, received diploma, 1959; Pontificia Universidad Católica del Perú, M.A., 1963, Ph. D., 1965; Harvard University, postdoctoral study, 1965-67.

*ADDRESSES: Home*—1459 18th St. #138, San Francisco, CA 94107-2801. *Office*—School of Education, University of San Francisco, 2130 Fulton St., San Francisco, CA 94117-1071.

*CAREER:* Colegio A. von Humboldt, Lima, Perú, head of Spanish department, 1963-65, 1967-69; Emory University, Atlanta, GA, associate professor of Romance languages, 1970-72; Mercy College of Detroit, Detroit, MI, professor, 1973-75; University of San Francisco, San Francisco, CA, professor of education, 1976—, and director of Center for Multicultural Literature for Children and Young Adults. University of Guam, Agana, Guam, visiting professor, summer, 1978; University of Texas, El Paso, TX, visiting professor, summer, 1979, winter, 1991; Universidad Complutense, Madrid, Spain, visiting professor, summers, 1989, 1990, 1991; St. Thomas University, Houston, TX, visiting professor, summers, 1992, 1993; Fundación José Ortega y Gassett, Madrid, Spain, summers, 1996, 1997, 1998. Member of selection committee, Fulbright Overseas Fellowship Program, 1968-69, 1977-78; chairperson, National Seminar on Bilingual education, 1974, National Policy Conference on Bilingualism in Higher Education, 1978, and International Congress of Children's Literature in Spanish, 1978, 1979, 1981; publishing consultant, 1975-95; member of the board, Books for Youth and Children's Television Workshop's *Sesame Street* in Spanish; *Loose Leaf; Between the Lions; Journal of Latinos in Education;* founder and first editor-in-chief of *Journal of the National Association for Bilingual Education;* Reading the World annual conference, University of San Francisco, faculty advisor.

*MEMBER:* International Reading Association; International Board on Books for Young Children (IBBY); National Association for Bilingual Education (founding member of the Michigan and Illinois branches); California Association for Bilingual Education.

*AWARDS, HONORS:* Fulbright scholar, 1965-67; grants from Institute for International Education, 1965-67, Emory University, 1971, and Michigan Endowment for the Arts, 1974; Mary Bunting Institute scholar at Radcliffe College and Harvard University, 1966-68; University of San Francisco Distinguished Research Award from the School of Education, 1984; Marta Salotti Gold Medal (Argentina), 1989, for *Encaje de piedra;* University of San Francisco Outstanding Teacher Award, 1985; Christopher Award (ages eighten), 1992, and Notable Children's Trade Book in the Field of Social Studies, National Council for the Social Studies/Children's Book Council, both for *The Gold Coin;* Parents' Choice Honor Book, 1995, for *Dear Peter Rabbit;* Aesop Accolade from the American Folklore Association and American Booksellers "Pick of the List," both 1995, for *Mediopollito/Half-Chicken;* Simon Wiesenthal Museum of Tolerance Award, 1998, for *Gathering the Sun;* Gold Medal, *Parenting* magazine, 1998, for *The Lizard and the Sun;* Marta Salotti Award (Argentina), for *Encaje de piedra;* California PTA Association Yearly Award; Latina Writers' Award, José Martí World Award (Costa Rica), and San Francisco Public Library Laureate, all 2000; Pura Belpré Award, American Library Association, 2000, for *Under the Royal Palms.*

*WRITINGS:*

*FOR CHILDREN*

(With Maria del Pilar de Olave) *El Enanito de la pared y otras historias* (title means "The Wall's Dwarf and Other Tales"), Editorial Arica (Lima, Peru), 1974.

(With Maria del Pilar de Olave) *Las Pintas de la mariquitas* (title means "The Ladybug's Dots"), Editorial Arica (Lima, Peru), 1974.

(With Maria del Pilar de Olave) *Saltarín y sus dos amigas y otras historias* (title means "Springy and His Two Friends and Other Stories"), Editorial Arica (Lima, Peru), 1974.

(With Maria del Pilar de Olave) *La Gallinita costurera y otras historias* (title means "The Little Hen Who Enjoyed Sewing and Other Stories"), Editorial Arica (Lima, Peru), 1974.

*Amigos/Friends,* illustrated by Barry Koch, Santillana USA Publishing (Miami, FL), 1989.

*Quien nacera aquí?/Who's Hatching Here?,* illustrated by Viví Escrivá, Santillana USA Publishing (Miami, FL), 1989.

*Me gustaría tener/How Happy I Would Be,* Santillana USA Publishing (Miami, FL), 1989.

*El Canto del mosquito/The Song of the Teeny-Tiny Mosquito,* Santillana USA Publishing (Miami, FL), 1989.

*Una Extraña visita/Strange Visitors,* Santillana USA Publishing (Miami, FL), 1989.

*The Gold Coin,* translated from the Spanish by Bernice Randall, illustrated by Neil Waldman, Atheneum (New York, NY), 1991, published as *La Moneda de oro,* Turtleback Books (Madison, WI), 1996.

(With Rosalma Zubizarreta) *Despues de la tormenta/After the Storm,* illustrated by Viví Escrivá, Santillana USA Publishing (Compton, CA), 1991.

(With Rosalma Zubizarreta) *La Piñata vacia/The Empty Piñata,* illustrated by Viví Escrivá, Santillana USA Publishing (Compton, CA), 1991.

(With Rosalma Zubizarreta) *La Jaula dorada/The Golden Cage,* illustrated by Viví Escrivá, Santillana USA Publishing (Compton, CA), 1991.

(With Rosalma Zubizarreta) *Como nació el arco iris/How the Rainbow Came to Be,* illustrated by Viví Escrivá, Santillana USA Publishing (Compton, CA), 1991.

(With Rosalma Zubizarreta) *No quiero derretirme/I Don't Want to Melt,* illustrated by Viví Escrivá, Santillana USA Publishing (Compton, CA), 1991.

(With Rosalma Zubizarreta) *La Hamaca de la vaca, o, Un amigo mas/In the Cow's Backyard,* illustrated by Viví Escrivá, Santillana USA Publishing (Compton, CA), 1991.

(With Rosalma Zubizarreta) *No fui yo . . ./It Wasn't Me,* illustrated by Viví Escrivá, Santillana USA Publishing (Compton, CA), 1991.

(With Rosalma Zubizarreta) *Rosa alada/A Rose with Wings,* illustrated by Viví Escrivá, Santillana USA Publishing (Compton, CA), 1991.

(With Rosalma Zubizarreta) *La Sorpresa de Mamá Coneja/A Surprise for Mother Rabbit,* illustrated by Viví Escrivá, Santillana USA Publishing (Compton, CA), 1991.

(With Rosalma Zubizarreta) *¿Pavo para la Cena de Gracias? ¡No, gracias!/Turkey for Thanksgiving? No Thanks!,* illustrated by Viví Escrivá, Santillana USA Publishing (Compton, CA), 1991.

(With Rosalma Zubizarreta) *El Susto de los fantasmas/What Are Ghosts Afraid Of?,* illustrated by Viví Escrivá, Santillana USA Publishing (Compton, CA), 1991.

*Los Seis deseos de la jirafa,* illustrated by Doug Roy, Hampton-Brown Books (Carmel, CA), 1992, translated by Shirleyann Costigan as *Giraffe's Sad Tale (with a Happy Ending),* Hampton-Brown Books (Carmel, CA), 1992.

*Una Semilla nada más,* illustrated by Frank Remkiewicz, Hampton-Brown Books (Carmel, CA), 1992, translated by Shirleyann Costigan as *Just One Seed,* Hampton-Brown Books (Carmel, CA), 1992.

*Serafina's Birthday,* illustrated by Louise Bates Satterfield, translated from the Spanish by Ana M. Cerro, Atheneum (New York, NY), 1992.

(With Rosalma Zubizarreta) *El Papalote/The Kite,* illustrated by Viví Escrivá, Santillana USA Publishing (Compton, CA), 1992.

(With Janet Thorne and Philip Wingeier-Rayo) *Choices and Other Stories from the Caribbean,* illustrated by Maria Antonia Ordonez, Friendship Press (New York, NY), 1993.

*Barquitos de papel/Paper Boats,* illustrated by Pablo Torrecilla, Laredo Publishing (Beverly Hills, CA), 1993.

*Barriletes/Kites,* illustrated by Pablo Torrecilla, Laredo Publishing (Beverly Hills, CA), 1993.

*Canción de todos los niños del mundo* (title means "Song of All Children of the World"), Houghton Mifflin (Boston, MA), 1993.

*Días de circo,* Laredo Publishing (Beverly Hills, CA), 1993, translation by Rosalma Zubizarreta published as *Circus Time,* Laredo Publishing (Beverly Hills, CA), 1993.

*La Tataranieta de cucarachita Martina/The Great-great-granddaughter of La Cucarachita Martina,* illustrated by Ana López Escrivá, Scholastic (New York, NY), 1993.

*Me gusta . . .* (title means, "I Like . . ."), illustrated by Denise y Fernando, Houghton Mifflin (Boston, MA), 1993.

*¡Me gusta jugar!* (title means, "I Like to Play!"), illustrated by Jon Godell, McGraw-Hill (New York, NY), 1993.

(With Rosalma Zubizarreta) *Olmo y la mariposa azul,* illustrated by Viví Escrivá, Laredo Publishing (Torrance, CA), 1992, translation by Rosalma Zubizarreta published as *Olmo and the Blue Butterfly,* Laredo Publishing (Beverly Hills, CA), 1995.

*El Pañuelo de seda,* illustrated by Viví Escrivá, Laredo Publishing (Torrance, CA), 1993, translation by Rosalma Zubizarreta published as *The Silk Scarf,* Laredo Publishing (Beverly Hills, CA), 1995.

*Pin, pin, sarabín,* illustrated by Pablo Torrecilla, Laredo Publishing (Beverly Hills, CA), 1993.

*Pregones,* illustrated by Pablo Torrecilla, Laredo Publishing (Torrance, CA), 1993, translation by Rosalma Zubizarreta published as *Vendor's Calls,* Laredo Publishing (Beverly Hills, CA), 1995.

*El Reino de la geometría,* illustrated by José Ramón Sánchez, Laredo Publishing (Torrance, CA), 1993, translation by Rosalma Zubizarreta published as *The Kingdom of Geometry,* Laredo Publishing (Beverly Hills, CA), 1995.

(Reteller) *The Rooster Who Went to His Uncle's Wedding: A Latin American Folktale,* illustrated by Kathleen Kuchera, Putnam (New York, NY), 1993, published as *El Gallo que fue a la boda de su tio,* PaperStar (New York, NY), 1998.

(With Rosalma Zubizarreta) *Dear Peter Rabbit,* illustrated by Leslie Tryon, Atheneum (New York, NY), 1994, published as *Querido Pedrin,* Turtleback Books (Madison, WI), 1997.

*En el barrio/In the Barrio,* illustrated by Liliana Wilson Grez, Scholastic (New York, NY), 1994.

(With Rosalma Zubizarreta) *El Unicornio del oeste/ The Unicorn of the West,* illustrated by Abigail Pizer, Atheneum (New York, NY), 1994.

*Me encantan los sabados . . . and Saturdays too,* illustrated by Michael Bryant, Atheneum (New York, NY), 1994, English translation published as *I Love Saturdays . . . y Domingos,* illustrated by Elivia Savadier, Atheneum (New York, NY), 1998.

*El Ratón de la ciudad y el ratón del campo,* Grosset & Dunlap (New York, NY), 1994.

*Los Tres gatitos,* Grosset & Dunlap (New York, NY), 1994.

*Y colorín colorado,* Turtleback Books (Madison, WI), 1995.

(With Pam Schiller) *A Chance for Esperanza/La oportunidad de Esperanza,* McGraw-Hill (New York, NY), 1995.

*Bernice the Barnacle/Más poderoso que yo,* illustrated by Viví Escrivá, McGraw Hill (New York, NY), 1995.

(With Rosalma Zubizarreta) *Mediopollito/Half-Chicken: A New Version of a Traditional Story* (bilingual edition), illustrated by Kim Howard, Doubleday (New York, NY), 1995.

*Mi mamá siembra fresas/My Mother Plants Strawberries,* illustrated by Larry Ramond, McGraw-Hill (New York, NY), 1995.

*El Vuelo de los colibríes* (title means "The Hummingbirds' Flight"), illustrated by Judith Jacobson, Laredo Publishing (Beverly Hills, CA), 1995.

*Jordi's Star,* illustrated by Susan Gaber, Putnam (New York, NY), 1996.

(With Rosalma Zubizarreta) *The Lizard and the Sun/La Lagartija y el sol: A Folktale in English and Spanish,* illustrated by Felipe Dávalos, Doubleday (New York, NY), 1997.

*El Árbol de Navidad/The Christmas Tree* (bilingual edition), illustrated by Viví Escrivá, Santillana USA Publishing (Miami, FL), 1997, new edition, illustrated by Terry Ybanez, Hyperion (New York, NY), 1997.

*The Malachite Palace,* illustrated by Leonid Gore, translation by Rosalma Zubizarreta, Atheneum (New York, NY), 1998.

*Yours Truly, Goldilocks,* illustrated by Leslie Tryon, Atheneum (New York, NY), 1998.

*En la playa* (title means "At the Beach"), illustrated by Roberta Ludlow, Harcourt (Orlando, FL), 1999.

*Three Golden Oranges,* illustrated by Reg Cartwright, Atheneum (New York, NY), 1999.

*Daniel's Mystery Egg,* illustrated by G. Brian Karas, Harcourt (San Diego, CA), 2000.

*Friend Frog,* illustrated by Lori Lohstoeter, Harcourt (San Diego, CA), 2000.

*Daniel's Pet,* illustrated by G. Brian Karas, Harcourt, (San Diego, CA), 2001.

*En el mar* (title means "In the Ocean"), illustrated by Richard Bernal, Harcourt (Orlando, FL), 2001.

*With Love, Little Red Hen,* illustrated by Leslie Tryon, Atheneum (New York, NY), 2001.

(With Douglas Hill) *Brujas y magos,* Santillana USA Publishing (Miami, FL), 2002.

Also author of *Así pasaron muchos años; Canción y alegría; Cieto abierto; En un lugar muy lejano; Erase que se era; Letters; ¿Quién cuidara al cocodrilo?; ¿Quieres que te cuente?; The New Hamster;* and *Y fueron felices.*

*POETRY*

*Una Vez en el madio del mar* (title means "Once Upon a Time in the Middle of the Sea"), illustrated by Ulises Wensell, Escuela Española (Madrid, Spain), 1987.

*A la sombra de un ala* (title means "Under the Shade of a Wing"), illustrated by Ulises Wensell, Escuela Española (Madrid, Spain), 1988.

*Abecedario de los animales* (title means "An Animal ABC"), illustrated by Viví Escrivá, Espasa-Calpe (Madrid, Spain), 1990.

(With Rosalma Zubizarreta) *Gathering the Sun: An ABC in Spanish and English,* illustrated by Simón Silva, English Lothrop (New York, NY), 1997.

*Coral y espuma* (title means "Coral and Foam"), illustrated by Viví Escrivá, Espasa-Calpe (Madrid, Spain), 2003.

*CHAPTER BOOKS*

*Encaje de piedra* (title means "Stone Lace"), illustrated by Kitty Lorefice de Passalia, Editorial Guadalupe (Buenos Aires, Argentina), 1989.

*El Manto de pluma y otros cuentos* (title means "The Feather Cloak and Other Stories"), illustrated by Viví Escrivá, Alfaguara (Compton, CA), 1990.

*My Name Is María Isabel,* translated from the Spanish by Ana M. Cerro, illustrated by K. Dyble Thompson, Atheneum (New York, NY), 1993, published as *Me llamo María Isabel,* Macmillan (New York, NY), 1994.

*¿Quién cuida al cocodrilo?* (title means "Who Will Keep the Crocodile?"), illustrated by Viví Escrivá, Espasa-Calpe (Madrid, Spain), 1994.

(With F. Isabel Campoy) *Ecos del pasado* (title means "Echoes from the Past"), Harcourt Brace (Orlando, FL), 1996.

*PLAYS; WITH F. ISABEL CAMPOY*

*Primer Acto,* Harcourt School Publishers (Orlando, FL), 1996.

*Risas y aplausos,* Harcourt School Publishers (Orlando, FL), 1996.

*Escenas y alegrías,* Harcourt School Publishers (Orlando, FL), 1996.

*Actores y flores,* Harcourt School Publishers (Orlando, FL), 1996.

*Saludos al público,* Harcourt School Publishers (Orlando, FL), 1996.

*Ensayo general,* Harcourt School Publishers (Orlando, FL), 1996.

*Acto final,* Harcourt School Publishers (Orlando, FL), 1996.

*Rat-a-Tat,* Alfaguara (Miami, FL), 2000, published as *Rat-a-Tat Cat,* Santillana USA Publishing (Miami, FL), 2002.

*Roll 'n' Roll,* Alfaguara (Miami, FL), 2000, published as *Roll 'n Role,* Santillana USA Publishing (Miami, FL), 2002.

*Top Hat,* Alfaguara (Miami, FL), 2000.
*Curtains Up!,* Alfaguara (Miami, FL), 2000.

*FOR CHILDREN; WITH F. ISABEL CAMPOY*

*Sigue la palabra,* Harcourt School Publishers (Orlando, FL), 1995.

*Imágenes del pasado,* Harcourt School Publishers (Orlando, FL), 1995.

*Música amiga* (anthology of Hispanic folklore; includes tapes and teacher's guide), ten volumes, Del Sol (Westlake, OH), 1996-98.

*Una Semilla de luz* (title means "A Seed of Light"), illustrated by Felipe Dávalos, Alfaguara (Madrid, Spain), 2000.

*Tablado de Doña Rosita/Curtain's Up,* Santillana USA Publishing (Miami, FL), 2001.

*¡Feliz cumpleaños, Caperucita Roja!/Happy Birthday, Little Red Riding Hood!* (bilingual edition), illustrated by Ana López Escrivá, Alfaguara (Miami, FL), 2002.

*El Nuevo hogar de los siete cabritos/The New Home of the Seven Billy Goats,* illustrated by Viví Escrivá, Alfaguara (Miami, FL), 2002.

*A New Job for Pérez the Mouse/Ratoncito Perez, Cartero,* illustrated by Sandra López Escrivá, Alfaguara (Miami, FL), 2002.

*One, Two, Three, Who Can It Be?/Uno, dos, tres: ¡Dime quién es!,* illustrated by Viví Escrivá, Alfaguara (Miami, FL), 2002.

*On the Wings of the Condor/En alas del condor,* Alfaguara (Miami, FL), 2002.

*Eyes of the Jaguar/Ojos del jaguar,* Alfaguara (Miami, FL), 2002.

*Friends from A to Z: A Glossary of the Hispanic World/Amigos de la A a la Z: Un alfabeto del mundo hispánico,* Santillana USA Publishing (Miami, FL), 2002.

*The Quetzal's Journey/Vuelo del quetzal,* illustrated by Felipe Daválos, Santillana USA Publishing (Miami, FL), 2002.

(Adaptor) *Rosa Raposa,* illustrated by Ariane Dewey and Jose Aruego, Harcourt (New York, NY), 2002.

*POETRY; IN SPANISH; WITH F. ISABEL CAMPOY*

*Gorrión, Gorrión,* Harcourt School Publishers (Orlando, FL), 1996.

*El Verde limón,* Harcourt School Publishers (Orlando, FL), 1996.

*La Rama azul,* Harcourt School Publishers (Orlando, FL), 1996.

*Nuevo día,* Harcourt School Publishers (Orlando, FL), 1996.

*Huertos de coral,* Harcourt School Publishers (Orlando, FL), 1996.

*Ríos de lava,* Harcourt School Publishers (Orlando, FL), 1996.

*Dulce es la sal,* Harcourt School Publishers (Orlando, FL), 1996.

*Canta la letra,* illustrated by Ulises Wensell, Del Sol (Westlake, OH), 1998, with music by Suni Paz, 2003.

*Caracolí,* illustrated by Ulises Wensell, Del Sol (Westlake, OH), 1998, with music by Suni Paz, 2003.

*Con ton y son,* illustrated by Ulises Wensell, Del Sol (Westlake, OH), 1998, with music by Suni Paz, 2003.

*Corre al coro,* illustrated by Ulises Wensell, Del Sol (Westlake, OH), 1998, with music by Suni Paz, 2003.

*Do, re, mi, sí, sí!* illustrated by Ulises Wensell, Del Sol (Westlake, OH), 1998, with music by Suni Paz, 2003.

*El Camino de tu risa,* illustrated by Ulises Wensell, Del Sol (Westlake, OH), 1998, with music by Suni Paz, 2003.

*El Son de sol,* illustrated by Ulises Wensell, Del Sol (Westlake, OH), 1998, with music by Suni Paz, 2003.

*Qué rica la ronda!* illustrated by Ulises Wensell, Del Sol (Westlake, OH), 1998, with music by Suni Paz, 2003.

*Sigue la música,* illustrated by Ulises Wensell, Del Sol (Westlake, OH), 1998, with music by Suni Paz, 2003.

*"HAGAMOS CAMINOS" SERIES; WITH MARIA DEL PILAR DE OLAVE*

*Partimos* (title means "We Start"), illustrated by Ulises Wensell, Addison-Wesley (Reading, MA), 1986.

*Andamos* (title means "We Walk"), illustrated by Ulises Wensell, Addison-Wesley (Reading, MA), 1986.

*Corremos* (title means "We Run"), illustrated by Ulises Wensell, Addison-Wesley (Reading, MA), 1986.

*Volamos* (title means "We Fly"), illustrated by Ulises Wensell, Addison-Wesley (Reading, MA), 1986.

*Navegamos* (title means "We Sail"), illustrated by Ulises Wensell, Addison-Wesley (Reading, MA), 1986.

*Exploramos* (title means "We Explore"), illustrated by Ulises Wensell, Addison-Wesley (Reading, MA), 1986.

*"GATEWAYS TO THE SUN" SERIES; WITH F. ISABEL CAMPOY*

*Smiles/Sonrisas* (biographies of Pablo Picasso, Gabriela Mistral, and Benito Juarez), Alfaguara (Miami, FL), 1998.

*Steps/Pasos* (biographies of Rita Moreno, Fernando Botero, and Evelyn Cisneros), Alfaguara (Miami, FL), 1998.

*Voices/Voces* (biographies of Luis Valdez, Judith F. Baca, and Carlos J. Finlay), Alfaguara (Miami, FL), 1998.

*Paths/Caminos* (biographies of José Marti, Frida Kahlo, and Cesar Chavez), Alfaguara (Miami, FL), 1998.

*Yo/I Am,* Santillana USA Publishing (Miami, FL), 1999.

*Rimas/Rhymes,* Santillana USA Publishing (Miami, FL), 1999.

*Poemas/Poems,* Santillana USA Publishing (Miami, FL), 1999.

*Palabras,* Santillana USA Publishing (Miami, FL), 1999.

*Mis relatos/My Stories,* Santillana USA Publishing (Miami, FL), 1999.

*Mis recuerdos,* Santillana USA Publishing (Miami, FL), 1999.

*Mambru,* Santillana USA Publishing (Miami, FL), 1999.

*Letras,* Santillana USA Publishing (Miami, FL), 1999.

*Lapices/Pencils,* Santillana USA Publishing (Miami, FL), 1999.

*Crayones/Crayons,* Santillana USA Publishing (Miami, FL), 1999.

*Colores/Colors,* Santillana USA Publishing (Miami, FL), 1999.

*Así soy/This Is Me,* Santillana USA Publishing (Miami, FL), 1999.

*Acuarela,* Santillana USA Publishing (Miami, FL), 1999.

*Blue and Green/Azul y Verde,* Alfaguara (Miami, FL), 2000.

*Brush and Paint/Brocha y pinchel,* Alfaguara (Miami, FL), 2000.

*Artist's Easel/Caballete,* Alfaguara (Miami, FL), 2000.

*Canvas and Paper/Lienzo y Papel,* Alfaguara (Miami, FL), 2000.

(Selector) *Dreaming Fish/Pimpón* (poetry), Alfaguara (Miami, FL), 2000.

(Selector) *Laughing Crocodiles/Antón Pirulero* (poetry), Alfaguara (Miami, FL), 2000.

(Selector) *Singing Horse/Mambrú* (poetry), Alfaguara (Miami, FL), 2000.

(Selector and contributor) *Flying Dragon* (published in Spanish as *Chuchurumbé*), Alfaguara (Miami, FL), 2000.

*TEXTBOOKS AND EDUCATIONAL PUBLICATIONS*

*Sale el oso* ("Big Book, Rimas y Risas Green" series), illustrated by Amy Myers, Hampton-Brown Books (Carmel, CA), 1988.

*¡Manzano, Manzano!,* illustrated by Sandra C. Kalthoff, Hampton-Brown Books (Carmel, CA), 1989.

*El Oso mas elegante,* illustrated by Sandra C. Kalthoff, Hampton-Brown Books (Carmel, CA), 1989.

*Cassette Guide: Culture through Literature and Music* (Spanish Elementary series), illustrated by Jan Mayer, Addison-Wesley (Reading, MA), 1989.

*Sol Kit,* Addison-Wesley (Reading, MA), 1989.

*Whole Language and Literature: A Practical Guide,* Addison-Wesley (Reading, MA), 1990.

*Cinco pollitos y otras poesías favoritas: Tan Small Book Set* ("Días y Días de Poesía" series), Hampton-Brown Books (Carmel, CA), 1991.

*Classroom Set: Tan Set* ("Días y Días de Poesía" series), Hampton-Brown Books (Carmel, CA), 1991.

*El Patio de mi casa* ("Early Learning Packs" series), illustrated by Liz Callen, Hampton-Brown Books (Carmel, CA), 1991.

*Caballito blanco y otras poesías favoritas: Green Small Book Set* ("Días y Días de Poesía" series), Hampton-Brown Books (Carmel, CA), 1992.

*Chart Set: Green Set* ("Días y Días de Poesía" series), Hampton-Brown Books (Carmel, CA), 1992.

*Classroom Set: Green Set* ("Días y Días de Poesía" series), Hampton-Brown Books (Carmel, CA), 1992.

*Días y días de poesía: Complete Program* (available with small books or tapes), Hampton-Brown Books (Carmel, CA), 1992.

*Bear's Walk* ("ESL Theme Links" series), illustrated by Jan Myers, Hampton-Brown Books (Carmel, CA), 1993.

(With Violet J. Harris and Lee Bennett Hopkins) *A Chorus of Cultures: Developing Literacy through Multicultural Poetry* (anthology), illustrated by Morissa Lipstein, Hampton-Brown Books (Carmel, CA), 1993.

*Hampton-Brown Pre-K Program,* Hampton-Brown Books (Carmel, CA), 1993.

(Editor, with Josefina Villamil Tinajero) *The Power of Two Languages: Literacy and Biliteracy for Spanish-Speaking Students,* Macmillan/McGraw-Hill (New York, NY), 1993.

*Actividades para el hogar,* Santillana USA Publishing (Miami, FL), 2001.

*Teatro del gato garabato,* Santillana USA Publishing (Miami, FL), 2001.

*Teatrín de Don Crispin,* Santillana USA Publishing (Miami, FL), 2001.

*Stories the Year 'Round/Cuentos para todo el año,* Santillana USA Publishing (Miami, FL), 2001.

*Cuentos para todo el año: Cuaderno de actividades,* Santillana USA Publishing (Miami, FL), 2001.

*Stories for the Telling/Libros para contar,* Santillana USA Publishing (Miami, FL), 2001.

*Guía del Maestro,* Santillana USA Publishing (Miami, FL), 2001.

*Escenario de Polichinela,* Santillana USA Publishing (Miami, FL), 2001.

*A Magical Encounter: Latino Children's Literature in the Classroom,* Santillana USA Publishing (Compton, CA), 1994, 2nd edition, Allyn & Bacon (Boston, MA), 2003.

(With Pam Schiller) *DLM Pre-Kindergarten and Kindergarten Early Childhood Programs,* McGraw-Hill (New York, NY), 1995.

(With Colin Baker) *Guía para padres y maestros de niños bilingües,* Multilingual Matters (Clevedon, England), 2002.

(With F. Isabel Campoy and Rosalma Zubizarreta) *Authors in the Classroom: Transformative Education for Teachers, Students, and Families,* Allyn & Bacon (Boston, MA), 2004.

Also author of *Transformative Family Literacy: Engaging in Meaningful Dialogue with Spanish-Speaking Parents.*

*COMPILER*

*Poesía menuda* (anthology; title means "Tiny Poetry"), Editorial Arica (Lima, Peru), 1970.

*Poesía pequeña* (anthology; title means "Little Poetry"), Editorial Arica (Lima, Peru), 1973.

*Poesía niña* (anthology; title means "Child Poetry"), Editorial Arica (Lima, Peru), 1973.

*Poesía infantil* (anthology; title means "Poetry for Children"), Editorial Arica (Lima, Peru), 1974.

*Fabulas de siempre* (title means "Everlasting Fables"), Editorial Arica (Lima, Peru), 1974.

*Cuentos en verso* (title means "Stories in Verse"), Editorial Arica (Lima, Peru), 1974.

*Vamos a leer* (title means "Let's Read"), Editorial Arica (Lima, Peru), 1974.

*Adivina adivinador* (title means "A Collection of Traditional Riddles"), Editorial Arica (Lima, Peru), 1974.

*El Nacimiento del Imperio Incaico* (history; title means "The Origins of the Inca Empire"), Editorial Arica (Lima, Peru), 1974.

*El Descubrimiento de America* (history; title means "The Discovery of the New World"), Editorial Arica (Lima, Peru), 1974.

*El Sueño de San Martín* (history; title means "San Martin's Dream"), Editorial Arica (Lima, Peru), 1974.

*Las Aceitunas y la cuchara* (plays; title means "The Olives and the Wooden Spoon"), Editorial Arica (Lima, Peru), 1974.

*La Condesita peregrina y la desposada del rey* (plays; title means "The Wandering Countess and The King's Bride"), Editorial Arica (Lima, Peru), 1974.

*El Cuento del gato y otras poesías favoritas,* Hampton-Brown Books (Carmel, CA), 1992.

(With F. Isabel Campoy) *Pío peep!: Traditional Spanish Nursery Rhymes* (bilingual edition), illustrated by Viví Escrivá, English adaptations by Alice Schertle, HarperCollins (New York, NY), 2003.

*TRANSLATOR*

Lucille Clifton, *El Niño que no creía en la primavera,* illustrated by Brinton Turkle, Dutton (New York, NY), 1975 (originally published as *The Boy Who Didn't Believe in Spring*).

Evaline Ness, *¿Tienes tiempo, Lidia?,* illustrated by the author, Dutton (New York, NY), 1975 (originally published as *Do You Have Time, Lydia?*).

Norma Simon, *Cuando me enojo,* illustrated by Dora Leder, A. Whitman (Chicago, IL), 1976 (originally published as *When I Get Mad*).

Judith Vigna, *Gregorio y sus puntos,* illustrated by the author, A. Whitman (Chicago, IL), 1977 (originally published as *Gregory's Stitches*).

Barbara Williams, *El Dolor de muelas de Alberto,* illustrated by Kay Chorao, Dutton (New York, NY), 1977 (originally published as *Albert's Toothache*).

Barbara Brenner, *Caras,* photographs by George Ancona, Dutton (New York, NY), 1977 (originally published as *Faces*).

Mary Garcia, *The Adventures of Connie and Diego/Las Aventuras de Connie y Diego,* illustrated by Malaquis Montoya, Children's Book Press (San Francisco, CA), 1978.

Lila Perl, *Piñatas and Paper Flowers/Piñatas y flores de papel: Holidays of the Americas in English and Spanish,* illustrated by Victori de Larrea, Clarion Books (New York, NY), 1982.

Harriet Rohmer, *The Legend of Food Mountain/La Leyenda de la montaña del alimento,* illustrated by Graciella Carrillo, Children's Book Press (San Francisco, CA), 1982.

Judy Blume, *¿Estás ahí, Dios? Soy yo, Margaret,* Bradbury Press (Scarsdale, NY), 1983 (originally published as *Are You There, God? It's Me, Margaret*).

Judy Blume, *La Ballena,* Bradbury Press (Scarsdale, NY), 1983 (originally published as *Blubber*).

Donald Charles, *El Año de gato Galano,* illustrated by the author, Children's Book Press (San Francisco, CA), 1985 (originally published as *Calico Cat's Year*).

Judith Viorst, *Alexander y el día terrible, horrible, espantoso, horroso,* illustrated by Ray Cruz, Macmillan (New York, NY), 1989 (originally published as *Alexander and the Terrible, Horrible, No Good, Very Bad Day*).

Judith Viorst, *Alexander, que era rico el domingo pasado,* illustrated by Ray Cruz, Macmillan (New York, NY), 1989 (originally published as *Alexander, Who Was Rich Last Sunday*).

Robert Baden, *Y domingo, siete,* edited by Judith Mathews, illustrated by Michelle Edwards, A. Whitman (Chicago, IL), 1990.

Watty Piper, *La Pequeña locomotora que si pudo,* illustrated by Doris Hauman, Putnam (New York, NY), 1992 (originally published as *The Little Engine That Could*).

Ruth Heller, *Las Gallinas no son las unicas,* Grosset & Dunlap, 1992 (originally published as *Chickens Aren't the Only Ones*).

Val Willis, *El Secreto en la caja de fosforos,* illustrated by John Shelley, Farrar, Straus (New York,

NY), 1993 (originally published as *The Secret in the Matchbox*).

(With Rosalma Zubizarreta) Harriet Rohmer, *Uncle Nacho's Hat/El Sombrero del tío Nacho,* illustrated by Mira Reisberg, Children's Book Press (San Francisco, CA), 1993.

Karen Ackerman, *Al amanecer,* illustrated by Catherine Stock, Atheneum (New York, NY), 1994 (originally published as *By the Dawn's Early Light*).

Keith Baker, *¿Quíen es la bestia?,* Harcourt (San Diego, CA), 1994 (originally published as *Who Is the Beast?*).

Kristine L. Franklin, *El Niño pastor,* illustrated by Jill Kastner, Macmillan (New York, NY), 1994 (originally published as *The Shepherd Boy*).

James Howe, *Hay un dragón en mi bolsa de dormir,* illustrated by David S. Rose, Atheneum (New York, NY), 1994 (originally published as *There's a Dragon in My Sleeping Bag*).

Lynne Cherry, *El Gran capoquero,* Harcourt (San Diego, CA), 1994 (originally published as *The Great Kapok Tree*).

Nancy Luenn, *El Cuento de Nessa,* illustrated by Neil Waldman, Atheneum (New York, NY), 1994 (originally published as *Nessa's Story*).

Barbara Shook Hazen, *Fue el gorila,* illustrated by Ray Cruz, Atheneum (New York, NY), 1994 (originally published as *The Gorilla Did It*).

Barbara Shook Hazen, *Adiós! Hola!,* illustrated by Michael Bryant, Atheneum (New York, NY), 1995 (originally published as *Goodbye! Hello!*).

Nancy Luenn, *La Pesca de Nessa,* illustrated by Neil Waldman, Atheneum (New York, NY), 1995 (originally published as *Nessa's Fish*).

Carolyn S. Bailey, *El Conejito que queria tener alas rojas,* illustrated by Jacqueline Rogers, Putnam (New York, NY), 1995 (originally published as *The Little Rabbit That Wanted to Have Red Wings*).

Margery Williams, *El Conejito de pana,* illustrated by Florence Graham, Putnam (New York, NY), 1995 (originally published as *The Velveteen Rabbit*).

Ann Hayes, *Te presento a la orquesta,* illustrated by Karmen Thompson, Harcourt (San Diego, CA), 1995 (originally published as *Meet the Orchestra*).

Carol Snyder, *Uno arriba, uno abajo,* illustrated by Maxie Chambliss, Atheneum (New York, NY), 1995 (originally published as *One Up, One Down*).

Judith Viorst, *Alexander que de ninguna manera—¿le oyen?—¡lo dice en serio!—se va a mudar,* illustrated by Robin Preiss Glasser, Libros Colibri (New York, NY), 1995 (originally published as *Alexander Who Is Not—Do You Hear Me?—Going—I Mean It!—to Move*).

Judith Viorst, *Alexander se muda,* Atheneum (New York, NY), 1995 (originally published as *Alexander Moves*).

Audrey Wood, *La Casa adormecida,* illustrated by Don Wood, Harcourt (San Diego, CA), 1995 (originally published as *The Napping House*).

Julie Vivas, *La Natividad,* Harcourt (San Diego, CA), 1995 (originally published as *The Nativity*).

Sue Williams, *Sali de paseo,* Harcourt (San Diego, CA), 1995 (originally published as *I Went Walking*).

Jane Yolen, *Encuentro,* illustrated by David Shannon, Harcourt (San Diego, CA), 1996 (originally published as *Encounter*).

Cynthia Rylant, *Henry y Mudge: El Primer libro de sus aventuras,* illustrated by Suçie Stevenson, Aladdin (New York, NY), 1996 (originally published as *Henry and Mudge*).

Cynthia Rylant, *Henry y Mudge con barro hasta el rabo: Segundo libro de sus aventuras,* Suçie Stevenson, Aladdin (New York, NY), 1996 (originally published as *Henry and Mudge in Puddle Trouble*).

Cynthia Rylant, *Henry y Mudge y el mejor día del año,* illustrated by Suçie Stevenson, Aladdin (New York, NY), 1997 (originally published as *Henry and Mudge and the Best Day of All*).

Pat Hutchins, *El Paseo de Rosie,* Aladdin (New York, NY), 1997 (originally published as *Rosie's Walk*).

*TRANSLATOR; WITH F. ISABEL CAMPOY*

Lois Ehlert, *Plumas para almorzar,* illustrated by the author, Harcourt (San Diego, CA), 1996 (originally published as *Feathers for Lunch*).

Lois Ehlert, *A sembrar sopa de verduras,* illustrated by the author, Harcourt (San Diego, CA), 1996 (originally published as *Growing Vegetable Soup*).

Gary Soto, *¿Que montón de tamales!,* illustrated by Ed Martinez, PaperStar (New York, NY), 1996 (originally published as *Too Many Tamales*).

Ellen Stoll Walsh, *Salta y brinca,* Harcourt (San Diego, CA), 1996 (originally published as *Hop Jump*).

Henry Horenstein, *Béisobol en los barrios,* Harcourt (New York, NY), 1997.

Mem Fox, *Quienquiera que seas,* illustrated by Leslie Staub, Harcourt (San Diego, CA), 2002 (originally published as *Whoever You Are*).

Gerald McDermott, *Zomo el conejo: Un Cuento de Africa occidental,* illustrated by the author, Harcourt (San Diego, CA), 2002 (originally published as *Zomo the Rabbit*).

Peter Golenbock, *Compañeros de equipo,* illustrated by Paul Bacon, Harcourt (San Diego, CA), 2002 (originally published as *Teammates*)

Lois Ehlert, *Día de mercado,* illustrated by the author, Harcourt (San Diego, CA), 2003 (originally published as *Market Day*).

*FOR ADULTS; WITH F. ISABEL CAMPOY*

*Home School Interaction with Culturally or Language-diverse Families,* Del Sol (Westlake, OH), 1998.

*Ayudando a nuestros hijos* (title means "Helping Our Children"), Del Sol (Westlake, OH), 1998.

*Comprehensive Language Arts,* Del Sol (Westlake, OH), 1998.

*Effective English Acquisition for Academic Success,* Del Sol (Westlake, OH), 1998.

*OTHER*

*Where the Flame Trees Bloom* (memoir), illustrated by Antonio Martorell, Atheneum (New York, NY), 1994, also published as *Alla donde florecen los flamboyanes.*

*Under the Royal Palms: A Childhood in Cuba* (autobiography), Atheneum (New York, NY), 1998, also published as *Bajo las palmas reales.*

*A pesar del amor* (novel for adults; title means "Love Notwithstanding"), Alfaguara (Miami, FL), 2003.

*Escribiendo desde el corazón/Writing from the Heart* (video), Del Sol Publishing (Westlake, OH), 1996.

*Meeting an Author* (video), Del Sol Publishing (Westlake, OH), 1996.

*Aprender cantando I y II* (sound recording; title means "Learning through Songs"), voice and music by Suni Paz, Del Sol Publishing (Westlake, OH), 1998.

*Como una flor* (sound recording; title means "Like a Flower"), voice and music by Suni Paz, Del Sol Publishing (Westlake, OH), 1998.

Also author of *Pedro Salinal: El Diálogo creador,* and *Aserrin Aserran.* Author of introduction, Mayra Fernandez, *Barrio Teacher,* Sandcastle Publishing, 1992. Coauthor of "Cuentamundos" literature-based

reading series, Macmillan/McGraw-Hill, 1993. Contributor to *In Grandmothers' House,* edited by Bonnie Christiensen, HarperCollins, 2003.

*ADAPTATIONS: Andamos, Corremos, Exploramos, Navegamos, Partimos,* and *Volamos* were adapted for audiocassette by Addison-Wesley, 1987; *Gathering the Sun, Coral y espuma,* and *Abecedario de los animales/An Animal ABC* were voiced by Suni Paz for audio recording and produced by Del Sol (Westlake, OH), 1998; many of the author's books were adapted for audiocassette by Santillana USA Publishing, 1999-2000.

*SIDELIGHTS:* Alma Flor Ada wrote in her 1994 Atheneum press release: "My grandmother taught me to read before I was three by writing the names of plants and flowers on the earth with a stick. Reading and nature became very intertwined for me." She continued, "My grandmother and one of my uncles were great storytellers. And every night, at bedtime, my father told me stories he invented to explain to me all that he knew about the history of the world. With all of these storytellers around me, it is not a surprise that I like to tell stories." Ada is not only a prolific storyteller, but a prime mover in the bilingual education movement. Most of her picture books are available in bilingual Spanish and English editions that promote literacy in both tongues. Ada has also translated into Spanish a significant number of picture books written in English.

As an educator, Ada promotes the use of quality literature as an integral part of the curriculum (her recent book, *A Magical Encounter,* is dedicated to this topic) and emphasizes that everyone—teachers, students, and their families—has important stories, life experiences, and thoughts that deserve to be written and shared. A recent book, cowritten with F. Isabel Campoy (*Authors in the Classroom: Transformative Education with Teachers, Students, and Families*), describes their extensive work in this field. Through her many books, Ada also serves as a cultural liaison: she retells traditional Latin American tales (*The Rooster Who Went to His Uncle's Wedding; Half-Chicken*), presents stories set in Latin America (*The Gold Coin, Jordi's Star*), offers perspectives on life in Latin American countries (*Where the Flame Trees Bloom* and *Under the Royal Palms*), and describes the feelings of children as they confront cultural misunderstanding and learn to take pride in their heritage (*My Name Is Maria Isabel* and *I*

*Love Saturdays . . . y Domingos).* "My vocation as a writer started as a young child," Ada once told *CA*. "I couldn't accept the fact that we had to read such boring textbooks while my wonderful storybooks awaited at home. I made a firm commitment while in the fourth grade to devote my life to producing schoolbooks that would be fun—and since then I am having a lot of fun doing just that!"

Ada was born in Camaguey, Cuba, in 1938. After studying at the Universidad Complutense in Madrid, Spain, she earned her doctorate in Peru. Postdoctoral studies at Harvard and at the Radcliffe Institute as an Institute fellow and a Fulbright scholar led to a teaching position at Emory University. She has spent the major part of her career at the University of San Francisco, as both a professor of education and the director for the Center for Multicultural Literature for Children and Young Adults. Ada is well known as a writer and translator of picture books and poetry for Spanish-speaking children and young adults. Her materials are often used in classrooms where both English and Spanish are taught, and she has done much to give Hispanic culture a wider representation through her non-fiction children's books. At the same time, she has written a series of children's books consisting of letters written by traditional storybook characters to one another (*Dear Peter Rabbit; Yours Truly, Goldilocks;* and *With Love, Little Red Hen*) which have garnered a devoted following among English-speaking children and have taken her work to a broader audience.

Ada's work as a scholar of romance languages—she is the author of a major study on the Spanish poet Pedro Salinas—has been a strong influence on her writing. Another major influence has been her active promotion of bilingualism and multiculturalism. At the same time, the author credits her children as a "constant source of inspiration." She once told *CA:* "I was brought back to my childhood calling, when, in the midst of writing a very scholarly work, my daughter, who was three years old at the time, complained that I was writing very ugly books. One of my greatest joys is that my daughter has often collaborated with me in my work." Ada's daughter, Rosalma Zubizarreta, is an author in her own right and has translated many of her mother's books. Today, Ada's grandchildren continue to inspire and motivate Ada's writing, sometimes becoming characters in her books, just as their parents once did.

Ada created an "unusually appealing readaloud," according to a contributor to *Kirkus Reviews,* in *The*

*Rooster Who Went to His Uncle's Wedding,* an English retelling of a traditional Latin American folktale. In this humorous cumulative tale, a rooster spends so much time grooming himself in preparation for his uncle's wedding that he forgets to eat breakfast. On the way to the wedding, he cannot resist pecking at the kernel of corn he finds in a mud puddle. The rooster asks the grass to clean his muddy beak, but the grass will not help. A lamb refuses to eat the grass, and a dog refuses to bite the lamb . . . but at last the sun, who has always enjoyed the rooster's sunrise song, agrees to help the rooster. *School Library Journal* critic Lauralyn Persson recommended *The Rooster Who Went to His Uncle's Wedding* as a "solid addition to folklore collections."

In *The Three Golden Oranges,* a Spanish folktale, three brothers who wish to marry are instructed by a wise old woman to travel to a distant castle and return with three golden oranges. The two foolish older brothers refuse to follow the instructions they have received, but the faithfulness of the kind younger son is rewarded by marriage to Blancaflor, a beautiful princess, who helps the young man rescue his brothers. Reviewers detected a feminist twist in the ending, in which Blancaflor's sisters refuse to marry the foolish brothers, and praised Ada's simplified rendition of a fairly complex traditional tale.

Ada adapted a Mexican folktale for *The Lizard and the Sun/La Lagartija y el sol,* published in a bilingual edition with the Spanish original on the left side of the page and the English translation by Zubizarreta on the right. The sun has disappeared, and everyone has gone out to search for him. Long after all the others have given up, Lizard continues to search, eventually finding the sun curled up inside a rock. "Readers will cheer Lizard as she find the Earth's source of light and warmth," observed Vianela Rivas in *School Library Journal.*

Ada adapted another Spanish folktale in *Mediopollito/ Half-Chicken: A New Version of a Traditional Story.* Set in colonial Mexico, the Spanish and English bilingual text tells the story of how the weathervane came to be. The story begins with the birth of Half-Chicken, whose unusual appearance—he was born with only one wing and one leg—makes him something of a celebrity in his small village. In search of greater fame, Half-Chicken travels to Mexico City to meet the Viceroy. Along his journey, he befriends a stream, fire, and wind, all of whom end up coming to his aid when the Viceroy's cook decides that Half-Chicken would make a tasty soup. The story is "brimming with silliness and the simple repetition that children savor," remarked Annie Ayres in *Booklist*.

Ada's original fairy tale *The Malachite Palace* features a lonely young princess in search of a friend who captures a songbird. Yet when the songbird ceases to sing, she realizes she needs to release him. The bird helps the girl learn to venture her own cage and make friends with children her own age, regardless of their social differences. "Although the story is not highly original, youngsters will enjoy its gentle familiarity," remarked Denise E. Agosto in *School Library Journal*. Another lonely character is at the center of *Jordi's Star*, another original picture book by Ada. Here Jordi tends a herd of goats on a barren hillside. In his loneliness comes to believe that a star's reflection in a pool of water is a fallen star which has come to befriend him. Jordi tends the star with care, decorating the place where it dwells until the barren landscape is transformed by his love. "Written with strong emotion and a sense of wonder, this story has the tone and resonance of a folktale," noted Joy Fleishhacker in *School Library Journal*. In a star review for *Booklist*, Susan Dove Lempke called the book a "touching, lyrically told story."

Ada's original picture book *The Gold Coin* was honored with a Christopher Award in 1992 and was named a Notable Children's Trade Book. While a thief looks on greedily through the window, Doña Josefa admires a gold coin and tells herself aloud that she must be the richest woman in the world. Juan, the thief, decides to steal the elderly woman's wealth, and lies in wait until she departs. Yet he finds no treasure when he ransacks her home, so he begins to pursue the old woman, intending to force her to give him her gold. Since he is asking for Doña Josefa, everyone assumes he must be her friend, and Juan is gradually transformed as he encounters the friendship and goodwill of all the people that Doña Josefa has helped. As Ann Welton remarked in *School Library Journal*, *The Gold Coin* "makes an important point" about the nature of true wealth and the consequences of greed. A critic for *Publishers Weekly* described the story as "unusual" and "rewarding," concluding that it is "worthy of repeated readings."

*Where the Flame Trees Bloom*, as Ada explains in the book's introduction, is based on her own childhood memories of Cuba. In the evenings, family members would reminisce, telling the stories from which these eleven vignettes are drawn. One of the short stories in this collection offers a portrait of Ada's grandfather, who was confronted at the same time with his wife's imminent death and the collapse of the economy. Another story recounts how Ada's blind great-grandmother crafted dolls for poor children. Ada also recalls the time when her uncle, a schoolteacher, feared for his students' lives when the school was struck by lightning, an experience that helped him realize the significance of his job as a teacher. According to a critic in the *Bulletin of the Center for Children's Books*, Ada's writing "evokes the warmth and character of her family," and *School Library Journal* contributor Marilyn Long Graham described Ada's writing as "elegant."

*Under the Royal Palms* is a companion volume to *Where the Flame Trees Bloom* and is another celebration of Cuban life and culture in the 1940s. While in the first book, Ada recounts stories she remembers hearing in her childhood, in *Under the Royal Palms* she narrates her own childhood experiences. "At the core of the collection, there is a heartfelt portrayal of a quickly disappearing culture and a vastly beautiful land," observed a contributor to *Publishers Weekly*. The book received the Pura Belpré Award of the American Library Association in 2000.

Raising the self-esteem of Spanish-speaking children and children of Hispanic origin living in a society where Anglo culture dominates is the unstated goal of most of Ada's work, and several of her books take on this task explicitly. In *My Name Is María Isabel*, María Isabel's family has moved, and she must attend a new school. There are already two Marías in her class, so the teacher decides to call her "Mary Lopez" instead of María Isabel Salazar López. María Isabel has difficulty identifying herself as "Mary," which leads to some unhappy situations. Yet when María Isabel describes her difficulties in an essay she has been assigned, the teacher realizes her mistake and finds a way to remedy the situation. As Irvy Gilbertson wrote in *Five Owls*, the "link of María Isabel's name with her heritage is an important theme in this story," and various Spanish words are used to "expose the reader to a different culture."

Likewise, *I Love Saturdays . . . y Domingos* makes "a strong statement about cultural diversity and the universality of love," remarked Ann Welton in *School Li-*

*brary Journal.* In this book, a little girl recounts with joy the pleasures she experiences on the Saturdays she spends with her Grandma and Grandpa, as well as the Sundays (*domingos*) she spends with her Abuelito and Abuelita. Both sides come together to celebrate her birthday, showing the girl the blessing of belonging to two worlds. Reviewers also noted that the bilingual format encourages easy adoption of Spanish-language terms, and a contributor to *Kirkus Reviews* remarked that "children eager to explore their own heritage will enjoy watching as the heroine embraces all the diversity in her life."

Ada received a Parents' Choice Honor Award for *Dear Peter Rabbit,* a fantasy that weaves together the tales of various storybook characters, including the Three Little Pigs, the Big Bad Wolf, Little Red Riding Hood, Peter Rabbit, and Baby Bear. Goldilocks is also included in this story, recast as the daughter of Mr. McGregor, the farmer who almost catches Peter Rabbit in the beloved Beatrix Potter stories. Through the letters that they send to one another, readers learn about their various adventures and misadventures. "Children will be enchanted by this opportunity to meet familiar faces in new settings," commented *School Library Journal* reviewer Joy Fleishhacker. Pointing out that Ada's book belongs to the genre of fairy tale parodies, Roger Sutton asserted in *Bulletin of the Center for Children's Books* that *Dear Peter Rabbit* "is as clever as most in the genre." In *Yours Truly, Goldilocks,* Ada and illustrator Leslie Tryon provided a sequel for fans of *Dear Peter Rabbit.* The fairy tale characters continue corresponding in preparation for a housewarming party at the Three Little Pigs' new, wolf-proof home. "This is fairy-tale fun at its best," wrote Beth Tegart in *School Library Journal.* Another sequel, *With Love, Little Red Hen,* portrays the arrival of the Little Red Hen in the enchanted forest that provided the setting for the first two books. "Lovers of fractured fairy tales will be amused by this further peek into the personal letters of familiar characters," predicted a contributor to *Kirkus Reviews.*

Due to Ada's talent and persistence, fewer children learning either Spanish or English will have to endure the boring textbooks or second-rate stories she bemoaned as a child. The author spoke of the benefits of this bilingual approach in her publicity release: "Nothing can surpass the inherent musicality of the [Spanish] language, the deep cultural values incorporated in it," she noted. "Yet [Spanish-speaking] children also

need to read the literature that their peers are reading in English, so that their introduction to American culture occurs through the best medium the culture has to offer." One of Ada's successful ventures in providing bilingual education in a storybook format is *Gathering the Sun: An Alphabet in Spanish and English.* Ada wrote poems to celebrate aspects of farm laborers' lives for each letter of the alphabet, which were translated into English by Ada's daughter, Rosa Zubizarreta. The resulting book is more than a tribute to Cesar Chavez, hero of the migrant labor movement, noted Ann Welton in *School Library Journal;* "whether used to show the plight of migrant workers or the pride Hispanic laborers feel in their heritage, this is an important book," Welton concluded.

Ada is considered to have made a most important contribution to the education of both English and Spanish-speaking children in the United States since she began translating, adapting, and inventing stories for children in the 1970s. Her bilingual picture books are often credited as proof that bilingual education can be attractive and motivating for children while offering high aesthetic, literary, and human values. Ada's recent collection, *Puertas al Sol/Gateways to the Son,* coauthored with F. Isabel Campoy, consists of a number of different series, including poetry, theater, art, and biogrpahies of cultural leaders. This collection offers children the opportunity to enjoy the various contributions that have shaped Hispanic culture. Given the significant population of Americans with Latin American origin, Ada's evident pride in the Latin American heritage is considered a valuable contribution to the literature enjoyed by children in the United States.

*BIOGRAPHICAL AND CRITICAL SOURCES:*

BOOKS

*Children's Literature Review,* Volume 62, Gale (Detroit, MI), 2000.
*Notable Hispanic American Women,* Book II, Gale (Detroit, MI), 1998.
Zipes, Jack, editor, *The Oxford Companion to Fairy Tales,* Oxford University Press (New York, NY), 2000, p.1.

*PERIODICALS*

*American Book Review,* November-December, 1997, George R. Bodmer, review of *Gathering the Sun: An Alphabet in Spanish and English,* pp. 12-13.

*Booklist,* March 1, 1991, review of *The Gold Coin,* pp. 1395-1396; March 1, 1993, Graciela Italiano, review of *The Rooster Who Went to His Uncle's Wedding,* p. 1231; June 1, 1993, Ilene Cooper, review of *My Name Is María Isabel,* p. 1828; May 1, 1994, Ilene Cooper, review of *Dear Peter Rabbit,* p. 1606; February 1, 1995, Isabel Schon, review of *La Pesca de Nessa,* p. 1012; September 15, 1995, Annie Ayres, review of *Mediopollito/ Half-Chicken: A New Version of a Traditional Story,* p. 165; December 1, 1996, Susan Dove Lempke, review of *Jordi's Star,* p. 652; April 15, 1997, Annie Ayers, review of *Gathering the Sun,* p. 1431; December 15, 1997, Julie Corsaro, review of *The Lizard and the Sun/La Lagartija el sol,* p. 698; May 1, 1998, Ilene Cooper, review of *Yours Truly, Goldilocks,* p. 1520; May 15, 1998, Hazel Rochman, review of *The Malachite Palace,* p. 1629; November 15, 1998, Hazel Rochman, review of *Under the Royal Palms,* p. 582; May 15, 1999, Hazel Rochman, review of *The Three Golden Oranges,* p. 1698; September 15, 1999, review of *Under the Royal Palms,* p. 254; August, 2000, Isabel Schon, review of *Anton Pirulero,* p. 2154; July, 2001, Carolyn Phelan, review of *Daniel's Mystery Egg,* p. 2022; September 15, 2001, Lauren Peterson, review of *With Love, Little Red Hen,* p. 229; February 1, 2002, Annie Ayres, review of *I Love Saturdays . . . y Domingos,* p. 944.

*Book Report,* May-June, 1995, Sherry York, review of *Where the Flame Trees Bloom,* p. 45.

*Bulletin of the Center for Children's Books,* April, 1994, Roger Sutton, review of *Dear Peter Rabbit,* p. 249; February, 1995, Susan Dove Lempke, review of *Where the Flame Trees Bloom,* p. 190; December, 1996, Amy E. Brandt, review of *Jordi's Star,* p. 126; June, 1997, Janice M. Del Negro, review of *Gathering the Sun,* pp. 348-349; October, 1997, Janice M. Del Negro, review of *The Lizard and the Sun,* p. 40; March, 1998, Pat Matthews, review of *The Malachite Palace,* pp. 234-235.

*Five Owls,* September-October, 1993, Irvy Gilbertson, review of *My Name Is María Isabel,* p. 14.

*Horn Book,* January-February, 1988, Laurie Sale, review of *The Adventures of Connie and Diego/Las Aventuras de Connie y Diego,* p. 89; March-April, 1995, Martha V. Parravano, review of *Where the Flame Trees Bloom,* p. 218; November-December, 1995, Martha V. Parravano, review of *Mediopollito,* p. 749; January-February, 2002, Kitty Flynn, review of *I Love Saturdays . . . y Domingos,* p. 65.

*Horn Book Guide,* July-September, 1992, Caroline Ward, review of *Serafina's Birthday,* p. 18; January-June, 1993, Marcia Cecilia Silva-Diaz, review of *The Rooster Who Went to His Uncle's Wedding,* p. 324; July-December, 1994, Martha V. Parravano, review of *Where the Flame Trees Bloom,* p. 72; spring, 1997, Maria B. Salvadore, review of *Jordi's Star,* p. 17; spring, 1998, Rebecca Mills, review of *The Lizard and the Sun* and *Gathering the Sun,* p. 116; fall, 1998, Marilyn Bousquin, review of *Yours Truly, Goldilocks,* p. 282, and Kitty Flynn, review of *The Malachite Palace,* p. 282; spring, 1999, Gail Hedges, review of *Under the Royal Palms,* p. 134; fall, 1999, Martha Sibert, review of *Three Golden Oranges,* p. 322.

*Kirkus Reviews,* January 1, 1991, review of *The Gold Coin,* p. 42; May 1, 1993, review of *The Rooster Who Went to His Uncle's Wedding,* p. 591; March 1, 1994, review of *Dear Peter Rabbit,* p. 297; July 15, 1995, review of *Mediopollito,* p. 1020; July 1, 1997, review of *The Lizard and the Sun,* p. 1026; December 15, 1997, review of *El Arbol de Navidad/The Christmas Tree,* p. 1832; May 1, 1998, review of *The Malachite Palace,* p. 654; May 1, 1999, review of *The Three Golden Oranges,* p. 718; September 1, 2001, review of *Daniel's Mystery Egg,* p. 1284; October 1, 2001, review of *With Love, Little Red Hen,* p. 1418; December 1, 2001, review of *I Love Saturdays . . . y Domingos,* p. 1680.

*Language Arts,* November, 1995, Miriam Martinez and Marcia F. Nash, review of *Where the Flame Trees Bloom,* pp. 542-543; March, 1996, review of *Me llamo María Isabel,* p. 207.

*Library Journal,* August, 2001, Lucia M. Gonzalez, review of *Abecedario de los animales/Animal ABC,* p. S26.

*Publishers Weekly,* April 22, 1983, review of *Pinatas and Paper Flowers,* p. 126; June-July, 1987, review of *The Adventures of Connie and Diego,* p. 82; January 11, 1991, review of *The Gold Coin,* p. 103; February, 1991, review of *Y domingo, siete* and *Amigos,* p. 102; April 19, 1993, review of *My Name Is María Isabel,* p. 62; April 26, 1993, review of *The Rooster Who Went to His Uncle's Wedding,* p. 76; February 21, 1994, review of *Dear Peter Rabbit,* p. 253; November 4, 1996, review of *Jordi's Star,* p. 75; March 31, 1997, review of *Gathering the Sun,* p. 76; October 6, 1997, review of *The Christmas Tree,* p. 54; May 4, 1998, Jennifer M. Brown, review of *The Malachite Palace,* p. 212; May 25, 1998, review of *Yours Truly,*

*Goldilocks,* p. 89; December 7, 1998, review of *Under the Royal Palms,* p. 61; May 31, 1999, review of *Three Golden Oranges,* p. 93; December 10, 2001, review of *I Love Saturdays . . . y Domingos,* p. 69.

*Reading Teacher,* September, 1993, Kathy G. Short and Kathryn Mitchell Pierce, review of *The Gold Coin,* p. 46; September, 1998, review of *The Lizard and the Sun,* p. 58.

*School Library Journal,* January, 1981, L. Michael Espinosa, review of *El Niño que no creia en la primavera, Caras,* and *El Dolor de muelas de Alberto,* p. 33; February, 1988, Louise Yarian Zwick, review of *Volamos, Parmos, Exploramos, Corremos, Andamos,* and *Manzano, Manzano!,* p. 92; February, 1990, review of *Alexander y el día terrible, horrible, espantoso, horroso* and *Alexander, que era rico el domingo pasado,* p. 120; August, 1990, Louise Yarian Zwick and Mark Zwick, review of *Quien nacera aqui?, Me gustaria tener . . . , Una extrana visita, El Canto del mosquito,* and *Abecedario de los animales/Animal ABC,* p. 172; April, 1991, Ann Welton, review of *The Gold Coin,* p. 88; September, 1992, Alexandra Marris, review of *Serafina's Birthday,* p. 196; November, 1992, Rose Zertuche Trevino, review of *Olmo y la mariposa azul,* p. 133; April, 1993, Ann Welton, review of *My Name Is María Isabel,* p. 117; May, 1993, Lauralyn Persson, review of *The Rooster Who Went to His Uncle's Wedding,* p. 92; August, 1993, Rose Zertuche Trevino, review of *El Secreto en la caja de fosforos,* p. 204; June, 1994, Jane Marino, review of *The Unicorn of the West,* p. 94; July, 1994, Joy Fleishhacker, review of *Dear Peter Rabbit,* p. 73; August, 1994, Rose Zertuche Trevino, review of *El Unicornio del oeste,* p. 181; November, 1994, Rose Zertuche Trevino, review of *Quien es la bestia?* and *Querido Pedrin,* p. 130, and review of *La Natividad,* p. 131; February, 1995, Marilyn Long Graham, review of *Where the Flame Trees Bloom,* p. 96, and Rose Zertuche Trevino, review of *Hay un dragon en mi bolsa de dormir, Fue el gorila, Me llamo María Isabel,* and *Al amanecer,* p. 126; August, 1995, Rose Zertuche Trevino, review of *One Up, One Down* and *Good-Bye! Hello!,* p. 167; November, 1995, Graciela Italiano, review of *Mediopollito,* p. 87; February, 1996, Rose Zertuche Trevino, review of *Sali de paseo* and *Te presento a la orquesta,* pp. 128, 130; June, 1996, Cynthia R. Richey and Doreen S. Hurley, review of *The Gold Coin,* p. 54; August, 1996, Rose Zertuche

Trevino, review of *Alexander que de ninguna manera—le oyen?—lo dice en serio!—se va a mudar,* p. 179; December, 1996, Joy Fleishhacker, review of *Jordi's Star,* p. 84; March, 1997, Ann Welton, review of *Gathering the Sun,* pp. 169-170; August, 1997, Vianela Rivas, review of *The Lizard and the Sun/La Lagartija y el sol: A Folktale in English and Spanish,* p. 180; October, 1997, Jane Marino, review of *The Christmas Tree,* p. 40; May, 1998, Denise E. Agosto, review of *The Malachite Palace,* p. 106; July, 1998, Beth Tegart, review of *Yours Truly, Goldilocks,* p. 64; December, 1998, Sylvia V. Meisner, review of *Under the Royal Palms,* p. 132; July, 1999, Sally Bates Goodroe, review of *Three Golden Oranges,* p. 83; October, 2001, Bina Williams, review of *With Love, Little Red Hen,* p. 104; January, 2002, Ann Welton, review of *I Love Saturdays . . . y Domingos,* p. 89; February, 2002, Kathleen Simonetta, review of *Daniel's Mystery Egg,* p. 96.

*ONLINE*

*Alma Flor Ada Web Site,* http://www.almaada.com/ (April 8, 2002).

*Houghton Mifflin Reading,* http://www.eduplace.com/ kids/ (April 8, 2002).

*Little Chiles,* http://www.littlechilies.com/ada.htm/ (April 8, 2002).

*University of San Francisco,* http://www.soe.usfca. edu/childlit/ (April 8, 2002).

*OTHER*

Ada, Alma Flor, "Alma Flor Ada" (publicity release), Atheneum (New York, NY), 1994.

\*    \*    \*

## ALLPORT, Susan 1950-

*PERSONAL:* Born July 5, 1950, in New Haven, CT; daughter of Alexander Wise (an administrator) and Jane (Raible) Allport; married David C. Howell (an artist and product designer), September 10, 1978; children: Liberty, Cecil. *Education:* Pitzer College, B.A., 1972; Tulane University of Louisiana, M.S., 1977. *Politics:* Independent. *Religion:* None.

*ADDRESSES: Home*—New York. *Agent*—Virginia Barber, 101 Fifth Ave., New York, NY 10003.

*CAREER:* Writer.

*MEMBER:* National Association of Science Writers, American Medical Writers Association.

*AWARDS, HONORS:* Named Pennsylvania Art Educator of the Year, Pennsylvanian Art Education Association, 1996.

*WRITINGS:*

*Explorers of the Black Box: The Search for the Cellular Basis of Memory,* Norton (New York, NY), 1986.

*Sermons in Stone: The Stone Walls of New England and New York,* illustrated by David Howell, Norton (New York, NY), 1990.

*A Natural History of Parenting: From Emperor Penguins to Reluctant Ewes: A Naturalist Looks at Parenting in the Animal World and Ours,* Harmony (New York, NY), 1997, reprinted as *A Natural History of Parenting: A Naturalist Looks at Parenting in the Animal World and Ours,* Three Rivers (New York, NY), 1998.

*The Primal Feast: Food, Sex, Foraging, and Love,* Harmony Books (New York, NY), 2000.

(With Kevin Gardner) *The Granite Kiss: Traditions and Techniques of Building New England Stone Walls,* illustrated by Guillermo Nunez, Countryman Press (Woodstock, VT), 2001.

Also contributor to the *New York Times.*

*SIDELIGHTS:* Susan Allport is interested in the history of the things that surround her, and this interest is reflected in her writing. A frequent contributor to the *New York Times,* Allport is also the author of several nonfiction works, including *Explorers of the Black Box: The Search for the Cellular Basis of Memory, Sermons in Stone: The Stone Walls of New England and New York,* and *A Natural History of Parenting: From Emperor Penguins to Reluctant Ewes: A Naturalist Looks at Parenting in the Animal World and Ours.*

In 1990 Allport published *Sermons in Stone: The Stone Walls of New England and New York* in which she reported on the origins and reasons for the more than 250,000 miles of stone walls existing in New England and New York following the Civil War. *New York Times* reviewer Rolland Foster Miller explained that Allport "tells many stories. She traces a history of the eons, of the great glaciations that threw these stones in our path in the first place. She outlines the early need for walls, the laws that grew up around them and the dramatic shifts in agriculture that signaled the end of their early usefulness." Some of the old stone walls still exist throughout New England and New York, 1000 yards of which remain on Allport's land, noted Miller, "with some walls serving an old purpose—fencing the family's . . . sheep." In 2001 Allport revisited the subject of stone walls in a collaboration with stonemason Kevin Gardner, titled *The Granite Kiss: Traditions and Techniques of Building New England Stone Walls.* In addition to providing the history, aesthetics, and philosophy of wall building, this book also provides detailed instruction on constructing a good stone wall.

Allport's third publication, *A Natural History of Parenting: From Emperor Penguins to Reluctant Ewes: A Naturalist Looks at Parenting in the Animal World and Ours,* addresses the child-rearing practices of a wide variety of species. Inspired by her observations of ewes raised on her upstate New York property, Allport gives both personal perspectives and scientific information about a variety of parenting activities, from birthing the young to abandonment. Intermingling information about human behavior with that of other animals, such as bats, wasps, dolphins, and baboons, *A Natural History of Parenting* looks at various adaptations evolved by species related to parental care of offspring.

"Readers are taken on a journey of discovery," noted Gloria Maxwell in *Library Journal,* for example, "learning that . . . flamingos form daycare centers." Allport's "writing is clear and often lovely," proclaimed a *Publishers Weekly* reviewer who thought the work is "occasionally too technical for the average reader." Other reviewers, such as Maxwell and *Booklist* contributor Nancy Bent, thought the book was very readable. Bent noted "minor mistakes in detail" and wished for more direct citation for particular facts, but the critic concluded that in *A Natural History of Parenting* "Allport shows how well popular writing can explain science." Discussing the book in *Scotsman,* Fordyce Maxwell found it occasionally superficial, saying that at times the author seemed to have "skimmed the surface" of her subject "rather than waded through it." Yet Maxwell found much merit in Allport's book, particularly the author's exploration of "the question most human parents have asked themselves at some point in the best of families: why have children? She makes a brave, and entertaining, attempt at the answer."

In *The Primal Feast: Food, Sex, Foraging and Love,* Allport considers the ways in which food shapes the nature and rhythm of human and animal lives. Her focus is broad, and her book provides, "if not an exploration of the whole feast of nature," at least "a tasty excursion through some of its most intriguing dishes," reflected Susan Lumpkin in *Zoogoer.* "It will make happy any reader interested in the menu of items in the subtitle: food, sex, foraging, and love—and who isn't interested in at least one of these?" wrote Lumpkin. The reviewer also drew attention to Allport's "thoughtful discussion of food sharing," which examines the importance of food sharing in human relationships. In conclusion, Lumpkin recommended the book as full of "food for thought."

*BIOGRAPHICAL AND CRITICAL SOURCES:*

*PERIODICALS*

*Atlantic Monthly,* March, 1991.
*Booklist,* February 1, 1997.
*Boston Magazine,* November 30, 1990.
*Library Journal,* February 1, 1997.
*Los Angeles Times,* October 28, 1986.
*Nature,* January, 1987.
*New Yorker,* January 28, 1991.
*New York Times,* March 10, 1991.
*Publishers Weekly,* January 13, 1997.
*Scotsman,* March 2, 1998, Fordyce Maxwell, review of *A Natural History of Parenting,* p. 15.
*Washington Post Book World,* February 22, 1987.

*ONLINE*

*Zoogoer: Friends of the National Zoo,* http://www.fonz.org/ (October 15, 2002), Susan Lumpkin, review of *The Primal Feast: Food, Sex, Foraging and Love.*\*

## ANDERSON, Dave
  See ANDERSON, David (Poole)

\*      \*      \*

## ANDERSON, David (Poole) 1929-
  (Dave Anderson)

*PERSONAL:* Born May 6, 1929, in Troy, NY; son of Robert P. (an advertising executive) and Josephine (an insurance broker; maiden name, David); married Maureen Ann Young, October 24, 1953; children: Stephen, Mark, Mary Jo, Jean Marie. *Education:* Holy Cross College, B.A., 1951. *Hobbies and other interests:* Golf.

*ADDRESSES: Home*—8 Inness Rd., Tenafly, NJ 07670. *Office*—New York Times, 229 West 43rd St., New York, NY 10036.

*CAREER: Brooklyn Eagle,* Brooklyn, NY, sports writer, 1951-55; *New York Journal-American,* New York, NY, sports writer, 1955-66; *New York Times,* New York, NY, sports writer, 1966—, author of column "Sports of The Times," 1971—.

*AWARDS, HONORS:* Best Sports Stories Award, Dutton Press, 1965, for "The Longest Day of Sugar Ray," and 1972, for "Beaufort, SC Loves Joe Frazier . . . Now"; Page One Award from New York Newspaper Guild, 1972, for "Beaufort, SC Loves Joe Frazier . . . Now"; Best Sports News-Feature Prize, Dutton Press, 1972, for "I'll Forgive but I'll Never Forget"; Pro Football Writers Story of the Year Award, 1972; Nat Fleischer Award, 1974, for distinguished boxing journalism; Pulitzer Prize for distinguished commentary, 1981; Red Smith Award, 1994; Lifetime Achievement Award, Professional Golfers Association, 1988; McCann Memorial Award for distinguished football reporting, 1998; inducted into National Sportscasters and Sportswriters Hall of Fame, 1990; inducted into New York Sports Museum and Hall of Fame, 1991.

*WRITINGS:*

*UNDER NAME DAVE ANDERSON*

*Great Quarterbacks of the NFL* (juvenile), Random House (New York, NY), 1965.
*Great Pass Receivers of the NFL* (juvenile), Random House (New York, NY), 1966.

*Great Defensive Players of the NFL* (juvenile), Random House (New York, NY), 1967.

*Countdown to Super Bowl,* Random House (New York, NY), 1969.

(With Sugar Ray Robinson) *Sugar Ray,* Viking (New York, NY), 1970.

(With Larry Csonka and Jim Kiich) *Always on the Run,* Random House (New York, NY), 1973.

*Pancho Gonzalez: The Golden Year,* Prentice Hall (Tappan, NJ), 1974.

(With Frank Robinson) *Frank: The First Year,* Holt (New York, NY), 1976.

*The Yankees,* Random House (New York, NY), 1979.

*Sports of Our Times,* Random House (New York, NY), 1979.

(Editor and contributor) *The Red Smith Reader,* Random House (New York, NY), 1982.

(With John Madden) *Hey, Wait a Minute, I Wrote a Book,* Villard (New York, NY), 1984.

*The Cubs,* Random House (New York, NY), 1985.

*The Story of Football,* foreword by O. J. Simpson, Morrow (New York, NY), 1985, revised edition published with a foreword by Troy Aikman, 1997.

(With John Madden) *One Knee Equals Two Feet: And Everything Else You Need to Know about Football,* Villard (New York, NY), 1986.

*The Story of Basketball,* foreword by Julius Erving, Morrow (New York, NY), 1988, revised edition published with a foreword by Grant Hill, 1997.

(With John Madden) *One Size Doesn't Fit All: And Other Thoughts from the Road,* Villard (New York, NY), 1988.

*In This Corner: Great Boxing Trainers Talk about Their Art,* Morrow (New York, NY), 1991, published in England as *Ringmasters: Great Boxing Trainers Talk about Their Art.*

*Pennant Races: Baseball at Its Best,* Doubleday (New York, NY), 1994.

(With Sugar Ray Robinson) *Sugar Ray: The Sugar Ray Robinson Story,* Da Capo (New York, NY), 1994.

*The Story of the Olympics,* foreword by Carl Lewis, Morrow (New York, NY), 1996.

(Essayist) *The Hogan Mystique: Classic Photographs of the Great Ben Hogan,* American Golfer (Greenwich, CT), 1996.

(Essayist) *The Greatest of Them All: The Legend of Bobby Jones,* American Golfer (Greenwich, CT), 1996.

(With John Madden) *Hey, I'm Talking Pro Football!,* HarperCollins (New York, NY), 1996.

*The Story of Golf,* foreword by Jack Nicklaus, Morrow (New York, NY), 1998.

*The New York Yankees: An Illustrated History,* St. Martin's Press (New York, NY), 2002.

(Author of text) *Classic Baseball: The Photographs of Walter Iooss, Jr.,* Abrams (New York, NY), 2003.

Contributor of more than two hundred articles to magazines, including *Reader's Digest, Sports Illustrated, Saturday Evening Post,* and *New York Times Magazine.*

Contributor to numerous anthologies, including *Best Sports Stories 1959, 1963, 1964, 1965, 1966, 1967, 1972, 1973, 1974, 1977, 1978, The Armchair Quarterback,* and *The Fireside Book of Baseball.*

*SIDELIGHTS:* David Anderson "covers a multitude of sports and covers them well," according to *Dictionary of Literary Biography* essayist Jack Ziegler. A longtime sports reporter for New York-based newspapers, Anderson foregoes the statistical or sensational aspects of an athlete's life and "shows more concern for the content of his character," as Ziegler wrote.

Born in Troy, New York, Anderson grew up in Brooklyn, then the home of the beloved Dodgers baseball team. Though not particularly skilled in athletics, Anderson played street versions of baseball, football, and basketball; but there was another side to the young boy. Anderson's father used to bring home a half dozen newspapers daily, which the boy "would spread out and read on the living room floor," wrote Ziegler. "He was thus introduced to writings of Arthur Daley of the *New York Times,* Frank Graham of the *New York Journal-American,*" and other journalistic luminaries of the day.

As a teenager Anderson set his sights on sports writing and got his start in newspapers as a copyboy for the *New York Sun.* After graduation from Holy Cross College, Anderson found his career derailed slightly when the *Sun* folded. In 1951 he went to work for the *Brooklyn Eagle,* working on the racing charts. His "professional break," as Ziegler put it, "came in 1953 when the Dodgers beat reporter . . . broke his hip in Cincinnati. Anderson became a permanent fill-in, covering the 'boys of summer' until 1955," the year the *Eagle* folded. From there Anderson moved to the *New York Journal-American.* Eleven years later he was hired as a sports columnist for the *New York Times.*

Anderson quickly made his reputation. In 1964 he won an award from Dutton Press for his article "The Longest Day of Sugar Ray," a story about the life of boxer Sugar Ray Robinson after he left the ring. Robinson, a former champ, had no other skills to sustain him in retirement; "at age forty-four," noted Ziegler's article, "Robinson is reduced to filling halls in places such as Pittsfield, Massachusetts, against unknowns for small purses." Anderson's full-length biography of Robinson, written with the boxer, was published in 1994.

After the New York Jets' 1969 victory over the Baltimore Colts in Super Bowl III, quarterback Joe Namath announced that he would be interviewed only by New York reporters—among them, Dave Anderson. The columnist had covered the Jets when they were first known as the Titans and was an admirer of Namath's skill, in addition to harboring the idea that the Jets could beat Baltimore. *Countdown to Super Bowl,* Anderson's chronicle of the days prior to football's most prestigious event, was praised for its clear, concise, and unbiased sports presentation. Arthur Cooper of *Newsweek* noted that Anderson "has written a day-by-day account in an understated style that is mercifully free of sport clichés."

Anderson teamed up with the ebullient ex-football coach and television personality John Madden for a series of books, including *Hey, Wait a Minute, I Wrote a Book* and *One Knee Equals Two Feet: And Everything Else You Need to Know about Football.* In the latter work, Madden relates his life in coaching the Oakland Raiders, offering expert views that include the revelation of how "quarterbacks often tip off where they are planning to throw a pass by the way they hold their shoulders as they drop back," as Ralph Novak noted in *People.*

The author produced something of an oral history with *In This Corner: Great Boxing Trainers Talk about Their Art.* Indeed, noted *Sports Illustrated* reviewer Ron Fimrite, Anderson "merely sets the stage for his subjects with a few paragraphs. . .and then lets the subjects, on tape, take over the narrative." Among the interviews is former Mike Tyson cornerman Kevin Rooney, who "has a grand time taking potshots at Don King, Robin Givens (the former Mrs. Tyson) and Givens's mother," as Fimrite wrote.

In an interview with *Editor & Publisher,* Anderson was asked about sports writing. "I'd say it's generally good and sometimes excellent in the major cities and in many of the smaller cities," he said. "There are more realists than romantics now. The best way to improve sports writing is to hire the best writers and reporters available. Don't let them dismiss journalism as a profession because of its comparatively low pay scale. The better the pay, the better writers and reporters it will attract."

*BIOGRAPHICAL AND CRITICAL SOURCES:*

*BOOKS*

*Authors in the News,* Volume 2, Gale (Detroit, MI), 1976.

*Dictionary of Literary Biography,* Volume 241: *American Sportswriters and Writers on Sport,* Gale (Detroit, MI), 2001.

*PERIODICALS*

*Booklist,* July, 1996, Carolyn Phelan, review of *The Story of the Olympics,* p. 1820; January 1, 1998, Phelan, review of *The Story of Football,* p. 796; May 15, 1998, Bill Ott, review of *The Story of Golf,* p. 1622.

*Book Report,* March-April, 1989, Alice Wittig, review of *One Size Doesn't Fit All: And Other Thoughts from the Road,* p. 50; November-December, 1996, Michael Cabaya, review of *The Story of the Olympics,* p. 58; January-February, 1998, Ron Marinucci, review of *The Story of Football,* p. 55.

*Business Week,* August 16, 1982, review of *The Red Smith Reader,* p. 9.

*Child Life,* July-August, 1996, review of *The Story of the Olympics,* p. 34.

*Christian Science Monitor,* April 19, 1994, Larry Eldridge, review of *Pennant Races: Baseball at Its Best,* p. 14.

*Editor & Publisher,* April 6, 1974.

*Horn Book,* September-October, 1998, Elizabeth Watson, review of *The Story of Golf,* p. 618.

*Library Journal,* September 1, 1984, review of *Hey, Wait a Minute, I Wrote a Book,* p. 1683; March 15, 1991, Genevieve Stuttaford, review of *In This Corner: Great Boxing Trainers Talk about Their Art,* p. 51.

*Newsweek,* August 4, 1969, Arthur Cooper, review of *Countdown to Super Bowl;* August 9, 1982, William Plummer, review of *The Red Smith Reader,* p. 63; January 28, 1985, Jim Miller, review of *Hey, Wait a Minute, I Wrote a Book,* p. 70.

*New York,* September 29, 1969.

*New Yorker,* August 16, 1982, review of *The Red Smith Reader,* p. 92.

*New York Review of Books,* September 23, 1982, review of *The Red Smith Reader,* p. 45.

*New York Times,* February 25, 1970; July 15, 1982, John Leonard, review of *The Red Smith Reader,* p. 23; July 18, 1982, Donald Hall, review of *The Red Smith Reader,* p. 3; September 25, 1986, Edwin McDowell, review of *One Knee Equals Two Feet,* p. C23.

*New York Times Book Review,* April 15, 1979; July 18, 1982, Donald Hall, review of *The Red Smith Reader,* p. 3; December 5, 1982, review of *The Red Smith Reader,* p. 34; November 9, 1986, David Whitford, review of *One Knee Equals Two Feet,* p. 33; September 4, 1988, Diane Cole, review of *One Size Doesn't Fit All,* p. 17; May 12, 1991, Allen Barra, review of *In This Corner,* p. 25; April 10, 1994, Susan Jacoby, review of *Pennant Races,* p. 26; June 11, 1995, Gordon Thompson, review of *The Hogan Mystique: Classic Photographs of the Great Ben Hogan,* p. 63; October 20, 1996, Carolyn Hughes, review of *Hey, I'm Talking Pro Football!,* p. 23;

*Parents,* November, 1985, review of *The Story of Football,* p. 64.

*People,* November 26, 1984, review of *Hey, Wait a Minute, I Wrote a Book,* p. 21; September 22, 1986, Ralph Novak, review of *One Knee Equals Two Feet,* p. 16.

*Publishers Weekly,* June 3, 1988, Genevieve Stuttaford, review of *One Size Doesn't Fit All,* p. 78; March 21, 1994, Stuttaford, review of *Pennant Races,* p. 62.

*School Library Journal,* February, 1985, review of *Hey, Wait a Minute, I Wrote a Book,* p. 92; December, 1986, review of *One Knee Equals Two Feet,* p. 127; February, 1989, Elaine Fort Weischedel, review of *The Story of Basketball,* p. 83; April, 1996, Renee Steinberg, review of *The Story of the Olympics,* p. 144; July, 1998, Janice Hayes, review of *The Story of Golf,* p. 102; June, 2000, Michael McCullough, review of *The Story of the Olympics,* p. 157.

*Sporting News,* November 17, 1986, review of *One Knee Equals Two Feet,* p. 11.

*Sports Illustrated,* July 29, 1991, Ron Fimrite, review of *In This Corner,* p. 8; December 12, 1994, Fimrite, review of *The Hogan Mystique,* p. 7A.

*Time,* July 26, 1982, Stephen Smith, review of *The Red Smith Reader,* p. 61; September 24, 1984, John Leo, review of *Hey, Wait a Minute, I Wrote a Book,* p. 78.

*Times Literary Supplement,* December 20, 1991, Mike Phillips, review of *Ringmaster: Great Boxing Trainers Talk about Their Art,* p. 26.

*Wall Street Journal,* April 22, 1994, Frederick Klein, review of review of *The Hogan Mystique,* p. A11.*

\* \* \*

**ANDERSON, Sarah 1947-**

*PERSONAL:* Born May 17, 1947, in London, England; daughter of John Murray (a stockbroker) and Gillian Mary (Drummond) Anderson. *Education:* London School of Oriental and African Studies, London, degree in Chinese, 1977. *Religion:* Roman Catholic.

*ADDRESSES: Office*—Travel Bookshop, 13 Blenheim Cres., London W11 2EE, England. *Agent*—Clare Alexander, Gillon Aitken Associates, 29 Fernshaw Rd., London SW10 0TG, England. *E-mail*—sarah@umbrellabooks.com.

*CAREER:* Travel Bookshop, London, England, founder and owner, 1979—.

*WRITINGS:*

*Anderson's Travel Companion,* Scolar Press (Brookfield, VT), 1995.
*The Virago Book of Spirituality,* Virago (London, England), 1996, published as *Heaven's Gate Thinly Veiled,* Shambhala (Boulder, CO), 1998.
(With Miranda Davies) *Inside Notting Hill,* Portobello Publishing (London, England), 2001.

Contributor to periodicals.

*SIDELIGHTS:* Sarah Anderson told *CA:* "My first book, *Anderson's Travel Companion,* is a book of the bookshop I founded. It is a reference book arranged by country and recommending books in every category.

I wanted people unable to visit the shop to have an idea of how background reading about places makes travel more interesting.

"*The Virago Book of Spirituality* incorporates one of my other interests. I love doing books and articles on topics I know little about. It is a wonderful way of increasing knowledge and interest in different fields.

Anderson later added: "*Inside Notting Hill* was written to show how much more there is to the Notting Hill area than the film."

\* \* \*

**ARAKAWA, Yoichi 1962-**

*PERSONAL:* Born March 25, 1962, in Mexico City, Mexico; son of Tetsuo and Yuriko Arakawa. *Ethnicity:* "Asian." *Education:* University of California—Los Angeles, B.A., 1987; Berklee College of Music, graduated, 1992.

*ADDRESSES: Office*—c/o Six String Music Publishing, P.O. Box 7718-157, Torrance, CA 90504.

*CAREER:* Musician and author.

*MEMBER:* Publishers Marketing Association.

*WRITINGS:*

*ARRANGER; SONGBOOKS*

*Best of Red Hot Chili Peppers,* Warner Bros. Publications (Miami, FL), 1993.
*Best of Black Crowes,* Warner Bros. Publications (Miami, FL), 1993.
*You Too Can Play . . . Jazz Guitar,* Warner Bros. Publications (Miami, FL), 1993.
*You Too Can Play . . . Soft Rock Guitar,* Warner Bros. Publications (Miami, FL), 1993.
*Best of Miles Davis,* Warner Bros. Publications (Miami, FL), 1993.

*Best of Count Basie,* Warner Bros. Publications (Miami, FL), 1993.
*Top Hits of the Country Superstars,* Warner Bros. Publications (Miami, FL), 1994.
*Jim Croce: The Greatest Hits,* Warner Bros. Publications (Miami, FL), 1995.
(With John Stix) *Minor Pentatonic Scales for Guitar,* Hal Leonard Publishing (Milwaukee, WI), 1995.
(With John Stix) *Major Pentatonic Scales for Guitar,* Hal Leonard Publishing (Milwaukee, WI), 1995.
(With John Stix) *Basic Blues for Rock Guitar,* Hal Leonard Publishing (Milwaukee, WI), 1995.
(With John Stix) *Acoustic Rock for Guitar,* Hal Leonard Publishing (Milwaukee, WI), 1995.
(With John Stix) *Modes for Rock and Blues Guitar,* Hal Leonard Publishing (Milwaukee, WI), 1995.
*Jazz Riffs for Guitar,* with cassette or compact disc, Cherry Lane (Port Chester, NY), 1995.
*A Fingerstyle Christmas: Nineteen Beloved Contemporary and Standard Seasonal Favorites Arranged for Solo Fingerstyle Guitar,* Cherry Lane (Port Chester, NY), 1995.
(With John Stix) *Warm-up Exercises for Guitar,* Hal Leonard Publishing (Milwaukee, WI), 1996.
(With John Stix) *Rock Riffs for Guitar,* Hal Leonard Publishing (Milwaukee, WI), 1996.
*Guitar Chords and Accompaniment,* Six Strings Music Publishing (Torrance, CA), 1998, 2nd edition, 2001.
*101 Basic Reading for Guitar,* Six Strings Music Publishing (Torrance, CA), 1999.
*101 Basic Blues Scales for Guitar,* Six Strings Music Publishing (Torrance, CA), 1999.
*101 Basic Major Pentatonic Scales for Guitar,* Six Strings Music Publishing (Torrance, CA), 1999.
*101 Basic Minor Pentatonic Scales for Guitar,* Six Strings Music Publishing (Torrance, CA), 1999.
*101 Basic Guitar Chords,* Six Strings Music Publishing (Torrance, CA), 1999.
*Blues Guitar Chords and Accompaniment,* Six Strings Music Publishing (Torrance, CA), 2003.
*More Guitar Chords and Accompaniment,* Six Strings Music Publishing (Torrance, CA), 2nd edition, 2002.
*More Jazz Guitar Chords and Accompaniment,* Six Strings Music Publishing (Torrance, CA), 2002.
*Jazz Guitar Chords and Accompaniment,* Six Strings Music Publishing (Torrance, CA), 2nd edition, 2003.

## AUBIN, Henry (Trocmé) 1942-

*PERSONAL:* Born December 16, 1942, in New Brunswick, NJ; son of Robert Arnold (a professor) and Elisabeth Gabrielle (a teacher; maiden name, Trocmé) Aubin; married Penelope Morgan (a library editor), December 22, 1968; children: Seth André Morgan, Nishi Elisabeth, Nicolas Charles, Raphaëlle Trocmé. *Education:* Harvard University, B.A., 1964; studied at Washington Journalism Center, 1968, attended Université Laval, Quebec, Canada, 1981-82. *Religion:* Protestant.

*ADDRESSES: Home*—622 Victoria Ave., Westmount, Quebec, Canada H3Y 2R9. *Office*—Montreal Gazette, 1010 Ste. Catherine Street West, Montreal, Quebec H3B 5L1, Canada. *Agent*—Beverly Slopen Literary Agency, 131 Bloor Street west, Suite 711, Toronto, Ontario M5S 1S3.

*CAREER: Philadelphia Bulletin,* Philadelphia, PA, urban affairs reporter and Washington correspondent, 1966-70; *Washington Post,* Washington, DC, urban affairs reporter, 1970-71; *Montreal Gazette,* Montreal, Quebec, Canada, urban affairs reporter, editorial writer, and columnist, 1973—. *Military service:* U.S. Army Reserve, 1965-71.

*MEMBER:* Canadian Centre for Investigative Journalism (co-founder).

*AWARDS, HONORS:* B'nai B'rith Canadian Human Rights Award, 1973; Canadian National Newspaper Award, 1973, 1976, for enterprise in reporting and in 2000 for editorial writing; Canadian National Business Writing Award, 1974, 1975, 1976; Quebec Writers' Federation Award for history, 2002; Canadian Jewish history award, 2003.

*WRITINGS:*

*City for Sale: International Financiers Take a Major North American City by Storm,* James Lorimer & Co., 1977.
*Questions d'éthique: Jusqu'où peuvent aller les journalistes?* Québec-Amérique, 1991.
*The Rescue of Jerusalem: The Alliance between Hebrews and Africans in 701 B.C.,* Soho Press (New York, NY), 2002.

*City for Sale* has been translated into French.

*SIDELIGHTS:* American-born journalist and author Henry Aubin once commented to *CA* that working in Quebec allowed him "to be amidst as much cultural vigor as anywhere in North America" due to the fact that the eastern region of Canada "is trying to burst out on its own after centuries as a sat-upon backwater." Much of Aubin's work has been investigative journalism; his newspaper articles, were the foundation of his 1977 work *City for Sale: International Financiers Take a Major North American City by Storm.* Aubin's examination of "who owns Montreal" quickly became a best-seller in its French-language version, *Les Vrais proprietaires de Montreal.*

"Most of my stuff deals with economic power and who wields it rather than with politics," Aubin added, "since there are so many reporters who probe the latter and since without scrutiny business is all the more easily unaccountable. I am more interested in getting the facts out on how a society is being run and letting people form their own opinions than in trying to deliberately shape those opinions."

A conflict of the distant past is the subject of Aubin's 2002 book, *The Rescue of Jerusalem: The Alliance between Hebrews and Africans in 701 B.C.* When the Assyrian army approached the gates of Jerusalem, the city seemed fated to fall to the invader. But according to the Old Testament, God sent an "angel of the Lord" to save the fortress and devastate the Assyrians. In Aubin's reading, the "angel" came in the form of the African Kushite army, made up of warriors from the Sudan. That the African army remained uncelebrated, the author argues in his book, can be attributed to "a racist campaign over the last two centuries to erase the Kushite contribution to Israel's survival," as a *Kirkus Reviews* critic explained.

According to Clay Williams in *Library Journal,* Aubin asserts that "The Kushites played the decisive role in one of the most important conflicts in history." Much of *The Rescue of Jerusalem*'s critical response concerns this controversial finding, which, according to Donald Akenson of *The Globe and Mail,* suggest that "an entire century of scholarship—the twentieth—was dead wrong on one of the turning points in Western history . . . " He added that "Aubin has mastered the relevant Near Eastern, biblical, and Egyptological material . . . And he argues with real brilliance." A *Publishers Weekly* contributor, while labeling portions of the book "arduous," still found that Aubin "may offer the best solution to a biblical problem that has long troubled scholars."

*BIOGRAPHICAL AND CRITICAL SOURCES:*

*PERIODICALS*

*Globe and Mail,* June 1, 2002, Donald Harman Akenson, "Did Africa Save Monotheism?" p. D11.

*Kirkus Reviews,* February 1, 2002, review of *The Rescue of Jerusalem: The Alliance between Hebrews and Africans in 701 B.C.,* p. 152.

*Library Journal,* May 1, 2002, Clay Williams, review of *The Rescue of Jerusalem,* p. 116.

*National Post,* September 21, 2002, John Fraser, review of *The Rescue of Jerusalem,* p. SP9.

*Publishers Weekly,* April 29, 2002, review of *The Rescue of Jerusalem,* p. 52.

# B

**BARCLAY, Bill**
    **See MOORCOCK, Michael (John)**

\*    \*    \*

**BARCLAY, William Ewert**
    **See MOORCOCK, Michael (John)**

\*    \*    \*

**BARNES, Stephen Emory 1952-**
    **(Steven Barnes)**

*PERSONAL:* Born March 1, 1952, in Los Angeles, CA; son of Emory Flake (an employment counselor) and Eva Mae (a real estate broker; maiden name, Reeves) Barnes; married Tananarive Due (an author); children: one daughter. *Education:* Attended Pepperdine University, 1970-74. *Religion:* Episcopalian.

*ADDRESSES: Home*—13215 Southeast Mill Plain Rd., No. C8-243, Vancouver, WA 98684. *Agent*—Eleanor Wood, Spectrum Agency, 320 Central Park W., Suite 1-D, New York, NY 10025.

*CAREER:* Writer. Columbia Broadcasting System, Hollywood, CA, tour guide, 1974-76; Pepperdine University, Malibu, CA, manager of audio-visual and multi-media department, 1978-80; creative consultant to Don Bluth Productions, 1981; University of California, Los Angeles, currently instructor in creative writing.

*AWARDS, HONORS:* Second place in National Korean Karate championships, 1972; Hugo Award nomination, 1980, for short story "The Locusts."

*WRITINGS:*

*SCIENCE-FICTION NOVELS; UNDER NAME STEVEN BARNES*

(With Larry Niven) *Dream Park,* Ace Books (New York, NY), 1981.
(With Larry Niven) *The Descent of Anansi,* Tor Books (New York, NY), 1982.
*Streetlethal,* Ace Books (New York, NY), 1982.
*The Kundalini Equation,* Tor Books (New York, NY), 1986.
(With Larry Niven and Jerry Pournelle) *The Legacy of Heorot,* Simon & Schuster (New York, NY), 1987.
*Gorgon Child,* Tor Books (New York, NY), 1989.
(With Larry Niven) *The Barsoom Project,* Ace Books (New York, NY), 1989.
(With Larry Niven) *Achilles' Choice,* Tor Books (New York, NY), 1991.
(With Larry Niven) *Dream Park: The Voodoo Game,* Pan Books (London, England) 1991, published as *The California Voodoo Game,* Ballantine (New York, NY), 1992.
*Firedance,* Tor Books (New York, NY), 1993.
(With Larry Niven and Jerry Pournelle) *Beowulf's Children,* Tor Books (New York, NY), 1995.
*Blood Brothers,* Tor Books (New York, NY), 1996.
*Iron Shadows,* Tor Books (New York, NY), 1998.
(With Larry Niven) *Saturn's Race,* Tor Books (New York, NY), 2000.
*Charisma,* Tor Books (New York, NY), 2002.

*Lion's Blood: A Novel of Slavery and Freedom in an Alternate America,* Aspect/Warner Books (New York, NY), 2002.

*Zulu Heart,* Warner Books (New York, NY), 2003.

OTHER; UNDER NAME STEVEN BARNES

*Ki: How to Generate the Dragon Spirit* (nonfiction), Sen-do Publications, 1976.

*The Secret of NIMH* (animated cartoon), Don Bluth Productions, 1982.

Also author of screenplay *The Soulstar Commission,* 1987, and of television scripts, including *Little Fuzzy* (adaptation of the novel by H. Beam Piper), 1979; *The Test* (adaptation of the short story by Stanislaw Lem), 1982; and "Teacher's Aid" and "To See the Invisible Man" (adaptation of the short story by Robert Silverberg), both in *The Twilight Zone* series, 1985-86. Also author of scripts for *Real Ghostbusters* (television cartoon series), 1987, and *The Wizard,* 1987. Contributor of short stories to *Analog* and *Isaac Asimov's Science-Fiction Magazine.*

SIDELIGHTS: Steven Barnes is not only one of the more popular science-fiction authors on the current scene, he is also one of the few African-American writers to make his mark in the world of fantasy literature. Indeed, "the achievements of the versatile [Barnes] have remained virtually unnoticed both in African American literary circles and the broader academic community," maintained an essayist in *Notable Black American Men.*

A native of Los Angeles, Barnes turned to visual entertainment for his initial career, beginning as a tour guide at the CBS studios; eventually he went on to teach creative writing at the University of Southern California film school. Ultimately, the lure of fiction caught up with Barnes, who studied at Los Angeles area colleges but found fault with academia, feeling that college professors lacked the real-life advice a commercial writer needed to get established in the business. Abandoning college, Barnes chose instead to associate himself with successful writers, a strategy that paid off when he met award winning sci-fi novelist Larry Niven. The two exchanged manuscripts, then embarked on a collaboration that would last through several publications.

Barnes made the move to full-time writing in 1980, fulfilling a childhood ambition. "Before I wrote," he told a *Players* interviewer, "I told elaborate lies and decided that it would be more interesting to write them down than get the tar whaled out of me for lying. When I was 16, I decided I wanted to be a writer and I've been one ever since." In his science-fiction novels, Barnes usually pits "one talented and resourceful man against a decadent and/or evil social system," explained Don D'Ammassa in *St. James Guide to Science-Fiction Writers.* "Although the worlds he describes are bleak and repulsive, in each case the resolution of the story is hopeful, indicating that the indomitability of the human spirit will rise above temporary setbacks and persevere."

Barnes's novels *Streetlethal, Gorgon Child,* and *Firedance* all concern Aubry Knight, an assassin of the future who has harnessed his deadly talents into doing good in a ruined Los Angeles of the near future. In this ruined landscape, the result of a natural catastrophe, Knight battles the criminals who prey on the bedraggled citizenry. In *Streetlethal* he takes on drug dealers; in *Gorgon Child* he thwarts an evil religious cult; and in *Firedance* Knight leads a band called the Scavengers, who seek to rebuild the fallen city while being attacked by a dictator's hired killers. A critic for *Kirkus Reviews* described *Firedance* as ideal for "fans of futuristic martial-arts yarns," while a reviewer in *Library Journal* noted that *Firedance* contains "fast-paced action tinged with pseudomysticism." Barnes's interest in the martial arts is also reflected in *The Kundalini Equation.* In this 1986 novel Barnes tells of a martial arts practitioner whose mental training unleashes hidden mystical forces within, transforming the fighter into a potentially dangerous and inhuman creature.

Barnes's *Lion's Blood: A Novel of Slavery and Freedom in an Alternate America* is set in a fantasy version of the nineteenth century. In this book Barnes explores race relations—which he called "probably America's rawest unhealed wound" in a *Publishers Weekly* interview with M. M. Hall. In *Lion's Blood,* Irish Christian Aidan O'Dere and African Islamic Kai ibn Jalleleddin ibn Rashid create an uneasy alliance after the Africans have colonized the United States. O'Dere, kidnapped from his village, is sold into slavery, and is acquired by the wealthy and powerful Rashid. The lives of the two "connect on a battlefield both metaphorical and physical," as a *Publishers Weekly* critic put it. In the opinion of Zakia Carter in

*Black Issues Book Review,* the novel "is an ambitious undertaking, and Barnes ensures success through careful research, strong character development and detailed writing."

In addition to his solo novels, Barnes has also written a number of collaborations with fellow science-fiction writers Niven and Jerry Pournelle. The collaborative works with Niven include *Dream Park* and *The Barsoom Project,* both set in a futuristic theme park where reality is dangerously simulated.

Barnes once told *CA:* "My primary area of interest is human mental and physical development. To this end I research psychology, parapsychology, and kinesiology, practice and teach martial arts, and meditate and study comparative religious philosophy. My major viewpoint is that all human beings are perfect, but that we allow ourselves to dwell in our illusions of imperfection, creating fear, hate, and all negativity in human experience. At any moment we are capable of creating perfection in our lives merely by accepting our divinity. Virtually no Western discipline creates a proper balance between Body, Mind, and Spirit. To this end I have attempted to synthesize a belief system which enables me to grow without ceasing, love without reservation, and face life by accepting death. Life is too short to spend in sorrow or regret and too long to live without sober and informed evaluation.

"To say that 'all men are brothers' is to avoid the real point. We are all expressions of the same Life, call it God, Holy Spirit, Ki, ch'i, prana, kundalini, or anything else you please—these are merely words, symbols, and symbols are only shadows of the Truth. If I have any real goal in life it is to strip away the 'knowledge' I have learned and reenter the Void from which came all things and to which all things must inevitably return."

*BIOGRAPHICAL AND CRITICAL SOURCES:*

BOOKS

*Notable Black American Men,* Gale (Detroit, MI), 1998.
*St. James Guide to Science-Fiction Writers,* St. James Press (Detroit, MI), 1995.

PERIODICALS

*Analog,* August 17, 1981, p. 162; February, 1987, p. 181; October, 1991, p. 163; January, 1996, p. 273; December, 2000, Tom Easton, review of *Saturn's Race,* p. 132.

*Black Issues Book Review,* May-June, 2002, Zakia Carter, review of *Lion's Blood: A Novel of Slavery and Freedom in an Alternate America,* p. 42.
*Booklist,* November 15, 1993, p. 606; February 15, 1998, Eric Robbins, review of *Iron Shadows,* p. 990; July, 2000, Roland Green, review of *Saturn's Race,* p. 2015; January 1, 2002, Green, review of *Lion's Blood,* p. 824; June 1, 2002, Green, review of *Charisma,* p. 1659.
*Fantasy Review,* September, 1986, p. 20.
*Isaac Asimov's Science Fiction Magazine,* March, 1981.
*Kirkus Reviews,* October 15, 1993, p. 1298.
*Library Journal,* November 15, 1993, p. 103; February 15, 1998, Jackie Cassada, review of *Iron Shadows,* p. 174.
*Locus,* January, 1990, p. 49; February, 1991, p. 55; February, 1994, pp. 35, 56.
*Los Angeles Times,* August 2, 1987, p. B11.
*Publishers Weekly,* May 29, 1987, p. 67; August 11, 1989, p. 452; December 6, 1993, p. 61; October 16, 1995, p. 46; June 26, 2000, review of *Saturn's Race,* p. 55; January 21, 2002, review of *Lion's Blood,* p. 69, M. M. Hall, "PW Talks with Steven Barnes," p. 70; June 3, 2002, review of *Charisma,* p. 70.
*Science Fiction Review,* February 1985, p. 41.
*Tribune Books* (Chicago, IL), July 12, 1987, p. 7.*

*        *        *

**BARNES, Steven**
   **See BARNES, Stephen Emory**

*        *        *

**BARRINGTON, Michael**
   **See MOORCOCK, Michael (John)**

*        *        *

**BARRON, T(homas) A(rchibald) 1952-**
   **(Tom Barron)**

*PERSONAL:* Born March 26, 1952, in Boston, MA; son of Archibald (a hotel operator) and Gloria (a geologist and museum founder) Barron; married Currie Cabot; children: three boys, two girls. *Education:* Princeton University, B.A., 1974; attended Oxford University on a Rhodes scholarship, graduated, 1978; Harvard University, M.B.A. and J.D., both 1982. *Hobbies and other interests:* Reading, traveling, hiking, "playing any sports that my kids like to play."

*ADDRESSES: Home and office*—545 Pearl St., Boulder, CO 80302.

*CAREER:* Author and environmentalist. Businessman, c. 1979-89, positions included president of venture capital firm, New York, NY; general partner, Sierra Ventures; chairman, Swiss Army Corporation. Full-time writer, 1989—. Princeton University, Princeton, NJ, founder of environmental studies program and former university trustee. Trustee of Nature Conservancy of Colorado; has led workshops in environmental preservation and restoration for Wilderness Society and other groups. Speaker at schools, libraries, and conferences on literature, education, and the environment.

*MEMBER:* Wilderness Society (member of board).

*AWARDS, HONORS:* Best Books of the Year designation, *Parents* magazine, and *Voice of Youth Advocates,* 1992, Best Books for the Teen Age, New York Public Library, 1993, and Young-Adult Choice, International Reading Association, 1994, all for *The Ancient One;* Colorado Book Award, 1995, Texas Lone Star Book Award, 1997, Utah Book Award, Children's Literature Association of Utah, 1998, and Best of the Texas Lone-Star reading lists, 2000, all for *The Merlin Effect;* Robert Marshall Award, Wilderness Society, 1997, for environmental work; "Not Just for Children Anymore" award, Children's Book Council, 1997, and Oppenheim Portfolio Gold Award, 2000, both for *The Lost Years of Merlin;* "Not Just for Children Anymore" award, 1998, for *The Seven Songs of Merlin;* Best Books of the Year designation, *Voice of Youth Advocates,* and Best Fantasy Books list, *Booklist,* both 1999, both for *The Fires of Merlin;* Colorado Book Award nominee, 2000, for *The Mirror of Merlin* and *The Fires of Merlin.*

*WRITINGS:*

*To Walk in Wilderness: A Rocky Mountain Journal* (adult nonfiction), photographs by John Fielder, Westcliffe Publishers (Englewood, CO), 1993.

(With Enos Mills and John Fiedler) *Rocky Mountain National Park: A One-Hundred-Year Perspective* (adult nonfiction), photographs by Enos Mills and John Fielder, Westcliffe Publishers (Englewood, CO), 1995.

*Where Is Grandpa?* (picture book), illustrated by Chris K. Soenpiet, Philomel (New York, NY), 2000.

*Tree Girl* (middle-grade fiction), Philomel (New York, NY), 2001.

*The Hero's Trail: A Guide for a Heroic Life* (essays), Philomel (New York, NY), 2002.

*High as a Hawk: The Story of a Brave Young Girl and a Mountain Guide,* illustrated by Ted Lewin, Philomel (New York, NY), 2004.

Contributor to periodicals, including *Book Links, Parents,* and *Voice of Youth Advocates.* Some work also appears under the name Tom Barron. Barron's books have been translated into several languages, including German and Spanish.

*"HEROIC ADVENTURES OF KATE" SERIES*

*Heartlight,* Philomel New York, NY), 1990.

*The Ancient One,* Philomel (New York, NY), 1992.

*The Merlin Effect,* Philomel (New York, NY), 1994.

*"LOST YEARS OF MERLIN" SERIES*

*The Lost Years of Merlin* (also see below), Philomel (New York, NY), 1996.

*The Seven Songs of Merlin* (also see below), Philomel (New York, NY), 1997.

*The Fires of Merlin* (also see below), Philomel (New York, NY), 1998.

*The Mirror of Merlin,* Philomel (New York, NY), 1999.

*The Wings of Merlin,* Philomel (New York, NY), 2000.

*A T. A. Barron Collection* (omnibus; includes *The Lost Years of Merlin, The Seven Songs of Merlin,* and *The Fires of Merlin*), Philomel (New York, NY), 2001.

*ADAPTATIONS:* Listening Library has adapted several of Barron's novels for audiocassette, including *The Lost Years of Merlin,* 2001, and *The Seven Songs of Merlin,* 2002.

*WORK IN PROGRESS:* A fantasy for children; a nature book for adults; a book of essays for adults.

*SIDELIGHTS:* A popular, prolific author of fiction for children and young adults as well as informational books for general readers, T. A. Barron is regarded as both a master storyteller and a gifted nature writer. Writing in *School Library Journal,* Connie Tyrell Burns praised him as "a wonderful storyteller, a maker of myths and fables who creates magical places where characters learn wisdom and power." Barron is perhaps best known as the author of two series of coming-of-age fantasies for young adults, the "Heroic Adventures of Kate" trilogy and "The Lost Years of Merlin" series. The "Kate" series blends such elements as science fiction, history, mythology, metaphysics, and ecology in contemporary adventures that feature Kate Prancer Gordon, a courageous, resourceful teenager. The "Merlin" series focuses on the adolescent years of the legendary magician, a period that is not represented in traditional Arthurian literature. In addition, the author has been lauded his contributions to *To Walk in Wilderness: A Rocky Mountain Journal,* and *Rocky Mountain National Park: A One-Hundred-Year Perspective.*

Thematically, Barron is noted for addressing issues that relate directly to both his young audience and to the universal human condition. He explores such themes as the connections among people, cultures, and other forms of life; the ultimate meaning of existence; the power of love; death as part of a grand design; the bond between generations; the need to preserve the environment; and the acceptance of the light and darkness within ourselves. In the "Kate" and "Merlin" series, Barron takes his protagonists on both literal and figurative journeys. The teens face enormous—and often dangerous—obstacles that force Kate and Merlin to make difficult, sometimes life-threatening decisions which lead them to a greater degree of self-confidence and maturity as well as to a deeper sense of how they can contribute to the world. As a writer, Barron characteristically favors a clear, lyrical prose style. He is commended for his use of descriptive language; for his creation of exciting plots, which often include twists at the end; and for his inclusion of strong female and sensitive male characters. Although some observers have criticized Barron for overwriting, most critics applaud him as a talented author whose well crafted blend of adventure, fantasy, and spirituality has led to the creation of insightful, moving books.

Writing on the Web site for the National Resources Defense Council (NRDC), Barron stated, "My childhood was spent in two places: a New England town full of apple orchards, Native American lore, and Shaker craftspeople, and a ranch in Colorado where I learned to yip and yap like a coyote and hoot like a great horned owl." Barron credits his parents and several of his teachers with fostering his innate love and nature and interest in traditional cultures. His earliest memory is of being carried on his father's shoulders to an old chestnut tree near his home. In an article for *Book Links,* the author wrote, "I remember him lifting me up to peer into a dark hole in the trunk. To my surprise, a family of baby raccoons, their eyes as bright as lanterns, peered back at me. Whenever I think of that man, I think of all the places that we shared. And the memories, like the eyes of those raccoons, are lantern-bright. Small wonder that, for me, place is far more than landscape." Barron eventually used his father, and the man's passing, as the basis for *Where Is Grandpa?*

After the youngest of Barron's six brothers and sisters started school, his mother, Gloria Barron, returned to college to study geology. Later, she founded the Touch Museum, a hands-on nature museum for children, at the Colorado School for the Deaf and Blind. "By word and example," Barron recalled in a media piece titled "Colorado's Heroic Kids," Gloria Barron "instilled in each of her seven children the idea that one individual can make a lasting difference in the lives of others." In 2001 Barron established the Gloria Barron Prize for Young Heroes, a national award that celebrates young people who make a major contribution to their community or to the world at large.

In an article in *Voice of Youth Advocates,* Barron stated, "My own background as a writer is rooted in nature, having grown up reading Henry David Thoreau, Rachel Carson, and John Muir long before I ever dipped into Madeleine L'Engle, Lloyd Alexander, Ursula Le Guin, E. B. White, or J. R. R. Tolkien." After winning a national speech competition sponsored by the Scouts, he was sent to Washington, D.C., to meet the president of the United States. After high school, he attended Princeton University, where he founded two literary magazines and discovered Tolkien. During his senior year he won the Pyne Prize, the university's highest honor for an undergraduate, which honors outstanding service to Princeton by one of its students. Receiving a Rhodes scholarship, he then set off for Oxford University in England.

At Oxford, Barron studied, but also continued to write. He took a year off from school to travel, exploring the

British Isles, riding the Trans-Siberian railway, and traveling to the Arctic, Africa, India, Nepal, and Japan. Returning to Oxford, he wrote his first novel, and collected more than forty rejection letters for it. Once back in the United States, he enrolled at Harvard University Law School, hoping to become an environmental lawyer. He changed his mind, got his MBA, and went to New York City to work as a venture capitalist, acquiring small and medium-size businesses for his firm.

While working in New York, Barron married Currie Cabot, a woman whom he had met while cross-country skiing in the Catskill Mountains, and with whom he has raised their five children. After he sent a manuscript of his first novel for young people, *Heartlight,* to author Madeleine L'Engle, she passed it on to her agent, whereupon Currie suggested that the fledgling author quit his day job. In 1989 Barron resigned from his firm and moved his family to a Colorado ranch so that he could become a full-time writer. *Heartlight* was published the following year, beginning the "Heroic Adventures of Kate" series.

In *Heartlight,* thirteen-year-old Kate and her grandfather, an astrophysicist researching the nature of light and its relationship to the human soul, travel to a distant galaxy by liberating their souls (or "heartlights") to find out why the Earth's sun is losing power. Their discoveries there force them to battle a demonic force seeking eternal life. Kate's adventures continue in *The Ancient One,* as she and her great-aunt Melanie work to save a forest of redwood trees on Native American holy ground from being cut down. Transported five hundred years into the past, Kate encounters the Halamis, a tribe of Native Americans threatened with annihilation by a volcanic eruption caused by an evil being that wants to rule the world. Kate enlists the help of the Ancient One, the oldest living tree in the forest, to save the tribe. In the final book of the series, *The Merlin Effect,* Kate accompanies her Arthurian scholar father to the coast of Baja California. Here, he hopes to discover one of Merlin's lost treasures, a drinking horn that grants immortality that was supposedly aboard a sunken Spanish galleon. While rescuing a whale tangled in the expedition's equipment, Kate is caught in a whirlpool and dragged to the ocean floor, where she battles the enchantress Nimue and her demon army, who also seek the horn. In order to save her companions, Kate must find a way to shake Nimue's magic and return the horn to its rightful place.

Noted for its perceptive exploration of complex ideas, difficult choices, and adult/child relationships, the "Heroic Adventures of Kate" interweave mythological imagery, metaphysical philosophy, scientific theories, and environmental issues with the adventures—and personal growth—of its heroine. Reviewers generally lauded the series, a critic in *Publishers Weekly* writing that *Heartlight* "shines as a bold, original effort worthy of repeat readings."

Doing research for *The Merlin Effect,* Barron became intrigued, and planned a story covering the missing teen years of Merlin's life. Originally planned as a trilogy, the success of the first volumes prompted the author to add more books to the series, each covering one year of the teen's life. In the "Lost Years of Merlin" series readers meet Merlin before he realizes his calling as a sorcerer, following him in a series of adventures that prepare Merlin to become the greatest magician of all time. Merlin comes of age and gains humility and compassion while battling his own insecurities and shortcomings, and is aided on his quests by both natural and supernatural creatures.

In the first volume of the series, *The Lost Years of Merlin,* twelve-year-old Emerys has lost his memory but discovers he has magical powers; his mother, the witch Branwen, refuses to tell him about his past. When Branwen is about to be burned at the stake by a mob, Emerys saves her but is blinded in the process. Recovering in an abbey, he vows never to use his powers in anger, and after developing second sight to replace his lost eyesight he sets off on a journey to find out who he really is. On this quest, which takes him to Fincayra, an enchanted island between Heaven and the Otherworld, Emerys learns about his parents and his sister, Rhia, and discovers that he is Merlin. *The Seven Songs of Merlin* finds the thirteen-year-old magician appointed to heal the barren lands of Fincayra. When he uses his powers irresponsibly to bring Branwen to the island, she is threatened with death by the evil Rhita Gawr, and Merlin must find the potion that will save her. On his quest he finds the magical sword Excalibur that one day will belong to King Arthur.

In *The Fires of Merlin,* fourteen-year-old Merlin is learning wizardry, although his powers are still new. Through a plot to harm him, he is made the target of an angry dragon emperor, Valdearg, while Rhita Gawr conspires to gain Merlin's powers and steal Excalibur.

The fourth volume of the series, *The Mirror of Merlin,* finds fifteen-year-old Merlin searching for his stolen sword, now in the possession of the sorceress Nimue. She infects the teen with a deadly, condition, but a meeting with Ector—the boy destined to become King Arthur—sets Merlin on the path to a cure, a path that takes him into the future. There he meets his older self, trapped in the Crystal Cave by Nimue, and envisions the Round Table and the creation of a society based on justice. *The Wings of Merlin* finds Rhita Gawr preparing to invade Fincayra, forcing Merlin to arrange a defense of the island. Merlin and his followers are forced to flee to the Forgotten Island, a place considered fearsome by Fincayrans, although after a series of battles they prove victorious and the Forgotten Island is transformed into Avalon. Now Merlin must make the decision to leave his beloved Fincayra for the earthly island of Britannia, where he will become mentor to King Arthur as well as the celebrated wizard of story and song.

Barron's "Merlin" books have been praised for providing young readers with a unique depiction of the legendary character. In the *NAPRA Review,* Annette Botsford wrote, "Through the adventures of young Merlin and his fellow travelers, Barron—more than any other on my sagging shelf of Merlin books, helps readers of all ages confront . . . vital topics with renewed vigor and deepened insight." Writing about the series in *Newspapers in Education,* Laura Farrell maintained that "Barron has an extraordinary way with words that can be described as no less than magical," while Sara Pearce of the *Cincinnati Enquirer* urged young readers: "I know this is asking a lot, but I want you to set aside Harry Potter and pick up Merlin." Writing on his Web site, Barron explained that, for him, Merlin's story is a metaphor "for the idea that all of us, no matter how weak or confused, have a magical person down inside, just waiting to be discovered."

Other books by Barron include the stand-alone fantasy novel *Tree Girl* and the picture book *Where Is Grandpa?* In *Tree Girl,* nine-year-old orphan Rowanna fights her fear of the dark forest in order to learn about her mysterious past, and discovers a world inhabited by spirits from nature. While a *Publishers Weekly* contributor found the story "anticlimactic" and somewhat confusing, in *School Library Journal* Connie Tyrell Burns praised the book as a "stylistically rich and lyrical. . . . imaginative tale." *Where Is Grandpa?* explains the cycle of life through the perceptions of a

young boy, sitting with his family on the day that his grandfather has passed away. Each member of the family shares a memory of Grandpa: at the tree house, at the waterfall, and at the door, ready to carve Halloween pumpkins. The boy realizes that his grandfather can be with him in all of the places they have shared, that Grandpa is everywhere. A critic in *Kirkus Reviews* stated that Barron creates "a heartfelt tribute" to family, while in *School Library Journal* Virginia Golodetz called *Where Is Grandpa?* a "helpful introduction to death and the grieving process."

In *The Hero's Trail: A Guide for a Heroic Life,* Barron collects both real-life stories of individuals of accomplishment and fictional tales of personal heroism, and helps young readers differentiate between the five types of true heroism and "celebrity." Featuring people as diverse as Prometheus, Helen Keller, Lance Armstrong, and young Rubie Bridges, the author "likens the journey through life to a hike on a trail," explained *School Library Journal* contributor Wendy Lukehart, and posits that heros help all people realize that they are not "walking alone." Noting that Barron "makes his points in a lucid, direct way," a *Kirkus* reviewer praised *The Hero's Trail* as "compelling motivational reading."

On his Web site, Barron explained: "I write books I would like to read. That means each story must have a character, a relationship, a place, a dilemma, and an idea that I care about. A lot. I like a story where an individual must deal with personal issues as well as overarching issues. The mythic quest—call it fantasy if you prefer—allows me to incorporate all of these qualities" in an entertaining format. In his *Booklist* interview, Barron told Estes that, since he became a full-time writer, "I haven't had a moment of regret. I feel very, very lucky to get to follow my deepest passion in life."

*BIOGRAPHICAL AND CRITICAL SOURCES:*

*BOOKS*

Barron, T. A., *The Hero's Trail: A Guide for a Heroic Life,* Philomel (New York, NY), 2002.

*PERIODICALS*

*Booklist,* April 15, 2001, Sally Estes, "The *Booklist* Interview: T. A. Barron," p. 1560.

*Chicago Parent,* March, 1999, Ken Trainer, "Teaching the Difference between Celebrities and Heroes."

*Cincinnati Enquirer,* October 29, 1999, Sara Pearce, "Youngsters Can Find Magic in *Merlin.*"

*Denver Post,* October 28, 1998, Claire Martin, "Colorado Author Is Living His Dream."

*Emergency Librarian,* Volume 24, number 4, 1997, Kylene Beers, "Where Fantasy Flies: An Interview with T. A. Barron," pp. 61-63.

*Kirkus Reviews,* December 1, 1999, review of *Where Is Grandpa?* p. 1880; August 15, 2002, review of *The Hero's Trail,* p. 1215.

*NAPRA Review,* April, 1997, Antoinette Botsford, "Merlin in Our Midst."

*Parents,* November, 1998, T. A. Barron, "Merlin's Message."

*Publishers Weekly,* June 29, 1990, review of *Heartlight,* p. 102; January 11, 2000, review of *Where Is Grandpa?* p. 103; October 15, 2001, review of *Tree Girl,* p. 72.

*School Library Journal,* February, 2000, Virginia Golodetz, review of *Where Is Grandpa?* p. 91; October, 2001, Connie Tyrell Burns, review of *Tree Girl,* p. 148; December, 2002, Wendy Lukehart, review of *The Hero's Trail,* p. 153.

*Voice of Youth Advocates,* April, 1999, T. A. Barron, "Vision, Voice and the Power of Creation: A Young Adult Author Speaks Out."

ONLINE

*Book Links,* http://www.tabarron.com/ (July 24, 2001), T. A. Barron, "A Place for Love: The Story behind *Where Is Grandpa?*."

*Children's Book Page,* http://www.bookpage.com/ (July 24, 2001), "Meet the Kids' Author: T. A. Barron."

*NAPRA—ALA Web site,* http://www.napra.com/ (July 21, 2001), Antoinette Botsford, "To Think As a Tree, to Act As a Man."

*Natural Resources Defense Council Web site,* http://www.ndrc.org/ (July 24, 2001), "Profile—T. A. Barron."

*The Worlds of T. A. Barron* (T. A. Barron's official Web site), http://www.tabarron.com (July 24, 2001).

*Young Heroes Prize,* http://www.youngheroesprize.org/ (July 24, 2001), T. A. Barron, "Colorado's Heroic Kids."*

**BARRON, Tom**
**See BARRON, T(homas) A(rchibald)**

\*    \*    \*

**BARRY, Sebastian 1955-**

*PERSONAL:* Born July 5, 1955, in Dublin, Ireland; son of Francis (a poet and architect) and Joan (an actress; maiden name, O'Hara) Barry; married Alison Deegan (an actor), May 4, 1992; three children. *Education:* Trinity College, Dublin, B.A., 1977. *Hobbies and other interests:* Horses, American pool under Irish rules.

*ADDRESSES: Office*—27 Longford Terrace, Monkstown, Dublin, Ireland. *Agent*—Curtis Brown Ltd., 4th Floor, Haymarket House, 28-29 Haymarket St., London SW1Y 4SP, England.

*CAREER:* Writer. Honorary fellow in writing at the University of Iowa, 1984; writer-in-residence, Abbey Theatre (member of board of directors), Dublin, Ireland, 1990-91, and Trinity College, Dublin, 1995-96.

*AWARDS, HONORS:* Irish Arts Council bursary, 1982; BBC/Stewart Parker Award, 1988, for *Boss Grady's Boys;* Writers' Guild Best Fringe Play award, 1995, Critics' Circle Best Play award, and Christopher Ewart-Biggs Memorial Prize, both 1996, and Ireland Funds Literary Award, 1997, all for *The Steward of Christendom.*

*WRITINGS:*

*Macker's Garden* (novel), Irish Writers' Co-operative, 1982.

*The Water-Colourist* (poetry), Dolmen Press (Portlaoise, Ireland), 1983.

*Time out of Mind* (short novels; contains *Time out of Mind* and *Strappado Square*), Wolfhound Press, 1983.

*Elsewhere* (novel for children), Brogeen Books/Dolmen Press (Portlaoise, Ireland), 1985.

*The Rhetorical Town,* Dolmen Press (Portlaoise, Ireland),1985.

*Sebastian Barry*

*Fanny Hawke Goes to the Mainland Forever,* Raven Arts Press (Dublin, Ireland), 1989.

*Prayers of Sherkin; Boss Grady's Boys: Two Plays,* Methuen Drama (Portsmouth, NH), 1991.

*The Only True History of Lizzy Finn; The Steward of Christendom; White Woman Street: Three Plays,* with introduction by Fintan O'Toole, Heinemann Press (Portsmouth, NH), 1995.

*Plays* (includes *Prayers of Sherkin, Boss Grady's Boys,* and others) Methuen Press (Portsmouth, NH) 1997.

(Author of book) *Frank Loesser's Hans Christian Andersen* (musical), produced in San Francisco, CA, 2000.

*Our Lady of Sligo* (play; produced in New York, NY, 2000), Dramatists Play Service (New York, NY), 1999.

*The Whereabouts of Eneas McNulty,* Thorndike Press (New York, NY), 1999.

*Hinterland,* Faber (London, England), 2001.

*Annie Dunne,* Viking (New York, NY), 2002.

Contributor to anthologies, including *The Anthology,* Co-op Books, 1982; *Ireland's Living Voices,* Rainbow,

1985; and *The Inherited Boundaries: Younger Poets of the Republic of Ireland,* Dolmen Press, 1985. Contributor of poems and short fiction to periodicals, including *Irish Times, Irish Press, Cyphers, Paris/ Atlantic, Tracks, Poetry Ireland, London Magazine, Stand,* and *Literary Review.*

*SIDELIGHTS:* In his first decade as a playwright, poet and novelist Sebastian Barry became a new and respected voice in Irish drama. But even Barry himself dismisses the label of "Irish writer" as too confining. Indeed, wrote Fintan O'Toole in an introduction to the 1995 anthology of Barry's plays titled *The Only True History of Lizzy Finn; The Steward of Christendom; White Woman Street: Three Plays,* while the dramas seem "utterly Irish," they "also acknowledge the terrifying truth that Ireland is not a fixed place." In such works as *Boss Grady's Boys* and the award-winning *The Steward of Christendom* Barry explores his country's heritage and examines the impact of British rule in Ireland. Through it all, the playwright "employs an extremely personal voice, particularly in his evasion of conventional conflict-driving narrative and the main stage of history and contemporary politics," according to Margaret Llewellyn-Jones in a *Dictionary of Literary Biography* essay.

"Although Barry's plays may seem to some observers to allude to Irish canonical drama," Llewellyn-Jones explained, she added that "their fluid form and introspective elements disrupt the conventional realistic structures" typical of earlier Irish plays. In Barry's dramas, misfits take center stage. Such characters imbued with what Llewellyn-Jones called "ambiguous identities," are the focus of themes that involve "the spiritual journeying of individual human beings rather than overtly ideological issues."

Barry's reluctance to present the "typical" Irish point of view can perhaps be traced to his youth as a citizen of many countries. He was born in Dublin in 1955 to a bohemian family of actors and writers. A traveler's lifestyle took Barry from his B.A. at Trinity College to France, Switzerland, England, Greece, and Italy before the young man settled at the University of Iowa on a writing fellowship. Returning to his homeland in 1985, Barry found that "none of the available identities of Irishness seemed to fit," as he wrote in a memoir excerpted in *Dictionary of Literary Biography.* "Since I was now to be an Irishman, it seemed I would have to make myself up as I went along." To Llewellyn-Jones, this attitude "suggests two key elements in Barry's plays: the exploration of his wider family and ancestors as a means of clarifying his identity, and the elliptical relationship of personal memory to history that permeates his work and makes it different from that of Irish dramatists such as John Millington Synge, whose poetic style is often compared to Barry's."

After affiliating with Dublin's Abbey Theatre—where his mother, Joan Barry, was a featured actor—Barry completed his first full-length play, *Boss Grady's Boys,* which premiered in August, 1988. In his introduction to *Prayers of Sherkin [and] Boss Grady's Boys,* Barry acknowledges writing the latter play "to repay a human debt to a pair of real brothers in a real corner of Cork, where I had lived for a while in 1982." *Boss Grady's Boys* concerns itself with two brothers, aging and unmarried, living out their days together on a farm. Mick, at sixty, is concerned about his elder brother, Josey, who may be displaying the symptoms of Alzheimer's disease. Josey rants at length about a horse in the rain, or about a long-deceased dog; he thinks the boys' dead father will return from a fair. "I throw stones into the poor man that echo with a deep, lost sort of echo," says Mick at one point. "I love him, I love his idiocy."

The action in *Boss Grady's Boys* revolves largely around the brothers' remembrances—real or not—as compared to the reality of their poverty-stricken present. For example, "the brothers' repressed sexuality is shown in two encounters with girls, and it is not clear whether these scenes are fantasies or actual happenings in the past," as Llewellyn-Jones wrote. The brothers engage in reverie about the larger world as well: "Mick's memories of meeting Irish revolutionary leader Michael Collins creates the impression that the brothers' forgotten lives, like those of others in their rural community, are marginal to history." Lyn Gardner, reviewing *Boss Grady's Boys* for the London *Guardian,* wrote that its "prose leaks poetry and it quivers with luminous intensity."

In 1990 Barry premiered *Prayers of Sherkin,* a play set on a remote, tightly knit 1890s island community with characters based on the playwright's forebears. The heroine, Barry revealed in a preface, is modeled after his great-grandmother, Fanny Hawke, who left the security of her family to settle on Sherkin Island. In the play, Fanny is one of the few residents of mar-

riageable age; conflict arises when she chooses Patrick Kirwin, who not only lives off the island but is also of Jewish heritage. Marrying outside the community would bar Fanny from Sherkin Island permanently. While "other writers might have made the religious conflict central," noted Llewellyn-Jones of *Prayers of Sherkin,* "Barry emphasizes that reconciliation and forgiveness are essential."

Following the play *White Women Street,* Barry produced his most notable drama to date with his fifth play, *The Steward of Christendom.* Again the playwright reached into his family's history to create a character, in this case Thomas Dunne, head of the Dublin Metropolitan Police (DMP). "An Irish organization devoted to the British crown," as Greg Evans explained in his review of *The Steward of Christendom* for *Variety,* "the DMP found itself on the wrong side of history and its countrymen when Irish revolutionary Michael Collins rose to power in the early 1920s." This political shift leaves Thomas Dunne reviled; as the play opens, he is depicted at age seventy-five as cast-off and destitute, living in a mental asylum, a "Lear in long johns," to quote *Newsweek* reviewer Jack Kroll. Like Shakespeare's King Lear, Thomas has a tempestuous bond to his three daughters and ruminates about his past and his pride at his old position of authority. Also similar to Lear, noted *New Republic* reviewer Robert Brustein, "Thomas's madness is informed by deeper insights into the human condition than those of the sane. His 'sleepy sleepy' ramblings have some of the visionary power of the sleeper in [James Joyce's *Finnegans Wake*]."

While some reviewers expressed mild criticism, *The Steward of Christendom* opened to generally exultant notice and marked a turning point in Barry's career. The play won several awards and the production toured the United Kingdom and the United States, exposing Barry's work to new audiences. In 1998 he completed the play *Our Lady of Sligo.* The lead character, Mai O'Hara, is Barry's maternal grandmother, an aging woman dying of liver cancer but still possessed of the spirit of a young girl. "Mai died before Barry was born, and he knew of her only through the traumatised tales his mother told him," noted John Cunningham in a *Guardian* article. Mai's husband, Jack, also provided Barry with insight about the couple, both of whom were born English and lived a middle-class life under British rule in Ireland. "Barry, a Catholic married to a Presbyterian, makes the case for inclusiveness," added Cunningham.

Though parent-child relations and Irish-English conflicts are explored in *Our Lady of Sligo* as they were in *The Steward of Christendom*, Llewellyn-Jones described the more recent play as "less overtly political" than its predecessor. In a review for the *Guardian*, Michael Billington also compared the two plays, stating that Mai, like Thomas Dunne, "is blighted by events. He was a loyal servant of the British . . . she is a member of the Catholic middle class at a time when they are being marginalised by the new Free State. But Dunne's tragedy arose from a peculiar mixture of his private life and public role; with Mai it is harder to feel the oppressive weight of history." "This is a play in which a sense of national failure is reflected in a sense of private bankruptcy," declared London *Sunday Times* critic John Peter. "Barry understands how intensely aware people are, in nations with a history of oppression and exploitation, that they carry the burden of their race."

The acclaim heaped upon *The Steward of Christendom* and *Our Lady of Sligo* stood in sharp contrast to the criticism awarded Barry's next play, 2001's *Hinterland*. A controversial project from the start, the drama is based on the life of Irish nationalist Charlie Haughey. A former architect and real-estate broker, Haughey entered politics in 1957 as a member of Fianna Fail. He rose to the post of minister of finance, but was dismissed for allegedly running guns for the Irish Republican Army (IRA). He regained power as Taoiseach—prime minister—of the Republic of Ireland, but by 1992 his political career was over due to successive scandals. In *Hinterland* Haughey—the character Johnny Silvester in Barry's play—is presented as a man defeated, "holed up in a Georgian mansion, broken, angry, but still vainglorious," according to John Peter in a London *Sunday Times* review.

Peter was not alone in calling the play a disappointment; "windy and indigestible" is how Charles Spencer described it in a *Daily Telegraph* assessment, although Spencer added: "It pains me to write this way, because Sebastian Barry is one of Ireland's finest writers." Maintaining that his aim was not to "expose or hurt anybody," Barry told London *Sunday Times* interviewer Michael Ross that the backlash against *Hinterland* took him by surprise: "If it was prizefighting—which putting on a play often seems like—it was a [knockout] in the first round. I feel that if I was a Russian writer in those circumstances 30 years ago, I'd be in Siberia or dead. Every emotion one could go

through, I went through. I didn't find any of them particularly useful."

As a novelist, Barry has found a measure of success matching his work as a playwright. Reviewing Barry's 1998 novel *The Whereabouts of Eneas McNulty*, a *Publishers Weekly* contributor noted that "Barry brings all the attendant skills [of a playwright] to this stunning novel, with its evergreen theme of the parallels between a personal life and the political life of a country." The novel's title character is a boy who fights alongside the British during World War I, and finds himself a pariah in postwar Ireland for having done so. To *New Statesman* critic Maggie O'Farrell, "Eneas is a complex and tragic figure, at once deeply responsive and staggeringly naïve." She added that while some of the book's plot points are lacking, Barry's theatrical leanings serve his novel well: "Even if you've seen his plays, [the author's] dialogue will still astonish—it's dexterous, febrile and constantly challenging."

The 2002 novel *Annie Dunne* was similarly well received. "No one in Ireland can convey despair better than Sebastian Barry, and considering the hometown competition, that's a remarkable distinction," commented Ron Charles. In his *Christian Science Monitor* review of the novel Charles went on to say that "there's plenty of his signature despair in this new little masterpiece . . . but the emotional range is far broader, and the sparks of delight and love that shot through his previous work are given more oxygen here and encouraged to burn." Annie is a spinster, a sad fate for an Irish woman in the late 1950s. As a protagonist, though, she "is not a sweet, affecting woman," says Charles. "In fact, she's an unpleasant, cranky old hag." (She is also a daughter of Thomas Dunne, the disgraced ex-officer of *The Steward of Christendom*.) Anne lives with her single cousin, Sarah, until that existence is threatened by Sarah's potential love interest in the form of Billy, a farmhand. While Eamonn Sweeney, reviewing *Annie Dunne* for the *Guardian*, pointed to lapses in Barry's form and dubbed the book one "in which nothing happens many times," other critics found more to recommend in the novel. A *Publishers Weekly* reviewer, for instance, found it a "compassionate portrait of a distraught woman" and "a masterful feat of characterization." A writer for *Kirkus Reviews* called Barry's novel "tone-perfect and powerfully engaging."

In summing up Barry as a playwright and novelist, Llewellyn-Jones said that his works place him "as a key figure in the current renaissance of Irish drama. Barry's elliptical approach to history, which celebrates humanity through moments of grace and redemption, has an intensely lyrical, poetic quality that merits status within the Irish canon."

## BIOGRAPHICAL AND CRITICAL SOURCES:

*BOOKS*

*Dictionary of Literary Biography,* Volume 245: *British and Irish Dramatists since World War II,* Gale (Detroit, MI), 2001.

*PERIODICALS*

*Atlantic Monthly,* September, 1998, review of *The Whereabouts of Eneas McNulty,* p. 138.

*Back Stage,* February 7, 1997, David Sheward, review of *The Steward of Christendom,* p. 48; June 2, 2002, Diana Barth, "Our Lady of Ireland," p. 41; April 6, 2001, Victor Gluck, review of *Boss Grady's Boys,* p. 45.

*Booklist,* July, 1998, review of *The Whereabouts of Eneas McNulty,* p. 1855; February 1, 2002, Joanne Wilkinson, review of *The Whereabouts of Eneas McNulty,* p. 925.

*Boston Herald,* March 19, 1999, Terry Byrne, review of *The Steward of Christendom,* p. 7.

*Christian Science Monitor,* August 13, 1998, Ron Charles, "Dreaming of a Forbidden Home," p. B5; August 28, 1998, review of *The Whereabouts of Eneas McNulty,* p. B12; August 22, 2002, Charles, "Turn of the Shrew," p. 15.

*Daily Telegraph* (London, England), March 5, 2002, Charles Spencer, review of *Hinterland;* March 6, 2002, Michael Billington, review of *Hinterland,* p. 23.

*Economist,* June 13, 1998, review of *The Whereabouts of Eneas McNulty,* p. S17.

*Guardian* (London, England), March 14, 1998, Lyn Gardner, "Apocalypse Plough," p. 7; March 25, 1998, John Cunningham, "My Family, the Outcasts," p. 14; April 18, 1998, Michael Billington, "Conversation Piece," p. 7; March 5, 2002, Billington, review of *Hinterland,* p. 14; June 8, 2002, Angelique Chrisafis, "The Hay Festival," p. 6; June 29, 2002, Eamonn Sweeney, review of *The Steward of Christendom,* p. 27.

*Kirkus Reviews,* July 1, 2002, review of *Annie Dunne,* p. 897.

*Library Journal,* June 15, 1998, review of *The Whereabouts of Eneas McNulty,* p. 104.

*New Republic,* April 7, 1997, Robert Brustein, review of *The Steward of Christendom,* p. 28.

*New Statesman,* February 27, 1997, Maggie O'Farrell, "A Man Trapped for Life on the Wrong Side," p. 49.

*Newsweek,* February 17, 1997, Jack Kroll, review of *The Steward of Christendom,* p. 68.

*New York,* February 3, 1997, John Simon, review of *The Steward of Christendom,* p. 49; May 8, 2000, J. Simon, review of *Our Lady of Sligo,* p. 74.

*New Yorker,* October 2, 1995, John Lahr, review of *The Steward of Christendom,* p. 106; November 9, 1998, review of *The Whereabouts of Eneas McNulty,* p. 103.

*New York Review of Books,* summer, 1999, Des Traynor, review of *The Whereabouts of Eneas McNulty,* p. 157.

*New York Times,* January 19, 1997, Matt Wolf, "It's Ancestor Worship, but of a Dramatic Sort," p. H20; January 22, 1997, Ben Brantley, review of *The Steward of Christendom,* p. B1; February 2, 1997, Vincent Canby, review of *The Steward of Christendom,* p. H4; May 10, 1998, Benedict Nightingale, review of *Our Lady of Sligo,* p. AR9; April 21, 2000, B, Brantley, "One Life's Restless End," p. B1.

*New York Times Book Review,* November 1, 1987, Lois Gordon, review of *The Engine of an Owl-Light,* p. 24; October 18, 1998, Aoibheann Sweeney, review of *The Whereabouts of Eneas McNulty,* p. 26.

*Observer* (London, England), March 15, 1998, review of *The Whereabouts of Eneas McNulty,* p. 16.

*Publishers Weekly,* June 8, 1998, review of *The Whereabouts of Eneas McNulty,* p. 46; July 1, 2002, review of *Annie Dunne,* p. 53.

*San Francisco Chronicle,* September 9, 2000, Steven Winn, "Actors Fly, but 'Andersen' Remains Earthbound," p. B1.

*Spectator,* September 16, 1995, Sheridan Morley, review of *The Steward of Christendom,* p. 50; March 9, 2002, Toby Young, review of *Hinterland,* p. 59.

*Sunday Times* (London, England), March 1, 1998, Lindsey Duguid, "The Wandering Years," p. 3; April 26, 1998, John Peter, "The Year of Our Lady," p. 20; January 6, 2002, Peter, "Fast Forward 2002," p. 8; February 10, 2002, Karina Buckley, review of *Hinterland,* p. 29; March 10, 2002, J. Peter, review of *Hinterland,* p. 16; June 9, 2002,

Michael Ross, "The Anguish That Led to Hinterland" (interview), p. 4; July 28, 2002, Peter Parker, "The Farmer Wants a Life," p. 44.

*Theatre Journal,* May, 1997, Joan Fitzpatrick Dean, review of *The Steward of Christendom,* p. 233.

*Time International,* March 18, 2002, James Inverne, "Tragedy or Farce?," p. 68.

*Times* (London, England), May 21, 1997, Jeremy Kingston, "Devotion, Love, and Sects," p. 41; February 12, 1998, Roy Foster, "Rescued from the Ruin of Tenderness," p. 40; April 18, 1998, Benedict Nightengale, "Hearts of Darkness in Family History," p. 21; June 1, 2002, George Brock, "Country Stife," p. 19.

*Times Literary Supplement,* September 28, 1984; June 6, 1997, Maggie Gee, review of *Prayers of Sherkin,* p. 21; February 20, 1998, review of *The Whereabouts of Eneas McNulty,* p. 23; March 22, 2002, C. L. Dallat, "Hiding behind the Outskirts," p. 19; May 10, 2002, C. L. Dallat, "The Maiden Aunt," p. 25.

*Variety,* January 27, 1997, Greg Evans, review of *The Steward of Christendom,* p. 87; October 9, 2000, Dennis Harvey, review of *Hans Christian Andersen,* p. 36.

*Wall Street Journal,* July 24, 1998, Richard Tillinghast, review of *The Whereabouts of Eneas McNulty,* p. W10.

*Washington Post Book World,* December 6, 1998, review of *The Whereabouts of Eneas McNulty,* p. 10.

*Washington Times,* April 15 1998, Nelson Pressley, "A State of Insanity in 'Christendom,'" p. 11.*

\*     \*     \*

## BAUER, Erwin A. 1919-
### (Ken Bourbon, Nat Franklin, Tom Hardin, Charles W. North, Barney Peters)

*PERSONAL:* Born August 22, 1919, in Cincinnati, OH; son of Adam John (a safety engineer) and Louise (Volz) Bauer; married Doris Parker, April 26, 1941 (divorced); married Grace Margaret ("Peggy") Reid (a photographer), 1972; children: (first marriage) Parker, Robert, (stepchildren) Stephen, Paul, Charles. *Education:* Studied at the University of Cincinnati for three years. *Hobbies and other interests:* Camping, climbing, exploration, hunting, nature, boating, dogs, ecology, environment.

*ADDRESSES: Home and office*—Wildstock, P.O. Box 987, Livingston, MT 59047-0987.

*CAREER:* Former columnist, *Irontown Tribune* and other newspapers; free-lance writer specializing in outdoor travel and adventure; outdoor commercial photographer; author, illustrating own work (average fifty feature stories annually) with photographs. Public relations consultant for outdoor industries. *Military service:* U.S. Army, World War II and Korean Conflict; became first lieutenant; received Purple Heart and Croix de Guerre.

*MEMBER:* Society of Magazine Writers, American Society of Travel Writers, Ohio Outdoor Writers Association (former president).

*AWARDS, HONORS:* Awards from Ohio Outdoor Writers Association for best magazine articles by an Ohio writer, 1949, 1950, 1962, and for best photos, 1965, 1966, 1968, and 1969; Gold and Silver awards, Society of American Travel Writers, 1991, 1992; BBC Gas photography award, 1991; North American Nature Photography Association Life Achievement Award, 2000.

*WRITINGS:*

*Bass in America: The Haunts, Habits, and Other Secrets of One of the World's Finest Fresh-Water Game Fish,* includes photographs by Bauer and David Goodnow, Simon & Schuster (New York, NY), 1955.

*The Bass Fisherman's Bible,* Doubleday (New York, NY), 1961, revised edition, 1980, 3rd edition revised by Mark Hicks, 1989.

*The Salt-Water Fisherman's Bible,* Doubleday (New York, NY), 1962, revised, 1983, 3rd edition revised by Bob Stearns, 1991.

*Complete Book of Outdoor Photography,* Popular Science, 1964, published as *Outdoor Photography,* Harper (New York, NY), 1965, revised edition, Outdoor Life, 1975.

*The Duck Hunter's Bible,* Doubleday (New York, NY), 1965, revised edition by Robert Elman published as *The Waterfowler's Bible,* 1989.

(With George Laycock) *The New Archery Handbook,* Fawcett (New York, NY), 1965.

(With George Laycock) *Hunting with Bow and Arrow,* Arco (New York, NY), 1966.

*My Adventures with African Animals,* includes photographs by Bauer, Norton (New York, NY), 1968.

*The Sportsman on Wheels,* Popular Science, 1969.

(Illustrator) Charles F. Waterman, *The Hunter's World,* includes photographs by Bauer and others, Random House (New York, NY), 1970.

*Treasury of Big Game Animals,* Harper (New York, NY), 1972.

(Editor) *Hunter's Digest,* Follett (Chicago, IL), 1973, 2nd edition, 1979.

*Hunting with a Camera: A World Guide to Wildlife Photography,* Winchester Press (New York, NY), 1974.

(Editor) *Outdoor Photographer's Digest,* Follett (Chicago, IL), 1975, 2nd edition, 1980.

*Cross-Country Skiing and Snowshoeing,* Winchester Press (New York, NY), 1975.

*The Cross-Country Skier's Bible,* Doubleday (New York, NY), 1977.

*The Digest Book of Deer Hunting,* Follett (Chicago, IL), 1979.

*Erwin Bauer's Deer in Their World,* Outdoor Life Books (New York, NY); distributed by Stackpole Books (Harrisburg, PA), 1983.


*WITH WIFE, PEGGY BAUER*


(Editor) *Camper's Digest,* 2nd edition (Bauer not associated with first edition), Follett (New York, NY), 1974, 3rd edition, DBI Books (Northfield, IL), 1979.

(Editor) *The Digest Book of Camping,* DBI Books (Northfield, IL), 1979.

(Editor) *The Digest Book of Cross-Country Skiing,* DBI Books (Northfield, IL), 1979.

*Photographing the West: A State-by-State Guide,* Northland Press (Flagstaff, AZ), 1980.

*Wildlife Adventures with a Camera,* Harry N. Abrams (New York, NY), 1984.

*Photographing Wild Texas,* University of Texas Press (Austin, TX), 1985.

*Photographing the North American West,* Pacific Search Press (Seattle, WA), 1987.

*Denali: The Wild Beauty of Denali National Park,* Sasquatch Books (Seattle, WA), 2000.

(With Judy Jewell) *Camping! Oregon: The Complete Guide to Public Campgrounds for RVs and Tents,* Sasquatch Books (Seattle, WA), 2001.

*Glacier Bay: The Wild Beauty of Glacier Bay National Park,* Sasquatch Books (Seattle, WA), 2001.

*The Alaska Highway: A Portrait of the Ultimate Road Trip,* Sasquatch Books (Seattle, WA), 2002.

*Bears of Alaska: The Wild Bruins of the Last Frontier,* Sasquatch Books (Seattle, WA), 2002.

*The Last Big Cats: An Untamed Spirit,* Voyageur Press, 2003.


*PHOTOGRAPHER; WITH PEGGY BAUER*


*Erwin Bauer's Bear in Their World,* Outdoor Life Books (New York, NY), distributed by Stackpole Books (Harrisburg, PA), 1985.

*Erwin Bauer's Horned and Antlered Game,* Outdoor Life Books (New York, NY), distributed by Stackpole Books (Harrisburg, PA), 1986.

*Erwin Bauer's Predators of North America,* Outdoor Life Books (New York, NY), distributed by Stackpole Books (Harrisburg, PA), 1988.

*Erwin Bauer's Wild Alaska,* base maps by Joe LeMonnier, Outdoor Life Books (Danbury, CT), distributed by Stackpole Books (Harrisburg, PA), 1988.

Ron Hirschi, *Where Are My Bears?* (juvenile), Bantam Books (New York, NY), 1992.

Ron Hirschi, *Where Are My Puffins, Whales, and Seals?* (juvenile), Bantam Books (New York, NY), 1992.

Ron Hirschi, *Where Are My Swans, Whooping Cranes, and Singing Loons?* (juvenile), Bantam Books (New York, NY), 1992.

Ron Hirschi, *Where Are My Prairie Dogs and Black-Footed Ferrets?* (juvenile), Bantam Books (New York, NY), 1992.

(With others) *Whitetails: Behavior, Natural History, Conservation,* Voyageur Press (Stillwater, MN), 1993.

Ron Hirschi, *Save Our Forests* (juvenile), Delacorte Press (New York, NY), 1993.

Ron Hirschi, *Save Our Oceans and Coasts* (juvenile), Delacorte Press (New York, NY), 1993.

*Yellowstone,* Voyageur Press (Stillwater, MN), 1993, revised, 1999.

Ron Hirschi, *Save Our Prairies and Grasslands* (juvenile), Delacorte Press (New York, NY), 1994.

Ron Hirschi, *Save Our Wetlands* (juvenile), Delacorte Press (New York, NY), 1994.

*Wild Dogs: The Wolves, Coyotes, and Foxes of North America,* foreword by John Madson, Chronicle Books (San Francisco, CA), 1994.

Peggy Bauer, *Wild Kittens,* Chronicle Books (San Francisco, CA), 1995.

(And author) *Baja to Barrow: A Pacific Coast Wildlife Odyssey,* Willow Creek Press (Minocqua, WI), 1995.

(And author) *Antlers: Nature's Majestic Crown: A Spectacular Tribute to the Antlered Animas of North America and Europe,* Voyageur Press (Stillwater, MN), 1995.

*Elk: Behavior, Ecology, Conservation,* Voyageur Press (Stillwater, MN), 1995.

(And author) *Mule Deer: Behavior, Ecology, Conservation,* Voyageur Press (Stillwater, MN), 1995.

Peggy Bauer, *Wild Puppies,* (juvenile), Chronicle Books (San Francisco, CA), 1995.

*Bears: Behavior, Ecology, Conservation,* Voyageur Press (Stillwater, MN), 1996.

*Big Game of North America: Behavior, Ecology, Conservation,* Voyageur Press (Stillwater, MN), 2000.

Editor-at-large, *Outdoor Life,* 1973—.

*SIDELIGHTS:* Considered one of the premier wildlife photographers, Erwin Bauer has traveled across America and into many other countries in search of the perfect natural image with his wife and collaborator Peggy. As a youth, Bauer preferred spending his time in the wild lands adjoining his home in Cincinnati, Ohio. After finishing his stint in the Army as a decorated soldier, Bauer became an outdoors columnist for the *Irontown Tribune,* an Ohio paper, while also turning to freelancing. Though he considered himself a writer at that time, Bauer learned to use a camera out of necessity, as many publications demanded original photos to go with text. He drew upon his love of game sports to produce his first book, *Bass in America: The Haunts, Habits, and Other Secrets of One of the World's Finest Fresh-Water Game Fish,* in 1955. This volume went on to sell out its entire 7,500 first printing.

Following Bauer's 1972 marriage to Grace "Peggy" Reid, herself an accomplished photographer, the couple set out on a life of outdoor adventure, hunting animals with their cameras. Together they have produced numerous volumes aimed at both adult and youth audiences, usually with a conservationist's slant. Of *Bears: Behavior, Ecology, Conservation,* Wayne Trimm of *New York State Conservationist* said: "It is obvious that the Bauers are very pro-bear . . . [they] consider bears to be very intelligent animals with unusually keen senses." The book also lists the best places to find and photograph the animals, along with a safety guide to avoid unpleasant bear encounters. The "tough, resilient" whitetail deer, as *American For-*

*ests* writer Carl Reidel described it, is the focus of the Bauers' *Whitetails: Behavior, Ecology, Conservation.* Erwin Bauer's text covers the evolution and habits of the deer, leading Reidel to remark that this book "is, in the best sense of the word, an amateur's textbook—a 'lover's' textbook. It will charm and inform the most ardent deer watcher, hunter, or lover."

Similarly, the photo volume *Wild Dogs: The Wolves, Coyotes, and Foxes of North America* seeks to dispel some of the stereotypes of the continent's carnivorous canines. Kristin Hostetter of *Backpacker* recommended this Bauer book as one that "instills respect and understanding of these elusive animals."

*BIOGRAPHICAL AND CRITICAL SOURCES:*

*PERIODICALS*

*AB Bookman's Weekly,* June 17, 1996, review of *Mule Deer: Behavior, Ecology, Conservation,* and *Whitetails: Behavior, Ecology, Conservation,* p. 2404; June 23, 1997, review of *Bears: Behavior, Ecology, Conservation,* p. 2036.

*Alaska,* June, 1981, review of *Photographing the West,* p. 50.

*American Forests,* July-August, 1994, Carl Reidel, review of *Whitetales,* p. 58; spring, 2000, p. 17

*American West,* January-February, 1982, review of *Photographing the West,* p. 64; November-December, 1984, review of *Wildlife Adventures with a Camera,* p. 66; May, 1986, review of *Photographing Wild Texas,* p. 62; March-April, 1988, review of *Photographing the North American West,* p. 91.

*Audubon,* November, 1994, review of *Wild Dogs: The Wolves, Coyotes, and Foxes of North America,* p. 130.

*Backpacker,* December, 1989, "Erwin and Peggy Bauer: Some of the World's Most Beautiful Creatures Seem to Go out of Their Way to Let These Two Take Photographs," p. 44; February, 1995, Kristin Hostetter, review of *Wild Dogs,* p. 86.

*Booklist,* May 15, 1985, review of *Wildlife Adventures with a Camera,* p. 1286; October 15, 1992, Stephanie Zvirin, review of *Where Are My Bears? And Where Are My Puffins, Whales and Seals?* p. 434; March 15, 1993, Gilbert Taylor, review of *Yellowstone,* p. 1292; March 15, 1994, Ellen Mandel, review of *Save Our Oceans and Coasts,* p. 1339; April 15, 1994, Mary Harris Veeder, review of *Save Our Wetlands* and *Save Our Prairies and Grasslands,* p. 1530; April 1, 1996, Fred Egloff, review of *Mule Deer,* p. 1334; March 1, 1997, Nancy Bent, review of *Bears,* p. 1098; May 1, 1998, Egloff, review of *Big Game of North America,* p. 1485; January 1, 2000, Bent, review of *Denali: The Wild Beauty of Denali National Park,* p. 847; June 1, 2002, Bent, review of *Bears of Alaska: The Wild Bruins of the Last Frontier,* p. 1655.

*Bookwatch,* March, 1988, review of *Photographing the North American West,* p. 3; May, 1999, review of *Elk: Behavior, Ecology, Conservation,* p. 8.

*Canadian Book Review Annual,* 1997, *Bears,* p. 424.

*Choice,* July-August, 1988, review of *Big Game of North America,* p. 1878; November, 1996, review of Mule Deer, p. 484; March, 1997, review of *Elk,* p. 1185.

*Kliatt Young Adult Paperback Book Guide,* January, 1988, review of *Photographing the North American West,* p. 49; November, 1994, review of *Wild Dogs,* p. 43.

*Library Journal,* November 1, 1984, review of *Wildlife Adventures with a Camera,* p. 2070; November 1, 1994, Deborah Emerson, review of *Wild Dogs,* p. 106.

*Modern Photography,* February, 1985, Howard Millard, review of *Wildlife Adventures with a Camera,* p. 82.

*National Wildlife,* October-November, 1985, "Go Where the Pros Go," p. 49.

*Nature,* June 26, 1997, review of *Bears,* p. 866.

*Nature Canada,* winter, 1998, review of *Bears,* p. 51.

*New York State Conservationist,* August, 1998, Wayne Trimm, review of *Bears,* p. 23.

*Publishers Weekly,* July 27, 1984, Genevieve Stuttaford, review of *Wildlife Adventures with a Camera,* p. 134; April 5, 1993, review of *Yellowstone,* p. 57; February 5, 1996, review of *Mule Deer,* p. 74; June 17, 1996, review of *Elk,* p. 52.

*School Library Journal,* January, 1993, review of *Where Are My Puffins, Whales and Seals?, Where Are My Swans, Whooping Cranes, and Singing Loons?, Where Are My Prairie Dogs and Black-Footed Ferrets,* and *Where Are My Bears?,* p. 92; February, 1994, Amy Nunley, review of *Save Our Forests* and *Save Our Oceans and Coasts,* p. 110; May, 1994, Kathleen McCabe, review of *Save Our Prairies and Grasslands* and *Save Our Wetlands,* p. 123.

*Science Books and Films,* May, 1985, review of *Wildlife Adventures with a Camera,* p. 299; November, 1999, review of *Bears,* p. 273.

*SciTech Book News,* December, 1996, review of *Elk,* p. 33.

*Small Press Review,* June, 1993, review of *Yellowstone,* p. 8.

*Sports Afield,* August, 1984, review of *Erwin Bauer's Deer in Their World,* p. 88.

*Voice of Youth Advocates,* February, 1995, review of *Wild Dogs,* p. 354.

*Washington Post Book World,* February 26, 1984, review of *Deer in Their World,* p. 12; December 2, 1984, review of *Wildlife Adventures with a Camera,* p. 10.*

\*　　\*　　\*

## BECKER, Gary S(tanley) 1930-

*PERSONAL:* Born December 2, 1930, in Pottsville, PA; son of Louis W. and Anna (Siskind) Becker; married Doria Slote, 1955 (deceased); married Guity Nashat, 1979; children: (first marriage) Judith Sarah, Catherine Jean; two stepsons. *Education:* Princeton University, A.B. (summa cum laude), 1951; University of Chicago, A.M., 1953, Ph.D., 1955.

*ADDRESSES: Home*—1308 East 58th St., Chicago, IL 60637. *Office*—University of Chicago, Department of Economics, 1126 East 59th St., Chicago, IL 60637. *E-mail*—gbecker@uchicago.edu.

*CAREER:* University of Chicago, Chicago, IL, assistant professor of economics, 1954-57, visiting professor, 1969-70, university professor of economics, 1970-83, professor of economics and sociology, 1983—, chair of economic department, 1984-84; Columbia University, New York, NY, assistant professor, 1957-58, associate professor, 1958-60, professor of economics, 1960-68, Arthur Lehman Professor of Economics, 1968-69; Research associate, Economics Research Center and National Opinion Research Center, 1980—.

*MEMBER:* Union Internationale pour l'Etude Scientifique de la Population, National Academy of Sciences, American Economic Association (president, 1987), American Philosophical Society, American Statistical Association, American Academy of Arts and Sciences, National Academy of Education, Econometric Society, Mont Pelerin Society (director, 1985—, president, 1990-92), Phi Beta Kappa.

*Gary S. Becker*

*AWARDS, HONORS:* W. S. Woytinsky Award, University of Michigan, 1964, for *Human Capital;* John Bates Clark Medal from American Economic Association, 1967; professional achievement award, University of Chicago Alumni Association, 1968; Frank E. Seidman Distinguished Award in Political Economics, 1985; Merit Award from the National Institutes of Health, 1986; John R. Commons Award, and Nobel Prize in Economics, 1992. Honorary degrees from several institutions, including Hebrew University, Knox College, University of Illinois, State University of New York, and Princeton University.

*WRITINGS:*

*Economics of Discrimination,* University of Chicago Press (Chicago, IL), 1957, 2nd edition, 1971.
*Human Capital: A Theoretical and Empirical Analysis with Special Reference to Education,* Columbia University Press (New York, NY), 1964, 2nd edition, 1975.
*Human Capital and the Personal Distribution of Income: An Analytical Approach,* University of Michigan (Ann Arbor, MI), 1967.

*Economic Theory,* Knopf (New York, NY), 1971.
(Editor, with William M. Landes) *Essays in the Economics of Crime and Punishment,* Columbia University Press (New York, NY), 1974.
(With Gilbert Ghez) *The Allocation of Time and Goods over the Life Cycle,* Columbia University Press (New York, NY), 1975.
*The Economic Approach to Human Behavior,* University of Chicago Press (Chicago, IL), 1976.
*A Treatise on the Family,* Harvard University Press (Cambridge, MA), 1981.
(Contributor) *Discrimination, Affirmative Action, and Equal Opportunity: An Economic and Social Perspective,* coedited by W. E. Block and M. A. Walker, Fraser Institute (Vancouver, British Columbia, Canada), 1982.
(With Nigel Tomes) *Human Capital and the Rise and Fall of Families,* University of Western Ontario (London, ON), 1985.
*An Economic Analysis of the Family,* Economic and Social Research Institute (Dublin, Ireland), 1986.
*The Essence of Becker,* edited and with an introduction by Ramon Febrero and Pedro S. Schwartz, foreword by John Raisian, Hoover Institution (Stanford, CA), 1995.
*The Economic Way of Looking at Behavior: The Nobel Lecture,* Stanford University (Stanford, CA), 1996.
*Accounting for Tastes,* Harvard University (Cambridge, MA), 1996.
(With Guity Nashat Becker) *The Economics of Life: From Baseball to Affirmative Action to Immigration, How Real-World Issues Affect Our Everyday Life,* McGraw-Hill (New York, NY), 1997.
(With Kevin M. Murphy) *Social Economics: Market Behavior in a Social Environment,* Belknap Press (Cambridge, MA), 2000.

Also editor of *Essays in Labor Economics in Honor of H. Gregg Lewis,* 1976; contributor of columns to *Business Week.*

*SIDELIGHTS:* Gary S. Becker is one of the most respected economists of the famous Chicago school. Mentored by Milton Friedman, Becker helped move the study of economics into territory previously unexplored with his many books about subjects such as racial discrimination, crime, and the family unit. This body of work garnered Becker the Nobel Prize in Economics in 1992.

Becker recalled some of his pioneering research for a Web site on Nobel Prize winners. Speaking of his first book, 1957's *Economics of Discrimination,* he explained: "The book contains the first systematic effort to use economic theory to analyze the effects of prejudice on the earnings, employment, and occupations of minorities. . . . [It] was very favorably reviewed in a few major journals, but for several years it had no visible impact on anything." Becker added that "most economists did not think racial discrimination was economics, and sociologists and psychologists generally did not believe I was contributing to their fields." By 1983, however, Becker's wide-ranging interests were acknowleged when the University of Chicago made him a professor of both economics and sociology.

In 1996 Becker published *Accounting for Tastes,* a collection of several of the economist's essays, "including his Nobel lecture," reported Edward J. Smith in *Business Economics.* As Smith explained, "Becker's thesis is that basic consumption needs, such as food and shelter, have relatively minor importance in the developed world." Instead, Smith continued, "most consumption is unrelated to these basic needs and is profoundly influenced by factors not normally considered in economic models." The factors cited by Becker include peer-group influence and cultural upbringing. Smith felt that each essay in *Accounting for Tastes* is "lucid" and "thought-provoking." Even reviewers who disagreed with Becker's political viewpoint complimented his work. *Journal of Economic Issues,* reviewer Wilfred Dolfsman, for instance, concluded that "Becker has helped us to better formulate our own ideas."

Becker collaborated with his second wife, history professor Guity Nashat Becker, on 1997's *The Economics of Life: From Baseball to Affirmative Action to Immigration, How Real-World Issues Affect Our Everyday Life.* In this volume, the Beckers advocate such controversial social solutions as drug legalization, the auction of immigration slots to the highest bidder, and school vouchers.

Becker collaborated with colleague Kevin M. Murphy on the 2000 publication, *Social Economics: Market Behavior in a Social Environment.* According *Times Literary Suppplement,* reviewer David Throsby, "Becker and Murphy analyse the implications of the extended model of rational choice for decisions such as whom to marry, where to live and whether or not to collect art." Throsby went on to praise *Social Economics* because he felt it "marks another step in bringing economic theory closer to social reality."

## BIOGRAPHICAL AND CRITICAL SOURCES:

*BOOKS*

Blaug, Mark, *Great Economists since Keynes,* Barnes & Noble (Totowa, NJ).

*PERIODICALS*

*American Journal of Sociology,* September, 1983, review of *A Treatise on the Family,* p. 468.
*Business Economics,* October, 1997, Edward J. Smith, review of *Accounting for Tastes,* pp. 72-73.
*Choice,* April, 1982, review of *A Treatise on the Family,* p. 1100.
*Contemporary Sociology,* March, 1993, Debra Friedman, review of *A Treatise on the Family,* p. 225.
*Journal of Economic Issues,* September, 1997, Wilfred Dolfsman, review of *Accounting for Tastes,* p. 854.
*Journal of Economic Literature,* March, 1982, review of *A Treatise on the Family,* pp. 52, 65; December, 1994, p. 1990; September, 1996, review of *The Essense of Becker,* p. 1444; March, 1997, review of *Accounting for Tastes,* p. 199; December, 1998, review of *The Economics of Life: From Baseball to Affirmative Action to Immigration, How Real-World Issues Affect Our Everyday Life,* p. 2204; September, 2001, review of *Social Economics: Market Behavior in a Social Environment,* p. 1054.
*Journal of Economic Perspectives,* spring, 1994, Victor R. Fuchs, p. 183.
*Journal of Economic Studies,* June, 1992, Stephen P. Jenkins, review of *A Treatise on the Family,* p. 666.
*Population and Development Review,* September, 1992, review of *A Treatise on the Family,* p. 563.
*Reference and Research Book News,* July, 1996, review of *The Essence of Becker,* p. 28.
*Review of Black Political Economy,* spring, 1984, Marcus Alex, p. 41.
*Social Forces,* June, 1997, Eric M. Leifer, review of *Accounting for Tastes,* p. 1463.
*Times Literary Supplement,* March 22, 2002, David Throsby, "Humans Can Apply," p. 28.
*University of Chicago Law Review,* spring, 1997, Jon Elster, review of *Accounting for Tastes,* pp. 749-764.

*ONLINE*

*Nobel E-Museum,* http://www.nobel.se/economics/ laureates/ (July 29, 2002) "Gary S. Becker."\*

\*   \*   \*

## BELL, Clare (Louise) 1952-
## (Clare Coleman, a joint pseudonym)

*PERSONAL:* Born June 19, 1952, in Hitchin, Hertfordshire, England; immigrated to the United States, 1957; daughter of Ronald Lancelot Bell and Edna Kathleen (Wheldon) Steward; partner of M. Coleman Easton. *Education:* University of California, Santa Cruz, B.A., 1975; postgraduate studies at University of California, Davis, c. 1978; Stanford University, M.S.M.E., 1983. *Politics:* Green Party. *Hobbies and other interests:* Electric cars, music, hiking, cycling, swimming.

*ADDRESSES: Home and office*—5680 Judith St., San Jose, CA 95123. *Agent*—c/o Author Mail, Margaret K. McElderry Books, 866 Third Ave., New York, NY 10022. *E-mail*—Ce96ed@aol.com.

*CAREER:* U.S. Geological Survey, Menlo Park, CA, field assistant, 1976-78; International Business Machines (IBM), San Jose, CA, test equipment engineer, 1978-89; freelance writer, c. 1983—. *Current Events* (newsletter of Electric Auto Association), San Jose, managing editor, c. 1995—.

*MEMBER:* American Civil Liberties Union, National Writers Union, Science Fiction Writers of America, Electric Vehicle Association, San Jose Peace Center.

*AWARDS, HONORS:* PEN Los Angeles Award and American Library Association (ALA) Best Book for Young People Award, both 1983, and International Reading Association's Children's Book Award, 1984, all for *Ratha's Creature;* ALA Best Book for Young People Award, 1984, for *Clan Ground,* and 1990, for *Ratha and Thistle-Chaser.*

*WRITINGS:*

*Tomorrow's Sphinx* (juvenile), M. K. McElderry (New York, NY), 1986.
*People of the Sky,* Tor (New York, NY), 1989.

(With M. Coleman Easton, under joint pseudonym Clare Coleman) *Daughter of the Reef,* Jove (New York, NY), 1992.
*The Jaguar Princess,* Tor (New York, NY), 1993.
(With M. Coleman Easton, under joint pseudonym Clare Coleman) *Sister of the Sun,* Jove (New York, NY), c. 1993.
(With M. Coleman Easton, under joint pseudonym Clare Coleman) *Child of the Dawn,* Jove (New York, NY), 1994.
(Author of text, with Al Hirschfeld) *Hirschfeld's New York,* H. N. Abrams (New York, NY), 2001.

*JUVENILE FANTASY NOVELS; "RATHA" SERIES*

*Ratha's Creature,* Atheneum (New York, NY), 1983.
*Clan Ground,* Atheneum (New York, NY), 1984.
*Ratha and Thistle-Chaser,* M. K. McElderry (New York, NY), 1990.
*Ratha's Challenge,* M. K. McElderry (New York, NY), 1995.

*SIDELIGHTS:* A respected author of fantasy, Clare Bell came to the United States from England at age five. A master's candidate in engineering, Bell began her career as a geologist assistant and as a test engineer for International Business Machines (IBM). But she also embarked on a future creating fantasy fiction, and published her first novel, *Ratha's Creature,* in 1983. This book marked the beginning of a series for young readers featuring highly evolved felines who explore such sophisticated themes as mother/daughter relationships, the nature of leadership, and the need for spiritual expression. By 1989 her fiction was successful enough for her to leave engineering. In addition to three other books about Ratha and her friends, Coleman has penned fantasy novels for older audiences, including *People of the Sky* and *The Jaguar Princess.* She is also the coauthor, with M. Coleman Easton, of two novels under the joint pseudonym Clare Coleman.

As Ratha's story begins in *Ratha's Creature,* Ratha is a year-old cat in a clan which calls themselves the Named. The Named herd and practice agriculture; their traditional enemies, the Unnamed, do not, and often live by raiding the herds of the Named. Ratha is due to become one of the clan's herders, but her discovery of how to harness fire threatens the leader of the Named, and she is exiled. She lives for a time with the Unnamed, and breeds with one of them, but the resulting kittens are unintelligent, and she and they are exiled yet again. She eventually persuades the Named to accept her gift of fire, and becomes their queen.

A *Booklist* contributor hailed *Ratha's Creature* as a "powerful, moving, and memorable story" and predicted it "will draw readers right in." Trev Jones in *School Library Journal* praised it as well, noting that Bell's novel "is charged with powerful emotions" and that its characters "will come vividly alive to readers." Mary Ellen Baker in *Voice of Youth Advocates* called *Ratha's Creature* "moving," and gave the novel that periodical's highest rating for quality.

In *Clan Ground* Ratha's leadership is challenged by Shongshar, a male cat who turns the Named's use of fire into a strong and threatening religious cult. This sequel gained the favor of Hazel Rochman in *School Library Journal,* who observed that "Bell creates characters that are authentically wild and feline and also sensitive, intelligent and complicated." In *Ratha and Thistle-Chaser,* "the queen's long-lost daughter comes to light," according to a contributor to the *St. James Guide to Fantasy Writers.* Ratha is reunited with the daughter that she once tried to kill in the mistaken belief that the kitten was a throwback to a more mindless race of cats. Instead, it turns out that Thistle-Chaser and others like her are the next evolutionary step in sentient cats—kittens who take longer to come to maturity. By 1995's *Ratha's Challenge,* the mother and daughter are still creeping toward reconciliation, but they join forces to deal with and understand another clan of sentient cats controlled by a communal song.

Jeanne Triner declared in *Booklist* that "readers [of *Ratha's Challenge*] will find enough suspense, adventure, and even romance to satisfy them." Carolyn Polese, reviewing the same novel in *School Library Journal,* lauded its "vivid descriptions of . . . life on the veldt," while Leslie Acevedo in *Voice of Youth Advocates* concluded that the novel's themes "are presented in a well-paced and thought-provoking manner."

Bell also weaves her interest in cats into *Tomorrow's Sphinx,* a novel for children that explores the lives of two black cheetahs, one in Egypt during the reign of the pharaoh Tutankhamen, the other in a future devastated by environmental waste. Another novel of Bell's,

*The Jaguar Princess,* is an historical fantasy set during the time of the Aztecs. *The Jaguar Princess* concerns Mixcatl, a slave girl who turns out to be descended from a royal race of shape-changers. A *Kirkus Review* critic found *The Jaguar Princess* to be "thinly plotted," but a *Publishers Weekly* reviewer praised it as "vivid."

In *People of the Sky,* a fantasy novel written for all ages, Bell introduces Kesebe Temiya, a young woman of the twenty-third century. Preceding the start of the story, Kesebe's ancestors had fled a failing Earth several hundred years earlier to preserve their Puerto Rican traditions. After her airplane goes down in a storm, Kesebe is rescued by Imiya, a young boy from an interstellar colony called People of the Sky, and a descendent of the Hopi nation. When Kesebe unwittingly foments a cultural crisis by helping Imiya avoid enduring the rite of passage required by his culture, she resolved the problem. Reviewing this volume, *Booklist* contributor Roland Green stated that Bell "seems to be working the anthropological sf territory of [Ursula] Le Guin and [C. H.] Cherryh with a skill that promises a bright future."

*Daughter of the Reef,* Bell's first collaboration with M. Coleman Easton published under the joint pseudonym Clare Coleman, is set during ancient times on an island of the South Pacific. Tepua, the book's royal heroine, is washed away from the celebration of her own wedding by a tropical storm. In the place where she washes up, she must learn to fit in with a new society, and learns to dance for her new tribe. Her dancing also brings her a new love interest in Matopahu. A *Publishers Weekly* reviewer assessed that the novel has "a dynamism that keeps it afloat."

## BIOGRAPHICAL AND CRITICAL SOURCES:

### BOOKS

*St. James Guide to Fantasy Writers,* St. James Press (Detroit, MI), 1996.

### PERIODICALS

*Booklist,* March 15, 1983, Sally Estes, review of *Ratha's Creature,* pp. 956-957; October 15, 1986, S. Estes, review of *Tomorrow's Sphinx,* p. 344;

December 15, 1989, Roland Green, review of *People of the Sky,* p. 815; January 1, 1995, Jeanne Triner, review of *Ratha's Challenge,* pp. 814-816; December 15, 1997, S. Estes, review of *Ratha's Creature,* p. 695.

*English Journal,* September, 1984, Beth Nelms, review of *Ratha's Creature,* p. 102; February, 1986, Beth Nelms, review of *Clan Ground,* p. 106.

*Kirkus Reviews,* September 1, 1986, review of *Tomorrow's Sphinx,* p. 1372; November 1, 1989, review of *People of the Sky,* p. 1567; August 15, 1993, review of *The Jaguar Princess,* p. 1034.

*Publishers Weekly,* December 26, 1986, Diane Roback, review of *Tomorrow's Sphinx,* p. 57; October 27, 1989, Sybil Steinberg, review of *People of the Sky,* p. 60; November 9, 1992, p. 78; October 4, 1993, review of *The Jaguar Princess,* p. 68; November 9, 1993, review of *Daughter of the Reef,* p. 78.

*School Library Journal,* September, 1983, Trev Jones, review of *Ratha's Creature,* p. 130; October, 1984, review of *Clan Ground,* p. 164; November, 1986, Lyle Blake Smythers, review of *Tomorrow's Sphinx,* p. 96; June, 1990, Carolyn Polese, review of *Ratha and the Thistle-Chaser,* p. 136; January, 1995, Carolyn Polese, review of *Ratha's Challenge,* p. 134.

*Voice of Youth Advocates,* October, 1983, Mary Ellen Baker, review of *Ratha's Creature,* p. 196; June, 1990, Catherine Moorhead, review of *Ratha and the Thistle-Chaser,* p. 112; June, 1995, Leslie Acevedo, review of *Ratha's Challenge,* p. 101.*

\*   \*   \*

## BERNSTEIN, Michael Andre 1947-

*PERSONAL:* Born August 31, 1947, in Innsbruck, Austria; immigrated to Canada, 1956; naturalized Canadian citizen, 1956; son of John Vladimir (a diplomat) and Marion (Sklarz) Bernstein; married Jeanne Wolff von Amerongen (a clinical psychologist), November 3, 1980; children: Anna-Nora. *Education:* Princeton University, B.A., 1969; Oxford University, B.Litt., 1973, D.Phil., 1975.

*ADDRESSES: Home*—44 Highgate Rd., Kensington, CA 94707. *Office*—Department of English, University of California, Berkeley, CA 94720.

*CAREER:* University of California, Berkeley, assistant professor, 1975-81, associate professor, 1981-87, professor of English and comparative literature, 1987—.

*AWARDS, HONORS:* Danforth fellowship, 1969-75; fellowships from Association of Commonwealth Universities, 1969-73, Canada Council, 1973-75, American Council of Learned Societies, 1977-78 and 1981, and University of California, 1977-89; Koret Israel Prize, 1989; President's Research in the Humanities fellowship, 1991; Guggenheim Memorial fellowship, 1993; American Academy of Arts and Sciences (fellow), 1995.

*WRITINGS:*

*The Tale of the Tribe: Ezra Pound and the Modern Verse Epic,* Princeton University Press (Princeton, NJ), 1980.

*Prima della Rivoluzione* (poems; title means "Before the Revolution"), National Poetry Foundation/University of Maine Press (Orono, ME), 1984.

*Bitter Carnival: Ressentiment and the Abject Hero,* Princeton University Press (Princeton, NJ), 1992.

*Foregone Conclusions: Against Apocalyptic History,* University of California Press (Berkeley, CA), 1994.

*Five Portraits: Modernity and the Imagination in Twentieth-Century German Writing,* Northwestern University Press (Evanston, IL), 2000.

Contributor to numerous books, including *George Oppen: Man and Poet,* edited by B. Hatlen, National Poetry Foundation/University of Maine Press (Orono, ME), 1981; *Ezra Pound and History,* edited by Marianne Korn, National Poetry Foundation/University of Maine Press (Orono, ME), 1985; *Bakhtin: Essays and Dialogues on His Work,* edited by Gary Saul Morson, University of Chicago Press (Chicago, IL), 1986; *Ruth Francken: Antlitze,* edited by Wolfgang Horn, Kunsthalle Nürnberg (Nürnberg, Germany), 1986; *Ezra Pound: Modern Critical Views,* edited by Harold Bloom, Chelsea House (New Haven, CT), 1987; *Politics and Poetic Value,* edited by Robert von Hallberg, University of Chicago Press (Chicago, IL), 1987; *Rethinking Bakhtin: Extensions and Challenges,* edited by Morson and Caryl Emerson, Northwestern University Press (Evanston, IL), 1989; Shimon Attie, *Die Schrift an der Wand,* Edition Braus (Heidelberg,

Germany), 1993, translation published as *The Writings on the Wall: Projections in Berlin's Jewish Quarter,* Edition Braus, 1994; and *World War II: Fifty Years Later,* edited by Alvin Rosenfeld, Indiana University Press (Bloomington, IN), 1995.

Also contributor of critical essays, poems, and reviews to various American and European journals, including *Via, Poetics and Theory of Literature, University Publishing, St. Andrews Review, Yale Review, Critical Inquiry, Sagetrieb, Yeats Annual, TriQuarterly, New Orleans Review, Times Literary Supplement, New Republic, Modern Philology,* and *Modernism/Modernity.*

*WORK IN PROGRESS: Progressive Lenses,* a novel.

*SIDELIGHTS:* Michael Andre Bernstein's writings reflect his interest in literature and how it is influenced by philosophy, psychology, and history. In *Foregone Conclusions: Against Apocalyptic History,* Bernstein makes the argument that people and societies are weakened by the tendency to consider their paths to be determined by fate. He uses literary examples of foreshadowing to bolster his case. Bernstein introduces various illustrations of this idea, including the Holocaust. In *The New Republic,* Michael Ignatieff remarked, "Michael Andre Bernstein's splendid book is a hearteningly affirmative product of this new age of uncertainty and self-doubt." In response to the book's handling of the Holocaust and foreshadowing in literature, Ignatieff observed, "These forms of thought betray an effort to avoid the full weight of sorrow, to find some form of thought, however cruel, that would shield us, the living, from what we have lost. We would rather believe that it could not have happened otherwise than to entertain the still more agonizing thought that it need not have happened at all." David H. Hirsch of *Criticism,* however, found many failings in Bernstein's arguments. He found that Bernstein's book suffers from the author's "academic vanity" and inability to recognize his own strong biases. He particularly noted what he called "highly oversimplified terms" and a disregard for historical accuracy in the discussion of the Holocaust.

*Five Portraits: Modernity and the Imagination of Twentieth-Century German Writing* tackles the writing careers and influences of five important German writers. Shorter versions of the profiles were first pub-

lished in *The New Republic,* and Bernstein expanded them to create a single volume for reference by students, academics, and readers who admire German literature. Ulrich Baer of *Library Journal* concluded that this book of "deftly written essays is sure to knock many a full-length study of any of the five German writers under discussion off the shelf."

Bernstein once told *CA:* "I consider all of my writing, from my volume of poetry to my three critical works as well as my novel-in-progress, to be part of the same constellation of concerns, and in that sense, even part of the same project. The intersection of the imagination with history, and the search for an ethical language that engages moral issues without being moralistic is at the heart of my work.

"My writing stresses that in our culture it is not the attractiveness of extreme risk nor the darkest teachings of violence and domination that are repressed. Exactly these issues have long constituted an enormous, if not actually the major, portion of our intellectual conversation about history as well as about the human psyche. What *is* repressed, though, is the value of the quotidian, the counter-authenticity of the texture and rhythm of our daily routines and decisions, the myriad of minute and careful adjustments that we are ready to offer in the interest of a habitable social world. It is those adjustments, the moment-by-moment way we experience our lives and make our plans that most grip my imagination and inspire all of my writing."

*BIOGRAPHICAL AND CRITICAL SOURCES:*

*PERIODICALS*

*Choice: Current Reviews for Academic Libraries,* April, 1995, p. 1294; April, 2001, pp. 1467-1468.
*Commentary,* October 1, 1993, Gary Saul Morson, review of *Bitter Carnival: Ressentiment and the Abject Hero,* p. 62.
*Criticism,* March 22, 1995, David H. Hirsch, review of *Foregone Conclusion: Against Apocalyptic History,* p. 348.
*Library Journal,* August, 1980, p. 1634; May 1, 1992, p. 80; October 1, 2000, Ulrich Baer, review of *Five Portraits: Modernity and the Imagination in Twentieth-Century German Writing,* p. 94.
*Modern Fiction Studies,* winter, 1996, p. 929.

*Modernism/Modernity,* April, 2001, p. 359.

*Modern Philology,* November, 1996, p. 276.

*New Republic,* February 13, 1995, Michael Ignatieff, review of *Foregone Conclusions: Against Apocalyptic History,* p. 29.

*New York Times Book Review,* September 25, 1994, p. 24; October 30, 1994, p. 40.

*Times Literary Supplement,* March 6, 1981; March 3, 1995, p. 12; March 5, 1999, p. 4; January 12, 2001, p. 27.*

*    *    *

**BERTLING, Tom 1956-**

*PERSONAL:* Born June 21, 1956; son of Richard and Josephine (Caputo) Bertling; married Valerie Jo Bemis, August, 1992; children: Rikki Sage (daughter). *Ethnicity:* "English, Italian, German." *Politics:* Democrat. *Religion:* "Agnostic." *Hobbies and other interests:* Astronomy, astrophysics, physics, architecture, politics, music.

*ADDRESSES: Office*—Kodiak Media Group, P.O. Box 1029, Wilsonville, OR 97070.

*CAREER:* Kodiak Media Group, Wilsonville, OR, president, 1989—.

*WRITINGS:*

*A Child Sacrificed,* Kodiak Media Group (Wilsonville, OR), 1994.

*No Dignity for Joshua,* Kodiak Media Group (Wilsonville, OR), 1997.

(Editor) *American Sign Language: Shattering the Myth,* Kodiak Media Group (Wilsonville, OR), 1998.

(Editor) *An Intellectual Look at American Sign Language,* Kodak Media Group (Wilsonville, OR), 2001.

(Editor) *Communicating with Deaf Children,* Kodak Media Group (Wilsonville, OR), 2002.

*WORK IN PROGRESS:* Several projects related to signed languages and deafness; research on American Sign Language and signed English, sexual abuse among the deaf, deaf cultural issues, and astrophysics research.

*SIDELIGHTS:* Tom Bertling once told *CA:* "My primary reason for undertaking the difficult task of writing my books is the simple fact that most of the published material on deafness, in particular deaf culture, deaf education, and American Sign Language, was either completely biased or simply flat-out wrong. Because I attended a residential school for the deaf and also have a large 'deaf of deaf' family, I feel I am able to present a perspective on matters that, until now, were mostly hidden from society in general.

"There is a vocal minority—which claims to represent *all* deaf or hard-of-hearing people—that prefers I keep quiet about these matters, but they are in fact part of the problem, not the solution. My contribution to society is to continue the process of bringing things out into the open for full public scrutiny.

"In the beginning, I was discouraged by many so-called esteemed deaf leaders from writing about these emotional and political topics. After the first book, however, I was approached by numerous educators who encouraged me to keep writing and ignore the nay-sayers. A large number of individuals commented that they appreciated my direct, to-the-point style. English is, however, a lifelong learning process for me. I want to note that it was the late Dr. Otto Menzel, editor of *Life after Deafness,* who sped up the process for me. I am greatly indebted to him for making up for the educational shortcomings of my school years."

*    *    *

**BIGHAM, Darrel E. 1942-**

*PERSONAL:* Born August 12, 1942, in Harrisburg, PA; son of Paul and Ethel (Brandt) Bigham; married Polly Hitchcock (a program director), September 23, 1965; children: Matthew, Elizabeth. *Ethnicity:* "Caucasian." *Education:* Messiah College, B.A., 1964; attended Harvard University, 1964-65; University of Kansas, Ph.D., 1970. *Politics:* Democrat. *Religion:* Episcopalian. *Hobbies and other interests:* Travel, gardening.

*ADDRESSES: Office*—Department of History, University of Southern Indiana, 8600 University Blvd., Evansville, IN 47712; fax: 812-465-7061. *E-mail*—dbigham@usi.edu.

*CAREER:* University of Southern Indiana, Evansville, assistant professor, 1970-75, associate professor, 1975-81, professor of history, 1981—, director of Historic Southern Indiana program, 1986—. Indiana State University—Evansville, codirector of regional archives, 1972-74. Indiana Historical Bureau, member of historical marker advisory committee; Indiana Council for History Education, past chair; National Council for History Education, Indiana representative; member of Indiana Council for Social Studies and National Council for Social Studies; U.S. Abraham Lincoln Bicentennial Commission, member, 2000—; appointed Vanderburgh County Historian. Leadership Evansville, executive director, 1976-79; Southern Indiana Rural Development Project, member of board of directors; past president of board of directors of Volunteer Action Center, Evansville Arts and Education Council, Evansville Museum of Arts and Science, and Democrats for Better Government; past member of board of directors of Evansville Museum, Conrad Baker Foundation, and Evansville Vanderburgh County Public Library.

*MEMBER:* Organization of American Historians, American Historical Association, National Trust for Historic Preservation, American Association for State and Local History, Indiana Association of Historians (past president), Indiana Historical Society, Vanderburgh County Historical Society (past president of board of directors), Rotary Club of Evansville.

*AWARDS, HONORS:* Grant from National Endowment for the Humanities, 1989-91; Paul Harris fellow, Rotary Club of Evansville, 1992.

*WRITINGS:*

*Reflections on a Heritage: The German Americans in Southwestern Indiana,* Indiana State University (Evansville, IN), 1980.
*We Ask Only a Fair Trial: A History of the Black Community of Evansville, Indiana,* Indiana University Press (Bloomington, IN), 1987.
*An Evansville Album: Perspectives on a River City, 1812-1988,* Indiana University Press (Bloomington, IN), 1988.
*Indiana Resource Book,* Glencoe/McGraw (New York, NY), 1997.
*Towns and Villages of the Lower Ohio,* University Press of Kentucky (Lexington, KY), 1998.

*Evansville,* Arcadia Publishing (Mount Pleasant, SC), 1998.
*Southern Indiana,* Arcadia Publishing (Mount Pleasant, SC), 2000.
(Editor) *Indiana Territory, 1800-2000: A Bicentennial Perspective,* Indiana Historical Society (Indianapolis, IN), 2001.

Contributor to books, including *Their Infinite Variety: Essays on Hoosier Politicians,* Indiana Historical Bureau (Indianapolis, IN), 1981; *Always a River: An Anthology,* edited by Robert L. Reid, Indiana University Press (Bloomington, IN), 1991; *Indiana's African-American Heritage: Essays from Black History News and Notes,* edited by Wilma Dulin, Indiana Historical Society (Indianapolis, IN), 1993; and *The Black Press in the Middle West,* edited by Henry Lewis Suggs, Greenwood Press (Westport, CT), 1996. Contributor of articles and reviews to journals, including *Traces of Indiana and Midwestern History, Black History News and Notes, Old Northwest, Peace and Change, Journal of American History, American Historical Review,* and *Alabama Review.* Member of editorial board, *Indiana Magazine of History,* 1982-86; member of editorial advisory board, Evansville Press, 1983-86, and *Organization of American Historians Newsletter,* 2001—.

*WORK IN PROGRESS: On Jordan's Banks: Emancipation and Black Community Life on the Lower Ohio.*

*SIDELIGHTS:* Darrel E. Bigham once told *CA:* "In brief, I have sought to explain the place in which I have lived since 1970: how and why the towns and cities of the lower Ohio are what they are; how and why the people of this region think, believe, and act as they do. My audience is general—mostly regional—though I seek to reach academics, also, with a reliable and valid narrative."

\*     \*     \*

**BIRIMISA, George 1924-**

*PERSONAL:* Born February 21, 1924, in Santa Cruz, CA; son of Charles and Anna (Gjurovich) Birimisa; married Nancy Linden, 1952 (divorced, 1961). *Education:* Attended New School for Social Research; studied with Uta Hagen at Herbert Berghof Studios, New York, NY, 1965-66.

*George Birimisa*

ADDRESSES: *Home*—627 Page St., Apt. 6, San Francisco, CA 94117. *E-mail*—gbirimisa@aol.com.

CAREER: Actor, director, and playwright. Worked in a factory, as a disc jockey, health studio manager, clerk, bartender, bellhop, page for National Broadcasting Co., and in sales; Howard Johnson's, New York, NY, counter person, 1952-56; Laurie Girls, New York, NY, typist, 1969-70; Theatre of All Nations, New York, NY, artistic director, 1974-76; full-time writer, 1966—. *Military service:* U.S. Naval Reserve, 1942-43.

AWARDS, HONORS: Rockefeller grant, 1969; award from *DramaLogue,* 1978, for *A Rainbow in the Night.*

WRITINGS:

PLAYS

*Degrees,* produced in New York, NY, 1966.
*17 Loves and 17 Kisses,* produced in New York, NY, 1966.
*Daddy Violet,* produced in New York, NY, 1967.

*How Come You Don't Dig Chicks?,* produced in New York, NY, 1967.
*Mister Jello* (two-act), produced in New York, NY, 1968, revised version produced in New York, NY, 1974.
*Georgie Porgie,* produced in New York, NY, 1968.
*Adrian,* produced in New York, NY, 1974.
*Will the Real Yoganga Please Stand Up?,* produced in New York, NY, 1974.
*A Dress Made of Diamonds,* produced in Los Angeles, CA, 1976.
*Pogey Bait!,* produced in Los Angeles, CA, 1976, produced in New York, NY, 1977.
*A Rainbow in the Night,* produced in Los Angeles, CA, 1978.
*A Rose and a Baby Ruth,* produced in San Francisco, CA, 1981.
*The Man with Straight Hair,* produced in San Francisco, CA, 1993.
*Looking for Mr. America,* produced in San Francisco, CA, 1994, produced in New York, NY, 1995.

OTHER

(And director) *Looking for Mr. America: A Portrait of George Birimisa* (videotape), Harvey Milk Institute, 2003.

Work appears in anthologies, including *More Plays from Off-Off-Broadway,* Bobbs-Merrill (Indianapolis, IN), 1972. Contributor to *Drummer, Alternate, Prism International,* and other periodicals.

A collection of Birimisa's manuscripts is housed at Joe Cino Memorial Library, Lincoln Center Library of the Performing Arts, New York, NY.

SIDELIGHTS: According to Michael T. Smith in *Contemporary Dramatists,* George Birimisa "is a fiercely moral writer; his plays are filled with compassionate rage against needless suffering, furious impatience with the human condition, desperately frustrated idealism. He links the pain of human isolation to economic and social roots."

Birimisa's most popular play, *Georgie Porgie,* for example, contains nine scenes dealing with homosexual encounters, each scene interspersed with choral quotations from communist Friedrich Engels. "The contrast," wrote Smith, "between Engels' idealistic vision of human liberty and Birimisa's variously stupid, contemptible, pitiful, self-despising characters, all imprisoned in their own compulsions, is powerful and painful." According to a critic for *Variety,* the play is an advance in its field, and "unlike many of its stage predecessors, . . . Birimisa's play minces few images or words in describing the plight of its characters."

*BIOGRAPHICAL AND CRITICAL SOURCES:*

BOOKS

*Contemporary Dramatists,* 5th edition, St. James Press (Detroit, MI), 1993.

PERIODICALS

*New York Times,* August 11, 1971.
*Variety,* September 1, 1971.
*Village Voice,* September 4, 1969.

\*      \*      \*

**BLOM, Jan**
    **See BREYTENBACH, Breyten**

\*      \*      \*

**BOURBON, Ken**
    **See BAUER, Erwin A.**

\*      \*      \*

**BOWKER, John (Westerdale) 1935-**

*PERSONAL:* Born July 30, 1935, in London, England; son of Gordon Westerdale and Marguerite Bowker; married Margaret Roper (a university lecturer), June 22, 1963; children: David Charles. *Education:* Oxford University, B.A., 1958. *Hobbies and other interests:* Books, painting, poetry.

*ADDRESSES: Home*—14 Bowers Croft, Cambridge CB1 8RP, England.

*CAREER:* Corpus Christi College, Cambridge, England, fellow, 1962-74, assistant lecturer, 1965, lecturer, 1969; University of Lancaster, Lancaster, England, professor of religious studies, 1974-85; Trinity College, Cambridge, dean, 1984-91; Gresham College, London, England, professor of divinity, 1992-97, fellow, 1997—. Wilde Lecturer, 1972-77 and Hanson Lecturer, Oxford University,; Staley Lecturer, Rollins College, 1978-78; also lecturer at University of Cardiff, Newcastle University, University of Toronto, and other schools.

*MEMBER:* Institute on Religion in an Age of Science (vice president, 1980); Christian Action on AIDS (president, 1987-91); Culture and Animals Foundation, 1984-92.

*AWARDS, HONORS:* HarperCollins Religious Book Award, 1993, for *The Meanings of Death.*

*WRITINGS:*

*The Targums and Rabbinic Literature: An Introduction to Jewish Interpretations of Scripture,* Cambridge University Press (New York, NY), 1969.
(Contributor) *Making Moral Decisions,* SPCK (London, England), 1969.
*Problems of Suffering in Religions of the World,* Cambridge University Press (New York, NY), 1970.
*The Sense of God: Sociological, Anthropological, and Psychological Approaches to the Origin of the Sense of God,* Oxford University Press (New York, NY), 1973, 2nd edition, Oneworld (Rockport, MA), 1995.
*Uncle Bolpenny Tries Things Out,* Faber (London, England), 1973.
*Jesus and the Pharisees,* Cambridge University Press (New York, NY), 1973.
*The Religious Imagination and the Sense of God,* Oxford University Press (New York, NY), 1978.
*Worlds of Faith: Religious Belief and Practice in Britain Today,* Ariel Books, 1983.
(Editor) *Senses and Culture: The Function and Management of Aggression and Cooperation in Biocultural Evolution,* Zygon, 1983.
*Licensed Insanities: Religions and Belief in God in the Contemporary World,* Darton, Longman & Todd (London, England), 1987.

*Is Anybody out There?: Religions and Belief in God in the Contemporary World,* Christian Classics (Westminster, MD), 1988.

*Hallowed Ground: Religions and the Poetry of Place,* SPCK (London, England), 1993.

*Is God a Virus?* SPCK (London, England), 1995.

*The Meanings of Death,* Cambridge University Press (New York, NY), 1993.

*World Religions: The Great Faiths Explored and Explained,* DK (New York, NY), 1997, revised edition, 2003.

(Editor) *The Oxford Dictionary of World Religions,* Oxford University Press (New York, NY), 1997, published as *The Concise Oxford Dictionary of World Religions,* 2000.

*What Muslims Believe,* Oneworld (Boston, MA), 1998.

*The Complete Bible Handbook,* DK (New York, NY), 1998.

*The Religious Imagination and the Sense of God,* Clarendon Press (New York, NY), 2000.

(Editor) *The Cambridge Illustrated History of Religions,* Cambridge University Press (New York, NY), 2002.

*God: A Brief History,* DK (New York, NY), 2002.

*EDITOR, WITH JEAN HOLM*

*Attitudes to Nature,* Pinter (New York, NY), 1994.

*Human Nature and Destiny,* Pinter (New York, NY), 1994.

*Making Moral Decisions,* Pinter (New York, NY), 1994.

*Picturing God,* Pinter (New York, NY), 1994.

*Rites of Passage,* Pinter (New York, NY), 1994.

*Sacred Place,* Pinter (New York, NY), 1994.

*Sacred Writings,* Pinter (New York, NY), 1994.

*Women in Religion,* Pinter (New York, NY), 1994.

*Worship,* Pinter (New York, NY), 1994.

*Myth and History,* Pinter (New York, NY), 1994.

**SIDELIGHTS:** Theologian and educator John Bowker released two simultaneous studies in 1997, *World Religions: The Great Faiths Explored and Explained* and *The Oxford Dictionary of World Religions,* the latter of which he edited. The two books complement each other, providing overviews of varying detail on the wide range of worldwide faith. *Library Journal* reviewer Glenn Masuchika found that while *The Oxford Dictionary of World Religions* is essentially "a one-volume desktop encyclopedia for ready reference," in

"World Religions," Bowker is "freed to range over what he wants to say and how he wants to say it." Gervase Rosser, writing in *Journal of Ecclesiastical History,* lauded Bowker's dictionary as an "extraordinary" achievement: "Individual entries, often thumbnail sketches of highly complex issues, are written with a marvelous combination of intelligence, clarity and vividness."

To *Times* critic John Hapgood, *The Oxford Dictionary of World Religions* reflects its editor's sensibilities. "Those who know and admire John Bowker's other work will not be surprised to find it centring on information theory. He argues that religions are protective systems designed to transmit well-tested information about explorations of human possibility."

In *God: A Brief History* Bowker offers a book "chock-full of facts, stories, legends and illustrations" on religious traditions around the world, as a *Publishers Weekly* contributor noted. Explaining that the work cites philosophers, psychologists, and scholars through the centuries to explain God's place in society, the *Publishers Weekly* critic cited "numerous problems" in Bowker's reading, specifying that the author "never explains what he means" by the term God. But Gary Gillum in a review for *Library Journal* found more to like, characterizing *God* as "a fascinating, all-purpose book." David Edwards in *Times Literary Supplement* called the book "a clear-minded and unifying masterpiece."

*BIOGRAPHICAL AND CRITICAL SOURCES:*

*PERIODICALS*

*American Reference Books Annual,* 1998, review of *The Oxford Dictionary of World Religions,* p. 591.

*Booklist,* July, 1997, review of *The Oxford Dictionary of World Religions,* p. 1837; October 15, 1999, Barbara Bibel and J. Christopher McConnell, review of *The Oxford Dictionary of World Religions* and *World Religions,* p. 472.

*Book Report,* September-October, 1997, review of *World Religions: The Great Faiths Explored and Explained,* p. 65.

*Catholic Library World,* December, 1997, review of *The Oxford Dictionary of World Religions,* p. 66; September, 1999, review of *The Complete Bible Handbook,* p. 35.

*Choice,* January, 1992, January, 1992, review of *The Meanings of Death,* p. 762; October, 1997, review of *The Oxford Dictionary of World Religions,* p. 273; May, 1999, D. D. Siles, review of *The Complete Bible Handbook,* p. 1590; March, 2001, J. R. Luttrell, review of *The Concise Oxford Dictionary of World Religions,* p. 1241.

*Christian Century,* March 8, 1989, review of *Is Anybody out There?,* p. 268; November 6, 1991, review of *The Meanings of Death,* p. 1044.

*Journal of Asian Studies,* August, 1992, review of *The Meanings of Death,* p. 621.

*Journal of Ecclesiastical History,* April, 1999, Gervase Rosser, review of *The Oxford Dictionary of World Religions,* p. 314.

*Journal of the American Academy of Religion,* spring, 1998, Russell McCutcheon, review of *Myth and History* and *Rites of Passage,* p. 147.

*Kliatt Young Adult Paperback Book Guide,* November, 2001, review of *The Complete Bible Handbook,* p. 24.

*Library Journal,* July, 1991, review of *The Meanings of Death,* p. 102; May 1, 1997, Glen Masuchika, review of *The Oxford Dictionary of World Religions,* p. 94; November 15, 2001, Martha Cornog and Eliabeth Plantz, review of *What Muslims Believe,* p. 82; June 1, 2002, Gary Gillum, review of *God: A Brief History* and William Collins, review of *The Cambridge Illustrated History of Religion,* p. 158.

*Medical Humanities Review,* fall, 1993, review of *The Meanings of Death,* p. 31.

*Middle East Journal,* summer, 1994, review of *The Meanings of Death,* p. 564.

*New Statesman,* April 14, 1995, review of *Is God a Virus?* p. 40.

*New Statesman & Society,* October 11, 1991, review of *The Meanings of Death,* p. 23.

*Observer* (London, England), June 20, 1993, review of *The Meanings of Death,* p. 62.

*Publishers Weekly,* November, 30, 1998, review of *The Complete Bible Handbook,* p. 65; June 10, 2002, review of *God: A Brief History,* p. 58.

*Quill & Quire,* December, 1998, review of *The Complete Bible Handbook,* p. 20.

*Religious Studies,* December, 1993, review of *The Meanings of Death,* p. 559.

*Religious Studies Review,* October, 1992, review of *The Meanings of Death,* p. 311; October, 1997, review of *The Oxford Dictionary of World Religions,* p. 367.

*School Library Journal,* December, 1997, review of *The Oxford Dictionary of World Religions,* p. 154.

*Theology Today,* July, 1998, Terry Muck, review of *The Oxford Dictionary of World Religions,* p. 271.

*Times* (London, England), March 27, 1997, John Hapgood, "Heart of a Heartless World," p. 41.

*Times Higher Education Supplement,* April 25, 1997, Anthony Freeman, review of *The Oxford Dictionary of World Religions,* p. 24.

*Times Literary Supplement,* November 1, 1991, John McManners, review of *The Meanings of Death,* p. 27; November 8, 2002, David L. Edwards, "Manifestations of the One," p. 15.

*Tribune Books* (Chicago, IL), August 25, 1991, review of *The Meanings of Death,* p. 5.

*Voice of Youth Advocates,* October, 1997, review of *The Oxford Dictionary of World Religions,* p. 258; June, 1999, review of *The Complete Bible Handbook,* p. 138.

*Zygon,* December, 1999, review of *Is God a Virus?* p. 713.

\* \* \*

## BOWLER, Peter J(ohn) 1944-

*PERSONAL:* Born October 8, 1944, in Leicester, England; son of Wallace (a mechanic) and Florence (Moon) Bowler; married Sheila Mary Holt, September 24, 1966; children: Caroline Margaret, Ian Peter. *Education:* King's College, Cambridge, B.A., 1966; University of Sussex, M.Sc., 1967; University of Toronto, Ph.D., 1971.

*ADDRESSES: Home*—17A Hillsborough Rd., Moira, Craigavon BT67 OHQ, Northern Ireland. *Office*—Department of History, Queen's University of Belfast, Belfast BT7 1NN, Northern Ireland.

*CAREER:* University of Toronto, Toronto, Ontario, Canada, assistant professor of history of science, 1971-72; Universiti Sains Malaysia, Penang, lecturer in history, 1972-75; University of Winnipeg, Winnipeg, Manitoba, assistant professor of history, 1975-79; Queen's University of Belfast, Belfast, Northern Ireland, lecturer, 1979-87, reader, 1987-92, professor of history of science, 1992—.

*MEMBER:* Royal Irish Academy (chairperson, National Committee for History and Philosophy of Science, 1996—), History of Science Society, British So-

*Peter J. Bowler*

ciety for the History of Science, Canadian Society for History and Philosophical Science, Canadian Science and Technical History Association.

*WRITINGS:*

*Fossils and Progress: Paleontology and the Idea of Progressive Evolution in the Nineteenth Century,* Science History Publications (New York, NY), 1976.

(Contributor) Sanborn C. Brown and Alexandra Oleson, editors, *The Pursuit of Knowledge in the Early American Republic,* Johns Hopkins University Press (Baltimore, MD), 1976.

*The Eclipse of Darwinism: Anti-Darwinian Evolution Theories in the Decades around 1900,* Johns Hopkins University Press (Baltimore, MD), 1983.

*Evolution: The History of an Idea,* University of California Press (Berkeley, CA), 1984, revised edition, 1989, revised and expanded edition, 2003.

*Theories of Human Evolution: A Century of Debate, 1844-1944,* Johns Hopkins University Press (Baltimore, MD), 1986.

*The Non-Darwinian Revolution: Reinterpreting a Historical Myth,* Johns Hopkins University Press (Baltimore, MD), 1988.

*The Mendelian Revolution,* Johns Hopkins University Press (Baltimore, MD), 1989.

*The Invention of Progress: The Victorians and the Past,* Blackwell (Cambridge, MA), 1989.

*Charles Darwin: The Man and His Influence,* Blackwell (Cambridge, MA), 1990.

*The Fontana/Norton History of the Environmental Sciences,* Fontana/Norton (New York, NY), 1992.

*Life's Splendid Drama: Evolutionary Biology and the Reconstruction of Life's Ancestry, 1860-1940,* University of Chicago Press (Chicago, IL), 1996.

(Editor, with Nicholas Whyte) *Science and Society in Ireland: The Social Context of Science and Technology in Ireland, 1800-1950,* Queen's University of Belfast, Institute of Irish Studies (Belfast, Northern Ireland), 1997.

*Reconciling Science and Religion: The Debate in Early Twentieth-Century Britain,* University of Chicago Press (Chicago, IL), 2001.

Contributor to history journals.

*SIDELIGHTS:* Peter J. Bowler once told *CA:* "Perhaps because most of my writing concerns the development of a very controversial scientific theory (evolution), I try to avoid an 'ivory tower' mentality. I think it is vital that scientists (and all who deal with science) communicate their views as widely as possible. The scientific method doesn't guarantee the production of 'truth'—and it would be much less interesting if it did. We need to celebrate the freedom from dogmatism implied by the 'questioning' nature of science. Failure to communicate this point may lose us the fight against the anti-science movements—and against dogmatism." Indeed, the majority of Bowler's writing does concern theories of evolution and Darwinism, and he provides opportunities to examine both sides of this controversial topic with such titles as *The Eclipse of Darwinism: Anti-Darwinian Evolution Theories in the Decades around 1900; Evolution: The History of an Idea,* which he has revised twice since the original publication in 1984; *Theories of Human Evolution: A Century of Debate, 1844-1944; The Non-Darwinian Revolution: Reinterpreting a Historical Myth;* and *Charles Darwin: The Man and His Influence.*

*Life's Splendid Drama: Evolutionary Biology and the Reconstruction of Life's Ancestry, 1860-1940* chronicles the history of ideas on the origins of vertebrates in the post-Darwinian era and also offers case studies on the origins of amphibians, birds, mammals, and arthropods. "It surveys events in the U.S., Britain, and Germany effortlessly and without evident bias . . . it succeeds admirably and impressively in providing what is not readily available anywhere else," commented T. J. Horder in a *Quarterly Review of Biology* review.

In the end of the nineteenth century, Darwinism caused a split in the intellectual world where science and religion previously had been closely linked, creating two opposing sides: Christianity and scientific materialism. In *Reconciling Science and Religion: The Debate in Early Twentieth-Century Britain,* published in 2001, Bowler advances the opinion that the impetus bringing the two camps together came from within each side, as scientists began to resent a rigid materialist philosophy that allowed no consideration of religious reasons for natural occurrences and Christian leaders became more willing to contemplate modern scientific views. With profiles of the leading thinkers, examinations of the inner controversies that caused dissention, descriptions of the political and economic atmosphere of the country and the world, and considerations of other influences, Bowler describes what caused these changes on both sides. *Times Literary Supplement* reviewer Mathew Thomson called it an "important and scholarly book . . . [that] provides us with a serious analysis of religion's position within the intellectual culture of twentieth-century Britain." An *Economist* contributor noted that Bowler "describes in scholarly detail different strategies for harmonizing faith and knowledge: the sought-after alliance between liberal theologians in the Church of England and religious-minded scientists, and the rather different efforts of science-minded writers such as Julian Huxley and George Bernard Shaw to foster a modern, non-Christian religion. All the while . . . the conservative faithful on the one side and the atheists on the other . . . resisted calls for reconciliation of any kind."

## BIOGRAPHICAL AND CRITICAL SOURCES:

### PERIODICALS

*American Historical Review,* June, 1977.

*Booklist,* July, 1993, review of *The Norton History of the Environmental Sciences,* p. 1930.

*Choice,* December 1988, review of *Fossils and Progress: Paleontology and the Idea of Progressive Evolution in the Nineteenth Century,* p. 610.

*Economist,* November 10, 2001, "The Perils of Religious Correctness; Religion and Science."

*English Historical Review,* October, 1993, review of *The Invention of Progress: The Victorians and the Past,* pp. 1046-47.

*Historian,* November, 1984, review of *The Eclipse of Darwinism: Anti-Darwinian Evolution Theories in the Decades around 1900,* p. 106; November, 1988, review of *Theories of Human Evolution: A Century of Debate, 1844–1944,* p. 114.

*History Today,* November, 2001, Anne Pointer, review of *Reconciling Science and Religion: The Debate in Early Twentieth-Century Britain,* p. 58

*Isis,* March, 1993, review of *Charles Darwin: The Man and His Influence,* pp. 113-14; June, 1993, review of *The Invention of Progress: The Victorians and the Past,* pp. 391-392; September, 1996, review of *Biology and Social Thought: 1850-1914,* p. 560.

*Library Journal,* March 1, 1984, review of *The Eclipse of Darwinism: Anti-Darwinian Evolution Theories in the Decades Around 1900,* p. 436; October 15, 1986, review of *Theories of Human Evolution,* p. 103.

*London Review of Books,* October, 15, 1987, review of *Theories of Human Evolution,* p. 13.

*Nature,* April 30, 1987, review of *Theories of Human Evolution,* p. 897; September 27, 2001, Geoffrey Cantor, review of *Reconciling Science and Religion,* pp. 363-364.

*New York Times Book Review,* October 17, 1993, review of *The Norton History of the Environmental Sciences,* p. 34.

*Quarterly Review of Biology,* March, 1991, review of *The Mendelian Revolution,* p. 68; December, 1993, review of *The Eclipse of Darwinism,* p. 564; *The Non-Darwinian Revolution: Reinterpreting a Historical Myth,* p. 83; June, 1998, T. J. Horder, review of *Life's Splendid Drama: Evolutionary Biology and the Reconstruction of Life's Ancestry, 1860-1940,* pp. 175-188.

*Science,* January 19, 1990, review of *The Mendelian Revolution,* p. 348; November 16, 2001, Thomas Dixon, review of *Reconciling Science and Religion,* pp. 1467-68.

*Times Literary Supplement,* June 17, 1977; December 9, 1983; August 2, 1985; February 14, 1992, review of *Charles Darwin: The Man and His Influence,* p. 26; March 29, 2002, Mathew Thomson, "Together and Apart," p. 6.

*Victorian Studies,* winter, 1989, review of *Theories of Human Evolution,* p. 276; summer, 1991, review of *The Invention of Progress,* p. 496.

\* \* \*

**BRADBURY, Edward P.**
**See MOORCOCK, Michael (John)**

\* \* \*

**BRADING, D. A. 1936-**

*PERSONAL:* Born August 26, 1936, in Ilford, Essex, England; son of Ernest Arthur and Mary Amy (Driscoll) Brading; married January 27, 1966; wife's name Celia W. V. (an historian); children: Christopher. *Education:* Attended University of San Francisco, 1950-55. *Religion:* Roman Catholic. *Hobbies and other interests:* Music, walking.

*ADDRESSES: Home*—28 Storey's Way, Cambridge CB3 0DT, England. *Office*—History Faculty Building, Cambridge University, West Rd., Cambridge, England.

*CAREER:* University of California, Berkeley, assistant professor of history, 1965-71; Yale University, New Haven, CT, associate professor of history, 1971-73; Cambridge University, Cambridge, England, lecturer in history, 1973-92; director of Centre of Latin-American Studies, 1975-90. Honorary professor, University of Lima, 1993.

*MEMBER:* United Oxford and Cambridge University.

*AWARDS, HONORS:* D.Litt., Cambridge University, 1991.

*WRITINGS:*

*Miners and Merchants in Bourbon Mexico,* Cambridge University Press (New York, NY), 1971.
*Haciendas and Ranchos in Mexican Bajio,* Cambridge University Press (New York, NY), 1979.

*Caudillo and Peasant in the Mexican Revolution,* Cambridge University Press (New York, NY), 1980.
*Myth and Prophecy in Mexican History,* Cambridge University Press (New York, NY), 1984.
*The Origins of Mexican Nationalism,* Cambridge University Press (New York, NY), 1985.
*The First America, 1492-1867,* Cambridge University Press (New York, NY), 1991.
(Translator and editor) *Generals and Diplomats: Great Britain and Peru, 1820-40,* Cambridge University Press (Cambridge, England), 1991.
*Church and State in Bourbon Mexico: The Diocese of Michoaca, 1749-1810,* Cambridge University Press (New York, NY), 1994.
*Marmoreal Olympus: José Enrique Rodo and Spanish-American Nationalism,* Cambridge University Press (Cambridge, MA), 1998.
*Mexican Phoenix: Our Lady of Guadalupe: Image and Tradition across Five Centuries,* Cambridge University Press (New York, NY), 2001.

*SIDELIGHTS:* D. A. Brading, a British-born professor of history, writes on topics religious, cultural, and political as they pertain to Mexico. In his 1991 work *The First America, 1492-1867,* Brading "first discussed the role of the Guadalupe cult in Mexican history," according to a *Contemporary Review* contributor. Since then Brading has produced a full-length study of Guadalupe—the apparition of the Virgin Mary—in *Mexican Phoenix: Our Lady of Guadalupe: Image and Tradition across Five Centuries.* In this book he provides what Paul Vanderwood of *History* called a "magnificent exposition of the central icon of the nation's religiosity" in "a study certain to be considered the crown jewel of [Brading's] distinguished career."

*Mexican Phoenix* explores the mystery of Guadalupe, beginning with the figure's first reported appearance, to Aztec native Juan Diego on December 9, 1531. The Virgin asked that a temple be built on the site of Tepeyac; to prove her presence to a skeptical bishop she is said to have imprinted her image on Diego's cloak. "Veneration began," noted Vanderwood. "Rome officially named the Virgin the principal patron . . . of all Latin America." But over the next centuries, the Virgin's intricately detailed image on the rough-hewn cloak—itself a religious icon—has been the subject of much debate. In the words of *New York Times Book Review* critic Garry Wills, Brading "recounts in detail the many struggles around this fascinating cult, whose authority grows as its authenticity diminishes."

Brading "offers a way to move beyond the debate centered on declarations and counter declarations of the veracity of scientific fact, by contemplating the significance of Guadalupe from the heart of Mexican faith and history," explained *National Catholic Reporter* writer Teresa Maya. In the same article, Maya noted that *Mexican Phoenix* "is not an easy read"; indeed, "the uninitiated reader will not find the answers to all his or her Guadalupe questions easily." Still, Maya praised the author's "exquisite new approach" to the subject, and maintained that those readers with a thorough grounding in Mexican religious history "will find the second half of the book most illumination, particularly the post-independence treatment of Guadalupe."

*BIOGRAPHICAL AND CRITICAL SOURCES:*

PERIODICALS

*American Historical Review,* June, 1992, Peter Bakewell, review of *The First America: The Spanish Monarchy, Creole Patriots, and the Liberal State, 1492-1867,* p. 966.

*Americas,* October, 1995, Mark Burkholder, review of *Church and State in Bourbon Mexico: The Diocese of Michoaca, 1749-1810,* p. 9.

*Catholic Historical Review,* October, 1997, Caroline Williams, review of *Church and State in Bourbon Mexico,* p. 810; October, 2001, Stafford Poole, review of *Mexican Phoenix: Our Lady of Guadalupe: Image and Tradition across Five Centuries,* p. 773.

*Church History,* March, 1997, Robert Matter, review of *Church and State in Bourbon Mexico,* p. 136.

*Contemporary Review,* October, 2001, review of *Mexican Phoenix,* p. 251.

*Eighteenth-Century Life,* November, 1996, Peter Mason, review of *The First America,* p. 107.

*Eighteenth-Century Studies,* spring, 1992, William Callahan, review of *The First America,* p. 421.

*Hispanic American Historical Review,* May, 2002, William Taylor, review of *Mexican Phoenix,* p. 357.

*Historical Journal,* September, 1992, Sabine McCormack, review of *The First America,* p. 753.

*History,* October, 1992, John Fisher, review of *The First America,* p. 464; fall, 2001, Paul Vanderwood, review of *Mexican Phoenix,* p. 16.

*Journal of Ecclesiastical History,* October, 1992, J. S. Cummins, review of *The First America,* p. 647.

*Journal of Latin American Studies,* May, 1992, review of *The First America,* p. 437; May, 1995, Margaret Chowning, review of *Church and State in Bourbon Mexico,* p. 472.

*Latin American Research Review,* winter, 1998, Susan Deans-Smith, review of *Church and State in Bourbon Mexico,* p. 257.

*Modern Studies,* winter, 1993, Timothy Anna, review of *The First America,* p. 119.

*National Catholic Reporter,* October 26, 2001, Teresa Maya, review of *Mexican Phoenix,* p. 34.

*New York Times Book Review,* April 28, 2002, Garry Willis, "Mexico's Miracle," p. 18.

*Sixteenth Century Journal,* summer, 2002, Lois Ann Lorentzen, review of *Mexican Phoenix,* p. 491.

*Times Literary Supplement,* August 16, 1991, p. 9.*

\*          \*          \*

**BRADLEY, Will**
**See STRICKLAND, (William) Brad(ley)**

\*          \*          \*

**BREYTENBACH, Breyten 1939(?)-**
**(Jan Blom)**

*PERSONAL:* Born September 16, 1939 (one source says 1940), in Bonnievale (one source says Wellington), South Africa; naturalized French citizen; married Yolande Ngo Thi Hoang Lien, 1964. *Education:* Attended University of Cape Town until 1959.

*ADDRESSES: Home*—Paris, France. *Office*—College of Arts and Science, New York University, 25 West 4th St., New York, NY 10012. *E-mail*—BB43@nyu. edu.

*CAREER:* Political activist, painter, and writer. New York University, New York, NY, currently global distinguished professor of creative writing.

*AWARDS, HONORS:* A. P. B. Literary Prize for *Die ysterkoei moet sweet* and Afrikaans Press Corps Prize for *Die ysterkoei moet sweet* and *Katastrofes,* both 1964; South African Central News Agency prizes, 1967, for *Die huis van die dowe,* 1969, for *Kouevuur,*

*Breyten Breytenbach*

and 1970, for *Lotus;* Lucie B. and C. W. Van der Hoogt prize from Society of Netherlands Literature, 1972, for *Skryt;* prize from Perskor newspaper group, 1976, for *Voetskrif;* Pris des Sept (international publisher's prize to provide funding for six foreign translations of Breytenbach's work), 1977; Hertzog Prize from South African Academy of Science and Arts, 1984; Rapport Prize for Literature from Afrikaans newspaper *Rapport,* 1986, for *YK.*

*WRITINGS:*

*Die ysterkoei moet sweet* (poetry; title means "The Iron Cow Must Sweat"), Afrikaanse Pers-Boekhandel (Johannesburg, South Africa), 1964.

*Katastrofes* (short stories), Afrikaanse Pers-Boekhandel (Johannesburg, South Africa), 1964.

*Die huis van die dowe* (poetry; title means "House of the Deaf"), Human & Rousseau (Cape Town, South Africa), 1967.

*Kouevuur* (poetry; title means "Gangrene"), Buren-Uitgewers (Cape Town, South Africa), 1969.

(Under pseudonym Jan Blom) *Lotus* (poetry), Buren-Uitgewers (Cape Town, South Africa), 1970.

*Om te vlieg: Ñopstel in vyf ledemate en ñ ode,* Buren-Uitgewers (Cape Town, South Africa), 1971.

*Skryt: Om ñ sinkende skip blou te verf* (title means "Sky/Write: To Paint a Sinking Ship Blue"), Meulenhoff Nederland (Amsterdam, Netherlands), 1972.

*Met ander woorde: Vrugte van die droom van stilte* (poetry; title means "In Other Words"), Buren (Cape Town, South Africa), 1973.

*Voetskrif* (poetry; title means "Footscript"), Perskor (Johannesburg, South Africa), 1976.

*Ñ seisoen in die Paradys* (poetry and prose), [South Africa], 1976, translation by Rike Vaughan published as *A Season in Paradise,* introduction by Andre Brink, Persea Books (New York, NY), 1980.

(Under name Breyten Breytenbach and pseudonym Jan Blom) *Blomskryf: Uit die gedigte van Breyten Breytenbach en Jan Blom* (selected poetry; title means "Flower Writing"), introduction by A. J. Coetzee, Taurus (Emmarentia, South Africa), 1977.

*Sinking Ship Blues* (selected poetry), Oasis (Toronto, Ontario, Canada), 1977.

*And Death White As Words: An Anthology of the Poetry of Breyten Breytenbach,* edited with an introduction by A. J. Coetzee, Collings (London, England), 1978.

*In Africa Even the Flies Are Happy: Selected Poems, 1964-1977,* English translation by Denis Hirson, J. Calder (London, England), 1978, Riverrun Press (New York, NY), 1982.

*Miernes* (short stories), Taurus (Johannesburg, South Africa), 1980.

*Eklips* (poetry), Taurus (Johannesburg, South Africa), 1983.

*Mouroir: Bespieeelende notas van ñ roman* (sketches in English and Afrikaans), Taurus (Johannesburg, South Africa), 1983, complete English translation published as *Mouroir: Mirrornotes of a Novel,* Farrar, Straus (New York, NY), 1984.

*The True Confessions of an Albino Terrorist,* Taurus (Johannesburg, South Africa), 1984, Faber (New York, NY) 1984, Farrar, Straus (New York, NY), 1985.

*YK* (poetry), Meulenhoff (Amsterdam, Netherlands), 1985.

*Lewendood* (poetry), Taurus (Johannesburg, South Africa), 1985.

*End Papers: Essays, Letters, Articles of Faith, Workbook Notes,* Farrar, Straus (New York, NY), 1986.

*Boek: Dryfpunt* (essays), Taurus (Johannesburg, South Africa), 1987.

*Judas Eye* (poetry and essays), Penguin (New York, NY), 1988.

*Memory of Snow and of Dust* (novel), Taurus (Johannesburg (South Africa), 1989; Farrar, Straus (New York, NY), 1989.

*Soos Die So,* Taurus, (Bramley, South Africa), 1990.

(With Marilet Sienaert) *Breyten: Breytenbach: Painting the Eye,* D. Philip (Cape Town, South Africa), 1993.

*Return to Paradise,* Harcourt (New York, NY), 1993.

*The Memory of Birds in Times of Revolution,* Harcourt (New York, NY), 1996.

*Boklied: Ǹ vermaaklikheid in drie bedrywe* (play; Oudtshoorn, Klein Karoo National Arts Festival), Human & Rousseau (Cape Town, South Africa), 1998.

*Dog Heart: A Memoir,* Harcourt (New York, NY), 1999.

*Johnny Cocroach: A Lament for Our Times* (play), produced in Grahamstown, South Africa, at the Standard Bank Arts Festival, 1999.

*Woordwerk: Die kantskryfjoernaal van ǹ swerwer,* Human & Rousseau (Cape Town, South Africa), 1999.

*Ysterkoei-blues: Versamelde gedigte, 1964-1975,* Human & Rousseau (Cape Town, South Africa), 2001.

*Lady One: Of Love and Other Poems* (poetry), Human & Rousseau (Cape Town, South Africa), 2000, Harcourt (New York, NY), 2002.

Also author of *Oorblyfsels* (title means "Remnants"), 1970. Author of introduction to *Unwrapped: Irrelevant Fiction for a Post-Calvinist South Africa,* edited by Ted Leggett, University of Natal, Center for Creative Arts, 1998; and *Afrikaner Afrikaan: Anekdotes en Analise,* by F. van Zyl Slabbert, Tafelberg, 1999. Contributor to periodicals, including *Poetry International* and *Raster.* Translator of numerous works into Afrikans. Works have been translated into many languages, including English, Dutch, French, and Portuguese.

*SIDELIGHTS:* At the height of his literary acclaim, Breyten Breytenbach, South Africa's leading Afrikaner poet, was imprisoned by the government of his fellow Afrikaners for clandestine activities against its apartheid system of racial laws. Although he was released in December, 1982, Breytenbach remained an outspoken critic of the oppression of blacks and other minorities. Much of his writing is in his native Afri-

kaans, the language evolved from the Dutch spoken by the first white settlers in South Africa and the first language of three million white Afrikaners—the group that ruled South Africa from 1948 until the early 1990s.

Descended from a distinguished old Cape Province family—the Breytenbachs were among the early settlers of the seventeenth century who called themselves Afrikaners—Breytenbach graduated from high school in the Afrikaner heartland. He became interested in art and poetry, and, impressed by the reputation of the fine arts faculty of the University of Cape Town, he enrolled in that English-language university instead of Stellenbosch University, the traditional center of Afrikaner higher education. At the age of twenty, however, Breytenbach left school and set out for Europe, drifting into a variety of jobs in England and on the Continent. In 1961 he settled in Paris, where he painted, wrote, and taught English, and where he married Yolande Ngo Thi Hoang Lien, who was born in Vietnam. In 1964 Breytenbach published *Die ysterkoei moet sweet,* his first book of poems, followed by *Die huis van die dowe* in 1967, *Kouevuur* in 1969, and, under the pseudonym Jan Blom, *Lotus* in 1970.

When Breytenbach wanted to return to South Africa to collect awards he had won in 1967 and 1969, his wife was refused an entry visa as a "non-white" and Breytenbach was told he could face arrest under the Immorality Act, which made interracial marriage a crime. Then in 1973, when *Met ander woorde* was published, the Breytenbachs were both issued three-month visas to visit South Africa. That journey back to his homeland after twelve years of exile in Paris both rekindled warm childhood memories and reinforced his anger at the violence and injustice of apartheid. Breytenbach recorded his homecoming impressions in what Richard Rathbone described in the *Times Educational Supplement* as "an inspired and sometimes ecstatic book" published in a censored version in South Africa in 1976 as *Ǹ seisoen in die Paradys* and in English translation in 1980 as *A Season in Paradise.* According to *Washington Post Book World* contributor Stanley Uys, the book, a mixture of poetry and prose, is "an intensely personal narrative, nostalgic and bitter at the same time. The images of South Africa—of friends and familiar places—are vivid. [Breytenbach] gazes upon everything with the heightened perception of the artist and leaves the reader to make what he can of it." *Los Angeles Times*

*Book Review* critic Malcolm Boyd called *A Season in Paradise* "an ode to freedom, an existential work about the tension between belonging and transcendence" in which Breytenbach reveals himself as "angry, sensuous, ironical."

By the end of his three-month stay, Breytenbach had so exasperated authorities with his scathing public criticism of the Afrikaner nationalist government that authorities told him not to come back. Upon his return with his wife to Paris, Breytenbach, however, lost no time renewing his ties with anti-apartheid groups. Ultimately he founded—with other white South Africans in exile—an anti-apartheid organization called Okhela. They decided that Breytenbach should travel incognito to South Africa to contact sympathetic whites and some black spokesmen in order to channel money from European church groups to black trade unionists in South Africa.

In August, 1975, with the help of a French anti-apartheid organization that supplied a forged French passport, Breytenbach shaved off his beard and flew to Johannesburg under an assumed name. But the French group had apparently been infiltrated, because from the time Breytenbach obtained his visa the South African security police had him under surveillance. The police shadowed the poet in Johannesburg and Cape Town, noting his contacts, before arresting him and charging him under the Terrorist Act. Initially Breytenbach was not unduly concerned about his imprisonment because he believed he had not done anything more illegal than use a false passport. But he was sentenced to nine years in prison for the intent with which he had entered the country. The court took the view that trade union campaigns against apartheid constituted a threat to the safety of the state.

In November, 1975, Breytenbach began his solitary confinement in Pretoria's maximum security section. Then he was brought to trial under the Terrorism Act for a second time in June, 1977. Breytenbach, however, was acquitted of all charges except smuggling letters out of prison, for which he was fined the equivalent of fifty dollars. While in detention and awaiting trial, he managed to get out the poems that were published in a volume called *Voetskrif* in 1976, which won a prize from the Perskor newspaper group. Johan van Wyk, writing in *Dictionary of Literary Biography,* described the book as containing "remarkable poetry, evoking the prison environment." One poem, title

translated as "Aim—a Canto for E.P." van Wyk called "a beautiful poem exploring the similarities between his own situation and Ezra Pound's imprisonment during World War II and points to the intense concern with words, poetry, and language that dominate Breytenbach's prison work."

The poet was taken a thousand miles, from Pretoria to Pollsmoor Prison, near Cape Town, where he spent the next five years of his captivity. After Breytenbach was sentenced, none of his new writing could be published. However, his imprisonment generated renewed attention from Europe and North America, and this led to the publication of earlier, preprison work. *Bloomskrif,* published in 1977 and including older unpublished material, some of which he wrote under his pseudonym of Jan Blom, was his last book of poetry published in South Africa while he was jailed. With the publication of English-translation titles *Sinking Ship Blues,* published in Canada in 1977, and *And Death White As Words* and *In Africa Even the Flies Are Happy: Selected Poems, 1964-1977,* both published in Great Britain in 1978, as well as translations in French, Dutch, and Portuguese of other work, Breytenbach earned international acclaim and won an international award, the Prix des Sept.

During this period, the French government brought diplomatic pressure to bear on Pretoria, pressure that intensified when the socialist government of Francois Mitterand came to power. In December, 1982, the South African government finally relented and commuted Breytenbach's sentence from nine years to seven, to which the South African authorities attached no conditions beyond requiring that he leave the country. He was allowed a brief visit with his father and was then flown with his wife to Johannesburg and on to Paris.

Breytenbach had permission to write while he was in prison, and when he was released, his work was returned to him, but it was under these conditions: prison authorities took what he wrote each day and read it over. Beginning in 1983, the first of five volumes of Breytenbach's prison poems, collectively titled *Die ongedanste dans,* was published, called *Eklips,* poems from 1977 to 1979, when he was in Pollsmoor Prison and out of solitary confinement. It was followed by *YK,* poems written right after 1979, also published in 1983; *Buffalo Bill,* poems from June, 1976, to June, 1977, and published in 1984, and *Lewendood,* poems written before 1977 while he was in solitary confinement in Pretoria, published in 1985. Many of these poems were collected in English translation in 1988 as *Judas Eye.* According to van Wyk, critics in general praised Breytenbach's prison poetry for "his ability to manipulate language, to achieve multiple significations through exploiting the ambiguities inherent in words. But this linguistic manipulation leads to a certain amount of verbosity, which often is also pointed out as one of the shortcomings of his poetry." The isolated prison life "obviously led to an intense preoccupation with language, with what is referred to as metapoetry or poetry referring to the process of writing poetry," van Wyk remarked.

Breytenbach also composed during prison the semifictional pieces subsequently published and translated under the title *Mouroir: Mirrornotes of a Novel.* Not really a novel at all, the book is a series of loosely connected stories or sketches that present an imagistic, surreal portrait of Breytenbach's psyche as a prisoner. *New York Times Book Review* contributor John Wideman called *Mouroir* a "complex, demanding, haunting book" that "contains characters, themes and images which occur and reoccur, creating the illusion of narrative, continuity, reality unfolding." Fellow South African writer Nadine Gordimer, an *Atlantic Monthly* contributor, described its images as "exquisite, chilling, aphoristic, witty"; and Grace Ingoldby, reviewing *Mouroir* for *New Statesman,* judged it "a beautifully written, grappling, difficult book" in which "the mirror images both elucidate and confuse; at times it is too obscure to be successful, at others, far too plain to be forgotten." Other critics likewise found *Mouroir* difficult to read. "Breytenbach's writing . . . is astonishingly vigorous and agile," noted Neal Ascherson in *New York Review of Books.* "It can also become lush, indigestible." Similarly, Judy Cooke observed in the *Times Educational Supplement,* "*Mouroir* is an uneven, fragmentary, unforgettable piece of writing."

On his release from prison, Breytenbach felt compelled to publish a more direct account of his experiences. The result was *The True Confessions of an Albino Terrorist,* in which Breytenbach recounts how he was trapped by his captors, describes his years of physical and psychological deprivation, and outlines the prospects for South Africa's future as he sees them. Breytenbach's narrative of his prison experiences was disturbing to several critics. Among them were Malcolm Boyd, whose *Los Angeles Times Book*

*Review* article described Breytenbach's book as "a harrowing, unrelenting, searing account of a writer's survival in an experience of hell" and *Detroit News* contributor Charles R. Larson, who remarked, "I've read a lot from journals of people who have been jailed for their political beliefs, and a lot of South African literature as well. But nothing I have read in either category upset me as much as Breytenbach's account of his imprisonment. The details of bestiality, crime and murder, ritual cannibalism and even the daily routines of prison life have never been as revolting as they are here."

According to Joseph Lelyveld, writing in the *New York Times Book Review, The True Confessions of an Albino Terrorist* tells the story of Breytenbach's "personal misadventure in revolutionary politics and the nightmarish quality of the South African penal system." The book, Lelyveld added, also represents "the final stage of a major cultural rupture, the poet's apostasy from the creed of an Afrikaner nationalism. This did not begin in prison but, inevitably, it was completed there." Lelyveld further speculated that Breytenbach's "confessions" are "an important contribution to a corpus of South African prison literature that has been steadily, painfully accumulating over the last quarter-century; and they are especially important since his is the first such memoir to have been written by an Afrikaner." Rob Nixon, writing in *American Book Review,* came to a similar conclusion. In the confessions themselves, he posited, Breytenbach "meticulously recreates his spell in prison, interrogating with undiminished insight, not only his own shifting selves but also his jail-mates and the motley flunkeys of apartheid whose job it was to ensure that he remained solitary but not private."

Like Lelyveld, Nixon viewed *The True Confessions of an Albino Terrorist* as an important document in South Africa's rich "traditions of prison literature . . . partly because Breyten Breytenbach is firstly an established writer and only secondarily a political activist . . . and partly because he is a rare and important defector from Afrikanerdom." Continued Nixon, "The book is largely an account of the unmaking of an Afrikaner. . . . Some of the finest passages evoke the pathos of being a poet born into a policeman's language and of having to concede," the critic quoted Breytenbach, that "'To be an Afrikaner in the way *they* define it is to be a living insult to whatever better instincts we human beings possess.'"

Several critics commented as well on the literary merits of *The True Confessions of an Albino Terrorist.* For example, *New York Times* reviewer John Gross remarked: "Given the ordeal it chronicles, *The True Confessions of an Albino Terrorist* could hardly fail to make a powerful impression, but it displays considerable artistry as well. The writing is sharp, restless, often raspingly sarcastic; a little mannered here and there, perhaps, but no matter—Mr. Breytenbach succeeds brilliantly in depicting the horror and squalor and near-madness . . . of the prison world into which he was thrust."

*Observer* contributor Bernard Levin underscored the influence of Breytenbach's background as a poet in what the critic called "the savage rhythms and psychedelic colours of his prose." And Robert Cox, reviewing *The True Confessions of an Albino Terrorist* for the *Washington Post Book World,* was particularly generous in his praise. He called the book "a testament of suffering and exultation—a powerful document, full of humanity, expressing a limitless love for life," noting that Breytenbach's "literary achievement is so considerable that the political impact of *The True Confessions of an Albino Terrorist* is like the blast of a truck bomb. He holds up a mirror to the South African penal system, which in turn reflects the self-destructive madness of apartheid." Cox pronounced Breytenbach "a remarkable man" and *The True Confessions of an Albino Terrorist* "a magnificent book."

Breytenbach insists that his prison experiences have scarred him forever. "Resistance," Nixon quoted the activist's words in *The True Confessions of an Albino Terrorist,* "if that is what you want to call survival, is made up of a million little compromises and humiliations, so subtle that the human eye cannot perceive them." Yet, to the astonishment of those familiar with his history, Breytenbach returned to South Africa in the spring of 1986 to receive the *Rapport* prize for literature. But more importantly, as he has stated, he returned because he identified with the struggle of South Africans for liberation.

Breytenbach's 1993 memoir, *Return to Paradise,* chronicles his 1991 return visit to his homeland. According to the author, this title, along with *A Season in Paradise* and *The True Confessions of an Albino Terrorist,* are meant to be read as a series comprising the writer's intercessions with South Africa: "exile, incarnation, and return," noted Lynn Freed in the *Washing-*

*ton Post Book World.* Breytenbach finds South Africa in a state of turmoil, surrounding the fall of F. W. De Klerk and the white-controlled government. J. M. Coetzee, a fellow South African novelist, writing in the *New York Review of Books,* described Breytenbach's analysis as "not . . . original." However, along with other reviewers, he praised Breytenbach's narrative: "An immensely gifted writer, he is able to descend effortlessly into the Africa of the poetic unconscious and return with the rhythm and the words, the words in the rhythm, that give life." Freed also praised the author's writing, noting of his descriptions in particular, "Breytenbach's portraits themselves are extraordinary, resonant." About Breytenbach's emotional ties to his subject, Freed wrote, "The book is written with a wild heart and an unrelenting eye, and is fueled by the sort of rage that produces great literature." Adam Kuper in the *Times Literary Supplement* concurred, "The best parts of this book have nothing to do with politics. They are the occasional descriptions of landscapes, rendered with the intensity of a painter, and the portraits of his Afrikaner friends." William Finnegan, in *The New York Times Book Review,* noted that "purposeful reporting is not Mr. Breytenbach's forte" but declared the book to be "protean, funny, bitchy, beautifully written and searingly bleak." *The Memory of Birds in Times of Revolution,* published in 1996, is a collection of Breytenbach's essays and talks on apartheid, South Africa, and writing. While a *Kirkus Reviews* critic found it "an outdated, awkward collection . . . [lacking] the saving humanism and insight . . . that would have kept them otherwise readable and trenchant," a *Library Journal* reviewer described it as "an important addition to his narrative essays." "Though . . . he is not above the political cliches and moral posturing for which he criticizes others, Breytenbach's passionate desire to know and serve the truth . . . is deeply admirable," concluded Bruce Bawer in the *Washington Post Book World.*

In 1989, Breytenbach published the novel *Memory of Snow and of Dust,* described by Carli Coetzee in *Encyclopedia of World Literature* as "a reflection on exile by means of three characters living in Paris, one of them a white author who comes to South Africa and is arrested and sentenced to death for a murder he did not commit." The *Oxford Companion to Twentieth-Century Literature in English* contributor referred to the novel as "allusive and complex in its imagery . . . [it] examines the conflicts within Breytenbach's own psyche between spiritual yearning and the need to be politically effective."

Breytenbach recounted another return to South Africa and to his hometown, Bonnieville, this time after the end of apartheid, in *Dog Heart: A Memoir,* published in 1999. Stated *San Francisco Chronicle* reviewer David Tuller, it is "a thorny, complex, difficult book: difficult to read, difficult to forget. By turns haunting, elegiac, bitter, sardonic and horrifying, it is Breytenbach's compelling effort to reconcile his memories of the land he left forty years ago with the reality of post-apartheid existence." The form Breytenbach uses to stir up his memories comprises unconnected snippets of folk tales, meditations on the country's history, flashes of his own personal history, bits of social commentary, lists of atrocities committed in past and present. Commented *Booklist* reviewer Hazel Rochman, "It is in his lyrical evocation of place, the particulars of rock, mountain, sky, animals, and plants, that he speaks most eloquently about the search for home." Though critics agree that readers unfamiliar with the details of South Africa's politics, geography, or folklore may find Breytenbach's ruminations difficult to follow, they also concur that the book is, as Anthony O. Edmonds in *Library Journal* wrote, "beautifully written"; Tuller remarked that readers who stayed with it would be "richly rewarded. The book's fractured structure clearly reflects the author's own tortured ambivalence toward his homeland and his disillusionment with what is happening there now." A *Publishers Weekly* reviewer wrote, "Throughout, the writing is artful and some passages soar."

"Image-rich free-verse catalogues share space with dream-or folktale-like stories, at their best . . . combining love with political rage," is how the *Publishers Weekly* reviewer described *Lady One: Of Love and Other Poems,* published in 2000. Breytenbach offers love poems to his wife and depicts images of southern Africa, east Asia, and Morocco. Because his wife is Vietnamese, their marriage was taboo under South Africa's apartheid laws, leading to Breytenbach's initial exile from his homeland. "The poems' combination of the private and the global and . . . the political—that sense of being alone together in no-man's land—gives them their power," reflected Hazel Rochman in *Booklist.*

## BIOGRAPHICAL AND CRITICAL SOURCES:

### BOOKS

Breytenbach, Breyten, *The True Confessions of an Albino Terrorist,* Farrar, Straus (New York, NY), 1985.

Breytenbach, Breyten, with Marilet Sienaert, *Breyten Breytenbach: Painting the Eye,* D. Philip (Cape Town, South Africa), 1993.

Coetzee, Carli, *Encyclopedia of World Literature in the 20th Century,* Volume 1, St. James Press (Detroit, MI), 1999.

*Contemporary Literary Criticism,* Gale (Detroit, MI), Volume 23, 1983, Volume 37, 1986, Volume 126, 2000.

Golz, Hans-Georg, *Staring at Variations: The Concept of 'Self' in Breyten Breytenbach's "Mouroir: Mirrornotes of a Novel,"* P. Lang (New York, NY), 1995.

Jolly, Rosemary Jane, *Colonization, Violence, and Narration in White South African Writing: Andre Brink, Breyten Breytenbach, and J. M. Coetzee,* Ohio University Press (Athens, OH), 1995.

Stringer, Jenny, editor, *Oxford Companion to Twentieth-Century Literature in English,* Oxford University Press (New York, NY), 1996.

Van Wyk, Johan, *Dictionary of Literary Biography,* Volume 225, Gale (Detroit, MI).

### PERIODICALS

*American Book Review,* January-February, 1983, review of *In Africa Even the Flies Are Happy,* p. 16; January-February, 1986, Rob Nixon, review of *The True Confessions of an Albino Terrorist,* p. 21.

*Atlantic Monthly,* July, 1984, Nadine Gordimer, review of *Mouroir: Mirrornotes of a Novel,* p. 114; September, 99, review of *Dog Heart: A Memoir,* p. 105.

*Best Sellers,* September, 1984, review of *Mouroir,* p. 203.

*Biography,* winter, 2001, Tim Trengrove Jones, review of *Dog Heart,* p. 317.

*Booklist,* July, 1999, Hazel Rochman, review of *Dog Heart,* p. 1890; February 15, 2002, Hazel Rochman, review of *Lady One: Of Love and Other Poems,* p. 985.

*Detroit News,* March 31, 1985, Charles R. Larson, review of *The True Confessions of an Albino Terrorist.*

*Globe and Mail* (Toronto, Ontario, Canada), October 8, 1988.

*Kirkus Reviews,* December 1, 1995, review of *The Memory of Birds in Times of Revolution,* p. 1677.

*Library Journal,* February 15, 1996, review of *The Memory of Birds in Times of Revolution,* p. 152; August, 1999, Anthony O. Edmonds, review of *Dog Heart,* p. 106.

*Los Angeles Times,* June 27, 1984.

*Los Angeles Times Book Review,* February 10, 1985; August 17, 1986, review of *End Papers,* p. 1.

*New Statesman,* October 3, 1980, review of *And Death White As Words,* p. 20; review of *A Season in Paradise,* p. 20; May 4, 1984, Grace Ingoldby, review of *Mouroir.*

*New York Review of Books,* October 25, 1984, Neal Ascherson, review of *Mouroir,* p. 23; November 23, 1993, p. 3; September 23, 1999, review of *Dog Heart,* p. 51-52.

*New York Times,* February 5, 1985, review of *The True Confessions of an Albino Terrorist,* p. 27.

*New York Times Book Review,* March 30, 1980, review of *A Season in Paradise,* p. 8; April 13, 1980; February 10, 1985, review of *The True Confessions of an Albino Terrorist;* April 6, 1986, review of *The True Confessions of an Albino Terrorist;* November 22, 1987, review of *End Papers,* p. 50; November 28, 1993, review of *Return to Paradise,* p. 3; September 12, 1999, Ariel Dorfman, "Truth and Reconciliation: Breyton Breytenbach Returns to a South Africa Greatly Changed from the One He Left," p. 14; December 5, 1999, review of *Dog Heart,* p. 88.

*Poetics Today,* summer, 2001, Simon Lewis, p. 435.

*Publishers Weekly,* June 21, 1999, review of *Dog Heart,* p. 44; April 29, 2002, review of *Lady One,* p. 65.

*Research in African Literatures,* spring, 2001, Robert Elliot Fox, review of *The Memory of Birds in Times of Revolution,* p. 158.

*San Francisco Chronicle,* December 12, 1999, David Tuller, "Expatriate Surveys the Post-Apartheid Landscape in a Fierce Memoir," p. 5.

*Sunday Times* (London, England), November 28, 1999, Anthony Sattin, review of *Dog Heart,* p. 2.

*Times Educational Supplement,* July 13, 1984, Judy Cooke, review of *Mouroir,* p. 24; December 20, 1985, review of *The True Confessions of an Albino Terrorist,* p. 17; June 24, 1988, review of *Judas Eye,* p. 27.

*Times Literary Supplement,* December 24, 1993, Adam Kuper, review of *Return to Paradise,* p. 22.

*Wall Street Journal,* October 4, 1999, review of *Dog Heart,* p. A40.

*Washington Post,* February 9, 1985.

*Washington Post Book World,* April 20, 1980, Stanley Uys, review of *A Season in Paradise,* p. 4; June 24, 1984; May 5, 1985, review of *The True Confessions of an Albino Terrorist,* p. 5; April 6, 1986, review of *The True Confessions of an Albino Ter-*

*rorist,* p. 12; November 28, 1993, Lynn Freed, review of *Return to Paradise,* p. 4; May 5, 1996, Bruce Bawer, review of *The Memory of Birds in Times of Revolution,* p. 5; December 19, 1999, review of *Dog Heart,* p. 7.

*World Literature Today,* spring, 1977; winter, 1978; summer, 1978; autumn, 1978; winter, 1979; summer, 1981, review of *A Season in Paradise,* p. 520; winter, 1982, review of *Miernes,* p. 166; summer, 1984, review of *Mouroir,* p. 460; summer, 1987, review of *End Papers,* p. 482.*

\*   \*   \*

**BRISCOE, Connie 1952-**

*PERSONAL:* Born December 31, 1952, in Washington, DC; daughter of Leroy Fabian and Alyce Levinia (Redmond) Briscoe; married, 1980 (marriage ended). *Education:* Hampton University, B.S., 1974; American University, M.P.A., 1978.

*ADDRESSES: Agent*—c/o Author Mail, Doubleday, 1745 Broadway, New York, NY 10019.

*CAREER:* Analytic Services Inc., Arlington, VA, research analyst, 1976-80; Joint Center for Political and Economic Studies, Washington, DC, associate editor, 1981-90; *American Annals of the Deaf,* Gallaudet University, Washington, DC, managing editor, 1990-94; novelist, 1994—.

*WRITINGS:*

NOVELS

*Sisters and Lovers,* HarperCollins (New York, NY), 1994.

*Big Girls Don't Cry,* HarperCollins (New York, NY), 1996.

*A Long Way from Home,* HarperCollins (New York, NY), 1999.

*P. G. County,* Doubleday (New York, NY), 2002.

*SIDELIGHTS:* Connie Briscoe is the author of novels focusing on the personal and professional struggles of middle-class African-American women in Washington,

D.C. Briscoe's debut novel, *Sisters and Lovers,* centers on three women, each of whom has to resolve difficulties in her personal life. Thirty-year-old Beverly works as an editor, and as the novel opens she is reeling from the infidelity of her boyfriend. In the course of the novel she dates a series of unsuitable black men, eventually embarking on a doomed relationship with a white man. Her sister Charmaine is married to a charming but indolent liar whose debts mount while she works as a secretary to support the family. The third sister, Evelyn, a successful psychologist, is married to a lawyer who wants to give up his well-compensated position as a partner in a prominent law firm to start his own practice, a move which she fears will jeopardize their comfortable lifestyle.

Discussing *Sisters and Lovers,* Stephanie Goldberg of the *Chicago Tribune* wrote, "Even though the tenor of this book is mostly comic, there are serious undertones." She noted that "Briscoe's women have abundant drive and determination" and concluded that *Sisters and Lovers* is "the perfect commentary on postmodern romance: In the '90s, the object isn't to be rescued by a handsome prince but merely to meet one's equal." In an assessment in *Kirkus Reviews,* a commentator described the book as "smoothly readable, but flat and uninventive," and compared it to Terry McMillan's *Waiting to Exhale* "without the sex, the sizzle, and the funky humor." Roz Spafford, in the *Washington Post Book World,* wrote that "more complexity in [Briscoe's] characters' evolution as well as in the structure of the book itself" was needed, but noted that "Briscoe's message is a warm one and the novel is entirely readable."

*Big Girls Don't Cry,* Briscoe's second novel, treats major issues of contemporary African-American history through the story of Naomi Jefferson, who is a middle-class, Washington, DC, adolescent as the novel opens in the early 1960s. Against the backdrop of the Civil Rights movement, Briscoe presents Naomi's coming-of-age while exploring such topics as radicalism, racism, sexism, teen pregnancy, and drug use. At school Naomi learns that it is preferable to date someone light-skinned, and her new friend, the light-skinned Jennifer snubs Naomi's best friend, Debbie, because her skin is too dark. Later, Naomi's older brother, Joshua, becomes involved in the radical protest movement while at college and is killed while en route to a rally. Naomi herself drops out of college after experiencing racial and gender discrimination in her technical curriculum and experiments with drugs in the aftermath of a failed romance. Eventually Naomi completes her education and wins a position with a prominent computer-consulting firm in Washington. However, she leaves to start her own business when it becomes apparent that her race and gender present insurmountable obstacles to climbing the corporate ladder in the white, male-dominated firm.

Emily Listfield observed in a *Washington Post Book World* review that in Briscoe's book "the recipe for success is simple, if not simplistic: Stop whining and start earning." Listfield concluded that "the obstacles that Naomi faces are genuine," but noted "they are drawn here with a sketchiness that undermines their impact." Listfield concluded that "Briscoe, a talented writer, is not afraid to take on serious concerns: racism, the glass ceiling, [and] the importance of personal responsibility." Corrine Nelson, in a favorable review in *Library Journal,* concluded, "This believable and wonderfully written novel is highly recommended for all fiction collections."

Briscoe reached farther back in time for her novel *A Long Way from Home,* based on three generations of her ancestry. The inspiration for the book, Briscoe told *Essence,* came from researching her family's slave background. "I came across the usual grim tales of whipping, sales and miscegenation," she remarked. "But I also uncovered stories of love and hope."

In antebellum Virginia, light-skinned slave Susan (Briscoe's great-great-grandmother) grows up on a plantation but is sold to a new master in big-city Richmond. She can pass for white there, and "although she is treated better," noted *Library Journal* contributor Catherine Swenson, "she is still unable to fulfill her own dreams." Susan falls in love with the freeman Oliver as talk of a Civil War looms. When the South surrenders in 1865, Susan is also granted freedom, and now embarks on a journey to locate the members of her fragmented family. A reviewer for *Publishers Weekly* found that "Briscoe's characters, especially Susan, are largely appealing, and the novel's extended chronology is informative." Harriet Klausner, in *Under the Covers,* praised *A Long Way from Home* as "another winning, gut-wrenching family drama."

Changing course, Briscoe produced a satire of contemporary African-American upper crust in *P. G. County.* "Remember Peyton Place? Dynasty? Now fast forward to 2002 and paint the characters black," remarked Robin Green-Cary in *Black Issues Book Review*. The five very different women living in upscale Prince Georges County, Maryland, include Barbara, described by a *Kirkus Reviews* writer as "the alcoholic wife of a self-made millionaire," and Candice, a white woman whose son is dating the black daughter of hardworking hairdresser Pearl. Examining her family records on microfiche, Candice is shocked to discover an "old census record with a capital M on the line for race. As in mulatto." To Green-Cary, "readers will likely run out of angst over [Candice's] problems long before she does." That said, "*P. G. County* is thoroughly and delightfully enjoyable. Briscoe's quick wit and obvious love of language shine brightly in this twisted tale."

Briscoe, who gradually lost her hearing as an adult due to a genetic condition, discussed her career with Victoria Valentine in a May, 1996, interview conducted by TDD (a telecommunications relay system used by the hearing impaired) and published in *Emerge*. Briscoe revealed that *Big Girls Don't Cry* "was a little bit harder to write because I had to dig deeper. . . . *Sisters* was sort of out there on the surface. It almost wrote itself. It has a lot of me and some of my friends in it." She did not rule out a deaf character in a future work, noting "I'm still dealing with my feelings about it. So to write, I would have to work those feelings and thoughts out. Maybe once I do that, I will feel comfortable including a deaf character."

## BIOGRAPHICAL AND CRITICAL SOURCES:

### PERIODICALS

*Black Issues Book Review*, September-October, 2002, Robin Green-Cary, review of *P. G. County*, p. 24.

*Booklist*, April 15, 1994, Denise Perry Donavin, review of *Sisters and Lovers*, p. 1484; February 15, 2000, Deborah Taylor, review of *A Long Way from Home*, p. 1096; April 1, 2001, Brad Hooper, review of *A Long Way from Home*, p. 1456; August, 2002, Mary Frances Wilkens, review of *P. G. County*, p. 1883.

*Bookwatch*, May 1, 1994, review of *Sisters and Lovers*, p. 11; April 28, 1996, review of *Big Girls Don't Cry*, p. 11.

*Chicago Tribune*, July 31, 1994, Stephanie Goldberg, review of *Sisters and Lovers*, p. 4.

*Christian Science Monitor*, July 1, 1994, review of *Sisters and Lovers*, p. 10.

*Emerge*, May, 1996, Victoria Valentine, review of *Big Girls Don't Cry*, pp. 66-67.

*Entertainment Weekly*, August 20, 1999, review of *A Long Way from Home*, p. 120.

*Essence*, July, 1999, Martha Souhtgate, "Speaking Volumes," p. 95.

*Jet*, September 5, 1994, review of *Sisters and Lovers*, p. 24.

*Kirkus Reviews*, March 1, 1994, review of *Sisters and Lovers*, p. 227; March 1, 1996, review of *Big Girls Don't Cry*, p. 310; May 15, 1999, review of *A Long Way from Home*, p. 739; July 1, 2002, review of *P. G. County*, p. 897.

*Kliatt*, March, 1995, p. 57.

*Library Journal*, April 1, 1994, Angela Washington-Blair, review of *Sisters and Lovers*, p. 130; April 15, 1995, p. 144; June 1, 1996, Corrine Nelson, review of *Big Girls Don't Cry*, pp. 146, 148; February 15, 2000, Catherine Swenson, review of *A Long Way from Home*, p. 214; January 1, 2001, Nancy Pearl, "Waiting for Terry: African American Novels," p. 200; August, 2002, Jennifer Baker, review of *P. G. County*, p. 140.

*Los Angeles Times Book Review*, June 2, 1996, review of *Big Girls Don't Cry*, p. 14; September 26, 1999, review of *A Long Way from Home*, p. 9.

*Mademoiselle*, May, 1994, Elizabeth Berg, review of *Sisters and Lovers*, p. 102.

*Newsweek*, April 29, 1996, Malcolm Jones, Jr., review of *Big Girls Don't Cry*, p. 79.

*New York Times*, September 2, 1999, Felicia R. Lee, "A Novelist Fills in Slavery's Blanks with Imagination," p. B1.

*New York Times Book Review*, September 18, 1994, review of *Sisters and Lovers*, p. 20.

*People Weekly*, June 10, 1996, Clare McHugh, review of *Big Girls Don't Cry*, p. 37.

*Publishers Weekly*, March 28, 1994, review of *Sisters and Lovers*, p. 81; June 20, 1994, Paul Nathan, "Three Lives," p. 28; March 11, 1996, review of *Big Girls Don't Cry*, p. 41; July 26, 1999, review of *A Long Way from Home*, p. 65; August 26, 2002, review of *P. G. County*, p. 43.

*School Library Journal*, April, 2003, Joyce Fay Fletcher, review of *P. G. County*, p. 195.

*Tribune Books* (Chicago, IL), July 31, 1994, review of *Sisters and Lovers*, p. 4; March 19, 1995, p. 8.

*Washington Post Book World*, May 1, 1994, Roz Spafford, review of *Sisters and Lovers*, p. 11; April 28,

1996, Emily Listfield, review of *Big Girls Don't Cry,* p. 11; August 15, 1999, review of *A Long Way from Home,* p. 6.

*ONLINE*

*Connie Briscoe Web site,* http://www.conniebriscoe. com/ (October 12, 2002).
*Under the Covers,* http://www.silcom.com/~manatee/ briscoe_long.html/ (July 4, 1999), Harriet Klausner, review of *A Long Way from Home.**

\*          \*          \*

## BURRIDGE, Kenelm (Oswald Lancelot) 1922-
## (James Casing)

*PERSONAL:* Born October 31, 1922, in St. Julians, Malta; son of William (a professor of physiology) and Jane (Cassar-Torregiani) Burridge; married Rosabelle Griffiths (marriage ended); married Anna Emslie; children: (first marriage) Julian Langford. *Ethnicity:* "English." *Education:* Oxford University, B.A., 1948, diploma in anthropology, 1949, M.A., 1950, B.Litt., 1950; Australian National University, Ph.D., 1953.

*ADDRESSES: Home*—231 Prince John Way, Xlanaimo, British Columbia V9T 4L4, Canada. *E-mail*—kenannabur@shaw.ca.

*CAREER:* University of Malaya, Kuala Lumpur, Malaysia, research fellow, 1954-56; University of Baghdad, Baghdad, Iraq, professor of anthropology, 1956-58; Oxford University, Oxford, England, lecturer in ethnology, 1958-68; University of British Columbia, Vancouver, British Columbia, Canada, professor of anthropology, 1968—, head of anthropology and sociology department, 1973—. University of Western Australia, visiting lecturer, 1968; International Christian University, Tokyo, Japan, visiting professor, 1988-89. *Military service:* Royal Navy, 1939-46; became lieutenant.

*MEMBER:* Royal Society of Canada, Royal Anthropological Institute of Great Britain and Ireland.

*AWARDS, HONORS:* Guggenheim fellow, 1972-73; fellow of Social Sciences and Humanities Research Council of Canada, 1979-80; Killam fellow, 1979-80.

*Kenelm Burridge*

*WRITINGS:*

(Under pseudonym James Casing) *Submariners,* Macmillan (London, England), 1951.
*Mambu: A Melanesian Millennium,* Methuen (London, England), 1960, Harper Torchbooks (New York, NY), reprinted with revised preface, Princeton University Press (Princeton, NJ), 1995.
*Tangu Traditions: A Study of the Way of Life, Mythology, and Developing Experience of a New Guinea People,* Clarendon Press (Oxford, England), 1969.
*New Heaven, New Earth: A Study of Millenarian Activities,* Schocken (New York, NY), 1969.
*Encountering Aborigines: A Case Study: Anthropology and the Australian Aboriginal,* Pergamon Press (New York, NY), 1973.
*Someone, No One: An Essay on Individuality,* Princeton University Press (Princeton, NJ), 1979.
*In the Way: A Study of Christian Missionary Endeavors,* University of British Columbia Press (Vancouver, British Columbia, Canada), 1991.

Contributor of more than 100 articles and reviews to learned journals.

Some of Burridge's writings have been translated into Spanish and Japanese.

*SIDELIGHTS:* Anthropology is frequently defined as the comparative study of humankind. The word comparative carries special significance for many contemporary cultural anthropologists, including Kenelm Burridge. Burridge believes that a culture must not be arbitrarily criticized through another's standards. Nevertheless, it is vital to realize a culture's relevance to every other society. Burridge takes this position in *Encountering Aborigines: A Case Study: Anthropology and the Australian Aboriginal.* Though suggested by the title, his work is not totally devoted to the aborigine; rather, it is "concerned with the way the anthropological enterprise has been shaped by the context of Western civilization, as that enterprise is revealed through its praxis among the Aborigines," explained Philip L. Newman in *Science.*

Burridge begins *Encountering Aborigines* with a cumulation of much of the published information available on the migratory tribe to date. He then draws generalizations on the society as a whole, leading directly into "motives" or "themes" applicable to any culture. The aborigine is seen as "everyman," reacting in his own unique way to the basic biological and sociological stimuli faced by all humankind. By not taking into account alien cultures such as this one, Burridge insists we cannot ultimately understand our own. And to gain this intrinsic knowledge, the overwhelming conceit in the virtue of our own morals and traditions with its condescending opinion of other cultures must be eradicated.

Burridge's "critique of evolutionary theory [in *Encountering Aborigines*] is particularly interesting in terms of his general thesis," commented Newman. However, "most of the standard works on the history of anthropological theory [are not mentioned,]" reported a *Choice* critic, noting that "Burridge's command of Aboriginal data seems limited, although 'extensive field work' is claimed. A convoluted and ponderous style makes for obscurity and leads Burridge into errors." Nevertheless, Newman wrote, "Burridge can count the book a success insofar as it moves its reader into a greater awareness of whence he came intellectually and where, possibly, he might go."

Burridge sees the unfortunate trend of anthropology today leaning toward "professionalism" rather than "humanism." Cultures are statistically and categori-

cally analyzed with little apparent regard for inherent motivating factors. Rituals and routines alike are duly recorded, but the spirit of the people themselves never emerges. As in most human endeavor, however, a reversal is in sight. Burridge believes the current attitude will soon run its course, with a more humanistic approach resulting.

Critics of *Tangu Traditions: A Study of the Way of Life, Mythology, and Developing Experience of a New Guinea People* praised the methodology Burridge used in exploring the Tangu people. "Besides adding to what we know of [the Tangu] culture, it presents an interesting and innovative mode of analysis. . . . Both substantively and methodologically the book is a valuable addition to a library collection in anthropology," claimed a *Choice* contributor. A *Times Literary Supplement* reviewer wrote: "Here we have an ideal combination of the empiricism of British anthropology and the metaphysics of French structuralism. Following from his field research in the early 1950s, Dr. Burridge has found and developed a theoretical framework that has resulted in this most important contribution to social anthropology so far. He has tackled one of the most complex aspects of the discipline but with undoubted competence and with invaluable results."

Another Burridge accomplishment, *New Heaven, New Earth: A Study of Millenarian Activities,* "is a thoughtful, provocative, and exciting book that will encourage a fresh approach not only to millenarian activities but to the question of dynamics generally," according to *Pacific Affairs* contributor D. G. Bettison. In this work Burridge reviews and criticizes existing literature as well as providing his own theories; it "presents a model of the social process responsible for that type of millennial movement in which transition to a money economy presents a crucial challenge to male integrity," described A. F. C. Wallace in *American Anthropology.* Burridge "is intent on using millenarian activities as a test case in the search for a new objective validity to the interpretation of social relations," explained Bettison. "Although the model is too narrow for application to all revitalization movements, it permits a penetrating analysis of some movements," maintained Wallace. "When Burridge turns to the task of explanation, he does this in a way that is singularly appropriate for the present stage of sociological and anthropological enquiries," reported Alasdair MacIntyre in *Encounter,* concluding: "This is one of the most interesting books in the field of the human sciences for some time."

Burridge told *CA:* "I write because, in a sense, I have to. Sometimes, on putting pen to paper, something entirely unexpected comes on to the paper. Difficulties arise in sticking to the point.

"I suppose the influence on my work that I am most aware of is that of E. E. Evans-Pritchard: a certain honesty, trying to be led by the material rather than attempting to control it so as to conform to a 'genre' or more popular point of view.

"Inspiration and the writing process really go together. I ask myself what material do I have? What do I need to know to make sense of it? I listen to people's direct ('You ought to write a book about . . .') and indirect ('There ought to be a book about . . .') suggestions. I plot out what might make a book—which goes through many changes—and then I start writing. However, I am doing very little writing these days."

*BIOGRAPHICAL AND CRITICAL SOURCES:*

*PERIODICALS*

*American Anthropology,* October, 1970, A. F. C. Wallace, review of *New Heaven, New Earth: A Study of Millenarian Activities.*
*Choice,* September, 1970, review of *Tangu Traditions: A Study of the Way of Life, Mythology, and Developing Experience of a New Guinea People;* May, 1974, review of *Encountering Aborigines: A Case Study: Anthropology and the Australian Aboriginal.*
*Encounter,* March, 1970, Alasdair MacIntyre, review of *New Heaven, New Earth.*
*Pacific Affairs,* summer, 1970, D. G. Bettison, review of *New Heaven, New Earth.*
*Science,* June 28, 1974, Philip L. Newman, review of *Encountering Aborigines: A Case Study.*
*Times Literary Supplement,* March 5, 1970, review of *Tangu Traditions.*

\*    \*    \*

## BURROWS, William E. 1937-

*PERSONAL:* Born March 27, 1937, in Philadelphia, PA; son of Eli and Helen (Marino) Burrows; married Joelle Hodgson (an art historian), November 19, 1966; children: Lara. *Education:* Columbia University, B.A., 1960, M.A., 1962. *Politics:* "Ultra right-wing liberal."

*ADDRESSES: Home*—154 Burns St., Forest Hills, NY 11375. *Office*—Department of Journalism, New York University, 100 Washington Sq. East, New York, NY 10003. *E-mail*—william.burrows@nyu.edu.

*CAREER:* Journalist, educator, and author. *New York Times,* New York, NY, news assistant, 1962-65, reporter, 1967-68; *Richmond Times-Dispatch,* Richmond, VA, reporter, 1965-66; *Washington Post,* Washington, DC, reporter, 1966-67; *Wall Street Journal,* New York, NY, reporter, 1968-70; Puerto de Pollensa, Mallorca, Spain, travel writer, 1971-73; New York University, New York, NY, assistant professor of journalism, beginning 1974, and founder/director of Science and Engineering Reporting Program.

*MEMBER:* American Academy of Political and Social Science, Authors Guild, Association for Education in Journalism, National Political and Science Honor Society, Pi Sigma Alpha, Kappa Tau Alpha.

*WRITINGS:*

*Richthofen: A True Story of the Red Baron,* Harcourt (New York, NY), 1969.
*Vigilante!,* Harcourt (New York, NY), 1976.
*On Reporting the News,* New York University Press (New York, NY), 1977.
*Deep Black: Space Espionage and National Security,* Random House (New York, NY), 1986.
*Exploring Space: Voyages in the Solar System and Beyond,* Random House (New York, NY), 1990.
*Mission to Deep Space: Voyager's Journey of Discovery,* Scientific American Books for Young Readers (New York, NY), 1993.
(With Robert Windrem) *Critical Mass: The Dangerous Race for Superweapons in a Fragmenting World,* Simon & Schuster (New York, NY), 1994.
*This New Ocean: The Story of the First Space Age,* Random House (New York, NY), 1998.
*The Infinite Journey: Eyewitness Accounts of NASA and the Space Age,* Discovery Books (New York, NY), 2000.
*By Any Means Necessary: America's Secret Air War in the Cold War,* Farrar, Straus (New York, NY), 2001.

Contributing editor, *Air & Space.* Contributor of articles to periodicals.

*SIDELIGHTS:* The Cold War between the United States and the former Soviet Union was still in the headlines when journalist William Burrows published *Deep Black: Space Espionage and National Security.* In this 1986 work, Burrows examines how the two superpowers "know all about each other's deployment and can infer about each other's intentions," as an *Economist* reviewer explained. The two reigning superpowers used their respective overhead reconnaissance equipment, which in the case of the United States was a sophisticated satellite nicknamed "Keyhole," "KH" for short. In 1984 the KH-11 craft picked up a "sunlit orbital photograph of the first large Soviet aircraft carrier, under construction on the Black Sea" from 500 miles away, according to Philip Morrison in a *Scientific American* review. The Soviets, meanwhile, reportedly launched similar crafts "routinely every couple of weeks," as Morrison wrote, "and when events suggest it, one every few days. Their style is that of the assembly line: each device delivers relatively low performance, but each is simpler [than its U.S. counterpart], less expensive, adaptable and quickly replaced."

Calling Burrows a "responsible and savvy journalist," Morrison praised *Deep Black* as "an up-to-date, thoughtful, nontechnical, factual study of a topic that lies behind much of the news." A related volume by Burrows and Robert Windrem, *Critical Mass: The Dangerous Race for Superweapons in a Fragmenting World,* came out in 1993, three years after India and Pakistan narrowly averted atomic combat. That conflict and others are recounted in what *Booklist* contributor Gilbert Taylor called a "hair-raising reality check on the status of nuclear proliferation." "Terrifying" is how Eric Nadler of *Nation* described the authors' argument that "while the end of the cold war lessened chances of a global nuclear war, the proliferation of nuclear weapons and the expertise to build them have accelerated dangerously." Burrows and Windrem list the nuclear-capable countries as of 1993; they included Ukraine, Kazakhstan, China, Israel, India, and North Korea, as well as then-"active programs" in Iraq, Iran, Libya, and Algeria.

In *Critical Mass* the authors finger U.S. foreign policy as a contributing factor in worldwide nuclear proliferation. "The last two Republican administrations," said Nadler, referring to the Ronald Reagan and George (H.) Bush years, "acted with subjectivity

and short-sightedness. President Reagan, for example, fended off tough Congressional restrictions on Pakistan as it constructed what that nation's leaders said was an 'Islamic bomb.'"

Burrows reaches back into history for another real-life drama. *By Any Means Necessary: America's Secret Air War in the Cold War* was released just weeks following the terrorist attacks of September 11, 2001. As a shocking and history-making event, the attacks against America were compared to the Japanese storming of Pearl Harbor in December, 1941. As Burrows recounts, U.S. intelligence in 1960 scrambled to stop "a second Pearl Harbor," as Michael Beschloss noted in his *New York Times Book Review* piece, by sending "American aircraft into the Soviet periphery or, more dangerously, into Soviet airspace to gain crucial information on border installations." Though these flights had been secretly going on since 1946, the spy missions drew international headlines in 1960 when the U-2 plane piloted by Francis Gary Powers crashed in Soviet territory, sparking fears of an all-out retaliation.

*Critical Mass* tells the stories of the pilots and crews who risked their lives in these covert campaigns. While noting that the volume might have benefitted by being a more "ambitious" work, Beschloss concluded that "Burrows's book provides a service by giving names and human faces" to the people behind the flights, people whose role in national defense was "often officially denied by [the U.S.] government, who flew crucial missions during the cold war."

"My primary motivations," Burrows once told *CA,* "are to contribute to my society while challenging myself through my writing and teaching. That means trying to get the best out of myself all the time. I have come to understand in the course of my professional life that ultimate competition is not with others, but with myself, and that is the toughest competition imaginable. I have to live with myself, and be responsible to myself, so if I care about my integrity as an artist and a human being, I need to push up my level of competence all the time. I try to do that by avoiding what is easy or only commercial, and instead attacking what is important and challenging."

*BIOGRAPHICAL AND CRITICAL SOURCES:*

*PERIODICALS*

*Air & Space* December 2001, review of *By Any Means Necessary: America's Secret Air War in the Cold War,* p. 81.

*Air Power History,* winter, 2001, Rick Sturdevant, review of *The Infinite Journey: Eyewitness Accounts of NASA and the Space Age,* p. 59.

*American History,* June, 2002, Steven Martinovich, *By Any Means Necessary,* p. 70.

*Annals of the American Academy of Political and Social Science,* May, 1989, Leonard Cole, review of *Deep Black: Space Espionage and National Security,* p. 148.

*Astronomy,* August, 1987, review of *Deep Black,* p. 148; April, 2001, review of *The Infinite Journey,* p. 90.

*Booklist,* December 15, 1990, review of *Exploring Space: Voyages in the Solar System and Beyond,* p. 799; November 15, 1993, Carolyn Phelan, review of *Mission to Deep Space: Voyager's Journey of Discovery,* p. 615; December 15, 1993, review of *Critical Mass: The Dangerous Race for Superweapons in a Fragmenting World,* p. 725; October 1, 1998, Roland Green, review of *This New Ocean: The Story of the First Space Age,* p. 299.

*Books,* January, 1988, review of *Deep Black,* p. 14.

*Bookwatch,* March, 1994, review of *Critical Mass,* p. 1.

*Choice,* July, 1987, review of *Deep Black,* p. 1750; June, 1991, review of *Exploring Space,* p. 1658; July-August, 1994, review of *Critical Mass,* p. 1783; April, 1999, review of *This New Ocean,* p. 1478; May, 2002, K. Eubank, review of *By Any Means Necessary,* p. 1646.

*Christian Science Monitor,* August 7, 1987, review of *Deep Black,* p. B3; November 1, 2001, review of *By Any Means Necessary,* p. 18.

*Commentary,* May, 1987, Angelo Codevilla, review of *Deep Black,* p. 77.

*Comparative Strategy,* April-June, 2000, Steven Lambakis, review of *This New Ocean,* p. 197.

*Economist,* March 19, 1988, review of *Deep Black,* p. 96.

*Encounter,* March, 1988, review of *Deep Black,* p. 36.

*Far Eastern Economic Review,* May 12, 1994, Ahmed Rashid, review of *Critical Mass,* p. 46.

*Foreign Affairs,* number 4, 1987, review of *Deep Black,* p. 893; May, 1994, review of *Critical Mass,* p. 157.

*Guardian Weekly* (London, England), February 26, 1995, review of *Critical Mass,* p. 36.

*International Affairs,* October, 1994, Simon Henderson, review of *Critical Mass,* p. 769.

*Issues in Science and Technology,* winter, 1988, Robert Pirie, Jr., review of *Deep Black,* p. 11.

*Journal of American History,* March, 1992, Richard Hallion, review of *Exploring Space,* p. 1527.

*Journal of Military History,* July, 1994, review of *Critical Mass,* p. 566.

*Kirkus Reviews,* November 15, 1986, review of *Deep Black,* p. 1694; November 1, 1999, review of *Exploring Space,* p. 1507; December 15, 1993, review of *Critical Mass,* p. 1560; September 1, 1998, review of *This New Ocean,* p. 1248; July 15, 2001, review of *By Any Means Necessary,* p. 992.

*Library Journal,* March 1, 1992, review of *Exploring Space,* p. 44; January, 1994, review of *Critical Mass,* p. 140; September 15, 1998, review of *This New Ocean,* p. 108; February 1, 1999, review of *This New Ocean,* p. 56; August, 2001, review of *By Any Means Necessary,* p. 129.

*London Review of Books,* October 27, 1988, review of *Deep Black,* p. 22.

*Los Angeles Times Book Review,* December 28, 1986, review of *Deep Black,* p. 7; April 10, 1994, review of *Critical Mass,* p. 3.

*Nation,* March 21, 1994, Eric Nadler, review of *Critical Mass,* p. 382.

*Nature,* March 4, 1999, review of *This New Ocean,* p. 35.

*New Scientist,* June 2, 1988, Norman Dombey, review of *Deep Black,* p. 58; April 2, 1994, review of *Critical Mass,* p. 35; February 25, 1995, review of *Critical Mass,* p. 41; March 6, 1999, review of *This New Ocean,* p. 46.

*New York Times Book Review,* February 15, 1987, review of *Deep Black,* p. 14; June 16, 1991, review of *Exploring Space,* p. 13; February 6, 1994, review of *Critical Mass,* p. 7; November 15, 1998, Alex Roland, review of *This New Ocean,* p. 72; December 16, 2001, Michael Beschloss, "Spies in the Skies," p. 18.

*Orbis,* summer, 1987, Adam Garfinkle, review of *Deep Black,* p. 247.

*Publishers Weekly,* December 12, 1986, review of *Deep Black,* p. 47; November 9, 1990, review of *Exploring Space,* p. 49; December 20, 1993, review of *Critical Mass,* p. 58; September 14, 1998, review of *This New Ocean,* p. 63; August 13, 2001, review of *By Any Means Necessary,* p. 295.

*School Library Journal,* December, 1993, John Peters, review of *Mission to Deep Space,* p. 120.

*Science Books & Films,* September, 1987, review of *Deep Black,* p. 24; March, 1994, review of *Mission to Deep Space,* p. 46.

*Science Fiction Studies,* July, 2000, Doris Witt, "The Final Frontier?," p. 349.

*Science Teacher,* May, 2001, Sue LeBeau, review of *The Infinite Journey,* p. 69.

*Scientific American,* May, 1987, Philip Morrison, review of *Deep Black,* p. 22.

*Sky & Telescope,* July, 1991, Mark Washburn, review of *Exploring Space,* p. 43; April, 1999, review of *This New Ocean,* p. 84.

*Tribune Books* (Chicago, IL), February 12, 1989, review of *Deep Black,* p. 9.

*Wall Street Journal,* January 23, 1991, review of *Exploring Space,* p. A10.

*Washington Post Book World,* February 15, 1987, review of *Deep Black,* p. 6; February 3, 1991, review of *Exploring Space,* p. 13; June 12, 1994, review of *Critical Mass,* p. 4; November 8, 1998, John Schwartz, review of *This New Ocean,* p. 8.

*West Coast Review of Books,* number 4, 1988, review of *Deep Black,* p. 40.

*Wilson Quarterly,* spring, 1988, review of *Deep Black,* p. 149.*

# C

## CANEMAKER, John 1943-

*PERSONAL:* Born John Cannizzaro, May 28, 1943, in Waverly, NY; son of John F. (in hospital maintenance) and Rose (a nurse's aid; maiden name, Laux) Cannizzaro. *Education:* Marymount Manhattan College, B.A., 1974; New York University, M.F.A., 1976.

*ADDRESSES: Home*—New York, NY. *Office*—New York University, Tisch School of the Arts, Department of Film and Television, 721 Broadway, New York, NY 10003. *Agent*—Robert Cornfield, 145 West 79th St., New York, NY 10024.

*CAREER:* Worked as actor, singer, and dancer on television commercials and on stage, 1961-71; WCBS-TV, New York, NY, teacher, cartoonist, and performer on "Patchwork Family" series, 1972-75; animation teacher at workshops in New York City, 1973-76, and Nassau County Arts Development Center, Long Island, 1976; William Paterson College, Wayne, NJ, instructor in animation techniques, 1978—; Adelphi University, Garden City, NY, instructor in animation history, 1978—. Lecturer in animation at School of Visual Arts, New York City, 1976, New York University, 1977-78, Adelphi University, 1978, and Los Angeles International Film Exposition (Filmex), 1978. Host for CBS Camera Three, 1975-77; artistic director and master of ceremonies at New York International Animation Festival, 1975; coordinated the first U.S. retrospectives of the classic animated films of Winsor McCay, 1975; arranged the first U.S. retrospective "Felix the Cat" tribute to Otto Messmer at Whitney Museum of American Art, 1976. Held drawing exhibi-

*John Canemaker*

tion in 1978; held cartoon screenings at New York Film Festival, Museum of Modern Art, Carpenter Center for Visual Arts, and John F. Kennedy Center. Freelance animator for producers of "Sesame Street," "Electric Company," "Captain Kangaroo," "Patchwork Family," American Broadcasting Co. (ABC)-TV's special "Days of Liberty," and in-house video for Merrill Lynch Pierce Fenner & Smith, Inc; New York University Tisch School of the Arts, professor of film and television, head of animation area. *Military service:* U.S. Army, 1965-67.

*AWARDS, HONORS:* Award for best film in nostalgia category, Association of Animators, 1973, for "Lust"; third prize from Association of Animators, 1973, for "Greed"; grant from American Film Institute to produce, write, and direct "Remembering Winsor McCay," 1976; "The 40's" was selected for 1977 New York Film Festival American Program; National Education Association grant, 1981, Public Broadcasting System grant, 1983, 1984, for *What Do Children Think of When They Think of the Bomb?;* Museum of Modern Art, "Cineprobe" retrospective, 1984. Designed and directed animation for Academy Award-winning documentary *You Don't Have to Die* and the Peabody Award-winning documentary, *Break the Silence: Kids against Child Abuse.*

*WRITINGS:*

*The Animated Raggedy Ann & Andy: An Intimate Look at the Art of Animation; Its History, Techniques and Artists,* Bobbs-Merrill (Indianapolis, IN), 1977.
(Author of introduction) Walt Disney Productions, *Treasures of Disney Animation Art,* Abbeville Press (New York), 1982.
*Winsor McCay, His Life and Art,* Abbeville Press (New York), 1987.
*Felix: The Twisted Tale of the World's Most Famous Cat,* Pantheon Books (New York), 1991.
*Before the Animation Begins: The Art and Lives of Disney Inspirational Sketch Artists,* Hyperion (New York), 1996.
*Tex Avery: The MGM Years, 1942-55,* Turner Publications (Atlanta, GA), 1996.
(Illustrator) Joseph Kennedy, *Lucy Goes to the Country,* Alyson Wonderland (Los Angeles, CA), 1998.
*Paper Dreams: The Art and Artists of Disney Storyboards,* Hyperion (New York), 1999.
*Walt Disney's Nine Old Men and the Art of Animation,* Disney Editions (New York), 2001.
*The Art and Flair of Mary Blair,* Disney Press, 2003.

TELEVISION PROGRAMS

*The Boys from Termit Terrance,* Columbia Broadcasting System (CBS)-TV, 1975.
*The Animated Art of Oskar Fischinger,* CBS-TV, 1977.

SHORT SUBJECT FILMS

*Animation: Its History and Uses,* 1959.
*Lust,* 1973.
*The 40's,* 1974.
*Street Freaks,* 1974.
*Remembering Winsor McCay,* 1976.
*Otto Messmer and Felix the Cat,* 1977.
*Confessions of a Stardreamer,* 1978.
*Bottom's Dream,* 1983.
*The Hunger Project,* 1987.
*You Don't Have to Die,* 1988.
*John Canemaker: Marching to a Different Toon,* 2001.

Contributor of articles to periodicals, including *New York Times, Print, Film Comment, Filmmakers Newsletters, Variety,* and *Cinefantasique.* Animation editor of *Millimeter,* 1975—; created the animation segment for the movie *The World According to Garp,* 1981; made several Children's Television Workshop films.

New York University's Fales Library houses the collection of Canemaker's documentary and graphic materials, which contain information on personalities and subjects, both American and international, who have significantly contributed to film animation.

*SIDELIGHTS:* John Canemaker is a professional animator who has written extensively about his field. He is not only an award-winning cartoonist, he is also an internationally recognized historian of animation. Some of his more noted publications include studies of the early Walt Disney Studio artists such as Tex Avery, Albert Hurter, Bill Peet, as well as Disney himself; pioneer animator Winsor McCay; and the creator of the cartoon character Felix the Cat, Otto Messmer.

Canemaker was born John Cannizzaro on May 28, 1943, in Waverly and then reared in Elmira, both towns located near the Finger Lakes region of upstate New York. He became interested in animation in high school and even produced a film, but upon graduation, he decided to move to the big city and try to make a living as an actor. After gaining several lucrative positions as actor, singer, and dancer for television commercials and off-Broadway plays, Canemaker decided, at age twenty-eight, to enroll in college. It was at Marymount Manhattan College (New York City) that Canemaker met a teacher who would turn his career back to his original fascination with animation.

Sister Dymphna Leonard learned that Canemaker had made an animated film in high school, so she offered him an opportunity in the summer of 1973 to travel to Disney Studios and research the lives and careers of some of the original Disney cartoonists. In an article posted at the *Animated World Network* website, Mike Lyons reported that when Canemaker arrived at the studios, he met all of the "Nine Old Men" [a group of of original Disney animators], all of whom were still alive. During his stay at the studios, Canemaker told Lyons, "they showed me films and I saw Albert Hurter's drawings and I flipped [the animation drawings of] the Mushrooms from *Fantasia* and I was gone!" Afterwards, not only was Canemaker's interest in animation reawakened, he also became fascinated with the history of animation. Since then, he has authored several books on this topic. Lyons reported, "Canemaker says he strives to uncover the background of the artist in his writing and how their lives impacted on their work. 'I'm interested in the humanist aspects, the human story.'"

*Winsor McCay, His Life and Art* was the first book that Canemaker wrote in which he focused on a single artist. John Gross commented in *New York Times:* "John Canemaker's biography should go a long way toward putting McCay firmly back on the map. . . . He satisfies your curiosity about McCay's life, sets him in the context of his times, and comments perceptively on his art." Michael Barrier in *Comics Journal* called the book "Probably the best biography ever written . . . John Canemaker's text is that great and most welcome rarity, a genuine work of scholarship about a cartoonist . . . A model for other books about comic art."

McCay's contribution to the field of animation was considerable. Beckerman emphasizes "the high level of art that no one had approached previously and few have attained in the years since." Early animated films demanded thousands of drawings, and McCay had the gift for accuracy and quickness. Beckerman noted that Canemaker effectively demystifies his subject's life by providing important facts that had eluded historians and artists who wanted to know more about him and his colleagues.

Canemaker researched the story of another important figure in animation, Otto Messmer, for his next book. *Felix: The Twisted Tale of the World's Most Famous Cat* relates the story of Messmer's creation of the first cartoon character to express an individualized personality in a film series. Felix started quite unpretentiously as a rush job for Paramount. The studio was so impressed with the little black cat that they asked for a whole series of the cartoon character, who was first called Master Tom. Messmer's boss, Pat Sullivan, took credit for the creation, but after the death of Sullivan, Messmer received his long overdue credit.

While conducting interviews of the old-time animators, people kept telling Canemaker that he should seek out Messmer. According to Lyons's article, "The meetings between Canemaker and Messmer would change both men's lives." After his interviews with Messmer, Canemaker wrote a book and produced a documentary film about the classic animator.

In *Tex Avery: The MGM Years, 1942-55,* Canemaker chronicles the life of a man who, according to *Booklist* reviewer Gordon Flagg, preferred the creative freedom of highly imaginative animation. Flagg adds that "today's cartoons owe far more to Avery's over-the-top style than to Disney's staidness." Walt Disney believed in making his characters lifelike. Avery did not. Instead, Avery created the character Bugs Bunny and other Warner Brothers animated stars. His influence remains popular in more contemporary animated cartoons.

After almost thirty years of working with animation, as an artist, as a teacher, and as a historian, Canemaker wrote *Walt Disney's Nine Old Men and the Art of Animation,* going back to those first interviews that he conducted while an undergraduate student. The nine people he interviewed were Les Clark, Woolie Reitherman, Eric Larson, Ward Kimball, Milt Kahl, Frank Thomas, Ollie Johnston, John Lounsbery, and Marc Davis, cartoonists and animators responsible for Disney Studios' early successes. This was Canemaker's third book on the topic of Disney Studio artists; the first two were *Before the Animation Begins: The Art and Lives of Disney Inspirational Sketch Artists* and *Paper Dreams: The Art and Artists of Disney Storyboards.*

Interviewer Amid Amidi of the Web site *Animation Blast* asked Canemaker what drew him to the project of writing *Walt Disney's Nine Old Men and the Art of Animation.* Canemaker responded, "I wanted to delve into great detail about each of the Nine, personally and professionally. I was interested in discovering their individual approaches to animation techniques, their philosophy of entertainment and communication, etc. I also wanted to know them as people, what their personal lives and personalities were like, and how that affected their work and relationships."

Canemaker's book was "highly recommended" by *Library Journal*'s David M. Lisa, who wrote that this work would appeal to readers interested in "the creative forces" responsible for bringing to life "some of the most recognizable characters and sequences" in Disney's history.

*BIOGRAPHICAL AND CRITICAL SOURCES:*

*PERIODICALS*

*Atlanta Journal-Constitution,* November 18, 1978.
*Back Stage,* July 10, 1987, Volume 28, Howard Beckerman, review of *Winsor McCay, His Life and Art,* pp. 46-47.
*Booklist,* November 15, 1996, Volume 93, number 6, Gordon Flagg, review of *Tex Avery: The MGM Years, 1942-1955,* p. 562; October 1, 1999, Volume 96, number, 3, Mike Tribby, review of *Paper Dreams: The Art and Artists of Disney Storyboards,* p. 333.
*Chronicle of Higher Education,* April 4, 1997, Zoe Ingalls, "Designs That Come to Life: The Basic Magic of Animation."
*Comics Journal,* March, 1988, Michael Carrier, review of *Winsor McCay, His Life and Art.*
*Film News,* November and December, 1976, summer, 1977.
*Hollywood Reporter,* August 12, 1977.
*Library Journal,* October 1, 1999, Volume 124, number 16, Kelli N. Perkins, review of *Paper Dreams,* p. 95; February 1, 2002, Volume 127, number 2, David M. Lisa, review of *Walt Disney's Nine Old Men and the Art of Animation,* p. 94.
*Los Angeles Times,* May 26, 1978.
*New York Daily News,* February 2, 2003, Chrissy Persico, "That Old Walt Disney Magic."
*New York Times,* June 9, 1987, John Gross, review of *Winsor McCay, His Life and Art,* p. 24; May 4, 2001, Wendy Noonan, "When Mickey Was Just a Minor Mouse."

*New York Times Book Review,* March 31, 1991; Michael Cart, review of *Felix: The Twisted Tale of the World's Most Famous Cat,* p. 11.
*Print,* July-August, 1992, Volume 46, number 4, Steven Heller, review of *Felix,* p. 285; July-August, 1997, Volume 51, number 4, James McMullan, review of *Before the Animation Begins: The Art and Lives of Disney Inspirational Sketch Artists,* pp. 28-29B; January, 2000, Volume 54, number 1, Joe Sedelmaier, review of *Paper Dreams,* p. 40A.
*Publishers Weekly,* September 20, 1999, Volume 246, number 38, "Inside the Mouse," review of *Paper Dreams,* p. 68.
*Southampton Press,* October 15, 1998, Ellen Keiser, "'Bridgehampton' Colorful Art Potpourri in Cinematic Animation."

*ONLINE*

*Animated World Network,* http://www.awn.com/ (July 26, 2002), Mike Lyons, "The Animated World of John Canemaker."
*Animation Blast,* http://www.animationblast.com/ (July 26, 2002), Amid Amidi, "Then Questions about Nine Old Men: An Interview with John Canemaker."
*Entertainment Geekly,* http://www/entertainment geekly.com/ (June, 2002).
*Laughing Place,* http://www.laughingplace.com/ (May 7, 2002), "An Interview with John Canemaker and a Look at Walt Disney's Nine Old Men."
*Turner Classic Movies,* http://www.turnerclassic movies.com/ (September 4, 2003), "John Canemaker—Marching to a Different Toon."

*         *         *

## CARLSON, Lewis H(erbert) 1934-

*PERSONAL:* Surname changed in infancy; born August 1, 1934, in Muskegon, MI; son of Robert and Margaret (Carlson) Lavine; married Simone Conrad (a teacher), December 26, 1960; children: Ann Margaret Thomas, Linda Louise Dietz. *Education:* University of Michigan, B.A., 1957, M.A., 1962; Michigan State University, Ph.D., 1967. *Politics:* Democrat. *Hobbies and other interests:* Trout fishing, wine tasting.

*Lewis H. Carlson*

*ADDRESSES: Home*—306 South Ferry St., #10, Ludington, MI 49431; (winter) 114 Javelin Dr., Lakeway, TX 78734. *E-mail*—lewis.carlson@wmich.edu; LHCarlson@att.net.

*CAREER:* High school teacher in Muskegon, MI, 1960-61, Los Angeles, 1962-63; Ferris State College, Big Rapids, MI, assistant professor of history, 1965-68; Western Michigan University, Kalamazoo, assistant professor, 1968-71, associate professor, 1971-79, professor of history, 1979-99, professor emeritus, 1999—. *Military service:* U.S. Army, 1957-59.

*MEMBER:* National Association of Popular Culture.

*AWARDS, HONORS:* Western Michigan University Alumni Teaching Award, 1972.

*WRITINGS:*

(Contributor) Joseph S. Roucek and Thomas Kiernan, editors, *The Negro Impact on Western Civilization*, Philosophical Library, 1970.

*We Were Each Other's Prisoners: An Oral History of World War II American and German Prisoners of War,* Basic Books (New York), 1997.

(With James M. Ferreira) *Beyond the Red, White, and Blue: A Student's Introduction to American Studies,* McGraw-Hill (New York, NY), 1999.

*Remembered Prisoners of a Forgotten War: An Oral History of the Korean War POWs,* St. Martin's Press (New York, NY), 2002.

(With Richard M. Bassett) *And the Wind Blew Cold: The Story of an American POW in North Korea,* Kent State University Press (Kent, OH), 2002.

(With Angelo M. Spineli) *Life behind Barbed Wire: The Secret World War II Photographs of Angelo M. Spinelli,* Fordham University Press (New York, NY), 2003.

*EDITOR*

(Editor, with Colburn George) *In Their Place: White America Defines Her Minorities, 1850-1950* introduction by George McGovern, Wiley (New York, NY), 1972.

(Editor, with John J. Fogarty) *Tales of Gold: An Oral History of the Summer Olympic Gales Told by America's Gold Medal Winners,* Contemporary Books (Chicago, IL), 1987.

(Editor, with Kevin B. Vichcales) *American Popular Culture at Home and Abroad,* Western Michigan University (Kalamazoo, MI), 1996.

*WRITTEN IN GERMAN*

(With Frank Unger) *Amerika—der gespaltene Traum* (title means "America the Fragmented Dream"), Aufbau Verlag (Berlin, Germany), 1992.

(With Frank Unger) *Highland Park oder Stadt der Zukunft* (title means "Highland Park: City of the Future?"), Aufbau Verlag (Berlin, Germany), 1994.

(With Norbert Haase) *Warten auf Freiheit: Deutsche und Amerikanische Kriegsgefangene des Zweiten Weltkrieges Erzahlen* (title means "Waiting for Freedom: An Oral History of World War II German and American Prisoners of War"), Aufbau Verlag (Berlin, Germany), 1996.

Also wrote and produced *Images in Black and White: A Documentary Film on Racial Images in Popular Culture,* 1988.

*SIDELIGHTS:* Lewis H. Carlson writes about a range of topics that include popular American culture, prisoners of war, American studies, and sports. In addition to writing, he has also enjoyed a long professional career as a college professor, teaching history and American studies at Western Michigan University since the late 1960s. His fluency in German has resulted in a number of German-language books and experience as a lecturer in Germany.

In 1987 Carlson collected stories from fifty-seven Olympic gold medalists and one silver medalist to trace the history of the Olympic Games from 1912 to the late 1980s in *Tales of Gold: An Oral History of the Summer Olympic Games Told by America's Gold Medal Winners.* Through the oral history of these athletes, Carlson (and his coeditor John J. Fogarty) has recorded, as Craig Neff for *Sports Illustrated* described, "stories of tragedy, humor and unexpected challenge." Some of these stories reflect the times in which the games were played, such as the story of Harrison Dillard, who tells of a track in Britain composed of the rubble of war-ravaged buildings in the 1948 Games. Another Olympiad, sprinter Helen Stephens relates how she had to escape an orgy sponsored by Hitler sidekick Hermann Göring, during the 1936 Berlin Games. Neff concluded that *Tales of Gold* "makes a lively and valuable tapestry."

Carlson's dual interest in the United States and Germany led to his role as coeditor, with Kevin B. Vichcales, of *American Popular Culture at Home and Abroad.* For this book, Carlson collected twenty-one essays from both German and American scholars whose unifying theme is American culture and the effect it has had on both the United States and Germany.

One year later, Carlson saw publication of *We Were Each Other's Prisoners: An Oral History of World War II American and German Prisoners of War.* This is the first book ever to compare the experiences of American and German POWs. In *We Were Each Other's Prisoners,* Carlson interviews more than 150 survivors, including a German soldier who surrendered rather than fight for Hitler, a Jewish soldier who was sent to a slave labor camp, and an American soldier who was captured twice before successfully escaping on the third attempt. Carlson gets his subjects to talk openly about what it was like physically and psychologically to be a prisoner of war. Critics recognized in these stories an enduring will to survive. "The

interviewees were eager to talk to Carlson," according to a reviewer for *Publishers Weekly,* "and many unlocked painful memories of the dreadful events they had repressed for years."

In his 2002 book *Remembered Prisoners of a Forgotten War: An Oral History of the Korean War POWs,* Carlson takes up a similar theme, with a different angle. The Korean War POWs endured accusations of having turned on their fellow soldiers after being brainwashed by the Korean enemy. They did not receive a hero's welcome upon returning home, at least not for many years following the war. In his book Carlson attempts to bring the prisoners' stories alive, giving the soldiers the space to relate their experiences. Of more than 7,000 prisoners, only sixty percent survived. This book is a tribute to the survivors. Edwin B. Burgess of *Library Journal* observed that the prisoners' "survival, under conditions of extreme privation, torture, and psychological pressure, is nothing short of amazing." A reviewer for *Publishers Weekly* found that "while the book is probably too weighted toward testimony to find general readers, buffs and survivors will take it to heart."

*BIOGRAPHICAL AND CRITICAL SOURCES:*

*PERIODICALS*

*Choice,* October 1997, Volume 35, G. H. Davis, review of *We Were Each Other's Prisoners: An Oral History of World War II American and German Prisoners of War,* p. 345.

*Kirkus Reviews,* February 15, 2002, Volume 70, number 4, review of *Remembered Prisoners of a Forgotten War: An Oral History of Korean War POWs,* pp. 232-33. *Library Journal,* November 15, 1987, Volume 112, number 19, Dennis Dillon, review of *Tales of Gold: The Oral History of the Olympic Games Told by American's Gold Medal Winners,* p. 88; March 15, 2002, Volume 127, number I5, Edwin B. Burgess, review of *Remembered Prisoners of a Forgotten War,* p. 93.

*New York Times Book Review,* March 20, 1988, Michael Janofsky, review of *Tales of Gold,* p. 27.

*Oral History Review,* summer-fall, 1999, Volume 26, number 2, Ronald E. Marcello, review of *We Were Each Other's Prisoners,* p. 169.

*Publishers Weekly,* October 23, 1987, Volume 232, Genevieve Stuttaford, review of *Tales of Gold,* p. 43; March 24, 1997, Volume 244, number 12,

review of *We Were Each Other's Prisoners,* pp. 70-71; February 11, 2002, Volume 249, number 6, review of *Remembered Prisoners of a Forgotten War,* p. 171.
*Sports Illustrated,* April 25, 1988, Volume 68, number 17, Craig Neff, review of *Tales of Gold,* pp. 10-11.

\*     \*     \*

**CASING, James**
   **See BURRIDGE, Kenelm (Oswald Lancelot)**

\*     \*     \*

**CHUNG, Lily**

*PERSONAL:* Born in Hong Kong; naturalized U.S. citizen; daughter of Ping Kwan and Meilen (Ling) Chung; married Glen Wan, February, 1975. *Education:* Chinese University of Hong Kong, B.A., 1963; Kent State University, M.A., 1967; University of Minnesota—Twin Cities, Ph.D., 1972. *Religion:* "Multi." *Hobbies and other interests:* Natural law, metaphysics.

*ADDRESSES: Home and office*—Pacifica, CA. *Agent*—c/o Author Mail, Llewellyn Worldwide, P.O. Box 64383, St. Paul, MN 55164-0383. *E-mail*—lwanju@aol.com.

*CAREER:* High school teacher in Hong Kong, 1963-65; instructor in geography at colleges in Hong Kong and Pennsylvania, 1969-75; Wells Fargo Bank, San Francisco, CA, employee, 1976-95; City College of San Francisco, San Francisco, CA, instructor in Chinese metaphysics, 1996-97. Practitioner of *feng shui* and divination; instructor in Chinese metaphysics and talk show host for Sinocast (Chinese radio station), 1996-97; also workshop presenter.

*MEMBER:* Society of Metaphysicians (London, England).

*WRITINGS:*

*Human Geography for Hong Kong,* 1977.
*The Path to Good Fortune: The Meng,* Llewellyn Worldwide (St. Paul, MN), 1997.

*Easy Ways to Harmony,* Gold Medal Books (Pacifica, CA), 1999.
*Calendars for Feng Shui and Divination* (e-book), iuniverse.com (Lincoln, NE), 2000.

Columnist, *Asian Week,* 1992—; also author of a *feng shui* column for *California Property.*

*WORK IN PROGRESS: Natural Laws: The Wisdom of I Ching.*

*SIDELIGHTS:* Lily Chung once told *CA:* "My motivation for writing began with frustration about the uncontrollable changes in our lives. Why does our luck change beyond our control while our endowment does not change? If we are so smart, why can't we succeed all the time? The answer is cyclical cosmic flows.

"This is not a new topic. The formulas on how the flows of the five elements affect human destiny have been applied and proven by the huge Chinese population for more than a thousand years. Chinese are blessed with three mysterious metaphysical documents: the lunar calendar which registers the timely cosmic flows, *I Ching* which preaches natural law, and the number plate from which *feng shui* was originated. These tools have to come out to benefit the world. Authentic Chinese metaphysicians who have mastered the subject through a lifetime of devotion don't speak English. Those who are making waves on the global stage on this subject don't read Chinese. I feel the need to bridge the gap.

"I first completed the most important task by converting the lunar calendar into English. It is a Bible for all Chinese metaphysicians, a tool with which to chart the personal flow and the grand cosmic flow in order to design the best possible environment for the individual. None of the western practitioners on Chinese *feng shui* are aware of this procedure, because the tool only recently became available.

"My research on many great political leaders in the western world, hundreds of Nobel Prize winners and Olympic gold medalists, and many others has supported these formulas. Luck plays the key! This is the subject of my book, *The Path to Good Fortune: The Meng.*

"As an advocate of natural law, I have also completed a manuscript on the most functional *I Ching* divination system. It is a vital key to learn the natural law. My second book, *Easy Ways to Harmony,* summarizes some of these findings. All of us want and try hard to be successful, but the privilege is assigned to only a few by birth. Can we do something about it? My system offers some help. We can identify our endowment and the problem spot that keeps us from fulfilling our goals. By attuning to the flows, we can turn our luck into success. My passion is to find out the truth about luck."*

"Every good mystery writer should make a concerted effort expand the perimeters of the genre, instead of expanding upon pre-existing plots. Doing so makes their work new and different and helps showcase the author's talent. The mystery genre has been around for quite a while, but the scientific and technological techniques used today have not. It should be incumbent upon every mystery author to reflect these changes in his or her novel. Readers deserve something new and exciting!"

\*     \*     \*

### COLE, Susan Letzler 1940-

*PERSONAL:* Born June 4, 1940, in Washington, DC; daughter of Alfred (an attorney) and Alice (a teacher and volunteer; maiden name, Parson) Letzler; married David Cole (a playwright), June 28, 1969. *Education:* Duke University, B.A. (summa cum laude), 1962; Harvard University, M.A., 1963, Ph.D., 1968. *Hobbies and other interests:* Theater, music, travel.

*ADDRESSES: Home*—137 Cottage St., Apt. E6, New Haven, CT 06511-2457. *Office*—Department of English, 318 Aquinas Hall, Albertus Magnus College, 700 Prospect St., New Haven, CT 06511-2457; fax: 203-773-3117.

*CAREER:* Cleveland State University, Cleveland, OH, assistant professor of English, 1968-69; Southern Connecticut State College, New Haven, lecturer in English, 1969; Yale University, New Haven, CT, tutor in English, 1969-70; Quinnipiac College, New Haven, CT, assistant professor of English, 1970-71; Albertus Magnus College, New Haven, CT, assistant professor, 1971-76, associate professor and department head, 1977-83, professor of English and academic director of concentration in creative writing and drama concentration in English, 1983—, dramaturg for college plays, 1988—. University of Virginia, Northern Virginia Center, instructor, summers, 1964, 1966; Yale University, visiting fellow, 1978-79, 1980-81.

*MEMBER:* Modern Language Association of America, Shakespeare Association of America, American Association of University Professors, New York Shakespeare Society, Columbia University Seminar in Shakespeare.

*AWARDS, HONORS:* Woodrow Wilson fellow, 1962-63.

*     *     *

### CLARKE, Kenneth 1957-

*PERSONAL:* Born March 22, 1957, in Wichita, KS; son of Carolyn Gunnels Clarke. *Ethnicity:* "Caucasian." *Education:* El Centro Junior College, A.A.S., 1981; East Texas State University, B.S., 1986. *Politics:* Republican. *Religion:* Protestant. *Hobbies and other interests:* Collecting vintage radio tapes, 1925-65; learning to speak French.

*ADDRESSES: Home*—3130 Royal Gable Dr., Dallas, TX 75229-3787. *E-mail*—kclarke5@juno.com.

*CAREER:* Spring Corp., Dallas, TX, customer service associate and departmental assistant, 1987-2001; writer.

*MEMBER:* Mystery Writers of America, National Writers Association.

*WRITINGS:*

*The Case of the Magnolia Murders* (mystery novel), 1stBooks Library (Bloomington, IN), 1998.
*Deadly Justice* (mystery novel), 1stBooks Library (Bloomington, IN), 2002.

*SIDELIGHTS:* Kenneth Clarke told *CA:* "I've always liked mystery books. It's because of the challenge involved with solving a crime which baffles everyone else and bringing the criminal to justice.

*WRITINGS:*

*The Absent One: Mourning Ritual, Tragedy, and the Performance of Ambivalence,* Pennsylvania State University Press (University Park, PA), 1985.

*Directors in Rehearsal: A Hidden World,* Routledge (New York, NY), 1992.

*Playwrights in Rehearsal: The Seduction of Company,* Routledge (New York, NY), 2001.

Contributor to books, including *Figuring Age: Women, Bodies, Generations,* Indiana University Press (Bloomington, IN), 1998; *The Theater of Maria Irene Fornes,* edited by Marc Robinson, Johns Hopkins University Press (Baltimore, MD), 1999; and *Conducting a Life: Reflections on the Theatre of Maria Irene Fornes,* Kraus & Smith, (Lyme, NH), 1999. Contributor to journals, including *Signs.*

*WORK IN PROGRESS: Missing Alice: In Search of a Mother's Voice,* an "experimental memoir."

\*     \*     \*

**COLEMAN, Clare**
    **See BELL, Clare (Louise)**

\*     \*     \*

**COLLICOTT, Sharleen 1937-**
    **(Sharleen Pederson)**

*PERSONAL:* Born April 10, 1937, in Los Angeles, CA; married Con Pederson (a special effects designer; divorced, 1985); children: Eric. *Education:* University of California at Los Angeles, B.A., 1969.

*ADDRESSES: Home and office*—2960 Bel Air Dr., Las Vegas, NV 89109-1581. *E-mail*—rubincolli@aol.com.

*CAREER:* Writer, illustrator, ceramist, sculptor, and educator. Duntog Foundation, artist-in-residence, 1983; Otis/Parson Design Institute, teacher, 1983; California State University, Long Beach, teacher, 1983-84. National Endowment for the Arts, panelist, 1985; affiliated with India Ink Galleries, 1985-86, and Every Picture Tells a Story (art gallery), 1991-95. Has also

worked on special effects for motion pictures. *Exhibitions:* Exhibitor at galleries in Los Angeles, CA, including India Ink Gallery, 1983; Los Angeles City College, 1984; Every Picture Tells a Story, 1991, 1994; and Storyopolis, 1997.

*AWARDS, HONORS:* Society of Illustrators, Los Angeles awards; Art Directors Club of Los Angeles awards; *Advertising Age* awards.

*WRITINGS:*

FOR CHILDREN; SELF-ILLUSTRATED

*Seeing Stars,* Dial (New York, NY), 1996.
*Mildred and Sam,* HarperCollins (New York, NY), 2002.
*Toestomper and the Caterpillars,* Houghton Mifflin (Boston, MA), 2002.
*Toestomper and the Bad Butterflies,* Houghton Mifflin (Boston, MA), 2003.

ILLUSTRATOR

(As Sharleen Pederson) Michael Hallward, *The Enormous Leap of Alphonse Frog,* Nash Publishing (Los Angeles, CA), 1972.

(As Sharleen Pederson) Suzanne Klein, *An Elephant in My Bed,* Follett (Chicago, IL), 1974.

*Mouse, Frog, and Little Hen,* DLM, 1990.

Sharon Lucky, *The Three Dinosaurs Dreadly,* DLM, 1991.

Karen Radler Greenfield, *The Teardrop Baby,* HarperCollins (New York, NY), 1994.

Laura Joffe Numeroff, *The Chicken Sisters,* HarperCollins (New York, NY), 1997.

Judith Barrett, *Which Witch Is Which?* Atheneum (New York, NY), 2001.

Also contributor of illustrations to *Elementary Math Series,* Addison-Wesley, *Frickles and Frackles,* DLM, and *Pattern Palace,* DLM. Contributor of illustrations to periodicals, including *Psychology Today, Westways, National Wildlife Federation, Human Behavior, Lady Bug,* and *Ranger Rick.*

*SIDELIGHTS:* Highly regarded illustrator Sharleen Collicott has been creating picture-book images since the early 1970s. After working for over twenty years teaching, illustrating the work of children's book authors, and exhibiting her paintings sculpture, and ceramics at art galleries, Collicott decided to expand her creative talents even further. In 1996 she published *Seeing Stars,* the first of her works containing both original art and text. Her pictures—colorful, detailed paintings that range from intimate views to double-page spreads—characteristically feature fantastic animals and have been compared to such artists as Hieronymous Bosch for their imaginative quality and attention to detail.

Born in 1937, Collicott enjoyed drawing even as a child, and animals were among her favorite subjects. She graduated from the University of California at Los Angeles in 1969 with a degree in sculpture, then went to live in England for several years, where she worked on special effects for motion pictures. Although ceramics and welded steel were originally her artistic media of choice, she began to draw seriously during her stay in England when, because of rainy weather, she spent many days indoors at the London Zoo. In an interview with Marv Rubin in *Communication Arts,* Collicott explained that being at the zoo "put me much closer to the animals than I had ever been. That inspired me to try sketching in my notebook, and to discover how much I enjoyed it." Attending a centennial exhibit of nineteenth-century British illustrator Beatrix Potter's work convinced her "that drawing the things I imagined was indeed legitimate." After filling the pages of her notebook, she showed them to others, including director Stanley Kubrick, for whom she was sculpting alien creatures for the film *2001: A Space Odyssey.* Although Collicott's aliens were ultimately cut from the film, Kubrick encouraged her to add background to her animal sketches for exhibition or publication. She took his advice and has been illustrating ever since. "When I paint now," she told Rubin, "I'm revealing something from my imagination as realistically as possible."

Collicott began her new career as a professional artist by illustrating advertising copy, magazine articles, educational material, and record covers. One of her most recognizable works was the first wide-screen version of the "Columbia Lady," the image of a woman holding a torch that is featured at the beginning of movies produced by Columbia Pictures. Collicott has also taught art at the university level, served as an artist-in-residence in the Philippines, and formed affiliations with several Los Angeles art galleries. However, by the early 1990s she had decided to focus her efforts on illustrating and writing picture books.

Many of Collicott's initial book illustrations were done for educational publications, such as the easy-readers *An Elephant in My Bed* and *Mouse, Frog, and Hen.* The first children's picture book she contributed to was Karen Greenfield's *The Teardrop Baby,* published in 1994. In this original fairy tale, a childless couple meet a magical woman who creates a child for them from their tears. When the boy is seven, the old woman comes back to claim him and makes him her servant; after tricking the woman with a fortune baked into a loaf of bread, the boy returns to his parents. "Collicott's illustrations, with many-eyed flowers and a deliciously scary depiction of the edge of the world, realize and enhance Greenfield's cryptic tale," declared a contributor to *Publishers Weekly.* In a review for *School Library Journal,* Lisa Dennis called *The Teardrop Baby* an "unusual picture book" and noted that the illustrations "suit the fairy-tale flavor of the story." Collicott's "decision to paint eyes on the flowers creates a distinctly creepy atmosphere," concluded Dennis.

Collicott's 1996 work *Seeing Stars* marked her debut as a children's book author. The story describes how two small animals, Motley and Fuzzball, build a makeshift spaceship out of parts found in a junkyard in an attempt to reach the stars in outer space. Through Collicott's illustrations, the reader knows exactly where the ship lands: in the ocean. However, the befuddled pair thinks they are in space and that the starfish are actually stars. Writing in *School Library Journal,* Jane Marino noted that "younger readers may forgive the lapses in the story to enjoy the beautiful illustrations and may even sympathize with these two wayward passengers." A *Publishers Weekly* reviewer found *Seeing Stars* "impressive for its eye-catching visuals," and noted that Collicott "adroitly pulls off the kid-pleasing contrivance" of letting young readers in on a secret of which her characters are unaware.

As is characteristic in Collicott's books, animals take center stage in *Mildred and Sam,* the author/illustrator's 2002 easy-read chapter book. Mildred and Sam are fieldmice who make their home under a patch of daffodils, but the overwrought homemaker Mildred despairs of their tiny home ever being big enough for company. Although at first Sam is totally in the dark as to what his anxious mousewife means, he eventually understands when a litter of eight tiny mouse babies makes its appearance. "A well-balanced narrative with plenty of judiciously repeated phrases" make *Mildred and Sam* "a fine choice for beginning readers," remarked a *Publishers Weekly* contributor, who also praised Collicott's "fetching graphics." Praising the book's "whimsical" illustrations, a *Kirkus* reviewer wrote that the book's "fanciful themes and vibrant illustrations make this an enjoyable romp to share as a read-aloud."

Collicott's self-authored *Toestomper and the Caterpillars* and its sequel, *Toestomper and the Bad Butterflies*, feature a trio of bad-mannered rodents—Barfy, Basher, and Nightmare—who call themselves the Rowdy Ruffians and whose leader, the bullying Toestomper, suffers a change of heart when faced by small animals in peril. Actually, the peril in *Toestomper in the Caterpillars* is Toestomper himself; the uncouth rat crushes the bush a caterpillar family calls home before pangs of conscience kick in and he makes the homeless insects his friends. While a *Publishers Weekly* reviewer found the book's storyline "mediocre," the reviewer went on to dub Collicott's illustrations "cuddly" and the Rowdy Ruffians' behavior "funny."

In addition to illustrating her own texts, Collicott has continued to contribute highly praised illustrations to books by other authors. Among these are Laura Joffe Numeroff's 1997 work *The Chicken Sisters,* which features three sister hens whose hobbies—baking, knitting, and singing—annoy a neighboring wolf because of the talent (or lack thereof) of their practitioners. The story "comes brilliantly alive in Collicott's pictures," declared *Booklist* contributor Ilene Cooper, who added that the artist's work "is chock-full and pretty darn adorable." In *School Library Journal* Jane Marino commented that the illustrations for *The Chicken Sisters* "reinforce the text, giving personality to the feathered siblings," while a *Publishers Weekly* contributor predicted that toddlers would enjoy "the bright colors in Collicott's intricately detailed art." Collicott's contribution to Judith Barrett's *Which Witch Is Which?* were hailed by *Booklist* contributor Connie Fletcher as "eye-popping gouache paintings [that] deliver just the right kind of creepy-crawly landscapes" for Barrett's rhyming wordplay.

Collicott works from her artist's studio in Las Vegas, Nevada, where she has lived for several years. Although when she began illustrating she used colored pencils, she has since expanded her medium to include water colors, egg tempera—a blend of ground pigment powder and egg yolk made using recipes and techniques dating from the Middle Ages—and gouache, an

opaque form of water color. In her interview with Marv Rubin in *Communication Arts,* she explained that in individual illustrations every area is "equally important. I don't like empty areas or unimportant areas." Collicott spends almost as much time preparing for an illustration as she does painting it. "I plan the pictures and their 'stories' carefully," she explained to Rubin. "I 'cast' all the characters before I begin. I do research on them and on their settings. I know all about them."

## BIOGRAPHICAL AND CRITICAL SOURCES:

*PERIODICALS*

*Artist,* October, 1994.
*Booklist,* May 1, 1997, Ilene Cooper, review of *The Chicken Sisters,* p. 1497; November 1, 2001, Connie Fletcher, review of *Which Witch Is Which?,* p. 480.
*Communication Arts,* January-February, 1983, Marv Rubin, "Sharleen Pederson," pp. 66-70.
*Crayola Kids,* June-July, 1998.
*Kirkus Reviews,* May 1, 1997, review of *The Chicken Sisters;* September 14, 1999, review of *Toestomper and the Caterpillars,* p. 1498; November 15, 2002, review of *Mildred and Sam,* p. 1689.
*Publishers Weekly,* August 15, 1994, review of *The Teardrop Baby,* p. 95; April 29, 1996, review of *Seeing Stars,* p. 70; April 7, 1997, review of *The Chicken Sisters,* p. 90; September 27, 1999, review of *Toestomper and the Caterpillar,* p. 104; December 23, 2002, review of *Mildred and Sam,* p. 68.
*School Library Journal,* September, 1994, Lisa Dennis, review of *The Teardrop Baby,* p. 184; April, 1996, Jane Marino, review of *Seeing Stars,* p. 105; May, 1997, J. Marino, review of *The Chicken Sisters,* p. 109.
*Today's Art,* Volume 27, number 8.

*OTHER*

Collicott, Sharleen, interview in promotional piece, DLM Publishing.*

\*     \*     \*

**COLVIN, James
See MOORCOCK, Michael (John)**

# D

## DEICHMANN, Ute 1951-

*PERSONAL:* Born December 23, 1951, in Düsseldorf, Germany. *Education:* University of Heidelberg, M.A., 1975; University of Cologne, Ph.D., 1991.

*ADDRESSES: Home*—Weissenburgstrasse 44, D-50670 Cologne, Germany. *Office*—Institut für Genetik, University of Cologne, Weyertal 121, D-50931 Cologne, Germany; fax: +49-221-470-5170. *E-mail*—ute.deichmann@uni-koeln.de.

*CAREER:* Schoolteacher, 1975-87; University of Cologne, Cologne, Germany, research fellow and lecturer, 1987-96, 1997-98, privatdozent, beginning 2001; Beckman Center for the History of Chemistry, Philadelphia, PA, Edelstein International fellow in the History of the Chemical Sciences, 1996-97; Hebrew University of Jerusalem, Jerusalem, Israel, research fellow, 1997; Ben-Gurion University of the Negev, Israel, guest lecturer, 1998—.

*AWARDS, HONORS:* Ladislaus Laszt International and Social Concern Award, Ben-Gurion University of the Negev, 1995.

*WRITINGS:*

*Biologen unter Hitler: Vertreibung, Karrieren, Forschung,* Campus (New York, NY), 1992, expanded edition published as *Biologen unter Hitler: Porträt einer Wissenschaft im NS-Staat,* Fischer (Frankfurt am Main, Germany), 1995, translation by Thomas Dunlop published as *Biologists under Hitler,* Harvard University Press (Cambridge, MA), 1996.

*Flüchten, Mitmachen, Vergessen: Chemiker und Biochemiker in der NS-Zeit,* Wiley/UCH, 2001.

Contributor to journals.

*WORK IN PROGRESS:* Studying protein research in Germany, 1920-60; research on German-Jewish scientists in the nineteenth and twentieth centuries.

\*     \*     \*

## DENIM, Sue
### See PILKEY, Dav

\*     \*     \*

## de PALCHI, Alfredo 1926-

*PERSONAL:* Born December 13, 1926, in Verona, Italy; son of Carlo Giop and Ines de Palchi; married Sonia Raiziss, 1952 (deceased); married Rita di Pace (a curator of art), June 23, 1989; children: Luce. *Ethnicity:* "Caucasian."

*ADDRESSES: Home*—33 Union Square W., New York, NY 10003; fax: 212-989-3083. *E-mail*—katpoet13@aol.com.

*CAREER:* Chelsea Associates, Inc., editor of *Chelsea* and publisher of Chelsea Editions; poet and translator. Prisoner of war, 1945-51.

*WRITINGS:*

(Editor of Italian section, with Sonia Raiziss) *Modern European Poetry,* Bantam (New York, NY), 1966.

*Sessioni con l'analista* (poetry), Mondadori (Milan, Italy), 1967, translation by I. L. Salomon published as *Sessions with My Analyst,* October House (Stonington, CT), 1970.

*Mutazioni* (poetry), Campanotto (Udine, Italy), 1988.

*The Scorpion's Dark Dance = La buia danza di scorpione* (poetry), English translation by Sonia Raiziss, Xenos Books (Riverside, CA), 1993, 2nd edition, 1995.

*Anonymous Constellation* (poetry), translated by Sonia Raiziss, Xenos Books (Riverside, CA), 1997.

(Editor, with Michael Palma) Luciano Erba, *The Metaphysical Streetcar Conductor: Sixty Poems,* Gradiva Publications, 1998.

*Addictive Aversions = Le Viziose Avversioni,* English translation by Michael Palma, Xenos Books (Riverside, CA), 1999.

*Paradigma* (poetry), Caramanica (Marino di Mintuano, Italy), 2001, English translation by Barbara Carle, forthcoming.

Contributor of poetry and translations to magazines, including *American Poetry Review, Chicago Review, New Letters,* and *TriQuarterly.*

*SIDELIGHTS:* Alfredo de Palchi told *CA:* "My primary motivation for writing is that I consider myself an artist—from the beginning. My work is influenced by a thought, an image—the so-called inspiration. My writing is inspired by my early life as a political prisoner, and the beauty of women, and my voluntary exile.

"My writing process is: after having written a poem of twenty lines, I strip it down to five to ten lines. I found my voice in the beginning, but one can hear it and see it in all my writings in various intonations. Each book is different—doesn't repeat itself."

## DUBOST, Thierry 1958-

*PERSONAL:* Born June 4, 1958, in Cherbourg, France; son of Jacques (a teacher) and Thérèse (a manager; maiden name, Pruvost) Dubost; married Elaine Fontaine (a deputy headmistress), August 26, 1983; children: Clarissa, Valentin. *Education:* University of Caen, M.A., 1982; Sorbonne, University of Paris IV, Ph.D., 1993.

*ADDRESSES: Home*—Falaise, France. *Office*—Departement d'Anglais, Universite de Caen, Esplanade de la Paix, 14032 Caen Codex, France. *E-mail*—Dubost@ cte.unicaen.fr.

*CAREER:* Schoolteacher in France, 1985-93; University of Caen, Caen, France, assistant professor, 1993-94, associate professor, 1994-2001, professor of English, 2001—. Open University of Caen, dean of Distance Learning Center and former head of English studies.

*MEMBER:* Eugene O'Neill Society, SOFEIR, RADAC, SAES.

*WRITINGS:*

(Translator) Wole Soyinka, *Death and the King's Horseman,* Hatier, 1986.

*Struggle, Defeat, or Rebirth: Eugene O'Neill's Vision of Humanity,* McFarland (Jefferson, NC), 1997.

(Editor, with Alice Mills) *La Femme noire americaine: Aspects d'une crise d'identite* (title means "Black American Women: Aspects of an Identity Crisis"), Presses Universitaires de Caen (Caen, France), 1997.

(Editor, with Paul Brennan) *Regards croises sur G. B. Shaw* (title means "G. B. Shaw: Crossing Lines"), Presses Universitaires de Caen (Caen, France), 1998.

*Le Théâtre de Thomas Kilroy,* Presses Universitaires de Caen (Caen, France), 2001.

*WORK IN PROGRESS:* Research on the plays of Eugene O'Neill and on contemporary American and Irish drama.

\*     \*     \*

## DUNCAN, Patrick Sheane 1947(?)-

*PERSONAL:* Born c. 1947; father worked as a migrant farmer; married (separated). *Education:* Grand Valley State College, earned history degree.

*ADDRESSES: Agent*—c/o Author Mail, Putnam Berkley Group Inc., 375 Hudson St., New York, NY 10014.

*CAREER:* Former district manager of a movie-theatre chain and accountant for film producer Roger Corman. Screenplay writer, director, and novelist, 1989—. *Military service:* U.S. Army, served in Vietnam.

*WRITINGS:*

*Courage under Fire* (novel), Putnam (New York, NY), 1996.
*A Private War* (novel), Putnam (New York, NY), 2002.

*SCREENPLAYS*

(And director) *Eighty-four Charlie Mopic,* New Century/Vista, 1989.
(And director) *Live! From Death Row* (teleplay), Fox, 1992.
(And executive producer) *A Home of Our Own,* Gramercy Pictures, 1993.
(And director) *The Pornographer,* Charlie MoPic Co., 1994.
*Nick of Time,* Paramount, 1995.
*Mr. Holland's Opus,* Buena Vista, 1996.
*Courage under Fire* (adapted from his novel), Twentieth Century-Fox, 1997.

*SIDELIGHTS:* After growing up under trying circumstances, Patrick Sheane Duncan has made steady advances throughout his career, becoming, in the mid-1990s, one of the most highly sought-after screenwriters in Hollywood. Among the films to his credit are *Nick of Time, Mr. Holland's Opus,* and *Courage under Fire,* the last based on his 1996 novel.

As a child in Los Angeles, Duncan endured both poverty—his father was a migrant farm worker—and tragedy. When Duncan was ten, his father was stabbed to death in a barroom brawl; the boy's mother packed the growing family off to Michigan, where she worked picking fruit for a living. Duncan grew up helping raise his eleven younger siblings. After high school he enlisted in the U.S. Army, but soon found himself in a stockade, sentenced for "assault with intent" after a fight with another soldier. "I'm not proud" of that episode, the writer later told Gary Arnold of *Insight on*

*the News.* "But if you're poor in this country, you get angry. You're bombarded with images of stuff you don't have that other people seem to have." Eventually Duncan found himself in Vietnam, where he got a different education in class consciousness: "Bullets don't discriminate between rich and poor," he told a *People* interviewer.

Duncan's Vietnam experiences matured him to the point where he was named a squadron leader. He graduated from college on his return home, and got his first show-business job booking movies for a theatre chain. "I'd often go to New York and see several movies in a day," Duncan recalled to Arnold. "Most of them [were] pretty rotten, so I'd bitch and moan. I repeatedly told my wife that I could write better crap than what I was seeing. Being the kind of woman she is, she called my bluff." To prove he was right, Duncan began drafting his first script.

Ambition brought Duncan to Hollywood, where he got an accounting job with producer/director Roger Corman. By the late 1980s Duncan had started his film career with low-budget movies he directed from his own scripts. The first, *Eighty-four Charlie Mopic,* was termed "one of the more remarkable films about Vietnam" by *Variety* reviewer Emanuel Levy. In 1992 Duncan wrote and directed the television film *Live! From Death Row,* a criticism of television news sensationalism. The premise is that a convict on death row takes a newswoman as hostage, threatening to execute her on live TV if not freed. The film starts off "sharply" in the opinion of *People* contributor David Hiltbrand, but then succumbs to flaws which included miscasting. For *Entertainment Weekly* critic Ken Tucker, the film lacks originality in its presentation of the stories of convicts. *Variety*'s Van Gordon Sauter found the plot premise hard to swallow, and felt that the prison scenes are marred by unreality and by the characters' philosophizing. He maintained, as well, that it is impossible to decide whether the film is social criticism with exploitative overtones, or vice versa.

Duncan's next project was the working-class melodrama *A Home of Our Own,* directed by Tony Bill with Duncan acting as executive producer. In this film Kathy Bates stars as a divorced mother who, in 1962, quits her assembly-line job because of sexual harassment, then drives with her six children to Idaho, where she buys a rundown house. She succeeds in setting up a good life for her family, despite obstacles, with the assistance of a kindly Asian-American neighbor. *Variety* contributor Levy found the story idea excessively familiar, comparing *A Home of Our Own* to such film successes as *Places in the Heart* and *Alice Doesn't Live Here Anymore. Entertainment Weekly* critic Ty Burr wrote, "Duncan's memory-movie at least feels honest in its sentimentality."

In 1994 Duncan wrote and directed the low-budget *Pornographer,* which Levy interpreted as a "meditation on art vs. commerce in American life." Levy found this tale to be "intellectually pretentious" and "simplistic," its screenplay overloaded with "stereotypes and cliches." Although he enjoyed the first half-hour of the film, the script is in need of "dramatic streamlining" to rid it of trite Freudian and melodramatic aspects, Levy maintained.

Duncan's career got new impetus in the mid-1990s with the commercial success of three screenplays: *Nick of Time,* a 1995 thriller starring Johnny Depp; *Mr. Holland's Opus,* a 1996 tearjerker in which Richard Dreyfuss plays a high school music teacher; and *Courage under Fire,* a 1997 film starring Meg Ryan and Denzel Washington about the Persian Gulf War that was based on Duncan's own 1996 novel. In *Mr. Holland's Opus,* Dreyfuss, in the title role, has seen his lifelong dream of becoming a serious composer diverted into a career of helping youngsters learn a bit about music, and about themselves; in the process, he has, however, shunned his deaf son. Through a series of learning experiences, the movie covers his career from 1965 to the 1990s, climaxing at his retirement ceremony, when his grateful former students unite to play Holland's own composition, conducted by him. In talking to Duncan, Arnold decided that "Holland's origins are far more personal than topical." Though he faced rough times, the screenwriter described himself in the interview as an optimist: "Life is difficult and tough, but you can achieve a lot if you want it badly enough and apply some common sense."

Both a *New Yorker* reviewer and Richard Corliss of *Time* responded to the film as a successfully crafted but unsubtle melodrama—a "schmalz fest," in the *New Yorker* critic's words—that would succeed at the box office due to its ability to make audiences cry. Calling the script "reductive and repetitive," Corliss labeled the movie, which boasted a fully loaded soundtrack, "a greatest-hits album, with Kleenex," and wryly ob-

served that foremost among the lessons of the film, audiences "will learn that films avoid the problems they pretend to confront."

Duncan's next major project, *Courage under Fire,* was greeted with considerably more respect by critics. It is a *Rashomon*-like story of attempts to discover the truth about a military skirmish during which several soldiers are killed by investigating different participants' versions of the same events. The investigator, Lieutenant Colonel Nat Serling (Denzel Washington), has been drinking hard and alienating himself from his family because of his guilt after a friendly-fire incident in which he was involved. Now he is assigned to investigate the case of a female pilot (Meg Ryan), killed in action and now in line to become the first female combat soldier ever to receive the Medal of Honor. Suspecting that the deceased pilot is being used posthumously for political purposes, Serling asks tough questions of her crew, and finds complicated truths about courage and cowardice underlying the facts of her death. Calling *Courage under Fire* the "first major film [of the Persian Gulf War]," *New Republic* critic Stanley Kauffmann remarked that the "real subject" of Duncan's screenplay "is not a specific war but the military ethos itself." "What's interesting about Duncan's take," said David Ansen of *Newsweek,* "is that it's neither a knee-jerk put-down of the military nor simply a patriotic salute. He has bones to pick with the army's duplicitous protection of its own image, but it's the critique of an insider who believes in military values."

Duncan based the *Courage under Fire* screenplay on his own novel, which a *Publishers Weekly* reviewer found to be "exciting" and constructed "with the slick cinematic skill that has made [Duncan] a top Hollywood screenwriter." *Booklist* contributor Gilbert Taylor and *Library Journal* reviewer Charles Michaud viewed the book as a slickly conceived prelude to the movie, which, on release, was widely applauded as a serious and well-crafted piece of work. In 2002, Duncan released the novel *A Private War.* In this tale Lieutenant Colonel Meredith Cleon "arrives at Fort Hazelton, Indiana, half-convinced that someone important doesn't like her," as a *Kirkus Reviews* contributor put it. The soldier—a law-enforcement officer—faces even more worry when a woman's corpse is found on the firing range. It is up to Meredith to solve the crime and cope with army politics, sexual harassment, and the hijacking of guns. A *Publishers Weekly* reviewer noted that Duncan's "most pointed observations are those of a military run like a corporation," adding that this whodunit seems "practically begging to be made into a film."

## BIOGRAPHICAL AND CRITICAL SOURCES:

*PERIODICALS*

*Book,* July-August, 2002, Michael Phillips, review of *A Private War,* p. 78.

*Booklist,* February 15, 1996, Gilbert Taylor, review of *Courage under Fire,* p. 990.

*Commonweal,* May 5, 1989, p. 278.

*Current Cinema,* January 29, 1996, p. 93.

*Entertainment Weekly,* April 3, 1992, Ken Tucker, review of *Live! From Death Row,* p. 40; November 19, 1993, Ty Burr, review of *A Home of Our Own,* p. 70; February 7-13, 1994, p. 40; July 26, 1996, Owen Gleiberman, review of *Courage under Fire,* p. 32.

*Insight on the News,* February 19, 1986, Gary Arnold, review of *Mr. Holland's Opus* and author interview, p. 32.

*Kirkus Reviews,* January 1, 1996, p. 9; April 15, 2002, review of *A Private War,* p. 513.

*Library Journal,* February 15, 1996, Charles Michaud, review of *Courage under Fire,* p. 174; October 1, 1996, p. 47.

*National Catholic Reporter,* August 23, 1996, Joseph Cunneen, review of *Courage under Fire,* p. 10.

*New Republic,* July 29, 1996, Stanley Kauffmann, review of *Courage under Fire,* p. 24.

*Newsweek,* July 15, 1996, David Ansen, review of *Courage under Fire,* p. 59.

*New York,* July 22, 1996, p. 94.

*New Yorker,* January 29, 1996, review of *Mr. Holland's Opus,* p. 93.

*People,* April 6, 1992, David Hiltbrand, review of *Live! From Death Row,* p. 13; February 12, 1996, "Mr. Duncan's Opus" (author interview), p. 24.

*Publishers Weekly,* January 22, 1996, review of *Courage under Fire,* p. 61; May 6, 2002, review of *A Private War,* p. 34.

*Rolling Stone,* August 8, 1996, p. 68.

*Time,* January 22, 1996, Richard Corliss, review of *Mr. Holland's Opus,* p. 64; July 22, 1996, Richard Schickel, review of *Courage under Fire,* p. 94.

*Variety,* March 30, 1992, Van Gordon Sauter, review of *Live! From Death Row,* p. 81; November 1, 1993, Emanuel Levy, review of *The Pornographer,* p. 37.*

\*    \*    \*

## DUSSLING, Jennifer 1970-

*PERSONAL:* Born May 8, 1970, in Lima, PA; daughter of John and Ricky (Pfeifer) Dussling. *Education:* University of Delaware, B.A.; College of William and Mary, M.A.

*ADDRESSES: Home*—Highland Park, NJ. *Agent*—c/o Author Mail, Kane Press, 240 W. 35th St., Suite 300, New York, NY 10001.

*CAREER:* Writer; children's book editor.

*AWARDS, HONORS:* Big-Three Book Award, Nottingham City Libraries (Nottingham, England), 2003, for *A Very Strange Doll's House.*

*WRITINGS:*

*FOR CHILDREN*

*Finger Painting,* illustrated by Carrie Abel, Grosset & Dunlap (New York, NY), 1995.

*In a Dark, Dark House,* illustrated by Davy Jones, Grosset & Dunlap (New York, NY), 1995.

*Under the Sea,* illustrated by Marcos Monteiro, Grosset & Dunlap (New York, NY), 1995.

*Bossy Kiki,* illustrated by Matthew Fox, Grosset & Dunlap (New York, NY), 1996.

*Stars,* illustrated by Mavis Smith, Grosset & Dunlap (New York, NY), 1996.

*Kermit's Teeny Tiny Farm,* illustrated by Rick Brown, Grosset & Dunlap (New York, NY), 1996.

*Creep Show,* illustrated by Jeff Spackman, Grosset & Dunlap (New York, NY), 1996.

*Don't Call Me Names,* illustrated by Tom Brannon, Grosset & Dunlap (New York, NY), 1996.

*A Very Strange Doll's House,* Macmillan Children's Books (London, England), 1996, published as *A Very Strange Dollhouse,* illustrated by Sonja Lamut, Grosset & Dunlap (New York, NY), 1996.

*Don't Call Me Names!* illustrated by Tom Brannon, Grosset & Dunlap (New York, NY), 1996.

*The Princess Lost Her Locket,* illustrated by Jerry Smath, Grosset & Dunlap (New York, NY), 1996.

*Muppet Treasure Island,* Grosset & Dunlap (New York, NY), 1996.

*Top Knots: The Ultimate Bracelet and Hair-wrapping Kit,* illustrated by Edward Heins, Grosset & Dunlap (New York, NY), 1996.

*The Bunny Slipper Mystery,* illustrated by Joe Ewers, Grosset & Dunlap (New York, NY), 1997.

*A Simple Wish,* Grosset & Dunlap (New York, NY), 1997.

*Bug Off!,* illustrated by Amy Wummer, Grosset & Dunlap (New York, NY), 1997.

*The Dinosaurs of the Lost World, Jurassic Park,* Grosset & Dunlap (New York, NY), 1997.

*A Dozen Easter Eggs,* illustrated by Melissa Sweet, Grosset & Dunlap (New York, NY), 1997.

*Jewel the Unicorn,* illustrated by Rebecca McKillip Thornburgh, Grosset & Dunlap (New York, NY), 1997.

*Construction Trucks,* illustrated by Courtney, Grosset & Dunlap (New York, NY), 1998.

*Tall Tale Trouble,* illustrated by Lyndon Mosse, Grosset & Dunlap (New York, NY), 1998.

*Small Soldiers: The Movie Storybook,* Grosset & Dunlap (New York, NY), 1998.

*A Heart for the Queen of Hearts,* illustrated by Lynn Adams, Grosset & Dunlap (New York, NY), 1998.

*Slinky, Scaly Snakes,* Dorling Kindersley (New York, NY), 1998.

*The Magic Carpet Ride,* illustrated by Jerry Smath, Grosset & Dunlap (New York, NY), 1998.

*Bugs! Bugs! Bugs!,* Dorling Kindersley (New York, NY), 1998.

*Pink Snow and Other Weird Weather,* illustrated by Heidi Petach, Grosset & Dunlap (New York, NY), 1998.

*Gargoyles: Monsters in Stones,* illustrated by Peter Church, Grosset & Dunlap (New York, NY), 1999.

*Giant Squid: Mystery of the Deep,* illustrated by Pamela Johnson, Grosset & Dunlap (New York, NY), 1999.

*The 100-Pound Problem,* illustrated by Rebecca McKillip Thornburgh, Kane Press (New York, NY), 2000.

*Planets,* illustrated by Denise Ortakales, Grosset & Dunlap (New York, NY), 2000.

*Dinosaur Eggs,* illustrated by Pamela Johnson, Scholastic (New York, NY), 2000.

(Adapter) L. M. Montgomery, *Anne of Green Gables,* illustrated by Lydia Halverson, Grosset & Dunlap (New York, NY), 2001.

*Looking at Rocks,* illustrated by Alan Drew-Brook-Cormack and Tim Haggerty, Grosset & Dunlap (New York, NY), 2001.

*The Rainbow Mystery,* illustrated by Barry Gott, Kane Press (New York, NY), 2002.

*Lightning: It's Electrifying,* illustrated by Lori Osiecki, Grosset & Dunlap (New York, NY), 2002.

*Gotcha!* illustrated by John A. Nez, Kane Press (New York, NY), 2003.

*Fair Is Fair!* illustrated by Diane Palimisciano, Kane Press (New York, NY), 2003.

*SIDELIGHTS:* Jennifer Dussling, a children's book editor for a New York City publishing house, is also a prolific author of children's picture books and early readers, with more than thirty titles to her credit since 1995. She has written movie storybooks based on such popular films as *Muppet Treasure Island* and *Small Soldiers,* as well as titles in the "All Aboard Reading" and "Science Solves It" series, an adaptation of the novel *Anne of Green Gables* for younger readers, and a number of stand-alone picture books.

While growing up outside of Philadelphia, Dussling read avidly, but dreamed of becoming an artist. In college she studied both art and English literature, paving her way to a career in children's book publishing. Among her titles are several books about insects, including *Bugs! Bugs! Bugs!* for the "Eyewitness Readers" series. According to Patricia Manning of *School Library Journal, Bugs! Bugs! Bugs!* is a "chatty" book with the visually interesting, "user-friendly format" made famous by Dorling Kindersley Publishing. Also in this series is Dussling's *Slinky, Scaly Snakes,* which Jackie C. Horne called a "good" beginner nonfiction book in her *Horn Book Guide* review. Another "bug book," this time part of the "Eek! Stories to Make You Shriek" series, is *Bug Off!* Several reviewers doubted the book's ability to make anyone "shriek," and in *Horn Book Guide* Maeve Visser Knoth termed the early reader merely "serviceable."

In the "All Aboard Reading" series Dussling is responsible for several titles, including *Planets,* a "satisfying" introduction to our solar system featuring "kid-friendly examples" to quote *Booklist* contributor Gillian Engberg. Another title in this series is *Gargoyles: Monsters in Stone,* about the fanciful waterspouts featured in Gothic architecture. Writing in *School Library Journal,* Lisa Smith thought the text somewhat "choppy" yet the work generally "adequate" overall, while *Booklist* reviewer Ilene Cooper deemed *Gargoyles* a "fine treatment of an intriguing topic" and gave the book a starred review. For the "Science Solves It" series, Dussling contributed *The Rainbow Mystery* in which Annie and her friend Mike discover the science secret behind the rainbows that form on Annie's wall when the sun shines. Praising this work, Carolyn Phelan explained in her *Booklist* review that not only do the stories and illustrations appeal, they go over the top in showing the solve-the-mystery aspect of scientific investigation.

### BIOGRAPHICAL AND CRITICAL SOURCES:

*PERIODICALS*

*Booklist,* October 1, 1999, Ilene Cooper, review of *Gargoyles: Monsters in Stone,* p. 365; December 1, 2000, Gillian Engberg, review of *Planets,* p. 735; September 15, 2002, Carolyn Phelan, review of *Rainbow Mystery,* p. 239.
*Bulletin of the Center for Children's Books,* July, 1996, p. 368.
*Horn Book Guide,* spring, 1998, Maeve Visser Knoth, review of *Bug Off!,* p. 55; spring, 1999, Danielle J. Ford, review of *Bugs! Bugs! Bugs!,* p. 110; fall, 1999, Jackie C. Horne, review of *Slinky, Scaly Snakes,* p. 344; fall, 2001, Harry Clement Stubbs, review of *Planets,* p. 354; fall, 2001, Carolyn Shute, review of *Anne of Green Gables,* p. 293.
*School Library Journal,* January, 1999, Patricia Manning, review of *Bugs! Bugs! Bugs!,* p. 114; August, 1996, pp. 121, 134; February, 1998, Gale W. Sherman, review of *Bug Off!,* p. 85; November, 1999, Lisa Smith, review of *Gargoyles,* p. 136.

*ONLINE*

*Big Three Book Award,* http://kotn.ntu.ac.uk/big3/ (May 14, 2003), "Jennifer Dussling."

*   *   *

## DYJA, Thomas 1962-

*PERSONAL:* Born July 31, 1962, in Chicago, IL; son of Edward S. (a pharmacist) and Margaret (a teacher; maiden name, Hartman) Dyja; married Suzanne Gluck (a literary agent), May 12, 1990; children: Nicholas E., Kaye A. *Education:* Columbia University, B.A., 1984. *Hobbies and other interests:* Sports, film, design, history.

*ADDRESSES: Agent*—Lisa Bankoff, ICM, 40 West 57th St., New York, NY 10019.

*CAREER:* Worked at bookstores in Chicago, IL, and New York, NY, 1978-84; International Creative Management (literary agency), New York, NY, assistant agent, 1984-85; Bantam Books, New York, NY, began as assistant editor, became editor, 1988-92; Balliett & Fitzgerald (book packagers), New York, NY, began as executive editor, became partner, 1993-2002. Lecturer on Civil War topics.

*WRITINGS:*

(With Lynne Arany and Gary Goldsmith) *The Reel List* (nonfiction), Dell (New York, NY), 1995.
*Play for a Kingdom* (fiction), Harcourt (Orlando, FL), 1997.
*Meet John Trow* (novel), Viking (New York, NY), 2002.

*EDITOR*

(With Will Balliett) *The Hard Way: Writing by the Rebels Who Changed Sports,* Thunder's Mouth Press (New York, NY), 1999.
*Awake: Stories of Life-changing Epiphanies,* Marlowe (New York, NY), 2001.
*Life-changing Stories of Coming of Age,* Marlowe (New York, NY), 2001.
*Life-changing Stories of Forgiving and Being Forgiven,* Marlowe & Co. (New York, NY), 2001.

Senior editor, Illumina Books, 2000-01.

*ADAPTATIONS: Play for a Kingdom* was adapted to audio cassette. Film rights to *Meet John Trow* were optioned by New Regency.

*WORK IN PROGRESS:* Researching the early years of the National Association for the Advancement of Colored People (NAACP).

*SIDELIGHTS:* Thomas Dyja writes on the topics of personal interest to him, including sports and history. In the former category he has produced *The Hard Way: Writing by the Rebels Who Changed Sports.* This book features more than a dozen case histories of men and women who influenced their respective sports and societies, from Billie Jean King and Jim Bouton to Dennis Rodman and Babe Didrickson. Wes Lukowsky of *Booklist* found that "race is a dominant theme" in the book, which spotlights the life of early twentieth-century heavyweight Jack Johnson, who overcame racial prejudice to rise in boxing, as well as "Jackie Robinson's struggles nearly a half-century later."

In 2002 Dyja parlayed his expertise in U.S. Civil War history to publish the novel *Meet John Trow*. Set in 1999, the book features protagonist Steven Armour, a middle-aged executive tired of the rat race and frustrated by his distracted and increasingly distant wife and children. He transplants his yuppie brood from New York City to rural Connecticut, where Steven finds what he needs in a Civil War re-enactment society. Assigned the role of John Trow, a "nondescript soldier," as a *Kirkus Reviews* contributor described him, Steven finds the man's "unheroic life nevertheless begins to exert a strong fascination." This is compounded when Steven discovers Trow's secret romance with the wife of a superior officer. A contributor to *Publishers Weekly* praised Dyja's handling of the story, saying the author "charts Steven's identity crisis with sympathy and a healthy hint of sarcasm."

Dyja once told *CA:* "I have an old-fashioned view of literature: it is meant to educate and entertain. A great book is not about expression as much as it helps the reader understand other lives, other ways of life, other ways to live his or her own life. Literature exists not by its simple existence, but by what it does. I hope my work will always make readers think about how they live and how they can participate in a generous and beneficent vision of life. My favorite writers are Nelson Algren, Sherwood Anderson, E. M. Forster, and Graham Greene."

*BIOGRAPHICAL AND CRITICAL SOURCES:*

*PERIODICALS*

*Aethlon*, fall, 1998, review of *Play for a Kingdom*, p. 203.
*Booklist*, January 1, 2000, Wes Lukowsky, review of *The Hard Way: Writing by the Rebels Who Changed Sports*, p. 860.
*Boston Herald*, June 11, 2002, Judith Wynn, "Remembrance of Things Past Propels Delightful 'John Trow,'" p. 48.
*Kirkus Reviews*, June 15, 2001, review of *Awake: Stories of Life-changing Epiphanies*, p. 842; May 1, 2002, review of *Meet John Trow*, p. 595.
*Library Journal*, March 15, 1998, review of *Play for a Kingdom*, p. 44; December, 1999, Morey Berger, review of *The Hard Way*, p. 144; August, 2002, Susan Zappia, review of *Awake*, p. 106.
*New York Times Book Review*, July 14, 2002, Adam Mazmanian, review of *Meet John Trow*, p. 20.
*Publishers Weekly*, May 27, 2002, review of *Meet John Trow*, p. 34.*

# E

## EDWARDS, Clive D. 1947-

*PERSONAL:* Born March 24, 1947, in England; son of Douglas (a company secretary) and Mary (a private secretary) Edwards; married July 5, 1993; wife's name Lynne; children: Nicholas, Philip, Matthew, Tom. *Education:* Royal College of Art, doctorate, 1992.

*ADDRESSES: Home*—122 Outwoods Dr., Loughborough LE11 3LU, England. *Office*—School of Art and Design, Loughborough University, Epinal Way, Loughborough LE11 0QE, England. *E-mail*—c.edwards@lboro.ac.uk.

*CAREER:* Perrings Furnishings, London, England, retail manager, 1965-85; Victoria and Albert Museum, London, England, staff member, 1989-91; Loughborough University, Loughborough, England, began as lecturer, senior lecturer in art and design history, 1991—.

*MEMBER:* Royal Society of Arts (fellow).

*WRITINGS:*

(Author of revision) John Gloag, *Dictionary of Furniture,* expanded and revised edition, Unwin Hyman, 1990, Overlook Press (Woodstock, NY), 1991.
*Victorian Furniture: Technology and Design,* Manchester University Press (New York, NY), 1993.
*Twentieth-Century Furniture: Its Materials, Manufacture, and Markets,* Manchester University Press (New York, NY), 1994.

*Eighteenth-Century Furniture,* Manchester University Press (New York, NY), 1996.
*Encyclopaedia of Furniture Materials, Trades, and Techniques,* Ashgate (Brookfield, VT), 2000.
*Turning Houses into Homes: Retailing and Consumption of the Domestic Interior,* Ashgate (Brookfield, VT), 2003.

Contributor to books, including *Conservation of Furniture and Related Wooden Objects,* Butterworth-Heinemann (London, England), 1998; and *Dictionary of Interior Design.* Contributor of articles and reviews to periodicals, including *Studies in the Decorative Arts, Art History, Journal of Design History, Country Life, Furniture History, Burlington, History of Technology,* and *Antique Collecting.*

*WORK IN PROGRESS: Encyclopedia of Textile Furnishings,* for Ashgate, completion expected in 2004.

\*        \*        \*

## EMERSON, Earl W. 1948-

*PERSONAL:* Born July 8, 1948, in Tacoma, WA; son of Ralph W. and June (Gadd) Emerson; married Sandra Evans, April 25, 1968; children: Sara, Brian, Jeffrey. *Education:* Attended Principia College, 1966-67, and University of Washington, Seattle, 1967-68.

*ADDRESSES: Home*—North Bend, WA. *Agent*—Dominick Abel, Dominick Abel Literary Agency Inc., 146 West 82nd St., Suite 1B, New York, NY 10024. *E-mail*—author@earlemerson.com.

*CAREER:* Writer. Seattle Fire Department, Seattle, WA, lieutenant, 1978—.

*MEMBER:* Mystery Writers of America, Private Eye Writers of America.

*AWARDS, HONORS:* Shamus Award, Private Eye Writers of America, 1985, for *Poverty Bay.*

*WRITINGS:*

*MYSTERY NOVELS*

*The Rainy City,* Avon (New York, NY), 1985.
*Poverty Bay,* Avon (New York, NY), 1985.
*Nervous Laughter,* Avon (New York, NY), 1986.
*Fat Tuesday,* Morrow (New York, NY), 1987.
*Black Hearts and Slow Dancing,* Morrow (New York, NY), 1988.
*Deviant Behavior,* Morrow (New York, NY), 1988.
*Help Wanted: Orphans Preferred,* Morrow (New York, NY), 1990.
*Yellow Dog Party,* Morrow (New York, NY), 1991.
*Morons and Madmen,* Morrow (New York, NY), 1993.
*The Portland Laugher,* Ballantine (New York, NY), 1994.
*The Vanishing Smile,* Ballantine (New York, NY), 1995.
*Going Crazy in Public: A Mac Fontana Mystery,* Morrow (New York, NY), 1996.
*The Million-Dollar Tattoo,* Ballantine (New York, NY), 1996.
*Deception Pass,* Ballantine (New York, NY), 1997.
*The Dead Horse Paint Company: A Mac Fontana Mystery,* Morrow (New York, NY), 1997.
*Catfish Café,* Ballantine (New York, NY), 1998.
*Vertical Burn,* Ballantine (New York, NY), 2002.
*Into the Inferno: A Novel of Suspense,* Ballantine (New York, NY), 2003.

*SIDELIGHTS:* Earl W. Emerson has brought the crime novel into the Pacific Northwest with his books set in or near Seattle, Washington. He has created two distinctive series heroes: Thomas Black, a hard-core private detective with a strong sense of justice and morals; and Mac Fontana, a small town fire chief with more than his share of extraordinary conflagrations to fight. In his *St. James Guide to Crime and Mystery Writers* essay on Emerson, John M. Muste noted that

in all of Emerson's work, his prose "is clean and his narratives always move with considerable momentum. His plots are complicated, sometimes perhaps overly so, but the resolutions are clear." Muste added, "As a body of work, Emerson's novels provide an interesting setting, some relaxed humor and a different perspective for plots that are not always entirely fresh."

Emerson's first protagonist, Thomas Black, has appeared in almost a dozen titles. Early Black stories emphasize his toughness and independence as an ex-policeman solving crimes not for financial profit but for the satisfaction of helping to right wrongs. Through the series, Black is joined in his crime-fighting efforts by an attorney named Kathy Birchfield, for whom he develops an attraction that deepens over time. From a platonic but sexually tinged relationship through the early books, Black and Birchfield move into romance and marriage, often facing dangerous situations together. "A typical Black case," said Muste, "begins with Kathy Birchfield coming to him with fears about the fate of a friend, or bringing him a client. The novels all contain high levels of violence, and Black himself, although adept at the martial arts, comes in for beatings; like many fictional detectives, he sometimes loses the first fight but he never loses the last one."

Although one *Publishers Weekly* critic dismissed a Black novel for its "substandard Chandlerisms and a barrage of wisecracks," Emerson's works have received positive reviews. *The Portland Laugher,* for instance, was cited in *Publishers Weekly* for its "superbly worked-out plot, a narrator with a likable voice, and Emerson's clean, witty prose." Another *Publishers Weekly* reviewer praised the way the detective's personal relationships "show a vulnerable side of the tough, resourceful Black." The same reviewer noted the novels' "gritty panache."

In the more recent Black story *Catfish Café* some critics noted that Emerson departs somewhat from witty repartee to take on a more serious tone about family relationships. *Catfish Café* is about Black's investigation into a murder that might have been committed by the daughter of his one-time partner, Luther Little. Gradually, after sorting all the complicated relationships in Little's African-American family, Black surmises that the murder was the end result of an incident that occurred long ago at the café of the title. "Part social study, part whodunnit, the elegantly written *Catfish Café* does well by both," said Dick Lochte in the

*Los Angeles Times.* A *Publishers Weekly* critic similarly noted that the murder mystery itself is not the most compelling part of the novel, which "will likely leave readers more interested in the mysteries and variety of human behavior than in explications."

Beginning in 1978, Emerson has been employed as a professional firefighter in Seattle. This career led to the development of his second hero, Mac Fontana. Fontana heads a small fire department in a town near Seattle. Sometimes he must also moonlight as the town's sheriff, and he does so with great determination. From his debut appearance in *Black Hearts and Slow Dancing,* Fontana has proven a hit with the critics. A *Publishers Weekly* correspondent described him as "a no-nonsense and likable guy" whose actions show "that fire departments aren't just a bunch of guys and a couple of Dalmatians hanging out at the station." Another *Publishers Weekly* reviewer called *The Dead Horse Paint Company,* Fontana's fifth mystery, "deftly constructed [and] compelling." The reviewer continued, "Fontana . . . sifts through the rubble of broken lives to find a killer as Emerson constructs a brooding, engaging tale of personal and professional conflict."

Since character Fontana and author Emerson are both firefighters, some of the most vivid scenes in the Fontana books are, not surprisingly, of firefighters bravely performing their jobs. This is especially the case in *Vertical Burn,* according to a number of reviewers. In the opening scene, Fontana is caught in a blaze set off by arsonists that causes a wall to fall and kill his partner Finney. Although Fontana is not formally charged with wrongdoing, his peers suspect that he panicked during the incident and that this led to Finney's death. Fontana then sets out to prove his innocence and find out how the fire was started. Praising the fire scenes in the book, *Los Angeles Times* contributor Lochte felt that Emerson's descriptions were so convincing that "readers may wind up struggling to breathe," adding that the "roaring fires [are] so stunningly depicted that you can feel the heat and smell the acrid smoke." Although Michael Prager in the *Houston Chronicle* felt the story is marred by "implausibility," *Booklist* contributor Dennis Dodge called it a "thriller that delivers on thrills."

*BIOGRAPHICAL AND CRITICAL SOURCES:*

BOOKS

*St. James Guide to Crime and Mystery Writers,* 4th edition, St. James Press (Detroit, MI), 1996.

PERIODICALS

*Booklist,* June 1, 1998, Dennis Dodge, review of *Catfish Café,* p. 1731; April 1, 2002, Dennis Dodge, review of *Vertical Burn,* p. 1309.
*Denver Post,* December 7, 1997.
*Houston Chronicle,* June 30, 2002, Michael Prager, "Smoke Eater's Serenade: Firefighting Author Writes from Experience," p. 35.
*Kirkus Reviews,* June 15, 1998, review of *Catfish Café,* p. 846.
*Library Journal,* March 15, 2002, Roland Person, review of *Vertical Burn,* p. 108.
*Los Angeles Times,* August 23, 1998, Dick Lochte, "Mysteries," p. 5; June 5, 2002, Dick Lochte, "Mysteries: Sleuth Goes to Blazes to Nab Arsonists," p. E2.
*New York Times Book Review,* March 16, 1986, p. 31; March 8, 1987, p. 29; March 6, 1988, p. 22; March 18, 1990, p. 33; June 9, 2002, Marilyn Stasio, "Book Review Desk," p. 18.
*Publishers Weekly,* April 26, 1993, p. 60; August 8, 1994, p. 390; September 4, 1995, p. 52; April 29, 1996, p. 54; August 12, 1996, p. 67; May 12, 1997, p. 61; September 1, 1997, p. 100; June 1, 1998, review of *Catfish Café,* pp. 48A, 56; May 6, 2002, review of *Vertical Burn,* p. 34.*

\*          \*          \*

## EMERSON, Ken 1948-

*PERSONAL:* Born October 29, 1948, in Huntington, WV; son of Robert K. (an attorney) and Roberta Esther (a museum director; maiden name, Shinn) Emerson; married Ellen Ketchum O'Meara (a teacher), June 27, 1981; children: Maude. *Education:* Attended Groton School, Harvard University, Yale University, and Rutgers University.

*ADDRESSES: Home*—140 Bellevue Ave., Montclair, NJ 07043. *Agent*—Gloria Loomis, Watkins Loomis Agency, 133 East 35th St., Suite 1, New York, NY 10016. *E-mail*—Emersonrk@aol.com.

*CAREER: Boston Phoenix,* Boston, MA, writer and editor, 1968-77; *New York Times Magazine,* New York, NY, articles editor, 1980-89; *New York Newsday,* New York, NY, "op-ed" editor, 1990-95.

*AWARDS, HONORS:* Anschutz Distinguished Fellowship in American Studies, Princeton University, 1998-99; Writers Guild of America Award nomination, outstanding script for a documentary other than current events, 2001, for "Stephen Foster."

*WRITINGS:*

*Doo-dah!: Stephen Foster and the Rise of American Popular Culture,* Simon & Schuster (New York, NY), 1997.
(With others) "Stephen Foster" (television special), *The American Experience,* Public Broadcasting Service, 2001.
(Editor, with others) *Rethinking the Urban Agenda: Reinvigorating the Liberal Tradition in New York City and Urban America,* Century Foundation Press (New York, NY), 2001.

Contributor to periodicals, including *Wall Street Journal, Washington Post, Los Angeles Times, New York Times, Nation, New Republic,* and *Sports Illustrated.*

*WORK IN PROGRESS:* A history of popular songwriting in New York City, 1957-68, for Viking.

*SIDELIGHTS:* Ken Emerson delves into the life of one of the most influential songwriters in American history in his 1997 book *Doo-dah!: Stephen Foster and the Rise of American Popular Culture.* Foster wrote about 200 songs, including "Oh! Susannah," "Old Folks at Home" (also known as "Swanee River"), "Camptown Races," "My Old Kentucky Home," "Jeanie with the Light Brown Hair," "Beautiful Dreamer," and "Old Black Joe." As Emerson reveals, Foster also wrote songs for minstrel shows that featured white performers in blackface and skits about slavery. Emerson also recounts that Foster often sold the rights to his songs for very little money, and died an alcoholic, in poverty, at the age of thirty-seven. Yet Foster's songs remain popular, and Emerson describes their influence on the development of an American music that incorporates qualities of both European and African-American music.

Commentators noted Emerson's thorough research when reviewing *Doo-Dah!* A *Publishers Weekly* contributor called Emerson's studies "exhaustive" and ob-

served that his findings have "been meticulously worked into a vivid portrait of nineteenth-century America." Writing in *Library Journal,* Michael Colby noted that *Doo-dah!* "goes a long way towards dispelling the myths that have surrounded the composer." However, David Thigpen, writing in Chicago *Tribune Books,* maintained that the exhaustive approach has a downside, noting that "to dig deeply into Foster's life is to scrape away much of the magic of his magnificent songs." According to Thigpen, Foster's pro-slavery sympathies should be understood within the climate of his times: "Even as we are made aware of the many skeletons rattling around in Foster's closets, Emerson places him in a historical context that makes his life and art compelling."

*BIOGRAPHICAL AND CRITICAL SOURCES:*

PERIODICALS

*Atlantic,* June, 1997, p. 122.
*Kirkus Reviews,* March 15, 1997, p. 433.
*Library Journal,* May 1, 1997, Michael Colby, review of *Doo-dah!: Stephen Foster and the Rise of American Popular Culture,* p. 105.
*Los Angeles Times Book Review,* May 4, 1997, p. 4.
*New York Times Book Review,* June 22, 1997, p. 5.
*Publishers Weekly,* March 31, 1997, review of *Doo-Dah!,* pp. 53-54.
*Tribune Books* (Chicago, IL), May 4, 1997, review of *Doo-Dah!,* p. 5.
*Village Voice,* June 17, 1997, pp. 55-56.
*Washington Post Book World,* May 11, 1997, p. 3.

\*    \*    \*

**EMERY, Tom 1971-**

*PERSONAL:* Born July 27, 1971, in Urbana, IL; son of Janice Ann (Evans) Emery. *Ethnicity:* "Caucasian." *Education:* Blackburn College, B.A., 1993; Southern Illinois University—Edwardsville, M.B.A., 1995. *Politics:* Democrat. *Religion:* Presbyterian. *Hobbies and other interests:* Reading, travel, sports, the U.S. Civil War.

*ADDRESSES: Home and office*—337 East Second South St., Carlinville, IL 62626.

*CAREER:* Blackburn College, Carlinville, IL, sports information director, 1993-94, instructor in economics, 2000; *Macoupin County Enquirer,* Carlinville, IL, reporter, 1994-96; History in Print, Carlinville, IL, owner and general manager, 1997—. Monterey Coal Co., journalist, 1994-95. Melberger Award voting panel, member, 1996—; USA III football panel, member, 1997—.

*MEMBER:* Illinois State Historical Society, Macoupin County Genealogical Society, Macoupin County Civil War Round Table.

*AWARDS, HONORS:* Certificate of Excellence, Illinois State Historical Society, 1999.

*WRITINGS:*

*Richard Rowett: Thoroughbreds, Beagles, and the Civil War,* History in Print (Carlinville, IL), 1997.
*The Other John Logan: Colonel John Logan and the 32nd Illinois,* History in Print (Carlinville, IL), 1998.
*Ninteenth-Century Echoes: The Carlinville City Cemetery,* History in Print (Carlinville, IL), 2000.
*The Beagle: Its Beginnings in America,* History in Print (Carlinville, IL), 2001.
*The Memorable Month: Minor-League Baseball in Staunton, Illinois,* History in Print (Carlinville, IL), 2001.
*Hold the Fort: The Battle of Allatoona Pass,* History in Print (Carlinville, IL), 2001.
*The Macoupin County Courthouse: Scandalous Symbol,* History in Print (Carlinville, IL), 2002.
*Eddie: Lincoln's Forgotten Son,* History in Print (Carlinville, IL), 2002.

*WORK IN PROGRESS: Major Civil War Battles of Missouri;* research on Civil War history in the central Midwest.

*SIDELIGHTS:* Tom Emery once told *CA:* "When I write, I want to make a statement on subjects that have never been covered before. I like pioneering research and ideas that are brought to light for the first time or written in a way that has never been done before. Talking about new material in the best way possible is a key goal for my work.

"Like many others, I am influenced by the leaders in research who have come before me, but I draw my greatest influence from some of the historians and writers who are not mainstream. Many definitive works have been written on subjects that are not household words by authors who aren't commonplace, and I often look to them for inspiration. Likewise, the thought of doing something that's never been done is an inspiration in itself.

"I don't know that my writing process is different or unique from that of anyone else, but I pride myself on thought and planning. I spend a considerable amount of time just thinking about writing and how I'm going to do it. It helps me when I sit down to do it, because I have an established, yet flexible, plan that my writing follows. I also try to play on what I feel are my strengths, to compensate for the areas in which I am trying to improve.

"My first book is a biography of Richard Rowett, a Civil War hero and nationally recognized thoroughbred breeder who introduced the beagle hound to this country. Only a few paragraphs had ever been written about him, and he had fallen into obscurity. His was a fascinating story that deserved mention, and that was motivation enough for me."

*BIOGRAPHICAL AND CRITICAL SOURCES:*

*PERIODICALS*

*Alton Telegraph* (Alton, IL), May 1, 2001.
*Chicago Tribune,* January 16, 1998.
*St. Louis Post-Dispatch,* January 31, 2002.
*State Journal-Register* (Springfield, IL), December 28, 1997.

\*     \*     \*

## EVANS, Greg 1947-

*PERSONAL:* Born November 13, 1947, in Los Angeles, CA; son of Herman (an electrical inspector) and Virginia (a homemaker; maiden name, Horner) Evans; married Betty Ransom (a teacher and city council member), December, 1970; children: Gary, Karen.

*Education:* California State University—Northridge, B.A., 1970. *Hobbies and other interests:* Movies, plays, writing music, golf.

*ADDRESSES: Office*—c/o United Media, 200 Madison Ave., New York, NY 19916.

*CAREER:* High school art teacher in California and Australia, 1970-74; radio and television station promotion manager in Colorado Springs, CO, 1975-80; author of comic strip "Luann," 1985—. Participated in Cartoonists for Literacy campaign, 2001.

*MEMBER:* National Cartoonists Society.

*AWARDS, HONORS:* Reuben Award nomination, National Cartoonists Society, 1995 and 2002, both for "Luann."

*WRITINGS:*

*SELF-ILLUSTRATED*

*Meet Luann,* Berkeley (New York, NY), 1986.
*Why Me?,* Berkeley (New York, NY), 1986.
*Is It Friday Yet?,* Berkeley (New York, NY), 1987.
*Who Invented Brothers Anyway?,* Tor (New York, NY), 1989.
*School and Other Problems,* Tor (New York, NY), 1989.
*Homework Is Ruining My Life,* Tor (New York, NY), 1989.
*So Many Malls, So Little Money,* Tor (New York, NY), 1990.
*Pizza Isn't Everything but It Comes Close,* Tor (New York, NY), 1991.
*Dear Diary: The Following Is Top Secret,* Tor (New York, NY), 1991.
*Will We Be Tested on This?,* Tor (New York, NY), 1992.
*There's Nothing Worse Than First Period P.E.,* Tor (New York, NY), 1992.
*If Confusion Were a Class I'd Get an A,* Tor (New York, NY), 1992.
*School's OK If You Can Stand the Food,* Tor (New York, NY), 1992.
*I'm Not Always Confused, I Just Look That Way,* Tor (New York, NY), 1993.

*My Bedroom and Other Environmental Hazards,* Tor (New York, NY), 1993.
*Sometimes You Just Have to Make Your Own Rules,* Rutledge Hill Press (Nashville, TN), 1998.
*Luann,* Rutledge Hill Press (Nashville, TN), 1998.
*Passion! Betrayal! Outrage! Revenge!,* Rutledge Hill Press (Nashville, TN), 1999.

*ADAPTATIONS:* The musical play *Luann* was adapted from Evans's comic strip by Eleanor Harder and published by Pioneer Drama Service (Denver, CO), 1985.

*SIDELIGHTS:* Cartoonist Greg Evans is the creative talent behind the popular comic strip "Luann," featuring the trials and traumas of an American high school student. "Simplistically drawn, *Luann* remains a sympathetic record of the changing lifestyles of contemporary youth," maintained essayist Dennis Wepman in *One Hundred Years of American Newspaper Comics.* "Teenagers of both sexes find in the strip much that is familiar and the reassurance that they are not alone."

Evans describes himself as quite similar to the title character of his comic strip, "Luann." "She's not exceptional in any way; she's just an average kid and I was very average all through school," Evans once commented to interviewer Deborah A. Stanley. A typical teen, Luann agonizes over her appearance, spends countless hours at the mall, fights with her older brother, and loves high school heartthrob Aaron Hill from afar. School is a source of endless frustration, but Luann takes solace in friends Delta and Bernice, guidance counselor Ms. Phelps, and Puddles, her dog, to help her keep things in perspective. Of course, there is also Luann's classmate Tiffany, her snobby teen rival and source of much tension.

Born in Los Angeles, California, in 1947, Evans was a doodler since childhood and eventually studied art while a student at California State University—Northridge during the late 1960s. He began his career as an art teacher working with teens in both the United States and Australia. Other creative jobs included work as a graphic artist and promotions manager for a Colorado television station and creating a promotional robot character for use at fairs and trade shows. Although he worked at developing saleable cartoon strips for years, nothing he submitted for publication ever caught the interest of editors; nothing until "Luann," that is.

Evans began to draw the "Luann" strip in 1985, after experimenting with several other comic-book characters. As he recorded on the United Media Web site, "I began developing comic strip ideas when I was in college. Over the years, I submitted a dozen or so strips, all rejected (for good reason: they were lousy). Finally, I came up with Luann and it was accepted." The character of Luann DeGroot began with Evans's observations of his daughter. As he shared in his interview with Stanley, "I was playing around with the idea of a strip about a saucy little five-year-old, because you know how little girls are at that age—they like to put on lipstick and Mom's big high-heeled shoes and clop around the house. As I was working around those lines, I began to realize that five was so young—you don't really have any life experiences—so I kept aging the character. Finally I said, 'Oh, I'll make her a teenager because I can remember being a teenager, and I'll have something to draw upon from my school teaching experiences.'"

The "Luann" strip has evolved over the years since its debut in 1985. "Part of that was intentional and part of it just happens over the years," Evans remarked to *CA*. Some changes were the result of the artist's growing skill; others came from boredom or frustration with the material. "You'll suddenly say, 'I don't like the way I'm doing this. I'm going to figure out a better way,'" Evans explained. Luann's personality is one of several things that have changed. "In the beginning Luann was a little more cartoony and simpler, a caricature of a teenager," Evans recalled, noting that by the early 1990 she was a "much more authentic" thirteen-year-old. Timely topics introduced in the strip include drug abuse, the onset of menstruation, birth control, and teen drinking; Luann has also changed her hairstyle and had her ears pierced. In 1999, Luann aged three years, moving from junior high to high school. "I wanted her to have more adventures," Evans told interviewer Laura Groch in *Editor and Publisher*, although hastening to add that his popular character would never leave her teens. "She'll be getting her own car, so that opens up a whole can of worms."

A nationally syndicated cartoonist, Evans and fellow members of the National Cartoonists Society get together once a year to recognize the best among them with the Reuben Awards. "It's kind of like our version of the Academy Awards," Evans revealed. "The ballots go out to cartoonists around the world and we vote to nominate in various categories such as greeting card cartooning, animation, and comic strips. Then we all get together somewhere in the country and have a three-day bash and have the award ceremony. That's the place where most of the cartoonists see one another, which is nice because it's a very solitary profession. It's really good to get together with your peers and talk shop and just see everyone." In both 1995 and 2002, Evans was pulled from the crowd at the Reuben Awards reception as one of only four finalist for the as-yet-illusive honor.

While fellow artists provide a nudge to Evans's creativity, much of his inspiration has come from his children, who while growing into their teen years provided him with ready-made story lines acted out each day in his home. Before and since the home-grown teen was available, Evans relied on his and his wife's experiences as teachers. To continue to fuel "Luann," he remains a keen teen-watcher, and spends a lot of time observing teens at shopping malls and other popular hangouts. He summed up the guiding philosophy of "Luann" for interviewer Kenneth R. Shepherd, "It's tough being a teenager, but you will survive. Billions of people have survived it. Just try to have a sense of humor. And don't let anyone tell you these are the best years of your life."

## BIOGRAPHICAL AND CRITICAL SOURCES:

*BOOKS*

Evans, Greg, in an interview with Deborah A. Stanley, *Something about the Author,* Volume 73, 1992, pp. 53-56.
Evans, Greg, in an interview with Kenneth R. Shepherd, *Authors and Artists for Young Adults,* Volume 23, Gale (Detroit, MI), 1998.
*One Hundred Years of American Newspaper Comics,* edited by Maurice Horn, Random House (New York, NY), 1996.

*PERIODICALS*

*Editor and Publisher,* October 16, 1999, David Astor, "Luann Ages Three Years in Twenty-four Hours," p. 42; March 27, 2000, Laura Groch, "Small Number of Comic Strips Have Plenty of New Wrinkles," p. 33.
*Voice of Youth Advocates,* August, 1997, p. 159.

*ONLINE*

*United Media,* http://www.unitedmedia.com/comics/ (April 5, 2003), "About the Artist: Greg Evans."*

# F

## FALCK, (Adrian) Colin 1934-

*PERSONAL:* Born July 14, 1934, in London, England; son of Frederick Walter (an orphanage secretary and Baptist minister) and Jessie Dorothy (a secretarial worker; maiden name née Edmonds) Falck; married Linda Diane (a painter), 1977 (divorced 1984); married Sonja Esterhuyse (a psychotherapist), 1999; children: (first marriage) Diana, (second marriage (Damon). *Education:* Magdalen College, Oxford, B.A. (philosophy, politics, and economics), 1957, B.A. (philosophy, psychology, and physiology), 1959, M.A., 1986; University of London, Ph.D. (literary theory), 1988. *Politics:* Labour Party. *Religion:* None.

*ADDRESSES: Home*—20 Thurlow Rd., London NW3 5PP, Englang. *Agent*—John Johnson Ltd., Clerkenwell House, 45-47 Clerkenwell Green, London EC1R OHT, England.

*CAREER:* University of London, London School of Economics, London, England, lecturer in sociology, 1961-62; University of Maryland, European Division, London, part-time lecturer in philosophy, 1962-64; University of London, Chelsea College, lecturer in modern literature, 1964-84; Syracuse University, London program, part-time lecturer in literature, 1985-89; Antioch University, London program, part-time lecturer in literature; York College, York, PA, associate professor, 1989-99. The *Review* (poetry magazine), co-editor, 1962, coeditor, 1965-72; poetry editor, the *New Review,* 1974-78. *Military service:* British Army, Royal Artillery, 1952-54; Royal Air Force Volunteer Reserve, 1954-56.

*WRITINGS:*

*The Garden in the Evening: Poems from the Spanish of Antonio Machado* (pamphlet), The Review (Oxford, England), 1964.

*Promises* (poetry pamphlet), The Review (London, England), 1969.

*Backwards into the Smoke* (poetry), Carcanet (Cheadle, Cheshire, England), 1973.

(Editor, with Ian Hamilton) *Poems since 1900: An Anthology of British and American Verse in the Twentieth Century,* Macdonald & Janes (London, England), 1975.

*In This Dark Light* (poetry pamphlet), TNR (London, England), 1978.

(Editor) *Robinson Jeffers: Selected Poems,* 1987.

*Myth, Truth, and Literature: Towards a True Post-Modernism,* Cambridge University Press (New York, NY), 1989, second edition, 1994.

(Editor) *Edna St. Vincent Millay: Selected Poems: The Centenary Edition,* HarperCollins (New York, NY), 1991, Carcanet Press (Manchester, England), 1992.

*Memorabilia* (poems), Stride (Exeter, England), 1992.

*Post-Modern Love: An Unreliable Narration* (poems), Stride (Exeter, England), 1997.

*American and British Verse in the Twentieth Century: The Poetry That Matters* (critical history), Ashgate (Burlington, VT, 2003.

Contributor to literary and philosophical journals in England and the United States.

*SIDELIGHTS:* Beginning in the 1960s, Colin Falck was among the English poets who, through their association with the the poetry magazine the *Review,* tried to revive some of the ideas and methods of Imagism. Falck's earlier poems attempted to capture the emotional impact and inward truth of particular moments in time, and were often very short. His first publication was a collection of verses adapted from the Spanish of Antonio Machado in *The Garden in the Evening: Poems from the Spanish of Antonio Machado*, which a contributor to *The Oxford Companion to Twentieth-Century Poetry in English* described as "the best of the many that have been attempted. In his later work, he has moved towards more traditional verse-patterns. His *Post-Modern Love* is a sequence of fifty Petrarchan sonnets, which tells the story of a marriage."

Falck has also edited centenary selections of the American poets Robinson Jeffers and Edna St. Vincent Millay. He has written extensively about philosophy, his most ambitious contribution to this field of study so far is his *Myth, Truth, and Literature: Towards a True Post-Modernism*, which according to to a *Religious Studies* contributor discusses "the relationship between theology and literature." "*Myth, Truth, and Literature* argues that literature can reveal truths otherwise inexpressible through the use of myth," commented James Seaton in *Philosophy and Literature*. *Myth, Truth, and Literature* opposes post-structionalist and post-modernist literary theory and calls for a return to the principles of German and British romanticism.

In *American and British Verse in the Twentieth Century: The Poetry That Matters*, Falck offers a critical history of twentieth-century poetry in terms of these ideas. He aims to show—despite all its recent actual failings—what ought to be the place of poetry (and more generally of literature) in the modern human world.

Falck once commented, "My main literary interest is in poetry and is divided between 1) writing it, 2) criticizing it, and 3) trying to explain why almost no one reads it except people who i) write it, ii) criticize it, or iii) (etc. etc.)."

## BIOGRAPHICAL AND CRITICAL SOURCES:

### PERIODICALS

*Acumen*, April, 1992, William Oxley, review of *Myth, Truth, and Literature: Towards a True Post-Modernism*; October, 1992, review of *Edna St. Vincent Millay*; April, 1993, review of *Memorabilia*; January 1998, Glyn Pursglove, review of *Post-Modern Love*, p. 107.

*Agenda*, 1990, Robert Stein, review of *Myth, Truth, and Literature*, pp. 73-73; summer, 1992, Philip Hoy, review of *Memorabilia*, pp. 36-42.

*Chapman*, June, 1993, review of *Memorabilia*.

*Commentary*, June, 1992, Evelyn Toynton, review of *Edna St. Vincent Millay: Selected Poems: The Centenary Edition*, p. 59.

*Houston Post*, July, 1993, Robert Phillips, review of *Edna St. Vincent Millay*.

*Independent*, May, 1992, Jill Neville, review of *Edna St. Vincent Millay*.

*Irish Times*, June, 1992, Eavan Boland, review of *Edna St. Vincent Millay*.

*Journal of Aesthetics and Art Criticism*, winter, 1991, review of *Myth, Truth, and Literature*, p. 102.

*Literature and Theology*, April, 1991, Graham Ward, review of *Myth, Truth, and Literature*.

*London Review of Books*, June, 1992, review of *Memorabilia*.

*Modern Language Review*, April, 1992, Steven Connor, review of *Myth, Truth, and Literature*, p. 422.

*New Criterion*, April, 1992, Mary Jo Slater, review of *Edna St. Vincent Millay*, pp. 23-29.

*New Republic*, January 6, 1992, Amy Clampitt, review of *Edna St. Vincent Millay*, p. 44.

*New York Times Book Review*, March 15, 1992, Liz Rosenberg, review of *Edna St. Vincent Millay*, p. 3.

*Philosophy*, April, 1990, Martin Warner, review of *Myth, Truth, and Literature*, p. 237.

*Philosophy and Literature*, 1990, Richard Eldridge, review of *Myth, Truth, and Literature*, pp. 227-228; 1996, James Seaton, review of *Myth, Truth, and Literature*, pp. 264-266.

*PN Review*, November, 1993, review of *Memorabilia*.

*Poetry Review*, summer, 1989, Edna Longley, review of *Myth, Truth, and Literature*, pp. 15-16; summer, 1992, review of *Memorabilia*.

*PQS*, spring, 1998, review of *Post-Modern Love: An Unreliable Narration*, pp. 75-76.

*Referatedienst zur Literaturwissenschaft*, March, 1990, Rainer M. Wallat, review of *Myth, Truth, and Literature*.

*Religious Studies*, September, 1995, review of *Myth, Truth, and Literature*, p. 413.

*Reviewing Sociology*, 1990, Andrew Travers, review of *Myth, Truth, and Literature*, pp. 35-38

*St. Louis Post-Dispatch*, December, 1991, Charles Guenther, review of *Edna St. Vincent Millay*.

*Sewanee Review,* spring, 1996, Judith Weissman, review of *Myth, Truth, and Literature,* p. 35.

*Stand,* summer, 1993, review of *Memorabilia.*

*Sunday Telegraph,* April, 1992, Hugo Williams, review of *Memorabilia.*

*Theology,* August, 1991, Graham Ward, review of *Myth, Truth, and Literature.*

*Times,* May, 1992, Robert Nye, review of *Edna St. Vincent Millay.*

*Times Literary Supplement,* December 22, 1989, Michael Walters, review of *Myth, Truth, and Literature,* p. 1419; August 21, 1992, Nicholas Everett, review of *Edna St. Vincent Millay,* p. 19; January, 1998, Hugo Williams, review of *Post-Modern Love;* September 4, 1998, Janet Montefiore, "Post-Modern Love: An Unreliable Narration," p. 22.

*Zeitschrift für Anglistik and Amerikanistik,* Volume 40, 1992, Wolfgang Wicht, review of *Myth, Truth, and Literature.*

\* \* \*

**FANCHI, John R(ichard) 1952-**

*PERSONAL:* Born November 17, 1952, in Pontiac, IL; son of John Anton (a printer) and Shirley Mae (a homemaker; maiden name, Andersen) Fanchi; married Katherine Frances Goedecke, August 22, 1976; children: Anthony Clifford, Christopher John. *Education:* University of Denver, B.S. (physics), 1974; University of Mississippi, M.S., 1975; University of Houston, Ph.D. (theoretical physics), 1977.

*ADDRESSES: Home*—180 Eagle Dr., Golden, CO 80403. *Office*—Department of Petroleum Engineering, Colorado School of Mines, Golden, CO 80401. *E-mail*—jfanchi@mines.edu.

*CAREER:* Writer and educator. Worked as a reservoir management expert in North Sea, Persian Gulf, Gulf of Mexico, Alaska, and elsewhere; employed by Marathon Oil Company, Cities Service, and Getty Oil, Inc. in technology centers; Colorado School of Mines, Golden, professor of petroleum engineering; technology consultant. Principal creator, U.S. Department of Energy BOAST and BOAST II simulators; designer of computer software. Fanchi Enterprises, co-owner. Vice president of board of trustees, Littleton (CO) Public Schools, 1993-95.

*MEMBER:* International Association for Relativistic Dynamics (president).

*WRITINGS:*

*Parametrized Relativistic Quantum Theory,* Kluwer Academic (Hingham, MA), 1993.

*Principles of Applied Reservoir Simulation,* Gulf Publishing (Houston, TX), 1997, 2nd edition, Butterworth-Heinemann (Boston, MA), 2001.

*Math Refresher for Scientists and Engineers,* Wiley (New York, NY), 1997, 2nd edition, 2000.

*Integrated Flow Modeling,* Elsevier (Amsterdam, Netherlands), 2000.

*Flashpoint: Sakhalin* (fiction), Access FE Publishers (Golden, CO), 2001.

*Shared Earth Modeling,* Butterworth-Heinemann (Boston, MA), 2002.

Contributor to professional journals.

*WORK IN PROGRESS: Energy in the Twenty-first Century: The Science, Origin, Technology, and Future of Energy;* independent research into relativistic quantum theory.

*SIDELIGHTS:* John R. Fanchi once told *CA:* "The books I have written appear to be quite diverse, yet they are in fact part of my effort to understand the reality of nature. I have sought truth in every realm that I have encountered, ranging from academia to industry to public service. This search, which often feels like a Quixotic quest, has become a lifelong endeavor.

"I have found that truth is a precious commodity that many believe should be hoarded or distorted for personal gain. Publishing is a means of disseminating a perspective that can help others in their search for understanding in a complex world. The beauty of publishing is the opportunity it gives me to communicate the lessons I have learned during my quest.

"Authorship can provide tangible rewards, but I have found the intangible rewards to be much more rewarding. I have been able to communicate with others in both space and time. Authorship is like teaching: you can touch the future.

"My work is not yet done. More than twenty years ago I wrote a manuscript about a search for truth that predated the explosion of titles on the subject of universal creation and the evolution of life. I was in my early twenties and an unwelcome challenger of the status quo. Today, publishing gives me an opportunity to participate in the debate.

"The issues that appeal to me are contentious, but they are also the issues in life that matter. My publications represent my engagement in activities that are important and intellectually stimulating. They embody my effort to contribute to humanity's store of knowledge for the good of future generations."

*BIOGRAPHICAL AND CRITICAL SOURCES:*

*ONLINE*

*John R. Fanchi Home Page,* http://www.mines.edu/ ~jfanchi/ (May 21, 2003).

*Paula S. Fass*

\*    \*    \*

## FASS, Paula S. 1947-

*PERSONAL:* Born May 22, 1947, in Hannover, West Germany (now Germany); immigrated to United States, 1951; naturalized citizen, 1960; daughter of Harry (in business) and Bluma Fass; married John E. Lesch (a professor of history), July 13, 1980; children: Bluma Jessica, Charles H. T. *Education:* Barnard College, A.B. (with high honors), 1967; Columbia University, M.A., 1968, Ph.D., 1974.

*ADDRESSES: Home*—Berkeley, CA. *Office*—Department of History, University of California—Berkeley, Berkeley, CA 94720; fax: 510-643-5323. *E-mail*—psfass@socrates.berkeley.edu.

*CAREER:* U.S. Department of Health, Education, and Welfare, Office of Education, Washington, DC, intern, 1968; Rutgers University, New Brunswick, NJ, lecturer, 1972-73, assistant professor of history, 1973-74; University of California—Berkeley, assistant professor, 1974-77, associate professor, 1977-87, professor of history, 1987—, Chancellor's Professor, 1998-2001, Preston Hotchkis Professor, 2001—.

*MEMBER:* American Historical Association, Organization of American Historians, Society for the History of Childhood and Youth, Phi Beta Kappa.

*AWARDS, HONORS:* Woodrow Wilson fellow, 1967, 1971; Rockefeller Foundation humanities fellow, 1977-78; National Endowment for the Humanities fellow, 1985-86, 1994-95; Center for Advanced Study in the Behavioral Sciences, Palo Alto, CA, fellow, 1991-92.

*WRITINGS:*

*The Damned and the Beautiful: American Youth in the 1920s,* Oxford University Press (New York, NY), 1977.

*Outside In: Minorities and the Transformation of American Education,* Oxford University Press (New York, NY), 1989.

*Kidnapped: Child Abduction in America,* Oxford University Press (New York, NY), 1997.

(Coeditor) *Childhood in America,* New York University Press (New York, NY), 2000.

(Editor-in-chief) *Child and Childhood Encyclopedia,* three volumes, Macmillan (New York, NY), 2003.

Contributor to books, including *The Hofstadter Aegis,* edited by Stanley Elkins and Eric McKitrick, Knopf (New York, NY), 1974; *Television As a Cultural Force,* edited by Douglass Cater and Richard Adler, Praeger (New York, NY), 1976; *School Days, Rule Days: The Legalization of Education,* edited by David L. Kirp and Donald Jensen, Falmer Press (Philadelphia, PA), 1986; *All Our Families: New Policies for a New Century,* edited by Mary Ann Mason, Arlene Skolnick, and Stephen Sugarman, Oxford University Press (New York, NY), 1998; and *American Places: Encounters with History,* edited by William E. Leuchtenburg, Oxford University Press, 2000. Contributor to history and education journals.

*SIDELIGHTS:* Paula S. Fass once told *CA:* "In my work I have been concerned with how deviant or marginal behaviors among groups (for example, youth, immigrants, or blacks) have been incorporated into and have recreated the mainstream culture. More recently I have become interested in crimes against and by children. In my first book, *The Damned and the Beautiful: American Youth in the 1920s,* I examined deviant behavior among mainstream (and largely privileged) youth in colleges and universities. In *Outside In: Minorities and the Transformation of American Education* I argued that American education in the twentieth century cannot properly be understood without looking carefully at how various subgroups (immigrants, blacks, women, and Catholics, for example) have been incorporated by schools, and how they have changed schools. More recently, in *Kidnapped: Child Abduction in America,* I have examined how the heinous crime of child kidnapping was embedded in larger social issues to become the most feared threat to children in contemporary America.

"I was drawn to write *Kidnapped* by the need to understand why I, as a parent, had become terrified that my children might be abducted. I was clearly not alone, since the fear of kidnapping was widespread among American parents. As a historian, my first thought was to locate the source of both the phenomenon of child kidnapping and the fears in historical time. When did these start? How had they changed? Who was stealing our children? As I began to explore the subject, I realized that the problem of child kidnapping was deeply woven into the cultural fabric of the past 120 years and that to unravel the mystery of our own anxieties was to grapple with the formation of intimate emotions in the context of the evolution of the modern family and gender roles; policing, law, and court procedures; the media and the role of publicity; sexuality and the governing visions of psychology.

"At that point, my writing became an exciting exploration of the intersection of the personal and the social as I became deeply aware of the complex relationship between our crimes, our fears, and the great social changes of modern times—changes which are usually described in the most impersonal and abstract terms by historians and other social analysts. That recognition made clear to me that the book had to be written as it was experienced—as very personal stories about abducted children and their parents. It was my role as a historian to tell their stories while locating them in their full social, cultural, and historical space. For me this was a profoundly important revelation that made the writing itself a great fulfillment of vision. For the first time in my career I believed that I was the instrument of a book that had to be written and that it was my role to make sure that this happened."

*BIOGRAPHICAL AND CRITICAL SOURCES:*

*PERIODICALS*

*American Historical Review,* December, 1977; October, 1991, Miriam Cohen, review of *Outside In: Minorities and the Transformation of American Education,* p. 1311.
*American Journal of Sociology,* July, 1990, David Tyack, review of *Outside In,* p. 253.
*Booklist,* October 15, 1997, Grace Fill, review of *Kidnapped: Child Abduction in America,* p. 366.
*Historian,* winter, 2000, E. Wayne Carp, review of *Kidnapped,* p. 408.
*Journal of American History,* December, 1998, Michael Grossberg, review of *Kidnapped,* p. 1114.
*Journal of Social History,* summer, 1991, Glenn C. Altschuler, review of *Outside In,* p. 834; spring, 1999, Daniel A. Cohen, review of *Kidnapped,* p. 677.
*Library Journal,* August, 1989, Jeffrey R. Herold, review of *Outside In,* p. 146; November 15, 1997, Sandra Isaacson, review of *Kidnapped,* p. 68.
*New Republic,* March 15, 1999, Margaret Talbot, "Against Innocence," p. 27.
*New York Times,* May 4, 1977.
*New York Times Book Review,* April 24, 1977.

*ONLINE*

Banker, John V., editor, *The Worlds around Us: Conversations with University of California—Berkeley Professors* (e-book), Archpublishing.com, 1999.

\* \* \*

**FIGUEIRA, Thomas J. 1948-**

*PERSONAL:* Born December 30, 1948, in New York, NY; son of Charles P. (a salesperson) and Marion (a social worker and case aide; maiden name, Gentile) Figueira; married Sarah George (a computer text editor), August 14, 1976; children: Elizabeth Anne, Julie Rose, Charles Francis. *Education:* Fordham University, B.A. (humanities), 1970; attended University of Chicago, 1970-72; University of Pennsylvania, Ph.D. (ancient history), 1977. *Politics:* "Maverick Conservative." *Religion:* Roman Catholic.

*ADDRESSES: Home*—4 Barnett Rd., Lawrenceville, NJ 08648. *Office*—Department of Classics and Archaeology, Rutgers University, 131 George St., New Brunswick, NJ 08901-1414. *E-mail*—figueira@rci.rutgers.edu.

*CAREER:* Stanford University, Stanford, CA, acting assistant professor of classics, 1977-78; Dickinson College, Carlisle, PA, assistant professor of classics, 1978-79; Rutgers University, New Brunswick, NJ, assistant professor, 1979-85, associate professor, 1985-90, professor of classics and ancient history, 1991-99, Professor (II) of Classics and Ancient History, 1999—. Visiting scholar, School of Historical Studies, Institute for Advanced Study, Princeton University, 1985-86.

*MEMBER:* American Philological Association, American Historical Association, Archaeological Institute of America, Association of Ancient Historians.

*AWARDS, HONORS:* Fulbright research fellowship, 1976-77; National Endowment for the Humanities fellowship, 1981; Center for Hellenic Studies fellowship, Harvard University, 1982-83; research fellowship, John Simon Guggenheim Memorial Fund, 1984-85; grant from American Council of Learned Societies, 1985; travel grant, Exxon Education Foundation, 1985.

*WRITINGS:*

*Aegina: Economy and Society,* Arno (New York, NY), 1981.
(Editor, with Gregory Nagy) *Theognis and Megara: Poetry and Polis,* Johns Hopkins University Press (Baltimore, MD), 1985.
*Athens and Aegina in the Age of Imperial Colonization,* Johns Hopkins University Press (Baltimore, MD), 1991.
*Excursions in Epichoric History,* Rowman & Littlefield, 1993.
*The Power of Money: Coinage and Politics in the Athenian Empire,* University of Pennsylvania Press (Philadelphia, PA), 1998.
(With T. Corey Brennan, Rachel Hall Sternburg, and Julia Heskel) *Wisdom from the Ancients: Enduring Business Lessons from Alexander the Great, Julius Caesar, and the Illustrious Leaders of Ancient Greece and Rome,* edited by Julia Heskel, Perseus (Cambridge, MA), 2001.

Contributor to books, including *Sparta: New Perspectives,* edited by S. Hodkinson and A. Powell, 1999; contributor of articles and reviews to journals, including *Transactions of the American Philological Association.*

*WORK IN PROGRESS: Aiakos: Myth and Cult; State University Gulag: Travels in the Rutgers Archipelago* (tentative title).

*SIDELIGHTS:* Thomas J. Figueira told *CA:* "For a child who spent his formative years in Manhattan, Greek myths and history provided a passport to a richly textured world of experience. That cultural empowerment would have enriched any career, but it is my good fortune to have transformed my passion for the ancient world into a career that transcends vocation to become avocation. My early professional life has been devoted to writing on as many aspects of Greek culture as I could find time for out of my responsibilities as a teacher and colleague. Research, writing, and teaching are intimately conjoined functions in my life.

"Because I teach at a bureaucratized and politicized state university, the recovery and imparting of classical civic humanism becomes perforce a controversial endeavor. I find that much of my most eloquent prose appears in letters and documents on behalf of colleagues who are buffeted for their individuality, their unconventional views, and their commitment to their students by a depersonalized, custodial, and adversarial educational system. Over the last several years, my writing has begun to branch out from its disciplinary origins to include an exploration of educational realities and prospects, as well as the practical predicaments of the American academic. A project that will take on some of these writings has the working title *State University Gulag: Travels in the Rutgers Archipelago.*

*BIOGRAPHICAL AND CRITICAL SOURCES:*

*PERIODICALS*

*American Journal of Archaeology,* October, 1999, Harold B. Mattingly, review of *The Power of Money: Coinage and Politics in the Athenian Empire,* p. 712.
*Booklist,* November 15, 2001, Eileen Hardy, review of *Wisdom from the Ancients: Enduring Business Lessons from Alexander the Great, Julius Caesar, and the Illustrious Leaders of Ancient Greece and Rome,* p. 530.
*Classical Review,* February, 1994, p. 331.
*Classical World,* January, 1999, p. 305.
*Coin World,* June 29, 1998, p. 80.
*History: Review of New Books,* winter, 1999, Richard M. Berthold, review of *The Power of Money,* p. 87.
*Journal of Economic History,* June, 2000, Michael Clark, review of *The Power of Money,* p. 546.
*Mnenosyne,* October, 2001, Richard J. Evans, review of *The Power of Money,* p. 619.
*Religious Studies Review,* January, 1999, p. 84.
*Times Literary Supplement,* December 15, 2000, Paul Millett, review of *The Power of Money,* p. 26.*

\*      \*      \*

# FLORIDA, Richard (L.) 1957-

*PERSONAL:* Born November 26, 1957, in Newark, NJ; son of Louis and Eleanor (De Cicco) Florida; married Joye-Nathalie Davis. *Education:* Rutgers University, B.A., 1979; graduate study at Massachusetts Institute of Technology; Columbia University, Ph.D., 1986.

*ADDRESSES: Home*—411 South Highland Ave., Pittsburgh, PA 15206. *Office*—J. John Heinz III School of Public Policy and Management, Carnegie-Mellon University, 5000 Forbes Ave., Pittsburgh, PA 15213-3890. *E-mail*—florida@cmu.edu.

*CAREER:* Carnegie-Mellon University, Pittsburgh, PA, associate professor of public policy and management at J. John Heinz III School of Urban and Public Affairs and faculty member of department of engineering and public policy, 1987—. Also taught at Ohio State University. Consultant to multinational corporations and government agencies.

*AWARDS, HONORS:* Grants from National Science Foundation, Ford Foundation, Joyce Foundation, U.S. Economic Development Administration, and U.S. Department of Agriculture

*WRITINGS:*

*The Breakthrough Illusion: Corporate America's Failure to Move from Innovation to Mass Production,* Basic Books (New York, NY), 1990.
(With Martin Kenney) *Beyond Mass Production: The Japanese System and Its Transfer to the United States,* Oxford University Press (New York, NY), 1993.
*Industrializing Knowledge: University-Industry Linkages in Japan and the United States,* MIT Press (Cambridge, MA), 1999.
*The Rise of the Creative Class: And How It's Transforming Work, Leisure, Community, and Everyday Life,* Basic Books (New York, NY), 2002.

Coauthor or editor of other books. Contributor of articles to scholarly journals and trade periodicals. North American editor, *Regional Studies.*

*SIDELIGHTS:* Richard Florida once told *CA:* "My main research interests revolve around foreign direct investment in U.S. manufacturing, the Japanese 'transplant' manufacturers and U.S.-Japan joint ventures, technological innovation, industrial competitiveness, venture capital, and the structure and organization of regional innovation complexes such as Silicon Valley and the Route 128 area around Boston. I spent several years working closely with state, regional, and national officials to develop new directions for industrial, technological, and economic development policy, especially to revitalize the Rust Belt states."

Florida and coauthor Martin Kenney published *Beyond Mass Production: The Japanese System and Its Transfer to the United States* in 1994. This study illustrates the commercial and cultural impact of the arrival of Japanese "transplant" factories in the 1980s. In the authors' view, Japan "is at the centre of an epoch-making new model of technology, work and production organisation that is now being transferred to the United States and elsewhere around the globe," according to Steven Tolliday in *Business History*. Japanese-style labor practices include work teams, job rotation, and "multiskilling," as well as "quality control and quality circles, low management hierarchies and management by walking around," in the words of *Economic Geography* contributor Richard Walker.

In the first part of *Mass Production* Florida and Kenney define the Japanese industrial system; in Tolliday's opinion, "they establish a clear case that information and skills flow relatively freely in the Japanese system and that this is central to Japanese success." However, the critic added, "conduits for these flows . . . are only sketchily mapped out." To Tolliver, "the lack of definition" underlies the authors' argument, that the Japanese system has been successfully integrated into the U.S. factory culture. Walker similarly had some doubts about Florida and Kenney's argument, noting that the authors don't acknowledge the flaws in Japan's system, but overall deemed *Beyond Mass Production* "an exceedingly good book and a vital contribution to the debates over the changing face of industry and the global economy in the late twentieth century."

In 2002's *The Rise of the Creative Class: And How It's Transforming Work, Leisure, Community, and Everyday Life,* Florida theorizes that the U.S. cities enjoying the most economic growth are the ones welcoming the artistic and the offbeat. He adds that the creative class comprises gays and "bohemians" such as authors, painters, musicians, computer programmers, and entrepreneurs. "Creativity has come to be valued," Florida writes, "because new technologies, new industries, new wealth and all other good economic things flow from it."

Florida is not the first economist to make the case for creativity enhancing a community, noted Emily Eakin in her *New York Times Book Review* article. But where

the author "adds a new twist . . . is to argue that while the creative class is unquestionably a blessing to the economy as a whole, at the regional level the picture is hardly so rosy." Indeed, Florida takes to task members of the creative elite who enter a city and leave over-gentrification in their wake. "The rise of the creative class, Florida says, not only leaves the endemic injustices of American life untouched, it probably makes them worse," *Adweek* columnist Debra Goldman commented.

For those cities willing to embrace a creative class, the community must be willing to welcome creative types who seek "tolerant environments and diverse populations as well as good jobs," as Eakin explained. "In essence, Florida's advice is what any savvy consultant might tell a brand trying to boost market share: Attract lots of young people, project an image of authenticity, and generate buzz," remarked Goldman. "It works for TV networks, soft drinks and cars. Why not cities?" Using his own creativity index, Florida determines the top-five larger U.S. cities that have benefitted from the creative class: San Francisco, Austin, Texas; San Diego, Boston, and Seattle. At the bottom of Florida's list are Buffalo, New York; Las Vegas; Norfolk, Virginia; and Memphis.

## BIOGRAPHICAL AND CRITICAL SOURCES:

*BOOKS*

Florida, Richard, *The Rise of the Creative Class: And How It's Transforming Work, Leisure, Community, and Everyday Life,* Basic Books (New York, NY), 2002.

*PERIODICALS*

*Adweek,* July 15, 2002, Debra Goldman, "Consumer Republic," p. 16.

*Booklist,* June 1, 2002, Mary Whaley, review of *The Rise of the Creative Class: And How It's Transforming Work, Leisure, Community, and Everyday Life,* p. 1651.

*Business History,* October, 1994, Steven Tolliday, review of *Beyond Mass Production: The Japanese System and Its Transfer to the United States,* p. 170.

*Choice,* July-August, 1993, J. W. Leonard, review of *Beyond Mass Production,* p. 1812.

*Crain's New York Business,* November 20, 2000, Alice Lipowicz, "Do Large Gay Populations Help Build Tech Centers?," p. 22.

*Economic Geography,* January, 1994, Richard Walter, review of *Beyond Mass Production,* p. 76.

*Journal of Asian Studies,* February, 1994, Koji Taira, review of *Beyond Mass Production,* p. 212.

*Journal of Engineering and Technology Management,* June, 1994, Carl Dassbach, review of *Beyond Mass Production,* p. 171.

*Journal of Japanese Studies,* winter, 1995, Michael Smitka, review of *Beyond Mass Production,* p. 167.

*New York Times,* June 1, 2002, Emily Eakin, "The Cities and Their New Elite," p. A15.

*Planning,* July, 2002, Philip Langdon, "The Coming of the Creative Class," p. 22.

*Times Higher Education Supplement,* January 28, 1994, Tom Kemp, review of *Beyond Mass Production,* p. 25.

ONLINE

*Richard Florida Web Site,* http://www2.heinz.cmu.edu/ (September 7, 2002).*

*      *      *

# FRANCO, Jean 1924-

*PERSONAL:* Born March 31, 1924, in Dukinfield, England; naturalized United States citizen; daughter of William (a shopkeeper) and Ella (Newton) Swindells; married Juan Antonio Franco (marriage ended); children: Alexis Parke. *Education:* University of Manchester, B.A. (first-class honors), 1944, M.A., 1946; King's College, London, B.A. (first-class honors), 1960, Ph.D. (Spanish), 1964. *Hobbies and other interests:* Swimming, horse racing.

*ADDRESSES: Home*—440 Riverside Dr., New York, NY 10027. *E-mail*—jf29@columbia.edu.

*CAREER:* Educator and cultural critic. University of London, London, England, lecturer at Queen Mary College, 1960-64, reader at King's College, 1964-68; University of Essex, Colchester, England, professor of Latin-American literature, 1968-72; Stanford University, Stanford, CA, professor of Spanish and comparative literature, 1972-82; Columbia University, New York, NY, professor of Spanish, beginning 1982, then professor emerita, 1996—.

*MEMBER:* Latin-American Studies Association (founding member; treasurer, 1965-67; vice chairman, 1967-68), Modern Language Association.

*AWARDS, HONORS:* Guggenheim fellowship, 1976-77.

*WRITINGS:*

(Editor) *Cuentos americanos de nuestros dias,* Harrap (London, England), 1965.

(Editor) *Short Stories in Spanish,* Penguin (Harmondsworth, England), 1966.

*The Modern Culture of Latin America: Society and the Artist,* Praeger, 1967, revised edition, Penguin (Harmondsworth, England), 1970.

(Editor) Horacio Quiroga, *Cuentos escogidos,* Pergamon Press, 1968.

*An Introduction to Spanish-American Literature,* Cambridge University Press (Cambridge, England), 1969.

*A Literary History of Spain,* Volume VII: *Spanish-American Literature since Independence,* Harper (New York, NY), 1973.

*Poetry and Silence: César Vallejo's Sermon upon Death: The Seventeenth-Annual Lecture Delivered at Canning House, on 10th May, 1972,* Grant & Cutler, 1973.

*César Vallejo: The Dialectics of Poetry and Silence,* Cambridge University Press (New York, NY), 1976.

*Plotting Women: Gender and Representation in Mexico,* Columbia University Press (New York, NY), 1989.

(Editor, with Juan Flores and George Yúdice) *On Edge: The Crisis of Contemporary Latin-American Culture,* University of Minnesota Press (Minneapolis, MN), 1992.

*Critical Passions: Selected Essays,* edited by Mary Louise Pratt and Kathleen Newman, Duke University Press (Durham, NC), 1999.

*The Decline and Fall of the Lettered City: Latin America in the Cold War,* Harvard University Press (Cambridge, MA), 2002.

Contributor of introductions to books, including W. H. Hudson, *La Tierra purpurea; Alla lejos y hace tiempo* (translation of *Far away and Long Ago*), Biblioteca Ayacucho (Caracas, Venezuela), 1980; *In Other Words: Literature by Latinas of the United States,* edited by Roberta Fernandez, Arté Público Press (Houston, TX), 1994; and *Ecrire le Mexique,* Presses de la Sorbonne Nouvelle, 1999. Editor of Latin-American section, *Penguin Companion to Literature,* Volume III: *United States and Latin America.* Contributor of essays to journals and other periodicals, including *Times Literary Supplement, TDR,* and *Spectator.* Editor of *Tabloid* (journal), beginning 1980.

Franco's works have been translated into Spanish.

*WORK IN PROGRESS: The Absent Bourgeois,* a series of essays on the relation between literature and popular and mass culture in Latin America.

*SIDELIGHTS:* Jean Franco is an academic as well as a respected specialist on Latin-American culture and literature. She has written and edited many books in her area of expertise, ranging from literary history to poetry to gender issues in Latin America. Franco's *César Vallejo: The Dialectics of Poetry and Silence,* published in 1976, was the first full-length study in English of this major Peruvian poet.

In 1999 a collection of Franco's essays from the last three decades was published as *Critical Passions: Selected Essays.* Marcial Godoy-Anativia, writing for the *NACLA Report on the Americas,* called the book "an impressive chronicle of the work of the one of the foremost critics of Latin American culture and literature." The book is separated into four sections, highlighting the main topics of Franco's work: feminism, popular culture, literature, and Mexico. Godoy-Anativia also noted that this compilation gives the reader a close look at the skills of a "feminist critic whose commitment to social justice and uncompromising insistence on the historical and political dimensions of aesthetics and culture" have greatly influenced the work of other scholars focused on cultural criticism of Latin America. Marcus Vinicius Freitus,

writing in *World Literature Today,* remarked that *Critical Passions* "well represents the poststructuralist approach to literature."

*The Decline and Fall of the Lettered City: Latin America in the Cold War* presents Franco's theories regarding the shifts that took place within Latin-American literature during the cold war era of the mid-twentieth century. In this work she contends that these changes came about because literature suddenly became a component of the region's political environment as writers focused on topics surrounding Socialist Realism and couched within their books arguments for the preservation of cultures and the granting of political freedom. This shift toward a politicized, localized focus resulted in a declining appreciation for Latin-American literature just as it was gaining recognition among a world audience. Mark L. Grover of *Library Journal* praised *The Decline and Fall of the Lettered City* as "well-crafted and so original."

*BIOGRAPHICAL AND CRITICAL SOURCES:*

*PERIODICALS*

*American Quarterly,* September, 2001, review of *Critical Passions,* p. 511.

*Comparative Literature,* winter, 1993, Sharon Larisch, review of *Plotting Women: Gender and Representation in Mexico,* p. 92.

*Feminist Review,* autumn, 1992, Carmen Ramos Escandon, review of *Plotting Women,* p. 105.

*Hispanic American Historical Review,* May, 1979; November, 1990, Silvia M. Arrom, review of *Plotting Women,* p. 681; November, 1995, Helen Delpar, "Mediating Two Worlds: Cinematic Encounters in the Americas," p. 653; August-November, 2001, p. 771.

*Journal of Latin American Studies,* May, 1990, Judith Adler Hellman, review of *Plotting Women,* p. 412.

*Library Journal,* May 1, 2002, Mark L. Grover, review of *The Decline and Fall of the Lettered City: Latin America and the Cold War,* p. 100.

*Modern Fiction Studies,* summer, 1992, Pamela Finnegan, review of *Plotting Women,* p. 501.

*Modern Language Journal,* September, 1978.

*NACLA Report on the Americas,* May, 2000, Marcial Godoy-Anativia, review of *Critical Passions,* p. 48.

*New Statesman and Society,* December 15, 1989,
    Amanda Hopkinson, review of *Plotting Women,*
    p. 35.
*New York Review of Books,* December 21, 1978.
*Signs,* review of *Plotting Women,* p. 382.
*Times Literary Supplement,* July 14, 1989, Michael
    Wood, review of *Plotting Women,* p. 778.
*World Literature Today,* spring, 1990, Sonja Karsen,
    review of *Plotting Women,* p. 282; summer, 2000,
    Marcus Vinicius Freitas, review of *Critical Pas-
    sions,* p. 691.

\*     \*     \*

**FRANKLIN, Nat**
**See BAUER, Erwin A.**

\*     \*     \*

**FRASER, Robert (H.) 1947-**

*PERSONAL:* Born May 10, 1947, in London, England;
son of Harry McKenzie (a lawyer) and Ada Alice
(Gittins) Fraser; married Catherine Birkett (a lecturer
in law), 1987; children: Benedict Joseph. *Ethnicity:*
British. *Education:* Attended Winchester Cathedral
Choir School, 1956-60; University of Sussex, B.A.,
1968, M.A., 1970; Royal Holloway College, London,
Ph.D., 1984. *Religion:* Anglican.

*ADDRESSES: Home*—19 Belvedere Rd., London
SE19 2HJ, England. *Office*—Literature Dept., The
Open University, Walton Hall, Milton Keynes MK7
6AA, England. *E-mail*—Fras999@yahoo.co.uk.

*CAREER:* University of Cape Coast, Cape Coast,
Ghana, lecturer in English, 1970-74; University of
Leeds, Leeds, England, lecturer in English, 1974-78;
University of London, London, England, research associate at Royal Holloway and Bedford New College,
1986-91, research fellow in School of Advanced Study,
1997—; Cambridge University, Trinity College, Cambridge, England, lecturer in English, 1991-93, director
of studies in English, 1992-93; The Open University,
Milton Keynes, England, senior research fellow in literature, 1999—. Visiting professor, University of Ku-
wait, 1988, and University of Sao Paulo, 1990.

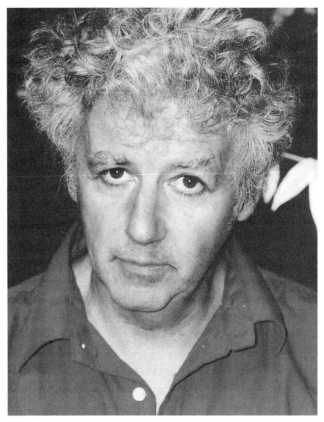

*Robert Fraser*

*MEMBER:* International PEN (England).

*AWARDS, HONORS:* Wingate scholar, Harold Hyam
Wingate Foundation, 1989-92.

*WRITINGS:*

*The Novels of Ayi Kwei Armah,* Heinemann (New
    York, NY), 1980.
*West African Poetry: A Critical History,* Cambridge
    University Press (New York, NY), 1986.
(Editor) *The Collected Poems of George Barker,* Faber
    (New York, NY), 1987.
*The Making of "The Golden Bough": The Origins and
    Growth of an Argument,* Macmillan (New York,
    NY), 1990.
*Sir James Frazer and the Literary Imagination,* Mac-
    millan (New York, NY), 1990.
*Proust and the Victorians: The Lamp of Memory,* St.
    Martin's Press (New York, NY), 1994.
(Editor and author of introduction) James George
    Frazer, *The Golden Bough: A Study in Magic and
    Religion,* Oxford University Press (New York,
    NY), 1994.

(Editor) *The Selected Poems of George Barker*, 1995.

*Victorian Quest Romance: Stevenson, Haggard, Kipling, and Conan Doyle,* Northcote House (Plymouth, England), 1998.

*Lifting the Sentence: The Poetics of Postcolonial Fiction,* Manchester University Press (Manchester, England), 1999.

*The Chameleon Poet: A Life of George Barker,* Jonathan Cape (London, England), 2001.

*Ben Okri: Towards the Invisible City,* Northcote House (Tavistock, England), 2002.

Literary editor, *West Africa,* 1978-81; contributing editor, *Wasafiri,* 1984—.

PLAYS

*Kwame's Aunt,* 1972.

*Soul Brother,* 1973.

*Gesualdo (The Life and Death of Carlo Gesualdo, Prince of Venosa): A Madrigal Show for Voices and Actor-Narrator,* produced on a tour of South Wales and the west of England by Welsh Theatre Company, 1974.

*The Last Supper,* produced in Leeds, England, at University of Leeds, 1975.

*January and May: A Chaucerian Carnival,* produced in Leeds, England, at Swarthmore Centre, 1976.

*Something in the Air,* produced in Leeds, England, at Leeds Workshop Theatre, 1977.

*A Mistress Not So Coy: A Dialogue for Two Torsos,* produced in Leeds, England, at Swarthmore Centre, 1978.

*"God's Good Englishman": An Investigation into the Life and Opinions of Dr. Samuel Johnson,* produced in Oxford, England, at Oxford Playhouse, 1984.

*"Pessima O . . .": Lord Byron and the Contessa Teresa Guiccioli,* produced in Nottinghamshire, England, 1988.

*The Parisian Painter,* produced at Buxton Opera Festival, 1989.

Thirty-six interviews with Frasier, conducted from 1993 through 1997, are stored in the British Library National Sound Archive.

*WORK IN PROGRESS:* Book with the working title *Culture and Migration.*

*SIDELIGHTS:* Former Cambridge Don, currently a fellow at the University of London and senior research fellow at The Open University in England, Robert Fraser has written a number of literary studies on a variety of authors, such as Sir James Frazer and the poet George Barker. Critics have praised his works for helping bring to light some of the forgotten, lost, or unnoticed aspects of England's literature. For example, his book *The Making of the Golden Bough,* an evocation of the imaginative genesis behind Sir James Frazer's monumental comparative study of magic and religion, was lauded by Roger Just in the *Times Literary Supplement* for its "care, precision, good sense and, given the complexity of the task, an admirable lightness of touch." Later, in editing Frazer's *The Golden Bough,* Fraser reinserted passages that had been extirpated by Frazer's wife in the 1922 version of the book because they were too controversial for the time. "Fraser's selection reinstates the passages on ancient sexuality and restores those addressing the crucifixion to their original place in the 1900 edition," according to Stan Smith in the *Review of English Studies.* This is important not only to remain true to the original work, but also because it will help readers to understand what T. S. Eliot meant when he said that Frazer's work influenced his most famous poem, *The Waste Land.* "Exegetes of The Waste Land will benefit from easy access to the mesmeric descriptions of cultic religion in the Middle East," said Smith, who added that "Robert Fraser has done a great service in thoroughly historicizing a text which remains 'one of the great classics of the world.'"

In 2001, Fraser published an extensive biography of the poet George Barker, who lived from 1913 to 1991. A largely forgotten poet today, Barker was once the darling of the literary community. He was compared to Dylan Thomas and was much admired by such giants as William Butler Yeats and T. S. Eliot, although others criticized him for the unevenness of his work. A profligate man who had several lovers and wives, and who sired fifteen children, Barker was also known for his abrupt fits of temper and almost juvenile attitude that others owed him a living. Nevertheless, his exceeding charm won him many friends and loyal followers. Fraser, who had known Barker during his later years, has the advantage of offering a personal perspective to *The Chameleon Poet: A Life of George Barker.* As Lloyd Evans wrote in the *Daily Telegraph,* "Fraser has created a fascinating tribute. His prose is of the best kind—fluent, lucid and with no 'style' peeping through anywhere. . . . The book is crammed with gossip and quotable anecdotes." However, another reviewer, *Guardian* contributor Ian Sansom, noted that Fraser's personal take on the poet paints somewhat of a one-sided story: The author "gives Barker the benefit of the doubt at every twist and turn of his extraordinary life story, absolving him of all responsibility in wrong-doing." *Sunday Times* critic Humphrey Carpenter questioned if the lengthy biography, which is over six hundred pages long, was really "justified for someone as ultimately unimportant as Barker." Nevertheless, poet Carol Ann Duffy commented in *Mail on Sunday* that Fraser's "close, shoulder-to-shoulder empathy with his subject" enlivened the book, and in *Financial Times* Poet Laureate Andrew Motion mused, "Imagine being Barker's biographer, and picking your way, unravelling . . ."

Robert Fraser told *CA:* "I was brought up within the fold of the high Anglican church, and ever since I have been preoccupied with questions of religious truth and the meeting or friction between religion and other sources of human energy, such as art, music, or sexuality. I think that much of my work could also be seen as characterized by a certain obliqueness. In *Proust and the Victorians,* for instance, I attempted a paroroma of one of the great periods of English, Scottish, and Irish culture, but viewed it through the unusual lens of Proust's imagination. Early in 2003 I offered a warning in the *Times Literary Supplement* on the dangers of the impending Iraq war, a subject that I approached sideways via the Bellicose Strain in some of Handel's oratorios. (Music has always been an importan nexus, in my theater work as elsewhere.) I believe, however, that the final justification of all good writing lies, not so much in its content, as in its form. You make a basket out of wicker; the end product, however, is not wicker: it is a basket."

*BIOGRAPHICAL AND CRITICAL SOURCES:*

*PERIODICALS*

*Daily Telegraph* (London, England), February 2, 2002, Lloyd Evans, "Give Tongue, Give Tongue: Lloyd Evans Admires a Poet Who Was Lucky to Be Given Anything."

*Financial Times* (London, England), February 9, 2002, Andrew Motion, "Equally Devoted to the Gutter and the Stars," p. 4.

*Guardian* (London, England), March 2, 2002, Ian Sansom, "Master of the Red Martini: Ian Sansom on a Lucky Poet Who Partied His Way to Posterity," p. 8.

*Mail on Sunday* (London, England), February 24, 2002, Carol Ann Duffy, "Rhapsody on a Bohemian," p. 64.

*Modern Language Review,* October, 1993, Colin Nicholson, review of *The Making of "The Golden Bough": The Origins and Growth of an Argument,* p. 954; October, 1995, W. I. Hodson, review of *Proust and the Victorians: The Lamp of Memory,* p. 1018.

*Nineteenth-Century Literature,* December, 1992, review of *Sir James Frazer and the Literary Imagination,* p. 399.

*Reference & Research Book News,* September, 1994, review of *Proust and the Victorians,* p. 40.

*Review of English Studies,* November, 1996, Stan Smith, review of *The Golden Bough: A Study in Magic and Religion,* p. 627.

*Spectator,* July 7, 1990; February 23, 2002, Frederic Raphael, "An Old Bohemian, Amoral and Fiercely Moralising," p. 37; November 16, 2002, D. J. Taylor, "Books of the Year," p. 48.

*Sunday Telegraph* (London, England), February 3, 2002, Vernon Scannell, "Faithful to His Muse, Not to His Women: Vernon Scannell on a Readable If Over-long Life of George Barker, Whose Fecundity Was Not Limited to His Poetry."

*Sunday Times* (London, England), March 17, 2002, Humphrey Carpenter, "A Pugilist Poet with a Taste for Danger," p. 44; April 27, 2003, John Hegley, "A Little Night Reading," p. 40.

*Times* (London, England), February 20, 2002, Robert Nye, "The Roaring Boy's Delinquent Spirit, in Verse and in Life," p. 18.

*Times Literary Supplement,* January 11, 1991, Roger Just, "*The Making of the Golden Bough:* The Origins and Growth of an Argument," p. 3; August 26, 1994, Edward Hughes, review of *Proust and the Victorians,* p. 11; February 22, 2002, Anthony Thwaite, "In Love with the Muse: The Early Fame and Later Neglect of George Barker," pp. 3-4; January 17, 2003, Robert Fraser, "'Whatever Is, Is Right': Handel's Penultimate Oratorio and the Pity of War," pp. 13-14.

*Victorian Studies,* spring, 1992, Robert Ackerman, review of *The Making of "The Golden Bough,"* p. 337.

*ONLINE*

*Open University Web site,* http://www.open.ac.uk/ (September 15, 2003), faculty page.

*OTHER*

*The Priest of Nemi,* BBC Radio 3, January 3, 1991.

\*   \*   \*

**FREDRICKSON, George M(arsh) 1934-**

*PERSONAL:* Born July 16, 1934, in Bristol, CT; son of George (a merchant) and Gertrude (Marsh) Fredrickson; married Helene Osouf, October 16, 1956; children: Anne Hope, Laurel, Thomas, Caroline. *Ethnicity:* "Swedish-American." *Education:* Harvard University, A.B., 1956, Ph.D., 1964; University of Oslo, graduate study, 1956-57. *Politics:* Progressive Democrat. *Hobbies and other interests:* Crossword puzzles, jazz, tennis.

*ADDRESSES: Home*—741 Esplanada Way, Stanford, CA 94305. *Office*—Department of History, Stanford University, Stanford, CA 94305. *E-mail*—fredrick@ stanford.edu.

*CAREER:* Harvard University, Cambridge, MA, instructor in history, 1963-66; Northwestern University, Evanston, IL, associate professor, 1966-71, professor of history, 1971-84, William Smith Mason professor of American history, 1979-84; Stanford University, Stanford, CA, Edgar E. Robinson professor of U.S. history, 1984—. Moscow University, Fulbright professor, 1983; Oxford University, Harmsworth Professor of American History, 1988-89. *Military service:* U.S. Navy, 1957-60; became lieutenant junior grade.

*MEMBER:* American Academy of Arts and Sciences, American Antiquarian Society, American Historical Association, Organization of American Historians (past president), Society of American Historians (fellow), Southern Historical Association.

*AWARDS, HONORS:* Guggenheim fellowship, 1967-68; Anisfield-Wolf Award in race relations, 1972, for *The Black Image in the White Mind: The Debate on*

*Afro-American Character and Destiny;* National Endowment for the Humanities fellowship, 1973-74, 1985-86; Center for Advanced Studies in the Behavioral Sciences fellowship, 1977-78; Ralph Waldo Emerson Award from Phi Beta Kappa, 1981, and Avery Craven Prize from Organization of American Historians, 1982, both for *White Supremacy: A Comparative Study in American and South African History;* Ford senior fellowship, Dubois Institute of Harvard University, 1993.

*WRITINGS:*

*The Inner Civil War: Northern Intellectuals and the Crisis of the Union,* Harper (New York, NY), 1965, with a new preface, University of Illinois Press (Urbana, IL), 1993.

*The Black Image in the White Mind: The Debate on Afro-American Character and Destiny, 1817-1914,* Harper (New York, NY), 1971.

(Contributor) Nathan I. Huggins, Martin Kilson, and Daniel M. Fox, editors, *Key Issues in the Afro-American Experience,* Harcourt (New York, NY), 1971.

*White Supremacy: A Comparative Study in American and South African History,* Oxford University Press (New York, NY), 1981.

(Contributor) *Prejudice,* Belknap Press (Oxford, England), 1982.

(With Robert A. Divine and others) *America: Past and Present,* Scott, Foresman (Glenview, IL), 1984, 4th edition, 1995.

*The Arrogance of Race: Historical Perspectives on Slavery, Racism, and Societal Inequality,* Wesleyan University Press (Middletown, CT), 1988.

*Black Liberation: A Comparative History of Black Ideologies in the United States and South Africa,* Oxford University Press (New York, NY), 1995.

*Why the Confederacy Did Not Fight a Guerrilla War after the Fall of Richmond: A Comparative View* (lecture), Gettysburg College (Gettysburg, PA), 1996.

*The Comparative Imagination: On the History of Racism, Nationalism, and Social Movements,* University of California Press (Berkeley, CA), 1997.

*Racism: A Short History,* Princeton University Press (Princeton, NJ), 2002.

*EDITOR*

Albion Tourgee, *A Fool's Errand,* Torchbooks (New York, NY), 1966.

Hinton R. Halper, *The Impending Crisis of the South,* Harvard University Press (Cambridge, MA), 1968.

*William Lloyd Garrison,* Prentice-Hall (Englewood Cliffs, NJ), 1968.

*A Nation Divided: Problems and Issues of the Civil War and Reconstruction,* Burgess (Minneapolis, MN), 1975.

Maurice Evans, *Black and White in the Southern States,* University of South Carolina Press (Columbia, SC), 2000.

*OTHER*

Contributor to *American Historical Review, Dissent, Journal of American History, Journal of Southern History, New York Review of Books,* and other periodicals.

*WORK IN PROGRESS: Difference and Power: A Short History of Racism,* for Princeton University Press; a book on the transformation of American society, 1865-1900.

*SIDELIGHTS:* In *White Supremacy: A Comparative Study in American and South African History,* George M. Fredrickson systematically analyzes the similarities and differences between the histories of the two countries. Although *New York Times Book Review* critic David Brion Davis maintained that such a comparison "evokes resistance," Robert Dawidoff suggested in his review of *White Supremacy* for the *Los Angeles Times Book Review* that Fredrickson "illustrates how clarifying and absorbing and how challenging comparative history can be. . . . [He] has written about white European domination of native and imported, slave and otherwise, unfree nonwhite people in South Africa and the United States." And, in doing so, concluded *Washington Post Book World* writer Jim Hoagland, Fredrickson "deftly picks apart the tangled threads of two brands of white power and traces them back to their sources."

In both the United States and South Africa, white supremacy began in the 1600s with the subjugation of natives who were not black; in both cases, reactions to these native groups were preceded by "rehearsals" elsewhere on the part of the parent nations. "In England," explained C. Vann Woodward in the *New York Review of Books,* "the brutal subjugation of the 'Wild Irish' . . . was such a rehearsal. At the same time the Dutch commercially exploited the East Indies with the

milder motives of trade, without the need for expropriation of the land or extermination of the natives. The English repeated their experience in colonizing America, treating the Indians as they had the 'Wild Irish.' The Dutch repeated theirs at the Cape of Good Hope." Neither the English nor the Dutch considered the indigenous populations their social or intellectual equals, and both groups found the natives unsuitable as sources of cheap labor or slaves.

Both societies solved their labor problems by importing slaves: Americans from West Africa, Cape colonists from East Africa, Madagascar, and the East Indies. Kathryn Marshall in *Commonweal* observed Fredrickson's contention that "the institution of racial slavery was intimately linked to tensions within the white social order, with the dehumanization of blacks creating a basis for inter-class unity among whites," an important consideration when dealing with the chaos of a frontier society. Eventually both slave societies developed an ideology of what Fredrickson calls "*Herrenvolk* democracy"—or as Woodward explained it, "the equality of all white males—to justify white supremacy, and each developed its own style of patriarchalism."

Despite these and other similarities, there were also important differences in the way each country developed. The Boer descendants of South Africa's Dutch settlers, for instance, were primarily herdsmen, while the white Americans were farmers who wanted to clear, cultivate and claim title to the vast lands of North America. Responsive to the demands of its citizens, the U.S. government committed itself to the spread of "civilization" and did little to protect helpless minorities. According to *New York Times Book Review* critic Davis, "these distinctive conditions of American settlement and expansion, when compared with those of South Africa, led at first to a more ruthless dispossession of the indigenes, to a more thoroughgoing commitment to Negro slavery and to a much earlier insistence on a rigid and impermeable color line." On the other hand, maintained *Washington Post Book World* reviewer Hoagland, "South Africans will also have to register Fredrickson's conclusions that for all its imperfections and fitful halts, the United States has since the Civil War worked hard at eliminating the legalized 'dominative racism' while a new central government in South Africa has moved in exactly the opposite direction, with disastrous results."

Despite the temptation to moralize, Fredrickson restrains himself "and thereby fuels the reader's thinking on the issues he raises," _Los Angeles Times Book Review_ critic Dawidoff noted. "Without saying what should or will happen, he does show what can happen here, because it did. He also suggests . . . that it might all have been different and therefore may yet be."

In 1995 Fredrickson wrote yet another book contrasting the United States and South Africa. In _Black Liberation: A Comparative History of Black Ideologies in the United States and South Africa_ he outlines the challenges faced by blacks in both countries, as they dealt with white supremacy. He also looks at the influence of communism on black leaders and black movements in the 1920s and 1930s.

Fredrickson's _The Comparative Imagination: On the History of Racism, Nationalism, and Social Movements_ proved its author to be a leading scholar on the racial struggles in the United States and South Africa. This 1997 book collects the author's essays from the past twenty years that focus on race issues in the two countries. Anthony W. Marx, reviewing _The Comparative Imagination_ for the _Journal of Interdisciplinary History,_ explained that Fredrickson "explores how and why to employ comparison, as well as its implications for the study of race generally and for the specific contrasts and similarities between South Africa and the United States." Marx went on to call the book a "crucial bridge between historical narrative and the social science analysis."

In his 2002 work, _Racism: A Short History,_ Fredrickson tracks racial enmity back to medieval days and reports that anti-Semitism had some influence on how African slave-traders rationalized their actions. He continues to follow discrimination—often referred to as the "disease"—through the European expansion and the Enlightenment of the nineteenth century. Racism climaxed in both Germany and the United States with World War II, although it continued to persist long afterward, Fredrickson explains. John Dunn, reviewing _Racism_ for the _Times Literary Supplement,_ felt that what sets Fredrickson apart from other scholars on the topic of race is "his continuing urge to widen the comparative framework he uses to understand why these relations have developed as they did."

_BIOGRAPHICAL AND CRITICAL SOURCES:_

_PERIODICALS_

_Chicago Tribune Book World,_ April 5, 1981.
_Commonweal,_ June 5, 1981.

_Comparative Sociology,_ Ivan Evans, review of _The Comparative Imagination: On the History of Racism, Nationalism, and Social Movements,_ p. 637.
_Journal of African History_ July, 2001, Shula Marks, review of _The Comparative Imagination,_ p. 330.
_Journal of American History,_ December, 1989, p. 894.
_Journal of Interdisciplinary History,_ autumn, 1998, Anthony W. Marx, review of _The Comparative Imagination,_ pp. 285-287.
_Journal of Southern History,_ August, 1990, p. 575; August, 1999, John W. Cell, review of _The Comparative Imagination,_ p. 677.
_Journal of the Society of Historians,_ spring, 1990, p. 648.
_Los Angeles Times Book Review,_ March 29, 1981.
_New York Review of Books,_ March 5, 1981; May 23, 2002, William H. McNeill, review of _Racism: A Short History,_ pp. 56-58.
_New York Times Book Review,_ January 25, 1981; March 30, 1989, p. 29; May 10. 2002, p. 16; August 11, 2002, review of _Racism,_ p. 22.
_Reviews in American History,_ June, 1990, p. 256; December, 1999, Mia Bay, review of _The Black Image in the White Mind,_ p. 646.
_Times Literary Supplement,_ June 17, 1988, p. 667; May 10, 2002, John Dunn, review of _Racism,_ p. 16.
_Washington Post Book World,_ March 1, 1981.

_ONLINE_

_Stanford University History Department Web Site,_ http://history-db.stanford.edu/ (September 7, 2002).

\*    \*    \*

## FRIEDMAN, Thomas L(oren) 1953-

_PERSONAL:_ Born July 20, 1953, in Minneapolis, MN; son of Harold Abraham and Margaret (a retired real estate broker; maiden name, Philips) Friedman; married Ann Louise Bucksbaum (a copyeditor), November 23, 1978. _Education:_ Brandeis University, B.A. (summa cum laude), 1975; St. Antony's College, Oxford, M.Phil., 1978. _Religion:_ Jewish.

_ADDRESSES: Office_—New York Times, 1627 I Street NW, Washington, DC 20006.

*Thomas L. Friedman*

*CAREER:* United Press International, correspondent in London, England, 1978-79, and Beirut, Lebanon, 1979-81; *New York Times,* New York, business reporter, 1981-82, Beirut bureau chief, 1982-84, Jerusalem bureau chief, 1984-89, Washington, DC, bureau, chief diplomatic correspondent, 1989-95, foreign affairs columnist, 1995—.

*MEMBER:* Phi Beta Kappa.

*AWARDS, HONORS:* Overseas Press Club award, 1980, for best business reporting from abroad; George Polk Award, 1982, and Pulitzer Prize and Livingston Award for Young Journalists, both 1983, all for coverage of war in Lebanon; Page One Award, New York Newspaper Guild, 1984; Colonel Robert D. Heinl, Jr., Memorial Award in Marine Corps History, Marine Corps Historical Foundation, 1985; Pulitzer Prize, 1988, for coverage of Israel; National Book Award, National Book Foundation, 1989, for *From Beirut to Jerusalem;* Pulitzer Prize, 2002, for commentary; New Israel Fund Award for Outstanding Reporting from Israel.

*WRITINGS:*

(Author of text) *War Torn* (photo collection), Pantheon, 1984.
*From Beirut to Jerusalem,* Farrar, Straus (New York, NY), 1989.
(With Richard Rhodes) *Writing in an Era of Conflict,* Library of Congress (Washington, DC), 1990.
*Israel, a Photobiography: The First Fifty Years,* Simon & Schuster (New York, NY), 1998.
*The Lexus and the Olive Tree: Understanding Globalization,* Thorndike Press (Thorndike, ME), 1999.
*Longitudes and Attitudes: Exploring the World after September 11,* Farrar, Strauss (New York, NY), 2002.

Contributor to *New York Times Magazine.*

*SIDELIGHTS:* Having survived five years of reporting from one of the most war-torn areas of the Middle East, Thomas L. Friedman decided he had had enough when he awoke one night in 1984 to find his Beirut neighborhood under mortar attack. *Chicago Tribune* reporter Kenneth R. Clark related Friedman's reaction: "I said to myself, 'This is really crazy. I'm the *New York Times* bureau chief in Beirut and my neighborhood is being shelled and it's not news. It's time to go home.'" From his assignment in Beirut, Friedman moved on to a posting in Jerusalem, where he remained until 1989. Two Pulitzer Prizes and innumerable war stories later, Friedman returned to the United States as chief diplomatic correspondent for the Washington, D.C., bureau of the *New York Times.*

*From Beirut to Jerusalem* represents the culmination of Friedman's experiences covering the Middle East, with glimpses of his youth and background. As a Jewish American, Friedman brings an enlightening perspective to discussions of Middle Eastern affairs. Barbara Newman said in the *Los Angeles Times Book Review* that Friedman "has written an intimate portrait of his ten years of reporting in the Middle East, chronicling his change from awe-struck lover of Israel to outspoken critic." Friedman's infatuation with Israel began at the age of fifteen, when he visited the country with his parents. In the introductory chapter of *From Beirut to Jerusalem,* Friedman relates an anecdote from his high school days: "I was insufferable. When the Syrians arrested thirteen Jews in Damascus,

I wore a button that said, 'Free the Damascus 13,' which most of my classmates thought referred to an underground offshoot of the Chicago 7."

*From Beirut to Jerusalem* is divided into two sections consisting of discussions of Beirut and of Jerusalem, corresponding to Friedman's assignments first as Beirut bureau chief and later as Jerusalem bureau chief for the *New York Times.* "Mr. Friedman is different when writing of Beirut than he is when writing of Jerusalem," said Roger Rosenblatt in the *New York Times Book Review.* "When he arrives in Jerusalem for the second stage of his assignment, and for the second half of the book, he becomes the political and historical analyst. Reporting from Beirut, he is, for the most part, Pandemonium's correspondent, detailing scenes of pathos and hysteria."

Rosenblatt praised Friedman's treatment of his subject. "For a writer to appear evenhanded discussing the Jews and Arabs in this situation takes little more than giving each equal space in print and ascribing as many errors and atrocities to one as to the other. Mr. Friedman, who leaves no question as to the ardor of his Jewishness, is more interestingly evenhanded in that he rarely makes judgments on specific actions. When he delivers opinions, the judgments are so cosmic and melancholy that the question of fairness does not arise. First and last he is a reporter."

Conor Cruise O'Brien said in the *New York Times,* "I warmly recommend *From Beirut to Jerusalem.* But I do have some reservations. Mr. Friedman is splendid when he is interpreting events of which he has first-hand experience. His grasp on the previous history of the Arab-Israeli conflict is not so sure." O'Brien cited a section of the book that documents Egyptian President Anwar el-Sadat's efforts to negotiate a peace treaty with Israel only after waging war in 1973. O'Brien contended that Sadat made an unreciprocated attempt for peace in 1971. "Most Israelis have forgotten that episode," O'Brien said. "It is odd that so staunch a critic of Israel as Mr. Friedman should share in that Israeli amnesia."

Friedman concluded in *From Beirut to Jerusalem* that the situation in the Middle East is not hopeless, but will require the intervention of the United States for its resolution. "Only a real friend tells you the truth about yourself," he wrote. "An American friend has to help jar these people out of their fantasies by constantly holding up before their eyes the mirror of reality."

Over the years, Friedman began to expand his focus and concentrate his attention on issues encompassing not only the Middle East, but the entire world. The hotly debated subject of globalization formed the thesis for his book *The Lexus and the Olive Tree: Understanding Globalization.* In it, he writes that, because it is driven by technology, globalization is inevitable; and he discusses the changes, some of them painful, that technology brings as the world becomes smaller and more interconnected. "We all increasingly know how each other lives. And when we all increasingly know how each other lives, we all start to demand the same things. And when we don't get them, we get mad. . . . Oh, in globalization you get mad!" He further sees globalization and access to technology as empowering the individual.

*The Lexus and the Olive Tree,* partly because of its timeliness and partly because of its controversial topic, received massive critical attention from the business, political, and technology communities, as well as the literary community. *New York Times* critic Richard Eder called *The Lexus and the Olive Tree* "a spirited and imaginative exploration of our new order of economic globalization." Christopher Farrell commented in *Business Week* that "the global economy is still evolving, and Friedman's work in progress is a timely read."

*BIOGRAPHICAL AND CRITICAL SOURCES:*

*PERIODICALS*

*American Spectator,* December, 1995, p. 38.
*Book,* July 1999, p. 83.
*Booklist,* March 1, 1999, Vernon Ford, review of *The Lexus and the Olive Tree: Understanding Globalization,* p. 1100; January 1, 2000, review of *The Lexus and the Olive Tree,* p. 816.
*Business and Society,* June, 2001, Denis Collins, review of *The Lexus and the Olive Tree,* p. 226.
*Business Economics,* July, 2000, Robert D. Shriner, review of *The Lexus and the Olive Tree,* p. 78.

*Chicago Tribune,* December 1, 1989.

*Christian Century,* November 3, 1999, John B. Cobb, Jr., "Globalization with a Human Face," p. 1054.

*Christian Science Monitor,* November 18, 1999, p. 14.

*Commentary,* October, 1999, Christopher Caldwell, review of *The Lexus and the Olive Tree,* p. 68.

*Computerworld,* January 15, 2001, Kevin Fogarty, "Moving with the Herd," p. 42.

*Detroit News,* April 19, 1983.

*Economist,* June 19, 1999, "Globalization," p. 8

*Europe,* November, 1999, Robert J. Guttman, review of *The Lexus and the Olive Tree,* p. 47.

*Foreign Affairs,* May, 1999, Barry Eichengreen, review of *The Lexus and the Olive Tree,* p. 118.

*Foreign Policy,* fall, 1999, "Dueling Globalization," p. 110.

*Globe and Mail,* June 26, 1999, p. D12.

*Harper's,* October, 1999, Thomas Frank, review of *The Lexus and the Olive Tree,* p. 72.

*Harvard Business Review,* July, 1999, p. 173.

*Kirkus Reviews,* March 15, 1999, p. 427.

*Library Journal,* April 15, 1999, Patrick J. Brunet, review of *The Lexus and the Olive Tree,* p. 112; March 15, 2000, Susan C. Awe, "Web Vision Comes of Age," p. 44.

*London Review of Books,* September 2, 1999, p. 11.

*Los Angeles Times Book Review,* July 16, 1989, p. 2; May 23, 1999, p. 3.

*Multicultural Review,* December, 1993, p. 18.

*National Journal,* May 22, 1999, Clive Crook, "The Golden Arches Theory of Metaphor Inflation," p. 1383.

*New Leader,* June 14, 1999, Peter B. Kenen, review of *The Lexus and the Olive Tree,* p. 8.

*New Republic,* June 14, 1999, David S. Landes, "Show Me the Money," p. 39.

*New Statesman,* July 5, 1999, p. 53.

*Newsweek,* July 24, 1989, p. 57.

*New Yorker,* May 10, 1999, p. 86.

*New York Review of Books,* July 15, 1999, Benjamin M. Friedman, review of *The Lexus and the Olive Tree,* p. 404.

*New York Times,* February 27, 1983; April 19, 1983; July 6, 1989; April 26, 1999, Richard Eder, "The Global Village Is Here. Resist at Your Peril," p. E8; December 5, 1999, p. 92.

*New York Times Book Review,* July 9, 1989, pp. 1, 26; April 25, 1999, Josef Joffe, review of *The Lexus and the Olive Tree,* p. 14; June 6, 1999, p. 39.

*Observer,* (London, England) June 27, 1999, p. 13.

*Progressive,* July, 1999, Amitabh Pal, review of *The Lexus and the Olive Tree,* p. 41.

*Publishers Weekly,* April 15, 1988; June 2, 1989, pp. 73-74; July 14, 1989; July 10, 1995, p. 55; March 1, 1999, review of *The Lexus and the Olive Tree,* p. 48.

*Tikkin,* July-August, 1999, David C. Korten, review of *The Lexus and the Olive Tree,* p. 71.

*Time,* July 10, 1989, p. 62.

*Times* (London, England), February 22, 1990.

*Times Literary Supplement,* June 29, 1990.

*Wall Street Journal,* May 3, 1999, p. A20.

*Washington Post,* April 18, 1999, Lester C. Thurow, "Players and Spectators," p. X05.

*Washington Post Book World,* July 16, 1989, pp. 1, 11.

*Wilson Quarterly,* summer, 1999, Robert Wright, review of *The Lexus and the Olive Tree,* p. 127.

*World Policy Journal,* winter, 1999, Sanjib Baruah, "Globalization—Facing the Inevitable?," p. 105.*

\*     \*     \*

## FRIST, Bill
### See FRIST, William H.

\*     \*     \*

## FRIST, William H. 1952-
### (Bill Frist)

*PERSONAL:* Born February 22, 1952, in Nashville, TN; son of Thomas F., Sr. (a physician) and Dorothy Harrison (a homemaker; maiden name, Cate) Frist; married March 14, 1981; wife's name Karyn (a homemaker); children: Harrison, Jonathan, Bryan. *Education:* Princeton University, A.B., 1974; Harvard University, M.D. (with honors), 1978. *Politics:* Republican. *Religion:* Presbyterian. *Hobbies and other interests:* Flying (commercial, instrument, and multi-engine ratings).

*ADDRESSES: Home*—Nashville, TN. *Office*—United States Senate, 416 Russell Senate Office Bldg., Washington, DC, 20510-4205; fax: 202-228-1264. *Agent*—Richard S. Pine, Arthur Pine Associates, Inc., 1780 Broadway, New York, NY 10019. *E-mail*—senator_frist@frist.senate.gov.

*CAREER:* Licensed to practice medicine in Massachusetts, California, Tennessee, and Washington, DC; Massachusetts General Hospital, Boston, resident in surgery, 1978-83, research fellow in surgery, 1983, chief resident and fellow in cardiothoracic surgery, 1984-85; Southampton General Hospital, Southamp-

*William H. Frist*

ton, England, senior registrar in cardiothoracic surgery, 1983; Stanford University, Stanford, CA, senior fellow and chief resident in cardiovascular surgery at Cardiac Transplant Service, 1985-86; Nashville Veterans Administration Hospital, Nashville, TN, staff surgeon, 1986-93; Vanderbilt University, Nashville, TN, assistant professor of cardiac and thoracic surgery, 1986-93, director of heart and heart-lung transplantation and surgical director of Vanderbilt Multi-Organ Transplant Center and chair of the center's executive committee, 1989-93; United States Senate, senator from Tennessee, 1995—. Diplomate, National Board of Medical Examiners, 1979, American Board of Surgery, 1990, American Board of Thoracic Surgery. National Academy of Sciences, member of Advisory Committee on Strategies for Prevention of Disease and Promotion of Health, Institute of Medicine, 1977; Tennessee Donor Services, member of board of advisers, 1986-94; United Network for Organ Sharing, chair of Communications Committee, 1989-91; Battelle Research Center, member of advisory committee, 1989-90; National Kidney Foundation of Middle Tennessee, member of board of directors, 1990-93, vice-president, 1991-92; Alliance for Health Reform, vice chair, 1995; National Heart Assist Transplant Fund, member of ad-

visory board; National Heart Transplantation Network, member of clinical advisory panel. Princeton University, member of board of trustees, 1974-78, 1991-2001; Cumberland Science Museum, member of board of directors, 1989-92; American Lung Association of Tennessee, member of board of directors, 1989-91; Leadership Nashville, member, 1990-91; Third National Bank, member of board of directors, 1990-94; American Heart Association, member of board of directors, 1990-94; Frist Center for the Visual Arts, member of board of directors, 2001—; Center for Excellence in Education, honorary board of trustees, 2001—; Center for Strategic and International Studies, member of advisory board, 2001—; Library of Congress Center for Russian Leadership Development, member of board of trustees, 2001—; National Endowment for Democracy, member of board of directors, 2001—; member of Council on Foreign Relations.

*MEMBER:* International Society for Heart and Lung Transplantation, American College of Surgeons, American Medical Association, American Society of Transplant Physicians, American Society of Transplant Surgeons, Association for Academic Surgery, Smithsonian Institution (chairman of Board of Regents, 2001—), Transplantation Society, Society of Thoracic Surgeons, Cum Laude Society, Flying Physicians' Association, American Running Association (honorary board of directors, 2001—), Southern Thoracic Surgical Association, Southeastern Surgical Congress, Tennessee Medical Association, Tennessee Transplant Society, Massachusetts Medical Society, Nashville Academy of Medicine, Nashville Cardiovascular Society, Nashville Surgical Society, Rotary Club of Nashville, Alpha Omega Alpha.

*AWARDS, HONORS:* Woodrow Wilson scholar, 1974; first place award, Texas affiliate awards competition, American Heart Association, 1978; Mead Johnson Excellence in Research Award, National Student Research Forum, 1978; President's Award for best scientific paper, Southern Thoracic Surgical Association, 1986, 1992; Distinguished Service award, Tennessee Medical Association, 1992; President's Award for Volunteer Service, 1992; Distinguished Alumnus Award, Montgomery Bell Academy, 1993; Leadership Award, Nashville Academy of Medicine and Davidson County Medical Society, 1995; Nashville Hero Award, 1996; National Public Service award, American Heart Association, 1997; Joseph F. Boyle, M.D. award for distinguished public service, American Society of Internal Medicine, 1997; Congressional Initiatives Award, American Horticultural Industry Council of the American Horticultural Therapy Association, 1997; American Chemical Society Public Service Award, 1998; National Association of Geriatric Education Centers Award, 1998; honorary doctorate of medicine, Meharry Medical College, 1999; honorary doctorate of civil laws, Rhodes College, 1999; Good Guys Award, Nashville Women's Political Caucus, 1999; Science Coalition Champion of Science Award, 1999; Hero of the Taxpayer Award, Americans for Tax Reform, 1999, 2000, 2001; First Annual Public Policy Leadership award, American Society of Transplantation, 2000; Outstanding Commitment to Local Governance of Education, special recognition award, National School Board Association, 2000; Congressional Champion award, Rotary International, 2000; Jefferson Award, American Institute for Public Service, 2000; Commitment to Parks and Recreation on a National Level Award, Tennessee Recreation and Parks Association, 2000; Award for Support of Science, Council of Scientific Society Presidents, 2000; Certificate of Merit, Tennessee Historical Commission, 2000; Legislative Recognition Award, American Ambulance Association, 2000; George E. Brown, Jr. Science-Engineering-Technology Leadership Award, Science-Engineering-Technology Work Group and the Coalition for Technology Partnerships, 2000; Spirit of Enterprise Award, 2000, 2001; Year of the Senior Award, 60-Plus Association, 2000; Champion of the Small Business Community, Small Business Survival Committee, 2000; Guardian of Small Business Award, National Federation of Independent Business, 2000; Legislator of the Year, Biotechnology Industry Association, 2000; Jefferson Award, Citizens for a Sound Economy, 2000; William V. Corr Award, Tennessee Primary Care Association, 2000; Senior Legislative Achievement Award, Seniors Coalition, 2000; SEDC Legislative Honor Roll Award, Southern Economic Development Council, 2000; Service Award for Defending America's Flag, Citizens Flag Alliance, 2000; Guardian of Small Business Award, National Federation of Independent Business, 2001; honorary doctorate of laws, Maryville College, 2001; Public Service Award, National Association of County and City Health Officials, 2001; Public Service Award, Association of Air Medical Services, 2001; Silvio Conte Award for Public Awareness and Education, Brain Injury Association, 2001; Distinguished Community Health Champion Award, National Association of Community Health Centers, 2001; Golden Plate Award, American Academy of Achievement,

2001; Congressional Service Award, InterAction American Council for Voluntary International Action, 2001; Eagle Award, Tennessee Associated Builders and Contractors, 2001; Honor Roll of Legislative Achievement in Economic Development Award, Southern Economic Development Council, 2001; Special Recognition for Service of Veterans and Veterans Programs, Disabled American Veterans, 2001; Pioneer Award for E-Mail Constituent Care, EchoMail, 2002; Publius Award for Distinguished Leadership, Center for the Study of the Presidency, 2002; Honor Award, Oncology Nursing Society, 2002; TechNet Founders Circle Award, 2002.

*WRITINGS:*

*Transplant: A Heart Surgeon's Account of the Life-and-Death Dramas of New Medicine,* Atlantic Monthly Press (New York, NY), 1989.

(Editor, with J. Harold Helderman) *Grand Rounds in Transplantation,* Chapman & Hall (New York, NY), 1995.

(With J. Lee Annis, Jr.) *Tennessee Senators, 1911-2001: Portraits of Leadership in a Century of Change,* Madison Books (Lanham, MD), 1999.

(As Bill Frist) *When Every Moment Counts: What You Need to Know about Bioterrorism from the Senate's Only Doctor,* Rowman & Littlefield (Lanham, MD), 2002.

Work represented in anthologies, including *New Frontiers of U.S. Health Policy,* Rutgers University Press, 1986; *Organ Transplantation and Replacement,* edited by G. J. Cerilli, Lippincott, 1987; *The Impact of Cardiac Surgery on the Quality of Life: Neurological and Psychological Aspects,* edited by A. Wilnee and G. Rodewald, Plenum, 1991; and *Heart and Lung Transplantation,* edited by N. Shumway and S. Shumway, 1992; *Postoperative Critical Care Procedures of the Massachusetts General Hospital,* Little, Brown, 1992; *Cardiac Anesthesia for Infants and Children,* Mosby-Year Book, 1994; *Grand Rounds in Transportation,* Chapman & Hall, 1995; *Thoracic Transplantation,* Blackwell Scientific Publications, 1995; *Disease Management: A Systems Approach to Improving Patient Outcomes,* American Hospital Publishing, 1997; and *Nashville Medicine: A History,* Association Publishing, 1999. *Transplant Science,* editorial board, 1991—. Contributor of articles to medical journals, including *American Journal of Physiology, American Journal of*

*Surgery, Cardiac Surgeon, Journal of Thoracic Cardiovascular Surgery, Annual of Thoracic Surgery, Transplantation,* and *Surgical Forum.*

*SIDELIGHTS:* After the threat of bioterrorism escalated because of the attacks on September 11, 2001, William H. Frist, a practicing physician and U.S. Senator, answered questions relating to bioterrorism in *When Every Moment Counts: What You Need to Know about Bioterrorism from the Senate's Only Doctor.* The book contains "levelheaded replies" and "quality information" according to Anne C. Tomlin, a reviewer for *Library Journal.* As a doctor and policy maker, Frist told *Chicago Tribune* writer Peter Gorner that "bioterrorism . . . meshes into public policy and health care." As the only guide to deal with bioterrorism, *When Every Moment Counts* includes answers and guidance for laypeople while interjecting candid information about the status of America's health care system by the Senate's only doctor. A reviewer for *Publishers Weekly* called the book a "reassuring, thorough resource."

## BIOGRAPHICAL AND CRITICAL SOURCES:

*PERIODICALS*

*Chicago Tribune,* April 29, 2002, Peter Gorner, "Tennessee Senator Bill Frist: Practicing Medicine in Congress," p. K0171.
*Library Journal,* May 1, 2002, Anne C. Tomlin, review of *When Every Moment Counts: What You Need to Know about Bioterrorism from the Senate's Only Doctor,* p. 126.
*Publishers Weekly,* March 25, 2002, review of *When Every Moment Counts,* p. 58.

*ONLINE*

*Bill Frist, M.D.,* http://www.senate.gov/~frist/ (June 4, 2003).*

# G

## GALBRAITH, Stuart IV 1965-

*PERSONAL:* Born December 29, 1965, in Detroit, MI; son of Stuart E. and Mary A. Galbraith; married Anne Sharp, 1990 (divorced, 1994). *Education:* Eastern Michigan University, B.A. (magna cum laude); University of Southern California, M.A., 1997.

*ADDRESSES: Home*—7400 Hollywood Blvd., No. 516, Hollywood, CA 90046.

*CAREER:* Writer.

*WRITINGS:*

*Motor City Marquees,* McFarland (Jefferson, NC), 1994.

*Japanese Science Fiction, Fantasy, and Horror Films,* McFarland (Jefferson, NC), 1994.

*The Japanese Filmography, 1900-1994,* McFarland (Jefferson, NC), 1996.

*Monsters Are Attacking Tokyo!: The Incredible World of Japanese Fantasy Films,* Feral House (Venice, CA), 1997.

*The Emperor and the Wolf: The Lives and Films of Akira Kurosawa and Toshiro Mifune,* Faber & Faber (New York, NY), 2001.

Author of "Video View," a weekly home video column in the *Ann Arbor News,* 1989-93. Contributor to magazines and newspapers, including *Filmfax, Cult Movies, Agenda,* and *Current.*

*WORK IN PROGRESS:* A book on the science fiction genre, 1977-1997.

*SIDELIGHTS:* Stuart Galbraith IV conducted extensive research on the lives of Japanese director Akira Kurosawa and actor Toshiro Mifune to write his book *The Emperor and the Wolf.* The book is a biography of two men in Japanese cinema who collaborated on sixteen films together, including *Rashomon* and *The Seven Samurai.* Galbraith extensively describes each man's background and the events that led them into cinema just after World War II. He goes into great detail explaining their cooperation on projects, the critics' responses to Kurosawa and Mifune's cinematic creations together, and the end of their friendship. With Kurosawa as director and Mifune as his leading man, they were leaders of Japanese cinema. However, after completing *Red Beard,* their last picture together, both men's careers went into decline. They died estranged and never finding the same success they experienced when working with one another.

Peter Biskind, writing in the *New York Times,* called Galbraith's book a "rare feast for lovers of Japanese cinema." But *Variety*'s Nicholas Riccardi considered the length and depth of Galbraith's description of plot synopses in *The Emperor and the Wolf* overwhelming and smothering. He concluded that *The Emperor and the Wolf* is a "disappointment" and fans of Kurosawa "will have to wait for the great [biography]." Nevertheless, *Library Journal* contributor Stephen Rees praised Galbraith's effort to tell "a little-known, sometimes inspiring story [that provides] astute reading of major themes in the work of Kurosawa and Mifune."

Galbraith once told *CA:* "Movies are my great passion, and my books and magazine articles are a means to learn more about those film areas of which I am especially fond. Also, I am attracted to subjects of which little has been written. In the case of my Japanese cinema books, I was frustrated that there was so little on this subject, other than film theory-type books or books that focus almost exclusively on so-called 'art house' films. I am amazed, for instance, there is yet to appear an English-language biography or filmography of Japan's greatest star, Toshiro Mifune.

"My interests and areas of expertise include classical Hollywood cinema, especially science fiction, horror, fantasy, comedies, musicals, and westerns; wide-screen and sound technologies and film exhibition or historic film theaters; postwar American film; and Japanese and British cinema. My influences include writers Bill Warren, Leonard Maltin, Kevin Brownlow, Donald Richie, the late Ron Haver, and Thomas Schatz; in any event, they have written some of the film books I like most. Several other associates of mine, notably writers Steve Ryfle, Ted Okuda, and R. M. Hayes, have also been major influences, as have my film history professors Rick Jewell, David Shepard, and Drew Casper. The best film book I've read in a long time was Shawn Levy's *The King of Comedy;* I would like to write something as good as that some day.

"I write in a very straightforward, matter-of-fact style. I abhor pretentiousness, particularly writing about film that ignores or dismisses the realities of how and why motion pictures are produced, released, and received by contemporary audiences and critics. I believe in exhaustive research, and for me the biggest kick about writing lies in finding those little nuggets of heretofore unknown information. I also try to inject my passion for film into my writing, while providing the reader with an entertaining and useful tool that he or she will want to keep near the video cassette recorder, one that will inspire people to seek out films they might otherwise overlook.

"Ultimately, I would like to be able to live reasonably from my writing, while working in the environment of a film archive or library."

*BIOGRAPHICAL AND CRITICAL SOURCES:*

*PERIODICALS*

*Booklist,* January 1, 2002, Gordon Flagg, review of *The Emperor and the Wolf: The Lives and Films of Akira Kurosawa and Toshiro Mifune,* p. 790.

*Choice,* September, 1996, review of *The Japanese Filmography,* p. 98.
*Economist,* February 2, 2002, review of "Dynamic Duo: Japanese Cinema."
*Film Quarterly,* winter, 1997, review of *The Japanese Filmography,* p. 64.
*Library Journal,* May 15, 1996, review of *The Japanese Filmography,* p.54; January, 2002, Stephen Rees, review of *The Emperor and the Wolf,* p. 106.
*New York Times,* April 14, 2002, Peter Biskind, "Samurai Cinema," p.23.
*Reference and Research Book News,* May, 1994, review of *Japanese Science Fiction, Fantasy and Horror Films,* p. 48; July, 1996, review of *The Japanese Filmography,* p. 60.
*RQ,* winter, 1996, review of *The Japanese Filmography,* p. 298.
*Sunday Times* (London, England), March 3, 2002, Christopher Silvester, "Japanese Cinema's Greatest Double Act; Cinema," p.42.
*TCI,* October, 1994, review of *Motor City Marquees,* p. 53.
*Times Higher Education Supplement,* March 15, 2002, Donald Richie, "Director's Cut Leaves Scars," p. 25.
*Variety,* January 28, 2002, 1995, Nicholas Riccardi, review of *The Emperor and the Wolf,* p. 40.*

*       *       *

**GARRISON, Webb B(lack) 1919-2000**
**(Gary Webster)**

*PERSONAL:* Born July 19, 1919, in Covington, GA; died July 20, 2000; son of Pinkney Jefferson and Lorena (Black) Garrison; married Mary Elizabeth Thomson, 1938; children: Carol Patricia, Webb Black, Jr., William Thomson. *Education:* Emory University, Ph.B., 1940, B.D., 1949; McKendree College, D.D., 1957.

*CAREER:* The Methodist Church, South Carolina Conference, Timmonsville, SC, pastor, 1940-49; Emory University School of Theology, Atlanta, GA, assistant dean, 1950-54; Methodist General Board of Education, Nashville, TN, staff member, 1955-57; McKendree College, Lebanon, IL, president, 1957-60; Roberts Park Methodist Church, Indianapolis, IN, pastor, 1960-63; Central Methodist Church, Evansville, IN, pastor, 1963-80; freelance writer, beginning 1980. Lecturer on communication at Methodist pastors' schools in twenty-eight states.

*WRITINGS:*

*The Preacher and His Audience,* Revell (New York, NY), 1954.

*Why You Say It,* Abingdon (Nashville, TN), 1955.

*Improve Your Church Bulletins,* Revell (New York, NY), 1957.

*Sermon Seeds from the Gospel,* Revell (New York, NY), 1958.

(Under pseudonym Gary Webster) *Codfish, Cats, and Civilization,* Doubleday (New York, NY), 1959.

(Under pseudonym Gary Webster) *Laughter in the Bible,* Bethany (Minneapolis, MN), 1960.

*Creative Imagination in Preaching,* Abingdon (Nashville, TN), 1960, published as *Taking the Drudgery Out of Sermon Preparation,* Baker Book (Grand Rapids, MI), 1975.

*Women in the Life of Jesus,* Bobbs-Merrill (Indianapolis, IN), 1962.

*A Guide to Reading the Entire Bible in One Year,* Bobbs-Merrill (Indianapolis, IN), 1963, reprinted, Rutledge Hill Press (Nashville, TN), 1999.

*The Biblical Image of the Family,* Tidings (Nashville, TN), 1965.

*What's in a Word?,* Abingdon (Nashville, TN), 1965.

*Ten Paths to Peace and Power,* Abingdon (Nashville, TN), 1966.

*Strange Bonds between Animals and Men,* Ace (New York, NY), 1966.

*Giving Wings to a Warm Heart,* Methodist Commission on Promotion and Cultivation (Evanston, IL), 1968.

*Strange Facts about the Bible,* Abingdon (Nashville, TN), 1968, reprinted Testament Books (New York, NY), 2000.

*The Ignorance Book,* Morrow (New York, NY), 1970.

*Disasters That Made History,* Abingdon (Nashville, TN), 1973.

*Sidelights on the American Revolution,* Abingdon (Nashville, TN), 1974.

*Devotions for the Middle Years,* Upper Room (Nashville, TN), 1974.

(With Halford E. Luccock) *Endless Line of Splendor,* revised edition, United Methodist Commission on Communications (Evanston, IL), 1975.

*Lost Pages from American History,* Stackpole (Harrisburg, PA), 1976.

*Strange Facts about Death,* Abingdon (Nashville, TN), 1978.

*Oglethorpe's Folly: The Birth of Georgia,* Copple House (Lakemont, GA), 1982.

*Behind the Headlines: American History's Schemes, Scandals, and Escapades,* Stackpole (Harrisburg, PA), 1983.

*A Treasury of Georgia Tales,* Rutledge Hill Press (Nashville, TN), 1987.

*The Legacy of Atlanta: A Short History,* Peachtree Publishers (Atlanta, GA), 1987.

*A Treasury of Carolina Tales,* Rutledge Hill Press (Nashville, TN), 1988.

*A Treasury of Civil War Tales,* Rutledge Hill Press (Nashville, TN), 1988.

*A Treasury of Florida Tales,* Rutledge Hill Press (Nashville, TN), 1989.

*A Treasury of White House Tales,* Rutledge Hill Press (Nashville, TN), 1989, updated edition with Beth Wieder, 2002.

*A Treasury of Christmas Stories,* Rutledge Hill Press (Nashville, TN), 1990.

*Great Stories of the American Revolution,* Rutledge Hill Press (Nashville, TN), 1990.

*A Treasury of Virginia Tales,* Rutledge Hill Press (Nashville, TN), 1991.

*Civil War Trivia and Fact Book,* Rutledge Hill Press (Nashville, TN), 1992.

*A Treasury of Ohio Tales,* Rutledge Hill Press (Nashville, TN), 1993.

*The Lincoln No One Knows: The Mysterious Man Who Ran the Civil War,* Rutledge Hill Press (Nashville, TN), 1993.

*Civil War Curiosities: Strange Stories, Oddities, Events, and Coincidences,* Rutledge Hill Press (Nashville, TN), 1994.

*More Civil War Curiosities,* Rutledge Hill Press (Nashville, TN), 1995.

*Atlanta and the War,* Rutledge Hill Press (Nashville, TN), 1995.

*White House Ladies: Fascinating Tales and Colorful Curiosities,* Rutledge Hill Press (Nashville, TN), 1996.

*A Treasury of Pennsylvania Tales,* Rutledge Hill Press (Nashville, TN), 1996.

*Unusual Persons of the Civil War,* Sergeant Kirland's (Fredericksburg, VA), 1996.

*A Treasury of Texas Tales,* Rutledge Hill Press (Nashville, TN), 1997.

*Creative Minds in Desperate Times: The Civil War's Most Sensational Schemes and Plots,* Rutledge Hill Press (Nashville, TN), 1997.

*Southern Tales,* Galahad Books (New York, NY), 1997.

*Lincoln's Little War,* Rutledge Hill Press (Nashville, TN), 1997.

*Civil War Stories: Strange Tales, Oddities, Events, and Coincidences,* Promontory Press (New York, NY), 1997.

*A Treasury of Titanic Tales,* Rutledge Hill Press (Nashville, TN), 1998.

*The Amazing Civil War,* Rutledge Hill Press (Nashville, TN), 1998.

*A Treasury of Minnesota Tales,* Rutledge Hill Press (Nashville, TN), 1998.

*Two-Thousand Questions and Answers about the Civil War: Unusual and Unique Facts about the War between the States,* Gramercy Books (New York, NY), 1998.

*True Tales of the Civil War: A Treasury of Unusual Stories During America's Most Turbulent Era,* Gramercy Books (New York, NY), 1998.

*Amazing Women of the Civil War,* Rutledge Hill Press (Nashville, TN), 1999.

*Friendly Fire in the Civil War: More Than 100 True Stories of Comrade Killing Comrade,* Rutledge Hill Press (Nashville, TN), 1999.

*Why You Say It,* MJF Books (New York, NY), 1999.

*A Treasury of Iowa Tales,* Rutledge Hill Press (Nashville, TN), 2000.

*The Unknown Civil War: Odd, Peculiar, and Unusual Stories of the War between the States,* Cumberland House (Nashville, TN), 2000.

*Civil War Hostages: Hostage Taking in the Civil War,* White Mane Books (Shippensburg, PA), 2000.

*Love, Lust, and Longing in the White House: The Romantic Relationships of America's Presidents,* Cumberland House (Nashville, TN), 2000.

*True Tales of the Civil War,* Gramercy Books (New York, NY), 2000.

*Brady's Civil War: A Collection of Memorable War Images Photographed by Mathew Brady and His Assistants,* Lyons Press (New York, NY), 2000.

(With Cheryl Garrison) *The Encyclopedia of Civil War Usage: An Illustrated Compendium of the Everyday Language of Soldiers and Civilians,* Cumberland House (Nashville, TN), 2001.

*Mutiny in the Civil War,* White Mane Books (Shippensburg, PA), 2001.

*445 Fascinating Word Origins,* Galahad Books (New York, NY), 2001.

*FOR CHILDREN*

(Under pseudonym Gary Webster) *Wonders of Science,* Sheed (London, England), 1956.

(Under pseudonym Gary Webster) *Wonders of Man,* Sheed (London, England), 1957.

(Under pseudonym Gary Webster) *The Man Who Found Out Why: The Story of Gregor Mendel,* Hawthorn (New York, NY), 1963.

(Under pseudonym Gary Webster) *Journey into Light: The Story of Louis Braille,* Hawthorn (New York, NY), 1964.

(Under pseudonym Gary Webster) *Wonders of Earth,* Sheed (London, England), 1967.

*How It Started,* Abingdon (Nashville, TN), 1972.

*Why Didn't I Think of That?,* Prentice-Hall (Old Tappan, NJ), 1977.

*OTHER*

Author of "Dixie Scrapbook," a weekly feature in *Atlanta Journal/Atlanta Constitution,* beginning 1981. Contributor to books, including *Reaching beyond Your Pulpit,* Revell (New York, NY), 1962, and *History of American Methodism,* Abingdon (Nashville, TN), 1963. Contributor to juvenile anthologies, including *Builders for Freedom,* Beckley-Cardy (Chicago, IL), 1949; *Builders for Progress,* Beckley-Cardy (Chicago, IL), 1950; *Latin American Leaders,* Beckley-Cardy (Chicago, IL), 1951; *Leaders of the Frontier,* Beckley-Cardy (Chicago, IL), 1952; *John Kieran's Treasury of Great Nature Writing,* Hanover House (New York, NY), 1957; *Illustrated Library of the Natural Sciences,* four volumes, Simon & Schuster (New York, NY), 1958; *The Bible Story Library,* Bobbs-Merrill (New York, NY), 1963; and *Audubon Nature Library,* Simon & Schuster (New York, NY), 1969. Also contributor to most annual volumes of *The Upper Room Companion* and *Upper Room Disciplines,* beginning 1959. Contributor of over 1,200 articles to numerous scientific, religious, and general periodicals, including *Christianity Today, Mature Years, Catholic Digest, St. Anthony Messenger,* and *National Enquirer.* Columnist for *Indianapolis News,* 1960-78, and *Evansville Press,* 1963-78.

*ADAPTATIONS: Wonders of Science* has been made into filmstrips and records; *Codfish, Cats and Civilization* has been made into a talking book for the blind by the Library of Congress.

*SIDELIGHTS:* Pastor and Civil War buff Webb B. Garrison wrote many books on practicing religion faithfully and even more books on the Civil War. Garrison sorted through approximately six thousand photographs taken by Mathew Brady and his team during the Civil War before selecting three hundred images for *Brady's Civil War.* The result, according to Harry Frumerman in *Library Journal,* is a book that will "appeal to Civil War buffs" that includes photos ranging from the dead and dying during battle to official portraits of commanders and political leaders.

"Friendly fire," or the killing of comrade by comrade, occurred approximately once every ten days of the Civil War, according to Garrison's research in *Friendly Fire in the Civil War.* He found that the confusion due to similarities in uniform and flags created numerous cases of mistaken identity. *Friendly Fire in the Civil War* covers famous stories of friendly fire, as well as lesser-know stories, but Garrison was not able to "add new information" to the topic, according to *Civil War History* contributor Michael P. Gray, who added that the book might be better for those with a general interest in the subject rather than academics.

Days before Webb B. Garrison's death in 2000, he and his daughter, Cheryl, completed *The Encyclopedia of Civil War Usage.* By using personal correspondence, eyewitness accounts, and official government documents and reports, the Garrisons spent thirty years compiling an encyclopedia of slang and standard English that was used by the two armies during the Civil War. A *Publishers Weekly* reviewer called the book a "delight," especially for those interested in Civil War history and linguistic origins.

Garrison once told *CA:* "Though writing is hard work, it also has strong recreational aspects. I find great satisfaction in dealing with historical and scientific topics in such fashion that the typical reader's interest is captured and held—while scholarly specialists can find no fault with the research. *The Ignorance Book* attracted little attention in the original edition, but found a large and faithful audience in Japan."

*BIOGRAPHICAL AND CRITICAL SOURCES:*

*PERIODICALS*

*Civil War History,* March, 2000, Michael P. Gray, review of *Friendly Fire in the Civil War: More Than 100 True Stories of Comrade Killing Comrade,* p.66.
*Come-All-Ye,* spring, 1992, review of *A Treasury of Florida Tales,* p. 12; fall, 1996, review of *A Treasury of Pennsylvania Tales,* p. 3; fall, 1997, review of *A Treasury of Tales Ohio Tales,* p. 10; fall, 1997, review of *A Treasury of Virginia Tales,* p. 10.
*Library Journal,* January 1, 2001, Harry Frumerman, review of *Brady's Civil War: A Collection of Memorable War Images Photographed by Mathew Brady and His Assistants,* p. 130.
*Publishers Weekly,* May 14, 2001, "Grim Glory," p. 71.*

\* \* \*

## GEORGE, Emery E(dward) 1933-

*PERSONAL:* Born May 8, 1933, in Budapest, Hungary; son of Larry H. (a tool designer) and Julianna (Deutsch) George; married Mary G. Wiedenbeck (a librarian), 1969. *Education:* University of Michigan, B.A., 1955, M.A., 1959, Ph.D., 1964.

*ADDRESSES: Home*—16 Buckingham Avenue, Trenton, NJ 08618. *E-mail*—eegeorge@hotmail.com

*CAREER:* Educator and poet. University of Illinois at Urbana-Champaign, instructor, 1964-65, assistant professor of German, 1965-66; University of Michigan, Ann Arbor, assistant professor, 1966-69, associate professor, 1969-75, professor, 1975-88, professor emeritus of German, 1988—. *Military service:* U.S. Army, 1955-58.

*MEMBER:* International Academy of Poets (Cambridge, England), Modern Language Association of America, Poetry Society of America, Hölderlin-Gesellschaft.

*AWARDS, HONORS:* Hopwood Major Award for Poetry, 1960; International Research and Exchanges Board fellowship to Hungary, 1981; Deutsche Forschungsgemeinschaft travel and research grant, 1986; *Kenyon Review* nonfiction award for literary excellence, 1991, for "The Allegory of Spandau."

*WRITINGS:*

(Editor) *Friedrich Hölderlin: An Early Modern,* University of Michigan Press (Ann Arbor, MI), 1972.

*Hölderlin's "Ars Poetica,"* Mouton (The Hague, Netherlands), 1973.

(Editor, with L. T. Frank) *Husbanding the Golden Grain: Studies in Honor of Henry W. Nordmeyer,* Department of German, University of Michigan (Ann Arbor, MI), 1973.

(Editor and contributor of translations) *Contemporary East European Poetry: An Anthology,* Ardis (Ann Arbor, MI), 1983, expanded edition, Oxford University Press (New York, NY), 1993.

*The Poetry of Miklós Radnóti: A Comparative Study,* Karz-Cohl (New York, NY), 1986.

(Editor, with D. E. Sattler) Friedrich Hölderlin, *Sämtliche Werke: Homburger Folioheft,* Stroemfeld/Roter Stern (Frankfurt am Main, Germany/Basle Switzerland), 1986.

*Hölderlin and the Golden Chain of Homer: Including an Unknown Source,* Edwin Mellen Press (Lewiston, NY), 1992.

*Hölderlin's Hymn "Der Einzige": Sources, Language, Context, Form,* Bouvier (Bonn, Germany), 1999.

*Iphigenie in Czestochowa: A Play in Five Acts,* Kylix Press (Princeton, NJ), 2001.

*Iphigenie in Manhattan: A Play in Five Acts,* Kylix Press (Princeton, NJ), 2001.

*Orest: A Play in Five Acts,* Kylix Press (Princeton, NJ), 2001.

*Iphigenie in Auschwitz: A Play in Five Acts,* Kylix Press (Princeton, NJ), 2001.

*POETRY*

*Mountainwild,* Kylix Press (Ann Arbor, MI), 1974.

*Black Jesus,* Kylix Press (Ann Arbor, MI), 1974.

*A Gift of Nerve: Poems, 1966-1977,* Kylix Press (Ann Arbor, MI), 1978.

*Kate's Death: A Book of Odes,* Ardis (Ann Arbor, MI), 1980.

*The Boy and the Monarch: Sonnets and Variations,* Ardis (Ann Arbor, MI), 1987.

*Voiceprints,* Ardis (Ann Arbor, MI), 1987.

*Blackbird: A Book of Poems on the World and Work of Franz Kafka,* Mellen Poetry Press (Lewiston, NY), 1993.

*Valse Triste: Songs and Ballads,* Mellen Poetry Press (Lewiston, NY), 1997.

*Compass Card: One Hundred Villanelles,* Mellen Poetry Press (Lewiston, NY), 2000.

*TRANSLATOR*

Miklós Radnóti, *Subway Stops: Fifty Poems,* Ardis (Ann Arbor, MI), 1977.

Miklós Radnóti, *The Complete Poetry,* Ardis (Ann Arbor, MI), 1980.

(And editor) János Pilinszky, *Metropolitan Icons: Selected Poems in Hungarian and English,* Edwin Mellen Press (Lewiston, NY), 1995.

Contributor of poems to books, including *Lyrics of Love: A Treasury of Romantic Poetry,* Young Publication, 1972; *The Ardis Anthology of New American Poetry,* Ardis, 1977; *Shaping: New Poems in Traditional Prosodies,* Dryad, 1978; *Anthology of Magazine Verse and Yearbook of American Poetry,* Monitor Book, 1980, 1981, 1984, 1985; *The Hopwood Anthology: Five Decades of American Poetry,* University of Michigan Press (Ann Arbor, MI), 1981; *A Year in Poetry: A Treasure of Classic and Modern Verses for Every Date on the Calendar,* Crown (New York, NY), 1995; and *Gods and Mortals: Modern Poems on Classical Myths,* Oxford University Press (New York, NY), 2001. Contributor to periodicals, including *Blue Unicorn, Denver Quarterly, Poetry, Partisan Review, Beloit Poetry Journal, College English, Colorado Quarterly, Kansas Quarterly, Kenyon Review, Literary Review, Modern Poetry Studies, Poetry Northwest, South Dakota Review,* and *Journal of New Jersey Poets.*

Contributor of translations to *Modern European Poetry,* edited by Willis Barnstone, Bantam (New York, NY), 1966; Anna Akhmatova, *Sochineniia tom vtoroi* (title means "Works: Volume II"), Interlanguage Literary Associates, 1968; *Baltic Literature,* edited by Aleksis Rubulis, University of Notre Dame Press, 1970; *Voices within the Ark: The Modern Jewish Poets,* Avon (New York, NY), 1980; *New Directions in Prose and*

*Poetry,* no. 42, New Directions (New York, NY), 1981; *Against Forgetting: Twentieth-Century Poetry of Witness,* W. W. Norton (New York, NY), 1993 and subsequent reprintings.

Contributor of articles and reviews to journals, including *Kenyon Review, Saturday Review, Michigan Quarterly Review, Germanic Review, Hölderlin-Jahrbuch, Journal of English and Germanic Philology, Language and Style, Michigan Germanic Studies, The Modern Language Review, Orbis litterarum, Publications of the Modern Language Association of America,* and *Texas Studies in Literature and Language.* Associate editor, *Russian Literature Triquarterly,* 1972-84; founding editor, *Michigan Germanic Studies,* 1975-76; coeditor, *Frankfurter Hölderlin-Ausgabe,* beginning 1978.

*WORK IN PROGRESS:* A book on Goethe's poetic language; translations of Hungarian poems.

*SIDELIGHTS:* Emery E. George, an author and professor emeritus of German, has written numerous books on the writings of German poet Friedrich Hölderlin. His 1992 book *Hölderlin and the Golden Chain of Homer: Including a Unknown Source* focuses on the idea of *the Great Chain,* which is the belief that the universe is made up of a hierarchically connected cycle of creatures, ranging from lowest to highest. George connects this belief with the works of Hölderlin by referring to writings of Cardinal Bellarmino (published in 1615). George also offers evidence asserting that the *golden chain* found in the works of Homer is a metaphor for the *Great Chain of Being.* Timothy Torno, reviewing the book in *Journal of English and Germanic Philology,* maintained that while George clearly conducted excellent research on his topic, "in order to be convincing, the author needs to develop specific images in Hölderlin's own work."

Among George's numerous volumes of poetry is a collection of villanelles titled *Compass Card: One Hundred Villanelles.* This collection is seen as quite an accomplishment, as a proper villanelle is a very structured, somewhat difficult poem to compose. This type of poem, explained by E. J. Czerwinski in *World Literature Today,* includes structured repetition, which "augments the musicality of the form and provides the artist with a forum for his ideas." Czerwinski acknowledged that George's "range of subject matter is impressive," and noted that the collection exhibits the presence of "profound thought" behind its poetry.

In addition to publishing his own verse, George has also translated various works by other poets, among them *Miklós Radnóti: The Complete Poetry.* Of this book *Times Literary Supplement* reviewer Henry Gifford noted that George "has given five years to rendering the complete poems into an American English that nearly always rises to the occasion. . . . Aiming at 'versions that have power and beauty as English poems', with the closest possible fidelity to form, he makes Radnoti a genuine presence. This says much for the energy and truth of Radnoti's own writing which takes command of an attentive translator. It also speaks for the translator's devotion, exemplified further in his introduction and careful notes."

In 2001 George published a cycle of plays composed of *Iphigenie in Manhattan, Iphigenie in Czestochowa, Orest,* and *Iphigenie in Auschwitz.* (The actual writing of the four plays took place between August 1992 and January 1996.) The plays are a modern-day version of the myth of Iphigenia, the daughter of Agamemnon and Clytemnestra. The main character is a girl who has emigrated from the Ukraine to New York City, pursuing a career in acting. Iphigenie chose a hard-luck year to be in New York—1938—and an even worse year—1939—to return to Poland. Although World War II is beginning, Iphigenie stays in order to find her brother, Orest. In the final play, the brother and sister, along with Orest's friend Pavel Rózencveig (who is also Iphigenie's fiancé and corresponds to the Pylades of the classical Greek plays), end up working—and dying—in Auschwitz. Bernard F. Dick, reviewing the four-play cycle for *World Literature Today,* found the works "intellectually exhilarating" to read; they forced him to "rethink an ancient myth in terms of the most horrific event of the last century." However, Dick also surmised that the plays would fail on stage because of undeveloped characters and tiresome exposition.

George once commented to *CA:* "By background I am both a European and an American; by training and inclination, both a scholar and a writer. In my academic profession—German language, literature, and culture taught at the university level—great emphasis is placed upon the missionary nature of our activity. In scholarship I aim at finding and training the exceptional student; in my writing, on the other hand, I hope to reach people everywhere. Despite widespread feeling among the best of us that, as one distinguished poet recently put it, everyone writes poetry and yet no one buys or reads it, I remain impressed by the number of people in all walks of life who do in fact read, and read perceptively."

George told *CA:* "To try to field the question of what writers have influenced me: the list would have to be long. I do not wish to be remembered as a 'follower' of anyone. Like any real writer, I absorb influences from all quarters and strive to give originality in exchange. To name a few poets who have made an impact, though: like Friedrich Hölderlin (German, 1770-1843) and Miklós Radnóti (Hungarian, 1909-1944), I regard myself as a classicist contemporary. My deep admiration extends also to W. H. Auden, T. S. Eliot, W. S. Merwin, Richard Howard, Ezra Pound; my admirations extend from the Sumerians to the present. Among living novelists, I particularly admire Russell Banks, Saul Bellow, and William Styron. In the genre of drama, I learn from playwrights from Aeschylus to Arthur Miller. As Goethe said, we writers are what we owe to others; yet it is also urgently true that we are unrepeatable individuals."

*BIOGRAPHICAL AND CRITICAL SOURCES:*

*BOOKS*

*Encyclopedia of Literary Translation into English,* Fitzroy Dearborn Publishers (Chicago, IL), 2000.

Scharrar, Jack F., *Avery Hopwood: His Life and Works,* University of Michigan Press (Ann Arbor, MI), 1989.

*Twentieth-Century Literary Criticism,* volume 16, Gale (Detroit, MI), 1985.

*PERIODICALS*

*Choice,* December, 1972; March, 1978.

*Journal of English and Germanic Philology,* October, 1994, Timothy Torno, review of *Hölderlin and the Golden Chain of Homer,* pp. 618-620.

*Library Journal,* May 15, 1994, Daniel L. Guillory, review of *Contemporary East European Poetry,* p. 76.

*Michigan Quarterly Review,* winter, 1998, John R. Carpenter, review of *Metropolitan Icons,* p. 166-175.

*Modern Language Review,* October, 2001, p. 1138.

*Publishers Weekly,* June, 1977; February 28, 1994, review of *Contemporary East European Poetry,* p. 78.

*Times Literary Supplement,* October 10, 1980; July 13, 1984.

*World Literature Today,* winter, 1979; autumn, 1981; winter, 1982; autumn, 1983; summer, 1994, E. J. Czerwinski, review of *Contemporary East European Poetry,* p. 644; spring, 2001, E. J. Czerwinski, review of *Compass Card,* p. 337; spring, 2002, Bernard F. Dick, review of *Iphigenie in Manhattan, Iphigenie in Czestochowa, Orest,* and *Iphigenie in Auschwitz,* p. 155.

\*     \*     \*

## GERARD, Philip 1955-

*PERSONAL:* Born April 7, 1955, in Wilmington, DE; son of Felix A. Sczubelek (a cost accountant) and Margaret Clementine Herel (a homemaker); married Kathleen Ann Johnson (a translator), June 3, 1989. *Education:* University of Delaware, B.A., 1977; University of Arizona, M.F.A., 1981. *Hobbies and other interests:* Acoustic fingerstyle guitar, running his dogs, sailing, the outdoors.

*ADDRESSES: Home*—6231 Tortoise Ln., Wilmington, NC 28409. *Office*—Department of English, University of North Carolina at Wilmington, Wilmington, NC 28403. *Agent*—Jeffrey M. Kleinman, Esq., Graybill & English, LLC, 1875 Connecticut Avenue, N.W., Suite 712, Washington, D.C., 20009. *E-mail*—gerardp@ uncw.edu.

*CAREER:* Arizona State University, Tempe, visiting assistant professor of English, 1981-82, writer-in-residence, 1983-85; Lake Forest College, Lake Forest, IL, assistant professor of English, 1986-89; University of North Carolina at Wilmington, associate professor of creative writing, 1989—, acting director of professional and creative writing, 1990-91, director, 1991—. Managing editor, *North Carolina Humanities,* 1993-94. Serves on faculty of writers workshops; writer-in-residence in numerous academic settings; member of academic and fellowship boards.

*MEMBER:* Phi Beta Kappa.

*AWARDS, HONORS:* Bread Loaf scholar in fiction, 1982, fellow, 1987; *Quarterly West* novella competition finalist, 1986; Ernest Hemingway First Novel Prize nomination, 1986; Blumenthal Series winner, 1989; Emerging Artist grant from Arts Council of the Lower Cape Fear, 1991; University of North Carolina English Department Service Award, 1992-93, College of Arts and Sciences Excellence in Teaching Award, 1992, Chancellor's Excellence in Teaching Award, 1993;North Carolina Arts Council individual artist's fellowship, 1993; University of North Carolina board of Trustees Excellence in Teaching Award, 2001; Graduate Mentor Award, 2001.

*WRITINGS:*

*Hatteras Light* (novel), Scribner (New York, NY), 1986.

*Brilliant Passage* (nonfiction), Mystic Seaport Museum Press (Mystic, CT), 1989.

*Cape Fear Rising* (novel), John F. Blair (Winston-Salem, NC), 1994.

*Desert Kill* (novel), Morrow (New York, NY), 1994.

*Creative Nonfiction: Researching and Crafting Stories of Real Life,* Story Press (Cincinnati, OH), 1996.

*Writing a Book That Makes a Difference,* Story Press (Cincinnati, OH), 2000.

(Editor, with Carolyn Forché) *Writing Creative Nonfiction: Instruction and Insights from Teachers of the Associated Writing Programs,* Story Press (Cincinnati, OH), 2001.

*Secret Soldiers: The Story of World War II's Heroic Army of Deception* (nonfiction), Dutton (New York, NY), 2002.

Author of television documentary scripts, including *River Run: Down the Cape Fear to the Sea, Hong Kong: A Little England in the Eastern Seas, Hong Kong: An Absolute Money Machine,* and *Hong Kong: The Future of Freedom.* Author and performer of radio essays for public radio. Contributor of stories and articles to periodicals, including *Soundings East, Puerto Del Sol, New England Review, Bread Loaf Quarterly, Amherst Review, permafrost, Hayden's Ferry Review, Arts Journal, Crescent Review, Carolina Style, World & I, Associated Writing Programs Chronicle,* and *Hawaii Review.*

*SIDELIGHTS:* Philip Gerard's debut novel, *Hatteras Light,* was nominated for the Ernest Hemingway First Novel Prize in 1986. According to Maurice C. York in

*North Carolina Libraries, Hatteras Light* "received favorable reviews." Gerard's two subsequent novels, both published in 1994, received perhaps more widespread attention due to their subject matter. In *Cape Fear Rising* the author explores an historical incident that took place in Wilmington, North Carolina, where Gerard teaches at the local university. The story he relates in his novel—that of the 1898 uprising of white supremacists against an elected city government that included blacks, white Republicans, and other liberals—sparked animated discussions in Wilmington and throughout the surrounding area. Though Gerard made it clear that he took certain liberties with the facts in order to create better fiction, he did include the actual names of those men and women involved in the incident, causing descendants of those portrayed unfavorably to complain. As Pama Mitchell reported in the *Atlanta Journal/Constitution:* "'Sufficient unto the day is the evil thereof,' says Walker Taylor III, a white Wilmington native whose grandfather plotted and profited from the 1898 reordering of the city's power structure. 'We've got to deal with the problems of 1994.'"

Despite some negative local publicity, the response from critics to *Cape Fear Rising* was overwhelmingly favorable. Paul Howle, reviewing the novel in the *Atlanta Journal/Constitution,* hailed it as "an interesting story of an important event well told," and particularly observed that "the book's real protagonist is the riot itself, and it is here that Gerard shines." York noted that the author's "bedrock sense of place and knowledge of human character serve him well" in the novel; Phil Rubio in the *Prism* declared that "Gerard perfectly captures the contrasts, ironies and hypocrisies of turn-of-the-[twentieth-]century Wilmington."

*Desert Kill,* Gerard's taut novel about a psychotic serial killer in Arizona, also garnered much praise for its author. John Dillon explained in *Mostly Murder* that the book is "thrilling not only for its fast action, gory details, and hair-raising ending, but because it's also a stylistic tour de force. It's as if Ernest Hemingway and Thomas Harris [author of *Silence of the Lambs*] have teamed to write a short, nasty police procedural shamelessly designed to give you the creeps." Other reviewers lauded *Desert Kill*'s well-delineated characters, which include investigator Paul Pope, his college professor nephew Roy, and Roy's wife, Eileen, who suffers the psychological aftermath of a brutal rape.

In his more recent work, Gerard has turned to the art of his craft, and penned books aimed at a target audience of would-be writers. In addition to writing the instruction manuals *Creative Nonfiction: Researching and Crafting Stories of Real Life* and *Writing a Book That Makes a Difference,* he also coedited a book with poet Carolyn Forché. This book, *Writing Creative Nonfiction,* gathers information from over thirty writers and teachers who are part of the Associated Writing Programs. Each expert presents an aspect of writing, using his or her own work as an example.

Gerard returned to historical events with his 2002 book *Secret Soldiers: The Story of World War II's Heroic Army of Deception.* The book profiles a covert military unit whose story was hidden for fifty years. The 23rd Headquarters Special Troops was the only deception outfit ever created by the U.S. Army. Comprised of artists, sound technicians, designers, musicians, and electronic specialists, the outfit's job was to convince the Nazis of the existence of American units, in order to throw them off track. The troop's primary weapons were sound-effect machines, camouflage, and inflatable tanks. Gerard pieced the outfit's story together using memoirs, diaries, veteran recollections, and recently declassified archives. As Terry Teachout commented in his review of *Secret Soldiers* for *Book,* Gerard tells his fact-based story "straightforwardly and admiringly, with no shortage of vivid material." A *Kirkus Reviews* contributor felt that the account offers "intriguing evidence of a unique and selfless service that resonates poignantly in today's crisis-filled world."

Gerard once told *CA:* "The more I write, the more writing becomes like reading—I finish a novel to find out what happens next, whether I'm reading it or writing it. I'm always anxious to make my story happen in somebody else's imagination. I write relentlessly, every day when I can manage it, except for interludes between long projects.

"The writers I admire are versatile and full of energy, trying new and daring things but always grabbing the reader by the collar and hauling him along with them: Tim O'Brien, Carolyn Forché, Martin Cruz Smith, Ron Hansen, Don DeLillo, Bob Reiss, Randall Kenan, and Gore Vidal.

"The themes I return to in my own writing again and again are community, the need for courage, the ethical lines we draw in our lives and when and why we are willing to step over them. When I am old and eloquent enough, I will write about the beautiful act of teaching, which at its best is an act of love.

"Lately, too, I have become very interested in the way stories are told out loud—in my essays for local and nationwide National Public Radio broadcast, I have tried to discover the possibilities of the spoken word.

"My wife, Kathleen A. Johnson, is an eloquent and well-published scholar of narrative in the French novel of the twentieth century, especially in the works of George Semprun, a Spaniard who writes in French and Spanish. She is my best and toughest critic, and the best judge of whether a story is working."

Gerard more recently added: "I spend a lot more time planning my writing now than in the past—thinking ideas through, making notes, daydreaming, pushing and probing the material. Then I write with great discipline—in all seasons, on holidays usually six or more hours per day when I am on a long project. Meantime I accumulate subjects and ideas in journals and files. I relentlessly revise—revision is the heart of good writing.

"Each book I write humbles me all over again before the demands of the subject and the craft. Writing uses your whole personality—all your virtues, and talents, and faults—maybe especially your faults. It is bottomless, which makes it satisfying to pursue.

"Every writer's favorite is the next book—that's where the passion is always directed. But *Cape Fear Rising* had an immediate effect on the community here. It caused African Americans and Whites to talk about their past; it provoked a healing discussion.

"I want to give the reader an adventure in words, take him someplace he never would have gotten to on his own. I want her to live in my world awhile and feel as if her experience has been enlarged. I want to share the excitement of my discovery and feel passionately hopeful about the possibilities of the human soul.

*BIOGRAPHICAL AND CRITICAL SOURCES:*

*PERIODICALS*

*Atlanta Journal/Constitution,* March 6, 1994, Paul Howle, review of *Cape Fear Rising,* pp. A3, N11.

*Book,* July-August, 2002, Terry Teachout, review of *Secret Soldiers: The Story of World War II's Heroic Army of Deception,* p. 77.

*Booklist,* April 1, 2001, Mary Carroll, review of *Writing Creative Nonfiction,* p. 1443; May 15, 2002, Gilbert Taylor, review of *Secret Soldiers,* p. 1570.

*Kirkus Reviews,* April 1, 2002, review of *Secret Soldiers,* p. 468.

*Library Journal,* June 1, 2002, Denise S. Sticha, review of *Writing Creative Nonfiction,* p. 178; May 15, 2002, Jim Doyle, review of *Secret Soldiers,* p. 108.

*Mostly Murder,* July-August-September, 1994.

*North Carolina Libraries,* summer, 1994, p. 81.

*Prism,* April, 1994, p. 3.

*Publishers Weekly,* May 6, 2002, review of *Secret Soldiers,* p. 49.

ONLINE

*Philip Gerard Home Page,* http://www.philipgerard.com/ (September 9, 2002).

\*     \*     \*

# GLASSMAN, Bernard Tetsugen 1939-
## (Bernie Glassman)

*PERSONAL:* Born January 18, 1939, in Brooklyn, NY; son of Otto Isaac (a composer) and Pauline (Finkelstein) Glassman; married Helen Silverberg (a Buddhist priest), August 25, 1963; children: Alisa, Marc. *Education:* Polytechnic Institute of New York, B.S., 1960; University of California, Los Angeles, M.A., 1968, Ph.D., 1970.

*ADDRESSES: Home*—Greyston Seminary, 690 West 247th St., Riverdale, NY 10471. *Office*—Zen Community of New York, 5720 Mosholu Ave., Riverdale, NY 10471.

*CAREER:* Buddhist monk, teacher, and author. Douglas Aircraft Co., Inc., Santa Monica, CA, associate engineer, 1960-62, aerodynamicist, 1963-69; McDonnell Douglas Astronautics, Inc., Huntington Beach, CA, senior scientist and acting branch chief of performance analysis, guidance, and flight mechanics, 1971-76. Ordained Soto Zen Buddhist monk, 1970; Zen Center of Los Angeles, head monk and head of meditation center, 1973, executive vice president, assistant spiritual director, and director of Center Publishing's "Zen Writing Series," 1976-79; Institute for Transcultural Studies, Los Angeles, CA, executive vice president, 1976-79; Zen Community of New York, Riverdale, chairman of board of directors, president, and spiritual director, 1980—. Member of *Soto Zenshu,* Soto Zen Buddhist School of Japan; presenter at workshops, conferences, and seminars; lecturer at colleges and universities, including University of California, Los Angeles, Occidental College, Haverford College, Swarthmore College, University of Pennsylvania, Syracuse University, Herbert H. Lehman College of the City University of New York, and Hofstra University; guest on radio programs.

*WRITINGS:*

*Three-Degree-of-Freedom Trajectory Simulation Computer Program AB60,* McDonnell Douglas Aircraft (Huntington Beach, CA), Volume I: *Derivation of Equations,* Volume II: *User's Manual,* 1966.

*Space Flight Handbook,* Volume III: *Planetary Flight Handbook,* National Aeronautics and Space Administration, 1969.

*Computer Program Management Technique: CPMT Manual,* McDonnell Douglas Aircraft (Huntington Beach, CA), 1973.

(With Taizan Maezumi) *The Hazy Moon of Enlightenment,* Center Publishing (Los Angeles, CA), 1978.

(With Rick Fields) *Instruction to the Cook: A Zen Master's Lessons in Living Life That Matters,* Bell Tower (New York, NY), 1996.

(Under name Bernie Glassman) *Bearing Witness: A Zen Master's Lessons in Making Peace,* Bell Tower (New York, NY), 1998.

(Under name Bernie Glassman) *Infinite Circle: Teachings in Zen,* Shambala (Boston, MA), 2002.

EDITOR

*On Zen Practice,* Center Publishing (Los Angeles, CA), 1976.

*On Zen Practice II: Body, Breath, Mind,* Center Publishing (Los Angeles, CA), 1977, revised edition, under name Bernie Glassman, Wisdom Publications (Boston, MA), 2002.

John Buksbazen, *To Forget the Self,* Center Publishing (Los Angeles, CA), 1978.

Maezumi Loori and John Loori, *The Way of Everyday Life,* Center Publishing (Los Angeles, CA), 1978.

Thomas Cleary, *Sayings and Doings of Pai-Chang,* Center Publishing (Los Angeles, CA), 1979.

Francis Cook, *How to Raise an Ox,* Center Publishing (Los Angeles, CA), 1979.

*SIDELIGHTS:* Prior to his ordination as a Buddhist monk in 1970, Bernard Tetsugen Glassman worked in the aerospace industry, and developed the General Performance Analysis Tool Trajectory Simulation computer program. He authored three texts related to the aerospace field, but the bulk of his writing career has been as author or editor of works on subjects relating to Zen Buddism.

Glassman's 1998 book *Bearing Witness* instructs readers in how to make peace with the world and the past. When discussing the state of world affairs, as Raul Nino noted in *Booklist,* Glassman offers a "centered . . . and balanced perspective." His *Infinite Circle: Teachings in Zen* is another educational book on the topic, and this time Glassman takes a much more in-depth look at three important Zen texts. He guides the reader through an understanding of the poem "Heart Sutra," as well as of *The Identity of Relative Absolute* and the *Zen Bodhisattva Precepts.* His contention is that an understanding these writings is crucial for all Zen practitioners. A contributor to *Publishers Weekly* commented that Glassman's "style and thinking are like thick, polished glass: clear, compact and strong."

Glassman once told *CA:* "I was principal investigator on an independent study to develop new parameter hunting and optimization procedures and supervised the engineering effort that provided trajectory optimization programs for the National Aeronautics and Space Administration at Goddard and the Comsat Corporation.

"I directed trajectory and mission analyses for lunar and interplanetary mission studies and was in charge of the preparation of the planetary flight handbook for Mars stopover missions using Venus swingbys. I also worked on studies related to Thor system space vehicles, and range safety studies and capability studies in connection with the Delta space vehicle.

"During this time, I maintained a parallel career in my religious practice and involvement with the development of Zen Buddhism in America, having first encountered Zen in 1958 during a college course on religions. This began an odyssey of study through books and personal contacts with teachers in Japan and the United States, including Yasutani Roshi, Koryu Roshi, and Taizan Maezumi Roshi.

"I began full-time practice with Taizan Maezumi Roshi in 1968. Maezumi Roshi is a Dharma successor in the Soto tradition, as well as in two lines of the Rinzai tradition. He trained me in a wide range of personal studies in addition to various administrative, liturgical, and training positions connected with a Zen center and training *dojo.* He allowed me to work closely with him in the development of the Zen Center of Los Angeles.

"I became a monk in 1970 and in 1976 left the aerospace industry to devote myself entirely to Zen practice. I helped found the Institute of Transcultural Studies (now the Kuroda Institute) and Center Publications. In 1976 I completed *koan* study, and in 1977 formal training for the priesthood in the Soto tradition, becoming the first Dharma successor of Maezumi Roshi. The occasion was celebrated in Japan in August, 1978, when I officiated at *zuisse* ceremonies at the two head temples of the Soto sect, Eiheiji and Sojiji.

"In 1980 I moved to New York City to establish the Zen Community of New York, an interreligious Zen practice center. The community offers regularly scheduled meditation, Dharma meetings, retreats, workshops, classes, seminars, and month-long intensive training periods, each with its unique emphasis. In addition, the Zen Community of New York began its first livelihood, Greyston Bakery and Café, in 1982. I developed a full-time, comprehensive training program consisting of daily meditation, of work-practice within the bakery, café, and offices of the community, of communal living-practice, and of study of root texts and sutras. I also hold private interviews with my students and give Dharma talks several times monthly, some on the meaning of work-practice."

*BIOGRAPHICAL AND CRITICAL SOURCES:*

*PERIODICALS*

*Booklist,* April, 1998, Raul Nino, review of *Bearing Witness: A Zen Master's Lessons in Making Peace,*

p. 1280; April 15, 2002, Donna Seaman, review of *Infinite Circle: Teachings in Zen,* p. 1364.

*Publishers Weekly,* April 15, 2002, review of *Infinite Circle,* p.61; July 1, 2002, review of *On Zen Practice,* p. 72.

*Tikkun,* January-February, 1998, "Buddhism, Activism, and Unknowing: A Day With Bernie Glassman" (interview), Christopher Queen, p. 64.


\*      \*      \*

**GLASSMAN, Bernie**
    **See GLASSMAN, Bernard Tetsugen**


\*      \*      \*

**GLATZER, Hal 1946-**

*PERSONAL:* Born January 31, 1946, in New York, NY; son of Harold (an attorney) and Glenna (a teacher; maiden name, Beaber) Glatzer. *Education:* Syracuse University, B.A. (English), 1968; University of Hawaii, M.A. (communications), 1979; also attended graduate courses at Hilo College. *Politics:* Democrat. *Hobbies and other interests:* Playing banjo, guitar, fiddle, mandolin, autoharp, and dulcimer in the style of traditional mountain music and Bluegrass; reading, watching television, gardening.

*ADDRESSES: Home*—476 Hickory St., San Francisco, CA 94102-5607.

*CAREER: Honolulu Advertiser,* Hilo, HI, bureau chief, 1971; *Orchid Isle* (magazine), Hilo, HI, editor, 1972-74; KITV-News, Hilo, HI, reporter, 1975; Oceanic Cablevision, Honolulu, HI, news director, 1976; television producer in Honolulu and Seattle, 1976; *People,* New York, NY, Hawaii correspondent, 1976-80; *The Printout,* Honolulu, editor, 1979-80; Words and Pictures, Seattle, WA, chief executive officer, 1980; computer consultant in Seattle, 1980; *Software News,* Westborough, MA, West Coast correspondent, 1983; Key Thinkers, Inc., Oakland, CA, partner, 1985. Former member of Big Island Committee on Crime Prevention. Delegate for the Democratic Convention in Kansas City, MO, 1974.

*MEMBER:* American Association for the Advancement of Science, Union of Concerned Scientists, Insti-

tute of Electrical and Electronic Engineers, Computer Press Association (vice president, 1985-87), Hawaii Professional Writers.

*AWARDS, HONORS:* Media Award, American Cancer Society, 1978.

*WRITINGS:*

*Kamehameha County* (journalistic novel), Friendly World Enterprises (Pepeekeo, HI), 1974.
*Introduction to Word Processing,* Sybex (Berkeley, CA), 1981.
*The Birds of Babel: Satellites for a Human World,* H. W. Sams (Indianapolis, IN), 1983.
*Who Owns the Rainbow?: Conserving the Radio Spectrum,* H. W. Sams (Indianapolis, IN), 1984.
*The Trapdoor,* 1986.
*Murder on the Kona Coast,* 1987.
*Too Dead to Swing: A Katy Green Mystery,* John Daniel (Santa Barbara, CA), 2002.

Also contributor to local magazines and to *Christian Science Monitor.*

*ADAPTATIONS: Too Dead to Swing* was originally performed as an audio play for Audio-Playwrights in 2000.

*SIDELIGHTS:* Hal Glatzer is a former journalist who has often written books on technical subjects such as computers. However, he has also penned mystery fiction. His *Too Dead to Swing,* for example, was originally performed as an audio-play, but it was based on an unpublished novel from the 1940s. The story centers around an all-girl 1940s swing band. When one of the members is attacked, musician and amateur sleuth Katy Green joins the band. As the band travels by train, members of the band are murdered one by one. *Library Journal* reviewer Rex E. Klett wrote that the novel's "simple, easy-going style" was engaging and recommended *Too Dead to Swing* to fans of Forties noir mysteries.

Glatzer once told *CA:* "I am an eclectic radical thinker. . . . I believe in God and Mankind. I do not believe in owning land. I believe in beating swords into ploughshares and spears into pruning hooks. I do not study war."

*BIOGRAPHICAL AND CRITICAL SOURCES:*

PERIODICALS

*Booklist,* April 15, 1982, review of *Introduction to Word Processing,* p. 1052; May 1, 2001, review of *Too Dead to Swing,* p. 1617.

*Book World,* October 3, 1982, review of *Introduction to Word Processing,* p. 11.

*Journalism Quarterly,* autumn, 1985, review of *The Birds of Babel,* p. 675; summer, 1985, review of *Who Owns the Rainbow?,* p. 425; spring, 1986, review of *The Telecommunications Revolution,* p. 204.

*Library Journal,* March 1, 2002, Rex E. Klett, review of *Too Dead to Swing,* p. 143.

*Publishers Weekly,* December 4, 2000, review of *Too Dead to Swing,* p. 32.

*San Francisco Review of Books,* September, 1982, review of *Introduction to Word Processing,* p. 30.*

\*　　\*　　\*

**GODFREY, Peter 1917-1992**

*PERSONAL:* Born September 8, 1917, in Vereeniging, South Africa; died, 1992; son of Louis (an entrepreneur) and Bessie (a homemaker; maiden name, Gluckman) Godfrey; married Naomi Cowan (an office consultant), July 3, 1941; children: Dennis Etien, Ronald Marcus. *Education:* University of the Witwatersrand, B.A. (literature), 1938; University of South Africa, B.A. (psychology; with honors), 1942.

*CAREER:* Journalist. Worked for various newspapers and magazines in South Africa, including editorships of anti-apartheid weekly *Cape Standard* and magazine *Spotlight* in Capetown and Johannesburg, 1933-61; *Drum,* London, England, editor in chief of East, Central, and West African editions, 1961-63; Odhams Press Ltd., London, England, subeditor of *Daily Herald* and *Sun,* 1963-69; IPC Business Press, London, England, chief subeditor of *Industry Week,* 1970; Clerical and Administrative Workers' Union, Wimbledon, England, public relations officer, 1970-71; *Times,* London, England, subeditor of "Business News," 1971-81; freelance writer, beginning 1981. *Military service:* South African Army, Counter Intelligence, 1939-43.

*MEMBER:* Crime Writers Association (past member of council), Mystery Writers of America.

*AWARDS, HONORS:* Ellery Queen Short Story Award, *Ellery Queen's Mystery Magazine,* 1948, for "The Lady and the Dragon," 1949, for "The Newtonian Egg," and 1953, for "Hail and Farewell."

*WRITINGS:*

*Death under the Table* (short stories), South African Scientific Publishers, 1954.

*Four o'Clock Noon* (three-act play), first produced in Johannesburg, South Africa, at Library Theatre, 1961.

*The Newtonian Egg: And Other Cases of Rolf Le Roux* (short stories), Crippen & Landru (Norfolk, VA), 2002.

Also author of radio, television, and stage plays. Work represented in anthologies, including *John Creasey's Crime Collection,* St. Martin's Press (New York, NY), 1978-86; *Ellery Queen's Scenes of the Crime,* Dial (New York, NY); *Best Detective Stories of the Year,* Dutton (New York, NY), 1978, 1980. Contributor of more than 2,000 stories to periodicals.

*ADAPTATIONS:* Godfrey's novella "Wanton Murder" was adapted into the film "The Girl in Black Stockings," starring Anne Bancroft.

*SIDELIGHTS:* Peter Godfrey was a South African journalist who wrote mystery stories on the side. A fairly prolific author of plays for stage and screen, he only published one collection of his stories, *Death under the Table,* before his death in 1992. His skills as a mystery writer were nevertheless rewarded with three Ellery Queen awards.

Many of Godfrey's stories that featured his recurring character, master sleuth Rolf le Roux, remained uncollected until the more recent publication of ten tales written between the years 1948 and 1986 in *The Newtonian Egg: And Other Cases of Rolf Le Roux.* Set in his native South Africa, which the author later left for England in protest of apartheid, the le Roux mysteries are somewhat in the spirit of Sherlock Holmes in that they feature a brilliant detective faced with bizarre cases, which he solves using his amazing powers of ratiocination. Some of the stories in *The Newtonian Egg* include the title story, in which le Roux must figure out how poison was put inside a boiled egg without cracking its shell, a story about a cable car conductor who is apparently murdered by an invisible assailant, and the strange case of a murdered Shakespearian actor that can only be solved by someone with an expert's knowledge of the play *Macbeth*. "The stories' apartheid regime background lends an extra dimension" to the book, commented a *Publishers Weekly* critic, who concluded that mystery fans "will eagerly devour this cunning author's work."

*BIOGRAPHICAL AND CRITICAL SOURCES:*

*PERIODICALS*

*Kirkus Reviews,* February 15, 2002, review of *The Newtonian Egg: And Other Cases of Rolf le Roux,* p. 223.

*Publishers Weekly,* March 25, 2002, review of *The Newtonian Egg,* p. 45.*

\*      \*      \*

**GOLDSCHMIDT, Arthur (Eduard), Jr. 1938-**

*PERSONAL:* Born March 17, 1938, in Washington, DC; son of Arthur Eduard (a United Nations administrator) and Elizabeth (a professor of public policy and welfare consultant; maiden name, Wickenden) Goldschmidt; married Louise Robb (a homemaker), June 17, 1961; children: Stephen Robb Gold, Paul William. *Ethnicity:* "German and English." *Education:* Colby College, A.B., 1959; attended American University of Beirut; Harvard University, A.M., 1961, Ph.D., 1968. *Politics:* Democrat. *Religion:* Unitarian-Universalist. *Hobbies and other interests:* Reading, exercise, cooking.

*ADDRESSES: Home*—1173 Oneida St., State College, PA 16801-5938. *Office*—c/o Pennsylvania State University, University Park, PA 16802-1503; fax: 814-863-7840. *E-mail*—axg2@psu.edu.

*CAREER:* Pennsylvania State University, University Park, assistant professor, 1965-73, associate professor, 1973-89, professor of Middle East history, 1989-2000,

professor emeritus, 2000—. Haifa University, visiting associate professor, 1973-74; University of Cairo, visiting professor, 1981-82; New Jersey Scholars Program, academic dean, 1985; Semester at Sea Program, visiting lecturer, 1987, 2001. *Voices of Central Pennsylvania,* founder, 1993, president, 1993-97.

*MEMBER:* American Historical Association, Middle East Studies Association, American Research Center in Egypt.

*AWARDS, HONORS:* Class of 1933 Award for outstanding contributions to the humanities, 1972; AMOCO Teaching Award, 1981; Warnock Award for service to fraternities, 1993; Mentoring Award, Middle East Studies Association, 2000.

*WRITINGS:*

*A Concise History of the Middle East,* Westview Press (Boulder, CO), 1979, 7th edition, 2002.

*Modern Egypt: The Formation of a Nation State,* Westview Press (Boulder, CO), 1988.

(Translator and annotator) *The Memoirs and Diaries of Muhammad Farid,* Edwin Mellen Press (Lewiston, NY), 1992.

*Historical Dictionary of Egypt,* Scarecrow Press (Metuchen, NJ), 1994, new edition, 2003.

*Biographical Dictionary of Modern Egypt,* Lynne Rienner (Boulder, CO), 2000.

Contributor to periodicals, including *Voices of Central Pennsylvania.*

*WORK IN PROGRESS: They Drank from the Nile: Foreign Sojourners in Egypt; Modern Egypt: The Formation of a Nation State.*

*SIDELIGHTS:* Arthur Goldschmidt once told *CA:* "My parents and grandmother told me that I started writing before I knew the alphabet, having devised a code that enabled me, if asked, to read aloud the same story from what I had scribbled. I was a slow talker and stuttered or stammered as a child. Even now I often prefer to express my thoughts in writing, rather than in speech, even though others think I can lecture or chair meetings well. To me, writing allows me to put something down and, if it sounds wrong, change it; whereas, once one has said something, there is no way one can strike it out. My first ambition was to become a famous author; only later did I choose a career of research and writing history.

"The book for which I am best known, *A Concise History of the Middle East,* grew out of my frustration with available textbooks for beginning students in Islamic and Middle East history, the subject that I have taught throughout my career. I believe that it is possible to write a textbook that students will read with pleasure. Among the writers of my formative years, who may have influenced my interest in didactic writing, I can recall Mark Twain, Donald Culross Peattie, Carlton Coon, and David Thompson; but there must have been others I am forgetting.

"Unfortunately for my scholarly career, I have not developed much facility for monographic research and writing, a flaw that would have been fatal had I gone into academic life any later than I did. Before computers were available, I used to write drafts on the backs of used sheets of paper, using a clipboard and sitting (or lying) wherever I could, but rarely at a desk. I often wrote first and then checked my facts afterwards, before rewriting my draft on a typewriter. The word processor has greatly facilitated my writing process and made me much more productive, although I must carefully check my work for discursiveness.

"The topics of my writing have usually been dictated by my academic training in Middle East history, with a special interest in Egypt in the nineteenth and early twentieth centuries. Throughout my career, however, I have also done some journalistic writing, initially for my college newspaper, later for various dailies. For the past few years I have been writing in *Voices of Central Pennsylvania,* which I founded as a liberal and monthly journal of news and opinion in a fairly conservative region. Initially I wanted to refute a conservative, anti-feminist, and homophobic biweekly called *Lionhearted,* which has not survived. I also enjoy writing letters, whether sent in envelopes or via the Internet, and take pride in my letters of recommendation for students and, when needed, of counsel to them."

\*        \*        \*

### GOMES, Peter J(ohn) 1942-

*PERSONAL:* Born May 22, 1942, in Boston, MA; son of Peter Lobo (an agricultural worker) and Orissa Josephine (a civil servant; maiden name, White) Gomes. *Education:* Bates College, B.A., 1965; Harvard Uni-

*Peter J. Gomes*

versity, S.T.B., 1968. *Politics:* Republican. *Religion:* Baptist. *Hobbies and other interests:* Music, antiques, cigars.

*ADDRESSES: Home*—Sparks House, 21 Kirkland St., Cambridge, MA 02138-2001. *Office*—Memorial Church, Harvard University, Cambridge, MA 02138.

*CAREER:* Minister, historian, church musician, and author. Ordained Baptist minister, 1968; Tuskegee Institute, Tuskegee, AL, instructor of history and director of freshman experimental program, 1968-70; Memorial Church, Harvard University, Cambridge, MA, assistant minister to acting minister, 1970-74, minister, 1974—, Plummer Professor of Christian Morals, 1974—, W. E. B. DuBois Institute for Afro-American History, acting director, 1990—. Visiting professor, Duke University, 1993-94. National chaplain, American Guild of Organists, 1978-82. Director of the English-Speaking Union; trustee of the Pilgrim Society, Donation to Liberia, 1973—, Bates College, 1973-78, 1980—, Charity of Edward Hopkins, 1974—, Boston Freedom Trail, 1976—, Plymouth Plantation, 1977—, Roxbury Latin School, 1982—, Wellesley

College, 1985—, Boston Foundation, 1985—, Plymouth Public Library, 1985—, Handel and Haydn Society, and the International Fund for Defense and Aid in South Africa (and president), 1977—. Member of the Farmington Institute of Christian Studies.

*MEMBER:* Royal Society of Arts (fellow), Royal Society of Church Music, American Baptist Historical Society, Unitarian Historical Society, Country Day School Headmasters Association (honorary), Signet Society (president), Colonial Society of Massachusetts, Massachusetts Historical Society, Harvard Musical Association (president), Phi Beta Kappa.

*AWARDS, HONORS:* Rockefeller Fellow, 1967-68; Pilgrim Society award for history, 1970; D.D. (hon.), New England College, 1974, University of the South, 1989, and Bates University, 1997; L.H.D., Waynesburg College, 1978, Duke University, 1997, and University of Nebraska, 1997; Hum.D., Gordon College, 1985; Litt.D., Knox College, 1987; fellow, Emmanuel College, Cambridge University.

*WRITINGS:*

(With Lawrence D. Geller), *The Books of the Pilgrims,* Garland (New York, NY), 1975.
(And editor) *History of Harvard Divinity School,* Harvard University (Cambridge, MA), 1992.
*Proclamation Series,* Lent, 1995.
*The Good Book: Reading the Bible with Mind and Heart,* Morrow (New York, NY), 1996.
*Sermons: Biblical Wisdom for Daily Living,* Morrow (New York, NY), 1998.
*The Good Life: Truths That Last in Times of Need,* HarperCollins (New York, NY), 2002.

Editor of *History of the Pilgrim Society,* 1970. Author of *Proclamation Series Commentaries,* Lent, 1985. Author of introduction to *Narrative of the Life of Frederick Douglass, an American Slave,* by Frederick Douglass, Signet Classic (New York, NY), 1997, and *The Courage to Be,* by Paul Tillich, second edition, Yale University Press (New Haven, CT), 2000. Editor, *Parnassus,* 1970; member of editorial board, *Pulpit Digest.*

*SIDELIGHTS:* After ministering to the congregation of Harvard University's Memorial Church for more than twenty years, Peter J. Gomes stepped into contro-

versy in late 1991 when he challenged a student magazine's anti-homosexual propaganda in a speech, during which he declared himself gay. "Gay people are victims *not* of the Bible, *not* of religion, and *not* of the church, but of people who use religion as a way to devalue and deform those whom they can neither ignore nor convert," he told the crowd of hundreds, as quoted by Robert S. Boynton in the *New Yorker.*

Gomes, a conservative, Republican, African-American clergyman who had delivered the benediction at Ronald Reagan's second presidential inauguration and the sermon at George H. Bush's inauguration, quickly found himself hailed by progressive elements on campus—some of whom left notes and flowers at the church door—and vilified by reactionaries who called for his resignation. National magazines and television news programs picked up the story. Concerning his new celebrity, Gomes told Boynton: "I don't like being the main exhibit, but this was an unusual set of circumstances, in that I felt I had a particular resource that nobody else there possessed." With a personal dislike for such terms as "gay activist" and "homosexual chaplain," Gomes bracketed for possible deletion in the printed text of his speech the phrase in which he referred to himself as "a Christian who happens as well to be gay." Nevertheless, after giving the full speech, he asserted confidently to the *New Yorker,* "I have no regrets."

Gomes has been an ardent individualist all his life, with a style, however, that has enabled him to fit into the most exalted institutional circles of the Ivy League: he collects antiques, throws exquisite dinner parties, smokes expensive cigars, and dresses like a model of patrician good taste. He grew up in Plymouth, Massachusetts, the son of a highly intelligent father who was a farm laborer, and a mother who, as a descendant of Boston's black aristocracy, was the first African-American woman to work in the Massachusetts State House as a clerk, as well as being organist and choir director for a predominately white church. As the only child of late-marrying parents, Gomes grew up in a nurturing environment and was exposed to literature, the arts, and science from an early age. Educated mainly in the company of white children, he was often selected by them as class president and was noted for his activities in school (and later, college) organizations.

Gomes loved to play church as a boy, giving sermons in emulation of the pastor of his family's church. As he would later tell Boynton, "Church for me was what the basketball court is to most black kids: a place where my imagination was unleashed and I was given free reign on a stage." After studying history at Bates College in Maine, he was persuaded by a religion professor there to experience the intellectual stimulation offered at Harvard Divinity School. Upon being ordained, Gomes took a teaching position at traditionally black Tuskegee Institute in Alabama, where, by his own admission, "I saw more black people in my first half hour . . . than I had ever seen in my entire life."

The conservatively dressed, New England-accented Gomes became a favorite of Tuskegee's students. Two years later, he successfully embraced the opportunity to become a favorite at Harvard, an institution he regards as having, historically, a civilizing moral obligation toward society. At Harvard, where by virtue of his benedictions and commencement speeches he is, according to Boynton, "the first and last official voice that every Harvard student hears," Gomes gained a reputation as a stirring, memorable orator who combined the mellifluous verbal play of African-American preachers with the rigorous rhetoric of a New England intellectual. Nobel Prize-winning poet and Harvard professor Seamus Heaney, describing Gomes's oratory, told Boynton: "He embraces this old-fashioned grandiloquent style in a manner that is always on the edge of carnival. . . . His style is full of cadence, roguery, and scampishness, which is itself redemptive."

An energetic worker and a much sought-after member of organizations, Gomes—who told Boynton that he has never had a gay partner and expected never to have one—professes himself relatively unexposed to what mainstream America perceives as the gay community. Nevertheless, his position as a well-placed clergyman who had come out lent special weight to his 1996 book, *The Good Book: Reading the Bible with Mind and Heart.* In this volume, Gomes attempts to refute the literalism, culturalism, and, in his words "bibliolatry" of right-wing fundamentalists who use selected passages from the Bible to inveigh against homosexuality, abortion, and the science of evolution. Gomes's work is intended to be a readable introduction to the Bible for general readers who may have regretted their comparative ignorance of that source of moral and spiritual guidance. "People have a hunger and look to the bible for answers that they can't find elsewhere. And that is a problem," Gomes told Boynton. He explained, "They attribute to the Bible a kind of functional credibility that it was never designed to have. They idolize it."

*The Good Book* is organized into three parts. In the first, Gomes discusses the Bible's background, its composition, and related basic issues. In the second part, he deals with twelve specific contemporary public issues on which the Bible's words had been used as ammunition; these include wealth, race, and the equality of women, as well as homosexuality and other issues. The third part is titled "The True and Lively Word"; *Washington Post Book World* contributor Diana L. Hayes, a theologian from Georgetown University, found this section to be where "Gomes's creativity is fully revealed." Here, he argues for the individual's use of "moral imagination" in evaluating issues with the help of Biblical scripture. The book at this point "invites the reader . . . into an unending dialogue with God's word as interpreted by humanity," said Hayes. Presbyterian minister and philosopher John C. S. Kim, writing in the *Los Angeles Times Book Review,* also welcomed Gomes's work, calling it "a noble, though sometimes ambivalent, attempt to suggest how one can live by God's law in a complicated, secular age." John Moryl of Yeshiva University, commenting on *The Good Book* for *Library Journal,* thought that Gomes succeeded in reaching readers with his "honest, down-to-earth, personal, and thoughtful" approach and added that the book was "not preachy, pietistic, or fundamentalist." Lord Runcie, the Archbishop of Canterbury, remarked, as quoted by Boynton, that Gomes's opus was "easily the best contemporary book on the Bible for thoughtful people." Gomes himself greeted the critical and financial success of his book—which had earned a three hundred thousand dollar advance—with equanimity, thus perhaps adding another unusual aspect to his own self-characterization: "The oddest thing about being an oddity is that there are very few oddities like you," he told Boynton.

Gomes followed the success of *The Good Book* with *The Good Life: Truths That Last in Times of Need,* which seeks to convince readers that happiness in life cannot be obtained through material possessions or career accomplishments but rather is found by the pursuit of more noble purposes. He was inspired to write the book after observing that many of the students at Harvard were redefining what they wanted in life. Rather than viewing college as a place to obtain a degree with the purpose of getting a high-paying job, they instead want to gain personal satisfaction by living more moral lives. As a conservative, Gomes feels that some of the answers to the questions posed by today's generation can be found in the Western tradition going back to Aristotle and Plato. It is a tradition, he asserts, that has been largely lost in America because of ignorance and cultural plurality; however, one must not simply look to the past for answers but instead should use the wisdom passed down to us to help build the future. *The Good Life,* Richard Higgins further explained in *Christian Century,* "dissects the 'plausible lies' of our materialistic culture and argues that we need to revivify the cardinal virtues of prudence, justice, temperance and fortitude and the great theological virtues of faith, hope and love." "Gomes," added *Christian Century* contributor Jennifer E. Copeland, "defines success as 'doing something that is worth doing.' This is not groundbreaking news but, rather, a confirmation that good living takes a lot of hard work." A *Library Journal* critic concluded that with its "clear thinking and writing" *The Good Life* "promises to be another best seller." And *Booklist* reviewer June Sawyers wrote that "in writing about things that matter, [Gomes] has written a book that matters."

*BIOGRAPHICAL AND CRITICAL SOURCES:*

*PERIODICALS*

*Booklist,* October 1, 1996, p. 296; April 15, 1998, Ray Olson, review of *Sermons: Biblical Wisdom for Daily Living,* p. 1397; March 15, 2002, June Sawyers, review of *The Good Life: Truths That Last in Times of Need,* p. 1187.

*Christian Century,* May 22, 2002, Jennifer E. Copeland, "Tools for Life," p. 18, and Richard Higgins, "Polishing the Truth," p. 19.

*Christianity Today,* April 7, 1997, p. 42.

*Harvard Business Review,* September, 2001, David A Light, "Is Success a Sin?," p. 63.

*Hudson Review,* winter, 1998, Bruce Bawer, review of *The Good Book: Reading the Bible with Mind and Heart,* p. 691.

*Library Journal,* December 1996, John Moryl, review of *The Good Book,* pp. 99-100; May 1, 1998, Bernandette McGrath, review of *Sermons: Biblical Wisdom for Daily Living,* p. 106; May 15, 2002, John Moryl, review of *The Good Life,* p. 102.

*Los Angeles Times Book Review,* January 5, 1997, John C. S. Kim, review of *The Good Book,* p. 8.

*New Yorker,* November 11, 1996, Robert S. Boynton, pp. 64-73.

*People,* March 3, 1997, p. 65.

*Publishers Weekly,* September 16, 1996, p. 66.

*Time,* January 27, 1997, p. 77.

*Washington Post Book World,* March 23, 1997, Diana L. Hayes, review of *The Good Book,* p. 7.*

\*          \*          \*

**GORDON, Robert Ellis 1954-**

*PERSONAL:* Born May 25, 1954, in Boston, MA; son of Mark (in sales) and Joan (a teacher; maiden name, Strumph) Gordon. *Education:* Harvard College, B.A. (cum laude), 1977; Iowa Writers Workshop, M.F.A., 1979.

*ADDRESSES: Home*—P.O. Box 20129, Seattle, WA 98102.

*CAREER:* Novelist. Washington State Prison Writers Project, workshop director and writing teacher, 1989-96.

*AWARDS, HONORS:* James Michener Creative Writing fellow, 1983-84; Artist Trust grant, 1992; King County Arts Commission Publication Award for Fiction, 1993, for *When Bobby Kennedy Was a Moving Man.*

*WRITINGS:*

*When Bobby Kennedy Was a Moving Man,* Black Heron Press (Seattle, WA), 1993.

(With the inmates of the Washington Correction System) *The Funhouse Mirror: Reflections on Prison,* Washington State University Press (Pullman, WA), 2000.

Contributor of short stories to periodicals, including *Fiction, Ploughshares, Other Voices,* and *Seattle Review.*

*WORK IN PROGRESS: Between Worlds,* "a nonfiction account of my experiences teaching in the prisons."

*SIDELIGHTS:* In Robert Ellis Gordon's 1993 novel *When Bobby Kennedy Was a Moving Man,* Robert F. Kennedy is reincarnated as a moving man. Endowed by the gods who returned him to Earth with such magical powers as the ability to levitate furniture and the power to read people's thoughts, Kennedy defies the gods' orders and seeks out the gangster he believes murdered his brother, former U.S. President John F. Kennedy. Bobby is incarcerated, and is severely punished for sins he committed in his former life, as well as for the sins he has committed in his present life; ultimately, however, the gods forgive him and he is allowed to ascend to heaven. A contributor to *Publishers Weekly* praised Gordon's combination of "messianic novel and Kennedy tell-all," while in *Kirkus Reviews* a critic dubbed *When Bobby Kennedy Was a Moving Man* "the yarn to end all Kennedy yarns." In her review in the *Philadelphia Inquirer,* Madeline Crowley commented that the novel "dissects a human heart, shadowed by evil, rent by corruption and yet brilliantly lit by a heartfelt passion for social justice. As fiction, it plays fast and loose with facts, but it is scrupulous in its refusal to simplify the fine and the malign facets of Bobby Kennedy's character."

Gordon once told *CA:* "When I stumbled into prison teaching in 1988 (I was afraid of teaching in prison, but the job was offered and I needed the money), I discovered a second passion, right up there with writing. Clearly, my incarcerated students have problems with boundaries. Indeed, they have, on occasion, destroyed lives through their impulsiveness and rage. Still, when this same absence of inhibition is put in the service of story, the results can be penetrating, dazzling, profoundly moving in a way that 100 well-crafted stories in *Atlantic Monthly* will never be. My students teach me a lot about the literary perils of risk-aversion, about how to reach for the stories that matter. When I hear about critics or professors of literature proclaiming the death of literature, I think that these people are simply looking in the wrong places. Stories will live so long as the human race lives. We are a storytelling species, and that is all there is to it.

"I am a terribly slow writer, and I do not know what to do about that except to proceed, slowly, sentence by sentence, year by year. I pay as little attention as possible to the folks (there are so many of them!) who believe it is a writer's job to write about the world as they wish to see it. I can't even write about the world as *I* wish to see it. A writer's job, I believe, is to be as true to his or her own vision as possible; to bring all the craft (and then some) at his or her disposal to bear upon the vision, and to hope, over time, that the vision

and the craft will evolve. Time, not current intellectual fashion, will determine if a story has staying power, if it is one that matters."

After nearly a decade of teaching writing to inmates in the Washington state prison system, Gordon had enough fodder for a new book, and *The Funhouse Mirror: Reflections on Prison* was published in 2000. The volume contains Gordon's powerful account of teaching behind prison walls, and is complete with stories and essays by six prisoners. When explaining why he teaches these students, Gordon writes in his book: "When we give voice to the voiceless; when we give souls to formerly anonymous convicts; when we can no longer deny their humanity, we have no choice but to lay claim to them. And if and when we do that—if and when we peer into the funhouse mirror and conclude that our criminals belong to us and that they're made of the same stuff as us—well then we will . . . begin, as a society, to grow up." Trish Ready, a critic for *The Stranger.com,* described *The Funhouse Mirror* as "a timely, beautifully crafted, persistent book in its efforts to uncover the Third World of America's ever-expanding prison system." Dick Lehr agreed in his review for the *Houston Chronicle,* noting that Gordon has an "edgy and introspective style" in this "unvarnished examination of a prison culture that is as distant to most of us as the dark side of the moon."

## BIOGRAPHICAL AND CRITICAL SOURCES:

*PERIODICALS*

*Houston Chronicle,* April 29, 2001, Dick Lehr, "At the Steel Hotel, No Smiles in the Funhouse Mirrors," p. 21.
*Kirkus Reviews,* August 1, 1993.
*New York Times Book Review,* November 28, 1993, p. 26.
*Philadelphia Inquirer,* January 9, 1994.
*Publishers Weekly,* August 30, 1993, p. 90; August 14, 2000, review of *The Funhouse Mirror,* p. 344.

*ONLINE*

*The Stranger.com,* http://www.thestranger.com/ (September 24, 2002), Trisha Ready, review of *The Funhouse Mirror.**

**GOSDEN, Roger 1948-**

*PERSONAL:* Born September 23, 1948, in Ryde, England; married August 7, 1971; wife's name Carole Ann (divorced, 2003); children: Matthew, Thomas. *Ethnicity:* "English." *Education:* University of Bristol, B.Sc., 1970; Cambridge University, Ph.D., 1974; University of Edinburgh, D.Sc., 1989. *Religion:* Protestant.

*ADDRESSES: Office*—Jones Institute for Reproductive Medicine, Eastern Virginia Medical School, 601 Colley Ave., Norfolk, VA 23507; fax: 757-446-5905. *Agent*—Maggie Pearlstine, 31 Ashley Gardens, London SW1P 1QE, England. *E-mail*—gosdenrg@evms.edu.

*CAREER:* Cambridge University, Cambridge, England, research scholar, 1970-74; Duke University, Durham, NC, Population Council research fellow, 1974-75; Cambridge University, Cambridge, England, research fellow, 1975-76; University of Edinburgh, Edinburgh, Scotland, began as lecturer, became senior lecturer in physiology, 1970-94; University of Leeds, Leeds, England, professor of reproductive biology, 1994-99; McGill University, Montreal, Quebec, Canada, research director for obstetrics and gynecology at Royal Victoria Hospital, 1999-2001; Eastern Virginia Medical School, Norfolk, VA, scientific director of Jones Institute for Reproductive Medicine, 2001—.

*MEMBER:* European Society for Human Reproduction and Embryology, American Society for Reproductive Medicine, British Fertility Society, Society for the Study of Fertility.

*WRITINGS:*

*Biology of Menopause,* Academic Press (London, England), 1985.
*Transplantation of Ovarian and Testicular Tissues,* R. G. Landes (Austin, TX), 1996.
*Cheating Time: Science, Sex, and Aging,* W. H. Freeman (New York, NY), 1996.
*Designer Babies: The Brave New World of Reproductive Technology,* W. H. Freeman (New York, NY), 1999.
(With A. O. Trounson) *Biology and Pathology of the Oocyte,* Cambridge University Press (Cambridge, England), 2003.

Contributor to scientific journals.

*SIDELIGHTS:* Roger Gosden once told *CA:* "I write a large number of articles each year for scientific publications; they address technical subjects in reproductive medicine and biology. The books are written for fun and to expand my reading beyond the confines of biology. I choose to write about subjects from my professional life as a scientist, in the faint hope that I can bring a balanced view to subjects that all too often are sensationalized and aggravate public anxiety. Since I am a full-time academic, my writing is done in spare time and in the unsociable hours of the day and night."

*BIOGRAPHICAL AND CRITICAL SOURCES:*

*PERIODICALS*

*BioScience,* December, 1997, Avril D. Woodhead, review of *Cheating Time: Science, Sex, and Aging,* p. 804.
*Economist* (U.S.), March 9, 1996, review of *Cheating Time,* p. 87.
*New England Journal of Medicine,* February 20, 1997, James F. Fries, review of *Cheating Time,* p. 592.
*New Scientist,* February 10, 1990, Gail Vines, "Transplanted Eggs Can Create Ovaries," p. 30; March 30, 1996, Rosie Woodroffe, review of *Cheating Time,* p. 43.
*Publishers Weekly,* April 19, 1999, review of *Designing Babies: The Brave New World of Reproductive Technology,* p. 53.

\*     \*     \*

**GRAYSMITH, Robert 1942-**

*PERSONAL:* Born Robert Gray Smith, September 17, 1942, in Pensacola, FL; name legally changed, 1976; son of Robert Gray (a lieutenant colonel in the U.S. Air Force) and Frances Jane (Scott) Smith; married Margaret Ann Womack (a nurse), November 8, 1963 (divorced, June, 1973); married Melanie Krakower, November 26, 1975 (divorced, September, 1980); children: David Martin, Aaron Vincent, Margot Alexandra. *Education:* California College of Arts and Crafts, B.F.A., 1965. *Politics:* Democrat. *Religion:* Presbyterian. *Hobbies and other interests:* Collecting comic books and antique toys.

*Robert Graysmith*

ADDRESSES: *Home*—1015 Lincoln Way, San Francisco, CA 94122. *Office*—San Francisco Chronicle, 901 Mission St., San Francisco, CA 94103-2905. *Agent*—Dan Strone, William Morris Agency, 1350 Avenue of the Americas, New York, NY 10022.

CAREER: Oakland Tribune, Oakland, CA, political cartoonist, 1964-65; *Stockton Record,* Stockton, CA, staff artist, 1965-68; *San Francisco Chronicle,* San Francisco, CA, editorial cartoonist, 1968-80, illustrator, 1980-83; freelance illustrator and writer, 1983—.

AWARDS, HONORS: Foreign Press Club second place award, 1973, for cartoons; World Population Contest award, 1976, for "The Five Horsemen"; Pulitzer Prize nominee.

WRITINGS:

*NONFICTION, EXCEPT AS NOTED; SELF-ILLUSTRATED*

*Zodiac,* St. Martin's Press (New York, NY), 1986.
*The Sleeping Lady: The Trailside Murders above the Golden Gate,* Dutton (New York, NY), 1990.

*The Murder of Bob Crane,* Crown (New York, NY), 1992, published as *Autofocus: The Murder of Bob Crane,* Berkley Books (New York, NY), 2002.
*Unabomber: A Desire to Kill,* Regnery Publishing (Washington, DC), 1997, revised edition, Berkley Books (New York, NY), 1998.
*The Bell Tower: The Mystery of Jack the Ripper Finally Solved,* Regnery Publishing (Washington, DC), 1999.
*Zodiac Unmasked: The Identity of America's Most Elusive Serial Killer Revealed,* Berkley Books (New York, NY), 2002.
*Amerithrax: The Hunt for the Anthrax Killer,* Berkeley Books (New York, NY), 2003.

Illustrator of children's book *I Didn't Know What to Get You* by Penny Wallace, 1993; *Zodiac* has been translated into several languages.

ADAPTATIONS: *Autofocus: The Murder of Bob Crane* was adapted for film by Sony Classics and released as *Autofocus* in 2002; *Zodiac* has been adapted for film by Columbia TriStar.

WORK IN PROGRESS: *Melville and Gericault: Polished Shield, Dark Helmet,* the story of two great works of art and literature inspired by a shipwreck on the Equator; *Cape Disappointment,* a mystery novel; *Gluck,* a retelling of John Ruskin's *King of the Golden River* for children; *Torch Boys; Mocha Dick: The Man Who Painted Himself to Death; The Way-Car; The Vandeleur Moth;* and *Life in the Ghost Fleet.*

SIDELIGHTS: "After Jack the Ripper and before the Green River Killer came the Zodiac, one of the most deadly, elusive, and mysterious mass murderers in U.S. history," journalist Robert Graysmith once told *CA.* His popular first book, *Zodiac,* is an account of the numerous murders which haunted San Francisco during the late 1960s and early 1970s and was perpetrated by a person who called himself "Zodiac." "Like a political cartoon, I wanted this book to accomplish something, to effect a change," continued Graysmith. "Witchcraft, death threats, cryptograms, a hooded killer in consume, dedicated investigators, and a mysterious man in a white Chevy who is seen by all and known by no one are all parts of the Zodiac story—the scariest story I know. Slowly each arcane symbol and cipher broke away and I learned how the killer wrote the untraceable Zodiac letters (printed in their entirety for the first time in this book), why he killed when he did, and even the inspiration for his crossed-circle symbol and his executioner's costume."

"From my perspective as political cartoonist for the largest paper in northern California, the *San Francisco Chronicle,* I was there from the beginning as each cryptic letter, each coded message, each bloody swatch of victim's shirt came across the wood-grained editorial desk," recalled Graysmith. "At first the visual qualities of the Zodiac symbols drew me, but gradually a resolve grew within me to unravel the killer's clues and discover his true identity—and, failing that, to present every scrap of evidence available to ensure that someone, somewhere, might recognize the Zodiac and provide the missing piece to the puzzle."

The popularity of *Zodiac* pushed it on to national bestseller lists and ran it into thirteen printings and a French translation. Unfortunately, its popularity extended beyond mere readers. Graysmith told *CA* that in 1990 *Zodiac* again made the bestseller list after New York City officials announced that a mass-murderer dubbed "Zodiac" appeared to be "going by the book" that described the details of the killings that had once terrorized San Francisco. Investigators on the New York City Zodiac task force believed the gunman stalking their city had possibly copied methods outlined in Graysmith's book. "*Zodiac* was referred to as a 'handbook for death' and a 'blueprint for the killer's astrological shootings,'" Graysmith noted. "I spent a week in New York telling what I knew about the original case. The East Coast killer was undoubtedly a copycat and since he knew the birth signs of his victims, all strangers, before he shot them, I suspected he was a census taker."

In 2002 Graysmith published a follow-up to *Zodiac* titled *Zodiac Unmasked: The Identity of America's Most Elusive Serial Killer Revealed.* Here the author is able to positively identify the Zodiac killer, Arthur Leigh Allen. Allen, who died in 1992, had been near the top of a list of suspects during the investigation, but detectives Dave Toschi and Bill Armstrong were never able to build a convincing case for two main reasons: lack of sophisticated tools at the time, such as DNA testing, and because the police departments in San Francisco and Vallejo, California, where Allen lived, refused to cooperate with each other. Although this sequel offers readers a detailed account of the investigation, some reviewers noted that, other than re-

vealing the killer's true name, not much new information is provided. *San Francisco Chronicle* reviewer Bill Wallace commented that *Zodiac Unmasked* "is simply not as good as Graysmith's first effort, even though it is even longer and more detailed."

In addition to his books on the Zodiac killer, Graysmith has written several other true crime books, including works about Jack the Ripper, Theodore Kaczynski (also known as the Unabomber), and the murder of Bob Crane. *The Murder of Bob Crane* is a study of the mysterious unsolved murder of the star of the popular television series *Hogan's Heroes.* "I have always been enormously lucky in obtaining confidential documents and exclusive photos for my books," said Graysmith, "and the Crane book is no exception. I returned from Scottsdale, Arizona, where Bob was murdered, with over a thousand pages of police and D.A.'s documents." With a talent for both illustration and cartooning, Graysmith has provided the illustrations for each of his works of nonfiction. "*Crane* has twenty-nine illustrations and maps that I drew—it is my favorite part of the work," the author commented.

In *The Bell Tower: The Mystery of Jack the Ripper Finally Solved,* Goldsmith puts forth a theory that Jack the Ripper was, in fact, the Rev. Jack Gibson, a Canadian minister who was in England about the same time as the Jack the Ripper murders and who became a pastor in San Francisco just before two women were murdered in his parish. Although a *Publishers Weekly* reviewer stated that the author "makes a persuasive argument" that Gibson was the only one with the opportunity to kill the women, other critics of the book felt that Goldsmith does not present his case well. Michael Rogers, for one, wrote in *Library Journal* that Graysmith does not show "a single shred of hard evidence" that Gibson was the killer. In fact, another man was later tried and hanged for the crime. Rogers and the *Publishers Weekly* critic also both complained that very little of *The Bell Tower* is actually concerned with the Jack the Ripper case, instead wandering through other tangents, such as biographies of the journalists who covered the story. Nevertheless, a *Booklist* contributor praised Graysmith's "rat-a-tat, driving style," which makes for a compelling crime narrative.

Graysmith has also worked on a couple of books unrelated to true crime stories. *Gluck,* a work in progress, is a retelling of the Victorian classic, *King of the*

*Golden River,* by John Ruskin. And he has also illustrated *I Didn't Know What to Get You* by children's author Penny Wallace. These projects have provided Graysmith with yet another outlet for his talent. As he once told *CA,* "Children's book illustration is something I have dreamed of doing my entire life."

BIOGRAPHICAL AND CRITICAL SOURCES:

*PERIODICALS*

*Booklist,* July, 1999, Jay Freeman, review of *The Bell Tower: The Mystery of Jack the Ripper Finally Solved,* p. 1902.
*Kirkus Reviews,* June 15, 1999, review of *The Bell Tower,* p. 937.
*Library Journal,* March 1, 1986, p. 104; April 15, 1990, p. 108; June 15, 1999, Michael Rogers, review of *The Bell Tower,* p. 92; May 15, 2002, Michael Sawyer, review of *Zodiac Unmasked: The Identity of America's Most Elusive Serial Killer Revealed,* p. 112.
*Publishers Weekly,* June 28, 1999, review of *The Bell Tower,* p. 65; March 25, 2002, review of *Zodiac Unmasked,* p. 52.
*San Francisco Chronicle,* May 12, 2002, Bill Wallace, "The Murder Mystery That Wouldn't Die: Graysmith's Second Book on the Zodiac Reveals the Killer's Identity—but That's Not Really News," p. 6.

\*    \*    \*

**GRAYSON, Kristine**
   **See RUSCH, Kristine Kathryn**

\*    \*    \*

**GREENE, Stanley A. 1929-**

*PERSONAL:* Born April 27, 1929, in Rochester, NY; married Katherine Marine, November 1, 1959; children: Susan. *Education:* University of Arizona, B.S., 1952; University of Pennsylvania, M.B.A., 1954.

*ADDRESSES: Home*—829 Winter Rd., Rydal, PA 19046. *E-mail*—stanely.greene@att.net.

*CAREER:* Lawyers Co-operative Publishing Co., Rochester, NY, product manager, 1961-68; Auerbach Publishers, Philadelphia, PA, marketing manager for computer reference publications, 1968-73; *Legal Intelligencer,* Philadelphia, PA, general manager, 1975-80; Warman Publishing Co. (publisher of antique price guides), Philadelphia, PA, owner and president, 1980-89.

*AWARDS, HONORS:* Award for outstanding reference book, Reference Librarians Association, 1995.

*WRITINGS:*

(Editor, with Richard Pohanish) *Hazardous Materials Handbook,* Van Nostrand (New York, NY), 1996.
(Editor, with Richard Pohanish) *Rapid Guide to Chemical Incompatibilities,* Van Nostrand (New York, NY), 1997, second edition published as *Wiley Guide to Chemical Incompatibilities,* J. Wiley (Hoboken, NJ), 2003.
(Editor, with Richard Pohanish) *Hazardous Substances Resource Guide,* 2nd edition, Gale (Detroit, MI), 1997.
(Editor, with Richard Pohanish) *Electronic and Computer Industry Guide to Chemical Safety and Environmental Compliance,* Wiley (New York, NY), 1998.
(Editor, with Richard Pohanish) *Hazardous Chemical Safety Guide for the Machining and Metalworking Industries,* McGraw-Hill (New York, NY), 1999.
*McGraw-Hill's Hazardous Chemical Safety Guide for the Plastic Industry,* McGraw-Hill (New York, NY), 2000.
(Editor) *International Resources Guide to Hazardous Chemicals: Manufacturers, Agencies, Organizations, and Useful Sources of Information,* Noyes Publications (Norwich, NY), 2003.

\*    \*    \*

**GRIERSON, Philip 1910-**

*PERSONAL:* Born November 15, 1910, in Dublin, Ireland; son of Philip Henry (in business) and Roberta Ellen Jane (Pope) Grierson. *Ethnicity:* "White." *Education:* Gonville and Caius College, Cambridge, M.A., 1936. *Hobbies and other interests:* Science fiction.

*Philip Grierson*

ADDRESSES: *Office*—Gonville and Caius College, Cambridge University, Cambridge CB2 1TA, England; fax: 01223-33246.

CAREER: Cambridge University, Cambridge, England, fellow of Gonville and Caius College, 1935—, librarian, 1944-69, honorary keeper of coins at Fitzwilliam Museum, 1949—, lecturer, 1945-49, reader, 1959-71, professor of numismatics, 1971-78, president of the college, 1966-76, professor emeritus, 1978—. Free University of Brussels, professor, 1948-71; Oxford University Ford's Lecturer, 1956-57; University of London Creighton Lecturer, 1970. Dumbarton Oaks Center of Byzantine Studies, advisor in numismatics, 1955-98.

MEMBER: British Academy (fellow), Society of Antiquaries (fellow), Royal Numismatic Society (president, 1961-66), Royal Historical Society (literary director, 1945-55), Medieval Academy of America (corresponding fellow), Koninklijke Vlaamse Academie (corresponding member), Academie Royale de Belgique (associate member).

AWARDS, HONORS: Litt.D., University of Ghent, 1958; Cambridge University, Litt.D., 1971, LL.D., 1993; Litt D., University of Leeds, 1978.

WRITINGS:

(Editor and author of introduction and notes) *Les Annales de Saint-Pierre de Gand et de Saint Amand: Annales Blandinienses, Annales Elmarenses, Annales Formoselenses, Annales Elnonenses* (title means "The Annals of St. Peter's of Ghent and of St. Amand's"), Palais des Academies (Brussels, Belgium), 1937.

*Books on Soviet Russia, 1917-1942: A Bibliography and a Guide to Reading,* Methuen (London, England), 1943, reprinted, Anthony C. Hall (Twickenham, England), 1969.

*Numismatics and History,* G. Philip (London, England), 1951.

(Translator) F. L. Ganshof, *Feudalism,* Longman (London, England), 1952, revised edition, Harper (New York, NY), 1961, reprinted, University of Toronto Press (Toronto, Ontario, Canada), 1996.

(Editor) C. W. Previté-Orton, *The Shorter Cambridge Medieval History,* Cambridge University Press (Cambridge, England), 1952.

*Coins and Medals: A Select Bibliography,* Historical Association (London, England), 1954.

(Editor) H. E. Ives, *The Venetian Gold Ducat and Its Imitations,* American Numismatic Society (New York, NY), 1954.

(Editor, with John Ward Perkins) *Studies in Italian History Presented to Miss E. M. Jamison,* British School at Rome (Rome, Italy), 1956.

*Sylloge of Coins of the British Isles,* Volume I: *Fitzwilliam Museum: Early Ancient British and Anglo-Saxon Coins,* Oxford University Press (Oxford, England), 1958.

(With A. R. Bellinger) *Catalogue of the Byzantine Coins in the Dumbarton Oaks Collection and in the Whittemore Collection,* Dumbarton Oaks Center for Byzantine Studies (Washington, DC), Volume I: *Anastasius I to Maurice, 491-602,* 1966, Volume II: *Phocas to Theodosius III, 602-717,* two volumes, 1968, Volume III: *Leo III to Nicephorus III, 717-1081,* two volumes, 1973, Volume V: *Michael VIII to Constantine XI,* two volumes, 1999.

*English Linear Measures: An Essay in Origins,* University of Reading (Reading, England), 1972.

*Numismatics,* Oxford University Press (Oxford, England), 1975.

*Monnaies du Moyen Age* (title means "Coins of the Middle Ages"), Office du Livre (Fribourg, Switzerland), 1976.

*Les Monnaies,* Brepols (Turnhout, Belgium), 1977.

*The Origins of Money,* Athlone Press (London, England), 1977.

*Dark Age Numismatics,* Varorium Reprints (London, England), 1979.

*Later Medieval Numismatics (Eleventh-Sixteenth Centuries): Selected Studies,* Varorium Reprints (London, England), 1979.

*Bibliographie numismatique* (title means "Numismatic Bibliography"), 2nd edition, Cercle d'Etudes Numismatiques (Brussels, Belgium), 1979.

*Byzantine Coins,* University of California Press (Berkeley, CA), 1982.

(With Mark Blackburn) *Medieval European Coinage: The Early Middle Ages (Fifth-Tenth Centuries),* Cambridge University Press (Cambridge, England), 1986.

*The Coins of Medieval Europe,* Seaby's Numismatic Publications (London, England), 1990.

(Editor, with Ulla Westermark) Otto Morkholm, *Early Hellenistic Coinage,* Cambridge University Press (Cambridge, England), 1991.

(With Giuseppe Libero Mangieri) *Tari follari e denari,* translated by Alberto De Falco and Elio Venditti, Elea Press (Salerno, Italy), 1991.

(With Melinda Mays) *Catalogue of Late Roman Coins in the Dumbarton Oaks Collection and in the Whittemore Collection,* Dumbarton Oaks Center for Byzantine Studies (Washington, DC), 1992.

(With Lucia Travaini) *Medieval European Coinage,* Volume XIV: *Italy,* Part 3: *South Italy, Sicily, Sardinia,* Cambridge University Press (Cambridge, England), 1998.

Contributor to periodicals.

Author's works have been translated into several languages, including Italian.

*WORK IN PROGRESS: Medieval European Coinage,* Volume VII, *The Low Countries,* with Mark Blackburn, for Cambridge University Press (Cambridge, England).

*SIDELIGHTS:* Philip Grierson once told *CA:* "I am professionally a medieval historian, and medieval European history was what I taught at Cambridge University down to my retirement, but most of my publications over the past four decades have been in the field of numismatics.

"I became interested in coins at the quite advanced age of thirty-four, through finding a coin—from the era of the Byzantine emperor Phocas—in a box of junk belonging to my father. This started me collecting medieval European coins, initially as something to show to students, but in due course as material for research, so that I now possess what is probably the most representative collection of medieval European coins that exists. The collection is on indefinite loan to the Fitzwilliam Museum, Cambridge, so as to be available to scholars, and is bequeathed to the museum in my will.

"My more professional interest in the subject came about through a series of accidents. My early research had been concerned with medieval Flanders, and in 1947 I was invited to lecture at the universities of Brussels, Liege, and Amsterdam as part of a program of restoring scholarly links between the United Kingdom and the Low Countries after World War II. One of the lectures I gave had as its theme the light thrown by numismatics on the fall of the Roman Empire and the origins of medieval Europe. After giving the lecture at Brussels I was invited to apply for the professorship of numismatics in the university, a post I had not previously known to exist and that happened at the time to be vacant. I was appointed and gave an inaugural lecture on the historian and numismatics.

"I turned this lecture into a pamphlet that was published in England by the Historical Association. The president of the American Numismatic Society in New York read the pamphlet and conceived the idea for establishing a summer school in numismatics to be run by the society. In 1953 I was invited to assist in running the school and to stay in New York as the society's guest for six months. While I was there I visited the Dumbarton Oaks Center of Byzantine Studies in Washington, D.C. On a second visit in 1954 I was offered an honorary post as advisor in Byzantine numismatics, with the duty of turning their relatively small collection of Byzantine coins into one of international importance. I was also to have the privilege of publishing a catalogue when the time seemed ripe.

"The collection is now the best collection of Byzantine coins in the world, and in 1999, more than thirty years later, I completed the fifth and final volume of its catalogue's publication. I am also engaged in publishing a catalogue of the western medieval coins in the Fitzwilliam Museum in Cambridge, mainly ones in my own collection. Two volumes have already appeared. I do not expect to live to complete it, since fourteen volumes are planned, and it is already apparent that some of them will run to more than a single volume. But I am working with a sequence of younger research associates, funded jointly by the British Academy and my college in Cambridge, so I have every hope that the work will eventually be finished."

*BIOGRAPHICAL AND CRITICAL SOURCES:*

BOOKS

Brooke, C. N. L., editor, *Studies in Numismatic Method Presented to Philip Grierson,* Cambridge University Press (Cambridge, England), 1983.

PERIODICALS

*Caian,* November, 1978.
*Spink's Numismatic Circular,* September, 1991-March, 1992.

\*        \*        \*

## GRUBER, William E. 1943-

*PERSONAL:* Born September 26, 1943, in Hokendauqua, PA; son of William I. (a teacher) and Bessie (a teacher; maiden name, Hartman) Gruber; married Nancy Herrick, October 21, 1968; children: Elaine H., Laura K., Robert H. *Education:* Yale University, B.A., 1965; University of Idaho, M.A., 1974; Washington State University, Ph.D., 1979.

*ADDRESSES: Office*—Department of English, Emory University, Atlanta, GA 30322. *E-mail*—wegrube@emory.edu.

*CAREER:* Journalist and educator. *Courier-Post,* Camden, NJ, reporter, 1968-69; *Age,* Melbourne, Australia, reporter, 1969-70; Emory University, Atlanta, GA, professor of English, 1980—. *Military service:* U.S. Marine Corps, 1966-68.

*MEMBER:* Modern Language Association, South Atlantic Modern Language Association.

*AWARDS, HONORS:* Bread Loaf Writer's Conference Bakeless Prize, 2002, for *On All Sides Nowhere.*

*WRITINGS:*

*Comic Theaters* (novel), University of Georgia Press (Athens, GA), 1986.
*Missing Persons* (novel), University of Georgia Press (Athens, GA), 1994.
*On All Sides Nowhere: Building a Life in Rural Idaho* (memoir), Houghton Mifflin (Boston, MA), 2002.

*SIDELIGHTS:* William E. Gruber is a writer and professor of English whose third book, the memoir *On All Sides Nowhere: Building a Life in Rural Idaho,* takes him back to his days as a graduate student. In 1972 Gruber began graduate work at the University of Idaho while he and his wife homesteaded forty acres in the wilderness. Gruber reflects on how he eventually began to understand the lives of his neighbors, some of whom lived in crumbling shacks with junked cars in the yard, and good-naturedly pokes fun at their humorous idioms and simple yet magical way of perceiving the world. *Booklist* contributor Gilbert Taylor commended Gruber's characterization of his friends and neighbors, writing that they are "efficiently and honestly portrayed." A critic for *Publishers Weekly* agreed, noting that "While Gruber's writing is a gift, even better are the simple but profound truths he shares."

*BIOGRAPHICAL AND CRITICAL SOURCES:*

PERIODICALS

*Booklist,* August, 2002, Gilbert Taylor, review of *On All Sides Nowhere: Building a Life in Rural Idaho,* p. 1915.
*Kirkus Reviews,* June 15, 2002, review of *On All Sides Nowhere,* p. 854.
*Publishers Weekly,* June 3, 2002, review of *On All Sides Nowhere,* pp. 74-75.\*

# H

## HAGUE, Richard 1947-

*PERSONAL:* Born August 7, 1947, in Steubenville, OH; son of James R. (an engineer) and Ruth (a home-maker; maiden name, Heights) Hague; married Pamela C. Korte (a potter and teacher), June 24, 1980; children: Patrick, Brendan. *Ethnicity:* "White." *Education:* Xavier University, Cincinnati, OH, B.S., 1969, M.A., 1971. *Religion:* Roman Catholic. *Hobbies and other interests:* "Science, in particular local geology and archaeology, and the powers and functions of the brain and memory; gardening, which I practice compulsively and yet with great enjoyment."

*ADDRESSES: Office*—Purcell Marian High School, 2935 Hackberry, Cincinnati, OH 45206; fax: 573-751-1396. *E-mail*—haguekort@fuse.net.

*CAREER:* Purcell Marian High School, Cincinnati, OH, teacher of English, 1969—, department chair, 1975—. Xavier University, Cincinnati, adjunct lecturer; Southern Appalachian Writers Cooperative, co-coordinator, 1982, 1996; University of Louisville, literary artist at Kentucky Institute for Arts in Education, 1984; Ohio Arts Council, member of literary panel, 1984-87; Appalachian Writers Workshop, member of poetry staff, 1988, 1994; Green River Writers, member of advisory board, 1998—; Fitton Center for the Arts, John P. Kurlas Poet-in-Residence, 2000; Millikin University, visiting writer, 2001. Gives writing workshops and lectures on poetry; judge of writing competitions. Madisonville Community Garden, site manager, 1987-2001.

*MEMBER:* National Council of Teachers of English, Associated Writing Programs, Appalachian Teachers Network, Southern Appalachian Writers Cooperative, Ohio Council Teachers of English and Language Arts, Cincinnati Writers Project.

*AWARDS, HONORS:* President's Award in Poetry, *Ohio Journal,* 1979, for "An Unsent Letter of Darwin's," and 1981, for "Moose Ridge Apple Wine"; *Post*-Corbett Award in Literary Arts, *Cincinnati Post,* 1982, for continuing contribution to the arts in Cincinnati; grant from Greater Cincinnati Foundation, 1984; first prize in professional prose category, Ohio Educational and Library Media Association, 1985, for story "Whistling Woman and the Man of Light"; named Ohio co-poet of the year by Ohio Poetry Day Association, 1985, for *Ripening;* first prize in poetry, *Ambergris* Poetry and Fiction Contest, 1988; Black Swamp Poetry Prize, 1989; grant from National Endowment for the Humanities, 1990; National First Prize, English-Speaking Union, 1994, for writing program; Ohio Arts Council fellow, 1994, 1999; Council for Basic Education fellow, 1995; Marianist Education Consortium grants, 1996, 1998; Learning Links teacher's grants, Greater Cincinnati Foundation, 1996, 2002-03; National Book Award nomination, 1997, for *Milltown Natural: Essays and Stories from a Life;* Katherine Bakeless Scholar in Nonfiction, Bread Loaf Writer's Conference, 1997; first prize, Sow's Ear Poetry Contest, 1999; grants from Ohio Appalachian Arts Initiative and Southern Poverty Law Center, 1999; first prize, Sarasota Poetry Theater Poetry Contest, 1999, for "Soulspeak."

*WRITINGS:*

*Crossings* (poetry), Cincinnati Area Poetry Press, 1979.

*A Week of Nights down River* (poetry), privately printed, 1981.

*Ripening* (poetry), Ohio State University Press (Columbus, OH), 1984.

*Possible Debris* (poetry), Poetry Center, Cleveland State University (Cleveland, OH), 1988.

*Mill and Smoke Marrow* (poetry), Bottom Dog Press (Huron, OH), 1991.

*In a Red Shadow of Steel Mills* (poetry), Bottom Dog Press (Huron, OH), 1991.

*A Bestiary* (poetry), Pudding House Publications (Johnstown, OH), 1996.

*Milltown Natural: Essays and Stories from a Life,* Bottom Dog Press (Huron, OH), 1997.

*Greatest Hits, 1968-2000,* Pudding House Publications (Johnstown, OH), 2001.

*Garden* (poetry), Word Press (Cincinnati, OH), 2002.

*Into the Light* (poetry), Word Press (Cincinnati, OH), 2003.

Work represented in anthologies, including *Old Wounds, New Words,* Jesse Stuart Foundation, 1994; *Appalachia Inside Out,* University of Tennessee Press, 1995; *Coffeehouse Poetry Anthology,* Bottom Dog Press, 1996; *Down Home, down Town: Urban Appalachians Today,* Kendall-Hunt (Dubuque, IA), 1996; and *I Have My Own Song for It: Modern Poems of Ohio,* edited by Elton Glaser and William Greenway, University of Akron Press (Akron, OH), 2002. Columnist, *Word,* 1997-99; creativity columnist, *Personal Journaling,* 2001-02. Contributor of articles, essays, poetry, short stories, and reviews to periodicals, including *Appalachian Heritage, Country Journal, Creative Nonfiction, English Journal, Gambit, Kiosk, Laurel Review, Open Places, Poetry,* and *Wooster Review. Pine Mountain Sand and Gravel: Contemporary Appalachian Writing,* poetry editor, 1986, editor and publisher, 1996-2001; poetry editor, *Soaptown: Magazine of Cincinnati Writing* member of editorial board, *Appalachian Connection,* 1998-99, and *Down the River: A Collection of Ohio River Prose and Poetry.*

*WORK IN PROGRESS:* Poetry collections, including *Lives of the Poem* and *Alive in Hard Country; Aquavitae,* a short-story collection; *House Hold,* a creative nonfiction collection; *Earnest Occupation,* an essay collection.

*SIDELIGHTS:* Richard Hague once told *CA* that one of the most important events of his career "was the growing realization that I came from a specific and interesting place, that I was an Ohioan, a border Appalachian, and that these places had value and significance. Becoming aware of my own roots, I lived alone on Greenbrier Ridge in southeastern Ohio for several summers, and it was these stays, and their attendant lessons, that shaped me early in my career, and continue to do so now. Recently, I have centered even more: now I am a resident of Madisonville, an old neighborhood in Cincinnati, and I am a husband and father and gardener there. These, too, shape my work more and more. I try to celebrate the local; I try to find in the commonly overlooked or misapprehended detail some significance that may allow me to speak to people elsewhere, to reach them where they live.

"My major areas of vocational interest are the teaching of writing, both prose and poetry; studying and teaching the literature of place, so-called regional literature, discovering in it the universal."

*BIOGRAPHICAL AND CRITICAL SOURCES:*

*PERIODICALS*

*Appalachian Journal,* summer, 1985.
*Journal of Kentucky Studies,* September, 1993, pp. 57-65.
*Ohioana Quarterly,* spring, 1986.
*Western Ohio Journal,* spring, 1988.

\* \* \*

**HAMBLY, Barbara 1951-**

*PERSONAL:* Born August 28, 1951, in San Diego, CA. *Education:* University of California at Riverside, M.A. (medieval history); also studied at University of Bordeaux, France. *Hobbies and other interests:* Karate.

*ADDRESSES: Agent*—c/o Del Rey Books, 201 East 50th St., New York, NY 10022.

*CAREER:* Freelance writer. Has worked as a research assistant, high school teacher, and karate instructor.

*Barbara Hambly*

*MEMBER:* Science Fiction Writers of America (president, 1994-96).

*WRITINGS:*

NOVELS

*The Quirinal Hill Affair,* St. Martin's Press (New York, NY), 1983, published as *Search the Seven Hills,* Del Rey (New York, NY), 1987.

*Dragonsbane,* Del Rey (New York, NY), 1986.

*Those Who Hunt the Night,* Del Rey (New York, NY), 1988, published as *Immortal Blood,* Unwin (London, England), 1988.

*Beauty and the Beast* (novelization of television script), Avon (New York, NY), 1989.

*Song of Orpheus* (novelization of television script), Avon (New York, NY), 1990.

*Stranger at the Wedding,* Del Rey (New York, NY), 1994, published as *Sorcerer's Ward,* HarperCollins (London, England), 1994.

*Bride of the Rat God,* Del Rey (New York, NY), 1994.

*Traveling with the Dead* (sequel to *Those Who Hunt the Night*), Del Rey (New York, NY), 1995.

*Star Wars: Children of the Jedi,* Del Rey (New York, NY), 1995.

*Star Wars: Planet of Twilight,* Del Rey (New York, NY), 1997.

*Dragonshadow* (sequel to *Dragonsbane*), Del Rey (New York, NY), 1999.

*Knight of the Demon Queen* (sequel to *Dragonshadow*), Del Rey (New York, NY), 2000.

(With Marc Scott Zicree) *Magic Time,* EOS (New York, NY), 2001

*Sisters of the Raven,* Warner Books (New York, NY), 2002.

*"DARWATH" SERIES*

*The Time of the Dark,* Del Rey (New York, NY), 1982.

*The Walls of Air,* Del Rey (New York, NY), 1983.

*The Armies of Daylight,* Del Rey (New York, NY), 1983.

*Mother of Winter,* Del Rey (New York, NY), 1996.

*Icefalcon's Quest,* Del Rey (New York, NY), 1998.

*"SUN WOLF" SERIES*

*The Ladies of Mandrigyn,* Del Rey (New York, NY), 1984.

*The Witches of Wenshar,* Del Rey (New York, NY), 1987.

*The Unschooled Wizard,* (includes *The Ladies of the Mandrigyn* and *The Witches of Wenshar*), Doubleday (New York, NY), 1987.

*The Dark Hand of Magic,* Del Rey (New York, NY), 1990.

*"SUN-CROSS" SERIES*

*The Rainbow Abyss,* Del Rey (New York, NY), 1991.

*Magicians of the Night,* Del Rey (New York, NY), 1992.

*Sun-Cross* (includes *The Rainbow Abyss* and *Magicians of the Night*), Guild America, 1992.

*"WINDROSE CHRONICLES" SERIES*

*The Silent Tower,* Del Rey (New York, NY), 1986.

*The Silicon Mage,* Del Rey (New York, NY), 1988.

*Darkmage* (includes *The Silent Tower* and *The Silicon Mage*) Doubleday, 1988.
*Dog Wizard,* Del Rey (New York, NY), 1993.

*"STAR TREK" SERIES*

*Ishmael: A Star Trek Novel,* Pocket Books (New York, NY) 1985.
*Ghost Walker,* Pocket Books (New York, NY), 1991.
*Crossroad,* Pocket Books (New York, NY), 1994.

*"BENJAMIN JANUARY" SERIES*

*A Free Man of Color,* Bantam Books (New York, NY), 1997.
*Fever Season,* Bantam Books (New York, NY), 1998.
*Graveyard Dust,* Bantam Books (New York, NY), 1999.
*Sold down the River,* Bantam Books (New York, NY), 2000.
*Die upon a Kiss,* Bantam Books (New York, NY), 2001.
*Wet Grave,* Bantam Books (New York, NY), 2002.
*Days of the Dead,* Bantam Books (New York, NY), 2003.

*OTHER*

(Editor) *Women of the Night,* Warner Aspect, 1994.
(Editor) *Sisters of the Night,* Warner Aspect, 1995.

Contributor of short fiction to anthologies and other publications, including *Xanadu 2,* edited by Jane Yolen and Martin H. Greenberg, 1994; *South from Midnight,* Southern Fried Press, 1994; *Sandman: Book of Dreams,* 1996; and *War of Worlds: Global Dispatches,* 1996. Also author of scripts for animated cartoons.

*SIDELIGHTS:* While prolific novelist Barbara Hambly pens primarily sword-and-sorcery fantasies, she also writes in a variety of other genres: everything from vampire stories to mysteries to science fiction. Her novels include *Dragonshadow,* about a couple who must free their young son from a band of demons who have entered the human dimension to feed on the magic of dragons, wizards, and other fantastic creatures; she has also enjoyed success with a series of

historical mysteries featuring the free black man Benjamin January as he makes his way in pre-Civil War America. In addition, Hambly has created novelizations based on characters from popular films and television shows, among them *Beauty and the Beast, Star Wars,* and *Star Trek.* Considered a gifted storyteller, she has garnered a wide readership, and critics have praised her work. "Hambly's writing is witty and fast-paced," wrote Elizabeth Hand in the *Washington Post Book World,* while David Langford, in a *St. James Guide to Fantasy Writers* essay, remarked that Hambly "has a special talent for reclaiming and reworking familiar themes of fantasy, making them over into a seamless gestalt which is very much her own."

Hambly saw her writing career take shape in 1982 with publication of *The Time of the Dark,* the first book in her "Darwath" series. The series centers on a race of flying creatures known as the Dark Ones. Determined to take over a parallel Earth, the Dark Ones force graduate student Gil Patterson and auto mechanic Rudy Solis to defend the human race. Michael W. McClintock, reviewing *The Time of the Dark* in *Science Fiction and Fantasy Book Review,* found some faults, but wrote that Hambly "draws Gil and Rudy effectively, and the plot shows at least the possibility of interesting development." In contrast, Susan L. Nickerson in *Library Journal* described *The Time of the Dark* as a "heart stopping" and "unusually effective" fantasy work. *The Walls of Air* continues the adventure of Rudy and Gil, who have been taken to the Dark Ones' parallel world and transformed into a wizard and an elite guard respectively. While reviews for this novel were also mixed, Nickerson praised *The Walls of Air* for its "brisk action" and a feeling of impending menace which "keeps the reader deeply involved." *The Armies of Daylight* and *Mother of Winter* continue the "Darwath" saga, the latter novel drawing praise from a *Publishers Weekly* contributor who found "the story . . . involving, and the narrative intelligent."

In 1988 Hambly crafted a London-based vampire story with an odd twist: vampires as victims. *Those Who Hunt the Night* deals with a mysterious being who opens the coffins of vampires, exposing the nightstalkers to lethal sunlight and killing them as it drinks the vampire's blood. A frightened vampire enlists the help of ex-secret agent James Asher to find the culprit. Susan M. Schuller, writing in *Voice of Youth Advocates,* stated that Hambly "delves into vampire lore with gusto, detailing the lust for blood and the killing urge among the undead." *Traveling with the Dead* continues the adventures of Asher and his wife, Lydia, who battle together to prevent an alliance between human governments and the living dead. A *Library Journal* critic believed that *Traveling with the Dead* "captures both the subtle ambiance of turn-of-the-[twentieth-]century political intrigue and the even more baroque pathways of the human and the inhuman heart." A reviewer for *Publishers Weekly* remarked that Hambly's "vivid portraits" of the vampires "allow them to emerge as memorable personalities distinct from the viewpoints they represent."

Hambly has gained a strong following among mystery readers with her series of historical novels begun with 1997's *A Free Man of Color*. Set in early-nineteenth-century New Orleans, the book follows the exploits of Benjamin January, a free Creole with dark brown skin. January, a trained surgeon and pianist, returns to Louisiana after living in Paris and promptly becomes a murder suspect. Hambly does extensive research in preparation for each installment in the series, and her attention to detail pays off handsomely for readers. Marilyn Stasio, in the *New York Times Book Review*, praised *A Free Man of Color* as a "stunning first mystery"; Dick Adler described the novel in Chicago's *Tribune Books* as "magically rich and poignant." Commenting on Hambly's "seductive," detailed plots and vivid settings, Stasio maintained that Hambly paints her antebellum New Orleans setting as "a city that glitters with the sinister beauty of a snake."

In *Fever Season*, the second novel in the "Benjamin January" series, Hambly's talented musician/physician/sleuth works at a New Orleans charity hospital at a time when the city is in the grip of a cholera epidemic. January also realizes that free men of color are disappearing, and his investigations into the matter lead to a horrifying conclusion. According to a *Publishers Weekly* critic, *Fever Season* is "complex in plotting, rich in atmosphere, and written in powerful, lucid prose." A *Booklist* reviewer also praised the novel, calling it "rich, intense, and eye-opening."

January returns in several more novels by Hambly, among them *Graveyard Dust, Die upon a Kiss*, and *Days of the Dead*. In *Graveyard Dust* he confronts the power of Voodoo while attempting to free his sister from a murder rap and protect a young child from abuse. The year is 1834, and the free black man must also deal with racism and the still-raging cholera out-

break devastating New Orleans in a novel praised by a *Publishers Weekly* contributor for its "emotional authenticity, varied cast and rich historical trappings." Music enters the mix in *Die upon a Kiss* as pianist January performs in a production of the opera *Othello* with the orchestra of an opera company whose Italian cast members seem marked for murder. While noting that the plot is sometimes confusing, a *Publishers Weekly* contributor praised Hambly's "exquisite evocation" of the "exotic culture and menacing politics of antebellum New Orleans." Murder and mayhem continue to cross January's path in *Days of the Dead*, as the black sleuth and his new wife, Rose, travel south to Mexico to help a friend suspected of murder. January's efforts to exonerate his friend for the murder of the son of wealthy and eccentric Don Prospero de Castellon make for a characteristically intricate plotline in which Hambly introduces readers to a Mexico that a *Publishers Weekly* contributor described as "frighteningly alive, from its rampant poverty and self-serving politicians to the nation's preoccupation with and devotion to its dead." Praising not only *Days of the Dead* but the entire "Benjamin January" series, David Pitt noted in *Booklist* that Hambly's black protagonist is among the mystery genre's "most unusual and interesting protagonists" in a series that is tantamount to "literary time travel."

Other books by the prolific Hambly include several novels based on the popular *Star Wars* films as well as two based on the *Star Trek* television series created by the late Gene Roddenberry. In *Ishmael: A Star Trek Novel*, the Starship *Enterprise*'s First Officer Spock travels back in time to visit the earth in 1867 in an effort to thwart a Klingon plan to change human history. Roland Green of *Booklist* praised Hambly's effort, recommending it "not only for Star Trek collections but as a good novel in its own right." *Ishmael* grabs the reader's attention throughout "with humor, action and personal interplay," according to Roberta Rogow in a review for *Voice of Youth Advocates*.

*BIOGRAPHICAL AND CRITICAL SOURCES:*

*BOOKS*

*Detecting Women*, Purple Moon Press (Dearborn, MI), 1996, p. 88.
*Encyclopedia of Science Fiction, 1975-1991*, Gale (Detroit, MI), 1992.
*St. James Guide to Fantasy Writers*, St. James Press (Detroit, MI), 1996, pp. 261-263.

*PERIODICALS*

*Booklist,* September 1, 1983, p. 31; July, 1985, p. 1519; April 1, 1995, p. 1355; February 1, 1997, p. 907; May 15, 1998, review of *Fever Season;* February 8, 1999, p. 199; February 15, 1999, Roberta Johnson, review of *Dragonshadow,* p. 1048; April 15, 1999, Sally Estes, review of *Graveyard Dust,* p. 1478; May 15, 1999, p. 1678; February 1, 2000, Roberta Johnson, review of *Knight of the Demon Queen,* p. 1011; May 1, 2000, GraceAnne A. De Candido, review of *Those Who Hunt the Night* and *Traveling with the Dead,* p. 1599, and Jenny McLarin, review of *Sold down the River,* p. 1617; March 15, 2001, David Pitt, review of *Die upon a Kiss,* p. 1333; October 12, 2001, Regina Schroeder, review of *Magic Time,* p. 388; May 1, 2003, David Pitt, review of *Days of the Dead,* p. 1545.

*Davis Enterprise* (Davis, CA), October 29, 1995.

*Kirkus Reviews,* August 1, 1996, p. 1107; May 15, 1997, review of *A Free Man of Color,* p. 741; November 15, 1997, p. 1678; January 15, 1999, p. 110; June 15, 1999, p. 921; September 15, 2001, review of *Magic Time,* p. 1331.

*Kliatt,* January, 1999, p. 18.

*Library Journal,* May 15, 1982, Susan L. Nickerson, review of *The Time of the Dark,* p. 1014; March 15, 1983, p. 603; March 15, 1985, Janet Cameron, review of *The Ladies of Mandrigyn,* p. 599; March 15, 1995, p. 101; August, 1995, review of *Traveling with the Dead,* p. 122; September 15, 1996, p. 101; June 1, 1997, p. 148; March 15, 1999, Jackie Cassada, review of *Dragonshadow,* p. 112; July, 1999, Shirley Gibson Coleman, review of *Graveyard Dust,* p. 131; January, 2000, Jackie Cassada, review of *Knight of the Demon Queen,* p. 167; March 1, 2000, review of *Sold down the River,* p. S8; June 1, 2001, Rex Klett, review of *Die upon a Kiss,* p. 222; December, 2001, Jackie Cassada, review of *Magic Time,* p. 180; August, 2002, Jackie Cassada, review of *Sisters of the Raven,* p. 151.

*New Statesman,* November 28, 1986, p. 35.

*New York Times Book Review,* August 2, 1998, Marilyn Stasio, review of *Fever Season,* p. 24; July 25, 1999, Marilyn Stasio, review of *Graveyard Dust,* p. 20; July 23, 2000, Marilyn Stasio, review of *Sold down the River,* p. 20; July 8, 2001, Marilyn Stasio, review of *Die upon a Kiss,* p. 18; July 21, 2002, Marilyn Stasio, review of *Wet Grave,* p. 16.

*Publishers Weekly,* March 13, 1995, p. 63; September 4, 1995, review of *Traveling with the Dead;* September 16, 1996, p. 74; May 5, 1997, p. 197; April 27, 1998, p. 48; February 8, 1999, review of *Dragonshadow,* p. 199; May 31, 1999, review of *Graveyard Dust,* p. 69; January 3, 2000, review of *Knight of the Demon Queen,* p. 61; June 5, 2000, review of *Sold down the River,* p. 75; April 23, 2001, review of *Die upon a Kiss,* p. 52; October 8, 2001, review of *Magic Time,* p. 48; May 13, 2002, review of *Wet Grave,* p. 53; June 9, 2003, review of *Days of the Dead,* p. 40.

*Science Fiction and Fantasy Book Review,* September, 1982, pp. 30-31.

*Tribune Books* (Chicago, IL), July 6, 1997, Dick Adler, review of *A Free Man of Color,* p. 2.

*Voice of Youth Advocates,* February, 1986, pp. 393-394; August-October, 1986, p. 162; April, 1989, p. 42; October, 1995, p. 232; August, 1998, p. 210; April, 1999, p. 13.

*Washington Post Book World,* January 29, 1989, p. 6.

*ONLINE*

*Official Barbara Hambly Web site,* http://www.barbarahambly.com/ (July 25, 2003).*

\*    \*    \*

**HARDIN, Tom**
**See BAUER, Erwin A.**

\*    \*    \*

**HARRINGTON, Kent (Michael) 1945-**

*PERSONAL:* Born January 24, 1945, in Rochester, NY; son of Joseph Michael and Sally (Berkley) Harrington; married Antoinette Camille Roser (a hospital administrator), March 27, 1967. *Education:* Duke University, B.A., 1966; Johns Hopkins School of Advanced International Studies, M.A. (with distinction), 1968. *Hobbies and other interests:* Sailing, skiing, tennis.

*ADDRESSES: Home*—6909 Winners Circle, Fairfax Station, VA 22039. *Office*—Harrington Group, Suite 508, 1011 Arlington Blvd., Apt. 314, Arlington, VA 22209-2243. *Agent*—Sue Katz, Sue Katz and Associates, 928 Fifth Ave., New York, NY 10010.

*CAREER:* Citibank, New York, NY, loan officer, 1968-69; Embassy of Japan, Washington, DC, research counsel, 1972-73; Central Intelligence Agency, Washington, DC, intelligence officer, 1974-97, also held positions as director of public affairs, chief of station, analyst, and division chief; Arnold International, Washington, DC, president, beginning 1997; Harrington Group, Washington, DC, chairman, 1997—. Lecturer and guest speaker. *Military service:* U.S. Air Force, 1969-72; became first lieutenant.

*MEMBER:* Asia Society, Japanese-American Society, Authors Guild, Authors League of America.

*WRITINGS:*

FICTION

*The Gift of a Falcon,* McGraw-Hill (New York, NY), 1988.
*A Brother to Dragons,* Donald I. Fine (New York, NY), 1993.
*Dark Ride,* St. Martin's Press (New York, NY), 1996.
*Dia de los Muertos,* Dennis McMillan (Tucson, AZ), 1997.
*The American Boys,* Dennis McMillan (Tucson, AZ), 2000.
*The Tattooed Muse,* Dennis McMillan (Tucson, AZ), 2001.

Also contributor to periodicals.

*SIDELIGHTS:* Kent Harrington is a former CIA intelligence officer who has turned to writing noir and suspense novels that feature down-and-out protagonists who are often responsible for their own misfortunes. In *Dark Ride,* for example, Jimmy Rogers was a star athlete in school and heir to his father's fortune. Most people in his hometown thought that he would become a great success, but when his father writes him out of his will, Jimmy has to take a lowly job selling insurance. Things turn from bad to worse when his lover, a married woman who is addicted to sex and drugs, promises Jimmy a share of the wealth if he will murder her husband, Phil. Committing the crime does not improve his situation, however, because Phil's brother, an ex-convict named Nigel, finds out about the arrangement. From this point on, events in the novel spin out of control as Jimmy commits crime af-ter heinous crime in a desperate attempt to untangle the web he has woven. "Readers who like their humor black and their action noir should enjoy" *Dark Ride,* wrote one *Publishers Weekly* writer.

Harrington's *Dia de los Muertos* is set in Tijuana during the Day of the Dead celebrations. The protagonist, DEA agent Vince Calhoun, is suffering from gambling debts, dengue fever, a nasty ex-girlfriend, a gay agent who has fallen in love with him, and an investigation against his suspected involvement in smuggling illegal aliens into the United States. In a desperate attempt to release himself from his problems, Calhoun sets out on one last big smuggling caper. A *Publishers Weekly* reviewer wrote that Calhoun seemed to be "a parody of the noir hero" and that "most readers won't care" as they watch him destroy himself.

Harrington was on familiar ground in 2000 with his well-received spy thriller, *The American Boys,* before venturing into a mainstream mystery with *The Tattooed Muse* in 2001. The former title features CIA spy Alex Law, who, after twenty years of service to the agency, is on the outs as alcoholism takes its toll. But when he stumbles into a huge conspiracy involving drug cartels, high-ranking security agents, a plot against the American president, and even danger for his wife and son, Law gets a chance to redeem himself. "This literate thriller is edge-of-the-seat reading from start to finish," wrote one *Publishers Weekly* reviewer. In *The Tattooed Muse* the author once again studies a man who has had his circumstances suddenly reversed from good to bad. Writer Martin Anderson's fortunes seem to be on the rise when one of his books is accepted by a publisher and movie rights have been sold as well. However, someone seems to be trying to drive Martin insane, and when he starts to have memory lapses he starts to believe that he may have killed a movie producer. Although *Booklist* critic Thomas Gaughan liked Harrington's earlier noir pieces better, he noted that *The Tattooed Muse* is "worth the ride."

*BIOGRAPHICAL AND CRITICAL SOURCES:*

PERIODICALS

*Booklist,* December 15, 1995, Thomas Gaughan, review of *Dark Ride,* p. 688; November 15, 2001, Thomas Gaughan, review of *The Tattooed Muse,* p. 557.

*Kirkus Reviews,* December 15, 1995, review of *Dark Ride,* p. 1719.

*Publishers Weekly,* December 4, 1995, review of *Dark Ride,* p. 53; November 10, 1997, review of *Dia de los Muertos,* p. 56; April 17, 2000, review of *The American Boys,* p. 49.\*

ONLINE

*Under the Covers,* http:www.silicon.com/ (September 3, 1997), Kathee S. Card, review of *Dark Ride.*\*

\* \* \*

## HARRISON, Helen A(my) 1943-

*PERSONAL:* Born December 4, 1943, in Richmond Hill, NY; daughter of Joseph and Helen (Quortrup) Harrison; married Roy William Nicholson (an artist), August 26, 1967. *Education:* Adelphi University, A.B., 1965; attended Brooklyn Museum Art School, 1965-66, and Hornsey College of Art, 1966-67; Case Western Reserve University, M.A., 1975.

*ADDRESSES: Home*—R.D. 1, Box 447A, Sag Harbor, NY 11963. *Office*—Guild Hall Museum, 158 Main St., East Hampton, NY 11937.

*CAREER:* Artist, curator, and writer. Sculptor, 1967-73; independent researcher and curator, 1975-77; Parrish Art Museum, Southampton, NY, curator, 1977-78; *New York Times,* New York, NY, art critic, 1978—. Guest curator at Queens Museum, Flushing, NY, 1979-81; consultant curator at Guild Hall Museum, 1982—. Executive director of Public Art Preservation Committee, 1981-82.

*MEMBER:* Association International des Critiques d'Art, American Association of Museums, American Studies Association.

*WRITINGS:*

*Dawn of a New Day: The New York World's Fair, 1939-1940,* New York University Press (New York, NY), 1980.

*Larry Rivers* (monograph), Harper (New York, NY), 1984.

(With Lucy R. Lippard) *Women Artists of the New Deal Era: A Selection of Prints and Drawings,* National Museum of Women in the Arts (Washington, DC), 1988.

*Silkscreen: Arnold Hoffmann, Jr. and the Art of the Print,* Museums at Stony Brook (Stony Brook, NY), 1995.

(Editor) *Such Desperate Joy: Imagining Jackson Pollock,* Thunder's Mouth Press (New York, NY), 2000.

(With Constance Ayers) *Hamptons Bohemia: Two Centuries of Artists and Writers on the Beach,* Chronicle Books (San Francisco, CA), 2002.

Contributor of articles and reviews to art journals, exhibition catalogs, and newspapers, including *New York Times.*

*WORK IN PROGRESS:* Research on Sara and Gerald Murphy and their surrealist circle in East Hampton prior to World War II.

*SIDELIGHTS:* Helen A. Harrison is an art critic and curator as well as a writer. She writes about the world of art, those who inhabit it, and its history. In 2000 she edited a book titled *Such Desperate Joy: Imagining Jackson Pollock.* Pollock, who died in 1956, was always seen as a troubled and radical artist, though in more recent years he has been hailed as brilliant. Harrison compiled a collection of writings, interviews, and even personal responses from Pollock about his life and paired them with photos of his work in an attempt to demystify the artist.

*Hamptons Bohemia: Two Centuries of Artists and Writers on the Beach* is a chronicle of the artistic legacy of the Hamptons from the mid-nineteenth century to the 1960s and 1970s. The Hamptons developed into a traditional summer and weekend haven for artists, and Winslow Homer, Andy Warhol, James Fenimore Cooper, and John Steinbeck were among those who visited there. Harrison recounts beach trips, art gallery openings, and everyday life, complete with photographs. Mark Rozzo, reviewing the book for the *New Yorker,* praised *Hamptons Bohemia* as "a colorful ode to the Hamptons' often overlooked cultural legacy."

Describing her career in the arts, Harrison once told *CA*: "During my original career as an artist, a period of residence in England stimulated my curiosity about public art patronage and ultimately led me to return to the United States to pursue a graduate degree in art history, concentrating on the federal patronage programs of the New Deal era. This is my major area of scholarly research.

"Work on catalogs and exhibitions developed out of my graduate study, and my critical writings began as a consequence of my curatorial activities. Thus, each aspect of my professional life has been vital to the growth and development of my career, and I consider my early training in art to be an essential part of my life as a scholar, critic, and curator. Without this preparation, I would not have the practical background I believe to be essential to my work today.

"The role of art critic is perhaps the most challenging aspect of my professional life, for it involves the publication of subjective judgments based on personal experience, rather than the disinterested examination of historical facts or the rigorous objectivism of scholarly discourse. It does not necessarily involve interest in and curiosity about the artists themselves, but in my case, I am familiar with many of the artists about whose work I write.

"The fact that I write primarily for newspaper readers implies that my audience is broad and general, and I feel it is my responsibility to speak to them in terms they can understand without 'talking down' and presuming them naive. My function, I feel, is to stimulate interest in and appreciation of art without offering hard-and-fast rules for interpretation or evaluation.

"I stress that art must be experienced before it can be judged, and that only through exposure and open-minded examination can the viewer form a valid opinion. On the other hand, I do not shrink from expressing my own opinions but I feel obliged to back them up with solid reasoning. In this way, I hope to encourage readers to think for themselves and arrive at their own conclusions."

*BIOGRAPHICAL AND CRITICAL SOURCES:*

*PERIODICALS*

*Art in America,* July, 2002, p. 23.
*New Yorker,* May 27, 2002, p. 21.
*Publishers Weekly,* May 27, 2002, p. 47.*

## HARRISON, Kathryn 1961-

*PERSONAL:* Born March 20, 1961, in Los Angeles, CA; daughter of Edward M. and Carole Cecile (Jacobs) Lang; married Colin Harrison (an editor and novelist); children: two. *Education:* Attended Stanford University and University of Iowa Writers' Workshop.

*ADDRESSES: Home*—Brooklyn, NY. *Agent*—Amanda Urban, International Creative Management, 40 West 57th St., New York, NY 10019. *E-mail*—thebindingchair@yahoo.com.

*CAREER:* Writer. Former editor at Viking Publishers, New York, NY.

*AWARDS, HONORS:* James Michener Fellowship, 1989; artists' fellowship, New York Foundation for the Arts, 1994.

*WRITINGS:*

*Thicker Than Water,* Random House (New York, NY), 1991.
*Exposure,* Random House (New York, NY), 1993.
*Poison,* Random House (New York, NY), 1995, published as *A Thousand Orange Trees,* Fourth Estate (London, England), 1995.
*The Kiss* (memoir), Random House (New York, NY), 1997.
*The Binding Chair; or, A Visit from the Foot Emancipation Society,* Random House (New York, NY), 2000.
(Author of introduction) Nathaniel Hawthorne, *The Scarlet Letter,* Modern Library (New York, NY), 2000.
*The Seal Wife,* Random House (New York, NY), 2002.
*Seeking Rapture: Essays and Occasional Pieces,* Random House (New York, NY), 2003.

*SIDELIGHTS:* With the publication of her 1997 memoir, *The Kiss,* Kathryn Harrison placed herself at the center of a firestorm of controversy. In this personal tale, the novelist tells the story of how with a passionate kiss her father started an incestuous relationship with her that lasted four years, until the death of her mother. What made Harrison's story different from other exposes of incest, and what raised the contro-

*Kathryn Harrison*

versy, was that Harrison was twenty years old when the kiss occurred. Over the next four years, the once estranged father and daughter carried on an affair, secret meetings in places far from Harrison's college and her father's community, where he had a new wife and family, and a position as a preacher.

Harrison's frank talk about this incestuous affair drew immediate and pointed criticism. One line of criticism accused the author of using this serious breach of social mores to titillate the masses in order to sell more books, increasing her financial and literary capital. Jonathan Yardley's blunt assessment of Harrison's book represented this view. He wrote in the *Washington Post,* "*The Kiss* is trash from the first word to the last, self-promotion masquerading as literature." Other critics faulted Harrison for turning a cathartic confrontation of past demons into an exercise in raising the kiss-and-tell bar to absurd heights. "The point is," maintained James Wolcott in the *New Republic,* "just because she wrote it doesn't mean she had to publish it. It is assumed today that all secrets are bad, that withholding them is unhealthy; secrets denied the light of day will only fester." But, according to Wolcott,

"There is a big difference between getting something out of your system and putting it on the market." Similarly, for other reviewers, *The Kiss* represented an act of narcissism and evasion of responsibility on Harrison's part.

Harrison and *The Kiss* were not without their defenders, however. "What's really going on in this memoir," suggested Diane Roberts in the *Atlanta Journal and Constitution,* "has to do with the shifty issues of power, possession, how families live and lie, how the role of parent is not God-given or inviolate, how a child can be both victim and collaborator." And, according to Christopher Lehmann-Haupt in the *New York Times,* Harrison did not sidestep the issues of narcissism and responsibility. "Ms. Harrison," he wrote, "while not analytical, spins a complex web of clues involving narcissism, repressed desire, her mother's emotional inaccessibility, her father's hunger to recapture the past and her own need for substantiation."

*Harper's Bazaar* contributor Mary Gordon rejected the notion that Harrison's novel was just another kiss-and-tell expose contrived to appeal to the basest of human instincts. "*The Kiss* stands out from a welter of recent sensational memoirs because of the complexity of Harrison's moral views," she maintained; "her refusal to allow her carefully crafted 'I' the simple role of victim; and her near absolute avoidance of the prurient—the description of the kiss and another scene . . . are the extent of the sexual specifics." It is not "trash" in Roberts's view. Rather, she declared *The Kiss* "an extraordinary book," "exquisite" and written "the way a poet writes." Noted Lehmann-Haupt, "Her narrative is spare and stark, written in a present tense that perfectly conveys how her experience happened." Harrison stood by her effort to write about that experience and to publish it. As she told Gordon, "There is only one real incest taboo: talking about it. . . . The people who judge me about this book don't judge me for what I did, just for talking about it."

In addition to stirring a controversy among critics, *The Kiss* also confirmed in the minds of some reviewers that, despite the author's prior comments to the contrary, Harrison was mining her own family experience for the material for her first two novels. *Los Angeles Times* critic Carolyn See described the plot of Kathryn Harrison's first novel, *Thicker Than Water,* as "the story of a particular California nightmare: The child who is born in easy, even luxurious circumstances, and soon, way too soon, notices that her fate on Earth is to be discarded and loathed." Isabel, the protagonist of *Thicker Than Water,* is abandoned first by a father she's never met and then by her mother, who is not interested in taking care of a child. She is raised quietly by her grandparents in a wealthy suburb of Los Angeles and subjected to regular and frequent visits from her mother, who abuses her. When her father appears late in her adolescence, he completes a pattern of sexual assault by raping her repeatedly over the two-year period during which her mother struggles with cancer.

Scott Spencer characterized *Thicker Than Water* in his *New York Times Book Review* article as "odd but beautifully written." The novel similarly struck other reviewers, who point to Harrison's lyrical prose, which encompasses such horrifying acts as incest and physical degradation. Sally Emerson explained in the *Washington Post Book World* that "it is . . . not so much the plot which is compelling, but the mesmeric writing and the control with which the author moves back and forth through different time frames." Michiko Kakutani of the *New York Times* called the effect of Harrison's writing "devastating." Kakutani added that *Thicker Than Water* "is a story written in hallucinatory, poetic prose, yet a story that possesses the harrowing immediacy—and visceral impact—of a memoir." Similarly, Spencer commented: "[Harrison] has produced a beautifully written, unsparingly honest novel."

Spencer then wondered in his 1991 review of *Thicker Than Water* (six years before Harrison's public admission in *The Kiss*) if this first novel was more honest than the author was willing to admit. "The first two words of *Thicker Than Water* are 'In truth,'" Spencer wrote, "and as the novel plunges into a woman's painfully frank and unsparing revelations about her miserable childhood, and her struggle to awaken from its dank, hypnotic spell, this reader felt, at times, that he was reading a harrowing, fully imagined work of nonfiction. There is very little traditional narrative flow, yet the reader remains spellbound not only by the artistry of the writing but by its persistent and often horrifying matter-of-factness." Kakutani echoed this observation, writing, "There is almost no authorial distance between Isabel and her creator, almost no indication that this is a novel we're reading." Even so, as Kakutani found remarkable, the story successfully

presents more than just the tragedy experienced by a child, "it also manages to wring from its heroine's story the hope and possibility of transcendence."

Harrison's second novel, *Exposure,* also centers on an abnormal relationship between a parent and child; in this case, a photographer-father takes eerily suggestive and morbid pictures of his daughter throughout her childhood and adolescence. Harrison told Patricia A. O'Connell in *Publishers Weekly:* "I wrote about a photographer because I wanted a relationship between a parent and a child in which the former stole something from the latter, and the thing taken was somewhat slippery." The main action of the story takes place during the weeks before a retrospective of Edgar Rogers's work is scheduled at the Museum of Modern Art. Through a variety of perspectives, including first-person monologues, court and private detective reports, and newspaper articles, Harrison constructs the demise of the daughter as she becomes addicted to crystal methedrine and begins to shoplift. The author explained this choice of narrative exposition to O'Connell: "I had a character who was going through crisis and change; although intelligent, she was not self-aware. I needed a number of mechanisms by which we could see into her . . . because she's not good at telling us about herself."

Critical response to *Exposure* was warm, both for the issue of artistic freedom versus artistic integrity the novel raises and for Harrison's unconventional method of exposition. Mindi Dickstein of the *Chicago Tribune Book World* remarked: "At their best, stories expose the secrets we live with but cannot utter, and the best writers preserve the unsayable nature of those secrets while capturing them long enough for us to gaze upon their mystery. Kathryn Harrison is such a writer." While noting that "at times Ms. Harrison is heavy-handed and comes close to making a didactic look-what-you've-done-to-this-girl argument," Howard Coale concluded in the *New York Times Book Review* that "Ms. Harrison does not allocate blame without a full analysis of all the ironies and all the nooks and crannies of responsibility." *Washington Post Book World* contributor Wendy Smith described Harrison's "accomplishment" in *Exposure* as "the delineation, in superbly modulated prose, of a woman's painful, tentative journey toward self-knowledge." Of her own work, Harrison commented to O'Connell: "I'm not a doctor, so clinical diagnosis is not my realm. But both physical and mental illnesses are factors in my work. I hope that my imagination in some way illuminates the human condition."

In her third work of fiction, *Poison,* Harrison achieves some artistic distance between herself and her work by setting the story in seventeenth-century Spain. Her blending of historical fact and fiction impressed a number of reviewers. "The historical novel is a vigorously evolving form," observed Laura Argiri in the *Village Voice.* "And Kathryn Harrison's *Poison* is a lively example of that evolution." For *New York Times Book Review* contributor Janet Burroway, "Ms. Harrison's voluminous research is everywhere evident, but so seamlessly matched by invention that the reader neither knows nor cares which is which." Ron Hansen offered a similar evaluation in the *Los Angeles Times Book Review:* "It's gratifying to find that in this book she's handled the forbidding obligations of historical fiction so well."

Harrison's story follows two women, Maria Luisa and Francisca, who lead very different lives; even so, both women are consumed by a Spain in a period of decline. Maria Luisa (born Marie Louise de Bourbon, the niece of France's King Louis XIV) is an historical figure. She is sent from her homeland to become the queen to Spain's Carlos II and to bear him an heir. Carlos is a boy, retarded and crippled, who lives off of breast milk supplied to him by a team of wet nurses. The daughter of one of these wet nurses and a failed silkworm farmer is Francisca de Luarca. Maria Luisa fails to produce an heir for her incompetent or impotent husband and is poisoned. Francisca pursues forbidden love with a priest and is imprisoned. From her prison cell, Francisca becomes Maria Luisa's biographer, reconstructing the story of the queen, abandoned and destroyed in a strange land. "In a novel of less authority this might be clumsy," commented Burroway, "but in Ms. Harrison's hands it raises, instead, serious questions about the power of imagination and the nature of history."

*Poison* captures the events of Spanish history swirling around these two women as well as the public lives that they live in the Spanish capital; but it also offers insight into the intimate lives of women in the seventeenth century. For Francisca, there is love. And, in the opinion of Judith Dunford in *Tribune Books,* Harrison's portrayal of this love is "remarkable—crystalline prose perfumed (but not too much; she knows just when to stop) with musky eroticism, bigger

enough than life to carry you away." For Maria Luisa, there is no love; there is only duty. "If Harrison writes meltingly about sexual love," added Dunford, "she does even better at sexual loathing . . . the mixture of disgust, longing, pity and duty in the couplings of Charles [Carlos] and Maria Luisa."

The result of Harrison's blending of fact and fiction to create the lives and loves of these two women "is a fascinating, feminist princess-and-pauper story, gorgeously written and hauntingly told," concluded Hansen. "It is a tale of passion, hopelessness and thwarted ambitions in a harsh and hate-filled century that was, as in all fine historical fiction, quite different than and disturbingly like our own."

Harrison's fourth novel, *The Binding Chair,* tells the story of a woman whose feet were crushed and bound per the Chinese aesthetic of beauty. May-li, the book's protagonist, had her feet ritually bound as a child. The ritual left her virtually a cripple, but her physical disfigurement is only an outward display of female subservience to men in nineteenth-century China. Following an unhappy arranged marriage, May-li flees and goes into prostitution. As a prostitute, she meets an Englishman and marries into his very Western family. Although she is cold and manipulative, May-li becomes a mentor to her young English niece, Alice.

Although *Times* reviewer Christina Koning said that Harrison accurately described Shanghai and the period, "conjuring up a wonderfully vivid image of the city and its inhabitants," the darkness and misery May-li faces becomes "a bit relentless." Other critics felt differently. Eleanor J. Bader, for example, asserted in *Library Journal* that even though the subject matter is brutal and tragic, Harrison is an "extremely gutsy writer" and *The Binding Chair* is "ambitious." *Booklist* reviewer Donna Seaman similarly said that Harrison is an "inventive" and "provocative" author. The critic also described the plot as "sinuous" and "surprising." A *Publishers Weekly* reviewer further called *The Binding Chair* Harrison's "best work to date. . . . [It is] intricately and elegantly constructed."

*The Seal Wife* also deals with a cross-cultural love affair. Set in Alaska during the early part of the twentieth century, the novel features a young American meteorologist who goes to Alaska to set up a weather station. In the mysterious, provocative land, Bigelow falls deeply in love with a silent Aleut woman who barely acknowledges him, and who ends the affair inexplicably. Hopelessly obsessed, Bigelow desperately desires to get the silent woman back. Critics generally responded to *The Seal Wife* positively. Donna Seaman, writing again in *Booklist,* called the love story "provocative" and the tale itself "delectably moody," while Vince Passaro of *O: The Oprah Magazine* declared the story "elegant and brief" and "profoundly reverent." A *Publishers Weekly* reviewer noted that "Harrison writes mesmerizing, cinematically vivid scenes."

Commenting on Harrison's writing in general, Maria Russo described her in the *New York Times* as an author who possesses "a real talent for conjuring far-flung times and places." Relying on the themes of female oppression, victimhood, and martyrdom, Harrison has demonstrated an ability to describe the minute details of particular eras and the torment her characters experience throughout each of her novels.

*BIOGRAPHICAL AND CRITICAL SOURCES:*

BOOKS

*Contemporary Literary Criticism,* Volume 70, Gale (Detroit, MI), 1992.

PERIODICALS

*Atlanta Journal and Constitution,* March 30, 1997, p. K12.
*Book,* May-June 2002, Kera Bolonik, "Keeping Secrets," p. 13.
*Booklist,* May 1, 1995, p. 1551; March 1, 1997, p. 1094; February 15, 2000, Donna Seaman, review of *The Binding Chair,* p. 1051; April 1, 2002, Donna Seaman, review of *The Seal Wife,* p. 1306.
*Chicago Tribune,* June 4, 1995, p.3.
*Chicago Tribune Book World,* February 21, 1993, p. 5.
*Cosmopolitan,* May, 1995, p. 44.
*Daily Telegraph* (London, England), May 13, 2000, Victoria Lane, review of *The Binding Chair,* p. 05.
*Entertainment Weekly,* May 26, 1995, p. 79; March 21, 1997, pp. 30-31.
*Glamour,* May, 1995, p. 172.
*Guardian Weekly,* July 31, 1994, p. 28.

*Harper's Bazaar,* April, 1997, p. 136.
*Insight in the News,* June 26, 1995, pp. 24-25.
*Kirkus Reviews,* February 15, 2002, review of *The Seal Wife,* p. 209.
*Library Journal,* March 15, 2000, Eleanor J. Bader, review of *The Binding Chair,* p. 127; April 1, 2002, Colleen Lougen, review of *The Seal Wife,* p. 138.
*Los Angeles Times,* March 18, 1991, p. E3.
*Los Angeles Times Book Review,* June 18, 1995, p. 8.
*New Republic,* March 31, 1997, p. 32.
*New Statesman & Society,* July 28, 1995, p. 40.
*Newsweek,* February 17, 1997, p. 62.
*New York,* May 15, 2000, Daniel Mendelsohn, review of *The Binding Chair,* p. 70.
*New York Times,* April 26, 1991, p. C30; February 27, 1997, p. C18; May 26, 2000, Michiko Kakutani, "Willful Sensation yet Not Soap Opera," pp. B42, E44; April 30, 2002, Michiko Kakutani, "Sexual Obsession in Frontier Alaska," pp. B8, E8; May 5, 2002, Maria Russo, "Which Way the Wind Blows," p. 12.
*New York Times Book Review,* April 21, 1991, pp. 13-14; March 14, 1993, p. 10; December 5, 1993, p. 60; May 29, 1994, p. 20; May 14, 1995, p. 12; September 8, 1996, p. 36; March 30, 1997, p. 11; June 14, 1998, review of *The Kiss,* p. 32; May 21, 2000, review of *The Binding Chair,* p.9; June 7, 2000, Susan Hall-Balduf, review of *The Binding Chair,* p. 24; May 12, 2002, review of *The Seal Wife,* p. 26; June 2, 2002, review of *The Seal Wife,* p. 24.
*O: The Oprah Magazine,* May, 2002, Vince Passaro, "Love in a Very Cold Climate," p. 190.
*People Weekly,* May 29, 1995, p. 27; March 17, 1997, p. 33; May 15, 2000, V. R. Peterson, review of *The Binding Chair,* p. 59.
*Publishers Weekly,* March 1, 1993, pp. 33-34; March 6, 1995, p. 53; February 10, 1997, p. 71; March 15, 2000, review of *The Binding Chair,* p. 59; February 25, 2002, review of *The Seal Wife,* p. 37.
*Sunday Times,* November 7, 1999, "Postmodernist Homage," p. 37.
*Time,* May 29, 1995, p. 71; March 10, 1997, p. 90.
*Times* (London, England), May 6, 2000, Christina Koning, "Shanghai Surprise," p. 22.
*Times Literary Supplement,* May 12, 2000, Ruth Scurr, review of *The Binding Chair,* p. 21.
*Tribune Books* (Chicago, IL), July 17, 1994, p. 8; June 4, 1995, p. 3; December 10, 1995, p. 1.
*USA Today,* May 25, 1995, p. D4; March 13, 1997, p. D4.

*US Weekly,* May 29, 2000, Melanie Rehak, review of *The Binding Chair,* p. 51.

*Vanity Fair,* February, 1997, pp. 54-58.

*Village Voice,* May 16, 1995, p. 82.

*Wall Street Journal,* March 4, 1997, p. A16; May 12, 2000, Gabi Taub, review of *The Binding Chair,* p. W8.

*Washington Post,* June 9, 1991, p. 11; June 16, 1993, pp. B1, B4; March 5, 1997, p. D2.

*Washington Post Book World,* March 7, 1993, p. 7; April 30, 1995, p. 9.*

\*      \*      \*

## HEYLIN, Clinton (M.) 1960-

*PERSONAL:* Born April 8, 1960, in Urmston, Manchester, England; son of Stanley Alexander (an insurance broker) and Maisie (a perfumery consultant; maiden name, Stone) Heylin. *Education:* Bedford College, London, B.A. (with honors), 1981; University of Sussex, M.A., 1983. *Religion:* Church of England.

*ADDRESSES: Home*—203 Northenden Rd., Sale, Cheshire M33 2JB, England.

*CAREER:* Codirector of an insurance brokerage, 1983-89; writer.

*WRITINGS:*

*Rain Unravelled Tales,* privately printed, 1982.

*More Rain Unravelled Tales,* privately printed, 1984.

(With Craig Wood) *Form and Substance,* Sound Publishing (Denver, CO), 1988.

*Stolen Moments,* Wanted Man (London, England), 1988.

*Rise/Fall,* Omnibus Press (New York, NY), 1989.

*Gypsy Love Songs and Sad Refrains,* privately printed, 1989.

*Bob Dylan: Behind the Shades,* Penguin (New York, NY), 1991.

*Dylan,* Viking (New York, NY), 1991.

(Editor) *The Penguin Book of Rock and Roll Writing,* Viking (London, England), 1992, published as *The Da Capo Book of Rock and Roll Writing,* Da Capo Press (Boulder, CO), 2000.

*From the Velvets to the Voidoids: A Pre-Punk History for a Post-Punk World,* Penguin (New York, NY), 1993.

*Bootleg: The Secret History of the Other Recording Industry,* St. Martin's Press (New York, NY), 1995.

*Bob Dylan: The Recording Sessions, 1960-1994,* St. Martin's Press (New York, NY), 1995.

*Bob Dylan: A Life in Stolen Moments, Day by Day, 1941-1995,* Schirmer (New York, NY), 1996.

(With Nina Antonia) *Never Mind the Bollocks, Here's the Sex Pistols,* Schirmer (New York, NY), 1998.

*Going to the Wars,* Macmillan (New York, NY), 2000.

*Bob Dylan: Behind the Shades, The Biography—Revisited,* Morrow (New York, NY), 2001.

Contributor to magazines, including *Q, Goldmine, Record Collector,* and *Spiral Scratch.*

*SIDELIGHTS:* Clinton Heylin is an author who has specialized in writing about popular music. In *Bootleg: The Secret History of the Other Record Industry,* he chronicles the story of the music pirates who make illegal copies of legally released music or record and sell completely unavailable music, such as live concerts or studio recordings dubbed substandard by record producers. Such "bootleg" versions of recorded music violate copyright laws and steal millions of dollars from both the recording companies and the artists themselves. But they also make available to the public music that would otherwise never have been offered for sale. A critic for *Publishers Weekly* called Heylin's effort an "exhaustively researched and absorbing volume," while Gordon Flagg said in *Booklist* that "Heylin seems to labor out of love . . . as he celebrates the underground entrepreneurs responsible for freeing otherwise lost recordings."

Heylin tackles one of the leading bands of the British punk movement in *Never Mind the Bollocks, Here's the Sex Pistols,* cowritten with Nina Antonia. Taking its title from the Sex Pistols' only album, the book focuses on the band's limited number of recorded songs rather than on their personal scandals. *Library Journal* contributor Lloyd Jansen found that "the authors leave the reader with a surprising appreciation for the Sex Pistols' musical ability and pop craftsmanship."

Singer and songwriter Bob Dylan has been the subject of four of Heylin's books, including *Bob Dylan: A Life in Stolen Moments, Day by Day, 1941-1995,* and

**CONTEMPORARY AUTHORS • New Revision Series, Volume 122**

*Bob Dylan: Behind the Shades, The Biography—Revisited.* The first title contains "every documented concert, recording date, personal appearance, notable private activity, and other significant event" in Dylan's life, according to Flagg in another *Booklist* review. A *Publishers Weekly* reviewer found the book to be "an offbeat yet compelling portrait of Dylan as a restless, shape-shifting artist."

In *Bob Dylan: Behind the Shades, The Biography—Revisited,* Heylin reworks his earlier title *Bob Dylan: Behind the Shades.* Some eighty percent of the more recent title is new material covering the singer's career during the 1990s. Flagg believed that the book offered "detailed information and insight into a still-vital artist," while Jansen claimed that it is "the most authoritative Dylan biography available." *New Statesman* contributor Julian Keeling concluded that "every serious Dylan fan should find space for it on their shelves."

Heylin once told *CA:* "Though my previous reputation has been derived primarily from my work on singer Bob Dylan, I have written on rock acts as diverse as Public Image Limited, Joy Division, and Richard Thompson. My . . . anthology of the best rock-and-roll writings and the history of the CBGBs scene, should prove that I work from a wider spectrum."

*BIOGRAPHICAL AND CRITICAL SOURCES:*

*PERIODICALS*

*Booklist,* April 15, 1995, Gordon Flagg, review of *Bootleg: The Secret History of the Other Recording Industry,* p. 1458; August, 1996, Gordon Flagg, review of *Bob Dylan: A Life in Stolen Moments, Day by Day, 1941-1995,* p. 1871; April 15, 1998, Gordon Flagg, review of *Never Mind the Bollocks, Here's the Sex Pistols,* p. 1409; October 15, 2000, Gordon Flagg, review of *Bob Dylan: Behind the Shades: The Biography—Revisited,* p. 404.
*Globe and Mail* (Toronto, Ontario, Canada), May 25, 1991, p. C8.
*Library Journal,* May 1, 1998, Lloyd Jansen, review of *Never Mind the Bollocks, Here's the Sex Pistols,* p. 100; October 1, 2000, Lloyd Jansen, review of *Bob Dylan: Behind the Shades: The Biography—Revisited,* p. 102.

*New Statesman,* October 23, 2000, Julian Keeling, "Road to Nowhere," p. 56.
*Publishers Weekly,* September 28, 1992, review of *The Penguin Book of Rock and Roll Writing,* p. 60; April 10, 1995, review of *Bootleg,* p. 47; July 1, 1996, review of *Bob Dylan: A Life in Stolen Moments, Day by Day, 1941-1995,* p. 52; September 25, 2000, review of *Bob Dylan: Behind the Shades: The Biography—Revisited,* p. 103.
*Times Literary Supplement,* May 10, 1991, p. 28.*

\* \* \*

## HILL, Elizabeth Starr 1925-

*PERSONAL:* Born November 4, 1925, in Lynn Haven, FL; daughter of Raymond King (a science-fiction novelist) and Gabrielle (Wilson) Cummings; married Russell Gibson Hill (a chemical engineer), May 28, 1949 (died, 1999); children: Andrea van Waldron, Bradford Wray. *Ethnicity:* Caucasian. *Education:* Attended Finch Junior College, 1941-42; attended Columbia University, 1970-73. *Politics:* Independent. *Religion:* Episcopalian. *Hobbies and other interests:* Music, theatre, art.

*ADDRESSES: Home*—Langford Apartments, P.O. Box 940, Winter Park, FL 32790. *Agent*—Wendy Schmalz Agency, P.O. Box 831, Hudson, NY 12534.

*CAREER:* Freelance writer. Former actress in radio and summer-stock productions. Adult education teacher at Princeton Adult School. Painter, with work exhibited in metropolitan New York.

*MEMBER:* University Club of Winter Park.

*AWARDS, HONORS:* Notable Children's Book citation, American Library Association, 1967, for *Evan's Corner;* Pick-of-the-Lists citation, American Book Association, 1992, for *Broadway Chances;* award for outstanding achievement in children's books, *Parents' Guide to Children's Media,* and Parents' Choice gold Medal award, both 1999, both for *Bird Boy;* Parents' Guide to Children's Media award, for *Chang and the Bamboo Flute.*

*WRITINGS:*

*FOR CHILDREN*

*The Wonderful Visit to Miss Liberty,* illustrated by Paul Galdone, Holt (New York, NY), 1961.

*The Window Tulip,* illustrated by Hubert Williams, F. Warne (New York, NY), 1964.

*Evan's Corner,* illustrated by Nancy Grossman, Holt (New York, NY), 1967, revised edition illustrated by Sandra Speidel, Viking (New York, NY), 1990.

*Master Mike and the Miracle Maid,* Holt (New York, NY), 1967.

*Pardon My Fangs,* Holt (New York, NY), 1969, revised as *Fangs Aren't Everything,* illustrated by Larry Ross, Dutton (New York, NY, 1985.

*Bells: A Book to Begin On* (nonfiction), illustrated by Shelly Sacks, Holt (New York, NY), 1970.

*Ever-after Island,* Dutton (New York, NY), 1977.

*When Christmas Comes,* Penguin (New York, NY), 1989.

*The Street Dancers,* Viking (New York, NY), 1991.

*Broadway Chances* (sequel to *The Street Dancers*), Viking (New York, NY), 1992.

*The Banjo Player,* Viking (New York, NY), 1993.

*Curtain Going Up!* (sequel to *Broadway Chances*), Viking (New York, NY), 1995.

*Bird Boy,* illustrated by Lesley Liu, Farrar, Straus (New York, NY), 1999.

*Chang and the Bamboo Flute* (sequel to *Bird Boy*), illustrated by Lesley Liu, Farrar, Straus (New York, NY), 2002.

Contributor to *Encyclopaedia Britannica.* Contributor of stories and articles to periodicals, including *New Yorker, Reader's Digest, Harper's Bazaar, Seventeen, Woman's Day, Woman's Home Companion, Good Housekeeping, Collier's, Cricket, New World Writing, Faith Today,* and other magazines in the United States, Britain, and France.

*ADAPTATIONS: Evan's Corner* was adapted as a film and produced by Stephen Bosustow in 1969.

*WORK IN PROGRESS: Wildfire!* for Farrar, Straus.

*SIDELIGHTS:* Although she is best known as the author of the picture book *Evan's Corner,* Elizabeth Starr Hill has written books for young readers of a variety of reading levels. Including both fiction and nonfiction among her published works, Hill excels at creating believable characters who often grow in self-knowledge through their interaction with the natural world. "I find the natural world amazing, fascinating, endlessly absorbing—and people are as much a part of it as a tree or a chipmunk," the author once commented to *CA.*

"There are stories in every country morning; and also in every city afternoon, and every frightened naptime. The important thing is to pay attention to life."

First published in 1967 and reissued with new illustrations in 1990, Hill's *Evan's Corner* focuses on an African-American boy who tries to find a quiet place in his family's noisy apartment. His mother gives him a subtle lesson in sharing after she allows him to claim a corner of the apartment as his own. Praising the story in *School Library Journal,* Luann Toth noted that Hill presents young readers with a "sensitive and thoughtful" protagonist and shows the value of "the support and encouragement of a loving family" in learning that things gain in value when they are shared with others.

Beginning readers are the intended audience of Hill's *Bird Boy,* which takes place in China and focuses on a young mute boy named Chang. Living on a houseboat, Chang has developed a special love for water birds, and when his father helps him raise one of the cormorant chicks through which the family makes their living, Chang gains in self-confidence. In addition to introducing readers to Chang's family's unique way of life, Hill "effortlessly weaves in multiple themes of courage, responsibility and friendship," explained a *Publishers Weekly* contributor. Praising the story for inspiring young readers with disabilities, Lauren Peterson added in her *Booklist* review that *Bird Boy* imparts an important lesson: that "friendship and trust must be given only to those who earn it." Praising Hill's "excellent little novel," Elaine A. Bearden noted in her review for the *Bulletin of the Center for Children's Books* that "readers will identify with Chang and his desire to do grownup things." Hill continues Chang's story in 2002's *Chang and the Bamboo Flute.*

Among Hill's novels for middle-grade readers is the three-book series that includes *The Street Dancers, Broadway Chances,* and *Curtain Going Up!* The series focuses on a girl who lives an unsettled life due to her parents' theatrical careers. In *The Street Dancers* readers meet Fitzi Wolper, who lives in New York but is home-schooled because of the moves required by her parents' acting stints. Because the family's fortunes fluctuate with their ability to land roles on Broadway, nothing seems normal to the increasingly self-conscious teen, and normal is what Fitzi wants. Citing *The Street Dancers* for its "good balance of realism and glamor," *Bulletin of the Center for Children's Books* reviewer Kathryn Pierson Jennings added that Hill's "characters are believable." Calling the novel a "charming" tale that "grows out of the author's own stage experience," a *Kirkus* contributor praised the work for presenting a realistic picture of life behind the theater curtain.

Fitzi's teen years continue to be explored in the two sequels to *The Street Dancers.* In *Broadway Chances* Fitzi's grandfather lands a small role in a Broadway musical and her parents are offered small roles as well. After she auditions for the child's lead and loses to an arch-rival, Fitzi nonetheless wins a dancer's role and helps to thwart a kidnaping between rehearsals. "Hill presents an enthralling look at a theatrical production," in the opinion of a *Kirkus* reviewer, and Jennings added in her *Bulletin of the Center for Children's Books* review that the author includes the requisite "good old Broadway happy ending." A love interest enters the picture in the series conclusion, *Curtain Going Up!,* as Fitzi wins a dance solo in a Broadway show but loses her heart to Mark Hiller, the show's charismatic young lead.

Other novels Hill has written for middle-grade readers include *When Christmas Comes* and *The Banjo Player.* In *When Christmas Comes* a young girl named Callie attempts to come to terms with her parents' divorce, but is upset when the family breakup leaves her living in a trailer park with her father and his new wife. The fact that everyone is busy celebrating the approaching holiday season doesn't improve her mood, but when she and a friend find and care for an abandoned pup Callie finally begins to come to terms with the changes in her life. Praising the novel's characters, a *Kirkus* reviewer noted that the stepmother, Fran, "is both creative and patient with her new charge," and praised the novel's ending as "satisfyingly heartwarming." Citing the relationship between Callie and her father and new stepmother as "well drawn," *Booklist* contributor Kay Weisman noted that young readers would find *When Christmas Comes* "a satisfying read." A work of historical fiction that focuses on the Orphan Trains of the late 1800s, *The Banjo Player* also features a teen protagonist in young Jonathan. Moving to New Orleans, the teen becomes a street musician, and later an actor on a showboat. Praising Hill's protagonist as commendable, *School Library Journal* contributor Bruce Anne Shook called *The Banjo Player*

"upbeat reading" that "provides plenty of colorful details about the late 1800s in New Orleans and vicinity."

Describing her writing process, Hill once commented to *CA:* "Story ideas are a combination of knowledge and imagination. I believe the use of our senses is as important to writing as the actual setting of pencil to paper. If we know—*really* know—how things look and sound and smell and feel, the daydreams that come to us will be rooted in life, recognizable to young readers.

"When I was a little girl, my mother told me, 'Learn to love nature. Then you'll always be happy.' It was good advice. Some of my happiest hours are spent in relative idleness, watching storms or butterflies or the coming of a new season. The wonder of growth and change never diminishes, and I try to express some of that wonder in my writing."

## BIOGRAPHICAL AND CRITICAL SOURCES:

*PERIODICALS*

*Booklist,* November 15, 1989, Kay Weisman, review of *When Christmas Comes,* p. 668; October 1, 1992, Kay Weisman, review of *Broadway Chances,* p. 326; January 15, 1995, Ilene Cooper, review of *Curtain Going Up!,* p. 928; April 15, 1999, Lauren Peterson, review of *Bird Boy,* p. 1528; October 15, 2002, GraceAnne A. DeCandido, review of *Chang and the Bamboo Flute,* p. 405.

*Books for Keeps,* May, 1991, review of *Evan's Corner* p. 29.

*Bulletin of the Center for Children's Books,* July, 1991, Kathryn Pierson Jennings, review of *The Street Dancers,* pp. 264-265; June, 1992, K. Jennings, review of *Broadway Chances,* pp. 263-264; March, 1995, Deborah Stevenson, review of *Curtain Going Up!,* pp. 237-238; July, 1999, Elaine A. Bearden, review of *Bird Boy,* p. 389;

*Children's Book Review Service,* May, 1985, Jeanette Cohn, review of *Fangs Aren't Everything,* p. 110.

*Horn Book,* September-October, 1991, Ethel L. Heins, review of *Evan's Corner,* p. 618.

*Kirkus Reviews,* August 15, 1989, review of *When Christmas Comes,* p. 1246; May 15, 1991, review of *The Street Dancers,* p. 672; May 15, 1992, review of *Broadway Chances,* p. 671; July 1, 1993, review of *The Banjo Player,* p. 861; October 1, 2002, review of *Chang and the Bamboo Flute,* p. 1470.

*Publishers Weekly,* November 1, 1991, review of *When Christmas Comes,* p. 82; May 3, 1991, review of *The Street Dancers,* p. 73; May 18, 1992, review of *Broadway Chances,* p. 71; June 28, 1993, review of *The Banjo Player,* p. 78; April 10, 1995, review of *Curtain Going Up!,* p. 63; March 29, 1999, review of *Bird Boy,* p. 105.

*School Library Journal,* May, 1985, review of *Fangs Aren't Everything,* p. 90; March, 1991, Luann Toth, review of *Evan's Corner,* p. 173; June, 1991, Tatiana Castleton, review of *The Street Dancers,* p. 106; May, 1992, Jennifer Kraar, review of *Broadway Chances,* p. 114; July, 1993, Bruce Anne Shook, review of *The Banjo Player,* p. 85.

\*       \*       \*

## HILL, Reginald (Charles) 1936-
### (Dick Morland, Patrick Ruell, Charles Underhill)

*PERSONAL:* Born April 3, 1936, in West Hartlepool, England; son of Reginald and Isabel (Dickson) Hill; married Patricia Ruell, August 30, 1960. *Education:* St. Catherine's College, Oxford, B.A. (with honors), 1960. *Politics:* "Agnostic." *Religion:* "Cynic."

*ADDRESSES: Home*—Oakbank, Broad Oak, Ravenglass, Cumbria CA18 1RN, England. *Agent*—A. P. Watt, 20 John St., London WL1N 2DR, England.

*CAREER:* Worked as a secondary school teacher in England, 1962-67; Doncaster College of Education, Doncaster, England, lecturer in English literature, 1967-82; full-time writer, 1982—. *Military service:* British Army Border Regiment, 1955-57.

*MEMBER:* Crime Writers Association, Mystery Writers of America.

*AWARDS, HONORS:* Edgar Award nomination, Mystery Writers of America, 1981, for *The Spy's Wife;* Crime Writers Association, Gold Dagger Award for best novel of the year, 1990, for *Bones and Silence;* and Cartier Diamond Dagger, lifetime contribution to crime writing, 1995.

*WRITINGS:*

*CRIME NOVELS*

*A Clubbable Woman,* Collins (London, England), 1970, Countryman Press (Woodstock, VT), 1984.

*Fell of Dark,* Collins (London, England), 1971.

*An Advancement of Learning,* Collins (London, England), 1971, Countryman Press (Woodstock, VT), 1985.

*A Fairly Dangerous Thing,* Collins, 1972, Countryman Press (Woodstock, VT), 1983.

*Ruling Passion: A Dalziel and Pascoe Novel,* Collins (London, England), 1973, Harper (New York, NY), 1977.

*A Very Good Hater,* Collins (New York, NY), 1974, Countryman Press (Woodstock, VT), 1982.

*An April Shroud: A Dalziel and Pascoe Novel,* Collins (London, England), 1975, Countryman Press (Woodstock, VT), 1986.

*Another Death in Venice,* Collins (London, England), 1976.

*A Pinch of Snuff: A Dalziel and Pascoe Novel,* Harper (New York, NY), 1978.

*Pascoe's Ghost,* Collins (London, England), 1979.

*The Spy's Wife,* Pantheon (New York, NY), 1980.

*A Killing Kindness: A Dalziel and Pascoe Novel,* Collins (London, England), 1980, Pantheon (New York, NY), 1981.

*Who Guards the Prince?,* Pantheon (New York, NY), 1982.

*Traitor's Blood,* Collins (London, England), 1983, Countryman Press (Woodstock, VT), 1986.

*Deadheads: A Dalziel and Pascoe Novel,* Collins (London, England), 1983, Macmillan (New York, NY), 1984.

*Exit Lines,* Collins, 1984, Macmillan (New York, NY), 1985.

*No Man's Land,* St. Martin's Press (New York, NY), 1985.

*Child's Play,* Macmillan (New York, NY), 1987.

*The Collaborators,* Collins (London, England), 1987, Countryman Press (Woodstock, VT), 1989.

*Underworld,* Scribner (New York, NY), 1988.

*Bones and Silence,* Delacorte (New York, NY), 1990.

*One Small Step,* HarperCollins (New York, NY), 1990.

*Recalled to Life,* Delacorte (New York, NY), 1992.

*Blood Sympathy,* St. Martin's Press (New York, NY), 1993.

*Pictures of Perfection,* Delacorte (New York, NY), 1994.

*Born Guilty,* St. Martin's Press (New York, NY), 1995.

*The Wood Beyond,* Delacorte (New York, NY), 1996.

*Killing the Lawyers,* St. Martin's Press (New York, NY), 1997.

*Beulah Height,* Delacorte (New York, NY), 1998.

*Singing the Sadness: A Private Eye Joe Sixsmith Mystery,* St. Martin's Minotaur (New York, NY), 1999.

*Arms and the Women: An Elliad,* Delacorte (New York, NY), 1999.

*Arms and the Woman,* HarperCollins (New York, NY), 2000.

SCIENCE FICTION NOVELS UNDER PSEUDONYM DICK MORLAND

*Heart Clock,* Faber & Faber (Winchester, MA), 1973.

*Albion! Albion!,* Faber & Faber (Winchester, MA), 1976.

ADVENTURE NOVELS UNDER PSEUDONYM PATRICK RUELL

*The Castle of the Demon,* Hutchinson, 1971, Hawthorne (New York, NY), 1972.

*Red Christmas,* Hutchinson, 1972, Hawthorne (New York, NY), 1973.

*Death Takes the Low Road,* Hutchinson (London, England), 1974, Mysterious Press (New York, NY), 1987.

*Urn Burial,* Hutchinson, 1975, Countryman Press (Woodstock, VT), 1987.

*The Long Kill,* Methuen (New York, NY), 1986, Countryman Press (Woodstock, VT), 1988.

*Death of a Dormouse,* Mysterious Press (New York, NY), 1987.

*Dream of Darkness,* Methuen (New York, NY), 1989, Countryman Press (Woodstock, VT), 1990.

HISTORICAL ADVENTURE NOVELS UNDER PSEUDONYM CHARLES UNDERHILL

*Captain Fantom: Being an Account of Sundry Adventures in the Life of Carlo Fantom, Soldier of Misfortune, Hard Man and Ravisher,* Hutchinson (London, England), 1978, St. Martin's Press (New York, NY), 1980.

*The Forging of Fantom,* Hutchinson (London, England), 1979.

OTHER

*Crime Writers: Reflections on Crime Fiction* (nonfiction), British Broadcasting Corp. (London, England), 1978.

*There Are No Ghosts in the Soviet Union: A Novella and Five Short Stories,* Collins (London, England), 1987, Countryman Press (Woodstock, VT), 1988.

SIDELIGHTS: Reginald Hill is a former lecturer in English whose passion for writing crime novels became a full-time occupation in 1981. Hill once told *CA:* "I became a full-time writer because I realised that's what I was, no matter what other activity I was ostensibly pursuing." With a reputation as a "writer of wit and precision, with a sensitivity for place and atmosphere," as one London *Times* reviewer remarked, Hill is best known for the characters Superintendent Dalziel (pronounced Dee-ell) and Detective-Inspector Peter Pascoe, who appear in a number of his procedural novels.

Hill once told *CA:* "I lead a quiet life punctuated by loud bursts of laughter at its absurdity. My wife and I devote ourselves to looking after two Siamese cats and a Labrador dog who are the only living creatures whose lot I envy."

BIOGRAPHICAL AND CRITICAL SOURCES:

BOOKS

Magill, Frank N., editor, *Critical Survey of Mystery and Detective Fiction,* Volume 2, Salem Press (Englewood Cliffs, NJ).

PERIODICALS

*Globe and Mail* (Toronto, Ontario, Canada), November 3, 1984; July 30, 1988.

*Los Angeles Times,* March 27, 1981.

*New York Times Book Review,* January 18, 1981; April 5, 1981; June 24, 1984; March 2, 1986; June 1, 1986; November 30, 1986; March 15, 1987.

*Spectator* (London, England), February 11, 1984; September 26, 1987.

*Time,* November 4, 1985.

*Times* (London, England), July 7, 1983; March 31, 1990.
*Times Literary Supplement,* November 6, 1970; July 9, 1971; February 4, 1972; November 10, 1972; August 15, 1975; March 24, 1978; April 18, 1980; December 26, 1980; July 2, 1982; March 30, 1984; October 30, 1987; August 17, 1990.
*Tribune Books* (Chicago, IL), August 5, 1990.
*Village Voice,* July 3, 1984.
*Village Voice Literary Supplement,* July, 1986.
*Washington Post Book World,* April 19, 1971; January 15, 1978; March 18, 1979; June 16, 1985; August 11, 1985; August 21, 1988.*

\*      \*      \*

**HILL, Tobias 1970-**

*PERSONAL:* Born March 30, 1970, in London, England; son of George (a journalist) and Caroline (a book designer) Hill. *Education:* Sussex University, B.A., 1992. *Politics:* Liberal. *Religion:* Agnostic.

*ADDRESSES: Home and office*—Flat 4, 1 Minster Rd., London NW2 3SD, England. *Agent*—Victoria Hobbs, Toby Eady Associates, 9 Orme Ct., London W2 4RL, England.

*CAREER:* Apex School, Anjo, Aichi, Japan, teacher, 1993-94; writer, editor, and music critic.

*AWARDS, HONORS:* Poetry Book Society Recommendation, shortlisted for Forward Prize for best poem, and Cambridge University Harper-Wood Studentship for Literature, all 1996, all for *Midnight in the City of Clocks;* Eric Gregory Award, National Poetry Foundation, 1996, for *Year of the Dog;* PEN/Macmillan Award for Fiction and Ian St. James Award, both 1997, both for *Skin.*

*WRITINGS:*

*Year of the Dog* (poetry), National Poetry Foundation (Orono, ME), 1995.
*Midnight in the City of Clocks* (poetry), Oxford University Press (Oxford, England), 1996.
*Skin* (short stories), Faber (London, England), 1997.

*Zoo* (poetry), Oxford University Press (Oxford, England), 1998.
*Underground* (novel), Faber (London, England), 1999.
*The Love of Stones* (novel), Faber (London, England), 2001.

Poetry editor of *Richmond Review* and books editor of *Don't Tell It* magazine, both 1995-96; contributor to London *Observer,* London *Times,* and *Telegraph;* music critic, *Telegraph on Sunday,* 1994—.

*SIDELIGHTS:* British writer Tobias Hill is one of England's rising young literary stars. Son of a London *Times* journalist and a book designer, and still only in his mid-twenties when he began to earn recognition, Hill studied English literature at Sussex University, and from 1993 to 1994 taught overseas at a school for children with learning difficulties. His experiences in Japan had a decided influence upon his poetry, and many of the works that would later bring him success recall the spare, formal constructions of Japanese verse. Back in England in 1995, Hill began to publish his work and read it on the radio. That same year his first collection, *Year of the Dog,* which won top honors in the National Poetry Foundation competition, was published. The book also won him a generous financial prize with the Eric Gregory Award.

Hill began to win several freelance assignments for publications, including from the London *Times* and *Telegraph.* His next collection, *Midnight in the City of Clocks,* was published by Oxford University Press in 1996. The laudatory reviews were matched by several literary accolades for this title, including a Poetry Book Society Recommendation. The book's thirty-seven poems are drawn primarily from Hill's experiences in Japan. A *Times Literary Supplement* reviewer praised the collection as solid, and called Hill's approach "austerely sensual. . . . Hill specializes in the type of ripple-effect found in haiku and tanka, where intuitions seem to glow and multiply in the unstated."

The short stories in 1997's *Skin* take place in locales as varied as Las Vegas, Tokyo, and a warm sea in which a French war veteran is decimated by a shark. The title story concerns a Japanese gangster on the run who is trying to rid himself of identifying tattoos, and the detective who pursues him. Another story, "Zoo," is about the disappearance of dead animals from the London Zoo and the Finnish immigrant who finally discovers the culprit. "No One Comes Back from the Sea" leads the reader backward through a sad tale about a set of parents who communicate with their two dead children via the Internet. Reviewers of *Skin* noted the successful transition Hill seemed to have made from poetry to prose, and remarked upon the spare, lyrical nature of the tales. For example, Ra Page, writing in the *Spectator,* noted that Hill's "first collection of short stories is . . . a smooth translation of his poetic aptitudes." "His attention to visual detail," wrote Hal Jensen in the *Times Literary Supplement,* "results in some resonant images: a pencil-case seething with larvae; acid burning the skin off a tattooed arm; a beautifully presented plate of wafer-thin horse innards."

Similar attention to descriptive prose marked Hill's first novel, *Underground,* which *New Statesman* reviewer Douglas McCabe considered evocative and "atmospheric." The book is set in London's Camden Town subway station, where Casimir, a Polish exile, works. A serial killer who preys on blonde women is at large in this huge labyrinth of transit tunnels, and Casimir must try to prevent homeless Alice, with whom he has fallen in love, from being targeted. Though McCabe felt that the novel's structure was sometimes too schematic, he praised Hill's "portrait of [the Underground] as a fragile subterranean city," adding that "it delivers a considerable emotional punch, as if this underground and its hideous crimes are telling us something uncomfortable about ourselves and the city we choose to live in."

Hill's second novel, *The Love of Stones,* received significant attention and was the author's first book to be published in the United States. It presents the story of Katharine Sterne and her obsessive quest for a famous piece of jewelry called The Three Brethren, an arrangement of three balas rubies around a huge diamond. The gems were brought to London in the early 1800s by two Iraqi Jewish brothers, Daniel and Salman, whose story—along with the tumultuous six hundred-year history of the coveted stones—is interwoven with Katharine's. As many critics pointed out, Hill's characters are tough, hard, and single-minded in their pursuit of the gems—qualities unlikely to capture readers' sympathy. "This saga," wrote Adam Nicolson in the London *Daily Telegraph,* "is burdened with its central coldness and, eventually, with the banality of its central preoccupation. . . . This is a loveless book." Similarly, a contributor to the *Economist* ob-

served that "Katharine never comes to life off the page, and the question 'Why is she doing this?' is not satisfactorily answered." Yet several reviewers felt that the strengths of the novel—brilliant descriptive passages and deeply imagined themes—more than make up for unsympathetic characters. "*The Love of Stones* is an admirable achievement," wrote Robert MacFarlane in the *Times Literary Supplement.* "Densely detailed and densely imagined throughout, [the] novel is an object lesson in how fascination can harden into love, or be mistaken for it." According to *New York Times Book Review* contributor Nell Freudenberger, the novel "often has the controlled beauty of a sestina." Jerome Boyd Maunsell, writing in the *Times,* described the book as "an eerie parable of greed that is even more precious than its glittering subject." And a reviewer for *Publishers Weekly* praised the novel's "dexterous combination of historical scope, lush yet precise storytelling, and twist-and-turn subterfuge and intrigue."

Hill once told *CA:* "I have always been and will always be a poet first and foremost: It is what I do for most of my working time; it is what I take the greatest pleasure in and put most of my energies into; and it is also what I do best. Although I take great enjoyment from spinning a yarn, from trying to tell a good story, I feel like a part-time writer of fiction. What works in my prose tends to come from poetic strengths; the collection *Skin,* it seems to me, has the organization, lyricism and interrelated structure of a collection of poems. In my first novel, *Underground,* I tried to step away from the finished quality and 'completeness' of the poems and stories. It is a big, rambling old ruin of a novel, like the archaic subterrannea it describes. The temptation was to clarify the image—the emergence of a central character from psychological burial, the underworld of homelessness, the subsumed racial tensions of postwar Poland. I chose not to even out the narrative, and when the novel works, I think it does so in a way entirely different from the other work I have done.

"I believe in the gift principle of writing. It is something I can do for people; I give poems away like birthday presents. I think the best writing gives something to the reader the first time it is read and the last—whether that be the first or hundredth time. In the best writing there is joy and beauty, even in the act of facing darkness. I look to combine some or all of this with the simpler action of giving pleasure."

*BIOGRAPHICAL AND CRITICAL SOURCES:*

*PERIODICALS*

*Booklist,* December 15, 2001, Elsa Gaztambide, review of *The Love of Stones,* p. 703.

*Daily Telegraph* (London, England), January 20, 2001, Adam Nicolson, review of *The Love of Stones;* March 10, 2001, Tom Payne, "Little Gem of a Novel."

*Economist,* February 10, 2001, review of *The Love of Stones,* p. 9.

*Guardian* (London, England), February 3, 2001, James Hopkin, review of *The Love of Stones,* p. 10.

*Kirkus Reviews,* November 1, 2001, review of *The Love of Stones,* p. 1507.

*Los Angeles Times,* January 29, 2002, Bernadette Murphy, review of *The Love of Stones,* p. E3.

*New Statesman,* April 26, 1999, Douglas McCabe, review of *Underground,* p. 49.

*New York Times Book Review,* February 3, 2002, Nell Freudenberger, review of *The Love of Stones,* p. 26; February 10, 2002, "And Bear in Mind," p. 22.

*Observer* (London, England), September 29, 1996, p. 18.

*Publishers Weekly,* November 5, 2001, review of *The Love of Stones,* p. 38.

*Spectator,* June 28, 1997, p. 45; May 1, 1999, Andrew Barrow, review of *Underground,* p. 38.

*Times* (London, England), January 31, 2001, Naomi Gryn, review of *The Love of Stones,* p. 14; February 11, 2001, review of *The Love of Stones,* p. 45; February 24, 2001, Jerome Boyd Maunsell, review of *The Love of Stones,* p. 23; February 25, 2001, "You Really Must Read," p. 47; March 16, 2002, Eve Peasnall, review of *The Love of Stones,* p. 14.

*Times Literary Supplement,* May 30, 1997, p. 25; June 20, 1997, p. 22; February 2, 2001, Robert Mac-Farlane, review of *The Love of Stones,* p. 21.

*Virginia Quarterly Review,* spring, 1997, p. 65.*

*　　　*　　　*　　　**

## HINES, Anna Grossnickle 1946-

*PERSONAL:* Born July 13, 1946, in Cincinnati, OH; daughter of Earl Stanton (a mathematical analyst) and Ruth Marie (a personnel service representative; maiden name, Putnam) Grossnickle; married Steve Carlson, August 12, 1965 (divorced, 1973); married Gary Roger Hines (a forest ranger, writer, and musician), June 19, 1976; children: (first marriage) Bethany, Sarah; (second marriage) Lassen. *Education:* Attended San Fernando State College (now California State University—Northridge), 1965-67; Pacific Oaks College, B.A. (human development), 1974, M.A. (human development), 1979. *Hobbies and other interests:* Needlework, quilting, knitting, gardening, grandparenting.

*ADDRESSES: Home*—R.R. 4, Box 8057, Milford, PA 18337. *Office*—c/o Author Mail, Greenwillow Books, 1350 Avenue of the Americas, New York, NY, 10019-4702, and Clarion Books, 215 Park Ave. S, New York, NY 10003-1603.

*CAREER:* Los Angeles City Children's Centers, Los Angeles, CA, preschool teacher, 1967-70; Columbia Elementary School, Columbia, CA, third-grade teacher, 1975-78; full-time writer and illustrator, 1978—.

*MEMBER:* International Reading Association, National Association for the Education of Young Children, Society of Children's Book Writers and Illustrators.

*AWARDS, HONORS:* Children's Book of the Year list, Child Study Association of America, 1985, for *All by Myself;* Children's Choice Award, International Reading Association and the Children's Book Council (IRA/CBC), 1987, for *Daddy Makes the Best Spaghetti;* Children's Choice Award, IRA/CBC, 1990, for *Grandma Gets Grumpy;* Outstanding Science Book for Children, National Science Teachers Association, 1991, for *Remember the Butterflies;* Children's Books of the Year list, Bank Street College, 1991, for *Tell Me Your Best Thing;* Notable Children's Trade Book, National Council for the Social Studies, 1993, for *Flying Firefighters;* Carolyn W. Field Award Honor Book, Pennsylvania Library Association, 1995, for *What Joe Saw.* Other titles by Hines have been selected for the Junior Literary Guild, Book-of-the-Month Club, and other book clubs.

*WRITINGS:*

*FOR CHILDREN; SELF-ILLUSTRATED, EXCEPT AS NOTED*

*Taste the Raindrops,* Greenwillow (New York, NY), 1983.

*Come to the Meadow,* Clarion (Boston, MA), 1984.

*Maybe a Band-Aid Will Help,* Dutton (New York, NY), 1984.

*All by Myself,* Clarion (New York, NY), 1985.

*Bethany for Real,* Greenwillow (New York, NY), 1985.

*Cassie Bowen Takes Witch Lessons* (juvenile novel), illustrated by Gail Owens, Dutton (New York, NY), 1985.

*Daddy Makes the Best Spaghetti,* Clarion (New York, NY), 1986.

*Don't Worry, I'll Find You,* Dutton (New York, NY), 1986.

*I'll Tell You What They Say,* Greenwillow (New York, NY), 1987.

*It's Just Me, Emily,* Clarion (New York, NY), 1987.

*Keep Your Old Hat,* Dutton (New York, NY), 1987.

*Grandma Gets Grumpy,* Dutton (New York, NY), 1988.

*Boys Are Yucko!* (sequel to *Cassie Bowen Takes Witch Lessons*), illustrated by Pat Henderson Lincoln, Dutton (New York, NY), 1989.

*Sky All Around,* Clarion (New York, NY), 1989.

*Big Like Me,* Greenwillow (New York, NY), 1989.

*They Really Like Me,* Greenwillow (New York, NY), 1989.

*The Secret Keeper,* Greenwillow (New York, NY), 1990.

*Mean Old Uncle Jack,* Clarion (New York, NY), 1990.

*The Greatest Picnic in the World,* Clarion (New York, NY), 1991.

*Remember the Butterflies,* Dutton (New York, NY), 1991.

*Tell Me Your Best Thing* (juvenile novel), illustrated by Karen Ritz, Dutton (New York, NY), 1991.

*Jackie's Lunch Box,* Greenwillow (New York, NY), 1991.

*Moon's Wish,* Clarion (New York, NY), 1992.

*Rumble Thumble Boom!,* Greenwillow (New York, NY), 1992.

*Moompa, Toby and Bomp,* Clarion (New York, NY), 1993.

*Gramma's Walk,* Greenwillow (New York, NY), 1993.

*Even If I Spill My Milk?,* Clarion (New York, NY), 1994.

*What Joe Saw,* Greenwillow (New York, NY), 1994.

*Big Help!,* Clarion (New York, NY), 1995.

*When the Goblins Came Knocking,* Greenwillow (New York, NY), 1995.

*When We Married Gary,* Greenwillow (New York, NY), 1996.

*Miss Emma's Wild Garden,* Greenwillow (New York, NY), 1997.

*My Own Big Bed,* illustrated by Mary Watson, Greenwillow (New York, NY), 1998.

*What Can You Do in the Rain?,* illustrated by Thea Kliros, Greenwillow (New York, NY), 1998.

*What Can You Do in the Wind?,* illustrated by Thea Kliros, Greenwillow (New York, NY), 1999.

*What Can You Do in the Snow?,* illustrated by Thea Kliros, Greenwillow (New York, NY), 1999.

*What Can You Do in the Sunshine?,* illustrated by Thea Kliros, Greenwillow (New York, NY), 1999.

*Not without Bear,* Orchard Books (New York, NY), 2000.

*William's Turn,* Children's Press (New York, NY), 2001.

*Got You!,* Children's Press (New York, NY), 2001.

*Pieces: A Year in Poems and Quilts,* Greenwillow (New York, NY), 2001.

*Whose Shoes?,* illustrated by LeUyen Pham, Harcourt (San Diego, CA), 2001.

*Which Hat Is That?,* Harcourt (San Diego, CA), 2002.

*My Pat-a-Cake Grandma,* Candlewick Press (Cambridge, MA), 2003.

*FOR CHILDREN; ILLUSTRATOR*

Gary Hines, *A Ride in the Crummy,* Greenwillow (New York, NY), 1991.

Gary Hines, *Flying Firefighters,* Clarion (New York, NY), 1993.

Gary Hines, *The Day of the High Climber,* Greenwillow (New York, NY), 1994.

Sarah Hines-Stephens, *Bean,* Harcourt/Red Wagon Books (San Diego, CA), 1998.

Sarah Hines-Stephens, *Bean's Games,* Harcourt (New York, NY, 1998.

Sarah Hines-Stephens, *Bean's Night,* Harcourt (New York, NY), 1998.

Jackie French Koller, *Bouncing on the Bed,* Orchard Books (New York, NY), 1999.

Sarah Hines-Stephens, *Bean Soup,* Harcourt (San Diego, CA), 2000.

Gary Hines, *Soup Too?,* Harcourt (San Diego, CA), 2000.

Gary Hines, *Soup's Oops!,* Harcourt (San Diego, CA), 2000.

Also contributor to magazines, including *Society of Children's Book Writers Bulletin.*

ADAPTATIONS: *Daddy Makes the Best Spaghetti* and *It's Just Me, Emily* have been adapted for audio cassette.

*SIDELIGHTS:* Anna Grossnickle Hines is an award-winning author and illustrator of both picture books and chapter books for primary graders. She blends her accomplished art with stories about family and sibling relations, first friendships, and the delights of nature, among other subjects. "My stories come mostly from my experiences and feelings as a child and with my own children," Hines once told *CA.* "The stories are mostly about the discovery, imagination, playfulness, and wonder in young children's everyday lives, so often missed by busy adults." Praised for her understanding of her young audience and depiction of family relationships as well as for her skill as an artist, Hines is acknowledged as the creator of pleasant, positive, and reassuring works, several of which are noted as especially useful books on their subjects.

Hines resolved at an early age to become a writer of children's books, and although discouraged at times, she accomplished her goal. "In early college I was discouraged from pursuing my interest in picture books," Hines told *CA.* "I was told it was not a worthy interest because a picture book was not truly 'fine art' on the one hand or 'commercial' on the other. To me, the art of the picture book, which can be held in the hands, carried about, taken to bed, is much more personal and intimate than the art which hangs in galleries or museums." "Now I have lots of published books," she concluded in *Sixth Book of Junior Authors and Illustrators,* "and I'm still learning things and trying to do my best to make the books better and better. Parts of the job are frustrating, but mostly it's just as much fun as I always thought it would be."

Initially, she thought she would simply do illustrations for others, but as she read these books she began to see that she had her own stories to tell. "I remembered things about myself when I was a child and how I felt as a little girl," Hines wrote in *Sixth Book of Junior Authors and Illustrators,* "and I started writing poems and then short stories." At first she shared these with family and friends, and then slowly she began submitting them to publishers, collecting over a hundred rejection slips. She reported to *CA,* "It was a few months after the birth of my third child that I decided I should either pursue my goal of doing children's books more seriously or give it up." After about twenty months, her renewed efforts paid off. She sold her first picture book, *Taste the Raindrops,* the story of a little child who loves to walk in the rain even though Mother warns against it at first. Since that first publication,

she has produced dozens of additional books, most written and illustrated by herself, as well as a few collaborative efforts with her husband and her daughter, Sarah.

Hines's second picture book, *Come to the Meadow,* is the tale of little Mattie, who desperately wants to go play in a meadow, but everyone in the family is too busy, except for Granny. Granny finally proposes a picnic there, enticing the rest of the family to find the spare time to go. A *Publishers Weekly* critic called this early effort a "poetic, unpretentious story," with pictures in "clear green and yellow offset with pristine-white spaces." This theme of the value of extended family, especially including grandparents, comes back in other titles by Hines. *Grandma Gets Grumpy* tells the story of five cousins who spend the night with their grandmother, but they quickly learn that she has rules too. "This slice of real life is depicted with such humor and affection that kids are sure to enjoy recognizing themselves and their elders," noted a critic for *Kirkus Reviews,* who added, "The soft, realistic pictures make each character an individual." Writing in *Horn Book,* Ellen Fader commented that Hines uses her "familiar, gentle, colored-pencil illustrations to bring this pleasant story to life," and added that Hines has the "envious ability to focus on the most ordinary situation, mix in a bit of gentle humor, and create, as the result, a charming and intimate glimpse into a preschooler's world." A different grandparent is featured in *Gramma's Walk,* a picture book about young Donnie and Gramma, who is in a wheelchair, and their imagined walk to the seashore. The bond between a boy and his grandfather is explored in *Moompa, Toby and Bomp,* "a charming tale of simple pleasures," according to Anna DeWind in *School Library Journal.*

Another favorite subject for Hines is child development. In *All by Myself,* she writes about a child taking "a step toward independence," as she described it for *CA,* by giving up night diapers and going unassisted to the bathroom in the middle of the night. Noting that "*All by Myself* holds a unique position in the growing genre of self-help books for young children," *School Library Journal* reviewer B. P. Goldstone concluded that the book is "a welcome addition to library collections that will help children cope with this problem as well as help to define a growing sense of worth." In *Even If I Spill My Milk?* Hines deals with children's fear of separation. Young Jamie doesn't want his parents to go to a party and leave him with a babysitter, and so he tries to delay their departure with a litany of questions. Childhood fear of thunder is dealt with in *Rumble Thumble Boom!,* which is about a boy and his dog who are afraid of such loud noises. Andrew W. Hunter commented in *School Library Journal* that Hines's "colorful effects enhance the book's use for storytelling with either a group or with a single child." *Booklist*'s Hazel Rochman concluded, "This is one of those read-alouds that will evoke smiles of wry recognition in adults without condescending to kids." The job of introducing a new sibling into the home is explored in *Big Like Me,* as a boy tells his baby sister all the things he will show her when she gets bigger. Denise Wilms concluded in *Booklist* that "Hines has an eye for pint-size anatomy," and that the book is an "affectionate and refreshingly positive celebration of a new infant." *Horn Book*'s Fader noted that the "watercolor and pencil illustrations have a gentle, cozy, and contented feeling which reinforces the mood of this distinctly useful book."

Hines has also explored the world of older children with several juvenile novels. *Cassie Bowen Takes Witch Lessons* tells the story of fourth-grader Cassie, who learns about not only herself, but also about the real meaning of friendship when she is paired with an unpopular girl to do a class assignment. Phyllis Ingram noted in *School Library Journal* that "readers will suffer along with Cassie as she strives to make the right decisions about friendship and loyalty." A reviewer for *Booklist* felt that Hines "carefully constructs a conflict that is true to life, injecting her story with realistic characterizations and dialogue and a solid understanding of the problems of growing up." The sequel, *Boys Are Yucko!,* finds Cassie planning her tenth birthday party, hoping that her divorced father will come, and also dealing with the insistence of her boy-crazy friend Stacy to invite the opposite sex to the event. *Tell Me Your Best Thing* is a story that looks at a young girl's decision to stand up to a class bully. A *Publishers Weekly* contributor commented that "the story's quick pace and believable portrayal of third-grade angst will appeal to the chapter book set."

Although she has written about a variety of childhood experiences, Hines's major subject would seem to be her own family. The author took inspiration from her own daughter, Sarah, for a trio of books about a young girl and her doll, Abigail. In *Maybe a Band-Aid Will Help* the doll's leg comes off and the mother is too busy to help Sarah fix it right away. Sarah and Abigail

get lost in a shopping mall in *Don't Worry, I'll Find You,* and *Keep Your Old Hat* has Sarah falling out with her friend, Mandy, over who gets to play mother. The author's daughter Bethany inspired *Bethany for Real,* which Hines told *CA* is "a fun story of the mix-up that results when Bethany pretends to be somebody else." Hines's husband, Gary, was the model for the father in *Daddy Makes the Best Spaghetti,* a tale of a nurturing dad. The resulting book, according to Mary M. Burns in *Horn Book,* is "a natural for picture-book programs. . . . Precise, fine lines combined with clear colors on snowy white backgrounds capture the circumscribed world of the preschooler while celebrating the joys to be found in daily events." A *Kirkus Reviews* critic concluded that "Daddy is bound to steal the hearts of many young readers." Hines again used personal family experience—her remarriage—for *When We Married Gary.* Young Sarah does not remember her father, but Beth does, and when a new man comes into their mother's life, adjustments need to be made. "Hines has done a superb job of tackling a realistic subject—remarriage—without oversimplifying it," noted Lisa Marie Gangemi in *School Library Journal.* Carolyn Phelan, writing in *Booklist,* commented, "Once again, Hines gets the child's perspective and the emotional tone of the story just right."

Hines's *My Own Big Bed* captures a little girl's excitement and fear when she moves from her baby crib to a bed of her very own. "In confronting her fears, she also discovers inner reserves of self-reliance," according to a critic for *Publishers Weekly.* Karen Simonetti in *Booklist* found that "even the youngest pre-reader will point along and chime in to the soothing, reassuring story."

Hines has also teamed up with her writer-husband on several titles, mostly having to do with the outdoors and forestry work. Two of these books are nostalgic reminiscences: in *A Ride in the Crummy,* two boys have an exciting ride in the caboose of a large train, while in its companion volume, *The Day of the High Climber,* two brothers spend the summer at their father's logging camp and marvel at the work of the high climber who must chop top branches off a tree. Donna L. Scanlon, writing in *School Library Journal,* noted that the latter title has a "coziness that is nostalgic but not cloying."

For the book *Pieces: A Year in Poems and Quilts,* Hines illustrates her free-verse poems about the seasons with photographs of quilts she made especially for the book. A critic for *Publishers Weekly* thought that the quilts were "worthy of exhibition," while Nina Lindsay, writing in the *School Library Journal,* believed that they "will certainly inspire young quilters or artists to try something similar." *Booklist*'s Ilene Cooper concluded that *Pieces* was "a thoughtful, lovely offering."

*BIOGRAPHICAL AND CRITICAL SOURCES:*

PERIODICALS

*Booklist,* February 1, 1986, p. 810; October 1, 1989, p. 350; September 15, 1992, pp. 154-155; March 1, 1996, Carolyn Phelan, review of *When We Married Gary,* p. 1188; March 1, 1997, Ilene Cooper, review of *Miss Emma's Wild Garden,* p. 1172; October 15, 1998, Karen Simonetti, review of *My Own Big Bed,* p. 427; June 1, 1999, Hazel Rochman, review of *What Can You Do in the Rain?,* p. 1842; January 1, 2001, Ilene Cooper, review of *Pieces: A Year in Poems and Quilts,* p. 951.

*Boston Herald,* March 25, 2001, Rosemary Herbert, "Editor's Choice," p. 58.

*Bulletin of the Center for Children's Books,* December, 1984, p. 67; May, 1985, p. 167; February, 1986, p. 110; September, 1987, p. 9; June, 1988, p. 206; February, 1989, p. 148; February, 1991, p. 142; September, 1995, p. 16.

*Horn Book,* January, 1985, p. 45; July, 1985, p. 439; July, 1986, p. 440; September-October, 1986, pp. 580-581; July, 1987, p. 453; July-August, 1988, pp. 479-480; May, 1989, p. 358; September-October, 1989, pp. 611-612; November, 1994, p. 760; July-August, 1996, Maeve Visser Knoth, review of *When We Married Gary,* p. 450.

*Kirkus Reviews,* February 15, 1986, p. 303; April 1, 1988, p. 539; August 1, 2001, review of *Whose Shoes?,* p. 1124.

*New York Times Book Review,* September 22, 1985, p. 32; September 7, 1986, p. 26; May 8, 1988, p. 30; September 8, 1996, p. 28.

*Publishers Weekly,* March 30, 1984, p. 56; March 21, 1986, p. 86; April 25, 1986, p. 72; August 28, 1987, p. 76; September 25, 1987, p. 107; April 28, 1989, p. 76; July 28, 1989, p. 220; February 23, 1990, p. 219; August 2, 1991, pp. 72-73; February 12, 1996, review of *When We Married Gary,* p. 77; November 9, 1998, review of *My Own Big Bed,* p. 76; January 8, 2001, review of *Pieces,* p. 67.

*School Library Journal,* May, 1985, p. 76; January, 1986, p. 68; February, 1993, p. 72; September, 1993, p. 208; June, 1994, p. 101; May, 1996, p. 92; March, 2001, Nina Lindsay, review of *Pieces,* p. 236; August, 2001, Anne Parker, review of *Whose Shoes?,* p. 153.

*Times Educational Supplement,* November 20, 1987, p. 30.

*Virginian Pilot,* June 22, 1999, Krys Stefansky, "Good Reads for Kids," p. E3.*

\*    \*    \*

## HOFFMAN, Mary (Margaret) 1945- (Mary Lassiter)

*PERSONAL:* Born April 20, 1945, in Eastleigh, Hampshire, England; daughter of Origen Herman (in telecommunications) and Ivegh (a homemaker; maiden name, Lassiter) Hoffman; married Stephen James Barber (a social worker), December 22, 1972; children: Rhiannon, Rebecca, Jessica. *Education:* Newnham College, Cambridge, B.A. (with honors), 1967; University of London, diploma in linguistics, 1970. *Politics:* "Green." *Religion:* Anglo-Catholic.

*ADDRESSES: Home*—28 Crouch Hall Rd., London N8 8HJ, England. *Agent*—Deborah Rogers, Rogers, Coleridge and White, 20 Powis Mews, London W11 1JN, England. *E-mail*—marushka@worldash.demon.co.uk.

*CAREER:* The Open University, Milton Keynes, England, lecturer in education, 1975-80; writer, 1980—. Member of The Other Award Panel, 1980-87; reading consultant to BBC-TV.

*MEMBER:* International Board on Books for Young People, National Union of Journalists, Society of Authors.

*WRITINGS:*

FOR ADULTS

*Reading, Writing, and Relevance,* Hodder & Stoughton (London, England), 1976.

(Under pseudonym Mary Lassiter) *Our Names, Our Selves,* Heinemann (London, England), 1983.

Also author of course materials for The Open University. Former columnist for *Mother.* Contributor to periodicals.

*FOR CHILDREN*

*White Magic,* Rex Collings (London, England), 1975.

(With Chris Callery) *Buttercup Busker's Rainy Day,* Heinemann (London, England), 1982.

(With Willis Hall) *The Return of the Antelope,* Heinemann (London, England), 1985.

*Beware, Princess!,* Heinemann (London, England), 1986.

*The Second-Hand Ghost,* Deutsch (London, England), 1986.

*A Fine Picnic,* Macdonald (London, England), 1986.

*King of the Castle,* Hamish Hamilton (London, England), 1986.

*Animal Hide and Seek,* Macdonald (London, England), 1986.

(With Trevor Weston) *Dangerous Animals,* Brimax Books (London, England), 1986.

*Whales and Sharks,* Brimax Books (London, England), 1986.

*The Perfect Pet,* Macdonald (London, England), 1986.

*Clothes for Sale,* Silver Burdett (London, England), 1986.

*Nancy No-Size,* Methuen (London, England), 1987.

*Specially Sarah,* Methuen (London, England), 1987.

*My Grandma Has Black Hair,* Dial (New York, NY), 1988.

*Dracula's Daughter,* Heinemann (London, England), 1988.

*All about Lucy,* Methuen (London, England), 1989.

*Min's First Jump,* Hamish Hamilton (London, England), 1989.

*Mermaid and Chips,* Heinemann (London, England), 1989.

*Dog Powder,* Heinemann (London, England), 1989.

*Catwalk,* Methuen (London, England), 1989.

*Just Jack,* Methuen (London, England), 1990.

(Editor) *Ip, Dip, Sky Blue,* Collins (London, England), 1990.

*Leon's Lucky Lunchbreak,* Dent (London, England), 1991.

*The Babies' Hotel,* Dent (London, England), 1991.

*Amazing Grace,* illustrated by Caroline Binch, Dial (New York, NY), 1991.

*Max in the Jungle,* Hamish Hamilton (London, England), 1991.

*The Ghost Menagerie,* Orchard Books (New York, NY), 1992.

*The Four-Legged Ghosts,* illustrated by Laura L. Seeley, Orchard Books (New York, NY), 1993.

*Amazing Mammals Kit,* Dorling Kindersley (London, England), 1993.

*Henry's Baby,* Dorling Kindersley (London, England), 1993.

*Cyril MC,* Viking (New York, NY), 1993.

*Bump in the Night,* Collins (London, England), 1993.

*Boundless Grace,* illustrated by Caroline Binch, Dial (New York, NY), 1995, published as *Grace and Family,* Frances Lincoln (London, England), 1995.

*Earth, Fire, Water, Air,* illustrated by Jane Ray, Dutton (New York, NY), 1995, published as *Song of the Earth,* Orion (London, England), 1995.

*Trace in Space,* Hodder & Stoughton (London, England), 1995.

*A Vanishing Tail,* Orchard Books (New York, NY), 1996.

*Quantum Squeak,* Orchard Books (New York, NY), 1996.

*Special Powers,* Hodder & Stoughton (London, England), 1997.

*A First Bible Storybook,* Dorling Kindersley (London, England), 1997.

*An Angel Just Like Me,* Frances Lincoln (London, England), 1997, Dial (New York, NY), 1998.

*Comet,* Orchard Books (New York, NY), 1997.

(Editor) *Stacks of Stories,* Hodder & Stoughton (London, England), 1997.

*Sun, Moon, and Stars,* Orion (London, England), 1998.

*A Twist in the Tail,* Frances Lincoln (London, England), 1998.

*Virtual Friend,* Barrington Stoke (London, England), 1998.

*Clever Katya,* Barefoot Books (London, England), 1998.

*Sun, Moon, and Stars,* Dutton Children's Books (New York, NY), 1998.

*A First Book of Myths: Myths and Legends for the Very Young from around the World,* Dorling Kindersley (London, England), 1999.

*Three Wise Women,* Phyllis Fogelman Books (New York, NY), 1999.

*Starring Grace,* Phyllis Fogelman Books (New York, NY), 2000.

*Women of Camelot: Queens and Enchantresses at the Court of King,* Abbeville Press (New York, NY), 2000.

*Parables: Stories Jesus Told,* Phyllis Fogelman Books (New York, NY), 2000.

*The Barefoot Book of Brother and Sister Tales,* Barefoot Books (London, England), 2000.

*A Grace Note,* Penguin (New York, NY), 2000.

*Miracles: Wonders Jesus Worked,* Phyllis Fogelman Books (New York, NY), 2001.

*A First Book of Fairy Tales,* DK Publishing (New York, NY), 2001.

*A First Book of Jewish Bible Stories,* DK Publishing (New York, NY), 2002.

*Stravaganza: City of Masks,* Bloomsbury (New York, NY), 2002.

*The Color of Home,* Putnam (New York, NY), 2002.

*Animals of the Bible,* Phyllis Fogelman Books (New York, NY), 2003.

*"ANIMALS IN THE WILD" SERIES*

*Animals in the Wild: Tiger,* Belitha/Windward (London, England), 1983.

*Animals in the Wild: Monkey,* Belitha/Windward (London, England), 1983.

*Animals in the Wild: Elephant,* Belitha/Windward (London, England), 1983.

*Animals in the Wild: Panda,* Belitha/Windward (London, England), 1983.

*Animals in the Wild: Lion,* Belitha/Methuen (London, England), 1985.

*Animals in the Wild: Zebra,* Belitha/Methuen (London, England), 1985.

*Animals in the Wild: Hippo,* Belitha/Methuen (London, England), 1985.

*Animals in the Wild: Gorilla,* Belitha/Methuen (London, England), 1985.

*Animals in the Wild: Wild Cat,* Belitha/Methuen (London, England), 1986.

*Animals in the Wild: Snake,* Belitha/Methuen (London, England), 1986.

*Animals in the Wild: Giraffe,* Belitha/Methuen (London, England), 1986.

*Animals in the Wild: Bear,* Belitha/Methuen (London, England), 1986.

*Animals in the Wild: Wild Dog,* Belitha/Methuen (London, England), 1987.

*Animals in the Wild: Seal,* Belitha/Methuen (London, England), 1987.

*Animals in the Wild: Antelope,* Belitha/Methuen (London, England), 1987.

*Animals in the Wild: Bird of Prey,* Belitha/Methuen (London, England), 1987.

*SIDELIGHTS:* "Whenever I write, I am in touch with the five-year-old or seven-year-old or nine-year-old who is still inside me," Mary Hoffman wrote for *Something about the Author Autobiography Series (SAAS)*. In her long essay, she described many of the memorable childhood events and friendships that molded the writer she is today. A recurring motif in the essay is Hoffman's ongoing fascination with play-acting and the invention of playlets and pantomimes. In the traditional British pantomime, she explained, there is always (at least) a leading male character (played by a woman) and an unappealing female character (played by a man). Hoffman's problem, she commented, was that she always wanted to play the lead, or all of the "good" parts combined, leaving her companions with the leftovers. She also noticed that many of the best parts were intended for boys.

The book that has won Hoffman the greatest recognition, on both sides of the Atlantic, is *Amazing Grace.* "Grace is really me," she declared in *SAAS*, "a little girl who loved stories and who loved acting them out." Grace also wanted to play the leading parts, even when people told her she could not appear in a male role. Hoffman once told *CA*, "I am a feminist and first got involved in children's books by assessing them in terms of their attitudes toward sex roles." In her recent essay, she commented, "Because things have moved on a bit in equality between the sexes since I was Grace's age, I added another level of challenge by making her Black." This gave people even more opportunities to try to dissuade Grace from pursuing her goal of playing Peter Pan.

According to an essayist for the *St. James Guide to Children's Writers,* "Although Mary Hoffman had written over forty books when she wrote *Amazing Grace* in 1991, it was this picture book that catapulted her into the limelight. In this she hit on something that touched so many people—that stereotypes of sex and colour, and particularly the limitations that are placed on people because of them. Her heroine Grace is always acting out her favourite stories, so naturally wants the star part in the school play of Peter Pan. As well as being a girl, Grace is black, both reasons why her classmates think she could not be Peter Pan. Grace auditions, gets the part, and plays it brilliantly, proving 'You can be anything you want, if you put your mind to it.' It is . . . sensitively and intelligently written, and . . . beautifully illustrated by Caroline Binch." *Amazing Grace* was also adapted for the stage and produced by the Children's Theatre Company in Minneapolis, Minnesota. *Horn Book* reviewer Mary M. Burns called the story "a dynamic introduction to one of the most engaging protagonists in contemporary picture books."

Hoffman wrote a sequel, *Boundless Grace,* because, as she stated in her *SAAS* essay, "Grace had become a role model for hundreds of thousands of children around the world, and if she could come to terms with a situation experienced by . . . many children today, it could really be helpful." Grace, now twelve years old, must face the separation and divorce of her parents. Hoffman and her illustrator, Caroline Binch, had to travel to the West African nation of Gambia to meet with the girl who had served as a photographic model for the first "Grace" book. Because of the photographic technique involved in creating the illustrations, no other model would do. It was natural, then, for the older Grace to move to Africa, too, to visit her father and his new wife and two step-siblings. She flies there with her grandmother, filled with anxiety about her reception into this new family. The lesson of the story, wrote a *Publishers Weekly* reviewer, is that "that families are what you make of them," concluding that *Boundless Grace* "is as assured and uplifting as its predecessor." Burns reported that "this story, like Grace, transcends social, cultural, and geographic boundaries."

"In the sequel . . . ," wrote the essayist for the *St. James Guide to Children's Writers,* "Mary Hoffman follows the same characters back to their native country of Gambia, and explores the difficult feelings that are aroused when families are kept apart by divorce. Grace's father was not in the first book, and the sequel shows him living in Africa. Once again, Mary Hoffman is honest in her portrayal of this situation, and the book is a touching and powerful portrait of a family who, though divided, feel deeply about each other."

In *Starring Grace,* the energetic youngster leads her friends as they play a series of imaginative games, including circus and ghost busters, all of which prepare them for roles in a local theatrical production. The first chapter book featuring the popular picture book character, *Starring Grace* presents "the excitement of dressing up and being part of a show," according to Hazel Rochman in *Booklist.* The reviewer for *Horn Book* found that "Grace is as appealingly irrepressible as ever."

*Stravaganza: City of Masks* is set in an alternate version of Renaissance Italy and tells the story of fifteen-year-old Lucien, who awakens in the strange city of Bellezza and finds himself in the midst of deadly political intrigue. Back home in England, Lucien is suffering from cancer. But in Bellezza, he is healthy once again. The *Publishers Weekly* reviewer believed that the "complex, at times slow-moving and somber story line . . . will likely intrigue more sophisticated readers." The critic for *Kirkus Reviews* found that the "fast-paced plot tightly integrates the fantastic with the historical, and frequent cuts between viewpoints ratchet up the suspense."

While her character Grace introduced many American readers to Hoffman, she had written nearly forty books by the time Grace first appeared. More than a dozen of these are titles in the "Animals in the Wild" series. "I have been a vegetarian since 1969," Hoffman once told *CA,* "and I like animals, particularly cats and reptiles." According to her *SAAS* essay, Hoffman's first book was *White Magic,* a story "about two cousins, a boy and a girl . . . who find a unicorn and have to look after it." Recent titles include *The Four-Legged Ghosts,* the tale of a pet mouse who somehow revives the ghosts of all past animal residents of the house where he lives, to the consternation of his "keepers" Carrie and Alex. A *Publishers Weekly* reviewer recommended the fantasy: "Readers will enjoy the mounting tension . . . and they will eagerly anticipate the resolution." Hoffman also wrote *Earth, Fire, Water, Air,* a wide-ranging miscellany of facts, poems, and stories about the elements that reflect what a *Publishers Weekly* critic called "a general reverence for the natural world." She followed this with *Sun, Moon, and Stars,* a similar collection of material on the luminaries of the sky.

Hoffman once told *CA:* "I have three daughters, and I have a good marriage. I worked through the whole period of having and raising babies, and have never had a nanny or au pair. I'm proud of my achievements and could never imagine not working."

*BIOGRAPHICAL AND CRITICAL SOURCES:*

*BOOKS*

*St. James Guide to Children's Writers,* 5th edition, St. James Press (Detroit, MI), 1999.
*Something about the Author Autobiography Series,* Volume 24, Gale (Detroit, MI), 1997.

*PERIODICALS*

*Booklist,* February 15, 2000, Hazel Rochman, review of *Starring Grace,* p. 1112; November 15, 2000, Gillian Engberg, review of *The Barefoot Book of Brother and Sister Tales,* p. 641.

*Horn Book,* July-August, 1995, p. 450; March, 2000, review of *Starring Grace,* p. 196

*Kirkus Reviews,* August 15, 2002, review of *The Color of Home,* p. 1225; September 15, 2002, review of *Stravaganza: City of Masks,* p. 1392.

*Publishers Weekly,* July 12, 1993, p. 80; May 8, 1995, p. 294; December 18, 1995, p. 54; September 27, 1999, review of *Three Wise Women,* p. 61; May 15, 2000, "A Grace Note," p. 119; July 24, 2000, review of *Parables: Stories Jesus Told,* p. 91; October 9, 2000, review of *The Barefoot Book of Brother and Sister Tales,* p. 90; July 30, 2001, review of *Miracles: Wonders Jesus Worked,* p. 82; September 30, 2002, review of *Stravaganza,* p. 72.*

\*　　\*　　\*

## HOLLISTER, C(harles) Warren 1930-1997

*PERSONAL:* Born November 2, 1930, in Los Angeles, CA; died September 14, 1997, in Santa Barbara, CA; son of Nathan and Carrie (Cushman) Hollister; married Edith Elizabeth Muller, April 12, 1952; children: Charles Warren, Jr. (deceased), Lawrence Gregory, Robert Cushman. *Education:* Harvard University, A.B., 1951; University of California, Los Angeles, M.A., 1957, Ph.D., 1958.

*CAREER:* University of California, Santa Barbara, instructor, 1958-60, assistant professor, 1960-63, associate professor, 1963-64, professor of history, 1964-97, chairman of department, 1967-70, became professor emeritus. Visiting assistant professor, Stanford University, 1962-63; visiting fellow, Merton College, Oxford, 1965-66, and Australian National University, 1978, 1993. Visiting lecturer, Oxford University, 1965, Cambridge University, 1966, University of Ghent, 1966, University of the Netherlands, 1966, University of Leyden, 1966, University of Utrecht, 1966, University of Bologna, 1967, University of Melbourne, 1978 and 1993, University of Sidney, 1978, University of Auckland, 1978 and 1993, University College, Dublin,

1986, University of Toronto, 1988, and Arizona Center for Medieval and Renaissance Studies, 1995. *Military service:* U.S. Air Force, 1951-53; became second lieutenant.

*MEMBER:* International Wizard of Oz Club (member of board of directors, 1978-86), North American Conference on British Studies (vice president, 1983-85; president, 1985-87), American Historical Association (member of executive council, Pacific Coast branch, 1968-71; vice president for teaching, 1974-76; chairman of program committee, 1984), Royal Historical Society (fellow), Mediaeval Academy of America (fellow), Medieval Academy of Ireland (fellow), Pacific Coast Conference on British Studies (president, 1968-70), Medieval Association of the Pacific (member of executive council, 1971-73), Charles Homer Haskins Society (cofounder and president, 1982-97).

*AWARDS, HONORS:* Haynes Foundation fellowship, 1959; Social Science Research Council grant-in-aid, 1961; American Council of Learned Societies grant-in-aid, 1962-63, 1963-64; Triennial Book Prize, North American Conference on British Studies, 1963, for *Anglo-Saxon Military Institutions on the Eve of the Norman Conquest;* Guggenheim fellow, 1965-66; Fulbright research fellow, 1965-66; E. Harris Harbison Award for Distinguished Teaching, Danforth Foundation, 1966; Walter D. Love Memorial Prize, North American Conference on British Studies, 1980; Alumni teacher of the year, University of California, Santa Barbara, 1983.

*WRITINGS:*

*Anglo-Saxon Military Institutions on the Eve of the Norman Conquest,* Clarendon Press (Oxford, England), 1962.

*Medieval Europe: A Short History,* Wiley (New York, NY), 1964, 5th edition, Knopf (New York, NY), 1982.

*The Military Organization of Norman England,* Clarendon Press (Oxford, England), 1965.

*A History of England,* Volume I: *The Making of England, 55 B.C.-1399,* Heath, 1966, 8th edition, Houghton Mifflin (Boston, MA), 2001.

*Roots of the Western Tradition: A Short History of the Ancient World,* Wiley (New York, NY), 1966, 4th edition, 1982.

(With John L. Stipp and Alan Dirrum) *The Rise and Development of Western Civilization,* two volumes, Wiley (New York, NY), 1967, 2nd edition, 1972.

(Editor) *Landmarks of the Western Heritage,* two volumes, Wiley (New York, NY), 1967, 2nd edition, 1973.

(Editor) *The Impact of the Norman Conquest,* Wiley (New York, NY), 1969.

(Editor) *The Twelfth-Century Renaissance,* Wiley (New York, NY), 1969.

(With Judith Pike) *The Moons of Meer* (juvenile fantasy), Walck, 1969.

(With others) *River through Time: The Course of Western Civilization* (also see below), Wiley (New York, NY), 1974.

*Odysseus to Columbus: A Synopsis of Classical and Medieval History* (contains slightly revised version of first fifteen chapters of *River through Time*), Wiley (New York, NY), 1974.

(Editor, with others) *Medieval Europe: A Short Sourcebook,* Knopf (New York, NY), 1982.

*Monarchy, Magnates, and Institutions in the Anglo-Norman World,* Hambledon Press, 1986.

(Editor) *Anglo-Norman Political Culture and the Twelfth-Century Renaissance: Proceedings of the Borchard Conference on Anglo-Norman History, 1995,* Boydell Press (Rochester, NY), 1997.

(With J. Sears McGee and Gale Stokes) *The West Transformed: A History of Western Civilization,* Harcourt College Publishers (Fort Worth, TX), 2000.

*Henry I,* edited and completed by Amanda Clark Frost, Yale University Press (New Haven, CT), 2001.

General editor, "Major Issues in World History," Wiley, 1968—. Contributor of articles to professional journals, including *Baum Bugle, Speculum, English Historical Review, Journal of British Studies,* and *American Historical Review.* Associate editor, *Viator;* member of editorial boards of *American Historical Review* and *Journal of Medieval History.*

*SIDELIGHTS:* C. Warren Hollister spent most of his academic career as a professor of medieval history at the University of California, Santa Barbara. In 1962 he accepted a commission to write a biography on England's Henry I, the youngest son of William the Conqueror, a project that became Hollister's lifelong endeavor. After his first draft, along with all his notes and research, were destroyed in a house fire in 1990, he rewrote the book and got as far as the last two

chapters before he died unexpectedly in 1997. His student, Amanda Clark Frost, used the outline Hollister left behind to finish the book.

In *Henry I* Hollister argues that the king who ruled England and Normandy for over thirty years in the twelfth century was one of the most effective leaders in England's early history due to his ability to maintain peace and consolidate the country's power in the process. Prior scholars have generally agreed that Henry I was a ruthless tyrant who dispensed with his enemies violently and without regret—a man so hated that his own daughter tried to assassinate him with a crossbow. Hollister provides evidence to suggest that Henry's preferred form of punishment was exile, not death, and that he kept the kingdom intact by using his army to successfully defeat those who attacked him, rather than by trying to conquer other lands. Hollister also sheds light on Henry's disagreements with the Catholic Church, notably the Archbishop of Canterbury, which conflicts were eventually ironed out and paved the way for Henry to establish two more dioceses in England, thereby strengthening the Church's power. Even Henry's legendary sexual exploits are explained as the king's way of ensuring his legacy. Hollister further details Henry's advances in law and administration, which enabled him to govern more effectively by establishing more formal education and an organized court that centralized and strengthened the government. These are significant achievements, Hollister maintains, in an era known for its lawlessness and treachery.

Critics were divided in their assessment of *Henry I.* Fred A. Cazel, Jr., of *History: Review of New Books,* called the volume "a work of outstanding scholarship" that "is a joy to read." Similarly, Nigel Tappin in a review for *Library Journal* praised the authors' "good narrative flow" and heralded the book as the definitive source on its subject. A writer for *Publishers Weekly* noted that the details of such a large cast of characters requires "a scorecard to keep track of the players," and George Garnett of the *Times Literary Supplement* wrote that "the book reads like a medieval work, cobbled together from a disparate collection of sources, with joints which are too obvious." In creating a work of scholarship so at odds with the prevailing notions of Henry, Hollister's "case for Mr Anglo-Norman Nice Guy is argued unremittingly, chapter after chapter, as if the wrong done to his reputation by historians biased in favor of brutal methods cried aloud for redress," wrote Eric Christiansen in the *Spectator*, who nevertheless concluded that Hollister writes "with a confidence that can exasperate, and insights which enlighten."

Aside from history, Hollister's other passions were music and the book *The Wizard of Oz.* He was purported to have amassed one of the largest collections of rare first editions of *The Wizard of Oz* in the world, a collection that took precedence over his *Henry I* manuscript when his house went up in flames and was thus spared a similar charred fate. In addition to the time it took for his work to come to fruition, wrote Christiansen, Hollister will be remembered for "his clear and sometimes humorous style" and the respect he won "by not bowing the knee to received opinion when it failed to meet his own standard of verification."

*BIOGRAPHICAL AND CRITICAL SOURCES:*

BOOKS

Abels, Richard P., and Bernard S. Bachrach, editors, *The Normans and Their Adversaries at War: Essays in Memory of C. Warren Hollister,* Boydell Press (Rochester, NY), 2001.

PERIODICALS

*Albion,* summer, 1998, review of *Anglo-Norman Political Culture and the Twelfth-Century Renaissance,* p. 257.
*American Historical Review,* February 2002, Frank Barlow, review of *Henry I,* p. 265.
*Choice,* June, 1965; July, 1965; February, 1967; July, 1969; January, 2002, S. Morillo, review of *Henry I,* p. 951.
*Contemporary Review,* July, 2001, review of *Henry I,* p. 61.
*English Historical Review,* February, 1999, Christopher Allmand, review of *Anglo-Norman Political Culture and the Twelfth-Century Renaissance,* p. 146.
*History: Review of New Books,* fall, 2001, Fred A. Cazel, Jr., review of *Henry I,* p. 20.
*Library Journal,* July, 2001, Nigel Tappin, review of *Henry I,* p. 102.

*New York Review of Books,* November 17, 1966.
*Publishers Weekly,* May 14, 2001, review of *Henry I,* p. 61.
*Spectator,* August 4, 2001, Eric Christiansen, review of *Henry I,* p. 35.
*Times Literary Supplement,* April 22, 1965; February 27, 1987; April 19, 2002, George Garnett, "A Wicked Businessman," p. 27.*

\*    \*    \*

## HOWARD, Michael (Eliot) 1922-

*PERSONAL:* Born November 29, 1922, in London, England; son of Geoffrey Eliot and Edith (Edinger) Howard. *Education:* Attended Wellington College, 1936-40; Christ Church, Oxford, B.A., 1946, M.A., 1948. *Religion:* Anglican. *Hobbies and other interests:* Music, weeding.

*ADDRESSES: Home*—The Old Farm, Eastbury, Hungerford, Berkshire RG17 7JN, England.

*CAREER:* King's College, University of London, London, England, assistant lecturer, 1947-50, lecturer in history, 1950-53, lecturer in war studies, 1953-61, reader, 1961-63, professor of war studies, 1963-68; Oxford University, Oxford, England, fellow of All Souls College, 1968—, Ford's Lecturer in English History, 1971, Chichele Professor of the History of War, 1977-80, Regius Professor of Modern History, 1980-89, professor emeritus of modern history, beginning 1993; Yale University, New Haven, CT, Robert A. Lovett Professor of Naval and Military History, 1989-93. Visiting professor of European history, Stanford University, 1967; Radcliffe lecturer, University of Warwick, 1975; Trevelyan lecturer, Cambridge University, 1977; Leverhulme lecturer, 1996; Lee Kuan Yew Distinguished Visiting professor, National University of Singapore, 1996. President and cofounder, International Institute for Strategic Studies; vice president, Council on Christian Approaches to Defence and Disarmament; chairman of army educational advisory board, 1966-71; chairman of academic advisory council, Royal Military Academy, 1969-75. Trustee of Imperial War Museum and British National Army Museum. Governor, Wellington College. *Military service:* British Army, Coldstream Guards, 1942-45; became captain; received Military Cross, 1943.

*MEMBER:* British Academy (fellow), Royal Historical Society (fellow), Institute for Strategic Studies (life president), American Academy of Arts and Sciences, Athenaeum Club, Garrick Club, Pratts Club.

*AWARDS, HONORS:* Duff Cooper Memorial Prize, 1962, for *The Franco-Prussian War: The German Invasion of France, 1870-1871;* Wolfson Foundation History Award, 1972, for *Grand Strategy,* Volume 4; Memorial Gold Medal, Royal United Services Institute for Defence Studies, 1973; Commander of the Order of the British Empire, 1977; NATO Atlantic Award, 1989; Companion of Honor, 2002; Friedrich Ebert Prize, 2002, for the *Invention of Peace: Reflections on War and International Order,;* honorary degrees from Leeds University, University of London, and Lehigh University.

*WRITINGS:*

(With John Sparrow) *The Coldstream Guards, 1920-1946,* Oxford University Press (London, England), 1951.

*Proud Heritage: A Portrait of Greatness,* edited by Richard Livingstone, Bernard Paget, and H. Imrie Swainston, J. Dron, 1951.

(Editor) *Soldiers and Governments: Nine Studies in Civil-Military Relations,* Eyre & Spottiswoode (London, England), 1957, Indiana University Press, 1959, reprinted, Greenwood Press, 1978.

*Disengagement in Europe,* Penguin (London, England), 1958.

(Editor) *Wellingtonian Studies: Essays on the First Duke of Wellington by Five Old Wellingtonian Historians,* Gale & Polden, 1959.

*The Franco-Prussian War: The German Invasion of France, 1870-1871,* Macmillan, 1961, revised edition, Methuen (London, England), 1981.

(Editor) *The Theory and Practice of War: Essays Presented to Captain B. H. Liddell Hart on His Seventieth Birthday,* Cassell (London, England), 1965, Praeger, 1966.

*Lord Haldane and the Territorial Army* (monograph), Birkbeck College, 1967.

(With Robert Hunter) *Israel and the Arab World: The Crisis of 1967,* Institute for Strategic Studies, 1967.

*Strategy and Policy in Twentieth-Century Warfare* (monograph), United States Air Force Academy, 1967.

*The Mediterranean Strategy in the Second World War,* Praeger, 1968.

*The Central Organisation of Defence,* Royal United Service Institute, 1970.

*Studies in War and Peace,* Maurice Temple Smith, 1970, Viking (New York, NY), 1971.

*The Continental Commitment: The Dilemma of British Defence Policy in the Era of the Two World Wars,* Maurice Temple Smith, 1972.

*Grand Strategy,* Volume 4: *August 1942-September 1943,* H.M.S.O., 1972.

*The British Way in Warfare: A Reappraisal,* J. Cape (London, England), 1975.

*War in European History,* Oxford University Press (New York, NY), 1976.

(Editor and translator, with Peter Paret) Carl von Clausewitz, *On War,* Princeton University Press (Princeton, NJ), 1976, reprinted, Library of Congress (Washington, DC), 1998.

*War and the Nation State,* Clarendon Press (Oxford, England), 1978.

*War and the Liberal Conscience,* Rutgers University Press (Rutgers, NJ), 1978.

(Editor) *Restraints on War: Studies in the Limitation of Armed Conflict,* Oxford University Press (New York, NY), 1979.

*The Lessons of History: An Inaugural Lecture Delivered before the Vice Chancellor and Fellows of the University of Oxford on Friday, 6 March 1981,* Clarendon Press (New York, NY), 1981.

*Clausewitz,* Oxford University Press (New York, NY), 1983.

*The Causes of Wars and Other Essays,* 2nd edition, enlarged, Harvard University Press (Cambridge, MA), 1983.

*The Lessons of History,* Yale University Press (New Haven, CT), 1991.

(Editor, with R. Ahmann and A. M. Birke) *The Quest for Stability: Problems of West European Security, 1918-1957,* Oxford University Press (New York, NY), 1993.

(Editor, with George J. Andreopoulos and Mark R. Shulman) *The Laws of War: Constraints on Warfare in the Western World,* Yale University Press (New Haven, CT), 1994.

(With John F. Guilmartin, Jr.) *Two Historians in Technology and War,* Strategic Studies Institute (Carlisle Barracks, PA), 1994.

(Editor, with William Roger Louis) *The Oxford History of the Twentieth Century,* Oxford University Press (New York, NY), 1998.

*The Invention of Peace: Reflections on War and International Order,* Yale University Press (New Haven, CT), 2001.

*The First World War,* Oxford University Press (New York, NY), 2002.

Author of foreword, *The Shield of Achilles: War, Peace, and the Course of History,* by Philip Bobbitt, Knopf, 2002. Contributor to periodicals, including *Encounter, Journal of the Royal United Service Institute,* and *English History Review.*

*SIDELIGHTS:* As an academic specializing in military and naval history, Michael Howard has focused much of his writing on interpreting the events of the early twentieth century as they relate to war. In *The Invention of Peace: Reflections on War and International Order,* Howard won praise from critics for his concise explanation of how the twentieth century ushered in a new era in human history—one in which peace, rather than constant war, is an actual possibility. The roots of this sea change reached back to the Enlightenment of the eighteenth century, and its feasibility strengthened by two world wars. Even though the book, which is an expanded essay based on one of Howard's lectures, sounds encouraging, critic Robert F. Drinan noted in the *National Catholic Reporter* that, in fact, it is "unsettling," mostly because Howard understands "the mentality of extremists who are determined to impose their views on others," as the new century dawns.

Writing in the *English Historical Review,* Brian Bond noted that Howard explains how the formation of an international community and increasing globalization makes peace an option, but that religious fundamentalism and terrorism, conjoined with the apathy of citizens in democratic states, may quite possibly undermine any chance for peace in the coming years. John Dear of *America* called *The Invention of Peace* a "brief but sweeping survey of the past 2,000 years of European-based warmaking" that, despite its title, makes clear "that there is little hope that we will ever be free of war." Rather than peace, wrote Dear, Howard focuses on the "re-invention of war" as it evolves with ever new weapons of mass destruction and greater possibility for annihilation. Gilbert Taylor of *Booklist* echoed Dear's sentiment, saying that "Howard's analytically sharp discourse is ultimately pessimistic," especially when he outlines growing anti-American sentiment in other parts of the world. A

writer for *Publishers Weekly* credited Howard's ability to distill information, concluding that "for all its brevity, this book is extraordinarily ambitious in scope."

In *The First World War* Howard summarizes the defining moment of the twentieth century in only 154 pages. Critics gave Howard high marks for his brevity in explaining the causes and complications of World War I in a way that makes the events sound inevitable. Starting with the geopolitical situation on the eve of the war in 1914, Howard outlines the reasons each country had for entering into the conflict. He also explains how countries formed alliances with one another, a new concept at the time but one that has characterized most global conflicts since. Trench warfare and modern machinery, which lengthened the war and transformed it into one of attrition, are also explained in Howard's book. Finally, the war ended with a major migration of refugees, an unbearable number of casualties, and the Versailles Treaty, which, Howard claims, laid the groundwork for the rise of Adolf Hitler. With each new development, says Howard, generals were sure the war would end, but the reverse happened. Taylor, writing in *Booklist,* called *The First World War* "succinctly expressive," a sentiment shared by other reviewers. Ian McGibbon wrote in the *New Zealand International Review* that *The First World War* is "written with great clarity and authority" and "focuses unabashedly on the events on the battlefield, which, Howard explains, ultimately transformed the social and political structures of Europe." A writer for *Kirkus Reviews* said that Howard "engages and educates . . . with clarity, craft, and precision."

*BIOGRAPHICAL AND CRITICAL SOURCES:*

*BOOKS*

Freedman, Lawrence, Paul Hayes, and Robert O'Neill, *War, Strategy, and International Politics: Essays in Honour of Sir Michael Howard,* Oxford University Press (New York, NY), 1992.

*PERIODICALS*

*America,* April 9, 2001, John Dear, review of *The Invention of Peace,* p. 40.

*Booklist,* March 1, 2001, Gilbert Taylor, review of *The Invention of Peace,* p. 1211; September 15, 2002, Gilbert Taylor, review of *The First World War,* p. 198.

*English Historical Review,* April, 1997, Brian Bond, review of *The Laws of War,* p. 550; November, 2000, Brian Bond, review of *The Invention of Peace,* p. 1349.

*Journal of Modern History,* September, 1997, Mathias Schmoeckel, review of *The Laws of War,* p. 570.

*Kirkus Reviews,* February 15, 2001, a review of *The Invention of Peace,* p. 235; August 1, 2002, review of *The First World War,* p. 1096.

*Los Angeles Times Book Review,* June 3, 2001, review of *The Invention of Peace,* p. 3.

*National Catholic Reporter,* August 24, 2001, Robert F. Drinan, review of *The Invention of Peace,* p. 18.

*New York Times Book Review,* September 6, 1981, review of *The Franco-Prussian War,* p. 19; January 29, 1984, Linda Robinson, review of *The Causes of Wars and Other Essays,* p. 23.

*New Zealand International Review,* September-October, 2002, Ian McGibbon, review of *The First World War,* p. 29.

*Orbis,* winter, 1996, Eugene V. Rostow, review of *The Laws of War,* p. 145.

*Publishers Weekly,* February 26, 2001, review of *The Invention of Peace,* p. 69.

\*    \*    \*

## HOYT, Richard (Duane) 1941-
### (Nicholas Van Pelt)

*PERSONAL:* Born January 28, 1941, in Hermiston, OR; son of Clyde Lorrain (a railroad laborer) and Nellie Beryl (a school cafeteria manager; maiden name, Allen) Hoyt; married Carole Lindell, 1967 (divorced, 1978); married, Sheila Burgard, 1980 (divorced, 1981); married Teresita Artes, 1992; children: Laura Lynne Dell, Teresita Nelli. *Ethnicity:* "Caucasian of Western European" *Education:* Columbia Basin College, A.A., 1961; University of Oregon, B.S. (journalism), 1963, M.S. (journalism), 1967; University of Hawaii, Ph.D., 1972. *Politics:* Independent *Hobbies and other interests:* "Speculation on the nature of folly and delusion, staying out of the noonday sun."

*ADDRESSES: Home*—#18 Garden Grove Villa, Sapangdaku, Guadeloupe, Cebu City 6000, Philippines. *Agent*—Jacques de Spoelberch, 9 Shagbark Rd., Wilson Pt., South Norwalk, CT 06854. *E-mail*—richardhoyt2001@yahoo.com.

*CAREER:* Novelist, journalist, and educator. *Honolulu Star Bulletin,* Honolulu, HI, reporter, 1967-70; *Newsweek,* New York, NY, correspondent, 1969-72; *Honolulu Advertiser,* Honolulu, HI, reporter, 1970-72; University of Maryland at College Park, assistant professor of journalism, 1973-76; Lewis and Clark College, Portland, OR, associate professor of communications, 1976-1982. Freelance writer, 1982—. *Military service:* U.S. Army, 1963-66, Intelligence Corps.

*MEMBER:* Authors Guild.

*AWARDS, HONORS:* Washington Journalism Center fellow, 1967; American Mystery Award for best espionage, 1987, for *Siege.*

*WRITINGS:*

*The Manna Enzyme,* Morrow (New York, NY), 1982.
*Darwin's Secret,* Doubleday (New York, NY), 1989.
*Old Soldiers Sometimes Lie,* Forge (New York, NY), 2001.

UNDER PSEUDONYM NICHOLAS VAN PELT

*The Mongoose Man,* Forge (New York, NY), 1998.
*Stomp!* Forge (New York, NY), 1999.

"JIM QUINT" SERIES

*Cool Runnings,* Viking (New York, NY), 1984.
*Vivienne,* Forge (New York, NY), 2000.

"JOHN DENSON" SERIES

*Decoys,* M. Evans (New York, NY), 1980.
*Thirty for a Harry,* M. Evans (New York, NY), 1981.
*The Siskiyou Two-Step,* Morrow (New York, NY), 1983.
*Fish Story,* Viking (New York, NY), 1985.
*Whoo?* T. Doherty (New York, NY), 1991.
*Bigfoot,* Tor (New York, NY), 1993.
*Snake Eyes,* Forge (New York, NY), 1995.
*The Weatherman's Daughter,* Forge, (New York, NY), 2003.

*"JAMES BURLANE" SERIES*

*Trotsky's Run,* Morrow (New York, NY), 1982.

*Head of State,* Tor (New York, NY), 1985.

*The Dragon Portfolio,* Tor (New York, NY), 1986.

*Siege,* Tor (New York, NY), 1987.

*Marimba,* Tor (New York, NY), 1992.

*Red Card: A Novel of World Cup 1994,* Forge (New York, NY), 1994.

*Japanese Game,* Forge (New York, NY), 1995.

(With Neil Abercrombie) *Blood of Patriots,* Forge (New York, NY), 1996.

*Tyger! Tyger!,* Forge (New York, NY), 1996.

*WORK IN PROGRESS: Pony Girls,* a "John Denson" mystery, for Forge (New York, NY), May 2004; *Sonja's Run,* a romantic novel of high adventure set in the Urals, Siberia, and the Asian steppe in 1853, for Forge, (New York, NY), 2005; *Poor Do,* a "John Denson" mystery; *The Death of Magellan.*

*SIDELIGHTS:* Richard Hoyt began writing mystery and suspense novels in 1980, and his books have been well received by critics in both genres. His writing style is characterized by well-plotted stories enhanced by attention to detail and skill in creating atmosphere. Curtis S. Gibson of *Twentieth-Century Crime and Mystery Writers* praised Hoyt's economical use of words, which guides the reader through the narrative easily and unobtrusively. Gibson added, "Hoyt has a considerable gift for comic writing but indulges it only where appropriate, that is to say, in the dialogue, which is generally trenchant and frequently hilarious."

In his first novel, *Decoys,* Hoyt introduces John Denson, a private investigator based in Seattle, Washington. Hired by a second investigator—attractive but duplicitous Pamela Yew—to help locate a vicious San Francisco-based pimp, Denson eventually becomes Yew's competitor in a race to retrieve a valuable Chinese vase from smugglers. *New York Times Book Review* critic Newgate Callendar welcomed Hoyt's "tough but attractive" protagonist, predicting that he "could well turn out to be a valuable addition to the private-eye genre." The reviewer deemed Hoyt "an expert writer" moving securely "within [the] established parameters" of his craft as well. Also judging Denson a "shamus who has promise" in a review for the *Washington Post Book World,* Jean M. White related: "Humor and witty dialogue lighten the grim proceedings of drugs, several slashed throats and kinky sex."

A former newspaper reporter, Hoyt exhibits his journalism background in *Thirty for a Harry,* his second Denson adventure. A *Seattle Star* investigative reporter is suspected of taking bribes and suppressing a news story that reveals corruption (such a journalist is called a "harry"). Denson is asked to investigate the matter and uncovers murder, corporate misdeeds, and police wrongdoing. While critics acknowledged a complicated plot in *Thirty for a Harry,* they also found much in the novel to admire. White, for example, commented that "Hoyt more than redeems his over-manipulated plot with his newsroom scenes and reporter's talk. He knows the newspaper business and its people." Hoyt "goes into a city room with the kind of authority that only experienced hands have," concurred Callendar, adding that *Thirty for a Harry* "is really a grand job." Writing that "the Seattle background provides a happy departure from the customary sleaze of southern California," *New Republic* reviewer Robin W. Winks decided that, despite the predictability inherent in detective fiction, *Thirty for a Harry* is "a good ride." "The story is well-written, tough, amusing, and highly readable," agreed Alice Cromie in her review for the *Chicago Tribune Book World.*

Private investigator Denson reappears in *The Siskiyou Two-Step,* drawn into a case involving an Elizabethan play that could definitively identify playwright William Shakespeare as the earl of Oxford. As the Federal Bureau of Investigation, British intelligence, and other operatives vie for control over the manuscript, violence and murder ensue. Reviewing the novel in the *New York Times,* Walter Goodman wrote that Hoyt "has plainly overdosed on Raymond Chandler and Dashiell Hammett. Denson is so tough that he passes off with an aside an attempt on his life. . . . Obviously, [he] is a jerk, and he keeps getting into enough trouble to satisfy the conventions of his craft." Callendar, however, came away with a more favorable impression of the novel: "The story unfolds in a good-humored, relaxed, cynical style," remarked the critic. "Nobody is going to take the hectic goings-on seriously, but the book is a lot of fun."

In *Fish Story* Denson tries to help a Cowlitz Indian friend—currently involved in a court case to reinstate his tribe's salmon-fishing rights—find the opposition fanatics who are using threats, beatings, murder, and dismemberment to strong-arm the decision. White observed that Hoyt "is back in . . . top form, . . . offer-[ing] a difficult blend of bawdy comedy satire with hard-boiled detective fiction" that "works most of the time." While noting that the plot stretches plausibility, the critic offered commendations as well: "Some of the best moments in *Fish Story* . . . come when author Hoyt delves into Indian lore or history," stated White. "Seattle adds its own distinctive character to a private eye yarn . . . [that] ends with an eerie, thrilling case-confrontation in [a] 'buried' city of underground tunnels." "Confusing at times, but never dull" is how Cromie described *Fish Story,* deeming this tale "of far-out multiple mayhem . . . macabre but fast-moving." And, like White, Callendar particularly appreciated the novel's "eerie sequences" in Seattle's "city beneath the city," deciding that *Fish Story* "is a neat job, up to the high standard previously established by Mr. Hoyt."

Denson shows up again in *Whoo?,* a comical title for a mystery revolving around the murder of an ecologist who is studying the spotted owl population in Washington. Denson falls in love with the ecologist while on a marijuana investigation in the same area, motivating him to solve the crime. A *Publisher's Weekly* reviewer called the plot "complicated" and felt that while the book was suspenseful, it was "impeded by macho humor." In *Snake Eyes,* Denson and his sidekick William Pretty-Bird are hired by the lawyer of an anti-environmentalist rancher whose cows have contracted anthrax. Again, Denson gets the woman—this time a young widowed Native American—and there are murders to be solved among the dying cows. A critic for *Publishers Weekly* gave this mystery a mixed review, concluding that although the story is "observant and funny," "Hoyt needs either more satire or more suspense to carry his weak plot." In *The Weatherman's Daughter,* another Denson outing, the detective is hot on the trail of bear poachers in a novel *Booklist* contributor Frank Sennett dubbed "full of delightful surprises."

In the Toronto *Globe and Mail* Derrick Murdoch described Hoyt's spy novel *Cool Runnings* as "a thriller, a satire, a burlesque entertainment [and] a bawdy parable." Involving a Dutch pacifist organization whose reconstruction of a nuclear bomb is stolen and armed with plutonium, the novel has at its center Jim Quint, a roving *Rolling Stone* reporter who is chosen by a nuclear weapons monitoring consortium as the unlikely—and reluctant—principal agent in the case (he had been covering the Dutch group for an article). Also the pseudonymous author of thrillers about a

James Bond-like superspy, Quint learns that real-life espionage is not nearly so straightforward or glamorous; "nothing about it makes anything remotely approximating sense," observed *Washington Post Book World* reviewer Jonathan Yardley; "each episode is more improbable that the one that went before, and most of it is quite thoroughly hilarious." Noting that Hoyt lampoons such targets as "pacifist extremists . . . British espionage professionals . . . the dope culture, . . . [and] the genre novel of macho sex and violence," the critic decided that *Cool Runnings* is "a clever, sophisticated, irreverent and witty send-up of just about everything worth sending up these days, and into the bargain it's a diverting suspense novel in its own right."

Writing in the *New York Times Book Review* that the premise of *Cool Runnings* "is not exceptionally outlandish," reviewer Arthur Krystal determined, "What makes this tale different from other similar scenarios is Mr. Hoyt's sense of humor, which is applied in the broadest possible strokes." With "none of [the] characters . . . presented seriously, and . . . the narrative . . . riddled with arch or just plain silly vignettes," continued the reviewer, "Mr. Hoyt does not require that we suspend belief, only that we find him amusing. Sometimes we do, sometimes we don't." Yardley was more taken with the novel, however, remarking that "there are enough wackos and weirdos in *Cool Runnings* to satisfy the most demanding appetite." He concluded that "if they gave out medals for skillful, intelligent light reading . . . *Cool Runnings* would be a leading contender for 1984 honors."

Jim Quint returns in 2000's *Vivienne,* a novel called a "masterful work, not for the faint of heart" by *Affaire de Coeur* critic Heather Nordahl. The book is set in 1968 and journalist Quint is now covering the Vietnam War. Vivienne is the Vietnamese wife of Colonel Del Lambert, an intelligence officer. The two men meet in Vietnam at a dinner where Lambert tries to bribe Quint with his wife's sexuality. Lambert offers to give Vivienne to Quint if the reporter can get her to reveal a secret: the location of a missing documentary on a Viet Cong massacre of a small village. The ensuing psychosexual thriller "weaves a vivid tapestry around the day-to-day headlines of the crucial presidential election year of 1968," explained a *Publishers Weekly* critic. Davis Pitt of *Booklist* remarked that this novel is "an intelligent rumination on the Vietnam War."

During the early 1960s Hoyt was a U.S. Army intelligence agent, an experience he draws on in his writings.

His cold war-era thriller *The Manna Enzyme* tells of a biochemist who has discovered an enzyme capable of making all plant life edible and of the American, British, and Soviet agents—as well as Cuban dictator Fidel Castro—who pursue him during an Oregon fishing vacation. The focus of *Trotsky's Run* is infamous British traitor/Soviet spy Kim Philby—who in Hoyt's fictional account has information that America's president-elect is a puppet of the Soviet secret police; U.S. agent James Burlane is charged with secreting Philby out of Russia. Callendar wrote that the plot of *Trotsky's Run* "is a bit complicated, though always logically handled," adding, "[The book] is a stunner—superbly written, . . . a bit scary but believable despite its far-out premise." Also noting the author's "good deal of irony and cynicism . . . [and] realistic view of the fencing that goes on between American and Soviet intelligence agents," *New York Times Book Review* critic Callendar deemed *Trotsky's Run* "a potent package," instructing readers: "Put this book at the top of your list." Burlane is again a main character in *Marimba,* where he goes undercover as a cocaine cargo pilot and finds that other deep-cover officers are also consuming large quantities of the drug. "The plot quickly takes on a satisfying who's-with-who insolubility," noted a *Publishers Weekly* critic. The same reviewer said that the mystery has a "cheeky, over-the-top quality that makes it memorable."

Reviewing *Head of State,* another Hoyt thriller featuring Burlane, for the Toronto *Globe and Mail,* Margaret Cannon determined that it again shows the author's "ability to turn the conventional sex-and-action elements into a bizarre romp." Russian poet Isaac Ginsburg hatches a plan to avenge his years of Siberian exile by stealing Lenin's head from the revolutionary's Moscow sarcophagus and forcing the Soviet Union to declare a year of unrestricted emigration for its citizens; the incident necessitates the return of U.S. intelligence agent Burlane. While maintaining that Hoyt's zany "premise and people . . . should keep the reader guessing about what's next," the reviewer also noted: "Hoyt's research into the Soviet Union's past and present ideological currents is well done. . . . His descriptions, whether real or imagined, have the ring of authenticity." Cannon decided that "beneath the surface glitter . . . *Head of State* is a conventional action-thriller with all the expected confrontations and cliches," but added, "[It] is a brilliant twist to the old plot and readers will be charmed by Hoyt's macabre wit."

Central Intelligence Agency operative Burlane reappears in *The Dragon Portfolio,* accompanied by beautiful female agent Ellen Nidich; the spies are involved in purchasing Chinese secret documents—a pursuit complicated by the schemes of two kung-fu movie stars and a pair of rich, oil-dealing Texans. In his review for the *New York Times Book Review,* Stephen McCauley observed that "early on . . . it becomes clear that Mr. Hoyt is more interested in exercising his satiric wit than boiling a thoroughly plausible plot," adding, "His best scenes have the wild comic energy of very good farce," "leaving the reader little time to worry about political or emotional credibility." Cannon likewise observed that "as with all Hoyt novels the plot is enormously complicated"; noted too was the author's "tendency to overkill," with "some of the snide asides going on too long, turning into rants." Still, the critic decided that "for sheer inventive craziness, Hoyt is . . . difficult to beat"—his "unforgettable characters engaged in wild and wacky capers." In *Siege* Burlane and Nidich foil Arab terrorists occupying British Gibraltar. The novel pokes fun at assorted targets, including spy novelists, ratings-driven television employees, and Britain's prime minister.

In the mid-1990s Hoyt embarked on another string of mysteries featuring maverick ex-CIA man James Burlane. In *Redcard,* which a *Booklist* critic called a "terrific murder mystery," Burlane is hired by the international soccer organization to stop a terrorist who is killing star soccer players. A writer for *Publishers Weekly* thought that one of the most notable things about this novel was the fact that Hoyt clearly knows much about soccer and "manages to educate as he entertains." *Japanese Game* has Burlane tracking down the U.S. vice president's daughter, who has been kidnapped and sold to Japanese gangsters. The gangsters use the girl to blackmail Americans into halting their crackdown on unfair Japanese trade practices. A critic from *Booklist,* who said Hoyt should "return to his earlier approach," and one from *Publishers Weekly* both agreed that Hoyt seems to have abandoned his sense of humor in the recent Burlane mysteries. The *Publishers Weekly* writer related that the author "seems torn between farce and melodrama." Burlane goes after tiger poachers in *Tyger! Tyger!* and meets up with a German detective tracking a serial killer who paints his victims with tiger stripes. Hoyt weaves magic and myth into the plot as Burlane travels to Siberia, Hong Kong, and the Philippines. The mystery was called "edifying and spirited entertainment" by a *Booklist* critic.

Continuing with the adventures of CIA operative Burlane, Hoyt tries something new, teaming up with U.S.

Congressman-turned-writer Neil Abercrombie in writing *Blood of Patriots*. Abercrombie's personal insight into Washington, D.C., and its political environs enhanced the authors' story of terrorists who attack the House of Representatives and kill 124 people. A *Publishers Weekly* writer said that the politician's input "allows for some fresh local coloring," but admitted that the story feels "flat" and the dialogue "stilted."

A departure from his detective and spy novels, Hoyt's *Darwin's Secret* is an adventure story that takes place on the Amazon river boat *Barco Igaranha*. Its assortment of passengers includes an American physician, a writer, a Catholic priest, and a witch doctor; gold, a sacred object with healing powers, and a lost band of European utopians are the various grails these travelers seek. Their hostile journey culminates in the discovery of "a stunning secret" of "sheer terror," according to *New York Times Book Review* critic Ross Thomas, who added, "Hoyt handles [this development] very well indeed." Deeming *Darwin's Secret* a "wild, witty and often caustic novel" that targets religion, American medicine, and the destruction of Brazil's rain forest, the reviewer commented that "[Hoyt] blends accurate scientific facts with nicely confected ones into an intoxicating mixture that almost induces complete suspension of disbelief." Praising its author as "facile and energetic," Thomas concluded: "*Darwin's Secret* . . . is the best trip I've ever taken up the Amazon."

## BIOGRAPHICAL AND CRITICAL SOURCES:

### BOOKS

*Twentieth-Century Crime and Mystery Writers,* 3rd edition, St. James Press (Detroit, MI), 1991.

### PERIODICALS

*Armchair Detective,* fall, 1993.
*Booklist,* July, 1992, Thomas Gaughan, review of *Marimba,* p. 1917; May 15, 1994, Thomas Gaughan, review of *Red Card,* p. 1667; June 1, 1994, Bill Ott, review of *Marimba,* p. 1778; January 15, 1995, Thomas Gaughan, review of *Japanese Game,* p. 899; December 1, 1995, Thomas Gaughan, review of *Snake Eyes,* p. 612; March 1, 1996, Thomas Gaughan, review of *Tyger! Tyger!,* p. 1124; October 15, 2000, David Pitt, review of *Vivienne,* p. 424; May 1, 2003, Frank Sennett, review of *The Weatherman's Daughter,* p. 1545.
*Chicago Tribune Book World,* September 20, 1981; March 24, 1985; November 3, 1991.
*Globe and Mail* (Toronto), August 18, 1984; October 19, 1985; December 6, 1986.
*Library Journal,* November, 1, 1991, Rex E. Klett, review of *Whoo?,* p. 135; July, 1992, Elsa Pendleton, review of *Marimba,* p. 124; March 1, 1995, Maria A. Perez-Stable, review of *Japanese Game,* p. 102.
*Los Angeles Times Book Review,* August 4, 1985; July 9, 1989.
*New Republic,* August 22, 1981.
*New Yorker,* August 26, 1985.
*New York Times,* August 6, 1983.
*New York Times Book Review,* January 4, 1981; November 15, 1981; August 22, 1982; August 7, 1983; November 13, 1983; September 9, 1984; June 9, 1985; December 21, 1986; July 26, 1992, review of *Marimba,* p. 13; June 26, 1994, Newgate Callendar, review of *Red Card,* p. 19; February 26, 1995, Newgate Callendar, review of *Japanese Game,* p. 29; July 20, 2003, Marilyn Stasio, review of *The Weatherman's Daughter.*
*Publishers Weekly,* September 20, 1991, review of *Whoo?,* p. 123; May 25, 1992, review of *Marimba,* p. 24; November 16, 1992, review of *Bigfoot,* p. 50; May 23, 1994, review of *Red Card,* p. 81; January 2, 1995, review of *Japanese Game,* p. 60; November 13, 1995, review of *Snake Eyes,* p. 51; February 19, 1996, review of *Tyger! Tyger!,* p. 243; April 15, 1996, review of *Blood of Patriots,* p. 51; October 16, 2000, review of *Vivienne,* p. 47; October 14, 2002, review of *Old Soldiers Sometimes Lie,* p. 66.
*Seattle Times,* March 28, 1999, p. B5.
*Washington Post Book World,* September 21, 1980; October 18, 1981; July 8, 1984; June 16, 1985; June 11, 1989; July 26, 1992; May 19, 1996.

### ONLINE

*Affaire de Coeur,* http://www.affairedecoeur.com/ (June 26, 2002).
*Stop You're Killing Me,* http://stopyourekillingme.com/ (March 7, 2001).

## HYMAN, Timothy 1946-

*PERSONAL:* Born April 17, 1946, in Hove, Sussex, England; son of Alan (a screenwriter and author) and Noreen (Gypson) Hyman; married Judith Ravenscroft (a fiction writer), March 22, 1982. *Education:* Slade School of Fine Art, London, diploma, 1967. *Politics:* "Left/anarchist." *Hobbies and other interests:* The novels of John Cowper Powys, Italian cinema.

*ADDRESSES: Home*—62 Myddelton Sq., London EC1R 1XX, England.

*CAREER:* Artist (painter), writer, curator, and lecturer.

*AWARDS, HONORS:* Leverhulme Award, 1993; Wingate Award, 1997.

*WRITINGS:*

*Bonnard,* Thames & Hudson (London, England), 1998.
*Bhupen Khakhar,* Mapin (India), 1998.
*Carnivalesque,* University of California Press (Berkeley, CA), 2000.
*Stanley Spencer,* Tate Gallery (London, England), 2001.
*Sienese Painting,* Thames & Hudson (London, England), 2003.

Contributor of numerous articles to magazines and newspapers, including *London, Artscribe, Modern Painters,* and *Times Literary Supplement.*

*SIDELIGHTS:* Timothy Hyman once told *CA:* "For the past twenty years I've been in the awkward category of a 'painter who writes.' Most of my energies have been devoted to painting (which remains my chief source of income). I began to write as a crusader—in defense of artists unregarded or misunderstood—and that remains my central motivation. Of course I am also writing about the artists from whom I have learned the most and to whom I feel closest, and that quest for self-understanding determines my critical viewpoint.

"The focus of my book on Bonnard is a subjective pictorial space—a new space for the self—which obviously links to my own practice as a painter. It is partly my interest in the representation of the city (that is, London) that now fuels my research on Ambrogio Lorenzetti and Sienese painting. For me, the writing and the painting are integral and interdependent—even if the gear changes are sometimes troublesome!"

# J

## JACKSON, Guida M. 1930-

*PERSONAL:* Given name is pronounced "*Guy*-da"; born August 29, 1930, in Amarillo, TX; daughter of James Hurley (a merchant) and Ina (Benson) Miller; married Prentice Lamar Jackson (an anesthesiologist), June 15, 1951 (divorced, 1986); married William H. Laufer (an artist), February 14, 1986; children: (first marriage) Jeffrey Allen, William Andrew, James Tucker, Annabeth. *Ethnicity:* Caucasian. *Education:* Attended Musical Arts Conservatory, Amarillo, TX, 1945-47; Texas Technological College (now Texas Tech University), B.A. (journalism), 1951; attended University of Houston, 1953; California State University, M.A. (third world literature), 1985; attended Union Graduate School, 1986; International Institute of Advanced Studies, Ph.D. (comparative literature), 1990.

*ADDRESSES: Home*—116 Tree Crest Cir., The Woodlands, TX 77381. *E-mail*—guidamj@flex.net.

*CAREER:* English teacher at public high schools in Houston, TX, 1951-54; music teacher and freelance writer in Houston, 1956-71; Monday Shop (antiques store), Houston, owner, 1971-75; *Texas Country* (magazine), Houston, editor, 1976-78; freelance writer, 1978—. Lecturer, University of Houston, 1985-90; writing instructor, Montgomery College, 1990-98. Publisher, Panther Creek Press, 2000—.

*MEMBER:* International Women's Writing Guild, Dramatists Guild, Women in Communications, PEN, Woodlands Writers Guild, Authors Unlimited of Houston, Houston Writers Guild, Houston Writers Consortium, Writers Forum.

*Guida M. Jackson*

*WRITINGS:*

*Passing Through* (novel), Simon & Schuster (New York, NY), 1979.
*A Common Valor,* Simon & Schuster (New York, NY), 1980.
*The Lamentable Affair of the Vicar's Wife* (play), I. E. Clark (Schulenburg, TX), 1980.

*Heart to Hearth,* Prism (New York, NY), 1988.

*African Women Write,* Touchstone Books (New York, NY), 1990.

*Women Who Ruled,* American Bibliographical Center-Clio Press (Santa Barbara, CA), 1990.

*Favorite Fables,* Prism (New York, NY), 1991.

*Virginia Diaspora: Southern Bensons and Related Families,* Heritage Books (Bowie, MD), 1992.

*Encyclopedia of Traditional Epics,* ABC-CLIO (Santa Barbara, CA), 1994.

*Traditional Epics: A Literary Companion,* Oxford University Press (New York, NY), 1995.

*Encyclopedia of Literary Epics,* ABC-CLIO (Santa Barbara, CA), 1996.

(Editor, with Jackie Pelham) *Fall from Innocence: Memoirs of the Great Depression,* Page One Publications, 1997.

*Women Rulers throughout the Ages: An Illustrated Guide,* ABC-CLIO (Santa Barbara, CA), 1999.

Contributor to *The Three-Ingredient Cookbook,* compiled by Phyllis Stillwell Prokop, Broadman (Nashville, TN), 1981. Contributor to magazines. Editor, *TSA Newsletter,* 1974-82, and *Touchstone Literary Quarterly,* 1976—; contributing editor, *Houston Town and Country,* 1975.

*ADAPTATIONS: Women Who Ruled* was adapted for CD-ROM by ABC-Clio as "Women Leaders: Rulers throughout History"; *Virginia Diaspora: Southern Bensons and Related Families* was adapted for CD-ROM by Heritage Books as "Heritage Books Archives: Southern Bensons by Guida M. Jackson-Laufer, Ph. D."

*WORK IN PROGRESS:* A novel.

*SIDELIGHTS:* Guida M. Jackson told *CA:* "I consider more carefully, these days, whether or not what I write is worth destroying even one tree in order to publish it. Still, there are stories that beg to be told, lives that need to be chronicled. There are noble and courageous people whose histories are the heritage of our children, stories that will be forgotten if someone doesn't preserve them. Writers are like switchboard operators: we plug cultures together; we plug generations together. When my writing accomplishes this, I figure there will be a tree for me."

*BIOGRAPHICAL AND CRITICAL SOURCES:*

BOOKS

Fanning, Diane and Susie Kelly Flatau, *Red Boots and Attitude: The Spirit of Texas Women Writers,* Eakin Press (Austin, TX), 2002.

PERIODICALS

*Biography,* fall, 2001, Bella Vivante, review of *Women Rulers throughout the Ages: An Illustrated Guide,* p. 1014.

*Booklist,* November 1, 1994, review of *Encyclopedia of Traditional Epics,* p. 539; December 15, 1999, review of *Women Rulers throughout the Ages,* p. 804; May 15, 2000, Dona Helmer, review of *Encyclopedia of Traditional Epics,* p. 1774.

*Book Report,* September-October, 1997, Kate Clarke, review of *Encyclopedia of Literary Epics,* p. 59.

*Bookwatch,* November, 1999, p. 10.

*Book World,* February 18, 1996, p. 12.

*Choice,* April, 1995, C. Reik, review of *Encyclopedia of Traditional Epics,* p. 1277; July-August, 1997, J. R. Luttrell, review of *Encyclopedia of Literary Epics,* p. 1780.

*Dallas Morning News,* October 7, 1979, review of *Passing Through.*

*Durham Morning Herald,* October 14, 1979, review of *Passing Through.*

*History,* winter, 1992, p. 82.

*Houston Chronicle,* December 16, 1979.

*Houston Post,* November 4, 1979.

*Houston Reporter,* February 28, 1979, review of *Passing Through.*

*Journal of World History,* fall, 2001, Bella Vivante, review of *Women Rulers throughout the Ages,* p. 460.

*Kirkus Review,* July 15, 1979, review of *Passing Through.*

*Library Journal,* April 15, 1991, review of *Women Who Ruled;* September 1, 1994, Patricia Dooley, review of *Encyclopedia of Traditional Epics,* p. 173; December, 1999, Bonnie Collier, review of *Women Rulers throughout the Ages,* p. 108.

*Publishers Weekly,* July 24, 1979, review of *Passing Through.*

*Reference and Research Book News,* March, 1995, p. 43; August, 1997, p. 145.

*Reference Books Bulletin,* January 15, 1991, review of *Women Who Ruled.*

*RQ,* summer, 1995, Martin R. Kalfatovic, review of *Encyclopedia of Traditional Epics,* p. 517.

*School Library Journal,* May, 1991, review of *Women Who Ruled;* February, 2000, J. B. MacDonald, review of *Women Rulers throughout the Ages,* p. 80.

*South Bend Tribune,* November 18, 1979, review of *Passing Through.*

*Texas Monthly,* November, 1979.

*Washington Post,* September 22, 1979.

*Wilson Library Bulletin,* March, 1995, James Rettig, review of *Encyclopedia of Traditional Epics,* p. 78.

OTHER

*Heritage Books Archives: Southern Bensons* (CD-ROM), Heritage Books.

*Women Leaders: Rulers throughout History* (CD-ROM), ABC-CLIO.

\*　　\*　　\*

## JAMES, Philip
### See MOORCOCK, Michael (John)

\*　　\*　　\*

## JESSEL, Camilla (Ruth) 1937-

*PERSONAL:* Born December 7, 1937, in Bearsted, Kent, England; daughter of Richard Frederick (a naval officer) and Winifred May (Levy) Jessel; married Andrzej Panufnik (a symphonic composer), November 27, 1963; children: Roxanna Anna, Jeremy James. *Education:* University of Paris, Sorbonne, degree superieur, 1959. *Hobbies and other interests:* Music, theatre, art, ballet, literature, international politics.

*ADDRESSES: Home*—Riverside House, Twickenham TW1 3JD, England. *Agent*—David Higham Associates Ltd., 5-8 Lower John St., London W1R 4HA, England.

*CAREER:* Photographer and author. Former vice chairperson of Home Welfare Committee; Save the Children United Kingdom child care committee, member and vice chairperson, 1969-84; Cranborne Chase School, Wiltshire, England, school governor; Park Lane Group (for young musicians), council member. *Exhibitions:* Work shown in group and solo photographic exhibitions in England at Royal Festival Hall, Arts Theatre Club, Photographers Gallery, and Royal Photographic Society.

*AWARDS, HONORS:* Grant from Nuffield Foundation, 1972; Royal Photographic Society fellowship, 1980.

*WRITINGS:*

FOR CHILDREN; AND PHOTOGRAPHER

*Manuela Lives in Portugal* ("Children Everywhere" series), Hastings House (New York, NY), 1967.

*Paul in Hospital,* Methuen Children's Books (London, England), 1972.

*Mark's Wheelchair Adventures,* Methuen Children's Books (London, England), 1975.

*Life at the Royal Ballet School,* Methuen Children's Books (London, England), 1979, revised, 1985.

*The Puppy Book,* Methuen Children's Books (New York), 1980.

*The New Baby,* Methuen Children's Books (London, England), 1981.

*Moving House,* Methuen Children's Books (London, England), 1981.

*Going to the Doctor,* Methuen Children's Books (London, England), 1981.

*Away for the Night,* Methuen Children's Books (London, England), 1981.

*Lost and Found,* Methuen Children's Books (London, England), 1983.

*At Playgroup,* Methuen Children's Books (London, England), 1983.

*Going to Hospital,* Methuen Children's Books (London, England), 1983.

*The Baby-sitter,* Methuen Children's Books (London, England), 1983.

*Learner Bird,* Methuen Children's Books (London, England), 1983.

*If You Meet a Stranger,* Walker Books (London, England), 1990.

*The Puppy Book,* Walker Books (London, England), 1991, revised edition, 1993, Candlewick Press (Cambridge, MA), 1994.

*The Kitten Book,* Walker Books (London, England), 1991, revised edition, 1993, Candlewick Press (Cambridge, MA), 1994.

*Ballet School: What It Takes to Make a Dancer,* Hamish Hamilton (London, England), 1999, Viking (New York, NY), 2000.

*"BABYDAYS" SERIES; AND PHOTOGRAPHER*

*Baby's Day,* Methuen Children's Books (London, England), 1985.
*Baby's Toys,* Methuen Children's Books (London, England), 1985.
*Baby's Bedtime,* Methuen Children's Books (London, England), 1985.
*Baby's Clothes,* Methuen Children's Books (London, England), 1985.
*Baby's Food,* Methuen Children's Books (London, England), 1986.
*Where Is Baby?,* Methuen Children's Books (London, England), 1986.

*PHOTOGRAPHER*

Dorothy Shuttlesworth, *The Tower of London: Grim and Glamorous,* Hastings House (New York, NY), 1970.
Susan Harvey, *Play in Hospital,* Faber (London, England), 1972.
David Watkins, *Complete Method for the Harp,* Boosey & Hawkes (London, England), 1972.
Penelope Leach, *Baby and Child: A Modern Parent's Guide,* Knopf (New York, NY), 1978.
Sheila Kitzinger, *Pregnancy and Childbirth,* Knopf (New York, NY), 1980.
David Moore, *Multi-Cultural Britain* (booklet), Save the Children, 1980.
Miriam Stoppard, *Fifty-plus Life Guide: How to Ensure Fitness, Health, and Happiness in the Middle Years and Beyond,* Dorling Kindersley (London, England), 1983.
Esther Rantzen and Desmond Wilcox, *Baby Love,* Rainbird, 1985.

Contributor of photographs to newspapers.

*OTHER*

(Lyricist) Andrej Panufnik, *Thames Pageant* (cantata for children), Boosey & Hawkes (London, England), 1969.
(Lyricist) Andrej Panufnik, *Winter Solstice* (cantata), Boosey & Hawkes (London, England), 1972.

*The Joy of Birth: A Book for Parents and Children,* Dial Press (New York, NY), 1982.
*Catching the Moment: Photographing Your Child,* Dutton (New York, NY), 1985.
*The Taste of Spain: Traditional Spanish Recipes and Their Origins,* St. Martin's Press (New York, NY), 1990.
*Birth to Three: A Parents' Guide to Child Development,* Bloomsbury (London, England), 1990, published as *From Birth to Three: An Illustrated Journey through Your Child's Early Physical and Emotional Development,* Delta (New York, NY), 1991.

SIDELIGHTS: Photographer and author Camilla Jessel has enjoyed a career that allows her to explore her wide-ranging interests and share them with young children. Interested in child welfare and development, Jessel has created several series of toddler-sized books designed to assist youngsters in making connections, understanding abstract concepts, and learning the how-to's of life, while in photo-essays for older children and teens she explores personal health and safety issues. Among her many titles for children are *The Joy of Birth, The Puppy Book,* and *If You Meet a Stranger,* while *From Birth to Three: An Illustrated Journey through Your Child's Early Physical and Emotional Development* presents parents with photographs that provide what *Booklist* contributor Tracie Richardson dubbed a "beautiful and convincing depiction . . . of a child's growth."

Jessel was born in Kent, England, in 1937. Because of her father's career in the Royal Navy, her family was required to move, and by the time she was a teen she was living in South India and would soon spend a year in Paris studying French literature and civilization. "At the age of twenty," Jessel once noted, "I went to America with about one hundred dollars and had twenty-six different temporary secretarial jobs in six cities in one year: Princeton, Washington, New York, New Orleans, Dallas, and San Francisco."

Jessel's illustration career began by chance, after she shot some promotional photographs for the organization Save the Children, where she worked. The organization's press officer "liked the amateur shots I'd done of the organization's work. These fund-raising photos were followed by lots of hard work and lucky breaks." Working as a freelancer, Jessel sold photo-essays to newspapers such as the *Times Educational Supplement,* and after two of her photographs made it to the pages of the London *Guardian,* she was offered her first book contract with Methuen, where she created *Manuela Lives in Portugal* for their "Children Everywhere" series.

Jessel's first books, as well as many of her books since, were inspired by her interest in child development. "Doing color slides for a lecture on the psychology of play of children in the hospital, I got the idea of doing a photographic book to overcome children's fears of the hospital," she once explained. After *Paul in Hospital* was published, Jessel was given a grant for *Mark's Wheelchair Adventure,* a similar project that focuses on a young boy with a disability. Her 1982 work *The Joy of Birth: A Book for Parents and Children* features more than 100 photographs among its text outlining conception, birth, and the proper care of newborns. Praising Jessel's text as "well-written," a *Junior Bookshelf* contributor added that the "beautifully produced book" would be invaluable to parents seeking to educate their children about "the wonder and joy of motherhood." In *Booklist,* Denise M. Wilms praised *The Joy of Birth* as "a warm, realistic straighforward presentation" of "sensitive material."

Jessel's career as a photographer has allowed her to continue traveling, and assignments have taken her throughout both Africa and Europe. Her marriage in 1963 to an internationally known orchestra conductor and composer has also allowed her to explore parts of South America. Her love of music, art, and the dance also inspired her popular books *Life at the Royal Ballet School* and *Ballet School: What It Takes to Make a Dancer* which feature actual students of the dance. The more recent, *Ballet School,* takes readers on a year-long stay behind the scenes at England's Royal Ballet School, and reveals what a *Magpies* reviewer described as "the dedication, passion and training required in becoming a professional ballet dancer." From the audition process through classes building dance technique and academic skills through recitals and performances, *Ballet School* "succinctly and honestly describes the unrelenting practice and commitment required to participate in the school's program," according to the *Magpies* contributor. A *Kirkus* reviewer praised Jessel's "brisk" text and "realistic attitude" about most students' chance of ultimate success in the field of professional dance, and recommended *Ballet School* as a top choice for parents to give to "the artistic aspirants they care about most deeply."

As Jessel explained, "Some books have just 'happened.'" *The Puppy Book,* for instance, was photographed when Saffy, her family's Labrador retriever, gave birth to nine puppies. Jessel's children also figure in the story, as they watch the pups develop and, as *School Library Journal* reviewer Carol Kolb Phillips noted, "sadly say goodbye when the animals leave for new homes." An accompanying volume, *The Kitten Book,* focuses on a Burmese mother cat and her adorable litter. Praising both books for their "caring, supportive tone," a *Publishers Weekly* contributor added that Jessel's photographs are "captivating" and "well-composed," while Phillips dubbed *The Puppy Book* "truly charming."

Another book with its roots in Jessel's family is *Learner Bird,* which follows the fate of a baby thrush rescued by the photographer's then-eleven-year-old son. Citing Jessel's approach to the animal rescue as "totally unsentimental and accurate," a *Growing Point* reviewer noted that in *Learner Bird* the message for readers is that "wild birds are not pets." In her review for the *Times Educational Supplement,* Francesca Greenoak praised the factual information Jessel provides about the natural world, and pronounced *Learner Bird* "a super book."

In addition to building her own career as a successful photographer and illustrator, Jessel has also managed to raise her two children and work as her husband's business manager. "I enjoy being domestic—cooking, dressmaking—as well as having a career," she once noted. "I believe it's possible to be both liberated and a dedicated wife and mother."

Jessel's inspiration for her work is an "interest in children and my wish to use photography to combat prejudice and fear, such as the prejudice against the disabled or members of other races; I also want to use photography to educate children and to educate adults to be of more use to children. There is also my sheer enjoyment of photography and an attempt to heighten my own aesthetic standards."

## BIOGRAPHICAL AND CRITICAL SOURCES:

### PERIODICALS

*Booklist,* June 15, 1983, Denise M. Wilms, review of *The Joy of Birth,* p. 1340; Marcy 15, 1991, Tracie Richardson, review of *From Birth to Three: An Illustrated Journey through Your Child's Early*

*Physical and Emotional Development,* p. 1439; October 15, 1991, Sally Estes, review of *The Taste of Spain,* p. 393; February 1, 1992, Stephanie Zvirin, review of *The Puppy Book* and *The Kitten Book,* p. 1032; January 1, 2000, Carolyn Phelan, review of *Ballet School,* p. 910.

*Books for Your Child,* autumn, 1986, review of *Life at the Royal Ballet School,* p. 14.

*Daily Telegraph* (London, England), August 24, 1979.

*Growing Point,* September, 1983, review of *Learner Bird,* pp. 4127-4128; May, 1990, review of *If You Meet a Stranger,* pp. 5353-5354.

*Guardian* (London, England), August 24, 1979.

*Junior Bookshelf,* February, 1983, review of *The Joy of Birth,* p. 27; December, 1983, review of *Lost and Found,* pp. 244-245; February, 1984, review of *Learner Bird,* p. 24; February, 1986, review of *Baby's Bedtime,* p. 24; April, 1990, review of *If You Meet a Stranger,* p. 86.

*Kirkus Reviews,* February 1, 1992, review of *The Kitten Book,* p. 185; December 15, 1999, review of *Ballet School,* p. 1958.

*Magpies,* May, 2001, review of *Ballet School,* p. 42.

*Publishers Weekly,* February 3, 1992, review of *The Puppy Book* and *The Kitten Book,* p. 81.

*School Librarian,* March, 1982, Cliff Moon, review of *Away for the Night,* p. 28; August, 1990, review of *If You Meet a Stranger,* p. 102.

*School Library Journal,* April, 1992, review of *The Kitten Book,* p. 106; July, 1992, Carol Kolb Philips, review of *The Puppy Book,* p. 69; February, 2000, Ann W. Moore, review of *Ballet School,* p. 134.

*Times Educational Supplement,* March 9, 1984, Francesca Greenoak, review of *Learner Bird,* p. 54; October 25, 1985, Victoria Neumark, review of *Baby's Toys,* p. 31; March 7, 1986, Jenny Gilbert, review of *Baby's Clothes,* p. 25.

*Times Literary Supplement,* August 2, 1985, Frances Spalding, review of *Baby's Day,* p. 862.

*Voice of Youth Advocates,* December, 1983, Elizabeth Paddock, review of *The Joy of Birth,* p. 292.

*Wilson Library Bulletin,* May, 1992, review of *The Puppy Book* and *The Kitten Book,* p. 138.*

\*     \*     \*

## JOHNSON, Susan (Ruth) 1956-

*PERSONAL:* Born December 30, 1956, in Brisbane, Queensland, Australia; daughter of John Joseph Alister (in business) and Barbara Ruth (a homemaker; maiden name, Bell) Johnson; married John Patrick Burdett, September 10, 1989 (divorced, 1991); married Leslie William Webb, 1994; children: two. *Education:* Attended Clayfield College and University of Queensland, 1975-77. *Hobbies and other interests:* Reading, travel, films, food, surfing.

*ADDRESSES: Agent*—Margaret Connolly and Associates, P.O. Box 48, Paddington, New South Wales 2021, Australia.

*CAREER: Courier-Mail,* Brisbane, Australia, cadet journalist, 1975-77; *Australian Women's Weekly,* Sydney, Australia, journalist, 1977-78; *Sun-Herald,* Sydney, Australia, journalist, 1980; *Sydney Morning Herald,* Sydney, Australia, feature writer, 1980-82; *National Times,* correspondent from Queensland, Australia, 1982-84. Novelist, 1984—. Resident at Keesing Studio, Cité Internationale des Arts, Paris, France, until 1992.

*MEMBER:* International PEN, Australian Journalists' Association, Australian Society of Authors.

*AWARDS, HONORS: Flying Lessons* was short-listed for Victorian Premier's Literary Prize, 1990; fellowships from Literature Board, Australia Council, 1986-92.

*WRITINGS:*

(Coeditor) *Latitudes: New Writing from the North,* University of Queensland Press (Queensland, Australia), 1986.

*Messages from Chaos* (novel), Harper & Row (New York, NY), 1987.

*Flying Lessons* (novel), Faber & Faber (London, England), 1990.

*A Big Life* (novel), Faber & Faber (London, England), 1993.

*Hungry Ghosts* (novel), Washington Square Press (New York, NY), 2002.

*A Better Woman: A Memoir,* Washington Square Press (New York, NY), 2002.

Contributor of short stories to literary magazines.

*SIDELIGHTS:* Susan Johnson made her American debut with *Flying Lessons,* a novel about two women and their individual quests. The story centers on Ria

Lubrano, who is unsatisfied with her life in Sydney and moves to Queensland, where she hopes to find her brother. Queensland is also where Ria's father and grandmother were born, and she relates her grandmother's story to members of the commune where she lives. She feels a kinship with her grandmother, Emma, who, as Ria understands it, defied her family and married a man of whom they did not approve. "Ms. Johnson's prose is charged with feeling, insight and rambunctious wit," wrote Andy Solomon in the *New York Times Book Review.* ". . . Ria and Emma's shared desire to take wing feels so universal that it evokes recognition rather than surprise." A critic for *Kirkus Reviews,* however, found that "Ria and her flight are too minor in key for the significance that Johnson tries to attach to them. Evocative descriptions of Australia, but this is too laden with unfulfilled intellectual ambitions to really take off."

*A Big Life* is the story of Billy Hayes, who is sold by his father to a group of traveling tumblers. An accomplished gymnast of his own making, Billy is taken from his native Australia to England with the increasingly popular acrobatic show. The novel follows Billy through his growing up in a vaudeville setting and through a bad marriage that ends in divorce. As an adult, he must face the fact that the world can be harsh despite his loving nature. Linda Barrett Osborne commented in the *New York Times Book Review* that the book is "written with a touch so gentle that its sadness grows slowly, imperceptibly, like the passage from youth to middle age." In *Kirkus Reviews* a critic commented that in this novel the reader will find "not, in the end, your average hero, or your average story, as Johnson movingly celebrates the resilience of the human spirit."

*Hungry Ghosts* examines the rise and fall of a friendship. Friends from childhood, inhibited Rachel and exuberant Anne-Louise exemplify opposite personalities. Rachel is a successful artist and Anne-Louise is recovering from a psychotic breakdown when they reconnect and renew their friendship in Hong Kong. The "ghosts" of the title refers to the Chinese term for Westerners, and these two, joined by a troubled futures broker, drift through the city looking for something to fill their emptiness. When both women fall in love with the man, himself a tortured soul, the inevitable outcome is tragic. In her review for *Booklist* Margaret Flanagan wrote, "The deceptively matter-of-fact narrative provides a compelling

examination of love, dependency, and loss." Willa Williams, writing in *Library Journal,* thought the plot predictable and the women's characters unsympathetic and clichéd, but added that "Anne-Louise's emotional self-destruction is finely drawn and heartbreaking."

After the birth of her second child, Johnson wrote a book of memoirs documenting her transformation to motherhood. *A Better Woman: A Memoir* recalls what she thought it would be like to be a mother and describes the ensuing jolt into reality. In addition, her second birth left her with a painful injury that required perseverance to have acknowledged and repaired. Margaret Connolly, writing for *Publishers Weekly,* said Johnson's "voice [is] at once literate and excruciatingly intimate. . . . Johnson provides an affecting memoir of loss and pain, strength and survival, fear and despair, love and joy. She successfully captures the unique season of her life that made her 'a better woman,' through both the living and the writing of it."

*BIOGRAPHICAL AND CRITICAL SOURCES:*

*PERIODICALS*

*Aethlon,* spring, 1994, p. 161.
*Australian Book Review,* October, 1993, p. 5; July, 1994, p. 32; October, 1996, p. 42; October, 1999, p. 6.
*Booklist,* April 15, 2002, Margaret Flanagan, review of *A Better Woman: A Memoir,* p. 1375, and *Hungry Ghosts,* p. 1382.
*Kirkus Reviews,* September 1, 1991; July 15, 1993, p. 878; February 1, 2002, reviews of *Hungry Ghosts,* p. 128, and *A Better Woman,* p. 160.
*Library Journal,* August, 1993, Elizabeth Mellett, review of *A Big Life,* p. 151; April 1, 2002, Wilda Williams, review of *Hungry Ghosts,* p. 140; May 1, 2002, Rachel Collins, review of *A Better Woman,* p. 120.
*New York Times Book Review,* November 17, 1991, p. 20; December 19, 1993, Linda Barrett Osborne, review of *A Big Life,* p. 18.
*Observer* (London, England), September 12, 1993, p. 53.
*Publishers Weekly,* August 31, 1992, p. 72; September 6, 1993, p. 85; February 18, 2002, review of *Hungry Ghosts,* p. 73; March 4, 2002, review of *A Better Woman,* p. 68.
*Times Literary Supplement,* September 3, 1993, Roz Kaveney, review of *A Big Life,* p. 24.*

## JOHNSTON, Julie 1941-

*PERSONAL:* Born January 21, 1941, in Smiths Falls, Ontario, Canada; daughter of J. A. B. (a lawyer) and Sarah Mae (a homemaker; maiden name, Patterson) Dulmage; married Basil W. Johnston (an orthopedic surgeon), 1963; children: Leslie, Lauren, Andrea, Melissa. *Education:* University of Toronto, diploma (physical and occupational therapy), 1963; Trent University, B.A. (honors English), 1984. *Hobbies and other interests:* Old wooden boats, vegetable gardening, bicycling, hiking, traveling, reading, stonemasonry.

*ADDRESSES: Agent*—c/o Author Mail, Tundra Books, P.O. Box 1030, Plattsburgh, NY 12901. *E-mail*—julie.johnston@sympatico.ca.

*CAREER:* Occupational therapist at a school for mentally handicapped children, Smiths Falls, Ontario, Canada, 1963-65; Rehabilitation Centre, Kingston, Ontario, Canada, occupational therapist, 1965-69. Writer, 1980—. Peterborough Board of Education, Continuing Education Department, creative writing instructor, 1988-89.

*MEMBER:* Canadian Society of Children's Authors, Illustrators, and Performers (CANSCAIP), Canadian Children's Book Centre, Writer's Union of Canada, PEN Canada.

*AWARDS, HONORS:* Runner-up, *Chatelaine* Fiction Contest, 1979, for the short story "Canadian Content"; first prize, Solange Karsh Award, Birks Gold Medal, and cash prize, Canadian Playwriting Competition, Ottawa Little Theatre, 1979, for *There's Going to Be a Frost;* Kawartha Region Best Play award, 1980, for *There's Going to Be a Frost* and co-winner for best play, 1984, for *Lucid Intervals;* Canadian Library Association Young Adult Honour Book, 1993, shortlisting for Mister Christie's Book Award, 1993, National Chapter of Canada Independent Order Daughters of the Empire (IODE) Violet Downey Book Award, 1993, Governor General's Literary Award for children's literature, 1992, *School Library Journal* Best Book, 1994, New York Public Library's 1994 Books for the Teen Age list selection, Ontario Library Association Silver Birch Award nomination, 1994, and American Library Association notable book selection, all for

*Julie Johnston*

*Hero of Lesser Causes;* Governor General's Literary Award for children's literature, 1994, and Ruth Schwartz Children's Book Award, 1995, both for *Adam and Eve and Pinch-Me;* CLA Young Adult Book Award, Canadian Library Association, 1995, for *Adam and Eve and Pinch-Me;* honorary doctor of letters, Trent University, 1996; nominated for Governor General's Literary Award for children's literature and Geoffrey Bilson Award, both for *The Only Outcast,* both 1998; shortlisted for Young Adult Canadian Book Award, 2001, the Governor General's Literary Award for Children's Literature, 2001, the Ruth Schwartz Award, 2002, Mister Christie's Book Award, 2002, and the Silver Birch Award, 2002, for *In Spite of Killer Bees;* shortlisting for Vicky Metcalf Award, 2003, for her body of work.

*WRITINGS:*

*There's Going to Be a Frost* (one-act play), first produced at the Sears Drama Festival, 1980.
*Lucid Intervals* (one-act play), first produced at the Sears Drama Festival, 1984.

*Hero of Lesser Causes* (young adult novel; also see below), Lester Publishing, 1992, Little, Brown (Boston, MA), 1993.

*Adam and Eve and Pinch-Me* (young adult novel), Little, Brown (Boston, MA), 1994, Lester Publishing (Toronto, Ontario, Canada), 1994.

*The Only Outcast,* Tundra Books (Plattsburgh, NY), 1998.

(Editor) *Love Ya Like a Sister: A Story of Friendship: From the Journals of Katie Ouriou,* Tundra Books (Plattsburgh, NY), 1999.

*In Spite of Killer Bees* (young adult novel), Tundra Books (Plattsburgh, NY), 2001.

Contributor of the novella *The Window Seat* to *Women's Weekly Omnibus,* 1984, and the story "Mirrors" to the anthology *The Blue Jean Collection,* Thistledown Press, 1992. Contributor of fiction to periodicals, including *Women's Weekly Buzz, Chatelaine, Woman and Home,* and *Matrix;* contributor of nonfiction to periodicals, including *Wine Tidings, Homemakers, Doctor's Review,* and *Canadian Author and Bookman.* Johnston's works have been translated into French.

*ADAPTATIONS:* Johnston adapted her novel *Hero of Lesser Causes* as a screenplay, commissioned by Roy Krost Productions, 1994.

*WORK IN PROGRESS:* Historical fiction based on the early life of Susanna Moodie.

*SIDELIGHTS:* Julie Johnston won praise for her first novel for young adults, *Hero of Lesser Causes,* which reviewer Deborah Stevenson described in *Bulletin of the Center for Children's Books* as a "touching and funny story of sibling maturation." Set in Canada in 1946, the book begins as twelve-year-old Keely sees her brother Patrick paralyzed by polio after swimming in a public pool. Keely and her brother, just a year apart in age, are close friends, and Keely cannot imagine her life without him. Yet Patrick seems a different person as he becomes more and more bitter about his disease. Patrick's frustration and depression moves Keely to concoct wild plans to cheer and heal him. One of these plans is to find the fiance of Patrick's nurse, who is missing and presumed dead in World War II. Despite her efforts, Patrick's emotional condition grows increasingly serious. Finally, after an attempted suicide, Patrick begins to understand that his life is worth living, and he responds to Keely's optimism.

*Hero of Lesser Causes* was well received. A *Kirkus Reviews* writer noted that the book was "a fine first novel," while a *Publishers Weekly* reviewer found that the book "accelerates into a spectacular novel, balancing coming-of-age angst with the grief from a sudden, devastating affliction." Cindy Darling Codell praised the book in *School Library Journal* as being "wonderfully simple, yet layered with meaning." Nancy Vasilakis, a reviewer for *Horn Book,* appreciated the "unique period details" which "create a strong sense of the place and the time without slowing down the action." *Hero of Lesser Causes* earned Johnston Canada's prestigious Governor General's Literary Award in 1992.

In Johnston's next book, *Adam and Eve and Pinch-Me,* the author gave readers Sara Moone, a fifteen-year-old girl who has lived in foster homes since birth. Sara is hardened by her experiences and waits impatiently for the day she will turn sixteen so she can strike out on her own. She speaks little to her latest "family," a farm couple with two other foster children in their care; but, in a metaphor that continues throughout the book, she pours out her feelings into a computer that does not have the capacity to print. "With a wry eye, keen pacing, and a wonderfully nimble narrative, the author of *Hero of Lesser Causes* stirs up something saucy and fresh," declared a *Kirkus Reviews* contributor. Christy Tyson, a reviewer for *Voice of Youth Advocates,* affirmed: "Johnston has created a powerful examination of a young woman who must give up years of hard-won survival techniques in order to choose involvement with other people. Sara is a frequently unlikable but completely real character that young adult readers will understand, respect, and ultimately admire as she begins to re-contact her feelings for other people." And Carolyn Noah stated in *School Library Journal* that "this novel speaks volumes about the complexity of relationships and human affection."

Johnston's 1998 effort, *The Only Outcast,* also won acclaim from critics. In it she uses the actual short diary entries of a sixteen-year-old boy, written in 1904, as a framework for the novel. She fleshes out the character and story of the protagonist, Fred Dickinson, with her own novelization of his experiences at a summer cabin near a Canadian lake. Fred has the usual teenage angst, such as a crush on a sophisticated older girl who has accidentally seen him naked, but he must also deal with a stutter, the recent loss of his mother, and a harsh father. As a reviewer for the *Horn Book* magazine reported, however, "Johnston adeptly lets [Fred] grow from liking himself not at all to a quiet self-confidence and assertiveness." The year following *The Only Outcast,* Johnston again published a book involving a diary. This time she served as the editor of *Love Ya Like a Sister: A Story of Friendship: From the Journals of Katie Ouriou.* Ouriou was a Canadian teenager who died from leukemia before she turned seventeen.

Johnston again received Canadian literary award nominations for her 2001 young adult novel, *In Spite of Killer Bees.* Its story centers on fourteen-year-old Aggie, who lives with her older sisters since her father's death. Her mother abandoned the family long ago. When word arrives that Aggie's grandfather has died, leaving the family homestead to the girls, they travel to the small town in Ontario where it is located. Aggie's sisters have dreams of selling it and escaping into independent, adult lives, but the stipulations of their grandfather's will do not allow for such an easy out. Eventually, the family comes to realize that their grandfather's house and his town is exactly where they all belong—together. As Joan Marshall, reviewing *In Spite of Killer Bees* in *Resource Links,* put it, the novel's "satisfying ending sneaks up on the reader the way it sneaks up on Aggie." Martha V. Parravano in *Horn Book* concluded that *In Spite of Killer Bees* is "a signature Julie Johnston story: complex, subtle, and engaging."

"I once made a wish that I could be a busy writer, so busy with writing and writing concerns that I wouldn't have time to agonize over trifles or analyse the state of my mental health," Johnston confided in *Something about the Author Autobiography Series.* "Most of my wish came true. My time is almost completely taken up with writing, traveling to do readings, to give speeches, and to take part in workshops."

Explaining her approach to writing, Johnston once commented: "Fiction is about developing characters who never existed but might have, and allowing them to do things that never happened but could have. It's making up the truth. What I enjoy most about writing fiction is burrowing so deeply into these characters that I am in tune with how they think, how they sound, and how they see the world. The only way I can do this is to explore every facet of myself and use bits for every character—good, bad, or ridiculous. Creating a character is like going on an archeological dig of the

soul. Truth is what I'm digging for; the trick is in recognizing it. When I agonize over my own flaws and failures, or rejoice in chunks of good fortune, I find myself storing it all away in some closet in my mind to use as a hand-me-down for a future character. While I'm grubbing around under the surface of things I sometimes find the one true passion that rules a character's life."

## BIOGRAPHICAL AND CRITICAL SOURCES:

### BOOKS

*Children's Literature Review,* Volume 41, Gale (Detroit, MI), 1997.

Rae, Arlene Perly, *Everybody's Favourite: Canadians Talk about Books That Changed Their Lives,* Viking (New York, NY), 1997.

*Something about the Author, Autobiography Series,* Volume 24, Gale (Detroit, MI), 1997.

### PERIODICALS

*Booklist,* July, 1993, p. 1966; May 15, 1994, p. 1678.

*Book World,* December 23, 2001, review of *In Spite of Killer Bees,* p. 15.

*Bulletin of the Center for Children's Books,* April, 1993, p. 254; May, 1994, p. 290.

*Canadian Children's Literature,* number 77, 1995, pp. 33-38; spring, 1997, review of *The Only Outcast,* p. 47.

*Children's Book News,* spring, 1992, p. 17.

*CM: Canadian Materials for Schools and Libraries,* October, 1992, p. 272.

*Emergency Librarian,* March, 1993, p. 14.

*Globe and Mail* (Toronto, Ontario, Canada), October 6, 2001, review of *In Spite of Killer Bees,* p. D22.

*Horn Book,* August, 1993, p. 457; September-October, 1994, pp. 599, 626; January, 1999, review of *The Only Outcast,* p. 65; January-February, 2002, Martha V. Parravano, review of *In Spite of Killer Bees,* pp. 78-79.

*Kirkus Reviews,* May 15, 1993, p. 663; May 15, 1994, p. 700.

*Kliatt Young Adult Paperback Book Guide,* March, 1996, pp. 8, 10.

*Publishers Weekly,* May 24, 1993, p. 89; July 12, 1993, p. 24; April 18, 1994, p. 64; April 5, 1999, review of *Love Ya Like a Sister: A Story of Friendship: From the Journals of Katie Ouriou,* p. 242.

*Quill and Quire,* April, 1992, p. 31; May, 1994, p. 37; February, 1999, review of *The Only Outcast,* p. 43; October, 2001, review of *In Spite of Killer Bees,* p. 42.

*Resource Links,* December, 2001, Joan Marshall, review of *In Spite of Killer Bees,* pp.38-39.

*School Library Journal,* June, 1993, p. 107; July, 1994, p. 119; January, 1999, review of *The Only Outcast,* p. 128; May, 1999, review of *Love Ya Like a Sister* p. 141; December, 2001, Susan Geye, review of *In Spite of Killer Bees,* p. 138.

*Toronto Star,* December 22, 1992; March 16, 2003, Deirdre Baker, "Delicious, Subversive."

*Voice of Youth Advocates,* August, 1994, pp. 146-47; February, 1999, review of *The Only Outcast,* p. 435; December, 2001, review of *In Spite of Killer Bees,* p. 360.

ONLINE

*CANSCAIP,* http://www.canscaip.org/ (August 12, 2003).

*Tundra Books,* http://www.tundrabooks.com/ (August 12, 2003).

\*   \*   \*

## JONES, Gayl 1949-

*PERSONAL:* Born November 23, 1949, in Lexington, KY; daughter of Franklin (a cook) and Lucille (Wilson) Jones; married Bob Higgins, who later took the name Bob Jones (deceased). *Education:* Connecticut College, B.A., 1971; Brown University, M.A., 1973, D.A., 1975.

*ADDRESSES: Home*—Lexington, KY. *Agent*—c/o Author Mail, Beacon Press, 25 Beacon St., Boston, MA 02108.

*CAREER:* University of Michigan, Ann Arbor, 1975-83, began as assistant professor, became professor of English; writer.

*MEMBER:* Authors Guild, Authors League of America.

*AWARDS, HONORS:* Award for best original production in the New England region, American College Theatre Festival, 1973, for *Chile Woman;* grants from Shubert Foundation, 1973-74, Southern Fellowship Foundation, 1973-75, and Rhode Island Council on the Arts, 1974-75; fellowships from Yaddo, 1974, National Endowment of the Arts, 1976, and Michigan Society of Fellows, 1977-79; award from Howard Foundation, 1975; Fiction Award from *Mademoiselle,* 1975; Henry Russell Award, University of Michigan, 1981.

*WRITINGS:*

*Chile Woman* (play), Shubert Foundation (New York, NY), 1974.

*Corregidora* (novel), Random House (New York, NY), 1975.

*Eva's Man* (novel), Random House (New York, NY), 1976.

*White Rat* (short stories), Random House (New York, NY), 1977.

*Song for Anninho* (poetry), Lotus Press (Detroit, MI), 1981.

*The Hermit-Woman* (poetry), Lotus Press (Detroit, MI), 1983.

*Xarque and Other Poems,* Lotus Press (Detroit, MI), 1985.

*Liberating Voices: Oral Tradition in African American Literature* (criticism), Harvard University Press (Cambridge, MA), 1991.

*The Healing* (novel), Beacon Press (Boston, MA), 1998.

*Mosquito* (novel), Beacon Press (Boston, MA), 1999.

Contributor to anthologies, including *Confirmation,* 1983, *Chants of Saints, Keeping the Faith, Midnight Birds,* and *Soulscript.* Contributor to periodicals, including *Massachusetts Review.*

*WORK IN PROGRESS:* Research on sixteenth-and seventeenth-century Brazil and on settlements of escaped slaves, such as Palmares.

*SIDELIGHTS:* Gayl Jones's novels *Corregidora* and *Eva's Man,* in addition to many of the stories in her collection *White Rat,* offer stark, often brutal accounts of black women whose psyches reflect the ravages of accumulated sexual and racial exploitation. In *Corregidora* Jones reveals the tormented life of a woman whose female forebears—at the hands of one man—endured a cycle of slavery, prostitution, and incest over three generations. *Eva's Man* explores the deranged mind of a woman institutionalized for poisoning and sexually mutilating a male acquaintance. And in "Asylum," a story from *White Rat,* a young woman is confined to a mental hospital for a series of bizarre actions that, in her mind, protests a society she sees as bent on her personal violation. "The abuse of women and its psychological results fascinate Gayl Jones, who uses these recurring themes to magnify the absurdity and the obscenity of racism and sexism in everyday life," commented Jerry W. Ward, Jr., in *Black Women Writers (1950-1980): A Critical Evaluation.* "Her novels and short fictions invite readers to explore the interior of caged personalities, men and women driven to extremes." Keith Byerman elaborated in the *Dictionary of Literary Biography.*: "Jones creates worlds radically different from those of 'normal' experience and of storytelling convention. Her tales are gothic in the sense of dealing with madness, sexuality, and violence, but they do not follow in the Edgar Allan Poe tradition of focusing on private obsession and irrationality. Though her narrators are close to if not over the boundaries of sanity, the experiences they record reveal clearly that society acts out its own obsessions often violently."

*Corregidora,* Jones's first novel, explores the psychological effects of slavery and sexual abuse on a modern black woman. Ursa Corregidora, a blues singer from Kentucky, descends from a line of women who are the progeny, by incest, of a Portuguese slaveholder named Corregidora—the father of both Ursa's mother and grandmother. "All of the women, including the great-granddaughter Ursa, keep the name Corregidora as a reminder of the depredations of the slave system and of the rapacious natures of men," Byerman explained in the *Dictionary of Literary Biography.* "The story is passed from generation to generation of women, along with the admonition to 'produce generations' to keep alive the tale of evil." Partly as a result of this history, Ursa becomes involved in abusive relationships with men. The novel itself springs from an incident of violence; after being thrown down a flight of stairs by her first husband and physically injured so that she cannot bear children, Ursa "discharges her obligation to the memory of Corregidora by speaking [the] book," noted John Updike in the *New Yorker.* The novel emerges as Ursa's struggle to reconcile her heritage with her present life. *Corregidora* "persuasively fuses black history, or the mythic consciousness that must do for black history, with the emotional nuances of contemporary black life," Up-

dike continued. "The book's innermost action . . . is Ursa's attempt to transcend a nightmare black consciousness and waken to her own female, maimed humanity."

*Corregidora* was described as a novel of unusual power and impact. "No black American novel since Richard Wright's *Native Son* in 1940," wrote Ivan Webster in *Time,* "has so skillfully traced psychic wounds to a sexual source." Darryl Pinckney in *New Republic* called *Corregidora* "a small, fiercely concentrated story, harsh and perfectly told. . . . Original, superbly imagined, nothing about the book was simple or easily digested. Out of the worn themes of miscegenation and diminishment, Gayl Jones *excavated* the disturbingly buried damage of racism." Critics particularly noted Jones's treatment of sexual detail and its illumination of the central character. "One of the book's merits," according to Updike, "is the ease with which it assumes the writer's right to sexual specifics, and its willingness to explore exactly how our sexual and emotional behavior is warped within the matrix of family and race." In the book's final scene, Ursa comes to a reconciliation with her first husband, Mutt, by envisioning an ambivalent sexual relationship between her great-grandmother and the slavemaster Corregidora. *Corregidora* is a novel "filled with sexual and spiritual pain," wrote Margo Jefferson in *Newsweek;* "hatred, love and desire wear the same face, and humor is blues-bitter. . . . Jones's language is subtle and sinewy, and her imagination sure."

Jones's second novel, *Eva's Man,* continues her exploration into the psychological effects of brutality, yet presents a character who suffers greater devastation. Eva Medina Canada, incarcerated for the murder and mutilation of a male acquaintance, narrates a personal history that depicts the damaging influences of a sexually aggressive and hostile society. Updike described the exploitative world that has shaped the mentally deranged Eva: "Evil permeates the erotic education of Eva Canada, as it progresses from Popsicle-stick violations to the witnessing of her mother's adultery and a growing awareness of the whores and 'queen bees' in the slum world around her, and on to her own reluctant initiation through encounters in buses and in bars, where a man with no thumb monotonously propositions her. The evil that emanates from men becomes hers." In a narrative that is fragmented and disjointed, Eva gives no concrete motive for the crime committed; furthermore, she neither shows remorse nor any signs of rehabilitation. More experimental than *Corregidora*, *Eva's Man* displays "a sharpened starkness, a power of ellipsis that leaves ever darker gaps between its flashes of rhythmic, sensuously exact dialogue and visible symbol," according to Updike. John Leonard added in the *New York Times* that "not a word is wasted" in Eva's narrative. "It seems, in fact, as if Eva doesn't have enough words, as if she were trying to use the words she has to make a poem, a semblance of order, and fails of insufficiency." Leonard concluded that "*Eva's Man* may be one of the most unpleasant novels of the season. It is also one of the most accomplished."

*Eva's Man* was praised for its emotional impact, yet some reviewers found the character of Eva extreme or inaccessible. June Jordan in the *New York Times Book Review* called *Eva's Man* "the blues that lost control. This is the rhythmic, monotone lamentation of one woman, Eva Medina, who is nobody I have ever known." Jordan explained that "Jones delivers her story in a strictly controlled, circular form that is wrapped, around and around with ambivalence. Unerringly, her writing creates the tension of a problem unresolved." In the end, however, Jordan found that the fragmented details of Eva's story "do not mesh into illumination." On the other hand, some reviewers regard the gaps in *Eva's Man* as appropriate and integral to its meaning. Pinckney called the novel "a tale of madness; one exacerbated if not caused by frustration, accumulated grievances" and commented on aspects that contribute to this effect: "Structurally unsettled, more scattered than *Corregidora*, *Eva's Man* is extremely remote, more troubling in its hallucinations. . . .The personal exploitation that causes Eva's desperation is hard to appreciate. Her rage seems never to find its proper object, except, possibly, in her last extreme act." Updike likewise held that the novel accurately portrays Eva's deranged state, yet he points out that Jones's characterization skills are not at their peak. "Jones apparently wishes to show us a female heart frozen into rage by deprivation, but the worry arises, as it did not in *Corregidora,* that the characters are dehumanized as much by her artistic vision as by their circumstances."

Jordan raised a concern that the inconclusiveness of *Eva's Man* harbors a potentially damaging feature. "There is the very real, upsetting accomplishment of Gayl Jones in this, her second novel: sinister misinformation about women—about women, in general, about black women in particular." Jones commented in *Black Women Writers (1950-1980)* on the predicament faced in portraying negative characters: "To deal with such a character as Eva becomes problematic in the way that 'Trueblood' becomes problematic in [Ralph Ellison's] *Invisible Man.* It raises the questions of possibility. Should a Black writer ignore such characters, refuse to enter 'such territory' because of the 'negative image' and because such characters can be misused politically by others, or should one try to reclaim such complex, contradictory characters as well as try to reclaim the idea of the 'heroic image'?" Jones elaborated in an interview with Claudia Tate for *Black Women Writers at Work:* "'Positive race images' are fine as long as they're very complex and interesting personalities. Right now I'm not sure how to reconcile the various things that interest me with 'positive race images.' It's important to be able to work with a range of personalities, as well as with a range within one personality. For instance, how would one reconcile an interest in neurosis or insanity with positive race image?"

Although Jones's subject matter is often charged and intense, a number of critics have praised a particular restraint she manages in her narratives. Regarding *Corregidora*, Updike remarked, "Our retrospective impression of *Corregidora* is of a big territory—the Afro-American psyche—rather thinly and stabbingly populated by ideas personae, hints. Yet that such a small book could seem so big speaks well for the generous spirit of the author, unpolemical where there has been much polemic, exploratory where rhetoric and outrage tend to block the path." Similarly, Jones maintains an authorial distance in her fiction which, in turn, makes for believable and gripping characters. Byerman commented, "The authority of [Jones's] depiction of the world is enhanced by [her] refusal to intrude upon or judge her narrators. She remains outside the story, leaving the reader with none of the usual markers of a narrator's reliability. She gives these characters the speech of their religion, which, by locating them in time and space, makes it even more difficult to easily dismiss them; the way they speak has authenticity, which carries over to what they tell. The results are profoundly disturbing tales of repression, manipulation, and suffering."

Reviewers have also noted Jones's ability to innovatively incorporate Afro-American speech patterns into her work. In *Black Women Writers (1950-1980)*, Melvin Dixon noted that "Gayl Jones has figured among the best of contemporary Afro-American writers who have used Black speech as a major aesthetic device in their works. Like Alice Walker, Toni Morrison, Sherley Williams, Toni Cade Bambara, and such male writers as Ernest Gaines and Ishmael Reed, Jones uses the rhythm and structure of spoken language to develop authentic characters and to establish new possibilities for dramatic conflict within the text and between readers and the text itself." In her interview with Tate, Jones remarked on the importance of storytelling traditions to her work: "At the time I was writing *Corregidora* and *Eva's Man* I was particularly interested—and continue to be interested—in oral traditions of storytelling—Afro-American and others, in which there is always the consciousness and importance of the hearer, even in the interior monologues where the storyteller becomes her own hearer. That consciousness or self-consciousness actually determines my selection of significant events."

In 1977 Jones published a collection of short stories, *White Rat.* A number of critics noted the presence of Jones's typical thematic concerns, yet also felt that her shorter fiction did not allow enough room for character development. Diane Johnson commented in the *New York Review of Books* that the stories in *White Rat* "were written in some cases earlier than her novels, so they confirm one's sense of her direction and preoccupations: sex is violation, and violence is the principal dynamic of human relationships." Mel Watkins wrote about Jones's short fiction in the *New York Times:* "The focus throughout is on desolate, forsaken characters struggling to exact some snippet of gratification from their lives. . . . Although her prose here is as starkly arresting and indelible as in her novels, except for the longer stories such as 'Jeveta' and 'The Women,' these tales are simply doleful vignettes— slices of life so beveled that they seem distorted."

While Jones's writing often emphasizes a tormented side of life—especially regarding male-female relationships—it also raises the possibility for more positive interactions. Jones pointed out in the Tate interview that "there seems to be a growing understanding—working itself out especially in *Corregidora*—of what is required in order to be genuinely tender. Perhaps brutality enables one to recognize what tenderness is." Some critics have found ambivalence at the core of Jones's fiction. Dixon wrote that "Redemption . . . is most likely to occur when the resolution of conflict is forged in the same vocabulary

as the tensions which precipitated it. This dual nature of language makes it appear brutally indifferent, for it contains the source and the resolution of conflicts. . . .What Jones is after is the words and deeds that finally break the sexual bondage men and women impose upon each other."

In 1991, Jones published her first book of literary criticism, *Liberating Voices: Oral Tradition in African American Literature.* Here Jones argues that all literatures, not just African-American, develop in relation to and must come to terms with their own culture's oral storytelling practices. With this point in mind, she compares the poetry, short fiction, and novels of African-American authors—including Paul Laurence Dunbar, Jean Toomer, Zora Neale Hurston, Ralph Ellison, Amiri Baraka, Alice Walker, Langston Hughes, and Toni Morrison—with the works of longstanding canonical authors from a wide variety of historical eras and cultures, from Chaucer and Cervantes to Joyce. M. Giulia Fabi, in *American Literature,* called this a "daring and insightful study."

*BIOGRAPHICAL AND CRITICAL SOURCES:*

*BOOKS*

*Contemporary Black Biography,* Volume 37, Gale (Detroit, MI), 2003.
*Contemporary Literary Criticism,* Gale (Detroit, MI), Volume 6, 1976, Volume 9, 1978.
*Contemporary Novelists,* 7th edition, St. James Press (Detroit, MI), 2001.
Coser, Stelamaris, *Bridging the Americas: The Literature of Paula Marshall, Toni Morrison, and Gayl Jones,* Temple University Press (Philadelphia, PA), 1995.
*Dictionary of Literary Biography,* Volume 33: *Afro-American Fiction Writers after 1955,* Gale (Detroit, MI), 1984.
Evans, Mari, editor, *Black Women Writers (1950-1980): A Critical Evaluation,* Anchor Press/ Doubleday (Garden City, NY), 1984.
Robinson, Sally, *Engendering the Subject: Gender and Self-Representation in Contemporary Women's Fiction,* State University of New York Press (Albany, NY), 1991.
Tate, Claudia, editor, *Black Women Writers at Work,* Continuum (New York, NY), 1986.

*PERIODICALS*

*African American Review,* winter, 1994, p. 559; spring, 1994, p. 141; summer, 1994, p. 223; summer, 2000, Candice M. Jenkins, review of *The Healing,* p. 365, Laurie Champion, review of *Mosquito,* p. 366.

*American Literature,* June, 1993.

*Artforum International,* March, 1998, Jacqueline Woodson, review of *The Healing,* p. S24.

*Belles Lettres,* summer, 1992.

*Black World,* February, 1976.

*Book World,* February 22, 1987.

*Canadian Literature,* winter, 1992.

*Choice,* November, 1991.

*College Literature,* February, 1992.

*Comparative Literature Studies,* summer, 1999, Bernard W. Bell, reviews of *Liberating Voices: Oral Traditions in African American Literature* and *The Healing,* p. 247.

*Esquire,* December, 1976.

*Guardian,* November 16, 1998, Michael Ellison, review of *The Healing,* p. T8.

*Journal of American Folklore,* winter, 1993.

*Kliatt,* spring, 1986.

*Library Journal,* January, 1999, Eleanor J. Bader, review of *Mosquito,* p. 152.

*Literary Quarterly,* May 15, 1975.

*Massachusetts Review,* winter, 1977.

*Michigan Quarterly Review,* spring, 2001, Arlene R. Keizer, review of *Mosquito,* p. 431.

*Modern Fiction Studies,* fall, 1993, p. 825.

*Nation,* May 25, 1998, Jill Nelson, review of *The Healing,* p. 30.

*National Review,* April 14, 1978.

*New Republic,* June 28, 1975; June 19, 1976.

*Newsweek,* May 19, 1975; April 12, 1976.

*New Yorker,* August 18, 1975; August 9, 1976.

*New York Review of Books,* November 10, 1977.

*New York Times,* April 30, 1976; December 28, 1977.

*New York Times Book Review,* May 25, 1975; May 16, 1976; March 15, 1987; May 10, 1998, Valerie Sayers, review of *The Healing,* p. 28.

*Publishers Weekly,* November 23, 1998, review of *Mosquito,* p. 57.

*Time,* June 16, 1975.

*Times* (London, England), April 1, 2000, Scott Bradfield, review of *The Healing,* p. 22, February 8, 1999, Tamala M. Edwards, review of *Mosquito,* p. 72.

*Washington Post,* October 21, 1977.

*Women's Review of Books,* March, 1998, Judith Grossman, review of *The Healing,* p. 15, March, 1999, Deborah McDowell, review of *Mosquito,* p. 9.

*Yale Review,* autumn, 1976.

*ONLINE*

*Voices from the Gaps,* http://voices.cla.umn.edu/ authors/ (August 2, 2003), "Gayl Jones."*

\*     \*     \*

## JONES, Jack P(ayne) 1928-

*PERSONAL:* Born November 20, 1928, in Timmonsville, SC; son of Ed M. (a farmer) and Laura L. (a homemaker) Jones; married Ernestine Ryals, October 5, 1955; children: Gregory, Kenneth, Ronald, Laura. *Ethnicity:* "Caucasian." *Education:* LaSalle Extension University, LL.B., 1948. *Politics:* Conservative Republican. *Religion:* Protestant. *Hobbies and other interests:* Travel.

*ADDRESSES: Home and office*—2395 Hawkinsville Highway, Golden Isle Parkway N, Eastman, GA 31023; fax: 478-374-9720. *E-mail*—jackjones@ progressivetel.com.

*CAREER:* U.S. Air Force, worked as investigator, chief of investigations, and chief of police in central Georgia, 1954-70; Jack P. Jones and Associates, Inc., Eastman, GA, general contractor and construction consultant, 1970-82; writer, 1982—. *Military service:* U.S. Air Force, intelligence specialist, 1950-54.

*MEMBER:* Authors Guild.

*WRITINGS:*

*NOVELS*

*Wagons in the Wind,* Exposition (Smithtown, NY), 1953, reprinted, Writers Club Press (Lincoln, NE), 2000.

*Three across Texas,* Walker (New York, NY), 1984.

*Three across Kansas,* Walker (New York, NY), 1986.

*Three across Wyoming,* R. Hale (London, England), 1996.

*Under a Lone Sky,* Writers Club Press (Lincoln, NE), 2002.

*Iron Spur,* Writers Club Press (Lincoln, NE), 2002.

*Three across Montana,* Writers Club Press (Lincoln, NE), 2002.

*Three across the Northern Plains,* Writers Club Press (Lincoln, NE), 2002.

Author of "The Siege of Canton," a novella published in the *Darlington Times,* 1989.

*OTHER*

*Manual of Professional Remodeling,* Craftsman (Carlsbad, CA), 1982.

*Spec Builder's Guide,* Craftsman (Carlsbad, CA), 1984.

*Handbook of Construction Contracting,* Volumes I-II, Craftsman (Carlsbad, CA), 1986.

*Remodeling Kitchens and Baths: A Contractor's Guide,* Craftsman (Carlsbad, CA), 1989.

*Creating Space without Adding On,* TAB Books (Blue Ridge Summit, PA), 1993.

*Small Space/Big Bucks: Converting Home Space into Profits,* McGraw-Hill (New York, NY), 1995.

*House Framing,* McGraw-Hill (New York, NY), 1995.

*Builder's Guide to Room Additions,* Craftsman (Carlsbad, CA), 1996.

*Garages and Carports,* Creative Homeowner (Passaic, NJ), 1997.

*The Third Season* (contemporary fiction), Golden Isle Publishers (Eastman, GA), 1999.

*WORK IN PROGRESS:* A contemporary novel; a book on construction estimating integrated into a computer software program.

*SIDELIGHTS:* Jack P. Jones told *CA:* "My primary motivations for writing are personal satisfaction, love of the language, and the music in words. My work is influenced by day-to-day living, books I've read, and the languages of the heart. I begin with an idea—a dream, a desire to 'paint' a different view. I also hope to earn money."

*BIOGRAPHICAL AND CRITICAL SOURCES:*

*ONLINE*

*Jack P. Jones Web Site,* http://www.jackpjones.org/ (June 28, 2003).

**JONES, Pirkle 1914-**

*PERSONAL:* Born January 2, 1914, in Shreveport, LA; son of Alfred Charles (a fine-cabinet maker) and Wilie (Tilton) Jones; married Ruth-Marion Baruch (a photographer and writer), January 15, 1949. *Education:* San Francisco Art Institute (formerly California School of Fine Arts), 1946-49, received certificate in photography. *Politics:* Peace and Freedom Party.

*ADDRESSES: Home and office*—663 Lovell Ave., Mill Valley, CA 94941. *E-mail*—pirkle@earthlink.net.

*CAREER:* Machine operator for Lima Sole and Heel Company, 1933-41; freelance photographer, 1949—; assistant to Ansel Adams, San Francisco, CA, 1949-52; California School of Fine Arts, San Francisco, photography instructor, 1953-58; San Francisco Art Institute, San Francisco, CA, photography instructor, 1971-97. Conducted and participated in many photographic workshops at University of California, Santa Cruz and Ansel Adams workshops in Yosemite, CA. Work represented in several major art museums, including Metropolitan Museum of Art and Museum of Modern Art, New York, NY, Amon Carter Museum of Western Art, TX, Chicago Art Institute, and San Francisco Museum of Art. Member of Mill Valley Architectural Advisory Committee, 1963-67. *Exhibitions:* Ansel Adams Gallery, San Francisco, CA, 1952; International Museum of Photography, George Eastman House, Rochester, NY, 1955; "Building an Oil Refinery," San Francisco Academy of Sciences, 1957; "California Roadside Council Exhibition," The Capital, Sacramento, CA, 1960; "Death of a Valley," San Francisco Museum of Art, 1960; "The Story of a Winery," Smithsonian Institution, Washington, DC, 1963; "Walnut Grove: Portrait of a Town," San Francisco Museum of Art, 1964; American Federation of Arts, Carmel, CA, 1965; Bay Window Gallery, Mendocino, CA, 1967; Photography Center, Carmel, CA, 1967; "Portfolio Two," California Redwood Gallery, San Francisco, CA, 1968; "Photographic Essay on the Black Panthers," De Young Museum, San Francisco, CA, 1968; Underground Gallery, New York, NY, 1969, "Gate Five," Ikon Gallery, Monterey, CA, 1970; Tintype Gallery, Tiburon, CA, 1971; "Portfolio Two," The Studio Gallery, Bolinas, CA, 1972; The Photography Place, Berwyn, PA, 1973; Shado' Gallery, Oregon City, OR, 1973; "Portraits of Adams, Lange, Sheeler, Weston," San Francisco Art Institute, 1977; "The

Sculpture of Annette Rosenshine," San Francisco Art Institute, 1977; and "Vintage Years," Vision Gallery, San Francisco, CA, 1984. Has also participated in group exhibitions. *Military service:* U.S. Army, 1941-46; served as a warrant officer in Signal Corps, 37th Infantry Division; fought in South Pacific; received Bronze Star.

*AWARDS, HONORS:* Photographic Excellence Award, National Urban League, New York, 1961; National Endowment for Arts photography fellowship, 1977; Award of Honor, Arts Commission of the City of San Francisco, 1983, for exceptional achievement in the field of photography; Citizen of the Day Award, KABL Radio, San Francisco, 1983.

*WRITINGS:*

*Portfolio One,* text by Charles P. Johnson, [San Francisco, CA], 1955.
(With Dorothea Lange) *Death of a Valley,* [Millerton, NY], 1960.
*Portfolio Two,* introduction by Ansel Adams, [Mill Valley, CA], 1968.
(With wife, Ruth-Marion Baruch) *The Vanguard: A Photographic Essay on the Black Panthers,* Beacon Press (Boston, MA), 1970.
(With Dorothea Lange) *Berryessa Valley: The Last Year* (exhibition catalogue), Vacaville Museum (Vacaville, CA), 1995.
(With Tim Wride) *Pirkle Jones: California Photographs,* Aperture Foundation (New York, NY), 2001.
(With Ruth-Marion Baruch) *Black Panthers 1968,* Greybull Press (Los Angeles, CA), 2002.

Also contributor to *Encyclopedia of Photography,* 1957, and to periodicals, including *Pacific Discovery* and *Darkroom Magazine.*

*SIDELIGHTS:* Pirkle Jones is a photographer whose books bring natural wonders to life for readers who would never otherwise encounter subjects such as the Black Panthers and the California landscape. His technical knowledge of film, paper, and developing was gained in the 1940s when he studied at the California School of Fine Arts with Ansel Adams and Minor White. In a review of *Pirkle Jones: California Photographs,* Sylvia Andrews of *Library Journal* observed

that Jones's "style fuses documentary photography with poetic emotion." Suzanne Muchnic of the *Los Angeles Times* wrote, "Philosophically, Jones is akin to [Minor] White, who conceived of photography as a spiritual discipline and valued meaning as much as composition."

In an interview for *Contemporary Photographers,* Jones commented on his work: "I am interested in the single image as an aesthetic expression and in documentary photography. I demand content in my work, and am not interested in style for its own sake."

*BIOGRAPHICAL AND CRITICAL SOURCES:*

BOOKS

*Contemporary Photographers,* 3rd edition, St. James (Detroit, MI), 1996.
Katzman, Louise, *Photography in California, 1945-1980,* [San Francisco, CA], 1984.

PERIODICALS

*Aperture,* Volume 4, number 2, 1956, Nancy Newhall, "Pirkle Jones Portfolio."
*British Journal of Photography,* October 17, 1980, Robert Holmes, "Pirkle Jones."
*Choice,* June, 2002, S. Spencer, review of *Pirkle Jones: California Photographs,* p. 1760.
*Darkroom,* December, 1977.
*Examiner and Chronicle Living,* January 13, 1985, Jack McCarty, "Poet of Images."
*Image,* March, 1957, Minor White, "Short Run Color."
*Library Journal,* March 1, 2002, Sylvia Andrews, review of *Pirkle Jones: California Photographs,* p. 94.
*Los Angeles Times,* December 2, 2001, Suzanne Muchnic, "Art: The Focus of a Lifetime," p. F6.
*Pacific Discovery,* January-February, 1967.
*U.S. Camera Magazine,* October, 1952, Ansel Adams, "Pirkle Jones, Photographer."

ONLINE

*The Davis Virtual Market,* http://www.dcn.davis.ca.us/vme/ (June 2, 2003).*

## JUSTICE, Donald (Rodney) 1925-

*PERSONAL:* Born August 12, 1925, in Miami, FL; son of Vascoe J. (a carpenter) and Mary Ethel (Cook) Justice; married Jean Catherine Ross (a writer), August 22, 1947; children: Nathaniel Ross. *Education:* University of Miami, Coral Gables, FL, B.A., 1945; University of North Carolina—Chapel Hill, M.A., 1947; attended Stanford University, 1947-48; University of Iowa, Ph.D., 1954. *Hobbies and other interests:* Composition in music, drawing and painting.

*ADDRESSES: Home*—338 Rocky Shore Dr., Iowa City, IA 52246.

*CAREER:* Educator, poet, and painter. University of Miami, Coral Gables, FL, instructor, 1947-48, 1949-51; University of Missouri—Columbia, visiting assistant professor of English, 1955-56; Hamline University, St. Paul, MN, assistant professor of English, 1956-57; University of Iowa, Iowa City, visiting lecturer, 1957-59, assistant professor, 1959-63, associate professor, 1963-66, professor of English, 1971-82; Syracuse University, Syracuse, NY, associate professor, 1966-67, professor of English, 1967-70; University of California—Irvine, visiting professor of English, 1970-71; University of Florida, Gainesville, professor of English, 1982-92. Reed College, poet-in-residence, 1962; Princeton University, Bain-Swiggett Lecturer, 1976; University of Virginia, visiting professor, 1980. Painter, including cover illustrations for books.

*MEMBER:* American Academy and Institute of Arts and Letters, Academy of American Poets (chancellor).

*AWARDS, HONORS:* Rockefeller Foundation fellow in poetry at University of Iowa, 1954-55; Academy of American Poets Lamont Poetry Selection, 1959, for *The Summer Anniversaries,* and fellow, 1988; *Poetry* Inez Boulton Prize, 1960, and Harriet Monroe Award; Ford Foundation fellowship in theater, 1964-65; National Endowment for the Arts grants, 1967, 1973, 1980, and 1989; National Book Award nominations, 1973, for *Departures,* and 1995, for *New and Selected Poems;* Guggenheim fellowship in poetry, 1976-77; Pulitzer Prize in poetry, 1979, for *Selected Poems;* Harriet Monroe Award, University of Chicago, 1984; National Book Critics Circle Award nomination, 1988, for *The Sunset Maker: Poems/Stories/A Memoir;* Bol-

*Donald Justice*

lingen Prize for poetry, 1991, for *A Donald Justice Reader: Selected Poetry and Prose;* Lannan Literary Award for poetry, 1996; also received awards for short fiction.

*WRITINGS:*

*POETRY COLLECTIONS*

*The Old Bachelor and Other Poems,* 1951.
*The Summer Anniversaries,* Wesleyan University Press (Middletown, CT), 1960, revised edition, University Press of New England (Hanover, NH), 1981.
*A Local Storm,* Stone Wall Press (Iowa City, IA), 1963.
*Night Light,* Wesleyan University Press (Middletown, CT), 1967, revised edition, University Press of New England (Hanover, NH), 1981.
(With Tom McAfee, Donald Drummond, and R. P. Dickey) *Four Poets,* Central College of Pella (Pella, IA), 1968.
*Sixteen Poems,* Stone Wall Press (Iowa City, IA), 1970.
*From a Notebook,* Seamark Press (Iowa City, IA), 1971.

*Departures,* Atheneum (New York, NY), 1973.

*Selected Poems,* Atheneum (New York, NY), 1979.

*Tremayne,* Windhover Press (Iowa City, IA), 1984.

*New and Selected Poems,* Knopf (New York, NY), 1995.

*Poems to Go,* Knopf (New York, NY), 1995.

*Orpheus Hesitated beside the Black River: Poems, 1952-1997,* Anvil Press Poetry (London, England), 1998.

*EDITOR*

*The Collected Poems of Weldon Kees,* Stone Wall Press (Iowa City, IA), 1960, revised edition, University of Nebraska Press (Lincoln, NE), 1992.

(With Alexander Aspel) *Contemporary French Poetry: Fourteen Witnesses of Man's Fate,* University of Michigan Press (Ann Arbor, MI), 1965.

*Syracuse Poems,* Department of English, Syracuse University (Syracuse, NY), 1968.

(With Robert Mezey, and coauthor of introduction) *The Collected Poems of Henri Coulette,* University of Arkansas Press (Fayetteville, AR), 1990.

(With Cooper R. Mackin and Richard D. Olson, and author of introduction) *The Comma after Love: Selected Poems of Raeburn Miller,* University of Akron Press (Akron, OH), 1994.

Joe Bolton, *The Last Nostalgia: Collected Poems, 1982-1990,* University of Arkansas Press (Fayetteville, AR), 1999.

*OTHER*

(Translator) Eugène Guillevic, *L'Homme qui se ferme/ The Man Closing Up,* Stone Wall Press (Iowa City, IA), 1973.

*Platonic Scripts* (essays), University of Michigan Press (Ann Arbor, MI), 1984.

*The Sunset Maker: Poems/Stories/A Memoir,* Atheneum (New York, NY), 1987.

*The Death of Lincoln: A Documentary Opera* (libretto), A. Thomas Taylor, 1988.

*A Donald Justice Reader: Selected Poetry and Prose,* University Press of New England (Hanover, NH), 1991.

*Oblivion: On Writers and Writing,* Story Line Press (Ashland, OR), 1998.

Author of librettos and one-act plays. Contributor to books, including *On Creative Writing,* edited by Paul Engle, Dutton (New York, NY), 1964; *New Poets of England and America; Twentieth-Century American Poetry,* edited by Conrad Aiken; *Contemporary American Poetry,* edited by A. J. Poulin; *The Direction of Poetry,* edited by Robert Richman; and *Contemporary American Poetry,* edited by Donald Hall. Contributor of essays and short stories to literary journals, including *Poetry, Antaeus, New Yorker,* and *New Criterion.* Poetry recordings include *Childhood and Other Poems,* Watershed, 1983; selections recorded by Archive of Recorded Poetry and Literature (Washington, DC), 1973, 1992.

A collection of Justice's manuscripts is housed at the University of Delaware Library, Dover.

*SIDELIGHTS:* "Those in a position to appreciate craft" in poetry have long admired the works of Donald Justice, Cathrael Kazin wrote in the *Dictionary of Literary Biography Yearbook: 1983.* Justice's first published book, *The Summer Anniversaries,* was the 1959 Lamont Poetry Selection, while his more recent *Departures* received a National Book Award nomination in 1973 and *Selected Poems* won the Pulitzer Prize in 1979. Added Kazin: "Justice has come to be recognized not only as one of America's most elegant and distinctive contemporary poets but also as one of its most significant." Technical prowess "never calls attention to itself in Justice's understated work," claimed *Southern Review* contributor Dana Gioia. While the poet's presence is implied by his control of form, according to reviewers, Justice uses the poems to efface the self rather than to vaunt it. Because one way of diminishing the self is to relax its control over form, Justice has sometimes used chance methods—such as shuffling word cards together—to compose poems. Thus, wrote Gioia, "Justice has published very little, but he has also distilled a decade of writing and experimentation in each new volume."

Published in 1960, *The Summer Anniversaries* established Justice's reputation for attention to craft. The book, related Greg Simon in the *American Poetry Review,* "consists of flawless poems, moving as inexorably as glaciers toward beautiful comprehension and immersion in reality." *Night Light,* published in 1967, presents poems that "are not so . . . manicured as those in *The Summer Anniversaries,*" noted Joel O. Conarroe in a *Shenandoah* review, while in *Departures* critics praised Justice for a command of poetic technique that surpassed much of his earlier work.

"The new Justice poem is no longer a set piece or still life, forced into shape," added Simon in his review of the 1973 volume, "but a vigorous and rhythmical composition, prosody at the limit of its kinetic potential. This remarkable new intention in Justice's work accounts for the fact that the forms of the best poems in *Departures* are invisible architecture. . . . It is intoxicating to see Justice now unfettered by the forms that circumscribed and dictated the action in his early poems; and to see him working with sources that are not only naturally energetic and new, but demanding in conception and daring in stance."

In subsequent books Justice has experimented with deliberate mistranslations of poems in other languages, or with methods of composition that combine words at random until they suggest a statement or a form. These methods help the poet to focus more on his materials than on his conscious control over them. Justice himself sees such "chance" methods as "in its way, a formal approach," one which allows him "to see images a little differently." Paul Ramsey, writing in the *Sewanee Review,* commented that Justice's poems composed in this way are prone "to fragmentation . . . [yet] his fragments sound completed. . . . His gift for order is an irresistible gift."

Gioia suggested that no other American poet has perfected as many poetic styles. Justice's 1979 *Selected Poems* "reads almost like an anthology of the possibilities of contemporary poetry," Gioia noted. "There are sestinas, villanelles and ballads rubbing shoulders with aleatory poems [composed using chance methods], surreal odes, and . . . free verse. . . . A new technique is often developed, mastered, and exhausted in one unprecedented and unrepeatable poem." During the selection process credited in the title, Justice rewrote some poems and gave them a new sequence to make *Selected Poems* a "nearly perfect volume," according to Gioia. In a *Parnassus* review, Vernon Young noted, "I doubt if there are six poems in [*Selected Poems*] which could be claimed for the public sensibility. But Justice has written a dozen lyrics I'd call virtually incomparable."

Autobiography figures little in Justice's work. "The principles of composition . . . really occupy him, not his own life," explained *Yale Review* contributor Richard Wertime. For the poet, his art functions as a hedge against death and loss. In his essay "Meters and Memory," reprinted in *Oblivion: On Writers and Writ-*

*ing,* Justice explains how writing about loss enables him to endure: "To remember an event is almost to begin to control it, as well as to approach an understanding of it; incapable of recurring now, it is only to be contemplated rather than acted on or reacted to. . . . The terror or beauty or, for that matter, the plain ordinariness of the original event, being transformed, is fixed and thereby made more tolerable. That the event can recur only in its new context, the context of art, sheers it of some risks, the chief of which may anyhow have been its transitory character." Submitting his materials to metrical structures is part of this process. As Robert Peters noted in the *American Book Review,* because "art endures while life is brief," Justice's elegies mitigate the total loss of death. Observed Kazin, "In the guise of lamenting a loss, [the poems] perform acts of preservation"; resurrected by memory and ensconced in art, the lost friends of childhood, suicides, and other casualties gain an extended life. Justice succeeds, explained Edward Hirsch in the *New York Times Book Review,* because "he counters our inevitable human losses with an unforgettable and permanent music."

Piano lessons Justice enjoyed as a child provide the central motif of *The Sunset Maker: Poems/Stories/A Memoir.* In this work Justice closely relates music and poetry through both verse and prose. "On the whole," Bruce Bawer commented in the *Washington Post Book World,* "*The Sunset Maker* is a deeply affecting volume—a beautiful, powerful meditation by a modern master upon the themes of aging, lost innocence, and the unalterable, terrifying pastness of the past."

*A Donald Justice Reader: Selected Poetry and Prose* gathers into one volume seventy-three poems and six prose pieces: three essays, two stories, and a memoir of Justice's Miami childhood. Felix Stefanile, writing in the *Christian Science Monitor,* called this collection "a real gift" since "it is a sign of Donald Justice's clear, retentive mind that so many of these works, assembled over decades—verse and prose—talk to each other." The essay "The Invention of Free Verse" proposes that a commemorative tablet be erected in Crawfordsville, Indiana, at Wabash College, to acknowledge Ezra Pound, and to celebrate the time (1907) and the place (Crawfordsville) of the invention of modern poetry. The collection also includes examples of Justice's poems about time and place, among them "Crossing Kansas by Train." A reviewer for the *Virginia Quarterly Review* commented that "Justice certainly deserves the wider audience this selection from his poems and prose . . . is designed to produce" since he is "revered by other poets as a virtuoso craftsman."

*New and Selected Poems,* published four years later in 1995, offers another collection of Justice's poems. Reviewing the work, Michael Hoffman, in the *New York Times Book Review,* deemed Justice's writing "skillful and musical" and maintained that Justice "probably has few peers when it comes to the musical arrangement of words in a line." A writer for *Publishers Weekly* acknowledged the work as a timeless retrospective on the work of an award-winning poet, and concluded: "Until we see a complete collected works, this is probably the definitive Justice."

*BIOGRAPHICAL AND CRITICAL SOURCES:*

BOOKS

*Contemporary Poets,* 7th edition, St. James Press (Detroit, MI), 2001.
*Contemporary Southern Writers,* St. James Press (Detroit, MI), 2001.
*Dictionary of Literary Biography Yearbook: 1983,* Gale (Detroit, MI), 1984.
*Encyclopedia of World Literature in the Twentieth Century,* Volume 2, St. James Press (Detroit, MI), 1999, pp. 583-584.
Gioia, Dana, and William Logan, editors, *Certain Solitudes: On the Poetry of Donald Justice,* University of Arkansas Press (Fayetteville, AR), 1998.
Hoy, Philip, *Donald Justice in Conversation with Philip Hoy,* Between the Lines (London, England), 2001.

PERIODICALS

*American Book Review,* January, 1982; April-May, 1993, p. 26.
*American Poetry Review,* March-April, 1976, Greg Simon, "On Donald Justice"; May, 1988, p. 9; January-February, 1996, interview with Dana Gioia.
*Antaeus,* spring-summer, 1982.
*Antioch Review,* winter, 1988, p. 102; summer, 1996, p. 377.
*Booklist,* January 1, 1992, p. 805; September 15, 1995, p. 132.
*Boston Review,* June, 1987, p. 27.

*Choice,* February, 1985, p. 815.
*Christian Science Monitor,* April 20, 1992, Felix Stefanile, review of *A Donald Justice Reader: Selected Poetry and Prose,* p. 13.
*Economist,* March 13, 1999, review of *New and Selected Poems,* p. S14.
*Hollins Critic,* October, 1992, Lewis Turco, "The Progress of Donald Justice."
*Hudson Review,* spring, 1974.
*Iowa Review,* spring-summer, 1980, pp. 1-21; winter, 1999, Jerry Harp, review of *Oblivion: On Writers and Writing,* p. 167.
*Library Journal,* February 1, 1967; May 1, 1987, p. 71; December, 1991, p. 144; September 15, 1995, p. 72; April 1, 1997, p. 95.
*Los Angeles Times,* August 12, 1987, Frances Ruhlen McConnel, review of *The Sunset Maker: Poems/ Stories/A Memoir.*
*Missouri Review,* fall, 1980, pp. 41-67.
*Modern Language Studies,* winter, 1978-79.
*Modern Poetry Studies,* spring, 1980, pp. 44-58.
*Nation,* December 26, 1987, p. 803.
*New Statesman,* August 22, 1980, pp. 17-18; August 23, 1987, p. 28.
*New York Herald Tribune Books,* September 4, 1960.
*New York Review of Books,* October 16, 1975.
*New York Times Book Review,* February 19, 1961; March 9, 1980, pp. 8, 16; August 23, 1987, p. 20; December 27, 1992, p. 2; December 10, 1995, Michael Hoffman, review of *New and Selected Poems,* pp. 13-14; September 19, 1996, p. 49.
*Notes on Contemporary Literature,* November, 1996, James A. McCoy, "'Black Flowers, Black Flowers': Meta-Criticism in Donald Justice's 'Bus Stop.'"
*Ohio Review,* spring, 2001, Wayne Dodd and Stanley Plumly, "The Effacement of Self: An Interview with Donald Justice," p. 405.
*Paris Review,* March, 1988, p. 490.
*Parnassus,* fall-winter, 1979, Vernon Young, review of *Selected Poems,* pp. 227-237.
*Partisan Review,* Volume 47, number 4, 1980, pp. 639-644.
*Perspective,* spring, 1962.
*Poetry,* October, 1974; October, 1984; September, 1989, p. 342; June, 1993, pp. 160-166; June, 1994, pp. 167-171; June, 1996, p. 168; June, 1996, p. 168; August, 1999, Christian Wiman, review of *Oblivion,* p. 286.
*Prairie Schooner,* Volume 47, 1973.
*Publishers Weekly,* August 28, 1995, review of *New and Selected Poems,* p. 108.
*Punch,* January 15, 1988, p. 44.

*Saturday Review,* October 14, 1967, pp. 31-33, 99.

*Sewanee Review,* spring, 1974; summer, 1980, pp. 474-478; fall, 1980; winter, 2001, David C. Ward, review of *Oblivion,* p. 147.

*Shenandoah,* summer, 1967, Joel O. Conarroe, review of *Night Light.*

*Southern Review,* summer, 1981; autumn, 1994, Charles Wright, "Homage to the Thin Man."

*Southwest Review,* spring, 1980, pp. 218-220.

*Times Literary Supplement,* May 18, 1967; March 29, 1974; April 16, 1976; May 30, 1980, p. 620; April 15-21, 1988, p. 420; July 30, 1999, N. S. Thompson, reviews of *Orpheus Hesitated beside the Black River: Poems, 1952-1957* and *Oblivion,* p. 23.

*Tribune Books* (Chicago, IL), June 21, 1987, p. 3.

*Verse,* winter-spring, 1992.

*Virginia Quarterly Review,* summer, 1992, review of *A Donald Justice Reader,* p. 101.

*Wallace Stevens Journal,* fall, 1993, Clive Watkins, "Some Reflections on Donald Justice's Poem 'After a Phrase Abandoned by Wallace Stevens.'"

*Washington Post Book World,* February 10, 1980, p. 11; January 3, 1988, Bruce Bawer, review of *The Sunset Maker.*

*Western Humanities Review,* summer, 1974.

*Yale Review,* June, 1960, pp. 589-598; summer, 1985, Richard Wertime, review of *Platonic Scripts,* p. 602; autumn, 1987, p. 124; spring, 1988.

# K

## KAMEN, Henry (Arthur Francis) 1936-

*PERSONAL:* Born October 4, 1936, in Rangoon, Burma; son of Maurice (an engineer) and Agnes (Frizelle) Kamen; married Eulalia Vila (a teacher), April, 1990. *Education:* Oxford University, B.A. (first class honors), 1960, D.Phil., 1963. *Religion:* Roman Catholic.

*ADDRESSES: Home*—Paseo de San Juan 48, 08010 Barcelona, Spain. *Agent*—Peters, Fraser & Dunlop Group, Ltd., Drury House, 34-43 Russell St., London WC2B 5HA, England. *E-mail*—hkamen@hotmail.com.

*CAREER:* Educator and historian. University of Edinburgh, Edinburgh, Scotland, lecturer, 1963-66; University of Warwick, Coventry, England, reader, 1966-90; Higher Council for Scientific Research, Barcelona, Spain, professor, 1991—.

*WRITINGS:*

*The Spanish Inquisition,* Weidenfeld & Nicolson (London, England), 1965, New American Library (New York, NY), 1966.

*The Rise of Toleration,* McGraw-Hill (New York, NY), 1967.

(Contributor) Hugh Trevor-Roper, *The Age of Expansion: Europe and the World, 1559-1660,* McGraw-Hill (New York, NY), 1968.

*The War of Succession in Spain, 1700-15,* Indiana University Press (Bloomington, IN), 1969.

*The Iron Century: Social Change in Europe, 1550-1660,* Praeger (New York, NY), 1971.

*A Concise History of Spain,* Scribner (New York, NY), 1973.

(With Joseph Pérez) *La Imagen internacional de la España de Flipe II: "Leyenda negra" o conflicto de intereses,* University de Valladolid (Valladolid, Spain), 1980.

*Spain in the Later Seventeenth Century, 1665-1700,* Longman (New York, NY), 1980.

*Spain, 1469-1714: A Society of Conflict,* Longman (New York, NY), 1983.

*European Society, 1500-1700,* Hutchinson (London, England), 1984.

*Inquisition and Society in Spain in the Sixteenth and Seventeenth Centuries,* Indiana University Press (Bloomington, IN), 1985.

*Vocabulario básico de la historia moderna: España y América, 1450-1750,* Crítica (Barcelona, Spain), 1986.

*Golden Age Spain,* Humanities Press International (Atlantic Highlands, NJ), 1988.

*The Phoenix and the Flame: Catalonia and the Counter Reformation,* Yale University Press (New Haven, CT), 1993.

*Crisis and Change in Early Modern Spain,* Variorum (Brookfield, VT), 1993.

*Philip of Spain,* Yale University Press (New Haven, CT), 1997.

*The Spanish Inquisition: A Historical Revision,* Yale University Press (New Haven, CT), 1998.

*Early Modern European Society,* Routledge (New York, NY), 2000.

(Editor and contributor) *Who's Who in Europe, 1450-1750,* Routledge (New York, NY), 2000.

*Philip V: The King Who Reigned Twice,* Yale University Press (New Haven, CT), 2001.

*SIDELIGHTS:* Professor Henry Kamen "has done more than any other modern historian to reverse the old Anglo-Saxon prejudice against Spain and to destroy the 'black legend' created by many eloquent but facile nineteenth-century writers," noted Maria Isabella Garcia in *Contemporary Review.* Kamen, who writes in English, is an authority on the Spanish Inquisition and on the history of Spain from the Renaissance era into the Industrial Revolution. Since he first published *The Spanish Inquisition* in 1965 he has led the push to revise early modern Spanish history in English and remove biases that had existed in scholarly and popular books for more than a century. Observed Eric C. Rust in the *Journal of Church and State,* "Connoisseurs of Spanish history require no introduction to Henry Kamen. Bringing a wealth of factual knowledge, scholarly integrity, and sensitivity to his subject, Kamen always stirs his readers as he transports them back to Spain's Golden Age."

Kamen has written three separate books on the Inquisition, each one adding more research and observations on the controversial topic. According to John Edwards in the *Journal of Modern History,* "Generations of students have been brought up on Henry Kamen's two earlier versions of the history of the Spanish Inquisition, which were published in 1965 and 1985 respectively, and which brought a refreshing independence of mind to what had often appeared to be a subject that lent itself to the adoption of fixed and tedious positions." *The Spanish Inquisition: A Historical Revision,* published in 1998, introduces new findings that in some cases alter Kamen's previous conclusions on the conduct and scope of the Inquisition. To quote Carla Rahn Phillips in *Renaissance Quarterly,* "Here Kamen adds a wealth of recent scholarship and presents a forceful and gracefully written narrative that is consciously aimed at the general reader." Carl L. Bankston III in *Commonweal* wrote: "Kamen's new book is a rewriting and extension of his original one that incorporates the findings of three-and-a-half decades of research. . . . [It] is a major contribution to the history of religion and the history of Spain. The clarity of the writing will make it appealing to interested general readers, as well as to specialists. . . . [Kamen] succeeds in reinterpreting a dark legend of torture and persecution as a series of human attempts to deal with issues of belief and social conflict."

In addition to his works on the Inquisition, Kamen has written biographies of two important Spanish kings, Philip II—who ruled in the sixteenth century—and

Philip V, the first Bourbon king of Spain. In both cases the scholar has sought to dispel myths about the kings in question, especially Philip II, who sent the Spanish Armada against England in 1588. A reviewer for the *Economist* felt that *Philip of Spain* "is formidably learned, impartial and just: a worthy achievement." Andrew A. Chibi, writing in *Historian,* stated: "What emerges from Kamen's book is a prince trying to do what is best for Spain, his family, and his religion. . . . Indeed, this is a book that all early modernists should read, particularly historians of Tudor England." *Renaissance Quarterly* reviewer M. N. Carlos Eire maintained that *Philip of Spain* "is a stunning achievement, not only because of its revisionist outlook and its use of sources, but also because of its style and structure. This is an exemplary piece of scholarship that reads very much like a good novel." Maria Isabella Garcia, reviewing *Philip V of Spain: The King Who Reigned Twice,* declared that the biography, "well research and well-written, provides a good introduction to the problems that bedeviled an eighteenth-century King of Spain." A *Publishers Weekly* contributor styled the book "a humane work, as well as a provocative one."

Kamen once told *CA:* "As a historian, my task is simply to investigate the past through an intelligent use of both scholarship and imagination."

*BIOGRAPHICAL AND CRITICAL SOURCES:*

*PERIODICALS*

*American Historical Review,* December, 1995, Gary W. McDonogh, review of *The Phoenix and the Flame: Catalonia and the Counter Reformation,* p. 1598; June, 1998, Richard L. Kagan, review of *Philip of Spain,* p. 912; December, 1999, Thomas F. Glick, review of *The Spanish Inquisition: A Historical Revision,* p. 1773. *Atlantic Monthly,* August, 1997, Francis X. Rocca, review of *Philip of Spain,* p. 85.

*Biography,* fall, 2001, Richard Herr, review of *Philip V of Spain: The King Who Reigned Twice,* p. 1003.

*Booklist,* April 1, 2000, Mary Ellen Quinn, review of *Who's Who in Europe, 1450-1750,* p. 1494; May 1, 2001, Brad Hooper, review of *Philip V of Spain,* p. 1660.

*Commonweal,* January 14, 1994, Carl L. Bankston III, review of *The Phoenix and the Flame,* p. 31; August 14, 1998, Carl L. Bankston III, review of *The Spanish Inquisition: A Historical Revision,* p. 22.

*Contemporary Review,* November, 2001, Maria Isabella Garcia, "Spain's First Bourbon King," p. 308.

*Economist* (U.S), October 18, 1997, review of *Philip of Spain,* p. S6; July 11, 1998, review of *The Spanish Inquisition: A Historical Revision,* p. S10.

*English Historical Review,* November, 1998, M. J. Rodriguez-Salgado, review of *Philip of Spain,* p. 1256.

*Historian,* summer, 1999, Andrew A. Chibi, review of *Philip of Spain,* p. 958.

*History Today,* July, 1994, Diarmaid MacCulloch, review of *The Phoenix and the Flame,* p. 58.

*Journal of Church and State,* spring, 1999, Eric C. Rust, review of *The Spanish Inquisition: A Historical Revision,* p. 381.

*Journal of Modern History,* June, 2000, John Edwards, review of *The Spanish Inquisition: A Historical Revision,* p. 549.

*New York Review of Books,* September 25, 1997, J. H. Elliott, review of *Philip of Spain,* p. 45.

*New York Times Book Review,* August 10, 1997, Hugh Thomas, review of *Philip of Spain,* p. 9; April 19, 1998, Richard L. Kagan, review of *The Spanish Inquisition: A Historical Revision,* p. 9; July 1, 2001, Richard Herr, "The Reigns in Spain: A Biography of the Founder of the Bourbon Dynasty Offers a New View," p. 21.

*Publishers Weekly,* February 9, 1998, review of *The Spanish Inquisition: A Historical Revision,* p. 85; April 9, 2001, review of *Philip V of Spain,* p. 65.

*Renaissance Quarterly,* spring, 1999, M. N. Carlos Eire, review of *Philip of Spain,* p. 243; autumn, 1999, Carla Rahn Phillips, review of *The Spanish Inquisition: A Historical Revision,* p. 891.*

\* \* \*

## KAN, Sergei 1953-

*PERSONAL:* Born March 31, 1953, in Moscow, USSR; son of Alexander S. Kan (a professor of history) and Elena Semeka-Pankratov (a professor of Russian); married Alla Glazman (a college administrator), December 19, 1976; children: Elianna. *Education:* Boston University, B.A. (summa cum laude), 1976; University of Chicago, M.A., 1978, Ph.D., 1982. *Politics:* "Conservative to moderate." *Religion:* Jewish.

*ADDRESSES: Home*—14 Village Green, West Lebanon, NH 03784. *Office*—Department of Anthropology, Dartmouth College, Hanover, NH 03755. *E-mail*—sergei.kan@dartmouth.edu.

*CAREER:* Educator and author. Northeastern University, Boston, MA, assistant professor of anthropology, 1981-83; University of Michigan, Ann Arbor, assistant professor of anthropology, 1983-89; Dartmouth College, Hanover, NH, assistant professor, 1989-92, associate professor of anthropology, 1992—. Ann Arbor Action for Soviet Jewry, co-chair, 1985-87.

*MEMBER:* American Anthropological Association, American Ethnological Society, American Society for Ethnohistory, American Association for the Advancement of Slavic Studies, Alaska Anthropological Association.

*AWARDS, HONORS:* Heizer Award, American Society for Ethnohistory, 1987, for journal article; American Book Award, Before Columbus Foundation, 1990, for *Symbolic Immortality.*

*WRITINGS:*

(Translator from Russian, and author of introduction and supplementary material) A. Kamenskii, *Tlingit Indians of Alaska,* University of Alaska Press (Fairbanks, AK), 1985.

*Symbolic Immortality: The Tlingit Potlatch of the Nineteenth Century,* Smithsonian Institution Press (Washington, DC), 1989.

*Memory Eternal: Tlingit Culture and Russian Orthodox Christianity through Two Centuries,* University of Washington Press (Seattle, WA), 1999.

*Strangers to Relatives: The Adoption and Naming of Anthropologists in Native North America,* University of Nebraska Press (Lincoln, NE), 2001.

*WORK IN PROGRESS:* Research on native cultures and Christianity in North America.

*SIDELIGHTS:* Sergei Kan once told *CA:* "In my research I try to combine detailed ethnography (study of native culture), social science theory, and history. I am particularly interested in change that takes place when different ideologies, such as religions, come into contact with each other. Recently I have also become interested in the plight of the indigenous peoples of Siberia, and I plan to do research and write on that subject."

Kan, who teaches Native American Studies and anthropology at Dartmouth College, has contributed to European understanding of the Tlingit culture in Alaska. His *Memory Eternal: Tlingit Culture and Russian Orthodox Christianity through Two Centuries* covers the history, economy, society, and traditions of the Tlingit and explores how the Russian Orthodox Church has influenced Tlingit beliefs over time. *Library Journal* contributors John Dockall and Bernice P. Bishop found the book "essential for . . . those deeply interested in the dynamics of traditional belief systems."

*BIOGRAPHICAL AND CRITICAL SOURCES:*

*PERIODICALS*

*American Anthropologist,* June, 1992, Robert Brightman, review of *Symbolic Immortality: The Tlingit Potlach of the Nineteenth Century,* p. 473.
*American Historical Review,* December, 2000, Gregory Freeze, review of *Memory Eternal: Tlingit Culture and Russian Orthodox Christianity through Two Centuries,* p. 1748.
*Current Anthropology,* August-October, 1990, Leland Donald, review of *Symbolic Immortality,* p. 481.
*Journal for the Scientific Study of Religion,* Dan W. Forsythe, review of *Symbolic Immortality,* p. 239.
*Journal of American History,* September, 2001, Kan Coates, review of *Memory Eternal,* p. 679.
*Library Journal,* January, 2000, John Dockall and Bernice P. Bishop, review of *Memory Eternal,* p. 126.
*Pacific Northwest Quarterly,* fall, 2001, Gunther Barth, review of *Memory Eternal,* p. 205.
*Russian Review,* July, 2000, Marjorie Mandelstam Balzer, review of *Memory Eternal,* p. 458.
*Western Historical Quarterly,* autumn, 2000, David Arnold, review of *Memory Eternal,* p. 385.*

\*       \*       \*

**KANIGEL, Robert 1946-**

*PERSONAL:* Born May 28, 1946, in Brooklyn, NY; son of Charles (an owner of a small factory) and Beatrice (a homemaker; maiden name, Wolshine) Kanigel; married Judith Schiff (a principal of a school for the retarded), June 28, 1981; children: David Saul. *Education:* Rensselaer Polytechnic Institute, B.S., 1966.

*ADDRESSES: Home and office*—2643 North Calvert St., Baltimore, MD 21218. *Agent*—Vicky Bijur Literary Agency, 333 West End Ave., New York, NY 10023.

*CAREER:* Mechanical engineer, 1966-67; Bendix Corporation, Towson, MD, mechanical engineer, 1968-69; freelance writer in Baltimore, MD, 1970-71 and 1976—, San Francisco, CA, 1971-74, and New York, NY, 1975. Instructor in writing at Johns Hopkins University, 1985-91; Yale Gordon College of Liberal Arts, professor of English and senior fellow of the Institute for language, technology, and publications design, 1991—.

*MEMBER:* American Society of Journalists, National Association of Science Writers, National Book Critics Circle, National Coalition of Independent Scholars, History of Science Society.

*AWARDS, HONORS:* A. D. Emmart Award for writing in the humanities, 1979, for "Orthodoxy's Invisible Wall"; Smolar Award for excellence in North American Jewish journalism, Council of Jewish Federations, 1978, for "Impressions of the Detlavs Trial," and 1980; Council for the Advancement and Support of Education, Citation Award, 1982, for "The Mentor Chain," Silver Award, 1985, for "An Intricate Edifice," and Gold Award, 1988, for "The Coming of Chaos"; second prize in Simon Rockower Memorial Writing Competition for excellence in Jewish journalism, American Jewish Press Association, 1982; Marine Biological Laboratory Science Writing fellowship, 1988; James T. Grady-James H. Stack Award for interpreting chemistry for the public, American Chemical Society, 1989; Outstanding Article of the Year award, American Society of Journalists and Authors, 1989, for "An Ordinary Miracle"; award for excellence in medical journalism, Medical-Chirurgical Faculty of Maryland, 1989, for "Getting a Fix on Nicotine Addiction"; National Book Critics Circle Award nominee, 1992, for *The Man Who Knew Infinity; Los Angeles Times* Book Prize, 1991.

*WRITINGS:*

*Apprentice to Genius: The Making of a Scientific Dynasty,* Macmillan (New York, NY), 1986.
*The Man Who Knew Infinity: A Life of the Indian Genius Ramanujan,* Scribner (New York, NY), 1991.

*The One Best Way: Frederick Winslow Taylor and the Enigma of Efficiency,* Viking (New York, NY), 1997.

*Vintage Reading: From Plato to Bradbury: A Personal Tour of Some of the World's Best Books,* Bancroft Press (Baltimore, MD), 1998.

*High Season: How One French Riviera Town Has Seduced Travelers for Two Thousand Years,* Viking (New York, NY), 2002.

Work represented in anthologies, including *Education and Opportunity,* edited by Gordon M. Seely, 2nd edition, Prentice-Hall, 1977; *Options in Rhetoric,* edited by Sylvia A. Holladay and Thomas M. Brown, Prentice-Hall, 1981; *Biology,* edited by John W. Crane, 4th edition, Dushkin, 1984.

Author of monthly literary review, "Vintage Reading," Baltimore *Evening Sun,* 1982-88. Contributor of nearly 400 articles, essays, and reviews to periodicals and newspapers, including *Chicago Tribune, Los Angeles Times, New York Times Magazine, New York Times Book Review, Psychology Today,* and *Sciences.* Contributing editor, *Johns Hopkins Magazine,* 1977—.

*SIDELIGHTS:* Robert Kanigel's first book, *Apprentice to Genius: The Making of a Scientific Dynasty,* is a study of the mentor system, which traces four members of the scientific elite as each matures from student to teacher. Throughout the book Kanigel refutes the stereotypical view that scientists are cold, rational automatons, revealing instead the creative and emotional influences that pervade their distinctly human endeavor to understand people and their world. The "dynasty" Kanigel scrutinizes began in the 1940s with eminent pharmacologist Bernard Brodie and his pupil, eventual Nobel Prize-winner Julius Axelrod. Next in succession is Solomon Snyder, Axelrod's pupil and the mentor of Candace Pert, whose research helped Snyder win the prestigious Albert Lasker Basic Medical Research Award for the discovery of opiate receptors in the mammalian brain. A controversy ensued when, despite her contributions, Pert was excluded from the award. What made these four scientists successful despite their personal and professional conflicts, argues Kanigel, is not that they passed along mere data but rather that in each case the mentor imbued the apprentice with an intuitive, daring attitude toward research. Such an attitude is perhaps best illustrated in *Apprentice to Genius* by Brodie's adventuresome expression, "Let's take a flier on it."

Critics cited *Apprentice to Genius* as a rarity in the realm of science writing. In the *Washington Post Book World,* reviewer Wray Herbert noted that *Apprentice to Genius* "contains some of the most lucid science writing I have read anywhere," calling it a "fascinating story" that is "skillfully" told by Kanigel. Lee Dembart, writing in the *Los Angeles Times,* noted that "Kanigel draws a riveting picture of scientists at work" and that the book "reveals more about people and how the world works than most psychology and sociology."

Kanigel's next book, *The Man Who Knew Infinity: A Life of the Indian Genius Ramanujan,* recounts the life and early death of the Indian genius Srinivasa Ramanujan, who grew up in poverty yet made his name in England and astounded the scientific community there with his amazing aptitude for solving formulas. In particular, the author focuses on Ramanujan's relationship with his British mentor, G. W. Hardy, a mathematics star in his own right who was the first to recognize the young Indian's natural-born talent. *New York Times Book Review* critic John Allen Paulos noted Kanigel "tells one of the most romantic stories in the history of mathematics." Indeed, even those readers not enamored of mathematics can enjoy this rags-to-riches parable, in Paulos's view. The book's "portrayal of Madras and the relaxed atmosphere and easy interaction of classes in the surrounding Talil villages where Ramanujan grew up is superbly evocative, as is its depiction of life in Cambridge during World War I." In a *Washington Post Book World* review, Shashi Tharoor called *The Man Who Knew Infinity* a "masterpiece." This work represents "a model of the biographer's art: Kanigel has taken a man, a social context and a specialist field and made each accessible and convincing. He has done so with a rare combination of skills—encyclopedic thoroughness, meticulous research, genuine sympathy for his subjects and first-rate writing of exceptional lucidity and verve." Some readers took exception to the author's penchant for detail; he has "exhaustively described every building that Ramanujan ever occupied, every tradition that Ramanujan ever encountered, every incident in which Ramanujan played even the tiniest role," Christopher Lehmann-Haupt wrote in the *New York Times.* "Did World War I descend upon England while Ramanujan was there? Mr. Kanigel expatiates on its causes. Did Ramanujan contract tuberculosis as a remotely indirect result? Mr. Kanigel holds forth on the bacillus Mycobacterium tuberculosis. One senses that if his hero had worn a wristwatch, the author would have told the history of Switzerland." Still, *Times Literary Supplement* writer A. W. Masters cited Kanigel for taking on the challenge: "Ramanujan is a troublesome subject for biography. Beyond the basic story of his relationship with Hardy during the five applauded years that preceded and largely accounted for his death, there isn't much for a non-mathematician to say. . . . For a journalist who is neither Indian nor English, and who, until 1987, had never even heard of Ramanujan, this book is a noteworthy performance."

In 1997, Kanigel delivered another noteworthy performance with his biography of Frederick Winslow Taylor (1856-1915), described by the author as "the first efficiency expert, the original time-and-motion man." *The One Best Way: Frederick Winslow Taylor and the Enigma of Efficiency* recounts the life of an industrial engineer whose name is not well known outside business circles but whose innovations at the turn of the twentieth century helped shape the way work is performed to this day. Born into affluence, Taylor was courted by top schools yet chose to toil among the men on the factory floor to learn how manual labor was accomplished—and how it could be sped up. Taylor would not stay a laborer for long. While rising through the management ranks he developed his formula for "scientific management," a way of working, based on quantifiable measures of established routines. "Taylorism," as it came to be known, "turned craft work into assembly line work," noted Robert Dowling in *Business Week*. "It presaged automation and the machine age, gave us speedups, downsizings, and rules for every job." Indeed, Taylor would gain a notorious reputation for his methods of research, which Kanigel discusses in *The One Best Way*. In the words of Benjamin Kline Hunnicutt, writing in the *Chicago Tribune,* "Those who hold the popular image of Taylor with his stopwatch timing the every move of a sweating, harassed worker, and of scientific management as a turn-of-the-century scheme to squeeze the last drop of effort out of employees before quitting time, will not be disappointed. Kanigel does not hide Taylor's warts; his authoritarianism, his hucksterism, his casual approach to facts, his disregard for the human side of work—all are displayed. [The author] fully describes labor's initial disgust with Taylor's scheme and the subsequent decline of his reputation." And if Lehmann-Haupt, in a generally favorable *New York Times* assessment, found Kanigel guilty of occasional "disorganized ambiguity," Bettyann Kevles felt that the author did well by his controversial subject. "With dry wit and scrupulous attention to detail, Kanigel draws the portrait of a man who understood the manufacture of

steel far better than he understood the people who worked it," she stated in a *Washington Post Book World* review. "He is no less thorough in describing Taylor's marriage, which was childless until, in his forties, he adopted three brutally orphaned children [lavishing upon them] love and attention that they never forgot."

Kanigel turned to some of the classics in his 1998 publication, *Vintage Reading: From Plato to Bradbury.* He has described his collection of essays, which Lisa J. Cihlar for *Library Journal* described as "light and amusing," not as a review of all the books on the established academic canon of literary works but rather as a personal tour of some of his favorites. Some of the books that he discusses include Henry James's *The Portrait of a Lady,* Isadora Duncan's *My Life,* Lewis Carroll's *Alice's Adventures in Wonderland,* and Jane Austen's, *Pride and Prejudice.* It is through his essays, according to *Booklist* reviewer GraceAnne A. DeCandido, that readers are inspired to pick up the old favorites and read them again. De Candido also recommended this book as "fine fodder for book-discussion groups."

In 2002, Kanigel published *High Season: How One French Riviera Town Has Seduced Travelers for Two Thousand Years,* a history of Nice. In what Eileen Hardy of *Booklist* called a "witty, humorous style," Kanigel has recounted the passage of time, from the years of the Roman Empire to the contemporary moment, of people who have passed through this sunny resort of warm temperatures and beautiful beaches. In Nice, which shares the influences of both France and Italy, no matter what kind of lifestyle or economic station in life one comes from, at the beach everyone is considered an equal compatriot. The only dark spot on the reputation of this town occurred during the German occupation of France, a time during which many Jewish people were turned over to the Nazis and ultimately sent to their deaths at concentration camps.

*Library Journal* contributor Joseph L. Carlson found *High Season* to be "insightful"; while a reviewer from *Publishers Weekly* pointed out that Kanigel made a strong argument for Nice as "an indicator of social mores and fashions." In other words, what is happening in Nice is indicative of what will soon happen in the rest of the world. The town, after all, has attracted, and continues to attract, some of the most influential and most creative people in the world. If one taps into the thoughts, the actions, and even the lifestyles of these imaginative and significant people, then, supposedly, one would also be able to tap into predictable trends for the future.

*BIOGRAPHICAL AND CRITICAL SOURCES:*

*PERIODICALS*

*American Enterprise,* November-December, 1997, Martin Morse Wooster, review of *The One Best Way: Frederick Winslow Taylor and the Enigma of Efficiency,* p. 84.

*American Scientist,* July-August, 1992, Krishnaswami Alladi, review of *The Man Who Knew Infinity: A Life of the Genius Ramanujan,* pp. 388-89.

*Booklist,* May 1, 1997, David Rouse, review of *The One Best Way,* p. 1467; February 15, 1998, GraceAnne A. DeCandido, review of *Vintage Reading: From Plato to Bradbury: A Personal Tour of Some of the World's Best Books,* p. 968; December 1, 1998, Gilbert Taylor, review of *The Man Who Knew Infinity,* p. 636; June 1, 2002, Eileen Hardy, review of *High Season: How One French Riviera Town Has Seduced Travelers for Two Thousand Years,* p. 1670.

*Business Week,* July 7, 1997.

*Chicago Tribune,* December 30, 1986; May 18, 1997.

*Commentary,* November, 1997, Christopher Caldwell, review of *The One Best Way,* pp. 62-63.

*Commonweal,* October 25, 1991, review of *The Man Who Knew Infinity,* p. 620.

*Fortune,* July 21, 1997, Alan Farnham, review of *The One Best Way,* p. 114.

*Historian,* spring, 1993, Ben Rogers, review of *The Man Who Knew Infinity,* pp. 545-46.

*Isis,* December, 2000, Steven W. Usselman, review of *The One Best Way,* p. 818.

*Journal of the American Medical Association,* June 5, 1987.

*Kirkus Reviews,* April 1, 2002, review of *High Season,* p. 471.

*Labor History,* February 1999, Howell John Harris, review of *The One Best Way,* p. 96.

*Library Journal,* April 15, 1997, Dale F. Farris, review of *The One Best Way,* p. 1467; April 15, 1998, Lisa J. Cihlar, review of *Vintage Reading,* p. 80; May 15, 2002, Joseph L. Carlson, review of *High Season,* p. 116.

*Los Angeles Times,* December 23, 1986.

*New Leader,* May 19, 1997, Roger Draper, review of *The One Best Way,* pp. 3-4.

*New Scientist,* December 21, 1991, John Fauvel, review of *The Man Who Knew Infinity,* p. 70.

*New York Review of Books,* December 5, 1991, Ian Stewart, review of *The Man Who Knew Infinity,* p. 12; November 20, 1997, review of *The One Best Way,* pp. 32-37.

*New York Times,* May 20, 1991; June 15, 1997; August 11, 1997.

*New York Times Book Review,* July 21, 1991, p. 11.

*Publishers Weekly,* May 6, 2002, review of *High Season,* p. 45.

*Reason,* January, 1998, Brink Lindsey, review of *The One Best Way,* pp. 48-52.

*School Library Journal,* September, 1998, Catherine Charvat, review of *Vintage Reading,* p. 232.

*Science,* July 19, 1991, Jonathan M. Borwein and Peter B. Borwein, review of *The Man Who Knew Infinity,* pp. 334-35; October 24, 1997, Glenn Porter, review of *The One Best Way,* pp. 594-95.

*Sewanee Review,* spring, 1995, David Miller, review of *The Man Who Knew Infinity,* p. 26.

*Smithsonian,* July, 1992, Nina Mehta, review of *The Man Who Knew Infinity,* p. 123.

*Times Literary Supplement,* February 21, 1992, p. 22.

*Washington Post Book World,* November 30, 1986; November 3, 1991, p. 4; July 13, 1997, p. 8.

*Wilson Quarterly,* winter, 1992, review of *The Man Who Knew Infinity,* p. 108.*

\*     \*     \*

## KAPLAN, Robert B. 1929-

*PERSONAL:* Born September 20, 1929; son of E. B. (a physician) and Natalie (Iretzky) Kaplan; married Audrey A. Lien, April 21, 1951; children: Robin Ann, Lisa, Robert Allen. *Education:* Willamette University, A.B., 1952; University of Southern California, M.A., 1957, Ph.D., 1963. *Hobbies and other interests:* Collecting conchological specimens, weapons, and rare books.

*ADDRESSES: Office*—P.O. Box 577, Port Angeles, WA 98362.

*CAREER:* University of Oregon, Eugene, instructor in English, 1957-60; University of Southern California, Los Angeles, instructor in English Communication

Program for Foreign Students, 1961-62, coordinator of program, 1962-63, director of program, 1966-73, assistant professor of English, 1963-65, associate professor of English and linguistics, 1965-73, professor of applied linguistics, 1973-95, professor emeritus, 1995—, chairman of department of linguistics, 1967-69 and 1977-78, associate dean of Continuing Education, 1973-76, director of American Language Institute, 1986-91, distinguished visiting professor of applied linguistics, Meikai University, Japan, 1998-2000. Editor-in-chief, *Annual Review of Applied Linguistics*, Newbury House, 1979-84, Cambridge University Press, 1984—. Speaker at national and international conferences on linguistics and related areas. *Military service:* U.S. Army, 1953-55; served in Japan and Korea.

*MEMBER:* International Cultural Society of Korea (honorary fellow), American Association for Applied Linguistics (president, 1993-94), Linguistics Society of America, American Anthropological Association, American Association for the Advancement of Science, American Council of Teachers of Foreign Languages, National Council of Teachers of English, Conference on College Composition and Communication, National Association for Foreign Student Affairs (field service consultant, 1966-86; president, 1983), American Association of University Professors, Association of Teachers of English as a Second Language (president, 1968), Teachers of English to Speakers of Other Languages (president, 1990), English-Speaking Union, Canadian Council of Teachers of English, Royal Anthropological Institute of Great Britain and Ireland (fellow), Australian Association for Applied Linguistics.

*WRITINGS:*

*Reading and Rhetoric,* Odyssey (New York, NY), 1963.
*Teachers Guide to Transformational Grammar,* English Language Services, 1968.
*Learning English through Typewriting,* English Language Services, 1969.
*The Anatomy of Rhetoric: Prolegomena to a Functional Theory of Rhetoric; Essays for Teachers,* Center for Curriculum Development (Philadelphia, PA), 1972.
(Editor) *On the Scope of Applied Linguistics,* Newbury House (Rowley, MA), 1980.

*The Language Needs of Migrant Workers,* New Zealand Council for Educational Research (Wellington, New Zealand), 1980.
(With Peter A. Shaw) *Exploring Academic Discourse: A Textbook for Advanced Level ESL Reading and Writing Students,* Newbury House (Rowley, MA), 1984.
(Editor, with Ulla Connor) *Writing across Languages,* Addison-Wesley (Reading, MA), 1986.
(With William Grabe) *Introduction to Applied Linguistics,* Addison-Wesley (Reading, MA), 1992.
(With William Grabe) *Theory and Practice of Writing: An Applied Linguistic Perspective,* Longman (New York, NY), 1996.
(With Richard B. Baldauf) *Language Planning from Practice to Theory,* Multilingual Matters (Philadelphia, PA), 1997.
(Editor, with Richard B. Baldauf) *Language Planning in Malawi, Mozambique, and the Philippines,* Multilingual Matters (Philadelphia, PA), 1999.
(Editor, with Richard B. Baldauf) *Language Planning in Nepal, Taiwan, and Sweden,* Multilingual Matters (Philadelphia, PA), 2000.
(Editor) *The Oxford Handbook of Applied Linguistics,* Oxford University Press (New York, NY), 2002.
(With Bauldauf) *Language and Language-in-Education Planning in the Pacific Basin,* Kluwer (Dordrecht), 2003.

*CONTRIBUTOR*

*Preparing the EFL Teacher: A Projection for the Seventies,* Center for Curriculum Development (Philadelphia, PA), 1970.
Harold B. Allen, editor, *Teaching English As a Second Language: A Book of Readings,* McGraw-Hill (New York, NY), 2nd edition, 1972.
Kenneth Croft, editor, *Readings on English As a Second Language for Teachers and Teacher-Trainees,* Winthrop, 1972.
William B. Brickman and Stanley Lehrer, editors, *Education and the Many Faces of the Disadvantaged: Cultural and Historical Perspectives,* Wiley (New York, NY), 1972.
E. C. Polome and others, editors, *Linguistic and Literary Studies,* Mouton (Paris, France), 1979.
John F. Povey, editor, *Language Planning and Language Teaching: Essays in Honor of Clifford H. Prator,* English Language Services, 1980.
H. M. Jenkins, editor, *Students and Scholars in International Educational Exchange,* Jossey-Bass (San Francisco, CA), 1983.

Also contributor to W. Enninger and L. M. Haynes, editors, *Studies in Language Ecology,* 1984; E. G. Barber, P. G. Altman, and R. G. Myers, editors, *Bridges to Knowledge,* 1984; J. Valdes, editor, *Culture Bound,* 1986; C. Purves, editor, *Writing across Languages and Cultures: Issues in Contrastive Rhetoric,* 1988; D. M. Johnson and D. H. Roen, editors, *Richness in Writing,* 1989; R. B. Baldauf and A. Luke, editors, *Language Planning and Education in Australasia and the South Pacific,* 1990; H. Schröder, editor, *Subject-oriented Text: Languages for Special Purposes and Text Theory,* 1991; W. Bright, et al., editors, *International Encyclopedia of Linguistics,* 1991; S. Sirangi and M. Coulthard, editors, *Discourse and Social Life,* 1999; R. D. Gonzalez and I. Melis, editors, *Language Ideologies: Critical Perspectives on the Official English Movement,* 2000; P. M. Ryan and R. Terborg, editors, *Language: Issues of Inequality,* 2003.

Contributor of numerous research articles and reviews to scholarly journals in the United States, Australia, Brazil, Canada, Great Britain, Germany, Japan, the Philippines, and New Zealand.

*WORK IN PROGRESS:* Research projects in applied linguistics, in text linguistics, and in language planning, as well as in English-as-a-second-language teaching and testing.

*SIDELIGHTS:* Robert B. Kaplan is "reasonably proficient" in Russian and French, though he does linguistic work in a number of languages. He once told *CA,* "The titles of my writings are technical, largely concerned with language, but in all of them there is a basic concern to improve the human condition through a better understanding of how and why human beings use written language."

In 1999 Kaplan and coeditor Richard B. Baldauf inaugurated a new series, "Current Issues in Language Planning." Titles in the series include *Language Planning in Nepal, Taiwan and Sweden* and *Language Planning in Malawi, Mozambique and the Philippines.* Mohamed Maamouri in the *Comparative Education Review* stated that the series "is an important and most welcome addition to the international language policy and planning literature." In his *Comparative Education Review* piece on *Language Planning in Nepal, Taiwan and Sweden,* Maamouri contended that the work "is strongly recommended for the amount of in-

formation it provides to scholars interested in international comparative education." The critic added, "I believe that the studies presented here, and similar ones in the other series volumes, will significantly contribute, in the long run, to developing useful language policy and planning theoretical guidelines."

*BIOGRAPHICAL AND CRITICAL SOURCES:*

PERIODICALS

*Comparative Education Review,* August, 2001, Mohamed Maamouri, review of *Language Planning in Malawi, Mozambique and the Philippines,* p. 430; November, 2001, Mohamed Maamouri, review of *Language Planning in Nepal, Taiwan and Sweden,* p. 632.\*

\*    \*    \*

## KEENAN, Brian 1950-

*PERSONAL:* Born September 28, 1950, in Belfast, Northern Ireland; son of John Keenan (a telephone engineer) and Minnie Elizabeth (a weaver; maiden name, McClean) Keenan; married Audrey Doyle (a physiotherapist), May 20, 1993; children: one son. *Education:* Ulster University, B.A. (with honors), 1974, M.A., 1984; Queens University (Belfast), Ph.D., 1993.

*ADDRESSES: Office*—Department of English, Trinity College, Dublin 1, Ireland.

*CAREER:* Orangefield Boys School, Belfast, Northern Ireland, teacher, 1975-77; Belfast City Council, Belfast, communnity development officer, 1977-84; American University, Beirut, Lebanon, instructor in English, 1985-86; Trinity College, Dublin, Ireland, writer in residence, 1993—.

*AWARDS, HONORS:* Named Commander of the British Empire; winner of the International *Time-Life* Non-Fiction prize and the Ewart Biggs Award, both 1993; recipient of the *Irish Times* Award and the Christopher Award, both 1994.

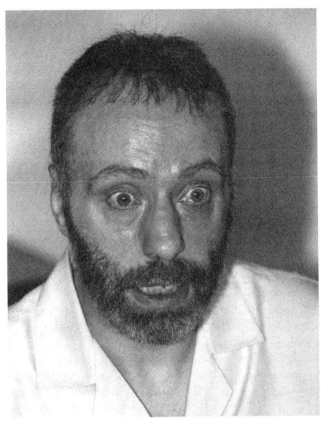

*Brian Keenan*

*WRITINGS:*

*An Evil Cradling: The Five-Year Ordeal of a Hostage* (an autobiography), Hutchinson, 1992, Viking (New York, NY), 1993.
(With John McCarthy) *Between Extremes* (nonfiction), Bantam Press (New York, NY), 1999.
*Turlough* (a novel), Jonathan Cape Random House (London, England), 2000.

Also author of *Blind Flight* (a screenplay), based on the experiences of both Keenan's and John McCarthy's imprisonment in Beirut.

*WORK IN PROGRESS: Swan upon a Darkening Flood.* Considering a book on Bernardo O'Higgins.

*SIDELIGHTS:* In his book *An Evil Cradling: The Five-Year Ordeal of a Hostage,* Brian Keenan writes of the fearful ordeal that catapulted him from obscurity into international headlines. A resident of Belfast, Northern Ireland, Keenan fled the ongoing civil strife there in

1985 for a change of scenery. He had accepted a teaching position in war-torn Lebanon at the American University in Beirut, but his academic year was interrupted when he was abducted by Islamic terrorists in April of 1986. Apparently simply looking for another Western citizen to add to a growing number of hostages, a group associated with the fundamentalist Islamic Jihad organization kidnapped Keenan, and he joined the infamous roster of English and American hostages held in the Middle East during the 1980s, including Church of England cleric Terry Waite and Associated Press bureau chief Terry Anderson. Keenan was released in August of 1990; *An Evil Cradling,* the chronicle of his harrowing experience, was published in England in 1992 and appeared the following year in the United States.

In the account of his captivity, Keenan attempts to describe the psychological trauma engendered by being blindfolded, beaten, starved, and confined to a filthy and minuscule cell for months on end. At a press conference shortly after his release, as quoted in the *Washington Post,* Keenan discussed the connotations hidden behind the word *hostage.* "'Hostage' is crucifying aloneness," he said. "There's a silent screaming slide into the bowels of despair. 'Hostage' is a man hanging by his fingernails over the edge of chaos, and feeling his fingers slowly straightening."

In *An Evil Cradling,* Keenan recounts the elaborate mental games he made up to keep his mind active and the ruses he and other captives invented to help relieve the stress of confinement. He narrates the occasional events of the long ordeal, such as the seventeen times that he was transferred to different holding locations throughout Lebanon and the daring but successful hunger strike he staged during the first months of captivity. Keenan also recounts the various relationships he developed both with other hostages and with the guards themselves. A good part of the book is devoted to his friendship with erstwhile cellmate John McCarthy, a British journalist, and the extreme sense of the absurd through which the two men began to see their world. This ironic detachment helped them to survive the darkest periods of depression during their captivity. Their detachment was also helped along by the sometimes bizarre behavior of their guards. Keenan describes the day one of his captors came into his cell to kindly offer him some peanuts, yet the man had disguised himself with an "ET" mask from the 1982 Hollywood film *ET: The Extra-Terrestrial.* Another time,

Keenan and other hostages were asked if they wished to convert and become Muslims, to which they held up their chains and replied, "No chance, pal."

Richard Beeston of the London *Times* deemed *An Evil Cradling* "a masterful chronicle of courage and resourcefulness." Beeston noted that published accounts of captivity are "a particularly difficult genre of narrative to master. But the wit and imagination which helped Keenan to survive his incarceration he also uses to bring alive his story." London *Observer* critic James Saynor remarked that the author "delivers some panoramic insights into human identity" in his account and thought Keenan's book "a story of mortification and self-mortification that's almost Scriptural in its resonances and its broad artistry, while being as gripping as an airport thriller."

Keenan once told *CA:* "As much as the five years confinement was a journey, the writing of the book was another journey into objective meaning. I promised myself when I sat down to write, 'be brutally honest' and 'don't descend into voyeurism.' The prophet Muhammad, in the Koran, advises his followers about hostage taking: 'Give them the Koran that they might take with them, when they leave, more than they possessed when they were first taken.' Ironically, that's what happened, no thanks to Muhammad or his followers. Though they stripped me of everything . . . I found treasure . . . a meaning for freedom that no man, nor the imaginings of mankind can ever take from me . . . not in ten thousand times, ten thousand years."

Six years after the publication of his first book, Keenan worked with John McCarthy, a fellow hostage, on a new book published in 1999, *Between Extremes: A Journey beyond Imagination,* which recounts their journey to Chile. As part of their desperate need to maintain their sanity during their four years in their Beirut prison cell, Keenan and McCarthy planned an imaginary trip to South America. They dreamed of moving there and raising yaks. Five years after being released, they realized at least part of their dream when they decided to visit the land that had sustained them; and *Between Extremes* is the result of that journey.

The authors alternate narratives in this book, recounting the extreme changes in geography as they travel from Arica to Tierra del Fuego. Their writing voices,

stated Margaret W. Norton in the *Library Journal,* were "filled with both humor and surprises." One of the more pleasant surprises for *New Statesman* reviewer John Hickman was not so much the details of their travels but rather "the appeal of their account" which "comprises the views of two people who understand each other so extraordinarily well."

Keenan also authored a book about an imaginary character who enticed him during his imprisonment, a story based on a seventeenth-century minstrel, whom Keenan claims also helped save his sanity while he was held all those long years in captivity. Turlough O'Carolan, an Irish musician, became the focus of Keenan's next book, a novel simply titled *Turlough,* published in 2000. Turlough, who played the harp and traveled all over Ireland, was blind, and in Keenan's mind, the bard visited him in his prison cell. For Keenan, Turlough became, according to Suzie Mackenzie for the London *Guardian,* "a way of distancing himself from what was happening to him. He helped to keep him sane." In the book, Keenan visits Turlough at his deathbed, and, as Mackenzie wrote, it is from this point that Keenan tells his story. Although there is much knowledge about the musician in terms of his art, little has been written about his emotions. This is the aspect of the Irish harpist's life that Keenan hoped to capture. "Turlough is reborn," wrote Mackenzie, "not as a musician, not as a historical character, but as a man." Although Turlough was a musician, the most prominent facet of his life that Keenan relates to is his blindness, according to John Morrish for London's *Independent Sunday.* Keenan himself spent many months blindfolded while he was a prisoner, and because of this experience, Keenan "is compelling on sightlessness, on the way it seems to foster the other senses and bring forward the inner life." The book has been widely praised.

In 2002, both Keenan and McCarthy agreed to recreate their four-year hostage ordeal in a feature film. Keenan has written the screenplay in collaboration with John Furse, the director. The film's working title is *Blind Flight.* Although filming was to begin in September, 2002, the terrorist attacks on the World Trade Center in New York City and the subsequent and continuing terrorist threats caused production to be postponed.

*BIOGRAPHICAL AND CRITICAL SOURCES:*

*PERIODICALS*

*Booklist,* September 15, 1993, Joe Collins, review of *An Evil Cradling,* pp. 121-22.

*Daily Telegraph* (London, England), October 7, 2000, Will Cohu, review of *Turlough.*

*Financial Times,* September 16, 2000, "A Genial Journey Dreamed Up in Hell," review of *Between Extremes,* p. 6.

*Guardian* (London, England), September 30, 2000, Suzie Mackenzie, "A Captive of History: In His Cell, Held Hostage in Beirut, Brian Keenan Had an Imaginary Companion," p. 36; November 11, 2000, Helen Falconer, "Terms of Imprisonment," review of *Turlough,* p. 12; December 1, 2001, p. 11.

*Independent Sunday* (London, England), September 12, 1999, "How We Met: John McCarthy and Brian Keenan," p. 59; September 26, 1999, "The Place That Changed Me: Brian Keenan; The Former Hostage and Now Author Looks for Inner Peace on the Western Edge of Ireland," p. 10; October 1, 2000, John Morrish, "Stirring Historical Stew; An Ambitious First Novel Pays Tribute to an Irish Harpist," p. 65.

*Library Journal,* March 15, 2002, Margaret W. Norton, review of *Between Extremes,* p. 99.

*Maclean's,* November 29, 1993, Scott Steele, review of *An Evil Cradling,* pp. 44-45.

*New Statesman,* November 1, 1999, John Hickman, review of *Between Extremes,* p. 57.

*New Yorker,* November 15, 1993, Michael Massing, review of *An Evil Cradling,* pp. 118-126.

*New York Times,* August 31, 1990, p. A3.

*Observer* (London, England), October 4, 1992, p. 60; September 24, 2000, Eldon King, review of *Between Extremes,* p. 14.

*Publishers Weekly,* August 30, 1993, review of *An Evil Cradling,* pp. 86-87.

*Time,* October 4, 1993, R. Z. Sheppard, review of *An Evil Cradling,* pp. 84-85.

*Times* (London, England), September 24, 1992.

*Times Literary Supplement,* March 12, 1993, p. 24.

*Washington Post,* September 1, 1990, p. A30.*

\*     \*     \*

**KENSINGTON, Kathryn Wesley**
**See RUSCH, Kristine Kathryn**

**KESSELL, John L(ottridge) 1936-**

*PERSONAL:* Born April 2, 1936, in East Orange, NJ; son of John S. (a physician) and Dorothy L. (a physician; maiden name, Lottridge) Kessell; married Marianne R., July 1, 1961; children: Kristen Anne. *Education:* Fresno State College (now California State University, Fresno), B.A., 1958; University of California, Berkeley, M.A., 1961; University of New Mexico, Ph.D. (history), 1969.

*ADDRESSES: Home*—823 Girard NE, Albuquerque, NM 87106.

*CAREER:* National Park Service, Washington, DC, historian at Saratoga National Historical Park, 1961-62, and Tumacacori National Monument, 1963-66; University of New Mexico, Albuquerque, visiting assistant professor of history, 1969-70; freelance historian and writer, 1970-80; University of New Mexico, Albuquerque, research associate to professor of history, beginning 1980.

*MEMBER:* Western Writers of America, Western History Association, Historical Society of New Mexico, Arizona Historical Society.

*AWARDS, HONORS:* Annual award from *New Mexico Historical Review,* 1966, for "The Puzzling Presidio: San Phelipe de Guevavi, alias Terrante"; Herbert E. Bolton Award, *Western Historical Quarterly,* 1973, for "Friars versus Bureaucrats: The Spanish Mission As a Threatened Institution on the Arizona-Sonora Frontier"; Spur Award, Western Writers of America, 1976, for *Friars, Soldiers, and Reformers;* award of honor, New Mexico Cultural Properties Review Committee, 1979, for *Kiva, Cross, and Crown;* Guggenheim fellowship, 1980-81.

*WRITINGS:*

(With Fay Jackson Smith and Francis J. Fox) *Father Kino in Arizona,* Arizona Historical Foundation (Tempe, AZ), 1966.

*Missions of Sorrows: Jesuit Guevavi and the Pimas, 1961-1767,* University of Arizona Press (Tucson, AZ), 1970.

*Friars, Soldiers, and Reformers: Hispanic Arizona and the Sonora Mission Frontier, 1767-1856,* University of Arizona Press (Tucson, AZ), 1976.

*Kiva, Cross, and Crown: The Pecos Indians and New Mexico, 1540-1840,* National Park Service (Washington, DC), 1979.

*The Missions of New Mexico since 1776,* University of New Mexico Press (Albuquerque, NM), 1980.

(With Sandra d'Emilio and Suzan Campbell) *Spirit and Vision: Images of Ranchos de Taos Church* (essays), Museum of New Mexico Press (Sante Fe, NM), 1987.

(Editor) *Remote beyond Compare: Letters of Don Diego de Vargas to His Family from Spain to New Mexico, 1675-1706,* University of New Mexico Press (Albuquerque, NM), 1989.

(Editor and author of introduction, with Rick Hendricks) *The Spanish Missions of New Mexico,* Garland (New York, NY), 1991.

(Editor, with Rick Hendricks) *By Force of Arms: The Journals of Don Diego de Vargas, New Mexico, 1691-1693,* University of New Mexico Press (Albuquerque, NM), 1992.

(With Rick Hendricks and Meredith D. Dodge) *Letters from the New World: Selected Correspondence of Don Diego de Vargas to His Family, 1675-1706,* University of New Mexico Press (Albuquerque, NM), 1992.

(Editor, with Rick Hendricks and Meredith D. Dodge) *To the Royal Crown Restored: The Journals of Don Diego de Vargas, New Mexico, 1692-94,* University of New Mexico Press (Albuquerque, NM), 1995.

(Editor, with Hendricks and Meredith D. Dodge) *Blood on the Boulders: The Journals of Don Diego de Vargas, New Mexico, 1694-97,* University of New Mexico Press (Albuquerque, NM), 1998.

(Editor, with others) *That Disturbances Cease: The Journals of Don Diego de Vargas, New Mexico, 1697-1700,* University of New Mexico Press (Albuquerque, NM), 2000.

(Editor, with others) *A Settling of Accounts: The Journals of Don Diego de Vargas, New Mexico, 1700-86,* University of New Mexico Press (Albuquerque, NM), 2002.

*Spain in the Southwest: A Narrative History of Colonial New Mexico, Arizona, Texas, and California,* University of Oklahoma Press (Norman, OK), 2002.

Contributor to *Reader's Encyclopedia of the American West.* Assistant editor of *New Mexico Historical Review,* 1970-72; editor of Vargas Project for the University of New Mexico, beginning 1980. Contributor to periodicals, including *Western Historical Quarterly.*

*SIDELIGHTS:* John L. Kessell is a career historian and professor whose writings explore the people and events of the early Southwest. One of his many roles at the University of New Mexico has been as the director of the Vargas Project, an effort to chronicle the life of pioneer Don Diego de Vargas. Kessell's work on this project and his access to journals has resulted in numerous books about Vargas. In the *American Indian Quarterly,* Peter L. Steere praised *By Force of Arms* for offering "excellent illustrations, maps, footnotes, a glossary, a bibliography, and an index," adding that the "Vargas project staff should be complimented for this . . . volume which provides an extraordinarily detailed picture of Don Diego de Vargas' official life."

Other books focus on how groups of people influenced the early years in regional history. *Friars, Soldiers, and Reformers: Hispanic Arizona and the Sonora Mission Frontier, 1767-1856,* for example, considers the role played by missionaries and other religious-minded pioneers in Arizona. Reviewing the books for the *Journal of San Diego History* Web site, Cynthia Radding Murrieta called the book "a masterpiece of the historian's craft" and a "major contribution to the historiography of Northwest Mexico and the U. S. Southwest," adding that it is "both a beautiful story and a model of historical research." Specifically, she concluded that "the book's greatest strength is the author's masterful use of voluminous Franciscan and civil documentation available in both Mexican and U. S. archives." In *Spain and the Southwest,* he integrates numerous accounts and narratives of the Spanish presence in the settlement and growth of the Southwest. A *Publishers Weekly* reviewer commended Kessell for his handling of more than 350 years of history, adding, "In an era of multiculturalism . . . this synthesis of the founding history of a large part of the nation not usually considered a seedbed of American culture is surely welcome."

Kessell once told *CA:* "After ten years as a freelance historical researcher, or contract historian, I do not recommend it as a career. It has been precarious. I have achieved neither fame nor financial security. I have done local history, which I feel deserves one's best shot. Never presuming that it might free the locals from repeating their errors, I do reckon that it may at times enlighten and reassure them, even make them laugh. It has been good fun. And there is something to be said for getting out on one's cross-country skis right when the snow falls, especially in the Southwest."

*BIOGRAPHICAL AND CRITICAL SOURCES:*

*PERIODICALS*

*American Historical Review,* June, 1989, p. 838.
*American Indian Quarterly,* summer, 1993, Peter L. Steere, review of *By Force of Arms: The Journals of Don Diego de Vargas, New Mexico, 1691-1693,* p. 414.
*American West,* January, 1980, p. 50.
*Catholic Historical Review,* January, 1980, p. 99; January, 1983, p. 109.
*Choice,* December, 1980, p. 518.
*Church History,* September, 1980, p. 339; December, 1982, p. 496.
*Hispanic American Historical Review,* February, 1980, p. 115; August, 1981, p. 512.
*History,* April, 1980, p. 122.
*Mid-America,* January, 1980, p. 47.
*Museum News,* January, 1980, p. 71.
*Pacific Historical Review,* May, 1982, p. 211.
*Publishers Weekly,* April 1, 2002, review of *Spain in the Southwest: A Narrative History of Colonial New Mexico, Arizona, Texas, and California,* p. 63.
*Reference and Research Book News,* April, 1988, p. 5; June, 1993, p. 14.
*San Diego History,* spring, 1977.
*Southwest Review,* winter, 1981, p. R6.
*Western Historical Quarterly,* May, 1993, p. 237.

*ONLINE*

*Journal of San Diego History,* http://www.sandiego history.org/ (July 14, 2003), Cynthia Radding Murrieta, review of *Friars, Soldiers, and Reformers: Hispanic Arizona and the Sonora Mission Frontier, 1767-1856.*\*

## KIM, In S(oo) 1943-

*PERSONAL:* Born November 23, 1943, in Seoul, Korea; son of Young Soon (an architect) and Ock Ja (Han) Kim; married Jung Sook Chung, May 22, 1970; children: Soo Jin, Hye Jin. *Ethnicity:* "Korean/Asian." *Education:* Presbyterian Theological Seminary, M.Div., 1969; Dubuque Theological Seminary, S.T.M., 1975; Union Theological Seminary in Virginia, Ph.D., 1993. *Religion:* Presbyterian.

*ADDRESSES: Office*—Presbyterian College and Theological Seminary, 353 Kwang Jang-dong, Kwang Jin-ku, Seoul, Korea 143-756; fax: 02-446-3437. *E-mail*—iskim@acha.pcts.ac.kr.

*CAREER:* Presbyterian College and Theological Seminary, Seoul, Korea, professor of church history, dean of seminary, and director of museum, 1982—. *Military service:* Korean Army, chaplain; became captain.

*MEMBER:* Northeast Asia Accredited Theological Schools (general secretary), Korea Association of Accredited Theological Schools (general secretary), Society of Church History of Korea (president).

*WRITINGS:*

*Protestants and the Formation of Modern Korean Nationalism, 1885-1920: A Study of the Contributions of Horace G. Underwood and Sun Chu Kil,* Peter Lang (New York, NY), 1996.
*Han'guk Kidok kyohoesa,* Presbyterian College and Theological Seminary Press (Seoul, Korea), 1994, translated as *History of the Christian Church in Korea,* 1997.
*P'yongsindo wa kyohoe hakkyo kyosa rul wihan kanch'urin Han'guk kyohoe ui yoksa* (title means "Brief History of the Christian Church in Korea"), Presbyterian College and Theological Seminary Press (Seoul, Korea), 1998.
*History of the 100 Years of the Presbyterian College and Theological Seminary,* Presbyterian College and Theological Seminary Press (Seoul, Korea), 2002.

## KINSELLA, Thomas 1928-

*PERSONAL:* Surname accented on first syllable; born May 4, 1928, in Dublin, Ireland; son of John Paul (a trade unionist and brewery worker) and Agnes (Casserly) Kinsella; married Eleanor Walsh, December 28, 1955; children: Sara, John, Mary. *Education:* University College, Dublin, diploma in public administration, 1949.

*ADDRESSES: Home*—Killalane, Laragh, County Wicklow, Ireland. *Office*—English Department, Temple University, Philadelphia, PA 19103, and Peppercanister Press, 47 Percy Ln., Dublin 4, Ireland.

*CAREER:* Poet. Irish Civil Service, Dublin, Ireland, Land Commission, junior executive officer, 1946-50, Department of Finance, administrative officer, 1950-60, assistant principal officer, 1960-65; Southern Illinois University at Carbondale, poet-in-residence, 1965-67, professor of English, 1967-70; Temple University, Philadelphia, PA, professor of English, 1970-90, founding director, Temple-in-Dublin Irish Tradition program, 1976—. Founding director, Peppercanister Press, Dublin, 1972—; director, Dolmen Press Ltd. and Cuala Press Ltd., Dublin. Artistic director, Lyric Players Theatre, Belfast, Ireland.

*MEMBER:* Irish Academy of Letters.

*AWARDS, HONORS:* Guinness Poetry Award, 1958, for *Another September;* Irish Arts Council Triennial Book Award, 1961, for *Poems and Translations;* Denis Devlin Memorial Award, 1964-66, for *Wormwood,* 1967-69, for *Nightwalker and Other Poems,* and 1988 and 1994; Guggenheim fellowships, 1968-69, 1971-72; Before Columbus Foundation award, 1983; D.Litt., National University of Ireland, 1984. *Another September* and *Downstream* were Poetry Book Society choices.

*WRITINGS:*

*POETRY*

*The Starlit Eye,* Dolmen Press (Dublin, Ireland), 1952.
*Three Legendary Sonnets,* Dolmen Press (Dublin, Ireland), 1952.

*Per Imaginem,* Dolmen Press (Dublin, Ireland), 1953.
*The Death of a Queen,* Dolmen Press (Dublin, Ireland), 1956.
*Poems,* Dolmen Press (Dublin, Ireland), 1956.
*Another September,* Dolmen Press (Dublin, Ireland), 1958, revised edition, 1962.
*Moralities,* Dolmen Press (Dublin, Ireland), 1960.
*Poems and Translations,* Atheneum (New York, NY), 1961.
(With John Montague and Richard Murphy) *Three Irish Poets,* Dolmen Press (Dublin, Ireland), 1961.
*Downstream,* Dolmen Press (Dublin, Ireland), 1962.
*Wormwood,* Dolmen Press (Dublin, Ireland), 1966.
*Nightwalker and Other Poems,* Dolmen Press (Dublin, Ireland), 1967.
(With Douglas Livingstone and Anne Sexton) *Poems,* Oxford University Press (New York, NY), 1968.
*Nightwalker and Other Poems,* Dolmen Press (Dublin, Ireland), 1968, Knopf (New York, NY), 1969.
*Tear,* Pym-Randall (Cambridge, MA), 1969.
*Finistere,* Dolmen Press (Dublin, Ireland), 1971.
*Notes from the Land of the Dead: Poems,* Cuala Press (Dublin, Ireland), 1972, published as *Notes from the Land of the Dead and Other Poems,* Knopf (New York, NY), 1973.
*Butcher's Dozen: A Lesson for the Octave of Widgery,* Peppercanister (Dublin, Ireland), 1972, revised edition, 1992.
*A Selected Life,* Peppercanister (Dublin, Ireland), 1972.
*Vertical Man: A Sequel to A Selected Life,* Peppercanister (Dublin, Ireland), 1973.
*The Good Fight: A Poem for the Tenth Anniversary of the Death of John F. Kennedy,* Peppercanister (Dublin, Ireland), 1973.
*New Poems, 1973,* Dolmen Press (Dublin, Ireland), 1973.
*Selected Poems, 1956-1968,* Dolmen Press (Dublin, Ireland), 1973.
*One* (also see below), Peppercanister (Dublin, Ireland), 1974.
*A Technical Supplement,* Peppercanister (Dublin, Ireland), 1975.
*Song of the Night and Other Poems,* Peppercanister (Dublin, Ireland), 1978.
*The Messenger,* Peppercanister (Dublin, Ireland), 1978.
*Poems, 1956-1973,* Wake Forest University Press, 1979.
*Peppercanister Poems, 1972-1978* (also see below), Wake Forest University Press (Winston-Salem, NC), 1979.
*Fifteen Dead* (also see below), Dufour (Dublin, Ireland), 1979.

*Peppercanister Poems, 1972-1978* [and] *Fifteen Dead,* Wake Forest University Press (Winston-Salem, NC), 1979.

*One and Other Poems,* Dolmen Press (Dublin, Ireland), 1979.

*Poems, 1956-76,* Dolmen Press (Dublin, Ireland), 1980.

*One Fond Embrace,* Deerfield Press (Hatfield, MA), 1981.

*Songs of the Psyche,* Peppercanister (Dublin, Ireland), 1985.

*Her Vertical Smile,* Peppercanister (Dublin, Ireland), 1985.

*Out of Ireland,* Peppercanister (Dublin, Ireland), 1987.

*St. Catherine's Clock,* Peppercanister (Dublin, Ireland), 1987.

*Blood and Family,* Oxford University Press (New York, NY), 1989.

*Personal Places,* Dedalus (Dublin, Ireland), 1990.

*Poems from Centre City,* Dedalus (Dublin, Ireland), 1990.

*Open Court,* Peppercanister (Dublin, Ireland), 1991.

*Madonna and Other Poems,* Peppercanister (Dublin, Ireland), 1991.

*Collected Poems, 1956-1994,* Oxford University Press (New York, NY), 1996.

*The Pen Shop,* Dufour Editions (Chester Springs, PA), 1997.

*The Familiar,* Dufour Editions (Chester Springs, PA), 1999.

*Godhead,* Dufour Editions (Chester Springs, PA), 1999.

*Citizen of the World,* Dufour Editions (Chester Springs, PA), 2000.

*Littlebody,* Dufour Editions (Chester Springs, PA), 2000.

*TRANSLATOR FROM THE GAELIC*

*The Breastplate of Saint Patrick,* Dolmen Press (Dublin, Ireland), 1954, published as *Faeth Fiada: The Breastplate of Saint Patrick,* 1957.

*Longes Mac n-Usnig, Being the Exile and Death of the Sons of Usnech,* Dolmen Press (Dublin, Ireland), 1954.

*Thirty Three Triads,* Dolmen Press (Dublin, Ireland), 1955.

*The Tain,* Dolmen Press (Dublin, Ireland), 1969, Oxford University Press (New York, NY), 1970, reprinted, 1985.

(With Sean O'Tuama) Sean O'Tuama, editor, *An Duanaire—An Irish Anthology: Poems of the Dispossessed, 1600-1900,* Dolmen Press (Dublin, Ireland), 1980, University of Pennsylvania Press (Philadelphia, PA), 1981.

*OTHER*

(Contributing editor) *The Dolmen Miscellany of Irish Writing,* Dolmen Press (Dublin, Ireland), 1962.

(With W. B. Yeats) *Davis, Mangan, Ferguson?: Tradition and the Irish Writer* (essays), Dolmen Press (Dublin, Ireland), 1970.

(Editor) Austin Clarke, *Selected Poems,* Wake Forest University Press (Winston-Salem, NC), 1976.

(Editor) Sean O'Riada, *Our Musical Heritage* (lectures on Irish traditional music), Gael-Linn, 1981.

(Editor and translator from the Gaelic) *The New Oxford Book of Irish Verse,* Oxford University Press (New York, NY), 1986.

(With John Montague and Brendan Kennelly) *Myth, History, and Literary Tradition,* Dundalk Arts (Dundalk, Ireland), 1989.

*The Dual Tradition: An Essay on Poetry and Politics in Ireland,* Carcanet (Manchester, England), 1995.

Also contributor of poetry to *Six Irish Poets,* edited by Robin Skelton, Oxford University Press (New York, NY), 1962. Recorded *Patrick Galvin and Thomas Kinsella Reading Their Poems* (sound cassette), 1980.

*SIDELIGHTS:* In a *New York Times Book Review* article, Calvin Bedient maintained that Thomas Kinsella "can hardly write a worthless poem." He is "probably the most accomplished, fluent, and ambitious Irish poet of the younger generation," according to *New York Times Book Review* critic John Montague, while *Dictionary of Literary Biography* essayist Thomas H. Jackson judged that Kinsella's "technical virtuosity and the profound originality of his subject matter set him apart from his contemporaries." He "seems to me to have the most distinctive voice of his generation in Ireland, though it is also the most versatile and the most sensitive to 'outside' influences," M. L. Rosenthal indicated in *The New Poets: American and British Poetry since World War II.*

Kinsella has described himself as coming from "a typical Dublin family," Jackson reported. His father, a longtime socialist, was a member of the Labour Party and the Left Book Club, and by means of a series of grants and scholarships Kinsella pursued a science degree at University College in Dublin, where he ultimately obtained a diploma in public administration. He entered the Irish civil service in 1946, but, with the encouragement of his wife in particular, also pursued his craft. During those early years, he met Liam Miller, founder of Dolmen Press, who published several of Kinsella's works; later, Kinsella became a director of the press. He also established an important friendship at that time with Sean O'Riada, a musician described by a *Times Literary Supplement* critic as "the most distinguished of modern Irish composers," who became, in Jackson's words, "a much-loved participant in [Kinsella's] growing intellectual life. O'Riada expressed in his life as much as in his music what seems to be a current Irish ambition in the arts—namely, to contain the world in the capacious and elegant vessel of the Irish imagination and tradition," explained the *Times Literary Supplement* critic.

Kinsella, too, "has explored Irish themes more and more in his later verse," wrote Jackson, "but only in terms of exploring his own consciousness and consciousness in general." His poems since 1956, Kinsella once told *CA,* have been "almost entirely lyrical—have dealt with love, death and the artistic act; with persons and relationships, places and objects, seen against the world's processes of growth, maturing and extinction." By the time he wrote *Nightwalker and Other Poems,* which was first published in 1968, he had become "more and more concerned—in longer poems—with questions of value and order, seeing the human function (in so far as it is not simply to survive the ignominies of existence) as the eliciting of order from experience—the detection of the significant substance of the individual and common past and its translation imaginatively, scientifically, bodily, into an increasingly coherent and capacious entity; or the attempt to do this, to the point of failure." A *Times Literary Supplement* reviewer characterized Kinsella's earlier poems as "on the whole less distraughtly introspective than [his more] recent work" but indicated that "they display the same fine knack of delving deeply into self-communion while staying nervously responsive to an actual world."

"All Kinsella's finest [early] poems are written in partial forfeiture to the inevitable destruction of life and pleasure," Calvin Bedient stated in *Eight Contemporary Poets.* The theme of his first major collection *An-*

*other September,* according to Jackson, "is order, the fruit of art, which in Kinsella's view is one major form of the mind's stance against mutability and corruption." Most of the poems in that volume, particularly "Baggot Street Deserta," confront "with stoic acceptance the grim fact of loss as a chief keynote of life," Jackson commented. In Kinsella's eyes "life is a tide of loss, disorder, and corruption, and the poetic impulse is an impulse to stem that tide, to place form where time leaves disorder and pain." Kinsella's collection *Downstream,* which includes five poems published earlier as *Moralities,* also conveys a "preoccupation with the passing of time—change as dying, change as birth—that has marked Kinsella's poetic mind from very early on," noted Jackson.

In *Downstream* Kinsella "turns more to the things people actually do in and with their lives. That many of the poems' titles refer to jobs, types of people, and life choices signals the linkage of the temporal and the abstract, the deeply buried and the visibly lived." This volume includes the "earliest of Kinsella's journey poems," pointed out Jackson, including "A Country Walk" and "Downstream." And in the opinion of John D. Engle in *Parnassus,* these are Kinsella's "most lasting early poems."

Beginning with *Downstream* and continuing with the short sequence *Wormwood* and the cumulative *Nightwalker and Other Poems,* "Kinsella emerged as a master not of slick verse but more saddened, more naked, more groping—of a poetry of subdued but unrelenting power," Bedient stated. "Here surfaced a poetry that, if almost completely without a surprising use of words, all being toned to a grave consistency, has yet the eloquence of a restrained sorrow, a sorrow so lived-in that it seems inevitable. With its sensitive density of mood, its unself-conscious manner, there is nothing in this poetry for other poets to imitate. Its great quality is the modesty and precision of its seriousness."

The poem "Nightwalker" itself is "a long nocturnal meditation on Ireland past and present, on the poet's consciousness as a source of order amid decay and betrayal," Jackson related. In the view of Dennis Paoli, writing in *Encyclopedia of World Literature in the Twentieth Century,* through the *Nightwalker* collection Kinsella laments "the near destruction of the Irish language in the [eighteenth century] and satirizes its institutionalization in the [twentieth]."

The culminating entry in *Nightwalker and Other Poems,* "Phoenix Park," is a journey poem described by

Jackson as "an ambitious composition that shows how far the poet has come since his earliest work. The title is the name of Dublin's largest park, but it bears connotation of the phoenix itself, the bird that rises from the ashes of its own cremation to live another millennium." John Montague, writing in *New York Times Book Review,* referred to the poem as the poet's "farewell to Ireland, in the shape of a drive with his wife along the Liffey [River], as well as an extension of the theme of married love." The poet and his wife, who are about to leave Dublin, drive past "various places meaningful to them," according to Jackson, and "the poet recalls their significance or associations . . . ; he reviews symbolic moments of his life, where he partook of possibilities which his children came to pursue or re-enact."

Modern travel poems like these face "a solitary consciousness towards place and time yet do not, as it were, sit still, are not even ostensibly at rest, but move through the world, continually stimulated to new observations, reactions, associations," Bedient observed. "Cast through space, these poems bring a flutter to the tentativeness of consciousness, which they heighten. They ride on motion the way, and at the same time as, the mind floats on duration. . . . They say that life is only here and now, and fleeting, a thing that cannot stand still," Bedient explained, "and more, that space is as unfathomably deep as time, in time's body, but at least outside ourselves, both mercifully and cruelly outside. The poems increase the sense of exposure to existence as actual travel renews and magnifies the sensation of living."

As the couple in "Phoenix Park" pass by familiar landmarks, Jackson reported, "the lovers' marriage is seen as a powerful form which overcomes loss and the chaos of life. Their love is 'the one positive dream' to which the speaker of 'Phoenix Park' refers as the exception to the fact that 'There's a fever now that eats everything.' . . . He expatiates on the implications of their love as evincing the 'laws of order,' on their love as ordeal, a continual wounding and healing, and a continual growing, and arrives at a sense of existence as a necessary ordeal—when we think we have attained some abstract 'ultimate,' living must end."

After the publication of *Nightwalker and Other Poems,* Kinsella left the civil service to enter academic life and become a full-time writer. He also set up Peppercanister Press at his home in Dublin, primarily to

publish limited editions of his works in progress. *Butcher's Dozen: A Lesson for the Octave of Widgery,* the press's first publication, was described by M. L. Rosenthal in the *New York Times Book Review* as a "rough-hewn, deliberately populist dream-visionary poem" on the 1972 shooting-down of thirteen demonstrators in Derry by British troopers and the investigation that followed. But, according to Edna Longley in the *Times Literary Supplement,* "despite these latent social and political contours," Kinsella's writing "overwhelmingly takes the traditional form of self-searching. (It is a deeper question whether the extreme isolation of his poetic persona owes more to culture than to idiosyncrasy.)"

*Butcher's Dozen* was revised in 1992 to mark the twentieth anniversary of the slayings. In 1999 *Explicator* critic Neville Newman revisited the poem and found that "phantoms represent the dead civilians and address a variety of national and cultural issues." In the poem, the bitter irony Kinsella uses to describe the attack takes the form of a satire on the children's rhyme "Tom, Tom the Farmer's Son." "The pig of the children's verse becomes the acronym by which the armored personnel carriers of the type deployed against the protesters are known," noted Newman. A reference to a "hooligan" running away puns on the Irish surname Houlihan, reflecting "the way that a long-established anti-Irish bias on the part of the British has passed into day-to-day language." And Kinsella's poetic assessment of the official investigation—which failed to prove that the Irish protesters were armed at the time they were killed—provides "observation that a life was lost for nothing more than 'throwing stones,'" as Newman quoted Kinsella, and "emphasizes the overreaction of the British to the incident."

Kinsella once indicated to *CA* that his poetry of this time begins to involve a turning "downward into the psyche toward origin and myth," and that it is "set toward some kind of individuation." The theme of his next major work, *Notes from the Land of the Dead and Other Poems,* according to a *Times Literary Supplement* critic, "is the spiritual journey from despair and desolation, 'nightnothing,' to a painful self-renewal." The poems in this work abandon syntax, Jackson commented, "because they have left the world to which syntax is relevant and moved to the world of dream, phantasm, and myth, the world in short of psychic exploration."

The volume includes an untitled prologue that Jackson described "as a mystical version of a Kinsellan wandering poem [which] recounts the speaker's descent into a psychic underworld, a reversion to the embryo stage." And "the low point of coherent consciousness in this exploration is [the poem] 'All Is Emptiness and Must Spin,'" related Jackson. John D. Engle explained in *Parnassus* that in *Notes from the Land of the Dead and Other Poems,* "Kinsella heads down, a quest hero, into the past and subconscious; he would retrieve the scary flotsam of memory, a dying old harpy of a grandmother or, perhaps, obsessive shadowplays drawn from a childhood reading of the *Book of Invasions,* Ireland's ancient and wild Genesis. After the confusing bobs and weaves of something like a plot, he bears back his prize: a new awareness, at once modest and enough to change one's life."

Discussing *Notes from the Land of the Dead and Other Poems* in the *New York Times Book Review,* Bedient found Kinsella's style "an almost constant pleasure," but also complained that, here, "Ireland's best living poet has brooded himself to pieces." Vernon Young mentioned in *Parnassus* the fact that, for many years, Kinsella translated "The Tain," an eighth-century Irish epic, "and in that translation you can find both the savage emblems and the bleak outlook of the independent poems [in *Notes from the Land of the Dead and Other Poems*]: as if the repetitive sanguinary deeds of the epic (to my mind a monotonously vindictive chronicle without a tremor of mercy or grace) had been used to compound the lethal evidence of mindless struggle forecast by the origin of the species."

However, Engle remarked that "the poetry of *Notes* is not as extravagantly disheveled as it occasionally seems, and what comes dressed as nihilism turns out to be something else." Kinsella was influenced by Jung, according to Jackson, and "where the earlier work was so concerned with the idea of suffering and pain as the motives of growth, the ordeal as a linear meeting of successive tests, these new poems take up the Jungian idea of a creative union of opposites. The ordeal of suffering and growth becomes the more comprehensive rhythm of destruction and creation, decay and regeneration, death and birth."

Kinsella continues in the same thematic direction with *Peppercanister Poems, 1972-1978,* which, along with the poem "Butcher's Dozen," includes meditations on the deaths of Kinsella's father and his friend, Sean O'Riada, and, according to Jackson, several poems "dealing with the poet's family history and himself as artist." And in an eight-poem sequence "One," Engle commented, Kinsella "plunges again through the crust of appearance into this region of process and origin. The eight poems send his thoughts again into a hoard of personal and common memory, back to his own childhood and further still to merge with those of Ireland's first wave of settlers. . . . This is Jung country."

"Jung and Kinsella's idea that creation and destruction, love and hate, life and death are interinvolved is an attempt to reclaim the wholeness of existence, not to deny its beauty," Jackson commented. "The poems here actually enact that stance: out of the death of a friend, of a father, or political matters comes poetry before our very eyes. Nor is being rooted in the prerational the same as being confined to it." Kinsella, Engle indicated, "is at home now in darkness, the secret shadows where we create and were created. If he invites us into a world that at times proves too elaborately personal, if he tries to do too much with his poems, these are generous blunders. They shouldn't obscure the fact that Kinsella is a serious poet of invention and honesty." Rosenthal concluded that "he is among the true poets, not only of Ireland but among all who write in English in our day."

*Blood and Family* is a collection of five of Kinsella's pamphlets, originally published by his own Peppercanister Press. The sections (originally pamphlets) of the book, which "include a sequence about the poet's childhood, a homage to Mahler, and an elegy for . . . Sean O'Riada, find their orders in disorder," noted William Logan in the *New York Times Book Review.* Noting the popularity of younger Irish poets, Logan continued, "Mr. Kinsella can still entertain the tragic possibilities, and his powerful recollective passions serve as an affront to a present that can only serve the past. His new poems are his darkest, and the least vulnerable to easy understanding." Kieran Quinlan, writing for *World Literature Today,* also commented on the complexity of the work, concluding, "This is difficult poetry that will offer only to some its hard-won satisfactions."

*Personal Places* and *Poems from Centre City,* both published in 1990, "extend and enrich" the poet's "focal emphasis on the most immediate and vivid data of concrete personal experience," found Tom Halpin in his review for the *Irish Literary Supplement.* To Halpin "the former deals with endings and beginnings, the dislocations inseparable from any attempt at continuity," while *Poems from Centre City* focuses on Kinsella's life in Dublin, including his writing mentors and family memories. Of *Poems from Centre City,* Elizabeth Gaffney stated in the *New York Times Book Review* that "the visions of Ireland in this idiosyncratic, melancholy collection ultimately cohere around the suggestion that another path might have permitted fulfillment of greater passion," while *Times Literary Supplement* contributor Steven Matthews felt that "the concentrated, vigorous, passionate sense of loss and betrayal in this book promises a revelatory renewal beyond the limits of our foul ascending city." Adam Thorpe, writing in the *Listener,* praised both volumes as "worth their weight in gold," finding them "both harrowing and uplifting." Halpin concluded, "In *Personal Places* and *Poems from Centre City* the sure-footed control of Kinsella's voice—a variegated blend of sorrow, compassion, love, anger and humor—earns at the end of each sequence its right to affirm and celebrate, however paradoxically but with no hint of irony, the capacity of poetry to face the worst within and without, and more than weather it in the process of imaginative transformation."

In *The Dual Tradition: An Essay on Poetry and Politics in Ireland,* Kinsella examines the concept that "Literature in Ireland is not divided but dual, and to consider either of its parts in isolation from the other is to diminish both," as Patricia Craig wrote in the *Times Literary Supplement.* This refers in part to "the hidden Ireland," or the Ireland unknown to the non-Irish speaker. Kinsella, like Yeats, writes about this "hidden Ireland," but is not a Gaelic speaker. According to Carol Rumens in the *New Statesman & Society,* Kinsella had examined this personal divide in his 1966 composition for the Modern Language Association, but she found that "his prose [in *The Dual Tradition*] carries little of that earlier energy and conviction." "He offers a politically sensitized historic overview that nevertheless reflects a poet's primary concerns," felt Rosenthal, this time writing for *Ploughshares.* In a review for *World Literature Today,* William Pratt recommended *The Dual Tradition* to "any reader who is not Irish, since it makes distinctions that are exclusively ethnic, unrelated to artistic merit." Craig concluded that the book adds up to "a succinct history of poetry in Ireland, in Irish and English—a brisk run through the centuries."

As the twentieth century drew to a close, Kinsella produced the 1997 collection *The Pen Shop* and followed

that with such *fin-de-siècle* works as *The Familiar, Godhead,* and *Citizen of the World. The Pen Shop* finds the poet on a "leisurely stroll though Dublin," according to Pratt of *World Literature Today,* where Kinsella writes of such places as the O'Connell Bridge, Bewley's Oriental Café, and the titular Pen Shop. Pratt found all this "evocative of [James] Joyce's Dublin," particularly in Kinsella's mixing of reality and fantasy. But the reviewer also wondered if Kinsella had deliberately set out to produce poems Pratt characterized as "slight." In the critic's view, "Kinsella seems to be frittering away his talents in trivialities at this late point in his career." "Slight," though, was hardly the word David Lloyd used to describe the 2001 collection, *Citizen of the World.* Indeed, "this is [poetry] that doesn't pander to the reader," wrote Lloyd. "Few people or places are identified beyond the briefest phrase, few situations fleshed out, or social or historical contexts illuminated." The title piece is a portrait of the English novelist Oliver Goldsmith, using a quote from the writer to explore the theme of a mind "not at ease."

The poetry of Kinsella, as George O'Brien summed up in the *Reference Guide to English Literature,* "is a commitment to negotiate the leap of artistic faith which alone can overcome the abyss of unjustifiable unknowing that is the mortal lot." O'Brien singled out Kinsella's "composed and graceful suspension" and concluded that his "anti-romantic conception of poetry, which entails giving tongue to darkness rather than to fire, identifies Kinsella as a crucial reviser of the Irish poetic tradition and a major figure in the problematic history of poetry in English during the postwar years."

## BIOGRAPHICAL AND CRITICAL SOURCES:

*BOOKS*

Badin, Donatella Abbate, *Thomas Kinsella,* Twayne, 1996.

Bedient, Calvin, *Eight Contemporary Poets,* Oxford University Press (New York, NY), 1974.

*Contemporary Literary Criticism,* Gale (Detroit, MI), Volume 4, 1975, Volume 19, 1981.

*Dictionary of Literary Biography,* Volume 27: *Poets of Great Britain and Ireland, 1945-1960,* Gale (Detroit, MI), 1984.

Dunn, Douglas, editor, *Two Decades of Irish Writing,* Dufour, 1975.

*Encyclopedia of World Literature in the Twentieth Century,* St. James Press (Detroit, MI), 1999, pp. 639-640.

Harmon, Maurice, *The Poetry of Thomas Kinsella: "With Darkness for a Nest,"* Wolfhound Press, 1974.

Jackson, Thomas H., *The Whole Matter: The Poetic Evolution of Thomas Kinsella,* Syracuse University Press (Syracuse, NY), 1995.

John, Brian, *Reading the Ground: The Poetry of Thomas Kinsella,* Catholic University of America Press, 1996.

Kersnowski, Frank L., *The Outsiders: Poets of Contemporary Ireland,* Texas Christian University Press, 1975.

Kinsella, Thomas, *Nightwalker and Other Poems,* Knopf (New York, NY), 1969.

Kinsella, Thomas, *Notes from the Land of the Dead and Other Poems,* Knopf (New York, NY), 1973.

Orr, Peter, editor, *The Poet Speaks: Interviews with Contemporary Poets,* Routledge, 1966.

*Reference Guide to English Literature,* second edition, St. James Press (Detroit, MI), 1991, pp. 817-818.

Rosenthal, M. L., *The New Poets: American and British Poetry since World War II,* Oxford University Press (New York, NY), 1967.

Rosenthal, M. L., *Poetry and the Common Life,* Oxford University Press (New York, NY), 1974.

*Viewpoints: Poets in Conversation with John Haffenden,* Faber, 1981.


PERIODICALS


*Agenda,* autumn, 1997, review of *The Pen Shop,* p. 191.

*America,* March 16, 1974; March 18, 1995, review of *Poems from Centre City,* p. 30.

*Books in Canada,* June, 1988, review of *Notes from the Land of the Dead,* p. 4.

*Choice,* February, 1996.

*Commonweal,* June 6, 1980.

*Eire-Ireland,* number 2, 1967; spring, 1968, p. 108; summer, 1979, pp. 80-82.

*Explicator,* spring, 1999, Neville Newman, "Kinsella's 'Butcher's Dozen,'" p. 173.

*Genre,* winter, 1979.

*Hollins Critic,* October, 1968, John Rees Moore, review of *Nightwalker,* pp. 11-12.

*Hudson Review,* winter, 1968-69; spring, 1996, review of *Poems from Centre City,* p. 170.

*Irish Literary Supplement,* fall, 1988, review of *St. Catherine's Clock* and *Out of Ireland,* p 34; fall, 1990, Tom Halpin, review of *Poems from Centre City* and *Personal Places,* p. 19; spring, 1998, review of *The Dual Tradition: An Essay on Poetry and Politics in Ireland,* p. 13.

*Kirkus Reviews,* November 15, 1999, review of *Godhead* and *The Familiar,* p. 1773.

*Kliatt Young Adult Paperback Book Guide,* January, 1990, review of *The New Oxford Book of Irish Verse,* p. 27.

*Listener,* July 5, 1990, Adam Thorpe, review of *Poems from Centre City* and *Personal Places.*

*Literary Review,* winter, 1979, pp. 139-140.

*Nation,* June 5, 1972.

*New Statesman,* November 9, 1973; January 16, 1987, review of *Poems, 1956-1973,* p. 30.

*New Statesman & Society,* December 23, 1988, review of *Blood and Family,* p. 36; June 2, 1995, Carol Rumens, review of *The Dual Tradition,* p. 46.

*New York Times Book Review,* August 18, 1968; June 16, 1974; February 24, 1980; May 28, 1989, William Logan, review of *Blood and Family,* p. 24; December 24, 1995, p. 11; December 31, 1995, Elizabeth Gaffney, review of *Poems from Centre City,* p. 11.

*Parnassus,* spring-summer, 1975; spring, 1981.

*Ploughshares,* fall, 1996, M. L. Rosenthal, review of *The Dual Tradition,* p. 243.

*Poetry,* January, 1975.

*Publishers Weekly,* June 18, 2001, review of *Citizen of the World,* p. 78.

*Shenandoah,* summer, 1998, review of *Collected Poems, 1956-1994,* p. 116.

*Stand,* spring, 1990, review of *One Fond Embrace* and *Blood and Family,* p. 14; autumn, 1995, review of *Poems from Centre City,* p. 72.

*Times Literary Supplement,* October 5, 1967; December 18, 1969; December 8, 1972; August 17, 1973; November 23, 1973; December 19, 1980; May 30, 1986, review of *Songs of the Psyche* and *Her Vertical Smile,* p. 585; September 13, 1991, Steven Matthews, review of *Poems from Centre City* and *Personal Places,* p. 26; July 3, 1992, review of *Open Court,* p. 28; August 27, 1993, review of *Butcher's Dozen: A Lesson for the Octave of Widgery,* p. 12; June 17, 1994, review of *Poems from Centre City,* p. 28; September 13, 1996, p. 26; January 26, 1996, Patricia Craig, review of *The Dual Tradition,* p. 26.

*Village Voice,* March 14, 1974.

*World Literature Today,* winter, 1991, review of *Blood and Family,* p. 123; autumn, 1996, William Pratt, review of *The Dual Tradition,* p. 967; winter, 1998, William Pratt, review of *The Pen Shop,* p. 147; summer, 1998, Kieran Quinlan, review of *Collected Poems, 1956-1994,* p. 622; winter, 2002, David Lloyd, review of *Citizen of the World,* p. 153.

*Yale Review,* spring, 1962, Thom Gunn, review of Poems and Translations, pp. 486-487.*

\*    \*    \*

## KITAMURA, Satoshi 1956-

*PERSONAL:* Born June 11, 1956, in Tokyo, Japan; moved to England, 1983; son of Testuo (a retail consultant) and Fusae (Sadanaga) Kitamura; married Yoko Sugisaki (an interior designer), December 15, 1987. *Education:* Attended schools in Japan.

*ADDRESSES: Agent*—c/o Author Mail, Farrar, Straus, 19 Union Square West, New York, NY, 10003.

*CAREER:* Freelance illustrator and author, 1975—.

*AWARDS, HONORS:* Mother Goose Award, Books for Children Book Club, 1983, for *Angry Arthur;* Signal Award, 1984, for *Sky in the Pie; What's Inside* selected one of *New York Times* Notable Books, 1985; Children's Science Book Award (Great Britain) and Children's Science Book Award, New York Academy of Sciences, both 1987, both for *When Sheep Cannot Sleep.*

*WRITINGS:*

*SELF-ILLUSTRATED*

*What's Inside: The Alphabet Book,* Farrar, Straus (New York, NY), 1985.

*Paper Jungle: A Cut-out Book,* A. & C. Black (London, England), 1985, Holt (New York, NY), 1986.

*When Sheep Cannot Sleep: The Counting Book,* Farrar, Straus (New York, NY), 1986.

*Lily Takes a Walk,* Dutton (New York, NY), 1987.

*Captain Toby,* Dutton (New York, NY), 1987.

*UFO Diary,* Andersen (London, England), 1989, Farrar, Straus (New York, NY), 1990.

*From Acorn to Zoo,* Andersen (London, England), 1991, published as *From Acorn to Zoo and Everything in between in Alphabetical Order,* Farrar, Straus (New York, NY), 1992.

*Sheep in Wolves' Clothing,* Andersen (London, England), 1995, Farrar, Straus (New York, NY), 1996.

*Paper Dinosaurs: A Cut-out Book,* Farrar, Straus (New York, NY), 1995.

*Squirrel Is Hungry,* Farrar, Straus (New York, NY), 1996.

*Cat Is Sleepy,* Farrar, Straus (New York, NY), 1996.

*Dog Is Thirsty,* Farrar, Straus (New York, NY), 1996.

*Duck Is Dirty,* Farrar, Straus (New York, NY), 1996.

*Bath-time Boots,* Andersen (London, England), 1997, Farrar, Straus (New York, NY), 1998.

*A Friend for Boots,* Andersen (London, England), 1997, Farrar, Straus (New York, NY), 1998.

*Goldfish Hide-and-Seek,* Farrar, Straus (New York, NY), 1997.

*Me and My Cat?* Andersen (London, England), 1999, Farrar, Straus (New York, NY), 2000.

*Comic Adventures of Boots,* Farrar, Straus (New York, NY), 2002.

*ILLUSTRATOR*

Hiawyn Oram, *Angry Arthur,* Harcourt (New York, NY), 1982.

Hiawyn Oram, *Ned and the Joybaloo,* Anderson (London, England), 1983, Farrar, Straus (New York, NY), 1989.

Roger McGough, *Sky in the Pie* (poems), Viking (New York, NY), 1983.

Hiawyn Oram, *In the Attic,* Andersen (London, England), 1984, Holt (New York, NY) 1985.

*The Flying Trunk* (anthology), Andersen (London, England), 1986.

Pat Thomson, *My Friend Mr. Morris,* Delacorte (New York, NY), 1987.

Alison Sage and Helen Wire, compilers, *The Happy Christmas Book* (anthology), Scholastic (New York, NY), 1986.

Andy Soutter, *Scrapyard,* A. & C. Black (London, England), 1988.

*A Children's Chorus* (anthology), Dutton (New York, NY), 1989.

Hiawyn Oram, *A Boy Wants a Dinosaur*, Andersen (London, England), 1990, Farrar, Straus (New York, NY), 1991.

Hiawyn Oram, *Speaking for Ourselves* (poems), Methuen (London, England), 1990.

Carl Davis and Hiawyn Oram, *A Creepy Crawly Song Book*, Farrar, Straus (New York, NY), 1993.

Mick Fitzmaurice, *Morris Macmillipede: The Toast of Brussels Sprout*, Andersen (London, England), 1994.

Stephen Webster, *Inside My House*, Riverswift (London, England), 1994.

Stephen Webster, *Me and My Body*, Riverswift (London, England), 1994.

Richard Edwards, *Fly with the Birds: An Oxford Word and Rhyme Book*, Oxford University Press (Oxford, England), 1995, published as *Fly with the Birds: A Word and Rhyme Book*, Orchard Books (New York, NY), 1996.

Brenda Walpole, *Hello, Is There Anyone There?*, Riverswift (London, England), 1995.

Brenda Walpole, *Living and Working Together*, Riverswift (London, England), 1995.

John Agard, *We Animals Would Like a Word with You*, Bodley Head (London, England), 1996.

John Agard, *Points of View with Professor Peekaboo* (poems), Bodley Head (London, England), 2000.

John Agard, *Einstein, the Girl Who Hated Maths*, Hodder Wayland (London, England), 2002.

Kitamura's books have been translated into Spanish.

*ADAPTATIONS: From Acorn to Zoo and Everything in between in Alphabetical Order* was published in Braille and also made into a take-home literacy pack that includes an audiocassette and activity book. Several books have been translated into Braille, including *When Sheep Cannot Sleep* and Oram Hiawyn's *Ned and the Joybaloo.*

*SIDELIGHTS:* Praised for his ability to interweave Japanese and Western visual traditions within the engaging illustrations he has contributed to the works of numerous writers, Satoshi Kitamura has also become known as an author of children's books. With strong technical abilities and a gift for visual humor, Kitamura adds a whimsical, often unconventional touch to traditional children's-book formats such as alphabet and counting books. He is widely recognized for his use of simplified, angular shapes and a rich palette of earth and sky tones. As David Wiesner noted in the *New York Times Book Review*, Kitamura's books "are suffused with both warmth and wit. . . . The simplicity of Mr. Kitamura's art is deceptive. A superb draftsman and colorist, he uses pen and brush to create remarkably lush and textured illustrations." Among the author/illustrator's most well-received titles are the award-winning counting book *When Sheep Cannot Sleep, Sheep in Wolves' Clothing*, and *UFO Diary*, a 1989 work that *School Librarian* contributor Sue Smedlcy praised as "a sophisticated book acknowledging that children deserve quality texts and illustrations."

"I am interested in different angles of looking at things," Kitamura once told *CA*. "I find great potential in picture books where visual and verbal fuse to experience and [I also] experiment with these angles. Also, there is an advantage of universality of expression in this medium due to the clarity required for young readers."

Kitamura was born and raised in Tokyo, Japan. In 1983 he moved to England, making his permanent home in London. By the time he became a resident of Great Britain, Kitamura's first children's book-illustration project, Hiawyn Oram's *Angry Arthur*, had already been published in both England and the United States. An award-winning book, *Angry Arthur* caused publishers to take notice of the young Japanese illustrator and his work; numerous projects were soon awarded Kitamura in quick succession.

In 1985 Kitamura published *What's Inside: The Alphabet Book*, the first of his many solo children's-book projects. Full of visual clues to help lead young prereaders through alphabetically ordered pairs of lower-cased letters, *What's Inside* was dubbed "gloriously exuberant" by a *Junior Bookshelf* critic and praised by *School Library Journal* contributor Patricia Homer as a book "which will delight readers who are up to a verbal and visual challenge." Denise M. Wilms echoed such praise in *Booklist*, maintaining that the "imaginative quality" of Kitamura's full-color line-and-wash illustrations "make for a fresh, engaging display of letters that will stand up to more than one close look."

In another alphabet book, Kitamura builds young readers' vocabulary, one letter at a time. *From Acorn to Zoo* features pages chock-full of illustrated objects that begin with the same letter, allowing children's vocabularies to be "expanded almost painlessly and [their] capacity for observation sharpened," in the opinion of a *Junior Bookshelf* reviewer. Each illustration features energetic pen-and-ink renderings of an unusual assortment of animals and objects, richly colored and positioned on the page in ways readers will find humorous. For example, on one page a hefty hippo tests the strength of a hammock by sitting in it and playing his harmonica while a harp and coat hanger can be found nearby. In a similar vein, Kitamura tackles introductory mathematics by illustrating the quandary of an insomniac named Woolly in *When Sheep Cannot Sleep*, a 1-2-3 book. Rather than lay about in the dark, Woolly goes on a search for objects grouped first in pairs, then in threes, fours, and so on up to twenty-two before tiring himself out and falling asleep in an abandoned country cottage. But Kitamura does not make things any too easy for his reader; on each page the object Woolly finds must also be discovered by the reader and its quantity totaled up. The work drew rave reviews. Calling *When Sheep Cannot Sleep* "a joy to look at," *Horn Book* contributor Anita Silvey added that Kitamura's "slightly primitive drawing style is delightful, making counting the objects or just looking at the book a great deal of fun." *Booklist* reviewer Ilene Cooper noted that the author/illustrator's "squared-off sheep has an endearingly goofy look that kids and adults will love," while Jane Doonan of the *Times Literary Supplement* dubbed *When Sheep Cannot Sleep* the "perfect picture book free from stereotype images, brimming with unforced humor." In *School Library Journal* Lorraine Douglas praised Kitamura for his "engaging and fresh approach." *School Librarian* reviewer Donald Fry also lauded *When Sheep Cannot Sleep,* concluding that no other such counting book is "so witty and enjoyable as this one."

Goofy-looking sheep serve as the focus of Kitamura's *Sheep in Wolves' Clothing.* Hubert, Georgina, and Gogol are sheep who hoof it on down to the seashore for one last dip in the ocean before the chill of winter sets in. Near the beach, they meet a group of wolves enjoying the fall afternoon by taking time off from work at their knitwear factory to take in a round of golf. The wolves generously offer to watch the sheep's warm wool coats while the seabound swimmers take their plunge; not surprisingly, neither wolves nor wool are anywhere to be found when the soaked sheep return. Fortunately, the sheep call in the services of Elliott Baa, a fully fleeced ace detective, who follows the woolly trail to its conclusion. "Younger children

will delight in the climactic brouhaha and will also find [*Sheep in Wolves' Clothing*] a satisfying mystery story," according to *Horn Book* reviewer Margaret Bush.

In *Lily Takes a Walk* young readers see the divergent perceptions of dog and child as an overactive imagination conjures up frightening sights. While on their routine evening walk, Nicky scares up shadows of everything from vampires to monsters, yet owner Lily sees none of Nicky's concerns. Several reviewers of the book praised Kitamura's combining of scariness and humor, such as a *Kirkus* reviewer who called *Lily Takes a Walk* "understated, subtle, and delightful," and Kay E. Vandergrift, who dubbed the work a "clever idea with an appropriately humorous ending" in *School Library Journal*. In conclusion, a *Publishers Weekly* contributor deemed this walk "well worth taking."

Other books by Kitamura that showcase his vivid imagination and ability to capture a child's attention include *UFO Diary*, the observations of an outer-space visitor who accidentally lands on Earth and is befriended by a young boy. Although never depicted in Kitamura's colorful drawings, the alien provides readers with an opportunity to "see our planet's natural abundance and beauty with fresh eyes," according to John Peters, a *School Library Journal* contributor. Among the book's enthusiasts are Liz Brooks of the *Times Literary Supplement,* who praised both Kitamura's artistry and simplicity, and Sue Perren of *Quill & Quire,* who noted that the illustrations "say it all." In the words of *Horn Book* contributor Nancy Vasilakis, *UFO Diary* is an "unusual" work, one that constitutes a "beautiful, quiet, respectful reminder of who we are and whence we come."

The picture book *Captain Toby* is also unusual in showing the aplomb of a young boy who takes charge in his imagination after he becomes convinced that the storm raging outside his bedroom window has blown his house out to sea. According to *School Library Journal*'s Patricia Pearl, "a clever premise is carefully realized in the illustrations," yet she found the plot less successful, particularly its denouement. On the other hand, a *Publishers Weekly* contributor called *Captain Toby* a "nautical romp," a voyage in which the creator melds "sweet charm and raucous revelry." Likening the book to a film that scrolls from frame to frame, Margery Fisher described the book as a "complete and believable fantasy" in her *Growing Point* review.

Cats play an important role in a handful of Kitamura's picture books. For example, his *Me and My Cat?*, which *Booklist* critic Amy Brandt described as "funny, frenetic, and insightful," revolves around the body-switch perpetrated by a witch's spell upon the boy Nicholas and his cat Leonardo. So while Leonardo in Nicholas's body goes off to school, Nicholas in Leonardo's body explores the varied activities of a cat with "high humor" and a "wickedly delightful twist at the end," to quote Ann Welton of *School Library Journal*. A *Horn Book* reviewer also praised the book's humor, describing it as "dry" and the book as a whole as "farcical comedy." In addition, in *Goldfish Hide-and-Seek* a cat stalks a goldfish that has left his bowl in search of a missing playmate, in what Lynne Taylor of *School Library Journal* termed "original, playful, absurd, superlative, inspired." And finally, a cat stars in one of a quartet of cardboard books for toddlers. Since they are geared to the youngest book users, *Cat Is Sleepy, Squirrel Is Hungry, Dog Is Thirsty,* and *Duck Is Dirty* feature fewer words and use illustrations that employ somewhat heavier lines than Kitamura's standard fare. Applauding these books for their appropriate humor and plots, *School Library Journal* contributor Ann Cook added, "No cutesy, patronizing stuff here." In fact, each story shows how an animal hero solves a simple, but not trivial, problem. According to a *Kirkus* reviewer, even the artwork in this quartet demonstrates more sophistication than is expected in books for such young readers.

Also showing Kitamura's feline fancy, a cat named Boots figures prominently in his fictional world. *Bathtime Boots, A Friend for Boots,* and *Comic Adventures of Boots* introduce readers to a memorable feline. The first two works are board books for toddlers in which a round-eyed cat tries to evade the bath and to find a friend, respectively. This duo "will hit home with small children," a *Kirkus Reviews* writer noted, because of their simple plot lines and the expressively depicted characters. For an older readership, children in grades two through four, the *Comic Adventures of Boots* is a collection of three cat stories that, to quote *Booklist* reviewer Susan Dove Lempke, are "equally goofy and laugh-out-loud funny." The first story, "Operation Fish Biscuit," shows how Boots gets back his best napping place, while in "Pleased to Meet You, Madam Quark" he takes swimming lessons from a duck, and in "Let's Play a Guessing Game" kittens play charades. The pages are broken up into panels like a comic book and use dialog balloons. This style elicited comment from Linda M. Kenton, who expressed concern in *School Library Journal* that some readers might be put off by such cluttered pages; even so, she praised the humor as "simultaneously sly and outrageous." Sometimes, as a *Kirkus Reviews* writer pointed out, words are unnecessary because Kitamura "captures an astonishing range of expressions and reactions" in the cats' features.

In assessing Kitamura's accomplishments for *Children's Literature*, Jane Doonan wrote: "Kitamura's work is notable . . . for the artist's material skills and for his distinctive relationship to the pictorial tradition of Japan. . . . In less than a decade Kitamura has made, and continues to make, a distinctive contribution to the art of the children's picture book. The fresh way of saying 'even something very commonplace' [to quote Maurice Sendak] is evident in all he does."

## BIOGRAPHICAL AND CRITICAL SOURCES:

### BOOKS

*Children's Literature Review,* Volume 60, Gale (Detroit, MI), 2000, pp. 82-103.

### PERIODICALS

*Booklist,* September 1, 1985, Denise M. Wilms, review of *What's Inside?: The Alphabet Book,* p. 64; October 1, 1986, Ilene Cooper, review of *When Sheep Cannot Sleep,* p. 273; April 15, 1991, Stephanie Zvirin, review of *A Boy Wants a Dinosaur,* p. 1651; July, 1992, Deborah Abbott, review of *From Acorn to Zoo,* p. 1943; May 1, 1996, p. 1512; March 1, 2000, Amy Brandt, review of *Me and My Cat?,* p. 1250; October 1, 2002, Susan Dove Lempke, review of *Comic Adventures of Boots,* p. 326.

*Books for Keeps,* September, 1988, Liz Waterland, review of *When Sheep Cannot Sleep,* pp. 8-9; July, 1995, Wendy Cooling, review of *Sheep in Wolves' Clothing,* pp. 24-25, 28.

*Children's Literature,* Volume 19, 1999, Jane Doonan, "Satoshi Kitamura: Aesthetic Dimensions," pp. 107-137.

*Growing Point,* January, 1987, Margery Fisher, review of *When Sheep Cannot Sleep,* p. 4745; January, 1990, Margery Fisher, "Picture-Book Adventures," pp. 5269-5272; February, 1990, p. 5269.

*Horn Book,* November, 1986, Anita Silvey, review of *When Sheep Cannot Sleep,* pp. 736-737; March, 1990, Nancy Vasilakis, review of *UFO Diary,* pp. 190-191; May, 1992, N. Vasilakis, review of *From Acorn to Zoo,* p. 330; January, 1994, N. Vasilakis, review of *A Creepy Crawly Song Book,* p. 83; July, 1996, Margaret Bush, review of *Sheep in Wolves' Clothing,* p. 450; March, 2000, review of *Me and My Cat?,* p. 187.

*Horn Book Guide,* July-December, 1997, Christine M. Heppermann, review of *Goldfish Hide-and-Seek,* p. 36; January-June, 1998, Christine M. Heppermann, reviews of *Bath-time Boots* and *A Friend for Boots,* p. 98.

*Junior Bookshelf,* October, 1982, A. Thatcher, review of *Angry Arthur,* p. 183; October, 1985, R. Baines, review of *What's Inside?,* p. 212; February, 1987, p. 21; August, 1989, p. 162; February, 1991, S. M. Ashburner, review of *Speaking for Ourselves,* p. 26.

*Kirkus Reviews,* May 15, 1985, review of *What's Inside?,* p. J26; November 1, 1987, review of *Lily Takes a Walk,* pp. 1575-1576; August 15, 1989, p. 1247; June 15, 1996, review of *Duck Is Dirty,* p. 906; June 15, 1997, review of *Gold Fish Hide-and-Seek,* p. 951; January 1, 1998, review of *Bath-time Boots,* p. 58; June 1, 2002, review of *Comic Adventures of Boots,* p. 806.

*New York Times Book Review,* June 16, 1985, Karla Kuskin, review of *What's Inside?,* p. 30; March 6, 1988, p. 29; May 21, 1989, John Cech, review of *Ned and the Joybaloo,* p. 41; May 19, 1991, Francine Prose, review of *A Boy Wants a Dinosaur,* p. 23; May 19, 1996, David Wiesner, review of "A Job for Elliott Baa, Private Eye," p. 27; May 14, 2000, David Small, review of *Me and My Cat?,* p. 21; June 1, 2002, review of *Comic Adventures of Boots,* p. 806.

*Publishers Weekly,* February 22, 1985, review of *In the Attic,* p. 158; September 11, 1987, review of *Lily Takes a Walk,* p. 92; June 24, 1988, review of *Ned and the Joybaloo,* p. 110; September 30, 1988, review of *Captain Toby,* p. 65; March 25, 1996, review of *Fly with the Birds: A Word and Rhyme Book,* p. 82; May 6, 1996, review of *Sheep in Wolves' Clothing,* p. 80; June 24, 1996, "Animal Pragmatism," p. 62; June 9, 1997, review of *Goldfish Hide-and-Seek,* p. 44; March 20, 2000, review of *Me and My Cat?,* p. 91; July 17, 2000, review of *Sheep in Wolves' Clothing,* p. 198.

*Quill & Quire,* October, 1989, Susan Perrin, review of *UFO Diary,* pp. 17-18.

*School Librarian,* December, 1986, Donald Fry, review of *When Sheep Cannot Sleep,* p. 337; February, 1988, Margaret Meek, review of *Lily Takes a Walk,* p. 16; November, 1989, Sue Smedley, review of *UFO Diary,* p. 145; November, 1990, Angela Redfern, review of *Speaking for Ourselves,* p. 156; February, 1991, Val Booler, review of *A Boy Wants a Dinosaur,* p. 20; August, 1992, I. Anne Rowe, review of *From Acorn to Zoo,* p. 97; November, 1997, Lynne Taylor, review of *Goldfish Hide-and-Seek,* p. 187.

*School Library Journal,* September, 1982, Holly Sanhuber, review of *Angry Arthur,* p. 110; August, 1984, Joan Wood Sheaffer, review of *Ned and the Joybaloo,* p. 63; September, 1985, Patricia Homer, review of *What's Inside?,* p. 120; December, 1986, Lorraine Douglas, review of *When Sheep Cannot Sleep,* pp. 90-91; November, 1987, Kay E. Vandergrift, review of *Lily Takes a Walk,* pp. 93-94; March, 1989, Patricia Pearl, review of *Captain Toby,* p. 164; January, 1990, John Peters, review of *UFO Diary,* p. 84; July, 1992, Mary Lou Budd, review of *From Acorn to Zoo,* p. 60; January, 1994, Jane Marino, review of *A Creepy Crawly Song Book* pp. 108-109; March, 1996, Sally R. Dow, review of *Fly with the Birds,* p. 173; August, 1996, Ann Cook review of *Cat Is Sleepy,* p. 124; August, 1996, Luann Toth, review of *Sheep in Wolves' Clothing,* p. 124; October, 1997, Karen James, review of *Goldfish Hide-and-Seek,* p. 100; March, 2000, Ann Welton, review of *Me and My Cat?,* p. 209; August, 2002, Linda M. Kenton, review of *Comic Adventures of Boots,* p. 159.

*Times Educational Supplement,* November 11, 1994, Mary Gribbin, review of *Inside My House,* p. 18.

*Times Literary Supplement,* November 28, 1986, Jane Doonan, review of *When Sheep Cannot Sleep,* p. 1345; July 7, 1989, Liz Banks, "Picturing Pets," p. 757.*

*          *          *

## KRANTZ, Steven G. 1951-

*PERSONAL:* Born February 3, 1951, in San Francisco, CA; son of Henry A. (a photographic engraver) and Norma O. (a bookkeeper) Krantz; married Randi D. Ruden (an independent scholar), September 7, 1974. *Education:* University of California—Santa Cruz, B.A. (with highest honors), 1971; Princeton University, Ph. D., 1974. *Hobbies and other interests:* Reading, music, cuisine.

*ADDRESSES: Home*—12 Princeton Pl., University City, MO 63130. *Office*—Department of Mathematics, Washington University, St. Louis, MO 63130; fax: 314-935-6839. *E-mail*—sk@math.wustl.edu.

*CAREER:* University of California—Los Angeles, assistant professor of mathematics, 1974-81; Pennsylvania State University, University Park, associate professor, 1980-84, professor of mathematics, 1984-86; Washington University, St. Louis, MO, professor of mathematics, 1986—. Texas A & M University, Frontiers Speaker, 1997; University of South Florida, Nagle Memorial Lecturer, 1998; visiting professor at Universite de Paris-Sud, 1977, Princeton University, 1980, Uppsala University and University of Beijing, 1984, University of Umeå and Universidad Autónoma de Madrid, 1986, Mittag-Leffler Institute and Université Paul Sabatier, 1988, Politecnico Torino, 1993, and Stanford University, 1997; guest lecturer at colleges and universities in the United States and abroad. American Institute of Mathematics, member of board of advisors, 1997—; software consultant to Natoli Engineering.

*MEMBER:* American Mathematical Society (member of executive committee, 1995-99), Mathematical Association of America, Textbook and Academic Authors Association.

*AWARDS, HONORS:* Grants from National Science Foundation, 1975—, and Fund for the Improvement of Post-Secondary Education, 1992-93; Mathematical Association of America, Chauvenet Prize, 1992, and Beckenbach Book Award, 1994; grant from Kemper Foundation, 1993-94; Richardson fellow, Australian National University, 1995; Outstanding Academic Book Award, *Current Review for Academic Libraries,* 1998.

*WRITINGS:*

(With Robert A. Bonic, Estelle Basor, and others) *Freshman Calculus,* Heath (Lexington, MA), 1971.

(With Robert A. Bonic and Estelle Basor) *Exercises and Sample Exams for Freshman Calculus,* Heath (Lexington, MA), 1971.

*Function Theory of Several Complex Variables,* Wiley (New York, NY), 1982, 2nd edition, Wadsworth Publishing (Belmont, CA), 1992.

(Editor) *Complex Analysis Seminar,* Springer-Verlag (New York, NY), 1987.

*Complex Analysis: The Geometric Viewpoint* (monograph), Mathematical Association of America (Washington, DC), 1990.

*Real Analysis and Foundations,* CRC Press (Boca Raton, FL), 1991.

(Editor, with E. Bedford, J. d'Angelo, and R. E. Greene) *Several Complex Variables and Complex Geometry,* three volumes, American Mathematical Society (Providence, RI), 1991.

*Partial Differential Equations and Complex Analysis,* CRC Press (Boca Raton, FL), 1992.

(With Harold R. Parks) *A Primer of Real Analytic Functions,* Birkhäuser (Basel, Switzerland), 1992.

*Geometric Analysis and Function Spaces,* American Mathematical Society (Providence, RI), 1993.

*How to Teach Mathematics,* American Mathematical Society (Providence, RI), 1993.

(With Stanley Sawyer) *TEX for Scientists,* CRC Press (Boca Raton, FL), 1994.

*The Elements of Advanced Mathematics,* CRC Press (Boca Raton, FL), 1995.

(Editor, with K. Rosen and D. Zwillinger) *The Standard Book of Tables and Formulas,* CRC Press (Boca Raton, FL), 1995.

*Techniques of Problem Solving,* American Mathematical Society (Providence, RI), 1996.

*A Primer of Mathematical Writing,* American Mathematical Society (Providence, RI), 1996.

(With R. E. Greene) *Function Theory of One Complex Variable,* Wiley (New York, NY), 1997.

(With E. Gavosto and W. McCallum) *Issues in Modern Mathematics Education,* Cambridge University Press (New York, NY), 1998.

(Coeditor) *Contemporary Issues in Mathematics Education,* Cambridge University Press (New York, NY), 1999.

*Handbook of Complex Variables,* Birkhäuser (Basel, Switzerland), 1999.

*A Panaroma of Harmonic Analysis,* Mathematical Association of America (Washington, DC), 1999.

(With Harold R. Parks) *The Geometry of Domains in Space,* Birkhäuser (Boston, MA), 1999.

(Coeditor) *Complex Geometric Analysis in Pohang: POSTECH-BSRI SNU-GARC International Conference on Several Complex Variables, June 23-27, 1997 at POSTECH,* American Mathematical Society (Providence, RI), 1999.

(Editor) *Dictionary of Algebra, Arithmetic, and Trigonometry,* CRC Press (Boca Raton, FL), 2000.

*Handbook of Typography for the Mathematical Sciences,* Chapman & Hall/CRC Press (Boca Raton, FL), 2001.

(With Harold R. Parks) *The Implicit Function Theorem: History, Function, and Applications,* Birkhäuser (Boston, MA), 2002.

*Handbook of Logic and Proof Techniques for Computer Science,* Birkhäuser (Boston, MA), 2002.

*Mathematical Apocrypha,* Mathematical Association of America (Washington, DC), 2002.

*A Handbook of Real Variables: With Applications to Differential Equations and Fourier Analysis,* Birkhäuser (Boston, MA), 2003.

*Calculus Demystified,* McGraw-Hill (New York, NY), 2003.

*A Mathematician's Survival Guide: Graduate School and Early Career Development,* American Mathematical Society (Providence, RI), 2003.

(With others) *Explorations in Complex and Reimannian Geometry: A Volume Dedicated to Robert E. Greene,* American Mathematical Society (Providence, RI), 2003.

Chief editor, "Carus Monograph Series," Mathematical Association of America (Washington, DC), 1997-2000; founder and consulting editor of "Studies in Advanced Mathematics" series, CRC Press (Boca Raton, FL). Contributor of numerous articles and reviews to mathematics journals. Founder and managing editor, *Journal of Geometric Analysis;* editor, *Complex Variables,* 1994—; member of editorial committee, *Notices* of the American Mathematical Society, 1995—, and *American Mathematical Monthly,* 1996—.

*WORK IN PROGRESS:* Revising *How to Teach Mathematics,* for American Mathematical Society (Providence, RI); books on calculus, geometry, complex analysis, and partial differential equations.

*SIDELIGHTS:* Steven G. Krantz once told *CA:* "I write in order to share my thoughts with a broad audience. My writing process is to sit down and do it. I do not believe in 'writer's block.'"

\*        \*        \*

## KRÜGER, Arnd 1944-

*PERSONAL:* Listed in some sources as Krueger; born July 1, 1944, in Muehlhausen, Germany; son of Walter (an owner and director of a textile mill) and Minna (an accountant; maiden name, Rose) Krüger; married

Barbara Weber, November 11, 1972; children: Julius, Myrthe, Noah. *Ethnicity:* "German." *Education:* Attended University of Mainz; University of California—Los Angeles, B.A., 1967; University of Cologne, Ph.D., 1971. *Politics:* "Liberal (FDP)." *Religion:* Lutheran. *Hobbies and other interests:* Running, cycling.

*ADDRESSES: Home*—3 Im Hacketal, Waake 37136, Germany. *Office*—University of Göttingen, 2 Sprangerweg, Göttingen 37075, Germany; fax: +49-551-395641. *E-mail*—akrueger@gwdg.de.

*CAREER:* German Sports Federation, Frankfurt, Germany, managing editor, 1971-74; Berlin Teachers Training College, Berlin, Germany, university assistant, 1976-78; University of Hamburg, Hamburg, Germany, associate professor, 1978-80; University of Göttingen, Göttingen, Germany, professor and department head, 1980—, and dean of School of Social Science. European Committee for Sport History, chair, 1995-97.

*MEMBER:* AAKPE (fellow), CESH (fellow), FIEP (member of board of directors), Lower Saxony Institute of Sport History (president), Willbald Gebhardt Institute for Sport and Society (president and member of research council).

*AWARDS, HONORS:* Eleven German national track-and-field championships.

*WRITINGS:*

*Sport und Politik,* Fackeltraeger, 1975.

*Sport und Gesellschaft,* Tischler (Berlin, West Germany), 1981.

(Editor, with John Marshall Carter) *Ritual and Record: Sports Records and Quantification in Pre-Modern Societies,* Greenwood Press (Westport, CT), 1990.

(Editor, with James Riordan) *The Story of Worker Sport,* Human Kinetics (Champaign, IL), 1996.

(Editor, with James Riordan) *The International Politics of Sport in the Twentieth Century,* Routledge (New York, NY), 1999.

(Editor, with William Murray)*The Nazi Olympics: Sport, Politics, and Appeasement in the 1930s,* University of Illinois Press (Champaign, IL), 2003.

Author of more than fifteen other books. Contributor of about 300 articles to scholarly journals.

*WORK IN PROGRESS: Tough As Krupp Steel.*

*SIDELIGHTS:* Arnd Krüger once told *CA:* "Too few people realize the social and political role of sports. More persons can be reached through sports than through any single other medium. After a long and relatively successful career as a middle-distance runner (from a world-record-breaking relay at the University of California—Los Angeles, to semifinals for the Olympic Games, and fifteen years on and off as German champion, 1962-76), I have learned that too few writers are actually aware of what is going on in the world of sports. In my books and learned papers I have shifted from regarding sport as a social and political phenomenon to seeing it as a cultural one, de-emphasizing somewhat the political use made of sport and putting more emphasis on the cultural distinguishing features of sport itself. This has changed the scope of sport as I look at it; it now includes a number of other bodily activities such as nudism, naturism, physical therapy, et cetera. The shift can also be seen in my practical work, in which I am now less active in preparing physical educators and coaches and more active in preparing sports journalists and sport managers."

# L

## LABER, Jeri (Lidsky) 1931-

*PERSONAL:* Born May 19, 1931, in New York, NY; daughter of Louis (an engineer) and Mae (Zias) Lidsky; married Austin Laber (an attorney), October 3, 1954 (divorced, 1978); married Charles M. Kuskin (a musician), June 19, 1994; children: Abigail, Pamela, Emily. *Education:* New York University, B.A., 1952; Columbia University, M.A., 1954.

*ADDRESSES: Home*—67 Riverside Dr., New York, NY 10024. *E-mail*—laberj@hrw.org.

*CAREER: Current Digest of Soviet Press,* New York, NY, foreign editor, 1954-56; Institute for Study of U.S.S.R., New York, NY, publications director, 1961-70; freelance writer and editor, 1970-75. Association of American Publishers, New York, NY, executive director of International Freedom to Publish Committee, 1977—; Fund for Free Expression, New York, NY, executive director, 1977-79; Helsinki Watch, a division of Human Rights Watch, New York, NY, executive director, 1979-95; senior advisor, Human Rights Watch, 1995-2001.

*MEMBER:* Amnesty International, Index on Censorship (member of board), Fund for Free Expression (member of board), Council on Foreign Relations (New York, NY), American Academy of Arts and Sciences.

*AWARDS, HONORS:* Grants from the John D. and Catherine T. MacArthur Foundation; Order of Merit from the Czech Republic; the Association of American Publishers established an annual monetary award in Laber's name starting in 2003 to honor a non-U.S. publisher "who has demonstrated courage and fortitude in the face of political persecution; Alumna of the Year, Harriman Institute, Columbia University, 2003."

*WRITINGS:*

*Czechoslovakia: Some Soviet People Protest,* Radio Liberty Committee, 1968.
(With Barnett R. Rubin) *Tears, Blood, and Cries: Human Rights in Afghanistan since the Invasion, 1979-1984,* Helsinki Watch Committee (New York, NY), 1984, supplement published as *To Die in Afghanistan,* Helsinki Watch Committee (New York, NY), 1985.
*To Win the Children: Afghanistan's Other War,* Helsinki Watch Committee (New York, NY), 1986.
(With Alice Henkin) *Freedom and Fear: Human Rights in Turkey,* U.S. Helsinki Watch Committee (New York, NY), 1986.
*Destroying Ethnic Identity: The Turks of Bulgaria,* Helsinki Watch Committee (New York, NY), 1987.
(With Lois Whitman) *State of Flux: Human Rights in Turkey,* Helsinki Watch Committee (New York, NY), 1987.
(With Barnett R. Rubin) *A Nation Is Dying: Afghanistan under the Soviets, 1979-87,* Northwestern University Press (Evanston, IL), 1988.
(With Lois Whitman) *Destroying Ethnic Identity: The Kurds of Turkey,* U.S. Helsinki Watch Committee (New York, NY), 1988.
(Editor, with Lois Whitman) Erika Dailey, *Human Rights in Moldova: The Turbulent Dniester,* Helsinki Watch (New York, NY), 1993.

(Editor, with Alexander Petrov) Erika Dailey, *Human Rights in Turkmenistan,* Helsinki Watch (New York, NY), 1993.

(Editor) Erika Dailey, *Human Rights in Uzbekistan,* Helsinki Watch (New York, NY), 1993.

(Editor) Ivana Nizich, *Civil and Political Rights in Croatia,* Human Rights Watch (New York, NY), 1995.

(Editor, with Sidney Jones) Mickey Spiegel, *China: State Control of Religion,* Human Rights Watch (New York, NY), 1997.

*The Courage of Strangers: Coming of Age with the Human Rights Movement* (memoir), preface by Václav Havel, PublicAffairs (New York, NY), 2002.

Contributor to numerous journals and newspapers, including the *New Republic, Commentary, Worldview, New York Times, Chicago Tribune, Washington Post,* and *Wall Street Journal.*

*SIDELIGHTS:* Jeri Laber's career as a human rights activist began in the 1970s, after years of being a middle-class homemaker and mother. With little experience in politics or international relations, Laber was appointed a founding member of the Association of American Publishers' International Freedom to Publish Committee. In her memoir *The Courage of Strangers: Coming of Age with the Human Rights Movement,* Laber recalls both the private and public facets of her life, from her sheltered upbringing to her efforts to free political dissidents up through the collapse of the Soviet Union in the late 1980s. As a founder of Helsinki Watch, which later became Human Rights Watch, Laber has lobbied governments throughout the world on behalf of political dissidents and those suffering under inhumane conditions and regimes. In her high-profile missions, she has consulted with world leaders such as Mikhail Gorbachev and made friends with former political prisoners, including Czech president Václav Havel. In *The Courage of Strangers,* Laber assesses the road she has traveled, concluding that "in my work to help others, I became free and independent myself."

Laber's upbringing foreshadowed little of her eventual career. Her parents were Russian-Jewish immigrants who wanted their daughter to enjoy the comforts of American life and did not encourage the exploration of her Russian heritage. Yet Laber was inspired as a teenager after reading *The Diary of Anne Frank,* and later by an article in the *New Republic* about victims of torture in Greece. By the 1970s, she traded her comfortable suburban life for a career in international relations by aligning herself with those in the publishing industry who sought to bring the right to free speech to all corners of the globe. She cofounded Helsinki Rights Watch, a group whose purpose was to monitor compliance with the Helsinki Accords of 1976, in which Soviet bloc countries agreed to extend basic human rights to all its citizens. The organization lobbied governments on behalf of those who had been silence or imprisoned, helping to bring a wider recognition of all sorts of violations perpetrated by governments against those who simply sought to express their opinions.

During her years with Helsinki Rights Watch, Laber wrote and edited many reports about human rights violations in a number of countries, particularly Afghanistan, which the Soviet Union invaded in 1978. Other countries, which Laber and her organization monitored, include Turkmenistan, Bulgaria, and Uzbekistan. The group's work was furthered by grants from the Ford Foundation, and Laber herself received a "genius" grant from the MacArthur Foundation. By 1988, the organization changed its name to Human Rights Watch and gained even wider recognition for its work in bringing to light the cruelty suffered by political prisoners in all countries, not just those under Soviet control.

Laber has not always been welcomed with open arms in her work. She writes of an incident with Elliot Abrams, chief of the U.S. Bureau of Human Rights and Humanitarian Affairs under President Reagan, who called her lobbying attempts on behalf of Turkish citizens "shrill and uninformed." But with time and history on her side, Laber's work eventually saved many lives, a fact spotlighted when Havel gave her the Czech Republic Order of Merit.

Critics who praised *The Courage of Strangers* enjoyed it as much for its insights into Laber's career as for the history of the human rights movement itself. Even as the nascent movement began to make inroads into the problem of human suffering, Laber was frequently the lone woman on a world stage dominated by men. Gilbert Taylor of *Booklist* wrote of Laber's courage in her travels behind the Iron Curtain during the 1970s and 1980s—even as she suffered feelings of guilt over neglecting her children—and said that Laber's "passion shines brightly" in the book. Claudia La Rocco of the *New York Times Book Review* said that "Laber rarely strikes a false note" in recounting the emotional punch of interviewing tortured prisoners, and a writer for the *Economist* called it "an honest, moving and simple memoir which shows self-knowledge without self-indulgence." Kathleen Caldwell, writing in the online magazine *Hope,* praised Laber's "gift for storytelling," and called *The Courage of Strangers* "a thoughtful, but usually fast-paced, inside view of Eastern Europe during a cataclysmic era."

Laber once told *CA,* "Holding two jobs in the human rights field is demanding, especially because of the nature of the work itself, since there is no end to what can and must be done. Nevertheless it is rewarding work to which I am deeply committed. My writings these days are mainly Op Ed articles and articles about my experiences travelling in Eastern Europe. I also review books on human rights and Soviet and East European affairs. One of these days I hope to publish a collection of my interviews with dissenters in Eastern Europe, and my photographs from these meetings."

*BIOGRAPHICAL AND CRITICAL SOURCES:*

*BOOKS*

Laber, Jeri, *The Courage of Strangers,* PublicAffairs (New York, NY), 2002.

*PERIODICALS*

*Booklist,* May 15, 2002, Gilbert Taylor, a review of *The Courage of Strangers,* p. 1559.
*Choice,* January, 1989, a review of *A Nation Is Dying,* p. 864.
*Christian Science Monitor,* April 1, 1988, a review of *A Nation Is Dying,* p. B3.
*Economist,* April 27, 2002, a review of *The Courage of Strangers.*
*Library Journal,* May 15, 1988, a review of *A Nation Is Dying,* p. 86.
*Los Angeles Times Book Review,* May 22, 1988, a review of *A Nation Is Dying,* May 22, 1988, p. 4.
*New York Times Book Review,* June 12, 1988, a review of *A Nation Is Dying,* p. 41; September 1, 2002, Claudia La Rocco, a review of *The Courage of Strangers,* p. 17.

*Times Literary Supplement,* June, 2003, review of *The Courage of Stangers.*
*Wall Street Journal,* December 11, 1989, "Destroying Ethnic Identity," p. A12.

*ONLINE*

*Hope Magazine,* http://www.hopemag.com/ (August 16, 2002), Kathleen Caldwell, "Mother Courage."
*Human Rights Watch Web Site,* http://www.hrw.org/ (December 13).

\*      \*      \*

## LAMB, David 1940-

*PERSONAL:* Born March 5, 1940, in Boston, MA; son of Ernest (a stockbroker) and Pauline (Ayers) Lamb; married Sandra L. Northrop (a filmmaker), February 14, 1977. *Education:* University of Maine, B.A., 1962.

*ADDRESSES: Agent*—Carl Brandt, Brandt & Brandt Literary Agents, Inc., 1501 Broadway, New York, NY 10036.

*CAREER: Los Angeles Times,* Los Angeles, CA, reporter in Vietnam, 1970-75, Nairobi bureau chief, 1976-80, Cairo bureau chief, beginning 1982, Southeast Asia bureau chief, Hanoi, North Vietnam, 1997-2001; writer. Writer-in-residence, University of Southern California School of Journalism. Narrator and host of documentary *Vietnam Passage: A Journey from War to Peace,* Public Broadcasting System, 2002. *Military service:* U.S. Army, 1963-64; became lieutenant.

*AWARDS, HONORS:* Nieman fellow, Harvard University, 1980; Alicia Patterson fellow; Pew fellow.

*WRITINGS:*

*The Africans,* Random House (New York, NY), 1983, published with a new preface and epilogue, Vintage Books (New York, NY), 1987.

*The Arabs: Journeys beyond the Mirage,* Random House (New York, NY), 1987, revised and updated edition, Vintage Books (New York, NY), 2002.

*Stolen Season: A Journey through America and Baseball's Minor Leagues,* Warner Books (New York, NY), 1991.

*A Sense of Place: Listening to Americans,* Times Books (New York, NY), 1993.

*Over the Hills: A Midlife Escape across America by Bicycle,* Times Books (New York, NY), 1996.

*Vietnam, Now: A Reporter Returns,* PublicAffairs (New York, NY), 2002.

Contributor to periodicals, including *National Geographic* and *Sports Illustrated.*

SIDELIGHTS: David Lamb spent the years 1976-1980 as *Los Angeles Times* correspondent in Nairobi, Kenya, traveling through forty-eight countries covering wars, coups, and other events. His impressions of the political and social situations in Africa are collected in *The Africans,* a survey divided by topics into sections on poverty, education, health, women, currencies, and trade. Writing in the *New York Times Book Review,* Alan Cowell predicted that Lamb would provoke debates with his argument that African society would benefit from the establishment of a middle class and his call for a "Marshall Plan" to replace undirected aid to Africa from Western nations. Nonetheless, Cowell called *The Africans* "a timely and valuable work that cuts through many of the distorted images propagated by Africans themselves, by the continent's apologists and by its detractors." He concluded: "*The Africans* is highly readable, uncluttered by statistics and marked by many an insight for the newcomer and more seasoned hand alike. Scholars may find that its very scope precludes detailed analysis of any one particular subject, but Mr. Lamb has nonetheless contributed to the relatively slim library of works that are essential reading for an understanding of modern-day Africa."

In subsequent years, Lamb has covered many major international events, from the Iranian revolution in the 1970s to the turmoil in East Timor in 1999. But it was Lamb's early assignment as a wartime reporter for the *Times* in Vietnam that provided him with an insider's perspective on a complex region. He was based in the Demilitarized Zone (DMZ) but spent most of his time in the bush with the soldiers. After six years as a

battlefield correspondent, Lamb left Vietnam in 1975, just days before the fall of Saigon. More than twenty years later, he returned to Hanoi to manage the *Times* Southeast Asia bureau, the first American to run a news bureau in peacetime Vietnam. This led to a new book, *Vietnam, Now: A Reporter Returns.* The volume's 2001 publication coincided with a television documentary shot by Lamb's wife, Sandra, and narrated by the author.

For many Americans Vietnam has remained an emotional issue, even decades after the Communist takeover. But Lamb's view was different: "I was never hooked by the war," he told Cindy Yoon of *AsiaSource.* "But I was always intrigued with Southeast Asia and what had happened to Vietnam when the war ended. To go back and to really bookend my career thirty years later was far too tempting and compelling to resist." *Vietnam, Now* focuses on the human aspect of the war and its aftermath; the author is also "not shy about sharing his personal feelings," as a *Publishers Weekly* reviewer noted. The author found the latter-day Vietnamese people friendly, even accepting of the events that shattered their country in the 1960s and '70s. Comparing what might in Asia be called the "American War" (much as the conflict was known as the "Vietnam War" in the U.S.), Lamb found that the Vietnamese people "have gotten over [it] in a far better way than how we [Americans] have tried to." As he continued in Yoon's interview, Lamb said that the war, put into Vietnam's historical perspective, "was really a small blip in their history. They fought the Chinese for thousands of years, the French for over [one] hundred, and they were occupied by the Japanese during World War II. Americans have basically come and gone in a decade."

Vietnam, in Lamb's book "emerges as a passionate yet patient country that is trying to adapt to . . . the needs of a new generation," suggested *Library Journal* reviewer Mike Miller. The author acknowledged that the first postwar baby boom of Vietnamese turned out to be "a whiz-kid generation that thirsts for knowledge," as he told Yoon. "They are so industrious and want to know about the world, but they really don't give a hoot about Communism and politics." Indeed, Americans and free enterprise in general are widely welcomed in the new Vietnam, a fact that the author attributed to the culture of the country: Animosity toward their former enemy, wrote Lamb in *Vietnam, Now,* "was replaced by a sense of relief that life was on the mend. Hating took energy—energy the Vietnamese wanted to expend in more productive pursuits." Robert Mann of the *New York Times Book Review* found that "it is this perplexing dichotomy—Vietnam's instinctive embrace of capitalism and western democracy mixed with toleration of moderately repressive Communism—that Mr. Lamb explains so skillfully."

*BIOGRAPHICAL AND CRITICAL SOURCES:*

*BOOKS*

Lamb, Robert, *Vietnam, Now: A Reporter Returns,* PublicAffairs (New York, NY), 2002.

*PERIODICALS*

*American-Arab Affairs,* summer, 1987, review of *The Arabs: Journeys beyond the Mirage,* p. 138.
*Best Sellers,* May, 1983, review of *The Africans,* p. 63.
*Booklist,* January 15 1983, review of *The Africans,* p. 656; March 1, 1991, review of *Stolen Season: A Journey through America and Baseball's Minor Leagues,* p. 1314; May 1, 1993, review of *A Sense of Place: Listening to Americans,* p. 1567; April 1, 1996, Janet St. John, review of *Over the Hills: A Midlife Escape across America by Bicycle,* p. 1340; May 1, 2002, Gilbert Taylor, review of *Vietnam, Now: A Reporter Returns,* p. 1501.
*Book Report,* November, 1991, review of *Stolen Season,* p. 62.
*Bookwatch,* March, 1988, review of *The Arabs,* p. 2.
*British Book News,* February, 1984, review of *The Africans,* p. 78.
*Business Week,* February 21, 1983, review of *The Africans,* p. 16; March 23, 1987, review of *The Arabs,* p. 15; June 29, 1992, review of *Stolen Season,* p. 14.
*Christian Science Monitor,* March 11, 1983, review of *The Africans,* p. 20; December 7, 1984, review of *The Africans,* p. B16; March 9, 1987, review of *The Arabs,* p. 28.
*Foreign Affairs,* number four, 1987, review of *The Arabs,* p. 912.
*Guardian Weekly,* August 21, 1983, review of *The Africans,* p. 21.
*Journal of Reading,* May, 1992, review of *Stolen Season,* p. 684.
*Kirkus Reviews,* December 1, 1982, review of *The Africans,* p. 1323; February 1, 1987, review of *The Arabs,* p. 203; January 1, 1991, review of *Stolen Season,* p. 32.
*Kliatt Young Adult Paperback Book Guide,* fall, 1984, review of *The Africans,* p. 55.
*Library Journal,* March 1, 1983, review of *The Africans,* p. 487; March 15, 1987, review of *The Arabs,* p. 71; February 15, 1991, review of *Stolen Season,* p. 201; April 15, 1993, review of *A Sense of Place,* p. 115; May 15, 2002, Mike Miller, review of *Vietnam, Now,* p. 109.
*London Review of Books,* December 1, 1983, review of *The Africans,* p. 24.
*Los Angeles Times Book Review,* May 3, 1987, review of *The Arabs,* p. 2; October 2, 1988, review of *The Arabs,* p. 14.
*Middle East Journal,* summer, 1989, review of *The Arabs,* p. 522.
*National Review,* May 27, 1991, review of *Stolen Season,* p. 52.
*Newsweek,* February 18, 1991, review of *The Arabs,* p. 62.
*New Yorker,* July 13, 1987, review of *The Arabs,* p. 89.
*New York Times,* May 29, 2002, Robert Mann, "Despite All Vietnam Still Likes Americans."
*New York Times Book Review,* February 6, 1983, Alan Cowell, review of *The Africans,* p. 7; March 18, 1984, review of *The Africans,* p. 34; April 5, 1987, review of *The Arabs,* p. 9; March 21, 1988, review of *The Arabs,* p. 34; April 7, 1991, review of *Stolen Season,* p. 27; March 29, 1992, review of *Stolen Season,* p. 28.
*Publishers Weekly,* December 3, 1982, review of *The Africans,* p. 51; January 20, 1984, review of *The Africans,* p. 87; February 20, 1987, review of *The Arabs,* p. 64; May 27, 1988, review of *The Arabs,* p. 59; January 15, 1991, review of *Stolen Season,* p. 43; March 2, 1992, review of *Stolen Season,* p. 63; February 19, 1996, review of *Over the Hills,* p. 194; April 29, 2002, review of *Vietnam, Now,* p. 54.
*San Francisco Review of Books,* May, 1983, review of *The Africans,* p. 15; March, 1993, review of *A Sense of Place,* p. 27.
*Times Educational Supplement,* September 23, 1983, review of *The Africans,* p. 25; September 27, 1985, review of *The Africans,* p. 26.
*Times Literary Supplement,* September 16, 1983.
*Tribune Books* (Chicago, IL), April 7, 1991, review of *Stolen Season,* p. 5.

*Virginia Quarterly Review,* autumn, 1991, review of *Stolen Season,* p. 140.

*Wall Street Journal,* April 19, 1991, review of *Stolen Season,* p. A13.

*Washington Post Book World,* March 13, 1983, review of *The Africans,* p. 4; March 22, 1987, review of *The Arabs,* p. 4; April 7, 1991, review of *Stolen Season,* p. 3; May 30, 1993, review of *A Sense of Place,* p. 3.

*Wilson Library Bulletin,* January, 1992, review of *Stolen Season,* p. S15.


ONLINE


*AsiaSource, http://www.asiasource.org/* (May 20, 2002), Cindy Yoon, author interview.*

\* \* \*

## LANGLEY, Charles P(itman) III 1949-

*PERSONAL:* Born April 6, 1949, in New Bern, NC; son of Charles P., Jr. and Eva (Connor) Langley; married Anne Smevog (an educational consultant), October 26, 1985; children: Catherine, Anna. *Ethnicity:* "Caucasian." *Education:* University of North Carolina—Chapel Hill, A.B., 1971, M.D., 1975. *Religion:* Presbyterian. *Hobbies and other interests:* Music, literature, foreign language.

*ADDRESSES: Home*—82 Fairview Farms, Shelby, NC, 28150. *Office*—711 North DeKalb St., Shelby, NC, 28150, fax. 704-482-0811. *E-mail*—cplffarms@aol.com.

*CAREER:* Shelby Medical Associates, Shelby, NC, physician (internal medicine), 1979—, and president.

*MEMBER:* American Medical Association, American Society of Internal Medicine, Phi Beta Kappa.

*WRITINGS:*

*Catherine and Geku: The Adventure Begins,* Research Triangle Press (Research Triangle Park, NC), 1996.

*Catherine, Anna, and Geku Go to the Beach,* Research Triangle Press (Research Triangle Park, NC), 1997.

*North, East, South, West: Catherine, Anna, and Geku Take a Long Trip,* Anacat Publications (Naperville, IL), 2001.

*SIDELIGHTS:* Charles P. Langley practices medicine in Shelby, North Carolina, where he lives with his wife, Anne, and two daughters, Catherine and Anna. In the hopes of stimulating his children's imaginations and teaching them values, Langley began telling them adventure stories with themes of trust and friendship. These stories grew to become the author's first two published works, *Catherine and Geku: The Adventure Begins* and *Catherine, Anna, and Geku Go to the Beach.* According to Langley, Geku, a fantastic giant bird featured in both books, "on one level . . . represents the inner spirit and imagination of the child. On another level, he represents the ideal in a parent figure: A companion who teaches, inspires, stimulates, builds confidence, and provides security."

\* \* \*

## LASSITER, Mary
### See HOFFMAN, Mary (Margaret)

\* \* \*

## LAVENDER, William D. 1921-

*PERSONAL:* Born 1921; son of Claud B. (a physician) and Maggie Mae (a homemaker; maiden name, Neel) Lavender; married Mary Bridget Kane (a research assistant); children: Debra, Larry, Randy. *Ethnicity:* "White." *Education:* Birmingham Southern Conservatory and College (Birmingham, AL), B. Music.; University of Southern California, M. Music.

*ADDRESSES: Home and office*—4210 Carney Ct., Riverside, CA 92507. *Agent*—Barbara Markowitz, Los Angeles, CA. *E-mail*—maryl@pe.net.

*CAREER:* Writer. Formerly employed by a U.S. government documentary film agency, scoring films and working on sound recording.

*WRITINGS:*

*Flight of the Seabird* (adult novel), Simon & Schuster (New York, NY), 1977.

*The Invisible People: A Musical Play,* Anchorage Press (Louisville, KY), 2000.

*Just Jane: A Daughter of England Caught in the Struggle of the American Revolution,* Harcourt (San Diego, CA), 2002.

Author of several novels for adults.

*WORK IN PROGRESS:* A historical novel set in San Francisco during the 1906 earthquake.

*SIDELIGHTS:* Author and composer William Lavender enjoyed several different careers—composing music, producing a musical show, and writing adult novels—before turning to writing fiction for children. After graduating from the Birmingham Conservatory, Lavender worked for several years composing music to accompany documentary films made by the U.S. government. He then began to create for a more general audience, writing the book, music, and lyrics for *The Invisible People,* a musical fantasy for children and family audiences that was successfully mounted throughout the United States. As Lavender told *CA,* "For years my wife and I made a sort of cottage industry out of promoting and handling the production arrangements of the play ourselves." Eventually Lavender offered *The Invisible People* for publication, and it appeared in print in 2000.

During the 1970s and 1980s Lavender wrote a handful of historical novels for adults, and one novel set in contemporary times. Although several of these novels were translated and brought out in foreign editions, by the turn of the millennium, all were out of print. Yet in the writing of them Lavender had honed his skills as a creator of historical fiction, a talent he was to put to good use in writing for children. "No longer feeling comfortable with the direction in which adult fiction was moving, I then discontinued writing for some time while engaging in other activities," he explained. "But recently I have returned to the novel form, now aiming my work at the Younger Reader genre." His 2002 offering, *Just Jane: A Daughter of England Caught in the Struggle of the American Revolution,* is Lavender's first novel for young readers, and as the title indicates, he returned to his favorite genre—historical fiction.

Lavender decided to base *Just Jane,* about an orphaned girl of noble English birth, in South Carolina, for as he continued, "Hardly any other American colony in rebellion against England saw the fabric of its everyday life so tragically torn apart as did South Carolina. The abundance of dramatic material collected was the basis of my decision to set my Revolutionary War story in that area." In the novel, Lady Jane Prentice, who drops her aristocratic title to become "just Jane," is forced to make choices about her own independence as well as her allegiance to the new nation or the old. Not only does the narrative involve Jane's decision-making over a six-year period, it involves family feuds, political wrangling, and finally military action.

Like many writers of historical fiction, Lavender sets high value on the accuracy of his portrayal of past life. "Since historical accuracy is of enormous importance in this kind of writing, I consider myself extremely fortunate to have an outstandingly capable research assistant in my wife, Mary," Lavender explained. "For this project, as for others, she has gone all out to compile prodigious amounts of historical information, both from published materials and original sources. In collecting the background material for *Just Jane,* we spent an entire month in South Carolina, ranging from Charleston to remote locations in the back country." This attention to authenticity paid off for Lavender, as reviewers noted it in their comments on the novel's dialogue, characterizations, and subplots. In *School Library Journal,* Renee Steinberg called *Just Jane* "beautifully written" and praised Lavender's "vivid factual information," "rich prose," and "multilayered characters." Because the action of the novel takes place over a longer period than that in many novels for the young teen reading level, Lavender had to sometimes recap the action for readers, a technique that slows down the action. Yet according to a *Kirkus Reviews* critic, "it's a lively story nevertheless," one that makes both the "personal and the political [choices] . . . real and immediate." *Booklist* contributor Carolyn Phelan predicted that historical fiction enthusiasts would find *Just Jane* "refreshing" for its unusual location.

*BIOGRAPHICAL AND CRITICAL SOURCES:*

*PERIODICALS*

*Booklist,* November 1, 2002, Carolyn Phelan, review of *Just Jane: A Daughter of England Caught in the Struggle of the American Revolution,* p. 485.

*Kirkus Reviews,* July 15, 2002, review of *Just Jane,*
p. 1036.
*School Library Journal,* December, 2002, Renee Steinberg, review of *Just Jane,* pp. 143-144.

*       *       *

**LAWTON, Barbara (Perry) 1930-**

*PERSONAL:* Born August 26, 1930, in Springfield,
MA; daughter of Kenneth W. (an insurance executive)
and Elizabeth (a homemaker; maiden name,
McGovern) Perry; married Sanford Lawton, Jr.
(divorced, March, 1967); children: William C., Cynthia L., Mark R. (deceased). *Education:* Mount Holyoke College, B.A., 1952. *Politics:* Republican. *Religion:* Episcopalian.

*ADDRESSES: Home and office*—1430 Timberbrook
Dr., Kirkwood, MO 63122-6734.

*CAREER:* Missouri Botanical Garden, St. Louis, MO,
manager of publications and editor of *M.B.G. Bulletin,*
1967-72; *St. Louis Post-Dispatch,* St. Louis, weekly
columnist, 1972-90; Gary Ferguson, (public relations),
public relations counselor and partner, 1972-81; Daniel
J. Edelman (public relations), St. Louis, account supervisor, 1981-84; Lawton & Associates (public relations and writing services), Kirkwood, MO, public relations counselor and writer, 1984—; writer and
photographer. Kirkwood Planning and Zoning Commission, member, 1986-92; St. Louis Press Club,
newsletter editor, 1986-89, board member, 1986—.
Gaylord Foundation, trustee, 1987—; Garden Writers
Foundation, trustee; affiliated with Master Gardener
and Master Composter, 1993—.

*MEMBER:* American Society of Journalists and Authors, Garden Writers Association of America (past
president), Women in Communications, Missouri Press
Women, Junior League, Kirkwood Historical Society
(past president and garden restoration chairperson).

*AWARDS, HONORS:* Awards for writing and photography from Missouri Press Women, National Federated Press Women, Garden Writers Association of
America, and St. Louis Artists' Guild; Captain Donald

T. Wright Award in Maritime Journalism; *The Magic
of Irises* was nominated for the American Horticultural
Society Award.

*WRITINGS:*

*Improving Your Garden Soil,* illustrated by Paul Kratter, Ortho Information Services (San Ramon, CA),
1992.
(With George F. Van Patten) *Organic Gardener's Basics,* Van Patten Publishing (Seattle, WA), 1993.
*Seasonal Guide to the Natural Year: A Month by
Month Guide to Natural Events—Illinois, Missouri, and Arkansas,* Fulcrum (Golden, CO), 1994.
*The Magic of Irises,* Fulcrum (Golden, CO), 1998.
*Mints: A Family of Herbs and Ornaments,* foreword
by Steven Still, Timber Press (Portland, OR),
2002.

*SIDELIGHTS:* Barbara Lawton has combined her love
of gardening, writing, and photography into an award-
winning career. Her love of growing things began
when she was a child and cultivated small gardens to
satisfy her curiosity. As an adult, her work as editor of
and contributor to the Missouri Botanical Garden bulletin brought her into contact with horticulturists and
botanists from whom she learned a great deal. Today,
she is a master gardener in her own right.

Her 2002 *Mints: A Family of Herbs and Ornaments*
has garnered praise from a number of critics. Marianne Binetti of the *Seattle Post-Intelligencer* predicted
that the book would change the minds of people who
consider mints to be weeds that rapidly dominate
gardens. Alice Joyce of *Booklist* commented that gardeners will appreciate Lawton's sound recommendations and will value the "thoroughly serviceable guide"
to more than sixty-five kinds of mint.

Lawton once told *CA:* "I hope to write more books on
gardening, natural history, and also American rivers."

*BIOGRAPHICAL AND CRITICAL SOURCES:*

*PERIODICALS*

*Booklist,* March 15, 2002, Alice Joyce, review of
*Mints: A Family of Herbs and Ornaments,* p. 1199.
*Horticulture,* January, 1999, p. 82.

*St. Louis Post-Dispatch,* May 18, 2002, Becky Homan, "Go to the Mint: A Kirkwood Author's New Book Explains the Mint Family's Many Uses As Flowers, Herbs—Even Insect Repellents," p. 18.

*Seattle Post-Intillegencer,* May 9, 2002, review of *Mints,* p. E10.

ONLINE

*Timber Press,* www.timber-press.com/ (May 16, 2003).*

\* \* \*

**LESSING, Doris (May) 1919-**
  **(Jane Somers, a pseudonym)**

*PERSONAL:* Born October 22, 1919, in Kermanshah, Persia (now Iran); daughter of Alfred Cook Taylor (a farmer) and Emily Maude McVeagh; married Frank Charles Wisdom, 1939 (marriage dissolved, 1943); married Gottfried Anton Nicholas Lessing, 1945 (marriage dissolved, 1949); children: (first marriage) John (deceased), Jean; (second marriage) Peter. *Politics:* "Left-wing."

*ADDRESSES: Agent*—c/o Jonathan Clowes Ltd., 10 Iron Bridge House, Bridge Approach, London NW1 8BD, England.

*CAREER:* Writer. Worked as a nursemaid, a lawyer's secretary, a Hansard typist, and a Parliamentary Commissioner's typist while living in Southern Rhodesia, 1924-49.

*MEMBER:* National Institute of Arts and Letters, American Academy of Arts and Letters, Modern Language Association (honorary fellow), Institute of Cultural Research.

*AWARDS, HONORS:* Somerset Maugham Award, Society of Authors, 1954, for *Five: Short Novels;* short-listed for the Booker McConnell Prize, 1971, for *Briefing for a Descent into Hell,* 1981, for *The Sirian Experiments: The Report of Ambien II, of the Five,* and 1981, for *The Good Terrorist;* Prix Medici Award for work translated into French, 1976, for *The Golden Notebook;* Austrian State Prize for European Literature, 1981; German Federal Republic Shakespeare Prize, 1982; Australian Science Fiction Achievement Award (Ditmars) nomination, 1982, for *The Sirian Experiments;* W. H. Smith Literary Award, 1986, Palermo Prize, 1987, and Premio Internazionale Mondello, 1987, all for *The Good Terrorist;* Grinzane Cavour award (Italy), 1989, for *The Fifth Child;* honorary degree, Princeton University, 1989, and Harvard University, 1995; distinguished fellow, University of East Anglia, 1991; James Tait Black Memorial Book Prize, University of Edinburgh, and *Los Angeles Times* Book Prize, both 1995, both for *Under My Skin;* David Cohen British Literary Prize, 2001, for her life's work; Asturias Prize for literature, Prince of Asturias Foundation, 2001.

*WRITINGS:*

*FICTION*

*The Grass Is Singing,* Crowell (New York, NY), 1950, reprinted, Perennial Classics (New York, NY), 2000.

*This Was the Old Chief's Country* (stories), M. Joseph (London, England), 1952.

*Five: Short Novels,* M. Joseph (London, England), 1955.

*Retreat to Innocence,* M. Joseph (London, England), 1956.

*Habit of Loving* (stories), Crowell (New York, NY), 1958.

*The Golden Notebook,* Simon & Schuster (New York, NY), 1962, with an introduction by the author, Harper Perennial (New York, NY), 1994.

*A Man and Two Women* (stories), Simon & Schuster (New York, NY), 1963.

*African Stories,* M. Joseph (London, England), 1964, Simon & Schuster (New York, NY), 1965.

*Briefing for a Descent into Hell,* Knopf (New York, NY), 1971.

*The Temptation of Jack Orkney and Other Stories,* Knopf (New York, NY), 1972, published as *The Story of a Non-Marrying Man and Other Stories,* J. Cape (London, England), 1972.

*The Summer before the Dark,* Knopf (New York, NY), 1973.

*The Memoirs of a Survivor,* Random House (New York, NY), 1975.

*Stories,* Knopf (New York, NY), 1978, published in two volumes as *Collected Stories I: To Room Nineteen* and *Collected Stories II: The Temptation of Jack Orkney and Other Stories,* J. Cape (London, England), 1978.

(Under pseudonym Jane Somers) *The Diary of a Good Neighbor* (also see below), Knopf (New York, NY), 1983.

(Under pseudonym Jane Somers) *If the Old Could . . .* (also see below), Knopf (New York, NY), 1984.

*The Diaries of Jane Somers* (contains *The Diary of a Good Neighbor* and *If the Old Could . . .*), Random House (New York, NY), 1984.

*The Good Terrorist,* Knopf (New York, NY), 1985.

*The Fifth Child,* Knopf (New York, NY), 1988.

*The Doris Lessing Reader,* Knopf (New York, NY), 1989.

*The Real Thing: Stories and Sketches,* HarperCollins (New York City), 1992, published as *London Observed: Stories and Sketches,* HarperCollins (London, England), 1992.

*Love, Again,* HarperCollins (New York, NY), 1996.

*Mara and Dann: An Adventure,* HarperFlamingo (New York, NY), 1999.

*Ben, in the World* (sequel to *The Fifth Child*), HarperCollins (New York, NY), 2000.

*The Sweetest Dream,* HarperCollins (New York, NY), 2002.

"CHILDREN OF VIOLENCE" SERIES

*Martha Quest,* M. Joseph (London, England), 1952.

*A Proper Marriage,* M. Joseph (London, England), 1954.

*A Ripple from the Storm,* M. Joseph (London, England), 1958.

*Landlocked,* Simon & Schuster (New York, NY), 1966.

*The Four-Gated City,* Knopf (New York, NY), 1969.

"CANOPUS IN ARGOS: ARCHIVES" SERIES

*Re: Colonized Planet Five, Shikasta,* Knopf (New York, NY), 1979.

*The Marriage between Zones Three, Four, and Five,* Knopf (New York, NY), 1980.

*The Sirian Experiments: The Report of Ambien II, of the Five,* Knopf (New York, NY), 1981.

*The Making of the Representative for Planet Eight,* Knopf (New York, NY), 1982.

*Documents relating to the Sentimental Agents in the Volyen Empire,* Knopf (New York, NY), 1983.

*Canopus in Argos: Archives* (contains *Re: Colonized Planet Five, Shikasta; The Marriage between Zones Three, Four, and Five; The Sirian Experiments: The Report of Ambien II, of the Five; The Making of the Representative for Planet Eight;* and *Documents Relating to the Sentimental Agents in the Volyen Empire*), Vintage (New York, NY), 1992.

NONFICTION

*Going Home,* drawings by Paul Hogarth, M. Joseph (London, England), 1957, with a new afterword, HarperPerrennial (New York, NY), 1996.

*In Pursuit of the English: A Documentary,* Simon & Schuster (New York, NY), 1961, reprinted, 1996.

*Particularly Cats,* Simon & Schuster (New York, NY), 1967, revised edition published as *Particularly Cats—And Rufus,* Knopf (New York, NY), 1991.

*A Small Personal Voice: Essays, Reviews, Interviews,* Random House (New York, NY), 1975.

*Prisons We Choose to Live Inside,* Harper (New York, NY), 1987.

*The Wind Blows away Our Words,* Random House (New York, NY), 1987.

*African Laughter: Four Visits to Zimbabwe,* HarperCollins (New York, NY), 1992.

*Under My Skin* (autobiography), HarperCollins (New York, NY), 1994.

*Walking in the Shade: Volume Two of My Autobiography, 1949-1962,* HarperCollins (New York, NY), 1997.

PLAYS

*Mr. Dollinger,* produced in Oxford, England, 1958.

*Each in His Own Wilderness,* produced in London, England, 1958.

*The Truth about Billy Newton,* produced in Salisbury, England, 1961.

*Play with a Tiger* (produced in London, England, 1962; produced in New York, NY, 1964), M. Joseph (London, England), 1962.

Also author of a libretto based on *The Making of the Representative for Planet Eight,* for an opera by Philip Glass.

*OTHER*

*Fourteen Poems,* Scorpion Press, 1959.
*The Old Age of El Magnifico,* Flamingo (London, England), 2000.

*ADAPTATIONS: The Memoirs of a Survivor* was adapted into a film and released in 1983; *The Grass Is Singing* was adapted into a film by Michael Raeburn and released as *Killing Heat* in 1984.

*SIDELIGHTS:* Doris Lessing, whose long career as a novelist, short story writer, and essayist began in the mid-twentieth century, is considered among the most important writers of the modern postwar era. Since her birth in 1919 in Britain's sphere of influence in Persia (now Iran), Lessing has traveled widely, in geographical, social, political, psychological, and literary terms. These travels, as expressed in her writing, offer readers insights into life at distant outposts of the British Empire and at its core. Through her books—including novels and short-story collections—one can encounter people buffeted by personal, historical, and political forces, and can explore the major issues of the age: racism, communism, feminism, terrorism, and the destruction of the environment. "Lessing has written prolifically on everything from British colonialism . . . to the failure of ideology," commented Gail Caldwell in the *Boston Globe,* adding that during her long career the versatile author has "taken on the apocalyptic potential of a futuristic, Blade Runner London, the perils of the color bar in Africa, [and] the life of a young girl growing up on the veld."

Lessing's wide-ranging literary appetite is one of the defining characteristics of her work; another is her style. "The Lessing sentence is blunt," explained Philip Hensher in the *Spectator,* "quickly veering from concrete facts to abstract nouns, tempted briefly by the possibilities of rhapsody, but always turning back to the urgency of the urban demotic. . . . Its cadences are punchy. . . . she loves the grand, dramatic force of words like wisdom, and the vivid simplicity of the names of colours." "Critics have found it extremely hard to categorize Lessing," observed Fiona R. Barnes in the *Dictionary of Literary Biography,* "for she has at various stages of her life espoused different causes and been labeled over again."

In 1924 Lessing's father took the family to Southern Rhodesia (now Zimbabwe), hoping to make a fortune growing corn and tobacco and panning for gold. The family found little fortune on its new farm, located in a remote corner of the Rhodesian bush not far from the border with Mozambique. However, in her years growing up in the African wild, her stays in convent and government schools, and her brief career as a secretary and homemaker, Lessing found a wealth of literary inspiration. As Mark Mathabane noted in the *Washington Post Book World,* "The formidable problems of racial, social and economic injustice besieging the region of her formative years, its wondrous beauty and unfulfilled promise, left a permanent imprint on her. They molded her artistic temperament, politics and loyalties and made of her a highly original and activist writer." In 1949 Lessing left Africa behind for London, the heart of the British empire. She also left behind most of her family: her brother, her two failed marriages, and her two children from her first marriage. With her son from her second marriage, she embarked on a new life in London as a writer. Her first novel, *The Grass Is Singing,* was published the following year.

Like many of the novels and short stories that would follow its debut, *The Grass Is Singing* deals with settings, characters, and issues very close to its author's experience of Rhodesian society and its government's apartheid policies. The central character of the novel is Mary Turner, the wife of a farmer in the African bush, whose affair with an African servant ends in her murder. "Mary Turner is a strange, sad woman, suffering under the burden of obligations imposed upon her as a white woman by the sad, strange conventions of a colonial settler society," explained K. Anthony Appiah in the *New Republic,* the critic going on to add that "the novel is intensely humane in its attentiveness to the minutest details of the mental life of this central character." In the opinion of *New York Review of Books* contributor J. M. Coetzee, this book represents "an astonishingly accomplished debut, though perhaps too wedded to romantic stereotypes of the African for present-day tastes." At the time of Lessing's debut in 1950, however, Appiah observed, "reviewers pronounced her the finest new novelist" since World War II.

Lessing's major and most controversial novel is *The Golden Notebook,* first published in 1962, wherein she brilliantly explores, as a *New Statesman* reviewer noted, what it is like to be "free and responsible, a woman in relation to men and other women, and to struggle to come to terms with one's self about these things and about writing and politics." Lessing once explained that the work is "a novel about certain political and sexual attitudes that have force now; it is an attempt to explain them, to objectivize them, to set them in relation with each other. So in a way it is a social novel, written by someone whose training—or at least whose habit of mind—is to see these things socially, not personally." In its structure, the novel is really two novels, divided in four sections and "The Golden Notebook." Lessing split it into four parts in order to "express a split person. I felt that if the artist's sensibility is to be equated with the sensibility of the educated person, then it is logical to use different styles to express different kinds of people." She felt that the "personality is very much what is remembered; [the form] enabled me to say to the reader: Look, these apparently so different people have got so-and-so in common, or these things have got this in common. If I had used a conventional style, the old-fashioned novel, . . . I would not have been able to do this kind of playing with time, memory and the balancing of people. . . . I like *The Golden Notebook* even though I believe it to be a failure, because it at least hints at complexity."

After her initial flourishing as a writer, during which time she explored the Africa of her youth from her new home in London, Lessing turned away from the land of her past and toward new settings: inner space and outer space. *Briefing for a Descent into Hell* is a novel of ideas based on her interest in the views of British psychiatrist R. D. Laing. In subsequent novels, Lessing has continued to produce work critiquing modern society. In contrast to the realism that marked her earlier novels, Lessing's work of the late twentieth century—particularly her science-fiction series "Canopus in Argos: Archives"—would take startling new forms. In the five "Canopus" books she explores the destruction of life brought about by catastrophe and tyranny. Paul Schlueter in the *Dictionary of Literary Biography* noted that in this series Lessing's "high seriousness in describing earth's own decline and ultimate demise is as profoundly apocalyptic as ever."

Following her foray into science fiction, Lessing again surprised readers and critics by publishing two novels under a pseudonym, Jane Somers. *The Diary of a Good Neighbor* and *If the Old Could . . .* contain typical Lessing themes: relations between women, the question of identity, and psychological conflict. Though Lessing was able to get the "Somers" books

published in both England and the United States, they were generally ignored by critics and did not sell well. Lessing finally admitted that the works were her creation, saying that she had used the pseudonym to prove a point about the difficulties facing young writers. Without adequate marketing and publicity, noted Lessing, books by unknown writers are generally doomed to oblivion.

More recent fiction by Lessing includes *The Good Terrorist,* a satirical novel about romantic politics; *The Fifth Child,* a 1998 novel about a violent, antisocial child who wreaks havoc on his family and society; and *Love Again,* a reflection on the agonies and insufficiency of romantic love. Commenting on *Love Again* in the *New Yorker,* Brooks Appelbaum maintained that the book is "really about the sawdust sensation of knowing that one's darkest despair and brightest ecstasy have been felt and expressed before, and better; and that ultimately, their expression doesn't help." The book's protagonist, an older woman, dissects "her love and grief with the ruthless precision of a forensic pathologist" in passages that "radiate the analytical purity that has always been Lessing's greatest strength."

A sequel to *The Fifth Child* published over ten years later, *Ben, in the World* continues the story of middle-class Britisher Ben Lovatt, who has been treated as an outsider since birth due to his primitive, savage physique. Now eighteen, the muscular but apelike Ben looks much older than his age; with little education and fearful of society, he nonetheless flees his uncaring family for Brazil, where he attempts to come to terms with his savage spirit in a harsh world. Noting that the novel's plot borders on "bathetic melodrama," a *Publishers Weekly* contributor nonetheless commended Lessing for her efforts to show "how intellectuals acting in the name of art or science cruelly exploit simple people who can't defend themselves." Viewing the novel more positively in her *Christian Century* review, Trudy Bush called Lessing's approach a "fresh twist" on a traditional theme, and added that readers of *Ben, in the World* will never again "see those who are radically different from themselves in quite the same way."

Considered a semi-autobiographical novel, Lessing's *The Sweetest Dream* takes place during the 1960s and focuses on Julia, a widow living in a house in Hampstead who takes in her daughter-in-law and young grandsons after her son abandons his family in favor of the communist party. Due to the young mother's generosity, Julia's house is soon second home to a host of interesting characters, some of whom take advantage of the situation. In another part of the novel, a fictional African nation called Zimlia suffers through decolonization, and another political fiction is discredited as the new leaders show themselves to be as ruthless as their colonial predecessors were. In its examination of political systems gone awry and what *Booklist* contributor Donna Seaman dubbed the "sweet utopian dream of communism that went so nightmarishly wrong," Lessing's novel maintains what *New Criterion* contributor Paul Hollander called "a compelling focus on the timeless tension between idealistic social-political aspiration and the dark side of human failure. . . . As Lessing shows, 'the sweetest dream' . . . will likely continue to haunt and elude us." Calling Lessing "one of the great imaginative fantasists of our time," *Spectator* reviewer Hensher praised *The Sweetest Dream* as "loose, absorbing, urgent" in its focus on "the future of society and personal responsibility." Seaman praised the the work as "a realistic tour de force," adding that "the force of Lessing's vast knowledge and wisdom and the vigor and vision of her imagination and conviction are felt on every page."

Lessing has also produced nonfiction tomes, including *The Wind Blows away Our Words,* about war in Afghanistan during the 1980s. A nonfiction work and two volumes of autobiography marked her eventual return to her African homeland and to the preoccupations of her youth. After leaving Southern Rhodesia in 1949, Lessing had returned only once, in 1956, an experience she recounts in *Going Home.* After this first homecoming, the white minority government blocked any future returns because of Lessing's criticism of apartheid. It was not until the 1980s, after years of civil war and thousands of deaths brought the black majority to power in the newly christened Zimbabwe, that Lessing could return. In *African Laughter: Four Visits to Zimbabwe* she chronicles her trips to southern Africa in 1982, 1988, 1989, and 1992. On one level, this book offers the keen observations of a new nation's growing pains through the eyes of someone not an insider but not an outsider. She sees first a country trying to come to terms with the outcome of a long and bloody civil war based on race. In subsequent trips, she finds exuberance, corruption, and finally decline. "One is oneself fixed in the beam of Lessing's penetrating gaze from the first moments of the book," wrote Appiah.

In *African Laughter,* according to Mathabane, "Lessing gives us one of the most penetrating and even-handed critiques of Zimbabwe as a new nation." Her "portrait is without stereotype or sentimentality," the critic added, "and free of the overbearing shadow of South Africa and its larger-than-life problems of apartheid." For Appiah, however, Lessing's insights into the changes taking place in Zimbabwe are not complete because, as a white woman, she is unable to get inside the hearts and minds of blacks. "Lessing shows us only the exterior of the black Zimbabweans," he pointed out, "but still we are in her debt for what that view teaches us about what is happening in Zimbabwe." In Appiah's final analysis, "What we learn from this book, then, is not so much the political history of Zimbabwe in its first dozen years, but the psychic history of Southern Rhodesia, the inner history of the white settlers and what has become of them: the best of this book is the white man's story."

*Under My Skin,* the first volume of Lessing's autobiography, follows the writer from her birth in 1919 to 1949, the year she left Southern Rhodesia for London and her life as a single mother and aspiring writer. She recounts her very early years in Persia, the railway journey across a chaotic Soviet Russia, the promising voyage to Africa, and the years in the bush and in convent school. She also describes the lives of the Taylor family, their fellow whites, and the African majority around them. *Under My Skin* "is not so much a recollection of her early life in Southern Rhodesia as a dissection of it," commented Martha Duffy in *Time;* "The chapters on childhood are marvelously, sometimes frighteningly, detailed." Roberta Rubenstein commented in Chicago's *Tribune Books* that "*Under My Skin* makes for compelling reading because of Lessing's vivid reconstructions of decisive experiences and significant people of her childhood. Throughout, she juxtaposes descriptions of events that occurred in her youth—before she was capable of fathoming them—with her current unsentimental judgments of them." Although this is autobiography, it is Lessing, true to her strengths as an observer and writer. Duffy concluded: "Set down in blunt, fluent prose, it is the same mix of the practical and the speculative that marks all her writing. And, alas, the same lack of humor. But if that is a flaw, it also ensures the author's total engagement with any subject she tackles. That is what one reads Doris Lessing for: unsparing clarity and frankness."

*Walking in the Shade,* the second Lessing autobiography, covers life in London from her arrival in 1949 to the publication in 1962 of *The Golden Notebook,* which secured her reputation as a major postwar English writer. Much of the book deals with Lessing's love/hate relationship with the Communist Party, which she joined in 1952—"the most neurotic act of my life," she once wrote—and stuck with it for nearly twenty years despite deep misgivings. "Her . . . description of the Cold War years, the potent mixture of arrogance, emotionalism and naivety that kept her and others tied to the Party line, long after they knew it was nonsense, will not be bettered," wrote Anne Chisholm in the *Times Literary Supplement.* The book also recounts Lessing's disastrous love affairs, her struggles as a single mother with little money in grim, tattered postwar London, her writing habits, her relatively rapid entry into the city's intellectual circles, and her perceptions of the famous—and eccentric—who moved in those circles. Chisholm found the book to be "not Lessing's best-written or best-constructed book; it is repetitive, and the more gossipy sections have a perfunctory air, as if added under pressure from her publishers. But even its flaws testify to her seriousness of purpose." *Walking in the Shade* is "stingingly self-mocking," according to Claudia Roth Pierpont in the *New Yorker;* it "is about the admission of colossal, sickening error and defeat." But "it is surely Lessing's ability to hold fast to her goal even as she records every stumble and collapse along the way which has made her work of near-inspirational value to so many."

According to Mathabane, "whatever her subject, Lessing is a surefooted and convincing storyteller. Her work possesses a universality, range and depth matched by that of few other writers in our time." As Schlueter remarked of her career, Lessing's "work has changed radically in format and genre over the years, . . . and she has been more and more willing to take chances fictionally by tackling unusual or taboo subjects. . . . And while it is commonplace to note that Lessing is not a stylist, that she is repetitive, and that her fiction too easily reflects her own enthusiasms at particular moments, . . . the fact remains that she is among the most powerful and compelling novelists of our century."

*BIOGRAPHICAL AND CRITICAL SOURCES:*

*BOOKS*

Arora, Neena, *Nayantara Sahgal and Doris Lessing: A Feminist Study in Comparison,* Prestige Books/ Indian Society for Commonwealth Studies (New Delhi, India), 1991.

Bigsby, C. W. E., *The Radical Imagination and the Liberal Tradition,* Junction Books, 1981.

Cederstrom, Lorelei, *Fine-tuning the Feminine Psyche: Jungian Patterns in the Novels of Doris Lessing,* Peter Lang (New York, NY), 1990.

Christ, Carol P., *Diving Deep and Surfacing: Women Writers on Spiritual Quest,* Beacon Press (Boston, MA), 1980.

*Contemporary Literary Criticism,* Gale (Detroit, MI), Volume 1, 1973, Volume 2, 1974, Volume 3, 1975, Volume 6, 1975, Volume 10, 1979, Volume 15, 1980, Volume 22, 1982, Volume 40, 1986.

Dandson, Cathy N., and E. M. Brown, editors, *The Lost Tradition: Mothers and Daughters in Literature,* Ungar (New York, NY), 1980, pp. 207-216.

*Dictionary of Literary Biography,* Gale (Detroit, MI), Volume 15: *British Novelists, 1930-1959,* 1983, Volume 139: *British Short Fiction Writers, 1945-1980,* 1994.

*Dictionary of Literary Biography Yearbook: 1985,* Gale (Detroit, MI), 1986.

Fahim, Shadia S., *Doris Lessing: Sufi Equilibrium and the Form of the Novel,* St. Martin's Press (New York, NY), 1994.

Galin, Muge, *Between East and West: Sufism in the Novels of Doris Lessing,* State University of New York Press (Albany, NY), 1997.

Greene, Gayle, *Doris Lessing: The Poetics of Change,* University of Michigan Press (Ann Arbor, MI), 1994.

Holmquist, Ingrid, *From Society to Nature: A Study of Doris Lessing's "Children of Violence,"* Gothenburg Studies in English, 1980.

Ingersoll, Earl G., editor, *Doris Lessing: Conversations,* Ontario Review Press (Princeton, NJ), 1994.

Ingersoll, Earl G., editor, *Putting the Questions Differently: Interviews with Doris Lessing, 1964-1994,* Flamingo (London, England), 1996.

Laurenson, Diana, editor, *The Sociology of Literature: Applied Studies,* University of Keele Press (Newcastle on Tyne, England), 1978.

Myles, Anita, *Doris Lessing: A Novelist with Organic Sensibility,* Associated Publishing House (New Delhi, India), 1991.

Pickering, Jean, *Understanding Doris Lessing,* University of South Carolina Press (Columbia, SC), 1990.

Rigney, Barbara H., *Madness and Sexual Politics in the Feminist Novel: Studies in Brontë, Woolf, Lessing, and Atwood,* University of Wisconsin Press, 1978.

Robinson, Sally, *Engendering the Subject: Gender and Self-Representation in Contemporary Women's Fiction,* State University of New York Press (Albany, NY), 1991.

Rose, Ellen Cronan, *The Tree outside the Window: Doris Lessing's Children of Violence,* University Press of New England (Hanover, NH), 1976.

Rowe, Margaret Moan, *Doris Lessing,* St. Martin's Press (New York, NY), 1994.

Saxton, Ruth, and Jean Tobin, editors, *Woolf and Lessing: Breaking the Mold,* St. Martin's Press (New York, NY), 1994.

Seligman, Dee, *Doris Lessing: An Annotated Bibliography of Criticism,* Greenwood (Westport, CT), 1981.

Shapiro, Charles, editor, *Contemporary British Novelists,* Southern Illinois University Press (Carbondale, IL), 1964.

*Short Story Criticism,* Volume 6, Gale (Detroit, MI), 1990.

Whittaker, Ruth, *Doris Lessing,* St. Martin's Press (New York, NY), 1988.

*PERIODICALS*

*America,* December 7, 1996, p. 25.

*Antioch Review,* fall, 1996, p. 493.

*Ariel,* July, 1995, p. 176.

*Belles Lettres,* summer, 1993, p. 30.

*Book,* May, 2001, p. 86; January-February, 2002, Penelope Mesic, review of *The Sweetest Dream,* p. 63.

*Booklist,* November 15, 2001, Brad Hooper, review of *The Grass Is Singing,* p. 555; December 1, 2001, Donna Seaman, review of *The Sweetest Dream,* p. 605.

*Boston Globe,* July 29, 1992, p. 62; October 16, 1994, p. B18; November 13, 1994, p. B1.

*Choice,* April, 1995, p. 1298; October, 1995, p. 292; March, 1997, p. 1167.

*Christian Century,* December 13, 2000, Trudy Bush, review of *Ben, in the World,* p. 1313.

*Christian Science Monitor,* December 9, 1992, p. 13; November 17, 1994, p. 14.

*Critique,* spring, 2002, p. 228.

*Economist* (U.K.), December 22, 2001, review of *The Sweetest Dream,* p. 117.

*Frontiers,* June, 2001, Roberta Rubenstein, "Feminism, Eros, and the Coming of Age,", pp. 1-20.

*Globe and Mail* (Toronto, Ontario, Canada), November 24, 1984; April 6, 1985; December 21, 1985; August 6, 1988.

*Hudson Review,* spring, 2001, Alan Davis, review of *Ben, in the World,* p. 141.

*Library Journal,* February 1, 2002, Beth Anderson, review of *The Sweetest Dream,* p. 131.

*London Review of Books,* April 22, 1993, p. 22.

*Los Angeles Times,* March 1, 1983; July 6, 1983; May 10, 1984; January 14, 1988; June 25, 1992, p. E12; October 20, 1994, p. E8; December 8, 1994, p. E1.

*Los Angeles Times Book Review,* March 1, 1981; March 21, 1982; February 10, 1985; October 13, 1985; October 20, 1985; March 27, 1988; April 6, 1988; November 1, 1992, p. 2; September 5, 1993, p. 6.

*Maclean's,* January 9, 1995, p. 66; April 15, 1996, p. 64.

*Modern Fiction Studies,* summer, 1975; spring, 1980; spring, 1996, p. 194.

*Modern Language Quarterly,* March, 1974.

*Nation,* January 11, 1965; January 17, 1966; June 13, 1966; March 6, 1967; November 7, 1994, p. 528; May 6, 1996, p. 62; October 13, 1997, p. 31.

*New Criterion,* March, 2003, Paul Hollander, review of *The Sweetest Dream,* pp. 71-76.

*New Republic,* June 28, 1993, p. 30.

*New Statesman,* April 20, 1962; November 8, 1963; October 31, 1997, p. 43; October 1, 2001, Stephanie Merriman, review of *The Sweetest Dream,* p. 83.

*Newsweek,* October 14, 1985.

*New York,* October 26, 1992, p. 96.

*New Yorker,* June 10, 1996, p. 88; November 17, 1997, p. 108; February 18, 2002, Louis Menand, review of *The Sweetest Dream,* p. 193.

*New York Review of Books,* December 22, 1994, p. 51; April 18, 1996, pp. 13-15.

*New York Times,* October 21, 1972; October 23, 1979; March 27, 1980; January 19, 1981; January 29, 1982; March 14, 1983; April 22, 1984; October 5, 1984; October 23, 1984; July 14, 1985; September 17, 1985; March 30, 1988; June 14, 1988; June 16, 1992, p. C16; November 2, 1994, p. C1.

*New York Times Book Review,* March 14, 1971; May 13, 1973; June 4, 1978; November 4, 1979; March 30, 1980; January 11, 1981; February 2, 1982; April 3, 1983; September 22, 1985; January 24, 1988; April 3, 1988; April 12, 1992, p. 13; October 18, 1992, p. 13; November 6, 1994, p. 1; April 21, 1996, p. 13; September 14, 1997, p. 16.

*Partisan Review,* spring, 2002, Anthony Chennells, review of *The Sweetest Dream,* p. 297.

*Publishers Weekly,* September 19, 1994, p. 47; May 29, 2000, review of *Ben, in the World,* p. 46; January 21, 2002, review of *The Sweetest Dream,* p. 63.

*San Francisco Review of Books,* number 3, 1992, p. 25.

*Spectator,* October 31, 1992, p. 38; October 22, 1994, p. 48; April 20, 1996, p. 42; October 18, 1997, p. 55; September 1, 2001, Philip Hensher, review of *The Sweetest Dream,* p. 33.

*Time,* October 1, 1984; October 7, 1985; November 21, 1994.

*Times* (London, England), March 19, 1981; June 2, 1983; August 12, 1985; October 7, 1985.

*Times Literary Supplement,* November 23, 1979; May 9, 1980; April 17, 1981; April 2, 1982; June 3, 1983; September 13, 1985; May 8, 1987; October 17, 1987; April 22, 1988; December 18, 1992, p. 8; December, 2, 1994, p. 11; April 5, 1996, p. 27; December 5, 1997, p. 6.

*Tribune Books* (Chicago, IL), October 30, 1979; April 27, 1980; January 24, 1982; September 29, 1985; January 31, 1988; March 20, 1988; July 26, 1992, p. 3; January 3, 1993, p. 3; October 23, 1994, p. 1.

*USA Today,* December 1, 1994, p. D9.

*Village Voice,* January 4, 1973; October 2, 1978.

*Washington Post,* September 24, 1984; October 1, 1984; October 24, 1984; June 11, 1992, p. B2; December 29, 1994, p. C1.

*Washington Post Book World,* October 21, 1979; November 4, 1979; April 6, 1980; January 25, 1981; March 21, 1982; April 24, 1983; September 22, 1985; March 20, 1988; April 19, 1992, p. 15; January, 10, 1993, p. 5; October 16, 1994, p. 14; March 31, 1996, p. 7.

*Women's Review of Books,* March, 1995, p. 11; October, 1996, p. 11; November, 1997, p. 5.

*World Literature Today,* spring, 2002, Charles P. Sarvan, review of *The Sweetest Dream,* pp. 119-120.

*World Literature Written in English,* November, 1973; April, 1976.*

\*      \*      \*

# LEVINE, Judith 1952-

*PERSONAL:* Born September 20, 1952, in Queens, NY; daughter of Theodore (a psychologist) and Charlotte (an administrator; maiden name, Peterson) Levine. *Education:* City College of the City University of New York, B.A. (magna cum laude), 1974; Columbia University, M.S., 1979. *Politics:* "Feminist, socialist." *Religion:* "Jewish, non-practicing." *Hobbies and other interests:* Bicycling, cross-country skiing, swimming, film, theater, art, birdwatching.

*ADDRESSES: Home*—372 State St., Brooklyn, NY 11217. *Agent*—Diane Cleaver, 55 Fifth Ave., New York, NY 10003.

*CAREER:* Writer, 1979—. Worked variously as a waitress, daycare teacher, and bike messenger, 1972-79.

*MEMBER:* National Writers Union (vice president), Authors Guild, Feminist Anti-Censorship Taskforce (FACT), No More Nice Girls (founder).

*AWARDS, HONORS:* Richard J. Margolis Award, 1993.

*WRITINGS:*

*My Enemy, My Love: Man Hating and Ambivalence in Women's Lives,* Doubleday (New York, NY), 1992.

*Harmful to Minors: The Perils of Protecting Children from Sex,* University of Minnesota Press (Minneapolis, MN), 2002.

Contributor of articles and reviews to periodicals, including *Lears, Mirabella, New Woman, Philadelphia Inquirer Book Review, Village Voice,* and *Village Voice Literary Supplement.* Contributing editor, *New York Woman* (magazine), 1991-92.

*SIDELIGHTS:* Journalist Judith Levine's second book, *Harmful to Minors: The Perils of Protecting Children from Sex,* became the focus of a bitter controversy even before its publication in 2002. Levine intended the book to be a discussion about how reactionary laws and puritanical attitudes affect adolescents' development as sexual beings, but some critics branded it a rationalization for pedophilia and child molesting. The debate over the book was split along political lines, with those on the right inclined to view the book as a dangerous treatise on sexual relationships between children and adults, and those on the left, who believed it brought to light the failure of "abstinence only" sex education policies. At times, the controversy overshadowed meaningful discourse about Levine's ideas, which were controversial enough at the outset for her to have had trouble finding a publisher. Though University of Minnesota Press agreed to publish the book, the subsequent public outcry led them to form an independent review board to greenlight all subsequent projects. This controversy in part proved Levine's thesis, which is that American culture is ruled by a "politics of fear" that prevents a substantive discussion of sexuality and minors. For this and other reasons, the book quickly became, in the words of Beth Gillin of the *Philadelphia Enquirer,* "the most vilified book in America."

The controversy began in earnest after an interview in which Levine, commenting on the breaking scandal in the Roman Catholic Church involving the cover-up of pedophile priests, stated that it wasn't outside the realm of possibility that a sexual relationship between a child and a priest could be a positive one. In subsequent interviews, Levine strongly asserted that priests should not have sex with children, in addition to renouncing pedophilia, rape, and other illegal sex acts. But she stood firm in her assertion that "America's drive to protect kids from sex is protecting them from nothing," as Robert Stacy McCain of *Insight on the News* quoted her. The timing of the book's publication, which occurred just as the scandal in the Roman Catholic Church was making headlines, was hard to overcome. "The priest scandal," wrote JoAnn Wypijewski in the *Nation,* "has . . . limited the possibilities for thoughtful discussion on the real things people do and feel, the causes and effects and complex power exchanges of a human activity that does not and will never, operate according to the precepts of a textbook or lawbook."

Another topic in *Harmful to Minors* is the shifting age of consent, which in Levine's eyes is a legal construct that doesn't necessarily reflect the laws of nature. Many states determine the age of consent to be eighteen, but most European countries set it at fifteen. Either way, Levine argues, a seventeen-year-old is more sexually aware than an eight-year-old and should be treated as such, but this factor is not reflected in the law. Instead, the politics of fear come into play, and minors are bound by laws that determine that they have been victimized even if they don't see it that way. Regarding this and other ideas, John Leo of *U.S. News & World Report* wrote that "the real danger, [Levine] thinks, is not the pedophile, but parents and

parental figures who project their fears and their own lust for young flesh onto the mythically dangerous child molester." Rebecca Winters wrote in *Time* that Levine "argues that adults harm children by associating sex with danger . . . but not acknowledging that children and teens are capable of a measure of sexual pleasure."

Critics who did not view the book through a political lens were inclined to give credence to at least some of Levine's ideas. Among them are teaching high school students about the risks of sexually transmitted diseases, various forms of contraception, and the consequences of being sexually active—ideas that are often discouraged in "abstinence only" sex education programs. Levine also argues that feelings are important to any discussion of teen sexuality, and the debate about sex education often ignores the sometimes surprising maturity some teenagers have regarding their own sexuality. The book also takes issue with dangers that are given a disproportionate amount of attention in the media. For instance, Levine cites studies that indicate child pornography on the Internet is a relatively rare occurrence, and that child molesters do not routinely prey on unsuspecting children in online chat rooms. "Her well-documented horror stories of zealotry and incompetence are chilling," wrote Martha Cornog of *Library Journal,* but Leo took issue with Levine's reliance on the 1998 Rind study, which was widely seen by many as being soft on child sexual abuse, and called *Harmful to Minors* "a classic example of how disorder in the intellectual world leaks into the popular culture."

Other reviews were more positive. *Harmful to Minors* presents "a good start to confronting some vital questions," wrote a critic for *Publishers Weekly.* Deborah Roofman of *Psychology Today* qualified her praise: "Levine articulately addresses the moral issues intrinsic in sexual decision-making. Yet nowhere does she offer strategies for helping children and adolescents develop skills for moral thinking." She concluded that "Levine's call for a new approach to sex education is important—but inadequate." Louise Armstrong of the *Women's Review of Books* similarly stated that "Levine seems more enthused about the sex in sex ed than the safety," but that her "advocacy for sex education to encourage condom use, to provide reliable information on sexually transmitted diseases and the real danger of AIDS is both worthy and urgent." Wypijewski found some satisfaction in other elements of the book, concluding that "the greatest virtue in Levine's book is its hope that children might learn to find joy in the realm of the senses, the world of ideas and souls, so that when sex disappoints and love fails, as they will, a teenager, a grown-up, still has herself, and a universe of small delights and strong hearts to fall back on."

*BIOGRAPHICAL AND CRITICAL SOURCES:*

PERIODICALS

*Insight on the News,* May 20, 2002, Robert Stacy McCain, "Sex Isn't Just for Adults Anymore," p. 27.

*Library Journal,* June 1, 2002, Martha Cornog, review of *Harmful to Minors: The Perils of Protecting Children from Sex,* p. 176.

*Nation,* May 20, 2002, JoAnn Wypijewski, "The Wonder Years," p. 24.

*Philadelphia Inquirer,* April 16, 2002, Beth Gillin, "Book Blasted for Views on Childhood Sexuality."

*Psychology Today,* July-August, 2002, Deborah Roofman, "Sex: Friend or Foe?," p. 70.

*Publishers Weekly,* April 22, 2002, review of *Harmful to Minors,* p. 63.

*Time,* April 15, 2002, Rebecca Winters, "Child Sexuality: Challenging the Taboos," p. 22.

*U.S. News & World Report,* April 22, 2002, John Leo, "Apologists for Pedophilia," p. 53.

*Women's Review of Books,* June, 2002, Louise Armstrong, "Wishful Thinking," pp. 1-3.*

\*     \*     \*

**LEVINE, Lawrence W(illiam) 1933-**

*PERSONAL:* Born February 27, 1933, in New York, NY; son of Abraham and Anne (Schmookler) Levine; married Cornelia Roettcher, May 29, 1964; children: Alexander, Joshua, Isaac. *Education:* City College of New York, B.A., 1955; Columbia University, M.A., 1957, Ph.D., 1962. *Religion:* Jewish.

*ADDRESSES: Home*—431 Boynton St., Berkeley, CA 94707. *Office*—Department of History, George Mason University, B353 Robinson Hall, 4400 University Dr., Fairfax, VA 22030-4444. *E-mail*—llevine1@gmu.edu.

*CAREER:* City College of New York, New York, NY, lecturer, 1959-61; Princeton University, Princeton, NJ, instructor, 1961-62; University of California, Berkeley, assistant professor, 1962-67, associate professor, 1967-70, professor of history, 1970-84, became Margaret Byrne Professor, 1984; George Mason University, Fairfax, VA, currently professor of history and art history. Visiting professor at University of East Anglia, Norwich, England, 1967-68, and Free University of Berlin, West Germany, 1977. Member of national advisory board of the Center for American Culture Studies, Columbia University, 1983-84. President of Congregation Beth El, Berkeley, CA, 1979-82.

*MEMBER:* American Academy of Arts and Sciences, American Studies Association (member of national council, 1980-82), American History Association (member of council, 1987-90), Organization of American Historians (member of executive board, 1984-87; president, 1992), American Folklore Society, American Film Institute, Society of American Historians, Phi Beta Kappa (bicentennial fellow, 1973).

*AWARDS, HONORS:* Social Science Research Council fellow, 1965-66; Chicago Folklore Prize, 1977, for *Black Culture and Black Consciousness: Afro-American Folk Thought from Slavery to Freedom;* National Museum of American History Smithsonian Institution Regents fellow, 1981-82; Woodrow Wilson fellow, International Center for Scholars, 1982-83; MacArthur Foundation fellow, 1983-88; Center for Advanced Study in Behavioral Sciences fellow, 1990-91.

*WRITINGS:*

*Defender of the Faith: William Jennings Bryan; The Last Decade, 1915-1925,* Oxford University Press (New York, NY), 1965, reprinted, 1987.

(Editor, with Richard M. Abrams) *The Shaping of Twentieth-Century America: Interpretive Essays,* Little, Brown (Boston, MA), 1965.

(Editor, with Robert Middlekauff) *The National Temper: Readings in American Culture and Society,* Harcourt (New York, NY), 1968.

*Black Culture and Black Consciousness: Afro-American Folk Thought from Slavery to Freedom,* Oxford University Press (New York, NY), 1977.

*Highbrow/Lowbrow: The Emergence of Cultural Hierarchy in America,* Harvard University Press (Cambridge, MA), 1988.

(Contributor, with Alan Trachtenberg) *Documenting America, 1935-1943,* University of California Press (Berkeley, CA), 1988.

*The Unpredictable Past: Explorations in American Cultural History,* Oxford University Press (New York, NY), 1993.

*The Opening of the American Mind: Canons, Culture, and History,* Beacon Press (Boston, MA), 1996.

(With wife, Cornelia Levine) *The People and the President: America's Conversation with FDR,* Beacon Press (Boston, MA), 2002.

*ADAPTATIONS: Black Culture and Black Consciousness: Afro-American Folk Thought from Slavery to Freedom* was adapted for audiocassette, read by the author.

*SIDELIGHTS:* Professor Lawrence W. Levine has written books on various aspects of American culture. His first, *Defender of the Faith: William Jennings Bryan; The Last Decade, 1915-1925,* is a look at the last years of American politician and lawyer Bryan, who is best remembered for fighting to uphold the anti-evolution law during the "Monkey Trial" of teacher John Scopes in Dayton, Tennessee, during the 1920s. A *Washington Post Book World* reviewer of Levine's portrait of Bryan remarked that *Defender of the Faith* is "brilliantly and sympathetically reconstructed by the distinguished Berkeley historian."

Among the most critically acclaimed of Levine's works is *Black Culture and Black Consciousness: Afro-American Folk Thought from Slavery to Freedom,* which examines African-American culture and viewpoint from slavery to the twentieth century through religion, music, humor, folk tales, and superstitions. Levine points out that slaves, despite the horrible and depraved conditions thrust upon them, were nonetheless able to develop their own culture within the confines of slavery, enabling them to at least overcome their circumstances psychologically. Beginning with the era of slavery, Levine expounds upon the spiritual essence of slave songs, observing that the songs promised a better future, in this life or the next. Levine also relates slave jokes that reveal a determined effort by black Americans to laugh in the midst of their trials. This humor, according to Levine, also served as a means of liberating hostile feelings toward their white masters.

*Black Culture and Black Consciousness* was praised by critics such as the *Washington Post Book World* reviewer Al-Tony Gilmore, who deemed it "a thought-

fully organized, smooth reading, well researched study that ranks among the best books written on the Afro-American experience in recent years." In his *Nation* review, Jerry H. Bryant noted that *Black Culture and Black Consciousness* "is a fine book on a number of levels. It contains a tremendous store of information drawn from a huge array of sources, some readily available, some not. . . . Nevertheless, this is a book of history, albeit folk history, or social history. It examines the everyday experience of ordinary people. Levine comes to his work as a serious historian who believes that much important history has been lost because of the limits orthodoxy has placed upon its subjects and evidence, but this does not mean he abandons thorough and systematic research and presentation."

Levine's 1988 book, *Highbrow/Lowbrow: The Emergence of Cultural Hierarchy in America,* addresses the labels "highbrow," "middle-brow," and "lowbrow," used by certain intellectuals to categorize other members or elements of society. Levine was inspired to write *Highbrow/Lowbrow* by his learning that at one time, during the nineteenth century, Shakespearean plays were considered entertaining by virtually all segments of the population in America. Levine writes that the values espoused in Shakespeare's writings meshed with those of nineteenth-century Americans and that the love of Shakespeare's works, including burlesques and parodies of them, knew no cultural boundaries. Towards the end of the century, Levine proposes, lovers of European culture began to approach the arts as something exclusive that must be taught in order to be appreciated. The result: the fine arts eventually were reserved for a select group (the highbrows) and out of the ready reach of the common man (or lowbrows). Thus, Levine asserts, came the existing hierarchy of culture.

Reaction to *Highbrow/Lowbrow* was mixed, undoubtedly because its audience would largely be considered "highbrow." Nevertheless, several critics have expressed appreciation of Levine's effort, among them Carlin Romano, who wrote in the *Washington Post Book World:* "We can all appreciate a scholar who bites the process that feeds him. *Highbrow/Lowbrow* sinks its teeth into our smug cultural assumptions and holds on for dear life." *Los Angeles Times Book Review* critic Alex Raksin concluded that "Levine's elucidation of the dangers in denigrating other cultures without truly understanding them is sharp and unrefutable, while his overview of cultural hierarchies since the nineteenth century is spirited and entertaining."

The title of Levine's 1996 work *The Opening of the American Mind: Canons, Culture, and History* plays off the controversial bestseller of 1988, Allan Bloom's *The Closing of the American Mind.* In his book, which sparked widespread debate on just how students should be taught at the university level, Bloom gave the opinion that the modern-day educational system—with its growing curriculum of multiculturalism—was failing Americans. He argued for a politically conservative approach that stressed Western culture. In *The Opening of the American Mind,* Levine counters that conservatives like Bloom nurture "nostalgia for a past that never existed," as Gregory Streich noted in *Journal of American Ethnic History.* The author "illustrates that past changes in curricula that produced the canon that conservatives now defend—the addition of Shakespeare and Milton, the addition of American literature by Melville and Hawthorne—were all made despite fears that such changes would lead to declining standards and values."

*American Scholar* critic Seth Forman pointed to that perceived nostalgia as a failing of *The Opening of the American Mind.* "Most of the critics Levine discusses," including Bloom, Arthur Schlesinger, Jr., and Richard Bernstein, "do not long for some nonexistent past," Forman commented, "but merely for that period of American higher education before the late 1960s, when the university was shedding its former provincialism, dropping its discriminatory admissions policies for ones based primarily on academic merit, and generally realizing the liberal 'cosmopolitan' intellectual of that era."

In an article for *Locke Book Report,* Andrew Cline felt Levine "sees everything in black and white. . . . He pigeonholes everyone into either the conservative or the liberal camp. But his categories are too neatly drawn, and the inaccuracies of these neat boxes show in his treatment of Allan Bloom." Wilfred M. McClay, writing in the *Wilson Quarterly,* also held the view that Levine "repeatedly goes overboard in fulminating against critics and traditionalists" but also found that the author "correctly points out that many of the contemporary critics of higher education have themselves been guilty of sloppy research and excessive rhetoric." *Booklist* reviewer Donna Seaman found value in Levine's argument, saying that he "reminds us that to

understand the present, we must understand the past and not traffic in nostalgia."

With his wife, Cornelia, Levine turned from cultural history to political biography with their 2002 publication, *The People and the President: America's Conversation with FDR.* Franklin Delano Roosevelt, whose three-term administration spanned the Depression and World War II, was considered among the most accessible of presidents. He was famous for his "Fireside Chats" radio addresses given regularly beginning a week after FDR took office in 1933. "Tell me your troubles," he said during his first chat, and "so the nation did, flooding Washington with millions of letters," summarized a *Kirkus Reviews* contributor. Those letters make up the basis for the Levines' book, a compendium of correspondence on nearly every topic. Some of the missives complement the president; but many of the included letters are critical of FDR's alliance with England against Germany, for example. Other letter-writers were more personal in their complaints: "I would feel more confident if you didn't have so many smart alex young Jews and Irish around you," wrote a farmer in 1940, as quoted in a *Publishers Weekly* review. *Library Journal* contributor Thomas Baldino made special note of the "fascinating and touching letters [that] provide much more insight into the lives of average Americans . . . than simply reading a historical account."

## BIOGRAPHICAL AND CRITICAL SOURCES:

### PERIODICALS

*AB Bookman's Weekly,* May 29, 1989, review of *Highbrow/Lowbrow: The Emergence of Cultural Hierarchy in America,* p. 2411.
*American Ethnologist,* spring, 1992, review of *Highbrow/Lowbrow,* p. 818.
*American Historical Review,* June, 1994, review of *The Unpredictable Past: Explorations in American Cultural History,* p. 958; April, 1990, review of *Highbrow/Lowbrow,* p. 569; October, 1998, review of *The Opening of the American Mind: Canons, Culture, and History,* p. 1357.
*American Literature,* March, 1989, review of *Highbrow/Lowbrow,* p. 157.
*American Quarterly,* September, 1991, review of *Highbrow/Lowbrow,* p. 518.

*American Scholar,* fall, 1997, Seth Forman, review of *The Opening of the American Mind,* p. 619.

*Antioch Review,* winter, 1989, review of *Highbrow/Lowbrow,* p. 113.

*Booklist,* September 15, 1996, Donna Seaman, review of *The Opening of the American Mind,* p. 181.

*Books & Culture,* May, 1997, review of *The Opening of the American Mind,* p. 7.

*Choice,* July, 1989, review of *Highbrow/Lowbrow,* p. 1895; October, 1993, review of *The Unpredictable Past,* p. 354; March, 1997, review of *The Opening of the American Mind,* p. 1227.

*Christian Science Monitor,* July 12, 1989, review of *Highbrow/Lowbrow,* p. 13.

*College Literature,* February, 1991, review of *Highbrow/Lowbrow,* p. 111.

*Come-All-Ye,* summer, 1990, review of *Highbrow/Lowbrow,* p. 6.

*Contemporary Sociology,* July, 1990, review of *Highbrow/Lowbrow,* p. 508.

*Dissent,* winter, 1997, review of *The Opening of the American Mind,* p. 115.

*English Journal,* November, 1989, review of *Highbrow/Lowbrow,* p. 86.

*Georgia Review,* spring, 1989, review of *Highbrow/Lowbrow,* p. 179.

*History,* spring, 1989, review of *Highbrow/Lowbrow,* p. 109; summer, 1994, review of *The Unpredictable Past,* p. 148.

*Journal of American Ethnic History,* fall, 1997, Gregory Streich, review of *The Opening of the American Mind,* p. 86.

*Journal of American Folklore,* April, 1980, review of *Black Culture and Black Consciousness: Afro-American Folk Thought from Slavery to Freedom,* p. 187.

*Journal of American History,* September, 1989, review of *Highbrow/Lowbrow,* p. 565.

*Journal of American Studies,* August, 1990, review of *Highbrow/Lowbrow,* p. 292.

*Journal of Interdisciplinary History,* autumn, 1989, review of *Highbrow/Lowbrow,* p. 329.

*Journal of Popular Culture,* summer, 1989, review of *Highbrow/Lowbrow,* p. 143.

*Journal of Social History,* winter, 1989, review of *Highbrow/Lowbrow,* p. 387.

*Kirkus Reviews,* August 1, 1996, review of *The Opening of the American Mind,* p. 1124; April 1, 2002, review of *The People and the President: America's Conversation with FDR,* p. 472.

*Libraries and Culture,* summer, 1991, review of *Highbrow/Lowbrow,* p. 557.

*Library Journal,* May 15, 1993, review of *The Unpredictable Past,* p. 83; April 15, 2002, Thomas Baldino, review of *The People and the President,* p. 105.

*Los Angeles Times Book Review,* October 9, 1988, Alex Raksin, review of *Highbrow/Lowbrow,* p. 4.

*Modern Language Review,* October, 1990, review of *Highbrow/Lowbrow,* p. 934.

*Nation,* March 12, 1977, Jerry Bryant, review of *Black Culture and Black Consciousness,* pp. 311-313; October 7, 1996, review of *The Opening of the American Mind,* p. 25.

*New Leader,* December 16, 1996, review of *The Opening of the American Mind,* p. 7.

*New Republic,* December 3, 1977, p. 25.

*New York Times Book Review,* January 22, 1978; October 27, 1996, review of *The Opening of the American Mind,* p. 14.

*Nineteenth-Century Literature,* June, 1990, review of *Highbrow/Lowbrow,* p. 120.

*Partisan Review,* no. 2, 1990, review of *Highbrow/Lowbrow,* p. 317.

*Publishers Weekly,* June 22, 1996, review of *The Opening of the American Mind,* p. 221; April 15, 2002, review of *The People and the President,* p. 49.

*San Francisco Review of Books,* number 4, 1989, review of *Highbrow/Lowbrow,* p. 33.

*Shakespeare Quarterly,* fall, 1991, review of *Highbrow/Lowbrow,* p. 373.

*Sociological Review,* August, 1990, review of *Highbrow/Lowbrow,* p. 608.

*Southern Humanities Review,* summer, 1999, review of *The Opening of the American Mind,* p. 297.

*Theatre Journal,* October, 1990, review of *Highbrow/Lowbrow,* p. 391.

*Times Literary Supplement,* May 25, 1967, p. 468; July 14, 1989, review of *Highbrow/Lowbrow,* p. 767.

*Virginia Quarterly Review,* summer, 1989, review of *Highbrow/Lowbrow,* p. 97; spring, 1998, review of *The Opening of the American Mind,* p. 368.

*Washington Post Book World,* April 10, 1977; February 19, 1978, Al-Tony Gilmore, review of *Black Culture and Black Consciousness,* p. E7; July 5, 1987; January 8, 1989, Carlin Romano, review of *Highbrow/Lowbrow,* pp. 3, 6; September 29, 1996, review of *The Opening of the American Mind,* p. 3.

*Wilson Quarterly,* summer, 1993, review of *Black Culture and Black Consciousness,* p. 30; autumn, 1996, Wilfred M. McClay, review of *The Opening of the American Mind,* p. 94.

*ONLINE*

*Locke Book Review,* http://www.johnlocke.org/ (July 16, 2002), Andrew Cline, review of *The Opening of the American Mind.**

\* \* \*

### LINK, (Eugene) Perry (Jr.) 1944-

*PERSONAL:* Born August 6, 1944, in Gaffney, SC; son of Eugene (a professor) and Beulah M. (a teacher; maiden name, Meyer) Link; married Yi Tong, April 5, 2003; children: Monica, Nathan. *Education:* Harvard University, B.A., 1966, M.A., 1969, Ph.D., 1976.

*ADDRESSES: Office*—Department of Asian Studies, 215 Jones Hall, Princeton University, Princeton, NJ 08544. *E-mail*—eplink@princeton.edu.

*CAREER:* Princeton University, Princeton, NJ, assistant professor/lecturer, 1973-76, assistant professor of East Asian studies, 1976-77, became professor; University of California, Los Angeles, assistant professor, 1977-80, associate professor of Oriental languages, c. 1980, organizer and chairman of interdisciplinary workshop on modern China, 1977-78. Instructor at Middlebury College, 1971, lecturer-in-charge, 1972, 1978, and 1979. Chair of Harvard University's East Asian Colloquium, 1970-71; co-chair of Columbia University's workshop on writers and publics in modern China, 1974-76; chair of program committee of Southern California China Colloquium, 1979. Visiting scholar at East Asian Institute, 1975-76; visiting associate research linguist at Center for Chinese Studies, 1981. Member of board of trustees of Princeton-in-Asia Foundation, 1976-78; member of advisory committee of Hong Kong's Universities Service Center, 1977—.

*MEMBER:* Phi Beta Kappa.

*AWARDS, HONORS:* Michael C. Rockefeller memorial traveling fellowship from Harvard University, 1966-67; Fulbright fellowship, 1972-73; grant from American Council of Learned Societies, 1977; National Academy of Sciences fellowship for China, 1979-80; grant from American Council of Learned Societies and Social Science Research Council, 1980.

*Perry Link*

*WRITINGS:*

*Mandarin Ducks and Butterflies: Popular Urban Fiction in Early Twentieth-Century Chinese Cities,* University of California Press (Berkeley, CA), 1981.

(Editor) *Chinese Literature, 1979-80,* Indiana University Press (Bloomington, IN), 1982.

(Editor) *Stubborn Weeds: Popular and Controversial Chinese Literature after the Cultural Revolution,* Indiana University Press (Bloomington, IN), 1983.

(Editor) Liu Binyan, *People or Monsters?: And Other Stories and Reportage from China after Mao,* Indiana University Press (Bloomington, IN), 1983.

(Editor) *Roses and Thorns: The Second Blooming of the Hundred Flowers in Chinese Fiction, 1979-80,* University of California Press (Berkeley, CA), 1984.

(Editor, with Richard P. Madsen and Paul G. Pickowicz) *Unofficial China: Popular Culture and Thought in the People's Republic,* Westview Press (Boulder, CO), 1989.

*Evening Chats in Beijing: Probing China's Predicament,* W. W. Norton (New York, NY), 1992.

*The Uses of Literature: Life in the Socialist Chinese Literary System,* Princeton University Press (Princeton, NJ), 2000.

(Editor, with Andrew J. Nathan) *The Tiananmen Papers,* compiled by Zhang Liang, Public Affairs (New York, NY), 2001.

(Editor, with Richard P. Madsen and Paul G. Pickowicz) *Popular China: Unofficial Culture in a Globalizing Society,* Rowman & Littlefield (Lanham, MD), 2002.

*CONTRIBUTOR*

*The Indochina Story,* Bantam, 1971.

Merle Goldman, editor, *Modern Chinese Literature in the May Fourth Era,* Harvard University Press, 1977.

George Kao, editor, *Two Writers and the Cultural Revolution,* University of Washington Press, 1980.

K. Y. Hsu, editor, *Literature on the People's Republic of China,* Indiana University Press, 1980.

Joseph Lau and Leo Lee, editors, *Modern Chinese Stories,* Columbia University Press, 1981.

*Chinese Primer: Character Text,* Princeton University Press (Princeton, NJ), 1994.

*Chinese Primer: Volumes 1-3 (Pinyin),* Princeton University Press (Princeton, NJ), 1994.

*Chinese Primer: Volumes 1-3 (GR),* Princeton University Press (Princeton, NJ), 1994.

*Oh, China! Elementary Reader of Modern Chinese for Advanced Beginners,* Princeton University Press (Princeton, NJ), 1997.

*Nanking 1937: Memory and Healing,* M. E. Sharpe (Armonk, NY), 2001.

Author of *The College of Emporia,* 1982. Contributor of articles, translations, and reviews to scholarly journals in the United States and abroad. Coeditor of *Bulletin of Concerned Asian Scholars,* 1971-72.

*SIDELIGHTS:* Perry Link is a scholar of China and its culture. His publications have added to the growing field of Sinology, which involves analyzing Chinese politics and culture in an effort to gain a better understanding of the historically inscrutable land.

Link was involved with the publication of the controversial book *The Tiananmen Papers,* which a *Publishers Weekly* writer called "one of the most significant works of scholarship on China in decades." The book purports to be a collection of transcribed documents that recount Chinese leaders' debate over how to handle the democratic uprisings in the spring of 1989 that culminated in the takeover of Tiananmen Square in Beijing. The papers were smuggled out of the country by a person operating under the pseudonym Zhang Liang; both Link and coeditor Andrew Nathan have gone to great lengths to ensure Liang's safety by concealing his identity. Liang claims to have been a participant in the uprising as well as a member of the Communist party, who gained access to the papers years after the uprising was put down by the government. Nathan and Link worked with several translators to ensure the accuracy of the translated documents and they claim that the documents are real, although they cannot release proof of their veracity because it would compromise their sources.

*The Tiananmen Papers* tells the story of a power struggle between China's moderates and hardliners, with the hardliners eventually winning out. Borne out in the debate was the recognition that the uprisings were illegal, and the students should be dealt with, but also that more freedom was necessary in China if the country wished to compete in the emerging global economy. Ultimately, the leaders decided to enact martial law, and the uprisings, which began peacefully, ended in bloodshed and the death of over two hundred people. Implicit in Liang's actions, and the documents themselves, is that reform in China must come from within the Communist party; Link and coeditor Andrew Nathan argue that had China's decision been different, the country today might be a democracy.

The controversy over *The Tiananmen Papers* stems from the possibility that the documents transcribed in the book could have been forged, simply because China's notorious secrecy makes such a huge leak uncharacteristic. Even Link and Nathan themselves acknowledge a rich tradition of forged documents in China. As George Walden of the *National Interest* said, "with China, you never know," but that "if this is a forgery it is brilliantly done." The papers illustrate that initially, many members of the Politburo were willing to negotiate with the students and entertain their demands for a freer press, among other things. But the moderates were ultimately overruled by Prime Minister Li Peng, who called on elder members of the government to stand true to their belief in the ideology of China's Communist revolution. Because consensus is important to the Chinese, in subsequent debates, other leaders were not willing to express dissenting opinions, and the students' fate was sealed.

Despite Link and Nathan's claims of having authenticated the documents, some critics remained unconvinced. Edward Jay Epstein, writing in the *Nation* cautioned that "we do not know why [the documents] were transcribed or who transcribed them. We do not know who directed this process—or why—and who selected, or wrote, the 516 pages delivered for publication. All we know for sure is that some anonymous person from China delivered for publication in America a computer file that cannot be authenticated." Regardless, the papers "contain no startling revelations," according to Andrew Scobell in the journal *Parameters.*

Other critics disagreed. Walden said the papers "should help our China policy mature." Gerald F. Kreyche of *USA Today Magazine* called the papers "an entrée to the inscrutable minds of Politburo members" and concluded that "the expose will probably have repercussions on some of those who are governing China today." Concurring with this view, with the caveat of allowing for whether or not the papers are real, was Danny Schechter of the *Economist,* who said the book "may contain an impetus, perhaps a powerful one, for future change." More pragmatically, Jonathan Spence of the *New York Times Book Review* stated that "what Zhang Liang and his American editors seem to have pulled off is a no-lose situation: if this book succeeds in provoking the Chinese authorities to try to rebut its conclusions by bringing into the public domain a still wider range of sources, so much the better. And if the authorities don't attempt a rebuttal, it may be taken as a kind of acquiescence to the genuineness of the materials published here."

In *The Uses of Literature: Life in the Socialist Chinese Literary System,* Link examines Chinese literature from roughly the period of 1970 through 1980, in the waning days of the Cultural Revolution after the death of Chairman Mao. Link likens this period to a post-Stalin USSR, when writers were subtly rebelling from generations of being told what to write and how to write it. Works examined include Chen Rong's novella *At Middle Age,* Zhang Yang's *The Second Handshake,* as well as a look at popular fiction of detective stories, romance, and pornography. The debate over literature in China, Link writes, usually took place between the

audience and top ranking members of the Communist Party, who frequently assessed whether or not a published work of fiction was "correct" or not. Timothy C. Wong, writing in *World Literature Today,* took issue with Link's definition of "uses of literature," but nevertheless said that "his book stands as a significant contribution to our understanding of Chinese literature."

In *Evening Chats in Beijing: Probing China's Predicament,* Link talks with leading Chinese intellectuals and reports that they are nearly unanimous in their desire to leave China permanently for the West. Furthermore, dissidents who have made it to the West usually do not wish to return to China, or even fight for political reforms from the safety of exile in the West. Research for the book was conducted in 1988 and 1989 while Link served as the director of the National Academy of Science Office on Scholarly Exchange in Beijing. Through his interviews with intellectuals from several generations, "Link displays a remarkable grasp of China's recent history," wrote Timothy Tung in the *New Leader.* Link discovers that most high-ranking Chinese officials have sent their children to the United States and that support for Marxism is almost nonexistent even within the country. Tung further complimented Link's explanation of the Chinese language, particularly in the subtle double meanings of many words. The book, Tung concluded, "shows Link to be exceptionally versed in the complexities of Chinese thought—no mean feat for a Western scholar."

*BIOGRAPHICAL AND CRITICAL SOURCES:*

*PERIODICALS*

*Choice,* April, 1994, reviews of *Evening Chats in Beijing, Unofficial China, Stubborn Weeds,* and *Roses and Thorns,* p. 1249.
*Economist,* March 3, 2001, Danny Schechter, "China's Lost Decade: The Legacy of Tiananmen," p. 1.
*Foreign Affairs,* March-April, 2001, Lucian W. Pye, "Appealing the Tiananmen Verdict: New Documents from China's Highest Leaders," p. 148.
*Nation,* February 5, 2001, Edward Jay Epstein, review of *The Tiananmen Papers,* p. 6.
*National Interest,* summer, 2001, George Walden, "Communist Crowd Control," p. 121.
*New Leader,* September 21, 1992, Timothy Tung, review of *Evening Chats in Beijing,* p. 17.

*New York Review of Books,* August 2, 1992, review of *Evening Chats in Beijing,* p. 6; March 8, 2001, review of *The Uses of Literature,* p. 41.

*New York Times Book Review,* January 21, 2001, Jonathan Spence, "Inside the Forbidden City," p. 10.

*Pacific Affairs,* winter, 2000, Richard King, review of *The Uses of Literature,* p. 580.

*Parameters,* autumn, 2001, Andrew Scobell, review of *The Tiananmen Papers,* p. 165.

*Publishers Weekly,* June 1, 1992, review of *Evening Chats in Beijing,* p. 43; January 15, 2001, review of *The Tiananmen Papers,* p. 64.

*Time International,* January 15, 2001, Jen Wei Ting, "What Really Happened?," p. 14.

*USA Today Magazine,* May, 2001, Gerald F. Kreyche, review of *The Tiananmen Papers,* p. 79.

*World Literature Today,* winter, 2001, Timothy C. Wong, review of *The Uses of Literature,* p. 102.

# M

## MARES, Michael A(llen) 1945-

*PERSONAL:* Surname is pronounced "*Mah*-riss"; born March 11, 1945, in Albuquerque, NM; son of Ernesto Gustavo and Rebecca Gabriela (Devine) Mares; married Lynn Ann Brusin (an attorney), August 27, 1966; children: Gabriel Andres, Daniel Alejandro. *Education:* University of New Mexico, B.S. (biology), 1967; Fort Hays Kansas State College (now University), M.S. (zoology), 1969; University of Texas at Austin, Ph.D. (zoology), 1973.

*ADDRESSES: Home*—3930 Charing Cross Ct., Norman, OK 73072-3201. *Office*—Oklahoma Museum of Natural History, University of Oklahoma, 1335 Asp Ave., Norman, OK 73019-6070. *E-mail*—mamares@ou.edu.

*CAREER:* University of Pittsburgh, Pittsburgh, PA, 1973-81, began as assistant professor, became associate professor; University of Oklahoma, Norman, associate professor, 1981-85, professor of zoology, 1985—, Oklahoma Museum of Natural History curator of mammals, 1981—, and director of museum, 1983—. Adjunct professor, Universidad Nacional de Cordoba, Argentina, 1971-72; visiting professor, Universidad Nacional de Tucuman, Argentina, 1972; research fellow, Chicano Council on Higher Education, 1978, and Ford Foundation Minority Research, 1980-81; University of Arizona, Tucson, visiting scientist, 1980-81. Member of American Republics Board, Fulbright Commission, 1983-86, 1988-91; U.S. Fish and Wildlife Service, Oklahoma representative to Endangered Mammal Species Committee, 1987—; Council for the International Exchange of Scholars, member of board of directors, 1988-91; Systematics Agenda 2000, co-chair of International Programs Committee. Consultant to NUS in Venezuela, 1980-81, Argentine National Science Foundation, Institute for Arid Zone Research, 1983, World Wildlife Fund in Brazil, 1986, and White House Biodiversity, Ecology, and Ecosystems group, 1992-94; member of advisory board, Center for Biological Diversity, Department of the Interior; member of Commission on the Future of the Smithsonian Institutions, 1993-96, and the Smithsonian Council, 2000.

*MEMBER:* Interamerican Association for the Advancement of Science, American Association for the Advancement of Science, American Society of Mammalogists (vice president, 1990-94), American Ecological Society, American Institute for the Biological Sciences, American Society of Naturalists, Society for the Study of Evolution, Paleontological Society, Association of Systematics Collections, Southwestern Association of Naturalists, Sigma Xi, Phi Kappa Phi, Beta Beta Beta.

*AWARDS, HONORS:* National Science Foundation grants, 1974-79, 1982-93, 1999-2000; Brazilian National Academy of Sciences research award, 1975-78; Fulbright-Hayes research fellowship, 1976; National Chicano Council on Higher Education Postdoctoral Research fellowship, Sigma Xi, 1978; Ford Foundation Minority Postdoctoral fellowship, 1980; University of Oklahoma Associates' Distinguished Lectureship Awards, 1984, 1987; Mid-America State University Honors Lecturer Designation, 1985; Don W. Tinkle Research Excellence Award, Southwestern Association of Naturalists, 1989; University of Oklahoma Regents Award, 1990, for superior accomplishment in professional and university service; National Geological Society grants, 1992-95, 1999; Alumni Achievement Award, Ft. Hays State University, 1998; C. Hart Merriam Award, American Society of Mammalogists, 2000, for outstanding service to mammalogy.

*WRITINGS:*

(With Daniel F. Williams) *A New Genus and Species of Phyllotine Rodent,* Carnegie Museum of Natural History (Pittsburgh, PA), 1978.

*Convergent Evolution among Desert Rodents: A Global Perspective,* Carnegie Museum of Natural History (Pittsburgh, PA), 1980.

*Mammalian Biology in South America: A Symposium Held at the Pymatuning Laboratory of Ecology, May 10-14, 1981,* Pymatuning Laboratory of Ecology (Linesville, PA), 1982.

(With Ricardo A. Ojeda and Rubén M. Barquez) *Guide to the Mammals of Salta Province,* illustrated by Enrique Guanuco, Patricia Capllonch de Barquez, and Norbeto Giannini, University of Oklahoma Press (Norman, OK), 1989.

*The Mammals of Oklahoma,* University of Oklahoma Press (Norman, OK), 1989.

(With Ricardo A. Ojeda) *A Biogeographic Analysis of the Mammals of Salta Province Argentina,* Texas Tech University Press (Lubbock, TX), 1989.

*Latin American Mammalogy: History, Biodiversity, and Conservation,* University of Oklahoma Press (Norman, OK), 1991.

*The Mammals of Tucuman,* Oklahoma Museum of Natural History (Norman, OK), 1991.

*Encyclopedia of Deserts,* University of Oklahoma Press (Norman, OK), 1999.

(With Rubén M. Barquez and Janet K. Braun) *The Bats of Argentina,* Museum of Texan Tech University (Lubbock, TX), 1999.

*A Desert Calling: Life in a Forbidding Landscape,* Harvard University Press (Cambridge, MA), 2002.

Contributor to and editor of periodicals.

*WORK IN PROGRESS: A Key to the Skulls of South American Mammals; Field Guide to the Mammals of South America;* research on systematics, distribution, and ecology of Argentina's mammals; research on applications of geographic information systems (GIS) in mammalogy.

*SIDELIGHTS:* In Michael A. Mares's research, he examines convergent evolution, adaptation, and community organization of desert rodents of the world, as well as ecology, conservation, evolution, and systematics of South American mammals. His work as a zoologist and ecologist has taken him all over the world, and his books reflect the depth of his work.

Several of Mares's books deal specifically with the mammals and climate of the desert. His book *A Desert Calling* is his effort to bring together his scientific insights alongside his personal reflections on life in the desert. Critics such as Tim Markus of *Library Journal* were impressed by the study tools presented in the book. Markus praised the maps and photographs, adding, "this unique books also includes a thorough bibliography and should appeal to both lay readers and scholars." In *Science News,* a reviewer praised Mares for bringing the desert ecosystem to life: "he paints amazing portraits of the ways rodents and other creatures . . . adapt to this hot, dry terrain." In a review for *Booklist,* Nancy Bent commented on Mares's process, noting that "the wonder of field research and of the discoveries that results shines through his matter-of-fact tone." Chip Ward of *Washington Post* remarked on the personal nature of the book: "*Desert Calling* is the autobiography of Mares's own evolution as a naturalist woven into a lively tapestry that includes fascinating science and eloquent advocacy." Ward concluded, "Deserts have long been regarded as places of exile where you go to wrestle with your demons and bring back revelations. Mares's exile was thirty years of hard fieldwork, and *A Desert Calling* is his gift of revelation to us."

*BIOGRAPHICAL AND CRITICAL SOURCES:*

*PERIODICALS*

*Agricultural History,* winter, 2000, review of *Encyclopedia of Deserts,* p. 127.

*Booklist,* April 1, 2002, Nancy Bent, review of *A Desert Calling: Life in a Forbidding Landscape,* p. 1290.

*Choice,* November, 1999, p. 510.

*Library Journal,* April 15, 2000, Brian E. Coutts and John B. Richard, review of *Encyclopedia of Deserts,* p. 55; April 1, 2002, Tim Markus, review of *A Desert Calling,* p. 135.

*Science News,* June 22, 2002, review of *A Desert Calling,* p. 399.

*SciTech Book News,* June, 1999, p. 5.

*Washington Post,* April 21, 2002, Chip Ward, review of *A Desert Calling,* p. BW9.

ONLINE

*Harvard University Press Web Site,* http://www.hup. harvard.edu/ (May 16, 2003).

*University of Oklahoma Web Site,* www.ou.edu/ (May 16, 2003).*

\*　　\*　　\*

**McCALL, Wendell**
**See PEARSON, Ridley**

\*　　\*　　\*

**McGOOGAN, Ken 1947-**

*PERSONAL:* Born January 18, 1947, in Montreal, Quebec, Canada. *Education:* Attended Concordia University, 1964-69; Ryerson Polytechnical University, B.A., 1974; University of British Columbia, M.F.A., 1976.

*ADDRESSES: Home*—185 Willow Ave., Toronto, Ontario M4E 3K4, Canada. *Office—Calgary Herald,* P.O. Box 2400, Station M, Calgary, Alberta T2N 0G3, Canada.

*CAREER:* Journalist, essayist, novelist, and biographer. *Calgary Herald,* Calgary, Alberta, Canada, literary editor. Worked as a journalist for Montreal *Star* and Toronto *Star.*

*MEMBER:* Writers Union of Canada.

*AWARDS, HONORS:* Award for best nonfiction book, Writers Guild of Alberta, 1991, for *Canada's Undeclared War;* Alberta Freedom of Expression Award; Wolfson College Fellowship, University of Cambridge, 1998; Christopher Award, Grant MacEwan Author's

Award (co-winner), History Award, Canadian Authors' Association, and Drainie-Taylor Biography Prize, Writers' Trust of Canada, all 2001, all for *Fatal Passage.*

*WRITINGS:*

*Canada's Undeclared War: Fighting Words from the Literary Trenches,* Detselig (Calgary, Alberta, Canada), 1991.

*Visions of Kerouac: A Novel,* Pottersfield Press, 1993, revised as *Kerouac's Ghost,* R. Davies Publishing (Montreal, Quebec, Canada), 1996.

*Calypso Warrior,* R. Davies Publishing (Montreal, Quebec, Canada), 1995.

*Chasing Safiya,* Bayeux Arts (Calgary, Alberta, Canada), 1999.

*Fatal Passage: The Untold Story of John Rae, the Arctic Adventurer Who Discovered the Fate of Franklin,* HarperFlamingo (Toronto, Ontario, Canada), 2001, published as *Fatal Passage: The True Story of John Rae, the Arctic Hero That Time Forgot,* Carroll & Graf (New York, NY), 2002.

*Ancient Mariner: The Amazing Adventures of Samuel Hearne, the Sailor Who Walked to the Arctic Ocean,* HarperFlamingo (Toronto, Ontario, Canada), 2003, Carroll & Graf (New York, NY), 2004.

*SIDELIGHTS:* Ken McGoogan is a journalist and author in Calgary, Alberta. His recent creative nonfiction works have won him major awards and international acclaim. These successes arose after McGoogan honed his craft as both a journalist and a novelist. After working at The Toronto Star and The Montreal Star, he became literary editor at the *Calgary Herald* a position he held for more than fifteen years. By rising at 5 a.m. and writing before he went into the newspaper, he wrote several books, publishing four of them. *Canada's Undeclared War: Fighting Words From the Literary Trenches* was a controversial work that won the best non-fiction-book award from the Writers' Guild of Alberta.

In 1993 McGoogan published his first novel, *Visions of Kerouac,* a coming-of-age story about a young boy named Frankie who hits the road just like Beat author Jack Kerouac. In 1996 the book was released in a revised version titled *Kerouac's Ghost.* The original story is narrated by an adult Frankie, who has gone back to visit the places he traveled as a boy and is now accompanied by his wife. The point of view shifts radically in McGoogan's rewrite, with the actual ghost of Jack Kerouac telling the story. Ann Ireland noted in *Quill and Quire* that this shift in narrator could be problematic. She explained that "many readers know Kerouac's work intimately and will be convinced they know how his prose sounds and thinks. Comparisons are inevitable." However, Ireland was impressed with McGoogan's attempt to better his own writing, noting "How often do we get to see the process of novel making?"

McGoogan himself is on record as being uncertain which version of the novel he prefers: *Visions of Kerouac* or *Kerouac's Ghost*. McGoogan told *CA* that he would "like to take another run" at *Calypso Warrior,* his 1995 novel, which is set in Quebec and treats the politics of language. Aesthetically, he remains happier with *Chasing Safiya.* Called a metaphysical romp and a supernatural quest, McGoogan used a fast-paced narrative while employing both flashbacks and flashforwards. Though the book did not sell well, the writing of it prepared McGoogan for his next project—the breakthrough book *Fatal Passage: The True Story of John Rae, the Arctic Hero That Time Forgot.*

In 2002, McGoogan attracted international attention with *Fatal Passage.* That best-selling work of creative nonfiction won four major awards and was short-listed for three others. With *Fatal Passage,* McGoogan drew for the first time on both the fact-gathering skills he had honed during as a journalist and the narrative artistry he had developed while writing three novels. The book tells the story of John Rae, a young Scottish doctor and outdoorsman who sailed to Hudson Bay in 1832 and went on to become a leading northern explorer. He conducted a series of four expeditions between 1846 and 1854, on which he explored and mapped the Arctic coast. During that time the famed British expedition group, the Franklin party, arrived in the area in search of the Northwest Passage. The entire party died and the men were hailed as brave heroes back in Great Britain. Meanwhile, Rae located the passage and in the mid-1850s returned to Great Britain to tell the story of what actually happened to the Franklin party: they had resorted to cannibalism. This news was not well received by Britain's high society, especially Franklin's widow, and she and others saw to it that Rae never received the credit he deserved for his explorations.

McGoogan's biography is a work of "creative nonfiction," in which he uses fictional techniques—scenes, dialogue, point of view—to explore factual material. This approach, an historical variation on a tradition that includes landmark books by Truman Capote, Tom Wolfe, Norman Mailer, and Piers Paul Read, remains controversial. Sherrill Grace questioned his use of this format in her review for *Books in Canada,* commenting that the author "should have pushed further and created a character of flesh and blood—a truly fictional hero—or he should have stuck to the documentary record." Other critics were more open to the technique. A *Publishers Weekly* critic acknowledged that "McGoogan's extensive research reveals compelling evidence," while David F. Pelly praised *Fatal Passage* in his review for *Canadian Geographic,* writing that "McGoogan's account of Rae's career is faultless, both seamlessly and engagingly told."

In 2003, McGoogan published a second volume employing the same narrative strategies: *Ancient Mariner: The Amazing Adventures of Samuel Hearne, the Sailor Who Walked to the Arctic Ocean.*

## BIOGRAPHICAL AND CRITICAL SOURCES:

### PERIODICALS

*Beaver: Exploring Canada's History,* October, 2001, William Barr, review of *Fatal Passage,* p. 44; December, 2001-January, 2002, Ken McGoogan, letter to the editor, p. 3.

*Books in Canada,* summer, 1995, Roger Burford Mason, review of *Calypso Warrior,* p. 41; November-December, 2001, Sherrill Grace, review of *Fatal Passage,* pp. 25-27.

*Canadian Geographic,* September, 2001, David F. Pelly, review of *Fatal Passage,* p. 84.

*Kirkus Reviews,* February 1, 2002, review of *Fatal Passage,* p. 164.

*New York Times Book Review,* April 7, 2002, Roland Huntford, review of *Fatal Passage,* p. 8.

*Publishers Weekly,* April 1, 2002, review of *Fatal Passage,* p. 66.

*Quill and Quire,* July, 1995, Mark Noel Cosgrove, review of *Calypso Warrior,* p. 51; September, 1996, Ann Ireland, review of *Kerouac's Ghost,* p. 64.

## MILLS, Stephanie (Ellen) 1948-

*PERSONAL:* Born September 11, 1948, in Berkeley, CA; daughter of Robert C. and Edith (Garrison) Mills; married Philip Thiel (divorced, July, 1990). *Education:* Mills College, B.A., 1969. *Politics:* "Bioregional." *Religion:* "Animist." *Hobbies and other interests:* Swimming, cooking.

*ADDRESSES: Agent*—Katinka Matson, Brockman, Inc., 5 East 59th St., New York, NY 10022.

*CAREER:* Planned Parenthood, campus organizer in Alameda, San Francisco, and Oakland, CA, 1969-70; *Earth Times,* San Francisco, CA, editor in chief, 1970; *Earth,* San Francisco, CA, story editor, 1971; Mills College, Oakland, CA, conference facilitator, 1973-74; Emory University, Atlanta, GA, writer for Family Planning Program, 1974; Friends of the Earth, San Francisco, CA, director of Outings Program, 1975-76, director of membership development, 1976-78, editor in chief, 1977-78; Foundation for National Progress, San Francisco, CA, fellow, 1978-80; *CoEvolution Quarterly,* Sausalito, CA, began as assistant editor, became guest editor and editor, 1980-82; California Tomorrow, San Francisco, CA, editor in chief and research director, 1982-83; World College West, San Rafael, CA, director of development, 1983-84; freelance writer and lecturer, 1984—. Farallones Institute, member of board of directors, 1976-78; Earth First! Foundation, vice president, 1986-89; Northern Michigan Environmental Action Council, president, 1987-88; Great Lakes Bioregional Congress, member of planning committee, 1991; Oryana Natural Foods Cooperative, president of board of directors, 1992-93; member of board of advisors, Center for Sustainable Development and Alternative World Futures, Alliance for a Paving Moratorium, Northwoods Wilderness Recovery, The Onion Society, and Wildlands Center for Preventing Roads.

*MEMBER:* Planned Parenthood Federation of America (member of board of directors, 1970-76).

*AWARDS, HONORS:* Award from *Mademoiselle,* 1969; grant for Sweden from Point Foundation, 1972; resident of Blue Mountain Center, 1983, 1986; award from Friends of the United Nations Environment Program, 1987; grant from IRA-HITI Foundation, 1992; named as an *Utne Reader* Visionary, 1996.

*WRITINGS:*

(Editor, with Robert Theobald) *The Failure of Success: Ecological Values vs. Economic Myths,* Bobbs-Merrill (Indianapolis, IN), 1973.
*Whatever Happened to Ecology?* (memoir), Sierra Books (San Francisco, CA), 1989.
(Editor and contributor) *In Praise of Nature,* Island Press (Washington, DC), 1990.
*In Service of the Wild: Restoring and Reinhabiting Damaged Land,* Beacon Press (Boston, MA), 1995.
(Editor) *Turning away from Technology: A New Vision for the 21st Century,* Sierra Club Books (San Francisco, CA), 1997.
*Epicurean Simplicity,* Island Press (Washington, DC), 2002.

Also author of *Hay Foot, Straw Foot.* Correspondent for *Wild Earth.* Contributor to magazines. Editor, *Not Man Apart,* 1977-78; editorial adviser for *E* magazine.

*WORK IN PROGRESS:* Collected essays, for University of Georgia Press, 2002.

*SIDELIGHTS:* Author, activist, and lecturer Stephanie Mills first came to public attention in 1969 when, as commencement speaker at Mills College in Oakland, California, she raised eyebrows by predicting a bleak future in which "humanity was destined for suicide, the result of overpopulation and overuse of natural resources," as the author was paraphrased by *First Monday* interviewer Ed Valauskas. The address made national headlines, with a *New York Times* reporter calling it "perhaps the most anguished [valedictory] statement" of the year.

Mills's interest in the fate of the Earth has not waned in the subsequent decades. She is the author of several works that address environmental issues and the rise of technology. Regarding the latter issue, Mills has acknowledged herself as a Luddite, a word popularly used for a person who rejects forms of modern gadgetry in favor of a more technologically unencumbered lifestyle. "It's not that I'm proud of being a Luddite, it's that I'm content with the pace, volume and style of communication I do enjoy," she explained in the *First Monday* piece. Noting that the rise of technology, from moveable type to cyberspace, has made a quantitative change in communications, "whether technological change actually enhances human relationships and social organizations is not so clear." *First Monday* also noted that the interview between Mills and Valauskas took place via postcards, since Mills "does not use a computer or the Internet."

The author elaborated on her ideas in the 2002 book *Epicurean Simplicity*. In recent times the word epicurean has come to be equated with gourmet; Mills reaches farther back to refer to the philosopher Epicurus, who focused on the basic joys of life. "The pleasures and riches of simplicity, it seems to me, arrive mainly through the sense, through savoring the world of a given moment," Mills writes. Though Mills does not "offer us much hope for the future," commented Reeve Lindbergh in a review for *Washington Post Book World, Epicurean Simplicity* does provide "a bouquet of simple pleasures." Continuing a somewhat mixed review, Lindbergh cited "one or two awkward places" in the book, but added that overall *Epicurean Simplicity* is graced with "clear and simple language, along with much beautifully phrased wisdom." To *Booklist* contributor Donna Seaman, the author's messages about the consequences of consumerism run wild "are grounded in deep ecological understanding and sensitivity to the demanding realities of people's lives"; Seaman also noted that Mills's book projects "simplicity without undue simplification."

Living in harmony with the land is the subject of Mills's *In Service of the Wild: Restoring and Reinhabiting Damaged Land.* For this book the author visited five restoration sites and describes the people involved in the site's rehabilitation; her own site in the Leelanau Peninsula in Michigan was also chronicled. In writing the story of nature returning to its original state, said Anne Bell in *Alternatives Journal,* Mills offers "an uncommonly lyrical account of the possibilities inherent in ecological restoration." A *Whole Earth* critic called Mills a "tutelary sprit, guiding her heart, the reader's, and the heart of place; shepherding them through watersheds of ideas as well as landscapes."

*BIOGRAPHICAL AND CRITICAL SOURCES:*

*PERIODICALS*

*Alternatives Journal,* spring, 1997 Anne Bell, review of *In Service of the Wild: Restoring and Reinhabiting Damaged Land,* p. 34.

*Booklist,* March 15, 2002, Donna Seaman, review of *Epicurean Simplicity,* p. 115.
*Washington Post Book World,* April 21, 2002, Reeve Lindbergh, "Less Is More," p. 9.
*Whole Earth,* summer, 2000, Jay Kinney, review of *Hay Foot, Straw Foot,* p. 49; spring, 2001, review of *In Service of the Wild,* p. 32.

*ONLINE*

*First Monday,* http://www.firstmonday.dk/ (June 13, 2002), Ed Valauskas, "FM Interviews Stephanie Mills."*

\*          \*          \*

**MINEHAHA, Cornelius**
    **See WEDEKIND, (Benjamin) Frank(lin)**

\*          \*          \*

**MITZMAN, Arthur Benjamin 1931-**

*PERSONAL:* Born September 18, 1931, in Newark, NJ; married, 1956; children: two. *Education:* Columbia University, B.S., 1956, M.A., 1959, Brandeis University, M.A., 1959, Ph.D. (history), 1963.

*ADDRESSES: Office*—Historisch Seminarium, University of Amsterdam, Herengracht 286, Amsterdam-C, Netherlands.

*CAREER:* Brooklyn College of the City University of New York, Brooklyn, NY, instructor in history, 1962-64; Goddard College, Plainfield, VT, instructor in history, 1964-65; University of Rochester, Rochester, NY, assistant professor of history, 1965-69; Simon Fraser University, Burnaby, British Columbia, associate professor of social theory, 1969-71; University of Amsterdam, Amsterdam, Netherlands, professor of history, 1971—, emeritus professor of modern history.

*MEMBER:* American Historical Association.

*WRITINGS:*

*The Iron Cage: An Historical Interpretation of Max Weber,* Alfred A. Knopf (New York, NY), 1969; with new introduction by the author, preface by Lewis A. Coser, Transaction Books (New Brunswick, NJ), 1985.

*Sociology and Estrangement: Three Sociologists of Imperial Germany,* Alfred A. Knopf (New York, NY), 1973; with new introduction by the author, Transaction Books (New Brunswick, NJ), 1987.

*Michelet, Historian: Rebirth and Romanticism in Nineteenth-Century France,* Yale University Press (New Haven, CT), 1990.

*Michelet ou la subversion du passé: Quatre leçons au Collège de France,* Boutique de l'histoire (Paris, France), 1999.

*Prometheus Revisited: The Quest for Global Justice in the Twenty-first Century,* University of Massachusetts Press (Amherst, MA), 2003.

Contributor to *Encyclopaedia Britannica.* Contributor to history and sociology journals.

*SIDELIGHTS:* Commenting on Arthur Mitzman's psychobiography titled *Michelet, Historian: Rebirth and Romanticism in Nineteenth-Century France,* Edward K. Kaplan offered a rather extensive review and summary of the text for *Clio:* "This fascinating book successfully combines literary, psychological, sociological, and historical analysis as it traces the development of Jules Michelet (1798-1874), France's exemplary populist historian. Arthur Mitzman's accomplishment is significant, for his emphasis on Michelet's *Le Peuple* (1846), the seven-volume *Histoire de la Revolution,* (1847-1853), and *Le Banquet* (written in 1854), defines how the 'artist-historian' became an ideological model of the Third Republic." Kaplan explained that the chronological order of Mitzman's book "traces in remarkable detail the conditions under which Michelet wrote his most influential works. . . . Mitzman's subtle and detailed biography of Michelet's crucial middle years would have pleased his subject who strove, himself, to render, in his vivid and subjective histories, the inseparability of his nation's intimate and crucial events."

Irene Collins explained in the *English Historical Review* that Michelet's reputation as one of France's finest historians is partially because of his heavy influence on nineteenth-century French thought and his encouragement of the myths surrounding the French Revolution. Among his peers, Michelet's legacy is the strides he made in the field of historiography, considering issues such as the historian's relation to his subject and the psychological elements of historical trends and events. Collins concluded that students of European history "have reason to be grateful to Mitzman for untangling the threads which made up the complicated skein of thought known as social romanticism, for explaining the connection between Michelet's social and historical ideas, and for many fascinating insights into his view of nationhood." In *Journal of European Studies* Hazel Mills wrote, "Mitzman's book will appeal more to the specialist than the general reader, but it is vigorously entertaining, and represents something of a landmark in the development of psycho-history."

*Prometheus Revisited: The Quest for Global Justice in the Twenty-first Century* addresses the interpretation of the myth of Prometheus by the industrial world as a metaphor for humankind's dominance over nature through technology, industrialization, and human resourcefulness. In his book, Mitzman turns this perspective on its ear, pointing out that many European romantics, especially the English poet Shelley, defined the Promethean myth as a symbiotic relationship between humankind and nature. Mitzman purports that the growth and power premise behind socialism, nationalism, and consumer capitalism suppresses and suffocates the original impetus of Promethean creativity. He also believes that the inability of our ecology to sustain unbridled exploitation, along with the ever-widening socioeconomic division—both of which are created by the modern Promethean perspective—threaten the existence of all humankind. While the globalization mentality of this age may seem irreversible, Mitzman explores the possibility of attaining an entirely different world view, one in which individual communities are completely self-governing, creativity is encouraged and valued, and the premise behind economy outstrips the current mentality of scarcity and insecurity.

*BIOGRAPHICAL AND CRITICAL SOURCES:*

*PERIODICALS*

*Clio,* fall 1992, Edward K. Kaplan, review of *Michelet, Historian: Rebirth and Romanticism in Nineteenth-Century France,* p. 91.

*English Historical Review,* February 1994, Irene Collins, review of *Michelet, Historian,* p. 217.

*Journal of European Studies,* December 1992, Hazel Mills, review of *Michelet, Historian,* p. 357.*

## MOORCOCK, Michael (John) 1939-

(Bill Barclay, William Ewert Barclay, Michael Barrington, Edward P. Bradbury, and James Colvin, pseudonyms; Philip James, joint pseudonym; Desmond Reid, house pseudonym)

*PERSONAL:* Born December 18, 1939, in Mitcham, Surrey, England; son of Arthur Edward and June (Taylor) Moorcock; married Hilary Denham Bailey (a writer), October 25, 1962 (divorced, April, 1978); married Jill Riches, May 7, 1978 (divorced, 1983); married Linda Mullens Steele, September 23, 1983; children: (first marriage) Sophie, Katherine, Max. *Education:* Michael Hall, Sussex, Pitman's College, Croydon, Surrey, England.

*ADDRESSES: Home*—P.O. Box 1230, Bastrop, TX 78602. *Agent*—Howard Morhaim, Howard Morhaim Literary Agency, 841 Broadway, Ste. 604, New York, NY 10003.

*CAREER:* Writer. Has also worked as a singer-guitarist. *Tarzan Adventures* (juvenile magazine), editor, 1956-58; Amalgamated Press, London, England, editor and writer for the *Sexton Blake Library* and for comic strips and children's annuals, 1959-61; Liberal Party, editor and pamphleteer, 1962; *New Worlds* (science fiction magazine), London, England, editor and publisher, 1964—; worked with rock and roll bands Hawkwind and Blue Oyster Cult; member of rock and roll band Michael Moorcock and the Deep Fix.

*MEMBER:* Authors Guild, Society of Authors, Royal Overseas League, Amnesty International, Southern Poverty Law Center, Fawcett Society.

*AWARDS, HONORS:* Nebula Award, Science Fiction Writers of America, 1967, for *Behold the Man;* British Science Fiction Association award and Arts Council of Great Britain award, both 1967, both for *New Worlds;* August Derleth awards, British Fantasy Society (London, England), 1972, for *The Knight of the Swords,* 1973, for *The King of the Swords,* 1974, for *The Jade Man's Eyes,* 1975, for *The Sword and the Stallion,* 1976, for *The Hollow Lands, Legends from the End of Time,* and *The Sailor on the Seas of Fate,* 1977, for *The Weird of the White Wolf,* 1978, for *Gloriana; or, The Unfulfill'd Queen,* 1979, for *The Golden*

*Michael Moorcock*

*Barge,* 1981, for *The Entropy Tango,* 1985, for *The Chronicles of Castle Brass,* 1986, for *The Dragon in the Sword,* 1987, for *Wizardry and Wild Romance,* and 1988, for *Fantasy;* International Fantasy awards, 1972 and 1973, for fantasy novels; *Guardian* Literary Prize, 1977, for *The Condition of Muzak;* John W. Campbell Memorial Award, 1978, and World Fantasy Award, World Fantasy Convention, 1979, both for *Gloriana; or, The Unfulfill'd Queen.*

*WRITINGS:*

(With James Cawthorn, under house pseudonym Desmond Reid) *Caribbean Crisis,* Sexton Blake Library (London, England), 1962.

*The Sundered Worlds,* Compact Books (London, England), 1965, published as *The Blood Red Game,* Sphere Books (London, England), 1970.

*The Fireclown,* Compact Books (London, England), 1965, published as *The Winds of Limbo,* Sphere Books (London, England), 1970.

(Under pseudonym James Colvin) *The Deep Fix,* Compact Books (London, England), 1966.

*The Wrecks of Time* (bound with *Tramontane* by Emil Petaja), Ace Books (New York, NY), 1966, revised edition published as *The Rituals of Infinity,* Arrow Books (London, England), 1971.

*The Twilight Man,* Compact Books (London, England), 1966, Berkley Publishing (New York, NY), 1970, published as *The Shores of Death,* Sphere Books (London, England), 1970.

*Behold the Man,* Allison & Busby (London, England), 1969.

*The Ice Schooner,* Sphere Books (London, England), 1968, Berkley Publishing (New York, NY), 1969, revised edition, Harrap (London, England), 1985.

(With wife, Hilary Bailey) *The Black Corridor,* Ace Books (New York, NY), 1969.

*The Time Dweller,* Hart-Davis (London, England), 1969, Berkley Publishing (New York, NY), 1971.

(With James Cawthorn, under joint pseudonym Philip James) *The Distant Suns,* Unicorn Bookshop (London, England), 1975.

*Moorcock's Book of Martyrs,* Quartet Books (London, England), 1976, published as *Dying for Tomorrow,* DAW Books (New York, NY), 1978.

*Sojan* (juvenile), Savoy Books (Manchester, England), 1977.

*Epic Pooh,* British Fantasy Society (London, England), 1978.

*Gloriana; or The Unfulfill'd Queen,* Allison & Busby (London, England), 1978, Avon (New York, NY), 1979.

*The Real Life Mr. Newman,* A. J. Callow, 1979.

*The Golden Barge,* DAW Books (New York, NY), 1980.

*My Experiences in the Third World War,* Savoy Books (Manchester, England), 1980.

*The Retreat from Liberty: The Erosion of Democracy in Today's Britain,* Zomba Books (London, England), 1983.

(With others) *Exploring Fantasy Worlds: Essays on Fantastic Literature,* edited by Darrell Schweitzer, Borgo, 1985.

*Letters from Hollywood,* Harrap, 1986.

(With James Cawthorn) *Fantasy: The One Hundred Best Books,* Carroll & Graf (New York, NY), 1988.

*Mother London,* Harmony (New York, NY), 1989.

*Wizardry and Wild Romance: A Study of Heroic Fantasy,* Gollancz (London, England), 1989.

*Casablanca,* Gollancz (London, England), 1989.

*Tales from the Texas Woods,* Mojo Press, 1997.

*Sailing to Utopia,* illustrated by Rick Berry, White Wolf (Stone Mountain, GA), 1997.

*King of the City,* Scribner (New York, NY), 2000.

(With Storm Constantine) *Silverheart,* Simon & Schuster (London, England), 2000.

*London Bone* (short stories), Scribner (New York, NY), 2001.

(With China Mieville, Paul de Fillipo, and Geoff Ryman) *Cities,* Gollancz (London, England), 2003.

*"NICK ALLARD/JERRY CORNELL" SERIES*

(Under pseudonym Bill Barclay) *Printer's Devil,* Compact Books (London, England), 1966, published under name Michael Moorcock as *The Russian Intelligence,* Savoy Books (Manchester, England), 1980.

(Under pseudonym Bill Barclay) *Somewhere in the Night,* Compact Books (London, England), 1966, revised edition published under name Michael Moorcock as *The Chinese Agent,* Macmillan (New York, NY), 1970.

(Ghostwriter) Roger Harris, *The LSD Dossier,* Compact Books (London, England), 1966.

*"ELRIC" SERIES; "ETERNAL CHAMPION" BOOKS*

*The Stealer of Souls, and Other Stories* (also see below), Neville Spearman (London, England), 1963, Lancer Books (New York, NY), 1967.

*Stormbringer,* Jenkins (England), 1965, Lancer Books (New York, NY), 1967.

*The Singing Citadel* (also see below), Berkley Publishing (New York, NY), 1970.

*The Sleeping Sorceress,* New English Library (London, England), 1971, Lancer Books (New York, NY), 1972, published as *The Vanishing Tower,* DAW Books (New York, NY), 1977.

*The Dreaming City,* Lancer Books (New York, NY), 1972, revised edition published as *Elric of Melnibone,* Hutchinson (London, England), 1972.

*The Jade Man's Eyes,* Unicorn Bookshop (London, England), 1973.

*Elric: The Return to Melnibone,* Unicorn Bookshop (London, England), 1973.

*The Sailor on the Seas of Fate,* DAW Books (New York, NY), 1976.

*The Bane of the Black Sword,* DAW Books (New York, NY), 1977.

*The Weird of the White Wolf* (contains some material from *The Stealer of Souls, and Other Stories* and *The Singing Citadel*), DAW Books (New York, NY), 1977.

*Elric at the End of Time,* DAW Books (New York, NY), 1985.

*The Fortress of the Pearl,* Ace Books (New York, NY), 1989.

*The Revenge of the Rose,* Ace Books (New York, NY), 1991.

"ALBINO" SEQUENCE; "ELRIC" SERIES

*The Dreamthief's Daughter: A Tale of the Albino,* Warner Books (New York, NY), 2001.

*The Skrayling Tree: The Albino in America,* Warner Books (New York, NY), 2003.

"VON BEK FAMILY" SERIES

*The War Hound and the World's Pain,* Timescape, 1981.

*The Brothel in Rosenstrasse,* New English Library (London, England), 1982, Tigerseye Press, 1986.

*The City in the Autumn Stars,* Ace Books (New York, NY), 1986.

*Lunching with the Antichrist: A Family History: 1925-2015* (short stories), Ziesing, 1995.

*Von Bek,* White Wolf (Stone Mountain, GA), 1995.

"MICHAEL KANE" SERIES; UNDER PSEUDONYM EDWARD P. BRADBURY

*Warriors of Mars* (also see below), Compact Books (London, England), 1965, published under name Michael Moorcock as *The City of the Beast,* Lancer Books (New York, NY), 1970.

*Blades of Mars* (also see below), Compact Books (London, England), 1965, published under name Michael Moorcock as *The Lord of the Spiders,* Lancer Books (New York, NY), 1971.

*The Barbarians of Mars* (also see below), Compact Books (London, England), 1965, published under name Michael Moorcock as *The Masters of the Pit,* Lancer Books (New York, NY), 1971.

*Warrior of Mars* (contains *Warriors of Mars, Blades of Mars,* and *The Barbarians of Mars*), New English Library (London, England), 1981.

*Kane of Old Mars,* White Wolf (Stone Mountain, GA), 1998.

"THE HISTORY OF THE RUNESTAFF" SERIES; "ETERNAL CHAMPION" BOOKS

*The Jewel in the Skull* (also see below), Lancer Books (New York, NY), 1967.

*Sorcerer's Amulet* (also see below), Lancer Books (New York, NY), 1968, published as *The Mad God's Amulet,* Mayflower Books (London, England), 1969.

*Sword of the Dawn* (also see below), Lancer Books (New York, NY), 1968.

*The Secret of the Runestaff* (also see below), Lancer Books (New York, NY), 1969, published as *The Runestaff,* Mayflower Books (London, England), 1969.

*The History of the Runestaff* (contains *The Jewel in the Skull, Sorcerer's Amulet, Sword of the Dawn,* and *The Secret of the Runestaff*), Granada (London, England), 1979.

*Hawkmoon,* White Wolf (Stone Mountain, GA), 1995.

"JERRY CORNELIUS" SERIES

*The Final Programme* (also see below), Avon (New York, NY), 1968, revised edition, Allison & Busby (London, England), 1969.

*A Cure for Cancer* (also see below), Holt (New York, NY), 1971.

*The English Assassin* (also see below), Allison & Busby (London, England), 1972.

*The Lives and Times of Jerry Cornelius* (also see below), Allison & Busby (London, England), 1976.

*The Adventures of Una Persson and Catherine Cornelius in the Twentieth Century* (also see below), Quartet Books (London, England), 1976.

*The Condition of Muzak* (also see below), Allison & Busby (London, England), 1977, Gregg (New York, NY), 1978.

*The Cornelius Chronicles* (contains *The Final Programme, A Cure for Cancer, The English Assassin,* and *The Condition of Muzak*), Avon (New York, NY), 1977.

*The Great Rock 'n' Roll Swindle,* Virgin Books (London, England), 1980.

*The Entropy Tango* (also see below), New English Library (London, England), 1981.

*The Opium General* (also see below), Harrap (London, England), 1985.

*The Cornelius Chronicles, Volume 2* (contains *The Lives and Times of Jerry Cornelius* and *The Entropy Tango*), Avon (New York, NY), 1986.

*The Cornelius Chronicles, Volume 3* (contains *The Adventures of Una Persson and Catherine Cornelius in the Twentieth Century* and *The Opium General*), Avon (New York, NY), 1987.

*The Cornelius Quartet,* Phoenix House (London, England), 1993, Four Walls Eight Windows (New York, NY), 2001.

*A Cornelius Calendar,* Phoenix House (London, England), 1993.

*Firing the Cathedral,* PS Publishing (Harrogate, England), 2002.

*"KARL GLOGAUER" SERIES*

*Behold the Man,* Allison & Busby (London, England), 1969, Avon (New York, NY), 1970.

*Breakfast in the Ruins: A Novel of Inhumanity,* New English Library (London, England), 1972, Random House (New York, NY), 1974.

*"CORUM" SERIES; "ETERNAL CHAMPION" BOOKS*

*The Knight of the Swords* (also see below), Mayflower Books (London, England), 1970, Berkley Publishing (New York, NY), 1971.

*The Queen of the Swords* (also see below), Berkley Publishing (New York, NY), 1971.

*The King of the Swords* (also see below), Berkley Publishing (New York, NY), 1971.

*The Bull and the Spear* (also see below), Berkley Publishing (New York, NY), 1973.

*The Oak and the Ram* (also see below), Berkley Publishing (New York, NY), 1973.

*The Sword and the Stallion* (also see below), Berkley Publishing (New York, NY), 1974.

*The Swords Trilogy* (contains *The Knight of the Swords, The Queen of the Swords,* and *The King of the Swords*), Berkley Publishing (New York, NY), 1977.

*The Chronicles of Corum* (contains *The Bull and the Spear, The Oak and the Ram,* and *The Sword and the Stallion*), Berkley Publishing (New York, NY), 1978, published as *The Prince with the Silver Hand,* Millennium Books, 1993.

*"JOHN DAKER" SERIES; "ETERNAL CHAMPION" BOOKS*

*The Eternal Champion,* Dell (New York, NY), 1970, revised edition, Harper (New York, NY), 1978.

*Phoenix in Obsidian,* Mayflower Books (London, England), 1970, published as *The Silver Warriors,* Dell (New York, NY), 1973.

*The Dragon in the Sword,* Granada (London, England), 1986.

*"OSWALD BASTABLE" SERIES*

*The Warlord of the Air* (also see below), Ace Books (New York, NY), 1971.

*The Land Leviathan* (also see below), Quartet Books (London, England), 1974.

*The Steel Tsar* (also see below), DAW Books (New York, NY), 1983.

*The Nomad of Time* (contains *The Warlord of the Air, The Land Leviathan,* and *The Steel Tsar*), Granada (London, England), 1984.

*"THE DANCERS AT THE END OF TIME" SERIES*

*An Alien Heat* (also see below), Harper (New York, NY), 1972.

*The Hollow Lands* (also see below), Harper (New York, NY), 1974.

*The End of All Songs* (also see below), Harper (New York, NY), 1976.

*Legends from the End of Time,* Harper (New York, NY), 1976.

*The Transformations of Miss Mavis Ming,* W. H. Allen (London, England), 1977, published as *A Messiah at the End of Time,* DAW Books (New York, NY), 1978.

*The Dancers at the End of Time* (contains *An Alien Heat, The Hollow Lands,* and *The End of All Songs*), Granada (London, England), 1981.

*"COUNT BRASS" SERIES; "ETERNAL CHAMPION" BOOKS*

*Count Brass* (also see below), Mayflower Books (London, England), 1973.

*The Champion of Garathorm* (also see below), Mayflower Books (London, England), 1973.

*The Quest for Tanelorn* (also see below), Mayflower Books (London, England), 1975, Dell (New York, NY), 1976.

*The Chronicles of Castle Brass* (contains *Count Brass, The Champion of Garathorm,* and *The Quest for Tanelorn*), Granada (London, England), 1985.

*"BETWEEN THE WARS" SERIES*

*Byzantium Endures,* Secker & Warburg (London, England), 1981, Random House (New York, NY), 1982.

*The Laughter of Carthage,* Random House (New York, NY), 1984.

*Jerusalem Commands,* Jonathan Cape (London, England), 1992.

*"SECOND ETHER" SERIES*

*Blood: A Southern Fantasy,* William Morrow (New York, NY), 1994.

*Fabulous Harbors,* Avon (New York, NY), 1995.

*The War amongst the Angels,* Avon (New York, NY), 1996.

*SCREENPLAYS*

*The Final Programme* (based on his novel of the same title; removed name from credits after dispute with director), EMI, 1973.

*The Land That Time Forgot,* British Lion, 1975.

*EDITOR*

(And contributor, under name Michael Moorcock and under pseudonym James Colvin) *The Best of "New Worlds,"* Compact Books (London, England), 1965.

*Best SF Stories from "New Worlds,"* Panther Books (London, England), 1967, Berkley Publishing (New York, NY), 1968.

*The Traps of Time,* Rapp & Whiting (London, England), 1968.

(And contributor, under pseudonym James Colvin) *The Best SF Stories from "New Worlds" 2,* Panther Books (London, England), 1968, Berkley Publishing (New York, NY), 1969.

(And contributor, under pseudonym James Colvin) *The Best SF Stories from "New Worlds" 3,* Panther Books (London, England), 1968, Berkley Publishing (New York, NY), 1969.

*The Best SF Stories from "New Worlds" 4,* Panther Books (London, England), 1969, Berkley Publishing (New York, NY), 1971.

*The Best SF Stories from "New Worlds" 5,* Panther Books (London, England), 1969, Berkley Publishing (New York, NY), 1971.

(And contributor) *The Best SF Stories from "New Worlds" 6,* Panther Books (London, England), 1970, Berkley Publishing (New York, NY), 1971.

*The Best SF Stories from "New Worlds" 7,* Panther Books (London, England), 1971.

*New Worlds Quarterly 1,* Berkley Publishing (New York, NY), 1971.

*New Worlds Quarterly 2,* Berkley Publishing (New York, NY), 1971.

*New Worlds Quarterly 3,* Sphere Books (London, England), 1971.

(With Langdon Jones and contributor) *The Nature of the Catastrophe,* Hutchinson (London, England), 1971.

*New Worlds Quarterly 4,* Berkley Publishing (New York, NY), 1972.

*New Worlds Quarterly 5,* Sphere Books (London, England), 1973.

*New Worlds Quarterly 6,* Avon (New York, NY), 1973.

*Before Armageddon: An Anthology of Victorian and Edwardian Imaginative Fiction Published before 1914,* W. H. Allen (London, England), 1975.

*England Invaded: A Collection of Fantasy Fiction,* Ultramarine (Hastings-on-Hudson, NY), 1977.

*New Worlds: An Anthology,* Fontana (London, England), 1983.

H. G. Wells, *The Time Machine,* Tuttle (Boston, MA), 1993.

(With Michael Butterworth) *Queens of Deliria,* Collector's Guide, 1995.

*RECORDINGS; UNDER NAME "MICHAEL MOORCOCK AND THE DEEP FIX"*

*The New Worlds Fair,* United Artists, 1975.

*Dodgem Dude/Starcruiser* (single), Flicknife, 1980.

*The Brothel in Rosenstrasse/Time Centre* (single), Flicknife, 1982.

(With others) *Hawkwind Friends and Relations,* Flicknife, 1982.

(With others) *Hawkwind & Co.,* Flicknife, 1983.

Also composer of songs recorded by others, including *Sonic Attack, The Black Corridor, The Wizard Blew His Horn, Standing at the Edge, Warriors, Kings of Speed, Warrior at the End of Time, Psychosonia, Coded Languages, Lost Chances, Choose Your Masks,* and *Arrival in Utopia,* all recorded by Hawkwind; *The Great Sun Jester, Black Blade,* and *Veteran of the Psychic Wars,* all recorded by Blue Oyster Cult.

Contributor, sometimes under pseudonyms William Ewert Barclay and Michael Barrington, among others, to *Guardian, Punch, Ambit,* London *Times,* and other publications. Contributor to anthologies, including *The Road to Science Fiction 5: The British Way* and *Year's Best SF 3.*

Many of Moorcock's novels have provided the story for graphic novels, including *Stormbringer, The Jewell in the Skull,* and *The Crystal and the Amulet,* which were adapted and drawn by James Cawthorn. Writer of comic strips in early 1960s and of the DC comic *Michael Moorcock's Multiverse,* 1-12, 1997—.

*ADAPTATIONS:* The character Elric is featured in role-playing games from the Avalon Hill Game Company and from Chaosium, in comic books published by Pacific Comics, Dark Horse Comics, and by Star Reach Productions, and in miniature figures marketed by Citadel Miniatures; the character Oswald Bastable is featured in a computer game.

*WORK IN PROGRESS: The Vengeance of Rome,* the final book in the "Colonel Pyat" series; the final book in the "Albino" series; *Love,* a memoir of Mervyn and Maeve Peake; a graphic novel about Elric's early life and training as a sorcerer; a book about Heaven's Gate for the British Film Institute.

*SIDELIGHTS:* Michael Moorcock was associated with the New Wave, an avant-garde science fiction movement of the 1960s, which introduced a wider range of subject matter and style to the science fiction field. As editor of *New Worlds,* the most prominent of the New Wave publications, Moorcock promotes the movement and provides a showcase for its writing.

The New Wave, wrote Donald A. Wollheim in *The Universe Makers,* was an "effort to merge science fiction into the mainstream of literature . . . The charges brought against old line science fiction were on the basis of both structure and content. Structurally, the charge was made that too much of the writing retained the flavor of the pulps [and] that science fiction writers were not keeping up with the experimental avant-garde. . . . Internally, the charge was made that science fiction actually was dead—because the future was no longer credible. The crises of the twentieth century . . . were obviously insurmountable. We would all never make it into the twenty-first century." In response to Wollheim's comments, Moorcock told

*CA* that this conclusion missed the point, for he and his fellow writers "loved the present" and were not, in fact, completely disillusioned with the future. In an interview with Ian Covell of *Science Fiction Review,* Moorcock said of the New Wave: "We were a generation of writers who had no nostalgic love of the pulp magazines, who had come to SF as a possible alternative to mainstream literature and had taken SF seriously. . . . We were trying to find a viable literature for our time. A literature which took account of science, of modern social trends, and which was written not according to genre conventions but according to the personal requirements of the individuals who produced it."

Moorcock has written science fiction adventures in the style of Edgar Rice Burroughs's Mars novels, sword-and-sorcery novels, comic and satirical science fiction, and time-travel science fiction. Some of Moorcock's fantasy novels have earned him major genre awards and an exalted position among fans. Tom Hutchinson in the London *Times,* for example, called Moorcock's sword-and-sorcery novel, *The Chronicles of Castle Brass,* "a masterpiece of modern high fantasy."

Despite their continuing popularity, some of these books, Moorcock admits, were written for the money. *New Worlds* was an influential magazine in the science fiction field, but it was never a financial success. When creditors needed to be paid it was Moorcock, as editor and publisher, who was held responsible. He was often forced to write a quick novel to pay the bills. Charles Platt recounted in his *Dream Makers: The Uncommon People Who Write Science Fiction,* that "it was not unusual for the magazine's staff to be found cowering on the floor with the lights out, pretending not to be home, while some creditor rang the bell and called hopefully through the mail slot in the front door—to no avail."

The genre books that brought Moorcock to critical attention, and those that he considers among his most important, combine standard science fiction trappings with experimental narrative structures. *Breakfast in the Ruins: A Novel of Inhumanity,* for instance, contains a number of historical vignettes featuring the protagonist Karl Glogauer. In each of these, Karl is a different person in a different time, participating in such examples of political violence as the French Revolution, the Paris Commune, a Nazi concentration camp, and a My Lai-style massacre. Interwoven with these vignettes is a homosexual love scene, involving Karl and a black Nigerian, that takes on a mystical connotation as the two lovers seem to merge into each other's identities. Helen Rogan of *Time* described the book as "by turns puzzling, funny, and shocking," and Moorcock as "both bizarrely inventive and highly disciplined." Writing in the *New York Times Book Review,* John Deck called the book "a dazzling historical fantasy."

In the books and stories featuring Jerry Cornelius, Moorcock has experimented with character as well as with narrative structure. Cornelius has no consistent character or appearance. He is, as Nick Totton wrote in *Spectator,* "a nomad of the territories of personality; even his skin color and gender are as labile as his accomplishments." Cornelius's world is just as flexible, containing a multitude of alternative histories, all contradictory, and peopled with characters who die and resurrect as a matter of course. Within this mutable landscape, Cornelius travels from one inconclusive adventure to another, trapped in an endless existence. As Colin Greenland maintained in the *Dictionary of Literary Biography,* Cornelius is "an entirely new kind of fictional character, a dubious hero whose significance is always oblique and rarely stable, equipped to tackle all the challenges of his time yet unable to find a satisfactory solution to any of them."

*The Condition of Muzak,* completing the initial Jerry Cornelius tetralogy, won the *Guardian* Literary Prize in 1977, bringing Moorcock added praise from the literary world. At the time of the award, W. L. Webb of the *Guardian* wrote, "Michael Moorcock, rejecting the demarcation disputes that have reduced the novel to a muddle of warring sub-genres, recovers in these four books a protean vitality and inclusiveness that one might call Dickensian if their consciousness were not so entirely of our own volatile times." Moorcock, according to Angus Wilson in the *Washington Post Book World,* "is emerging as one of the most serious literary lights of our time. . . . For me his Jerry Cornelius quartet [of novels] assured the durability of his reputation." Ralph Willett, writing in *Science-Fiction Studies,* claimed that during the late 1960s and early 1970s, Moorcock became "that rare phenomenon, the popular novelist whose work has also become a cult among the young and the avant-garde." Willett compared Moorcock to experimental novelist William Burroughs, "especially with respect to the Jerry Cornelius books . . . Moorcock lacks William Burroughs's ac-

curate and devastating satire, and his verbal experiments have been less radical, but in both artists can be observed a basic dissatisfaction with linear methods of representing space and time, a surreal sense of coexisting multiple worlds, and an emphasis on apocalyptic disaster."

After almost a decade-long rest, Moorcock brought back Jerry Cornelius in 2002 in *Firing the Cathedral.* In *Firing the Cathedral,* Cornelius responds to the September, 2001, terrorist attacks on America and their consequences, the realities of global warming, and other apocalyptic events. Patrick Hudson, writing for *The Zone,* stated that the new Cornelius book "finds Moorcock and Cornelius in fine form." He continued, "There's plenty for them to do in the post September 11th world of the war on terrorism, and once more life is cheap and weapons plentiful. Moorcock makes artful use of clippings from the last eighteen months . . . and bits and bobs from the archive throw the broad satirical sweeps into sharp relief."

Moorcock's literary standing was substantially enhanced with the publication of *Byzantium Endures* and *The Laughter of Carthage.* These two novels are the closest Moorcock came to conventional literary fiction, being the purported autobiography of Russian emigré, Colonel Pyat. Pyat was born on January 1, 1900, and the story of his life becomes a history of the twentieth century. Pyat survives the Russian revolution, travels throughout Europe and America, and participates in a number of important historical events. But he is a megalomaniac who imagines himself to be both a great inventor, the equal of Thomas Edison, and a major figure on the stage of world history. He is also an anti-Semite who sees true Christianity, as embodied in the Russian Orthodox Church, as engaged in a battle against the Jews, Orientals, Bolsheviks, and other destroyers of order. He likens Western Christianity to Byzantium, his enemies to Carthage. Naturally, Pyat's account of his life is self-aggrandizing and inaccurate.

*Byzantium Endures* focuses on the first twenty years of Pyat's life, telling of his opportunistic role in the Russian revolution. Pyat survives the upheaval of the revolution and the subsequent civil war by working first for one side and then another. As Frederic Morton wrote in the *New York Times Book Review,* his mechanical skills are put to good use "repairing the rifles of anarchist guerrillas, fixing the treads of White Army tanks [and] doctoring the engine in one of Trotsky's armed trains." Pyat claims to have invented the laser gun on behalf of Ukrainian nationalists fighting against the Red Army, but when the electrical power failed, so did his gun. "Pyat's self-serving recollections," Bart Mills stated in the *Los Angeles Times Book Review,* "contain a vivid picture of the events of 1917-1920, down to menus, street names and the color of people's moustaches." The novel, wrote Robert Onopa in the *Chicago Tribune Book World,* is "utterly engrossing as narrative, historically pertinent, and told through characters so alive and detail so dense that it puts to shame all but a few writers who have been doing this kind of work all along."

*The Laughter of Carthage* covers Pyat's life from 1920 to 1924, detailing his escape from Communist Russia and subsequent travels in Europe and America. His activities are sometimes unlawful, requiring him to change his residence and name frequently. He meets everyone from Dylan Thomas to Tom Mix and lives everywhere from Constantinople to Hollywood. Because of the scope of Pyat's adventures, *The Laughter of Carthage* is a sweeping picture of the world during the 1920s. "Moorcock provides an exotic itinerary, a robust cast of opportunists and scoundrels, and a series of dangerous adventures and sexual escapades," noted R. Z. Sheppard of *Time.* "This is epic writing," praised Valentine Cunningham in the *Times Literary Supplement,* adding, "As [D. W.] Griffith stuffed his movies with vast throngs and Promethean matter so Pyat's narration feeds hugely on the numerous people he claims to have met, the history he makes believe he has helped to shape, the many places his traveller's tales take him to."

Pyat's narration, because it is colored by his eccentric, offensive views and his distorted sense of self-importance, gives a fantastic sheen to the familiar historical events he relates. "This is Moorcock's achievement: he has rewritten modern history by seeing it in the distorting mirror of one man's perceptions so that the novel has the imaginative grasp of fantasy while remaining solidly based upon recognizable facts," Peter Ackroyd wrote in the London *Times.* "Moorcock has here created a fiction," Nigel Andrew said in the same paper, "that is seething with detailed life at every level—in the headlong narrative, in the bravura passages of scene-setting description, and, particularly, in the rendering of Pyat's vision of the world." Although Richard Eder of the *Los Angeles Times* found

Pyat's narrative to be an "extremely long-winded unpleasantness" because of his political views, the *New York Times Book Review*'s Thaddeus Rutkowski forgave the "sometimes tedious" nature of Pyat's narration. "Most often," he found, "Pyat's tirades are beguiling. They are the pronouncements of a singularly innocent intelligence gone awry."

Moorcock continued Pyat's story with the publication of *Jerusalem Commands.* In it, he recounts Pyat's life between the years of 1924 and 1929, in which he lives as minor celebrity Max Peters in Hollywood. "Moorcock's powers of description—especially when focused on the sights and smells of megalopoli—and his range of references are immense," remarked Mark Sanderson in the *Times Literary Supplement.* However, Sanderson noted, "Like Thomas Pynchon he can simultaneously be highly impressive and deeply boring. But his main achievement in this tetralogy . . . is to force the reader to afford the luckiest bastard in the whole damn universe (Colonel Pyat) a grudging respect. Even a little affection too." Julian Symons, a newcomer to the Colonel Pyat trilogy, found him less than enchanting. Writing for the *London Review of Books,* he said in a commentary on the length of Pyat's memoirs that "Michael Moorcock's purpose, I suppose, was to offer a picaresque view of history in the first half of this century as seen by a man, by no means a hero, shuttled from country to country. It's a pity he chose a narrator suffering from logorrhea."

In *Blood: A Southern Fantasy,* Moorcock returns to the New Wave style of his early writings. Tim Sullivan in the *Washington Post Book World* hailed the return, saying that "the New Wave style is so old it seems new again, adding a certain freshness to the mix." *Blood,* according to David V. Barrett in *New Statesman & Society,* "is both a fantasy and a literary novel" in which the characters (persons of color in a New South where Anglos are in the minority) are gamblers playing games that draw them into other realities. Moorcock borrows previous themes and elements of his earlier stories to create what he terms a "multiverse." In *World Literature Today* Carter Kaplan wrote, "His language is a post-poststructuralist pidgin of Christian humanism, New Age metaphysics, and pulp science fiction that increases in profundity as it becomes more ridiculous. *Blood* translates meaninglessness into epiphany."

*Lunching with the Antichrist: A Family History: 1925-2015* is a collection of Moorcock's short stories from his Von Bek family series. The various members of the Von Beks display Moorcock's concept of the "Seeker"—they are characters who spend their time pursuing meaning in their lives. The collection, noted Gerald Jonas in the *New York Times Book Review,* "satisfies the same high standards that [Moorcock] espoused as an editor." Roland Green in *Booklist* hailed Moorcock as "a master of his craft."

Moorcock combines mainstream fiction with a bit of fantasy in *The Brothel of Rosenstrasse,* a novel set in the imaginary city of Mirenburg. The city's brothel is the center of social life, as well as a "microcosm of *fin de siecle* Central Europe; hedonistic, decadent, deluded, and heedless of an inevitable future," as Elaine Kendall wrote in the *Los Angeles Times.* Narrated by an aging hedonist who relates the story of his long and dissipated life, the novel follows a handful of decadent characters to their eventual destruction during the bombardment of Mirenburg. Suffering makes the characters finally come alive in a way they have never been before. "They begin to engage our full attention," Kendall concluded, "and earn not only our sympathy but in some cases, our respect. By then it's too late; Mirenburg and all the good and evil it represented has vanished forever. If there's no parable here, surely there's a moral."

In *Mother London,* Moorcock presents a "complex, layered history of London since the war, seen through the stories of a group of psychiatric patients," explained Brian Applecart in the London *Times.* The novel earned high praise from several critics. Nigel Andrew of the *Listener* called *Mother London* "a prodigious work of imaginative archaeology . . . [in which Moorcock] displays the generosity of spirit, the sweep and sheer gusto of Dickens." Similarly, Gregory Feeler in the *Washington Post Book World* stated that *Mother London* "often indulges its author's crotchets and biases, [but] it also proves warm and humane, often surprisingly funny, and moving in a way Moorcock has never before succeeded in being." "If," wrote Andrew, "this wonderful book does not finally convince the world that [Moorcock] is in fact one of our very best novelists and a national treasure, then there is no justice."

Moorcock composed two more variations of the London theme with *King of the City* and *London Bone.* *King of the City* follows the life of Denny Dover, from his post-World War II childhood to his exploits as a paparazzo in the '80s and '90s. John Coulthart from *The Edge* wrote, "Art, culture and politics all blend together in a heady, gumbo-like brew. Like the novelists of old, this book has an epic sweep . . . and seeking to encompass all that's worth communicating. . . . . While others are concerned with literary games Moorcock's concern is with writing great books." *London Bone* is a collection of nine short stories that pursue ordinary characters whose lives take an extraordinary turn. Some of the stories are about the seedy side of the London tourist trade, Irish-Americans, and brave old ladies. Writing for *The Guardian,* Ian Penman commented that the UFO tales are really about love and family, "Family is the tie that binds these nine pieces together, rather than the nominal city." Penman also wrote that "Moorcock . . . remains a curiously old-fashioned visionary. Which is good, when it includes the 'old-fashioned' virtues of humane interest and the refusal to follow trend for trend's sake."

Moorcock's move from science fiction to mainstream fiction was welcomed by several critics. Observed Gregory Cent in the *Village Voice,* "It's wonderful to see Moorcock grow from a genre writer into, simply, a writer. . . . A mainstream novel gives him far more scope to nourish the obsessions (and also the passion, zaniness, and eye for detail) that made his science fiction both fun and worthwhile." Moorcock, Andrew said, "has had to come the long way to literary recognition. But now, with *The Laughter of Carthage,* he can surely no longer be denied his due; this enormous book—with its forerunner, *Byzantium Endures*—must establish him in the front rank of practising English novelists."

Evaluations of Moorcock's career often emphasize the sheer volume and variety of his work. "It is like trying to evaluate an industry," Philip Oakes noted in the London *Times Magazine.* Throughout his career, Moorcock has shown an impressive ability to write consistently well within a wide range of genres and styles. "I have read about half his prodigious output," Oakes wrote, "and on the strength of that sample Moorcock strikes me as the most prolific, probably the most inventive and without doubt the most egalitarian writer practicing today." Writing in the *Observer* of Moorcock's long career, John Clute described him as "a figure of revolutionary fervour in the British literary world for nearly thirty years." Wilson called Moorcock "one of the most exciting discoveries that I have been able to make in the contemporary English novel during the forty or so years that I have been publishing my own novels and reviewing those of my contemporaries. Exciting for myself and, as is becoming increasingly clear with the appearance of each Moorcock book, for a legion of other readers."

Moorcock moved to Texas in the mid-1990s. Mike Shea covered the 1998 San Antonio Science Fiction Conference, attended by Moorcock, and said that the author "was welcomed with open arms, and his most basic needs—a reasonable number of good bookstores and restaurants—were served. Still, he grumbles that Texas 'is, compared to London, a cultural wasteland. [But] I'm an old whore basically; I can adapt to anything.' He was intrigued by the voices of Texas fiction—literary and speculative—and the attention focused on Austin. He views contemporary Texas writers as myth builders who are 'creating a kind of fiction that is very much going to be characteristic fiction of the twenty-first century.'"

Moorcock brought together his characters Elric of Melnibone and Ulric von Bek in *The Dreamthief's Daughter: A Tale of the Albino,* which begins with the growing power of Hitler. A *Kirkus Reviews* contributor said that "the best arrives early on, during the rise of Nazi Germany; thereafter, series fans will enjoy the warm familiarity of Elric's bloodthirsty adventures." "Fans of the series should enjoy this addition," wrote a *Publishers Weekly* reviewer. "A topnotch fantasy adventure," was *Library Journal* reviewer Jackie Cassada's comment. *Booklist* contributor Paula Luedtke opened her review of the book with "Moorcock stalwarts, rejoice! The Eternal Champion is back," and concluded by calling *The Dreamthief's Daughter* "quite a romp."

Moorcock talked about his life and work in an article on the *Time Warner Bookmark* Web site, where he said, "I have always been engaged with politics. Tom Paine's my hero. I'd like to help try to make the world a better place. That's why people who know my politics are a little surprised my books have so much to do with kings and princes. I do point out that my heroes, by and large, although doomed to perpetual struggle, tend to triumph over the supernatural and even, sometimes, their aristocratic backgrounds." Moorcock went on to say, "Reality isn't simple. Fiction can be simpler, can offer a relief from that complex world. But no matter how it entertains and distracts us, the best fiction, in my view, whether fantastic or naturalistic,

acknowledges those realities. There's an urgent need for such realism. More than at any point in human history our planet's future is now very much in our own hands. I can't help feeling we'd be wise to embrace its complexity rather than pretend it doesn't exist."

Moorcock told *CA:* "Most of my work recently has been in terms of a moral and psychological investigation of Imperialism (Western and Eastern) seen in terms of fiction. Even my fantasy novels are inclined to deal with moral problems rather than magical ones. I'm turning more and more away from SF and fantasy and more towards a form of realism used in the context of what you might call an imaginative framework. Late Dickens would be the model I'd most like to emulate."

Writing in the *Contemporary Authors Autobiography Series,* Moorcock commented of the writing life: "The job of a novelist has its own momentum, its own demands, its own horrible power over the practitioner. When I look back I wonder what I got myself into all those years ago when I realised I had a facility to put words down on paper and have people give me money in return. For ages the whole business seemed ludicrous. I couldn't believe my luck. Frequently, I still can't but it seems an unnatural way of earning a living. Of course, it's no longer easy. It's often a struggle. It spoils my health. . . . I suppose it must be an addiction. I'm pretty sure, though I deny it heartily, that I could now no longer give it up. I'm as possessed as any fool I used to mock."

*BIOGRAPHICAL AND CRITICAL SOURCES:*

*BOOKS*

*Authors and Artists for Young Adults,* Gale (Detroit, MI), Volume 7, 1992, Volume 26, 1999.
Bilyeu, R., *Tanelorn Archives,* Pandora's Books, 1979.
Callow, A. J., compiler, *The Chronicles of Moorcock,* A. J. Callow, 1978.
Carter, Lin, *Imaginary Worlds,* Ballantine (New York, NY), 1973.
*Contemporary Authors Autobiography Series,* Volume 5, Gale (Detroit, MI), 1987.
*Contemporary Literary Criticism,* Gale (Detroit, MI), Volume 5, 1976, Volume 27, 1984, Volume 58, 1990.

*Dictionary of Literary Biography,* Volume 14: *British Novelists since 1960,* Gale (Detroit, MI), 1983.

Greenland, Colin, *The Entropy Exhibition: Michael Moorcock and the British "New Wave" in Science Fiction,* Routledge & Kegan Paul, 1983.

Harper, Andrew and George McAulay, *Michael Moorcock: A Bibliography,* T-K Graphics, 1976.

Platt, Charles, *Dream Makers: The Uncommon People Who Write Science Fiction,* Berkley Publishing (New York, NY), 1980.

Walker, Paul, editor, *Speaking of Science Fiction: The Paul Walker Interviews,* Luna Publications, 1978.

Wollheim, Donald A., *The Universe Makers,* Harper (New York, NY), 1971.

PERIODICALS

*Amazing Stories,* May, 1971.

*Analog,* February, 1970; March, 1990.

*Booklist,* November 1, 1991, p. 496; February 15, 1995, p. 1064; October 1, 1998, Ray Olson, review of *Behold the Man,* p. 293; March 15, 2001, Paula Luedtke, review of *The Dreamthief's Daughter: A Tale of the Albino,* p. 1361.

*Books and Bookmen,* June, 1971; September, 1971; October, 1972; May, 1974; August, 1978.

*Chicago Tribune Book World,* January 31, 1982.

*Commonweal,* August 1, 1975.

*Detroit News,* February 24, 1985.

*Encounter,* November, 1981.

*Extrapolation,* winter, 1989.

*Guardian Weekly,* April 10, 1969.

*Harper's Bazaar* (British edition), December, 1969.

*Ink,* August, 1971.

*Kensington News,* April 18, 1969.

*Kensington Post,* April 4, 1969.

*Kirkus Reviews,* October 1, 1995, p. 1387.

*Library Journal,* November 15, 1991, p. 111; April 15, 2001, Jackie Cassada, review of *The Dreamthief's Daughter,* p. 137.

*Listener,* June 23, 1988; January 18, 1990.

*Locus,* May, 1989; November, 1989; February, 1990; March, 1990; May, 1993, p. 21.

*London Review of Books,* September 10, 1992, p. 22.

*Los Angeles Times,* January 9, 1985; November 10, 1987.

*Los Angeles Times Book Review,* March 7, 1982; February 7, 1988.

*Luna Monthly,* November, 1975.

*Magazine of Fantasy and Science Fiction,* June, 1998, review of *The War amongst the Angels,* p. 39.

*New Republic,* June 15, 1974.

*New Statesman,* April 4, 1969; May 18, 1973; June 18, 1976; April 15, 1977.

*New Statesman & Society,* July 24, 1992, p. 38; January 13, 1995, p. 38.

*New Worlds,* March, 1969.

*New York Times Book Review,* April 5, 1970; May 19, 1974; April 25, 1976; February 21, 1982; February 10, 1985; November 23, 1986; March 12, 1995, p. 25.

*Observer,* April 4, 1976; April 3, 1977.

*Publishers Weekly,* January 16, 1995, p. 442; June 11, 1995, p. 30; October 30, 1995, p. 49; February 12, 2000, review of *The Dreamthief's Daughter,* p. 188.

*Punch,* January 16, 1985.

*Rapport,* Volume 9, number 2, p. 35.

*Saturday Review,* April 25, 1970.

*Science Fiction Chronicle,* May, 1998, review of *Kane of Old Mars,* p. 40, review of *The Prince with the Silver Hand,* p. 46.

*Science Fiction Monthly,* February, 1975.

*Science Fiction Review,* January, 1971; January, 1979.

*Science-Fiction Studies,* March, 1976.

*Spectator,* April 1, 1969; August 10, 1974; November 20, 1976; April 9, 1977; December 24, 1977; June 27, 1981; February 9, 1985.

*Speculation,* May, 1970; August, 1970.

*Texas Monthly,* July, 1998, Mike Shea, "Sci-Fi Fo Fum," p. 60.

*Time,* August 5, 1974; January 28, 1985.

*Time Out,* September 17, 1971.

*Times* (London), September 6, 1984; November 25, 1984; August 5, 1985; June 18, 1988.

*Times Literary Supplement,* October 27, 1972; November 9, 1973; May 31, 1974; May 7, 1976; June 30, 1978; July 3, 1981; September 7, 1984; July 1, 1988; February 23, 1990; July 10, 1992, p. 22.

*Times Magazine* (London), November 5, 1978.

*Tribune Books* (Chicago), March 26, 1989.

*Village Voice,* March 2, 1982.

*Virginia Quarterly Review,* spring, 1975.

*Washington Post Book World,* March 21, 1982; December 23, 1984; September 28, 1986; May 14, 1989; December 31, 1995, p. 9.

*World Literature Review,* autumn, 1995, p. 796.

ONLINE

*Edge,* http://www.theedge.abelgratis.co.uk/ (April 28, 2003), John Coulthart, review of *King of the City.*

*Guardian Online,* http://books.guardian.co.uk/ (April 28, 2003), Ian Penman, "Magical history tours."

*Michael Moorcock: Cartographer of the Multiverse,* http://www.eclipse.co.uk/sweetdespise/moorcock/ (June 4, 2001).

*Multiverse,* http://www.multiverse. org/ (April 7, 2003).

*PS Publishing,* http://www.pspublishing.co.uk/ (April 28, 2003).

*Time Warner Bookmark,* http://www.twbookmark.com/ (June 4, 2001), "Michael Moorcock Speaks."

*Zone,* http://www.zone-sf.com/ (April 28, 2003), Patrick Hudson, review of *Firing the Cathedral.*\*

\*     \*     \*

## MOOREHEAD, Caroline 1944-

*PERSONAL:* Born October 28, 1944, in London, England; daughter of Alan McCrae (a writer) and Lucy (Milner) Moorehead; married Jeremy Swift (an economist), May 27, 1967; children: Martha, Daniel. *Education:* University of London, B.A. (with honors), 1965. *Politics:* Labour. *Religion:* Church of England.

*ADDRESSES: Home*—36 Fitzroy Rd., London NW1 8TY, England. *Agent*—Anthony Sheil, 43 Doughty St., London WC1N 2LF, England.

*CAREER:* Neuropsychiatric Hospital, Rome, Italy, psychologist, 1966-68; *Time,* Rome, Italy, reporter, 1968-69; *London Telegraph,* London, England, feature writer, 1969-70; *Times Educational Supplement,* London, England, feature editor, 1970-73; *Times,* London, England, feature writer, 1973-88; *The Independent,* London, England, feature writer, 1988-93. Producer of television series *Dunant's Dream,* based on her book, for the British Broadcasting Corp.

*WRITINGS:*

(Editor and translator) *Legends of Britain,* Burke Publishing (London, England), 1968.

*Helping: A Guide to Voluntary Work,* Macdonald & Jane's (London, England), 1975.

(With Margaret Trudeau) *Beyond Reason,* Paddington Press (London, England), 1979.

*Hostages to Fortune: A Study of Kidnapping in the World Today,* Atheneum (New York, NY), 1980, published as *Fortune's Hostages: A Study of Kidnapping in the World Today,* Hamish Hamilton (London, England), 1980.

(Editor) *The Letters of Dame Freya Stark,* Michael Russell (London, England), 1983.

*Sidney Bernstein: A Biography,* J. Cape (London, England), 1984.

*Freya Stark: A Biography,* Viking (New York, NY), 1985.

*Troublesome People: The Warriors of Pacifism,* Adler & Adler (Bethesda, MD), 1987.

*School Age Workers in Britain Today,* Anti-Slavery Society for the Protection of Human Rights (London, England), 1987.

(Editor) *Over the Rim of the World: Selected Letters of Freya Stark,* John Murray (London, England), 1988.

*Namibia: Apartheid's Forgotten Children,* Oxfam (Oxford, England), 1988.

(Editor) *Betrayal: Child Exploitation in Today's World,* Barrie & Jenkins (London, England), 1989, published as *Betrayal: A Report on Violence toward Children in Today's World,* Doubleday (New York, NY), 1990.

*Bertrand Russell: A Life,* Sinclair-Stevenson (London, England), 1992.

*The Lost Treasures of Troy,* Weidenfeld & Nicolson (London, England), 1994, published as *Lost and Found: The 9,000 Treasures of Troy,* Viking (New York, NY), 1996.

*Dunant's Dream: War, Switzerland, and the History of the Red Cross,* Carroll & Graf (New York, NY), 1999.

*Iris Origo: Marchesa of Val d'Orcia,* John Murray (London, England), 1999, Godine (Boston, MA), 2001.

Contributor of articles and reviews to periodicals.

*SIDELIGHTS:* Caroline Moorehead is the author of several acclaimed biographies, including 1993's *Bertrand Russell: A Life.* This book describes one of the twentieth century's greatest philosophers from both a professional and personal point of view; its detail and depth led a *Publishers Weekly* reviewer to call

Moorehead's work "the most intimate portrait of Russell . . . to date." Born in 1882, Russell had a traumatic early childhood, losing both parents while still very young. A freethinker all his life, Russell was sent to Cambridge University, but could not fit in with its traditional ways. He ran for Parliament in 1907 as a women's suffrage candidate, "fighting for a seat he could not win in order to stick up for an unpopular cause," according to a *Wilson Quarterly* critic. During the patriotic fervor of World War I Russell became a pacifist, and was eventually jailed for insulting Britain's ally, the United States (Russell reportedly said the U.S. Army would stay in Europe following the war to shoot striking workers). In the following decades Russell would write some of his most notable books, including *A History of Western Philosophy,* which helped him win the Nobel Prize for literature.

But the "post-1945 Russell is the one Americans remember," noted the *Wilson Quarterly* writer. Following World War II, the philosopher fought on behalf of the Nuclear Test Ban Treaty, wrote world leaders demanding nuclear disarmament, and "led a last, bitter campaign against the Vietnam War," as the article related. Russell died in 1970, leaving behind a legacy that included several shattered marriages and failed affairs. "Moorehead only occasionally raises an eyebrow at the discrepancy between Russell's mastery of logic and his weak grasp of realities of other people's lives," as the *Wilson Quarterly* contributor said. *Antioch Review* contributor Albert Stewart felt that *Bertrand Russell* focuses too much on Russell's personal life at the expense of presenting his intellectual achievements so that Moorehead's subject "sticks in the mind [as] the philanderer and inconsistent lover, not the logician and writer." The *Publishers Weekly* reviewer, on the other hand, found the book "especially strong" in the areas of family, marriage, and friendship with such Russell contemporaries as D. H. Lawrence and T. S. Eliot.

*Booklist*'s Donna Seaman referred to Moorehead's "outstanding" work on *Bertrand Russell* when reviewing the author's 1996 publication, *Lost and Found: The 9,000 Treasures of Troy.* This book is the biography of Heinrich Schliemann, who in 1871 discovered the ruins of the fabled ancient city of Troy and recovered golden treasure of King Priam. Moorehead relates how Schliemann rose from grocer's apprentice to archeologist, describing him as a bold and boastful adventurer whose archeological methods put him at odds with the scholars of the day. What's more, Schliemann stole much of Priam's treasure, which in more recent years was recovered from Nazi Germany and put on display in Moscow's Pushkin Museum.

In *Dunant's Dream: War, Switzerland, and the History of the Red Cross,* Moorehead chronicles the life of Swiss philanthropist Henry Dunant, who founded what would become the International Committee of the Red Cross. The organization was based on a simple philosophy: "to assist victims of warfare without distinction or discrimination," as Hans-Peter Gasser described it in an online assessment for *International Review of the Red Cross.* The book goes on to chronicle the history of the ICRC, a compassionate if sometimes controversial group (during World War II, the overly cautious ICRC leadership failed to publicly protest the Nazi extermination of Jews). To *Library Journal* contributor David Keymer the book "unfolds a moral drama of the first rank encompassing world military and civil conflicts." A similar view was held by a *Publishers Weekly* reviewer, who praised *Dunant's Dream* as a "fluid, character-rich history" and said that Moorehead focuses, "with a good novelist's sense of moral complexity, on the messy intersection between reality and lofty ideals."

In 2002 Moorehead produced *Iris Origo: Marchesa of Val d'Orcia,* "an affectionate history of the writer and charmer" of the twentieth century, according to a *Publishers Weekly* reviewer. Origo was born in 1902 into a wealthy American family that became a fixture in Florence, Italy. Defying family tradition, she married out of her class—to Antonio Origo, the illegitimate son of a cavalry officer. The couple revitalized the Tuscan valley and made possible an agricultural recovery in that area. During World War II they risked their safety by offering refuge to Allied partisans and prisoners of war. Amid a very public life as a writer and publisher, Iris Origo faced personal demons, enduring the death of one child and engaging in "several heart-wrenching extramarital affairs," as *Booklist* critic Margaret Flanagan put it. While the *Publishers Weekly* writer thought that the author "waits too long to bring the full force of Origo's literary ambitions and achievements to bear," Flanagan welcomed the biography as "magnificent . . . so absorbing and so full of fascinating characters and descriptive details that it reads like fiction."

BIOGRAPHICAL AND CRITICAL SOURCES:

PERIODICALS

*Albion,* fall, 1994, review of *Bertrand Russell: A Life,* p. 564.

*Antioch Review,* spring, 1994, Albert Stewart, review of *Bertrand Russell,* p. 360.

*Atlantic Monthly,* October, 1993, review of *Bertrand Russell,* p. 123.

*Booklist,* November 15, 1993, review of *Bertrand Russell,* p. 582; June 1, 1996, Donna Seaman, review of *Lost and Found: The 9,000 Treasures of Troy,* p. 1671; April 15, 1999, Mary Carroll, review of *Dunant's Dream: War, Switzerland, and the History of the Red Cross,* p. 1490; April 1, 2002, Margaret Flanagan, review of *Iris Origo: Marchesa of Val d'Orcia,* p. 1300.

*Bookwatch,* August, 1996, review of *Lost and Found,* p. 3.

*Choice,* April, 1994, review of *Bertrand Russell,* p. 1308; May, 1995, review of *Troublesome People: The Warriors of Pacifism,* p. 1408; October, 1999, review of *Dunant's Dream,* p. 384.

*Christian Science Monitor,* July 25, 1996, review of *Lost and Found,* p. B4.

*Contemporary Review,* February, 2001, review of *Iris Origo,* p. 128.

*Economist,* September 12, 1998, review of *Dunant's Dream,* p. 6.

*Kirkus Reviews,* August 15, 1993, review of *Bertrand Russell,* p. 1053; May 1, 1996, review of *Lost and Found,* p. 670; April 15, 1999, review of *Dunant's Dream,* p. 609.

*Kliatt Young Adult Paperback Book Guide,* September, 1997, review of *Lost and Found,* p. 29.

*Library Journal,* September 15, 1992, review of *Bertrand Russell,* p. 85; August, 1996, review of *Lost and Found,* p. 90; April 1, 1999, David Keymer, review of *Dunant's Dream,* p. 113.

*London Review of Books,* November 19, 1992, review of *Bertrand Russell,* p. 8; January 21, 1999, review of *Dunant's Dream,* p. 27.

*Los Angeles Times Book Review,* June 6, 1999, review of *Dunant's Dream,* p. 4.

*New Statesman & Society,* October 2, 1992, review of *Bertrand Russell,* p. 44; December 16, 1994, review of *The Lost Treasures of Troy,* p. 67.

*Newsweek,* November 1, 1993, review of *Bertrand Russell,* p. 70.

*New York,* September 13, 1993, review of *Bertrand Russell,* p. 105.

*New York Review of Books,* December 19, 1996, review of *Lost and Found,* p. 15; June 24, 1999, review of *Dunant's Dream,* p. 40.

*New York Times Book Review,* October 21, 1993, review of *Bertrand Russell,* p. 7; July 14, 1996, review of *Lost and Found,* p. 7.

*Observer* (London, England), October 25, 1992, review of *Bertrand Russell,* p. 64; November 8, 1992, review of *Bertrand Russell,* p. 60; June 14, 1998, review of *Dunant's Dream,* p. 16; August 1, 1999, review of *Dunant's Dream,* p. 14.

*Publishers Weekly,* August 30, 1993, review of *Bertrand Russell,* p. 81; June 3 1996, review of *Lost and Found,* p. 71; March 1, 1999, review of *Dunant's Dream,* p. 47; March 18, 2002, review of *Iris Origo,* p. 91.

*Sewanee Review,* April, 1994, review of *Bertrand Russell,* p. 310.

*Spectator,* October 3, 1992, review of *Bertrand Russell,* p. 29; December 17, 1994, review of *The Lost Treasures of Troy,* p. 72; July 11, 1998, review of *Dunant's Dream,* p. 30.

*Times* (London, England), February 16, 1984; November 9, 1985.

*Times Educational Supplement,* June 26, 1998, review of *Dunant's Dream,* p. 8.

*Times Literary Supplement,* April 29, 1983; February 3, 1984; October 2, 1992, review of *Bertrand Russell,* p. 13; December 9, 1994, review of *The Lost Treasures of Troy,* p. 25; July 31, 1998, review of *Dunant's Dream,* p. 3.

*Tribune Books* (Chicago, IL), November 28, 1993, review of *Bertrand Russell,* p. 6.

*Washington Post Book World,* January 2, 1994, review of *Bertrand Russell,* p. 1; July 4, 1999, review of *Dunant's Dream,* p. 4.

*Wilson Quarterly,* spring, 1994, review of *Bertrand Russell,* p. 86.

ONLINE

*International Review of the Red Cross,* http://icrc.org/ (June 13, 2002), Hans-Peter Gasser, review of *Dunant's Dream.**

\*          \*          \*

**MORLAND, Dick**
**See HILL, Reginald (Charles)**

## MORPURGO, Michael 1943-

*PERSONAL:* Born October 5, 1943, in St. Albans, England; son of Tony Valentine Bridge (stepson of Jake Eric Morpurgo) and Catherine Noel Kippe; married Clare Allen, 1963; children: three. *Education:* Attended Sandhurst; King's College, London, B.A., 1967.

*ADDRESSES: Home*—Langlands, Iddesleigh, Winkleigh, Devon EX19 8SN, England. *Agent*—David Higham Associates, 5-8 Lower John Street, Golden Square, London W1R 4HA, England.

*CAREER:* Writer, teacher. Primary school teacher, 1967-75. Joint founder and director, Farms for City Children, 1976—; opened Nethercourt House farm, 1976, Treginnis Isaf, 1989, and Wick Court, 1998.

*AWARDS, HONORS:* Runner-up, Whitbread Award, 1982, for *War Horse;* runner-up, Carnegie Medal, 1988, for *King of the Cloud Forests;* runner-up, *Guardian* Award, 1991, for *Waiting for Anya;* Silver Pencil Award, Holland; Best Books selection, *School Library Journal,* 1995, and Top of the List selection for Youth Fiction, *Booklist,* 1995, both for *The War of Jenkins' Ear;* Whitbread Award, 1995, for *The Wreck of the Zanzibar;* Smarties Gold Medal Award, 1997, for *The Butterfly Lion;* Editor's Choice, *Books for Keeps,* 1999, for *Cockadoodle-Doo, Mr. Sultana!* Awarded the MBE, 1999, for work in creating Farms for City Children.

*WRITINGS:*

*FICTION; FOR CHILDREN*

*It Never Rained: Five Stories,* illustrated by Isabelle Hutchins, Macmillan (London, England), 1974.
*Thatcher Jones,* illustrated by Trevor Ridley, Macmillan (London, England), 1975.
*Long Way Home,* Macmillan (London, England), 1975.
(Compiler, with Graham Barrett) *The Story-Teller,* Ward Lock (London, England), 1976.
*Friend or Foe,* illustrated by Trevor Stubley, Macmillan (London, England), 1977.
*What Shall We Do with It?,* illustrated by Priscilla Lamont, Ward Lock (London, England), 1978.
*Do All You Dare,* photographs by Bob Cathmoir, Ward Lock (London, England), 1978.

(Editor) *All around the Year,* photographs by James Ravilious, drawings by Robin Ravilious, new poems by Ted Hughes, J. Murray (London, England), 1979.
*The Day I Took the Bull by the Horn,* Ward Lock (London, England), 1979.
*The Ghost-Fish,* Ward Lock (London, England), 1979.
*Love at First Sight,* Ward Lock (London, England), 1979.
*That's How,* Ward Lock (London, England), 1979.
*The Marble Crusher and Other Stories,* illustrated by Trevor Stubley, Macmillan (London, England), 1980.
*The Nine Lives of Montezuma,* illustrated by Margery Gill, Kaye & Ward (Kingswood, England), 1980.
*Miss Wirtles' Revenge,* illustrated by Graham Clarke, Kaye & Ward (Kingswood, England), 1981.
*The White Horse of Zennor: And Other Stories from below the Eagle's Nest,* Kaye & Ward (Kingswood, England), 1982.
*The War Horse,* Kaye & Ward (Kingswood, England), 1982, Greenwillow (New York, NY), 1983.
*Twist of Gold,* Kaye & Ward (Kingswood, England), 1983, Viking (New York, NY), 1993.
*Little Foxes,* illustrated by Gareth Floyd, Kaye & Ward (Kingswood, England), 1984.
*Why the Whales Came,* Scholastic (New York, NY), 1985.
*Tom's Sausage Lion,* illustrated by Robina Green, A. & C. Black (London, England), 1986, BBC Consumer Publishing, 2003.
*Jo-Jo, the Melon Donkey,* illustrated by Chris Molan, Simon & Schuster (New York, NY), 1987, illustrated by Tony Kerins, Heinemann (London, England), 1995.
*King of the Cloud Forests,* Viking (New York, NY), 1988.
*My Friend Walter,* Heinemann (London, England), 1988.
(With Shoo Rayner) *Mossop's Last Chance,* A. & C. Black (London, England), 1988.
*Mr. Nobody's Eyes,* Heinemann (London, England), 1989, Viking (New York, NY), 1990.
*Conker,* Heinemann (London, England), 1989.
(With Shoo Rayner) *Albertine, Goose Queen,* A. & C. Black (London, England), 1989.
(With Shoo Rayner) *Jigger's Day Off,* A. & C. Black (London, England), 1990.
*Waiting for Anya,* Heinemann (London, England), 1990, Viking (New York, NY), 1991.
*Colly's Barn,* Heinemann (London, England), 1991.

(With Shoo Rayner) *And Pigs Might Fly!*, A. & C. Black (London, England), 1991.

*The Sandman and the Turtles*, Heinemann (London, England), 1991, Philomel (New York, NY), 1994.

(With Shoo Rayner) *Martians at Mudpuddle Farm*, A. & C. Black (London, England), 1992.

*The War of Jenkins' Ear*, Heinemann (London, England), 1993, Philomel (New York, NY), 1995.

*Snakes and Ladders*, Heinemann (London, England), 1994.

(Editor) *Ghostly Haunts*, illustrated by Nilesh Mistry, Pavilion (London, England), 1994.

*Arthur, High King of Britain*, illustrated by Michael Foreman, Pavilion (London, England), 1994, Harcourt (San Diego, CA), 1995.

*The Dancing Bear*, illustrated by Christian Birmingham, Young Lion (London, England), 1994, Houghton Mifflin (Boston, MA), 1996.

(With Shoo Rayner) *Stories from Mudpuddle Farm* (including the previously published *And Pigs Might Fly!*, *Martians at Mudpuddle Farm*, and *Jigger's Day Off*), A. & C. Black (London, England), 1995.

(With Shoo Rayner) *Mum's the Word*, A. & C. Black (London, England), 1995.

(Editor) *Muck and Magic: Tales from the Countryside*, foreword by H.R.H. The Princess Royal, Heinemann (London, England), 1995.

*The Wreck of the Zanzibar*, illustrated by Christian Birmingham, Viking (New York, NY), 1995.

*Blodin the Beast*, illustrated by Christina Balit, Fulcrum (Golden, CO), 1995.

*Sam's Duck*, illustrated by Keith Bowen, Collins (London, England), 1996.

*The King in the Forest*, illustrated by T. Kerins, Simon & Schuster (New York, NY), 1996.

*The Butterfly Lion*, illustrated by Christian Birmingham, Collins (London, England), 1996.

*The Ghost of Grania O'Malley*, Heinemann (London, England), 1996, Viking (New York, NY), 1996.

*Robin of Sherwood*, illustrated by Michael Foreman, Harcourt (San Diego, CA), 1996.

(Editor) *Beyond the Rainbow Warrior*, Pavilion (London, England), 1996.

*The Marble Crusher* (includes *The Marble Crusher*, *Colly's Barn*, and *Conker*), Mammoth (London, England), 1997.

*Farm Boy*, illustrated by Michael Foreman, Pavilion (London, England), 1997.

*Red Eyes at Night*, illustrated by Tony Ross, Hodder & Stoughton (London, England), 1997.

*Wartman*, illustrated by Joanna Carey, Barrington Stoke (Edinburgh, Scotland), 1998.

*Escape from Shangri-La*, Philomel Books (New York, NY), 1998.

(Reteller) *Cockadoodle-doo, Mr. Sultana!*, illustrated by Michael Foreman, Scholastic (London, England), 1998.

(Reteller) *Joan of Arc of Domremy*, illustrated by Michael Foreman, Harcourt (San Diego, CA), 1999.

(Compiler) *Animal Stories*, illustrated by Andrew Davidson, Kingfisher (New York, NY), 1999.

*Kensuke's Kingdom*, illustrated by Michael Foreman, Heinemann (London, England), 1999, Scholastic (New York, NY), 2003.

*Rainbow Bear*, illustrated by Michael Foreman, Doubleday (London, England), 1999.

*Billy the Kid*, illustrated by Michael Foreman, Pavilion (London, England), 2000.

*Black Queen*, Corgi Juvenile (London, England), 2000.

(Compiler) *The Kingfisher Book of Great Boy Stories: A Treasury of Classics from Children's Literature*, Kingfisher (New York, NY), 2000.

*Wombat Goes Walkabout*, illustrated by Christian Birmingham, Candlewick Press (Cambridge, MA), 2000.

*The Silver Swan*, illustrated by Christian Birmingham, Phyllis Fogelman Books (New York, NY), 2000.

*From Hereabout Hill*, Mammoth (London, England), 2000.

*Who's A Big Bully Then?*, illustrated by Joanna Carey, Barrington Stoke (Edinburgh, Scotland), 2000.

*Mister Skip*, Roaring Good Reads, 2000.

*The King in the Forest*, Hodder & Stoughton (London England), 2001.

*Toro! Toro!*, illustrated by Michael Foreman, Collins (London, England), 2002.

*Out of the Ashes*, illustrated by Michael Foreman, Macmillan (London, England), 2002.

*Cool*, HarperCollins Canada (Toronto, Ontario, Canada), 2002.

*Because a Fire Was in My Head*, Faber (London, England), 2002.

*Beastman of Ballyloch*, HarperCollins Canada (Toronto, Ontario, Canada), 2002.

*Jim Davis: A High-Sea Adventure*, Scholastic (New York, NY), 2002.

*The Last Wolf*, illustrated by Michael Foreman, Doubleday (London, England), 2002.

*Sleeping Sword*, Egmont (London, England), 2003.

*Gentle Giant*, Picture Lions (London, England), 2003.

*Mairi's Mermaid*, Crabtree, 2003.

*OTHER*

(Compiler, with Clifford Simmons) *Living Poets,* J. Murray (London, England), 1974.
(Librettist) *Words of Songs,* music by Phyllis Tate, Oxford University Press (London, England), 1985.

Some of Morpurgo's books have been translated into Irish and Welsh.

*ADAPTATIONS: Why the Whales Came* was adapted for a movie titled *When the Whales Came,* 1989, by Golden Swan Films; *My Friend Walter* was adapted for a television movie by Portobello Films for Thames Television and WonderWorks, 1993; *Out of the Ashes* was adapted for a television movie.

*SIDELIGHTS:* "I write stories, not books," British author Michael Morpurgo told a school class in an interview for *Young Writer.* "And I write stories for me—for both the child and the adult in me. . . . My stories are about children, not for them, because I know children—they interest me, children of all ages, even adult ones." Morpurgo, since leaving childhood himself, has hardly spent a day out of the company of children: a father by twenty, he was a grandfather at forty-three; a teacher in primary schools for a decade, he has helped to run Farms for City Children—a venture that brings urban children to the countryside—since 1976. In his sixty-plus novels and picture books for young readers, Morpurgo has consistently demonstrated this knowledge of and appreciation for children.

"Undoubtedly a leading figure in the field of children's books," according to *Children's Fiction Sourcebook,* Morpurgo blends adventure, fantasy and moral drama in his lyrical yet always understated prose. Consistent themes for Morpurgo are the conquest of evil by good and the vindication of virtues such as loyalty, hard work and determination, things that might seem somewhat old-fashioned in the relativistic age of cyberspace. His books are generally uplifting and teach ethical lessons, but Morpurgo is never preachy; the story is primary in such books as *Why the Whales Came, War Horse, The War of Jenkins' Ear, Waiting for Anya, The Wreck of the Zanzibar, The Butterfly Lion, Escape from Shangri-La, Billy the Kid,* and *Out of the Ashes,* although each propounds a moral dilemma. Much of Morpurgo's fiction is historical, set in the recent past,

and in such exotic locales as the Scilly Islands, China, Renaissance Venice, and the Pyrenees. His subjects range from war to rural life, from the sea to the boarding school, and his writing combines stark realism with touches of fancy and magic.

Morpurgo was born on October 5, 1943, in St. Albans, England, into a country that had been at war for over four years. At the age of seven he went away to a grammar school in Sussex where he was introduced to "class war," as he told *Booklist*'s Ilene Cooper. "The schoolboys and the village boys had fights and difficulties; walking along cow paths, we'd hurl insults at each other. It was an indication that there were people out there who didn't like you because of the way you spoke, and we didn't like them either. And while things have changed since the 1950s, class still seems to me to be a cancer that riddles our society." As a young schoolboy Morpurgo was thought of "as good at rugby and a bit stupid," he remarked in *Young Writer.* "As a child I think I lived up to that expectation. . . . I never liked writing as a child." It was not until much later that Morpurgo began to love reading, especially the novels of Robert Louis Stevenson, Paul Gallico, and Ernest Hemingway, and the poetry of Ted Hughes, a poet laureate of England and a close friend of Morpurgo.

At age fourteen Morpurgo entered King's School in Canterbury, graduating in 1962. The following year he married Clare Allen, daughter of the well-known publisher of Penguin books. They ultimately had three children together, two sons and one daughter. Graduating from King's College in London in 1967, Morpurgo became a teacher for a time after graduation, and also served as an army officer. It was during his teaching career that he determined to become a writer. "I had a notion I could tell a tale when the children I was teaching really seemed to want to listen to the tales I told them," Morpurgo noted in *Young Writer.* "An acid test." Reading Ted Hughes's *Poetry in the Making* influenced Morpurgo to think that he too could string words together rhythmically and literally got him writing. "No better invitation to write was every written and I accepted," Morpurgo remarked in *Young Writer.* "I love the sound of words, the rhythm of a sentence."

Living in the countryside, Morpurgo also wanted to introduce city-born-and-bred kids to the wonders of nature. To that end, he and his wife started Farms for

City Children in the 1970s. Under this program, kids come to stay at the farm and work and take care of animals for several weeks. So popular has the program become, that the Morpurgos operate three farms where more than two thousand children per year have the opportunity to get in touch with nature and themselves. In 1999, Morpurgo and his wife were honored in the Queen's Birthday List with the MBE for their work with Farms for City Children.

Much of Morpurgo's early work has not been published in the United States. This includes both short novels for ten-to-twelve-year-olds, and picture books for younger readers. Already with this early work, however, Morpurgo was making a name for himself in England as a writer "successfully outside the mainstream," as Josephine Karavasil described his work in a *Times Literary Supplement* review of *Miss Wirtle's Revenge,* Morpurgo's tale about a little girl who competes successfully against a class full of boys. His 1980 *Nine Lives of Montezuma* is a short novel detailing nine narrow-escape adventures of a farmyard cat named Montezuma. Told from the cat's point of view, the book also details the farming year as a background story, with "continuity" being the theme of the book, according to Margery Fisher of *Growing Point.* When Montezuma dies, the cat knows that there is a descendant to take its place in the scheme of things on the farm. *Junior Bookshelf* critic D. A. Young noted that the story "is told without sentimentality, though not without sentiment," and concluded that the book could be "recommended with confidence to cat-lovers of any age."

This same characteristic—appealing writing about animals without sentimentality—was the hallmark of Morpurgo's first book to be published in the United States, *War Horse.* Inspired by a painting of a horse in the village hall near Morpurgo's home, the book is the story of the First World War seen through the eyes of Joey, a farm horse commandeered in 1914. Cavalry stood little chance against the mechanized horrors of modern war; Joey endures bombardment and capture by the Germans. He is set to work pulling ambulances and guns, worked by different masters but never forgetting young Albert, the kind son of his original owner back in England. In the end, persistence and courage pay off—Joey is reunited with Albert in Devon. Kate M. Flanagan, writing in *Horn Book,* noted that "the courage of the horse and his undying devotion to the boy" permeate this book, which she main-

tained was written with "elegant, old-fashioned grace." *Voice of Youth Advocates* contributor Diane G. Yates, noting that *War Horse* is based on a true story, commented: "The message about the futility and carnage of war comes across loud and clear. The characters, both human and animal, that die in the war are all the best and brightest of their generation." Margery Fisher of *Growing Point* highlighted similarities between *War Horse* and the classic, *Black Beauty,* and concluded her review by stating that Morpurgo's book "is a most accomplished piece of story-telling, full of sympathy for an animal manipulated by man but preserving its dignity." Warmly received on both sides of the Atlantic, *War Horse* helped win an international audience for Morpurgo.

Morpurgo's next book was *Twist of Gold,* set in both Ireland and the United States. When famine hits Ireland in the 1840s, Sean and Annie O'Brien set off for America to find their father, an adventurous journey that takes them first across the ocean and then across a continent by wagon train and river boat. A story of a childhood test, *Twist of Gold* is a "touching and inventive adventure story," according to Margery Fisher of *Growing Point.* Morpurgo's name became more widely recognized in the United States with the 1985 publication of *Why the Whales Came* and the book's subsequent adaptation for film. Set in 1914 on Bryher in the Scilly Islands off England's southwest coast, this is "a story full of compassion," according to *Children's Fiction Sourcebook.* Gracie and Daniel have been forbidden to associate with the strange old man on the far side of the island who is known as the Birdman to the locals. But soon the two youngsters learn that the old man is not some evil magician, but simply a person made lonely because of his deafness, and one who had to flee another of the islands as a youth because of a curse put on it. The three become fast friends with the war always hovering ominously in the background. Yet on Bryher there is a parallel war between the islanders and the sea and weather. When a whale washes ashore, the islanders must be convinced to help return it to the sea rather than butcher it, for it was the destruction of sea life that brought the curse to the Birdman's original island. "The success of Morpurgo's novel comes . . . from its portrait of the two children and from its exploration of the blend of superstition and communal spirit existing in an isolated settlement," noted reviewer Marcus Crouch in *The Junior Bookshelf.* Cindy Darling Codell, writing in *School Library Journal,* commented that Morpurgo's language "is lean, yet lyrical," and that his descriptive paragraphs "let readers taste the salt of the sea and feel the grit of the islander's lives." Margery Fisher of *Growing Point* concluded her review by dubbing the book "a forceful and exciting narrative." Another Morpurgo novel that was adapted for film is *My Friend Walter,* a whimsical story about the ghost of Sir Walter Raleigh.

The Scilly Islands also provide a setting for Morpurgo's 1995 Whitbread Award-winning *Wreck of the Zanzibar,* the story of a childhood on Bryher Island as told through the diary of Laura, and of her secret treasure, Zanzibar, a wooden tortoise. Laura's narrative is the record of a harsh life, of adversity and the will to overcome. *Junior Bookshelf* reviewer Marcus Crouch commented that *The Wreck of the Zanzibar,* while a short book, is "by no means a slight one," and praised the "beautiful timing throughout." *Horn Book*'s Elizabeth S. Watson noted that "The slight book makes a solid impact on the reader, who will finish [it] with a satisfied smile." A further tale with an island setting is Morpurgo's *Ghost of Grania O'Malley,* a 1996 work set off the coast of Ireland and involving young Jessie, her American cousin Jack, and the ghost of the female pirate, Grania O'Malley, as they battle to prevent the ecological destruction of the island.

Morpurgo returned to an animal-centered story with *Jo-Jo, the Melon Donkey,* a picture book for older children set in 16th-century Venice. Jo-Jo is a bedraggled old donkey who is laughed at when attempting to sell melons in the main square. The Doge's (chief magistrate's) daughter, however, sees the plaintive look in the animal's eyes and decides to be his friend. When the Doge offers to give his daughter any horse in the kingdom, she opts for Jo-Jo, to her father's disgust. But when Jo-Jo helps to save the city from a flood, he becomes a hero and the Doge allows his daughter her wish. Amy Spaulding in *School Library Journal* noted that the "writing style follows that of the literary fairy tale, being at once simple and elegant," and a *Kirkus Reviews* critic commented: "With a nice blend of humor and sadness, Morpurgo brings to life the vibrancy of 16th-century Venice." Other Morpurgo picture books include the "Mudpuddle Farm" series with Shoo Rayner, and for older children, *Blodin the Beast* and *The Dancing Bear,* the latter being the story of young singer Roxanne and the orphaned bear cub she has raised. When a film crew comes to her remote village to make a video, Roxanne is lured by bright lights, and decides ultimately to leave with the group, pursuing fame and fortune as an

entertainer. Her bear dies the following day. As the narrator of the story, Roxanne's former teacher, says, "There's a lesson to be learned, if one just listens to my tale." *School Library Journal* contributor Kathy East, however, felt Morpurgo's lesson "likely to appeal more to adults, who will relate to the elderly narrator and his style, than to children."

Morpurgo has continued with picture books throughout his career, often teaming with Michael Foreman or with Christian Birmingham. Working with the former, Morpurgo wrote the 1999 *The Rainbow Bear,* about a polar bear who decides to hunt rainbows rather than seals. The book is "a fable about the folly of trying to become something that you naturally are not," according to Kate Kellaway, writing in London's *Observer.* Kellaway further noted that the book is "gracefully told and elegantly concluded." Another picture book collaboration with Foreman is *Cockadoodle-Doo, Mr. Sultana!,* about a rooster who refuses to be cheated out of a button it finds. For Mary Medlicott, writing in *School Librarian,* this tale "is rumbustiously full of life," with language "as rich as a plum pudding."

Working with Birmingham, Morpurgo has created a number of picture books, including *Wombat Goes Walkabout* and *The Silver Swan.* Catherine McClellan of *Magpies* felt that the story of a young wombat who becomes lost from its mother after digging a hole and then sitting in it to have a think is a "beautiful picture book." The hapless wombat meets up with a number of Australian animals as it searches for its mother, all of whom shake their heads at his digging and thinking skills. However, these are the very skills that ultimately save them all when they are threatened by a wildfire. In *The Silver Swan,* a swan is killed by a fox, breaking the heart of the boy who revered the dead animal. "Morpurgo writes compassionately and convincingly," commented Nikki Gamble in *School Librarian.* Gamble also praised Birmingham's "stunning artwork" in this "reflective story for quiet moments."

Morpurgo's love of animals finds its way into many of his novels for young adult readers, as well. The protagonist of *Little Foxes,* young Billy, feels attracted to the wildlife inhabiting land by a ruined church; the mythic Yeti save a lost boy in *King of the Cloud Forests;* Ocky the chimpanzee becomes a companion for Harry Hawkins in *Mr. Nobody's Eyes;* and giant turtles populate the dreams of Mike in *The Sandman and the*

*Turtles.* In *King of the Cloud Forests,* young Ashley Anderson must make his way with a Tibetan Buddhist across China to India and safety, one step ahead of the invading Japanese. Crossing the Himalayas, he and his guide are separated. Lost and near starvation, Ashley is rescued by a band of the legendary Yeti, red-furred, ape-like creatures who revere the boy as a god. Ashley stays in their idyllic community for a time, but is finally reunited with his guide and ultimately makes it safely to England. Jacqueline Simms, writing in the *Times Literary Supplement,* noted that "this marvelous adventure story . . . will surely become a perennial favourite," while Roger Sutton of the *Bulletin of the Center for Children's Books* thought that this "brief and dramatic novel . . . may woo reluctant readers back to the fold."

Two of Morpurgo's most compelling novels with child protagonists are *Waiting for Anya* and *The War of Jenkins' Ear.* *Waiting for Anya* relates the story of the plight of Jewish children in World War II France. The novel is set in the Pyrenees just after the surrender of the French forces, and its protagonist, Jo, a young shepherd, becomes involved in a scheme to save the children when he discovers that a man named Benjamin is hiding them at a farm near the village of Lescun. Benjamin is smuggling the children across the border into Spain; he is also waiting for his own daughter to make her way to this safe house from Paris. Jo begins delivering supplies to the farm, a job made much riskier when the Nazis occupy Lescun and threaten to kill anyone aiding fugitives. Soon, however, the entire town of Lescun is helping to get the children across the border. Though Benjamin is captured and sent to die at Auschwitz, Anya does finally turn up at the farm and is saved at the end of this "gripping, clearly written story," as Ellen Fader described it in *Horn Book.* Marcus Crouch, in a favorable review for the *Junior Bookshelf,* commented that *Waiting for Anya* "is an intensely exciting story guaranteed to keep a sensitive reader on the edge of his chair." Crouch added that Morpurgo's story is "rich in the qualities which make for critical approval," concluding: "There have been many Second World War stories for the young, none which deals more convincingly with its perils and dilemmas."

*The War of Jenkins' Ear* is an English boarding school tale in which young Toby Jenkins meets a remarkable boy named Christopher who claims to be the reincarnation of Jesus. Christopher begins to develop a fol-

lowing before being betrayed by one of his friends and expelled from the school for blasphemy. *Quill and Quire* contributor Joanne Schott commented: "A strict school of forty years ago makes a credible setting and gives scope for the complex relationships Morpurgo uses to examine questions of belief and credulity, deception and self-deception, loyalty and the pressure of doubt, and much more." Tim Rausch, writing in *School Library Journal,* called *The War of Jenkins' Ear* a book that "tackles provocative themes, dealing with the issues of hate, revenge, prejudice, and especially faith in an intelligent and fresh manner."

Morpurgo's 1996 novel *The Butterfly Lion* is a blend of fantasy and fiction, a story within a story about a ten-year-old boy who runs away from his miserable school and ends up in a dusty house where an old widow shows him the figure of a giant lion cut into the chalk hillside. This woman tells the boy about her dead husband, Bertie, who, as a youth growing up in South Africa, had as his pet and only friend a white lion. When his father sold the lion one day, Bertie vowed to find him again. This he did during World War One and then brought the animal with him to England where it ultimately died. Bertie thereafter spent forty years carving its likeness in the hillside, a figure visited by thousands of butterflies after the rains. Returning to school, the young boy learns that both Bertie and his widow had died many years before. "The story sounds hokey," noted *Booklist*'s Kathleen Squires, "but Morpurgo evocatively captures the South African landscape and presents young, lonely Bertie's heartbreak and blossoming friendship and love . . . with genuine emotion and tender passion." Reviewing the novel in *School Library Journal,* Gebregeorgis Yohannes concluded, "In addition to being a successful adventure story, the book demonstrates the value of character—of keeping promises, standing up for one's beliefs, and courage under fire." *The Butterfly Lion,* "at once marvelous and matter-of-fact," according to a writer for *Kirkus Reviews,* won England's prestigious Smarties Gold Medal Award in 1997. "This dreamlike story is suffused with a man's lifelong love for a rare, gentle animal friend," the critic for *Kirkus Reviews* concluded.

Morpurgo has also breathed new life into old legends. His retelling of the Arthurian tales in *Arthur, High King of Britain* is "the real thing—darkness and all," according to Heather McCammond-Watts in *Bulletin of the Center for Children's Books.* McCammond-

Watts explained that the Arthur of Morpurgo's book, who rescues a young time-traveler from the modern era, "is a complex character: an impetuous youth, an august yet sometimes rash ruler, a jealous lover, and a tortured man trying to live up to his epic persona." *School Library Journal* contributor Helen Gregory concluded that Morpurgo's Arthur "stands with the best." With *Robin of Sherwood*, Morpurgo added twists to the old tale—an albino Marian for example—that creates an "outstanding new version of the Robin Hood legend," according to Nancy Zachary in *Voice of Youth Advocates*. "Shelve this treasure alongside Howard Pyle's and Ian Serraillier's classic folktales," concluded Zachary. Similarly, *Booklist*'s Carolyn Phelan found the book to be a "fine, original piece of story-telling, faithful to the legend of Robin Hood."

Additionally, Morpurgo has tackled the legend of the Maid of Orleans in his 1999 *Joan of Arc of Domremy,* a tale that begins in the modern day when young Eloise Hardy moves with her family to Orleans, France, and begins studying legends of Joan. Steeping herself in such lore, Eloise one day hears Joan's voice telling her the story of her life. "Morpurgo is an accomplished writer and storyteller," wrote Shirley Wilton in a *School Library Journal* review. "Facts and popular beliefs, history and legend are drawn upon to create an exciting tale." A reviewer for *Publishers Weekly* felt that Morpurgo's storytelling "is premised on faith," and concluded that the book's "polish and panoramic scope will lure and hold readers."

With *Farm Boy,* Morpurgo returned to the here and now to detail the memories of four generations of an English farming family. Set once again in Morpurgo's beloved Devon, the book tells on one level the story of a young boy who goes to visit his grandfather on the farm. His grandfather in turn enchants the boy with tales of how farming was done before mechanization, capturing the spirit of rural life before the internal combustion engine and agribusiness. "Morpurgo's storytelling style is unhurried," noted *School Library Journal*'s Lee Bock, "reflecting great skill at giving unique voices to his characters." Bock continued, "The memories of [Grandpa's] horse are particularly poignant, and readers will learn many details about life during the early part of this century and World War I." A critic for *Kirkus Reviews* called the book "a small gem" and an "expertly crafted reminder that stories can link generations."

Memories of World War II figure in *Escape from Shangri-La,* in which an old tramp, Popsicle, watching

Cessie's house, turns out to be her long-lost grandfather. When the old man has a stroke, he is put in the Shangri-La nursing home, but he is withering away there. Finally Cessie finds her grandfather's real home, an old lifeboat once used to evacuate the British forces from Dunkirk during the Second World War. From a photograph and news clippings, Cessie learns her grandfather took part in this heroic effort, and the sight of a faded photo of the Frenchwoman who hid him from the Germans when he fell off the boat rescuing others makes Popsicle recall the past. Cessie helps her grandfather and other residents of the home make a break for it; they head to France to track down this woman, only to discover she never returned from German arrest in 1940. Going back to England, the entire family is again happily reunited. "Readers will enjoy the climactic adventure and respond on a deeper level to the friendship between a spirited child and a life-long loner," wrote John Peters in a *Booklist* review.

Morpurgo may well be one of the most versatile children's writers at work. Into his fourth decade of writing, his production and range have neither slowed nor narrowed. His themes and topics of books from the new millennium take readers from a Robinson Crusoe-type adventure yarn to a young girl recording the tragedy of the outbreak of disease on her farm, to the reminiscences of an old man. Morpurgo does not miss a beat as he changes from one era to another or from adventure to social commentary. In *Kensuke's Kingdom* he sets a young boy adrift on an island, on his own except for a dog and a mysterious old Japanese man, the Kensuke of the title, who slowly allows the boy—who fell overboard from the family boat—into his heart. "This must be ranked alongside Morpurgo's best," declared Linda Newbery in a *School Librarian* review, "and like several of his most successful stories, has the feel of a fable." Julia Eccleshore, reviewing the audiobook of the same title in *Books for Keeps,* also had praise for this "excellent adventure," noting that it is a "story full of insight and mood changes."

The reflections of age are conveyed in several other Morpurgo titles. *The Last Wolf* features an old man who is researching his family tree on the computer that his granddaughter has persuaded him to use. While doing his research, he stumbles across a tale set during the Jacobite rebellion in Scotland in 1745, when a young boy whose parents have been killed finds a similarly orphaned wolf pup. Together the two manage to escape to Canada and a new life. In *Toro! Toro!* a grandfather tells his grandson how he once planned to save a bull from the bullfighting ring by setting the herd free. The very night he planned to do this, however, the horrors of the Spanish Civil War reached his village when bombs kill his entire family. A reviewer for the *Times Educational Supplement* called this an "elegantly told tale," while George Hunt, writing in *Books for Keeps* similarly noted that the book was both "moving and exciting." Another old man reflects on his life from boyhood to his years of soccer-playing as a youth, and then his time in the Second World War and his capture by, and subsequent escape from, enemy troops in *Billy the Kid*, a graphic novel in format, with illustrations by Foreman. Chris Brown, writing in *School Librarian*, noted that though the book was a "skeleton" of a novel, it was still a story of "tremendous life and liveliness." Brown praised Morpurgo's "masterly structure and telling," and found that the book had a profound emotional effect. "Inevitably the tale gets behind the eyes," Brown concluded.

More traditional in format is the 2001 novel *Out of the Ashes,* in which thirteen-year-old Becky Morley keeps a diary of the disastrous hoof-and-mouth disease outbreak in England in 2001. Becky is a farmer's daughter, proud of her dad and loving her country life and her horse. All this changes as the epidemic reaches their Devon farm—as it did all three of Morpurgo's own farms in his Farms for City Children, forcing him to close down operations for a time. Within a matter of months the work of a lifetime has been destroyed for the Morleys and other farmers like them, but the novel does end on a positive note, giving hope for the future. Brown, writing in *School Librarian*, felt that Morpurgo's book "leads us into the personal tragedies and awful aftermath of the foot and mouth epidemic." Brown also called Morpurgo a "master of his art." Hunt, writing in *Books for Keeps*, likewise found *Out of the Ashes* to be a "short novel powerfully told," while a contributor for the *Times Educational Supplement* dubbed it a "hard-hitting novel" as well as a "heartfelt account."

Morpurgo has, over the years, contributed original children's literature in historical fiction, animal stories, fantasies, picture books, easy readers, and retellings of legend and myth. Often employing the rural setting that he knows so well, he typically places his young male or female protagonist in challenging situations that call up the best in them—courage, loyalty, and

self-confidence. Often praised for the simple elegance of his prose style, Morpurgo's works are "heartwarming and sensitive," according to Jennifer Taylor in *St. James Guide to Young Adult Writers*. Taylor further commented, "Morpurgo's imaginative empathy, whether writing about animals or people, makes for pure gold. His novels certainly open up horizons for young readers."

*BIOGRAPHICAL AND CRITICAL SOURCES:*

*BOOKS*

*Children's Literature Review,* Volume 51, Gale (Detroit, MI), 1999, pp. 116-151.
*St. James Guide to Young Adult Writers,* 2nd edition, St. James Press (Detroit, MI), 1999, pp. 603-605.

*PERIODICALS*

*Booklist,* February 1, 1984, p. 814; September 15, 1985, p. 137; July, 1988, p. 1814; November 1, 1989, p. 564; May 1, 1990, p. 1708; August, 1990, p. 2178; March 15, 1992, p. 1364; April 1, 1993, p. 1425; September 1, 1994, p. 44; September 1, 1995, p. 53; November 15, 1995, p. 560; January 1, 1996, Ilene Cooper, "The *Booklist* Interview," p. 816; March 15, 1996, p. 1282; October 1, 1996, Carolyn Phelan, review of *Robin of Sherwood*, p. 350; June 1, 1997, Kathleen Squires, review of *The Butterfly Lion*, p. 1704; September 15, 1998, John Peters, review of *Escape from Shangri-La*, p. 231.
*Books for Keeps,* September, 1997, Clive Barnes, review of *Sam's Duck*, p. 23; May, 1998, Gwynneth Bailey, review of *Red Eyes at Night*, p. 24; March, 1999, Rosemary Stores, review of *Cockadoodle-Doo, Mr. Sultana!*, p. 21; May, 1999, review of *The Rainbow Bear*, p. 6; July, 2001, Julia Eccleshore, review of *Kensuke's Kingdom* (audiobook), p. 24; January, 2002, George Hunt, review of *Out of the Ashes*, p. 23; March, 2002, George Hunt, review of *Toro! Toro!*, p. 22.
*Bulletin of the Center for Children's Books,* July-August, 1988, Roger Sutton, review of *King of the Cloud Forests*, pp. 234-235; March, 1991, p. 172; March, 1993, p. 221; May, 1995, Heather McCammond-Watts, review of *Arthur, High King of Britain*, p. 317; December, 1995, p. 135; May, 1996, pp. 309-10; January, 1997, p. 181.

*Carousel,* spring, 1997, p. 17.

*Growing Point,* November, 1980, Margery Fisher, review of *The Nine Lives of Montezuma,* p. 3776; November, 1982, Margery Fisher, review of *War Horse,* p. 3989; January, 1984, Margery Fisher, review of *Twist of Gold,* pp. 4183-4184; January, 1987, Margery Fisher, review of *Why the Whales Came,* p. 4749; November, 1989, pp. 5240-5245.

*Horn Book,* December, 1983, Kate M. Flanagan, review of *War Horse,* pp. 711-712; July-August, 1991, Ellen Fader, review of *Waiting for Anya,* p. 458; March-April, 1996, Elizabeth S. Watson, review of *The Wreck of the Zanzibar,* p. 198.

*Junior Bookshelf,* December, 1980, D. A. Young, review of *The Nine Lives of Montezuma,* p. 294; December, 1985, Marcus Crouch, review of *Why the Whales Came,* p. 279; August, 1988, pp. 179-180; December, 1989, pp. 298-299; February, 1991, Marcus Crouch, review of *Waiting for Anya,* pp. 35-36; June, 1992, pp. 113-114; August, 1995, Marcus Crouch, review of *The Wreck of the Zanzibar,* p. 148.

*Kirkus Reviews,* December 1, 1987, review of *Jo-Jo, the Melon Donkey,* p. 1677; April 15, 1997, review of *The Butterfly Lion,* p. 645; December 15, 1998, review of *Farm Boy.*

*Magpies,* November, 1999, Catherine McClellan, review of *Wombat Goes Walkabout,* p. 6.

*Observer* (London, England), October 24, 1999, review of *Wombat Goes Walkabout,* p. 13, and Kate Kellaway, review of *The Rainbow Bear,* p. 13.

*Publishers Weekly,* May 12, 1997, pp. 76-77; February 12, 1999, review of *Joan of Arc of Domremy,* p. 95.

*Quill and Quire,* July, 1993, Joanne Schott, review of *The War of Jenkins' Ear,* p. 59.

*School Librarian,* February, 1997, p. 33; autumn, 1998, Norton Hodges, review of *Escape from Shangri-La,* p. 147; spring, 1999, Jam Cooper, review of *Joan of Arc of Domremy,* pp. 40-41; summer, 1999, Mary Medlicott, review of *Cockadoodle-Doo, Mr. Sultana!,* p. 79; winter, 1999, Linda Newbery, review of *Kensuke's Kingdom,* p. 192; spring, 2001, Chris Brown, review of *Billy the Kid,* pp. 47-48; summer, 2001, Nikki Gamble, review of *The Silver Swan,* p. 90; autumn, 2001, Chris Brown, review of *Out of the Ashes,* pp. 158-159.

*School Library Journal,* February, 1987, Cindy Darling Codell, review of *Why the Whales Came,* p. 82; September, 1987, p. 181; April, 1988, Amy Spaulding, review of *Jo-Jo, the Melon Donkey,* p. 87; September, 1988, p. 200; November, 1990, p. 117; April, 1991, p. 122; December, 1991, p. 31; February, 1993, p. 94; November, 1993, p. 156; July, 1995, Helen Gregory, review of *Arthur, High King of Britain,* p. 89; September, 1995, Tim Rausch, review of *The War of Jenkins' Ear,* p. 219; December, 1995, "SLJ's Best Books, 1995," p. 22; May, 1996, Kathy East, review of *The Dancing Bear,* p. 114; August, 1997, Gebregeorgis Yohannes, review of *The Butterfly Lion,* p. 158; March, 1999, Lee Bock, review of *Farm Boy,* p. 212; May, 1999, Shirley Wilton, review of *Joan of Arc of Domremy,* p. 128; April, 2001, Edith Ching, review of *The Kingfisher Book of Great Boy Stories,* p. 146.

*Times Educational Supplement,* January 14, 1983, p. 30; January 13, 1984, p. 42; June 6, 1986, p. 54; November 27, 1987, p. 48; February 5, 1988, pp. 54, 60; March 10, 1989, p. B16; November 24, 1989, p. 27; February 15, 1991, p. 32; May 24, 1991, p. 24; July 2, 1993, p. 11; November 4, 1994, p. 89; May 31, 1995, p. 15; February 8, 2002, review of *The Last Wolf, Toro! Toro!,* and *Out of the Ashes,* pp. 20-21.

*Times Literary Supplement,* March 26, 1982, Josephine Karavasil, "Matters of Rhythm and Register," p. 347; February 19, 1988, Jacqueline Simms, "Magic Man," p. 200.

*Voice of Youth Advocates,* April, 1984, Diane G. Yates, review of *War Horse,* p. 32; February, 1997, Nancy Zachary, review of *Robin of Sherwood,* p. 330; June, 1998, Kathleen Beck, review of *The War of Jenkins' Ear,* pp. 103-104.

ONLINE

*Achuka,* http://www.achuka.com/ (April 20, 2003), "Achuka's Special Guest #39: Michael Morpurgo."

*Young Writer,* http://www.mystworld.com/youngwriter/ (February 12, 2003), "Issue 12: Michael Morpurgo."*

\*    \*    \*

## MURAVCHIK, Joshua 1947-

*PERSONAL:* Born September 17, 1947, in New York, NY; son of Emanuel and Miriam (Kornfield) Muravchik; married Sally Golden, January 1, 1974; children: Stephanie, Madeline, Valerie. *Education:* City

*Joshua Muravchik*

College of the City University of New York, B.A., 1970; Georgetown University, Ph.D., 1984. *Religion:* Jewish.

*ADDRESSES: Home*—11504 Orebaugh Ave., Wheaton, MD 20902. *Office*—American Enterprise Institute for Public Policy Research, 1150 Seventeenth St. NW, Washington, DC 20036. *E-mail*—jmuravchik@aei.org.

*CAREER:* Young People's Socialist League (now Young Social Democrats), New York, NY, national chair, 1968-73; Coalition for a Democratic Majority, Washington, DC, executive director, 1974-79; freelance writer, 1984-87; American Enterprise Institute for Public Policy Research, Washington, DC, resident scholar, 1987—; Washington Institute for Near East Policy, Washington, DC, fellow in residence. Member of United States Commission on Civil Rights and Maryland State Advisory Committee.

*WRITINGS:*

*The Senate and National Security,* Sage Publications (Beverly Hills, CA), 1980.

*Perceptions of Israel in the American Media: Summary of a Conference,* Institute on American Jewish-Israeli Relations (New York, NY), 1985.

*The Uncertain Crusade: Jimmy Carter and Dilemmas of Human Rights Policy,* Hamilton Press (Lanham, MD), 1986.

*Nicaragua's Slow March to Communism,* Cuban American National Foundation (Washington, DC), 1986.

*News Coverage of the Sandinista Revolution,* American Enterprise Institute for Public Policy Research (Washington, DC), 1988.

*Exporting Democracy: Fulfilling America's Destiny,* American Enterprise Institute for Public Policy Research (Washington, DC), 1991.

*U.S. Foreign Policy Options and Australian Interests,* Pacific Security Research Institute (Sydney, Australia), 1992.

*The Imperative of American Leadership: A Challenge to Neo-Isolationism,* American Enterprise Institute for Public Policy Research (Washington, DC), 1996.

*Heaven on Earth: The Rise and Fall of Socialism,* Encounter Books (San Francisco, CA), 2002.

Contributor to *Democracy in the Middle East: Defining the Challenge,* edited by Yehudah Mirsky and Matt Ahrens, Washington Institute for Near East Policy (Washington, DC), 1993. Also contributor to periodicals, including *Commentary, New Republic,* and *New York Times;* editorial board member of *World Affairs* and *Journal of Democracy.*

*SIDELIGHTS:* A political activist, Joshua Muravchik has focused his work on advocating democracy. Muravchik believes that democracy is the missing ingredient for world peace, arguing that democratic nations do not go to war with each other. Viewing past American policy as "realist"—placing strategic interests over democratic values mainly in an attempt to stave off Communism—he suggests a future agenda with the promotion of democracy as the central theme.

Muravchik's book *Exporting Democracy: Fulfilling America's Destiny* encompasses his arguments and discusses America's role as a world organizer. Daniel Pipes described the book's ambition in *Washington Post Book World:* "It tackles a topic no less than America's place in the world. It succeeds brilliantly."

While he found Muravchik's policy recommendations too general, *New York Times Book Review* contributor David Callahan acknowledged that "the case for exporting democracy is powerful." Lauded for its magnitude and relevance, *Exporting Democracy* has been characterized as a portentous work. Summing up his thoughts on the book, *New York Times* writer A. M. Rosenthal proclaimed, "It will be lastingly important."

Muravchik's *The Imperative of American Leadership: A Challenge to Neo-Isolationism* urges the United States not to bend to what the author calls "the isolationist temptation." Published in 1997, the book proposes the continued involvement of the United States in world affairs, arguing that as the "wealthiest, mightiest, and most respected nation" in the world, the U.S. is obliged to "respond to crisis, to discourage or thwart aggression, to settle quarrels, and to uphold international law." However, even in the wake of the decline of Communism, Muravchik points out other factors, including nuclear proliferation and economic isolation, "that threaten U.S. interest and security," according to Gabriel Kikas in *Perspectives on Political Science*. Kikas acknowledged the author's premise that there are "no clear alternatives to democracy," using the United Nations peacekeeping operations as an example, and related the book's conclusion that the United States "must take sound, practical measures to secure a democratic world order." *Foreign Affairs* critic David Hendrickson pointed to the many sides of the isolationist argument, stating that critics of globalism "will not want to join the author" along the chain of contingency, while "skeptics of the aggressive promotion of democracy" may wonder about the consequences of America's involvement in areas like East Asia, "where such a posture seems likely to be counterproductive or destabilizing."

*Heaven on Earth: The Rise and Fall of Socialism* examines the tempestuous history of a social-political movement. Muravchik begins with the birth of socialism, which was touted by intellectuals as the wave of the future, certain to create abundant societies and give birth to the "New Man." By the end of the twentieth century, however, socialism was discredited even in Communist nations, many of which, following the fall of the Berlin Wall, were quick to adopt a more capitalist society. *Heaven on Earth* looks at some of the advocates of socialism, including Robert Owen, who used its principles to design a modern utopia in

the United States; Clement Attlee, who attempted to introduce the movement to Great Britain; and Mikhail Gorbechev, the former Soviet prime minister who endorsed socialism in the post-Communist state. "Muravchik pulls no punches," commented a contributor to the *National Review Book Service*. "He shows why socialism has failed wherever it has been tried." Moreover, the reviewer added, the author "is unafraid to explore socialism's appeal as man's great attempt to replace religion." *Booklist* contributor Jay Freeman, meanwhile, summed up *Heaven on Earth* as "an important work and an object lesson showing great harm is frequently done by those with the purest motives."

Joshua Muravchik once told *CA:* "I spent the first decade of my working life as a political activist and apparatchik. During the course of this experience I became ever more impressed with the impact of ideas and argument—as opposed to mere interest and influence—in shaping our political life. I concluded that I would rather be a wordman than an 'orgman.' So, after some further education, I began a new career reading and writing about politics, with a focus on foreign policy. I am especially interested in issues of right and wrong. I believe that political acts are subject to measurement against moral standards, and that the virtues of kindness, compassion, generosity, honor, and reason should guide public life as well as private."

*BIOGRAPHICAL AND CRITICAL SOURCES:*

*PERIODICALS*

*American Spectator,* January, 1992, review of *Exporting Democracy: Fulfilling America's Destiny,* p. 16.

*Booklist,* April 1, 2002, Jay Freeman, review of *Heaven on Earth: The Rise and Fall of Socialism,* p. 1278.

*Choice,* February, 1992, review of *Exporting Democracy,* p. 960; September, 1996, review of *The Imperative of American Leadership: A Challenge to Neo-Isolationism,* p. 211.

*Foreign Affairs,* July-August, 1996, David Hendrickson, review of *The Imperative of American Leadership,* p. 146.

*New Republic,* January 27, 1992, review of *Exporting Democracy,* p. 39.

*New York Times,* April 16, 1991, A. M. Rosenthal, review of *Exporting Democracy,* p. A23.

*New York Times Book Review,* April 21, 1991, David Callahan, review of *Exporting Democracy,* p. 11.

*Perspectives on Political Science,* summer, 1997, Gabriel Kikas, review of *The Imperative of American Leadership,* p. 170.

*Times Literary Supplement,* July 12, 1996, review of *The Imperative of American Leadership,* p. 27.

*Wall Street Journal,* May 31, 1996, review of *The Imperative of American Leadership,* p. A8.

*Washington Post Book World,* June 16, 1991, Daniel Pipes, review of *Exporting Democracy,* p. 5; September 29, 1996, review of *The Imperative of American Leadership,* p. 6.

ONLINE

*National Review Book Service,* http://www.nrbookservice.com/ (June 13, 2002), review of *Heaven on Earth: The Rise and Fall of Socialism.**

# N

## NADEL, Ira Bruce 1943-

*PERSONAL:* Born July 22, 1943, in Rahway, NJ; son of Isaac David and Francis (Sofman) Nadel; married Susan Matties, June 5, 1966 (died, February 23, 1975); married Josephine Margolis (a lawyer), July 4, 1976; children: (second marriage) Ryan Martin, Dara Vanessa. *Education:* Rutgers University, B.A., 1965, M.A., 1967; Cornell University, Ph.D. (English), 1970. *Hobbies and other interests:* Theater studies and parallels between visual and verbal presentation.

*ADDRESSES: Home*—646 W. 26th Avenue, Vancouver, British Columbia, Canada V5H 4H6. *Office*—#397-1873 East Mall, Department of English, University of British Columbia, Vancouver, British Columbia V6T 1Z1, Canada. *E-mail*—nadel@interchange.ubc.ca.

*CAREER:* Scholar. University of British Columbia, Vancouver, assistant professor, 1970-76, associate professor, 1977-85, professor of English, 1985—, chair, Department of English graduate program, 1992-95. Coeditor, *David Mamet Review;* advisory board member, *The Journal of Modern Literature* and *Joyce Studies Annual;* editorial board member, *English Literature in Transition,* and *Autobiographical/Biographical Studies.*

*MEMBER:* Canadian Association of University Teachers of English, Modern Language Association of America (chairman of Non-Fictional Prose Division, 1987; chair of Discussion Group on Biography and Autobiography, 1989; executive, Division on Methods of Literary Research, 1991-94), Victorian Studies Association of Western Canada (president, 1980-82), James Joyce Foundation, Phi Beta Kappa.

*AWARDS, HONORS:* Canada Council fellowship, 1975-76; leave fellowship from Social Sciences and Humanities Research Council, 1982; Lowell Prize nomination, Modern Language Association, 1985, for *Biography: Fiction, Fact and Form;* Killam research fellowship, 1989-90; NEH Travel Fellowship, 1990; Beinecke fellowship, Yale, April-May, 1991; Killam Research Prize, 1992; Mellon fellowship, University of Texas, 1996; Royal Society of Canada fellow, 1996; University of British Columbia Medal for Canadian Biography, 1996; Social Sciences and Humanities Research Council research grant, 1997.

*WRITINGS:*

(Editor, with F. S. Schwartzbach, and contributor) *Victorian Artists and the City,* Pergamon (Elmsford, NY), 1980.

*Jewish Writers of North America,* Gale (Detroit, MI), 1981.

*Biography: Fiction, Fact and Form,* Macmillan (London, England), 1984.

(Editor) *Victorian Fiction: A Collection of Essays from the Period,* Garland Publishing (New York, NY), 1986.

(Editor) *Victorian Biography: A Collection of Essays from the Period,* Garland Publishing (New York, NY), 1986.

(Editor, with S. Neuman) *Gertrude Stein and the Making of Literature,* Northeastern University Press (Boston, MA), 1988.

(Editor, with Peter Buitenhuis) *Orwell: A Reassessment,* St. Martin's Press (New York, NY), 1988.

*Joyce and the Jews: Culture and Texts,* University of Iowa Press (Iowa City, IA), 1989.

(Editor) *The Letters of Ezra Pound to Alice Corbin Henderson,* University of Texas Press (Austin, TX), 1993.

*Leonard Cohen: A Life in Art,* ECW Press (East Haven, CT), 1994.

*Various Positions: A Life of Leonard Cohen,* Pantheon Books (New York, NY), 1996.

(Editor and author of introduction and notes) *The Dead Secret, Wilkie Collins,* Oxford University Press (New York, NY), 1997.

(Editor) *The Cambridge Companion to Ezra Pound,* Cambridge University Press (New York, NY), 1999.

(Editor and contributor) *The Education of Henry Adams,* Oxford University Press (New York, NY), 1999.

(Editor and author of notes and introduction) Wilkie Collins, *Iolani, or, Tahiti As It Was: A Romance,* Princeton University Press (Princeton, NJ), 1999.

*Tom Stoppard: A Life,* Palgrave Macmillan (New York, NY), 2002, published as *Double Act: A Life of Tom Stoppard,* Palgrave Macmillan (London, England), 2002.

*EDITOR, WITH W. E. FREDEMAN*

*Victorian Novelists before 1885,* Gale (Detroit, MI), 1983.

*Victorian Novelists after 1885,* Gale (Detroit, MI), 1983.

*Victorian Poets before 1850,* Gale (Detroit, MI), 1984.

*Victorian Poets after 1850,* Gale (Detroit, MI), 1985.

(With John Stasny) *The Victorian Muse: Selected Criticism and Parody of the Period,* 39 volumes, Garland Publishing (New York, NY), 1986.

Contributor to numerous literary collections, including *Assessing the 1984 Ulysses,* edited by G. Sandulescue and C. Hart, and *Essays on Canadian Writing.* Contributor to literary journals, including *Victorian Poetry, Mosaic, Journal of Modern Literature, Paideuma, Modern Drama,* and *Joyce Studies Annual.* Editor, with W. E. Fredeman, *Journal of Pre-Raphaelite and Aesthetic Studies,* 1987-1990.

*WORK IN PROGRESS: Ezra!: A Literary Life of Ezra Pound,* Palgrave, 2004; *David Mamet* (biography); editing *Ezra Pound: Tthe Early Poetry,* for Penguin.

*SIDELIGHTS:* Ira Bruce Nadel is the author and editor of various works of nineteenth-and twentieth-century literature. He is particularly interested in the Victorian era, nonfiction prose (most notably biography), and the novel. He once told *CA:* "My concern with the relationship between literature and society has been sharpened by my interest in the evolution of biography as a literary genre. Through various comparative studies I have been exploring the link between an actual and written life as well as the importance of imagination in writing the narrative of another. The crucial question, however, may not be why one writes a biography, but what use is it?"

In *Various Positions: A Life of Leonard Cohen,* which was deemed "a definitive biography of Canada's best-known poet and angst-ridden singer" by Kerry Diotte of the *Edmonton Sun,* Nadel lays bare the life of this legendary singer, songwriter, poet, and novelist. His biography chronicles the artist's life from his early years in Montreal through his experiences in London, Nashville, Los Angeles, and New York. Nadel gathered first-hand information for Cohen's biography from interviews with Cohen and his friends and family, and by thoroughly researching Cohen's correspondence. Arnie Keller, writing for the *Globe and Mail,* noted that "Cohen is a relentless keeper of letters, drafts, and notebooks, and Nadel had good access to them and to Cohen. That may have been too much of a good thing, however. . . . The result is one-sided, too much Leonard Cohen's own take on Leonard Cohen." Similary, Morton Ritts wrote for *Maclean's,* "In Nadel, who documents rather than analyzes, [Cohen] has found less a biographer than a disciple." Diotte found the most impressive aspect of the biography to be the way in which Nadel "explores what mind frame the singer was in when many of his important songs and poems were penned." He added that Nadel's book is "exhaustive in its exploration . . . [and] is also exhausting. It is dryly written in straight chronological style . . . Yet, until we're treated to Cohen's autobiography, this is as good as it gets." Margot Mifflin critiqued the book for *Entertainment Weekly* as "a critically sharp, information-rich biography." A *Publishers Weekly* reviewer remarked, "The chief virtues of the book are its thorough research and its honesty."

In *Tom Stoppard: A Life* Nadel chronicles the life of Sir Thomas Stoppard, considered by many the greatest living English-language playwright. Stoppard is the author of more than twenty-five plays produced since 1965 and has won a plethora of awards, including several Tony Awards and an Oscar Award for the film *Shakespeare in Love.* Barry X. Miller commented in

*Library Journal* that Nadel's work represents "the best and most complete Stoppard biography available."

Nadel, who spent four years researching his subject, was granted several interviews with Stoppard, along with permission to peruse his papers. The biography begins with Stoppard's birth in the Czech Republic in 1937 and traverses his childhood in Singapore and India to his arrival in England where, in 1967, he experienced his first great theatrical success with *Rosencrantz and Gildenstern Are Dead.* The biography continues through Stoppard's successes on English and American stages, through to the trilogy, "Coast of Utopia," that opened in London in 2002. Adam Langer of *Book* quoted Nadel as saying, "The wonderful thing about Stoppard's plays is that it's the truth and not accuracy that he's most interested in. . . . Stoppard may not believe in the accuracy of biography, but it can be truthful, and that's what I'm trying to do."

A reviewer for the *Complete Review* Web site commented that Nadel's biography of Stoppard "is pleasantly straightforward: largely descriptive covering a great deal of Stoppard's personal and professional life without too much hypothesizing or analysis about what possibly motivates and moves the artist." The reviewer explained that, in what appears to be the first full-length study of this artist, Nadel presents Stoppard's life, work, and even personal opinions as being a double act (hence the British title). The same reviewer was impressed with Nadel's chronological methodology as he documents "each next step and work. It gets messy along the way—screenplays (often unproduced for great lengths of time) litter the way. . . . Still, overall Nadel stays in track and works his way through most everything of importance." The critic did fault the biography for "too little" about Stoppard's personal life and relationships, some repetition, and some "rough jumps in the narrative." Overall, however, he felt the book "reads easily and quickly, and there are few lulls. Forays into Stoppard's Jewish heritage go somewhat astray," he commented. However, Langer found this element of the biography especially vivid. "On the whole," commented the critic for the *Complete Review,* "Nadel presents Stoppard's life well." He called the book "a fine read," and said "we learned much about Stoppard from it that we didn't know. We certainly recommend it to anyone interested in Stoppard."

*BIOGRAPHICAL AND CRITICAL SOURCES:*

*PERIODICALS*

*Book,* July-August, 2002, Adam Langer, "Creating Drama," review of *Tom Stoppard: A Life,* p. 27.

*Booklist,* September 15, 1996, Mike Tribby, review of *Various Positions: A Life of Leonard Cohen,* p. 204.

*Edmonton Sun,* November 17, 1996, Kerry Diotte, "Biography of Leonard Cohen Long on Detail, Short on Flair."

*Entertainment Weekly,* October 25, 1996, Margot Mifflin, review of *Various Positions,* p. 108.

*Globe and Mail,* November 23, 1996, Arnie Keller, review of *Various Positions,* p. D12.

*Library Journal,* July, 2002, Barry X. Miller, review of *Tom Stoppard,* p. 83.

*Maclean's,* December 2, 1996, Morton Ritts, review of *Various Positions,* p. 91.

*Publishers Weekly,* August 12, 1996, review of *Various Positions,* p. 7.

*ONLINE*

*Complete Review,* http://www.complete-review.com/ (October 8, 2002), review of *Double Act: A Life of Tom Stoppard.*

*Salon,* http://www.salon.com/ (October 8, 2002), George Rafael, review of *Tom Stoppard,* September 10, 2002.

*University Press of Florida ,* http://www.upf.com/ (October 8, 2002), description of *Joyce and the Jews.*

\*  \*  \*

# NAGEL, Thomas 1937-

*PERSONAL:* Born July 4, 1937, in Belgrade, Yugoslavia; naturalized U.S. citizen, 1944; son of Walter and Carolyn (Baer) Nagel; married Doris G. Blum, June 19, 1954 (divorced, 1973); married Anne Hollander, June 26, 1979. *Education:* Cornell University, B.A., 1958; Oxford University, B.Phil., 1960; Harvard University, Ph.D., 1963.

*ADDRESSES: Office*—New York University School of Law, 418 Vanderbilt, 40 Washington Square, New York, NY 10012. *E-mail*—nagelt@turing.law.nyu.edu.

*CAREER:* University of California, Berkeley, assistant professor of philosophy, 1963-66; Princeton University, Princeton, NJ, assistant professor, 1966-69, associate professor, 1969-72, professor of philosophy, 1972-80; New York University, New York, NY, professor of philosophy, 1980—, chair of department, 1981-86, professor of philosophy and law, 1986—, Fiorello LaGuardia Professor of Law, 2001—. Visiting professor at Rockefeller University, 1973-74, University of Pittsburgh, 1976, Universidad Nacional Autonoma de Mexico, 1977, University of the Witwatersrand, 1982, University of California at Los Angeles, 1986-87, All Souls College, Oxford, 1990. Tanner Lecturer, Stanford University, 1977; Tanner Lecturer, Oxford University, 1979; Howison Lecturer, University of California at Berkeley, 1987; Thalheimer Lecturer, Johns Hopkins University, 1989; John Locke Lecturer, Oxford University, 1990; Hempel Lecturer, Princeton University, 1995; Whitehead Lecturer, Harvard University, 1995; Immanuel Kant Lecturer, Stanford University, 1995; Townsend Lecturer, University of California at Berkeley, 1999.

*MEMBER:* American Philosophy Association, American Academy of Arts and Sciences, British Academy.

*AWARDS, HONORS:* Guggenheim fellowship, 1966-67; National Science Foundation fellowship, 1968-70; National Endowment for the Humanities fellowship, 1978-79.

*WRITINGS:*

*The Possibility of Altruism,* Oxford University Press (New York, NY), 1970.
(Coeditor) *Equality and Preferential Treatment,* Princeton University Press (Princeton, NJ), 1977.
*Mortal Questions,* Cambridge University Press (New York, NY), 1979.
(Coeditor) *Marx, Justice, and History,* Princeton University Press (Princeton, NJ), 1980.
(Coeditor) *Medicine and Moral Philosophy,* Princeton University Press (Princeton, NJ), 1981.
*The View from Nowhere,* Oxford University Press (New York, NY), 1986.

*What Does It All Mean?: A Very Short Introduction to Philosophy,* Oxford University Press (New York, NY), 1987.
*Equality and Partiality,* Oxford University Press (New York, NY), 1991.
*Other Minds: Critical Essays, 1969-1994,* Oxford University Press (New York, NY), 1995.
*The Last Word,* Oxford University Press (New York, NY), 1997.
(With Liam Murphy) *The Myth of Ownership: Taxes and Justice,* Oxford University Press (New York, NY), 2002.
*Concealment and Exposure: And Other Essays,* Oxford University Press (New York, NY), 2002.

Associate editor of *Philosophy and Public Affairs,* 1971.

*SIDELIGHTS:* Thomas Nagel is one of the best-known philosophers of his generation. His writings have tackled familiar topics, such as the mind-body problem and religion, as well as pioneering new areas in philosophy, including bioethics and the morality of taxation. As a professor of philosophy, he often address difficult subject matter in his works, but several of his books, including *What Does It All Mean?* and *The Myth of Ownership: Taxes and Justice,* are aimed at a general audience. In discussing Nagel's book *The View from Nowhere,* P. F. Strawson of the *New Republic* defined Nagel as "an unrepentant realist," who "sees all the many questions he discusses as aspects of a single problem: the problem of how to combine an internal, or subjective view of the world with an external, or objective view that seeks to explain, and where necessary to correct, the former." Recognizing that Nagel consistently examines issues that many thinkers do not attempt, Gilbert Meilaender of the journal *First Things* wrote that "the questions that concern him are ones that we never simply settle once and for all."

In *The Last Word,* Nagel forms an argument against subjectivism—the idea that morality is defined by the individual—in favor of objectivism, which is the concept that reality exists outside the human mind and can be observed. Contrary to many popular theorists, from Hume to Kant to the purveyors of postmodernism, Nagel is comfortable in denying that reality is subjective. Furthermore, he asserts that the logic of subjectivists is unintelligible. This belief has made him popular among Christian philosophers. "Nagel argues that there is nothing philosophically presumptuous and certainly nothing arrogant, in simple assertions," wrote Ric Machuga in *Christianity Today,* who went on to say that few Christian readers "will dispute the seriousness of what is at stake." Ruth Lessl Shively of the *American Political Science Review* analyzed this point further, noting that "Nagel connects the appeal of subjectivism to a 'fear of religion' that preys upon modern intellectuals, himself included." Shively concluded that "Nagel's argument is impressive. . . . It provides a necessary challenge to the often uncritical privileging of subjectivism that pervades the discipline and calls attention to the many ways in which this tendency . . . undermines our ability to engage fruitfully in argument with others."

In *The Myth of Ownership,* Nagel and coauthor Liam Murphy join a tumultuous debate by applying philosophical thought to the concept of federal taxation. At the heart of their thesis are questions regarding personal and social obligations as well as liberty. One primary assertion the authors make is that it is wrong to consider gross income as belonging solely to the person who earned it. In that mindset, the government becomes an evil force that takes away someone's money. Nagel argues that only after-tax income belongs to the individual; pre-tax income is "morally insignificant," and an erroneous point from which to argue the justice of taxes. Government is necessary to prevent anarchy. Social chaos would make all income irrelevant, so only after the needs of the government are accounted for can individuals claim entitlement to their wages.

While critics were intrigued by the ideas Nagel and Murphy present, some recognized flaws in their argument that are bound to aggravate some readers. David Cay Johnston of the *New York Times Book Review,* for example, said that "Murphy and Nagel offer ideas that would improve the national debate over how we should tax ourselves," but they "ignore the morality of tax enforcement and its role in tax justice" and pay "too little attention to the role of taxes in creating wealth." Johnston, nevertheless sympathetic to the authors' arguments, concluded that, "unhappily," their "reasoned suggestions . . . will be drowned out in the din of mindless anti-tax sound bites."

For the novice philosopher, Nagel's *Other Minds: Critical Essays, 1969-1994* presents an overview of many of the author's ideas. The collection of twenty-two essays focuses on two issues that interest Nagel:

the philosophy of the mind and political philosophy. Though some of the works were written for readers well-versed in current issues of philosophy, Robert Pasnau of the *Review of Metaphysics* said that "Nagel writes clearly and with a certain flair," and that several chapters "make ideal introductions for a nonspecialist."

*Equality and Partiality* is a "clear, sometimes subtle and elegant book," according to Barry R. Gross of *Society.* The work concerns social and economic constructs of contemporary life, which Nagel says do not work because people do not agree on the roles individuals must play in a society. Moreover, liberalism and even capitalism are failures, he says, because of the "immorally vast inequities of wealth and power between citizens," explained Gross. However, Nagel also believes that because there is no agreement on how individuals must function in order to benefit the whole, it is understandable and acceptable that individuals act according to their vested interests. Even democracy is suspect in Nagel's view, which he calls "the enemy of comprehensive equality." In its place, Nagel proposes a type of classless egalitarianism in which "we do not have rights to every penny in our possession, but to the resources that we need to shape a life of our own in accordance with our own values," summarized Michael Walzer in the *New Republic.*

Even as Nagel rejects liberalism, capitalism, and utopianism, he also does not recommend socialism or Marxism. In praising the book, Gross concluded that "*Equality and Partiality* will repay its reader. It deals philosophically with important problems but, unlike much of contemporary philosophy, it is well written and relatively non-technical." Other critics agreed. Walzer called Nagel "one of the most interesting American philosophers. He is highly intelligent, sharply analytical, thoroughly clearheaded."

A *Times Literary Supplement* reviewer called *The Possibility of Altruism* "a book for philosophers, or at least for those with enough interest in the subject to work at it fairly hard; for its argument is intricate and sometimes hard to follow, and Mr. Nagel does not make many concessions. But it is an excellent, and even an important, book."

In a review of *Mortal Questions* for the *New York Times Book Review,* Jonathan Lear wrote that "Mr. Nagel's approach is reminiscent of Hume's argument that although on reflection we can see that many of our beliefs lack foundation we are nevertheless unable to give them up. What response can there be to Hume's analysis of the human condition? 'Be a philosopher,' Hume enjoined, 'but amidst all your philosophy be still a man.' Mr. Nagel's awareness that a philosophical being remains a man is what makes this collection of essays so compelling."

*BIOGRAPHICAL AND CRITICAL SOURCES:*

BOOKS

Nagel, Thomas, *Equality and Partiality,* Oxford University Press (New York, NY), 1991.

PERIODICALS

*American Political Science Review,* March, 1998, Ruth Lessl Shively, review of *The Last Word,* p. 208.
*Choice,* November, 1995, review of *The View from Nowhere,* p. 411.
*Christianity Today,* November 16, 1998, Ric Machuga, review of *The Last Word,* p. 89.
*Commonweal,* January 30, 1998, review of *The Last Word,* p. 22.
*First Things,* June, 1999, Gilbert Meilaender, review of *The Last Word,* p. 45.
*Guardian Weekly,* April 30, 1995, review of *What Does It All Mean?,* p. 28.
*Library Journal,* February 1, 1986, review of *The View from Nowhere,* p. 83; October 1, 1987, review of *What Does It All Mean?,* p. 96.
*New Republic,* October 27, 1986, P. F. Strawson, review of *The View from Nowhere,* p. 44; February 17, 1992, Michael Walzer, review of *Equality and Partiality,* p. 30.
*New York Review of Books,* March 5, 1981, review of *Mortal Questions,* p. 37; November 19, 1998, review of *The Last Word,* p. 40.
*New York Times Book Review,* July 22, 1979, review of *Mortal Questions,* p. 6; February 23, 1986, review of *The View from Nowhere,* p. 14; April 21, 2002, David Cay Johnston, "You Can't Take It with You," p. 23.
*Observer* (London), April 21, 1991, review of *Mortal Questions,* p. 61.
*Publishers Weekly,* August 21, 1987, review of *What Does It All Mean?,* p. 60.

*Review of Metaphysics,* September, 1997, Robert Pasnau, review of *Other Minds: Critical Essays, 1969-1994,* p. 166.
*Society,* January-February, 1993, Barry R. Gross, review of *Equality and Partiality,* p. 94.
*Times Literary Supplement,* May 21, 1970; January 4, 1980, review of *Mortal Questions,* p. 19; September 5, 1986, review of *The View from Nowhere,* p. 962; February 21, 1992, review of *Equality and Partiality,* p. 11; December 5, 1997, review of *The Last Word,* p. 3.
*Wall Street Journal,* December 9, 1987, review of *What Does It All Mean?,* p. 36.*

\*          \*          \*

**NASAR, Jack L. 1947-**

*PERSONAL:* Born March 31, 1947, in Great Neck, NY; son of Leon and Frieda (Dweck) Nasar; married Judy Johnson, June 20, 1983; children: Joanna. *Ethnicity:* "Caucasian." *Education:* Washington University, St. Louis, MO, A.B., 1969; New York University, M.U.P., 1973; Pennsylvania State University, Ph.D., 1979. *Religion:* Jewish. *Hobbies and other interests:* Running, swimming, skiing, piano, reading.

*ADDRESSES: Home*—3003 Sudbury Rd., Columbus, OH 43221. *Office*—Department of City and Regional Planning, 279B Brown, Ohio State University, 190 West 17th St., Columbus, OH 43210. *E-mail*—nasar.1@osu.edu.

*CAREER:* Pennsylvania State University, University Park, instructor in architecture, 1975-76; University of Tennessee, Knoxville, assistant professor of architecture, 1977-80; Ohio State University, Columbus, began as assistant professor, became professor of city and regional planning, 1980—. University of Sydney, visiting scholar, 1988-89. City of Yonkers, NY, worked as assistant planner.

*MEMBER:* Environmental Design Research Association, American Institute of Certified Planners.

*AWARDS, HONORS:* Lilly Endowment fellow, 1979; Ethel Chettel fellow, 1988-89.

*WRITINGS:*

*Environmental Aesthetics: Theory, Research, and Practice,* Cambridge University Press (New York, NY), 1988.

*The Evaluative Image of the City,* Sage Publications (Beverly Hills, CA), 1997.

*Design by Competition: Making Design Competition Work,* Cambridge University Press (New York, NY), 1999.

(Editor, with Wolfgang F. E. Preiser) *Directions in Person-Environment Research and Practice,* Ashgate (Brookfield, VT), 1999.

*SIDELIGHTS:* Jack L. Nasar once told *CA:* "I enjoy writing. In my nonfiction works I try to communicate technical information on social science research to the educated reader. As this research deals with ways to plan and design our environment to fit and satisfy people, the public is the consumer and intended audience. The public must act to bring about change.

"To write, I need solitude—a quiet place without interruptions—and a block of time. I write freely and easily, but I spend much time editing and revising what I've written. I find the computer helpful in this regard.

"In my fiction, I try to put the social science ideas into action, or I try to have some fun with humor."

\*        \*        \*

**NELSON, Kris**
  **See RUSCH, Kristine Kathryn**

\*        \*        \*

**NIX, Garth 1963-**

*PERSONAL:* Born 1963, in Melbourne, Victoria, Australia; married, 2000; wife's name Anna; children: Thomas Henry. *Education:* University of Canberra, B.A., 1986. *Hobbies and other interests:* Traveling, fishing, bodysurfing, book collecting, reading, and films.

*ADDRESSES: Home*—Sydney, Australia. *Agent*—c/o Author Mail, HarperCollins, 10 E. 53rd St., 7th Floor, New York, NY 10022. *E-mail*—garthnix@ozemail. com.au.

*CAREER:* Author, editor, publicist, public relations consultant, agent. Worked for the Australian government; worked in a Sydney, Australia, bookshop; senior editor for a multinational publisher; Gotley Nix Evans Pty. Ltd., Sydney, Australia, marketing communications consultant, 1996-98; part-time agent, Curtis Brown, Australia, 1999-2002. *Military service:* Served four years in the Australian Army Reserve.

*AWARDS, HONORS:* Best Fantasy Novel and Best YA Novel, Aurealis Awards, 1995, Notable Book and Best Book for Young Adults, American Library Association (ALA), Notable Book, CBCA, Recommended Fantasy Novel, *Locus* magazine, Books for the Teenage, New York Public Library, 1997, shortlisted for six state awards in the United States, all for *Sabriel;* "Books in the Middle: Outstanding Titles" selection, *Voice of Youth Advocates,* 1996, for *Sabriel,* and 1997, for *Shade's Children;* shortlisted, Aurealis Award, 1997, Best Book for Young Adults, ALA, Pick of the Lists, ABA, Notable Book, CBCA, shortlisted for the Heartland Prize, the Pacific Northwest Reader's Choice Awards, the South Carolina Reader's Choice Awards, the Evergreen YA Award, and the Garden State Young Reader's Awards, all for *Shade's Children;* Adelaide Festival Award for Children's Literature, 2002, Best Book for Young Adults, ALA, Recommended Reading Fantasy Novel, *Locus* magazine, shortlisted for Young Adult and Fantasy Novel categories, Aurealis Awards, 2002, shortlisted for the 2002 Australian Science Fiction Achievement Award, all for *Lirael: Daughter of the Clayr.*

*WRITINGS:*

FOR CHILDREN; EASY READERS

*Bill the Inventor,* illustrated by Nan Bodsworth, Koala Books (Sydney, New South Wales, Australia), 1998.

*Blackbread the Pirate,* Koala Books (Sydney, New South Wales, Australia), 1999.

*Serena and the Sea Serpent,* illustrated by Stephen Michael King, Puffin (New York, NY), 2001.

*FOR CHILDREN; "THE SEVENTH TOWER" SERIES*

*The Fall,* Scholastic (New York, NY), 2000.
*Castle,* Scholastic (New York, NY), 2000.
*Renir,* Scholastic (New York, NY), 2001.
*Above the Veil,* Scholastic (New York, NY), 2001.
*Into Battle,* Scholastic (New York, NY), 2001.
*The Violet Keystone,* Scholastic (New York, NY), 2001.

*FOR YOUNG ADULTS*

*The Ragwitch,* Pan Books (Sydney, New South Wales, Australia), 1990, Tor (New York, NY), 1995.
*Shade's Children,* HarperCollins (New York, NY), 1997.
*The Calusari* ("X Files" Series), HarperCollins (New York, NY), 1997.

*"THE OLD KINGDOM" TRILOGY; YOUNG ADULT*

*Sabriel,* HarperCollins (New York, NY), 1995.
*Lirael: Daughter of the Clayr,* HarperCollins (New York, NY), 2001.
*Abhorsen,* HarperCollins (New York, NY), 2003.

*"VERY CLEVER BABY" SERIES*

*Very Clever Baby's First Reader: A Simple Reader for Your Child Featuring Freddy the Fish and Easy Words,* Nix Books (Sydney, New South Wales, Australia), 1988.
*Very Clever Baby's Ben Hur: Starring Freddy the Fish As Charlton Heston,* Nix Books (Sydney, New South Wales, Australia), 1988.
*Very Clever Baby's Guide to the Greenhouse Effect,* Nix Books (Sydney, New South Wales, Australia), 1992.
*Very Clever Baby's First Christmas,* Text Publishing (Melbourne, New South Wales, Australia), 1998.

*OTHER*

*Mister Monday* ("Keys to the Kingdom" series), Scholastic (New York, NY), 2004.

Also author of short stories and coauthor of shows for dinner theater. Nix's works have been translated into Dutch, Japanese, German, Portuguese, Finnish, Russian, Spanish, and several other languages.

*WORK IN PROGRESS:* Additional books in the "The Keys to the Kingdom," a seven-book fantasy series for children nine to thirteen, for Collins; *A Confusion of Princes,* a young adult science fiction novel.

*SIDELIGHTS:* The author of over twenty books for children and young adults, Australian Garth Nix is best known for his fantasy novels in the "Old Kingdom" trilogy, including *Sabriel, Lirael,* and *Abhorsen.* Writing for a slightly younger audience, he has also penned a six-novel cycle, "The Seventh Tower" series, and is at work on another fantasy series, "The Keys to the Kingdom." Known for his engaging and finely detailed fiction, Nix told Kelly Milner Halls of *Teenreads* about the need for fantasy and magic in his own life that helps to fuel his popular fiction: "Like most fantasy authors, I would love to have magic in this world. It would be great to be able to fly, or summon a complete restaurant meal on a white tablecloth to a deserted beach, or to take the shape of an animal. But I wouldn't want the downside of most fantasy books— the enemies, evil creatures, and threats to the whole world—and my sense of balance indicates that you can't have the good without the bad." Nix has also explained the genesis of his novels on his own Web site. "Most of my books seem to stem from a single image or thought that lodges in my brain and slowly grows into something that needs to be expressed. That thought may be a 'what if?' or perhaps just an image. . . . Typically I seem to think about a book for a year or so before I actually start writing."

Born in 1963, in Melbourne, Australia, Nix grew up in Canberra with an older and a younger brother. His father worked in science, while his mother was an artist, working with papermaking. Both parents also wrote and read widely, so Nix had a firm foundation for his own future work. Nix has noted that his mother was reading J. R. R. Tolkien's *The Lord of the Rings* when she was pregnant with him, "so I absorbed this master work of fantasy *in utero,* as it were," he once commented. "I went all through school in Canberra," Nix remarked in an autobiographical sketch on his Web site, "but as with many authors, much of my education came from books. . . . My apprenticeship as an author began with reading." Nix grew up, as he once commented, in "a culture of reading," with books all over his home and with frequent trips to the local library. Early on he encountered the works of Ursula Le Guin, Robert Heinlein, Robert Louis Stevenson, John Masefield, Mary Stewart, Isaac Asimov, Madeleine L'Engle, and a variety of other fantasy and science fiction authors. He would much rather read a book than do his homework, but did well in school. "I was a smart and smart-mouthed kid," he remarked on his Web site, "but I got on pretty well with everyone, probably because my best friend was always the school captain in every school and he was friends with everybody."

At seventeen, Nix thought he might want to become an army officer, so he joined the Australian Army Reserve, serving for one weekend a month and one month per year in training. However, he discovered that he did not want to make the military his career, but enjoyed the part-time soldiering enough to stick with it, learning how to build bridges and then blow them up. He was also going to the University of Canberra during these years, and worked a paper-shuffling job with the government for a year. He saved enough money to go traveling for six months, hitting the roads in England. It was during this time away from Australia that he began writing, composing the short story "Sam, Cars and the Cuckoo" while on the road, but not learning of its sale until he was back in Australia and was contacted for reprint rights.

With this success, Nix decided he could become a professional writer. To that end, he earned a bachelor's degree in professional writing from the University of Canberra, and immediately took a job at Dalton's Bookshop in Canberra (not connected to the American chain of the same name). "I now believe that anyone who works in publishing should spend at least three months in a bookshop, where the final product ends up," he once commented. Nix spent six months at the job, and then went into publishing, working as a sales representative, publicist, and editor to gain knowledge of all ends of the publishing and writing industry. During the six years he spent in publishing, he also became a published novelist.

His earliest publications were far from fantasy, though they do include elements of the fantastical. His self-published "Very Clever Baby" books are parodies of an easy reader, exploring the wonders of Christmas or

the movie *Ben Hur* featuring Freddy the Fish, but are not yet available outside his homeland. "They're little books that I first made back in 1988 as presents for some friends expecting babies, on the basis that all parents think their babies are geniuses," Nix explained to Claire E. White on *Writers Write.* Greeting-card sized, the little books are intended for adults rather than children.

If the "Very Clever Baby Books" were intended as a joke, there was nothing joke-like about his first published novel, *The Ragwitch,* which he had worked on as part of his degree requirement. Published in Australia in 1990, the novel tells the story of Paul and his sister Julia who are exploring a prehistoric garbage dump. There they find a nest that contains a rag doll that has the power to enslave others; and Julia becomes its first victim. Paul must then go into a bizarre fantasy world in order to save his sister. Reviewing this first novel, Ann Tolman, writing in *Australian Bookseller and Publisher,* felt that Nix "skillfully relates a magical tale which begins in a nice and easy way, but soon develops into a compelling and involving story of a journey through evil times." Tolman further noted that the book provides "good adult mystic escapism with considerable imaginative experiences for the reader." Similarly, Laurie Copping, writing in the *Canberra Times,* found *The Ragwitch* an "engrossing novel which should be enjoyed by true lovers of high fantasy."

Nix traveled in Turkey, Syria, Jordan, Iran, and Pakistan in 1993. During the trip, be began his next novel, *Sabriel,* finishing it upon his return to Australia. Also on his return, he left publishing for the public relations firm he helped to establish. *Sabriel,* a young adult novel, was the first of what ultimately became a trilogy. "A vividly imagined fantasy," in the words of *School Library Journal* contributor John Peters, it is the first of Nix's works to receive acclaim in the United States. Sabriel is a young woman who has been trained by her father, Abhorsen, a necromancer who, unlike others of his trade, is skilled at putting uneasy souls to rest instead of calling them to life. Sabriel is in her last year of boarding school when she receives Abhorsen's necromancing tools and sword and realizes that her father's life is in danger—he has left the Land of the Living. Sabriel leaves the safety of her school to return to the Old Kingdom, which her father was supposed to protect, in order to rescue him. As she travels to the world beyond the Land of the Living to the Gates of Death, Sabriel is joined by Mogget, a powerful being in the form of a cat who has acted as her father's servant, and a young prince named Touchstone, whom she has brought back from the dead. With their help, Sabriel battles her way past monsters, beasts, and evil spirits until she finally reaches her father, "only to lose him permanently in the opening rounds of a vicious, wild climax," as Peters explained. However, Sabriel—whom critics acknowledged as an especially sympathetic heroine—realizes that she is her father's successor and that the future of the Old Kingdom depends on her. Peters concluded, "This book is guaranteed to keep readers up way past their bedtime." Other reviewers also reacted favorably. "Rich, complex, involving, hard to put down," claimed a critic in *Publishers Weekly,* who added that the novel "is excellent high fantasy." *Booklist* reviewer Sally Estes, who compared *Sabriel* favorably to English writer Philip Pullman's fantasy *The Golden Compass,* stated, "The action charges along at a gallop, imbued with an encompassing sense of looming disaster. . . . A pageturner for sure." Writing in the *Horn Book* magazine, Ann A. Flowers commented: "The story is remarkable for the level of originality of the fantastic elements . . . and for the subtle presentation, which leaves readers to explore for themselves the complex structure and significance of the magic elements." According to a critic for *Voice of Youth Advocates, Sabriel* is "one of the best fantasies of this or any other year."

After publication of *Sabriel,* Nix's publishers wanted him to capitalize on its popularity and continue the saga. Nix, however, had another darker book that he needed to write. *Shade's Children* is a science fiction novel for young adults that, according to a *Publishers Weekly* critic, "tells essentially the same story" as *Sabriel,* with its "desperate quest by a talented few." In this book, however, a psychic young boy, Gold-Eye, runs to escape the evil Overlords who use the body parts of children for their own insidious purposes. The novel is set in a future time when the earth has been taken over by the terrible aliens, who have destroyed everyone over fourteen; the only adult presence is Shade, a computer-generated hologram. Gold-Eye joins a group of teenagers who, working from Shade's submarine base, fight the Overlords. In addition to battling the aliens, the young people must deal with betrayal and with losing half their group; however, they learn about their special talents and achieve victory through their sacrifices.

Critical reception for this third novel was again positive. A *Publishers Weekly* reviewer concluded that

while *Shade's Children* "lacks some of the emotional depth of Nix's first work, it will draw (and keep) fans of the genre." According to a critic in *Kirkus Reviews,* the book "combines plenty of comic-book action in a sci-fi setting to produce an exciting read. . . . [An] action-adventure with uncommon appeal outside the genre." Ann A. Flowers of *Horn Book* praised Nix's characterization of his young protagonists, adding: "The author leaves the reader to draw many conclusions from scattered evidence, hence capturing and holding the audience's attention all the way to the bittersweet ending. Grim, unusual, and fascinating." Donna L. Scanlon, writing in *Voice of Youth Advocates,* had further praise for the title, noting that through "a fast-paced combination of narrative, transcripts, chilling statistical reports, and shifting points of view, Nix depicts a chilling future." For Scanlon, however, Nix's grim futuristic view is also "laced with hope." *Reading Time* contributor Kevin Steinberger similarly enthused: "Exciting action, cracking pace and absorbing intrigue, all in a vividly imagined world, marks *Shade's Children* as one of the best adolescent reads of the year."

Following publication of *Shade's Children,* Nix left his PR firm to devote his time to writing, and also met the woman who would become his wife. He quickly wrote the young adult *The Calusari,* a novelization of an episode from the television series *The X-Files.* The work "really did not suit me," Nix told White. As he set to work to complete the next novel in the "Old Kingdom" cycle, *Lirael: Daughter of the Clayr,* he also turned out several easy readers for young children, including *Bill the Inventor, Blackbread the Pirate,* and *Serena and the Sea Serpent.* Russ Merrin, reviewing *Blackbread the Pirate* in *Magpies,* felt it was "utterly delightful nonsense." *Serena and the Sea Serpent,* about a little girl who saves a town from a misunderstood vegetarian sea serpent, is a "great story," according to another *Magpies* contributor.

Nix also busied himself working part-time as a literary agent (a position he gave up for full-time writing in 2002), and with a six-part fantasy series for Scholastic and Lucas Films, "The Seventh Tower," a children's fantasy featuring young Tal, a Chosen one of Orange Order from the Castle of the Seven Towers and his adventures in search of the Sunstones which he needs to save not only his family but his future. Tal's world is in the dark, literally; the sun only shines above the mysterious Veil, high above in the atmosphere over the Seven Towers. Tal's father disappears in the first book of the series, *The Fall,* on the very day that Tal is ascending to the throne. And his father has taken the Sunstone, which Tal needs for the ascension. Without the Sunstone, Tal cannot bind himself to a Shadowspirit, and failing that, he will lose not only his Chosen status, but also will not be able to find a cure for his mother's illness. Joining Tal in much of his search is the young woman Milla.

"I had to write these books fairly quickly, faster than I normally would," Nix told White. Basically, he turned out each novel in the series in two months. The books became popular with readers in the targeted age range of middle graders, reaching an older audience as well. The fourth book in the series, *Above the Veil,* even made a short appearance on the *New York Times* bestseller list and the series as a whole was on the *Publishers Weekly* children's bestseller lists, both in 2001. Reviewing *Above the Veil,* a contributor for *Publishers Weekly* praised Nix's creation of a "very complex world," and noted that fans of the series would enjoy "plenty of narrow squeaks, exciting chase scenes, and stunning revelations."

Nix published *Lirael,* the long-awaited sequel to *Sabriel,* in 2001. This book takes place fourteen years later, but the Old Kingdom is still facing dangers, this time from an evil necromancer who wants to free a terribly evil being. The book focuses on a group of clairvoyant women, the Clayr, who are gifted with what is called the "Sight." One of these, however, Lirael, does not have such powers, partly due to the mystery of her birth. Turning fourteen, she fears that she will never gain the Sight and become an adult. Yet she does have magic powers, and in the company of the Disreputable Dog, she is able to complete a quest that wins her the trust of her fellow Clayr. They thus entrust her with an even more dangerous and seemingly impossible mission. At the same time, similar doubts have infected Prince Sameth, son of King Touchstone and Sabriel, who feels he is not fit to perform the duties of office after battling with the evil necromancer, Hedge. Sameth and Lirael ultimately team up to battle the evil force attacking the Old Kingdom in a book "outstanding" for its "imaginative magical descriptions, plot intrigues, and adventure sequences," according to *Horn Book*'s Anita L. Burkam. Similarly, Beth Wright, reviewing the novel in *School Library Journal,* praised the "fast-paced plot" as well as the intricacy of the "haunting and unusual, exhaus-

tively and flawlessly conceived connections among . . . rulers and guardians, and the magic that infuses them all." *Booklist*'s Sally Estes also lauded the book, noting that "the characterizations are appealing," and that Nix "not only maintains the intricate world he created for the earlier book but also continues the frenetic pace of the action and the level of violence." Janice M. Del Negro, writing in *Bulletin of the Center for Children's Books,* commended Nix for a book "filled with hair-raising escapes, desperate flights, relentless pursuits, and magical duels, described in sensual language that makes the scenes live." And a reviewer for *Publishers Weekly* likewise found Nix's creation of the Old Kingdom "entrancing and complicated." The same reviewer noted that *Lirael* ends in a "cliffhanger," to be resolved in the third novel of the series.

That novel, *Abhorsen,* appeared in 2003. In this final installment, Sameth and Lirael continue to do battle with the forces of the dead, brought together by the evil Hedge. Again Disreputable Dog and Mogget are on hand to help out their respective companions. Lirael is now Abhorsen-in-Waiting and must travel into death to foil plans to release the Destroyer from an age-old prison. Secrets are revealed and ends tied up in this concluding novel of the trilogy, a book at once "breathtaking, bittersweet, and utterly unforgettable," as a critic for *Kirkus Reviews* described it. A reviewer for *Publishers Weekly* was also impressed by Nix's achievement, calling *Abhorsen* a "riveting continuation" of the saga, and further remarking that the novel was both an "allegory regarding war and peace and a testament to friendship." Estes, writing in *Booklist,* similarly held that the "tension throughout the story is palatable" and the conclusion was "satisfying." One and all, reviewers hoped, as did Sharon Rawlins in her *School Library Journal* review, that "this may not be the last story about the Old Kingdom."

In the course of his twenty books for young readers, Nix has created amazing and intricate worlds, a cast of characters that stick in the imagination, and lessons of friendship and loyalty that resonate. However, Nix does not see himself as a didactic writer, or that he is writing for a particular audience. "To be honest," he told White, in *Writers Write,* "most of the time I don't think about the fact that I am writing for children or young adults. I simply enjoy telling the story and the way I naturally write seems to work well for both young and older audiences. . . . Because my natural writing voice seems to inhabit the Young Adult realm, . . . I haven't had to change it." As for theme or message in his work, Nix told White, "I subscribe to the belief that 'if you want to send a message, use Western Union.' In other words, if the values or moral messages are too overt, the story will suffer and no one will read it. Children don't like to be preached to any more than adults do. On the other hand, while I always try and tell a good story, I can't help but infuse my moral and ethical views into any book."

## BIOGRAPHICAL AND CRITICAL SOURCES:

*BOOKS*

*Children's Literature Review,* Volume 68, Gale (Detroit, MI), 2001, pp. 100-111.
*St. James Guide to Young Adult Writers,* 2nd edition, St. James Press (Detroit, MI), 1999, pp. 632-633.

*PERIODICALS*

*Australian Book Review,* September, 1996, p. 63.
*Australian Bookseller and Publisher,* November, 1990, Ann Tolman, review of *The Ragwitch.*
*Booklist,* October 1, 1996, Sally Estes, review of *Sabriel,* p. 350; April 15, 2001, Sally Estes, review of *Lirael,* p. 1557; July, 2001, Jennifer Hubert, review of *Shade's Children,* p. 1999; January 1, 2003, Sally Estes, review of *Abhorsen,* p. 871.
*Bookseller,* February 21, 2003, "Latest Deals in Children's Publishing," p. 34.
*Bulletin of the Center for Children's Books,* December, 1996, p. 146; November, 1997, p. 95; May, 2001, Janice M. Del Negro, review of *Lirael,* pp. 348-349.
*Canberra Times* (Canberra, Australia), June 2, 1991, Laurie Copping, review of *The Ragwitch.*
*Horn Book,* January-February, 1997, Ann A. Flowers, review of *Sabriel,* pp. 64-65; September-October, 1997, Ann A. Flowers, review of *Shade's Children,* pp. 576-77; July-August, 2001, Anita L. Burkam, review of *Lirael,* p. 459; November-December, 2002, Kristi Beavin, review of *Sabriel* and *Lirael* (audiobooks), p. 790.
*Kirkus Reviews,* August 15, 1997, review of *Shade's Children,* pp. 1309-1310; December 15, 2002, review of *Abhorsen,* pp. 1854-1855.

*Kliatt,* January, 1998, Lesley S. J. Farmer, review of *Sabriel,* p. 17.
*Magpies,* September, 1998, Annette Dale Meiklejohn, review of *Bill the Inventor,* p. 33; September, 1999, Russ Merrin, review of *Blackbread the Pirate,* p. 28; March, 2001, review of *Serena and the Sea Serpent,* p. 29.
*Publishers Weekly,* October 21, 1996, review of *Sabriel,* p. 84; June 16, 1997, review of *Shade's Children,* p. 60; March 19, 2001, review of *Lirael,* p. 101; March 18, 2002, John F. Baker, "Garth Nix," p. 16; May 27, 2002, review of *Lirael,* p. 62; November 25, 2002, review of *Abhorsen,* p. 70.
*Reading Time,* November, 1997, Kevin Steinberger, review of *Shade's Children,* p. 35.
*School Library Journal,* September, 1996, John Peters, review of *Sabriel,* p. 228; May, 1998, review of *Shade's Children,* p. 52; May, 2001, Beth Wright, review of *Lirael,* p. 157; September, 2001, John Peters, review of *Above the Veil,* p. 231; February, 2003, Sharon Rawlins, review of *Abhorsen,* p. 146.
*Voice of Youth Advocates,* June, 1997, review of *Sabriel;* February, 1998, Suzann Manczuk and Ray Barber, review of *Shade's Children,* p. 366; June, 1998, Donna M. Scanlon, review of *Shade's Children,* p. 132.

*ONLINE*

*Australian SF Online,* http://www.eidolon.net/ (August 5, 2003).
*Garth Nix Web Site,* http://www.garthnix.co.uk/ (August 5, 2003).
*Offical Garth Nix Site,* http://www.members.ozemail.com.au/ (April 21, 2003), Garth Nix, "How I Write: The Process of Creating a Book," and "A Biographical Whimsy."
*Teenreads,* http://www.teenreads.com/ (February 18, 2003), Kelly Milner Halls, "Garth Nix Interview."
*Writers Write,* http://www.writerswrite.com/ (July-August, 2000), Claire E. White, "A Conversation with Garth Nix."*

\*      \*      \*

**NORTH, Charles W.**
**See BAUER, Erwin A.**

## NULL, Gary

*PERSONAL:* Son of Robert C. and Blandenia J. (Whitehead) Null. *Education:* Edison State College, B.S.; Union Graduate School, Ph.D.

*CAREER:* Has taught at the New York College of Chiropractic and the New School for Social Research; Director of Nutrition Institute of America, New York, N.Y., 1976—; founder and director of the Health and Nutrition Certificate Program at Pratt Institute.

Past publisher of the *Natural Living Newsletter* and *Natural Living Journal.* Founder of the Natural Living Walking and Running Club. Has appeared on numerous television and radio programs, including his own PBS specials and series.

*MEMBER:* International Association of Clinical Nutritionists, International Association for Colon Therapy, International Academy of Oral Medicine and Toxicology, American Association of Clinical Nutritionists, American Academy of Anti-Aging Medicine, American Society for Parental and Eternal Nutrition, American Holistic Medical Association, National Association for Holistic Aromatherapy, Cancer Prevention Coalition (board member), Institute of Noetic Sciences.

*WRITINGS:*

(With Richard Simonson) *How to Turn Ideas into Dollars,* Pilot Books (New York, NY), 1969.

*The Conspirator Who Saved the Romanovs,* Prentice-Hall (Englewood Cliffs, NJ), 1971.

*Profitable Part-Time Home-Based Businesses: How You Can Make up to $150 a Week Extra Income,* Pilot Books (New York, NY), 1971, revised edition, 1978.

*Surviving and Settling in New York on a Shoestring,* Pilot Books (New York, NY), 1971.

(With Steve Null) *The Complete Handbook of Nutrition,* Speller (New York, NY), 1972.

(With others) *The Complete Question-and-Answer Book of General Nutrition,* Speller (New York, NY), 1972.

*Grow Your Own Food Organically,* Speller (New York, NY), 1972.

(With Steve Null) *Herbs for the Seventies,* Speller (New York, NY), 1972.

*The Natural Organic Beauty Book,* Speller (New York, NY), 1972.

*Body Pollution,* edited by James Dawson, Arco (New York, NY), 1973.

*Protein for Vegetarians,* Pyramid Publications (New York, NY), 1974, revised and enlarged edition, 1975.

*Foodcombing Handbook,* Pyramid Publications (New York, NY), 1974.

(With Steve Null) *Biofeedback, Fasting, and Meditation,* Pyramid Publications (New York, NY), 1974.

*Black Hollywood: The Negro in Motion Pictures,* Citadel (Secaucus, NJ), 1975.

(With Steve Null) *Alcohol and Nutrition,* Pyramid Publications (New York, NY), 1976.

*Whole Body Health and Nutrition Book,* Pinnacle Books (New York, NY), 1976.

*Successful Pregnancy,* Pyramid Publications (New York, NY), 1976.

*Handbook of Skin and Hair,* Pyramid Publications (New York, NY), 1976.

*Italio-Americans,* Stackpole (Harrisburg, PA), 1976.

*Man and His Whole Earth,* Stackpole (Harrisburg, PA), 1976.

*How to Get Rid of the Poisons in Your Body,* Arco (New York, NY), 1977.

(With Steve Null) *The New Vegetarian: Building Your Health through Natural Eating,* Morrow (New York, NY), 1978.

(With Steve Null) *Why Your Stomach Hurts: A Handbook of Digestion and Nutrition,* Dodd (New York, NY), 1979.

*The New Vegetarian Cookbook,* Collier Books (New York, NY), 1980.

*Gary Null's Nutrition Sourcebook for the Eighties,* Macmillan (New York, NY), 1983.

*Complete Guide to Health and Nutrition,* Delacorte (New York, NY), 1984.

*The Egg Project: Gary Null's Complete Guide to Good Eating,* Four Walls Press (New York, NY), 1987.

*The Vegetarian Handbook,* St. Martin's Press (New York, NY), 1987, revised, 1996.

(With Martin Feldman) *Good Food, Good Mood: Treating Your Hidden Allergies,* St. Martin's Press (New York, NY), 1988.

*Gary Null's Complete Guide to Healing Your Body Naturally,* McGraw-Hill (New York, NY), 1988.

(With Howard Robins) *How to Keep Your Feet and Legs Healthy for a Lifetime: The Only Complete Guide to Foot and Leg Care, with Sections for*

*Walkers, Joggers, and Runners,* Four Walls Press (New York, NY), 1990.

*The Complete Guide to Sensible Eating,* Four Walls Press (New York, NY), 1990, revised edition, Seven Stories Press (New York, NY), 1998.

*Clearer, Cleaner, Safer, Greener: A Blueprint for Detoxifying Your Environment,* Villard Books (New York, NY), 1990.

(With Shelly Null) *Vegetarian Cooking for Good Health,* BBS Publishing (New York, NY), 1991, revised edition, 1999.

*No More Allergies: Identifying and Eliminating Allergies and Sensitivity Reactions to Everything in Your Environment,* Villard Books (New York, NY), 1992.

*Healing Your Body Naturally: Alternative Treatments to Illness,* Four Walls Press (New York, NY), 1992, 2nd revised edition, Seven Stories Press (New York, NY), 1997.

*Black Hollywood: From 1970 to Today,* Carol Publishing (New York, NY), 1993.

(With Howard Null) *Change Your Life Now: Get Out of Your Head, Get into Your Life,* Health Communications (Deerfield Beach, FL), 1993.

(With Howard Robins) *Ultimate Training: Gary Null's Complete Guide to Eating Right, Exercising, and Living Longer,* St. Martin's Press (New York, NY), 1993.

(With Martin Feldman) *Reverse the Aging Process Naturally: How to Build the Immune System with Antioxidants, the Supernutrients of the Nineties,* Villard Books (New York, NY), 1993.

*The '90s Healthy Body Book: How to Overcome the Effects of Pollution and Cleanse the Toxins from Your Body,* Health Communications (Deerfield Beach, FL), 1994.

*Nutrition and the Mind,* Four Walls Press (New York, NY), 1995.

*Be Kind to Yourself: Explorations into Self-Empowerment,* Carroll & Graf (New York, NY), 1995.

*The Complete Idiot's Guide to Getting and Keeping Your Perfect Body,* Alpha Books (New York, NY), 1996.

*Who Are You, Really?: Understanding Your Life's Energy,* Carroll & Graf (New York, NY), 1996.

*The Women's Encyclopedia of Natural Healing: The New Healing Techniques of Over 100 Alternative Practitioners,* Seven Stories Press (New York, NY), 1996.

*Supercharge Your Health!: 150 Easy Ways to Get Strong, Feel Great, and Look Your Best,* Harper-Perennial (New York, NY), 1997.

(With Vicki Riba Koestler) *Choosing Joy: Change Your Life for the Better,* Carroll & Graf (New York, NY), 1998.

*Gary Null's International Vegetarian Cookbook,* Macmillan (New York, NY), 1998.

*The Clinician's Handbook of Natural Healing,* Kensington (New York, NY), 1998.

*Healing with Magnets,* Carroll & Graf (New York, NY), 1998.

*The Complete Encyclopedia of Natural Healing,* Kensington (New York, NY), 1998.

*Secrets of the Sacred White Buffalo: Native American Healing Remedies, Rites & Rituals,* Prentice Hall (Paramus, NJ), 1998.

*The New Vegetarian Cookbook,* Galahad (New York, NY), 1998.

*Gary Null's Ultimate Anti-Aging Program,* Kensington (New York, NY), 1999.

*The Healing Arts Bible,* Seven Stories Press (New York, NY), 1999.

(With Shelly Null) *Vegetarian Cooking for Good Health,* BBS Publishing (New York, NY), 1991, revised edition, 1999.

(With Barbara Seaman) *The Practice and Politics of Women's Health,* Seven Stories Press (New York, NY), 1999.

(With Barbara Seaman) *For Women Only: Your Guide to Health Empowerment,* Seven Stories Press (New York, NY), 1999.

*Get Healthy Now!: A Complete Guide to Prevention, Treatment, and Healty Living,* Seven Stories Press (New York, NY), 1999.

*Natural Pet Care,* Seven Stories (New York, NY) 2000.

*The Food-Mood-Body Connection: Nutrition-Based and Environmental Approaches to Mental Health and Physical Well-Being,* Seven Stories Press (New York, NY), 2000.

*Gary Null's Ultimate Lifetime Diet: A Revolutionary All-Natural Program for Losing Weight and Building a Healthy Body,* Broadway Books (New York, NY), 2000.

*Your Spectacular Pet: How to Care for Your Animal Naturally,* Seven Stories Press (New York, NY), 2001.

*AIDS: A Second Opinion,* Seven Stories Press (New York, NY), 2001.

(With Shelly Null) *The Joy of Juicing: Creative Cooking with Your Juicer,* Avery (New York, NY), 2001.

(With Vicki Riba Koestler) *The Baby Boomer's Guide to Getting It Right the Second Time Around,* Carroll & Graf (New York, NY), 2001.

*Women's Health Solutions,* Seven Stories Press (New York, NY), 2002.

(With James Feast) *Germs, Biological Warfare, Vaccinations: What You Need to Know,* Seven Stories Press (New York, NY), 2003.

*SIDELIGHTS:* Gary Null has penned many books on health, diet, and alternative medicine. He holds a doctoral degree in nutrition, and has appeared in specials and series about naturopathic health solutions on PBS. Book critics have been generally positive in their response to Null's volumes; for instance, a *Publishers Weekly* reviewer of *Women's Health Solutions* wrote that "anyone interested in alternative therapies will find this guide invaluable." Though noting that some of Null's advice on diet and medicine is controversial, another critic for *Publishers Weekly* felt that he "offers some helpful guidance for the challenges of living in our time" in *The Baby Boomer's Guide to Getting It Right the Second Time Around. Booklist* contributor Penny Spokes praised his *Secrets of the Sacred White Buffalo: Native American Healing Remedies, Rites, and Rituals* as "a well-written introduction to Native American cosmology, sacred practices and traditional remedies." *Library Journal* reviewer Rebecca Cress-Ingebo, discussing Null's *The Complete Encyclopedia of Natural Healing,* concluded that its "easy-to-use format will indeed appeal to the lay reader."

*BIOGRAPHICAL AND CRITICAL SOURCES:*

*PERIODICALS*

*Booklist,* August, 1998, Penny Spokes, review of *Secrets of the Sacred White Buffalo: Native American Healing Remedies, Rites, and Rituals,* p. 1945.

*Library Journal,* June 1, 1998, Rebecca Cress-Ingebo, review of *The Complete Encyclopedia of Natural Healing,* pp. 99-100; February 1, 2000, Barbara M. Bible, review of *For Women Only: Your Guide to Health Empowerment,,* p. 110; May 15, 2002, Jeffrey Beall, review of *AIDS: A Second Opinion,* p. 120.

*Publishers Weekly,* January 27, 1999, review of *The Women's Encyclopedia of Natural Healing: The New Healing Techniques of Over 100 Alternative Practitioners,* p. 100; December 20, 1999, p. 76; May 7, 2001, review of *The Baby Boomer's Guide to Getting It Right the Second Time Around,* p. 236; March 25, 2002, review of *Women's Health Solutions,* p. 60.

*ONLINE*

*Complete Health Network,* http://www.completehealth network.com/ (July 17, 2002), profile of Gary Null.

*Gary Null Home Page,* http://www.garynull.com/ (July 17, 2002).*

# O

## OAKLEY, John H(enry) 1949-

*PERSONAL:* Born November 6, 1949, in Elizabeth, NJ; son of Howard T. (a chemical engineer) and Marjorie D. (a librarian; maiden name, Deyo) Oakley; married Evi G. Hessler, May 8, 1990; children: Nicholas T., Jacob T. *Education:* Rutgers University, B.A. (with high honors), 1972, M.A., 1976, Ph.D., 1980.

*ADDRESSES: Home*—2864 Hidden Lake Dr., Williamsburg, VA 23185. *Office*—Department of Classical Studies, College of William and Mary, Williamsburg, VA 23187. *E-mail*—jxoakl@malthus.morton.wm.edu.

*CAREER:* American School of Classical Studies at Athens, Athens, Greece, regular member, 1976-77, associate member, 1978-79; College of William and Mary, Williamsburg, VA, assistant professor, 1980-86, associate professor, 1986-93, professor of classical studies and Chancellor Professor, 1993-2000, Forrest D. Murden, Jr. Professor, 2000—, department head, 1989-92, 2000—. University of Canterbury, Christchurch, New Zealand, visiting professor, 1997; American School of Classical Studies, Elizabeth G. Whitehead Visiting Professor, 1997-98. American School of Classical Studies at Athens, member of managing committee, 1982—, member of staff for Agora Excavations, 1984-86, senior research fellow, 1986-87, 1993-94, member of executive committee, 1991-95, 2001—; member of archaeological excavations and surveys in Wroxeter and Kelvedon, England, Via Gabina, Rome, Corinth and Athens, Greece, and Khania, Crete.

*MEMBER:* Archaeological Institute of America (cofounder and president of Williamsburg chapter, 1994-97).

*AWARDS, HONORS:* Grants from American Philosophical Society, 1981, National Endowment for the Humanities, 1984, and American Council of Learned Societies, 1985, 1987; fellow of Alexander von Humboldt-Stiftung at University of Würzburg, 1988-89, 1991-92; Getty grants, 1989, 1991; Phi Beta Kappa Faculty Award for the Advancement of Scholarship, 1990; fellow of National Endowment for the Humanities, 1997-98, and Metropolitan Museum of Art, 2000-01.

*WRITINGS:*

*The Phiale Painter, Kerameus Eight,* Philipp von Zabern (Mainz, Germany), 1990.

(With S. I. Rotroff) *Debris from a Public Dining Place in the Athenian Agora,* American School of Classical Studies (Princeton, NJ), 1992.

*Corpus Vasorum Antiquorum,* Walters Art Gallery (Baltimore, MD), 1992.

(With R. H. Sinos) *The Wedding in Ancient Athens,* University of Wisconsin Press (Madison, WI), 1993.

*The Achilles Painter,* Philipp von Zabern (Mainz, Germany), 1997.

(Chief editor, with W. D. E. Coulson and O. Palagia, and contributor) *Athenian Potters and Painters: The Conference Proceedings,* Oxbow Books (Oxford, England), 1997.

(With Jenifer Neils) *Coming of Age in Ancient Greece: Images of Childhood from the Classical Past,* Yale University Press/Hood Museum of Art, Dartmouth College (New Haven, CT), 2003.

*Picturing Death in Classical Athens: The Evidence of the White Lekythoi,* Cambridge University Press (New York, NY), 2004.

Contributor of articles and reviews to scholarly journals, including *Hesperia, Arts in Virginia, Classical World, Classical Review, Journal of Hellenic Studies,* and *American Journal of Archaeology.* Member of editorial committee, *Corpus Vasorum Antiquorum,* 1985—.

\* \* \*

## ODBER (de BAUBETA), Patricia (Anne) 1953-

*PERSONAL:* Born November 16, 1953, in Glasgow, Scotland; daughter of Leslie Frederick (a metallurgist) and Kathleen Mary (a chartered accountant) Odber; married Dardo Washington Baubeta (a baker), January 3, 1986. *Ethnicity:* "British." *Education:* University of Glasgow, M.A. (with first class honors), 1978, Ph.D., 1991. *Hobbies and other interests:* Reading, music, house plants, dogs.

*ADDRESSES: Home*—25 Regent St., Stirchley, Birmingham B30 2LG, England. *Office*—Department of Hispanic Studies, University of Birmingham, Birmingham, England. *E-mail*—user@olimar.softnet.co.uk.

*CAREER:* Worked as an English language assistant in France, 1973-74, and Spain, 1975-76; University of Glasgow, Glasgow, Scotland, lecturer in Portuguese, 1978-80; University of Birmingham, Birmingham, England, lecturer in Portuguese and linguistics, 1981—, senior lecturer in Hispanic studies, 1996—. Lecturer at other universities, including University of Oporto, University of Salford, Oxford University, University of Santiago de Compostela, Catholic University of Lisbon, New University of Lisbon, Queen's University, Belfast, Northern Ireland, University of the Republic, Montevideo, Uruguay, and University of Leeds. Served as a foster parent, 1987-97.

*MEMBER:* International Medieval Sermon Studies Society, International Hispanists Association, Associacao Internacional de Lusitanistas, Association of Hispanists of Great Britain and Ireland, Association of Contemporary Iberian Studies, Society of Latin American Studies, CELCIRP.

*AWARDS, HONORS:* Scholarship for Portugal, Instituto de Alta Cultura, 1975.

*WRITINGS:*

*Ingles: Curso basico para Portugueses,* with cassettes, IPU (Lucerne, Switzerland), 1990.

*Anticlerical Satire in Medieval Portuguese Literature,* Edwin Mellen (Lewiston, NY), 1992.

(Editor, with Trevor J. Dadson and R. J. Oakley, and contributor) *New Frontiers in Hispanic and Luso-Brazilian Scholarship: Como se fue el maestro; for Derek W. Lomax in Memoriam,* Edwin Mellen (Lewiston, NY), 1994.

(Editor, with Malcolm Coulthard, and contributor) *Theoretical Issues and Practical Cases in Portuguese-English Translation,* Edwin Mellen (Lewiston, NY), 1996.

(Editor, with Malcolm Coulthard) *The Knowledges of the Translator: From Literary Interpretation to Machine Classification,* Edwin Mellen (Lewiston, NY), 1996.

*Igreja, pecado, e satira social na idade media Portuguesa,* Imprensa Nacional-Casa da Moeda (Lisbon, Portugal), 1997.

(Editor, with Jackie Cannon and Robin Warner) *Advertising and Identity in Europe: The I of the Beholder,* Intellect Press (Bristol, England), 2000.

(Translator, with Ivana Rangel Carlsen) Miguel Torga, *The Creation of the World,* Carcanet (Manchester, England), 2001.

Contributor to books, including *Portuguese, Brazilian, and African Studies Presented to Clive Willis on His Retirement,* Aris & Phillips (Warminster, England), 1995; and *Gender, Ethnicity, and Class in Modern Portuguese-speaking Culture,* edited by Hilary Owen, Edwin Mellen (Lewiston, NY), 1996. Translations of short fiction are represented in anthologies. Contributor of articles and reviews to academic journals, including *Paremia, Journal of the Association for Contemporary Iberian Studies Revista de Estudos Anglo-Portugueses,* and *Portuguese Studies.* Guest editor, *Revista de Lingua e Literatura Estrangeiras,* 1996.

*WORK IN PROGRESS: Bread, Wine, and the Communion of Advertising,* to be published in England; *History of Portuguese Literature in English Translation,* to be published in England.

*SIDELIGHTS:* Patricia Odber once told *CA:* "I am interested in advertising language, translation and translating, and fairy tales. Research interests were medieval literature, preaching, and confession. What is becoming clear is how all of these come together in advertising. I also have an abiding interest in Uruguayan literature, especially the short story—which draws to a great extent on the fairy tale tradition."

Odber added: "My principal interest at present is in the way that works of Portuguese literature have been translated into English—when, by whom, for which readership."

\*    \*    \*

## OHRT, Wallace 1919-

*PERSONAL:* Born June 29, 1919, in Moose Jaw, Saskatchewan, Canada; U.S. citizen; son of Norman F. (a welder) and Sigfrid (a homemaker; maiden name, Eidsness) Ohrt; married Betty Jo Martin, April 29, 1955; children: Laurie Ohrt Semke, Stephen F. *Ethnicity:* "Norwegian-German-English." *Education:* Attended University of Oregon, 1937-38, Victoria College, Victoria, British Columbia, Canada, 1946, and University of Washington, Seattle, 1947-48. *Politics:* Independent. *Religion:* Presbyterian. *Hobbies and other interests:* Gardening, reading, studying history.

*ADDRESSES: Home*—1105 Southwest 166th St., Seattle, WA 98166. *E-mail*—wallyohrt@aol.com.

*CAREER:* Boeing Aircraft Co., Seattle, WA, parts fabricator, 1941-42; Boeing Co., Seattle, WA, personnel representative, staff assistant, job evaluator, procedures writer, contracts manager, and staff writer, 1950-74; freelance technical writer and consultant, 1975-91. Teacher of English as a second language, 1994-96. *Military service:* U.S. Army Air Force, armorer gunner; served in Pacific theater during World War II; became sergeant.

*AWARDS, HONORS:* Second-place award, nonfiction book category, Pacific Northwest Writers Conference, 1977, for *The Rogue I Remember.*

*WRITINGS:*

*The Rogue I Remember* (memoir), Mountaineers Books (Seattle, WA), 1979.

*The Accidental Missionaries: How a Vacation Turned into a Vocation,* Inter-Varsity Press (Downers Grove, IL), 1990.

*Defiant Peacemaker: Nicholas Trist in the Mexican War,* Texas A & M University Press (College Station, TX), 1997.

(With mother, Sigfid Ohrt) *Immigrant Girl* (memoir), privately printed, 2000.

*WORK IN PROGRESS: Logtown* (tentative title), a fictional account of a young boy's disappearance, based on "the author's experiences during high school and young adulthood in a mountain logging district in southern Oregon during the Great Depression"; *Touch Not My Children* (tentative title), the true "experiences of an Afghan widow and mother of seven who escaped to America after her husband was murdered and her own life was threatened."

*SIDELIGHTS:* Wallace Ohrt once told *CA:* "Several months after World War II, I was sent home from the Pacific theater on a hospital ship. As we slogged our way from Manila to San Francisco—a thirty-day voyage on the old *Dogwood*—I got acquainted with paperback novels, cheerfully passed out by a charming Red Cross lady. What joy! The deceptively easy style of Nordhoff and Hall, Kenneth Roberts, and Samuel Hopkins Adams made me think this was something I could do. I pursued that illusion through two more years of college and one year as a starving freelancer, then settled for the greater security of corporate life. The urge returned in midlife, and I took early retirement to settle the question: could I actually become a writer? Twenty-five years later, as I approach my eightieth birthday, with three nonfiction books published, I still count myself an apprentice.

"My original motivation for writing was, as I have indicated, to discover whether I *could* write professionally. With that question at least partially resolved, I am now motivated by a desire to discover forgotten or neglected heroes, present and past, and to bring them to the public's attention so they can receive the honor they deserve.

"I count all good writing as instructive: novels, biographies, history, short stories, articles, essays, even newspaper sports reports. Writers I particularly admire and seek to emulate include novelists Willa Cather, Conrad Richter, and A. B. Guthrie; biographer Marquis James; historian Samuel Eliot; and essayist E. B. White. I read everything I can get my hands on, including biographies by the score about everyone from Dr. Samuel Johnson to Wild Bill Hickok.

"My writing routine is not particularly novel. I seldom get started before 9:30 and work until about three o'clock, leaving enough daylight for a little gardening in season or a two-mile walk in decent weather. I write only five days a week, having become attached to the leisurely weekend during twenty-five years of corporate life. I become totally absorbed into the world I am writing about, almost to the point of losing touch with my real surroundings. Insomnia becomes chronic, but I hardly begrudge the lost sleep because it is usually compensated in increased creativity.

"A love of history has inspired me to write about historic subjects. My only complaint with history is that there is too much of it! As to one recent project, my mother spent seven years in her eighties writing her memoirs, concluding with the statement that this was her legacy to her descendants, including those yet unborn. It is a rich legacy, needing only polishing and organizing in a somewhat more book-like form. She died at age ninety-four in 1985, and I have inherited her notes, which she called her 'stories.' I committed myself to the necessary editing task and self-published the result."

More recently, Ohrt commented: "At this stage of my life my primary motivations for writing are to acquaint today's readers with the daily lives of those whom Tom Brokaw refers to—over-generously—as the Greatest Generation, and to share insights I have been privileged to gain into the struggles of refugees as they seek to survive and raise their families in twenty-first-century America.

"From earliest memory, I have been fascinated by words. Capturing ideas, feelings, and events verbally, with precision and honesty, has always seemed the most difficult and yet the most worthwhile endeavor of mankind. As evidenced by the relatively few writings of Thomas Jefferson and Abraham Lincoln, the whole course of human history is altered by the stirring language produced by noble minds. Conversely, I am grieved by the erosion of language that currently invades our culture, the so-called 'dumbing of America.' George Orwell expressed it well when he wrote, 'Political chaos is connected with the decay of language.'

"My writing process should serve as no model for anyone serious about writing. I am a hopeless procrastinator who finds infinite excuses to delay getting started, and by four o'clock I am looking for a convenient stopping point. I loathed, feared, and avoided the computer until I was in my seventies; fortunately, my daughter and others wore down my resistance. Now I happily avail myself of its marvelous editing capabilities, though I consider it an idiot on subjects such as long sentences and the passive voice. Our relationship, you might say, is distant though symbiotic.

"Choosing subjects to write about does not come easily to me. Sometimes they are suggested by others, and sometimes they thrust themselves upon me. I choose to write books rather than shorter works, such as magazine articles or short stories, because I like to have a good-sized project that will hold me in thrall for a reasonably long time. The novel project, *Logtown,* came into being slowly after a friend urged me to write the history of the Upper Rogue River in southern Oregon, where we both attended high school. The nonfiction project, *Touch Not My Children,* is a natural: my wife and I are volunteering our assistance to an Afghan widow and mother of seven children who fled to this country after the husband/father was murdered by the Taliban."

\* \* \*

## OLITZKY, Kerry M. 1954-

*PERSONAL:* Born December 22, 1954, in Pittsburgh, PA; son of Abraham Nathan (an engineering technician) and Frances (an inventory controller; maiden name, Reznick) Olitzky; married Sheryl Mandy Rosenblatt (a market researcher), August 28, 1977; children: Avi Samuel, Jesse Michael. *Education:* Attended American College in Jerusalem, 1971-72; University of South Florida, B.A., 1974, M.A., 1975; Hebrew Union College-Jewish Institute of Religion, Cincinnati, OH, rabbinic ordination, 1981, D.H.L., 1985. *Politics:* Democrat. *Religion:* Jewish.

*ADDRESSES: Office*—Jewish Outreach Institute, 1270 Broadway, Suite 609, New York, NY 10001. *E-mail*—KOlitzky@joi.org.

*CAREER:* Ordained rabbi, 1981. Beth Israel, West Hartford, CT, assistant rabbi and director of religious education for congregation, 1981-84; Hebrew Union

*Kerry M. Olitzky*

College-Jewish Institute of Religion, New York, NY, director of graduate studies program at School of Education, 1984-98, national director for research and educational development, 1991-96, national dean of adult Jewish learning and living, 1996-98; Wexner Heritage Foundation, vice president, 1998-1999; Jewish Outreach Institute, New York, NY, executive director, 2000—;. Mature Adult Day Care Center, St. Petersburg, FL, program manager, 1976; American Jewish Archives, assistant archivist, 1978-81; B'nai B'rith Youth Organization, assistant regional director, 1978-81. Conference on Alternatives in Jewish Education, member of steering committee, 1981; Hartford Jewish Federation, member of Older Adults Committee and Education Committee, 1981; Rabbinical Fellowship of Greater Hartford, member, 1981; Hartford Jewish Center, member of board of directors, 1981; Greater Hartford Jewish Educators Council, member, 1981-84; Center for Jewish Life, honorary member of board of directors; Union of American Hebrew Congregations, facilitator for National Liheyot Task Force, and member of Gerontology Committee, executive committee of Joint Commission on Jewish Education, Committee on the Jewish Family, and Day School Curriculum Advisory Committee; member of National Interfaith Coalition on Aging and United Jewish Appeal/Federation's Task Force on the Jewish Aged; Open University of Israel, member of education board; Stepping Stones National Institute, board member; Bay Area Jewish High School, San Francisco, CA, member of advisory council; advisor for Jewish Alcoholics, Chemically Dependent Persons, and Significant Others Council; Skirball Center for Adult Jewish Learning at Temple Emanu-El, New York, NY, member of advisory council; People Advocating Therapeutic Homes, national board member; member of Inter-Religious Project Advisory Council of Felician College; Baruch College/Jewish Resource Center, member of advisory board; member of Rabbinic Cabinet of the United Jewish Appeal. ABC-Radio, producer and moderator of *Message of Israel;* executive producer of *Torah Tapes: Contemporary Insights into the Weekly Torah Reading.*

*MEMBER:* Jewish National Fund (member of Young Associates, 1979-81), National Association of Temple Educators, National Association for Foreign Student Affairs (honorary life member), Coalition for the Advancement of Jewish Education, Association of Reform Zionists in America, Gerontology Society of America, Association for Supervision and Curriculum Development, Association of Jewish Studies, American Society of Aging (member of Forum on Religion and Aging), Association for Jewish Studies, Rabbinical Assembly (corresponding affiliate member), Central Conference of American Rabbis, Teachers of English to Speakers of Other Languages (honorary life member).

*AWARDS, HONORS:* Vice Chancellors' grants, Universities of London, 1977, and New Zealand Universities, 1978; research grant, New Zealand Council for educational research, 1979; Rabbi Ronald B. Gittelsohn Prize, Rabbi Emil William Ziegler Prize, and Mr. and Mrs. Alvin Ziegler Prize, all from Hebrew Union College-Jewish Institute of Religion, all 1981; Greater Hartford Jewish Federation Committee on Jewish Education incentive grant, 1983; senior fulbright scholar, Hong Kong, 1986; received first award given by Black Administrators' Alliance, County of Los Angeles, 1989; American Jewish Archives travel grant, 1990; institutional grants, Vaasa University, and University of Birmingham, both 1992; senior fulbright scholar, New Zealand, 1992; distinguished faculty service award, Academic Senate, University of Southern California, 1995; presidential colloquium in honor of Professor Emeritus Robert B. Kaplan, 1996; Philip C. Holland Lectureship, Washington State University, 1997; American Association for Applied Linguistics Award for distinguished scholarship and service, 1988; Twentieth-Century Award for Achievement, 2000; Willamette University Distinguished Alumni Award and Jason Lee Medallion, 2002; Sadei Iwataki Award for service to the profession, California Association of Teachers of English to Speakers of Other Languages, 2003.

*WRITINGS:*

*EDUCATION AND REFERENCE BOOKS*

*Aging and Judaism* (textbook), Alternatives in Religious Education (Denver, CO), 1980.

*Critical Issues Facing American Jewish Youth: A Resource Book for Educators, Experimental Edition,* Union of American Hebrew Congregations (Washington, DC), 1982.

*Come Dance with Me: Life in the Jewish Shtetl, Experimental Edition,* Union of American Hebrew Congregations (Washington, DC), 1983.

*I Am a Reform Jew* (student workbook), Behrman (West Orange, NJ), 1986.

*Explaining Reform Judaism* (teacher's guide), Behrman (West Orange, NJ), 1986.

*My Jewish Community* (student workbook), Alternatives in Religious Education (Denver, CO), 1986.

*A Jewish Mourner's Handbook,* KTAV (Hoboken, NJ), 1991.

(With Ronald H. Isaacs) *A Glossary of Jewish Life,* J. Aronson (Northvale, NJ), 1992.

*When Your Jewish Child Asks Why: Answers for Tough Questions,* KTAV (Hoboken, NJ), 1993.

*Reform Judaism in America: A Biographical Dictionary and Source Book, 1824-1980,* Greenwood Press (Westport, CT), 1993.

*The "How To" Handbook of Jewish Living,* KTAV (Hoboken, NJ), 1993.

*Sacred Celebrations: A Jewish Holiday Handbook,* KTAV Publishing (Hoboken, NJ), 1994.

*Eight Nights, Eight Lights,* Alef Design Group (Los Angeles, CA), 1994.

*Sacred Moments: Tales of the Jewish Life Cycle,* Jason Aronson (Northvale, NJ), 1995.

*The American Synagogue: A Historical Dictionary,* Greenwood Press (Westport, CT), 1996.

(With Rachel T. Sabath) *Preparing Your Heart for the High Holy Days,* Jewish Publication Society (Philadelphia, PA), 1996.

(With Ronald H. Isaacs) *The Second "How To" Handbook for Jewish Living,* illustrated by Dorcas Gilbert, KTAV (Hoboken, NJ), 1996.

(With Rachel T. Sabath) *Striving toward Virtue: A Contemporary Guide for Jewish Ethical Behavior,* KTAV (Hoboken, NJ), 1996.

*The Jewish Wedding Ceremony,* KTAV (Hoboken, NJ), 1996.

*I Believe . . . . : A Confirmation Textbook,* KTAV (Hoboken, NJ), 1999.

(With Ronald H. Isaacs) *I Believe: The Thirteen Principles of Faith,* KTAV (Hoboken, NJ), 1999.

*American Synagogue Ritual,* Greenwood Press (Westport, CT), 2000.

*An Encyclopedia of American Synagogue Ritual,* Greenwood Press (Westport, CT), 2000.

*Preparing Your Heart for Passover: A Guide for Spiritual Readiness,* Jewish Publication Society (Philadelphia, PA), 2002.

*SELF-HELP BOOKS*

*Twelve Jewish Steps to Recovery: A Personal Guide to Turning from Alcoholism and Other Addictions,* Jewish Lights Publishing (Woodstock, VT), 1991.

*Renewed Each Day: Daily Twelve-Step Recovery Meditations Based on the Bible,* two volumes, Jewish Lights Publishing (Woodstock, VT), 1992.

*Recovery from Codependence: A Jewish Twelve-Steps Guide to Healing Your Soul,* Jewish Lights Publishing (Woodstock, VT), 1993.

*One Hundred Blessings A Day: Daily Twelve-Step Recovery Affirmations, Exercises for Personal Growth and Renewal, Reflecting Seasons of the Jewish Year,* Jewish Lights Publishing (Woodstock, VT), 1993.

(Translator, with Leonard S. Kravitz) *The Journey of the Soul: Traditional Sources of Teshuvah,* J. Aronson (Northvale, NJ), 1995.

(Editor, with others) *Paths of Faithfulness: Personal Essays on Jewish Spirituality,* KTAV (Hoboken, NJ), 1996.

(With Carol Ochs) *Jewish Spiritual Guidance: Finding Our Way to God,* Jossey-Bass (San Francisco, CA), 1997.

*Anticipating Revelation: Counting Our Way through the Desert: An Omer Calendar for the Spirit,* Synagogue 2000, 1998.

*Grief in Our Seasons: A Mourner's Companion for Kaddish,* Jewish Lights Publishing (Woodstock, VT), 1998.

(Editor, with Lori Forman) *Sacred Intentions: Daily Inspiration to Strengthen Spirit, Based on Jewish Wisdom,* Jewish Lights Publishing (Woodstock, VT), 1999.

*Jewish Paths toward Healing and Wholeness: A Personal Guide to Dealing with Suffering,* Jewish Lights Publishing (Woodstock, VT), 2000.

(Editor, with Lori Forman) *Restful Reflections: Nighttime Inspiration to Calm the Soul: Based on Jewish Wisdom,* Jewish Lights Publishing (Woodstock, VT), 2001.

*OTHER*

*To Grow Old in Israel: A Survey of Recent Trends and Developments,* Human Sciences, 1988.

*In Celebration: An American Jewish Perspective on the Bicentennial of the U.S. Constitution,* University Press of America (New York, NY), 1988.

*An Interfaith Ministry to the Aged: A Survey of Models,* Human Sciences, 1988.

*The Synagogue Confronts the Jewish Family of the Twenty-first Century,* Union of American Hebrew Congregations/Hebrew Union College-Jewish Institute of Religion (Washington, DC), 1988.

(Editor) *The Safe Deposit Box: And Other Stories about Grandparents, Old Lovers, and Crazy Old Men,* Markus Wiener (New York, NY), 1989.

*Leaving Mother Russia: Chapters in the Russian Jewish Experience,* American Jewish Archives, 1990.

*The Discovery Haggadah,* KTAV (Hoboken, NJ), 1992.

*Hebrew, Heroes, and Holidays: The Great Jewish Fun Book,* Union of American Hebrew Congregations (Washington, DC), 1992.

*Pirke Avot: A New Translation and Commentary,* Union of American Hebrew Congregations (Washington, DC), 1993.

*Documents of Jewish Life,* J. Aronson (Northvale, NJ), 1993.

(With Ronald H. Isaacs) *Doing Mitzvot: Mitzvah Projects for Bar/Bat Mitzvah,* KTAV (Hoboken, NJ), 1994.

(Editor, with Ronald H. Isaacs) *Critical Documents of Jewish History: A Sourcebook,* J. Aronson (Northvale, NJ), 1995.

*Will the Real Hero of Purim Please Stand Up?,* Torah Aura Productions, 1995.

*Healing Essays,* KTAV (Hoboken, NJ), 1996.

(With Marc Lee Raphael) *The American Synagogue: A Historical Dictionary and Sourcebook,* Greenwood Press (Westport, CT), 1996.

*Rediscovering Judaism: Bar and Bat Mitzvah for Adults,* KTAV (Hoboken, NJ), 1997.

*From Your Father's House . . . : Reflections for Modern Jewish Men,* Jewish Publication Society (Philadelphia, PA), 1999.

*Shemonah Perakim: A Treatise on the Soul,* Union of American Hebrew Press (New York, NY), 2000.

Work represented in anthologies, including *The Jewish Principal's Handbook,* 1983; and *Visions of Excellence: The Reform Jewish Day School,* Union of American Hebrew Congregations, 1990. Contributor of articles, poems, and reviews to professional journals and popular magazines, including *Cobblestone* and *South Florida Review.* Columnist for *JVibe* (online magazine). Editor, *Journal of Aging and Judaism;* executive editor, *Shofar;* past executive editor, *COMPASS;* former special issue editor on aging and Judaism for *Journal of Psychology and Judaism;* contributing editor, *Sh'ma: A Journal of Jewish Responsibility;* member of editorial board, *Journal of Ministry in Addiction and Recovery;* coeditor of *T'shuva: Bringing the News of Jewish Recovery.*

*WORK IN PROGRESS: Tales of Jewish Life,* J. Aronson; *The Big Book of Teshuvah,* J. Aronson; *Sparks beneath the Surface: A Psycho-Spiritual Commentary on the Bible,* J. Aronson; "The Jewish Welfare Board," to be included in *Encyclopedia of World War I,* Garland Publishing; "A Jewish Theology of Aging," to be included in *Handbook on Religion and Aging.* Reform Judaism editor for the *Oxford Dictionary of Judaism.*

*SIDELIGHTS:* Kerry M. Olitzky is a rabbi, educator, and author of a wide variety of books with Jewish themes. While much of his writing deals with issues of Jewish education or history, his reference manuals provide a broader scope of information for children, parents, or general readers. Olitzky has also published four "twelve-step" books intended to guide Jewish readers through a spiritual healing process.

Unlike his nonfiction publications, Olitzky's work *The Safe Deposit Box: And Other Stories about Grandparents, Old Lovers, and Crazy Old Men* is a collection of tales, memoirs, and anecdotes concerning old age by Jewish writers. Issues such as Black-Jewish relations and attitudes toward the elderly are explored in some of the pieces. In addition to the title selection by Isaac Bashevis Singer, the book includes Grace Paley's "Dreamer in a Dead Language," Hugh Nissenson's "The Crazy Old Man," and short works by Dan Jacobson, Bruno Lessing, Anzia Yezierska, and Edna Ferber.

*A Glossary of Jewish Life* provides definitions of terms commonly used in Judaism, as well as biographical portraits of historical and contemporary figures. Divided into eight segments by subject matter, with headings including "Religious Practice" and "World Jewish History," the book also includes cross-references and a general index. About Olitzky's *The American Synagogue,* Gregory A. Crawford asserted in *RQ* that it is a "book [that] fills a definite niche in the literature of American Judaism and especially the literature of the synagogue in America." Crawford "highly recommended" the book "for both Jewish and Christian seminary libraries and for libraries serving sizable Jewish populations."

Olitzky once told *CA:* "I work in several areas. My work in education generally serves a particular need. Often, I use a book to translate into reality (especially in a Jewish context) a theoretical construct from secular education. I also write in order to bring individuals closer to their Jewish roots and, in the process, closer to God. I aim to help them make their lives holy and sacred. My work in history is based on interest in particular areas, often of an esoteric nature."

*BIOGRAPHICAL AND CRITICAL SOURCES:*

PERIODICALS

*Publishers Weekly,* October 13, 1989, p. 44.
*RQ,* spring, 1997, Gregory A. Crawford, review of *The American Synagogue,* pp. 448-449.

\*     \*     \*

## O'NEILL, Joseph 1964-

*PERSONAL:* Born February 23, 1964, in Cork, Ireland; son of Kevin (a construction manager) and Caroline (a teacher; maiden name, Dakad) O'Neill; married Sally Singer (an editor), December 30, 1994. *Ethnicity:* "Irish father, Turkish mother." *Education:* Girton College, Cambridge, B.A. (law), 1985; attended Inns of Court School of Law, 1986-87.

*ADDRESSES: Office*—Chambers of Mark Strachan Q.C., 1 Crown Office Row, Temple, London EC4Y 7MM, England. *Agent*—Gill Coleridge, Rogers, Coleridge, & White, 20 Powis Mews, London W11, England. *E-mail*—josephoneill@earthlink.com.

*CAREER:* London, England, barrister and novelist. Called to the Bar, 1987.

*WRITINGS:*

*This Is the Life* (novel), Farrar, Straus (New York, NY), 1991.
*The Breezes* (novel), Faber (Boston, MA), 1995.
*Blood-Dark Track: A Family History* (nonfiction), Granta (London, England), 2000.

*WORK IN PROGRESS: My Prisoners,* a nonfiction inquiry into the imprisonment of O'Neill's two grandfathers, for Grant Books.

*SIDELIGHTS:* A barrister by profession, Joseph O'Neill has written two well-received novels. The first, *This Is the Life,* revolves around a hapless hero, James Jones, who idolizes renowned international lawyer Michael Donovan. After finishing law school, Jones finds work in Donovan's chambers for six months, but, to his disappointment, ultimately fails to secure a permanent position. Jones begins work at a small firm, and years later Donovan calls upon Jones to act for him in a divorce case. Jones comes to terms with his own identity during his torture-wracked courtroom preparations. "People do not have stories, they have lives; they have a spell of sticking around in the flesh, an then they are no more," O'Neill wrote, summing up the book's underlying philosophy. According to a London *Observer* critic, the change which Jones undergoes from a cliché-ridden and dull character to "fiery self-discovery is wittily and powerfully handled." Eloise Kinney of *Booklist* considered *This Is the Life* "a humorous imbroglio of a disgruntled man's fantasies, with Jones coming full circle." A critic for *Kirkus Reviews,* who called Jones "a sort of Lucky Jim at sea in the law," agreed that the writing was "witty and perceptive," but felt that overall the book was "too drawn out, too carefully crafted, and too repetitive to really stun." However, the reviewer did feel that O'Neill showed much "promise."

Critics noted that O'Neill's writing had grown more cynical with his next novel, *The Breezes,* published in 1995. As in *This Is the Life,* O'Neill's second work depicts down-on-their-luck characters who, in this case, are a family who "seem oblivious to the blows which life continually and indiscriminately deals them," according to *Times Literary Supplement* critic Hal Jensen. Jensen noted that O'Neill seems to be questioning how people even get out of bed, when life offers so much misfortune. Told through the perspective of the son, John Breeze, the story details the various stumbling blocks that his family encounters. His mother is killed by a lightning bolt, his father is a bumbling soccer referee and a magnet for mishaps, his sister dates a loser, and even his dog Trusty runs away. O'Neill's captivating and unique writing style caught the eye of several critics. He "captures our peculiar mannerism and shifting moods with style and precision, and his depiction of the moments when hilarity drifts into hysteria, are always brilliant," according to Jensen. *Observer* critic Christina Patterson admired the "elegant and witty" prose, while stating she found that the book "explores relationships and survival strategies with poignancy and affection."

O'Neill turned to nonfiction for his third book, *Blood-Dark Track: A Family History.* Born in Cork, Ireland, the author was always more or less aware of his mixed Irish and Turkish ancestry. When he was eleven, however, he learned that both his grandfathers had spent time in prison during World War II. His family was always relatively closemouthed about the circumstances of each incarceration, so O'Neill decided to research the matter for himself. He published his findings in *Blood-Dark Track,* which reveals that his Irish grandfather was a member of the IRA terrorist organization, and that his Turkish grandfather may well have been the Axis spy the British imprisoned him for being.

Like his novels, O'Neill's works of family history have met with good reviews. Fred Rhodes in the *Middle East* thought *Blood-Dark Track* a "thrilling . . . narrative of murder, paranoia, espionage and fear," while a critic in the *Economist* concluded it to be "a gripping detective story, a thoughtful enquiry into nationalism, and a moving evocation of world war at the edges of its European theatre."

O'Neill once told *CA:* "I have a fairly orthodox disinclination to explain my novels, which speak, or ought to speak, for themselves. I can say, however, that my

two novels are concerned, to an important degree, with examining the fictions we construct to make ourselves tolerable. Sometimes these fictions can act like shackles—as is the case with James Jones, the hero of *This Is the Life.* Other times, they are more or less necessary to understand the accidental nature of things. *The Breezes*—a tragicomedy—explores the limits of the disillusioned life (as lived by the narrator, John Breeze) and of the life sustained by irrational beliefs (as lived by the narrator's father, Eustace Breeze)."

*BIOGRAPHICAL AND CRITICAL SOURCES:*

*BOOKS*

*This Is the Life,* Farrar, Straus (New York, NY), 1991.

*PERIODICALS*

*Booklist,* June 15, 1991, review of *This Is the Life,* p. 1932.

*Books,* September, 1995, review of *The Breezes,* p. 24.

*Economist,* February 17, 2001, "On the Edge; Family Loyalties; Family Memoir As Thriller," review of *Blood-Dark Track,* p. 3.

*Kirkus Reviews,* April 15, 1991, review of *This Is the Life,* p. 496; July 15, 2001, review of *Blood-Dark Track.*

*Library Journal,* May 15, 1991, review of *This Is the Life,* p. 44; August, 2001, Robert Moore, review of *Blood-Dark Track,* p. 123.

*London Review of Books,* March 8, 2001, review of *Blood-Dark Track,* p. 33.

*Middle East,* April, 2001, Fred Rhodes, review of *Blood-Dark Track,* p. 41.

*New Statesman,* February 26, 2001, p. 52.

*Observer* (London, England), May 24, 1992, review of *The Breezes,* p. 61; August 20, 1995, review of *The Breezes,* p. 17; August 25, 1996, p. 18.

*Publishers Weekly,* April 26, 1991, review of *This Is the Life,* p. 44; September 3, 2001, review of *Blood-Dark Track,* p. 77.

*Spectator* (London, England), March 23, 1991, p. 38.

*Times Literary Supplement,* March 1, 1991, review of *This Is the Life,* p. 21; August, 18, 1995, review of *The Breezes,* p. 201; March 16, 2001, review of *Blood-Dark Track,* p. 29; December 7, 2001, review of *Blood-Dark Track,* p. 8.

*Wilson Library Bulletin,* November, 1991, review of *This Is the Life,* p. S14.*

# P

## PADEL, Ruth 1946-

*PERSONAL:* Born May 8, 1946, in London, England; daughter of John Hunter (a psychoanalyst) and Hilda (a child welfare worker; maiden name, Barlow) Padel; married Myles Burnyeat (a professor of ancient philosophy), August, 1984; children: Gwen. *Education:* Lady Margaret Hall, Oxford, B.A. (honors), 1969; Wolfson College, Oxford, D.Phil., M.A., 1976. *Politics:* Labour. *Religion:* Church of England.

*ADDRESSES: Agent*—c/o Author Mail, A. P. Watt, 20 John St., London WC1N 2DR, England.

*CAREER:* Poet. Oxford University, Oxford, England, research fellow and lecturer, 1972-80; Birkbeck College, University of London, London, England, lecturer in classics, 1980-84; freelance writer and lecturer, 1984—.

*MEMBER:* International P.E.N., Poetry Society, Society of Hellenic Studies.

*WRITINGS:*

*Alibi* (poems), Many Press, 1985.
*Summer Snow* (poems), Century Hutchinson (London, England), 1990.
*In and out of the Mind: Greek Images of the Tragic Self,* Princeton University Press (Princeton, NJ), 1992.
*Angel* (poems), Dufour Editions (Chester Springs, PA), 1993.
*Whom Gods Destroy: Elements of Greek and Tragic Madness,* Princeton University Press (Princeton, NJ), 1995.
*Fusewire* (poems), Chatto & Windus (London, England), 1996.
*Rembrandt Would Have Loved You* (poems), Chatto & Windus (London, England), 1998.
*I'm a Man: Sex, Gods, and Rock 'n' Roll,* Faber (London, England), 2000.
*Voodoo Shop,* Chatto & Windus (London, England), 2002.
*Fifty-two Ways of Looking at a Poem; or, How Reading Poetry Can Change Your Life,* Chatto & Windus (London, England), 2002.

Work represented in anthologies. Contributor of articles, poems, and reviews to magazines and newspapers.

*WORK IN PROGRESS: Connexions: Mapping and Divinity in the Greek Tragic Self;* a book of poems, tentatively titled *The Gods of Nothing Else;* research on Greeks and Jews in Renaissance Venice and the Ottoman Empire, with a novel expected to result.

*SIDELIGHTS:* Ruth Padel is a poet and author of critical nonfiction. She wrote a newspaper column called "Sunday Poem" for the *Independent on Sunday* for three years in which she published a new poem each week and instructed readers on how to interpret it. The collection of these poems is in her book *Fifty-two Ways of Looking at a Poem.* Padel's poetry explores the highs and lows of human emotions, focusing largely on the narrative situations encountered by her subjects. Padel's collection *Rembrandt Would Have Loved You* also reveals the author's ability as a storyteller. In this compilation of love poems she creates both power and vulnerability in her characters, and shapes her narrative against numerous mythological and cultural references.

Padel's *Voodoo Shop* was published in 2002. The poems in this collection chronicle a love affair that moves from Brazil to Ireland and thence to other countries. Also included are three poems addressed to the ailing mother of the narrator. This type of juxtaposition is classic for Padel. N. S. Thompson noted in a review for the *Times Literary Supplement* that in *Voodoo Shop* is "a language lush and bold, exotic as well as erotic."

Padel's critical work revolves around analyses of Greek texts and ideas. Her *In and out of the Mind: Greek Images of the Tragic Self* looks at expressions of consciousness in Greek thought. The book is divided into sections; the first four chapters explain Greek words that refer to the human psyche, the fifth chapter discusses how specific bodily imagery is female in gender, and chapters six through eight describe language used in tragedy, especially violent emotions. Ann N. Michelini maintained in a review for the *American Journal of Philology* that Padel's book has a "zestful marshaling of physical metaphors," although the critic found some problems as well. Michelini noted that the author sometimes confuses the analytic terminology with what the word describes, and not the actual word itself. She also suggested that the book needs "a more careful weighing of the biases of the texts taken in evidence and a more sophisticated approach to archaic Greek culture." Malcolm Heath in the *British Journal of Aesthetics* thought that one must have read *In and Out of the Mind* in order to appreciate Padel's *Whom Gods Destroy: Elements of Greek and Tragic Madness,* as the latter work is a continuation of her argument on the individual and consciousness, using fifth-century Greeks as an example. Heath explained that one of the book's recurring themes is "the need for interpreters to adopt the anthropologist's commitment to understanding a culture on its own terms." The critic noted that the book's most valuable feature is "the wonderful accumulation of detailed observations, unexpected connections and illuminating analogies; through these Padel contrived to demonstrate just how profoundly alien Greek ways of thinking were, while at the same time conveying . . . how these patterns of thought made sense."

The author dips slightly into modern culture with her book *I'm a Man: Sex, Gods, and Rock 'n' Roll,* wherein she explores how the sex and drama of rock music is derived from the roots of Greek myth. From the outset, Padel admits she knows very little about rock music, which may explain the somewhat cool reviews. Steven Poole in the *Guardian* observed that while *I'm a Man* contains "several well-researched chapters about racism in rock music and its orientalist subculture," Padel never truly makes her argument stick.

Padel once told *CA:* "In my nonfiction, I have concentrated on ancient tragedy's notions of what is inside people. I have taught Greek and Latin and the writing of Greek verse and prose, as well as the criticism of it. I am now deeply concerned to communicate to readers who do not understand Greek the resonance and spread of meaning caged within specific Greek words. My academic work is informed by anthropology, psychoanalysis, and literary criticism. I have written on feminism and classical scholarship, George Seferis and Homer, madness, possession, images of women's inwardness in Greek tragedy, and George Steiner's readings of tragedy. In all my work, both poetry and prose, I seek to illuminate by juxtaposition and the making of new connections."

*BIOGRAPHICAL AND CRITICAL SOURCES:*

*BOOKS*

*Contemporary Poets,* 7th edition, St. James Press (Detroit, MI), 2001.

*PERIODICALS*

*American Journal of Philology,* fall, 1994, Ann N. Michelini, review of *In and out of Mind: Greek Images of the Tragic Self,* p. 464.
*British Journal of Aesthetics,* July, 1996, Malcolm Heath, review of *Whom Gods Destroy: Elements of Greek and Tragic Madness,* p. 323.
*Guardian,* July 8, 2000, Steven Poole, "Phallic Cymbals."

*Times Literary Supplement,* September 7-13, 1990, p. 954; April 19, 2002, N. S. Thompson, "Take the Fortune-teller in White," p. 24.

*ONLINE*

*New Hope International Review,* http://www.nhi.clara.net/ (August 20, 2002), "Ruth Padel."

*Richmond Review,* http://www.richmondreview.co.uk/ (August 20, 2002), Brian Dillon, review of *I'm a Man: Sex, Gods, and Rock 'n' Roll.*

*Ruth Padel Home Page,* http://www.rpadel.dircon.co.uk/ (August 20, 2002).*

*        *        *

**PARRY, Owen**
  **See PETERS, Ralph**

*        *        *

**PATTON, Phil 1952-**

*PERSONAL:* Born March 23, 1952, in Durham, NC; son of Lewis and Mildred (Dwyer) Patton; married Joelle Delbourgo (an editor), May 16, 1976; children: Caroline. *Education:* Harvard University, A.B., 1974; Columbia University, M.A., 1975. *Politics:* Democrat.

*ADDRESSES: Home and office*—92 Bellevue Ave., Upper Montclair, NJ 07043. *Agent*—Melanie Jackson, 250 West 57th St., New York, NY 10107.

*CAREER:* Writer. *Esquire,* New York, NY, editorial staff, 1975-76. Worked as a contributing editor of *ID* magazine, *Wired,* and *Esquire;* has taught at Columbia University's Graduate School of Journalism.

*MEMBER:* Authors Guild.

*WRITINGS:*

*Razzle-Dazzle: The Curious Marriage of Television and Professional Football,* Dial (New York, NY), 1984.

*Open Road: A Celebration of the American Highway,* Simon & Schuster (New York, NY), 1986.

(With Jeana Yeager and Dick Rutan) *Voyager,* Knopf (New York, NY), 1987; reprinted with new introduction, Adventure Library (North Salem, NY), 2001.

*Made in U.S.A.: The Secret Histories of the Things That Made America,* Grove Weidenfeld (New York, NY), 1992.

(With Bernd Polster) *Highway: America's Endless Dream,* photographs by Jeff Brouws, Stewart, Tabori & Chang (New York, NY), 1997.

(With Frank Del Deo) *Bill Traylor: High Singing Blue,* Hirschl & Adler Modern (New York, NY), 1997.

*Technofollies: An Anthology of B,* Holt (New York, NY), 1997.

*Dreamland: Travels inside the Secret World of Roswell and Area 51,* Villard (New York, NY), 1998.

*Bug: The Strange Mutations of the Volkswagen Beetle, the World's Most Famous Car,* Simon & Schuster (New York, NY), 2002.

Contributor to *Artforum, Esquire, Smithsonian, New York Times, Vogue,* and many other publications.

*SIDELIGHTS:* Phil Patton has written or cowritten a variety of books, primarily in the areas of design and the culture of technology. In addition to his many contributions to magazines and newspapers, Patton has appeared on numerous public television series, served as a commentator on CBS's "Up to the Minute," and appears on television's History Channel. Patton has also served as a consultant to corporations and museums, including the National Building Museum and the Museum of Modern Art, for which he was the cultural consultant for the exhibit, "Other Roads: Automobiles for the Next Century."

In his books, Patton has written about such ingrained aspects of the American culture as America's highways and the popularity of televised football. He also cowrote books about the first plan to circumnavigate the globe nonstop without refueling by husband and wife pilots Jeana Yaeger and Dick Rutan, and he looked at folk artist Bill Traylor in a book written with Frank Del Deo. In his book, *Made in U.S.A.: The Secret Histories of the Things That Made America,* Patton delves into the relationship between popular technology and American society, covering everything from the Bowie knife and paper bags to automobiles and high-tech computers. "Vastly informative and great fun to read," wrote a reviewer in *Publishers Weekly.*

Wendy Smith, writing in *Entertainment Weekly,* noted, "Patton tells this quintessentially American tale with intelligence and zest."

Patton, who has been fascinated with aviation since he was a child, touched on a strange and eccentric aspect of American pop culture with his book *Dreamland: Travels inside the Secret World of Roswell and Area 51.* Largely known as the place where UFO enthusiasts believe the U.S. government houses a wrecked alien spaceship and perhaps even an alien's dead body, Roswell, or Area 51, has been the subject of movies, television shows, and books. In his book, Patton provides a detailed history based on prodigious research of the government's use of Area 51 to test top-secret projects, such as the U2 spy plane and the Stealth Fighter. However, he does not ignore the conspiracy theorists' belief of government duplicity in hiding an alien ship as he interviews local residents, ex-workers, and UFO enthusiasts. In *Booklist,* George Eberhart commented that "Patton deftly separates the folklore from the history." And for Patton, the real story is the government's test planes, which are often mistaken for alien spaceships by those who see them flash across the sky. A *Publishers Weekly* contributor noted that "Patton often succeeds in illuminating military aviation and issues of secrecy, though he cannot offer any substantial revelations on what is or isn't at the base." Writing in the *Nation,* John Leonard commented that *Dreamland* "is a brilliant book in which nothing is as it seems, while everything has a rational explanation, and yet, even so, the 'rational' is its own sort of Dracula."

For his next book, Patton turned from aliens and secret aircraft to the more commonly encountered Volkswagen Beetle automobile. In fact, the "Bug" has been one of the most wide-selling and commonly recognized cars in the world. In *Bug: The Strange Mutations of the Volkswagen Beetle, the World's Most Famous Car,* Patton provides a history of the car, complete with numerous anecdotes—from its creation as an affordable, reliable car for the masses by Ferdinand Porsche to its disappearance and reappearance on the car market. In the course of the Bug's tale, Patton ties in such disparate events as the creation of the automobile assembly line to manufacture the early Ford automobiles, Hitler's invasion of Russia during World War II, and the 1960s counterculture. In the *Library Journal,* contributor Eric C. Shoaf noted that other books about the Volkswagen Beetle "have more depth"

and that Patton failed in his attempt "to combine history, social commentary, design analysis, and political intrigue in one package." However, a contributor to the *Economist* praised the book, saying, "Phil Patton, an American design writer, gives an engaging account of the car's history, from low-budget origins to new-tech reincarnation." Writing in *Kirkus Reviews,* another reviewer noted, "With brio and dash, Patton . . . charts the long strange trip of the little bug that became a grand cultural totem."

## BIOGRAPHICAL AND CRITICAL SOURCES:

### PERIODICALS

*Booklist,* August, 1998, George Eberhart, review of *Dreamland: Travels inside the Secret World of Roswell and Area 51,* p. 1927.

*Economist,* August 25, 2002, "Legless but Lovable; the VW Beetle," review of *Bug: The Strange Mutations of the Volkswagen Beetle, the World's Most Famous Car.*

*Entertainment Weekly,* March 13, 1992, Wendy Smith, review of *Made in U.S.A.: The Secret Histories of the Things That Made America,* p. 48.

*Kirkus Reviews,* July 15, 2002, review of *Bug,* p. 1014.

*Library Journal,* September 15, 2002, Eric C. Shoaf, review of *Bug,* p. 76.

*Nation,* June 215, 1998, John Leonard, review of *Dreamland,* p. 23.

*New York Times Book Review,* June 29, 1986; June 20, 1999, review of *Dreamland,* p. 24.

*Publishers Weekly,* December 20, 1991, review of *Made in U.S.A.,* p. 73; July 27, 1998, review of *Dreamland,* p. 66.

*Washington Post,* May 21, 1986.

### ONLINE

*Aliens on Earth Web Site,* http://www.aliensonearth. com/ (October 8, 2002), review of *Dreamland.*

*BookPage,* http://www.bookpage.com/ (October 8, 2002), Michael Sims, review of *Dreamland;* Martin Brady, "Beetle Mania Rolls On," review of *Bug.*

*Denver Post Online,* http://www.denverpost.com/ (October 8, 2002), William Porter, review of *Dreamland,* August 30, 2002.

*Phil Patton Home Page,* http://www.philpatton.com/ (October 8, 2002).*

## PEARSON, Ridley 1953-
### (Wendell McCall, Steven Rimbauer)

*PERSONAL:* Born March 13, 1953, in Glencove, NY; son of Robert G. (a writer) and Betsy (an artist; maiden name, Dodge) Pearson; married second wife, Marcelle Marsh; children: Paige, Storey (daughters). *Education:* Attended University of Kansas, 1972, and Brown University, 1974.

*ADDRESSES: Office*—P.O. Box 715, Boise, ID 83701. *Agent*—Albert Zuckerman, Writer's House, Inc., 21 West 26th St., New York, NY 10010.

*CAREER:* Novelist and screenwriter. Worked variously as a songwriter for a touring bar band, a dishwasher, and a housekeeper in a hospital surgery suite; composer of orchestral score for documentary film *Cattle Drive.* Bass guitarist for Rock Bottom Remainders (literary garage band), with Dave Barry, Amy Tan, and Stephen King.

*MEMBER:* Writers Guild of America.

*AWARDS, HONORS:* Raymond Chandler Fulbright fellowship in detective fiction, Oxford University, 1990.

*WRITINGS:*

*NOVELS*

*Never Look Back: A Novel of Espionage and Revenge,* St. Martin's Press (New York, NY), 1985.
*Blood of the Albatross,* St. Martin's Press (New York, NY), 1986.
*The Seizing of the Yankee Green Mall,* St. Martin's Press (New York, NY), 1987.
*Undercurrents,* St. Martin's Press (New York, NY), 1988.
*Probable Cause,* St. Martin's Press (New York, NY), 1990.
*Hard Fall,* Delacorte (New York, NY), 1992.
*The Angel Maker,* Delacorte (New York, NY), 1993.
*No Witnesses,* Hyperion (New York, NY), 1994.
*Chain of Evidence,* Hyperion (New York, NY), 1995.
*Beyond Recognition,* Hyperion (New York, NY), 1997.
*The Pied Piper,* Hyperion (New York, NY), 1998.

*The First Victim,* Hyperion (New York, NY), 1999.
*Middle of Nowhere,* Hyperion (New York, NY), 2000.
*Parallel Lies,* Hyperion (New York, NY), 2001.
(As Steven Rimbauer) *The Diary of Ellen Rimbauer: My Life at Rose Red,* foreword by Stephen King, Hyperion (New York, NY), 2001.
*The Art of Deception,* Hyperion (New York, NY), 2002.
*The Body of Peter Hayes,* Hyperion (New York, NY), 2004.

*OTHER*

*The Diary of Ellen Rimbauer* (television miniseries; based on the book of the same title), American Broadcasting Corp., 2003.

Author of screenplay adaptations of his novels *Probable Cause* and *Undercurrents.* Also author, under pseudonym Wendell McCall, of *Aim for the Heart,* St. Martin's Press. Contributor to the anthology *Diagnosis: Terminal,* edited by E. Paul Wilson, Forge (New York, NY), 1996.

*ADAPTATIONS: Angel Maker, No Witnesses,* and *Undercurrents,* were optioned for film by Home Box Office; *Hard Fall* was optioned for film by Amadeo Ursini; film rights to *Probable Cause* were acquired by Ted Hartley of RKO. Several books by Pearson have been adapted as audiobooks, including *Parallel Lies,* Brilliance, 2001.

*SIDELIGHTS:* Ridley Pearson writes police procedurals about serial killers that some critics consider masterpieces of taut plotting, fascinating forensic details, and enjoyable characters. Pearson's thrillers featuring detective Lou Boldt and police psychologist Daphne Matthews—whose on-again, off-again romance provides the series with a continuing subplot—are set in the author's former home town of Seattle, Washington. Although some deem the author's characterizations flat and his plots implausible, others find Pearson's novels impossible to put down. "Some procedurals stress forensic detail, while others emphasize the multidimensional humanity of the cops. Pearson does both, and the combination continues to be unbeatable," wrote *Booklist* contributor Bill Ott in his review of Pearson's *Chain of Evidence.*

Pearson's 1986 novel *Blood of the Albatross* features spies, F.B.I. agents, a naive sailor, and a mysterious woman, all stock figures in crime novels. Accordingly, Newgate Callendar commented in the *New York Times:* "There is nothing new here, but the writing is ebullient, the author has a good time with the conventions, and so should the reader." By the time *The Angel Maker,* was published, nearly ten years later, Pearson had become a celebrated writer of forensic thrillers whose recurring characters Boldt and Matthews and the often highly technical trails of evidence that wind through his work were now celebrated by some reviewers. "Pearson's engaging forensic detail—he makes complicated, potentially disgusting facts almost entertaining—and brisk prose will have readers racing to the cliffhanger climax," averred a critic for *Publishers Weekly* in a review of *The Angel Maker.*

Reviewers of more recent Pearson procedurals have continued to praise the author's ability to incorporate the latest technological aids to detective work without slowing down the action in his taut plots. In *No Witnesses* a serial killer bent on exacting revenge against a food company begins poisoning the company's products, faxing extortion notes, and using ATM's to retrieve ransom money, thereby leaving no physical trace for Detective Boldt to track down. "Mr. Pearson's grasp of investigative technology is truly impressive," noted Marilyn Stasio in the *New York Times,* quipping: "O brave new world, Mr. Pearson has your PIN." *Booklist* contributor Ott found Pearson's shift from forensic thriller to techno-thriller well executed. "As in past Boldt-Matthews adventures . . . the combination of meticulous investigative detail and excruciating, screw-tightening suspense is utterly riveting," Ott enthused in his review of *No Witnesses.*

Boldt and Matthews return in *Beyond Recognition,* a thriller about a serial killer who disposes of his victims' bodies with rocket fuel, which burn so hot it leaves almost no trace behind. "Moving from one punchy scene to the next, this fuse-burning suspense tale is wonderful reading for a wide audience," noted Molly Gorman in *Library Journal.* Although a *Publishers Weekly* reviewer complained that *Beyond Recognition* is not up to the standard of earlier Boldt-Matthews procedurals, *Booklist* contributor Ott again praised Pearson's ability to "never stop playing the reader's emotions," creating a rhythm to his plot that builds excitement to a fever pitch. "You have to be a bit of a masochist to give in to a Pearson plot, but when you do, it hurts so good," Ott concluded.

Pearson brings the suspense home to Detective Boldt in *The Pied Piper,* in which the detective's own daughter is kidnapped after Boldt begins to get close to identifying a serial kidnapper. "The plot begins simply and becomes wonderfully complex," wrote a *Publishers Weekly* reviewer, who recommended the book even to first-time Pearson readers "who may be tempted to pick up earlier novels to see whether they're all this good." The eighth novel in the series, *The Art of Deception* continues Boldt's adventures, as the detective investigates a pair of suspicious deaths that ultimately point to a murderer who may not be finished yet. With the help of forensic pathologist Matthews—who finds herself with an unwanted admirer in the person of a local deputy sheriff—Boldt follows the trail of both murderers only to find them intersect in a novel that a *Kirkus* contributor cited as "on top of the summer's pile of procedurals" due to Pearson's "handsome command of detail and breathless pace." Calling the novel's "atmospheric descriptions of Seattle . . . dead-on," *Library Journal* contributor Jeff Ayers dubbed *The Art of Deception* "hands-down one of the best thrillers of the year." In *Booklist,* Bill Ott also commended Pearson's setting, noting that the novelist's "detail-rich treatment goes well beyond the typical cliches of dark passages and abandoned storefronts" and praising the "Boldt and Matthews" novels as among "the mystery genre's greatest pleasures."

Pearson shifts the scene from Seattle to Connecticut and leaves Detective Boldt behind in *Chain of Evidence.* In this novel Detective Joe Dartelli suspects that a series of suicides may actually be murders committed by his former mentor, forensic specialist Walter Zeller, a troubled man seemingly intent on exacting revenge for the murder of his own wife years before. Although a critic for *Publishers Weekly* declared Pearson's plot unbelievable and his characters "generic, if appealing," this reviewer also stated: "What Pearson does better than any other current thriller writer is forensic detail," and *Chain of Evidence* "stands as one of the best novels yet by this author."

*New York Times* contributor Stasio remarked upon Pearson's facility with incorporating gadgets and difficult technical or medical information into his plots, but bemoaned the fact that this ability does not carry through to his characterizations: "For someone who can be so lucid about complicated technical subjects like DNA mapping, Mr. Pearson has his problems writing about life-forms," Stasio noted in a review of *Chain of Evidence.*

A friend of horrormeister Stephen King, Pearson "conspired" with King in a literary hoax in 2002. Following the television airing of King's *Rose Red,* about a haunted mansion built on a Native American burial ground by the wealthy Rimbauer family in the early twentieth century, *The Diary of Ellen Rimbauer: My Life at Rose Red* appeared on bookstore shelves. With an introduction by King, the book was purported to be the work of Steven Rimbauer, based on the diary of his late aunt, with editorial commentary by Joyce Reardon, Ph.D., an expert in the paranormal. Only after this book was dramatized as an ABC miniseries was Reardon announced as the actual author and perpetrator of the hoax. As a novel, *The Diary of Ellen Rimbauer* presents the backdrop to King's book, and focuses on the writer's marriage to a wealthy oil magnate who will not pay heed to Ellen's concerns about the otherworldly occurrences in their luxurious new home. Noting that the fictional *Diary* "stands well on its own," a *Book Haven* contributor commended Pearson's adoption of a diary format, which "gives readers a voyeuristic thrill."

*BIOGRAPHICAL AND CRITICAL SOURCES:*

PERIODICALS

*Booklist,* August, 1994, p. 1993; September 1, 1995, p. 6; December 15, 1996, p. 693; May 1, 2001, review of *Parallel Lies;* June 1, 2002, Bill Ott, review of *The Art of Deception,* p. 1646.
*Entertainment Weekly,* October 27, 1995, p. 83.
*Kirkus Reviews,* July 1, 2002, review of *The Art of Deception,* p. 911.
*Library Journal,* January, 1997, p. 149; May 1, 1998, p. 156; July, 2002, Jeff Ayers, review of *The Art of Deception,* p. 122.
*New York Times,* October 56, 1986, section 7, p. 28; August 1, 1993; November 20, 1994; October 22, 1995.
*Playboy,* December, 1995, p. 35.
*Publishers Weekly,* February 8, 1993, p. 74; April 5, 1993, p. 28; August 5, 1994, p. 85; June 19, 1995, p. 17; September 18, 1995, p. 11; June 3, 1996, p. 62; December 16, 1996, p. 42; July 13, 1998, p. 63; July 1, 2002, review of *The Art of Deception,* p. 53; July 8, 2002, Dena Croog, "'Rimbauer' Author Unmasked," p. 18.

ONLINE

*Book Haven,* http://www.thebookhaven.homestead.com/ (August 28, 2003), Amy Carother, review of *The Diary of Ellen Rimbauer.*

**PEDERSON, Sharleen**
**See COLLICOTT, Sharleen**

*       *       *

**PELECANOS, George P. 1957-**

*PERSONAL:* Born February 18, 1957, in Washington, DC; son of Peter G. (a restaurateur) and Ruby K. (an administrator) Pelecanos; married Emily Hawk (a magazine producer), October 26, 1985; children: Nick, Peter, Rosa. *Ethnicity:* "Greek American." *Education:* University of Maryland—College Park, B.A., 1980.

*ADDRESSES: Home*—737 Silver Spring Ave., Silver Spring, MD 20910. *Office*—Circle Films, 2445 M St. NW, Washington, DC 20037. *Agent*—Sloan Harris, ICM 40 West 57th St., New York, NY 10019.

*CAREER:* Worked as a waiter, bartender, salesman, and in management until 1990; Circle Films (producers and distributors of theatrical films), Washington, DC, manager and developer, 1990—; currently story editor/writer for HBO series *The Wire.*

*MEMBER:* Mystery Writers of America.

*AWARDS, HONORS:* Notable Books of 1998 citation, *Publishers Weekly,* for *The Sweet Forever;* International Crime Novel of the Year, in France, Germany, and Japan, for *Big Blowdown; Los Angeles Times* Book Award, 2003, for *Hell to Pay.*

*WRITINGS:*

*A Firing Offense,* St. Martin's Press (New York, NY), 1992.
*Nick's Trip,* St. Martin's Press (New York, NY), 1993.
*Shoedog,* St. Martin's Press (New York, NY), 1994.
*Down by the River Where the Dead Men Go,* St. Martin's Press (New York, NY), 1995.
*The Big Blowdown,* St. Martin's Press (New York, NY), 1996.
*King Suckerman,* Little, Brown (Boston, MA), 1997.
*The Sweet Forever,* Little, Brown (Boston, MA), 1998.
*Shame the Devil,* Little, Brown (Boston, MA), 2000.
*Right As Rain,* Little, Brown (Boston, MA), 2001.

(Author of introduction) *Cutter and Bone,* Serpent's Tail (London, England), reprinted, 2001.

*Hell to Pay,* Little, Brown, (Boston, MA), 2002.

(Contributor) *Measure of Poison,* edited by Dennis McMillan, Dennis McMillan Publications (Tucson, AZ), 2002.

*Soul Circus,* Little, Brown (Boston, MA), 2003.

*Hard Revolution: A Novel,* Little, Brown (Boston, MA), 2004.

Contributor of articles and reviews to magazines and newspapers, including *Cineaste, Armchair Detective,* and *Washington Post Book World;* also author of short fiction appearing in *Esquire* and collections such as the *Usual Suspects* and *Best American Mystery Stories of 1997.*

*ADAPTATIONS:* Several of the author's books have been optioned for film.

*SIDELIGHTS:* The son of Greek immigrants, George P. Pelecanos grew up in the Washington, DC, Mount Pleasant area, where he worked as a teenager at his father's lunch counter. He didn't start writing until the age of thirty-one after working at various jobs, such as shoe sales and construction. He wrote his first book, *A Firing Offense,* at night in his spare time. Since the book's 1992 publication, he has written a series of gritty detective "noir" novels set in Washington, DC, all of which have received glowing critical praise as groundbreaking crime fiction.

In an *Entertainment Weekly* article by Daniel Fierman, writer Dennis Lehane commented, "The thing I like about his writing is that it's true noir. It's concerned with people who live outside the margins." Commenting on Pelecanos's *The Sweet Forever,* Lehane noted, "That book was a more precise evocation of what was going on in cities in the 1980s than *The Bonfire of the Vanities* could ever hope to be."

Building on the success of *A Firing Offense,* Pelecanos stayed with the novel's main character, Nick Stefanos, for his next book, *Nick's Trip.* A *Publishers Weekly* contributor called the Stefanos character "offbeat . . . with his gruff sensibilities and fine taste in women and music."

In *Shoedog,* Pelecanos tells the tale of Constantine, a former marine who ends up taking part in an armed robbery that goes bad and results in his seeking

revenge. "All sinners, none saints, the small-time hoods in this authentic world are crisply limned here in their fallible humanity," wrote a contributor to *Publishers Weekly.* Pelecanos returned to Nick Stefanos for his next effort, *Down by the River Where the Dead Men Go,* in which a drunken Nick hears a murder being committed nearby and seeks to find the killer or killers. Emily Melton, writing in *Booklist,* said, "This is a powerful, shocking foray into an uncompromising, bleak world of depravity and decadence, a book that will stick with the reader long after the awful conclusion."

Although praised by critics and fellow writers, Pelecanos was still seeking to reach the upper echelon in terms of public recognition. "The release of *The Big Blowdown* in 1996 was the turning point," according to Fierman in *Entertainment Weekly,* pointing out that this book and the three that followed resulted in a steadily growing audience. "It was a very conscious effort to swing for the bleachers," Pelecanos told Fierman of his writing in *The Big Blowdown,* another Stefanos novel which also chronicles twenty-five years of immigrant life in the nation's capital following World War II. "With stylistic panache and forceful conviction, Pelecanos delivers a darkly powerful story of the American city," wrote a contributor to *Publishers Weekly.*

Bill Ott noted in *Booklist* that Pelecanos's next novel, *King Suckerman,* is "much more" than just a "fictional homage to the blaxploitation films of the 1970s." Here Pelecanos defines the seventies through drug deals, racial tensions, and soul music in a story of two friends, one black and one white, who together track down a merciless killer. In *The Sweet Forever,* Pelecanos finds a setting in the cocaine world of Washington, DC, in the 1980s. The characters of Dimitri Karras and Marcus Clay from *King Suckerman* return to face a local drug lord who tries to establish himself as the law in the neighborhood where Clay has just opened the newest of his chain of record stores. A reviewer writing in *Publishers Weekly* noted that *The Sweet Forever* "is a winner" due to Pelecanos's ability to fashion "the novel's sweeping neoepic scale" and provide a "multitude of nuanced character studies that populate this lavishly constructed canvas." In *Shame the Devil,* Pelecanos continues to delve into the gritty underbelly of Washington, DC, as the Farrow brothers arrive in town, rob a restaurant, and kill several of the workers there. Richard Farrow is killed by another cop and as his brother Frank escapes he runs over a young boy, whose father is the familiar Pelecanos character Dimitri Karras. Frank Farrow vows revenge for his brother, and Dimitri sets out to stop him.

*Right As Rain* revolves around family secrets and features the ex-cop Derek Strange, who now has his own detective agency. When a black policeman is accidentally slain by another white cop, Strange, who is black, investigates at the request of the slain officer's mother. Joined by Terry Quinn, who shot the other policeman, Strange enters a world of drug trades, racism in the police force, and cold-blooded killers. A writer in *Publishers Weekly* noted that the character of Strange is "a new urban gumshoe who's just as tantalizing to watch in action" as Nick Stefanos of earlier novels. "What is perhaps most remarkable about this outstanding novel . . . is the way his plot-rich, extremely violent stories parallel the turbulence of his characters' inner lives," wrote Bill Ott in *Booklist*. In *Hell to Pay*, Strange and Quinn return to find a teenage girl who has disappeared and, in the process, encounter a ruthless criminal called Worldwide Wilson. As in many of his books, music plays a large part in the characters' lives; Strange, for example, drives around town listening to Teddy Pendergrass and Al Green. "In fact, the characters' musical selections function almost like personal soundtracks," noted Ben Greenman in the *New Yorker*, calling the book a "classic crime novel."

Pelecanos, who has also worked as an independent film producer, once told *CA:* "It was in college, during the burgeoning years of the punk and post-punk movements, that I first became interested in hard-boiled fiction. My intent is to marry the two forms and update the genre so that it has relevance and resonance to my generation. I'll stay within the circle (I respect the tradition that much), but I'm going to subvert the conventional elements as often as I can. I don't want to write books that I've already read."

As for his entrance into mainstream readership, Pelecanos told Fierman, "All I want to do is shine a light on the working-class people of this city. . . . The racial divide here is in your face. And that interests me, because I have three mixed-race kids. I worry about them."

*BIOGRAPHICAL AND CRITICAL SOURCES:*

PERIODICALS

*Booklist*, April 15, 1995, Emily Melton, review of *Down by the River Where the Dead Men Go*, p. 1483; April 15, 1996, Emily Melton, review of *The Big Blowdown*, p. 1424; August, 1997, Bill Ott, review of *King Suckerman*, p. 1885; June 1, 1998, Bill Ott, review of *The Sweet Forever*, p. 1735; December 15, 2000, Bill Ott, review of *Right As Rain*, p. 763; December 1, 2001, Bill Ott, review of *Hell to Pay*, p. 606.

*Entertainment Weekly*, March 8, 2002, Daniel Fierman, "D.C. Confidential: Mystery Writer George Pelecanos Breaks Out of Washington's Mean Streets."

*Library Journal*, August, 1997, Susan A. Zappia, review of *The Big Blowdown*, p. 134; July, 1998, Rex E. Klett, review of *The Sweet Forever*, p. 140; November 1, 2000, Bob Lynn, review of *Right As Rain*, p. 136; December, 2001, Bob Lynn, review of *Hell to Pay*, p. 174; May 1, 2000, Paul Kaplan, review of *Shame the Devil*, p. 180.

*New Yorker*, April 8, 2002, Ben Greenman, "Washington Wizard," review of *Hell to Pay*, p. 90.

*Publishers Weekly*, January 18, 1993, review of *Nick's Trip*, p. 452; March 14, 1994, review of *Shoedog*, p. 65; April 24, 1995, review of *Down by the River Where the Dead Men Go*, p. 63; April 8, 1996, review of *The Big Blowdown*, p. 59; June 1, 1998, review of *The Sweet Forever*, p. 48A; January 8, 2001, review of *Right As Rain*, p. 51; December 10, 2001, review of *Hell to Pay*, p. 50.

ONLINE

*Authors on the Web*, http://www.authorsontheweb.com/ (October 8, 2002).

*BookReporter*, http://www.bookreporter.com/ (October 8, 2002), review of *Right As Rain*.

*George Pelecanos Home Page*, http://www.georgepelecanos.com/ (August 11, 2003).

*Houston Chronicle*, http://www.chron.com/ (October 8, 2002), John B. Clutterbuck, "George P. What's-His-Name Just Keeps Delivering," April 26, 2002.

*January Magazine*, http://www.januarymagazine.com/ (October 8, 2002), Karen G. Anderson, reviews of *Soul Circus* and *Hell to Pay*.

\*        \*        \*

**PERRY, Phyllis J(ean) 1933-**

*PERSONAL:* Born October 23, 1933, in Nevada City, CA; daughter of William H. (a miner) and Winifred (a homemaker; maiden name, Elliott) Penaluna; married David Louis Perry, February 8, 1953; children: Janet

Marie Perry Miller, Jill Louise Perry Fernandez. *Ethnicity:* "English." *Education:* University of California—Berkeley, A.B., 1955; San Francisco State College (now University), M.A., 1960; University of Colorado, Ed.D., 1980. *Politics:* Democrat. *Religion:* Methodist. *Hobbies and other interests:* Hiking in the mountains, acting in community theater, attending concerts, playing bridge, reading to grandchildren, amateur radio operation.

ADDRESSES: *Home*—3190 Endicott Dr., Boulder, CO 80305.

CAREER: Boulder Valley Public Schools, Boulder, CO, teacher, curriculum specialist, educational programs specialist, instructional design specialist, director of talented and gifted education, principal, 1968-91. Nomad Community Theater, member of board of directors.

MEMBER: International Reading Association (Colorado Council), National Association for Gifted Children, Society of Children's Book Writers and Illustrators, Colorado Authors League, Colorado Language Arts Society, Phi Delta Kappa (Boulder chapter), Phi Beta Kappa.

AWARDS, HONORS: Governor's Award for Excellence in Education, 1986; Top Hand Awards, Colorado Authors League, children's nonfiction category, 1999, for *Bats: The Amazing Upside-Downers,* special writing category, 1999, for *Exploring Our Country's History: Linking Fiction to Nonfiction,* and children's nonfiction category, 2001, for *Animals under the Ground.*

WRITINGS:

CHILDREN'S NONFICTION

*Spiders,* illustrated by Lawrence M. Spiegel, Denison (Minneapolis, MN), 1964.

*Let's Look at the Birds,* illustrated by Lawrence M. Spiegel, Denison (Minneapolis, MN), 1965.

*A Trip through the Zoo,* illustrated by Barbara Furan, Denison (Minneapolis, MN), 1968.

*One Dozen Swimmers,* illustrated by June Talarczyk, Denison (Minneapolis, MN), 1968.

*Let's Look at Moths and Butterflies,* illustrated by June Talarczyk, Denison (Minneapolis, MN), 1969.

*Let's Look at Frogs,* illustrated by June Talarczyk, Denison (Minneapolis, MN), 1969.

*Let's Look at Snails,* illustrated by Celeste K. Foster, Denison (Minneapolis, MN), 1969.

*Let's Look at Seashells,* illustrated by Celeste K. Foster, Denison (Minneapolis, MN), 1971.

*Let's Learn about Mushrooms,* illustrated by Haris Petie, Harvey House (New York, NY), 1974.

*Mexican American Sketches,* BVSP, 1976.

*A Look at Colorado,* illustrated by Dian Diggs and with photographs by David L. Perry, Pruett Publishing (Boulder, CO), 1976.

*The Fiddlehoppers: Crickets, Katydids, and Locusts,* Franklin Watts (New York, NY), 1995.

*Ballooning,* Franklin Watts (New York, NY), 1996.

*Sea Stars and Dragons,* Franklin Watts (New York, NY), 1996.

*Armor to Venom: Animal Defenses,* Franklin Watts (New York, NY), 1997.

*The Crocodilians: Reminders of the Age of the Dinosaur,* Franklin Watts (New York, NY), 1997.

*Hide and Seek: Creatures in Camouflage,* Franklin Watts (New York, NY), 1997.

*The Snow Cats,* Franklin Watts (New York, NY), 1997.

*Soaring,* Franklin Watts (New York, NY), 1997.

*Bats: The Amazing Upside-Downers,* Franklin Watts (New York, NY), 1998.

*Exploring the World of Sports: Linking Fiction to Nonfiction* (in "Literature Bridges to Social Studies" series), Teacher Ideas Press (Portsmouth, NH), 1998.

*Crafty Canines: Coyotes, Foxes, and Wolves,* Franklin Watts (New York, NY), 1999.

*Freshwater Giants,* Franklin Watts (New York, NY), 1999.

*Keeping the Traditions: A Multicultural Resource,* Fulcrum (Colorado), 2000.

*Boardsailing,* Capstone Books (Bloomington, MN), 2000.

*Animals That Hibernate,* Franklin Watts (New York, NY), 2001.

*Animals under the Ground,* Franklin Watts (New York, NY), 2001.

*Trains,* Enslow Publishers (Berkeley Heights, NJ), 2001.

*Jazz Up Your Journal: Writing for Grades 1-2,* Carson-Dellosa (Lancaster, CA), 2003.

*Jazz Up Your Journal: Writing for Grades 3-4,* Carson-Dellosa (Lancaster, CA), 2003.

*Jazz Up Your Journal: Writing for Grades 5-6,* Carson-Dellosa (Lancaster, CA), 2003.

*"LITERATURE BRIDGES TO SCIENCE" SERIES*

*Bridges to the World of Water: Linking Fiction to Non-fiction,* Teacher Ideas Press (Portsmouth, NH), 1995.

*Rainy, Windy, Snowy, Sunny Days: Linking Fiction to Nonfiction,* Teacher Ideas Press (Portsmouth, NH), 1996.

*The World's Regions and Weather: Linking Fiction to Nonfiction,* Teacher Ideas Press (Portsmouth, NH), 1996.

*Exploring the World of Animals: Linking Fiction to Nonfiction,* Teacher Ideas Press (Portsmouth, NH), 1997.

*Exploring Our Country's History: Linking Fiction to Nonfiction,* Teacher Ideas Press (Portsmouth, NH), 1998.


*FOR TEACHERS*

*Full Flowering: A Parent and Teacher Guide to Programs for the Gifted,* Wetherall (Minneapolis, MN), 1985.

*A Guide to Independent Research,* G.C.T., 1986.

*Colorado History: Creative Activities for Curious Kids,* Hi Willow Research (San Jose, CA), 1994.

*A Teacher's Science Companion: Resources and Activities in Science and Math,* TAB Books (New York, NY), 1994.

*Getting Started in Science Fairs: From Planning to Judging,* TAB Books (New York, NY), 1995.

(With Peter Rillero) *365 Science Projects and Activities,* illustrated by Ellen Joy Sasaki and Terri and Jo Chicko, Publications International, 1996.

*Guide to Math Materials: Resources to Support the NCTM Standards,* Teacher Ideas Press (Portsmouth, NH), 1997.

*Reading Activities and Resources That Work,* Highsmith Press (Fort Atkinson, WI), 1997.

*Myths, Legends, and Tales,* Highsmith Press (Fort Atkinson, WI), 1998.

*Science Fair Success with Plants,* Enslow Publishers (Berkeley Heights, NJ), 1999.

*Meeting Math Standards: Grades 2-3,* McGraw-Hill (New York, NY), 2002.

*Meeting Math Standards: Grades 4-5,* McGraw-Hill (New York, NY), 2002.

*Substitute's Own Survival Guide,* Carson-Dellosa (Lancaster, CA), 2002.

*Science Companion for Library, Home, and School,* Scarecrow Press (Lanham, MD), 2002.

*Ten Tall Tales: Origins, Activities, and More,* Upstart Books (Fort Atkinson, WI), 2002.

*Teaching the Fantasy Novel: From "The Hobbit" to "Harry Potter and the Goblet of Fire,"* Teacher Ideas Press (Portsmouth, NJ), 2003.


*OTHER*

*My Big Rock,* Bebop Books (New York, NY), 2002.

*The Musical ABC,* Piano Press, 2001.

*Beneath the Old Oak Tree* (children's fiction), Seedling (Lakewood, CO), 2003.

*Mr. Crumb's Secret: A Fribble Mouse Library Mystery,* Alleyside (Fort Atkinson, WI), 2003.

Contributor to *The Young Gifted Child: Potential and Promise,* edited by Joan Franklin Smutny, Hampton Press (Cresskill, NJ), 1998. Contributor to periodicals, including *Educational Leadership, Middle School Journal, Instructor, Challenge, Wee Wisdom, High Adventure, Story Friends, Day Care and Early Education, Child Life,* and *Humpty Dumpty.*

*SIDELIGHTS:* Phyllis J. Perry once told *CA:* "As I work with colleagues to develop innovative approaches or to create solid foundations for educational programs, I seek to share these with others. Children are precious, and they deserve the best possible education in settings that respect their worth and dignity and promote their happiness and success."

Perry's nonfiction books for children include a series for Franklin Watts about various animal families, and the habitats and behaviors of each kind of animal. *The Crocodilians: Reminders of the Age of the Dinosaur* features crocodiles, alligators, caimans, and gavials, while *The Snow Cats* discusses cats from the sabertooth tiger to snow leopards and lynxes. In a review of these books in *School Library Journal,* Jacqueline Elsner concluded, "These two books are sure to circulate."

Some of Perry's books guide teachers as they attempt to interest children in science and social studies. *Bridges to the World of Water: Linking Fiction to Nonfiction,* written for teachers of middle-grade children, provides fiction and nonfiction readings that discuss oceans, lakes, and rivers in four chapters. As a critic noted in *Appraisal,* the chapters also contain "a wealth of practical and relevant suggestions for in-depth discussion and additional work." The book also includes a list of projects, ideas, and additional resources.

In *Getting Started in Science Fairs: From Planning to Judging,* Perry not only guides elementary school teachers through the process of organizing a science fair, she discusses scientific methods and provides ideas for projects in various scientific categories (which may help students and parents as well). Bibliographies are included. Writing in *Appraisal,* Kathleen Dummer described Perry's work as an "excellent reference book." According to *Appraisal* contributor R. Smith, of the many books about science-fair projects, *Getting Started in Science Fairs* "is clearly one of the best."

*BIOGRAPHICAL AND CRITICAL SOURCES:*

PERIODICALS

*Appraisal,* autumn, 1995, p. 37.
*Booklist,* February 1, 1997, pp. 937-938; July, 1997, p. 1816.
*Library Journal,* May 15, 1968, p. 2108.
*School Library Journal,* August, 1997, pp. 173-174; February, 1997, p. 95.
*Science Books & Films,* August-September, 1995, p. 176; October, 1995, p. 199.
*Voice of Youth Advocates,* December, 1996, p. 296.

\*     \*     \*

**PETERS, Barney**
    **See BAUER, Erwin A.**

\*     \*     \*

**PETERS, Ralph 1952-**
    **(Owen Parry)**

*PERSONAL:* Born April 19, 1952, in Pottsville, PA; son of Ralph Heinrich and Alice Catherine (maiden name, Parfitt) Peters; married Marion Ann Martin, 1982 (marriage ended); married Katherine McIntire,

June 4, 1994. *Ethnicity:* "Welsh and German." *Education:* St. Mary's University, M.A. (international relations), 1988; attended U. S. Army Command and General Staff College, U.S. Army Russian Institute, and other military schools and institutions. *Politics:* Independent. *Hobbies and other interests:* Adventure travel, languages, hiking, Shakespeare.

*ADDRESSES: Home*—5831 Green Springs Dr., Warrenton, VA 20187-9324. *Agent*—Robert Gottlieb, Trident Media, 41 Madison Avenue, New York, NY 10010.

*CAREER:* U.S. Army, 1976-98, commissioned, 1980, reached rank of lieutenant colonel. Writer, 1981—.

*MEMBER:* Army and Navy Club

*AWARDS, HONORS:* Legion of Merit, U.S. Army, 1998; Herodotus Award for Best First U.S. Historical Mystery, 2000, for *Faded Coat of Blue;* Dashiell Hammett Award, 2003, for *Honor's Kingdom.*

*WRITINGS:*

NOVELS

*Brave Romeo,* Richard Marek (New York, NY), 1981.
*Red Army,* Pocket Books (New York, NY), 1989.
*The War in 2020,* Pocket Books (New York, NY), 1991.
*Flames of Heaven,* Pocket Books (New York, NY), 1993.
*The Perfect Soldier,* Pocket Books (New York, NY), 1995.
*Devil's Garden,* Avon Books (New York, NY), 1998.
*Traitor,* Avon Books (New York, NY), 1999.
*Twilight of Heroes,* Stackpole Books (Mechanicsburg, PA), 2003.

UNDER PSEUDONYM OWEN PARRY

*Faded Coat of Blue,* Avon Books (New York, NY), 1999.
*Shadows of Glory,* W. Morrow (New York, NY), 2000.
*Call Each River Jordan,* William Morrow (New York, NY), 2001.

*Our Simple Gifts: Civil War Christmas Tales,* Harper-Collins (New York, NY), 2002.

*Honor's Kingdom,* William Morrow (New York, NY), 2002.

*Bold Sons of Erin,* W. Morrow (New York, NY), 2003.

NONFICTION

*Fighting for the Future: Will America Triumph?,* Stackpole Books (Mechanicsburg, PA), 1999.

*Beyond Terror: Strategy in a Changing World,* Stackpole Books (Mechanicsburg, PA), 2002.

*Beyond Baghdad: Postmodern War and Peace,* Stackpole Books (Mechanicsburg, PA), 2003.

Also author of articles and essays on military subjects and contributor to *New York Post, Washington Post, Wall Street Journal,* and other newspapers.

*ADAPTATIONS: A Faded Coat of Blue* was made into a sound recording by Books on Tape, 2001.

*WORK IN PROGRESS:* More novels, including Abel Jones mysteries.

*SIDELIGHTS:* Ralph Peters, a former U.S. Army military intelligence officer, has achieved success as a writer of contemporary political thrillers and books on policy analysis. He has also written several historical novels about the Civil War under the pseudonym Owen Parry. Growing up in Pennsylvania's Schuylkill Haven, Peters said that his exposure to the Pennsylvania German and other accents common in the area has been an important part of his training as a writer. "When I was growing up in the Fifties and Sixties, you could usually tell what town in the county people were from by their accent," Peters told *Washington Post* contributor Ken Ringle. Peters, who learned Russian and German during his military career, went on to note, "It wasn't a highly literate culture, but they were all great storytellers, so I grew up mesmerized by the magic and power of language."

The author's first novel, *Brave Romeo,* concerns Jack Thorne, a poetry-writing guerrilla fighter who becomes an intelligence officer and uncovers evidence of a right-wing conspiracy in Germany. Unable to convince his superiors of the terrorist operation's grave threat to Western security, the hero teams instead with a left-wing student who personally challenges the conspirators after having been accused of masterminding an act of aggression that they conducted. Alan Cheuse, writing in the *New York Times Book Review,* deemed *Brave Romeo* "worth reading."

Peters followed up with *Red Army,* a story set during World War III in which Soviet forces in Central Europe overwhelm North Atlantic Treaty Organization (NATO) troops. But unlike similar works in the genre, the perspective in *Red Army* is that of the Soviet fighters: an infantryman, fearing separation from his fellow soldiers, charges into the darkness where the enemy, presumably, awaits; a tank commander, motivated by cowardice, commits a heroic act; and an accomplished general ponders the significance of his Jewish background. *Newsweek* reviewer Harry Anderson hailed *Red Army* as "a very engaging read" and added that "it is hard to imagine a better portrayal of modern war."

His third novel, *The War in 2020,* was described by Donovan Fitzpatrick in the *New York Times Book Review* as "a terrifying vision of global conflict in the Twenty-first century." In this novel Peters presents a chaotic, high-technology conflict in which Israel is destroyed by nuclear and chemical bombs, American forces are undone in Africa, and Moslems armed with Japanese weapons threaten to overwhelm the Soviet Union, which is already teetering towards civil war. *Washington Post* reviewer David Morrell, while objecting that *The War in 2020* "tends to reinforce national stereotypes," conceded that it serves as "a diverting action novel."

Peters went on to write *Flames of Heaven,* about the crumbling empire of the Soviet Union, and *The Perfect Soldier,* which tells the story of a counterintelligence expert assigned to help prove that the Russians were involved in the execution of American prisoners during the Korean War. In his novel *Twilight of Heroes,* the protagonist, Colonel John Church, assumes the blame for the massacre of a U.S. military team on a mission in Bolivia and then goes on to complete the mission. According to a reviewer in *Publishers Weekly,* the story "captivates even as it infuriates with its depiction of men betrayed."

After writing two more superpower thrillers, *The Devil's Garden* and *Traitor,* under his own name, Peters switched gears as he published his first Civil War novel under the pseudonym Owen Parry. In *Faded Coat of Blue,* winner of the Herodotus Award, the author introduces the character of Abel Jones, a clerk in the Union supply office who ends up solving the murder of a young abolitionist in Washington, DC, at the beginning of the Civil War. Calling the book a "solid historical thriller," a contributor to *Publishers Weekly* noted that the character of Jones incorporates "the best qualities of such famous detectives as Hercule Poirot and Sherlock Holmes—with a little Miss Marple thrown in."

Having found a winning character in Jones, the author continued to tell of the Welshman's exploits in a series of books that includes *Shadows of Glory, Call Each River Jordan,* and *Honor's Kingdom,* which received the Dashiell Hammett Award for literary excellence. As a a loyal confidant of President Abraham Lincoln, Jones sets out in *Shadows of Glory* to investigate the rumors of an Irish insurrection in New York and the murder of two federal undercover agents. "Parry has created a thoroughly likable and believable character and engages him here in a riveting adventure," wrote a reviewer in *Publishers Weekly.* Tom and Enid Schantz, writing in the *Denver Post,* noted that "what really sets this novel apart is the author's mastery of the language and his adroit characterizations." In *Call Each River Jordan,* Jones teams up with a Southern soldier to investigate the butchering of runaway slaves. In a review for *Publishers Weekly,* a commentator said, "It's a gripping story, told in the deceptively easygoing style that has become Parry's hallmark, a style that is if anything stronger and more assured than his previous two outings." Jones's next adventure in *Honor's Kingdom* takes place in London, where Jones is trying to prevent Great Britain from becoming involved in the Confederate cause while looking for the murderer of his predecessor, a federal agent whose body is found chewed up in a basket of eels.

"I had never wanted to write a series because I had never had a character I wanted to live with for that long," Peters told Ringle. "But Abel and the idea for the series came to me fully realized. I didn't know how many books there'd be—I think now maybe twelve—but I knew instantly that he was the one to tell the story of the war the way I wanted it told."

Using his expertise as a former intelligence and foreign service officer, Peters has also written about the future of America's military efforts and terrorism. In *Fighting for the Future: Will America Triumph?,* Peters discusses the future of military conflicts that are likely to involve social and political battles as well as the standard military confrontations. In the *Washington Monthly,* contributor Ernest Blazar noted that Peters comes to some "hasty conclusions" but that his "entertaining predictions and prescriptions serve as useful signs of how maddening it is for the world's sole remaining economic, cultural and military superpower to peer into the twenty-first century with little clue as to what's to come." Robert B. Adolph, Jr. of *Special Warfare* called Peters "the most gifted military theorist of his generation" and noted that he writes "with conviction, integrity and unusual artistry." *Beyond Terror: Strategy in a Changing World* addresses the development and future of international terrorism. Roland Green, writing in *Booklist,* called the book "useful and occasionally abrasive . . . this is good, intelligent stuff."

Peters once told *CA,* "Those who are unwilling to risk their lives usually don't have lives worth risking."

## BIOGRAPHICAL AND CRITICAL SOURCES:

*PERIODICALS*

*Armed Forces and Society: An Interdisciplinary Journal,* fall, 2000, Volker Franke, review of *Fighting for the Future: Will America Triumph?,* p.157.

*Booklist,* April 1, 1999, Joe Collins, review of *Traitor,* p. 1386; July, 2002, Roland Green, review of *Beyond Terror: Strategy in a Changing World,* p. 1804; July, 2002, Roland Green, review of *Fighting for the Future,* p. 1804.

*Denver Post,* September 3, 2000, Tom and Enid Schantz, "Union Officer's Probe of Revolt Rich with Dialect, Fact," review of *Shadows of Glory,* p. H-02.

*Library Journal,* January, 1998, review of *The Devil's Garden,* p. 144; January, 1999, Mark E. Ellis, review of *Fighting for the Future,* p. 129.

*Naval War College Review,* spring, 2001, Jan Van Tol, review of *Fighting for the Future,* p. 142.

*New Republic,* June 23, 1982.

*Newsweek,* May 22, 1989, pp. 88-89.

*New York Times Book Review,* March 22, 1981; June 18, 1989, p. 20; May 5, 1991, p. 25.

*Publishers Weekly,* February 22, 1993, review of *Flames of Heaven,* p. 80; July 3, 1995, review of *A Perfect Soldier,* p. 50; December 9, 1996, review of *Twilight of Heroes,* p. 65; December 22, 1997, review of *The Devil's Garden,* p. 38; August 16, 1999, review of *Faded Coat of Blue,* p. 59; July 31, 2000, review of *Shadows of Glory,* p. 70; September 24, 2001, review of *Call Each River Jordan,* p. 66; June 24, 2002, review of *Honor's Kingdom,* p. 40; November 4, 2002, review of *Our Simple Gifts: Civil War Christmas Tales,* p. 64.

*Record* (Bergen County, NJ), August 29, 2002, Ken Ringle (special from the *Washington Post,*), "An Immigrant's Civil War: Owen Parry's Mystery Novels Retell History from a Rare and Vivid Angle," p. F07.

*Special Warfare,* spring, 2000, Robert B. Adolph, Jr., review of *Fighting for the Future,* p. 48.

*Washington Monthly,* April, 1999, Ernest Blazar, review of *Fighting for the Future,* p. 53.

*Washington Post,* April 11, 1991, p. D3.

\*      \*      \*

## PETRO, Pamela J. 1960-

*PERSONAL:* Born June 10, 1960, in NJ; daughter of Stephen (a civil engineer) and Patricia (a secretary; maiden name, Dreher) Petro. *Ethnicity:* "European-American." *Education:* Attended Ecole du Louvre, University of Paris, 1980-81; Brown University, B.A. (magna cum laude), 1982; University of Wales, M.A., 1984. *Hobbies and other interests:* Tennis, kayaking, travel, reading, film.

*ADDRESSES: Home*—38 Glendale Ave., Providence, RI 02906. *E-mail*—10211.1121@compuserve.com.

*CAREER:* Limited Editions Club, New York, NY, editor, 1985-86; Brown University Learning Community, Providence, RI, instructor, 1993, 1994, and 1997. Rare book consultant to New York Public Library; member of Literacy Volunteers of America.

*WRITINGS:*

*The Newport and Narragansett Bay Book: A Complete Guide,* Berkshire House (Stockbridge, MA), 1994, second edition, 1998.

*Travels in an Old Tongue: Touring the World Speaking Welsh,* HarperCollins (London, England), 1997.

*Sitting Up with the Dead: A Storied Journey through the American South,* Arcade (New York, NY), 2002.

Contributor to periodicals, including *Atlantic Monthly, Islands, Women's Review of Books, Four Seasons, Endless Vacation,* and the *New York Times.*

*SIDELIGHTS:* Pamela J. Petro writes nonfiction with a strong regional focus. *The Newport and Narragansett Bay Book: A Complete Guide* is a travel book; *Travels in an Old Tongue: Touring the World Speaking Welsh* relates Petro's efforts to get at the heart of the Welsh language and its people; and *Sitting Up with the Dead: A Storied Journey through the American South* explores the colorful and vibrant oral tradition of the South.

Petro's interest in the Welsh language was sparked while attending the University of Wales. Years later, she wrote *Travels in an Old Tongue* because of her interest in perfecting her ability to speak it. Frustrated by the Welsh people's tendency to switch to English when she stumbled on their language, she sought areas and people with deep-rooted Welsh traditions. Her explorations of the language not only inspired her to write the book, but they have also made her a respected speaker on how Welsh and other cultures relate to each other from across the globe. In *Geographical Magazine* Melanie Train remarked, "Even if you have no comprehension of the language (only 18 percent of Wales' inhabitants can speak Welsh) it is worth picking up Petro's witty and unique debut novel."

*Sitting Up with the Dead* represents Petro's efforts to discover regional, cultural, and historical influences on the oral tradition in the American South. Rather than discuss the topic in broad terms, Petro wanted to offer readers a detailed view of this complex element of Southern culture and how it varies from region to region. Allen Weakland of *Booklist* commended Petro for showing that the United States still enjoys variation among regional cultures. He particularly enjoyed reading about the "eccentric and captivating" storytellers she encountered, concluding that the book as a whole is "greatly entertaining and informative." In *Library Journal,* Mary V. Welk described the book as a "delightful sampling of folklore" and an "eyeopening look at an oral art form that is still alive and well." A reviewer for *Publishers Weekly* found the book to be a valuable source of cultural information, but one that is sometimes limited by the reality that many of the stories lose something in written presentation. Still, the critic concluded, "The strength of this book lies in the fine balance between the individual voices of her storytellers and her own observations and commentary." Similarly, a *Kirkus Reviews* critic noted that while many of the stories are captivating, "not all stories are created equal, and weirdness alone seldom suffices. More than a few of the tales are lifeless (they beg to be heard, not read), and some of Petro's epiphanies never advance beyond the banal."

*BIOGRAPHICAL AND CRITICAL SOURCES:*

PERIODICALS

*Booklist,* April 15, 2002, Allen Weakland, review of *Sitting Up with the Dead: A Storied Journey through the American South,* p. 1366.
*Geographical Magazine,* September, 1997, Melanie Train, review of *Travels in an Old Tongue: Touring the World Speaking Welsh,* p. 82.
*Kirkus Reviews,* March 1, 2002, review of *Sitting Up with the Dead,* p. 314.
*Library Journal,* May 15, 2002, review of *Sitting Up with the Dead,* p. 104.
*Publishers Weekly,* April 15, 2002, review of *Sitting Up with the Dead,* p. 53.

ONLINE

*Berkshire House Publishers,* http://www.berkshirehouse.com/ (May 16, 2003).
*BBC News Online,* http://news.bbc.co.uk/ (July 14, 2003), "Welsh Culture Focus of Conference.*"

\*     \*     \*

# PHELPS, Donald (Norman) 1929-

*PERSONAL:* Born December 13, 1929, in Brooklyn, NY; son of Walter Sinclair and Anna (Bruckert) Phelps. *Education:* Brooklyn College (now Brooklyn College of the City University of New York), B.A., 1951. *Politics:* Conservative. *Religion:* Protestant.

*ADDRESSES: Home*—Cabrini Center, 542 East 5th Street, New York, NY, 10009. *Office*—c/o Author's Mail, Fantagraphics Books, 7563 Lake City Way NE, Seattle, WA, 98115.

*CAREER:* Writer, editor, publisher, and civil servant. Contributing editor, *Kulchur,* 1958-66; associate editor, *Second Coming,* 1959-64; editor and publisher of *For Now,* 1962—.

*AWARDS, HONORS:* American Book Award, 2002, for *Reading the Funnies.*

*WRITINGS:*

*Covering Ground: Essays for Now,* Croton Press (New York, NY), 1969.
(Editor, with Anne Heller) *Hearing Out James T. Farrell,* Smith (New York, NY), 1985.
*Reading the Funnies: Looking at Great Cartoonists throughout the First Half of the 20th Century,* Fantagraphics Books (Seattle, WA), 2001.

Contributor to numerous publications including *Film Content* and *Nemo.*

*WORK IN PROGRESS:* Essays on Paul Goodman and Harrison Cady (a children's illustrator and cartoonist); a screenplay on Jonathan Swift.

*SIDELIGHTS:* Although he worked for decades as a civil servant for the city of New York, Donald Phelps also wrote numerous critical essays on art, film, and popular culture for small literary magazines in his free time. By the 1960s he had developed a reputation as a well-respected critic in New York's literary world. "Donald Phelps is the sort of nonacademic critic whose crafted essays are way too pop for the scholarly journals and whose aesthetic interest are far too quirky to ever be freelance-worthy no matter how many times *Talk* magazine crawled back from the grave," wrote J. Hoberman in an article for the *Village Voice.* Nevertheless, Phelps is a prolific writer and finally received national recognition in 2002 with an American Book Award for his collection of essays called *Reading the Funnies: Looking at Great Cartoonists throughout the First Half of the 20th Century.*

Phelps's first book was a collection of essays called *Covering Ground.* Hoberman described the book as "a startling mix of pieces," talking about everything from noted author Isaac Bashevis Singer to the Supreme Court to Phelps's own teeth. Hoberman went on to note, "It is often pretty brilliant, especially the piece on the 'Muck School' of stand-up comedy." Phelps is also coeditor of *Hearing Out James T. Farrell,* which presents thirteen lectures that the novelist Farrell delivered to college students during the 1950s.

In *Reading the Funnies,* Phelps presents a series of new and reworked essays on the classic newspaper comic strips that he read during his childhood, from famous favorites such as *Dick Tracy, Little Orphan Annie, Popeye,* and *Gasoline Alley* to lesser-known cartoons and cartoonists, such as the *Thimble Theatre* cartoon and the cartoonist B. Kliban. Writing for the online film journal *Senses of Cinema,* William D. Routt commented that Phelps's writing voice is "as distinctive and pointed" as noted novelists Cormac McCarthy and Thomas Pynchon. Calling Phelps's book "really good criticism," Routt also said, "For reading Donald Phelps *Reading the Funnies* is an intensive course in how to write and think about any of the media in which words and images are mixed together." In his *Village Voice* article Hoberman noted, "*Reading the Funnies* evokes not just the comics but a whole Depression-era mentalité." The reviewer went on to wonder why no one has collected and published Phelps's many essays on movies that have appeared in *Film Comment.* Hoberman then asked, "Better yet, why don't they ask him to write some more?"

*BIOGRAPHICAL AND CRITICAL SOURCES:*

PERIODICALS

*Chicago Tribune Book World,* June 16, 1985.
*New York Times Book Review,* July 28, 1985.

ONLINE

*Senses of Cinema,* http://www.sensesofcinema.com/ (October 8, 2002), William D. Routt, review of *Reading the Funnies: Looking at Great Cartoonists throughout the First Half of the 20th Century.*
*Village Voice,* http://www.villagevoice.com/ (October 8, 2002), J. Hoberman, "Funny Boy," review of *Reading the Funnies.*

## PICKERING, David (Hugh) 1958-

*PERSONAL:* Born October 9, 1958, in Bromsgrove, Worcester, England; son of George Donald (a solicitor) and Valerie Maureen (a teacher and homemaker; maiden name, Hall) Pickering; married Janet Moyse (a teacher), July 30, 1988; children: Edward Sebastian, Charles Duncan. *Ethnicity:* "White." *Education:* St. Peter's College, Oxford, M.A. (with honors), 1980. *Politics:* "All parties and none of them." *Religion:* "Humanist." *Hobbies and other interests:* Painting, drawing, cultural activities of all kinds, family activities.

*ADDRESSES: Home and office*—25 Mitre St., Buckingham, Buckinghamshire MK18 1DW, England. *E-mail*—david@pickering96.freeserve.co.uk.

*CAREER:* Market House Books, Ltd., Aylesbury, England, assistant editor, 1984-92; freelance writer and editor of general reference books, 1992—.

*MEMBER:* English Civil War Society (sergeant of musket, 1981-83), Old Gaolers Music and Drama Society (cochair, 1990-92; chair, 1996-98, 2002—), Redditch Amateur Theatre Society, Oxford Union Society (life member).

*AWARDS, HONORS:* Festival awards for stage plays written for amateur production.

*WRITINGS:*

*EDITOR; EXCEPT AS INDICATED*

(With William Packard and Charlotte Savidge) *The Facts on File Dictionary of the Theatre,* Facts on File (New York, NY), 1988.
(With Alan Isaacs and Elizabeth Martin) *Brewer's Dictionary of Twentieth-Century Phrase and Fable,* Cassell (London, England), 1991.
*Concise English Dictionary,* Cassell (London, England), 1992.
(With others) *International Dictionary of Theatre,* St. James Press (Detroit, MI), three volumes, 1992-1996.
*Brewer's Theatrical Phrase and Fable,* Cassell (London, England), 1993.

*Dictionary of European Culture,* Cassell (London, England), 1993.

(And contributor) *Encyclopedia of Pantomime,* Gale (Detroit, MI), 1993.

(And contributor) *Brewer's Soccer Phrase and Fable,* Cassell (London, England), 1993.

*Brewer's Twentieth-Century Music,* Cassell (London, England), 1994.

*Cassell Dictionary of Superstitions,* Cassell (New York, NY), 1995.

*Cassell Dictionary of Witchcraft,* Cassell (New York, NY), 1996.

*Dictionary of Abbreviations,* Cassell (New York, NY), 1996.

*Cassell Companion to Twentieth-Century Music,* Cassell (London, England), 1997.

*Cassell Dictionary of Proverbs,* Cassell (London, England), 1997.

(Compiler, with Betty Kirkpatrick) *The Cassell Thesaurus,* Cassell (London, England), 1998.

*Cassell Dictionary and Thesaurus,* Cassell (London, England), 1999.

*A Dictionary of Folklore,* Facts on File (New York, NY), 1999.

*The Penguin Dictionary of First Names,* Penguin (London, England), 1999.

(With Rosalind Fergusson and Martin Manser) *The New Penguin Thesaurus,* Penguin (New York, NY), 2000.

*Cassell's Sports Quotations,* Cassell (London, England), 2000.

(With Jonathan Law) *The New Penguin Dictionary of the Theatre,* revised and enlarged edition, Penguin (London, England), 2001.

*Pear's Fact Finder 2002,* Penguin (London, England), 2001.

(Associate editor) *The Facts on File Dictionary of Foreign Words and Phrases,* Facts on File (New York, NY), 2002.

Contributor to approximately 170 reference books.

SIDELIGHTS: David Pickering, a "compilation maven," as a *Publishers Weekly* reviewer called him, has served as editor for more than a dozen volumes on topics ranging from the bible to music, sports to witchcraft. He is particularly noted for his contributions to books about the stage, of which the three-volume *International Dictionary of the Theatre* is an example.

In the *Cassell Dictionary of Proverbs,* a proverb is defined by Pickering as "a short pithy saying." The volume covers some 3,000 proverbs from worldwide sources. A *Booklist* reviewer that noted Pickering's "entertaining and informative writing style makes this easy-to-use dictionary a pleasant experience." The 2000 publication *A Dictionary of Folklore* explores "a wide range of subjects, form the mythology of real and magic creatures to rituals," a *Booklist* critic noted, adding that some "modern touches" of contemporary folklorists "would have been helpful." Katherine Kaigler-Koenig of *Library Journal* pointed to the book's inclusion of "herbal remedies" and folklore "associated with selected trees, plants, birds, and animals."

The wit and wisdom of sports figures make up the basis for Pickering's *Cassell's Sports Quotations.* A *Publishers Weekly* reviewer noted that the Englishman Pickering quotes extensively from the "fanatical views" of international names, including soccer's Bill Shankly, who, according to Pickering, says his game is more than merely "a matter of life and death."

BIOGRAPHICAL AND CRITICAL SOURCES:

BOOKS

*Cassell's Sports Quotations,* Cassell (London, England), 2000.

PERIODICALS

*American Reference Books Annual,* 2001, review of *Cassell's Sports Quotations,* p. 358, and review of *A Dictionary of Folklore,* p. 545.

*Booklist,* March 15, 1996, review of *International Dictionary of the Theatre,* p. 1315; February 1, 1998, review of *Cassell Dictionary of Proverbs,* p. 934; May 15, 2000, review of *A Dictionary of Folklore,* p. 1780, and Dona Helmer, review of *Cassell Dictionary of Proverbs,* p. 1772.

*Choice,* May, 1996, review of *International Dictionary of the Theatre,* p. 1450.

*Library Journal,* July, 1996, review of *International Dictionary of the Theatre,* p. 104; March 1, 1999, review of *Cassell Companion to Twentieth-Century Music,* p. 76; June 1, 2000, Katherine Kaigler-Koenig, review of *A Dictionary of Folklore,* p. 116.

*Publishers Weekly,* February 26, 2001, "Let the Games Begin," p. 79.

*Reference and Research Book News,* July, 1996, review of *Dictionary of Abbreviations,* p. 58.

*School Librarian,* August, 1997, review of *Bible Questions and Answers,* p. 153.

*Teaching Music,* August, 1995, review of *Brewer's Twentieth-Century Music,* p. 49.

*Times Educational Supplement,* April 14, 1989, review of *The Facts on File Dictionary of the Theatre,* p. B15.

*Times Literary Supplement,* August 23 1996, review of *Dictionary of Superstitions,* p. 33.

* * *

**PILKEY, Dav 1966-**
  **(Sue Denim)**

*PERSONAL:* First name is pronounced "dave"; born March 4, 1966, in Cleveland, OH; son of David M. (a sales manager) and Barbara (an organist; maiden name, Pembridge) Pilkey. *Education:* Kent State University. A.A., 1987.

*ADDRESSES: Home*—Eugene, OR. *Agent*—Amy Berkower, Writer's House, 21 West 26th St., New York, NY, 10010.

*CAREER:* Freelance writer and illustrator, 1986—.

*AWARDS, HONORS:* Cuffie Award for Funniest Book of the Year, *Publishers Weekly,* for *The Adventures of Captain Underpants;* Kent State University, National Written and Illustrated By. . . Award; California Young Readers Medal, for *Dog Breath;* Children's Choice Awards, International Reading Association-Children's Book Council, for "Dumb Bunnies" books; Caldecott Medal Honor Book, American Library Association, 1997, for *The Paperboy.*

*WRITINGS:*

CHILDREN'S BOOKS; SELF-ILLUSTRATED

*World War Won,* Landmark Editions (Kansas City, MO), 1987.

*'Twas the Night before Thanksgiving,* Orchard Books (New York, NY), 1990.

*Dav Pilkey*

*When Cats Dream,* Orchard Books (New York, NY), 1992.

*Kat Kong: Starring Flash, Rabies, and Dwayne and Introducing Blueberry As the Monster,* Harcourt (San Diego, CA), 1993.

*Dogzilla: Starring Flash, Rabies, Dwayne, and Introducing Leia As the Monster,* Harcourt (San Diego, CA), 1993.

(Under pseudonym Sue Denim) *The Dumb Bunnies,* Blue Sky Press (New York, NY), 1994.

*Dog Breath!: The Horrible Terrible Trouble with Hally Tosis,* Blue Sky Press (New York, NY), 1994.

(Under pseudonym Sue Denim) *The Dumb Bunnies' Easter,* Blue Sky Press (New York, NY), 1995.

*The Hallo-Wiener,* Blue Sky Press (New York, NY), 1995.

*The Moonglow Roll-o-Rama,* Orchard Books (New York, NY), 1995.

(Under pseudonym Sue Denim) *Make Way for Dumb Bunnies,* Blue Sky Press (New York, NY), 1996.

*God Bless the Gargoyles,* Harcourt (San Diego, CA), 1996.

*The Paperboy,* Orchard Books (New York, NY), 1996.

*The Silly Gooses,* Blue Sky Press (New York, NY), 1997.

(Under pseudonym Sue Denim) *The Dumb Bunnies Go to the Zoo,* Blue Sky Press (New York, NY), 1997.

*The Silly Gooses Build a House,* Blue Sky Press (New York, NY), 1998.

*'Twas the Night before Christmas Two: The Wrath of Mrs. Claus,* Blue Sky Press (New York, NY), 1998.

*The Adventures of Super Diaper Baby: The First Graphic Novel by George Beard and Harold Hutchkins,* Blue Sky Press (New York, NY), 2002.

*"DRAGON" SERIES; SELF-ILLUSTRATED*

*A Friend for Dragon,* Orchard Books (New York, NY), 1991.

*Dragon Gets By,* Orchard Books (New York, NY), 1991.

*Dragon's Merry Christmas,* Orchard Books (New York, NY), 1991.

*Dragon's Fat Cat,* Orchard Books (New York, NY), 1992.

*Dragon's Halloween,* Orchard Books (New York, NY), 1993.

*"CAPTAIN UNDERPANTS" SERIES; SELF-ILLUSTRATED*

*The Adventures of Captain Underpants,* Blue Sky Press (New York, NY), 1997.

*Captain Underpants and the Attack of the Talking Toilets,* Blue Sky Press (New York, NY), 1999.

*Captain Underpants and the Invasion of the Incredibly Naughty Cafeteria Ladies from Outer Space,* Blue Sky Press (New York, NY), 1999.

*Captain Underpants and the Perilous Plot of Professor Poopypants,* Blue Sky Press (New York, NY), 2000.

*Captain Underpants and the Wrath of the Wicked Wedgie Woman,* Blue Sky Press (New York, NY), 2001.

*Captain Underpants and the Big, Bad Battle of the Bionic Booger Boy, Part 1: The Night of the Nasty Nostril Nuggets,* Blue Sky Press (New York, NY), 2003.

*Captain Underpants and the Big, Bad Battle of the Bionic Booger Boy, Part 2: Revenge of the Ridiculous Robo-boogers,* Blue Sky Press (New York, NY), 2003.

*"BIG DOG AND LITTLE DOG" SERIES; SELF-ILLUSTRATED*

*Big Dog and Little Dog,* Harcourt (San Diego, CA), 1997.

*Big Dog and Little Dog Getting in Trouble,* Harcourt (San Diego, CA), 1997.

*Big Dog and Little Dog Going for a Walk,* Harcourt (San Diego, CA), 1997.

*Big Dog and Little Dog Wearing Sweaters,* Harcourt (San Diego, CA), 1998.

*Big Dog and Little Dog Guarding the Picnic,* Harcourt (San Diego, CA), 1998.

*Big Dog and Little Dog Making a Mistake,* Harcourt (San Diego, CA), 1999.

*The Complete Adventures of Big Dog and Little Dog,,* Harcourt (San Diego, CA), 2003.

*"RICKY RICOTTA" SERIES; ILLUSTRATED BY MARTIN ONTIVEROS*

*Ricky Ricotta's Mighty Robot: An Epic Novel,* Blue Sky Press (New York, NY), 2000.

*Ricky Ricotta's Giant Robot vs. the Mutant Mosquitos from Mercury: The Second Robot Adventure Novel,* Blue Sky Press (New York, NY), 2000.

*Ricky Ricotta's Giant Robot vs. the Voodoo Vultures from Venus: The Third Adventure Novel,* Blue Sky Press (New York, NY), 2001.

*Ricky Ricotta's Mighty Robot vs. the Mecha-Monkeys from Mars,* Blue Sky Press (New York, NY), 2002.

*Ricky Ricotta's Mighty Robot vs. the Jurassic Jackrabbits from Jupiter: The Fifth Robot Adventure Novel,* Blue Sky Press (New York, NY), 2002.

*Ricky Ricotta's Mighty Robot vs. Stupid Stinkbugs from Saturn,* Blue Sky Press (New York, NY), 2003.

*ILLUSTRATOR*

Adolph J. Moser, *Don't Pop Your Cork on Mondays!: The Children's Anti-Stress Book,* Landmark Editions (Kansas City, MO), 1988.

Jerry Segal, *The Place Where Nobody Stopped,* Orchard Books (New York, NY), 1991.

Angela Johnson, *Julius,* Orchard Books (New York, NY), 1993.

*SIDELIGHTS:* A highly regarded and popular author and illustrator of children's books, Dav Pilkey combines lowbrow humor and broad parodies with a subtle moral often thrown into the mix. Among his popular books are those from the "Dragon," "Captain Underpants," and "Big Dog and Little Dog" series. His individual creations have also garnered high praise, including *The Paperboy,* which was named a Caldecott Medal Honor Book.

Pilkey's irreverent and antiauthoritarian outlook on life began when he was in grade school, where his fellow students enjoyed his antics as a class clown and his teachers watched him closely, believing that he needed a serious attitude adjustment. The fidgety and disruptive Pilkey was eventually diagnosed with attention deficit disorder. The diagnosis, however, did little to change Pilkey's humorous take on life or his penchant for drawing and making up stories. Often his teachers would send him out to the hallway, where he even had a desk to sit at and draw. One of his creations would eventually be featured in his immensely popular future series of children's books about "Captain Underpants." In an interview in *Time* magazine, Pilkey commented on the appeal of the character: "I think kids feel trapped just by being kids. You can't do anything when you're a kid. Adults are always trying to spoil your fun and making you follow dumb orders. So, I think kids are drawn to these books because the main characters, George and Harold, get away with so much. They're always having great adventures, and the adults can't stop them. It's great escapism."

Pilkey's talents were discovered by the publishing industry early on when, as an art student at Kent State University, he won the National Written and Illustrated By . . . Award for students. Soon he found himself on a plane to Kansas City, Missouri, to meet the publishers of Landmark Editions, which would publish his prize-winning book *World War Won.* "It was the most exciting time in my life," Pilkey recalled on his personal Web site. "I'll never forget getting off the plane in Kansas City and meeting my new publisher for the first time. I tried to act normal, but I was so excited. It took every bit of self-control I had not to scream, jump up and down, and laugh hysterically. . . . I was going to be an author!"

Since then, Pilkey has illustrated and/or written approximately fifty books for children. Commenting on Pilkey in *Something about the Author,* contributor Gerard J. Senick noted that Pilkey "favors straightforward

but lively narratives that are filled with wordplay" and that his artwork ranges "from campy cartoons in bold fluorescent colors to sumptuous, detailed paintings in muted tones." In his "Dragon" series, Pilkey tells of a lovable but zany dragon and his many adventures. For example, in *Dragon Gets By,* nothing turns out right for Dragon, like his breakfast disaster of reading the egg and frying the paper. Writing in *Publishers Weekly,* reviewers Elizabeth Devereaux and Kit Alderdice called the series hero "affability incarnate."

Pilkey's popular "Captain Underpants" series probably best reveals the irreverent psyche of young Pilkey back in grade school, where he first created the character. The book features the kind of bathroom humor that appeals to young readers as the hero runs around in his underpants having various adventures from run-ins with the wicked school principal to alien cafeteria ladies who serve the schoolchildren lunches that turn them into zombie-like nerds. The books are interactive, and readers can flip the pages to see moving characters. There are also lessons on drawing cartoons. The books have also caused concern among some adults and were even banned from an elementary school in Connecticut. A writer for the *Dallas Morning News* reported the principal's explanation for banning the books: "The boys started getting whooped up at Captain Underpants, saying things like 'You're in your underpants.' The book was beginning to take on a life of its own." Nevertheless, the popularity of the series has been widespread, with more than 12.5 million "Captain Underpants" books in print. Writing in *Publishers Weekly,* a reviewer noted, "Those with a limited tolerance for the silly need not apply to the Captain Underpants fan club, yet its legion members will plunge happily into his latest bumbling adventure."

Pilkey's award-winning book *The Paperboy* presents a more sedate take on life than many of his more boisterous stories and heroes. In it, Pilkey tells the tale of a young boy who delivers papers every morning with his trusty dog by his side. The text and illustrations provide details about the process of delivering papers combined with the tale of how a boy and his dog live their lives. Mary M. Burns of *Horn Book* commented on Pilkey's "lyrical combination of text and pictures" as a "meditative evocation of the extraordinary aspects of ordinary living." Carolyn Phelan, writing in *Booklist,* noted that "the book's acrylic paintings include beautifully composed landscapes and interiors, ending with a Chagall-like dream scene on the last page."

Another of Pilkey's creations is Ricky Ricotta, a timid mouse who teams up with a robot to battle various forces of evil like vultures from the planet Venus who use a voodoo ray to hypnotize people through their televisions or mechanized monkeys from Mars who plan to swarm over the earth. In an unusual move for Pilkey, the books, which also feature "Flip-o-Rama" animation and cartoon lessons, are illustrated by Martin Ontiveros instead of Pilkey himself. Commenting in an interview on the *Scholastic* Web site, Pilkey said that he wanted to work with another illustrator because, even though he knew in his head what the illustrations should look like, he believed he needed a more suitable artist to do the illustrations. "My line-work is too loose, and I have very little experience with action scenes," said Pilkey. He chose Ontiveros for the work because he "thought Martin's style would be perfect" for the series. The collaboration has garnered the praise of many critics. Writing a review for the *School Library Journal,* Anne Connor noted, "In an accessible, highly illustrated format, Pilkey writes an adventure story with great appeal to lonely little guys everywhere."

Pilkey once commented to CA: "When I really got serious about writing children's books, I began reading everything I could by my favorite writers, Arnold Lobel, Cynthia Rylant, James Marshall, and Harry Allard. I read *Frog and Toad, Henry and Mudge, George and Martha,* and *The Stupids* over and over again, until I started to pick up rhythms and recognize patterns. Soon I began to see what really *worked* in these books—what made them great pieces of literature.

"One of my biggest inspirations as an illustrator is the drawings of children. Children often send me pictures that they've drawn, and I'm always amazed at the way they present shape and color. Children are natural impressionists. They're not afraid to make their trees purple and yellow, and it's okay if the sky is green with red stripes. A horse can be as tall as a building with seven fingers on each hoof—when children are drawing, anything goes! Of course you know that one day an art teacher is going to grab a hold of these kids and turn them all into accountants, but while they are still fresh and naive, children can create some of the liveliest and most beautiful art there is."

BIOGRAPHICAL AND CRITICAL SOURCES:

*BOOKS*

*Children's Literature Review,* Volume 48, Gale (Detroit, MI), 1998.
*Something about the Author,* Volume 115, Gale (Detroit, MI), 2000.

*PERIODICALS*

*Booklist,* March 1, 1996, Carolyn Phelan, review of *The Paperboy.*
*Dallas Morning News,* April 4, 2000, p. 1C.
*Horn Book,* July-August, 1996, Mary M. Burns, review of *The Paperboy.*
*Publishers Weekly,* September 20, 1993, Elizabeth Devereaux and Kit Alderdice, review of *Dragon's Halloween;* July 19, 1999, review of *Captain Underpants and the Invasion of the Incredibly Naughty Cafeteria Ladies from Outer Space,* p. 195.
*School Library Journal,* April, 2000, Anne Connor, review of *Ricky Ricotta's Giant Robot.*
*Time,* August 27, 2001, "A Hero In Briefs," brief interview with Dav Pilkey.

*ONLINE*

*BookPage,* http://www.bookpage.com/ (October 8, 2002), "Meet the Author: Dav Pilkey."
*Dav Pilkey Home Page,* http://www.pilkey.com/ (October 8, 2002).
*Scholastic,* http://www.scholastic.com/ (October 8, 2002), "Q & A with Dav Pilkey.*"

\*          \*          \*

## PRITCHARD, Melissa 1948-

*PERSONAL:* Born December 12, 1948, in San Mateo, CA; daughter of Clarence John (a comptroller) and Helen Lorraine (a homemaker and volunteer worker; maiden name, Reilly) Brown; married Daniel Hachez, June 30, 1973 (divorced, 1976); married Mark Pritchard (an industrial filmmaker), May 21, 1977

*Melissa Pritchard*

(divorced, 1989); children: (second marriage) Noelle, Caitlin. *Ethnicity:* "Caucasian." *Education:* University of California, Santa Barbara, B.A. (comparative religions), 1970; graduate study at University of New Mexico, 1975-76, and Western Washington University, 1976-77; Vermont College, M.F.A., 1995. *Politics:* Democrat. *Religion:* Roman Catholic. *Hobbies and other interests:* Nia, dance form.

*ADDRESSES: Home*—332 East La Diosa Dr., Tempe, AZ 85282. *Office*—Department of English, Arizona State University, P.O. Box 870302, Tempe, AZ 85287-0302; fax: 480-965-3451. *Agent*—Joy Harris, Joy Harris Literary Agency, 156 Fifth Avenue, New York, NY 10010. *E-mail*—melissap@asu.edu.

*CAREER:* Santa Fe Community College, Santa Fe, NM, instructor in creative writing, 1990, 1991; Arizona State University, Tempe, visiting assistant professor of creative writing, 1992-94, assistant professor of English and women's studies, 1994—; currently associate professor and director of M.F.A. program in creative writing; Spalding University, Louisville, KY, fac-ulty, M.F.A. program in creative writing. Taos Children's Theater, codirector and scriptwriter, 1990-91; Santa Fe Literacy Center, coordinator, 1991; Native American Circle, Enid, OK, member of board of directors, 1996—; Taos Art School, member of board of directors, 1996—. Kentucky Women Writers' Conference, guest faculty, 1990-91; Santa Fe Writers' Conference, director, 1991, 1992; New Mexico State University, guest faculty at Writers' Conference, 1992; Writer's Voice, writer in residence, 1996; instructor at fiction workshops, including presentations at Vermont College, Arizona State University's annual creative writing conference, Taos Art School, Yavapai College, Taos Institute of the Arts, University of Arizona, and Dickinson College; judge for writing awards; book reviewers; gives readings from her works.

*MEMBER:* Associated Writing Programs, Authors Guild, Authors League of America.

*AWARDS, HONORS:* Fiction awards, Illinois Arts Council, 1980, for "The Housekeeper," 1981, for "A Dying Man," 1983, for "La Bete: A Figure Study," 1988, for "Taking Hold of Renee"; fellowship, National Endowment for the Arts, 1982; James D. Phelan Award, San Francisco Foundation, 1982, for a collection of twelve stories; outstanding writer citation, Pushcart Prize competition, 1983, for "Companions"; International PEN Syndicated Fiction Project winner, 1985, for "With Wings Cross Water"; fellowship, Illinois Arts Council, 1986; Flannery O'Connor Short Fiction Award, University of Georgia Press, 1987, and Carl Sandburg Literary Arts Award for fiction, Friends of Chicago Public Library, 1988, James Phelan Award, and honorary citation, PEN/Nelson Algren Award, all for *Spirit Seizures;* Great Lakes Colleges New Writers honorable mention, 1988; outstanding writer citation, Pushcart Prizes XVI, 1992, for "El Ojito del Muerto"; Claudia Ortese Memorial Lecture Prize in North American Literature, University of Florence, 1995; Pushcart Prize, 1996, for story "The Instinct for Bliss"; Janet Heidinger Kafka Prize, 1996, for collection *The Instinct for Bliss;* fellowship, National Endowment for the Arts; writer-in-residence fellowship, Writers' Voice YMCA; Howard Foundation fellowship, Brown University, 1999; Barnes and Noble Discover Great New Writers selection, 1999, for *Selene of the Spirits;* O. Henry Award, 2000, for "Salve Regina"; Pushcart Prize, 2001, for "Funktionslust"; NPR's summer reading list, 2002, for *Disappearing Ingenue.*

*WRITINGS:*

*Spirit Seizures* (stories), University of Georgia Press (Athens, GA), 1987.

(Editor, with Diane Williams and Anne Brashler) *The American Story: Best of Story Quarterly,* Cane Hill Press (New York, NY), 1990.

*Phoenix* (novel), Cane Hill Press (New York, NY), 1991.

*The Instinct for Bliss* (short stories), Zoland Books (Cambridge, MA), 1995.

*Selene of the Spirits,* G. Braziller (New York, NY), 1998.

*Disappearing Ingenue: The Misadventures of Eleanor Stoddard,* Doubleday (New York, NY), 2002.

Work represented in numerous textbooks and anthologies, including *O. Henry Prize Stories,* 1984; *Prize Stories 2000: The O. Henry Awards; The Literary Ghost: Great Contemporary Ghost Stories,* Atlantic Monthly Press, 1991; *Three Genres: Fiction, Poetry, and Drama,* Prentice-Hall (Englewood Cliffs, NJ), 1992; *The Flannery O'Connor Award: Selected Stories,* University of Georgia Press, 1992; *Walking the Twilight: Women Writers of the Southwest,* Northland Publishing (Menomonie, WI), 1993; *Pushcart Prize XX: Best of the Small Presses,* Pushcart Press (Wainscott, NY), 1995; *Mothers: Twenty Stories of Contemporary Motherhood,* North Point Press (Berkeley, CA), 1996; *American Gothic Tales,* edited by Joyce Carol Oates, Dutton (New York, NY), 1996; and *Canadian Fiction Anthology,* 1997. Contributor of stories, essays, and reviews to periodicals, including *Indiana Review, Southern Review, Epoch, Ontario Review, Prairie Schooner, American Voice, Paris Review, Southern Review, Story, Kenyon Review, Blackbird,* and *Washington Square. Story Quarterly,* coeditor, 1984-88, advisory editor, 1988—; guest editor, *Taos Review,* 1992.

*WORK IN PROGRESS: Late Bloomer,* a novel for Doubleday, forthcoming March, 2004.

*SIDELIGHTS:* Melissa Pritchard is an award-winning short story writer and novelist. In her novel *Selene of the Spirits* she draws upon her research into the Victorian-era obsession with contacting the spirit world in a story that is loosely based upon the life of Florence Cook, a famous British medium of the late nine-

teenth century. Teenager Selene Cook discovers her ability to contact the spirit world while still a schoolgirl; she is soon taken up by a wealthy philanthropist and introduced to established spiritualists of the day, who teach her how to augment her natural abilities in performances that offer audiences what they expect. This kind of trickery, of course, leads to Selene's exposure as a fraud. When she challenges Sir William Herapath, an important scientist, to either prove her a fake or validate her authenticity, the two fall in love. Their romance, however, leads to the downfall of both, for he is already married and twice her age. "Pritchard enlivens her tale with characters who, for all their interest in the other world, are rich and complex human beings," remarked Caroline M. Hallsworth in *Library Journal.* Other reviewers likewise praised Pritchard's well-rounded characters, both major and minor, and remarked on her skillful blend of a melodramatic plot with intriguing theses on the role of women in Victorian society, as well as on the war that was beginning to rage between science and religion. "Meticulous research, elegant style and genial acceptance of human nature make . . . Pritchard a compelling narrator," wrote a *Publishers Weekly* critic.

Pritchard's next novel, *Disappearing Ingenue: The Misadventures of Eleanor Stoddard,* is a collection of eight interconnected stories about a person who is always striving to be good, and always failing. From a serious sixth-grader who sets herself the task of reading about the Holocaust over the summer but who willingly becomes the dupe of her compulsive liar of a best friend, to her first cotillion, where Eleanor retreats into the bathroom to say the rosary but fails to save her friend from being seduced, to a frustrating marriage in which her daughters' Nancy Drew novels inspire her investigations into her husband's infidelity, Pritchard's protagonist is the picture of good intentions gone awry. "With each story the collection gains momentum," declared a contributor to *Publishers Weekly.* The critic particularly praised the final two episodes, including "Funktionslust," which won the Pushcart Prize, and ends the volume on a note of surreal high adventure, with Eleanor in the jungles of Central America accompanied by a rescued primate.

Pritchard once told *CA:* "Until I was thirty years old, I did not attempt, with any great commitment, to write fiction. I had been an actress, a waitress, a drama teacher, a secretary, a plant nursery worker, an organic gardener, a house cleaner . . . and still am a mother. I am fascinated by mythology and science, by things of the physical world, by things of the spirit. Writing fiction has become my center as well as my path outward."

*BIOGRAPHICAL AND CRITICAL SOURCES:*

*PERIODICALS*

*Booklist,* November 15, 1998, Nancy Pearl, review of *Selene of the Spirits,* p. 568.

*Glimmer Train,* summer, 2003, Leslie A. Wooten, interview with Melissa Pritchard.

*Kirkus Reviews,* September 15, 1998, review of *Selene of the Spirits,* p. 1320.

*Library Journal,* October 1, 1998, Caroline M. Hallsworth, review of *Selene of the Spirits,* p. 135.

*Metro* (Phoenix, AZ), June/July, 2003, interview with Melissa Pritchard.

*New York Times Book Review,* November 22, 1987; January 10, 1999, Nora Krug, review of *Selene of the Spirits,* p. 16.

*Publishers Weekly,* September 21, 1998, review of *Selene of the Spirits,* p. 73; March 25, 2002, review of *Disappearing Ingenue: The Misadventures of Eleanor Stoddard,* p. 38.

*San Francisco Review of Books,* September, 1995.

*Story Quarterly,* fall, 1997.

*World & I,* March, 1999, review of *Selene of the Spirits,* p. 273.

*ONLINE*

*Arizona State University Web Site,* http://www.asu.edu/ (January 23, 2003).

*Rambles: A Cultural Arts Magazine,* http://www.rambles.net/ (June 14, 2002), Donna Scanlon, review of *Selene of the Spirits.*

*Spalding University Web Site,* http://www.spalding.edu/ (April 9, 2003).

# R

## REDSHAW, Peggy A(nn) 1948-

*PERSONAL:* Born September 4, 1948, in Beardstown, IL; daughter of Francis B. and Margaret (Lee) Redshaw; married Jerry Bryan Lincecum (a professor of English), September 28, 1985. *Education:* Quincy University, B.S. (cum laude), 1970; Illinois State University, Ph.D., 1974. *Hobbies and other interests:* Photography, travel.

*ADDRESSES: Home*—608 North Cleveland, Sherman, TX 75090. *Office*—Austin College, 900 North Grand Ave., Sherman, TX 75090; fax: 903-813-2420. *E-mail*—predshaw@austincollege.edu.

*CAREER:* St. Louis University, St. Louis, MO, postdoctoral fellow at Medical School, 1974-77; Wilson College, Chambersburg, PA, assistant professor of biology, 1977-79; Austin College, Sherman, TX, began as assistant professor, became professor of biology, 1979—. Council on Undergraduate Research, member. Telling Our Stories (autobiography writing project), codirector, 1990—.

*MEMBER:* American Society for Microbiology, American Association for the Advancement of Science, Association of Biology Laboratory Educators.

*AWARDS, HONORS:* Miss Ima Hogg Historical Achievement Award, Center for American History, University of Texas—Austin, and Ottis Lock Award, East Texas Historical Association, both 1998, for *Science on the Texas Frontier: The Observations of Dr. Gideon Lincecum.*

*WRITINGS:*

(With Edward Hake Phillips and husband, Jerry Bryan Lincecum) *Science on the Texas Frontier: The Observations of Dr. Gideon Lincecum,* Texas A & M University Press (College Station, TX), 1997.

(Coeditor) *Gideon Lincecum's Sword: Civil War Letters from the Texas Home Front,* University of North Texas Press (Denton, TX), 2001.

\*     \*     \*

## REICH, Steve 1936-

*PERSONAL:* Born October 3, 1936, in New York, NY; son of Leonard Reich (an attorney) and June (Sillman) Carroll (a singer and lyricist); married second wife Beryl Korot (an artist), 1976; children: two sons. *Education:* Cornell University, B.A. (with honors), 1957; graduate study, Juilliard School of Music, 1958-61; Mills College, M.A., 1963; additional graduate study, University of Ghana, 1970, and American Society for Eastern Arts, summers, 1973-74. *Religion:* Jewish.

*ADDRESSES: Home*—16 Warren St., New York, NY 10007. *Office*—Boosey & Hawkes, Inc., East 21st St. New York, NY 10010-6212. *Agent*—Lynn Garon Management, 1199 Park Ave., New York, NY 10028.

*CAREER:* Composer and performer in San Francisco, CA, 1963-65; composer and performer in his own music ensemble in New York, NY, 1965—. Has performed at Carnegie Hall, Town Hall, and Museum of Modern Art. Collaborated on music and dance concerts throughout Europe and at New York University, 1972-73.

*AWARDS, HONORS:* National Endowment for the Arts grant, 1974; New York State Council on the Arts grant, 1974; Rockefeller Foundation grants, 1975, 1979, and 1981; Guggenheim fellow, 1978; Koussevitzky International Recording Award, 1981; Grammy Awards, 1989, for best contemporary composition for *Different Trains,* and 1998, for *Music for 18 Musicians;* William Schuman Award, 2000, from Columbia University's School of the Arts; *Village Voice* called Reich "America's greatest living composer"; Pulitzer Prize for music nomination, 2003, for *Three Tales.*

*WRITINGS:*

*Writings about Music* (essays), New York University Press, 1974, enlarged French translation published as *Ecrits et entretiens sur la musique,* Bourgois, 1981.

*Eight Lines* (octet; sound recording), Boosey & Hawkes, 1980.

*Music for a Large Ensemble* (sound recording), Warner Brothers, 1980.

*Pendulum Music* (sound recording), Universal Edition, 1980.

*Tehillim* (sound recording), Warner Brothers, 1982.

*Sextet for Percussion and Keyboards, 1984* (sound recording), Boosey & Hawkes, 1984.

*The Desert Music* (sound recording), Nonesuch, 1985.

*New York Counterpoint* (sound recording), Hendon Music, 1985.

*Steve Reich, Composer* (sound recording), National Public Radio, 1986.

*Three Movements for Orchestra* (sound recording), Boosey & Hawkes, 1986.

*Different Trains; and, Electric Counterpoint* (sound recording), Elektra/Asylum/Nonesuch Records, 1989.

*New York Counterpoint: For Clarinet and Tape or Clarinet Ensemble* (sound recording), Boosey & Hawkes, 1986.

*The Four Sections Music for Mallet Instruments, Voices and Organ* (sound recording), Elektra Nonesuch, 1990.

*Six Pianos* (sound recording), Boosey & Hawkes, 1992.

*The Cave* (sound recording), Boosey & Hawkes, 1993.

(With Michael Tenzer) *Gamelan Gong Kebyar: The Art of Twentieth-Century Balinese Music,* University of Chicago Press (Chicago, IL), 2000.

*Writings on Music, 1965-2000,* edited by Paul Hillier, Oxford University Press (New York, NY), 2002.

Also author of various recorded compositions, including "Come Out," Odyssey, 1967; "It's Gonna Rain" and "Violin Phase," Columbia Records, 1969; "Four Organs," Angel Records, 1973; "Drumming," "Six Pianos," and "Music for Mallet Instruments, Voices, and Organ," Deutsche Grammophon, 1974; "Music for Eighteen Musicians," ECM Records, 1978; "Octet," "Music for a Large Ensemble," and "Violin Phase," ECM Records, 1980; and "Tehillim," ECM Records, 1982. Author of other compositions, including "Phase Patterns," "Clapping Music," "Music for Pieces of Wood," and "Variations for Winds, Strings and Keyboards." Composer of the video opera *Three Tales,* 2002, with video artist Beryl Korot.

*SIDELIGHTS:* Described by *Newsweek's* Annalyn Swan as one of the leading composers of "stripped-down, hypnotically repetitive, so-called 'minimal' music," Steve Reich is committed to making an original and personally satisfying statement as he blends new musical forms with old. Explained Reich: "I didn't become a composer so that someone would pat me on the back and say, 'That's a pretty good twelve-tone piece, almost as good as third-rate Berio or Stockhausen,' which I think can be said of much serial music in America. Instead, I opted to do what came naturally. Basically I was after music with a strong, clear pulse, a clear tonal center, and that was clearly mine. . . . The listener I'm most concerned with is myself. I feel obliged to do something that's going to engage me."

Reich's early, wide-ranging musical interests guided his development of what has become known as "phase" music, a style that experiments electronically with tape loops and gradual shifting of sounds. Although phase music is performed with Western instruments and focuses on western tonality, it arose from Reich's studies of African rhythms in the early 1960s. He formed the ensemble Steve Reich and Musicians to perform the music, a necessity in the conservative classical community of the 1960s when other musicians were wary of such untested experimentation.

The ensemble attracted controversy from their very first performance at Carnegie Hall, but by the mid-1970s they had cultivated a devoted following. By the early 1970s, however, Reich was through experimenting with phase music, and set about creating yet another new genre—pulse music—which was launched with the premiere of *Music for 18 Musicians* in 1976. The piece concentrated on a cycle of eleven chords and allowed the musicians the latitude to change chords at will. Many critics cite the work as one of the most important compositions of the 1970s. In the late 1980s, Reich experimented with human speech in his works, most notably with *Different Trains,* in which the taped voices of Holocaust survivors were incorporated electronically with live musicians.

Reich typically borrows elements from a wide variety of styles and composers. Bach and Stravinsky, for example, are among his more traditional sources of inspiration. As a teenager, however, he developed an interest in jazz, and later, in his twenties, he was intrigued by Terry Riley's innovative and repetitively patterned composition "In C." Reich's exposure to new forms of music continued throughout the 1970s. Early in the decade, he journeyed to Ghana to study with a master drummer of the Ewe tribe at the Institute of African Studies; in subsequent years, he received instruction in the cantillation (chanting) of Hebrew scripture and in the specialized tuned percussion music known as Balinese Gamelan Semar Pegulingan.

These diverse kinds of music have all made their mark on Reich's work, often to such an extent that, as Swan pointed out, "on first hearing, [his] music can seem maddeningly mindless and static to ears steeped in the classical and romantic traditions. . . . The initial effect is of a floating, somewhat amorphous cloud of sound. Gradually, however, you begin to distinguish the subtly varied patterns within the whole. . . . Like Eastern music, Reich's compositions use the most sophisticated of means to achieve the simplest of surfaces. They are at once exhilarating, because of the bright intensity of his timbres and musical colors, and tranquil, because of their seeming suspension in time."

After praising Reich's "lively percussion patterns," "gentle sustained chords," and "light, quick notes," Gregory Sandow declared in a *Village Voice* article that "surely Steve Reich is one of the best composers around. I can't agree with most of the critical remarks about him. I don't think his way of writing turns mu-

sicians into robots fit only to execute mechanical repeating patterns; not everyone might want to play his music, but the people who do play it sound inspired and at times even exalted. I don't worry that his pieces are too much like their African and Balinese influences or else not rhythmically complicated enough to be worthy of them; Reich is not writing African or Balinese music. To my ear—though he uses sounds taken from music he likes, just as any composer would, and for that matter is original in countless ways of his own—he is a *western* composer, working squarely in the tradition of western classical music."

"Reich's work has been called 'minimal music,'" observed the *New Yorker*'s Andrew Porter. "It is a label that can fairly be attached to some of his earlier compositions, . . . which are based on the rigorous working out of a single idea. It does not apply to his increasingly thoughtful and elaborately eloquent later pieces. The reflection that Beethoven and Reich seem to have worked at some of the same 'problems' can calm the uneasiness voiced [by those who feel the composer relies too heavily on simple harmonies and a steady beat]. His music has a joyful, very attractive surface; it may be that some of his admirers do not get beyond it. . . . But there is substance beneath." Concluded Swan: "In the 1960s he was all but unheard of outside Manhattan's Soho district. In the '70s he was often dismissed as little more than a cult figure. But in the '80s Steve Reich . . . is emerging as one of the central influences in experimental music."

Reich has published two collections of his essays on music, including *Writings on Music, 1965-2000,* which presents sixty-four short works ranging from his classic 1968 essay "Music as a Gradual Process" to one-paragraph reminiscences. In "Music As a Gradual Process," which became one of the seminal essays on minimalist music, Reich compares the idea of gradual—or phase—music to "pulling back a swing, releasing it and observing it gradually come to rest." Other essays in the collection profile some of his favorite composers, past and present, including John Cage and Kurt Weill, his changing influences from the 1960s through the end of the century, and even several interviews and photographs from his private collection. Reich also writes about both Balinese Gamelan and Hebrew cantillation, two forms of music on which he has based some of his compositions. Even though Reich's essays are aimed at readers knowledgeable about music, "most of the writing comes across as extemporaneous rather than studied," said David Valencia in *Library Journal.*

Several orchestras in the United States and abroad have performed Reich's compositions, including the Boston Symphony Orchestra, the San Francisco Symphony, the South German Radio Symphony, and the New York Philharmonic. He has also collaborated with his wife, Beryl Korot, in creating several video operas, including *Three Tales* and *The Cave. The Cave* incorporates film footage of Israelis, Palestinians, and Americans along with chants of verses from the Bible and the Koran. K. Robert Schwartz of *Opera News* called the composition "a unique hybrid—not quite docu-drama, not quite opera, but owing something to them all." In *Three Tales,* Reich incorporates visions of the Hindenburg disaster, Dolly the cloned sheep, and the nuclear bomb tests on the Bikini Atoll in the 1950s. The multimedia opera has been staged in several major cities, including New York, London, Berlin, and Vienna, and audiences and critics alike have reacted with enthusiasm. In fact, in 2003, Reich was nominated for a Pulitzer Prize in music for *Three Tales.* Alex Ross of the *New Yorker* called *Three Tales* "a major work, a sneaky sort of tragic masterpiece, whose sounds and images haunt the mind for days." Ross concluded that "Reich seems to be mourning a catastrophe that has not yet taken place. It is as if a superior, sensitive robot mind were looking to the time when the human race begins to be obliterated by machines." In examining both the opera's visual and musical elements, which Ross claimed work on a "subliminal" level, the critic pronounced that "Reich is the most original musical thinker of our time."

*BIOGRAPHICAL AND CRITICAL SOURCES:*

*BOOKS*

*Contemporary Musicians,* Volume 8, Gale (Detroit, MI), 1992.
*Encyclopedia of World Biography,* 2nd edition, Gale (Detroit, MI), 1998.

*PERIODICALS*

*Artforum,* May, 1972.
*Chicago Tribune,* March 4, 1979.
*Christian Science Monitor,* October 23, 1980, D. Sterritt, "Composer Steve Reich: Tradition Reseen."

*Musical America,* June, 1980.
*Musical Times,* March, 1971.
*Newsweek,* March 29, 1982.
*New York,* May 25, 1970.
*New Yorker,* November 6, 1978; January 6, 2003, Alex Ross, "Opera As History," p. 86-87.
*New York Times,* October 24, 1971; March 14, 1982.
*New York Times Biographical Service,* June, 1986, Tim Page, "Steve Reich, a Former Young Turk, Approaches 50," p. 724-725.
*Opera News,* October, 1993, K. Robert Schwarz, review of *The Cave.*
*Village Voice,* March 10, 1980.
*Washington Post,* February 24, 1972.

*OTHER*

"Steve Reich: A New Musical Language," *Great Performances,* PBS Television, 1987.*

\*          \*          \*

**REID, Desmond**
    **See MOORCOCK, Michael (John)**

\*          \*          \*

**REISS, Oscar 1925-**

*PERSONAL:* Born February 14, 1925, in Brooklyn, NY; son of Abraham (a butcher) and Rose (a homemaker; maiden name, Goldenberg) Reiss; married Elinor Shatzman (a newspaper columnist), October 3, 1953; children: Stephen, Marcia Reiss-Franklin, Michael, John, Alice Reiss Malone. *Ethnicity:* "Austrian-Hungarian-Jewish." *Education:* New York University, B.A. (cum laude), 1947; State University of New York—Downstate Medical Center, M.D., 1951. *Politics:* "Moderate." *Religion:* Jewish. *Hobbies and other interests:* Reading history.

*ADDRESSES: Home*—10305 Rue Chamberry, San Diego, CA 92131. *E-mail*—elinor@inetworld.net.

*CAREER:* Physician, educator, and author. Private practice of internal medicine in Bristol, CT, 1955-75; Veterans Administration Hospital, Phoenix, AZ, worked as ward physician, resident instructor, then chief of General Medical Service, 1976-83. Yale University, clinical assistant professor of internal medicine. *Military service:* U.S. Army, medic, 1943-46; served in European theater; became sergeant.

*MEMBER:* American College of Physicians (fellow), Phi Beta Kappa.

*WRITINGS:*

*Blacks in Colonial America,* McFarland (Jefferson, NC), 1997.

*Medicine and the American Revolution: How Diseases and Their Treatments Affected the Colonial Army,* McFarland (Jefferson, NC), 1998.

*Medicine in Colonial America,* University Press of America (Lanham, MD), 2000.

Contributor to *Journal of the American Medical Association.*

*WORK IN PROGRESS: The Great Land Grab: Native Americans in Colonial America; The Smallest Minority: Jews in Colonial America;* research for a book to supplement *Medicine in Colonial America.*

*SIDELIGHTS:* Oscar Reiss once told *CA:* "I left private practice due to poor health. I took a job at a Veterans' Administration hospital to help start a teaching program for interns and residents in internal medicine. I retired from that in 1983 due to a worsening of arthritis. I started to write so that my epitaph would say, 'He was a good doc and he wrote books.' If I had not become a physician, I would have wanted to be a history teacher in a small residential college. I became interested in colonial history from a college course."

Reiss later added: "I was born in the first quarter of the twentieth century in New York City, long before the technological and information revolutions. It was a period when old age was respected, and the eighteen-to thirty-four-year age group kept its silence. I received twenty-four years of education in that city with a three-year hiatus during World War II, where I served as a medic in the European theater. After the completion of my education, I took my then-small family to Bristol,

Connecticut, where I started a practice in internal medicine. My health deteriorated, and I moved my then-large family to Phoenix, Arizona. The dry heat in the desert helped me extend my productive life eight more years. I decided to retire when I found I had more pain than my patients. After many operations, I found I was able to walk and stand without pain and decided to embark on a second career—as a researcher and writer on American colonial history.

"I completed five books on colonial history. Three have been published, and two are in the hands of my agent. After a morning spent swimming, the only exercise permitted by my neurologist, I do research in the medical library of the University of California at San Diego. At the present time I am researching a supplement to my book on medicine in colonial America. I plan to contact the publisher to ask if I can add small anecdotes to the new manuscript to make it lighter and more rapid reading.

"My wife of nearly fifty years would say I was a workaholic during my years as a physician. Perhaps my writing is an attempt to avoid the loss of precious days at this late time of my life. I spend far more time researching than writing. After I have satisfied myself on the completeness of my research, I read and collate the material. It begins to fall into place, and the writing is relatively easy.

"Over fifty years ago, I took a college course in American colonial history. It was a new subject, and no textbooks were available. The professor told us to read one book, monograph, or essay on any subject pertaining to this era. Throughout my years in medicine, where I had to read many journals to keep up with the literature, I tried to find a little home for my avocation. Now, in retirement, I can spend as much time on the subject as my old eyes and brain will permit.

"I have achieved my wish for immortality in the numbers in the Library of Congress and books on a bookshelf in a public library."

\* \* \*

**RIMBAUER, Steven**
    **See PEARSON, Ridley**

## RIORDAN, James 1936-

*PERSONAL:* Born October 10, 1936, in Portsmouth, England; son of William (an engineer) and Kathleen (a cleaner; maiden name, Smith) Brown; married Annick Vercaigne, July 4, 1959 (divorced, 1964); married Rashida Davletshina (a teacher), July 1, 1965; children: Tania, Nadine, Sean, Nathalie, Catherine. *Education:* University of Birmingham, B.S., 1959, Ph.D., 1975; University of London, certificate in education, 1960; University of Moscow, diploma in political science, 1962. *Politics:* Socialist. *Religion:* "Faith in people, not gods."

*ADDRESSES: Home*—Portsmouth, England. *Office*—Department of Language and International Studies, University of Surrey, Guildford, Surrey GU2 5XH, England.

*CAREER:* Writer and educator. British Railways, Portsmouth, England, clerk, 1956-57; Progress Publisher, Moscow, USSR, senior translator, 1962-65; Portsmouth Polytechnic, Portsmouth, England, lecturer in Russian, 1965-69; University of Bradford, Bradford, England, senior lecturer and reader in Russian studies; University of Surrey, Guildford, England, professor of Russian studies and head of the department. *Military service:* Royal Air Force, 1954-56, served in Berlin, Germany; British Olympic Attaché at Moscow Olympic Games, 1980.

*MEMBER:* International Sports History Association (vice president).

*AWARDS, HONORS:* Kurt Maschler Award runner-up, 1984, for *The Woman in the Moon and Other Tales of Forgotten Heroines;* NASEN Award and Whitbread Children's Book Award shortlist, both 1998, both for *Sweet Clarinet.*

*WRITINGS:*

*FOR CHILDREN*

(With Eileen H. Colwell) *Little Grey Neck,* illustrated by Caroline Sharpe, Kestrel, 1975, Addison-Wesley (Reading, MA), 1976.

(Reteller) *Beauty and the Beast,* illustrated by Annabel Large, Macdonald Educational (London, England), 1979.
(Reteller) *Sleeping Beauty,* illustrated by Carol Tarrant, Macdonald Educational (London, England), 1979.
*The Three Magic Gifts,* Kaye & Ward (London, England), 1980, illustrated by Errol le Cain, Oxford University Press (New York, NY), 1980.
*The Secret Castle,* illustrated by Peter Dennis, Silver Burdett (Morristown, NJ), 1980.
*Flight into Danger,* illustrated by Gary Rees, Silver Burdett (Morristown, NJ), 1980.
*Changing Shapes,* Macmillan (London, England), 1982.
*The Little Humpback Horse,* illustrated by Andrew Skilleter, Hamlyn (London, England), 1983.
(Reteller) *Peter and the Wolf,* illustrated by Victor G. Ambrus, Oxford University Press (New York, NY), 1986.
(Reteller) *The Wild Swans,* illustrated by Helen Stratton, Hutchinson (London, England), 1987.
(Reteller) *Pinocchio,* illustrated by Victor G. Ambrus, Oxford University Press (New York, NY), 1988.
*Babes in the Wood,* illustrated by Randolph Caldecott, Hutchinson (London, England), 1988, Barron's Educational (Hauppage, NY), 1989.
(Reteller) *The Snowmaiden,* illustrated by Stephen Lambert, Hutchinson (London, England), 1990.
(Reteller) *Thumbelina,* illustrated by Wayne Anderson, Putnam (New York, NY), 1990.
(Reteller) *Gulliver's Travels,* illustrated by Victor G. Ambrus, Oxford University Press (New York, NY), 1992.
(Compiler) *A Book of Narnians: The Lion, the Witch, and the Others* (based on the work of C. S. Lewis), illustrated by Pauline Baynes, Collins (London, England), 1994, HarperCollins (New York, NY), 1995.
*My G-r-r-reat Uncle Tiger,* illustrated by Alex Ayliffe, Peachtree (Atlanta, GA), 1995.
(Reteller) *The Barnyard Band: A Story from the Brothers Grimm,* illustrated by Charles Fuge, Macmillan (London, England), 1996.
*Grace the Pirate,* illustrated by Steve Hutton, Oxford University Press (New York, NY), 1996.
*The Twelve Labors of Hercules,* illustrated by Christina Balit, Millbrook Press (Brookfield, CT), 1997.
*Sweet Clarinet* (novel), Oxford University Press (New York, NY), 1998.
*Little Bunny Bobkin,* illustrated by Tim Warnes, Little Tiger, 1998.

(Reteller) *King Arthur,*, illustrated by Victor G. Ambrus, Oxford University Press (New York, NY), 1998.

(Adaptor) *The Coming of Night: A Yoruba Tale from West Africa,* illustrated by Jenny Stow, Millbrook Press (Brookfield, CT), 1999.

*The Story of Martin Luther King* (biography), illustrated by Rob McCaig, Smart Apple Media (North Mankato, MN), 2001.

*The Story of Nelson Mandela* (biography), illustrated by Neil Reed, Smart Apple Media (North Mankato, MN), 2001.

*When the Guns Fall Silent* (young adult novel), Oxford University Press (London, England), 2001.

*War Song* (sequel to *When the Guns Fall Silent*), Oxford University Press (London, England), 2002.

*Match of Death,* Oxford University Press (New York, NY), 2002.

*Boxcar Molly: A Story from the Great Depression* ("Survivors" series), Barron's Educational (Hauppage, NY), 2002.

*The Enemy: A Story from World War II* ("Survivors" series), Barron's Educational (Hauppage, NY), 2002.

(Reteller) Charles Dickens, *Great Expectations,* illustrated by Victor G. Ambrus, Oxford University Press (New York, NY), 2002.

*COLLECTIONS FOR CHILDREN*

(Adapter and translator) *The Mistress of the Copper Mountain: Tales from the Urals,* Muller, 1974.

*Tales from Central Russia: Russian Tales, Volume I,* illustrated by Krystyna Turska, Kestrel (New York, NY), 1976.

*Tales from Tartary: Russian Tales, Volume II,* illustrated by Anthony Colbert, Kestrel (New York, NY), 1978.

*A World of Fairy Tales,* Hamlyn (London, England), 1981.

*A World of Folktales,* Hamlyn (London, England), 1981.

*Tales of King Arthur,* illustrated by Victor G. Ambrus, Rand-McNally (Chicago, IL), 1982.

*Tales from the Arabian Nights,* illustrated by Victor G. Ambrus, Hamlyn (London, England), 1983, Rand-McNally (Chicago, IL), 1995.

*The Boy Who Turned into a Goat,* illustrated by I. Ripley, Macmillan (London, England), 1983.

*Petrushka and Other Tales from the Ballet,* Stodder & Houghton (London, England), 1984.

*Stories of the Ballet,* illustrated by Victor G. Ambrus, foreword by Rudolf Nureyev, Hodder & Stoughton (London, England), 1984, published as *Favorite Stories of the Ballet,* Rand-McNally (Chicago, IL), 1984.

(Translator) *The Twelve Months: Fairy Tales by Soviet Writers,* illustrated by Fyodor Lemkul, Raduga (Moscow, USSR), 1984.

*The Woman in the Moon, and Other Tales of Forgotten Heroines,* illustrated by Angela Barrett, Hutchinson (London, England), 1984, Dial (New York, NY), 1985.

*A World of Myths and Legends,* Hamlyn (London, England), 1985.

(Translator) Yefim Drutètìs and Alexei Gessler, collectors, *Russian Gypsy Tales,* Canongate (Edinburgh, Scotland), 1986, Interlink Books (New York, NY), 1992.

(Reteller) *Korean Folk-Tales,* Oxford University Press, 1994 (New York, NY).

(With Brenda Ralph Lewis) *An Illustrated Treasury of Myths and Legends,* illustrated by Victor G. Ambrus, Hamlyn (London, England), 1987, Peter Bedrick Books (New York, NY), 1991.

(Collector and translator) *The Sun Maiden and the Crescent Moon: Siberian Folk Tales,* Canongate (Edinburgh, Scotland), 1991.

(Editor) *A Treasury of Irish Stories,* illustrated by Ian Newsham, Kingfisher (New York, NY), 1995.

*Stories from the Sea,* illustrated by Amanda Hall, Abbeville Press (New York, NY), 1996.

(Editor) *The Songs My Paddle Sings: Native American Legends,* illustrated by Michael Foreman, Trafalgar (New York, NY), 1996.

(Editor) *Young Oxford Book of Football Stories,* Oxford University Press (Oxford, England), 1999.

(Editor) *Young Oxford Book of Sports Stories,* Oxford University Press, 2000.

(Editor) *Young Oxford Book of War Stories,* Oxford University Press, 2000.

*Russian Folk-Tales,* illustrated by Andrew Breakspeare, Oxford University Press (New York, NY), 2000.

*The Storytelling Star: Tales of the Sun, Moon, and Stars,* illustrated by Amanda Hall, Trafalgar Square (New York, NY), 2000.

*NONFICTION*

*Sport in Soviet Society: Development of Sport and Physical Education in Russia and the USSR,* Cambridge University Press (New York, NY), 1977.

(Editor) *Sport under Communism: The USSR, Czecho-slovakia, the G.D.R., China, Cuba,* C. Hurst (London, England), 1978, revised second edition, 1981.

*Soviet Sport: Background to the Olympics,* Washington Mews Books (New York, NY) 1980.

(Adapter) George Morey, *Soviet Union: The Land and Its People,* MacDonald Educational (London, England), 1986, Silver Burdett Press (Morristown, NJ), 1987.

*Eastern Europe: The Lands and Their Peoples,* Silver Burdett Press (Morristown, NJ), 1987.

(Editor) *Soviet Education: The Gifted and the Handicapped,* Routledge (London, England), 1988.

(Editor) *Soviet Youth Culture,* Indiana University Press (Bloomington, IN), 1989.

*Sport, Politics, and Communism,* Manchester University Press (New York, NY), 1991.

(Editor and translator, with Susan Bridger) *Dear Comrade Editor: Readers' Letters to the Soviet Press under Perestroika,* Indiana University Press (Bloomington, IN), 1992.

(Editor) *Soviet Social Reality in the Mirror of Glasnost,* St. Martin's Press (New York, NY), 1992.

(With Victor Peppard) *Playing Politics: Soviet Sport Diplomacy to 1992,* JAI Press (Greenwich, CT), 1993.

(Editor, with Igor S. Kon) *Sex and Russian Society,* Indiana University Press (Bloomington, IN), 1993, revised as *The Sexual Revolution in Russia: From the Age of the Czars to Today,* Free Press (New York, NY), 1995.

*Russia and the Commonwealth of Independent States,* Silver Burdett Press (Morristown, NJ), 1993.

(Editor, with Christopher Williams and Igor Ilynsky) *Young People in Post-Communist Russia and Eastern Europe,* Dartmouth College/University Press of New England (Hanover, NH), 1995.

(Editor, with Petar-Emil Mitev) *Europe, the Young, the Balkans* (conference proceedings), International Centre for Minority Studies and Intercultural Relations (Sofia, Bulgaria), 1996.

(Editor, with Arnd Krüger) *The Story of Worker Sport,* Human Kinetics (Champaign, IL), 1996.

(Editor, translator, and contributor) Olga Litvinenko, collector, *Memories of the Dispossessed: Descendants of Kulak Families Tell Their Stories,* Bramcote Press (Nottingham, England), 1998.

(Editor, with Pierre Arnaud) *Sport and International Politics: The Impact of Fascism and Communism on Sport,* E. & F. Spon (New York, NY), 1998.

*Russia and the Commonwealth of Independent States,* Silver Burdett Press (Morristown, NJ), 1999.

(Editor, with Robin Jones) *Sport and Physical Education in China,* Routledge (New York, NY), 1999.

(Editor, with Arnd Krüger) *The International Politics of Sport in the Twentieth Century,* Routledge (New York, NY), 1999.

*SIDELIGHTS:* British author and educator James Riordan, an expert in Russian language, folklore, and culture, has made a contribution to children's literature by translating and retelling folktales from Eastern Europe and Asia. From Russia, he brings young readers *The Three Magic Gifts* and *The Snowmaiden,* as well as many shorter folktales included in the collections *Tales from Tartary* and *Russian Folk-Tales.* Presenting each tale with what a *Publishers Weekly* reviewer characterized as "a storyteller's bravado," Riordan has also mined other regions of the world for traditional tales, which have been published in such books as *A Treasury of Irish Stories, Korean Folk-Tales,* and *The Woman in the Moon, and Other Tales of Forgotten Heroines.* In more recent years he has also begun to publish original works, including picture books such as *Little Bunny Bobkin* and novels for older readers that focus on World War II.

Born in 1936, Riordan spent his early childhood in Portsmouth, England. During World War II he was sent to live with his grandparents, an experience that proved influential. As he once recalled to *CA:* "The household was big, twelve adults and me, very warm and friendly. Amid the doodle-bugs and air-raid sirens (Portsmouth was blown to bits), the all-pervasive tang of soot in mouth and nose, and the massive picture of Lord Kitchener dominating our living room, my lasting attitudes of faith in ordinary people and hatred of war were being formed."

After finishing school Riordan "became successively a barman, a cratestacker in a brewery, commercial salesman (of 'unbreakable tea sets'), double-bass player in a dance band, postman, railway clerk and junior technician in the Royal Air Force." Determined to gain an education, he took classes at the universities of Birmingham, London, and Moscow, and "travelled and worked in various countries," including France, Germany, and the former Soviet Union. Spending five years in the USSR, Riordan gained a good understanding of both Russia's language and people. Beginning his teaching career in England in 1965, he worked as a lecturer in Russian at Portsmouth Polytechnic, and eventually worked his way up to professor of Russian studies at Guildford University.

Riordan published his first folk-story adaptations in 1975. *Little Grey Neck: A Russian Folktale,* a collaboration between Riordan and Eileen Colwell, is about a little duck with an injured wing. The duck, who cannot migrate with the other ducks as winter approaches, worries that she will be eaten by a fox. Instead, she is rescued by a man who brings her home for a pet.

*Little Grey Neck* marked the beginning of what has become a prolific career as a children's writer for Riordan, and among his many works have been retellings of traditional Russian tales. *The Three Magic Gifts,* described by a critic for *Junior Bookshelf* as an "excellent folktale," recounts the fate of an impoverished, good brother—Ivan the Poor—and a wealthy, bad one—Ivan the Rich. A *Booklist* contributor noted that "Riordan spices the text with brief verses," and in *Publishers Weekly* a reviewer maintained that *The Three Magic Gifts* "should entrance little readers." *The Snowmaiden,* a retelling described by a *Junior Bookshelf* contributor as "highly charged," tells the story of the daughter of the Spring and Frost. She has been living with peasants for sixteen years, hidden from the god of the sun and keeping warmth from the land. When the Snowmaiden leaves the peasants who have raised her, spring returns to the earth. The Snowmaiden then finds herself loved by a shepherd boy. Disappointed because she lacks a heart and cannot love him back, she begs for one. After she gains the ability to love the shepherd, the Snowmaiden remains too long in the sun; she melts away, and flowers grow on the spot where she once stood.

In *Tales from Central Russia* Riordan presents traditional Russian stories, his translations and retellings presented with "flavor and directness," in the opinion of *Horn Book* contributor Virginia Haviland. Praising the book's accessibility to children, a critic for *Junior Bookshelf* commented, "Here's treasure." *Tales from Tartary* is the product of months spent at the homes of friends and relatives of Riordan's Tartar wife, Rashida. Influenced by Asian culture, these tales come from Tartarstan, Siberia, and the Crimea, and show what a *Junior Librarian* contributor called Riordan's "deep respect for the traditions" of the Tartar people. A more broad-ranging collection, *Russian Folk-Tales* features

ten stories than include "The Firebird" and a Baba Yaga tale as well as some more unfamiliar to Western readers. Noting that Riordan makes his selections carefully, *School Library Journal* contributor Denise Anton Wright noted that the stories included in *Russian Folk-Tales* "emphasize family relationships, clever main characters, magical gifts, and punishment for evil," and the authors retellings "beg to be shared aloud."

Riordan has not limited himself to collecting and retelling the stories of former Soviet societies. *The Songs My Paddle Sings: Native American Legends* contains twenty stories collected during Riordan's trip across the United States and present the myths of the Apache, Blackfoot, Pueblo, and Salish, among others, all told in "stately language eminently suited to reading aloud," according to a *Kirkus Reviews* critic. *Korean Folk-Tales* provides twenty stories from Korea, and, in the words of a critic for *Junior Bookshelf,* provides "riches . . . for the oral storyteller." These stories are, in the words of *School Library Journal* contributor Diane S. Marton, "for the most part clearly and pleasantly told." *The Boy Who Turned into a Goat* contains six stories from different cultures written with "freshness and vitality," as a *Junior Bookshelf* reviewer remarked. *A World of Fairy Tales* contains stories from Australia, China, Africa, India, Russia, North and South America, and Europe. *The Coming of Night: A Yoruba Tale from West Africa* provides a fanciful explanation of how night was first created, and draws readers back to a time when the sun never set. According to the story—"written in a style rich with descriptive language and images" according to *School Library Journal* contributor Paul Kelsey—when a powerful chief named Oduduwa marries the daughter of the river goddess, his young bride leaves the waterbound home where Night dwells, but soon tires of the perpetual daylight. Her husband commands some animals to fetch Night from the river and bring it to his wife, but to be sure Night is kept in a sack as it will otherwise cause mischief. True to folktale form, the animals succumb to curiosity, open the sack, and release Night to overshadow a portion of each day.

In addition to collecting, translating, and retelling folktales, Riordan has made other contributions to children's literature. *Tales from the Arabian Nights* presents readers with a children's classic, retold in Riordan's own words with "sympathy and dramatic flair," according to a *Booklist* critic. *The Twelve La-*

*bors of Hercules* starts with the ancient hero's birth and goes on to tell how he incurred the wrath of the jealous goddess Hera, and how Hera caused him to go mad and kill his family, causing the labors meted out as his punishment. In Riordan's retelling, which is punctuated by what *School Librarian* reviewer Mary Medlicott described as "occasional touches of humor," Hercules's "personality comes through, especially his impulsiveness," according to *School Library Journal* contributor Pam Gosner. In *King Arthur*, Riordan presents an account of the famous king in a style that *Voice of Youth Advocates* contributor Rebecca Barnhouse characterized as "formal and distant, as befits a legend." Citing Riordan's effective mix of myth and history—he includes notes on the origins of the Arthur myth—Hazel Towson praised the retelling for being "well researched" and "lucidly told." *A Book of Narnians: The Lion, the Witch and the Others* is a compilation which allows readers unfamiliar with the famous books of C. S. Lewis to get to know the series characters. "The words are largely Lewis's own, though plucked selectively," noted *School Library Journal* contributor Nancy Palmer, who added that the "selection is skillfully done."

Riordan's original fiction includes several diverse works. In *Flight into Danger,* a pair of twins takes a harrowing plane ride with their father, who falls ill during the flight. *The Secret Castle* follows the story of a boy and a girl who travel back in time to the Middle Ages, where they lead the lives of lord and lady. The picture book *Little Bunny Bobkin* appeals to the very young, as it presents simple counting through the experiences of a young rabbit. After no one in the family burrow wants to help him practice counting, little Bobkin wanders out into the forest, where a group of hungry foxes seem only too happy to humor the tasty bunny. Riordan has also contributed two original stories—*Boxcar Molly: A Story from the Great Depression* and *The Enemy: A Story from World War II*—to Barron's "Survivors" series for preteen readers.

World Wars I and II have figured not only in *The Enemy* but in several other works by Riordan, who himself has memories of the World War II years. He includes excerpts from poems, diaries, and fiction about war in his edited anthology *The Young Oxford Book of War Stories,* which also covers the Vietnam conflict in what *School Librarian* contributor Janet Fisher described as a "sombre tone" in keeping with the book's subject matter. The 1998 novel *Sweet Clarinet* intro-

duces readers to Billy Riley, an English boy who is touched personally by World War II when he is disfigured by burns after German bombs hit an air-raid shelter and his mother is killed. Sent to a children's hospital, the orphaned Billy withdraws until he meets an injured soldier whose gift to the lonely boy—a clarinet—allows Billy to express his sadness and put his bitterness behind him. Praising Riordan for his use of accurate period detail, Sandra Bennett added in her *School Librarian* review of *Sweet Clarinet* that within Riordan's "simply told" story the young teen's "isolation and unhappiness are convincingly portrayed."

*When the Guns Fall Silent* and *War Song* are linking novels that focus on World War I. In *When the Guns Fall Silent* Jack Loveless is forced to relive his memories of the Great War during a trip with his grandson to France's war cemeteries. Noting that Riordan "is good at showing the dreadful chauvinism" that existed in Great Britain toward those of German heritage during the war years, Dennis Hamley noted in *School Librarian* that *When the Guns Fall Silent* is "a necessary, powerful, outspoken but ultimately healing book" that brings to life for modern readers the true horrors and disillusionment caused by war. Calling Riordan's text "as jagged and staccato as a fusillade" a *Books for Keeps* contributor also praised the book for recapturing the emotions visited upon Jack as a naive sixteen-year-old volunteer of the Great War. Equally poignant reading is *War Song,* which follows two sisters who, left at home, determine to help the war effort through working as a nurse and in a munitions factory. Noting the tension built up through the novel as the young women witness the tragedies visited upon friends and their own families, Eileen Armstrong praised *War Song* in her *School Librarian* review as a "compelling" and "accessible but uncomfortable, make-you-stop-and-think story that should not be missed."

Riordan credits his five children for helping him ensure that his stories and story collections are appropriate for ethnically diverse children, whether they are boys or girls. He explained to *CA,* "I love children and test all my stories out on them before producing a final version; so I have to keep producing more children to keep up with my writing. My own multi-ethnic family (parts English/Irish/Tartar/Bashkir) is a useful touchstone for all my stories. And since I only have one son, I make sure that at least half the stories in all my collections are about girls (most folk and fairy tales have exclusively male heroes)."

*BIOGRAPHICAL AND CRITICAL SOURCES:*

PERIODICALS

*Booklist,* July 15, 1979, review of *Tales from Tartary,* p. 1629; March 1, 1981, review of *The Three Magic Gifts,* pp. 967-68; December 15, 1985, review of *Tales from the Arabian Nights,* p. 630; March 15, 1991, pp. 1494-1495; March 15, 1998, Karen Hutt, review of *The Song My Paddle Sings,* p. 1242; October 1, 1998, Carolyn Phelan, review of *King Arthur,* p. 330; February 15, 1999, Ilene Cooper, review of *The Coming of Night: A Yoruba Tale from West Africa,* p. 1072; April 1, 2001, Carolyn Phelan, review of *Russian Folk-Tales,* p. 1463.

*Books for Keeps,* March, 2001, George Hunt, review of *When the Guns Fall Silent,* p. 25.

*Bulletin of the Center for Children's Books,* February, 1983, p. 116; December, 1985, review of *The Woman in the Moon and Other Tales of Forgotten Heroines,* p. 76.

*Horn Book,* August, 1979, Virginia Haviland, review of *Tales from Central Russia* and *Tales from Tartary,* pp. 430-431.

*Junior Bookshelf,* February, 1977, review of *Tales from Central Russia,* pp. 24-25; December, 1978, review of *Tales from Tartary,* p. 320; April, 1981, review of *The Three Magic Gifts,* p. 60; December, 1982, review of *A World of Fairy Tales,* p. 226; October, 1983, review of *The Boy Who Turned into a Goat,* p. 210; February, 1985, review of *The Woman in the Moon,* p. 30; August, 1990, review of *The Snowmaiden,* p. 164; December, 1992, review of *Gulliver's Travels,* p. 262; February, 1995, review of *Korean Folk-Tales,* p. 43.

*Kirkus Reviews,* February 15, 1998, review of *The Song My Paddle Sings,* p. 273.

*Library Journal,* July, 1991, p. 106.

*Magpies,* March, 1993, review of *Gulliver's Travels,* p. 23.

*New York Times Book Review,* March 9, 1986, p. 37.

*Publishers Weekly,* December 12, 1980, review of *The Three Magic Gifts;* December 21, 1998, review of *Little Bunny Bobkin,* p. 66; March 19, 2001, review of *Russian Folk-Tales,* p. 101; November 4, 2002, review of *Boxcar Molly: A Story from the Great Depression,* p. 85.

*School Librarian,* spring, 1998, Mary Medlicott, review of *The Twelve Labours of Hercules,* p. 36; autumn, 1998, Hazel Towson, review of *King Arthur,* p. 148; spring, 1999, Sandra Bennett, review of *Sweet Clarinet,* pp. 47-48; spring, 2001, Dennis Harnley, review of *When the Guns Fall Silent,* p. 49; autumn, 2001, Janet Fisher, review of *The Oxford Book of War Stories,* p. 159; winter, 2001, Eileen Armstrong, review of *War Song,* p. 214.

*School Library Journal,* April, 1987, p. 89; June, 1991, p. 89; March, 1995, Diane S. Marton, review of *Korean Folk-Tales,* p. 218; October, 1995, Nancy Palmer, review of *A Book of Narnians,* pp. 148-149; February, 1998, Pam Gosner, review of *The Twelve Labors of Hercules,* pp. 122, 124; May, 1998, Lisa Mitten, review of *The Song My Paddle Sings,* p. 136; October, 1998, Carolyn Jenks, review of *Little Bunny Bobkin,* p. 112; April, 1999, Helen Gregory, review of *King Arthur,* p. 154; May, 1999, Paul Kelsey, review of *The Coming of Night,* p. 112; November, 2000, Nancy A. Gifford, review of *The Storytelling Star,* p. 148; July, 2001, Denise Anton Wright, review of *Russian Folk-Tales,* pp. 97-98; October, 2002, Patricia D. Lothrop, review of *Great Expectations,* p. 170.

*Times Educational Supplement,* November 5, 1999, "After the Fire," p. 11; April 20, 2001, review of *The Oxford Book of War Stories,* p. 20.

*Voice of Youth Advocates,* December, 1998, Rebecca Barnhouse, review of *King Arthur,* p. 368.*

\* \* \*

**ROEDIGER, David R(andall) 1952-**

*PERSONAL:* Born July 13, 1952, in Columbia, IL; son of Arthur E. (a quarry worker) and Mary Ann (a teacher; maiden name, Lind) Roediger; married Jean Marie Allman (a professor of African history), 1979; children: Brendan David, Donovan Joseph. *Education:* Northern Illinois University, B.S., 1975; Northwestern University, Ph.D., 1980. *Politics:* "Socialist internationalism." *Hobbies and other interests:* Tennis, travel.

*ADDRESSES: Office*—Department of History, 309 Gregory Hall, MC-466, 801 South Wright St., University of Illinois, Urbana, IL 61801; fax: 217-333-2297. *E-mail*—droedige@uiuc.edu.

*CAREER:* Yale University, New Haven, CT, assistant editor of Frederick Douglass Papers, 1979-80; Northwestern University, Evanston, IL, lecturer in history,

1980-81, Mellon assistant professor, 1981-83, assistant professor, 1984-85; American Council of Learned Societies and Exxon Educational Foundation, fellow, 1983-84; University of Missouri—Columbia, from assistant to associate professor, 1985-92, professor of history, 1992-94; University of Minnesota, professor of history, 1995-2000, chair of American Studies Program, 1996-2000; University of Illinois, Kendrick Babcock Professor of History, 2000—. Charles H. Kerr Publishing Co., president of board of directors, 1992—. Students for a Democratic Society, president, 1970; Workers Defense, vice-chairperson, 1978-80; participant in anti-apartheid activities in Chicago and Missouri, 1983—.

*MEMBER:* American Studies Association, Organization of American Historians, Missouri Conference on History.

*AWARDS, HONORS:* Fellow of American Council of Learned Societies, 1983-84; Lloyd Lewis fellow and grant from National Endowment for the Humanities, 1989-90; Purple Chalk Teaching Award, University of Missouri-Columbia, 1989; Gustavus Myers Award for the Study of Human Rights in the United States, Outstanding Book Award, 1992; Outstanding Academic Book Award, *Choice,* 1992; Merle Curti Prize, Organization of American Historians, 1992, for *The Wages of Whiteness;* McKnight Research Award, University of Minnesota, 1999-2000.

*WRITINGS:*

(Editor and author of introduction) Covington Hall, *Dreams and Dynamite: Selected Poems,* Charles H. Kerr (Chicago, IL), 1985.

(Editor, with Franklin Rosemont) *Haymarket Scrapbook,* Charles H. Kerr (Chicago, IL), 1986.

(With Philip S. Foner) *Our Own Time: A History of American Labor and the Working Day,* Greenwood Press (New York, NY), 1989.

(Editor, with Phyllis Boanes) Irving S. Abrams, *Haymarket Heritage: The Memoirs of Irving S. Abrams,* introduction by Joseph M. Jacobs, Charles H. Kerr (Chicago, IL), 1989.

*The Wages of Whiteness: Race and the Making of the American Working Class,* Verso (New York, NY), 1991, revised edition, 1999.

(Editor) *Fellow Worker: The Life of Fred W. Thompson,* Charles H. Kerr (Chicago, IL), 1993.

*Towards the Abolition of Whiteness: Essays on Race, Politics, and Working Class History,* Verso (New York, NY), 1994.

(Editor and author of introduction) *Black on White: Black Writers on What It Means to Be White,* Schocken Books (New York, NY), 1998.

(Editor, with Martin H. Blatt) *The Meaning of Slavery in the North,* Garland (New York, NY), 1998.

(Editor and author of introduction) Covington Hall, *Labor Struggles in the Deep South and Other Writings,* Charles H. Kerr (Chicago, IL), 2000.

(Editor and author of introduction) W. E. B. Du Bois, *John Brown,* Modern Library (New York, NY), 2001.

*Colored White: Transcending the Racial Past,* University of California Press (Berkeley, CA), 2002.

Contributor of articles and reviews to history journals and other magazines, including *Tennis Arsenal, Progressive, Massachusetts Review, Monthly Review, Southern Exposure,* and *New Left Review.* Books editor, *In These Times,* 1980-81; member of editorial board, *Gateway Heritage,* 1989—.

*SIDELIGHTS:* David R. Roediger's historical analyses of what it means in the United States to be white has placed him at the forefront of the ongoing debate on race and racism in America. His publications begin by linking race and class, and examine how white laborers in the New World benefited psychologically as well as monetarily by differentiating themselves from black laborers, that is, from slaves, an idea he borrowed from W. E. B. Du Bois. With the dawn of the revolutionary era came an end to indentured servitude (a kind of limited white slavery), Roediger explains in *The Wages of Whiteness: Race and the Making of the American Working Class,* and the attribute of whiteness took on additional value. In discussing the nineteenth century, the author examines such phenomena as minstrelsy, black-face riots, and the question of the ferocity of the Irish immigrant workers in their racist attacks on black workers. "This is powerful stuff, provocatively and boldly advanced in ways to which a short review cannot begin to do justice," remarked Daniel J. Walkowitz in the *Journal of American Ethnic History.* Indeed, *The Wages of Whiteness* did provoke intense debate in the decade following its publication. In a review of the revised edition in *Labor History,* Carl Nightingale dubbed this "the history book that got everybody talking about whiteness, from anthropologists to legal theorists to theologians to activists."

Among Roediger's several other books on the invention of whiteness and its role in American history is an anthology of writings on the topic by black writers. Gathering fifty pieces of poetry, essays, stories, and excerpts from an autobiography, a novel, and a play, works dating from revolutionary days to the present, *Black on White: Black Writers on What It Means to Be White* is a "trailblazing anthology," according to Donna Seaman in *Booklist*. A contributor to *Lip Magazine* online similarly called this volume "astounding in its scope, insightfulness, intensity, and power." This critic described Roediger's writings as part of "the new abolitionism," a growing disaffection with the institutionalization of white power: "Not yet a decade old, the new abolitionist movement—the organized effort to abolish the white race as a social category . . .—reflects a widespread and growing grassroots ferment." And of Roediger's place in this movement, this critic asserted: "he is unquestionably one of contemporary abolitionism's leading thinkers." Although Louis J. Parascandola, writing in *Library Journal*, noted that Roediger excludes Malcolm X and other Nation of Islam writers, the resulting volume is nonetheless one "that should go a long way in helping us to understand America's troubled racial relations," the critic concluded.

Roediger once told *CA*: "Growing up in a working class, trade union family during the civil rights movement, I knew early that laboring people wanted better lives and could, at times, act decisively to win them. My earliest historical writings, profoundly influenced by the Trinidadian writer C. L. R. James, centered on the ways in which American workers expressed a vision of a new society by casting their fight for a shorter working day as a fight for dignity, education, health, political participation, and, in a little-appreciated but revealing phrase, *free time*.

"At the same time, however, my youth and later experiences as a New Left, labor, and anti-apartheid activist also suggested the considerable extent to which race shaped and disfigured the dreams and aspirations of white workers. For a good while I mused on the curious combination of racism, love of soul music, and worship of African-American athletes which characterized those of us attending high school in the 1960s in the quarrying town in which I grew up. Only with long exposure to the sophisticated work of Sterling Stucky and W. E. B. Du Bois, however, and with the example of a growing body of feminist historiography which historicized masculinity, did I find a broad question which could frame my musings: How, when, and why did large numbers of U.S. workers get the terrible idea that it was important to think of themselves as white labor, rather than simply as labor?

"An early result of attempts to answer this question for the years prior to 1877 was *The Wages of Whiteness*. In the book I argued that whiteness 'paid off,' not only or mainly in wage differentials between the races, but also as a way for white workers who distanced white workers from black slaves to make peace with the sacrifices required by industrial capitalism.

"A book of my essays on race and class, *Toward the Abolition of Whiteness*, continues work on these themes with a special emphasis on race, gender, and ethnicity. *Shades of Pale* asks why many workers in our century continue to prize whiteness."

## BIOGRAPHICAL AND CRITICAL SOURCES:

*PERIODICALS*

*American Studies International*, October, 1998, review of *The Meaning of Slavery in the North*, p. 92.

*Booklist*, February 15, 1998, Donna Seaman, review of *Black on White*, p. 954; April 15, 2002, Vernon Ford, review of *Colored White*, p. 1366.

*Bookwatch*, August, 1998, review of *Black on White*, p. 11.

*Choice*, February, 1996, review of *Towards the Abolition of Whiteness*, p. 903.

*Hungry Mind Review*, spring, 1998, review of *Black on White*, pp. 21, 53, review of *Towards the Abolition of Whiteness*, p. 55, and review of *The Wages of Whiteness*, p. 56.

*Journal of American Ethnic History*, fall, 1994, Daniel J. Walkowitz, review of *The Wages of Whiteness*, p. 98.

*Journal of American History*, review of *Towards the Abolition of Whiteness*, p. 82.

*Labor History*, February, 2000, Carl Nightingale, review of *The Wages of Whiteness*, p. 93.

*Library Journal*, May 1, 1998, Louis J. Parascandola, review of *Black on White*, p. 98.

*Minnesota Review*, fall, 1996, review of *Towards the Abolition of Whiteness*, p. 49.

*New York Times Book Review,* March 11, 1990, p. 15.

*Reference and Research Book News,* August, 1998, review of *The Meaning of Slavery in the North,* p. 44; November, 1998, review of *Black on White,* p. 49.

*Village Voice Literary Supplement,* September, 1994, review of *The Wages of Whiteness,* p. 11.

ONLINE

*Lip Magazine,* http://www.lipmagazine.org/articles/ (June 14, 2002), review of *Black on White.**

\*          \*          \*

## RONELL, Avital 1956-

*PERSONAL:* Born April 15, 1956, in Prague, Czechoslovakia; daughter of Paul G. and Evelyn (Garfunkel) Ronell. *Education:* Princeton University, Ph.D. (Germanic languages and literature), 1979. *Politics:* "Left of left."

*ADDRESSES: Office*—Department of Germanic Languages and Literature, New York University, 736 Broadway, New York, NY 10003. *E-mail*—avital. ronell@nyu.edu.

*CAREER:* University of California, Berkeley, associate professor of comparative literature, beginning 1986; New York University, New York, NY, currently professor of German, English, and comparative literature and chair of Department of Germanic Languages and Literature. Summer seminar professor, European Graduate School, Saas-Fee, Switzerland.

*AWARDS, HONORS:* Fulbright-Hayes fellow; award from Alexander von Humboldt Foundation.

*WRITINGS:*

*Dictations: On Haunted Writing,* Indiana University Press (Bloomington, IN), 1986, revised with new preface, University of Nebraska Press (Lincoln, NE), 1993.

*The Telephone Book: Technology, Schizophrenia, Electric Speech,* University of Nebraska Press (Lincoln, NE), 1989.

*Crack Wars: Literature-Addiction-Mania,* University of Nebraska Press (Lincoln, NE), 1992.

*Finitude's Score: Essays for the End of the Millennium,* University of Nebraska Press (Lincoln, NE), 1994.

*Stupidity,* University of Illinois Press (Urbana, IL), 2002.

Contributor of numerous articles to periodicals. Contributor of essays to *Thirteen Alumni Artists,* by Lisa Philips, Middlebury College Museum of Art, (Middlebury, VT), 2000.

*WORK IN PROGRESS: The Test Drive.*

*SIDELIGHTS:* A native of Czechoslovakia, professor and writer Avital Ronell plays to a global classroom. She lived in Israel and completed her education in Berlin and Paris, where Ronell studied under the groundbreaking feminist Helene Cixous. She has taught on both coasts of the United States and in many countries, most notably Switzerland, where Ronell conducts seminars at the European Graduate School.

Ronell's writing takes on a diverse range of themes. In *The Telephone Book: Technology, Schizophrenia, Electric Speech,* she argues that "communication technology has changed human beings so deeply, irreversibly, and suddenly that we [are] mesmerized, unable to recognize the changes wrought in our way of living in the world," according to *Whole Earth Review* contributor Howard Rheingold. Ronell begins her thesis, fittingly enough, with Alexander Graham Bell's first long-distance phone call in October, 1875; "the precise moment," noted Rheingold, "at which the power of the technological world floods into human history and changes it irrevocably." In another significant event, the author recalls, the philosopher Martin Heidegger in 1934 received a call from officials of the Nazi Party asking him to cooperate in the identification and removal of Jewish faculty members from a German university where Heidegger worked. Such history-changing events, prompted by telephone calls, suggest a link to "a web of ideas, inventions, and power-relations that constitute a cryptic metaphysical infrastructure of the modern world," Rheingold stated.

*Crack Wars: Literature-Addiction-Mania* has as its
theme the phenomenon of what interviewer Alexander
Laurence called the "speed culture," in which one
makes "definite judgments in an instant and [moves]
on to the next problem." "We have judgments without
having really taken the time to consider what a definition of drugs might be," Ronell told Laurence in *Write
Stuff*. "We have categories and classifications. Soft or
hard drugs. Or the narcotic schedules, as they're called.
We have taxonomies. Before you make people serve
time no one has taken the time, or given the time, to
consider what it is that we're as a culture so phobic
about." In *Crack Wars* Ronell coins the word *Narcossism,* which she defined to Laurence as "narcissism
[that] has been recircuited through a relation to drugs.
Narcossism is supposed to indicate the way that our
relation to ourselves has now been structured, medi-
ated, that is, by some form of addiction and urge.
Which is to say, that to get off any drug, . . . precipi-
tates a major narcissistic crisis. Basically I wanted to
suggest that we need to study the way the self is
pumped up or deleted by a chemical prosthesis."

By 1994 Ronell had produced a *fin de siecle* work,
*Finitude's Score: Essays for the End of the Millennium*.
The topics include the AIDS crisis, the Gulf War, and
the tumult surrounding the case of the 1991 beating of
motorist Rodney King in Los Angeles. Bruce Hainley
of *Artforum International* found this work to be not
just "philosophy (about Kant, Nietzsche, and
Heidegger)" but also "about AIDS, music, the telephone, rumor, the state, torture, racism, war video,
television—in short, the speed of now, that future:
how to read it, which is 'the question of how to read'
at all." Hainley found that Ronell "intricately, amazingly, and disturbingly connected" the Gulf War to the
Rodney King case, and decided that one entry titled
"Trauma TV" offers "the most illuminating essay on
TV and video ever written."

Ronell published the provocatively titled *Stupidity* in
2001. True to its title, the book is "an investigation of
all things stupid," in the words of *Times Literary
Supplement* critic Jonathan Ree. "It is a large topic,
and Ronell is wise to have chosen to nibble at its edges
rather than trying to swallow it whole." Ree added
that stupidity, "as Ronell understands it is a kind of
black hole devouring the light of rationality itself."
The author cites philosophy and literature, including
the works of Kirkegaard, Kafka, Karl Marx, and
Nietzsche. But Ree noted in Ronell's view,

"Philosophy . . . is nothing but a monstrous despot
whose oppressive legalism has reigned supreme
throughout the entire history of 'the West'. . . . Philosophy, she goes on, has 'demonstrated a need to im-
pound those who cannot speak for themselves, who
have not reached a certain legislated majority.' Philosophy, it seems, has blood on its hands."

*BIOGRAPHICAL AND CRITICAL SOURCES:*

*PERIODICALS*

*American Book Review,* April, 1993, review of *Crack
Wars: Literature-Addiction-Mania,* p. 17.
*Artforum International,* November, 1994, Bruce Hain-
ley, review of *Finitude's Score: Essays for the End
of the Millennium,* p. 14S.
*Bloomsbury Review,* September, 1990, review of *The
Telephone Book: Technology, Schizophrenia, Elec-
tric Speech,* p. 17.
*College Literature,* June, 1995, review of *Finitude's
Score,* p. 191.
*Journalism Quarterly,* autumn, 1990, review of *The
Telephone Book,* p. 619.
*Journal of Popular Culture,* spring, 2001, Ray Browne,
review of *Finitude's Score,* p. 198.
*Journal of the History of Ideas,* January, 1995, review
of *Finitude's Score,* p. 173.
*Modern Language Notes,* December, 1989, review of
*The Telephone Book,* p. 1220; July, 1992, review
of *The Telephone Book,* p. 668; December, 1992,
Akira Mizuta Lippit, review of *Crack Wars,*
p. 1046.
*New Statesman and Society,* April 27, 1990, review of
*The Telephone Book,* p. 36; April 17, 1993, review
of *Crack Wars,* p. 46.
*New York Times Book Review,* June 3, 1990; Septem-
ber 22, 1991, review of *The Telephone Book.*
*Poetics Today,* spring, 1997, review of *Finitude's Score,*
p. 132.
*Times Literary Supplement,* December 6, 1991, review
of *The Telephone Book,* p. 3; March 22, 2002,
Jonathan Ree, "It's the Philosophy, Stupid," re-
view of *Stupidity,* p. 8.
*Virginia Quarterly Review,* spring, 1995, review of
*Finitude's Score,* p. 64; winter, 1997, review of
*Dictations: On Haunted Writing,* p. 16.
*Whole Earth Review,* winter, 1991, Howard Rhein-
gold, review *The Telephone Book,* p. 87.

*ONLINE*

*Write Stuff,* http://www.altx.com/ (July 17, 2002), Alexander Laurence, "Avital Ronell Interview."*

*     *     *

**RUELL, Patrick**
    **See HILL, Reginald (Charles)**

*     *     *

**RUSCH, Kris**
    **See RUSCH, Kristine Kathryn**

*     *     *

**RUSCH, Kristine Kathryn 1960-**
    **(Kristine Grayson; Kathryn Wesley Kensington; Kris Nelson; Kris Rusch; Sandy Schofield)**

*PERSONAL:* Born June 4, 1960, in Oneonta, NY; daughter of Carroll E. (a math professor) and Marian M. (a homemaker; maiden name, Beisser) Rusch; married Randall Thompson (divorced, 1986); married Dean Wesley Smith (a writer), December 20, 1992. *Education:* University of Wisconsin, B.A., 1982; Clarion Writers Workshop, Michigan State University, 1985. *Hobbies and other interests:* History, music, film, theater, needlework.

*ADDRESSES: Home*—P. O. Box 479, Lincoln City, OR. *Agent*—Merrilee Heifetz, Writers House, 21 West 26th St., New York, NY 10010. *E-mail*—krisrusch@sff.net.

*CAREER:* Freelance journalist, 1978-86; WORT Radio, Madison, WI, reporter, 1980-86, and news director, 1983-86; owner, Shire Frame Shop & Galleries, 1981-84; editorial assistant, Wm. C. Brown Publishers, 1984; secretary in Eugene, OR, 1986-89; founder, with Dean Wesley Smith, of Pulphouse Publishing, Eugene, OR, 1987, and editor of *Pulphouse: The Hardback Magazine,* 1987-91; editor of *Magazine of Fantasy & Science Fiction,* 1991-97; freelance author, 1982—.

*AWARDS, HONORS:* World Fantasy Award (with Dean Wesley Smith), 1989, for work with Pulphouse Publishing; John W. Campbell Award for Best New Writer, 1990; *Locus* Award for Best Nonfiction (with Dean Wesley Smith), 1991, for *Science Fiction Writers of America Handbook: The Professional Writer's Guide to Writing Professionally; Locus* and Homer Award for Best Novella, both 1992, both for *Gallery of His Dreams;* Hugo Award for Best Editor, 1994; Homer Award for Best Novelette and Readers Choice Award, *Asimov's Science Fiction Magazine,* both 1998, both for *Echea;* Readers Choice Award, *Ellery Queen's Mystery Magazine,* 1998, for *Details;* Readers Choice Award, *Science Fiction Age Magazine,* 1998, for *Coolhunting;* Herodotus Award for Best U.S. Historical Mystery, 2000, for *A Dangerous Road;* Hugo Award for Best Novelette, 2001, for *Millennium Babies; Deadly Pleasures* Best Books of 2001 citation, for *Smoke-Filled Rooms;* Reviewers Choice, *Romantic Times,* 2000, for *Utterly Charming,* and 2001, for *Thoroughly Kissed.*

*WRITINGS:*

*The White Mists of Power* (novel), Roc (New York, NY), 1991.
*The Gallery of His Dreams* (short novel), Axolotl Press (Eugene, OR), 1991, reprinted in *The Year's Best Science Fiction: Ninth Annual Collection,* edited by Gardner Dozois, St Martin's Press (New York, NY), 1992.
(With Kevin J. Anderson) *Afterimage* (novel), Roc (New York, NY), 1992.
*Traitors* (novel), Roc (New York, NY), 1993.
*Heart Readers* (novel), Roc (New York, NY), 1993.
*Facade* (novel), Dell Abyss (New York, NY), 1993.
*Alien Influences* (novel), Millennium [England], 1994.
(Editor, with Edward L. Ferman) *The Best from Fantasy & Science Fiction: A 45th Anniversary Anthology,* St. Martin's Press (New York, NY), 1994.
*Sins of the Blood* (novel), Dell (New York, NY), 1994.
*The Fey: The Sacrifice* (novel), Millennium [England], 1995, Bantam (New York, NY), 1996.
*The Devil's Churn* (novel), Dell (New York, NY), 1996.
*Star Wars: The New Rebellion* (novel), Bantam (New York, NY), 1996.
(Compiler) *Star Wars Diplomatic Corps Entrance Exam,* Ballantine (New York, NY), 1997.
(Contributor) Margaret Weis, editor, *Legends: Tales from the Eternal Archives,* (collected works), Penguin (New York, NY), 1998.

(With Kevin J. Anderson) *Afterimage; Aftershock,* Meisha Merlin (Decatur, GA), 1998.

(Contributor, with others) *Star Trek: Invasion! Omnibus,* (collected works), Simon & Schuster (New York, NY), 1998.

(Under name Kris Rusch) *Hitler's Angel* (novel), St. Martin's Press (New York, NY), 1998.

(Contributor) *Star Trek: Day of Honor Omnibus,* (collected works), Pocket Books (New York, NY), 1999.

(Under pseudonym Sandy Schofield) *Predator: Big Game,* Spectra (Dillon, CO), 1999.

(Contributor) *Strange New Worlds II,* (collected works), Simon & Schuster, (New York, NY), 1999.

*Black Throne: The Black Queen,* Bantam (New York, NY), 1999.

(Author of introduction) Mike Resnick, *A Safari of the Mind,* Wildside Press (Holicong, PA), 1999.

*The Black King,* Bantam (New York, NY), 2000.

*In the Shade of the Slowboat Man* (radio script; adapted from Dean Wesley Smith's story of the same name), produced by Seeing Ear Theatre, 2000.

*Stories for an Enchanted Afternoon,* foreword by Kevin J. Anderson, Golden Gryphon Press (Urbana, IL), 2001.

*Little Miracles and Other Tales of Murder,* Five Star (Waterville, ME), 2001.

(Under pseudonym Kathryn Wesley Kensington) *The Monkey King* (novelization), Kensington (New York, NY), 2001.

*The Retrieval Artist, and Other Stories,* Five Star (Waterville, ME), 2002.

*The Retrieval Artist: The Disappeared,* Roc (New York, NY), 2002.

*WITH HUSBAND, DEAN WESLEY SMITH*

(Editor) *Science Fiction Writers of America Handbook: The Professional Writer's Guide to Writing Professionally,* Writers Notebook Press (Eugene, OR), 1990.

(Under pseudonym Sandy Schofield) *Star Trek: Deep Space Nine: The Big Game* (novel), Pocket Books (New York, NY), 1993.

*Star Trek: Voyager: The Escape* (novel), Pocket Books (New York, NY), 1995.

(Under pseudonym Sandy Schofield) *Aliens: Rogue* (novel), Bantam/Dark Horse (New York, NY), 1995.

*Star Trek: Deep Space Nine: The Long Night* (novel), Pocket Books (New York, NY), 1996.

*Star Trek: Klingon!* (novel), Pocket Books (New York, NY), 1996.

*Klingon Immersion Studies* (CD-ROM), Simon & Schuster Interactive (New York, NY), 1996.

*Star Trek: Rings of Tautee* (novel), Pocket Books (New York, NY), 1996.

*Star Trek: The Next Generation: Invasion! Soldiers of Fear* (novel), Pocket Books (New York, NY), 1996.

(Under pseudonym Sandy Schofield) *Quantum Leap: The Loch Ness Monster* (novel), Ace (New York, NY), 1997.

(With Nina Kiriki Hoffman) *Star Trek: Voyager: Echoes* (novel), Pocket Books (New York, NY), 1997.

*Star Trek: Deep Space Nine; The Mist: The Captain's Table,* Pocket Books (New York, NY).

*Star Trek: Day of Honor—Book Four* (novel) Pocket Books (New York, NY), 1997.

*Double Helix: Vectors,* Pocket Books (New York, NY),

*The Tenth Planet,* Del Rey Books (New York, NY), 1999.

*The Tenth Planet: Oblivion,* Del Rey Books (New York, NY), 2000.

*X Men,* Ballantine (New York, NY), 2000.

*Star Trek: Thin Air,* Pocket Books (New York, NY), 2000.

*Black Throne, Book 2: The Black King,* Bantam (New York, NY), 2000.

*The Tenth Planet: Final Assault,* Ballantine (New York, NY), 2000.

*Star Trek Voyager: Shadow,* Pocket Books (New York, NY), 2001.

*Roswell: No Good Deed,* Pocket Books (New York, NY), 2001.

*Roswell: Little Green Men,* Pocket Books (New York, NY), 2002.

*Star Trek Enterprise: By the Book,* Pocket Books (New York, NY), 2002.

*"THE FEY SERIES"*

*The Sacrifice: The First Book of the Fey,* Bantam (New York, NY), 1996.

*The Fey: The Rival,* Bantam (New York, NY), 1997.

*The Fey: The Resistance,* Bantam (New York, NY), 1998.

*Victory: The Final Book of the Fey,* Bantam (New York, NY), 1998.

*UNDER PSEUDONYM KRISTINE GRAYSON*

*Utterly Charming,* Zebra Books (New York, NY), 2000.
*Thoroughly Kissed,* Zebra Books (New York, NY), 2001.
*Completely Smitten,* Zebra Books (New York, NY), 2002.

*UNDER PSEUDONYM KRIS NELSON*

*A Dangerous Road,* St. Martin's Press (New York, NY), 2000.
*Smoke-Filled Rooms,* St. Martin's Press (New York, NY), 2001.
*Thin Walls,* St. Martin's Press (New York, NY), 2002.

*"STAR TREK VOYAGER COMIC BOOK SERIES"*

*Encounters with the Unknown,* Wildstorm Productions, 2001.
*Planet Killer: Book One,* Wildstorm Productions, 2001.
*Planet Killer: Book Two,* Wildstorm Productions, 2001.
*Planet Killer: Book Three,* Wildstorm Productions, 2001.

*EDITOR; PULPHOUSE ANTHOLOGIES*

*Pulphouse: The Hardback Magazine, Issues One and Two,* Pulphouse Publishing (Eugene, OR), 1988.
*Pulphouse: The Hardback Magazine, Issues Three, Four and Five,* Pulphouse Publishing (Eugene, OR), 1989.
*Pulphouse: The Hardback Magazine, Issues Six, Seven, Eight and Nine,* Pulphouse Publishing (Eugene, OR), 1990.
*Pulphouse: The Hardback Magazine, Issues Ten and Eleven,* Pulphouse Publishing (Eugene, OR), 1991.
*The Best of Pulphouse: The Hardback Magazine,* St. Martin's Press (New York, NY), 1991.
*Pulphouse: The Hardback Magazine, Issue Twelve,* Pulphouse Publishing (Eugene, OR), 1992.

Also author of *Simply Irresistible* (novel), Zebra Books; and *Millennium Babies* (novella); author, with Dean Wesley Smith, of *Klingon!* script for computer game, produced in 1996.

Contributor of short stories to anthologies, including *Alternate Gettysburgs,* edited by Brian M. Thomsen and Martin H. Greenberg, Berkley Books, 2002. Contributor of numerous short stories to periodicals, including *Magazine of Fantasy & Science Fiction, Alfred Hitchcock's Mystery Magazine, Ellery Queen's Mystery Magazine, Analog Science Fiction, Asimov's Science Fiction Magazine, Science Fiction Age,* and *Amazing Stories.* Author of several booklets about writing style.

*ADAPTATIONS: Star Trek: Klingon!* was adapted to audiocassette, Simon & Schuster Audio (New York, NY), 1996.

*WORK IN PROGRESS: Fantasy Life,* for Pocket Books.

*SIDELIGHTS:* A prolific and popular writer, Kristine Kathryn Rusch has had a great deal of influence on the genres of science fiction and fantasy writing toward the end of the twentieth century. "In less than a decade," noted Sydonie Benet in *St. James Guide to Science Fiction and Fantasy Writers,* "she has risen from relative obscurity to a highly regarded presence as both an editor and an author."

The daughter of a college math professor, Rusch grew up in a literate home; two of her elder siblings became English professors. Rusch took the route of a writer instead, with stops in radio, retail, and office work. At age twenty-six, Rusch had completed the prestigious Clarion Science Fiction Workshop and an experimental writing course in Taos, New Mexico. In 1987 she published her first story, in *Aboriginal Science Fiction,* but more importantly, with Dean Wesley Smith, she cofounded Pulphouse Publishing.

For many years, Pulphouse's primary project was the publication of *Pulphouse: The Hardback Magazine,* a book-length anthology that came out quarterly. They also published other projects within or about the speculative fiction field, including a collaboration between Rusch and Smith on the nonfiction *Science Fiction Writers of America Handbook: The Professional Writer's Guide to Writing Professionally,* which garnered them an award from *Locus* magazine. After *Pulphouse: The Hardback Magazine* went on hiatus—to return briefly in the mid-1990s in a more conventional magazine format—Rusch served as the editor of another popular outlet for speculative fiction, the *Magazine of Fantasy & Science Fiction,* until the middle of 1997. In 1991, she published her first full-length novel, *The White Mists of Power.* Since then, Rusch has penned many other novels and edited several anthologies.

In the same year that Rusch won Best New Writer acclaim, Pulphouse published her novella *The Gallery of His Dreams.* This tale, some eighty pages in length, concerns the historical figure Mathew Brady, famed for his photographic record of the U.S. Civil War. In his dreams, Brady travels through time to photograph the horrors of more modern wars, such as the atomic bombing of Hiroshima, Japan, and the massacre at My Lai in Vietnam. Tom Easton, reviewing *The Gallery of His Dreams* in *Analog Science Fiction & Fact,* observed that Rusch "is quite explicit in contrasting Brady's vision of his work as the production of cautionary documents with the visions of his contemporaries, of his photographs of death and destruction as commercial commodities . . . of those photographs as art." In the same article, Easton also reviewed *The Best of Pulphouse: The Hardback Magazine,* an anthology which Rusch edited during roughly the same period. He described it as "good stuff, the best of a good series. Often outrageous and provocative. Always interesting." Edward Bryant in the *Bloomsbury Review* labeled it "a fine anthology." In a previous issue of *Analog,* Easton described Rusch's nonfiction collaboration with Smith, *Science Fiction Writers of America Handbook,* as "thorough, useful discussions" of issues pertaining to writers in the genre.

In *The White Mists of Power,* readers become acquainted with Bard Byron, who is really the long-lost prince of Kilot, and his traveling companion Seymour, an inexpert magician. War in Kilot between the upper and lower classes is predicted by the magical being Cache Enos, but young Byron has a plan to preserve his country despite the fact that his father, the king, dies before Byron can be identified as the true prince. *Voice of Youth Advocates* reviewer Denice Thornhill wrote, "I just loved this book and have raved about it to several people." She went on to note the story's "good characters that grow," and called it "a must buy." *Publishers Weekly* liked *The White Mists of Power* as well, citing Rusch's "beguiling characters" and describing it as "a fine first novel."

Rusch collaborated with Kevin J. Anderson on the 1992 novel, *Afterimage.* The plot of this tale hinges on the existence of shape shifters who can help people jump from one body to another. One such being is able to save the life of Rebecca, left for dead after being assaulted and raped by the Joan of Arc killer. Unfortunately, she is spirited into the body of the last image left upon her mind—that of her attacker. She must conceal her temporary form from the police while she seeks a way to return to her old body. Jody Hanson in *Kliatt* thought *Afterimage* was "an excellent, thoroughly enjoyable book," though she did caution readers about the graphic rape scenes. Hanson felt, however, that these were not gratuitous depictions, but rather that they helped readers understand "the horror of these crimes."

*Traitors,* Rusch's next novel, was published in 1993. Its protagonist, Diate, reluctantly gives up his talent for dance, a compromise he makes in order to live in safety among the island people of Golga. On Golga he waits for the right time to seek revenge upon the rulers of his native land, whom he believes slaughtered all his family members. Observing that the novel contains "elements both modern and medieval," *Kliatt* reviewer Joseph R. DeMarco wrote that "what [Diate] does to fulfill his desire for revenge is laid out neatly" by Rusch. A *Science Fiction Chronicle* reviewer described *Traitors* as "entertaining" and "a well concocted mix."

With Edward L. Ferman, the previous editor of the *Magazine of Fantasy and Science Fiction,* Rusch edited 1994's *Best from Fantasy & Science Fiction.* Gary K. Wolfe in *Locus* recalled that the magazine from which the anthology sprang "was bending traditional genre boundaries decades before . . . others broadened the scope of the competition," cited many stories as worthy of attention, and concluded: "In all, this latest addition to a distinguished series honors both the magazine's rich tradition and its interesting new directions." Deborah A. Feulner, writing in *Voice of Youth Advocates,* wrote that "readers . . . will be pleased with the variety of stories presented."

Rusch tried her hand at vampire fiction in the 1994 novel *Sins of the Blood.* This book proposes that in the United States everyone acknowledges the existence of vampires. In some states, they are treated as victims of disease; in others, they are legally hunted down and killed, primarily through the efforts of bounty hunters. One such killer is the protagonist in *Sins of the Blood,* a woman whose own father is a vampire. During the course of the novel, she seeks to find her long-estranged brother, and protect him from joining the vampiric world. A *Science Fiction Chronicle* contributor noted "the well delineated central character" of *Sins of the Blood,* and described Rusch's vampire world as "tantalizing."

In 1996, Rusch began an epic work about an evil people known as "the Fey" with *The Sacrifice.* In this novel, the target of the Fey is the magical Blue Isle, and Prince Rugar, the son of the Black King of the Fey, leads the attack. Because of the Blue Isle's magic, the attackers are repulsed by its denizens, but the Fey are unlikely to give up their quest for world domination. Though she warned readers about what she saw as "gruesome" warfare descriptions, Karen Ellis of *Kliatt Young Adult Paperback Book Guide* recommended *The Sacrifice,* saying that "the diversity of characterization, as shaped by contrasting cultures, is fascinating."

As for the origins of the Fey, Rausch told *Interzone* interviewer Jayme Lynn Blaschke that "I just tend to accumulate weird facts. . . . I got the idea for *The Fey* somewhere in 1981 or '82, but it wasn't anything really developed." When she began work in earnest, Rusch described the work to her editor as "a Hundred Years' War. Now, if you've read [the series] you realize I haven't gotten anywhere close to a hundred years." As she began volume one of the series, Rausch said she realized "I'd started in the wrong place. Essentially, I'd started in year fifty of my hundred years' war, and to explain what was going to happen, I had to go back. So really, we're talking 150 years, but I don't want to scare people."

In the same year *The Sacrifice* hit bookstands, Rusch also published a novel in the popular *Star Wars* series created by filmmaker George Lucas. Titled *The New Rebellion,* the story takes familiar characters such as Princess Leia Organa Solo into the first year that former leaders of the evil empire are allowed to hold seats in the Senate. *Booklist* contributor Roland Green assured readers that "everybody snatches triumph from the jaws of disaster in the nick of time and in the approved fashion." Rusch described her *Star Wars* and *Star Trek* tie-in books to Blaschke as "the ultimate fan fic[tion]." Such sagas, she added, "have taken over our love of space opera in many, many areas. Kids will come in and they'll start reading those books first."

Rusch entered the romance field in 2000 with the novels *Utterly Charming, Thoroughly Kissed,* and *Com-* *pletely Smitten,* a trio written under the pseudonym of Kristine Grayson. She's also written historical fiction, most notably *Hitler's Angel,* which began, the author told Blaschke, as "a historical, alternate history novella. Hitler's niece was murdered, in his apartment, under suspicious circumstances in 1931. If that case had been solved and Hitler had been found guilty—I have no doubt he was guilty of that murder—the entire history of the Western world would've been changed, and millions of lives would've been saved."

*BIOGRAPHICAL AND CRITICAL SOURCES:*

*BOOKS*

*St. James Guide to Science Fiction and Fantasy Writers,* 4th edition, St. James Press (Detroit, MI), 1995.

*PERIODICALS*

*Analog Science Fiction & Fact,* September, 1991, review of *Science Fiction Writers of America Handbook: The Professional Writer's Guide to Writing Professionally,* p. 161; May, 1992, Tom Easton, review of *The Gallery of His Dreams,* p. 161.

*Bloomsbury Review,* December, 1991, Edward Bryant, review of *The Best of Pulphouse,* p. 27.

*Booklist,* October 1, 1996, Roland Green, review of *Star Wars: The New Rebellion,* p. 292; April 15, 2001, Green, review of *Stories for an Enchanted Afternoon,* p. 1543.

*Bookwatch,* May, 1991, review of *Science Fiction Writers of America Handbook,* p. 6; April, 1992, review of *The White Mists of Power,* p. 6.

*Kirkus Reviews,* July 15, 1991, review of *The Best of Pulphouse,* p. 896.

*Kliatt Young Adult Paperback Book Guide,* November, 1992, Jody Hanson, review of *Afterimage,* pp. 18-19; January, 1995, p. 19; March, 1996, Karen Ellis, review of *The Sacrifice,* p. 20.

*Library Journal,* November 15, 1991, review of *The White Mists of Power,* p. 111.

*Locus,* February, 1991, review of *Science Fiction Writers of America Handbook,* pp. 38, 58; March, 1991, review of *Science Fiction Writers of America Handbook,* p. 25; May, 1991, review of *Science Fiction Writers of America Handbook,* p. 29; June, 1991, review of *The Best of Pulp-*

*house*, p. 29; July, 1991, review of *The Gallery of His Dreams*, pp. 23, 27, 48; September, 1991, review of *The White Mists of Power*, p. 25; October, 1991, review of *The White Mists of Power*, p. 15, and *The Best of Pulphouse*, p. 52; December, 1991, review of *The White Mists of Power*, p. 55; January, 1992, review of *The White Mists of Power*, p. 59; September, 1992, review of *Afterimage*, p. 62; October, 1992, review of *Afterimage*, p. 23, and *The Best of Pulphouse*, p. 54; October, 1994, Gary K. Wolfe, review of *Best from Fantasy & Science Fiction*, p. 58.

*Magazine of Fantasy & Science Fiction*, October, 1992, review of *The White Mists of Power*, p. 23.

*Publishers Weekly*, August 16, 1991, review of *The Best of Pulphouse*, p. 51; October 4, 1991, review of *The White Mists of Power*, p. 84; September 24, 2001, review of *Little Miracles and Other Tales of Murder*, p. 73.

*Science Fiction Chronicle*, April, 1991, review of *Science Fiction Writers of America Handbook*, p. 30; August, 1991, review of *The Gallery of His Dreams*, p. 24; November, 1991, review of *The Best of Pulphouse*, p. 33; March, 1992, review of *The White Mists of Power*, pp. 20, 30; August, 1992, review of *Afterimage*, p. 49; October, 1993, p. 36; February, 1995, p. 38.

*Voice of Youth Advocates*, April, 1992, Denice Thornhill, review of *The White Mists of Power*, pp. 46-47; December, 1994, Deborah Feulner, review of *Best from Fantasy & Science Fiction*, pp. 282-283.

*ONLINE*

*Bookbrowser*, http://www.bookbrowser.com/ (July 17, 2002), Harriet Klausner, review of *The Retrieval Artist: The Disappeared*.

*Interzone*, http://www.sfsite.com/ (December, 1998), Jayme Lynn Blaschke, "A Conversation with Kristine Kathryn Rusch."*

# S

## SAMPSON, Michael 1952-

*PERSONAL:* Born October 13, 1952, in Denison, TX; son of Roy (a carpenter) and Ida (a homemaker; maiden name, Bon) Sampson; married Mary Beth Glossup (a professor), 1973; children: Jonathan, Joshua. *Education:* East Texas State University, B.S., 1974, M.Ed., 1976; University of Arizona, Ph.D., 1980. *Politics:* Independent. *Religion:* Baptist.

*ADDRESSES: Home*—Route 2, Box 50-7, Campbell, TX 75422. *Office*—Department of Elementary Education, Texas A & M University—Commerce, Commerce, TX 75429-3011. *E-mail*—Michael@michaelsampson.com.

*CAREER:* Educator, author, and storyteller. Commerce Independent School District, Commerce, TX, teacher, 1974-76; Texas A & M University—Commerce, professor, 1979—. International Institute of Literacy Learning, executive director, 1980—. With Bill Martin, Jr., hosted Pathways to Literacy teaching workshops throughout the United States. National Reading Conference, member of technology committee, 2002; vice chair, Texas Education Agency Professional Practices Commission; member of governing board, National Association of Creative Adults and Young Children. Storyteller at schools and libraries.

*MEMBER:* International Reading Association (member, Las Vegas program committee), National Reading Conference, National Council of Teachers of English, Texas Association for the Improvement of Reading (state board member; state president), Phi Delta Kappa.

*WRITINGS:*

*FOR CHILDREN*

*The Football That Won . . . ,* illustrated by Ted Rand, Holt (New York, NY), 1996.

(With Bill Martin, Jr.) *Si Won's Victory,* Scott Foresman (Reading, MA), 1996.

(With Mary Beth Sampson) *Star of the Circus,* illustrated by Jose Aruego and Ariane Dewey, Holt (New York, NY), 1996.

(With Bill Martin, Jr.) *Yummy Tum Tee,* Scott Foresman (Reading, MA), 1996.

(With Bill Martin, Jr.) *City Scenes,* Learning Media Ltd. (Wellington, New Zealand), 1997.

(With Mary Beth Sampson) *Wild Bear,* Learning Media Ltd. (Wellington, New Zealand), 1997.

(With Bill Martin, Jr.) *Football Fever,* Learning Media Ltd. (Wellington, New Zealand), 1997.

(With Bill Martin, Jr.) *Swish!,* illustrated by Michael Chesworth, Holt (New York, NY), 1997.

(With Bill Martin, Jr.) *Adam, Adam, What Do You See?,* illustrated by Cathie Felstead, Tommy Nelson (Nashville, TN), 2000.

(With Bill Martin, Jr.) *The Little Squeegy Bug* (based on the book by Martin published in 1946), illustrated by Pat Corrigan, Winslow Press (Delray Beach, FL), 2001.

(With Bill Martin, Jr.) *Rock It, Sock It, Number Line!,* illustrated by Heather Cahoon, Holt (New York, NY), 2001.

(With Bill Martin, Jr.) *Little Granny Quarterback,* illustrated by Michael Chesworth, Boyds Mills Press, 2001.

(With Bill Martin, Jr.) *I Pledge Allegiance*, illustrated by Chris Raschka, Candlewick Press (Cambridge, MA), 2002.

(With Bill Martin, Jr.) *Trick or Treat?*, illustrated by Paul Meisel, Simon & Schuster (New York, NY), 2002.

(With Bill Martin, Jr.) *Caddie the Golf Dog*, illustrated by Floyd Cooper, Walker (New York, NY), 2002.

Sampson's books have been translated into Spanish.

*TEACHING MATERIALS*

(With T. Kelly) *Signs and Safety*, Kendall/Hunt (Dubuque, IA), 1986.

*School*, Kendall/Hunt (Dubuque, IA), 1986.

*My House*, Kendall/Hunt (Dubuque, IA), 1986.

*Transportation*, Kendall/Hunt (Dubuque, IA), 1986.

*Nutrition*, Kendall/Hunt (Dubuque, IA), 1986.

*Supermarkets*, Kendall/Hunt (Dubuque, IA), 1986.

*Jobs in the Family*, Kendall/Hunt (Dubuque, IA), 1986.

*Growing Up*, Kendall/Hunt (Dubuque, IA), 1986.

*All about Time*, Kendall/Hunt (Dubuque, IA), 1986.

*Pets*, Kendall/Hunt (Dubuque, IA), 1986.

*The Zoo*, Kendall/Hunt (Dubuque, IA), 1986.

*Insects*, Kendall/Hunt (Dubuque, IA), 1986.

Also contributor to teaching materials published by Developmental Learning Materials (Allen, TX), 1989.

*FOR ADULTS*

(Editor) *The Pursuit of Literacy: Early Reading and Writing*, Kendall/Hunt Publishing (Dubuque, IA), 1986.

*Experiences for Literacy*, SRA Technology Training (Chicago, IL), 1990.

(With Mary Beth Sampson and Roach Van Allen) *Pathways to Literacy: A Meaning-centered Perspective*, Holt, 1991, 2nd edition published as *Pathways to Literacy: Process Transactions*, Harcourt (New York, NY), 1995, 3rd edition published as *Total Literacy: Pathways to Reading, Writing, and Learning*, Wadsworth (San Francisco, CA), 2003.

Contributor of articles and reviews to professional journals and periodicals, including *Reading Teacher, ACT, Tender Years, Reading Improvement, Christian Life, Reading Horizons, Reading Research Quarterly, Living with Preschoolers, Industrial Education* and *Ohio Reading Teacher*. Contributor to books, including *Practical Classroom Applications of Language Experience: Looking Back and Looking Forward*, edited by O. G. Nelson and W. M. Linek, Allyn & Bacon (Boston, MA), 1999.

*SIDELIGHTS:* Michael Sampson is an author and educator who has devoted his career to helping kids read and love it. Both on his own and together with longtime collaborator, children's writer Bill Martin, Jr., Sampson has written humorous titles such as *Swish!, Rock It, Sock It, Number Line!,* and *Caddie the Golf Dog.* Published in 1997, *Swish!* tells the story of two rival girls' basketball teams, and is punctuated by the ebb and flow of an actual basketball game, while in *Trick or Treat?* puns, alliteration, and other wordplay provide fun for novice readers. In the pages of *Rock It, Sock It, Number Line!* a parade of strutting vegetables helps teach young readers the numbers one through ten. On a quieter note, *Caddie the Golf Dog* introduces young children to a stray dog who finds not one but two loving homes in a "touching story" by Sampson and Martin that *School Library Journal* contributor Linda Ludke maintained would "resonate with children." *Adam, Adam, What Do You See?* reflects its authors' Christian faith in its descriptions of Bible characters and Christian concepts as well as its inclusion of short verses from both the Old and New Testament. Calling the text "friendly and age-appropriate," a *Publishers Weekly* contributor deemed *Adam, Adam, What Do You See?* a picture book that encourages discussion and leads curious "readers to the biblical verses that serve as sources."

Sampson joined collaborator Bill Martin, Jr. to update Martin's first children's book, originally published in 1946. In *The Little Squeegy Bug* a small bug feels less important than the other insects around him, but his efforts to try to be something he's not—a bee with silver wings and a long stinger—only bring failure. Finally, a trip to the wise Haunchy the Spider brings a change to Squeegy: Haunchy weaves the small bug a pair of beautiful silver wings, and instead of a stinger puts a shining star on Squeegy's own tail, turning the formerly nondescript bug into a firefly. *The Little Squeegy Bug* also features the artistic talents of illustrator Pat Corrigan, whose artwork a *Publishers Weekly* contributor praised as "appealingly stylized."

Martin and Sampson's 2000 picture book *I Pledge Allegiance* is designed to introduce the Pledge to the many U.S. children who recite at the start of each school day. Including an explanation of many of the Pledge's significant words, as well as a history of the oath since its composition by Frances Bellamy, the book "emphasizes the importance" of reciting the Pledge, according to *School Library Journal* contributor Krista Tokarz.

Sampson once told *CA:* "During my elementary school years, my first stories were about 'The Hardy Boys' and 'Superman,' while my first publication was a joke published in a national magazine. During the 1980s and 1990s I wrote several books for teachers, including *Pathways to Literacy*. Finally, in 1996, I came full circle in my writing when *The Football That Won . . .* was published. The story is based on an experience I had as a seventh-grade football player. Actual experiences continue to guide my writing. *Star of the Circus* resulted from watching my kindergarten-aged son's classroom circus show. *Si Won's Victory* is based upon the struggle of a Korean child my son knew in grade school. *Swish!* was written after watching the drama of a cliffhanger finish to a girls' basketball game."

*BIOGRAPHICAL AND CRITICAL SOURCES:*

*PERIODICALS*

*Booklist,* September 1, 2002, Gillian Engberg, review of *I Pledge Allegiance,* p. 120; September 15, 2002, Stephanie Zvirin, review of *Trick or Treat?,* p. 246; December 1, 2002, Helen Rosenberg, review of *Caddie the Golf Dog,* p. 676.

*Children's Book Review Service,* August, 1996, p. 162.

*Kirkus Reviews,* August 1, 2001, review of *Rock It, Sock It, Number Line!,* p. 1128; September 1, 2001, review of *The Little Squeegy Bug,* p. 1297; October 1, 2001, review of *Little Granny Quarterback,* p. 1428; September 15, 2002, review of *Trick or Treat?,* p. 1395; September 15, 2002, review of *I Pledge Allegiance,* p. 1394; October 1, 2002, review of *Caddie the Golf Dog,* p. 1479.

*Publishers Weekly,* July 29, 1996, p. 87; September 25, 2000, review of *Adam, Adam, What Do You See?,* p. 113; August 20, 2001, review of *Rock It, Sock It, Number Line!,* p. 78; October 1, 2001, review of *The Little Squeegy Bug,* p. 63; August 26, 2002, review of *I Pledge Allegiance,* p. 68; .

*School Library Journal,* October, 1996, p. 105; December, 2000, Patricia Pearl Dole, review of *Adam, Adam, What Do You See?,* p. 134; December,

2001, Piper L. Nyman, review of *Rock It, Sock It, Number Line!,* p. 106; December, 2001, Barbara Buckley, review of *Little Granny Quarterback,* p. 106; October, 2002, John Peters, review of *Trick or Treat?,* p. 120; December, 2002, Linda Ludke, review of *Caddie the Golf Dog,* p. 108, and Krista Tokarz, review of *I Pledge Allegiance,* p. 127.

*ONLINE*

*Michael Sampson Home Page,* http://www.michaelsampson.com/ (May 5, 2003).*

\*          \*          \*

# SANDOZ, (George) Ellis (Jr.) 1931-

*PERSONAL:* Born February 10, 1931, in New Orleans, LA; son of George Ellis (a dentist) and Ruby (Odom) Sandoz; married Therese Alverne Hubley, May 31, 1957; children: George Ellis III, Lisa Claire Alverne, Erica Christine, Jonathan David. *Education:* Attended University of North Carolina, 1950; Louisiana State University, B.A., 1951, M.A., 1953; graduate study at Georgetown University, 1952-53, and University of Heidelberg, 1956-58; University of Munich, Dr.Oec.Publ. (magna cum laude), 1965. *Politics:* Democrat. *Religion:* Baptist.

*ADDRESSES: Home*—2843 Valcour Ave., Baton Rouge, LA 70820. *Office*—Eric Voegelin Institute for American Renaissance Studies, 240 Stubbs Hall, Louisiana State University, Baton Rouge, LA 70803-5466. *E-mail*—esandoz@lsu.edu.

*CAREER:* Louisiana Polytechnic Institute, Ruston, LA, instructor, 1959-60, assistant professor, 1960-66, associate professor, 1966-67, professor of political science, 1967-68, director of Center for International Studies, 1966-68; East Texas State University, Commerce, TX, professor of political science and head of department, 1968-78; Louisiana State University, Baton Rouge, LA, professor of political science, 1978-98, Herman Moyse, Jr. Distinguished Professor of Political Science, 1998—, chairman of department, 1980-81, director of Eric Voegelin Institute for America Renaissance Studies, 1987—. Fulbright scholar in Germany, 1964-65; visiting summer scholar, Hoover Institution on War, Revolution, and Peace, 1970 and 1973. Member of council, Southwest Alliance for Latin America, 1966-68 and 1973. Member of National Council on the Humanities, 1982-1988. Speaker at professional conferences. Consultant, National Endowment for the Humanities fellowship program, 1977-80. *Military service:* U.S. Marine Corps, 1953-56; became first lieutenant.

*MEMBER:* American Political Science Association (member of council, 1978-79), American Society for Political and Legal Philosophy, Conference for the Study of Political Thought, Southwestern Political Science Association (member of executive council, 1970-71; vice-president, 1972-73; president, 1974-75), Southern Political Science Association (member of executive council, 1982-85), Phi Delta Kappa, Sigma Nu, Tau Kappa Alpha, Pi Sigma Alpha.

*AWARDS, HONORS:* Germanistic Society of America fellowship, 1964-65; H. B. Earhart fellowship, 1964-65; Fulbright Achievement Award, 1965; National Endowment for the Humanities research grant, 1976-78; Distinguished Research Master Award for faculty research scholarship, and Faculty Medal, Louisiana State University, 1992; University Medal and Certificate for Education Leadership, Palacky University Olomouc (Czech Republic), 1994.

*WRITINGS:*

*The Grand Inquisitor: A Study in Political Apocalypse,* [Munich, Germany], 1967, revised edition published as *Political Apocalypse: A Study of Dostoevsky's Grand Inquisitor,* Louisiana State University Press (Baton Rouge, LA), 1971, second edition, ISI Books (Wilmington, DE), 2000.
*Conceived in Liberty: American Individual Rights Today,* Duxbury (North Scituate, MA), 1978.
(Editor, with Cecil V. Crabb, Jr.) *A Tide of Discontent: The 1980 Elections and Their Meaning,* Congressional Quarterly (Washington, DC), 1981.
*The Voegelinian Revolution: A Biographical Introduction,* Louisiana State University (Baton Rouge, LA), 1981, second edition, Transaction Publishers (New Brunswick, NJ), 2000.
(Editor and author of introduction) *Eric Voegelin's Thought: A Critical Appraisal,* Duke University Press (Durham, NC), 1982.

(Editor, with Cecil V. Crabb, Jr.) *Election 84: Landslide without a Mandate?,* New American Library (New York, NY), 1985.
(Editor and author of introduction) Eric Voegelin, *Autobiographical Reflections,* Louisiana State University Press (Baton Rouge, LA), 1989.
(Editor and author of introduction) *The Collected Works of Eric Voegelin,* multiple volumes, Louisiana State University Press (Baton Rouge, LA), 1989-2001.
*A Government of Laws: Political Theory, Religion, and the American Founding,* Louisiana State University Press (Baton Rouge, LA), 1990.
(Editor) *Eric Voegelin's Significance for the Modern Mind,* Louisiana State University Press (Baton Rouge, LA), 1991.
(Editor) *Political Sermons of the American Founding Era, 1730-1805,* two volumes, Liberty (Indianapolis, IN), 1991, 2nd edition, 1998.
(Editor and author of introduction) *The Roots of Liberty: Magna Carta, Ancient Constitution, and the Anglo-American Tradition of Rule of Law,* University of Missouri Press (Columbia, MO), 1993.
(Editor) *Index to Political Sermons of the American Founding Era, 1730-1805,* Liberty Fund (Indianapolis, IN), 1997, 2nd edition, 1998.
*The Politics of Truth and Other Untimely Essays: The Crisis of Civic Consciousness,* University of Missouri Press (Columbia, MO), 1999.
(Editor) Eric Voegelin, *Order and History,* Volume 5: *In Search of Order,* University of Missouri Press (Columbia, MO), 2000.

Contributor to books, including *The Post-Behavioral Era: Perspectives on Political Science,* edited by George J. Graham, Jr. and George W. Carey, McKay, 1972; *The Ethical Dimension of Political Life: Essays in Honor of John H. Hallowell,* edited by Francis Canavan, Duke University Press (Raleigh, NC), 1983; and *American Values Projected Abroad,* University of Virginia, 1984. General editor of "History of Political Ideas" series, University of Missouri Press (Columbia, MO), 1997-99. Author of weekly column "Southerner Abroad" for *Shreveport Journal,* 1956-58. Contributor of about twenty articles to political affairs journals. Member of board of editors, *Political Science Reviewer,* 1970—, *Modern Age,* 1971—, *Journal of Politics,* 1975—, *Interpretation,* 1980—, and *This World,* 1981—.

*SIDELIGHTS:* Ellis Sandoz has written and edited numerous books on various aspects of political science, but his specialty is collecting, editing, and explaining the work of Eric Voegelin, who has been rated "the twentieth century's greatest political philosopher" by Richard J. Bishirjian in the *Review of Politics*. According to Bishirjian, Voegelin is a complex thinker who draws readers in, but his work is so full of ideas that it frequently proves to be difficult to sort out. The reviewer warned that "attempts to distill Voegelin's thought are never entirely successful," but added that Sandoz's essay "Voegelin's Philosophy of History and Human Affairs" is "one of the best expositions of Voegelin's philosophy that I have read." This essay, along with nine others by Sandoz, are collected in *The Politics of Truth and Other Untimely Essays: The Crisis of Civic Consciousness.*

"Sandoz is clearly on the top of his game in this brief collection," noted Bishirjian. "Virtually every essay brings his reader to a full stop, and a desire to learn more." Besides specifically discussing Voegelin, Sandoz also ponders the origins of the United States, the founding fathers' vision of the divine, and how that comes to bear on the United States as it is today. "Sandoz writes that what attracts him—truth and a desire to affirm the common sense notion that all is not relative—is disdained by intellectual culture," reported Bishirjian. "The love of the divine as the source of the order of being defines his existence as a political philosopher, against which a battery of 'isms' are counterpoised to his love: Freudianism, positivism, Marxism, new totalitarian movements such as political correctness, radical feminism, critical legal studies, multiculturalism, and deconstructionism."

*BIOGRAPHICAL AND CRITICAL SOURCES:*

*PERIODICALS*

*American Political Science Review,* September, 1991, review of *A Government of Laws: Political Theory, Religion, and the American Founding,* p. 1005.

*Annals of the American Academy of Political and Social Science,* January, 1991, review of *A Government of Laws,* p. 105.

*Booklist,* November 1, 1989, review of *A Government of Laws,* p. 507.

*Choice,* October, 1990, review of *A Government of Laws,* p. 386.

*Christian Science Monitor,* July 3, 1990, review of *A Government of Laws,* p. 15.

*Ethics,* October, 1991, review of *A Government of Laws,* p. 189.

*Journal of American History,* June, 1992, review of *A Government of Laws,* p. 245; June, 1994, review of *The Roots of Liberty: Magna Carta, Ancient Constitution, and the Anglo-American Tradition of Rule of Law,* p. 224.

*Journal of Church and State,* winter, 1993, review of *Political Sermons of the American Founding Era, 1730-1805,* p. 163.

*Journal of Economic Literature,* March, 1992, review of *Political Sermons of the American Founding Era, 1730-1805,* p. 308.

*Journal of Politics,* May, 1987, review of *Election 84: Landslide without a Mandate?,* p. 581; February, 1993, review of *A Government of Laws,* p. 264.

*Journal of Religion,* April, 1999, Thomas Heilke, review of *The Collected Works of Eric Voegelin,* p. 291.

*Modern Age,* summer, 1992, review of *A Government of Laws,* p. 363.

*National Review,* October 9, 2000, Mike Potemra, review of *Political Apocalypse: A Study of Dostoevsky's Grand Inquisitor.*

*Perspectives on Political Science,* spring, 1991, review of *A Government of Laws,* p. 105; fall, 1992, review of *Eric Voegelin's Significance for the Modern Mind,* p. 232.

*Reference & Research Book News,* May, 1993, review of *The Roots of Liberty,* p. 29; May, 1999, review of *The Politics of Truth and Other Untimely Essays: The Crisis of Civic Consciousness,* p. 123.

*Review of Politics,* spring, 1991, Richard J. Bishirjian, review of *A Government of Laws,* p. 423.

*Reviews in American History,* September, 1991, review of *A Government of Laws,* p. 338.

*Social Science Quarterly,* December, 1991, review of *Eric Voegelin's Significance for the Modern Mind,* p. 865.

*University Bookman,* February, 1992, review of *Eric Voegelin's Significance for the Modern Mind* and *A Government of Laws,* p. 27.

*University Press Book News,* June, 1990, review of *A Government of Laws,* p. 22; June, 1991, review of *Eric Voegelin's Significance for the Modern Mind,* p. 2.

*Virginia Quarterly Review,* autumn, 1990, review of *A Government of Laws,* p. 136.

*William and Mary Quarterly,* April, 1993, review of *A Government of Laws,* p. 458.*

**SCHOFIELD, Sandy**
  See RUSCH, Kristine Kathryn

\*   \*   \*

**SCULL, Andrew 1947-**

*PERSONAL:* Born May 2, 1947, in Edinburgh, Scotland; came to the United States, 1969; son of Allan Edward (a civil engineer) and Marjorie (a college teacher; maiden name, Corrigan) Scull; married Nancy Principi (a lawyer), August 16, 1970; children: Anna Theresa, Andrew Edward, Alexander. *Education:* Balliol College, Oxford, B.A. (with first class honors), 1969; Princeton University, M.A. (Sociology), 1971, Ph.D., 1974. *Hobbies and other interests:* Gardening, travel.

*ADDRESSES: Office*—Department of Sociology, University of California at San Diego, La Jolla, CA 92037. *Agent*—Peters, Fraser, & Dunlop, Drury House, 34-43 Russell St., London WC2B 5HA, England; Sterling Lord, 65 Bleeker St., New York, NY 10012. *E-mail*—ascull@ucsd.edu

*CAREER:* University of Pennsylvania, Philadelphia, lecturer, 1973-74, assistant professor of sociology, 1974-78; University of California at San Diego, La Jolla, associate professor, 1978-82, professor of sociology, 1982—, chairman of department, 1985-89, professor of science studies, 1988—. Visiting fellow at University of London, 1977, Princeton University, 1978-79, and Wellcome Institute for the History of Medicine, 1981-82; Hannah Lecturer in the History of Medicine, 1983; Squibb Lecturer in the History of Psychiatry, University of London, 1986.

*MEMBER:* Phi Beta Kappa (honorary member).

*AWARDS, HONORS:* American Council of Learned Societies fellow, 1976-77; Shelby Cullom Davis Center for Historical Studies fellow, 1978-79; Guggenheim fellow, 1981-82; University of California President's Research Fellowship in the Humanities, 1989-90, 2001-2002.

*WRITINGS:*

*Decarceration: Community Treatment and the Deviant: A Radical View,* Prentice-Hall (Englewood Cliffs, NJ), 1977, 2nd edition, Rutgers University Press (New Brunswick, NJ), 1984.

*Museums of Madness: The Social Organization of Insanity in Nineteenth-Century England,* St. Martin's Press (New York, NY), 1979.

(Editor) *Madhouses, Mad-Doctors and Madmen: The Social History of Psychiatry in the Victorian Era,* University of Pennsylvania Press (Philadelphia, PA), 1981.

(With Steven Lukes) *Durkheim and the Law,* St. Martin's Press (New York, NY), 1983.

(With Stanley Cohen) *Social Control and the State: Historical and Comparative Essays,* St. Martin's (New York, NY), 1983.

*Social Order/Mental Disorder: Anglo-American Psychiatry in Historical Perspective,* University of California Press (Berkeley, CA), 1989.

(Editor and author of introduction) W. A. F. Browne, *The Asylum As Utopia: W. A. F. Browne and the Mid-Nineteenth Century Consolidation of Psychiatry* (from an 1837 volume entitled *What Asylums Were, Are, and Ought to Be*), Routledge (New York, NY), 1991.

*The Most Solitary of Afflictions: Madness and Society in Britain, 1700-1900,* Yale University Press (New Haven, CT), 1993.

(With Charlotte MacKenzie and Nicholas Hervey) *Masters of Bedlam: The Transformation of the Mad-Doctoring Trade,* Princeton University Press (Princeton, NJ), 1996.

(With Jonathan Andrews) *Undertaker of the Mind: John Monro and Mad-Doctoring in Eighteenth-Century England,* University of California Press (Berkeley, CA), 2001.

(With Jonathan Andrews) *Customers and Patrons of the Mad-trade: The Management of Lunacy in Eighteenth-Century London,* University of California Press (Berkeley, CA), 2002.

Coeditor, "Research in Law, Deviance, and Social Control" series, JAI Press, 1984—. Contributor to scholarly texts, including *Theoretical Perspectives on Deviance,* 1972; *Corrections and Punishment: Structure, Function, and Process,* 1977; and *The Power to Punish,* 1983. Contributor to sociology, psychiatry, and medical journals and other periodicals, including *Times Literary Supplement* and *London Review of Books.*

*WORK IN PROGRESS: Desperate Remedies: A History of Somatic Treatments in Psychiatry.*

*SIDELIGHTS:* Andrew Scull specializes in studies of the insane of the past and the present. The latter subject is the topic of his first book, *Decarceration: Community Treatment and the Deviant: A Radical View.* This volume is, according to a critic for *Working Papers for a New Society,* "not only the best overview of this decade's 'reforms' [in psychiatric care] but also the best analysis of how the reforms have failed." Kim Hopper of the *Health-PAC Bulletin* describes Scull as "an able and effective historian, a shrewd critic, and a clear, compelling writer," and calls *Decarceration* "closely documented and carefully argued, . . . [a book]without parallel in the recent literature on psychiatric and penal institutions."

Turning toward history, Scull produced two similarly themed volumes. The first, *Museums of Madness: The Social Organization of Insanity in Nineteenth-Century England,* was published in 1979. Fourteen years later came *The Most Solitary of Afflictions: Madness and Society in Britain, 1700-1900,* a study of asylums and their effects on the public. In the nineteenth century, pressure to bring down the cost of caring for the insane led to institutional overcrowding; at the same time, senior citizens whose overall health was failing were often admitted to asylums by their families. Comparing this work to *Museums of Madness,* T. H. Turner of the *British Medical Journal* found that *The Most Solitary of Afflictions* was not "a new book," though the critic also acknowledged that "the additions . . . are an improvement" on the earlier volume. Likewise, *Sociology* contributor Joan Busfield called *The Most Solitary of Afflictions* "essentially a revised version" of *Museum of Madness.* Turner pointed to "the opening review of the rise of asylum," which Turner called "both eclectic and thoughtful, the best summary of modern research yet available." In Busfield's view, *The Most Solitary of Afflictions* "is much more thorough and detailed than *Museums of Madness.*" The author, she added, "has clearly taken the opportunity of the fifteen years since the first book was published to examine a far broader range of historical sources." Busfield concluded that the latter book "provides a fuller and more historically grounded picture of the rise of asylums than its more schematic predecessor. Yet, precisely because of the greater substantive detail, the key arguments stand out less clearly."

The word *bedlam* originated from a slang name for London's New Bethlehem Hospital, a notorious insane asylum of centuries past. Andrew Scull examines the history and legacy of such institutions in his book *Masters of Bedlam: The Transformation of the Mad-*

*Doctoring Trade.* In Victorian times, noted an *Economist* reviewer, "mad people, a messy and embarrassing feature of society, were . . . rounded up, cleaned up and put away." Indeed, the transformation of London from an agrarian to an industrial society had produced the kind of wealth that enabled the upper classes to "afford new luxuries: soap, servants, painters, plays—and treatment for their mad relations." But despite the proliferation of asylums and the growth industry of medical reformers, real progress in treating the mentally ill was slow. Doctors who disapproved of such common treatments as leeches and manacles "were a minority," noted the *Economist* reviewer.

Oonagh Walsh of the *Historian* found *Masters of Bedlam* an "admirably collaborative volume" that "examines the lives of seven mad-doctors, or 'alienists,' as they preferred to be titled." These medical men challenged the system by advocating new and better research into their patients' conditions as part of the emerging science of psychiatry. "This is not a study of great men," Walsh pointed out. "Some of these figures are deservedly obscure—but their lives provide a useful commentary upon the acceptance of psychiatry as a worthy branch of the medical profession."

Scull and coauthor Jonathan Andrews came upon a valuable archival resource in the case-book of "mad-doctor" John Monro, who practiced in the eighteenth century. From that discovery came their 2001 study *Undertaker of the Mind: John Monro and Mad-Doctoring in Eighteenth-Century England.* "Neither a conventional biography nor simply a study of an emerging profession," stated *Times Literary Supplement* reviewer Chandak Sengoopta, "the book seeks to illuminate the lives, sorrows, crime and mores of a complex, changing society." During the eighteenth century, the reputations of Monro "depended far less on his ability to cure than on his management of his trade and social image," Sengoopta commented. "As Andrews and Scull show us, the death of reason was then regarded as even more frightening than physical death, and mad-doctors akin to undertakers in their commerce with madness."

*BIOGRAPHICAL AND CRITICAL SOURCES:*

*PERIODICALS*

*AB Bookman's Weekly,* April 26 1982, review of *Madhouses, Mad-Doctors and Madmen: The Social History of Psychiatry in the Victorian Era,* p. 3301.

*Albion,* spring, 1994, review of *The Most Solitary of Afflictions: Madness and Society in Britain, 1700-1900,* p. 166; spring, 1998, review of *Masters of Bedlam: The Transformation of the Mad-Doctoring Trade,* p. 138.

*American Historical Review,* June, 1982, review of *Museums of Madness: The Social Organization of Insanity in Nineteenth-Century England,* p. 780; April, 1991, review of *Social Order/Mental Disorder: Anglo-American Psychiatry in Historical Perspective,* p. 478; December, 1994, review of *The Most Solitary of Afflictions,* p. 1691; June, 1998, review of *Masters of Bedlam,* p. 886.

*American Journal of Psychiatry,* December, 1994, review of *The Most Solitary of Afflictions,* p. 1832.

*American Journal of Sociology,* March, 1982, review of *Museums of Madness,* p. 1232, review of *Decarceration: Community Treatment and the Deviant: A Radical View,* p. 1234.

*British Book News,* March, 1982, review of *Madhouses, Mad-Doctors and Madmen,* p. 160.

*British Medical Journal,* September 4, 1993, T. H. Turner, review of *The Most Solitary of Afflictions,* p. 632.

*Choice,* April, 1982, review of *Madhouses, Mad-Doctors and Madmen,* p. 1096; March, 1983, review of *Museums of Madness* and *Madhouses, Mad-Doctors and Madmen,* p. 946; October, 1989, review of *Social Order/Mental Disorder,* p. 395; May, 1997, review of *Masters of Bedlam,* p. 1580.

*Commonweal,* July 12, 1985, review of *Decarceration,* p. 412.

*Contemporary Psychology,* February, 1995, review of *The Most Solitary of Afflictions,* p. 109.

*Contemporary Sociology,* March, 1981, review of *Decarceration,* p. 289; May, 1981, review of *Museums of Madness,* p. 658; September, 1994, review of *The Most Solitary of Afflictions,* p. 747; January, 1998, review of *Masters of Bedlam,* p. 103.

*Economist,* March 15, 1997, review of *Masters of Bedlam,* p. S10.

*English Historical Review,* April, 1983, review of *Madhouses, Mad-Doctors and Madmen,* p. 388; February, 1996, L. S. Jacyna, review of *The Most Solitary of Afflictions,* p. 212.

*Guardian Weekly,* July 4, 1993, review of *The Most Solitary of Afflictions,* p. 29.

*Health-PAC Bulletin,* September-October, 1977, Kim Hopper, review of *Decarceration.*

*Historian,* November, 1980, review of *Museums of Madness,* p. 111; November, 1983, review of *Madhouses, Mad-Doctors and Madmen,* p. 97; spring, 2001, Oonagh Walsh, review of *Masters of Bedlam,* p. 693. *History,* April, 1982, review of *Madhouses, Mad-Doctors and Madmen,* p. 149.

*Isis,* March, 1992, review of *Social Order/Mental Disorder,* p. 152; September, 1994, review of *The Most Solitary of Afflictions,* p. 526; June, 1999, review of *Masters of Bedlam,* p. 378.

*Journal of American Folklore,* fall, 1992, review of *Social Order/Mental Disorder,* p. 518.

*Journal of Interdisciplinary History,* spring, 1990, review of *Social Order/Mental Disorder,* p. 663; winter, 1996, review of *The Most Solitary of Afflictions,* p. 496.

*Journal of Modern History,* September, 1983, review of *Madhouses, Mad-Doctors and Madmen,* p. 524; December, 1996, review of *The Most Solitary of Afflictions,* p. 982.

*Journal of Social History,* summer, 1991, review of *Social Order/Mental Disorder,* p. 881; summer, 1994, review of *The Most Solitary of Afflictions,* p. 883.

*Kirkus Reviews,* November 1, 1996, review of *Masters of Bedlam,* p. 1593.

*Library Journal,* September 15, 1981, review of *Madhouses, Mad-Doctors and Madmen,* p. 1732; October 15, 1996, review of *Masters of Bedlam,* p. 79; January, 2002, Eric Albright, review of *Undertaker of the Mind: John Monro and Mad-Doctoring in Eighteenth-Century England,* p. 141.

*London Review of Books,* March 6, 1997, review of *Masters of Bedlam,* p. 29.

*Los Angeles Times Book Review,* March 30, 1997, review of *Masters of Bedlam,* p. 7.

*Medical Humanities Review,* January, 1990, review of *Social Order/Mental Disorder,* p. 36.

*Nature,* July 15 1993, review of *The Most Solitary of Afflictions,* p. 200.

*New Scientist,* August 25, 1989, review of *Social Order/Mental Disorder,* p. 29; February 1, 1997, review of *Masters of Bedlam,* p. 45.

*New Statesman and Society,* August 25, 1989; May 21, 1993, review of *The Most Solitary of Afflictions,* p. 36.

*New York Review of Books,* December 16, 1982, review of *Madhouses, Mad-Doctors and Madmen,* p. 28.

*Publishers Weekly,* November 25, 1996, review of *Masters of Bedlam,* p. 65.

*Readings,* December, 1993, review of *The Most Solitary of Afflictions,* p. 28.

*Science Books and Films,* September, 1982, review of *Madhouses, Mad-Doctors and Madmen,* p. 24.

*SciTech Book News,* September, 1993, review of *The Most Solitary of Afflictions,* p. 31.

*Social Forces,* September, 1981, review of *Museums of Madness,* p. 261; December, 1998, review of *Masters of Bedlam,* p. 804.

*Sociological Review,* February, 1980, review of *Museums of Madness,* p. 195; August, 1990, review of *Social Order/Mental Disorder,* p. 602; February, 1995, review of *The Most Solitary of Afflictions,* p. 218.

*Sociology,* September, 1980, review of *Museums of Madness,* p. 171; May, 1994, Joan Busfield, review of *The Most Solitary of Afflictions,* p. 594.

*Spectator,* March 1, 1997, review of *Masters of Bedlam,* p. 33.

*Times Literary Supplement,* January 8, 1982, review of *Madhouses, Mad-Doctors and Madmen,* p. 23; July 7-13, 1989, review of *Social Order/Mental Disorder,* p. 74; July 30, 1993, review of *The Most Solitary of Afflictions,* p. 5; August 8, 1997, review of *Masters of Bedlam,* p. 36; March 22, 2002, Chandak Sengoopta, "Cruden's Discordance," p. 7.

*Victorian Studies,* autumn, 1982, review of *Madhouses, Mad-Doctors and Madmen,* p. 106; winter, 1997, review of *The Most Solitary of Afflictions,* p. 360.

*Virginia Quarterly Review,* autumn, 1993, review of *The Most Solitary of Afflictions,* p. 117.

*Washington Post Book World,* July 4, 1993, review of *The Most Solitary of Afflictions,* p. 13.

*Working Papers for a New Society,* May-June, 1978, review of *Decarceration.*

\* \* \*

## SHANNON, George (William Bones) 1952-

*PERSONAL:* Born February 14, 1952, in Caldwell, KS; son of David W. (a professor) and Doris (Bones) Shannon. *Education:* Western Kentucky University, B.S., 1974; University of Kentucky, M.S.L.S., 1976. *Hobbies and other interests:* Gardening.

*ADDRESSES: Agent*—c/o Author Mail, Greenwillow Books, 1350 Avenue of the Americas, New York, NY 10019. *E-mail*—zolizoli@rmi.net.

*CAREER:* Storyteller and author. Librarian at public schools in Muhlenberg County, KY, 1974-75; Lexington Public Library, Lexington, KY, librarian, 1976-78;

professional storyteller and lecturer, 1978—. Guest lecturer at University of Kentucky, 1977. Member, external advisory board, Cooperative Children's Book Center, Madison, WI.

*AWARDS, HONORS:* Notable Book designation, American Library Association, 1981, and Children's Choice Book, International Reading Association/ Children's Book Council, 1982, both for *The Piney Woods Peddler;* Friends of American Writers award, 1990, for *Unlived Affections.*

*WRITINGS:*

*FOR CHILDREN*

*Lizard's Song,* illustrated by Jose Aruego and Ariane Dewey, Greenwillow Books (New York, NY), 1981.

*The Gang and Mrs. Higgins,* illustrated by Andrew Vines, Greenwillow Books (New York, NY), 1981.

*The Piney Woods Peddler,* illustrated by Nancy Tafuri, Greenwillow Books (New York, NY), 1981.

*Dance Away!,* illustrated by Jose Aruego and Ariane Dewey, Greenwillow Books (New York, NY), 1982.

*The Surprise,* illustrated by Jose Aruego and Ariane Dewey, Greenwillow Books (New York, NY), 1983.

*Bean Boy,* illustrated by Peter Sis, Greenwillow Books (New York, NY), 1984.

*Oh, I Love,* illustrated by Cheryl Harness, Bradbury Press (New York, NY), 1988.

*Sea Gifts,* illustrated by Mary Azarian, David Godine (New York, NY), 1989.

*Dancing the Breeze,* illustrated by Jacqueline Rogers, Bradbury Press (New York, NY), 1991.

*Laughing All the Way,* illustrated by Meg McLean, Houghton Mifflin (Boston, MA), 1992.

*Climbing Kansas Mountains,* illustrated by Thomas B. Allen, Bradbury Press (New York, NY), 1993.

*Seeds,* illustrated by Steve Bjorkman, Houghton Mifflin (Boston, MA), 1994.

*April Showers,* illustrated by Jose Aruego and Ariane Dewey, Greenwillow Books (New York, NY), 1995.

*Heart to Heart,* illustrated by Steve Bjorkman, Houghton Mifflin (Boston MA), 1995.

*Tomorrow's Alphabet,* illustrated by Donald Crews, Greenwillow Books (New York, NY), 1995.

(Compiler) *Spring: A Haiku Story,* illustrated by Malcah Zeldis, Greenwillow Books (New York, NY), 1995.

*This Is the Bird,* illustrated by David Soman, Houghton Mifflin (Boston, MA), 1996.

*Lizard's Home,* illustrated by Jose Aruego and Ariane Dewey, Greenwillow Books (New York, NY), 1999.

*Frog Legs: A Picture Book of Action Verse,* illustrated by Amit Trynan, Greenwillow Books (New York, NY), 2000.

*Lizard's Guest,* illustrated by Jose Aruego and Ariane Dewey, Greenwillow Books (New York, NY), 2003.

*Tippy-Toe Chick, Go!,* illustrated by Laura Dronzek, Greenwillow Books (New York, NY), 2003.

*Wise Acres,* illustrated by Deborah Zemke, Handprint Books, 2004.

Several of Shannon's books have been translated into Spanish, Chinese, French, and German.

*FOLKLORE*

*Stories to Solve: Folktales from around the World,* illustrated by Peter Sis, Greenwillow Books (New York, NY), 1985.

*More Stories to Solve: Fifteen Folktales from around the World,* illustrated by Peter Sis, Greenwillow Books (New York, NY), 1990.

*Still More Stories to Solve: Fourteen Folktales from around the World,* illustrated by Peter Sis, Greenwillow Books (New York, NY), 1994.

*True Lies: Eighteen Tales for You to Judge,* illustrated by John O'Brien, Greenwillow Books (New York, NY), 1997.

*More True Lies: Eighteen Tales for You to Judge,* illustrated by John O'Brien, Greenwillow Books (New York, NY), 2001.

*OTHER*

*Humpty Dumpty: A Pictorial History,* Green Tiger Press, 1981.

*Folk Literature and Children: An Annotated Bibliography of Secondary Materials,* Greenwood Press (New York, NY), 1981.

(With Ellin Greene) *Storytelling: A Selected Annotated Bibliography,* Garland (New York, NY), 1986.

*Arnold Lobel* (criticism), Twayne (Boston, MA), 1989.

*Unlived Affections* (young-adult novel) Harper (New York, NY), 1989.

(Compiler) *A Knock at the Door: 35 Ethnic Versions of a Tale,* illustrated by Joanne Caroselli, Oryx Press (Phoenix, AZ), 1992.

Contributor of articles and reviews to magazines, including *Horn Book, Children's Literature in Education, School Library Journal,* and *Wilson Library Bulletin.*

*WORK IN PROGRESS: Busy in the Garden,* illustrated by Sam Williams, and *White Is for Blueberry,* illustrated by Laura Dronzek, both for Greenwillow.

*SIDELIGHTS:* Professional storyteller George Shannon combines his interest in folklore and the oral storytelling tradition with his love of literature for children in a series of picture books for the younger set that include *Lizard's Home, Frog Legs: A Picture Book of Action Verse,* and *Tippy-Toe Chick, Go!* the last a "sure pick for storytime" in the opinion of *Booklist* contributor Linda Perkins. In addition to several nonfiction works and a series of popular retellings of folktales, Shannon has written such well-received works as *The Piney Woods Peddler, Dancing the Breeze,* and *Climbing Kansas Mountains,* as well as an award-winning young adult novel titled *Unlived Affections,* which he published in 1989.

Born in Caldwell, Kansas, in 1952, Shannon acquired the knack for spinning yarns early in life, and by the seventh grade was writing his stories down. Throughout middle and high school Shannon's teachers encouraged his efforts at writing, and at college he continued his love affair with books and writing by studying children's literature and library science. He spent several years working as a children's librarian before devoting himself to storytelling and writing his own books for children beginning in 1978.

Shannon's first published work for children, *Lizard's Song,* is the tale of a lizard who sings joyfully of his unique place in the world and, after a foolish bear attempts to set up camp near his rock home rather than in a cave, teaches other animals to be equally celebratory of their own. A *Publishers Weekly* reviewer praised the picture book, which has also been translated for Spanish-speaking children, calling it "a jolly, amiable fancy about the value of finding one's own niche and being one's own self." *Lizard's Song,* which features the colorful illustrations of Jose Aruego and Ariane Dewey, has since been followed by two sequels, both illustrated by Aruego and Dewey. In *Lizard's Home,* which a *Publishers Weekly* contributor dubbed a "bouyant and affirming" tale, a snake decides that Lizard's rock makes the perfect home—without Lizard. The clever Lizard outwits the snake as easily as he had outwitted the bear in the previous volume, and sings a new song that Patricia Manning commented in *School Library Journal* "will roll off the tongue as trippingly as his original hit tune." *Lizard's Guest,* published in 2003, continues the saga of Shannon's small reptilian homebody.

*The Piney Woods Peddler* is an adaptation of the story of "Lucky Hans" collected by the Brothers Grimm. A trader on the road doing business resolves to bring his daughter a silver dollar at the end of his travels; as his luck wanes, each of his trades brings in less than the one before, leaving him with only a silver dime. Fortunately the young daughter is cheerfully pleased with her father's small gift, providing a happy ending to a humorous story Ethel L. Heins described in *Horn Book* as "a repetitive, lilting tale that incorporates elements of traditional American swapping songs."

Shorter folktales also find their way into several collections by Shannon, among them *Stories to Solve: Folktales from around the World,* the sequel *More Stories to Solve,* and *True Lies: Eighteen Tales for You to Judge.* The last book contains short tales from all over the world, each story featuring a character who manages to trick others by twisting or omitting certain facts. Including detailed notes discussing each of the stories, Shannon creates a collection that has enough "brevity, humor, and accessible language" to attract even the most reluctant of readers, in the opinion of *School Library Journal* contributor Grace Oliff.

Relationships between family members are central to many of Shannon's tales for young people. A father and daughter await the moon in their flower garden in the poetic *Dancing the Breeze,* while *Climbing Kansas Mountains* finds Sam and his dad scaling a grain elevator in their native Kansas, from which height they can see the vast prairie stretching out before them. While Carol Fox found the latter story "more description than plot," she praised *Climbing Kansas Moun-*

*tains* in her review for *Bulletin of the Center for Children's Books,* noting that the story's "tone is warm and intimate with childlike language and viewpoint." And in *This Is the Bird,* described by a *Kirkus* reviewer as "a moving tribute to familial bonds," a carved wooden bird links generations as it is passed from one family member to another. Close friendship is dealt with in *Seeds,* as young Warren moves away from neighboring artist and gardener Bill, but retains ties to his friend by planting a garden in Bill's honor at his new home. *Seeds* "is a warm, satisfying story about a different kind of friendship, about loss, and about new beginnings," noted Stephanie Zvirin in her *Booklist* review.

Animal characters take center stage in several of Shannon's stories. *Dance Away!* finds Rabbit with so much energy that he out-dances all of his friends; he also out-dances cunning Fox, who had planned to trap a rabbit for his supper but ultimately ends up trapped in Rabbit's choreography. And in *Laughing All the Way,* Duck has a pretty awful day, which reaches a low point when Bear decides to pluck the fowl's feathers and make a soft downy bed. Fortunately, Duck keeps his sense of humor and soon has Bear laughing so hard that he accidentally lets Duck go. "Children who love silliness, wordplay, and colorful language . . . will delight in this book," commented Lauralyn Persson in a *School Library Journal* review. Shannon's *Frog Legs* also promises plenty of silliness within its twenty-four poems that "hop, prance, and even can-can across the pages," according to *School Library Journal* interviewer Carol Schene. Enhanced by joyous pastel illustrations by Amit Trynan that depict frogs doing all manner of childlike things, Shannon's verses more than keep pace, serving as "good fun" packaged in "small doses," according to *Booklist* contributor Stephanie Zvirin.

In addition to penning books for youngsters, Shannon is the author of a young-adult novel. *Unlived Affections,* which won the Friends of American Writers award in 1990, is the story of eighteen-year-old Willie Ramsey. After the death of his grandmother, who raised him since his mother was killed in a car accident when he was two, Willie is determined to break with his oppressive past, sell everything in the family home, and start a new life at college in Nebraska. While cleaning out his grandmother's things in preparation for the sale, Willie comes upon a trove of old letters, many written by his unknown father to his mother. The letters reveal many things Willie was told about his family to be untrue: his father did not desert his family but left because he was grappling with his sexual identity; and Willie's mother never told her husband that he had a son. "Shannon has a story to tell, and it is an unusual and moving one, full of secrets, lies, and dreams," commented Betsy Hearne in *Bulletin of the Center for Children's Books.* A *Publishers Weekly* reviewer called the novel's narrative "honest and concise," adding that "readers will be moved by the sensitive portrayal of each character and the tragedies they endure."

When Shannon tells stories before an audience it is like "writing out loud," with each telling slightly different, slightly unique, he once explained to *CA.* Several of his books have sprung from the stories he has performed in public, repeated out loud many times prior to being committed to paper. An avid journal-keeper and letter-writer, Shannon also collects impressions, thoughts, and ideas that often make their way into his fiction. "I travel frequently to tell stories," he once noted, "and always at my side is the dog-eared journal filled with dreams, lines, phrases, plot snatches, and impressions that all feed into the next story I tell and the next book I write." "The sounds and rhythms of my stories are of major importance to me," Shannon also explained of his craft, "and I want them to flow on the tongue as if always being said aloud—always new to share."

*BIOGRAPHICAL AND CRITICAL SOURCES:*

PERIODICALS

*Booklist,* December 1, 1981, p. 506; December 1, 1985, p. 574; February 15, 1991, p. 1203; June 1-15, 1994, Stephanie Zvirin, review of *Seeds,* pp. 1844-45; April 15, 1996, p. 1444; January 1, 2003, Linda Perkins, review of *Tippy-Toe Chick, Go!,* p. 910.

*Bulletin of the Center for Children's Books,* October, 1984, pp. 34-35; September, 1989, Betsy Hearne, review of *Unlived Affections,* p. 20; May, 1991, p. 226; January, 1994, Carol Fox, review of *Climbing Kansas Mountains,* p. 168; April, 1996, p. 279.

*Horn Book,* February, 1982, Ethel L. Heins, review of *The Piney Woods Peddler,* pp. 36-37; June, 1982, p. 283; September-October, 1990, p. 627; May-

June, 1991, pp. 342-43; November-December, 1994, p. 750; May-June, 1995, p. 329; July, 2001, Roger Sutton, review of *More True Lies,* p. 465.

*Junior Bookshelf,* August, 1982, p. 129; June, 1983, p. 110; June, 1984, p. 120; February, 1986, p. 29.

*Kirkus Reviews,* April 1, 1981, p. 431; September 1, 1983, p. 155; August 1, 1989, p. 1168; April 15, 1991, p. 539; July 15, 1994, p. 995; April 15, 1995, p. 563; March 1, 1997, review of *This Is the Bird,* pp. 387-388; December 15, 2002, review of *Tippy-Toe Chick, Go!,* p. 1856.

*Library Journal,* August, 2001, Lucia M. Gonzalez, review of *Lizard's Song,* p. 27.

*New York Times Book Review,* July 14, 1996, p. 19.

*Publishers Weekly,* May 1, 1981, p. 67; September 11, 1981, review of *Lizard's Song,* p. 76; July 14, 1989, review of *Unlived Affections,* p. 80; August 9, 1993, p. 477; April 1, 1996, p. 76; September 13, 1999, review of *Lizard's Home,* p. 83; November 18, 2002, review of *Tippy-Toe Chick, Go!,* p. 59.

*School Library Journal,* October, 1992, Lauralyn Persson, review of *Laughing All the Way,* p. 95; May, 1996, p. 108; September, 1999, Patricia Manning, review of *Lizard's Home,* p. 206; May, 2001, Grace Oliff, review of *More True Lies,* p. 146; February, 2003, Joy Fleishhacker, review of *Tippy-Toe Chick, Go!,* p. 122.*

\*     \*     \*

## SIKOV, Ed 1957-

*PERSONAL:* Born January 11, 1957, in Natrona Heights, PA; son of Irving (a lawyer) and Betty (Cohen) Sikov; partner of Bruce Schackman. *Education:* Haverford College, B.A., 1979; Columbia University, Ph.D., 1986.

*ADDRESSES: Home*—10 West Fifteenth St., #1228, New York, NY 10011. *Agent*—Edward Hibbert, Donadio and Olson, 121 West Twenty-seventh St., New York, NY 10001. *E-mail*—edsikov@aol.com.

*CAREER:* Has worked as a freelance journalist, a film scholar, and a teacher of film studies at Colorado, Brooklyn, and Haverford Colleges, and Columbia University.

*Ed Sikov*

WRITINGS:

*Screwball: Hollywood's Madcap Romantic Comedies,*
   Crown (New York, NY), 1989.
*Faculty Guide for American Cinema,* McGraw-Hill
   (New York, NY), 1994.
*Study Guide for American Cinema,* McGraw-Hill (New
   York, NY), 1994.
*Laughing Hysterically: American Screen Comedy of
   the 1950s,* Columbia University Press (New York,
   NY), 1994.
*On Sunset Boulevard: The Life and Times of Billy
   Wilder,* Hyperion (New York, NY), 1998.
*Mr. Strangelove: A Biography of Peter Sellers,* Hype-
   rion (New York, NY), 2002.

Contributor of articles to periodicals, including *Pre-
miere, Architectural Digest, Film Quarterly, Village
Voice, New York Times Book Review,* and the Brazilian
edition of *Cosmopolitan.* Contributor to anthologies,
including *Friends and Lovers,* NAL/Dutton (New
York, NY), 1995; *Boys Like Us,* Avon (New York,
NY), 1996; *Queer Representations,* New York Univer-
sity Press (New York, NY), 1997, and *Citizen Sarris:
American Film Critic,* Scarecrow Press (Lanham,
MD), 2001.

SIDELIGHTS: Ed Sikov is a film scholar who specializes in Hollywood comedies from the 1930s through
the 1970s. His first book, *Screwball: Hollywood's
Madcap Romantic Comedies,* lavishly illustrated with
black-and-white photo stills, argues against the commonsense notion that the madcap romantic comedies
of the 1930s and 1940s were produced to alleviate the
sufferings of a nation weighed down by the Great
Depression. Instead, according to Sikov, the films were
a direct response to the restrictions the government
imposed on showing sexuality on-screen. The 1934
Production Code lead directors to replace sexual activity between romantically engaged characters with slap-
stick violence, according to Sikov's thesis. In language
John Belton praised in *Film Quarterly* as "jargon-
free," Sikov divides screwball comedies into three
subgenres, including newspaper screwballs like *Nothing Sacred* and *His Girl Friday,* screwball mysteries
such as the *Thin Man* series, and films about screwball
families—*Bringing up Baby* and *My Man Godfrey* are
two prominent examples. Throughout, readers are
treated to "the author's breezily perceptive opinions
and succinct plot encapsulations," remarked a contributor to *Publishers Weekly.*

*Laughing Hysterically: American Screen Comedy of
the 1950s* picks up roughly where *Screwball* leaves
off. The book is organized around the work of four
central directors: Howard Hawks, Alfred Hitchcock,
Billy Wilder, and Frank Tashlin, influential directors
whose comedies "attack moral hypocrisy, satirize the
powerful, and expose sexual repression and frustration," according to a *Publishers Weekly* critic. Sikov,
who self-identifies as a gay critic in this volume, shows
special interest in the ways in which the films he examines contend with gender and sexuality. He looks
closely at the way women are represented, intimations
of homosexuality, and the representation of the family
unit within the best comedic films these directors produced, including *Some Like It Hot* by Wilder, *Gentle-
men Prefer Blondes* by Hawks, and *Will Success Spoil
Rock Hunter?* by Tashlin. "At his best, Sikov is both
provocative and delightfully funny," remarked K. S.
Nolley in *Choice,* recommending the book for all academic libraries.

Billy Wilder, who began life in 1906 as a Polish Jew
and became one of the most influential film directors

in Hollywood in the 1940s, 1950s, and 1960s, moves to center stage in Sikov's next book, *On Sunset Boulevard: The Life and Times of Billy Wilder.* Although Wilder refused to be interviewed for this biography, and none of his closest associates would agree to talk to Sikov either, *On Sunset Boulevard* was praised by reviewers for its firm grounding in extensive research, research that revealed in part that while Wilder was guilty of embellishing the truth about nearly every aspect of his life, the facts of his life story are fascinating in their own right. For a contributor to *Entertainment Weekly,* who eventually became somewhat impatient with Sikov's approach to tracking down the factual details of Wilder's life, "[Sikov's] monumentally research-heavy approach proves a curiously satisfactory foil to Wilder's more outlandish bits of exaggeration." On the other hand, wrote Steve Kurtz in *Reason,* Sikov manages to inject the story of Wilder's life with enough intriguing film commentary that so that film buffs will stay interested. "Sikov, to his credit, keeps the story moving but stops long enough to critique the movies, which, after all, are why we're interested. His analysis is generally insightful, and he catches things that most critics get wrong," Kurtz concluded. Robert L. Pela, a reviewer for the *Advocate,* noted Sikov's tenacious refusal to be convinced by Wilder's long denial of a homosexual undertone in many of his films, describing *On Sunset Boulevard* as "bursting with new anecdotes from Old Hollywood about one of its legendary geniuses."

Another notoriously hard-to-pin-down icon of Hollywood comedies is at the center of Sikov's next book, *Mr. Strangelove: A Biography of Peter Sellers.* Sellers was a British comedic actor who came to prominence on a seminal radio program called *The Goon Show,* which has been identified as the inspiration for the Monty Python players. He is perhaps best known for his role in the *Pink Panther* films as Inspector Clouseau, but critics single out stellar performances in genre-bending films such as *Dr. Strangelove* and *Being There* as more memorable work. Sellers died in 1980, and extensive interviews with the actor's friends and colleagues reveal that his uncanny ability to imitate others was perhaps the natural outgrowth of a person so pathologically insecure that even those closest to him felt as though they knew him not at all. His behavior, including bouts with drugs and alcohol, wife battering, and child abuse, is faithfully recounted, leaving a critic in *Kirkus Reviews* to speculate that "despite all the talent, readers will be happy to have

known Sellers only as an image on the screen." While Gordon Flagg, writing in *Booklist,* complained that "Sikov devotes much of his text to amateur psychology," Flagg also adds that "with the near-certifiable Sellers [this] seems almost inevitable." For a contributor to *Publishers Weekly,* on the other hand, "Sikov . . . treats Sellers with just the right mix of awe, irritation and sympathy, giving readers a clearheaded, respectful tribute to a disturbed genius."

## BIOGRAPHICAL AND CRITICAL SOURCES:

### PERIODICALS

*Advocate,* March 2, 1999, Robert L. Pela, review of *On Sunset Boulevard: The Life and Times of Billy Wilder,* p. 67.

*Booklist,* November 1, 1998, Ray Olson, review of *On Sunset Boulevard,* p. 462; October 1, 2002, Gordon Flagg, review of *Mr. Strangelove: A Biography of Peter Sellers,* p. 295.

*Choice,* May, 1990, W. K. Huck, review of *Screwball: Hollywood's Madcap Romantic Comedies,* p. 1513; March, 1995, K. S. Nolley, review of *Laughing Hysterically: American Screen Comedy of the 1950s,* p. 1130; April, 1999, R. Blackwood, review of *On Sunset Boulevard,* p. 1465.

*Cineaste,* fall, 1999, John Belton, review of *On Sunset Boulevard,* p. 57.

*Entertainment Weekly,* December 11, 1998, "Wilder Than Ever," p. 69; October 25, 2002, review of *Mr. Strangelove,* p. 80.

*Film Quarterly,* spring, 1991, John Belton, review of *Screwball,* pp. 58-59.

*Kirkus Review,* August 15, 2002, review of *Mr. Strangelove,* p. 1206.

*Library Journal,* September 15, 1994, Carol J. Binkowski, review of *Laughing Hysterically,* p. 73; October 1, 2002, Barry X. Miller, review of *Mr. Strangelove,* p. 98.

*Modern Maturity,* October-November, 1989, Digby Diehl, review of *Screwball,* p. 84.

*New York Times,* December 27, 1998.

*Publishers Weekly,* November 17, 1989, review of *Screwball,* p. 42; August 15, 1994, review of *Laughing Hysterically,* p. 81; October 5, 1998, review of *On Sunset Boulevard,* p. 72; September 30, 2002, review of *Mr. Strangelove,* p. 62.

*Reason,* June, 1999, Steve Kurtz, review of *On Sunset Boulevard,* p. 70.

*ONLINE*

*Ed Sikov Web Site,* http://users.rcn.com/edsikov/ (May 28, 2003).

\*    \*    \*

## SMALL, Gary W(illiam) 1951-

*PERSONAL:* Born July 28, 1951, in Los Angeles, CA; son of Max (a physician) and Gertrude (a psychotherapist; maiden name, Axelrod) Small; married Giselle Vorgan, May 28, 1989; children: Rachel, Harrison. *Education:* University of California—Los Angeles, B.A. (summa cum laude), 1973; University of Southern California, M.D., 1977. *Hobbies and other interests:* Crossword puzzles, cinema, classical music.

*ADDRESSES: Home*—Sherman Oaks, CA. *Office*—Neuropsychiatric Institute, 760 Westwood Plaza, University of California, Los Angeles, CA 90024. *Agent*—Sandra Dijkstra, 1237 Camino Del Mar, Suite 515C, Del Mar, CA 92014.

*CAREER:* Psychiatrist, educator, author. Children's Hospital and Adult Medical Center, San Francisco, CA, intern, 1977-78; Massachusetts General Hospital, Boston, resident in psychiatry, 1978-81; University of California, Los Angeles, fellow in geriatric psychiatry, 1981-83, assistant professor of psychiatry and biobehavioral sciences and assistant chief of curriculum coordination for Section on Neuropsychogeriatrics, 1983—, member of professional staff at Neuropsychiatric Hospital, 1986—, director of Geriatric Consultation Liaison Service, 1988—, chairman of pharmacy and therapeutics committee, 1985—, professor of psychiatry, 1995—, director of Imaging and Genetics Core, Alzheimer's Disease Center, 1997—, associate investigator in Department of Energy Laboratory, 1997—; Parlow-Solomon Professorship on Aging, School of Medicine, 1998. Diplomate of and examiner for American Board of Psychiatry and Neurology; Harvard Medical School, clinical fellow in psychiatry, 1978-81, instructor, 1980-81; distinguished visiting professor at Wilford Hall U.S. Air Force Medical Center, 1985. Veterans Administration Medical Center, Brentwood, CA, attending physician, 1981—, staff psychiatrist in Psychogeriatrics Inpatient Unit, 1982-

83; member of medical staff of Jewish Homes for the Aging of Greater Los Angeles, 1984—; Geriatric Psychiatry Program, West L.A. VA Medical Center, 1990-96. Public speaker.

*MEMBER:* International Association of Biomedical Gerontology, International Psychogeriatric Association, World Psychiatric Association, American Psychiatric Association, American Geriatrics Society, American Society for Geriatric Psychiatry, Gerontological Society of America, American Psychosomatic Society, Association for Academic Psychiatry, American Medical Association, American Association of University Professors, American Psychopathological Association, American Association for the Advancement of Science, Authors Guild, Authors League of America, West Coast College of Biological Psychiatry, California Medical Association, Southern California Psychiatric Society, Los Angeles County Medical Association, Los Angeles Alzheimer's Disease and Related Disorders Association (member of board of directors, 1988—), University of California, Los Angeles Faculty Association, Sigma Xi, Alpha Omega Alpha.

*AWARDS, HONORS:* Grants from National Institute for Mental Health, 1982-83, 1985-86, and National Institute on Aging, 1983-88; Zenith Award, Alzheimer's Association, 1998; Jack Weinberg Memorial Award for Geriatric Psychiatry, American Psychiatric Association, 2000.

*WRITINGS:*

(Editor, with R. H. Coombs and D. S. Mays) *Inside Doctoring: Stages and Outcomes in the Professional Development of Physicians,* Praeger, 1986.

(With L. F. Jarvik) *Parentcare: A Commonsense Guide for Adult Children,* Crown, 1988.

(Contributor) Michael Swash and J. M. Oxbury, editors, *Clinical Neurology,* Churchill Livingstone, 1988.

(Contributor) B. T. Karasu, editor, *Treatment of Psychiatric Disorders,* American Psychiatric Association, 1989.

(Contributor) H. E. Kasplan and B. J. Sadock, editors, *Comprehensive Textbook of Psychiatry,* Volume V, Williams & Wilkins, 1989.

*The Memory Bible: An Innovative Strategy for Keeping Your Brain Young,* Hyperion (New York, NY), 2002.

Contributor to *Year Book of Geriatrics and Gerontology* and *American Psychiatric Association Annual Review.* Contributor of articles and reviews to medical journals. Associate editor of *Year Book of Geriatrics and Gerontology,* 1987—; book review editor and member of editorial board of *Alzheimer's Disease and Associated Disorders: An International Journal,* 1985—; member of editorial board of *Journal of Geriatric Psychiatry and Neurology,* 1986; member of editorial board of *Geriatric Times,* 2000.

*SIDELIGHTS:* Gary W. Small is a renowned neuroscientist who specializes in aging. He has lectured extensively throughout the world and appeared on numerous television shows, including the *Today* show and *CBS News.* In addition to his many professional journal articles, Small has written for the *New York Times, Wall Street Journal, Washington Post,* and other publications. He is also the author of books on aging directed to the general public.

In *Parentcare: A Commonsense Guide for Adult Children,* Small and a fellow psychiatrist write for adults who must care for their aging parents. They provide advice on solving problems and include numerous case histories based on the authors' own patients. The book also features questionnaires for readers and appendixes with information on drugs and nutrition, living wills, power of attorney, and other issues.

Small once told *CA:* "Adult children must face two major tasks when they have to confront the problems of caring for their own parents. Not only must they identify and solve the practical problems that arise, but they also face a psychological task. Throughout our lives, long after we become adults and have our own families and careers, a part of us still feels like a child. At a psychological level, we perceive our parents as a source of emotional support. When they need our help, when we must provide parentcare, that child in us is forced to grow up. None of us is prepared for this often sad and painful stage of life.

"*Parentcare: A Commonsense Guide for Adult Children* offers solutions for adult children who struggle with these practical and psychological tasks. It is a detailed guide for adult children who must care for their own parents. My coauthor, Lissy Jarvik, and I hope that one day parentcare will become as familiar a term as childcare is today. By solving the problems of parentcare, we can enjoy and care for that part of our parents that we do love and never want to give up."

In 2002, Small's book on "brain fitness" was published. In *The Memory Bible: An Innovative Strategy for Keeping Your Brain Young,* Small prescribes numerous steps for keeping the brain young, primarily in the area of counteracting memory loss. The book is based on Small's years of experience as a neuroscientist and on recent scientific discoveries in how food, medicines, exercise, stress, alcohol, and other lifestyle choices affect aging brains. In addition to his "ten commandments" for improving brain performance, Small includes a "brain diet" consisting of foods that may protect memory, effective drugs and other treatments, and a workbook and calendar for tracking your adherence to the fitness program.

Karen McNally of *Library Journal* thought that some of Small's "memory enhancing techniques . . . seem too cumbersome to be useful." But she also noted, "Small's approach is entertaining yet practical, and the numerous case histories are appealing." *BookPage* contributor Al Huebner noted, "Small goes beyond the basics to skills that both slow aging of the brain and enrich everyday life." "In a similar manner, his program provides guidelines for optimizing other influences on brain health, such as diet and lifestyle, that will also improve health more broadly."

"Misplacing your keys a couple of times doesn't mean you should start labeling your cabinets," Small said in an article on *ABC Online.* "Memory loss is not an inevitable consequence of aging. Our brains can fight back."

*BIOGRAPHICAL AND CRITICAL SOURCES:*

*PERIODICALS*

*BookPage,* July, 2002, review of *The Memory Bible: An Innovative Strategy for Keeping Your Brain Young,* p. 18.
*Library Journal,* July, 2002, review of *The Memory Bible,* p. 109.
*Los Angeles Times,* April 17, 1988.
*Publishers Weekly,* May 13, 2002, review of *The Memory Bible,* p. 67.

*ONLINE*

*ABC Online,* http://abc.net.au/ (October 9, 2002),"Grey Matters."*

**SOMERS, Jane**
    **See LESSING, Doris (May)**


                    *       *       *


**STILLSON, Alan 1945-**

*PERSONAL:* Born December 16, 1945, in New York, NY; son of Jacob (an educator) and Rose (an educator) Stillson; married June 17, 1967; wife's name Sandra (divorced, 1977); married Gail Surgerman (an administrative secretary), May 20, 1983; children: Jeff, Debi, Howard, Gary. *Ethnicity:* "Jewish." *Education:* Queens College of the City University of New York, B.A., 1967, M.S., 1970; University of New Mexico, M.B.A., 1974. *Politics:* Independent. *Religion:* "Messianic Jewish." *Hobbies and other interests:* Music, puzzles and games.

*ADDRESSES: Home*—5515 Keokuk Ave., Woodland Hills, CA 91367; fax: 818-592-6472. *E-mail*—stillson@jps.net.

*CAREER:* Mathematics teacher at public schools in Queens, NY, 1967-71, and in Albuquerque, NM, 1971-74; financial analyst, 1974-78; owner of commercial real estate finance company, Los Angeles, CA, 1978-95; Best Buy, Calabasas, CA, marketing coordinator, 1995-2001; mathematics instructor at public schools and colleges in Los Angeles, CA, 2001—.

*MEMBER:* Mensa, National Puzzlers League, National Scrabble Association, B'nai B'rith (past president).

*WRITINGS:*

*The Mensa Genius A-B-C Quiz Book,* Perseus Press (Oxford, England), 1998.
(With Marvin Grosswirth and Abbie F. Salny) *Match Wits with Mensa: The Complete Quiz Book,* introduction by Isaac Asimov, Perseus Press (Oxford, England), 1999.
*One-Minute Brainteasers,* Sterling (New York, NY), 2001.
(With Karen C. Richards and Bernardo Rucamán Santos) *Classic Brain Teasers,* Metrobooks (New York, NY), 2002.

*Alan Stillson*

*Middle-School Word Puzzles,* Stillsonworks (Woodland Hills, CA), 2002.
*What's Your CQ?,* Bridge-Logos Publishers (Gainesville, FL), 2003.
*Ninety-Second Brainteasers,* Sterling (New York, NY), 2003.

*WORK IN PROGRESS:* Puzzle and game books for adults and children.

*BIOGRAPHICAL AND CRITICAL SOURCES:*

*ONLINE*

*Stillsonworks,* http://www.stillsonworks.com/ (June 29, 2003).


                    *       *       *


**STRANGER, Joyce**
    **See WILSON, Joyce M(uriel Judson)**

## STRAUSS, Leo 1899-1973

*PERSONAL:* Born September 20, 1899, in Kirchhain, Germany; died of pneumonia, October 18, 1973, in Annapolis, MD; came to United States, 1938; son of Hugo and Jennie (David) Strauss; married Miriam Bernson, June 20, 1933; children: Jennie, Thomas. *Education:* University of Hamburg, Ph.D., 1921. *Religion:* Jewish.

*CAREER:* Academy for Jewish Research, Berlin, Germany, research assistant, 1925-32; New School for Social Research, New York, NY, professor, 1938-49; University of Chicago, Chicago, IL, Hutchins Distinguished Service Professor of political science, 1949-68; Claremont Men's College, Claremont, CA, professor of political science, 1968-69; St. John's College, Annapolis, MD, Scott Buchanan Scholar in residence, 1969-73. *Military service:* German Army; served in World War I.

*MEMBER:* American Political Science Association.

*WRITINGS:*

IN ENGLISH TRANSLATION

*Die religionskritik Spinozas als Grundlage seiner Bibelwissenschaft,* Akademie-Verlag, 1930, translation by Elsa M. Sinclair published as *Spinoza's Critique of Religion,* Schocken Books (New York, NY), 1965, reprinted, University of Chicago Press (Chicago, IL), 1997.

*The Political Philosophy of Hobbes: Its Basis and Its Genesis,* translation from the original German by Elsa M. Sinclair, Clarendon Press (Oxford, England), 1936, reprinted, University of Chicago Press (Chicago, IL), 1963.

*On Tyranny: An Interpretation of Xenophon's Hiero,* edited by Victor Gourevitch and Michael S. Roth, Political Science Classics (New York, NY), 1948, revised edition, University of Chicago Press (Chicago, IL), 2000.

*Natural Right and History,* University of Chicago Press (Chicago, IL), 1950.

*Persecution and the Art of Writing,* Free Press of Glencoe (New York, NY), 1952, reprinted, University of Chicago Press (Chicago, IL), 1988.

*Thoughts on Machiavelli,* Free Press of Glencoe (New York, NY), 1959.

*What Is Political Philosophy?: And Other Studies,* Free Press of Glencoe (New York, NY), 1959, reprinted, University of Chicago Press (Chicago, IL), 1988.

(Editor, with Joseph Cropsey) *History of Political Philosophy,* Rand McNally (Chicago, IL), 1963.

*The City and Man,* Rand McNally (Chicago, IL), 1964.

*Socrates and Aristophanes,* Basic Books (New York, NY), 1966.

*Liberalism: Ancient and Modern,* Basic Books (New York, NY), 1968.

*Xenonphon's Socratic Discourse: An Interpretation of the Oeconomicus,* Cornell University Press (Ithaca, NY), 1970.

*Xenophon's Socrates,* Cornell University Press (Ithaca, NY), 1972, reprinted, St. Augustine's Press (South Bend, IN), 1998.

*The Argument and the Action of Plato's Laws,* University of Chicago Press (Chicago, IL), 1975.

*Political Philosophy: Six Essays,* edited by Hilail Gilden, Pegasus (New York, NY), 1975.

*Studies in Platonic Political Philosophy,* University of Chicago Press (Chicago, IL), 1983.

*Philosophy and Law: Essays toward the Understanding of Maimonides and His Predecessors,* translation by Fred Baumann, Jewish Publication Society (Philadelphia, PA), 1987.

*An Introduction to Political Philosophy: Ten Essays by Leo Strauss,* edited by Hilail Gildin, Wayne State University Press (Detroit, MI), 1989.

*The Rebirth of Classical Political Rationalism: An Introduction to the Thought of Leo Strauss: Essays and Lectures,* selected by Thomas L. Pangle, University of Chicago Press (Chicago, IL), 1989.

*Faith and Political Philosophy: The Correspondence between Leo Straus and Eric Voegelin, 1934-1964,* edited and translated by Peter Emberley and Barry Cooper, Pennsylvania State University Press (University Park, PA), 1993.

*Jewish Philosophy and the Crisis of Modernity: Essays and Lectures in Modern Jewish Thought,* edited by Kenneth Hart Green, State University of New York Press (Albany, NY), 1997.

*Leo Strauss on Plato's Symposium,* edited by Seth Benardete, University of Chicago Press (Chicago, IL), 2001.

Also contributor to *Hobbes: Studies,* edited by Keith C. Brown, Harvard University Press (Cambridge, MA), 1965.

*IN GERMAN*

(Editor, with others) Moses Mendelssohn, *Gesammelte Schriften,* Akademie-Verlag, 1929.
*Philosphie und Gesetz,* Schocken (New York, NY), 1935.
*Hobbes politische Wissenschaft,* new edition, Luchterhand (Berlin, Germany), 1965.

*SIDELIGHTS:* A well-known scholar, Leo Strauss was noted for his lucid and insightful interpretations of classical political theories. A reviewer for the *New York Times* observed that "Strauss is credited with keeping the study of the political classics alive and for showing students that thinkers such as Plato, Machiavelli, and Hobbes were relevant to present-day political dilemmas." Most of Strauss's books were geared toward scholarly readers, but many of his works were of interest to general readers as well.

Reviewers throughout the years have stressed Strauss's role in the study of political philosophy. A *Choice* critic, for example, said that "Strauss was an eminent and stormy figure in recent American political theory and his comments are important." *Ethics* critic H. M. Lubasz also noted, "Professor Strauss's arguments are often illuminating and sometimes challenging, so much so that one regrets that he deals almost exclusively with scholarly, historical, textual, interpretative problems rather than with the systematic philosophical problems of contemporary politics."

*Leo Strauss on Plato's Symposium,* published posthumously, is based on the author's University of Chicago course titled "Plato's Political Philosophy." According to Terry Skeats in *Library Journal,* "the resulting publication is not only an excellent analysis of an introduction to the Symposium but a text that mirrors the mind and skills of a renowned teacher."

*BIOGRAPHICAL AND CRITICAL SOURCES:*

*BOOKS*

*Encyclopedia of World Biography,* 2nd edition, Gale (Detroit, MI), 1998.
Turner, Roland, editor, *Thinkers of the Twentieth Century,* 2nd edition, St. James Press (Detroit, MI), 1987.

*PERIODICALS*

*America,* September 7, 1963.
*American Academy of Political and Social Science Annals,* May, 1937; January, 1953; May, 1969.
*American Political Science Review,* June, 1954.
*American Scholar,* winter, 1997, Gregory Bruce Smith, "Who Was Leo Strauss?," pp. 95-104.
*Choice,* February, 1967; January, 1973; November, 1975.
*Commentary,* October, 1967; January, 1975.
*Commonweal,* November 4, 1960.
*Ethics,* April, 1960.
*Guardian* (London, England), September 19, 1996, Nicholas Lezard "Lezard at Large," p. 15.
*Library Journal,* June 15, 2001, Terry Skeats, review of *On Plato's Symposium,* p. 76.
*New Republic,* July 3, 1989, Charles Larmore, "The Rebirth of Classical Political Rationalism: Essays and Lectures," pp. 30-34.
*New York Times,* May 1, 1949.
*Political Science & Politics,* September 17, 1997, Regina F. Titunik, "Taking Exception," pp. 441-442.
*Political Theory,* April, 1998, Dana R. Villa, "The Philosopher versus the Citizen: Arendt, Strauss, and Socrates," pp. 147-172; June, 1998, Robb A. McDaniel, "The Nature of Inequality: Uncovering the Modern in Leo Strauss's Idealist Ethics," pp. 317-345.
*Reason,* November, 1998, Loren E. Lomasky, "Straussed Out," pp. 71-73.
*Washington Times,* November 29, 1997, Larry Witham, "Challenge for the Skeptics," p. 3.

*OBITUARIES:*

*PERIODICALS*

*National Review,* December 7, 1973.
*New York Times,* October 21, 1973.
*Social Research,* spring, 1974.
*Times Literary Supplement,* April 9, 1976.
*Washington Post,* October 23, 1973.*

\*    \*    \*

## STRAVINSKY, Igor Fedorovich 1882-1971

*PERSONAL:* Surname listed in some sources as Stravinski or Strawinsky; born June 17, 1882, in Oranienbaum, Russia; immigrated to France, 1920; naturalized French citizen, June 10, 1934; came to

*Igor Fedorovich Stravinsky*

United States, September 30, 1939; naturalized U.S. citizen, December 28, 1945; died of heart failure, April 6, 1971, in New York, NY; buried in Cemetery of San Michele, in Venice, Italy; son of Fedor Ignatievich (an opera singer) and Anna Stravinsky; married Catherine Gabrielle Nossenko, January 11, 1906 (died March, 1939); married Vera Arturovna de Bosset Sudekine (an actress and dancer), March 9, 1940; children: (first marriage) Theodore, Ludmilla (deceased), Soulima (born Sviatoslav), Maria Milena. *Education:* University of St. Petersburg, degree in law, 1905; studied music with Nikolai Rimsky-Korsakov. *Religion:* Russian Orthodox. *Hobbies and other interests:* Painting, art, book collecting, literature.

*CAREER:* Music composer, 1903-66; guest conductor of orchestras, including the New York Philharmonic and the Boston Symphony orchestras, 1914-66; and piano soloist, 1924-66. Charles Eliot Norton Professor of Poetry at Harvard University, 1939-40.

*MEMBER:* American Academy of Arts and Letters, National Institute of Arts and Letters.

*AWARDS, HONORS:* Gold medal for music from National Institute of Arts and Letters, 1951; gold medal of the Royal Philharmonic (London, England), 1954; Sibelius Gold Medal, 1955; International award, Sonning Foundation of Denmark, 1960; Sibelius Prize from Wihuri International Prize Foundation, 1963.

*WRITINGS:*

AUTOBIOGRAPHICAL, EXCEPT AS NOTED

(With Walter Nouvel) *Chroniques de ma vie,* two volumes, Denoel et Steele, 1935, published as *Igor Stravinsky: An Autobiography,* Simon & Schuster (New York, NY), 1936, published as *Chronicle of My Life,* Gollancz (London, England), 1936.

(With Roland-Manuel) *Poetique musicale sous forme de six lecons* (lectures), Harvard University Press (Cambridge, MA), 1942, translation by Arthur Knodel and Ingolf Dahl published as *Poetics of Music in the Form of Six Lessons,* Harvard University Press (Cambridge, MA), 1947, bilingual edition, preface by George Seferis, Harvard University Press (Cambridge, MA), 1970.

(With Robert Craft) *Avec Stravinsky,* [Monaco], 1958, published as *Conversations with Igor Stravinsky,* Doubleday (New York, NY), 1959, University of California Press (Berkeley, CA), 1980.

(With Robert Craft) *Memories and Commentaries,* Doubleday (New York, NY), 1960.

(With Robert Craft) *Expositions and Developments,* Doubleday (New York, NY), 1962.

(With Robert Craft) *Dialogues and a Diary,* Doubleday (New York, NY), 1963.

(With Robert Craft) *Themes and Episodes,* Knopf (New York, NY), 1966.

(With Robert Craft) *Retrospectives and Conclusions,* Knopf (New York, NY), 1969.

*Stravinsky: Selected Correspondence,* edited by Robert Craft, Knopf (New York, NY), 1982.

OMNIBUS VOLUMES; WITH ROBERT CRAFT

*Stravinsky in Conversation with Robert Craft* (contains *Conversations with Stravinsky* and *Memories and Commentaries*), Harmondsworth (London, England), 1962.

*Themes and Conclusions* (contains *Themes and Episodes* and *Retrospectives and Conclusions*), Faber (London, England), 1972.

*MUSICAL WORKS; BALLETS*

*L'Oiseau de feu,* completed May 18, 1910 (one-act; title means "The Firebird"; adapted from Russian folklore; first performed in Paris, France, at Paris Opera, June 25, 1910; performed in New York, NY, March 20, 1935), Jurgenson-Schott, 1910, B. Schott (Mainz, Germany), 1973.

(And author of text, with Alexandre Benois) *Petrouchka,* completed May 26, 1911 (four-act; title means "Peter"; adapted from Russian folklore; first performed in Paris, France, at Theatre du Chatelet, June 13, 1911; performed in New York, NY, at Century Theatre, January 25, 1916 [some sources say January 24]), Edition Russe (Paris, France), 1911, Norton, 1967, revised score, completed, 1947, edited by Charles Hamm, Boosey & Hawkes (London, England), 1948.

(And author of text, with Nicholas Roerich) *Le Sacre du printemps: Choreographic Scenes of Pagan Russia,* completed March 8, 1913 (two-act; title means "The Rite of Spring"; first produced in Paris, France, at Theatre des Champs-Elysees, May 29, 1913; produced in concert in Philadelphia, PA, at Academy of Music, March 3, 1922; produced in concert in New York, NY, at Carnegie Hall, January 24, 1924), Edition Russe (Paris, France), 1913, Boosey & Hawkes (London, England), 1921, revised score completed, 1943, Associated Music Publishers, 1945, facsimile edition with commentary by Robert Craft, 1969.

(And author of text) *Le Renard,* completed August 1, 1916 (one-act; title means "The Fox"; adapted from Russian folklore; first produced in Paris, France, at Paris Opera, May 18, 1922), J. & W. Chester (London, England), 1917, bilingual edition with translations of text by Rollo M. Meyers and C. F. Ramuz, J. & W. Chester (London, England), 1930.

*Le Chant du rossignol,* completed April 4, 1917 (three-act; title means "The Song of the Nightingale"; adapted from last two acts of composer's opera "Le Rossignol" [also see below]; first produced in concert in Geneva, Switzerland, December 6, 1919; produced in Paris, France, at Paris Opera, February 2, 1920; produced in New York, NY, at Carnegie Hall, November 2, 1923), Edition Russe (Paris, France), 1921.

*L'Histoire du soldat,* completed, 1918 (six-act; title means "The Soldier's Tale"; adapted from Russian folklore; first produced in Lausanne, Switzerland, at Theatre Municipal de Lausanne, September 28, 1918; produced in New York, NY, at Jolson Theatre, March 25, 1928), text by Charles-Fernandez Ramuz, J. & W. Chester (London, England), 1924, translation by Michael Flanders and Kitty Black, J. & W. Chester (London, England), 1955.

*Pulcinella: Ballet with Voice and Orchestra on Themes, Fragments, and Pieces by Pergolesi,* completed April 20, 1919 (one-act; adapted from music by Giovanni Battista Pergolesi; first produced in Paris, France, at Paris Opera, May 15, 1920; produced in Chicago, IL, 1933), vocal score with libretto by Leonide Massine published by J. & W. Chester (London, England), 1919, full score published by Edition Russe.

(And author of text) *Les Noces,* completed April 6, 1923 (four-act; title means "The Wedding"; adapted from Kirieievsky's collection of Russian folk poems; first produced in Paris, France, at Theatre de la Gaite-Lyrique, June 13, 1923; produced in New York, NY, at Metropolitan Opera, April 25, 1929), J. & W. Chester (London, England), 1923, with translation of libretto by D. Millar Craig, J. & W. Chester (London, England), c. 1957.

(And author of text) *Apollon-Musagete,* completed January, 1928 (two-act; title means "Apollo, Master of the Muses"; first produced in Washington, D.C., at Library of Congress, April 27, 1928), Edition Russe (Paris, France), 1928, revised score published as *Apollo,* completed, 1947, Boosey & Hawkes (London, England), 1949.

(And author of text) *Le Baiser de la fee,* completed October 30, 1928 (four-act; title means "The Fairy's Kiss"; adapted from story "The Ice Maiden" by Hans Christian Andersen and from music by Petr Ilich Tchaikovsky; first produced in Paris at Paris Opera, November 27, 1928 [some sources say November 28]; produced in New York, NY, at Metropolitan Opera, April 27, 1937), Edition Russe (Paris, France), 1928, revised score, completed, 1950, Boosey & Hawkes (London, England), 1952.

*Persephone,* completed January 24, 1934 (three-act; first produced in Paris, France, at Paris Opera, April 30, 1934; produced in Boston, MA, March

15, 1935), text by Andre Gide, Edition Russe (Paris, France), 1934, arrangement for opera, completed, 1949, Boosey & Hawkes (London, England), 1950.

(And author of text) *Jeu de cartes: Ballet in Three Deals,* completed December 6, 1936 (three-act; title means "A Card Game"; first produced in New York, NY, at Metropolitan Opera, April 27, 1937), Schott Music, 1936, reprinted, 1965.

*Orpheus,* completed September 23, 1947 (three-act; first produced in New York, NY, at New York City Center, April 28, 1948), with translation of text by Robert A. Hague, Boosey & Hawkes (London, England), 1948, published in *Agon [and] Orpheus,* Muzyka, 1972.

*The Cage,* (one-act), first produced in New York, NY, at New York City Center, June 10, 1951 (some sources say June 4).

*Agon,* completed April 27, 1957 (one-act; title means "Contest"; first produced in concert in New York, NY, at New York City Center, November 27, 1957), Boosey & Hawkes (London, England), 1957, published in *Agon [and] Orpheus,* Muzyka, 1972.

*The Flood; or, Noah and the Ark,* completed March 14, 1962 (adapted from Genesis; first televised June 14, 1962), text by Robert Craft, Boosey & Hawkes (London, England), 1963.

*ORCHESTRAL COMPOSITIONS*

*Symphony No. 1 in E-flat major,* completed, 1907 (first produced in St. Petersburg, Russia, April 27, 1907), Jurgenson-Schott, 1907.

*Feu d'Artifice,* completed, 1908 (first produced in St. Petersburg, Russia, June 17, 1908; produced in New York, NY, December 1, 1910), B. Schott (Mainz, Germany), 1908, published as *Fireworks,* International Music, 1948.

*Scherzo fantastique,* completed, 1908 (first produced in St. Petersburg, Russia, February 6, 1909), Jurgenson-Schott, 1908.

*Le Sacre du printemps Suite* (adapted from composer's ballet *Le Sacre du printemps* [also see above]; first produced in Paris, France, April 5, 1914), Kalmus, 1938, revised score, completed, 1943, Associated Music Publishers (New York, NY), 1945.

*Song of the Volga Boatmen for Wind Orchestra,* completed, 1917 (adapted from a Russian folksong; first produced in Rome, Italy, April 9, 1917), J. & W. Chester (London, England), 1920.

*Ragtime for Eleven Instruments,* completed November 11, 1918 (first produced in London, England, April 27, 1920), J. & W. Chester (London, England), 1920.

*Suite de L'Oiseau de feu,* completed, 1919 (adapted from composer's ballet *L'Oiseau de feu* [also see above]), J. & W. Chester (London, England), 1920, revised score published as *The Firebird Symphonic Suite,* completed, 1945, Leeds Music, 1947.

*Symphonies d'instruments a vent: To the Memory of Debussy,* completed, 1920 (title means "Symphonies of Wind Instruments"; first produced in London, England, June 10, 1921), Edition Russe (Paris, France), 1920, revised score completed, 1947, Boosey & Hawkes (London, England), 1952.

*Capriccio for Piano and Orchestra,* completed, 1929 (first produced in Paris, France, December 6, 1929), Edition Russe (Paris, France), 1929, revised score completed, 1949, Boosey & Hawkes (London, England), 1952.

*Four Etudes for Orchestra,* completed, 1930 (adapted from composer's *Three Pieces for String Quartet* and *Etude for Pianola* [see below]; first produced in Berlin, Germany, November 7, 1930), Edition Russe (Paris, France), 1930, Boosey & Hawkes (London, England).

(With Sam Dushkin) *Divertimento for Orchestra,* completed, 1934 (adapted from composer's ballet *Le Baiser de la fee* [also see above]), Edition Russe (Paris, France), 1934, revised score, completed, 1949, Boosey & Hawkes (London, England), 1950.

*Preludium for Jazz Band,* completed, 1937, revised version, completed, 1953, Boosey & Hawkes (London, England), 1968.

*Symphonie en ut,* completed August 19, 1940 (title means "Symphony in C"; first produced in Chicago, IL, November 7, 1940), Associated Music Publishers (New York, NY), 1940.

*Circus Polka for Orchestra or Piano,* completed February 15, 1942 (first produced in Boston, MA, January 13, 1944), Associated Music Publishers (New York, NY), 1944, arrangement for band, Associated Music Publishers, 1948.

*Norwegian Moods: Four Episodes for Orchestra,* completed, 1942 (first produced in Cambridge, MA, January 13, 1944), Associated Music Publishers (New York, NY), 1944.

*Scherzo a la Russe for Jazz Orchestra,* completed, 1944 (first produced in San Francisco, CA, March 22, 1946), Chappell (London, England), 1944, arrangement for jazz band with title *Scherzo a la Russe for Jazz Band,* first produced in radio concert, 1944, arrangement for two pianos, Associated Music Publishers (New York, NY), 1945.

*Scenes de ballet for Orchestra,* completed, 1944 (first produced as part of musical revue *The Seven Lively Arts* in New York, NY, December 7, 1944; produced in concert in New York, NY, in Carnegie Hall, February 3, 1945), Associated Music Publishers (New York, NY), 1945.

*Symphony in Three Movements,* completed, 1945 (first produced in New York, NY, January 24, 1946), B. Schott (Mainz, Germany), 1945, Associated Music Publishers (New York, NY), 1946.

*Greeting Prelude,* completed, 1955 (adapted from song *Happy Birthday to You* by C. F. Summy), Boosey & Hawkes (London, England), 1956.

*Movements for Piano and Orchestra,* completed, 1959 (first produced in New York, NY, January 10, 1960), Boosey & Hawkes (London, England), 1960.

*Variations: Aldous Huxley in Memoriam,* completed, October 28, 1964 (first produced in Chicago, IL, April 17, 1965), Boosey & Hawkes (London, England), 1965.

*Canon on a Russian Popular Tune,* completed, 1965 (adapted from finale of composer's ballet *L'Oiseau de feu*), Boosey & Hawkes (London, England), 1966.

*RELIGIOUS COMPOSITIONS*

*Le Roi des etoiles: Cantata for Chorus and Orchestra,* completed, 1911 (title means "The King of the Stars"; first produced in Brussels, Belgium, at Institut Nationale de Radio-diffusion Belge, April 19, 1939), text by Konstantin Balmont, Jurgenson, 1911, Boosey & Hawkes (London, England), 1952.

*Symphonie de Psaumes for Chorus and Orchestra,* completed August 15, 1930 (title means "Symphony of Psalms"; first produced in Brussels at Palais des Beaux Arts, December 13, 1930; produced in Boston, MA, December 19, 1931), vocal score published by Edition Russe (Paris, France), 1930, full score, Edition Russe (Paris, France), 1932, revised score, completed, 1948, Boosey & Hawkes (London, England), 1948.

*Pater Noster for Unaccompanied Chorus,* completed, 1926, Edition Russe (Paris, France), 1932, revised score with Latin text, Boosey & Hawkes (London, England), 1949.

*Credo for Unaccompanied Chorus,* completed, 1932, Edition Russe (Paris, France), 1933, revised score with Latin text, Boosey & Hawkes (London, England), 1947, second revised score with Slavic text, completed March, 1964.

*The Tower of Babel: Cantata for Reciter, Male Chorus, and Orchestra,* completed April 12, 1944 (adapted from Book of Moses; first produced in Los Angeles, CA, at Wilshire Ebell Theatre, November 18, 1945), [Hollywood, CA], 1944, Associated Music Publishers (New York, NY), 1953.

*Mass in C for Mixed Chorus and Double Woodwind Quintet,* completed March 15, 1948 (first produced in Milan, Italy, at Teatro alla Scala, October 27, 1948), Boosey & Hawkes (London, England), 1948.

*Cantata on Four Poems by Anonymous English Poets of the Fifteenth and Sixteenth Centuries,* completed August, 1952 (first produced in Los Angeles, CA, November 11, 1952), Boosey & Hawkes (London, England), 1952.

*Canticum sacrum ad honorem Sancti Marci nominis,* completed, 1955 (first produced in Venice, Italy, at St. Mark's Cathedral, September 13, 1956), Boosey & Hawkes (London, England), 1956.

*Threni; id est, Lamentationes Jeremiae prophetae,* completed March 21, 1958 (first produced in Venice at International Festival of Contemporary Music, September 23, 1958), Boosey & Hawkes (London, England), 1958.

*A Sermon, a Narrative, and a Prayer,* completed January 31, 1962 (triptych adapted from texts from Saint Paul, the Acts of the Apostles, and a poem by Thomas Dekker; first produced in Basel, Switzerland, February 23, 1962), Boosey & Hawkes (London, England), 1962.

*Abraham and Isaac: A Sacred Ballad for Baritone and Chamber Orchestra,* completed March 3, 1963 (first produced in Jerusalem, Israel, at Binyanei He' Ooma, August 23, 1964), Boosey & Hawkes (London, England), 1965.

*Requiem Canticles for Contralto and Bass Soli, Chorus, and Orchestra,* completed, 1966 (first produced in Princeton, NJ, at Princeton University, October 8, 1966), Boosey & Hawkes (London, England), 1967.

*VOCAL COMPOSITIONS*

*Trois Petites Chansons: Souvenir de mon enfance for Voice and Piano,* completed, c. 1906 (title means "Three Little Songs: Souvenirs of My Childhood";

contains *The Magpie, The Rook,* and *The Jackdaw*), revised score, completed November, 1913, Edition Russe (Paris, France), 1913, arrangement for chamber orchestra, completed, 1930, Edition Russe (Paris, France), 1934, Boosey & Hawkes (London, England), 1947.

*Le Faune et la bergere for Voice and Orchestra,* completed, 1907 (title means "Faun and Shepherdess"; based on three poems by Aleksander Pushkin; contains *The Shepherdess, The Faun,* and *The River*; first produced in St. Petersburg, Russia, April 27, 1907), Belaieff, 1907, Boosey & Hawkes (London, England), 1964.

*Three Songs for Voice and Piano* (contains *Novice* and *Sainte Rosee,* texts by S. Gorodetsky, and *Pastorale*), Jurgenson, 1908.

*Chant funebre,* completed June, 1908 (title means "Funeral Dirge"; first produced in St. Petersburg, Russia, autumn, 1908), manuscript lost.

*Deux poems de Paul Verlaine,* completed July, 1910 (title means "Two Songs of Paul Verlaine"; contains *Un Grand Sommeil noir* and *La Lune blanche*) Jurgenson, 1911, Boosey & Hawkes (London, England), 1954, arrangement for chamber orchestra, completed, 1951, Boosey & Hawkes (London, England), 1953.

*Two Poems of Konstantin Balmont,* completed, 1911 (contains *The Flower* and *The Dove*), Edition Russe (Paris, France), 1912, revised version, completed, 1954, Boosey & Hawkes (London, England), 1954.

*Trois poesies de la lyrique japonaise for Voice and Small Instrumental Ensemble,* completed, 1913 (title means "Three Poems from the Japanese"; contains *Akahito, Mazatsumi,* and *Tsaraiuki*; first produced in Paris, January 14, 1914), translation by A. Brandt, Edition Russe (Paris, France), 1913, Boosey & Hawkes (London, England).

*Berceuses du chat for Voice and Three Clarinets,* completed, 1916 (title means "The Cat's Cradle Songs"), Edition Russe (Paris, France), 1916, J. & W. Chester (London, England), 1917.

*Chansons plaisants: Pribaoutki for Voice and Eight Instruments,* completed, 1914 (title means "Pleasant Songs"), J. & W. Chester (London, England), 1917.

*Four a Cappella Choruses for Women's Voices,* Chester-Schott, 1914-17.

*Trois histories pour enfants,* completed June 21, 1917 (title means "Three Stories for Children"; contains *Tilimbom, Geese, Swans,* and *The Bear's Little Song*), J. & W. Chester (London, England), 1920,

arrangement for orchestra, completed, 1923, B. Schott (Mainz, Germany), 1923.

*Four Russian Songs for Voice and Piano,* completed October 23, 1919 (contains *The Counting Song, The Drake, Table-Mat Song,* and *Dissident Song*), J. & W. Chester (London, England), 1919.

*Ode: Elegiac Song in Three Movements,* completed June 25, 1943 (contains *Eulogy, Ecologue,* and *Epitaph*; first produced in Boston, MA, October 8, 1943 [some sources say October 1]), Associated Music Publishers (New York, NY), 1943.

*Russian Maiden's Song for Voice and Piano,* lyrics by B. Kochno, translation by R. Burness, Boosey & Hawkes (London, England), 1948.

*Three Songs from William Shakespeare,* completed autumn, 1953 (first produced in Los Angeles, CA, March 8, 1954), Boosey & Hawkes (London, England), 1954.

*In Memoriam: Dylan Thomas,* completed March, 1954 (first produced in Los Angeles, CA, September 20, 1954), Boosey & Hawkes (London, England), 1954.

*Four Russian Songs for Soprano, Flute, Harp, and Guitar,* completed, 1954 (contains *Tilimbom* and *Geese, Swans* [both adapted from composer's *Trois Histoires pour enfants*; also see above] and *The Drake* and *A Russian Spiritual; or, Dissident Song* [both adapted from composer's *Four Russian Songs for Voice and Piano*; also see above]; first produced in Los Angeles, February 21, 1955), J. & W. Chester (London, England), 1954.

*Anthem: The Dove Descending Breaks the Air,* completed, 1962.

*Elegy for J.F.K.,* completed March, 1964 (scored to a poem by W. H. Auden; first produced in Los Angeles, April 6, 1964), Boosey & Hawkes (London, England), 1964.

*Introitus: T. S. Eliot in Memoriam,* completed, 1965.

*The Owl and the Pussycat,* completed, 1966, Boosey & Hawkes (London, England), 1967.

*Concertos: Concertino for String Quartet,* completed September 24, 1920 (first produced in Salzburg, Austria, August 5, 1923), Wilhelm Hansen, 1923, arrangement for twelve instruments, completed, 1952 (first produced in Los Angeles, CA, November 11, 1952), Wilhelm Hansen (Leipzig, Germany, and Copenhagen, Denmark), 1953.

*Concerto for Piano, Wind, Contrabasses, and Timpani,* completed April, 1924 (first produced in Paris, France, May 22, 1924; produced in Boston, MA, January 23, 1925), Edition Russe (Paris, France), 1924, arrangement for piano and orchestra, completed, 1936, Edition Russe (Paris, France), revised score, completed, 1950, Boosey & Hawkes (London, England), 1950.

*Concerto in D for Violin and Orchestra,* completed, 1931 (first produced in a radio concert in Berlin, Germany, October 23, 1931), Associated Music Publishers (New York, NY), 1931, Boosey & Hawkes (London, England), 1961.

(With S. Dushkin) *Duo-Concertante for Violin and Piano,* completed July 15, 1932 (first produced in a radio concert in Berlin, Germany, October 28, 1932), Edition Russe (Paris, France), 1933, Boosey & Hawkes (London, England).

*Concerto for Two Pianos,* completed November 9, 1935 (some sources say September 1, 1935; first produced in Paris at Salle Gaveau, November 21, 1935), Associated Music Publishers (New York, NY), 1936.

*Concerto in E-flat major for Chamber Orchestra: Dumbarton Oaks Concerto,* completed March 29, 1938 (first produced in Washington, DC, at Dumbarton Oaks estate, May 8, 1938), Associated Music Publishers (New York, NY), 1938, arrangement for two pianos, Associated Music Publishers, 1938.

*Concerto for Wind Orchestra: Ebony Concerto,* completed December 1, 1945 (first produced in New York, NY, at Carnegie Hall, March 25, 1946), Charling Music, 1945, Edwin H. Morris (New York, NY), 1954.

*Concerto for String Orchestra: Basle Concerto,* completed August 8, 1946 (first produced in Basel, Switzerland, January 21, 1947), Boosey & Hawkes (London, England), 1947, Associated Music Publishers (New York, NY), 1959.

*OPERAS*

(And author of libretto with Stephen N. Mitusoff) *Le Rossignol,* completed, 1914 (three-act; title means "The Nightingale"; adapted from story *The Emperor and the Nightingale* by Hans Christian Andersen; first produced in Paris, France, at Paris Opera, May 26, 1914; produced in New York, NY, at Metropolitan Opera, March 6, 1926), Edition Russe (Paris, France), 1914, Boosey & Hawkes (London, England), 1947, revised score with translation of libretto by Robert Craft, Boosey & Hawkes, 1956.

*Marva,* completed, 1921 (one-act; adapted from verse story *The Little House in Kolomna* by Aleksander Pushkin; first produced in Paris, France, at Hotel Continental, May 29, 1922; first produced in United States in 1934), libretto by Boris Kochno, Edition Russe (Paris, France), 1925, with translation of libretto by Robert Craft, Boosey & Hawkes (London, England), 1956.

*Oedipus Rex,* completed May 10, 1927 (two-act; adapted from play with same title by Sophocles; first produced in concert in Paris, France, at Theatre Sarah Bernhardt, May 30, 1927; produced in concert in Boston, MA, February 24, 1928; produced in New York, NY, April 21, 1931), libretto by Jean Cocteau, Edition Russe (Paris, France), 1928, revised score with translation of libretto by e. e. cummings, completed, 1948, Boosey & Hawkes (London, England), 1949.

*The Rake's Progress,* completed, 1951 (three-act; first produced in Venice at Teatro La Fenice, September 11, 1951; produced in New York, NY, at Metropolitan Opera, February 14, 1953), libretto by W. H. Auden and Chester Kallman, Boosey & Hawkes (London, England), 1951.

*CHAMBER MUSIC*

*Three Pieces for String Quartet,* completed, 1914 (first produced in New York, NY, November 30, 1915), Edition Russe (Paris, France), 1914, Boosey & Hawkes (London, England), 1947.

*Three Pieces for Clarinet Solo,* J. & W. Chester (London, England), 1918.

*Suite No. 2 for Small Orchestra,* completed, 1921 (adapted from composer's *Trois pieces facile for Piano, Four Hands* [also see below]), J. & W. Chester (London, England), 1921.

*Suite from Pulcinella,* completed c. 1922 (adapted from composer's ballet *Pulcinella* [also see above]), Edition Russe (Paris, France), 1924, revised version completed, 1949, Boosey & Hawkes (London, England), 1949.

*Octet for Wind Instruments,* completed, 1923 (first produced in Paris, October 18, 1923, produced in New York, NY, at Aeolian Hall, January 25, 1925), Edition Russe (Paris, France), 1923, revised version, completed, 1952, Boosey & Hawkes (London, England), 1952.

*Suite No. 1 for Small Orchestra,* completed, 1925 (adapted from composer's *Cinq pieces faciles for Piano, Four Hands* [also see below]), J. & W. Chester (London, England), 1925.

*Danses Concertantes for Chamber Orchestra,* completed January 13, 1942 (first produced in Los An-

geles, CA, February 8, 1942), Associated Music
Publishers, 1942.

*Elegy for Viola (or Violin) Solo,* completed, 1944,
Chappell (London, England), 1945.

*Septet for Piano, String, and Wind Instruments,* com-
pleted, 1953 (first produced in Washington, DC,
January 23, 1954), Boosey & Hawkes (London,
England), 1953.

*Epitaphium for Prince Max of Furstenberg for Flute,
Clarinet, and Harp,* completed, 1959 (first produced in Donaueschingen, Germany, October 17,
1959), Boosey & Hawkes (London, England),
1959.

*Double Canon for String Quartet,* completed, 1959,
Boosey & Hawkes (London, England), 1960.

*Fanfare for a New Theatre for Trumpet Duet,* completed, 1964, Boosey & Hawkes (London,
England), 1968.

*PIANO COMPOSITIONS*

*Scherzo,* completed, 1902, G. Schirmer (New York,
NY), 1974.

*Sonata in F-sharp minor,* completed, 1904, edited by
Eric Walter White, G. Schirmer (New York, NY),
1974.

*Four Etudes for Piano,* Jurgenson, 1908.

*Valse des fleurs,* completed August 30, 1914 (first produced in New York, NY, 1949), manuscript lost.

*Trois pieces faciles for Piano, Four Hands,* completed,
1915 (title means "Three Easy Pieces"), J. & W.
Chester (London, England), 1917, International
Music Co. (New York, NY), 1970.

*Cinq pieces faciles for Piano, Four Hands,* completed,
1917 (title means "Five Easy Pieces"; contains
*Andante, Neapolitana, Espanola, Balaika,* and *Ga-
lop;* first produced in Lausanne, Switzerland, November 8, 1919), Henn, 1917, J. & W. Chester
(London, England), 1925.

*Etude for Pianola: Madrid,* completed, 1917 (first produced in London, England, at Aeolian Hall, October 13, 1921), Duo-Art-Aeolian, 1917, J. & W.
Chester (London, England), 1920, Boosey &
Hawkes (London, England), 1951.

*Piano-Rag-Music,* completed June 28, 1919 (first produced in Lausanne, Switzerland, November 8,
1919), J. & W. Chester (London, England), 1919.

*Les Cinq Doigts: Little Piano Pieces for Children,*
completed February 18, 1921 (title means "The
Five Fingers"), J. & W. Chester (London,

England), 1921, arrangement for small orchestra
with title *Eight Instrumental Miniatures,* completed, 1962 (first produced in Toronto, Ontario,
Canada, at Massey Hall, April 29, 1962), J. & W.
Chester (London, England), 1963.

*Sonata for Piano,* completed, 1924 (first produced in
Donaueschingen, Germany, July, 1925), Edition
Russe (Paris, France), 1924, Boosey & Hawkes
(London, England), 1925.

*Serenade in A for Piano,* completed autumn, 1925,
Edition Russe (Paris, France), 1926, edited by Al-
bert Spalding, Boosey & Hawkes (London,
England), 1947.

*Tango for One or Two Pianos,* completed, 1940, Mercury Music (New York, NY), 1940, arrangement
for orchestra, completed, 1953 (first produced in
Los Angeles, CA, October 19, 1953), Mercury
Music, 1954.

*Sonata for Two Pianos,* completed, 1944 (first produced in Madison, WI, at Dominican Sisters, July,
1944), Associated Music Publishers (New York,
NY, 1945.

*SIDELIGHTS:* Igor Fedorovich Stravinsky, whose innovative score for the ballet "Le Sacre du printemps"
precipitated a riot at its first performance, has been ap-
praised by many commentators as the most important
composer of the twentieth century. Composer Claude
Debussy, for example, once described Stravinsky as
"the most marvelous orchestral craftsman of our time."
But "Igor Stravinsky was more than an immensely
great composer," wrote Peter Heyworth in *Observer
Review.* "Like Beethoven and Wagner, he was one of
those giants who stamp their creative image on a
whole epoch."

The Russian-born son of an opera singer, Stravinsky
was discouraged in his pursuit of a career in music by
his parents, who insisted that he study law at the University of St. Petersburg. While on vacation from the
university, Stravinsky met the celebrated composer
and music educator Nicolai Rimsky-Korsakov, who
began giving the young law student private lessons in
composition and orchestration. Though he earned a
degree in law, Stravinsky never practiced that profession for he was determined to become a composer.

Performances of his early pieces, including "Scherzo
fantastique" and "Feu d'artifice," were well-received,
but it was his score for Sergei Diaghilev's production

of "L'Oiseau de feu" ("The Firebird") in 1910 that established Stravinsky's reputation as a composer of genius. Based upon a Russian folktale, the ballet was written in the tradition of Rimsky-Korsakov, and the nationalist school of music, but it was strikingly original in its orchestral treatment. A dazzling success, "L'Oiseau de feu" inspired Diaghilev's prediction that Stravinsky was destined for fame.

Stravinsky's twenty-year association with Diaghilev's Russian Ballet resulted in a series of extraordinary ballet productions, including "Petrouschka" and "Le Sacre du printemps." Like "L'Oiseau de feu," "Petrouschka" was enthusiastically greeted. The imaginative ballet, which employs such innovations as irregular meter and bitonalism, a technique whereby music is played simultaneously in two different keys, is regarded by some critics as the composer's masterpiece. It was Stravinsky's next ballet, "Le Sacre du printemps," however, that became his best-known work.

Based upon a pagan rite involving the sacrifice of a young virgin to the god of spring, "Le Sacre" caused one of the most tumultuous scandals in musical history when it was first performed in 1913. The opening night audience was divided between those who believed the composition was great art and those who felt it destroyed the very foundations of music. A riot erupted during the performance. Stravinsky described the scene in his autobiography: "I left the auditorium at the first bars of the prelude, which had at once evoked derisive laughter. I was disgusted. These demonstrations, at first isolated, soon became general, provoking counter-demonstrations and very quickly developing into a terrific uproar." Composer Lazare Saminsky described Stravinsky as "the father of the rebarbarization in music," reported *Saturday Review.* "He has," continued Saminsky, "reduced melody to the primitive, inarticulate refrain of a Zulu and has converted the orchestra into a gigantic rattle, the toy and mouthpiece of the new savage."

Since its riotous first performance "Le Sacre du printemps" has become universally regarded as a masterpiece. Though it is seldom performed as a ballet, the work is often played as a symphonic poem and appears on the repertory of every major orchestra. The work remains unique, however, since Stravinsky, upon completing the revolutionary ballet, was already exploring other styles of musical expression.

Abandoning the neoprimitive movement that he had initiated with "Le Sacre du printemps," Stravinsky became a proponent of neoclassicism, composing works such as the ballet "Pulcinella," which was based upon music by the eighteenth-century composer Giovanni Battista Pergolesi. Later works from Stravinsky's neoclassic period are the opera "Oedipus Rex" and the ballets "Apollon-Musagete," "Le Baiser de la fee," and "Orpheus." Though some critics view "Orpheus" as one of Stravinsky's most beautiful compositions, the composer's works from this period are generally regarded as inferior to his neoprimitive pieces.

Stravinsky also began writing smaller scale compositions for vocal and instrumental ensembles. These include his comic theatre pieces "Renard" and "Marva" and his chamber works "Suite No. 2 for Small Orchestra" and "Octet for Wind Instruments," all composed between 1916 and 1923.

Though Stravinsky is best known for his compositions for the stage, he also wrote numerous influential works of "pure" music. Some of these, including "Symphonies of Wind Instruments," exhibit an impersonal, albeit masterful, style. Others, such as "Symphony of Psalms," reveal the composer's ability to write music that is both moving and brilliant. Stravinsky also transcribed musical works by such well-known composers as Johann Sebastian Bach, Petr Tchaikovsky, Frederic Chopin, and Modest Musorgski.

The composer published *Stravinsky: An Autobiography* in order, he said in his book, to "present to the reader a true picture of myself, and to dissipate the accumulation of misunderstandings that has gathered about both my work and my person." The volume was described by P. H. Lang in *Saturday Review* as a valuable contribution "to the understanding of the most original and most powerful musician of our era. . . . No one who is interested in the destiny of musical art should miss this thought-provoking book." Two years later Stravinsky was invited to deliver the Charles Eliot Norton lectures at Harvard University. His remarks, wrote A. V. Berger in *Saturday Review,* contain "a plea for 'order and discipline,' melody, the limitations imposed by form, and a sense of tradition separable from habit and the artistic conservatism advocated by the Soviets." The lectures were published as a collection of essays entitled *Poetics of Music in the Form of Six Lessons.*

In 1939, aware that his music was more admired in the United States than in France, where he had lived since World War I, Stravinsky decided to take up residence in California. There he continued to write the cool, controlled music that characterized his neoclassical period. Though Stravinsky was, according to a *Time* writer, "a fierce and uncompromising pioneer who quite literally revolutionized the music of his century, he was also as modishly conscious of musical fashions as Picasso was addicted to changing taste in art and sculpture." In 1952 Stravinsky once again shocked the music world when he became a convert to Arnold Schoenberg's twelve-tone system, a form of musical composition that involves the use of all twelve notes in the chromatic scale and that rejects traditional melodic and harmonic patterns. This technique, which allows for discordant combinations of notes, sometimes produces harsh sounds that can jar the musical sensibilities of audiences.

Though his last works were written when Stravinsky was in his eighties, "he never composed a bar of what may be termed 'old man's music,'" asserted Simon Karlinsky in the *Nation.* Noel Goodwin, writing in *Books and Bookmen,* similarly hailed the composer as "a genius with the extraordinary faculty for growing younger in creative imagination as his body grew older." Consequently, Stravinsky's final years were unusually productive. "There flowed," reported Heyworth, "another series of masterpieces such as 'Agon' (1957), 'Threni' (1958), and, finally, in 1966, the 'Requiem Canticles.'" Stravinsky, thus, made outstanding contributions to each of the three styles of music in which he composed. Heyworth attributed Stravinsky's greatness to "the variety of music he wrote in each of these styles" and to "the fact that at a period of musical disintegration he wrote more masterpieces than anyone else and continued to do so throughout a period of almost sixty years."

Also during his last years, Stravinsky collaborated with Robert Craft, a long-time associate, on several volumes of autobiographical miscellanea. The first three books, *Conversations with Stravinsky, Memories and Commentaries,* and *Expositions and Developments,* present a question-and-answer format. They were assessed by David Drew in *New Statesman* as "a treasured contribution to the documentation of music in our time." The later collaborations, including *Dialogues and a Diary, Themes and Episodes,* and *Retrospectives and Conclusions,* feature extensive commentaries by Craft in addition to Stravinsky's remarks. "The series," wrote a *Time* reporter, "was born out of complementary needs: Stravinsky's need to get his

opinions and perceptions on paper, and Craft's need to nourish his own identity—as a conductor and writer—at the cornucopia of genius."

The collaboration caused Stravinsky to again become the subject of controversy when his personal representative and biographer, Lillian Libman, declared that the composer's contribution to the series was minimal. In *And Music at the Close: Stravinsky's Last Years,* which was published after the musician's death, Libman claimed that much of the published material alleged to be by Stravinsky was actually the work of Robert Craft. Though Craft acknowledged the words may not have been verbatim, he insisted that the opinions expressed in the volumes were those of Stravinsky. Goodwin concurred, noting that "the force of [Stravinsky's] personality is inescapable, however much the printed text may have been smoothed along by a blend of Craft and spontaneity."

Stravinsky, summarized Karlinsky, has become a legend, whose "evolution can now be seen for what it always was: the rich, purposeful, astoundingly fruitful search for a synthesis between the musical culture of the past and the gradually emerging musical forms, both serious and popular, of the 20th century."

## *BIOGRAPHICAL AND CRITICAL SOURCES:*

*BOOKS*

Boretz, Benjamin and Edward T. Cone, editors, *Perspectives on Schoenberg and Stravinsky,* Princeton University Press, 1968.

*Contemporary Musicians,* Volume 21, Gale (Detroit, MI), 1998.

Craft, Robert, *Chronicle of a Friendship,* Knopf (New York, NY), 1972.

DeLerma, Dominique-Rene, *Igor Fedorovitch Stravinsky, 1882-1971: A Practical Guide to Publications of His Music,* Kent State University Press, 1974.

Dobrin, Arnold, *Igor Stravinsky: His Life and Times,* Crowell, 1970.

*Encyclopedia of World Biograhy,* Volume 14, Gale (Detroit, MI), 1998.

Evans, Evans, *The Firebird and Petrouchka,* Oxford University Press, 1933.

*Igor Stravinsky: A Complete Catalogue of His Published Works,* Boosey & Hawkes (London, England), 1957.

*International Dictionary of Opera,* St. James Press (Detroit, MI), 1993.

Lang, Paul Henry, editor, *Stravinsky: A New Appraisal of His Work,* enlarged edition, McLeod, 1969.

Lederman, Minna, editor, *Stravinsky in the Theatre,* DaCapo Press, 1975.

Libman, Lillian, *And Music at the Close: Stravinsky's Last Years,* Norton (New York, NY), 1972.

Montagu, Nathan M., *Contemporary Russian Composers,* C. Palmer & Haywood, 1917.

Siohan, Robert, *Stravinsky,* translated by Eric Walter White, Grossman, 1970.

*Stravinsky and the Dance: A Survey of Ballet Productions, 1910-1962,* New York Public Library (New York, NY), 1962.

*Stravinsky: Classic Humanist,* three volumes, translated by Hans Rosenwald, DaCapo Press, 1973.

Stravinsky, Theodore, *Catherine and Igor Stravinsky: A Family Album,* Boosey & Hawkes (London, England), 1973.

Stravinsky, Ver, and Robert Craft, *Stravinsky in Pictures and Documents,* Simon & Schuster (New York, NY), 1978.

Tansman, Alexandre, *Igor Stravinsky: The Man and His Music,* translated by Therese and Charles Bleefield, Putnam (New York, NY), 1949.

Vlad, Roman, *Stravinsky,* translated by Frederick and Ann Fuller, Oxford University Press, 1960.

White, Eric Walter, *Stravinsky: A Critical Survey,* Greenwood Press (New Haven, CT), 1979.

White, Eric Walter, *Stravinsky's Sacrifice to Apollo,* Hogarth, 1930.

White, Eric Walter, *Stravinsky: The Composer and His Works,* enlarged edition, University of California Press (Berkeley, CA), 1979.


*PERIODICALS*


*American Record Guide,* March-April, 1999, Tom Godell, "Stravinsky: Firebird, Scriabin, Prometheus," pp. 232-233; May, 2001, Roget Hecht, "Overview: Igor Stravinsky," p. 53.

*Atlantic Monthly,* November, 1949; June, 1957; May, 1961.

*Books and Bookmen,* January, 1973.

*Commonweal,* July 23, 1971.

*Life,* November 25, 1957.

*Los Angeles Times,* December 15, 2001, Daniel Cariaga, "Music Review: Mehta and Stravinsky: An Intense Combination," p. F11.

*Musical Quarterly,* April, 1919; July, 1935; July, 1940; January, 1941; July, 1962.

*Nation,* June 15, 1970.

*National Observer,* March 9, 1970.

*New Republic,* January 10, 1970.

*Newsweek,* November 3, 1947; June 24, 1957; February 3, 1958; May 11, 1959; August 22, 1960; May 21, 1962; October 15, 1962; January 19, 1970; July 17, 1972; January 8, 1979.

*New Yorker,* January 5, 1935.

*New York Times,* March 25, 1970; March 3, 1972; April 24, 2001, Anthony Tommasini, "Hollywood Denizens, Like Stravinsky," p. E5.

*New York Times Book Review,* June 10, 1962.

*New York Times Magazine,* June 15, 1952.

*Nouvelle revue francaise,* November 1, 1913.

*Observer Review,* April 11, 1969.

*Punch,* February 13, 1970.

*Saturday Review,* May 3, 1947; June 26, 1954; March 12, 1960; July 29, 1961; May 29, 1971.

*Spectator,* June 28, 1957; September 20, 1975.

*Tempo,* summer, 1948; spring-summer, 1962; summer, 1967.

*Time,* February 4, 1946; November 3, 1947; July 26, 1948; June 24, 1957; January 4, 1960; May 6, 1966; December 19, 1969; September 18, 1972; June 8, 1998, Philip Glass, "Igor Stravinsky: The Classical Musician," pp. 141-142.

*Times Literary Supplement,* December 22, 1972; October 18, 1974; May 26, 1978.

*Vogue,* November 1, 1963; April 15, 1965.


*OBITUARIES:*


*BOOKS*


*Oxford Companion to Music,* 10th edition, Oxford University Press, 1974.


*PERIODICALS*


*Atlantic Monthly,* July, 1971.

*Commentary,* July, 1971.

*Dance Magazine,* May, 1971.

*Life,* April 16, 1971.

*Newsweek,* April 19, 1971.

*New Yorker,* May 1, 1971.

*New York Times,* April 7, 1971.

*Opera News,* June 12, 1971.

*Saturday Review,* April 24, 1971.
*Time,* April 19, 1971.
*Washington Post,* April 7, 1971.
*Yale Review,* December, 1971.*

\*   \*   \*

## STRICKLAND, (William) Brad(ley) 1947-
### (Will Bradley)

*PERSONAL:* Born October 27, 1947, in New Holland, GA; son of Silas Henry (a textile laborer) and Eavleen Hannah (a homemaker; maiden name, Watkins) Strickland; married Barbara Ann Justus (a teacher), June, 1969; children: Jonathan Bradley, Amy Elizabeth. *Education:* University of Georgia, A.B., 1969, M.A., 1971, Ph.D., 1977. *Politics:* Democrat. *Religion:* Baptist. *Hobbies and other interests:* Photography, travel, animated cartoons.

*ADDRESSES: Home*—5044 Valley Ct., Oakwood, GA 30566. *Office*—Box 1358, Gainesville College, Gainesville, GA 30503. *Agent*—Richard Curtis Associates, 171 East 74th St., New York, NY 10021. *E-mail*—bstrickland@gc.peachnet.edu.

*CAREER:* Author, educator. Truett-McConnell Junior College, Cleveland, GA, chair of humanities department, 1976-85; Georgia Governor's Honors Program, Valdosta, GA, head of language arts department, 1981-85; Lakeview Academy, Gainesville, GA, head of secondary English department, 1985-87; Gainesville College, Gainesville, GA, associate professor of English, 1987—. Has acted in radio plays with the Atlanta Radio Theater.

*MEMBER:* Horror Writers Association, Science Fiction and Fantasy Writers of America, Society of Children's Book Writers and Illustrators, American Association of University Professors.

*AWARDS, HONORS:* Regents' Scholar, 1969-74; Northeast Georgia Writers Award for short fiction, 1974; Phoenix Award, Deep South Science Fiction Convention, 1992, for achievement in science fiction; Schaumburg Township Young Reader's Choice Award, 1996; Georgia Author of the Year (children's division), 1999, 2001.

*WRITINGS:*

*To Stand beneath the Sun,* Signet (New York, NY), 1986.
*Shadowshow,* Onyx (New York, NY), 1988.
*Moon Dreams* ("Jeremy Moon" series; fantasy) Signet (New York, NY), 1988.
*Nul's Quest* ("Jeremy Moon" series; fantasy), Signet (New York, NY), 1989.
*Children of the Knife,* Onyx (New York, NY), 1990.
*Silver Eyes* (thriller), New American Library, 1990.
*Wizard's Mole* ("Jeremy Moon" series; fantasy), Roc (New York, NY), 1991.
*Dragon's Plunder* (young adult fantasy), illustrated by Wayne D. Barlowe, Atheneum (New York, NY), 1992.
(As Will Bradley) *Ark Liberty* (science fiction), Penguin/Roc (New York, NY), 1992.
(With Todd Cameron Hamilton) *The Star Ghost* (based on the *Star Trek: Deep Space Nine* television series), Pocket Books (New York, NY), 1993.
(With Todd Cameron Hamilton) *Stowaways* (based on the *Star Trek: Deep Space Nine* television series), Pocket Books (New York, NY), 1994.
(With Barbara Strickland) *The Tale of the Secret Mirror* (based on the *Are You Afraid of the Dark?* television series), Pocket Books (New York, NY), 1995.
(With Barbara Strickland and Todd Cameron Hamilton) *Nova Command* (based on the *Star Trek, the Next Generation* television series), Pocket Books (New York, NY), 1995.
(With Barbara Strickland) *Starfall* (based on the *Star Trek, the Next Generation* television series), Pocket Books (New York, NY), 1995.
(With Barbara Strickland and Todd Cameron Hamilton) *Crisis on Vulcan* (based on the *Star Trek* television series), Pocket Books (New York, NY), 1996.
*The Hand of the Necromancer* (young adult fantasy; based on the characters of John Bellairs), Dial (New York, NY), 1996.
(With Barbara Strickland) *The Tale of the Phantom School Bus* (based on the *Are You Afraid of the Dark?* television series), Pocket Books (New York, NY), 1996.
(With Barbara Strickland) *The Tale of the Deadly Diary* (based on the *Are You Afraid of the Dark?* television series), Pocket Books (New York, NY), 1996.
*The Bell, the Book, and the Spellbinder* (young adult fantasy; based on the characters of John Bellairs), Dial (New York, NY), 1997.

*You're History* (based on the *Sabrina, the Teenage Witch* television series), illustrated by Mark Dubowski, Pocket Books (New York, NY), 1998.

(With Barbara Strickland) *Frame-Up* (based on the *Mystery Files of Shelby Woo* television series), Pocket Books (New York, NY), 1998.

*The Specter from the Magician's Museum* (young adult fantasy; based on the characters of John Bellairs), Dial (New York, NY), 1998.

(With Barbara Strickland) *Man Overboard!* (based on the *Mystery Files of Shelby Woo* television series), Pocket (New York, NY), 1999.

*The Wrath of the Grinning Ghost* (based on the characters of John Bellairs), Dial (New York, NY), 1999.

*The Beast under the Wizard's Bridge,* Dial (New York, NY), 2000.

*When Mack Came Back,* Dial (New York, NY), 2000.

*The Tower at the End of the World,* Dial (New York, NY), 2001.

*Survive!* (based on the "Dinotopia" series by James Gurney), Random House (New York, NY), 2001.

(With Barbara Strickland) *No-Rules Weekend* (based on the *Full House* television series), Pocket (New York, NY), 2001.

Has written for radio with the Atlanta Radio Theater, adapting works by H. P. Lovecraft and others, as well as writing original scripts. Strickland's stories have appeared in *The Year's Best Horror,* Volumes 15 and 17.

*CHILDREN'S NOVELS; BEGUN BY JOHN BELLAIRS; COMPLETED BY BRAD STRICKLAND*

*The Vengeance of the Witch-Finder,* Dial (New York, NY), 1993.

*The Ghost in the Mirror* (also see below), Dial (New York, NY), 1994.

*The Drum, the Doll, and the Zombie,* Dial (New York, NY), 1994.

*The Doom of the Haunted Opera,* Dial (New York, NY), 1995.

*The House with a Clock in Its Walls* (contains *The Ghost in the Mirror* and John Bellairs's *The House with a Clock in Its Walls*), Puffin (New York, NY), 2002.

*The Whistle, the Grave, and the Ghost,* Dial (New York, NY), 2003.

*"ADVENTURES OF WISHBONE" SERIES; BASED ON THE CHARACTER CREATED BY RICK DUFFIELD*

*Be a Wolf!,* Big Red Chair (Allen, TX), 1997.

*Salty Dog,* Big Red Chair (Allen, TX), 1997.

(With Thomas E. Fuller) *Riddle of the Wayward Books,* Big Red Chair (Allen, TX), 1997.

(With Thomas E. Fuller) *The Treasure of Skeleton Reef,* Big Red Chair (Allen, TX), 1997.

(With Thomas E. Fuller) *The Disappearing Dinosaurs,* Big Red Chair (Allen, TX), 1998.

(With Thomas E. Fuller) *Disoriented Express,* Big Red Chair (Allen, TX), 1998.

(With Thomas E. Fuller) *Drive-In of Doom,* Big Red Chair (Allen, TX), 1998.

(With Barbara Strickland) *Gullifur's Travels,* Big Red Chair (Allen, TX), 1999.

(With Thomas E. Fuller) *Jack and the Beanstalk,* Little Red Chair (Allen, TX), 1999.

(With Thomas E. Fuller) *Terrier of the Lost Mines,* Little Red Chair (Allen, TX), 1999.

(With Anne Capeci and Carla Jablonski) *The Wishbone Halloween Adventure,* Lyric (Allen, TX), 2000.

*"PIRATE HUNTER" SERIES*

(With Thomas E. Fuller) *Mutiny!,* Aladdin (New York, NY), 2002.

(With Thomas E. Fuller) *The Guns of Tortuga,* Aladdin (New York, NY), 2003.

(With Thomas E. Fuller) *Heart of Steele,* Aladdin (New York, NY), 2003.

*PLAYS*

(With Ed Cabell and Roy Forrester) *The Tale of the Rooster,* produced in Georgia, 1990.

*C.O.'s D-Day,* produced in Georgia, 1991.

(With Ed Cabell and Roy Forrester) *Farewell to Joe and Jackie,* produced in Georgia, 1991.

*The House on Nowhere Road* (radio play; part of "Horror House" series), broadcast on National Public Radio Theatre, 1993.

(With Thomas E. Fuller) *The Great Air Monopoly,* produced in Georgia, 1993.

Also author of *The Rats in the Walls* with Thomas E. Fuller, an adaptation of a story by H. P. Lovecraft, 1990.

*SIDELIGHTS:* Brad Strickland began as a writer of fantasy novels centered on the character of Jeremy Moon, an advertising executive who accidentally travels to a magical parallel universe where the power of words is quite literal. The books in this series, *Moon Dreams, Nul's Quest,* and *Wizard's Mole,* employ stock elements of fantasy novels enlightened by Strickland's puckish sense of humor. Other early novels include *Dragon's Plunder,* a pirate story described by Chris Sherman in *Booklist* as "a real page-turner, with cliff-hanging chapters that are perfect for reading aloud," and *Shadowshow,* a horror novel set in the author's native Georgia in the 1950s.

However, Strickland is perhaps best known for his collaboration with John Bellairs, an acknowledged master of horror novels for young adults. After Bellairs's death, Strickland finished some of his incomplete novels, beginning with *The Ghost in the Mirror,* featuring Bellairs regulars Rose Rita Pottinger and her neighbor Mrs. Zimmermann, a witch. Eventually, Strickland wrote several original novels that featured Bellairs's characters. Critical response to Strickland's assumption of Bellairs's mantle, along with his characters, was generally positive.

In *The Ghost in the Mirror,* Rose Rita and Mrs. Zimmermann wind up in 1828 Pennsylvania Dutch country when they go in search of Mrs. Zimmermann's lost powers. In *The Vengeance of the Witch-Finder,* featuring Lewis Barnavelt and his uncle Jonathan, an accidentally released ghost seeks revenge on his seventeenth-century murderer. A third Bellairs novel that Strickland completed, *The Doom of the Haunted Opera,* finds Lewis and Rose Rita staging an opera in an abandoned theater only to discover that the opera is a kind of spell that will allow the composer to take over the world. Critical response to these works was generally favorable, with reviewers assuring faithful readers that Strickland had seamlessly carried out the stories Bellairs started but failed to complete before his death. While *School Library Journal* contributor Ann W. Moore felt that *The Vengeance of the Witch-Finder* was not as successful as Bellairs's earlier novels featuring Lewis Barnavelt, a contributor to *Publishers Weekly* described this novel as "chock-full of deliciously spooky details and narrated in a voice that is as cozy as it is ornery," concluding, "this tale is utterly spellbinding."

With the publication of *The Drum, the Doll, and the Zombie,* Strickland began to receive accolades for his consistently high-quality novels for young adults. Here, Johnny Dixon, Fergie Ferguson, Father Higgins, and Professor Childermass battle a legion of zombies unleashed by an evil sorceress. Unusual among the trappings of standard horror novel fare, however, are humor and well-rounded characters, critics noted. "This ably devised bit of supernatural fun . . . is perfect for the pre-Stephen King set," remarked Stephanie Zvirin in *Booklist.* Connie Tyrrell Burns made similar comments in *School Library Journal* about *The Hand of the Necromancer,* a novel that features some of Bellairs's characters in an original story by Strickland. Here Johnny Dixon becomes embroiled in a battle to save the world when an evil wizard arrives in town wanting to awaken the spirit of his powerful ancestor. Readers who enjoy traditional elements of horror fiction, such as haunted houses, bad weather, and the like, will appreciate *The Hand of the Necromancer,* noted Burns, concluding her review by claiming the story "is stylistically a treat as well, full of foreshadowing and figurative language."

"Strickland continues John Bellairs's series with great imagination," wrote Janet Mura in *Voice of Youth Advocates* in a review of *The Specter from the Magician's Museum.* In this story, Lewis and Rose Rita decide to perform a magic show for the school talent show and accidentally ensnare Rose Rita in the evil spell of an ancient sorceress. Krista Grosick, writing in *School Library Journal,* believed that while Strickland had managed to successfully imitate Bellairs's style, he "even improves upon the deceased author's well-rounded and dynamic characters." Strickland's imitation of Bellairs is so complete in *The Bell, the Book, and the Spellbinder,* in which Fergie's life is endangered via the agency of a magical library book, that Connie Tyrrell Burns quipped in *School Library Journal,* "could it be reincarnation or body snatching?" Likewise Kendra Nan Skellen, writing in a *School Library Journal* review of *The Wrath of the Grinning Ghost,* remarked that this latest book "reads so much like Bellairs's books that [his fans] won't believe he didn't write it." In this story, Johnny Dixon's father is possessed, and only an ancient, chameleon-like book of magic can save him. The quest for the book takes Johnny and his friends all over the world and even into the underworld. "This is good reading for adventure enthusiasts as well as for series fans," remarked Kay Weisman in *Booklist.*

*The Beast under the Wizard's Bridge* is an effective mix of horror, mystery, and adventure story, according to reviewers. Here, Lewis Barnavelt and Rose Rita Pottinger are back, and along with Uncle Jonathan and Mrs. Zimmermann, they have a bad feeling about the town's plans to tear down an old (and evil) bridge. It turns out that the bridge is the only thing subduing a horrific monster capable of destroying everything it meets. "This entertaining page-turner . . . will captivate readers whether or not they are already familiar with Lewis and his friends," remarked Deborah L. Dubois in *Voice of Youth Advocates.* Strickland's next Bellairs novel, *The Tower at the End of the World,* is billed as a sequel to Bellairs's *The House with a Clock in Its Walls.* Although a contributor to *Kirkus Reviews* found this entry into the series, which takes place in Michigan's Upper Peninsula, a disappointing addition, Janet Gillen, writing in *School Library Journal,* called it "a wonderful blend of suspense, adventure, ghost story, and friendship that is a sure-to-please page-turner."

In a departure from his genre-fiction writing, which includes entries in the "Star Trek" and "Wishbone" series as well as the many supernatural novels inspired by John Bellairs, Strickland published a seemingly semi-autobiographical young-adult novel called *When Mack Came Back* in 2000. In this story, set in Georgia during the 1950s, a young boy rescues the dog his brother gave away when he left to serve in World War II. At odds with the wishes of his stern father, the boy nurses the dog back to health and refuses to relinquish him when his father tries to give the dog away again. "Strickland's strengths are vivid setting details and character development," remarked Kay Weisman in *Booklist,* commenting that the story lacks the fast pace or exciting action that some readers may desire. Like Weisman, Coop Renner, writing in *School Library Journal,* praised Strickland's period details about rural life during the World War II era, suggesting "*Mack* is a well-done novel aimed at a younger audience, most of whom will find the story satisfying and involving."

Strickland has also tried his hand at historical fiction for young readers, working with Thomas E. Fuller on the "Pirate Hunter" series. The first two books of the series, *Mutiny!* and *The Guns of the Tortuga,* feature an adolescent orphan boy named Danny Shea who travels to Jamaica in search of his only remaining relative, a surgeon. While not exactly pleased with his new charge, Dr. Patrick "Patch" Shea nonetheless takes the young lad on as his apprentice aboard a ship in the British Royal Navy. In *Mutiny!,* Danny and his uncle become involved in a dangerous mission to rid the Caribbean of pirates by staging a mock rebellion on the *HMS Retribution,* while *The Guns of Tortuga* finds the duo on the trail of the particularly heinous pirate Jack Steele. Reviewing *Mutiny!* for *Publishers Weekly,* a critic claimed, "If this rip-roaring adventure is any indication, it looks like smooth sailing ahead for an enjoyable new series." Referring to *The Guns of Tortuga, School Library Journal* contributor Kathleen A. Nester recommended the "fast-paced, action-packed tale" for "reluctant readers as well as adventure seekers."

Strickland once recalled, "Like many readers of fantasy and science fiction, I began early—in my teens. Like many of them, I tried my hand at writing a story early—at age sixteen. Unlike many, I actually sold my story, for one hundred dollars, to *Ellery Queen's Mystery Magazine.* The sale was unfortunate, for it gave me the mistaken impression that I had proved myself as a writer and need to write no more. However, after a lapse of seventeen years in my writing career, a friend talked me into reading some recent fantasy and science fiction. I liked it, tried writing a story or two, and found modest success. That led to my first novel, and since then I have been writing constantly across the spectrum of fantasy literature, including science fiction, adventure fantasy, and horror. I don't intend to stop again until I have to."

Strickland once told *CA:* "Coming from the South, I grew up in a family of storytellers. My aunts, uncles, and grandparents told tales of enchantment and terror involving vanishing hitchhikers, spirits of the dead wandering graveyards in the form of flickering flames, buried Confederate gold, indelible bloodstains at the site of murders . . . topics to make a child's flesh creep. However, I always wanted more and never failed to listen.

"So it was perhaps inevitable that my own stories, when I came to write them, were tales of enchantment and terror, all about flights to strange planets, wonder-working magicians, ghost-haunted mirrors, vengeful sorcerers, dragon gold and pirate booty, and resourceful young people. I'm still telling the kind of stories my relatives told, still writing books because I want to read them and they haven't been written by anyone else. Kindred spirits are important to a writer because writing can be a lonely business. My chance to work with the late John Bellairs was wonderful, exciting, and challenging, and my opportunity to write stories set in the 'Star Trek' universe was both a joy and a fulfillment for a lifelong science-fiction fan like me. My chance to write in these series made at least one reader happy: myself.

"But, of course, no writer can write just to please himself or herself. The reading audience is very special, and it's always pleasant to discover these stories appeal to others. I hope the young people who read my work will enjoy it half as much as I enjoy writing it, and it's good to hope that perhaps some of them will go on to become tellers of tales, masters of terror, workers of wonder."

## BIOGRAPHICAL AND CRITICAL SOURCES:

### BOOKS

*St. James Guide to Fantasy Writers,* St. James Press (Detroit, MI), 1996.

### PERIODICALS

*Booklist,* January 15, 1993, Chris Sherman, review of *Dragon's Plunder,* p. 892; February 15, 1993, Kay Weisman, review of *Ghost in the Mirror,* p. 1059; July, 1994, Stephanie Zvirin, review of *The Drum, the Doll, and the Zombie,* p. 1942; August, 1995, Stephanie Zvirin, review of *Hand of the Necromancer,* p. 1946; September 1, 1997, Susan DeRonne, review of *The Bell, the Book, and the Spellbinder,* p. 127; October 1, 1998, John Peters, review of *The Specter from the Magician's Museum,* p. 330; September 15, 1999, Kay Weisman, review of *The Wrath of the Grinning Ghost,* p. 261; October 15, 2000, Kay Weisman, review of *When Mack Came Back,* p. 441; November 1, 2000, Carolyn Phelan, review of *The Beast under the Wizard's Bridge,* p. 542; September 1, 2001, Carolyn Phelan, review of *Tower at the End of the World,* p. 111: December 1, 2002, Todd Morning, review of *Mutiny!,* p. 668; February 1, 2003, Todd Morning, review of *The Guns of Tortuga,* p. 995.

*Book Report,* March-April, 1993, Sylvia Feicht, review of *Dragon's Plunder,* p. 44; November-December, 1993, Nancye Starkey, review of *Ghost in the Mirror,* p. 42; January-February, 1994, Patsy

Launspach, review of *The Vengeance of the Witch-Finder,* p. 42; May-June, 1995, Norma Hunter, review of *The Drum, the Doll, and the Zombie,* p. 37; March-April, 1997, Charlotte Decker, review of *Hand of the Necromancer,* p. 42; May, 1999, Anne Sushko, review of *The Specter from the Magician's Museum,* p. 68.

*Horn Book Guide,* spring, 1997, Christine Heppermann, review of *The Bell, the Book, and the Spellbinder,* p. 76.

*Journal and Constitution* (Atlanta, GA), January 20, 1993.

*Kirkus Reviews,* July 1, 1996, review of *The Bell, the Book, and the Spellbinder,* p. 974; August 1, 2001, review of *Tower at the End of the World,* p. 1133.

*Library Journal,* May 15, 1988, Jackie Cassada, review of *Moondreams,* p. 96; February 15, 1989, Jackie Cassada, review of *Nul's Quest,* p. 180.

*Publishers Weekly,* November 4, 1988, review of *Shadowshow,* p. 77; January 6, 1989, review of *Nul's Quest,* p. 98; July, 1992, p. 81; July 12, 1993, review of *The Vengeance of the Witch-Finder,* p. 81; November 18, 2002, review of *Mutiny!,* p. 60.

*School Library Journal,* April, 1993, Susan L. Rogers, review of *Dragon's Plunder,* p. 125; September, 1993, Ann W. Moore, review of *The Vengeance of the Witch-Finder,* p. 228; September, 1995, Mary Jo Drungil, review of *Doom of the Haunted Opera,* p. 199; September, 1996, Connie Tyrrell Burns, review of *Hand of the Necromancer,* pp. 206, 208; August, 1997, Connie Tyrrell Burns, review of *The Bell, the Book, and the Spellbinder,* p. 160; January, 1998, John Sigwald, review of *Be a Wolf,* p. 116; November 1, 1998, Krista Grosick, review of *The Specter from the Magician's Museum,* p. 129; October, 1999, Kendra Nan Skellen, review of *The Wrath of the Grinning Ghost,* p. 160; January, 2000, John Sigwald, review of *Jack and the Beanstalk,* p. 112; June, 2000, Coop Renner, review of *When Mack Came Back,* p. 154; December, 2000, Lana Miles, review of *The Beast under the Wizard's Bridge,* p. 150; September, 2001, Janet Gillen, review of *Tower at the End of the World,* p. 234; November, 2002, Rita Soltan, review of *Mutiny!,* p. 176; March, 2003, Kathleen A. Nester, review of *The Guns of Tortuga,* p. 241.

*Stone Soup,* March, 2001, Austin Alvermann, review of *When Mack Came Back,* p. 32.

*Voice of Youth Advocates,* June, 1999, review of *The Specter from the Magician's Museum,* p. 126; April, 2001, Deborah L. DuBois, review of *The Beast under the Wizard's Bridge,* p. 57.

# T

## TAMAR, Erika 1934-

*PERSONAL:* Accent is on last syllable of surname; born June 10, 1934, in Vienna, Austria; came to the United States at age four; daughter of Julius (a physician) and Pauline (a homemaker; maiden name, Huterer) Tamar; divorced; children: Ray, Monica, Michael. *Ethnicity:* Jewish-American. *Education:* New York University, Washington Square College, B.A.; Stanford University, TV/Film Institute graduate. *Politics:* "Sometimes Democrat, mostly independent." *Religion:* Jewish. *Hobbies and other interests:* Visual and performing arts; taking painting classes; volunteering at the Metropolitan Museum of Art.

*ADDRESSES: Home*—399 East 72nd St., New York, NY 10021.

*CAREER:* Author, 1982—; speaker and writing instructor. Previously Leo Burnett Co., Inc., New York, NY, production assistant/casting director for *Search for Tomorrow,* television serial. Play Troupe of Port Washington, Long Island (community theater), actress and director.

*MEMBER:* Authors Guild, PEN, Society of Children's Book Writers and Illustrators.

*AWARDS, HONORS:* Books for the Teen Age list, New York Public Library, 1983, for *Blues for Silk Garcia,* 1984, for *Good-bye, Glamour Girl,* and c. 1994, for *The Things I Did Last Summer;* Young Adult Books for Reluctant Readers list, American Library Associa-

*Erika Tamar*

tion (ALA), and International Readers Association (IRA) Young Adult's Choice, both 1990, for *It Happened at Cecilia's;* IRA Young Adult's Choice, 1991, for *High Cheekbones;* Best Book for Young Adults, ALA, Books for the Teen Age list, New York Public Library, both 1993, Nevada Young Readers' Award nominee, 1997, and Garden State Master list, all for *Fair Game;* California Young Readers' Medal winner,

Intermediate List, 1998, winner, Virginia Young Readers Award, 1998, South Carolina Children's Book Award nominee, 1997-98, third place, Sequoyah Children's Book Award, Oklahoma Library Association, 1998, Rebecca Caudill Young Readers' Award master list, Bank Street College Children's Books of the Year citation, Virginia Yoing Readers Award, and Maud HartLovelace Award nominee, Minnesota, all for *The Junkyard Dog;* Child Study's Children's Books of the Year citation, commended title, Consortium of Latin American Studies Programs (CLASP), and Rebecca Caudill Young Readers Award master list, Illinois, all for *Alphabet City Ballet;* Golden Kite Award nomination, Society of Children's Book Writers and Illustrators, Notable Trade Book in the Field of Social Studies citation, National Council of Social Studies-Children's Book Center, CLASP commended title citation, and Arkansas Diamond Book Award nominee all for *The Garden of Happiness;* Spur Award for Best Western Juvenile Fiction, Western Writers of America, 2001, for *The Midnight Train Home.*

*WRITINGS:*

YOUNG ADULT NOVELS

*Blues for Silk Garcia,* Crown (New York, NY), 1983.
*Good-bye, Glamour Girl,* Lippincott (Boston, MA), 1984.
*It Happened at Cecilia's,* Atheneum (New York, NY), 1989.
*High Cheekbones,* Viking (New York, NY), 1990.
*Out of Control,* Atheneum (New York, NY), 1991.
*The Truth about Kim O'Hara,* Atheneum (New York, NY), 1992.
*Fair Game,* Harcourt (New York, NY), 1993.
*The Things I Did Last Summer,* Harcourt (New York, NY), 1994.
*We Have to Talk,* Parachute Press/HarperCollins (New York, NY), 2000.

MID-GRADE NOVELS

*Soccer Mania!* (novella) Random House (New York, NY), 1993.
*The Junkyard Dog,* Knopf (New York, NY), 1995.
*Alphabet City Ballet,* HarperCollins (New York, NY), 1996.

*The Trouble with Guys,* Parachute Press/Pocket Books (New York, NY), 1997.
*My Ex-Best Friend,* Parachute Press/Pocket Books (New York, NY), 1998.
*The Midnight Train Home,* Knopf (New York, NY), 2000.
*Venus and the Comets,* (novella) Darby Creek Publishing (Plain City, OH), 2003.

PICTURE BOOKS

*The Garden of Happiness,* illustrated by Barbara Lambase, Harcourt (New York, NY), 1996.
*Donnatalee,* illustrated by Barbara Lambase, Harcourt (New York, NY), 1998.

*WORK IN PROGRESS: The Girls of Lighthouse Lane,* for Parachute Press/HarperCollins.

*SIDELIGHTS:* A teenage girl seeks the truth about her long-absent father; local athletes gang-rape a mentally handicapped girl and the town is eager to cover up the crime; a Jewish refugee from Nazi Europe adapts to her new land; a young girl learns there are hidden costs to becoming a model; a summer romance with an older woman teaches a teenage boy hard lessons about the difference between physical and emotional love. These are just some of the incidents that inform the young adult novels of Erika Tamar, whose books for young adults explore, as she commented, "the unexpected truth that lies under the perceived image of a person, as well as the many contradictory perceptions people have of the same event."

In titles such as *Blues for Silk Garcia, Good-bye, Glamour Girl, High Cheekbones, Out of Control, Fair Game,* and *The Things I Did Last Summer,* Tamar delves into the world of young adults with a "fine eye for urban adolescent *angst,*" as *Kirkus Reviews* noted in its review of *It Happened at Cecilia's.* Tamar has created a memorable male protagonist, Andy Szabo, whom she follows through three linked novels, *It Happened at Cecilia's, The Truth about Kim O'Hara,* and *The Things I Did Last Summer.* Tamar has also written novels for younger readers, including *Soccer Mania!* and the award winning *The Junkyard Dog* as well as the picture books, *The Garden of Happiness* and *Donnatalee.*

"I loved reading as long as I can remember," Tamar once commented, "and I've always liked telling a story. I think I always wanted to be a writer." Born in Vienna, Austria, Tamar came to the United States at the age of four. "I was young enough to pick up English very easily," Tamar recalled, "yet old enough to be conscious of learning another language; perhaps that contributed to my awareness of words and their nuances of meaning."

Tamar attended New York University where she majored in English with an emphasis on creative writing. However, a class in screenwriting led her to other classes in film production, and by the time of her graduation she was interested in television or film, "another way of telling a story," she explained. She became for five years a production assistant and casting director for a live television serial, *Search for Tomorrow.*

Marriage and children soon followed; with the birth of her first child, the family moved to Port Washington on Long Island. "I was a full-time mom," she related, "and satisfied my creative urge by getting involved with community theater. I didn't concentrate seriously on writing for many years; the necessary solitude of writing clashed with my rather gregarious and extroverted personality, and it took some maturity to muster the self-discipline. It was the young adult novels that my children brought home that spurred me—the 'I can do that' syndrome." A writing workshop at the New School with Margaret Gabel was very helpful. Her work with television and film gave her a keen visual sense. "I still find that my ideas for books start with visual images," she commented. And her work with community theater instilled the idea of character creation in her. "I see a strong correlation between acting and writing—the ability to slip into character is what I rely on when I'm working on a book." Soon Tamar had completed a novel in class, and submitting it to Crown, she was amazed when this first publisher took the book. "I was hooked!" Tamar recalled.

That first novel, *Blues for Silk Garcia,* not surprisingly, included large doses of personal experience. Set in a facsimile of Port Washington, the book also dealt with jazz, a favorite musical form of Tamar's. Her daughter's virtuosity with classical guitar was also built into the story. As Tamar said, "My experiences and feelings, people I've known, things that move me or make me laugh, go into my novels in big fictionalized chunks—and that's what makes writing so much fun."

The novel's protagonist, Linda Ann Garcia, fifteen, learns that her long-absent father, Silk Garcia, the noted guitarist, is dead. Linda's search for information takes her into the world of nightclub musicians, where she slowly pieces together new levels of truth about her dad. *Booklist*'s Ilene Cooper observed that Tamar "skillfully combines Linda's quest for her father with her first romance and thereby provides readers a full-blown, memorable heroine capable of growth and change," concluding that "in every respect [the book is] a well-crafted first novel." Christy Tyson, writing in *Voice of Youth Advocates,* noted that "this is a carefully developed coming-of-age story enriched by a credible rock/jazz background." *School Library Journal* contributor Linda Wicher felt that *Blues for Silk Garcia* "will be popular with young adults and is an admirable book for a first novel." Chosen as one of the New York Public Library's "books for the teen-aged," Tamar's first novel was on all accounts successful and encouraged her on to further writing.

With her second novel, *Good-bye, Glamour Girl,* Tamar mined her own life more closely, going back to her first years in America when she herself became assimilated via the movies. Liesl is a Jewish refugee from Nazi-occupied Vienna in *Good-bye, Glamour Girl.* She is determined to transform herself into an all-American glamour queen just like her movie idol, Rita Hayworth. When not busy reading movie magazines, Liesl joins her new boyfriend, the reckless Billy Laramie, in adventures. When Billy finally asks her to run away with him, Liesl is confronted with the final decision of choosing between her dreams and reality. A *Kirkus Reviews* contributor noted that "Tamar provides wry, touch-true details of Austrian refugee life" and "also gives a full-blown portrait of the movie-star cult." Sandra Dayton, writing in *Voice of Youth Advocates,* observed that "the reader . . . should be inspired by Liesl's consistently positive outlook and hope for a brighter tomorrow." A *Publishers Weekly* contributor summed up a positive review of the book by stating that Tamar "seems to write out of total recall for an era she brings to life in a vibrant novel."

For her third young adult novel, Tamar employed stories her own children had regaled her with when working in restaurants to help put themselves through college, and also introduced Andy Szabo, the male protagonist whom she would employ in two future titles. "The story concerns the ups and downs of a Cajun-Hungarian restaurant," Tamar recalled. The book was also set in New York's Greenwich Village, a locale dear to Tamar since her own college days at NYU. In *It Happened at Cecilia's,* Andy is fourteen, sensitive, a secret writer, and the son of the Hungarian half of Cecilia's, a Greenwich Village restaurant, a locale dear to Tamar since her own college days at NYU. In *It Happened at Cecilia's,* Andy is fourteen, the son of the Hungarian half of the Cecilia's, a Greenwich Village restaurant. His mother is dead, and soon a customer, the dancer Lorraine, becomes interested in his father. Marriage plans are announced and Andy fears displacement. Meanwhile, the restaurant has become ultra-popular after a review, so much so that the Mafia begins to show interest in it. Andy and Lorraine are forced to team up to protect the man they both love, creating the "beginnings of a warm family relationship," according to Cindy Darling Codell in *School Library Journal.* Codell also noted "the well-constructed dialogue, the absolutely hilarious restaurant antics, and the believable portrayal of a family restructuring itself," which all contribute to making this "an entertaining book." Shirley Carmony, writing in *Voice of Youth Advocates,* felt that this was a book with a male protagonist that "will appeal to a great many junior high age students," while Zena Sutherland observed in *Bulletin of the Center for Children's Books* that the "characters are distinctive . . . and the fairly happy ending is not made pat and incredible by having everything sugar-iced." A *Kirkus Reviews* critic concluded by noting that the "promised sequel will be welcome."

In fact, two sequels followed: *The Truth about Kim O'Hara* and *The Things I Did Last Summer.* Andy is fifteen in *The Truth about Kim O'Hara,* and in love with the girl of the title, a Vietnamese-born beauty. The only problem is that Kim keeps him at arm's length sexually, and soon Andy begins to suspect there is more to her reticence than shyness; that perhaps there are secrets she has brought with her from Vietnam that have her in their grip. *Booklist*'s Susan DeRonne noted that through the many incidents of the book, Andy learns that "the essence of a deep relationship is not just sex, but friendship." DeRonne concluded that the story "is compelling reading with a multicultural twist." *The Things I Did Last Summer* is "a poignant story of a boy's first love," according to Larry Condit in *Voice of Youth Advocates.* Andy is seventeen now and spending the summer with his pregnant stepmother on Bay Island. The first day on the beach he meets a beautiful *au pair* who works for the wealthy Carlyles, and he is smitten. If he's not

with the woman, Susan, he is working part-time as a journalist for the local paper. The older Susan initiates Andy to sex and soon he has dreams of the two of them sharing a life together. Such dreams are smashed, however, when Andy learns the truth about Susan—that she is actually Mrs. Carlyle. Marilyn Makowski observed in *School Library Journal* that "in the end [Andy] is wiser and headed for a better future," while Deborah Stevenson concluded in *Bulletin of the Center for Children's Books* that the novel is "a well-written, absorbing story about first love and disillusionment." A *Kirkus Reviews* critic summed up much critical opinion by stating that "Tamar (who has never written better) probes deeply into the emotions that make first love so wonderful and so terrible. A book that should win a wide readership among mature [young adults]."

Tamar also took a look at the perils of modeling in the award-winning *High Cheekbones,* and at the lives of members of a teen rock band in *Out of Control,* which a *Publishers Weekly* reviewer dubbed "Rashomon-like" for its narrative diversity. One of Tamar's hardest-hitting young adult novels, however, is *Fair Game,* the story of the gang-rape of a mentally handicapped girl by the athletes from a small-town baseball team. Patterned after true events, *Fair Game* is set on Long Island and is told from several points of view: Cara, the retarded girl; Laura Jean, the girlfriend of one of the athletes involved in the rape and who initially is out to protect her man; and Julio "Joe" Lopez, an athlete who refuses to take part in the rape, but does nothing to stop it, either. Cara is a five-year-old in an attractive teen body who wants only to fit in. She will do anything to please, and one day a group of all-American boys have her do it all, even assaulting her with a bottle and broom handle. At first the incident is covered-up, but soon the media get hold of the story, and it will not go away. Laura Jean thinks Cara is a "slut" and that it was all her fault that the boys did what they did, until she interviews Cara, trying to trick her into clearing the boys. Instead, she comes face to face with the truth and finally understands the brutality of what was done to Cara.

A *Publishers Weekly* reviewer thought *High Cheekbones* was "meticulously rendered and narrated in speedy, staccato language," and that it was a "must-read for any teen who has considered the implications of foul play." A *Kirkus Reviews* contributor decided the book was "well wrought and compelling" and

Stevenson, in *Bulletin of the Center for Children's Books,* concluded that "this is a challenging book dealing with the interconnection of many complicated issues (racism, sexism, violence)—a book that could provoke some heated discussions."

*The Midnight Train Home* tells of the orphan trains, an old practice in which children without parents were shipped out of the large East Coast cities into the rural states of the Midwest and West. There, the children would be adopted by families and raised in what was hoped would be healthier circumstances. In Tamar's story, three children who are shipped out are separated when they are adopted by three different families. Eleven-year-old Deirfre's efforts to find her brothers is the focus of the story. Linda Binder in *School Library Journal* felt that "Tamar does a wonderful job of incorporating the historical attitudes and realities of life for the poor during the late '20s." A critic for *Publishers Weekly* concluded that "Deidre's realization that she is in control of her destiny comes as an uplifting epiphany."

Tamar has also turned her hand to books for younger readers as well as picture books. In the first category, most notable is the 1995 title *The Junkyard Dog,* about eleven-year-old Katie who, with advice from her stepfather, takes on the care and feeding of an abandoned dog, building it a doghouse to survive the winter. It is, in fact, her stepfather's attitude toward the dog, Lucky, that begins to bring the new family close together. Reviewing the book in *School Library Journal,* Virginia Golodetz noted that it was "a satisfying coming-of-age story, especially for dog lovers," and a *Kirkus Reviews* critic concluded that Tamar "has created a wise, wonderful tale of an ordinary girl who is transformed by the power of love into a self-reliant individual."

In *Alphabet City Ballet,* Tamar explores both the inner-city world and the world of ballet. Ten-year-old Marisol wins a scholarship to the Manhattan Ballet School, but still has obstacles to overcome. Motherless, she needs someone to take her from her Puerto Rican neighborhood to the school; she also needs to scrape enough money together to buy her ballet clothes and also gather her courage to fend off the remarks of rich girls attending the school. "Written with warmth and optimism, this highly readable novel is an easy choice for ballerina hopefuls," concluded a *Publishers Weekly* contributor.

*The Garden of Happiness,* Tamar's first picture book, is set in the inner city with young Marisol pining to grow something. Her desire leads to the reclamation of a vacant lot for a community garden, in a book that is a "delight for the eye and the heart," according to a critic for *Kirkus Reviews.*

In another picture book, *Donnatalee,* Katie and her family leave the hot, crowded city for a day at a hot, crowded beach. Katie is transformed into the mermaid Donnatalee and slips into the cool, spacious ocean to frolic with goldfish, duel with sharks, and dive with King Neptune. In her review of *Donnatalee,* Ilene Cooper of *Booklist* concluded that "Tamar's evocative text is lovely."

Tamar has just completed the first two books of a four-book mid-grade series to be published in 2004 and 2005. *The Girls of Lighthouse Lane* takes place in 1905 and 1906 in a small fishing village in Massachusetts. Each book tells the story of one of four best friends.

Tamar now makes her home in the city. "I live in Manhattan again and I enjoy the restaurants, theater, art galleries, films, walking everywhere and observing street life," Tamar commented. "I often meet with other writers for critique. Sometimes it's really hard to spend long hours at my desk, yet my greatest interest, still and always, is writing."

*BIOGRAPHICAL AND CRITICAL SOURCES:*

*PERIODICALS*

*Booklist,* August, 1983, Ilene Cooper, review of *Blues for Silk Garcia,* pp. 1468-1469; February 1, 1990, pp. 1079-1080; September 15, 1991, pp. 142-143; December 1, 1992, Susan DeRonne, review of *The Truth about Kim O'Hara,* pp. 659, 662; November 15, 1993, p. 614; May 1, 1995, pp. 1575-1576; July, 1996, Ilene Cooper, review of *The Garden of Happiness,* p. 1825; September 15, 1996, Michael Cart, review of *Alphabet City Ballet,* p. 242; October 15, 1998, Ilene Cooper, review of *Donnatalee,* p. 430.

*Bulletin of the Center for Children's Books,* December, 1984, review of *Good-bye, Glamour Girl,* p. 75; March, 1989, Zena Sutherland, review of *It Happened at Cecilia's,* p. 183; November, 1993, review of *Fair Game,* p. 103; April, 1994, Deborah

Stevenson, review of *The Things I Did Last Summer,* p. 271; September, 1995, p. 31; January, 1997, p. 187.

*Horn Book,* May, 1994, pp. 358-361; July, 2000, review of *The Midnight Train Home,* p. 467.

*Kirkus Reviews,* November 1, 1984, p. 108; April 15, 1989, review of *It Happened at Cecilia's,* p. 631; September 15, 1993, review of *Fair Game;* June 15, 1994, review of *The Things I Did Last Summer,* p. 852; June 15, 1995, review of *The Junkyard Dog,* p. 864; April 1, 1996, review of *The Garden of Happiness,* pp. 537-538; September 1, 1996, p. 1329.

*Publishers Weekly,* October 12, 1984, review of *Goodbye, Glamour Girl,* p. 51; October 4, 1991, review of *Out of Control,* p. 89; October 25, 1993, review of *Fair Game,* p. 65; June 19, 1995, review of *The Junkyard Dog,* p. 59; May 6, 1996, review of *The Garden of Happiness,* p. 80; November 11, 1996, review of *Alphabet City Ballet,* p. 76; June 12, 2000, review of *The Midnight Train Home,* p. 74.

*School Library Journal,* May, 1983, Linda Wicher, review of *Blues for Silk Garcia,* p. 86; March, 1989, Cindy Darling Codell, review of *It Happened at Cecilia's,* p. 202; August, 1990, p. 165; April, 1994, Marilyn Makowski, review of *The Things I Did Last Summer,* p. 155; June, 1995, Virginia Golodetz, review of *The Junkyard Dog,* pp. 114-115; November 11, 1996, review of *Alphabet City Ballet,* p. 76; July, 1998, p. 84; July, 2000, Linda Bindner, review of *The Midnight Train Home,* p. 110.

*Voice of Youth Advocates,* October, 1983, Christy Tyson, review of *Blues for Silk Garcia,* p. 209; April, 1985, Sandra Dayton, review of *Good-bye, Glamour Girl,* p. 52; June, 1989, Shirley Carmony, review of *It Happened at Cecilia's,* p. 108; February, 1993, pp. 342-343; December, 1993, pp. 302-303; June, 1994, Larry Condit, review of *The Things I Did Last Summer,* p. 94.

\* \* \*

## TOLAN, Stephanie S. 1942-

*PERSONAL:* Born October 25, 1942, in Canton, OH; daughter of Joseph Edward and Mary (Schroy) Stein; married Robert W. Tolan (a theater director and producer), December 19, 1964; children: R. J.; step-children: Patrick, Andrew, Robert, Jr. *Education:* Purdue University, B.A., 1964, M.A., 1967.

*ADDRESSES: Home*—4511 Eagle Lake Dr., Charlotte, NC 28217. *Agent*—Elaine Markson, Elaine Markson Literary Agency, 44 Greenwich Ave., New York, NY 10011. *E-mail*—StefT@carolina.rr.com.

*CAREER:* Purdue University, Fort Wayne, IN, instructor in continuing education, 1966-70; State University of New York—Buffalo, Buffalo, NY, faculty member in speech and theater, 1972; Franklin and Marshall College, Lancaster, PA, adjunct faculty member in English, 1973-75, coordinator of continuing education, 1974-75; writer, 1975—. Lecturer at Indiana University, 1966-70; participant, Artists-in-Education, Pennsylvania, 1974, Ohio, 1975, and North Carolina, 1984; faculty member, Institute of Children's Literature, 1988-93; senior fellow, Institute for Educational Advancement; consultant to parents and educators on the needs of highly gifted children and prodigies. Member of literature panel, Ohio Arts Council, 1978-80. Actress, performing with Curtain Call Co., 1970-71.

*MEMBER:* Authors Guild, Authors League of America, Children's Book Guild of Washington, D.C.

*AWARDS, HONORS:* Individual artist fellowships, Ohio Arts Council, 1978, 1981, and 1997; Post-Corbett Awards finalist, 1981; Ohioana Book Award for juvenile fiction, 1981, for *The Liberation of Tansy Warner;* Bread Loaf Writers' Conference Fellowship, 1981; Media Award for Best Book of 1983, American Psychological Association, for *Guiding the Gifted Child;* Best Book of 1988, *School Library Journal,* Dorothy Canfield Fisher Award nominee, and Books for the Teen Age selection, New York Public Library, all for *A Good Courage;* Sequoyah Children's Book Award nomination, and Georgia Children's Book Award nomination, both for *Grandpa—and Me;* Virginia Young Readers Best Choices winner, 1992-1993, Sequoyah Young Adult Book Award nominee, 1992-1993, Nevada Young Readers Award, 1993-1994, and Books for the Teen Age selection, New York Public Library, all for *Plague Year;* Sequoyah Young Adult Book Award nominee, for *The Great Skinner Getaway;* South Carolina Children's Book Award nominee, for *The Great Skinner Homestead;* Mark Twain Award nominee, Rebecca Caudill Young Readers' Book Award nominee, 1992-1993, California Young

Reader's Award nominee, and South Carolina Junior Book Award nominee, 1996-1997, all for *Who's There?*; Best Books for Young Adults, YALSA, 1994, Sequoyah Children's Book Award nominee, Land of Enchantment Children's Book Award nominee, and Editor's Choice selection, *Booklist,* all for *Save Halloween!*; Ohio Arts Council Summer Writing Residency, Fine Arts Work Center, Provincetown, MA, 1998; Dorothy Canfield Fisher nominee, and Books for the Teen Age selection, New York Public Library, both for *Welcome to the Ark;* Dorothy Canfield Fisher nominee, Best Books on Religion, American Library Association (ALA), and Sequoyah Young Adult Book Award nominee, all for *Ordinary Miracles;* Books for the Teen Age selection, New York Public Library, for *Flight of the Raven;* Best Book of 2002, *School Library Journal,* Notable Children's Books selection, *Smithsonian* magazine, 2002, Volunteer State Book Award nominee, Dorothy Canfield Fisher Award, Books for the Teenage selection, New York Public Library, and Newbery Honor Book, ALA, 2003, all for *Surviving the Applewhites.*

*WRITINGS:*

NOVELS FOR YOUNG READERS

*Grandpa—and Me,* Scribner (New York, NY), 1978.
*The Last of Eden,* Warne (New York, NY), 1980.
*The Liberation of Tansy Warner,* Scribner (New York, NY), 1980.
*No Safe Harbors,* Scribner (New York, NY), 1981.
*The Great Skinner Strike,* Macmillan (New York, NY), 1983.
*A Time to Fly Free,* Scribner (New York, NY), 1983.
*Pride of the Peacock,* Scribner (New York, NY), 1986.
*The Great Skinner Enterprise,* Four Winds, (New York), NY, 1986.
*The Great Skinner Getaway,* Macmillan (New York, NY), 1987.
*A Good Courage,* Morrow (New York, NY), 1988.
*The Great Skinner Homestead,* Macmillan (New York, NY), 1988.
*Plague Year,* Morrow (New York, NY), 1990.
*Marcy Hooper and the Greatest Treasure in the World,* Morrow (New York, NY), 1991.
*Sophie and the Sidewalk Man,* Macmillan (New York, NY), 1992.
*The Witch of Maple Park,* Morrow (New York, NY), 1993.

*Save Halloween!,* Morrow (New York, NY), 1993.
*Who's There?,* Morrow (New York, NY), 1994.
*Welcome to the Ark,* Morrow (New York, NY), 1996.
*The Face in the Mirror,* Morrow (New York, NY), 1998.
*Ordinary Miracles,* Morrow (New York, NY), 1999.
*Flight of the Raven,* HarperCollins (New York, NY), 2001.
*Surviving the Applewhites,* HarperCollins (New York, NY), 2002.
*Bartholomew's Blessing,* illustrated by Margie Moore, HarperCollins (New York, NY), 2003.

PLAYS

*The Ledge* (one-act), Samuel French (New York, NY), 1968.
*Not I, Said the Little Red Hen* (one-act), first produced in New York, NY, 1971.
(With Katherine Paterson) *Bridge to Terabithia* (based on Paterson's novel; first produced in Louisville, KY, 1990), music by Steven Liebman, Samuel French (New York, NY), 1992.
(With Katherine Paterson) *The Tale of the Mandarin Ducks: A Musical Play,* music by Steven Liebman, Samuel French (New York, NY), 1999.
(With Katherine Paterson) *The Tale of Jemima Puddle-Duck: A Musical Play Based on the Story by Beatrix Potter,* music by Steven Liebman, Dramatists Play Service (New York, NY), 2002.

OTHER

(With James T. Webb and Elizabeth Meckstroth) *Guiding the Gifted Child: A Practical Source for Parents and Teachers,* Ohio Psychology Publishing (Columbus, OH), 1982.

Contributor of poems to more than a dozen literary magazines, including *Roanoke Review, Descant,* and *Green River Review.*

*ADAPTATIONS: The Great Skinner Strike* was adapted as *Mom's on Strike,* a 1988 ABC-TV *After-School Special.*

*SIDELIGHTS:* The author of over twenty novels for children and young adults as well as several musical plays, Stephanie S. Tolan often writes of children who are, in some way or another, special if not exceptional. These include the outsiders, misfits, and misunderstood; there are also kids who are extraordinarily intelligent and intuitive, who are plagued by scandal, who find refuge in imaginary kingdoms, or who discover dangerous family secrets. Tolan's adolescent and teen protagonists have to learn to deal with the world as well as with their own special situations: surviving a personal fear of nuclear war, getting through the final years of boarding school, dealing with the life of a twin and with fundamentalism, contending with the violence of the larger world. Tolan is concerned about the rights of young people in a society that she feels cares less and less about children and their needs. Poverty, education, housing, the environment, violence, and abuse are some of the social issues that concern her, and she has dealt with some of these concerns in her books. She also raises these issues when she speaks to parents, educators, librarians, and other audiences.

According to Tolan's Web site, her earliest memories involve books, "those that were read to her and those she read to herself often late at night with a flashlight under the covers." Born in Ohio and raised in Wisconsin, she early on discovered the magic and joy to be found between the covers of a book. In the fourth grade, she wrote her first story, discovering for herself the magic of such creation, and from that time on she knew she would be a writer. By the time she was eleven, Tolan had already received her first rejection slips, but continued to write throughout her junior and senior high school years.

Majoring in creative writing at Purdue University, she went on to complete a master's degree in English. Married in 1964, she became an instant mother of three stepsons and then her own son; writing took second place to the concerns of family for a time, though she continued in fits and spurts even as she began instructing in English at the university level. Poetry and adult plays became Tolan's focus for a time; with her husband's career as a director in professional theater, the family was on the move frequently. When Tolan worked in a Poets-in-the-Schools program in Pennsylvania, she suddenly rediscovered her early connection to the magic of books. Her students were eager readers. "They brought back to me that special reading joy that most adults—even readers among us—have lost," Tolan noted on her Web site, "and I wanted to try my hand at writing for those kids, so like myself at their age and yet so different."

Tolan began writing about significant social problems with her first published work, *Grandpa—and Me,* which discusses the issue of dealing with aging family members. The central character, Kerry, grows to understand how age is affecting her grandfather's behavior and also comes to a new understanding of her place within her family. In *Plague Year,* Tolan writes about prejudice, ignorance, and hysteria, creating a compelling but frightening story about a maverick high school student whose appearance and personal background inspire hostility from the community.

In *Pride of the Peacock,* Tolan tells the story of Whitney and her fear of nuclear disaster. Whitney becomes preoccupied with the way the value and beauty of the Earth are threatened by people. She meets a sculptor, Theodora Bourke, who is trying to escape the violent atmosphere of New York, where her husband lost his life. They meet at an abandoned estate where the neglected garden has become overgrown with weeds. Together they clean out the garden and their friendship helps both Whitney and Theodora to cope in a troubled world. According to an *English Journal* reviewer, teens should relate to Whitney and her strong emotions, "her fear in grappling with unsolvable real-life problems, and her inability to own the solutions acceptable to her parents and peers."

Tolan deals with a number of social problems even in her "Skinner" series of books, which are lighter in tone and have much more humor than her other works. One of her Skinner stories, *The Great Skinner Strike,* deals with Eleanor Skinner's involvement in a nationally-publicized strike, while *The Great Skinner Enterprise* centers around running a home business. These books focus on issues about making a living that many middle-class people face in times of changing technology. Even *The Great Skinner Getaway* touches on the disillusionments of traveling, exploring, camping, and small-town American life. But despite their serious undertones, the "Skinner" series aims to fulfill Tolan's interest in writing stories that will bring joy and adventure to reading for children.

*Marcy Hooper and the Greatest Treasure in the World,* a chapter book for young readers, is a fairy tale story with nymphs and dragons, but it also shows how a little girl can gain courage and become self-reliant. Marcy is having trouble at school and runs off toward the hills near her house to forget spelling tests, two-wheeled bikes, and tripping on jump ropes. She feels like a failure. By the end of her adventure, during which she finds a treasure and encounters a dragon who would swallow her up if given the chance, Marcy finds the treasure of her own courage. Jana R. Fine, reviewing the book in *School Library Journal,* noted that Tolan's story "will attract those searching for mild adventure."

As with *Marcy Hooper and the Greatest Treasure in the World, The Witch of Maple Park* is "a semi-scary story with a happy ending," as Kathryn Jennings described it in the *Bulletin of the Center for Children's Books.* The story is told by Casey, but the central character is her friend Mackenzie, who is a psychic. Mackenzie is afraid that Barnaby, the little boy she is baby-sitting, is in danger of being kidnapped by a "witch" who seems to be following them. All ends well when the "witch" turns out to be an herbalist who helps Mackenzie's mother in her failing catering business. *School Library Journal* contributor Lisa Dennis called the book "a light, engaging read, jammed full of incidents and mild excitement, well blended into a pleasing whole." A *Kirkus Reviews* critic also wrote that "quick pacing makes this a prime candidate for readers, including reluctant ones, who enjoy a frothy mystery." And Carolyn Phelan concluded in *Booklist* that "this entertaining book is a cut above most middle-grade fare."

In *Sophie and the Sidewalk Man,* Tolan tells the story of an eight-year-old girl who is saving her allowance and collecting cans to buy Weldon, a stuffed hedgehog she sees in the window of a toy store. On one of her visits to see Weldon before she has enough money to buy him, Sophie encounters a ragged, dirty man sitting on the sidewalk holding a sign that asks for help because he is hungry. Buying Weldon is important to Sophie because her mother suffers from allergies and, consequently, pets are not allowed in the house. To help get the forty dollars she needs to buy Weldon, Sophie begins to skip lunch to add her lunch money to her savings. As Sophie experiences hunger, she becomes sympathetic to the "sidewalk man." Her sympathy for the man grows even stronger one day when she sees him giving half a sandwich to a stray cat. After having a discussion with her mother about giving handouts to the homeless, Sophie makes her difficult choice and helps the man.

Tolan has received praise from several reviewers for *Sophie and the Sidewalk Man.* One *Kirkus Reviews* critic called the story "a thoughtful, intelligent, and

appealing book, with respect for its young readers and for the problem it explores." In *Horn Book Guide,* Elizabeth S. Watson commented that Sophie's progress toward growing up is admirable, and "no adult moralizing clouds the simple solution." Susannah Price, writing in *School Library Journal,* similarly found the story "a meaningful novel that is infused with the spirit of Christmas. . . . This story will really hit home, right where kids' feelings are." As *Booklist* contributor Deborah Abbott stated, "Tolan draws her characters carefully, making them believable and likable," and added that the story's theme is "a welcome change of pace."

Similarly, as in her books about the Skinner family, Tolan has also explored another family, the Filkins, in two novels, *Save Halloween!* and *Ordinary Miracles.* In the former, eleven-year-old Johnna is deeply involved in her school Halloween pageant, though her Evangelical Christian family and preacher-father consider it the devil's holiday. Johnna must soon choose between the two in this story with "no easy answers" and "no stock characters," according to a reviewer for *Publishers Weekly.* Maeve Visser Knoth, writing in *Horn Book Guide,* also praised Johnna as a "well-developed character," and further lauded the author for her thoughtful balance of "serious issues." Set about a year before this action, *Ordinary Miracles* focuses on two other members of the family: Mark and his twin brother, Matthew. Raised to become Evangelical preachers like other men in the family, Mark begins to find such a life claustrophobic. He begins pulling away from his brother and religion, befriended by a Nobel Prize-winning scientist whose genetic engineering work is anathema to Mark's family. "Tolan does not flinch from setting up a truly difficult dilemma for her character," wrote Susan Dove Lempke in a *Booklist* review. Lempke concluded, "Such well-written fiction exploring Christian themes is rare, and many libraries will want to snap this up." Writing in *Bulletin of the Center for Children's Books,* Elizabeth Bush noted that Tolan maintains a "deep respect of scientific and religious viewpoints and concludes that there are shadowy mysteries and miracles that, at least so far, elude our best attempts to illuminate them."

Chills are served up in *Who's There?,* a novel about fourteen-year-old Drew and her mute younger brother, both recently orphaned, who come to live with their deceased father's relatives. Here, they discover that the house is haunted by the ghosts of a potent family secret. Dubbed an "entertaining ghost story" by *Booklist*'s Stephanie Zvirin, the book produces "sufficiently creepy" ghostly encounters and characters "drawn with care," as Zvirin further commented. Reviewing the novel in *Book Report,* Charlotte Decker wrote, "Tolan is a skilled writer who manages to create a sense of terror in a story with a logical plot that flows smoothly to its suspenseful climax." Decker concluded, "Ideal for readers searching for a 'scary story.'"

"Sibling rivalry gets a pretty nasty portrayal" in the ghost tale *The Face in the Mirror,* according to Sally Margolis, writing in *School Library Journal.* Jared, the young son of two divorced and very much self-absorbed actors, has been living with his grandfather. But when this man becomes ill, Jared is sent to Michigan to live with the father he never met, a director who has started a Shakespearean company in a historical theater. Once there, Jared suddenly has to deal with his spoiled but very talented half-brother. Both are playing the children of Richard III, locked in the tower, but off-stage rivalries spill over on stage. A seemingly playful ghost befriends Jared, but soon the youth finds himself in over his head when this ghost of the nineteenth-century actor Garrick Marsden plots to involve him in the killing of his half-brother. Though a contributor for *Publishers Weekly* thought this "ghost yarn offers little in the way of thrills and chills," Kathleen Armstrong, writing in *Book Report,* felt that "lovers of mysteries will enjoy this suspenseful story, a good choice for reluctant readers." Reviewing the same novel, *Booklist*'s Chris Sherman commented, "Tolan artfully weaves Shakespeare's Richard III, sibling rivalry, revenge, and a haunted theater with a vindictive ghost into a suspenseful story." Sherman further predicted that her incorporation of the Shakespeare play into the action of *The Face in the Mirror* might inspire readers to look into the original play.

Tolan's experiences with her own son and working with other gifted children have inspired several of her novels, including the 1996 *Welcome to the Ark* and its 2001 sequel, *Flight of the Raven.* Four child prodigies transfer from a center for research to an experimental group home, and thereby must learn a different way to connect with their new environment and the rest of the world. All the children's special gifts have to do with communication, from Elijah, who is empathic; to Taryn, the poet and healer; Doug, the musician and mathematician; and Miranda, master of many languages at fifteen. Together the four develop a telepathic link with themselves and other children around the world. But when the hospital director secretly sabotages this communication project, the children are disbanded and sent their individual ways. "Tolan blends elements of science fiction with nonstop suspense in a provocative, disturbingly real story set in a near future when violence is pandemic," wrote *Booklist*'s Sherman. Also reviewing *Welcome to the Ark,* Jacqueline Rose noted in *Voice of Youth Advocates* that the novel "will be best appreciated by sophisticated readers who understand its subtleties," and *Kliatt*'s Claire M. Dignan praised "Tolan's sense of urgency, combined with her beautiful imagery and use of metaphor [which] make this an enjoyable page-turner." The sequel, *Flight of the Raven,* focuses on Elijah after the breakup of the home, or the Ark as it is referred to. The story also deals with twelve-year-old Amber and her father, the leader of a militia group that has just committed one devastating terrorist attack and is planning another. Elijah's empathic power is put to the test against this idealistic but misguided man who now plans to use biological weapons. A contributor for *Kirkus Reviews* felt this was "a slow-moving sequel" with "too much talk and not enough action." Hazel Rochman, however, writing in *Booklist,* felt that the "fear, the tenderness, and the evil seem very close to home," and Katie O'Dell, writing in *School Library Journal,* concluded that the novel will make "for a confrontational and thought-provoking read deserving much discussion."

A family of artistic geniuses is portrayed in *Surviving the Applewhites,* a "screwball comedy," according to *Booklist*'s Ilene Cooper, that takes a standard story about how a tough young kid is turned around by a new family and "pushes [it] to a whole new place." Juvenile delinquent Jake is given a final opportunity in his life, placed in the Creative Academy at the Applewhite farm, called Wit's End, along with the homeschooled siblings of that family who seem to set their own curriculum. Only the young daughter of the clan, E. D., is organized and decidedly non-artistic. The father is a theater director, the mother a mystery writer, and an uncle and aunt respectively carve wood and write poetry. Resistant at first to the new rural and creative environment, and "the outrageously eccentric Applewhite clan," as Faith Brautigam described the family in *School Library Journal,* Jake is ultimately turned around, even taking part in Mr. Applewhite's production of *The Sound of Music.* "Humor abounds in the ever-building chaos," wrote a reviewer for *Publishers Weekly,* who concluded, "In the end, it's the antics of the cast of characters that keep this show on the road." Similarly, a critic for *Kirkus Reviews* praised the madcap comedy, noting that the mixture of first-and third-person narration "result[s] in well-built characterizations held together in a structure that smoothly organizes the chaos that busy artistic geniuses create."

Tolan, who lives on a lake near Charlotte, North Carolina, with her husband and pets, is also a lecturer. In both her books and her speaking engagements, she is an outspoken proponent of children's rights and the development of positive self-awareness. "Most of the world is busy trying to tell children that they aren't good enough, aren't enough like other children, aren't really worthy of being loved," the author wrote on her Web site. "What every kid needs to know is that she is just exactly the person she is meant to be, and that—no matter what—she is absolutely and unconditionally worthy of love. If I could help even one boy or girl to begin to really believe that, I'd feel as if I'd done what I was meant to do."

*BIOGRAPHICAL AND CRITICAL SOURCES:*

*BOOKS*

Cullinan, Bernice E., and Diane G. Person, editors, *Encyclopedia of Children's Literature,* Continuum (New York, NY), 2001, p. 779.

Helbig, Alethea K., and Agnes Regan Perkins, editors, *Dictionary of American Children's Fiction, 1985-1989,* Greenwood Press (Westport, CT), 1993.

Hipple, Ted, editor, *Writers for Young Adults,* Scribner (New York, NY), 2000, pp. 315-324.

*PERIODICALS*

*Booklist,* March 1, 1992, Deborah Abbott, review of *Sophie and the Sidewalk Man,* p. 1281; September 1, 1992, Carolyn Phelan, review of *The Witch of Maple Park,* p. 125; September 1, 1994, Stephanie Zvirin, review of *Who's There?,* p. 45; October 15, 1996, Chris Sherman, review of *Welcome to the Ark,* p. 414; September 1, 1998, Chris Sherman, review of *The Face in the Mirror,* p. 111; October 1, 1999, Susan Dove Lempke, review of *Ordinary Miracles,* p. 370; October 15, 2001, Hazel Rochman, review of *Flight of the Raven,* p. 396; November 1, 2002, Ilene Cooper, review of *Surviving the Applewhites,* p. 494.

*Book Report,* September-October, 1994, Charlotte Decker, review of *Who's There?,* p. 47; March-April, 1999, Kathleen Armstrong, review of *The Face in the Mirror,* p. 64.

*Bulletin of the Center for Children's Books,* December, 1992, Kathryn Jennings, review of *The Witch of Maple Park,* p. 125; October, 1993, pp. 59-60; December, 1994, Deborah Stevenson, review of *Who's There?,* p. 146; October, 1999, Elizabeth Bush, review of *Ordinary Miracles,* p. 72.

*English Journal,* October, 1987, review of *Pride of the Peacock,* p. 97.

*Horn Book Guide,* fall, 1992, Elizabeth S. Watson, review of *Sophie and the Sidewalk Man,* p. 259; spring, 1994, Maeve Visser Knoth, review of *Save Halloween!,* p. 83.

*Kirkus Reviews,* March 15, 1992, review of *Sophie and the Sidewalk Man,* p. 400; September 15, 1992, review of *The Witch of Maple Park,* p. 1194; September 15, 1998, review of *The Face in the Mirror,* p. 1391; October 1, 2001, review of *Flight of the Raven,* p. 1435; July 15, 2002, review of *Surviving the Applewhites,* p. 1046.

*Kliatt,* January, 1999, Claire M. Dignan, review of *Welcome to the Ark,* p. 20.

*New York Times Book Review,* April 30, 1978.

*Publishers Weekly,* September 20, 1993, review of *Save Halloween!,* p. 31; November 16, 1998, review of *The Face in the Mirror,* p. 76; August 5, 2002, review of *Surviving the Applewhites,* p. 73.

*School Library Journal,* January, 1992, Jana R. Fine, review of *Marcy Hooper and the Greatest Treasure in the World,* p. 99; May, 1992, Susannah Price, review of *Sophie and the Sidewalk Man,* p. 116; October, 1992, Lisa Dennis, review of *The Witch of Maple Park,* p. 122; October, 1993, p. 133; October, 1994, p. 150; October, 1996, p. 150; November, 1998, Sally Margolis, review of *The Face in the Mirror,* pp. 130-131; October, 1999, Elaine Fort Weischedel, review of *Ordinary Miracles,* p. 160; October, 2001, Katie O'Dell, review of *Flight of the Raven,* pp. 173-174; September, 2002, Faith Brautigam, review of *Suriving the Applewhites,* pp. 235-236.

*Voice of Youth Advocates,* April, 1997, Jacqueline Rose, review of *Welcome to the Ark,* p. 34.

*Washington Post Book World,* June 10, 1990.

\* \* \*

## TRANTER, John Ernest 1943-

*PERSONAL:* Born April 29, 1943, in Cooma, Australia; son of Frederick (a teacher) and A. K. Tranter; married, 1968; wife's name Lynette (a typesetter and graphic artist); children: Kirsten, Leon. *Education:* University of Sydney, B.A., 1970; studied at Australian Centre for Photography, 1982.

*ADDRESSES: Home*—c/o Literature Board, Australia Council, P.O. Box 788, Strawberry Hills, New South Wales 2012, Australia.

*CAREER:* Australian Broadcasting Commission, Sydney, Australia, darkroom technician, 1967-68; Angus & Robertson Publishers, Singapore, senior editor in education division, 1971-73; Australian Broadcasting Commission, Sydney, Australia, script editor in radio drama and features department, 1970-74, radio scriptwriter, 1974-80, radio drama and features producer, 1975, in charge of radio drama and features production for Queensland in Brisbane, 1976-77; subeditor for Special Broadcasting Service Multicultural Television, 1981-86, coordinator of Radio Helicon (arts program), 1987-88; Transit Poetry, Sydney, publisher and editor of *Transit,* 1980—; *Bulletin,* poetry editor, 1990-93. Creative writing teacher at Sydney College of the Arts; writer in residence, Rollins College, Winter Park, FL, 1992, and Cambridge University, Cambridge, England, 2001. Guest lecturer at University of Sydney, Macquarie University, Canberra College of Advanced Education, 1982, Australian National University, and New South Wales Institute of Technology, 1982-83. Visiting fellow, Australian National University, 1981. With wife, owns and operates literary agency Australian Literary Management.

*AWARDS, HONORS:* Senior fellowships, Literature Board of Australia Council, 1974, 1978, 1979, 1980, and 1982; Kenneth Slessor Prize, New South Wales State Literary Award for Poetry, 1989, for *Under Berlin,* 2002, for *Ultra;* Australian Artists Creative fellowship.

*John Ernest Tranter*

WRITINGS:

*The Livin' Is Easy,* Oldbourne (London, England), 1964.

*Parallax and Other Poems,* South Head Press (Sydney, Australia), 1970.

*Red Movie and Other Poems,* Angus & Robertson (Sydney, Australia), 1972.

*The Blast Area* (poems), Makar Press (St. Lucia, Queensland, Australia), 1974.

*Looking for Hunter* (radio play), 1974.

*Le Morte d'Arthur* (radio play; based on the work by Thomas Malory), 1974.

*Knight-Prisoner: The Life of Sir Thomas Malory* (radio play), 1974.

*The Alphabet Murders: Notes from a Work in Progress* (poems), Angus & Robertson (Sydney, Australia), 1975.

*Sideshow People* (radio play), 1976.

*The Poetry of Frank O'Hara* (radio script), c. 1976.

*Crying in Early Infancy: One Hundred Sonnets* (poems), Makar (Brisbane, Australia), 1977.

*Dazed in the Ladies Lounge* (poems), Island Press (Sydney, Australia), 1979.

(Editor) *The New Australian Poetry,* Makar (Brisbane, Australia), 1979.

*Selected Poems,* Hale & Iremonger (Sydney, Australia), 1982.

*Gloria* (poems), privately printed, 1986.

(Editor) *The Tin Wash Dish,* ABC Books (Sydney, Australia), 1988.

*Under Berlin: New Poems 1988,* University of Queensland Press (St. Lucia, Queensland, Australia), 1988.

(Editor, with Philip Mead) *The Penguin Book of Modern Australian Poetry,* Penguin (Ringwood, Victoria, Australia), 1991.

*Days in the Capital* (poems), National Library of Australia (Canberra, Australia), 1992.

*The Floor of Heaven* (poems), Angus & Robertson (Pymble, New South Wales, Australia), 1992.

(Editor) *Martin Johnston: Selected Poems and Prose,* University of Queensland Press (St. Lucia, Queensland, Australia), 1993.

*At the Florida* (poems), University of Queensland Press (St. Lucia, Queensland, Australia), 1993.

(Editor) *Martin Johnson: Selected Poems and Prose,* University of Queensland Press (St. Lucia, Queensland, Australia), 1993.

(Editor, with Philip Mead) *The Bloodaxe Book of Modern Australian Poetry,* Bloodaxe Books (Newcastle-upon-Tyne, England), 1994.

*Gasoline Kisses,* Equipage (Cambridge, England), 1997.

*Different Hands: Seven Stories,* Folio/Fremantle Arts Centre Press (South Fremantle, Australia), 1998.

*Late Night Radio,* Polygon (Edinburgh, Scotland), 1998.

*Ultra,* Brandl & Schlesinger (Rose Bay, New South Wales, Australia), 2000.

*Heart Print,* Salt Publishing (Cambridge, England), 2001.

Contributor of about thirty articles and reviews to magazines and newspapers, including the *Australian* and *Age.* Associate editor of *Aspect;* past member of editorial boards of *New Poetry* and *Poetry Australia.* Publisher and editor of online poetry quarterly *Jacket Magazine,* 1997—.

SIDELIGHTS: Australian poet John Tranter told *CA:* "The two strongest influences on my work have been those of Rimbaud and T. S. Eliot, in their emphasis on both formal experiment and the reconstruction of intense personal experience. The cool welcome given to such ideas in the backward-looking Australian literary world is perhaps responsible for the note of melancholy evident in my later work. My current hobby is an interest in the question: 'Is there life after postmodernism?'"

Tranter was also influenced by later poets such as Frank O'Hara and Ted Berrigan, as his own work moved away from romanticism to a more elegant, stripped-down style. He contends that a poet must write poetry for ten years before he can call himself a poet, and believes that creative writing classes are anathema to the true art of poetry. In an interview with C. K. Tower in *Riding the Meridian,* Tranter said, "My ideal writing school would overload and torment the students so badly that only one or two out of every hundred would put up with it for the ten years it takes to learn to be a poet. They would end up with their degrees, but they would have to take an oath inscribed and signed in their own blood never to teach creative writing."

One of Tranter's pet projects is his online poetry magazine, *Jacket.* Citing the Internet as the medium of the future, Tranter sees it as a solution to the most difficult problem facing poetry magazines, that of distribution. Tranter publishes *Jacket* quarterly, pulling together contributions from poets all over the world and providing free access to their work. He hopes that it will provide creative connections for a fragmented writing community.

*BIOGRAPHICAL AND CRITICAL SOURCES:*

*PERIODICALS*

*Courier-Mail* (Brisbane, Australia), November 24, 2001, Simon Patton, "The Poet As Saviour of the People," p. M5.

*Makar,* December, 1976.

*Observer* (London, England), April 1, 1979.

*Publishers Weekly,* March 18, 2002, "Heart Print," p. 93.

*Time International,* April 23, 2001, "Free Verse: From His Sydney Study, Poet John Tranter Broadcasts to the Literary World," p. 14.

*Times Literary Supplement,* August 6, 1999, p. 25.

*Weekend Australian,* October 13, 2001, Barry Hill, "So Tragically Hip, Dad," p. R14.

*ONLINE*

*Jacket Magazine,* http://jacketmagazine.com/ (May 16, 2003).

*John Tranter Homepage,* http://www.austlit.com/jt/ (May 16, 2003).

*Riding the Meridian,* http://www.heelstone.com/ meridian/ (May 16, 2003).*

\* \* \*

## TRIMBLE, Marshall I(ra) 1939-

*PERSONAL:* Born January 16, 1939, in Mesa, AZ; son of Ira (a stock person and railroad worker) and Juanita (a waitress) Trimble. *Ethnicity:* "White." *Education:* Arizona State University, B.A., 1961, M.A., 1963.

*ADDRESSES: Home*—5748 North 78th Pl., Scottsdale, AZ 85250. *Office*—9000 East Chaparral Rd., Scottsdale, AZ 85256; fax: 480-423-6066. *E-mail*—marshall. trimble@sccmail.maricopa.edu.

*CAREER:* Historian, writer, teacher, and folksinger. Scottsdale Community College, Scottsdale, AZ, teacher of history, 1972—, and head of Southwest studies program. Sound recordings include *Legends in Levis* (old cowboy songs), 1989. Host of *Arizona Backroads* (television series), AZTV-Television, and *Trimble's Tales* (syndicated radio program); other media appearances include *Legends and Dreamers,* KAET-TV, *Good Morning America,* and *This Morning;* media spokesperson for Saba's Western Stores and for Palace Restaurant and Saloon, Prescott, AZ.

*AWARDS, HONORS:* Finalist, Ben Franklin Award for humor, for *It Always Rains after a Dry Spell;* named Arizona's official state historian, 1997.

*WRITINGS:*

*Arizona: A Panoramic History of a Frontier State,* foreword by Barry M. Goldwater, Doubleday (New York, NY), 1977.

*Discover Arizona Heritage,* Arizona Highways (Phoenix, AZ), 1979.

*Marshall I. Trimble*

*Arizona Adventure: Action-packed True Tales of Early Arizona,* Golden West Publishers (Phoenix, AZ), 1982.

*CO Bar: Bill Owen Depicts the Historic Babbitt Ranch,* foreword by John G. Babbitt, Northland Press (Flagstaff, AZ), 1982.

*In Old Arizona: True Tales of the Wild Frontier,* Golden West Publishers (Phoenix, AZ), 1985.

(With Bob Hirsch) *Outdoors in Arizona: A Guide to Camping,* illustrated by Joe Beeler, Arizona Department of Transportation (Phoenix, AZ), 1986.

*Roadside History of Arizona,* illustrated by Joe Beeler, Mountain Press (Missoula, MT), 1986.

*Diamond in the Rough: An Illustrated History of Arizona,* Donning (Norfolk, VA), 1988.

(With James E. Cook and Sam Negri) *Travel Arizona: The Back Roads: Twenty Back-Road Tours for the Whole Family,* Arizona Department of Transportation (Phoenix, AZ), 1989.

*Arizona: A Cavalcade of History,* Treasure Chest (Tucson, AZ), 1989.

*It Always Rains after a Dry Spell* (collected legends, tall tales, and humorous true stories), illustrated by Jack Graham, Treasure Chest (Tucson, AZ), 1992.

*Marshall Trimble's Original Arizona Trivia,* Golden West Publishers (Phoenix, AZ), 1996.

*Arizona 2000: A Yearbook for the Millennium,* Northland Press (Flagstaff, AZ), 1999.

*Never Give a Heifer a Bum Steer,* Arizona Highways (Phoenix, AZ), 1999.

*Arizoniana: Stories from Old Arizona,* Golden West Publishers (Phoenix, AZ), 2002.

Also author of *Pulling Legs Attached to Tenderfeet.* Contributor to *Arizona Highways Album: The Road to Statehood,* by Dean Smith, Arizona Highways (Phoenix, AZ), 1987. Author of "Ask the Marshall," a column in *True West.* Editor of Arizona Trivia (board game); scriptwriter for Arizona segment of *Portrait of America* television series. Contributor of short stories to periodicals, including *Arizona Highways* and *Western Horseman.*

*SIDELIGHTS:* Marshall I. Trimble once told *CA:* "I graduated from college in 1961 and became a teacher. During the evenings and in summer I worked as a folksinger. I cut four records in 1964.

"In 1972 I began teaching Arizona history at Scottsdale Community College. I'm still there. My first book, published by Doubleday and Company in 1977, was *Arizona: A Panoramic History of a Frontier State.* The book was a big seller and I went on the speaking circuit. That work led to convention shows and television and radio work. That makes up a major part of my career today.

"I visit a lot of schools, especially fourth-grade classrooms, to promote Arizona history to youngsters. I sing old cowboy songs and tell stories and tall tales."

*BIOGRAPHICAL AND CRITICAL SOURCES:*

*PERIODICALS*

*Arizona Highways,* April, 1976.

*Arizona Republic,* June 6, 1976; May 13, 1977; July 3, 1977; July 10, 1977.

*Phoenix,* November, 1976.

*Phoenix Business Journal,* January 13, 1986, p. 17; October 8, 1993, p. 18.

*Phoenix Gazette,* January 12, 1974.

*Scottsdale Progress,* June 24, 1976; August 3, 1977.

# U-V

**UNDERHILL, Charles**
    **See HILL, Reginald (Charles)**

\*     \*     \*

**U'REN, Andrea 1968-**

*PERSONAL:* Born August 16, 1968, in Palo Alto, CA; daughter of Richard C. (a psychiatrist) and Marjorie Jean (a professor of English) Burns; married Sean Healy (an artist), June, 2003; children: Sebastian. *Education:* Attended Rhode Island School of Design, 1986-87; Cooper Union, B.F.A., 1990; Whitney Museum of American Art, Independent Study Program, 1991-92.

*ADDRESSES: Home*—4115 Northeast 11th Ave., Portland, OR 97211. *E-mail*—andreauren@yahoo.com.

*CAREER:* Author and illustrator.

*MEMBER:* Society of Children's Book Writers and Illustrators.

*AWARDS, HONORS:* Parents' Choice Award for *Pugdog.*

*WRITINGS:*

*SELF-ILLUSTRATED*

*Pugdog,* Farrar, Straus (New York, NY), 2001.
*Mary Smith,* Farrar, Straus (New York, NY), 2003.

*SIDELIGHTS:* Andrea U'Ren told *CA:* "I wrote and illustrated my first full-length picture book at the age of twelve. It was about Mount St. Helens, the volcano in the Northwest that—back in 1981—had just erupted. Amazingly enough, a local publisher wanted to purchase it for 2,000 dollars, but they also wanted to use an illustrator other than me. Meeting after meeting, they asked me to consider different illustrators; I turned each one down. The book never did get published.

"I went to art school first at the Rhode Island School of Design in Providence, than transferred to the Cooper Union in New York, New York. After receiving my degree in 1991, I attended the Whitney Museum of American Art Independent Study Program for artists. I began to feel the artwork I was making was speaking to and reaching a very small and exclusive audience. I needed a break from the fine arts.

"My latent desire to make children's books returned. I decided to finally publish a children's book. That was not as easy as I'd thought. Four years and *several* stories later, *Pugdog* was picked up by Farrar, Straus & Giroux.

"*Pugdog* is the story of a guy named Mike who assumes his dog is a male. After Mike discovers his boy-dog is actually a girl, he tries to get Pugdog to act more feminine—which means no more activities like digging, chasing squirrels, rolling on the ground, et cetera. Of course, Pugdog doesn't like this new life, and in the end Mike realizes the error of his ways. He loves his dog for being just who she is, male or female.

"Some people find it unbelievable that a grown man wouldn't know the gender of his pet. But, in fact, the

416

story is based on a similar mistake my brother (a doctor!) made with a cat. When my brother first got his kitten, he was totally smitten with 'her.' Months later, I finally met the cat and hesitantly informed my brother that his little girl was in fact a little boy. My brother was floored—and he was never quite as smitten with his feline companion again.

"*Mary Smith* is about a woman in England who woke people (so they could make it to their jobs on time) by shooting dried peas at their windows. People who had this occupation were known as 'knocker-ups.'

"Writing is not an easy process for me—it's a serious struggle—and, for that matter, so is the process of illustrating. But, somehow, I can't keep myself from working on these succinct and intimate things known as picture books."

*BIOGRAPHICAL AND CRITICAL SOURCES:*

PERIODICALS

*Booklist,* March 1, 2001, Gillian Engberg, review of *Pugdog,* p. 1288.
*Horn Book,* March, 2001, Roger Sutton, review of *Pugdog,* p. 203.
*Publishers Weekly,* January 29, 2001, review of *Pugdog,* p. 88.
*School Library Journal,* June, 2001, Anne Parker, review of *Pugdog,* p. 131.

\*     \*     \*

**VAN PELT, Nicholas**
**See HOYT, Richard (Duane)**

\*     \*     \*

**VOEGELIN, Eric (Herman Wilhelm) 1901-1985**

*PERSONAL:* Given name sometimes cited in German as Erich; born January 3, 1901, in Cologne, Germany; immigrated to United States, 1938, naturalized citizen, 1944; died of congestive heart failure, January 19, 1985, in Palo Alto (some sources say Stanford), CA;

son of Otto and Elisabeth (Ruehl) Voegelin; married Lissy Onken, July 30, 1932. *Education:* University of Vienna, Dr. rer. pol., 1922; graduate study at Oxford University, University of Berlin, and University of Heidelberg. *Religion:* Lutheran.

*CAREER:* University of Vienna, Vienna, Austria, assistant in law faculty, 1923-24 and 1928, privatdozent, 1929-35, extraordinarius, 1936-38; Harvard University, Cambridge, MA, instructor and tutor in political science, 1938-39; Bennington College, Bennington, VT, instructor, 1939; University of Alabama, Tuscaloosa, AL, assistant professor, 1939-42; Louisiana State University, Baton Rouge, LA, associate professor, 1942-46, professor, 1946-52, Boyd Professor of Government, 1952-58; University of Munich, Munich, Germany, professor of political science, 1958-69; Hoover Institution on War, Revolution, and Peace, Stanford University, Palo Alto, CA, Henry Salvatori Distinguished Scholar, 1969-74, senior research fellow, 1974-85. Member of administrative board of Volkshochschule, Vienna, and of Austrian Commission of Civil Service Examiners, both 1936-38.

*MEMBER:* American Political Science Association, American Social Science Association.

*AWARDS, HONORS:* Laura Spelman Rockefeller fellow, 1924-27; Lippincott Award from American Political Science Association, 1980; Gold Medal from City of Munich, Germany, 1981; honorary doctorates from Colorado College, Emory University, Marquette University, University of Augsburg, and University of Notre Dame.

*WRITINGS:*

*Ueber die Form des amerikanischen Geistes,* Mohr (Tuebingen, Germany), 1928.
*Rasse und Staat,* Mohr (Tuebingen, Germany), 1933, translation by Ruth Hein published as *Race and State,* Louisiana State University Press (Baton Rouge, LA), 1997.
*Die Rassenidee in der Geistesgeschichte von Ray bis Carus,* Junker & Duennhaupt (Berlin, Germany), 1933.
*Der Autoritaere Staat: Ein Versuch ueber das oesterreichische Staatsproblem,* J. Springer (Vienna, Austria), 1936.

*Die politischen Religionen,* Bermann-Fischer (Stockholm, Sweden), 1939.

*The New Science of Politics,* University of Chicago Press (Chicago, IL), 1952.

*Order and History* (also see below), Louisiana State University Press (Baton Rouge, LA), Volume 1: *Israel and Revelation,* 1956, Volume 2: *The World of the Polis,* 1957, Volume 3: *Plato and Aristotle,* 1957, Volume 4: *The Ecumenic Age,* 1974, Volume 5: *In Search of Order,* 1987.

*Wissenschaft, Politik und Gnosis,* Koesel (Munich, Germany), 1959, translation by William J. Fitzpatrick published as *Science, Politics, and Gnosticism,* Regnery (Lanham, MD), 1968, reprinted, 1997.

(With others) *Christentum und Liberalismus,* Zink (Munich, Germany), 1960.

*Anamnesis: Zur Theorie der Geschichte und Politik,* Piper (Munich, Germany), 1966, translation by Gerhart Niemeyer published as *Anamnesis,* University of Notre Dame Press (South Bend, IN), 1978.

(Editor) *Zwischen Revolution und Restauration: Politisches Denken in England im 17. Jahrhundert,* List (Munich, Germany), 1968.

*From Enlightenment to Revolution,* Duke University Press (Durham, NC), 1975.

*Autobiographical Reflections,* Louisiana State University Press (Baton Rouge, LA), 1989.

*The Collected Works of Eric Voegelin,* University of Missouri Press (Columbia, MO), Volume 1: *On the Form of the American Mind,* Volume 2: *Race and State,* Volume 3: *The History of the Race Idea: From Ray to Carus,* Volume 4: *The Authoritarian State: An Essay on the Problem of the Austrian State,* Volume 5: *Modernity without Restraint; The Political Religions; The New Science of Politics; and Science, Politics, and Gnosticism,* Volume 6: *Anamnesis: On the Theory of History and Politics,* Volume 7: *Published Essays, 1922-1928,* Volume 9: *Published Essays, 1934-1939,* Volume 10: *Published Essays, 1940-1952,* Volume 11: *Published Essays, 1953-1965,* Volume 12: *Published Essays, 1966-1985,* Volume 13: *Selected Book Reviews,* Volume 14: *Order and History, Volume 1, Israel and Revelation,* Volume 15: *Order and History, Volume 2, The World of the Polis,* Volume 16: *Order and History, Volume 3, Plato and Aristotle,* Volume 17: *Order and History, Volume 4, The Ecumenic Age,* Volume 18: *Order and History, Volume 5, In Search of Order,* Volume 19: *History of Political Ideas, Volume 1, Hellenism, Rome,* and Early Christianity, Volume 20: *History of Political Ideas, Volume 2, The Middle Ages to Aquinas,* Volume 21: *History of Political Ideas, Volume 3, The Later Middle Ages,* Volume 22: *History of Political Ideas, Volume 4, Renaissance and Reformation,* Volume 23: *History of Political Ideas, Volume 5, Religion and the Rise of Modernity,* Volume 24: *History of Political Ideas, Volume 6, Revolution and the New Science,* Volume 25: *History of Political Ideas, Volume 7, The New Order and Last Orientation,* Volume 26: *History of Political Ideas, Volume 8, Crisis and the Apocalypse of Man,* Volume 27, *Nature of the Law and Related Legal Writings,* Volume 28: *What Is History? And Other Late Unpublished Writings,* Volume 31: *Hitler and the Germans,* 1989-2003.

*SIDELIGHTS:* Historian and political philosopher Eric Voegelin is regarded as one of the most important scholars of the twentieth century. He drew upon an immense knowledge of languages and academic disciplines to construct his theories about human civilization, impressing peers with thoughtful, well-documented arguments. In works such as *The New Science of Politics, From Enlightenment to Revolution,* and especially in his five-volume masterwork, *Order and History,* Voegelin explored modern political institutions in light of pre-modern forms, and in so doing he fashioned a comprehensive view of human history. A *National Review* obituary noted that Voegelin "reminded the West of the real stakes involved in thinking, even when we are attempting thoughts beyond the reaches of our souls—the only thinking worthy of men."

For his philosophy Voegelin articulated a specific opinion on the nature of reality. He argued that human civilization is part of a larger cosmos, divine but mysterious; that the world existed before humanity began and will exist after it ends as well. While human beings inevitably long to discover the secrets of their origin and fate, that longing is destined to remain unfulfilled. The desire to know that which is unknowable, though, produces a "tension" of existence that fuels all human activity and creation. For those who understand and accept that reality is open-ended, this inner conflict is a healthy one: the quest to unlock the secrets of existence gives meaning to life and makes progress possible.

The importance of accepting reality applies to society as well as to individuals, and it is this larger scale that

Voegelin sought to chronicle. By studying the symbols of civilization—evident in the art, literature, and political and religious institutions of all societies—he built a philosophy that integrates his theory of reality with the way societies have ordered themselves throughout history. In ancient cultures such as those in Egypt, Mesopotamia, and Greece, noted Voegelin, humans created political and social forms that recognized the existence of a world beyond everyday life. Those cultures strove to understand that world and align themselves in harmony with it. By the twentieth century, however, humanity had faltered, producing the totalitarian systems of nations such as Nazi Germany and the Soviet Union. These regimes claimed to have the keys to human perfectibility and earthly paradise and denied the existence of any world beyond the present one. In other words, such cultures exalted a "closed" existence, which precludes significant human achievement and leads inevitably to disorder and conflict. Voegelin himself was forced to flee from Germany in 1938, and critics have noted that much of his subsequent philosophy was a reaction to the political makeup of his native country.

Voegelin's theories encompassed both individual experience and larger societal forms and ranged across the whole of human history. He was particularly interested in the symbols created by societies to explain their existence, and because of his vast knowledge of languages he was able to explore those symbols by reading original sources, whether from ancient Greece or modern Russia. Thus, his arguments were always well documented, eliciting admiration from peers and critics. "He rarely hazards an important generalization which is not supported by a cautious reading of the primary sources," noted Dante Germino in a *National Review* article about *From Enlightenment to Revolution.* "Here is a man who speaks with intellectual authority, and the sources of that authority are displayed for all to see."

*Order and History* remains Voegelin's most important achievement. He published the first volume of the series in 1956 and was completing the final volume when he died in 1985. Critical comment about the series gives further indication of the esteem in which the author is held. Writing in the *Yale Review* in 1957, Russell Kirk called Voegelin "probably the most influential historian of our century, and certainly the most provocative." And *Christian Century* contributor R. L. Shinn commented that "[Voegelin's] is one of the monuments of scholarship of our time."

In 2002, The University of Missouri Press released *The Collected Works of Eric Voegelin,* a thirty-one-volume project that includes many texts previously unavailable in English translation. This includes reprints of *Order and History* as well as Voegelin's eight-volume *The History of Political Ideas.* According to Thomas Heilke in the *Journal of Church and State,* in these volumes—and particularly in his essays—Voegelin "raises the discipline of political science to a level of theoretical insight and sophistication that it rarely attains."

*BIOGRAPHICAL AND CRITICAL SOURCES:*

*BOOKS*

Dempf, A., H. Arendt, and F. Engel-Janosi, editors, *Politische Ordnung und menschlich Existenz: Festgabe fuer Eric Voegelin,* C. H. Beck (Munich, Germany), 1962.

*Encyclopedia of World Biography,* 2nd edition, Gale (Detroit, MI), 1998.

Germino, Dante L., *Political Philosophy and the Open Society,* Louisiana State University Press (Baton Rouge, LA), 1982.

Kirby, John, and William M. Thompson, editors, *Voegelin and the Theologian: Ten Studies in Interpretation,* Edwin Mellen (Lewiston, NY), 1983.

McKnight, Stephen A., editor, *Eric Voegelin's Search for Order in History,* Louisiana State University Press (Baton Rouge, LA), 1978.

O'Connor, Eric, editor, *Conversations with Eric Voegelin,* Thomas More Institute (Montreal, Quebec, Canada), 1980.

Opitz, Peter J., and Gregor Sebba, editors, *The Philosophy of Order: Essays on History, Consciousness and Politics; for Eric Voegelin on His Eightieth Birthday,* Klett-Cotta (Stuttgart, Germany), 1981.

Sandoz, Ellis, *The Voegelinian Revolution,* Louisiana State University Press (Baton Rouge, LA), 1982.

Sandoz, Ellis, editor, *Eric Voegelin's Thought: A Critical Appraisal,* Duke University Press (Durham, NC), 1982.

Webb, Eugene, *Eric Voegelin: Philosopher of History,* University of Washington Press (Seattle, WA), 1981.

*PERIODICALS*

*Christian Century,* September 17, 1958.

*Journal of Church and State,* summer, 2000, Thomas Heilke, review of *The Collected Works of Eric Voegelin, Volume 5,* p. 568.

*Journal of Religion,* January, 1999, Thomas Heilke, review of *History of Political Ideas, Volume 1, Hellenism, Rome, and Early Christianity,* p. 136; April, 1999, Thomas Heilke, review of *History of Political Ideas, Volume 2, The Middle Ages to Aquinas,* p. 291.

*Library Journal,* September 15, 1995, Leon H. Brody, review of *The Collected Works of Eric Voegelin, Volume 1* p. 72.

*National Review,* January 14, 1969; October 25, 1975.

*New Republic,* October 29, 1956.

*Times Literary Supplement,* August 7, 1953.

*Yale Review,* spring, 1957.

OBITUARIES:

PERIODICALS

*Los Angeles Times,* January 24, 1985.

*National Review,* February 22, 1985, "Eric Voegelin, RIP," p. 21.

*Newsweek,* February 4, 1985.

*New York Times,* January 23, 1985.

*Time,* February 4, 1985, p. 81.

*Times* (London, England), February 5, 1985.

*Washington Post,* January 25, 1985.*

# W

## WALDMAN, Neil 1947-

*PERSONAL:* Born October 22, 1947, in Bronx, NY; son of Abraham (a businessman) and Jessie (Herstein) Waldman; married Jeri Socol (an elementary schoolteacher), December 20, 1972 (divorced, 1988); children: Sarah, Jonathan. *Education:* Rochester Institute of Technology, B.F.A., 1969, M.A., 1970. *Politics:* Liberal. *Religion:* Jewish Reformed. *Hobbies and other interests:* Chess, guitar, classical music, travel, softball.

*ADDRESSES: Home*—Greenburgh, NY. *Agent*—c/o Boyds Mill Press, 815 Church St., Honesdale, PA 18431.

*CAREER:* Painter, stamp designer, and freelance writer/illustrator, 1971—. Has worked as package designer, art teacher, and border guard. Olive farmer in Israel, 1970-73, 1975-76; Linbry Products, Yonkers, NY, art director, 1971; member of faculty, William Paterson College of New Jersey, 1980-81; art instructor at Westchester Art Workshop, State University of New York, 1994—; designer of postage stamps (for governments of Sierra Leone, Grenada, and Antigua), record album covers, book dust covers, and theater posters. Waldman's paintings can be found in the capitol buildings of more than a dozen nations, as well as in the United Nations building, and in the offices of several major corporations, including American Airlines, Merrill Lynch, and Sony. *Exhibitions:* Artwork exhibited at galleries in New York, Michigan, Massachusetts, Pennsylvania, and Connecticut.

*MEMBER:* Graphic Artists Guild.

*AWARDS, HONORS:* Desi Award, 1980, for a poster for Sylvania; Grammy Award nomination, National Academy of Recording Arts and Sciences, 1982 and 1983, for record cover designs; United Nations Poster Award for International Year of Peace, 1986; Parents' Choice Award, 1990, for *Nessa's Fish,* written by Nancy Luenn, and 1994, for *Nessa's Story,* written by Nancy Luenn; Washington Irving Award for illustration, 1990, for *Bring Back the Deer,* and 1992, for *The Highwayman;* Christopher Award (ages 8-10), 1991, for *The Gold Coin,* written by Alma Flor Ada; Notable Book selection, American Library Association, and Children's Book of the Year selection, Bank Street College, both for *The Passover Journey: A Seder Companion,* written by Barbara Diamond Goldin; Best Books of the Year selection, *School Library Journal,* 1995, for *Bayou Lullaby,* written by Kathi Appelt; National Jewish Book Award, Jewish Book Council, for *Next Year in Jerusalem: 3000 Years of Jewish Stories,* retold by Howard Schwartz; American Storytellers Award, for *The Two Brothers: A Legend of Jerusalem;* Notable Books selection, *Smithsonian* magazine, 1998, for *Masada,* and 2000, for *Wounded Knee;* Sidney Taylor Honor Book for Younger Readers, Association of Jewish Libraries, 2000, for *The Wisdom Bird: A Tale of Solomon and Sheba,* written by Sheldon Oberman.

*WRITINGS:*

*SELF-ILLUSTRATED*

(With Jeri Waldman) *Pitcher in Left Field,* Prentice-Hall (New York, NY), 1981.
*The Golden City: Jerusalem's 3000 Years,* Atheneum (New York, NY), 1995.

*The Never-Ending Greenness,* Morrow (New York, NY), 1997.

(Reteller) *The Two Brothers: A Legend of Jerusalem,* Atheneum (New York, NY), 1997.

*Masada,* Morrow (New York, NY), 1998.

*The Starry Night,* Boyds Mills Press (Honesdale, PA), 1999.

*Wounded Knee,* Atheneum Books for Young Readers (New York, NY), 2001.

*They Came from the Bronx: How the Buffalo Were Saved from Extinction,* Boyds Mills Press (Honesdale, PA), 2001.

*The Promised Land: The Birth of the Jewish People,* Boyds Mills Press (Honesdale, PA), 2002.

*The Snowflake: A Water Cycle Story,* Millbrook Press (Brookfield, CT), 2002.

*Dream Makers: The Hopes and Aspirations of Children,* Boyds Mills Press (Honesdale, PA), 2003.

*ILLUSTRATOR*

Walter Harter, *Osceola's Head and Other Ghost Stories,* Prentice-Hall (New York, NY), 1974.

David C. Knight, *The Moving Coffins: Ghosts and Hauntings around the World,* Prentice-Hall (New York, NY), 1983.

Patricia T. Lowe, *The Runt,* Caedmon (New York, NY), 1984.

Michael Mark, *Toba,* Bradbury (New York, NY), 1984.

David C. Knight, editor, *Best True Ghost Stories of the Twentieth Century,* Prentice-Hall (New York, NY), 1984.

Lee P. Huntington, *Maybe a Miracle,* Coward (New York, NY), 1984.

(And editor) Edgar Allan Poe, *Tales of Terror: Ten Short Stories,* Prentice-Hall (New York, NY), 1985.

William Warren, *The Headless Ghost: True Tales of the Unexplained,* Prentice-Hall (New York, NY), 1986.

William Warren, *The Screaming Skull: True Tales of the Unexplained,* Prentice-Hall (New York, NY), 1987.

Jeffrey Prusski, *Bring Back the Deer,* Harcourt (San Diego, CA), 1988.

Margery Williams, *The Velveteen Rabbit: Or, How Toys Become Real,* Tom Doherty Associates (New York, NY), 1988.

(With Bryna Waldman) Sarah Leiberman, *A Trip to Mezuzah Land,* Merkos L'inyonei Chinuch (Brooklyn, NY), 1988.

Robert Orkand, Joyce Orkand, and Howard Bogot, *Gates of Wonder: A Prayerbook for Very Young Children,* Central Conference of American Rabbis (New York, NY), 1989.

Mark D. Shapiro, *Gates of Shabbat: Shaarei Shabbat: A New Shabbat Manual for the 1990s,* Central Conference of American Rabbis (New York, NY), 1990.

Alfred Noyes, *The Highwayman,* Harcourt (San Diego, CA), 1990.

Betty Boegehold, *A Horse Called Starfire,* Bantam (New York, NY), 1990.

Nancy Luenn, *Nessa's Fish,* Atheneum (New York, NY), 1990.

Robert Orkand, Howard Bogot, and Joyce Orkand, *Gates of Awe: Holy Day Prayers for Young Children,* Central Conference of American Rabbis (New York, NY), 1991.

Alma Flor Ada, *The Gold Coin,* Atheneum (New York, NY), 1991.

Ken Kesey, *The Sea Lion: A Story of the Sea Cliff People,* Viking (New York, NY), 1991.

Nancy Luenn, *Mother Earth,* Atheneum (New York, NY), 1992.

Ellen Blanker, *Down by the Seashore,* Silver Burdett and Ginn (New York, NY), 1992.

William Blake, *The Tyger,* Harcourt (San Diego, CA), 1993.

Katharine Lee Bates, *America the Beautiful,* Atheneum (New York, NY), 1993.

(Reteller) Sarah Waldman, *Light: The First Seven Days,* Harcourt (San Diego, CA), 1993.

Nancy Luenn, *Nessa's Story,* Atheneum (New York, NY), 1994.

Barbara Diamond Goldin, *The Passover Journey: A Seder Companion,* Viking (New York, NY), 1994.

Chaim Stern, editor, *On the Doorposts of Your House: A Mezuzot Beitecha—Prayers and Ceremonies for the Jewish Home, Hebrew Opening,* Central Conference of American Rabbis (New York, NY), 1994.

Kathi Appelt, *Bayou Lullaby,* Morrow (New York, NY), 1995.

Howard Schwartz, reteller, *Next Year in Jerusalem: 3000 Years of Jewish Stories,* Viking Penguin (New York, NY), 1996, reprinted as *Jerusalem of Gold: Jewish Stories of the Enchanted City,* Jewish Lights Publishing (Woodstock, VT), 2003.

Shulamith Levey Oppenheim, *And the Earth Trembled: The Creation of Adam and Eve,* Harcourt (San Diego, CA), 1996.

Dorothy Hinshaw Patent, *Quetzal: Sacred Bird of the Cloud Forest,* Morrow (New York, NY), 1996.

Sheldon Oberman, *By the Hanukkah Light,* Boyds Mills Press (Honesdale, PA), 1997.

Ellen Schecter, *The Family Haggadah,* Viking (New York, NY), 1999.

Sheldon Oberman, *The Wisdom Bird: A Tale of Solomon and Sheba,* Boyds Mills Press (Honesdale, PA), 2000.

Richard Michelson, *Too Young for Yiddish,* Talewinds (Watertown, MA), 2001.

*SIDELIGHTS:* Neil Waldman is a distinguished author and illustrator of children's books with eleven of his own self-illustrated titles and three dozen other books that he has illustrated for a myriad of authors. Waldman's solo efforts as author and illustrator include many books on the Jewish religion, tradition, and folklore, like the Holocaust tale *The Never-Ending Greenness* and explorations of Jewish history in *The Golden City: Jerusalem's 3000 Years, The Two Brothers: A Legend of Jerusalem, Masada,* and *The Promised Land: The Birth of the Jewish People.* In *Wounded Knee* and *They Came from the Bronx: How the Buffalo Were Saved from Extinction,* Waldman deals with Native-American and frontier history. Working with other authors, the illustrator has looked at similar themes, as in Jeffrey Prusski's *Bring Back the Deer* and Nancy Luenn's *Nessa's Story,* both of which deal with Native Americans, and Howard Schwartz's *Next Year in Jerusalem: 3000 Years of Jewish Stories* and *The Passover Story: A Seder Companion* by Barbara Diamond Goldin. Additionally, Waldman has proven an able illustrator for poems and stories by classic English and American authors, including Alfred Noyes's *The Highwayman,* William Blake's *The Tyger,* and a collection of horror stories by Edgar Allan Poe titled *Tales of Terror: Ten Short Stories.*

Waldman once told *CA:* "I was raised in a house where all the arts were encouraged. I sensed, as a small child, that finger paints and coloring books were more than just fun. They were important tools that led to a road of joy, discovery, and fulfillment.

"When I entered first grade, I learned very quickly that, within the classroom walls, the arts were 'secondary subjects,' not nearly as important as reading, math and science. I resented this deeply, and unconsciously began to rebel. Through twelve years of

school I was considered an 'underachiever.' In fact, I was doing the minimum possible to get by, while working on my art at home.

"When I graduated from high school (near the bottom of my class), I felt as though I had been liberated. I entered an art college, where I spent most of my time drawing and painting. Here, surrounded by other artists for the first time, I began to blossom. Though I'd always known that art was important too, now it was reinforced in my environment. Instead of struggling against the current, I was gliding freely, ever faster and deeper, to places I had never imagined."

Waldman studied illustration and painting at Rochester Institute of Technology. "During and after college there was never a plan for my life," the artist told John Dalmas in the *Sunday Journal-News.* "I wanted to travel since I was a kid, and I always wanted to draw and paint. It just never occurred to me I would end up doing what I like for a living." After graduation, Waldman added, "I began to work as an illustrator. This seemed a natural decision, because it would allow me to do what I love most, while earning a living. It was difficult at first, almost like learning a new language. But it was worth it."

Early in his illustration career, Waldman designed postage stamps for Sierra Leone, Granada, Antigua, and many other countries, and won the United Nations poster competition representing the International Year of Peace in 1986. He also designed book jackets and magazine covers, but never considered illustrating children's literature until an editor at Gulliver Books approached him about working on a book titled *Bring Back the Deer,* by Jeffrey Prusski. Illustrating that book changed Waldman's life. Erin Gathrid, the editor at Gulliver, chose Waldman because she had been drawn to his work and felt that it had the same mystical quality as the manuscript for *Bring Back the Deer.* Initially Waldman refused, but Gathrid talked him into reading the manuscript at least five times before he made a decision.

*Bring Back the Deer* is the story of a young Native American boy's search for identity. When his father goes to hunt for food and doesn't return, the boy follows after him, and in the process discovers the animal spirit inside himself. Waldman once recalled for *CA:* "As I began to read, I felt like I was entering a dark, winding cave. By the time I finished reading, I was totally confused. The story left me feeling that I had missed something. If I hadn't promised to read it five times, I would never have looked at it again. But then a strange thing happened. On my second reading, a few things were revealed to me that had escaped me the first time. And when I read it again, I saw even more. By the fifth time, not only did I begin to appreciate it . . . I began to love it."

Though he had never worked on a children's picture book before, he agreed to handle the project. After weeks of difficulty finding the right images, Waldman arranged to meet with Gathrid and Prusski in New York City. Prusski told Waldman of his experience with Shamanism, and how a Native-American spirit had written the story through him. Waldman once told *CA,* "As Jeff continued speaking, I felt myself being transported back . . . back . . . back into the story. Images began flooding my brain. I opened my napkin and began scribbling on it. When I got home later that afternoon, I unfolded the napkin and began to study it. One of my scribblings was the image of two rectangles, one inside the other. I envisioned the main subject of each page within the smaller rectangle, with secondary subjects floating around it. The larger rectangle became the frame for each page. The color within the smaller rectangle would be very bright, to focus the viewer's attention on the central image." After discovering the boy and the grandfather in the tale, "the paintings were flowing effortlessly. Each image was like a road sign, directing me to whatever came next. I created a tribe, with its own special clothing, dwellings, environment, and even its own language of pictographs. It was as if I was constructing an entire world, which I lived in as I continued to paint."

"I painted intensely for two months," Waldman continued, "and when I finished the book it was clear that my life had changed forever. I knew that I wouldn't be working for advertising agencies or design studios anymore. I wanted to do more picture books. I had tiptoed through the window, and my path lay clearly before me. Like a many-colored fan, my life was unfolding before my eyes, revealing colors I had never even dreamed of." A *Publishers Weekly* critic praised Waldman's "splendid debut" in *Bring Back the Deer,* noting that his illustrations "have a lyrical quality that is haunting." Since 1988, when *Bring Back the Deer* was published, Waldman has worked exclusively on children's literature, having illustrated numerous pic-

ture books and dust jackets, including several Newbery or Newbery Honor winners. The book prompted changes in Waldman's personal life as well, as he decided to leave his marriage and embark on a journey of self-discovery.

In 1990, Waldman brought his artistic vision to Alfred Noyes's famous poem *The Highwayman,* which had recently been illustrated twice: once by Charles Mikolaycak and once by Charles Keeping. Unlike his predecessors, Waldman brought a broad palette to the poem, prompting Roger Sutton of the *Bulletin of the Center for Children's Books* to observe: "[Waldman's] colors are often unlikely—plenty of aqua and magenta—but surprisingly effective, as in a moody painting of the highwayman upon his horse, a study in blue and black and gray." A *Publishers Weekly* reviewer characterized Waldman's style in *The Highwayman* as "both abstract and realistic," adding that his watercolors "capture the haunting, tragic spirit of the text." Eleanor K. MacDonald, writing for *School Library Journal,* praised the effect of Waldman's artwork, stating that "the strong sense of atmosphere and dramatic use of design reinforce the melodrama of the story."

In 1993, Waldman illustrated another classic poem, this time William Blake's *The Tyger.* In her *School Library Journal* review, Ruth K. MacDonald described Waldman's acrylic artwork as "modern, highly painterly, and formal." The final picture is a fold-out spread of the "tyger" that covers four pages, with each of the pages leading up to it featuring a section of the larger picture, each reproduced in black and shades of gray. MacDonald stated that "the focus on individual portions of the whole gives readers an opportunity to study *The Tyger* carefully, and to discuss the artist's interpretation."

*Nessa's Story,* by Nancy Luenn, features the story of an Inuit girl who learns from her grandmother how to participate in the cultural tradition of storytelling. *Booklist* contributor Isabel Schon asserted that Waldman's "original, luminous watercolor paintings," which use a wide range of settings, "are the best part of this story." *School Library Journal* contributor Roz Goodman noted that the "soft, cool colors in a variety of pastel pinks, blues, purples, greens, and browns blend into scenes both realistic and imaginary."

In *Booklist,* Stephanie Zvirin described *The Passover Journey: A Seder Companion* as "a beautiful wedding of the work of two talented individuals" that is "exquisitely designed." Author Barbara Diamond Goldin describes the history behind the Jewish holiday of Passover, and the symbolism behind the Seder meal, eaten in remembrance of the Jews' freedom from slavery in Egypt. Waldman's interpretation of this text features the "geometric borders and pastels characteristic of [his] work," according to Zvirin, and are combined with "stylized classic Egyptian hieroglyphic figures and set against softly tinted pages that actually glow." Hanna B. Zeiger, writing for *Horn Book*, commented that "the page design and stylized illustrations, in pleasing soft pastel colors, help make this book a welcome addition to holiday literature."

Waldman followed his work on *The Passover Journey* with another Jewish-themed book the following year, writing and illustrating *The Golden City. School Library Journal* contributor Susan Scheps noted that the book "successfully introduces the panorama of religions and cultures that have formed the city's heritage and created its mystique." A *Kirkus Reviews* critic, on the other hand, maintained that the writing "often overly romanticizes and is entirely subjective about a topic few people can approach objectively." Both reviewers, however, praised Waldman's watercolor-and-pencil illustrations featuring architecturally accurate portraits of Jerusalem during various time periods in its three-thousand-year history.

In 1995, Waldman lent his talents to a story written by Kathi Appelt, *Bayou Lullaby*. Judy Constantinides, writing in *School Library Journal*, commented that while the verse of this Cajun lullaby is enjoyable, "the true merit of the book lies in Waldman's double-page acrylic paintings." Waldman's figures are stylized and his palette includes rich jewel tones set against a black background. A *Publishers Weekly* reviewer called *Bayou Lullaby* "an inspired pairing of author and artist."

Turning his attention once again to Jewish themes, Waldman teamed with reteller Howard Schwartz to create a collection of Jewish folktales titled *Next Year in Jerusalem*. The tales are taken in part from the Talmud and Midrash, some from folklore, and others from mystical or Hasidic sources. Marcia W. Posner wrote in *School Library Journal* that "Waldman has suffused the pages with the peach-colored dawns, golden sunlit days, and turquoise and lavender twilights of Jerusalem." In *Horn Book*, Hanna B. Zeiger observed that "Waldman's watercolor illustrations enhance the handsomely produced volume."

Two more books illustrated by Waldman and published in 1996 deal with ancient myth. *Quetzal: Sacred Bird of the Cloud Forest*, by Dorothy Hinshaw Patent, draws upon Mexican myths of the beautiful bird which inhabits the cloud forests of Mexico and Central America. Waldman employed colored pencil on tinted paper for his illustrations, which, according to *School Library Journal* contributor Pam Gosner, "are quite lovely, with rich glowing tones." For Shulamith Levey Oppenheim's book *And the Earth Trembled: The Creation of Adam and Eve*, based on a traditional Islamic tale of creation, Waldman used the technique of pointillism, which Patricia Lothrop regarded in *School Library Journal* as "well suited to his subject." Lothrop continued: "The pages are brightly colored, the image of the Ibis is appropriately scary, and Paradise is a vision of order in green and blue."

In 1997, Waldman wrote and illustrated *The Never-Ending Greenness*, a story of holocaust survival. In this work, the Jewish narrator reflects on his childhood as he recalls being exiled to a ghetto along with his family at the hands of Nazi soldiers. The family escapes to the surrounding forest, and the boy later realizes his dream of planting trees in Israel. Waldman's story is told in simple language, and his illustrations feature his characteristic stylized palette, using bright blue, orange, pink, and turquoise. A *Publishers Weekly* critic noted that the "reference to Tu b'Shvat . . . might commend the book to families who observe that holiday." Betsy Hearne of the *Bulletin of the Center for Children's Books* called *The Never-Ending Greenness* "perfectly paced as an unfolding of personalized history reflected in a life cycle like an unfolding of leaves." Hearne added that the "intensity of the boy's project is magnetic enough to build a bridge of identification with today's young listeners." Focusing on the artwork in the same book, a contributor for *Reading Teacher* lauded the "pointillistic" acrylic paintings which accent "the colorful beauty of new growth."

Waldman continues with Jewish themes in several more of his titles. *The Two Brothers*, a retelling of the legend of how Solomon selected the site of Jerusalem for his temple, is a "moving" tale, according to Maeve Visser Knoth in *Horn Book Guide*. The 1998 title *Masada* is a "tribute to the legendary citadel," according to a contributor for *Publishers Weekly*, following two millennia of history about the fortress built on a high plateau in the Negev desert, which became a final stronghold for the Jewish people in the Holy Land. Here the Zealots made the stand against the Romans, fighting to the last and committing suicide rather than surrendering. Waldman traces the history of the place from its founding by King Herod up to the 1960s when much of the current knowledge about it was revealed by an archaeological expedition. But it is the final battle against the Romans that takes center stage and is "most compelling," as the *Publishers Weekly* reviewer noted. Janice M. DelNegro, writing in *Bulletin of the Center for Children's Books,* spoke highly of Waldman's "thrillingly dramatic and admiring prose," adding that it has "strong nationalistic undertones." Susan Scheps, reviewing the same title in *School Library Journal,* observed that Waldman bases his tale on the account of Josephius Flavius, a young Jewish man who took an oath to serve the Romans in order to save his life. Waldman also uses dialogue in his account, "a tactic that gives a fictional quality to the otherwise carefully researched text," according to Scheps.

A change of pace for Waldman is the 1999 *The Starry Night,* a "nifty little fantasy based on the life of painter Vincent Van Gogh," as *Booklist*'s GraceAnne DeCandido described the picture book. In Waldman's tale, the Dutch artist pops up in Manhattan, setting his easel in Central Park. Young Bernard makes his acquaintance and takes him on a tour of the city. Afterwards, Vincent takes the young boy to the Metropolitan Museum of Art and shows him the picture "Starry Night," which inspires the boy to sketch his own interpretation of the famous painting. Throughout, the artwork represents both Waldman's impression of what Van Gogh's colorful vision of the city perhaps might be as well as more realistic, sepia-toned illustrations. A reviewer for *Publishers Weekly* felt that "Waldman's paintings . . . cleverly imitate Van Gogh's feeling for color." Similarly, DeCandido praised the contrasting of "briliantly colored" paintings in Van Gogh's style with the "lively sepia-toned . . . sketches." Margaret A. Chang, writing in *School Library Journal,* similarly called the book a "showcase for Waldman's paintings of New York City."

Waldman deals with Native American and Western themes in two further solo efforts, *Wounded Knee* and *They Came from the Bronx.* In the former title—a "remarkable and well-written history," according to Linda Greengrass in *School Library Journal*—Waldman provides a "vivid description" of that Lakota Indian massacre in 1890. Waldman's book also details the history of the settlers and the Native Americans in the South Dakota region known as the Black Hills. Randy Meyer, writing in *Booklist,* found Waldman's account to be "balanced" and "succinct," accompanied by black-and-white and color portraits. Likewise, a reviewer for *Publishers Weekly* found Waldman's treatment a "moving yet balanced overview." A *Horn Book* critic also thought that Waldman "provides a clear and focused background" to the tragedy but complained that "the lack of documentation hampers readers who want to reconsider [Waldman's] opinions."

With *They Came from the Bronx,* Waldman presents something of a hybrid tale of the history of the American bison. This "articulate and informative volume," as a reviewer for *Publishers Weekly* described the picture book, begins with a Comanche boy in Oklahoma who asks his grandmother to tell him the story of the buffalo. The grandmother proceeds to tell the young boy of the amazing wild beast and its decimation at the hands of white settlers. Interspersed with this tale is a parallel one of how the herd was rebuilt from animals shipped west from the Bronx Zoo at the turn of the century. The same *Publishers Weekly* critic praised Waldman's "eloquent, sepia-tone watercolors." Mary L. Laub, reviewing the book in *Childhood Education,* found it "inspirational as well as informative," while Kate McDowell, writing in the *Bulletin of the Center for Children's Books,* reserved her praise for the illustrations, which, in her opinion, "provide some of the emotional appeal absent from the story."

Waldman returns to Jewish life and history with illustrations for Sheldon Oberman's *The Wisdom Bird: A Tale of Solomon and Sheba* and *Too Young for Yiddish,* by Richard Michelson. Patricia Pearl Dole of *School Library Journal* commended Waldman's illustrations for Oberman's book, noting that the artwork of "elegant abstract designs, the king and the queen, the city of Jerusalem, and the many beautiful birds shine forth in full splendor." A reviewer for *Publishers Weekly* also had kind words for Waldman's work on the intergenerational tale *Too Young for Yiddish,* noting that this volume was "handsomely illustrated . . . in a sepia-toned palette recalling old family albums."

In his self-illustrated *The Promised Land,* Waldman takes a look at the beginnings of the Jewish people, tracing the origins from the time of Abraham to Moses and Joshua. Waldman begins with an examination of the promise of the land that God made to Abraham, an act that seems to have sustained the people, according to Waldman, through their long and turbulent history, including the time in Egypt, the Exodus, and Diaspora. A *Kirkus Reviews* critic called this "a straightforward account that sticks to Biblical sources," while Amy Lilien-Harper of *School Library Journal* felt it was "beautifully written but rather obscure." Lilien-Harper further noted that the writing is "lyrical and lovely," but that it is also often rather complex and "requires a certain amount of familiarity of Jewish history." A reviewer for *Publishers Weekly* also noted the demanding text, but found the artwork "consistently moving." Similarly, *Booklist*'s Stephanie Zvirin felt that Waldman's "densely packed text is not quite as successful as his art," which she described as "gorgeous."

## BIOGRAPHICAL AND CRITICAL SOURCES:

*PERIODICALS*

*Booklist,* March 1, 1994, Stephanie Zvirin, review of *The Passover Journey: A Seder Companion,* p. 1260; February 1, 1995, Isabel Schon, review of *Nessa's Story,* p. 1012; November 1, 1999, GraceAnne DeCandido, review of *The Starry Night,* p. 541; March 15, 2001, Randy Meyer, review of *Wounded Knee,* p. 1389; March 1, 2002, Hazel Rochman, review of *Too Young for Yiddish,* p. 1142; October 1, 2002, Stephanie Zvirin, review of *The Promised Land: The Birth of the Jewish People,* p. 344.

*Bulletin of the Center for Children's Books,* December, 1990, Roger Sutton, review of *The Highwayman,* pp. 95-96; June, 1997, Betsy Hearne, review of *The Never-Ending Greenness,* pp. 347-348; October, 1998, Janice M. DelNegro, review of *Masada,* p. 76; December, 2001, Kate McDowell, review of *They Came from the Bronx: How the Buffalo Were Saved from Extinction,* pp. 154-155.

*Childhood Education,* spring, 2002, Mary L. Laub, review of *They Came from the Bronx,* p. 172.

*Horn Book,* May-June, 1994, Hanna B. Zeiger, review of *The Passover Journey,* p. 334; July-August, 1996, Hanna B. Zeiger, review of *Next Year in Jerusalem: 3000 Years of Jewish Stories,* p. 472; July-August, 2001, review of *Wounded Knee,* p. 478.

*Horn Book Guide,* spring, 1998, Maeve Visser Knoth, review of *The Two Brothers: A Legend of Jerusalem,* p. 114; fall, 2001, Maeve Visser Knoth, review of *The Golden City: Jerusalem's 3000 Years,* p. 425.

*Kirkus Reviews,* August 1, 1995, review of *The Golden City,* p. 1118; January 15, 2002, review of *Too Young for Yiddish,* p. 106; September 1, 2002, review of *The Promised Land,* p. 1322.

*Publishers Weekly,* October 14, 1988, review of *Bring Back the Deer,* pp. 71-72; September 14, 1990, review of *The Highwayman,* p. 124; February 13, 1995, review of *Bayou Lullaby,* p. 77; February 3, 1997, review of *The Never-Ending Greenness,* p. 107; August 10, 1998, review of *Masada,* p. 390; February 22, 1999, review of *The Family Haggadah,* p. 86; October 18, 1999, review of *The Starry Night,* p. 80; August 28, 2000, review of *The Wisdom Bird: A Tale of Solomon and Sheba,* p. 78; May 14, 2001, review of *Wounded Knee,* p. 83; August 13, 2001, review of *They Came from the Bronx,* p. 312; January 14, 2002, review of *Too Young for Yiddish,* p. 60; September 9, 2002, review of *The Promised Land,* p. 65.

*Reading Teacher,* April, 1998, review of *The Never-Ending Greenness,* p. 589.

*School Library Journal,* December, 1990, Eleanor K. MacDonald, review of *The Highwayman,* p. 118; January, 1994, Ruth K. MacDonald, review of *The Tyger,* p. 118; April, 1994, Roz Goodman, review of *Nessa's Story,* p. 108; April, 1995, Judy Constantinides, review of *Bayou Lullaby,* p. 97; November, 1995, Susan Scheps, review of *The Golden City: Jerusalem's 3000 Years,* p. 94; January, 1996, Marcia W. Posner, review of *Next Year in Jerusalem,* p. 125; September, 1996, Patricia Lothrop, review of *And the Earth Trembled: The Creation of Adam and Eve,* p. 219; October, 1996, Pam Gosner, review of *Quetzal: Sacred Bird of the Cloud Forest,* p. 138; November, 1998, Susan Scheps, review of *Masada,* pp. 143-144; June, 1999, Yapha Nussbaum Mason, review of *The Family Haggadah,* p. 120; October, 1999, Margaret A. Chang, review of *The Starry Night,* p. 129; October, 2000, Patricia Pear Dole, review of *The Wisdom Bird,* p. 132; May, 2001, Linda Greengrass, review of *Wounded Knee,* p. 172; September, 2002, Amy Lilien-Harper, review of *The Promised Land,* p. 255.

*Sunday Journal-News* (Rockland County, NY), December 30, 1984, John Dalmas, "Neil Waldman: He Has Designs on Postage Stamps."

*ONLINE*

*The Starry Night Web site,* http://www.thestarrynight.com/ (June 22, 2003).*

## WALKER, Pamela

*PERSONAL:* Born in Scottsville, KY.

*ADDRESSES: Home*—Brooklyn, NY. *Agent*—c/o Author Mail, Scholastic, 555 Broadway, New York, NY 10012-3999.

*CAREER:* Author, teacher, and librarian. Worked as a teacher and librarian for twelve years.

*WRITINGS:*

*Pray Hard* (young adult novel), Scholastic (New York, NY), 2001.

*SIDELIGHTS:* Pamela Walker's debut novel *Pray Hard* centers on twelve-year-old Amelia Forrest. It is one year after the sudden death of her father in a small-plane crash, a death for which Amelia secretly feels responsible, and Amelia and her mother have fallen apart in the interim. Her mother has gained fifty pounds and Amelia's grades in school have dropped. But on the morning that Amelia decides to regain control of their lives, sending her mother off to the beauty shop and herself sitting down to study, a mysterious stranger arrives at their door claiming to be a messenger from her father. This man, according to Sharon Grover in *School Library Journal,* "becomes the catalyst that allows Amelia and her mama to regain a sense of purpose in life, and more importantly, to regain their faith." Despite questioning the effectiveness of Walker's open-ended conclusion, *Booklist* reviewer Ilene Cooper called *Pray Hard* "a fine debut from a writer to watch." Writing in *Publishers Weekly,* a critic found Walker's ending "highly satisfying and accomplished in its deference to readers' imaginations."

*BIOGRAPHICAL AND CRITICAL SOURCES:*

PERIODICALS

*Booklist,* March 1, 2001, Ilene Cooper, review of *Pray Hard,* p. 1283.
*Publishers Weekly,* April 9, 2001, review of *Pray Hard,* p. 75.
*School Library Journal,* July, 2001, Sharon Grover, review of *Pray Hard,* p. 115.

ONLINE

*Southern Kentucky Festival of Books,* http://www.soky bookfest.org/Bookfest01/ (May 13, 2003).*

\*       \*       \*

## WATSON, Wendy (McLeod) 1942-

*PERSONAL:* Born July 7, 1942, in Paterson, NJ; daughter of Aldren Auld (an art editor, illustrator, and writer) and Nancy (a writer; maiden name, Dingman) Watson; married Michael Donald Harrah (an actor and opera singer), December 19, 1970; children: two, including Mary Cameron Harrah. *Education:* Bryn Mawr College, B.A. (magna cum laude; with honors; Latin literature), 1964; studied painting with Jerry Farnsworth, Cape Cod, MA, summers, 1961 and 1962, and drawing and painting at National Academy of Design, 1966 and 1967. *Religion:* Society of Friends (Quaker). *Hobbies and other interests:* Theater, music (plays the piano and cello), reading, gardening.

*ADDRESSES: Home*—Southern Vermont. *Agent*—c/o Author Mail, Farrar Straus & Giroux, 19 Union Square W., New York, NY 10001.

*CAREER:* Hanover Press, Hanover, NH, compositor and designer, 1965-66; freelance illustrator of books, 1966—.

*MEMBER:* Authors Guild, Authors League of America.

*AWARDS, HONORS: Fisherman Lullabies* was included in the American Institute of Graphic Arts Children's Book Show, 1967-68; *When Noodlehead Went to the Fair* was included in the Printing Industries of America Graphic Arts Awards Competition, 1969; *New York Times* Outstanding Books citation, 1971, Children's Book Showcase award, Children's Book Council, 1972, and National Book Award finalist, Association of American Publishers, 1972, all for *Father Fox's Pennyrhymes,* which was also included in the American Institute of Graphic Arts Children's Book Show, 1972, and the Biennial of Illustrations, Bratislava, 1973.

*WRITINGS:*

*FOR CHILDREN; SELF-ILLUSTRATED*

*Very Important Cat,* Dodd (New York, NY), 1958.

(Editor) *Fisherman Lullabies,* music by sister, Clyde Watson, World Publishing (Cleveland, OH), 1968.

(Adapter) Jacob Grimm and Wilhelm Grimm, *The Hedgehog and the Hare,* World Publishing (Cleveland, OH), 1969.

*Lollipop,* Crowell (New York, NY), 1976.

*Moving,* Crowell (New York, NY), 1978.

*Has Winter Come?,* Philomel (New York, NY), 1978.

*Jamie's Story,* Philomel (New York, NY), 1981.

*The Bunnies' Christmas Eve,* Philomel (New York, NY), 1983.

*Christmas at Bunny's Inn: A Three Dimensional Advent Calendar with Twenty-four Windows and Doors to Open from December First to Christmas Eve,* Philomel (New York, NY), 1984.

*Little Brown Bear,* Western Publishing (New York, NY), 1985.

*Tales for a Winter's Eve* (short stories), Farrar, Straus (New York, NY), 1988.

*Wendy Watson's Mother Goose,* Lothrop, Lee & Shepard (New York, NY), 1989.

*Wendy Watson's Frog Went A-Courting,* Lothrop, Lee & Shepard (New York, NY), 1990.

*Thanksgiving at Our House,* Houghton (Boston, MA), 1991.

*A Valentine for You,* Houghton (Boston, MA), 1991.

*Boo! It's Halloween,* Clarion (New York, NY), 1992.

*Hurray for the Fourth of July!,* Clarion (New York, NY), 1992.

*Happy Easter Day!,* Clarion (New York, NY), 1993.

*Fox Went Out on a Chilly Night,* Lothrop, Lee & Shepard (New York, NY), 1994.

*Holly's Christmas Eve,* HarperCollins (New York, NY), 2002.

*ILLUSTRATOR*

Yeta Speevach, *The Spider Plant,* Atheneum (New York, NY), 1965.

*A Comic Primer,* Peter Pauper (Mount Vernon, NY), 1966.

*Love Is a Laugh,* Peter Pauper (Mount Vernon, NY), 1967.

*The Country Mouse and the City Mouse,* Stinehour Press (Lunenburg, VT), 1967.

Alice E. Christgau, *Rosabel's Secret,* W. R. Scott, 1967.

Paul Tripp, *The Strawman Who Smiled by Mistake,* Doubleday (New York, NY), 1967.

Edna Boutwell, *Daughter of Liberty,* World Publishing (Cleveland, OH), 1967.

Ogden Nash, *The Cruise of the Aardvark,* M. Evans (New York, NY), 1967.

Henry Wadsworth Longfellow, *Henry Wadsworth Longfellow: Selected Poems,* edited by Clarence Merton Babcock, Peter Pauper Press (Mount Vernon, VT), 1967.

Miska Miles, *Uncle Fonzo's Ford,* Little, Brown (Boston, MA), 1968.

*The Best in Offbeat Humor,* Peter Pauper (Mount Vernon, NY), 1968.

Kathryn Hitte, *When Noodlehead Went to the Fair,* Parents' Magazine Press (New York, NY), 1968.

Nancy Dingman Watson (mother), *Carol to a Child,* music by Clyde Watson, World Publishing (Cleveland, OH), 1969.

Louise Bachelder, compiler, *God Bless Us, Every One,* Peter Pauper (Mount Vernon, NY), 1969.

*The Jack Book,* Macmillan (New York, NY), 1969.

Margaret Davidson, *Helen Keller,* Scholastic (New York, NY), 1969.

Mary H. Calhoun, *Magic in the Alley,* Atheneum (New York, NY), 1970.

Mabel Harmer, *Lizzie, the Lost Toys Witch,* Macrae Smith (Philadelphia, PA), 1970.

Louise Bachelder, compiler, *Happy Thoughts,* Peter Pauper Press (Mount Vernon, VT), 1970.

*How Dear to My Heart,* Peter Pauper (Mount Vernon, NY), 1970.

Clyde Watson, *Father Fox's Pennyrhymes* (verse; also see below), Crowell (New York, NY), 1971, HarperCollins (New York, NY), 2001.

*Life's Wondrous Ways,* Peter Pauper (Mount Vernon, NY), 1971.

*America! America!,* Peter Pauper (Mount Vernon, NY), 1971.

*A Gift of Mistletoe,* Peter Pauper (Mount Vernon, NY), 1971.

Charles Linn, *Probability,* Crowell (New York, NY), 1972.

Clyde Watson, *Tom Fox and the Apple Pie,* Crowell (New York, NY), 1972.

Clyde R. Bulla, *Open the Door and See All the People,* Crowell (New York, NY), 1972.

Bobbie Katz, *Upside Down and Inside Out: Poems for All Your Pockets,* F. Watts (New York, NY), 1973.

Nancy Dingman Watson, *The Birthday Goat,* Crowell (New York, NY), 1974.

Paul Showers, *Sleep Is for Everyone,* Crowell (New York, NY), 1974.

Clyde Watson, *Quips and Quirks,* Crowell (New York, NY), 1975.

Michael Holt, *Maps, Tracks, and the Bridges of Königsberg,* Crowell (New York, NY), 1975.

Nancy Dingman Watson, *Muncus Agruncus: A Bad Little Mouse,* Golden Press (New York, NY), 1976.

Clyde Watson, *Hickory Stick Rag* (verse), Crowell (New York, NY), 1976.

Florence Pettit, *Christmas All around the House: Traditional Decorations You Can Make,* Crowell (New York, NY), 1976.

Clyde Watson, *Binary Numbers* (nonfiction), Crowell (New York, NY), 1977.

Clyde Watson, *Catch Me and Kiss Me and Say It Again* (verse; also see below), Philomel (New York, NY), 1978.

Miska Miles, *Jenny's Cat,* Dutton (New York, NY), 1979.

Clyde Watson, *How Brown Mouse Kept Christmas,* Farrar, Straus (New York, NY), 1980.

Jan Wahl, *Button Eye's Orange,* Warne (New York, NY), 1980.

Anne Pellowski, *Stairstep Farm: Anna Rose's Story,* Philomel (New York, NY), 1981.

Anne Pellowski, *Willow Wind Farm: Betsy's Story,* Philomel (New York, NY), 1981.

Clyde Watson, *Applebet: An ABC,* Farrar, Straus (New York, NY), 1982.

Anne Pellowski, *Winding Valley Farm: Annie's Story,* Philomel (New York, NY), 1982.

Anne Pellowski, *First Farm in the Valley: Anna's Story,* Philomel (New York, NY), 1982.

Rebecca C. Jones, *The Biggest, Meanest, Ugliest Dog in the Whole Wide World,* Macmillan (New York, NY), 1982.

Clyde Watson, *Father Fox's Feast of Songs* (musical adaptations of poems from *Father Fox's Pennyrhymes* and *Catch Me and Kiss Me and Say It Again*), Philomel (New York, NY), 1983.

Anne Pellowski, *Betsy's Up-and-Down Year,* Philomel (New York, NY), 1983.

Carolyn Haywood, *Happy Birthday from Carolyn Haywood,* Morrow (New York, NY), 1984.

Elaine Edelman, *I Love My Baby Sister (Most of the Time),* Lothrop, Lee & Shepard (New York, NY), 1984.

Elizabeth Winthrop, *Belinda's Hurricane,* Dutton (New York, NY), 1984.

John Bierhorst, *Doctor Coyote: A Native American Aesop's Fables,* Macmillan (New York, NY), 1987.

Marcia Leonard, *Angry,* Bantam (New York, NY), 1988.

Marcia Leonard, *Happy,* Bantam (New York, NY), 1988.

Marcia Leonard, *Scared,* Bantam (New York, NY), 1988.

Marcia Leonard, *Silly,* Bantam (New York, NY), 1988.

Clyde Watson, *Valentine Foxes,* Orchard Books (New York, NY), 1989.

B. G. Hennessy, *A, B, C, D, Tummy, Toes, Hands, Knees,* Viking Kestrel (New York, NY), 1989.

Clement Clarke Moore, *The Night before Christmas,* Clarion (New York, NY), 1990.

Clyde Watson, *Love's a Sweet,* Viking Penguin (New York, NY), 1998.

John Bierhorst, *Is My Friend at Home?: Pueblo Fireside Tales,* Farrar Straus (New York, NY), 2000.

Patricia Hubbell, *Rabbit Moon: A Book of Holidays and Celebrations,* Marshall Cavendish (New York, NY), 2002.

Clyde Watson, *Father Fox's Christmas Rhymes,* Farrar Straus (New York, NY), 2003.

*SIDELIGHTS:* An author and illustrator of books for children under the age of ten, Wendy Watson is most often recognized for her artistic work, especially when it accompanies stories written by her sister, Clyde Watson. The sisters' award-winning collaboration *Father Fox's Pennyrhymes* was widely praised by critics, including *New York Times Book Review* contributor George A. Woods, who called the book "an American original." Watson has gone on to produce many more titles for young readers, a score of which are her own self-illustrated works, and the rest done in collaboration with writers such as her sister, her mother—the writer Nancy Dingman Watson—and other notable authors from Ogden Nash to Anne Pellowski.

Watson once told *CA:* "My parents provided, indirectly, a great deal of my basic training in drawing and books in general." Watson was born in New Jersey, but grew up on a farm in Putney, Vermont, with her seven siblings, her artist father, and writer mother. Surrounded by animals—goats, horses and chickens—Watson also grew up in the company of art, for her father, Aldren, had his studio on the third floor of the house. Books were present everywhere as well, including those published by her mother, Nancy. Watson's "cheerful, homey illustrations reflect this rural upbringing," according to a contributor for *Children's Books and Their Creators.*

Watson attended Bryn Mawr College, majoring in Latin literature and graduating in 1964. However, from the time she was a young child, she knew she wanted to become an illustrator; during her college summers and thereafter, she received formal training from Jerry Farnsworth, Helen Sawyer, and Daniel Greene both on Cape Cod and at the National Academy of Design in 1966 and 1967. Her father also helped in her art training. Following college graduation, Watson worked for a time at a small press in New Hampshire where she was a compositor and designer, learning much about typography and design that would be invaluable to her in her book-illustrating career. In 1970 Watson married the opera singer and actor, Michael Donald Harrah.

Watson's career as a professional author and illustrator got underway in 1958—when she was only sixteen—with the publication of the self-illustrated *Very Important Cat.* Throughout the 1960s, she went on to illustrate a score of titles by other others, until she made her name with *Father Fox's Pennyrhymes,* written by her sister, Clyde. This fox entertains his large family around the fire on wintry nights with rhymes, telling of love and family life, as well as topics including gluttony and the love of song. Watson's illustrations for her sister's title were warmly received by critics and helped win the book a nomination for a National Book Award as well as inclusion in the 1972 Children's Book Showcase. The contributor for *Children's Books and Their Creators* noted that "the pen-and-ink and watercolor illustrations" for this book "depict the changing seasons of rural New England life and the chaos and warmth of family life."

The drawings for *Father Fox's Pennyrhymes* are typical of the artist's style. Having spent most of her life in Vermont, Watson creates illustrations that exude a New England country charm—"cheerful, old-fashioned illustrations," as one *Publishers Weekly* contributor characterized them in a review of *A Valentine for You.* "Her colors have a real integrity that seems to derive from the New England light," Christina Olson observed of *Wendy Watson's Mother Goose* in a *New York Times Book Review* article.

Another quality of many of Watson's illustrations is their attention to small details. A picture by Watson is often filled with objects and bustling with activity that catches the reader's eye. This aspect of her work is especially evident in books like *Wendy Watson's Frog Went A-Courting.* But while a *Publishers Weekly* reviewer remarked that "youngsters will enjoy seeking out the many droll details" in the illustrations, Olson, writing in *New York Times Book Review,* felt in this case that the "frenetic" nature of the pictures does not mesh well with the "rhythms of the text." But, for Olson, this was a small complaint when compared to the quality of the artist's work in general. "Wendy Watson is, after all," the critic concluded, "an illustrator who knows what she is doing. There is a sweetness in her work that is unfailingly appealing, and she produces thoughtful and well-made books."

Other collaborative efforts with her sister include such titles as *Tom Fox and the Apple Pie, Catch Me and Kiss Me and Say It Again, How Brown Mouse Kept Christmas, Father Fox's Feast of Songs, Love's a Sweet,* and the 2003 *Father Fox's Christmas Rhymes.* Most of these have a simple rhyming text, easily memorized by young readers or listeners, accompanied by Watson's watercolor illustrations which reveal an appreciation for family life and the fine details of childhood. A reviewer for *Horn Book,* for example, praised her "jolly, decorative illustrations" for *Father Fox's Feast of Songs.* Teaming up on her sister's collection of poems showing the ups and downs of love, *Love's a Sweet,* Watson supplies "lively colored pencil drawing that skip across the pages," according to *Booklist*'s Kathy Broderick. A critic for *Publishes Weekly* found the artwork for that same title "sweetly misted but witty," as well as "serene and soothing."

Watson has also used her own rural background, growing up in a large, loving, and boisterous family, as inspiration for her illustrations for the works of Anne Pellowski about farm families in Wisconsin, including *First Farm in the Valley: Anna's Story, Stairstep Farm: Anna Rose's Story,* and *Willow Wind Farm: Betsy's Story.* With John Bierhorst, she has worked on a duet of books involving the Native American trickster, Coyote. The 1987 volume *Doctor Coyote: A Native American Aesop's Fables* presents a bevy of Aztec interpretations of Aesop's fables. Bierhorst returned to such Coyote tales with the 2001 title *Is My Friend At Home?: Pueblo Fireside Tales,* a compilation of seven trickster tales from the Hopi tradition. Rosalyn Pierini, writing in *School Library Journal,* felt that Watson's "child-centered, humorous illustrations enliven the text and lend a great deal of personality to these archetypal characters." Similarly, *Horn Book*'s Nell D. Beram noted that Watson's cartoon-like illustrations "capture the spirit of these disarmingly absurd, unexpectedly touching tales." Rabbits take center stage in a collaborative effort with writer Patricia Hubbell for the 2002 *Rabbit Moon: A Book of Holidays and Celebrations.* Piper L. Nyman wrote in *School Library Journal* that the "adorable characters cavort over the spreads."

Watson has produced several books around the theme of holidays and celebrations. Christmas is featured in Clement Clarke Moore's traditional poem *The Night before Christmas,* an "utterly charming version," as a contributor for *Publishers Weekly* observed. Gathering several well-known rhymes and songs about love in *A Valentine for You,* Watson created "a fetching gift for a young Valentine," according to a reviewer for *Publishers Weekly.* In *Thanksgiving at Our House,* she presents an original story which contains traditional songs and rhymes, along with full-page artwork in "a pleasantly cluttered book," as another *Publishers Weekly* contributor described the book. The extended family featured in that book prepares for the big feast, and Watson's illustrations manage to "capture the high-spirited anticipation," according to the same critic. Independence Day receives the same treatment in *Hurray for the Fourth of July!,* featuring the family in a "heartening portrait of a holiday celebration in a small American town," as a contributor for *Publishers Weekly* commented. Watson once again peppers her original tale with traditional rhymes and songs, as well as her own artwork. She reprises the same family in *Happy Easter Day,* as the clan prepares hot-cross buns and Easter eggs for the holiday. The birth of five kittens turns out to be the biggest Easter surprise of all. Virginia Opocensky, writing in *School Library Journal,* dubbed this effort "a delightful addition for holiday shelves," and further praised Watson's illustrations, which are "bustling with activity and details." An *Entertainment Weekly* contributor also lauded Watson's "jolly" illustrations in this same work.

Watson provides her own take on foxes in *Fox Went Out on a Chilly Night,* a retelling of an old folk song about the fox who manages to go out at night to provide food for its young brood of kits, evading and eluding all the townsfolk who are soon in hot pursuit. A contributor for *Kirkus Reviews* found Watson's ad-

aptation a worthwhile addition, especially because of the artwork "that gives the classic a heft you can almost bite into." While *Booklist*'s Mary Harris Veeder commented that Watson's illustrations "supply the motivation that sends [fox] out" in the evening, a *Publishers Weekly* reviewer suggested that "Watson's timeless illustrations offer abundant particulars to pore over."

With the self-illustrated 2002 *Holly's Christmas Eve,* Watson returns to holiday themes in a tale of a painted wooden ornament on the Christmas tree who goes in search of her missing arm. Holly is the most recent addition to the ornaments, but when the family cat crawls up the tree, Holly is knocked down, losing her arm in the process. The vacuum cleaner proceeds to gobble it up, but Holly, joined by other ornaments, including the Tin Horse and Cloth Bear, make an expedition to retrieve the lost arm. She finds the missing appendage and, with the help of Santa, manages to repair it. Once again, Watson scored a winner, both in text and artwork, according to the critics. In a *School Library Journal* review, Maureen Wade praised the "vivid, full page . . . artwork [that] captures the drama and satisfying ending." *Booklist*'s Ilene Cooper also commended Watson's illustrations, which have "the exuberance and simplicity of children's own art." And a *Kirkus Reviews* critic focused on the text, noting that though the story is "simple," Watson blends "amusing characters" and a "folksy narrative voice . . . into a satisfying, if unusual, Christmas Eve tale."

From foxes to chaotic and happy families, Watson has portrayed a myriad of characters and activities in her warm, family-oriented tales and illustrations. Blending humor and traditional scenes, Watson has created a body of work praised by critics and honored by awards committees. Watson's "honest, often wise stories and detailed country illustrations are full of joy and life," concluded the contributor for *Children's Books and Their Creators.*

*BIOGRAPHICAL AND CRITICAL SOURCES:*

*BOOKS*

Silvey, Anita, editor, *Children's Books and Their Creators,* Houghton Mifflin (Boston, MA), 1995.

*PERIODICALS*

*Booklist,* March 1, 1993, Deborah Abbott, review of *Happy Easter Day!,* p. 1233; September 1, 1994, Mary Harris Veeder, review of *Fox Went Out on a Chilly Night,* p. 47; August, 1997, Hazel Rochman, review of *Sleep Is for Everyone,* p. 1904; December 1, 1998, Kathy Broderick, review of *Love's a Sweet,* p. 668; September 15, 2002, Ilene Cooper, review of *Holly's Christmas Eve,* p. 247.

*Entertainment Weekly,* March 11, 1994, review of *Happy Easter Day!,* p. 72.

*Horn Book,* October, 1971, p. 474; January, 1989, p. 64; March-April, 1993, review of *Father Fox's Feast of Songs,* p. 232; September-October, 2001, Nell D. Beram, review of *Is My Friend Home?,* p. 600.

*Kirkus Reviews,* October 15, 1994, review of *Fox Went Out on a Chilly Night,* p. 1418; November 1, 2002, review of *Holly's Christmas Eve,* p. 1627.

*New York Times Book Review,* August 15, 1971, George A. Woods, review of *Father Fox's Pennyrhymes,* p. 8; May 27, 1990, Christina Olson, "Children's Books," p. 18.

*Publishers Weekly,* April 27, 1990, review of *Wendy Watson's Frog Went A-Courting,* p. 60; September 14, 1990, review of *The Night before Christmas,* p. 123; January 25, 1991, review of *A Valentine for You,* p. 56; July 25, 1991, review of *Thanksgiving at Our House,* pp. 52-53; March 9, 1992, review of *Hurray for the Fourth of July!,* p. 55; October 17, 1994, review of *Fox Went Out on a Chilly Night,* p. 80; October 26, 1998, review of *Love's a Sweet,* p. 65.

*School Library Journal,* April, 1993, Virginia Opocensky, review of *Happy Easter Day!,* p. 116; August, 1997, Marsha McGrath, review of *Sleep Is for Everyone,* pp. 150-151; October, 1994, Roseanne Cerny, review of *Fox Went Out on a Chilly Night,* p. 116; January, 1999, Marlene Gawron, review of *Love's a Sweet,* p. 122; September, 2001, Rosalyn Pierini, review of *Is My Friend Home?,* p. 211; June, 2002, Piper L. Nyman, review of *Rabbit Moon: A Book of Holidays and Celebrations,* pp. 97-98; October, 2002, Maureen Wade, review of *Holly's Christmas Eve,* pp. 64-65.

*ONLINE*

*VisitingAuthors,* http://www.visitingauthors.com/ (June 29, 2003), "Wendy Watson's Biography and Books."*

# WAYLAND, April Halprin 1954-

*PERSONAL:* Born April 20, 1954, in Los Angeles, CA; daughter of Leahn J. (a farmer) and Saralee (a concert pianist; maiden name, Konigsberg) Halprin; married Gary Carlton Wayland (a certified public accountant), October 17, 1981; children: Jeffrey. *Education:* University of California—Davis, B.S. (cum laude), 1976. *Religion:* Jewish.

*ADDRESSES: Home*—143 South Kenter Ave., Los Angeles, CA 90049. *Agent*—Curtis Brown, Ltd., 10 Astor Place, New York, NY 10003.

*CAREER:* Children's book writer and speaker. Worked variously as a farmer, a government housing study worker for the Rand Corporation, a governess for comedian and talk show host Joan Rivers's daughter, and a marketing manager for Pacific Bell. Cofounder, Positive Education Inc. (nonprofit tutorial agency).

*MEMBER:* Authors Guild, Authors League of America, PEN, Society of Children's Book Writers and Illustrators, Association of Booksellers for Children, Southern California Children's Booksellers Association, Southern California Council on Literature for Children and Young People, Santa Monica Traditional Folk Music Club (founder, 1978).

*AWARDS, HONORS: To RabbitTown* was named a Junior Literary Guild selection, 1989, and was selected as a "Book of the Year" by Mommycare.

*WRITINGS:*

*To RabbitTown,* illustrated by Robin Spowart, Scholastic (New York, NY), 1989.

*The Night Horse,* illustrated by Vera Rosenberry, Scholastic (New York, NY), 1991.

*It's Not My Turn to Look for Grandma!,* illustrated by George Booth, Knopf (New York, NY), 1995.

*Girl Coming in for a Landing: A Novel in Poems,* illustrated by Elaine Clayton, Random House (New York, NY), 2002.

Contributor to anthologies edited by Myra Cohn Livingston, including *Poems for Mothers,* Margaret McElderry Books (New York, NY), 1990; *If the Owl*

*Calls Again,* Margaret McElderry Books (New York, NY), 1990; *Poems for Brothers, Poems for Sisters,* Holiday House (New York, NY), 1991; and *Roll Along: Poems on Wheels,* Margaret McElderry Books (New York, NY), 1993.

*ADAPTATIONS:* Wayland's stories for children were adapted for radio broadcast on *Halfway down the Stairs,* KPFK-FM.

*WORK IN PROGRESS:* "A billion books."

*SIDELIGHTS:* April Halprin Wayland is the author of several picture books for young readers, as well as *Girl Coming in for a Landing: A Novel in Poems,* a book for older readers that a *Kirkus* reviewer described as "utterly fresh and winning." In the picture books *The Night Horse,* and *It's Not My Turn to Look for Grandma!* she explores children's relationships to animals and people using humor and whimsy. "I see my books as mixtures of colors," she once explained to *CA.* "I want each to be as clear and as strong and as beautiful as it can be. I love the picture book format."

"To rebel in my family, you had to join management in a Fortune 500 company and wear a suit every day," Wayland once quipped. The daughter of a farmer and a concert pianist, Wayland grew up in Santa Monica, California, and spent her holidays and vacations at the family farm in Yuba City, five hundred miles north. While she began writing when she was thirteen years old, music was also an abiding interest; she played violin as a child and founded the Santa Monica Traditional Folk Music Club in her late twenties.

After graduating from college, Wayland held an assortment of jobs. She helped run the family farm after her father's death, worked as a governess, and co-founded a nonprofit tutorial organization called Positive Education, Inc. She finally entered the corporate world by going to work for Pacific Bell, where she became a marketing manager. Despite the job security, she still held dreams of becoming a writer, and after creating a picture book for her nephew, Joshua, she was hooked. "It wasn't brilliant literature, but I illustrated, xeroxed, laminated, and bound it," she recalled. "The night I finished it, I was so jazzed, I couldn't sleep."

Wayland published *To RabbitTown,* her first book for children, in 1989, and has continued to add to the list in the years since. *To RabbitTown* follows a young girl who is magically transformed into a rabbit, while *The Night Horse* is a gentle tale of another young girl who travels through the night sky on a horse who feeds on the stars. Wayland's 1995 picture book *It's Not My Turn to Look for Grandma!* introduces young listeners to Woolie, whose grandmother can never be found when there is work to be done around the house. While Ma asks Woolie and his siblings to fetch the elderly woman to help with chores throughout the day, each child comes back empty-handed until the evening, when Ma asks fun-loving Grandma to pluck a tune on her banjo—words and music included! Praising the story's "lively mountain twang," *School Library Journal* reviewer Virginia E. Jeschelnig called *It's Not My Turn to Look for Grandma!* a "silly good time for all," while a *Kirkus Reviews* critic dubbed it a story with "so much pep readers will swear it's been handed down for generations."

In 2002 Wayland expanded into the novel format by penning *Girl Coming in for a Landing.* Written in free verse, the book follows a young teen's high school year. In what *Booklist* contributor Gillian Engberg called a "warm and authentic" voice, Wayland describes such universal female coming-of-age experiences as a first crush, boredom, sibling rivalry, shyness, starting to shave one's legs, getting one's period, and dreaming about the future—in a text that Engberg noted "get[s] right to the heart of situations and emotions." Praising Wayland for adding a section on reading and writing verse that provides encouragement to teens who would "otherwise find these tasks intimidating," a *Publishers Weekly* contributor maintained that *Girl Coming in for a Landing* successfully reflects "the voice of a sensitive girl approaching adolescence."

Wayland once remarked, "I can't say enough about the community of children's book writers in Southern California. Teachers have become mentors and friends—everyone generously shares his/her knowledge. I thrive in groups, and this community (in addition to my husband) has had much to do with the joy I find in my career." She added, "I once decided that I wanted to publish 133 children's books by my ninetieth birthday. Then I re-read *Charlotte's Web* by E. B. White and I realized that *one* wonderful book was enough. So my new goal is to write each book as brilliantly as I can."

*BIOGRAPHICAL AND CRITICAL SOURCES:*

PERIODICALS

*Booklist,* October 15, 2002, Gillian Engberg, review of *Girl Coming in for a Landing,* p. 400.
*Kirkus Reviews,* May 15, 1995, review of *It's Not My Turn to Look for Grandma!,* p. 717; June 15, 2002, review of *Girl Coming in for a Landing,* p. 889.
*Publishers Weekly,* January 13, 1989, p. 87; June 26, 1995, review of *It's Not My Turn to Look for Grandma!,* p. 106; July 8, 2002, review of *Girl Coming in for a Landing,* p. 50.
*School Library Journal,* April, 1989, p. 92; April, 1991, p. 104; August, 1995, Virginia E. Jeschelnig, review of *It's Not My Turn to Look for Grandma!,* p. 131; August, 2002, Lauralyn Persson, review of *Girl Coming in for a Landing,* p. 220.

ONLINE

*April Halprin Wayland Web Site,* http://www.april wayland.com/ (June 29, 2003).*

\*       \*       \*

**WEBSTER, Gary**
    **See GARRISON, Webb B(lack)**

\*       \*       \*

**WEDEKIND, (Benjamin) Frank(lin) 1864-1918**
    **(Cornelius Minehaha)**

*PERSONAL:* Born July 24, 1864, in Hanover, Germany; died March 9, 1918, in Munich, Germany; son of a physician and an actress; married Tilly Newes (an actress; died, 1917); children: two daughters. *Education:* Attended University of Lausanne, 1884, University of Munich, 1884-85, and University of Zurich, 1888.

*CAREER:* Playwright. Worked in advertising, 1866-68; secretary with a circus, 1888; also worked as a staff member of satirical magazine *Simplizissimus,* and as a singer and actor; acted in some of his own plays.

*Frank Wedekind*

*WRITINGS:*

PLAYS

*Frühlings Erwachen* (title means "Spring's Awakening"; produced in Berlin, Germany, November 22, 1906), Gross, 1891; translation by Francis J. Ziegler published as *The Awakening of Spring,* Brown, 1909; also translation by S. A. Eliot published as *Spring's Awakening* (also see below); translation by Eric Bentley published in *The Modern Theatre,* Volume 6, 1960; translation by Tom Osborn published as *Spring Awakening,* 1969; and translation by Edward Bond, 1980.
*Kinder und Narren: Lustspiel in vier Aufzugen,* Warth, 1891, revised as *Die junge Welt: Komödie in drei Aufzugen und einem Vorspeil* (first produced in Munich, Germany, April 22, 1908), Langen, 1896.
*Der Erdgeist* (title means "Earth Spirit"; produced in Leipzig, Germany, February 25, 1898), published as *Der Erdgeist: Eine Tragödie,* Langen, 1895; translation by S. A. Eliot published as *Erdgeist (Earth-Spirit): A Tragedy in Four Acts* (also see below), Boni, 1914.

*Der Kammersänger* (produced in Berlin, Germany, December 10, 1899), published as *Der Kammersänger: Drei Szenen,* Langen, 1899, translation published as *Heart of a Tenor,* 1913; translation by Alber Wilhelm Bösche published as *The Court Singer,* German Publication Society, 1914; translation by André Tridon published as *The Tenor,* 1921.

*Der Schnellmaler; oder, Kunst und Mammon* (first produced in Munich, Germany, July 29, 1916), Schnabelitz, 1889.

*Liebestrank* (first produced in 1900; produced in Nuremberg, Germany, October 24, 1903), published as *Der Liebestrank: Schwank in drei Aufzugen,* Langen, 1899.

*Der Marquis von Keith* (produced in Berlin, Germany, October 11, 1901), published as *Der Marquis von Keith (Münchner Scenen): Schauspiel in fünf Aufzugen,* Langen, 1901, translation by Beatrice Gottlieb published as *The Marquis of Keith,* University of Denver Press (Denver, CO), 1952, new edition edited by Wolfgang Hartwig, 1965; translation by Carl Richard Müller published in *The Modern Theatre,* edited by R. W. Corrigan, 1964.

*So ist das Leben* (produced in Munich, Germany, February 22, 1902, revised as *König Nicolo; oder, So ist das Leben,* produced in Leipzig, Germany, January 15, 1919), published as *So ist das Leben: Schauspiel in fünf Akten,* Langen, 1902, translation by Francis J. Ziegler published as *Such Is Life,* Brown, 1912.

*Die Kaiserin von Neufundland* (pantomime), first produced, 1902.

*Die Büchse der Pandora: Eine Tragödie in drei Aufzugen* (produced in Nuremberg, Germany, February 1, 1904; produced as *Die Büchse der Pandora: Eine Monstretragödie,* in Hamburg, Germany, February 13, 1988), Cassirer, 1904, revised edition, Müller, 1911; translation by Carl Richard Müller published as *Pandora's Box* (also see below), 1918.

*Hidalla; oder, Sein und Haben: Schauspiel in fünf Akten* (first produced, 1905), Larchlewski, 1904, revised as *Karl Hetmann, der Zwerg-Riese (Hidalla): Schauspiel in fünf Akten* (produced in Munich, Germany, February 18, 1905), Müller, 1911.

*Lulu* (produced in Nuremberg, Germany, April 18, 1905), published in *Lulu: Tragödie in fünf Aufzugen mit einem Prolog,* Müller, 1913; translation by Carl Richard Müller published as *The Lulu Plays,* 1967.

*Totentanz* (produced in Nuremberg, Germany, May 2, 1906, revised as *Tod und Teufel,* in Berlin, Germany, April 29, 1912), published as *Totentanz: Drei Szenen,* Langen, 1906; translation by Samuel Eliot published as *Damnation!;* translation by Stephen Spender and Frances Fawcett published as *Death and Devil* (also see below).

*Musik* (produced in Nuremberg, Germany, January 11, 1908), published as *Musik: Sittengemälde in vier Bildern,* Langen, 1908.

*Die Zensur* (produced in Munich, Germany, July 27, 1909), published as *Die Zensur: Theodizee in einem Akt,* Cassirer, 1908.

*Oaha: Die Satire der Satire* (produced in Munich, Germany, December 23, 1911, revised as *Till Eulenspiegel,* in Munich, Germany, December 1, 1916), published as *Oaha: Schauspiel in fünf Aufzugen,* Cassirer, 1908, revised as *Der Stein der Weisen; oder, Laute, Armbrust und Peitsche: Eine Geisterbeschworung* (produced in Vienna, Austria, January 23, 1911), Müller, 1920.

*In allen Sätteln gerecht: Komödie in einem Aufzug,* Müller, 1910.

*Mit allen Hunden gehetzt: Schauspiel in einem Aufzug,* Müller, 1910.

*In allen Wassern gewaschen: Tragödie in einem Aufzug,* Müller, 1910.

*Felix und Galathea* (produced in Munich, Germany, July 25, 1914), Meyer, 1911.

*Schloss Wetterstein* (produced in Zurich, Switzerland, November 17, 1917), Müller, 1912; translation by Stephen Spender and Frances Fawcett published as *Castle Wetterstein,* in *Five Tragedies of Sex* (also see below), 1952.

*Franziska* (produced in Munich, Germany, November 30, 1912), Müller, 1912.

*Simson; oder, Scham und Eifersucht* (produced in Berlin, Germany, January 24, 1914), Müller, 1914.

*Bismarck* (produced in Weimar, Germany, October 30, 1926), Müller, 1916.

*Überfurchtenichts* (produced, 1919), Müller, 1917.

*Herakles* (produced in Munich, Germany, September 1, 1919), Müller, 1917.

*Elins Erweckung,* produced in Hamburg, Germany, March 16, 1919.

*Das Sonnenspektrum* (produced in Berlin, Germany, September 23, 1922), translation by D. Faehl and E. Vaughn published as *The Solar Spectrum,* in *Tulane Drama Review,* Volume 4, 1959.

*Tragedies of Sex,* translation by Samuel A. Eliot, Jr., Henderson, 1923.

*Ein Genussmensch: Schauspiel in vier Aufzugen,* edited by Fritz Strich, Müller, 1924.

*Five Tragedies of Sex* (includes *Spring's Awakening, Earth-Spirit, Death and Devil,* and *Castle Wetterstein*); translation by Frances Fawcett and Stephen Spender, Vision, 1952, Theatre Arts, 1952, reprinted without *Spring's Awakening* as *The Lulu Plays and Other Sex Tragedies;* translation by Stephen Spender, Riverrun, 1977.

*The Lulu Plays* (includes *Pandora's Box*); translation by Carl Richard Müller, Fawcett (New York, NY), 1967.

*The First Lulu,* Applause Theatre Books, 1993.

COLLECTIONS

*Gesammelte Werke,* nine volumes, edited by Artur Kutcher and Joachim Friedenthal, Müller, 1912-21.

*Ausgewählte Werke,* five volumes, edited by Fritz Strich, Volksverband der Bücherfreunde, 1924.

*Prosa, Dramen, Verse,* two volumes, edited by Hans-Georg Maier, 1954-60.

*Werke,* three volumes, edited by Manfred Han, Aufbau, 1969.

*Frank Wedekind: Four Major Plays,* translation by Carl Richard Müller, Smith & Kraus (Lyme, NH), 2000.

OTHER

*Die Fürstin Russalka* (fiction), Langen, 1897, translation by Frederick Eisemann published as *Princess Russalka,* Luce, 1919.

*Mine-Haha; oder, Über die körperliche Erziehung der jungen Mädchen: Aus Helene Engels schriftlichem Nachlass heraugegeben* (fiction), Langen, 1903.

*Die vier Jahreszeiten: Gedichte* (poetry), Langen, 1905.

*Feuerwerk: Erzählungen* (short stories), Langen, 1906, translation by Francis Ziegler published as *The Grisley Suitor,* Brown, 1911.

*Schauspielkunst: Ein Glossarium* (nonfiction), Müller, 1910, translation by Carl Richard Müller published as "The Art of Acting: A Glossary," in *The Modern Theatre,* Macmillan, 1964.

*Rabbi Ezra; The Victim: Two Stories* (originally published in German as *Rabbi Esra*), translation by Francis J. Ziegler, Brown, 1911.

*Lautenlieder: 53 Lieder mit eigenen und fremden Melodien* (poetry), edited by Artur Kutscher, Drei Masken, 1920.

*Gesammelte Briefe* (correspondence), two volumes, edited by Fritz Strich, 1924.

*Das arme Mädchen: Ein Chanson* (song), Thorbecke, 1948.

*Chansons* (songs), Desch, 1951.

*Selbstdarstellung,* edited by Willi Reich, 1954.

*Ich hab meine Tante geschlachtet: Lautenlieder und "Simplizissimus": Gedichte* (poetry), edited by Manfred Hahn, 1967.

*Der vermummte Herr: Briefe, 1881-1917* (correspondence), edited by Wolfdietrich Rasch, 1967.

*Gedichte und Chansons* (poems and songs), Bucherei, 1968.

*Die Tagebücher: Ein erotisches Leben,* edited by Gerhard Hay, Athenaeum, 1986, translation by W. E. Yuill published as *Diary of an Erotic Life,* Blackwell, 1990.

*Lieder zur Gitarre* (songs), selected and edited by Johannes Tappert, Hofmeister (Leipzig, Germany), 2001.

Sometimes published under the name Cornelius Minehaha.

*SIDELIGHTS:* German playwright Frank Wedekind's dramas are primarily concerned with attacking the hypocrisies of society, particularly the prohibitions against discussing sexuality. Though Wedekind avoided identification with any literary movement, his attacks on naturalism and his theatrical innovations made him a forerunner of both expressionism and the theater of the absurd. Wedekind's works introduced many of the techniques of modern dramaturgy to the German stage, including stylized, nonrealistic dialogue, an episodic format, grotesque characters, and bizarre plots.

The son of a physician and an actress, Wedekind moved with his family to Switzerland to escape Germany's instability and social repression. As a young man he reluctantly obeyed his father's request to attend classes at the University of Zurich's law school, foregoing his literary interests, but his father's unexpected death freed Wedekind from his studies, and his inheritance allowed him to enjoy life in Paris and London for some time. Whether abroad or back home in Germany, Wedekind chose the bohemian life, expressing contempt for what he considered the repressed, hypocritical middle class.

One of Wedekind's first plays, *Frühlings Erwachen* (later translated as *Spring's Awakening*), shocked its audience, for it dealt graphically with adolescent sexuality. Critics commended the work for shedding light on a taboo subject; enraged citizens, however, attacked Wedekind's portrayal of parents and teachers as repressive for keeping children ignorant of basic biological facts. The theme of sex and its power recurs in many of Wedekind's works. In the "Lulu" plays, *Der Erdgeist* ("The Earth-Spirit") and *Die Büchse der Pandora: Eine Tragödie in drei Aufzugen* (translated as *Pandora's Box*) Lulu, the sensual, predatory female, attracts and destroys men through their own passions until she meets a grisly death at the hands of Jack the Ripper. Though Lulu is sexually adept, she is portrayed by Wedekind as a primitive individual in constant conflict with a hypocritical society. Such characters are found throughout Wedekind's works. Because his aim was to force his audience to recognize how distorted conventional views of life were, Wedekind's characters are not fully realized portraits but exaggerated caricatures that embody specific ideas. They speak not *to* each other, but *at* each other, suggesting the alienation of modern life. The plays themselves are often disjointed and loosely connected and invariably concern the confrontation between society and the social outcast. Because Wedekind considered antisocial behavior heroic, criminals and prostitutes are usually the most admirable characters in his dramas. For example, in *Der Marquis von Keith* (*The Marquis of Keith*) the protagonist is a clever conman who almost succeeds in duping society by preying upon its weaknesses.

The audience of Wedekind's day regarded his plays as pornographic, and his work was repeatedly banned by the German censors. In addition, he received a prison term in 1899 for writing a poem satirizing Kaiser Wilhelm. Although his professed aim was usually to shock, Wedekind did so with the hope of enlightening and reeducating the public; for this reason he became very outspoken in defense of his work. After the turn of the century his plays became more autobiographical, often portraying a misunderstood artist in revolt against society. He acted in major roles in these plays, and often entertained in cabarets by performing his ballads. The public eventually grew used to him and his later dramas were met with a modest level of acclaim.

Wedekind's work exerted a strong influence on twentieth-century German drama, particularly on the

plays and aesthetic theories of Bertolt Brecht, who called Wedekind "one of the great educators of the new Europe." His work forms a solid bridge between naturalistic realism and modern German drama. Though banned by the Nazis and neglected after World War II, his plays were frequently revived throughout the 1960s, when the shock value of his work had been dissipated and more serious attention could be paid to his ideas.

## BIOGRAPHICAL AND CRITICAL SOURCES:

*BOOKS*

*Encyclopedia of World Literature*, St. James Press (Detroit, MI), 1999.

*PERIODICALS*

*Boston University Journal,* Volume 23, number 2, 1975, pp. 40-47.
*Central European History,* September, 1979, pp. 203-236.
*Chicago,* May, 1992, pp. 71-72.
*Colloquia Germanica,* Volume 19, 1986, pp. 47-67.
*Germanic Review,* Volume 43, 1968, pp. 163-87; summer, 1982, pp. 115-122.
*German Life and Letters,* April, 1985, pp. 205-232; January, 1989, pp. 113-128.
*German Quarterly,* March, 1966.
*German Studies Review,* February, 1984, pp. 27-38.
*Modern Language Review,* July, 1979, pp. 631-647; April, 1984, pp. 336-355; January, 1987, pp. 119-141.
*Monatshefte,* Volume 72, 1980, pp. 26-38.
*New Literary History,* winter, 1983, pp. 359-372.
*New Statesman & Society,* March 22, 1991, p. 37; November 6, 1992, p. 45.
*New York,* August 22, 1988, pp. 141-142.
*New York Times Book Review,* November 18, 1990, p. 13.
*Opera News,* March 26, 1988, pp. 28-32.
*Oxford German Studies,* Volume 9, February, 1978, pp. 105-118.
*Performing Arts Journal,* Volume 30, number 10, 1986-87, pp. 102-117.
*Publications of the English Goethe Society,* Volume 56, 1987, pp. 56-73.
*Seminar,* spring, 1969, pp. 21-35; Volume 15, 1979, pp. 235-243, pp. 244-250.*

## WELTON, Jude 1955-

*PERSONAL:* Born February 13, 1955, in Hythe, England; daughter of John and Audrey Welton; partner of David Edgar (a university lecturer); children: John James. *Education:* Nottingham University, B.A. (honors first class), 1976 and M.A., 1980.

*ADDRESSES: Office*—c/o Author Mail, Dorling Kindersley, 9 Henrietta St., Covent Garden, London WC2E 8PS, England.

*CAREER:* Author of books for young adults. Worked in a children's home, 1976-78; Marshall Cavendish, London, England, editor, 1981-88; George Philip Ltd., London, editor, 1989; freelance author, 1990—.

*WRITINGS:*

*"EYEWITNESS ART" SERIES*

*Monet,* Dorling Kindersley (New York, NY), 1993.
*Impressionism,* Dorling Kindersley (New York, NY), 1993.
*Looking at Paintings,* Dorling Kindersley (New York, NY), 1994.
*Gauguin,* Dorling Kindersley (New York, NY), 1994.

*"ARTISTS IN THEIR TIME" SERIES*

*Henri Matisse,* Franklin Watts (New York, NY), 2002.
*Marc Chagall,* Franklin Watts (New York, NY), 2003.

*OTHER*

*Impressionist Gardens,* Studio Editions, 1993.
*Impressionist Landscapes,* Studio Editions, 1993.
*Mothers in Art,* Studio Editions, 1994.
*Drawing: A Young Artist's Guide,* Dorling Kindersley (London, England), 1994.

Contributor to children's literature series *Classic Adventure,* and periodicals, including *Discovering Opera.*

*SIDELIGHTS:* Author Jude Welton has contributed books to several children's series about art, including "Eyewitness Art" and "Artists in Their Time." Both her series and non-series titles intend to introduce children to the basics of appreciating art and artists, and creating their own art, as she explained to *CA:* "My aim is to introduce art and literature to children and adults who have no specialist knowledge. It is my hope that they will come to enjoy and truly appreciate the arts."

Several of Welton's books deal with Impressionism, which is a style of painting that involves expressing subtle nuances of color and light in the outdoors, and styles that derived from it. Nineteenth-century French painter Claude Monet, the subject of her first book, is remembered as one of the originators of Impressionism and gave the name to the movement with his 1874 painting *Impressionism: Soleil levant* (Impression of a Sun Rise). Using dabs of primary colors, impressionist artists sought to approximate the hue of reflected light and the cheerier aspects of the world. Their paintings are generally of a light and pleasant nature and are more concerned with bright emotion than realistic depiction. Writing about *Monet,* a critic for *Kirkus Reviews* called Welton's book "admirably lucid" and termed it "invaluable" to those seeking an understanding of art history.

An offshoot of Impressionism was the *fauvism,* or "wild" use of color employed by such artists as Frenchman Henri Matisse and Russian-born Frenchman Marc Chagall, who are subjects of later works by Welton. Frenchman Paul Gauguin, as Welton explains, made an even greater departure from Impressionism in his works, which harked back to European folkloric painting and then to the primitive art of the Caribbean islands, to which he emigrated. With his art, Gauguin demonstrated the validity of using primitive art as a basis for aesthetic experiment.

On a practical plan, Welton created *Drawing: A Young Artist's Guide* to offer children a "creative example that both instructs and inspires," according to *RQ*'s Betty Porter. Using examples from the Tate Gallery in London, she introduces readers to aspects of outline and pattern, color, light and shade, texture, perspective, and composition, as would an art teacher. She encourages children to bring their imaginations to bear on their work as they attempt progressively more difficult art projects.

*BIOGRAPHICAL AND CRITICAL SOURCES:*

*PERIODICALS*

*Booklist,* May 1, 1993, p. 1562; summer, 1995, Kay Weisman, review of *Drawing: A Young Artist's Guide,* p. 927.

*Books for Keeps,* March, 1993, p. 21.

*Kirkus Reviews,* June 1, 1993, p. 729.

*RQ,* summer, 1995, Betty Porter, review of *Drawing,* p. 526.

*School Library Journal,* February, 1993, p. 109; May, 1993, p. 144; March, 1995, Alexandra Morris, review of *Drawing,* p. 220.

*Times Educational Supplement,* February 19, 1993, p. R8.*

\*　　\*　　\*

## WESTCOTT, Wayne L. 1949-

*PERSONAL:* Born May 17, 1949, in Waverly, NY; son of Warren and Eva Westcott; married Claudia Gance (a director of a fitness center). *Ethnicity:* "White." *Education:* Pennsylvania State University, B.S., 1971, M.S., 1974; Ohio State University, Ph.D., 1977. *Politics:* Independent. *Religion:* Christian. *Hobbies and other interests:* Strength training, running, cycling, gardening, skiing.

*ADDRESSES: Home*—18 Pine St., Abington, MA 02351. *Office*—South Shore Young Men's Christian Association, 79 Coddington St., Quincy, MA 02169; fax: 617-471-2590 or 617-479-0257.

*CAREER:* South Shore Young Men's Christian Association, Quincy, MA, fitness research director. Also worked as teacher and track coach at public schools in Vestal, NY; as instructor and track coach at Pennsylvania State University, University Park; as professor and track coach at Eastern Connecticut State University, Willimantic, and as professor at Florida State University, Tallahassee. Presenter of weekly radio fitness program. National Youth Fitness Foundation, member of advisory board; consultant to National Young Men's Christian Association, National School Fitness Foundation, American Council on Exercise,

Wayne L. Westcott

National Academy of Sports Medicine, President's Council on Physical Fitness and Sports, and Governor's Committee on Physical Fitness and Sports.

*AWARDS, HONORS:* Association of Professional YMCA Directors service award, 1983, Roberts-Gulick Memorial Award, 1998; recognition award, American Heart Association, 1992; honor award, Massachusetts Association of Health, Physical Education, Recreation, and Dance, 1993; lifetime achievement award, International Association of Fitness Professionals, 1993; Healthy American Fitness Leader Award, President's Council on Physical Fitness and Sports, 1995; lifetime achievement award, Governor's Committee on Physical Fitness and Sports, 1999; fitness industry leader award, National Strength Professionals Association, 2000; presidential award, National School Fitness Foundation, 2001.

*WRITINGS:*

*Strength Fitness: Physiological Principles and Training Techniques,* Allyn & Bacon (Newton, MA), 1982, 4th edition, W. C. Brown (Dubuque, IA), 1995.

*Building Strength at the YMCA,* Human Kinetics (Champaign, IL), 1987.

*Keeping Fit,* George W. Prescott, 1987.

*Be Strong: Strength Training for Muscular Fitness for Men and Women,* W. C. Brown (Dubuque, IA), 1992.

*Nautilus Strength Training Certification Textbook,* Nautilus (Vancouver, WA), 1995.

*Building Strength and Stamina,* Human Kinetics (Champaign, IL), 1996, 2nd edition, 2003, U.S. Navy edition, 2003.

*Strength Training past Fifty,* Human Kinetics (Champaign, IL), 1998.

*Strength Training for Seniors,* Human Kinetics (Champaign, IL), 1999.

(With Pete Draovitch) *Complete Conditioning for Golf,* Human Kinetics (Champaign, IL), 1999.

(With Avery D. Faigenbaum) *Strength and Power for Young Athletes,* Human Kinetics (Champaign, IL), 2000.

*Specialized Strength Training,* Healthy Learning, 2001.

(With Avery D. Faigenbaum) *Youth Fitness,* American Council on Exercise (San Diego, CA), 2001.

(With Rita la Rosa Loud) *No More Cellulite: A Proven Eight-Week Program for a Firmer, Fitter Body,* Berkley (New York, NY), 2003.

(With Tracy D'Arpino) *High-Intensity Strength Training,* Coaches Choice (Monterey, CA), 2002.

Contributor to books, including *Personal Trainer Manual,* American Council on Exercise (San Diego, CA), 1991. Author of a weekly newspaper fitness column. Contributor of more than 400 articles to professional journals. Member of editorial board, *Fitness Management, Prevention, Men's Health, Fitness, American Fitness Quarterly, Club Industry, Shape,* and *Nautilus.*

*SIDELIGHTS:* Wayne L. Westcott once told *CA:* "My writing is an extension of my research, and my motivation is twofold. First, I want to learn more about exercise and its effects on youth, adults, and seniors. Second, I want to share relevant fitness information and tested training programs with people who can benefit from exercise participation. All of my books are essentially 'how-to' books designed to help individuals improve their physical fitness with safe, effective, and efficient training programs.

"My work is influenced most by the thousands of participants in my research studies. Their training results are the basis for my program design and exercise protocols. My writing process is to revise my research articles, combine the information in a logical manner, and present the most relevant material as clearly and concisely as possible. My main objective is to 'write tight' and present information that has practical application for the reader.

"I have always placed a high value on physical fitness as an athlete, coach, teacher, professor, researcher, and lecturer. It was therefore natural for me to write on this topic."

\* \* \*

## WILSON, Joyce M(uriel Judson) 1921-
### (Joyce Stranger)

*PERSONAL:* Born May 26, 1921, in London, England; daughter of Ralph (an advertising manager) and Beryl Judson; married Kenneth B. Wilson, February 28, 1944; children: Andrew Bruce, Anne Patricia and Nicholas David (twins). *Ethnicity:* British. *Education:* London University, B.Sc., 1942. *Religion:* Church of England. *Hobbies and other interests:* Dog shows—competes in breed, obedience and working trials; canine behavior consulting.

*ADDRESSES: Agent*—Gillon Aitken Associates Ltd., 29 Fernshaw Road, London SW10 0TG, England. *E-mail*—joycestranger@k9phoenix.freeserve.co.uk.

*CAREER:* Imperial Chemical Industries, Manchester, England, research chemist, 1942-46. Lecturer and writer on dog training.

*MEMBER:* Society of Authors, Institute of Journalists, United Kingdom Registry of Canine Behaviourists, Canine Concern England (honorary president), People and Dogs Society (honorary president).

*AWARDS, HONORS:* Short listed, 2001, for the Golden Bone Award for best dog writer of the year.

*WRITINGS:*

CHILDREN'S BOOKS; UNDER PSEUDONYM JOYCE STRANGER

*Wild Cat Island,* illustrated by Joe Acheson, Methuen (London, England), 1961.

*Circus All Alone,* illustrated by Sheila Rose, Harrap (London, England), 1965.

*Jason, Nobody's Dog,* illustrated by Douglas Phillips, Dent (London, England), 1970.

*The Honeywell Badger,* illustrated by Douglas Phillips, Dent (London, England), 1972.

*Paddy Joe,* Collins (London, England), 1973.

*The Hare at Dark Hollow,* illustrated by Charles Pickard, Dent (London, England), 1973.

*Trouble for Paddy Joe,* Collins (London, England), 1973.

*The Secret Herds: Animal Stories,* illustrated by Douglas Reay, Dent (London, England), 1974.

*Paddy Joe at Deep Hollow Farm,* Collins (London, England), 1975.

*The Fox at Drummer's Darkness,* illustrated by William Geldart, Dent (London, England), 1976, Farrar, Straus (New York, NY), 1977.

*The Wild Ponies,* illustrated by Robert Rothero, Kaye & Ward (London, England), 1976.

*Joyce Stranger's Book of Hanaák's Animals* (poetry), illustrated by Mirko Hanák, Dent (London, England), 1976.

*Paddy Joe and Thomson's Folly,* Pelham (London, England), 1979.

*The Curse of Seal Valley,* Dent (London, England), 1979.

*Vet on Call,* Carousel (London, England), 1981.

*Double Trouble,* Carousel (London, England), 1981.

*Vet Riding High,* Carousel (London, England), 1982.

*No More Horses,* Carousel (London, England), 1982.

*Dial V.E.T.,* Carousel (London, England), 1982.

*Marooned!,* Kaye & Ward (London, England), 1982.

*The Hound of Darkness,* Dent (London, England), 1983.

*Shadows in the Dark,* Kaye & Ward (London, England), 1984.

*The Family at Fools' Farm,* Dent (London, England), 1985.

*Spy, the No-Good Pup,* Dent (London, England), 1989.

*Midnight Magic,* Lions (London, England), 1991.

*Animal Park Trilogy,* Lions (London, England), 1992.

*The Runaway,* Lions (London, England), 1992.

*The Secret of Hunter's Keep,* Lions (London, England), 1993.

*The House of Secrets Trilogy,* Lions (London, England), 1994.

*A Cherished Freedom,* Severn House (London, England), 2001.

*Cry to the Moon,* Severn House (London, England), 2002.

ADULT BOOKS; UNDER PSEUDONYM JOYCE STRANGER

*The Running Foxes,* illustrated by David Rook, Hammond (London, England), 1965, Viking (New York, NY), 1966.

*Breed of Giants,* Hammond (London, England), 1966, Viking (New York, NY), 1967.

*Rex,* Harvill Press (London, England), 1967, Viking (New York, NY), 1968.

*Born to Trouble,* Viking (New York, NY), 1968, published as *Casey,* Harvill Press (London, England), 1968.

*The Wind on the Dragon,* Viking (New York, NY), 1969, published as *Rusty,* Harvill Press (London, England), 1969.

*One for Sorrow,* Corgi (London, England), 1969.

*Zara,* Viking (New York, NY), 1970.

*Chia, the Wildcat,* Harvill Press (London, England), 1971.

*Lakeland Vet,* Viking (New York, NY), 1972.

*Walk a Lonely Road,* Harvill Press (London, England), 1973.

*A Dog Called Gelert and Other Stories* (short stories), Corgi (London, England), 1973.

*Never Count Apples,* Harvill (London, England), 1974.

*Never Tell a Secret,* Harvill (London, England), 1975.

*Flash,* Collins & Harvill (London, England), 1976.

*Khazan, the Horse That Came Out of the Sea,* Collins & Harvill Press (London, England), 1977.

*A Walk in the Dark,* Michael Joseph (London, England), 1978.

*The January Queen,* Michael Joseph (London, England), 1979.

*The Stallion,* Michael Joseph (London, England), 1981.

*The Monastery Cat and Other Stories* (short stories), Corgi (London, England), 1982.

*Josse,* Michael Joseph (London, England), 1983.

*The Hounds of Hades,* Michael Joseph (London, England), 1985.

*The Hills Are Lonely,* Souvenir (London, England), 1993.

*Thursday's Child,* Souvenir (London, England), 1994.

*A Cry on the Wind,* Souvenir (London, England), 1995.

*Perilous Journey,* Souvenir (London, England), 1998.

*A Cherished Freedom,* Severn House (Surrey, England), 2001.

*Cry to the Moon,* Severn House (Surrey, England), 2001.

*Call of the Sea,* Severn House (Surrey, England), 2002.

*OTHER; UNDER PSEUDONYM JOYCE STRANGER*

*Kym: The True Story of a Siamese Cat,* illustrated by William Geldart, Michael Joseph (London, England), 1976, Coward, McCann (New York, NY), 1977.

*Two's Company,* Michael Joseph (London, England), 1977.

*Three's a Pack,* Michael Joseph (London, England), 1980.

*All about Your Pet Puppy,* Pelham (London, England), 1980.

*How to Own a Sensible Dog,* Corgi (London, England), 1981.

*Two for Joy,* Michael Joseph (London, England), 1982.

*Stranger Than Fiction: The Biography of Elspeth Bryce-Smith,* Michael Joseph (London, England), 1984.

*A Dog in a Million,* Michael Joseph (London, England), 1984.

*Dog Days,* Michael Joseph (London, England), 1986.

*Double or Quit,* Michael Joseph (London, England), 1987.

Wilson's manuscripts are held at Boston University.

*ADAPTATIONS: Jason* was filmed by Walt Disney Productions; *The Fox at Drummers' Darkness* was filmed as *The Wild Dog; The Honeywell Badger* and *The Hare at Dark Hollow* were adapted for television by the British Broadcasting Corp.

*WORK IN PROGRESS:* Short stories, serials, feature articles, book as yet untitled.

*SIDELIGHTS:* Joyce M. Wilson has written about animals for over thirty years under the pseudonym of Joyce Stranger. She studied to be a biologist, specializing in animal behavior. It is no surprise, therefore, that she calls the animal material in her books "autobiographical"; they are written about animals she has known—horses she used to ride, hares that lived near her house, or dogs she has owned. Wilson's books all promote the rewards of partnerships between humans and animals. She commented in *Twentieth-Century Children's Writers* that "for many people, an animal can provide a harmony lacking in day-to-day relationships with people."

Many of her books, including *Jason, Nobody's Dog, Walk a Lonely Road,* and *Spy, the No-Good Pup,* explore the theme of friendship between humans and animals. Other books tell of humans who, intentionally or otherwise, mistreat animals. *The Honeywell Badger,* for instance, is the story of two young children who are so set upon having a badger for a pet that they ignore the consequences of trying to tame such an animal. In the 1973 book *Trouble for Paddy Joe* it is Paddy Joe's poor training of his pet Alsatian, Storm, that causes the animal to become lost in the Scottish wilderness.

Several of Wilson's books are told from the animal's point of view. *The Hare at Dark Hollow,* for example, is the story of how a hare adapts to changes in its natural surroundings. "*The Hare at Dark Hollow* came from a hare that lived near us in the middle of a housing estate," Stranger once explained. "She reared her family on a tiny playing field and fed in the gardens. There were hares there until we moved to Anglesey, yet the field was only about an acre in size. Another hare was on our caravan site and used to lurk and watch stock car racing. There are hares all over Manchester airport."

One of Wilson's literary strengths, according to critics, is her ability to appeal to a wide audience of adults and children. A reviewer for *Junior Bookshelf,* writing about *The Hound of Darkness,* not only praised Wilson's "deep feeling for wild country and for nature in its harshest moods," but noted that it is "by no means a book for children alone, or even for them particularly."

Although Wilson's books concentrate on deepening her readers' understanding of animals and their needs, she does not go to extremes in defending animal rights. In *The Family at Fools' Farm,* for example, eighteen-year-old Jan is hampered in her attempts to keep her family together and make the farm profitable by the irresponsible activities of a group of animal rights activists. A critic in *Growing Point* called the book an "absorbing and stirring narrative," while a *Junior Bookshelf* reviewer stated that the book gives "an honest picture of what farming really means in daily repetitive hard work and disappointment when crops fail or animals are sick," but it also shows the joys and pleasures of "the fruition of plans followed out against all odds."

In *Midnight Magic* Wilson writes of twelve-year-old Mandy, who has been thrown from a horse and is now afraid to ride again. Wilson incorporates much information about horses and horse training into the story as Mandy takes riding lessons from Kristy, an elderly horsewoman who helps Mandy conquer her fear and learn to respond to each horse as an individual. In *Twentieth-Century Children's Writers,* essayist Gwen Marsh called the book "a remarkable *tour de force* even from a writer whose feeling for animals has always been her greatest strength."

One of Wilson's favorite themes is the uneasy but necessary balance that must be struck between people and animals, especially in rural or semi-rural areas. In *A Cherished Freedom,* for example, self-reliant Louise Pritchard learns how to accept help from friends and neighbors after her husband goes missing while delivering food aid in a war-torn country. The progress of her pregnancy makes keeping up their farm by herself especially difficult, but by giving a runaway teenager a place to live and a job, both are helped. Then a pack of dogs from a neighboring farm is let loose among her sheep, killing or maiming a significant number, and the farm is once again in jeopardy. Louise's neighbors come to her rescue, however, "in this lovely story that will enchant animal lovers with its vivid portrayal of farm life," remarked Patricia Engelmann in *Booklist.* Stranger again depicts the hardships of farm life in *Cry to the Moon* in which two approaches to land management in the Scottish Highlands are juxtaposed. Here, one farm is devoted to gamekeeping, a way of life that is in jeopardy because of the scarcity of game and the arrival of a family of wildcats on the property. Sheina, the gamekeeper's daughter, wants to save the wildcats, and is aided by Rob, who has turned the neighboring estate into an animal sanctuary. In Engelmann's *Booklist* review of *Cry to the Moon* she contended that "animals . . . are the true stars of Wilson's latest tale; people merely serve as facilitators." Again, young people who love animals will be intrigued by Wilson's close-up depiction of their lives, Englemann predicted.

Wilson told *CA:* "I have written since I was a small girl. I was given a bedroom of my own as I kept my sisters awake with stories at night. I love words and how they work. My father was a writer and wrote at night when he got home from the office. He used to give me a pad and pencil and tell me to write so he had peace to get on with his own writing. I did not begin writing for publication until my first child was about a year old (in 1948) and I needed some intellec-

tual stimulation and money. I have written over seventy books and many short stories and articles, always animal based.

"I have spent much of my life among animals; watched wild animals for years from hides; helped out on farms, worked with dogs and taught owners of around twenty dogs a week how to teach their dogs good manners. I have always been fascinated by trying to understand the animal and how its mind works and feel so many people miss so much by living divorced from countryside, season, and animals of all kinds. I live in an isolated place, and write about folk who live in the same sort of place, often a farm or breeding establishment where the animals are their livelihood.

"Wildlife is so diverse and their habits are so fascinating. On British TV I love David Attenborough's wildlife programs . . . he knows so much and has seen so much. I would have liked to farm and most of my friends either breed or farm so I write about the countryside and the animals I meet. Though many of my books now are social history as farming has changed so much.

"I find many authors only research about animals and get things wrong, I try to get them right. My first well known book, *The Running Foxes,* was triggered by a book, which included foxes but had their habits all wrong. My animal books work because I watched the animals and studied animal behavior. I knew where the foxes laired and bred their cubs; where the hare hid, and watched her as she moved around and when she was caught by a fox or dog; I listened to a goose on an island as it died when the fox caught it. I hid in trees to watch badgers; I ride horses and I am in daily contact with many dogs. Farm animals are all around me—I can see sheep and cattle as I write. The world beyond the human is vastly exciting; it has much to reveal to us.

"[My writing process] is difficult, I get an idea and toss it around, make a synopsis and then try to do a certain number of words each day until it is finished. I may work with a serial editor who reads what I have written and makes suggestions."

Wilson told *CA* the most surprising thing she learned as a writer was "mainly not to force a story as the characters often take over and change its thread.

Maybe a minor character suddenly takes the center stage and you have to change it. And also I don't argue with editors unless they are trying to make an animal do something it would not do. Oddly my life now has been shaped by my book's subjects as six of them were autobiographical on my dogs and provoked more fan mail than any. As a result a lot of what I write is to help people who have dogs and who wouldn't read nonfiction.

"People write and say they find [my books] helpful and often tell them things they didn't know, or reflect some part of their own lives, and make them feel better about things that have gone wrong in them. Such letters are very rewarding and I always hope that I do have something to say to my readers which will please and benefit them. The Stallion is about a woman suddenly widowed and how she makes a new and rewarding life for herself. I have had letters from so many widows who say it helped them to adjust and start again."

Although the choice is a difficult one, Wilson has a tendency to choose the book she's writing at the moment as her favorite. "Maybe it is the Call of the Sea, which I was writing in conjunction with my favorite serial editor. He died suddenly of a heart attack just before I finished it and never saw it. It is his memorial, as he taught me more than anyone else I have ever met. His name was Ian Sommerville and he was my editor for My Weekly (magazine), for over twenty-five years. That book has become special for me and is dedicated to him," she related to CA.

In a piece written for K9Phoenix, an online resource, Wilson talked about the role that animals, in particular dogs, play in her own life as an elderly adult: "In my own life, since my own family left home and married, my dogs have often helped me through traumas; the death of my parents; my husband's two strokes . . . the dogs were there to distract, needing care and attention, offering consolation in their own way, providing stability and affection. The animals in my books have always an important function, often changing the way in which people live."

BIOGRAPHICAL AND CRITICAL SOURCES:

BOOKS

St. James Guide to Children's Writers, 5th edition, St. James (Detroit, MI), 1999.

Something about the Author Autobiography Series, Volume 24, Gale (Detroit, MI), 1997, pp. 251-275.
Twentieth-Century Children's Writers, 4th edition, St. James (Detroit, MI), 1995.

PERIODICALS

Booklist, April 15, 1969, p. 944; July 15, 1977, p. 1731; April 1, 2002; April 15, 2001, Patricia Engelmann, review of A Cherished Freedom, p. 1537.
Growing Point, November, 1985, review of The Family at Fools' Farm, p. 4524.
Junior Bookshelf, October, 1983, p. 215; December, 1985, p. 281; October, 1989, p. 245.
Kirkus Reviews, March 1, 1967, p. 300.
Magpies, September, 1992, p. 31.
New York Times Book Review, May 1, 1977, p. 44.
Publishers Weekly, March 28, 1977, p. 79.
School Librarian, June, 1986, p. 174; February, 1992, p. 21.
Times Educational Supplement, January 18, 1980, p. 41; July 17, 1981, p. 26.
Times Literary Supplement, November 23, 1973, p. 1430.

ONLINE

K9Phoenix, http://www.k9phoenix.freeserve.co.uk/ (June 17, 2002), "About Joyce Stranger."

*     *     *

## WINTERS, Katharine 1936-
### (Kay Winters)

PERSONAL: Born October 5, 1936, in Trenton, NJ; daughter of Robert (an aerospace engineer) and Luella (a homemaker) Lanning; married Earl D. Winters (a consultant), August 27, 1960; children: Linda Lee. Ethnicity: Scotch, English, Welsh. Education: Beaver College, B.S. (elementary education), 1958; attended Boston University (graduate studies in public relations); Wheelock College, M.S. (education); attended Lehigh University and New School for Social Research. Politics: Democrat. Religion: Protestant. Hobbies and other interests: Reading, biking, walking, gardening, and traveling.

*Katharine Winters*

ADDRESSES: *Home*—P. O. Box 339, Richlandtown, PA. *Office*—Box 339, Richlandtown, PA 18955. *E-mail*—kaywinters@kaywinters.com.

CAREER: Children's book author and literacy consultant. Massachusetts Public Schools, Newton, MA, elementary education teacher, 1960-63; Palisades School District, Kintnersville, PA, elementary education teacher and supervisor, 1968-92. American International Schools, education consultant, 1970-80.

MEMBER: International Reading Association (IRA), Society of Children's Book Writers and Illustrators, Author's Guild.

AWARDS, HONORS: Best Book of 1998, Bank State College, and Pick of the List, American Booksellers Association, 1997, both for *Wolf Watch;* Best 100 Books of the Year citation, International Reading Association (IRA) special interest group, for *Tiger Trail;* children's choice citation, IRA, for *Whooo's Haunting the Teeny Tiny Ghost;* Junior Library Guild Selection,

for *Abe Lincoln: The Boy Who Loved Books;* Golden Circle Award, Arcadia University (formerly Beaver College), for distinguished career as teacher and writer.

WRITINGS:

UNDER NAME KAY WINTERS

*Did You See What I Saw?: Poems about School,* illustrated by Martha Weston, Viking (New York, NY), 1996.

*The Teeny Tiny Ghost,* illustrated by Lynn Munsinger, HarperCollins (New York, NY), 1997.

*Wolf Watch,* illustrated by Laura Regan, Simon & Schuster (New York, NY), 1997.

*Where Are the Bears?,* illustrated by Brian Lies, Bantam (New York, NY), 1998.

*How Will the Easter Bunny Know?,* ("First Choice Chapter Book"), illustrated by Martha Weston, Yearling (New York, NY), 1999.

*Whooo's Haunting the Teeny Tiny Ghost?,* illustrated by Lynn Munsinger, HarperCollins (New York, NY), 1999.

*Tiger Trail,* illustrated by Laura Regan, Simon & Schuster (New York, NY), 2000.

*But Mom, Everybody Else Does!,* illustrated by Doug Cushman, Dutton (New York, NY), 2002.

*Abe Lincoln: The Boy Who Loved Books,* illustrated by Nancy Carpenter, Simon & Schuster (New York, NY), 2003.

*Voices of Ancient Egypt,* illustrated by Barry Moser, National Geographic Society (Washington, DC), 2003.

OTHER; UNDER NAME KAY WINTERS

(With Marta Felber) *The Teachers Copebook: How to End the Year Better Than You Started,* Fearon (Belmont, CA), 1980.

Also author of reading textbooks for Scott Foresman and Houghton Mifflin. *The Teeny Tiny Ghost* has been translated into French.

WORK IN PROGRESS: *My Teacher for President,* illustrated by Denise Brunkus, for Dutton; *The Teeny Tiny Ghost and the Monster,* illustrated by Lynn

Munsinger, for HarperCollins; *John Appleseed: His Trail of Trees,* for National Geographic; *Amelia Earhart: And Fly She Did!* for National Geographic.

*SIDELIGHTS:* Katharine Winters has written a number of popular children's books, many of them involving young children confronting the fears and troubles of their daily lives. Drawing on her twenty-seven years of teaching elementary school, Winters wrote her first book, *Did You See What I Saw?: Poems about School,* a book of poems devoted to the day-to-day goings-on in a typical schoolroom. Everything is explored in lighthearted verse, from the pleasure evoked by a new box of crayons to snow days and passing notes in class. Poems, such as "Lots of Spots," about the travails of chicken pox, and "Groundhog Day," paint amusing pictures of school life. "The rhythms and sounds and wordplay . . . are part of the fun," wrote Hazel Rochman in *Booklist.*

In *The Teeny Tiny Ghost,* Winters addresses the importance of mastering one's fears. In this take on a well-known tale, a diminutive specter is afraid of his own boos and howls. On Halloween night, a rap on the door sends shivers through him and his teeny tiny kittens. But summoning up all his courage, he swears to protect his feline companions and opens the door to his ghostly pals, who have come to take him trick-or-treating. Janice M. Del Negro, writing in *Bulletin of the Center for Children's Books,* said, "Tucked into this humorously written and illustrated tale is the kernel of stout-heartedness that makes young children love the hero." "This tale of banishing fear has just the right blend of wit and supernatural suspense," stated a reviewer for *Publishers Weekly.*

In the award-winning *Wolf Watch,* Winters uses poetic quatrains to tell the story of four wolf pups from birth until their first foray out of the den. The habits of a wolf pack are introduced, from howling to hunting and protecting their young. Danger is present in the form of a golden eagle who awaits the chance to prey upon one of the defenseless pups. *School Library Journal* contributor Susan Scheps called *Wolf Watch* "a treasure of a book," and wrote that "there is a lot of information to be gleaned from this sparsely written visual masterpiece." A critic for *Kirkus Reviews* called *Wolf Watch* "a splendid complement to titles with a more fact-based approach to wolf life."

*How Will the Easter Bunny Know?* was inspired by a real-life incident. Winters told Jodi Duckett of the

*Morning Call* that her husband's friend had been asked by his young nephew, "Uncle John, if I come to your house for Easter, how will the Easter bunny know?" Using that question and its worry as her starting point, Winters tells the story of a six-year-old boy who figures out a variety of ways to inform the Easter bunny that he is staying at his grandmother's house. He draws a map to grandmother's apartment, even carefully including a picture of her green door, leaves a letter to the Easter bunny, and makes signs to guide him. "The child has to solve the problem by himself; that's an unwritten rule in children's books," Winters explained to Duckett. Carolyn Phelan in *Booklist* called *How Will the Easter Bunny Know?* the "likable story of a child-size dilemma."

Winters's character the Teeny Tiny Ghost returns in the book *Whooo's Haunting the Teeny Tiny Ghost?* This time he comes home from school to find the front door open and scary noises coming from inside the house. He must summon up all of his courage to go inside and discover just what is going on. According to Lauren Peterson in *Booklist,* "Both art and text convey a feeling of spookiness without being overtly scary." A *Publishers Weekly* reviewer called the story "a lesson in bravery, a spine-tingler and an all-out charmer, this is the treat of the Halloween season."

In *But Mom, Everybody Else Does!* a young girl tries to "convince her mother that her acts and desires are not only legitimate but also universal," as a *Kirkus Reviews* contributor wrote. All children have messy rooms, they all failed the test at school, they all get bigger allowances, and so on. The girl tells her mother that no one walks to school, everyone sleeps with the dog, nobody has to practice, and everybody can paint better than she can. Cushman's illustrations never push too hard for effect, supporting the girl's outrageous conjectures and her active imagination. *Booklist* reviewer Hazel Rochman believed that "this farce reinforces every kid's frustration about bossy grown-ups."

Winters turned to the story of a historical figure in *Abe Lincoln: The Boy Who Loved Books,* in which she recounts the president's life from his rural childhood to his time in the White House. Told in free verse, Winters's version of Lincoln's biography emphasizes his love of reading and his attainment of great heights not through formal schooling but through his own independent study. In a statement posted at her Web site,

Winters explained how she came to write Lincoln's story: "I was drawn to exploring the life of Abe Lincoln because I wondered how someone could be born in extreme poverty, lose his mother at age nine, have less than a year of education, few role models, yet overcome these obstacles to become a beloved President whose words we remember today. I was delighted to discover that books made the difference." A reviewer for *Kirkus Reviews* called *Abe Lincoln: The Boy Who Loved Books* "a moving tribute to the power of books and words." In like manner, a *Publishers Weekly* reviewer praised the book for dramatizing "the importance of words in shaping ideas and lives."

Winters once told *CA:* "From the time I was seven years old I was a writer. I kept diaries, journals, wrote for the school and camp newspapers, and the college magazine. When I graduated from Beaver College with a bachelor of science degree in elementary education and a minor in English, I took additional writing courses at Boston University. I submitted poems, essays, articles, and stories to educational journals and textbooks. Now and then they were published. But making a living by writing books did not seem like a viable possibility at that time. My husband and I were just out of graduate school, and we had a big educational debt to pay to Massachusetts Institute of Technology (MIT), as well as a new baby.

"For the next twenty-nine years I worked in public schools as a teacher, a reading specialist, an educational consultant, and a college instructor. And I loved it. At every conference I attended I always went to hear the authors instead of the latest theory on the wonder of phonics. I continued to send in manuscripts now and then, but teaching was very consuming. There was little time for writing. In 1980, I coauthored a book for teachers with Marta Felber, *The Teachers Copebook: How to End the Year Better Than You Started.* In order to finish that project, I had to get up every morning at 4 a.m., sneak downstairs to my frosty office, and garbed in a fur robe, woolen gloves, and fleece-lined boots, would type until it was time to teach.

"In 1992, my school board offered early retirement. My resignation was on the superintendent's desk the next day. This was my chance! I was taking it. I started to write full time the day after I retired. I imagined that the Palisades School District was paying me to stay home and write. And write I did. I wrote every day. I went to the New School [for Social Research] in New York and took classes in writing for children with instructors Margaret Gable and Deborah Brodie. I attended conferences and met editors. I went to New York to the Children's Book Council and read all of the picture books from the years 1991 and 1992 that they had on their shelves.

"Gradually, the rejection forms from publishers changed into personal letters. Finally, in 1994, I got a phone call from an editor at HarperCollins. They were interested in *The Teeny Tiny Ghost.* From there, my writing career began to take off. Publishers were soon interested in *Wolf Watch* and *Did You See What I Saw?: Poems about School.* In the meantime, I was also writing reading textbooks. Soon, *Where Are the Bears?* and *How Will the Easter Bunny Know?* were going to press and I was writing *Who's Haunting the Teeny Tiny Ghost,* a sequel to *The Teeny Tiny Ghost,* and *Tiger Trail,* the companion to *Wolf Watch.* I was researching *Voices of Ancient Egypt* and *Abe Lincoln: The Boy Who Loved Books,* and planning the pattern book, *But Mom, Everybody Else Does.*"

Winters continued: "I write because that's how I know what I think. When I see what I say, ideas that were fuzzy come clear to me. And sometimes I am surprised at what I find out about myself.

"I write because I love to read and I want to give others that pleasure. Some of my happiest moments are when I am curled up by the fire in our old stone farmhouse in Bucks County. My husband and I seldom watch television. On summer evenings we read in the gazebo, which looks out on our ten acres of meadows and woods. The hummingbird stops by for a sip from our feeder. Butterflies light on the cosmos. We have wild turkeys, deer, and pheasants who visit. I hope that children will become more aware of small wonders from my books.

"I write because I love to learn. Writers have the chance to play many parts, hear many voices, and dream many dreams. One of the exciting fringe benefits of being a writer is the ability to pursue what you care about. I am interested in so many things, nature, people, history, humor. Writing gives me a powerful motivation for learning. I loved finding out about wolves, presenting their warm family life, and dispelling the 'big bad wolf' myth in *Wolf Watch*. It's important to examine how to face fears and cope, as I explored in *The Teeny Tiny Ghost,* or how to observe and share experiences and memories, as in *Did You See What I Saw?: Poems about School*. I liked putting myself in the place of a six-year-old, as if I was going to Grandma's house for Easter and had no way of letting the Easter Bunny know of my whereabouts in *How Will the Easter Bunny Know?* Or imagining twin bear cubs, Sassy and Lum, in *Where Are the Bears?,* figuring out which activities they would copy as they met campers for the very first time. As I worked on the book about Abraham Lincoln I lost myself in the wilderness, suffered on his hundred-mile trek to Indiana and sympathized with Abe as he searched for books and learned to use words to lift himself out of grinding poverty. In *Tiger Trail,* I loved putting myself in the place of the mother tigress and feeling her fear, her concern, and her triumph as she taught her cubs survival skills. When I was writing my book on ancient Egypt, the workers seemed to come alive and walk right off the pages in their sandals. In *Voices of Ancient Egypt,* I loved taking on the role of an ordinary worker in that complex society that existed so long ago. Speaking in the voice of each worker helped me hear what the scribe, the birdnetter, and the dancer had to say. I hope that as youngsters meet the characters in my stories, they will realize that whatever their own circumstances may be, they can choose—to be brave, to forge ahead, to take positive risks, to be kind, to overcome severe obstacles, to appreciate the moment.

"My work habits are similar to those I used when I was teaching. I work every day. I am always on the watch for a story, even when we are on vacation, riding elephants in Thailand or sailing on Lake Nockamixon. I have been very influenced by writers who use poetic prose, such as Karen Hesse, Jane Yolen, and Byrd Baylor. I love poetry by Aileen Fisher. I think Patricia Reilly Giff gets into the heads of her characters in a way I admire. And even though I frequently try to use other genres, poetic prose seems to speak up the most often. I am more interested in character development than plot. The story comes from the characters, and they frequently have a mind of their own. Still, writing the book is only the beginning. I also visit schools, attend book signings, speak at colleges, conferences, and bookstores.

"My advice for aspiring writers is to work, revise, and persist. Treat writing like a job. Make contacts. Go to conferences. Read current children's books. Join a writer's group. I am lucky to have a husband who is an excellent editor. Don't send your manuscript right off when you finish it. Let it breathe. Look at it again. And be grateful that you have chosen a career that makes every day matter. Whatever is going on in your life today will fit somewhere, sometime, in a story.

"I hope that my books will reach out to people of all ages and encourage them to look around, to pay attention, to notice their world and the people in it, to realize the power of words and ideas, and to take the gift of reading and use it to make their days full of meaning, their hearts full of hope."

*BIOGRAPHICAL AND CRITICAL SOURCES:*

*PERIODICALS*

*Booklist,* August, 1996, Hazel Rochman, review of *Did You See What I Saw?: Poems about School,* p. 1903; September 1, 1997, Lauren Peterson, review of *The Teeny Tiny Ghost,* p. 141; November, 1, 1997, Julie Corsaro, review of *Wolf Watch,* p. 485; March 15, 1999, Carolyn Phelan, review of *How Will the Easter Bunny Know?,* p. 1339; September 1, 1999, Lauren Peterson, review of *Whooo's Haunting the Teeny Tiny Ghost?,* p. 151; October 15, 2000, Lauren Peterson, review of *Tiger Trail,* p. 448; December 15, 2002, Hazel Rochman, review of *But Mom, Everybody Else Does!,* p. 770; January 1, 2003, Kay Weisman, review of *Abe Lincoln: The Boy Who Loved Books,* p. 901.

*Bulletin of the Center for Children's Books,* November, 1997, p. 107.

*Kirkus Reviews,* October 1, 1997, p. 1539; August 15, 2002, review of *But Mom, Everybody Else Does!,* p. 1239; November 15, 2002, review of *Abe Lincoln,* p. 1703.

*Morning Call* (Allentown, PA), October 10, 1997, Jodi Duckett, "Spirited Endeavor: Ex-Palisades Teacher Attains Goal to Write Children's Books," p. D12; March 26, 1999, Jodi Duckett, "Kay Winters Shares a 'Great' Story Idea," p. D7.

*Publishers Weekly,* October 6, 1997, review of *The Teeny Tiny Ghost,* p. 48; October 27, 1997, review of *Wolf Watch,* p. 75; September 27, 1999, review of *Whooo's Haunting the Teeny Tiny Ghost?,* p. 47; September 24, 2001, review of *Whooo's Haunting the Teeny Tiny Ghost?,* p. 95; November 25, 2002, review of *Abe Lincoln,* p. 67.

*School Library Journal,* October, 1996, Marilyn Taniguchi, review of *Did You See What I Saw?,* p. 119; November, 1997, Meg Stackpole, review of *The Teeny Tiny Ghost,* p. 103, Susan Scheps, review of *Wolf Watch,* p. 104; April, 1999, Gale W. Sherman, review of *How Will the Easter Bunny Know?,* p. 110; September, 1999, Martha Link, review of *Whooo's Haunting the Teeny Tiny Ghost?,* p. 210; January, 2001, Sally Bates Goodroe, review of *Tiger Trail,* p. 112; September, 2002, Kathy Piehl, review of *But Mom, Everybody Else Does!,* p. 208.

*ONLINE*

*Kay Winters Home Page,* http://www.kaywinters.com/ (April 8, 2003).

\*　　\*　　\*

**WINTERS, Kay**
    **See WINTERS, Katharine**

# Y

## YEE, Paul (R.) 1956-

*PERSONAL:* Born October 1, 1956, in Spalding, Saskatchewan, Canada; son of Gordon and Gim May (Wong) Yee. *Education:* University of British Columbia, B.A., 1978, M.A., 1983. *Hobbies and other interests:* Cycling, swimming.

*ADDRESSES: Home*—2 Abermarle Ave., Toronto, Ontario M4K 1H7, Canada. *E-mail*—paulryee@interlog.com.

*CAREER:* Writer. City of Vancouver Archives, Vancouver, British Columbia, Canada, assistant city archivist, 1980-88; Archives of Ontario, Toronto, Ontario, Canada, portfolio manager, 1988-91; Ontario Ministry of Citizenship, policy analyst, 1991-97.

*MEMBER:* Writers Union of Canada, CANSCAIP.

*AWARDS, HONORS:* Honourable Mention, Canada Council Prizes for Children's Literature, 1986, for *The Curses of Third Uncle;* Vancouver Book Prize, 1989, for *Saltwater City;* British Columbia Book Prize for Children's Literature, I.O.D.E. Violet Downey Book Award, Sheila A. Egoff Children's Book Prize, and Parents' Choice Honor, all 1990, all for *Tales from Gold Mountain;* Ruth Schwartz Award, Canadian Booksellers Association, 1992, for *Roses Sing on New Snow,* and 1997, for *Ghost Train;* Governor General's Award, Canada Council, 1996, and Prix Enfantasie (Switzerland), 1998, for *Ghost Train;* Best Books for Young Adults List, Young Adult Library Services As-sociation of the American Library Association, 1998, for *Breakaway;* Books for the Teenage List, New York Public Library, 2003, for *Dead Man's Gold.*

*WRITINGS:*

FICTION FOR CHILDREN AND YOUNG ADULTS

*Teach Me to Fly, Skyfighter!, and Other Stories,* illustrated by Sky Lee, Lorimer (Toronto, Ontario, Canada), 1983.

*The Curses of Third Uncle* (novel), Lorimer (Toronto, Ontario, Canada), 1986.

*Tales from Gold Mountain: Stories of the Chinese in the New World,* illustrated by Simon Ng, Groundwood Books (Toronto, Ontario, Canada), 1989, Macmillan (New York, NY), 1990.

*Roses Sing on New Snow: A Delicious Tale,* illustrated by Harvey Chan, Macmillan (New York, NY), 1992.

*Breakaway* (novel), Groundwood Books (Toronto, Ontario, Canada), 1994.

*Moonlight's Luck,* illustrated by Terry Yee, Macmillan (New York, NY), 1995.

*Ghost Train,* illustrated by Harvey Chan, Groundwood Books (New York, NY), 1996.

*The Boy in the Attic,* illustrated by Gu Xiong, Groundwood Books (Toronto, Ontario, Canada), 1998.

*Dead Man's Gold, and Other Stories,* illustrated by Harvey Chan, Douglas & McIntyre (Toronto, Ontario, Canada), 2002.

*The Jade Necklace,* illustrated by Grace Lin, Interlink, 2002.

NONFICTION

*Saltwater City: An Illustrated History of the Chinese in Vancouver,* Douglas & McIntyre (Vancouver, British Columbia, Canada), 1988, University of Washington (Seattle, WA), 1989.
*Struggle and Hope: The Story of Chinese Canadians,* Umbrella Press (Toronto, Ontario, Canada), 1996.

Yee's books have been translated into several languages, including French.

ADAPTATIONS: *Roses Sing on New Snow* was adapted as a videocassette produced by the National Film Board of Canada, 2002.

WORK IN PROGRESS: *Bamboo* (picture book), expected publication, 2004; *A Song for Ba* (picture book), expected publication, 2004; *Chinatowns: Chinese Communities across Canada* (nonfiction), expected publication, 2005.

SIDELIGHTS: Paul Yee is a Canadian author whose Chinese heritage and experiences growing up in the Chinatown region of Vancouver, British Columbia, have inspired many of his highly acclaimed books for younger readers. While written primarily for Canadian children of Chinese ancestry who desire to learn about themselves and their heritage, his books have found audiences with children of many backgrounds from both Canada and the United States. Among Yee's books are the short-story collections *Tales from Gold Mountain: Stories of the Chinese in the New World* and *Dead Man's Gold, and Other Tales,* as well as a number of picture books and the novels *Breakaway* and *The Curses of Third Uncle.* Despite his relatively small output, Yee has "made a notable contribution to Canadian children's literature by fusing the unique details of ethnic experience with the universal concerns for identity and love," a *Canadian Children's Books* essayist maintained.

Born in Spalding, Saskatchewan, in 1956, Yee had what he once termed a "typical Chinese-Canadian childhood, caught between two worlds, and yearning to move away from the neighborhood." While he wrote short stories as a hobby, he never considered making writing his profession. Instead, after graduating from

high school he went on to the University of British Columbia, and ultimately earned his M.A. in history in 1983. Although Yee has taught informally at several institutions in British Columbia, the focus of his career has been on his work as an archivist and policy analyst, organizing and analyzing information to come up with options for government agencies in Canada. In 1988 Yee began work in Toronto as multicultural coordinator for the Archives of Ontario.

Although it seems a far cry from archivist/analyst to children's book author, Yee found the step to be a natural one, given his circumstances and interests. "Back in 1983, I was involved in doing work for Chinatown, such as organizing festivals, exhibits, and educational programs," he once explained. "Even though I had written some short stories, I had not done anything in children's literature. A Canadian publishing company, Lorimer, knowing about my work in the Chinese community, asked me to write a children's book that would employ my knowledge of Chinese-Canadian life as a background." The result of this request would be *Teach Me to Fly, Skyfighter!, and Other Stories,* Yee's first book for children.

*Teach Me to Fly, Skyfighter!* contains four interlinking stories about children living in the immigrant neighborhoods of Vancouver. Yee "has succeeded in portraying the personalities, interests, and dreams of four eleven-year-old friends whose voices ring true throughout," according to Frieda Wishinsky in *Quill & Quire.*

Yee's second short story collection, *Tales from Gold Mountain,* was published in 1989 to high praise from critics. Lee Galda and Susan Cox, writing in *Reading Teacher,* wrote that the eight tales included in the book "give . . . voice to the previously unheard generations of Chinese immigrants whose labor supported the settlement of the west coast of Canada and the United States." Yee includes stories about the conflict between the manager of a fish cannery and his greedy boss; a young man who arranges the burial of Chinese railroad workers after he meets his father's ghost; a young woman's gift of ginger root to save her fiancee's life; a wealthy merchant who exchanges his twin daughters for sons; and clashes between old traditions and new influences. Betsy Hearne noted in the *Bulletin of the Center for Children's Books* that "Yee never indulges in stylistic pretensions" in blending realism and legend, and praised the stories for containing "mythical overtones that lend the characters unforgettable dimension—humans achieving supernatural power in defying their fate of physical and cultural oppression." *School Library Journal* contributor Margaret A. Chang praised Yee for "further expand[ing] and enhanc[ing] understanding of the Chinese immigrant experience," while a *Horn Book* reviewer praised *Tales from Gold Mountain* for interweaving "the hardships and dangers of frontier life in a new country with the ancient attitudes and traditions brought over from China" and predicted that the images created "will stay with the reader for a long time."

Published in 2002, *Dead Man's Gold, and Other Stories* contains ten tales that combine real life and the supernatural. Against the backdrop of a harsh existence comprised of hard labor in gold mines, on railroads, and in family-run businesses, Yee's protagonists long for home and family as they face prejudices while trying to build a better life. In these stories, each accompanied by an appropriately haunting illustration by Harvey Chan, Yee's characters are also tested by unearthly horrors of one sort or another. Calling the collection "a remarkable piece of literature," Laura Reilly noted in her *Resource Links* review that Yee's tales "all have surprising twists that compel the reader to read on." Praising *Dead Man's Gold, and Other Tales*, *Booklist* contributor Hazel Rochman noted that Yee's "plain, beautiful words speak with brutal honesty" as he writes of immigrant life from the mid-1800s through the 1950s.

Yee's first novel, *The Curses of Third Uncle,* is a work of historical fiction that deals with the period of the early twentieth century in which Sun Yat-Sen's revolutionary movement fought against the Chinese Empire. Dr. Sun Yat-Sen, called the "Father of Modern China," had led nine uprisings against the Empire by the time he visited Vancouver in 1910 and 1911. Yee's protagonist, fourteen-year-old Lillian, lives in Vancouver's Chinatown and misses her father, who often travels back to China and throughout the British Columbia frontier—presumably to take care of his clothing business. He is actually a secret agent for Dr. Sun's revolutionary movement. At one point in his travels, Lillian's father fails to return. His absence is economically hard on the family, but Lillian will not believe her father has deserted them. Her third uncle, however, threatens to send Lillian's family back to China.

In her attempts to locate her father by traveling through British Columbia, Lillian discovers that he has been betrayed by his brother, who has been paid to turn him over to his enemies. Reviewing the novel in *Emergency Librarian*, Christine Dewar called it "a story that is exciting but contrived, with an attractive and reasonably motivated heroine." *Quill & Quire* writer Annette Goldsmith similarly commented that *The Curses of Third Uncle* is "an exciting, fast-pace, well-written tale," and praised Yee for his use of legendary Chinese female warriors to reinforce Lillian's story.

Set in Chinatown in 1932 during the Great Depression, *Breakaway* "explores questions of identity and belonging by detailing conflicts between generations and cultures," according to a *Canadian Children's Books* essayist. A senior in high school, Kwok-Ken Wong hopes a soccer scholarship will save him from an otherwise dismal future working on his father's farm. When his plans are dashed and racism prevents him from playing the sport he loves, Kwok-Ken grows disillusioned but ultimately grows in understanding as he begins to appreciate the strengths of his cultural heritage. Reviewing *Breakaway* in *Quill & Quire*, Patty Lawlor called the book "a well-written novel with staying power" that would be useful in discussions of racism. While noting that the novel's ending is "rather abrupt," *Canadian Materials* contributor Margaret Mackey praised Yee's novel for painting "a valuable picture of a fascinating and complex time and world."

In addition to novels and short fiction for older readers, Yee has also made the Chinese-Canadian heritage come vividly to life for younger readers. Maylin, the heroine of his 1989 picture book *Roses Sing on New Snow*, embodies the difference between the Old World and the New World when she explains to the governor of South China, who is visiting her father's Chinatown restaurant to learn the secrets of her delicious recipes, that "this is a dish of the New World. . . . You cannot re-create it in the Old." Although efforts are made to push Maylin aside and allow the men of the family to take credit for the restaurant's excellent fare, after her father and brothers cannot reproduce the meals served to the governor Maylin is called forth and ultimately shown to be one of the most talented cooks in Chinatown. Hearne noted in the *Bulletin of the Center for Children's Books* that "vivid art and clean writing are graced by a neatly feminist ending."

Other picture books by Yee include *The Jade Necklace, The Boy in the Attic,* and the award-winning *Ghost Train. The Jade Necklace* focuses on Yenyee, a young girl whose fisherman-father presents her with a necklace with a carved jade fish, then is lost at sea soon after. Giving the necklace to the sea in the hope that it will return her father to her, Yenyee goes on to immigrate to the New World as a nanny before the sea responds to her request in a surprising way. In *Quill & Quire* Sherie Posesorski praised *The Jade Necklace* as "a coming-of-age tale that's both contemporary and timeless, realistic and symbolic," and added that Yee's prose "seamlessly marries the formality of the storyteller's voice with the intimacy of a child's perspective."

Winner of Canada's prestigious Governor General's award, *Ghost Train* focuses on a talented young artist named Choon-yi, whose father, a railway worker, is killed only days before Choon-yi arrives from China to join him. In *The Boy in the Attic* seven-year-old Chinese immigrant Kai-ming discovers the ghost of a boy who died in Kai-ming's new Canadian home eighty years before. Through the intervention of a magic butterfly, the two boys are able to break through their language barrier and converse, helping Kai-ming make the transition to his new country. Praising Yee's use of the ghost as a metaphor, *Quill & Quire* contributor Freida Ling described *The Boy in the Attic* as a tale of "human courage, resourcefulness, and the adaptability required to uproot yourself from your homeland and start over in a strange country."

Although Yee's primary career was as a historian, he found no difficulty making the switch to fiction. Nevertheless, he once remarked that he finds fiction writing more "arduous because instead of merely reporting what has happened in nonfiction, fiction requires the creation of a story" that will be believable and enjoyable. "The difference between nonfiction and fiction is the difference between reliable reporting and imaginative creating," he concluded.

## BIOGRAPHICAL AND CRITICAL SOURCES:

### BOOKS

*St. James Guide to Children's Writers,* 5th edition, St. James Press (Detroit, MI), 1999, pp. 1148-1149.

Yee, Paul, *Saltwater City: An Illustrated History of the Chinese in Vancouver,* Douglas & McIntyre (Vancouver, British Columbia, Canada), 1988, University of Washington (Seattle, WA), 1989.

Yee, Paul, *Tales from Gold Mountain: Stories of the Chinese in the New World,* Groundwood Books (Toronto, Ontario, Canada), 1989, Macmillan (New York, NY), 1990.

### PERIODICALS

*Booklist,* March 15, 1990, Denise Wilms, review of *Tales from Gold Mountain: Stories of the Chinese in the New World,* p. 1464; March 1, 1999, Sally Estes, review of *Tales from Gold Mountain,* p. 1212; November 1, 2002, Hazel Rochman, *Dead Man's Gold, and Other Stories,* p. 494.

*Books in Canada,* December, 1983, p. 17; December, 1986, p. 18; May, 1989, p. 5.

*Bulletin of the Center for Children's Books,* January, 1990, Betsy Hearne, review of *Tales from Gold Mountain,* p. 178; March, 1990, p. 178; July, 1992, B. Hearne, review of *Roses Sing on New Snow: A Delicious Tale,* p. 307.

*Canadian Children's Literature,* autumn, 1996, Marie Davis, "A Backward Way of Thanking People: Paul Yee on His Historical Fiction," pp. 50-68; winter, 1996, James Greenlaw, "Chinese Canadian Fathers and Sons," pp. 106-108.

*Canadian Literature,* spring, 1988, "Different Dragons," p. 168; autumn, 1991, pp. 142-143; winter, 1999, review of *The Boy in the Attic,* p. 204.

*Canadian Materials,* September, 1994, Margaret Mackey, review of *Breakaway,* p. 139.

*Emergency Librarian,* May-June, 1995, David Jenkinson, "Portraits: Paul Yee," pp. 61-64; May, 1987, Christine Dewar, review of *The Curses of Third Uncle,* p. 51.

*Horn Book,* July, 1990, review of *Tales from Gold Mountain,* pp. 459-460; March-April, 1992, Elizabeth S. Watson, review of *Roses Sing on New Snow,* p. 196.

*Kirkus Reviews,* May 15, 2002, review of *The Jade Necklace,* p. 744.

*Quill & Quire,* October, 1983, Frieda Wishinsky, review of *Teach Me to Fly, Skyfighter!,* p. 16; December, 1986, Annette Goldsmith, "Illuminating Adventures with Young People from Long Ago," p. 14; April, 1994, Patty Lawlor, review of *Breakaway,* p. 39; February, 1997, p. 51; October, 1998,

Freida Ling, review of *The Boy in the Attic,* p. 42; May, 2002, Sherie Posesorski, review of *The Jade Necklace,* p. 32.

*Reading Teacher,* April, 1991, Lee Galda and Susan Cox, review of *Tales from Gold Mountain,* p. 585.

*Resource Links,* June, 2002, Rosemary Anderson, review of *The Jade Necklace,* p. 46; December, 2002, Laura Reilly, review of *Dead Man's Gold, and Other Stories,* p. 35.

*School Library Journal,* May, 1990, Margaret A. Chang, review of *Tales from Gold Mountain,* p. 121; December, 1998, Diane S. Marton, review of *The Boy in the Attic,* p. 96; September, 2002, Margaret A. Chang, review of *The Jade Necklace,* p. 209.

ONLINE

*Canadian Children's Book Centre Web site,* http://www.bookcentre.ca/ (March 11, 2003), "Paul Yee."